D0454498

PENGUIN BOOKS

THE PENGUIN
ROGET'S COLLEGE THESAURUS
IN DICTIONARY FORM

Philip Morehead is a lexicographer, an authority on games, and Head of Music Staff of the Lyric Opera of Chicago and the Lyric Opera Center for American Artists. His books include *Hoyle's Rules of Games* and *The New International Dictionary of Music*. He lives in Chicago.

THE PENGUIN
ROGET'S
COLLEGE
THESAURUS
IN
DICTIONARY FORM

Philip Morehead

PENGUIN BOOKS

PENGUIN REFERENCE

Published by the Penguin Group

Penguin Putnam Inc., 375 Hudson Street, New York, New York 10014, U.S.A.

Penguin Books Ltd, 80 Strand, London WC2R 0RL, England

Penguin Books Australia Ltd, 250 Camberwell Road, Camberwell, Victoria 3124, Australia

Penguin Books Canada Ltd, 10 Alcorn Avenue, Toronto, Ontario, Canada M4V 3B2

Penguin Books India (P) Ltd, 11 Community Centre,
Panchsheel Park, New Delhi – 110 017, India

Penguin Books (N.Z.) Ltd, Cnr Rosedale and Airborne Roads,
Albany, Auckland, New Zealand

Penguin Books (South Africa) (Pty) Ltd, 24 Sturdee Avenue, Rosebank,
Johannesburg 2196, South Africa

Penguin Books Ltd, Registered Offices:
Harmondsworth, Middlesex, England

First published in the United States of America under the title *The New American
Roget's College Thesaurus in Dictionary Form* by New American Library 1958
Fifth edition published as *The Penguin Roget's Thesaurus in Dictionary Form*
in hardcover format in Penguin Reference 2001
This paperback edition published 2003

1 3 5 7 9 10 8 6 4 2

Copyright © Philip D. Morehead, 2001
All rights reserved

THE LIBRARY OF CONGRESS HAS CATALOGED THE HARDCOVER EDITION AS FOLLOWS:
Morehead, Philip D.
The Penguin Roget's college thesaurus in dictionary form / Philip Morehead.
p. cm.
ISBN 0-670-03016-3 (hc.)
ISBN 0 14 20.0170 8 (pbk.)
1. English language—Synonyms and antonyms—Dictionaries. I Title: Roget's college
thesaurus in dictionary form. II. Title: Thesaurus in dictionary form. III. Title.
PE1591 .M75 2001
423'.1—dc21 2001036039

Printed in the United States of America
Set in Sabon
Designed by Joe Rutt

Except in the United States of America, this book is sold subject to the condition
that it shall not, by way of trade or otherwise, be lent, re-sold, hired out, or otherwise
circulated without the publisher's prior consent in any form of binding or cover other
than that in which it is published and without a similar condition including
this condition being imposed on the subsequent purchaser.

The scanning, uploading and distribution of this book via the Internet or via
any other means without the permission of the publisher is illegal and punishable by law.
Please purchase only authorized electronic editions, and do not participate in or encourage
electronic piracy of copyrighted materials. Your support of the author's rights is appreciated.

To my father

The editor would like to give special thanks to Hugh Rawson, my former editor at New American Library for almost twenty years, who initiated this project and guided me through many others over the years. Thanks are also due to Sarah Manges, who ably picked up this project from Hugh and has been of great help to me in its completion. Thanks to my long-suffering wife, Patricia Morehead, composer and oboist, who put up with my endless hours at the computer. And finally, I would like to acknowledge the hard work of my late father and mother, Albert H. Morehead and Loy Morehead, who together were responsible for the original work on which this volume is based.

HOW TO USE
THIS THESAURUS

Peter Mark Roget was an English physician who was born in 1779 and who died in 1869. As a hobby he liked to make lists of words and group them together when they were related to one another. Some were related because they were synonyms, such as *illegal* and *unlawful;* some because they were antonyms, such as *peaceful* and *warlike;* some because they were reminders of one another, such as *father* and *mother.* Altogether Mr. Roget made a thousand different groups, or categories, of related words. Every word he knew or could find in the dictionaries he had was classified in one or more of these categories. In 1852, Mr. Roget's list of words was published. He called the book a thesaurus, or treasury, of words. There were not many words in the first *Roget's Thesaurus* compared to the number in a volume like this, but his book was the first collection of synonyms, antonyms, and other related words. Not only writers, but also many others found it invaluable. Dozens of editors, beginning with Mr. Roget's son, have revised the original *Thesaurus,* added to it, and brought it up to date (for many of the words in the original Roget list are now obsolete and many common words of today were unknown in his time); but virtually every edition is still called *Roget's Thesaurus* in honor of the man who first had the idea.

This edition of *Roget's Thesaurus* is both a dictionary of synonyms and a thesaurus, or "treasury," of related words. It combines in one easy-to-use alphabetical list categories (very much like those in Roget's original thesaurus) and a list of words with their close synonyms. For clarity, each category is printed the full width of the page and set off in a box while the synonym listings are printed at half-page width.

To find *synonyms* for a word, first look up the word in the alphabetical list. In most cases, you will find what you are looking for immediately under that word. Reference to more synonyms is indicated by words printed in SMALL CAPITALS. If you look up the word or words referred to, you will find additional synonyms and other words related to the word you were looking up. Most references are to categories, where you will also find words of related meaning but different parts of speech. *Antonyms* are listed for many synonym entries, and at the end of each category entry you will find references to sources for antonyms.

A special feature of this edition is the inclusion of many phrases and quotations, both contemporary and historical, appropriate to a certain category.

Frequently only one form of a word is entered in the alphabetical word list. You will find synonyms for the other forms by referring to the entries printed in SMALL CAPITALS under the listed word. For example, to find synonyms for *proximate,* look under *proximity* in the alphabetical word list and refer to the category NEARNESS, where you find *adjacent, adjoining* and other related adjectives.

A word or phrase in parentheses—( )— is explanatory or shows how the preceding word is to be used in a sentence. Brackets—[ ]—indicate that the bracketed letters, word, or phrase might or might not be used with the adjoining word, depending on the preference of the writer.

In the listings, synonyms for different senses of the listed word are separated by semicolons (;). Informal and slang *senses* of the entry word are labeled *informal* or *slang* at the beginning of each sense; informal and slang *synonyms* for all senses of the entry word are listed separately, headed by *Informal* or *Slang,* respectively. Moreover, entry words or individual synonyms might be labeled to indicate special or substandard usage. The most commonly used labels—in addition to *informal* and *slang*—are *dial.* (dialectal), *Brit.* (British), *poetic,* and *archaic.*

In the category entries, numbered senses are often preceded by a contextual gist label in parentheses and italics that indicate the meaning being covered in that paragraph. These labels can help you find the right word more quickly.

Familiar dictionary abbreviations are used for parts of speech: *n.,* noun; *v.,* verb; *v.i.,* intransitive verb; *v.t.,* transitive verb; *adj.,* adjective; *adv.,* adverb; *pron.,* pronoun; *prep.,* preposition; *conj.,* conjunction; *interj.,* interjection.

This is not a dictionary. It does not define words except to the extent that they are defined in their synonyms. A word that has no natural synonyms is not entered merely to define it. Moreover, alternate spellings for a word are generally not given. The publishers of this thesaurus also publish a companion volume, *The New American Webster Handy College Dictionary,* which was the authority for the preferred spellings used herein and in which may be found definitions of the words in this book.

Antonyms formed by simply adding *un-, in-, dis-,* etc., are generally not given, nor are words listed when they are simple negatives of other words. For example, such a word as *unloved* is not entered because one may merely look up the positive term, but *unbearable* is entered because the positive term has various dissimilar meanings.

The editor appreciates readers' suggestions for additions to the word list, phrases, and quotations, and any other comments. Comments and suggestions can be sent to the editor by e-mail at pmorehead@philsbooks.com.

THE PENGUIN
ROGET'S
COLLEGE
THESAURUS
IN
DICTIONARY FORM

A

aback, *adv.* rearward, behind. See REAR, DIFFICULTY. —**taken aback,** disconcerted (see DISCONTENT).

abaft, *adv.* aft, astern, behind. See REAR.

abandon, *v.t.* relinquish, resign, give up, forgo, surrender, discontinue, waive, abdicate; leave, quit, evacuate, withdraw (from); desert, forsake, maroon, discard, drop; let go, throw up, pull out of, have done with, turn one's back on, wash one's hands of; pull out on. See RELINQUISHMENT, RESIGNATION, DISUSE. —*n.* RASHNESS, recklessness, impetuosity, impulsiveness, audacity. *Ant.,* retain; continue; restraint.

abandoned, *adj.* dissipated, immoral, reprobate, dissolute, depraved; lost; unbridled. See IMPURITY, RASHNESS, RELINQUISHMENT, DISUSE.

abase, *v.t.* humble (see ABASH); demean, degrade; dishonor; cast down. See HUMILITY, SERVILITY. *Ant.,* uplift, exalt.

abash, *v.t.* humiliate, humble, shame; embarrass, disconcert; mortify, crush, take down a peg. See HUMILITY. *Ant.,* hearten, rally.

abate, *v.* DECREASE, lessen, moderate, diminish, subside; allay, slake, slacken, subdue; curtail, remit; let down (on), take off the edge (of). *Ant.,* INCREASE.

abattoir, *n.* slaughterhouse (see KILLING).

abbé, abbess, abbot, *n.* See CLERGY.

abbey, *n.* See TEMPLE.

abbreviate, *v.* abridge, condense, contract, shorten, curtail, digest, truncate, prune. See SHORTNESS, DEDUCTION. *Ant.,* expand, lengthen.

ABCs, *n.* alphabet; basics, rudiments. See INTRINSIC, WRITING.

abdicate, *v.* relinquish, resign, renounce, abandon, quit, surrender. See RELINQUISHMENT, RESIGNATION. *Ant.,* retain, maintain.

abdomen, *n.* belly, paunch, epigastrium, venter; midriff; corporation, solar plexus, guts (*all inf.*). See INTERIOR, BODY.

abduct, *v.t.* kidnap, carry off, steal, spirit away, shanghai, snatch. See STEALING.

abeam, *adv.* sideways (see SIDE).

aberration, *n.* DEVIATION, variation, distortion, disorientation; aberrance, INSANITY; ERROR.

abet, *v.t.* AID, assist, support; encourage. *Ant.,* impede, discourage.

abeyance, *n.* suspension. See END, LATENCY. *Ant.,* renewal, operation.

abhor, *v.t.* HATE. *Ant.,* LOVE.

abide, *v.* dwell, reside, live, stay; tolerate, endure, submit (to); remain, stay. See ABODE, DURABILITY, FEELING. *Ant.,* proceed, depart.

ability, *n.* POWER, SKILL, competency, capacity, capability, aptitude, faculty, talent (*inf.*), know-how; what it takes (*sl.*). *Ant.,* inability, incompetency.

ab initio, *Lat.,* from the BEGINNING.

abject, *adj.* servile, contemptible; miserable, wretched, hangdog; base. See SERVILITY, IMPROBITY, CONTEMPT. *Ant.,* exalted, noble.

abjure, *v.* forswear, renounce, repudiate. See NEGATION, NULLIFICATION. *Ant.,* maintain.

ablaze, *adj.* afire, burning; aglow. See HEAT, LIGHT, RESENTMENT.

able, *adj.* capable, competent, skillful, talented. See POWER, SKILL. *Ant.,* incompetent; weak.

able-bodied, *adj.* fit, robust. See STRENGTH, HEALTH.

abloom, *adj.* blossoming; in blossom *or* flower. See PROSPERITY.

ablution, *n.* cleansing, washing. See CLEANNESS. *Ant.,* pollution.

abnegate, *v.* See NEGATION.

abnormal, *adj.* unusual, aberrant, eccentric, irregular, anomalous; insane; monstrous. See UNCONFORMITY, INSANITY. *Ant.,* normal.

aboard, *adv. & prep.* on, on board. *Informal,* astride. See PRESENCE, SHIP.

ABODE
Place of residence

Nouns—1, *(living place)* abode, dwelling, residence, accommodations, domicile, address, habitation, berth, nest, seat, lodging[s], lodging place, roof over one's head, quarters, headquarters, base, depot, housing, place; habitat; open housing; barracks, dormitory; harem; stigmatized house; time-share. *Informal,* place to hang one's hat. *Slang,* dump, joint, digs, [crash]pad, [laid] crib, pilch, shebang. See LOCATION.

2, *(home)* home, homeplace, homestead, hearth, hearthstone, fireside, inglenook, ingleside, household, ménage, roof, *lares et penates;* ancestral hall[s], fatherland, native land *or* soil, country. *Informal,* roost; repent pad.

3, *(refuge)* retreat, asylum, cloister, hermitage, hideaway, hiding-place, sanctuary, arbor, sanctum sanctorum, cave, nest, den, cell, dugout, hive, hole, lair, haunt. *Slang,* hangout, hideout, stamping ground *or* place. See SECLUSION.

4, *(outdoor camp)* camp, barrack[s], bivouac, encampment, casemate; stopover; tourist camp, trailer camp; caravan, mobile home; cave, cliff dwelling; houseboat (see NAVIGATION). *Slang,* [hobo] jungle, squats.

5, *(structure)* house, dwelling[-place], building; hall; chalet, bungalow, maisonette, manor-house; brownstone [house], semidetached, flat, apartment [house], two- *(etc.)*family house, farmhouse, ranch house, split- *or* bi-level, duplex, triplex, townhouse, pied-à-terre, condominium, cooperative, time-share; penthouse, tenement, loft, ark; temple; rectory; [residential] hotel; skyscraper; [housing] development, [building] project; trailer; cliff dwelling; outbuilding; pueblo. *Informal,* diggings, digs; condo, co-op. *Slang,* pad, cheesebox, go-up, jam house, repent pad. See ARCHITECTURE, BUILDING.

6, *(modest structure)* hut, adobe, bunkhouse, hogan, cabin, cottage, hovel, igloo, tupek, lean-to, log cabin, Quonset *or* Nissen hut, rancho, shack, shanty, tent, tepee, hogan, earth lodge, wickiup, wigwam, balok, sweat lodge, kiosk, jacal. *Slang,* rathole.

7, *(commercial dwelling)* inn, caravansary, club, hospice, pension, posada, roadhouse, hostel, hostelry, hotel, motel, motor hotel, motor court, motor inn, rooming house, bread and breakfast, boardinghouse; resort, spa. *Slang,* scratch-crib; cherry orchard.

8, *(animal dwelling)* barn, cowshed, doghouse, kennel, pound, henhouse, hutch, warren, pen, [pig]sty, apiary, shed, stable, stall, booth, coop, dovecote, aviary, birdcage, birdhouse, roost, beehive.

9, *(palatial dwelling)* casa, mansion, manor, manse, palace, château, villa, alcázar, dacha, lodge, castle (see DEFENSE), palace, hall, estate, hacienda, palazzo, ranch, plantation, farm, domain, country seat.

10, *(town)* community; village, hamlet, burg, dorp, thorp, town, pueblo, shtetl, kampong, kraal; municipality, metropolis, conurbation, dynapolis, megalopolis, city, suburb, purlieu, satellite, exurb (see REGION); inner city, ghetto, slum, quarter; colony; commune, kolkhoz; shantytown. *Informal,* one-horse town, whistle stop, Podunk. *Slang,* duckburg; Hooverville, projects.

11, *(dwelling for the ill, etc.)* sanatorium, sanitarium, asylum, [health] resort, [convalescent, nursing, *or* rest] home. *Informal,* old folks' home. See REMEDY.

12, dweller (see INHABITANT).

13, *(domestic arts)* domestic arts, homemaking, home economics, human ecology. See ENVIRONMENT.

Verbs—1, *(live in)* inhabit, domesticate, colonize, naturalize; take root, sit down, settle [down], take up one's abode, establish oneself, squat, perch, pitch one's tent, put up at, keep *or* set up house; bivouac, stop over, encamp, rough it.

2, *(make one's home)* abide, occupy, people, dwell, reside, stay, sojourn, live, put up, tenant, lodge, nestle, board, live in, camp out. *Informal,* roost. *Slang,* shack up, cohabit. See INHABITANT.

3, *(provide dwelling for)* accommodate, lodge, put up, board.

Adjectives—**1,** *(making one's residence)* dwelling, residing, in residence, at home.

2, *(of dwelling centers)* urban, suburban, provincial; metropolitan, cosmopolitan; domestic, foreign.

3, downhome.

Phrases—home is where the heart is; East, West, home's best; there's no place like home.

Quotations—A man's house is his castle (*James Otis*); There's no place like home (*John Howard Paine*); A house is a machine for living in (*Le Corbusier*), The city is not a concrete jungle, it is a human zoo (*Desmond Morris*), Slums may be the breeding-grounds of crime, but middle-class suburbs are incubators of apathy and delirium (*Cyril Connolly*), Home is the girl's prison and the woman's workhouse (*G. B. Shaw*), Home is where you come to when you have nothing better to do (*Margaret Thatcher*).

---

abolish, *v.t.* annul, cancel, abrogate; exterminate, wipe out. See NULLIFICATION, DESTRUCTION. *Ant.,* establish, reinstate.

abolitionist, *n. & adj.* emancipator, freer (see NULLIFICATION, LIBERATION).

abominable, *adj.* detestable. See HATE, UNCLEANNESS. *Ant.,* likable. —**Abominable Snowman,** yeti.

aboriginal, *adj.* primitive, primeval; indigenous. See OLDNESS, INHABITANT.

abortion, *n.* miscarriage; premature delivery *or* birth; FAILURE, fiasco; monstrosity, freak. See END.

abound, *v.i.* teem, swarm, be plentiful; be filled (with). See SUFFICIENCY. *Ant.,* be short of, lack.

about, *adv.* around, round, on all sides; approximately; nearly, almost. —*prep.* concerning, regarding, anent, respecting. See RELATION, NEARNESS.

about-face, *n.* turnabout, reversal, volteface. See INVERSION.

above, *adv.* aloft, overhead, up; earlier, before. See HEIGHT. —*prep.* over, beyond; surpassing; more than, exceeding.

aboveboard, *adj.* candid (see PROBITY).

abracadabra, *n.* mumbo-jumbo (see SORCERY).

abrade, *v.t.* wear (away), grind. See FRICTION.

abrasive, *adj. & n.* —*adj.* rough, frictional; unpleasant. —*n.* grinder; sandpaper, corundum, *etc.* See DISCOURTESY, FRICTION.

abreast, *adv.* side by side; to the same degree. See SIDE, EQUALITY.

abridge, *v.* CONDENSE, shorten, compress, contract. See SHORTNESS. *Ant.,* expand, extend.

abroad, *adv.* overseas, away, outside; roaming, wandering, at large. See TRAVEL, ABSENCE, DISTANCE.

abrogate, *v.t.* repeal, annul, retract. See REJECTION, NULLIFICATION.

abrupt, *adj.* sudden, precipitate, short, curt; steep, precipitous, sheer; sudden *or* sharp (turn, *etc.*); jerky. See INSTANTANEITY. *Ant.,* gradual.

abscess, *n.* ulcer, boil. See DISEASE.

abscond, *v.i.* decamp, bolt, run away, flee, fly, take off. See AVOIDANCE, ESCAPE. *Ant.,* abide, stay.

ABSENCE
State of being away

Nouns—**1,** *(not being here)* absence, nonresidence, noninhabitance, nonpresence, nonattendance, absenteeism, truancy, hooky, family leave; French leave; NONEXISTENCE.

2, *(lack of contents)* emptiness, void, vacuum, vacuity, vacancy; blank, clean slate; aching void. See SPACE, INSUBSTANTIALITY.

3, *(one who is not present)* absentee, truant; missing person, MIA; absentee landlord *or* owner. *Informal,* no-show.

4, *(phrases)* nobody present, not a soul, nary a soul, nobody under the sun, nary a one, no one, no man, never a one.

5, lack (see INSUFFICIENCY).

Verbs—be absent, absent oneself, stay *or* keep away, keep out of the way, play truant, play hooky, take French leave, go AWOL, absent oneself without [official] leave; slip away (see ESCAPE); keep *or* hold aloof; withdraw, vacate (see DEPARTURE). *Informal,* not show up, make oneself scarce. *Slang,* cut [out].

Adjectives—1, *(not present)* absent, nonattendant, not present, away, nonresident, missing, missing in action, lost, wanting, omitted, nowhere to be found, out of sight, gone, lacking, away from home, truant, absent without [official] leave, AWOL; abroad, oversea[s], on vacation; gone with the wind. *Informal,* minus.

2, *(having no contents)* empty, vacant, void, vacuous, untenanted, unoccupied, uninhabited, tenantless; devoid, bare, hollow, blank.

Adverbs—nowhere; elsewhere; neither here nor there, neither hide nor hair; somewhere else, not here. *Dial.,* nowheres.

Prepositions—in absentia, without, less, minus, sans; wanting (see INSUFFICIENCY).

Phrases—absence makes the heart grow fonder; out of sight, out of mind; when the cat's away, the mice will play; absence is the mother of disillusion; a little absence does much good; nature abhors a vacuum.

Antonyms, see PRESENCE.

---

absentminded, *adj.* preoccupied, forgetful. See INATTENTION.

absolute, *adj.* complete, perfect, thorough; sheer; fixed, positive; unrestricted, unbounded, full, plenary; despotic, autocratic, supreme. See COMPLETION, GREATNESS, CERTAINTY. *Ant.,* relative; qualified.

absolution, *n.* cleansing, FORGIVENESS, shrift, dispensation; discharge. See ACQUITTAL, EXEMPTION.

absolutism, *n.* despotism, autocracy; dogmatism. See AUTHORITY, CERTAINTY.

absolve, *v.t.* forgive, cleanse, shrive, pardon, discharge. See FORGIVENESS, ACQUITTAL, EXEMPTION. *Ant.,* accuse, blame.

absorb, *v.* assimilate, take in, suck up; incorporate, integrate; engross, preoccupy, obsess. See THOUGHT, RECEIVING, ATTENTION, USE, COMBINATION, LEARNING.

abstain, *v.i.* forbear, refrain. See AVOIDANCE, MODERATION, ASCETICISM, DISUSE. *Ant.,* indulge.

abstemious, *adj.* abstaining, abstinent; temperate, sober. See MODERATION, ASCETICISM.

abstract, *adj.* theoretical, metaphysical; abstruse, recondite. —*v.* excerpt (from); remove, steal. —*n.* compendium, summary, epitome, précis, abridgment. See SUPPOSITION, STEALING, SHORTNESS. *Ant.,* restore; combine; concrete.

abstracted, *adj.* absentminded, inattentive. See INATTENTION. *Ant.,* alert.

abstraction, *n.* preoccupation; abridgment. See INATTENTION, SHORTNESS, THOUGHT.

abstruse, *adj.* profound, recondite, esoteric, subtle, deep; obscure, enigmatical. See UNINTELLIGIBILITY, OBSCURITY.

ABSURDITY
Quality of being absurd

Nouns—1, *(nonsensical quality)* absurdity, absurdness, nonsense; paradox, inconsistency; inanity (see FOLLY); ludicrousness, ridiculousness, comicality; koan, oxymoron, doublethink.

2, *(ridiculous quality)* muddle, [Irish] bull; bathos; song and dance; travesty (see RIDICULE).

3, *(nonsensical talk)* jargon, doubletalk, twaddle, gibberish, fustian, empty talk, galimatias. *Informal,* poppycock, stuff and nonsense. *Slang,* hot air, crapola, doodly-squat, horse feathers, crock, bull[shit], bushwah, flummadiddle, blarney, blather, jive, moonshine, piffle. See UNMEANINGNESS.

4, *(one who talks nonsense) Slang,* blowhard, bullshit artist.

5, *(art of nonsense)* theater of the absurd; dada[ism].

Verbs—1, *(act foolishly)* play the fool, talk nonsense, talk through one's hat, go from the sublime to the ridiculous.

2, *(make to look absurd)* make a fool of, make absurd, burlesque (see RIDICULE).

Adjectives—absurd, nonsensical, preposterous, senseless, inconsistent, illogical, paradoxical, ridiculous, extravagant, fantastic, silly, funny, comic[al], unmeaning, without rhyme or reason, fatuous, ludicrous, laughable. *Slang,* screwy, cockamamie, cock-and-bull.

Quotations—The intolerable absurdities of life (*Michael Wreszin*), There is nothing so absurd but some philosopher has said it (*Cicero*), No matter how you slice it, it's still baloney (*Al Smith*).

Antonyms, see MEANING.

---

abundance, *n.* plenty, SUFFICIENCY, profusion, luxuriance, fullness; affluence, opulence, wealth. *Ant.,* scarcity.

abuse, *v.t.* misuse, misapply; mistreat, injure, damage; malign, scold, berate, vilify, curse; flay. —*n.* injury, desecration; insult. See DISAPPROBATION, BADNESS, DECEPTION, IMPURITY, WRONG. *Ant.,* praise, flattery.

abut, *v.* touch, border (on). See CONTACT.

abysmal, *adj.* abyssal; deficient, below par, miserable. See DEPTH, INFERIORITY.

abyss, *n.* abysm, deep, DEPTH[s], gulf, chasm, [bottomless] pit, chaos, HELL. See INTERVAL.

academe, *n.* academia, SCHOOL; pedant, academician. See LEARNING, AFFECTATION.

academic, *adj.* scholastic, collegiate; educational; scholarly, erudite; theoretical. See TEACHING, LEARNING, SUPPOSITION.

academy, *n.* SCHOOL, college, preparatory *or* finishing school; [learned] society.

a cappella, *adj.* unaccompanied; solo. See MUSIC, UNITY.

accede, *v.i.* agree, ASSENT, CONSENT, acquiesce, yield, comply; attain. See SUBMISSION, ACQUISITION. *Ant.,* protest, deny.

accelerate, *v.* hasten, expedite, anticipate, speed (up), quicken. See EARLINESS, HASTE. *Ant.,* decelerate, retard.

accelerator, *n.* gas pedal, throttle. See VEHICLE, VELOCITY.

accent, *v.* accentuate, emphasize, stress. —*n.* emphasis, stress, tone; dialect, pronunciation; diacritic[al mark]. See SPEECH, SOUND, INDICATION, IMPORTANCE.

accept, *v.* ASSENT; take; adopt, believe; honor, admit. See RECEIVING, BELIEF, CONSENT, INCLUSION. *Ant.,* reject, refuse.

acceptable, *adj.* tolerable, adequate, OK. See MEDIOCRITY, SUFFICIENCY. *Ant.,* unwelcome, repugnant.

acceptation, *n.* sense, MEANING.

access, *n.* APPROACH, avenue, way; admittance, entrée. *Informal,* (an) in; a line (to). See PASSAGE, INGRESS, POSSIBILITY. —*v.t.* CONTACT; locate, find. See ACQUISITION.

accession, *n.* acceding, ASSENT; increase, ADDITION, ACQUISITION; attainment. See TRANSFER.

accessory, *adj.* contributory; helping; AUXILIARY, incident (to). —*n.* accomplice, assistant, confederate; jewelry, *etc.* See AID, ACCOMPANIMENT, ORNAMENT, CLOTHING.

accident, *n.* mishap, injury, casualty; CHANCE, fortuity. See ADVERSITY, OCCURRENCE. *Ant.,* PLAN, design.

acclaim, *v.t.* applaud; praise, hail, salute. —*n.* praise. See APPROBATION.

acclamation, *n.* acclaim, applause; unanimity. See APPROBATION, UNITY.

acclimate, acclimatize, *v.t.* accustom, inure, habituate. See HABIT.

acclivity, *n.* ASCENT, rise, incline, pitch, slope, grade.

accolade, *n.* honors, laurels, tribute, reward; decoration, embrace, kiss; brace, bracket. See APPROBATION, MUSIC.

accommodate, *v.* adapt, adjust, conform, fit, suit; oblige, help out; lend money (to); put up; lend (to). See AID, AGREEMENT, DEBT, PACIFICATION, ABODE. *Ant.,* inconvenience, impede.

ACCOMPANIMENT
Subordinate addition

Nouns—**1,** *(something that accompanies)* accompaniment, concomitance, company, association, companionship, [co]partnership, fellowship, coefficiency; sidebar. See SYNCHRONISM, SEQUENCE, MUSIC, EFFECT.

2, *(related idea)* concomitant, accessory, adjunct, corollary, coefficient.

3, *(person who accompanies)* companion, attendant, fellow, associate, consort, spouse, colleague, comrade, compadre; accompanist; [co]partner, satellite, hanger-on, shadow; convoy, cortege, escort, bodyguard, chaperon (see SAFETY); retainer[s], retinue, entourage, court, following (see SERVANT); cavalier, squire; fellow traveler, camp follower. *Slang,* pard, sidekick. See FRIEND, MARRIAGE.

Verbs—accompany, attend, hang on, wait on, go along with, go hand in hand with, keep company, row in the same boat, associate *or* consort with, take up with, hang around; string along; escort, usher, chaperon, conduct, convoy, squire, see out. *Informal,* take out. See EFFECT.

Adjectives—accompanying, attendant, concomitant, fellow, associated, coupled, accessory, peripheral.

Adverbs—hand in hand, arm in arm, side by side, cheek to cheek, hand in glove, together, at one's side; in tow; on one's coattails; in a body, in company. *Informal,* cheek by jowl.

Prepositions—with, together with, along with, in company with.

Conjunctions—and, both, also.

Phrases—a man is known by the company he keeps.

Antonyms, see DISJUNCTION.

---

accomplice, *n.* accessory, abettor, confederate, associate, crony; partner, colleague, sidekick (*inf.*). See AUXILIARY.

accomplish, *v.t.* do, complete, fulfill, perform, effect, execute, achieve, consummate. See COMPLETION. *Ant.,* fail, disappoint.

accomplished, *adj.* proficient, versed; talented. See SKILL.

accord, *v.i.* harmonize, conform, agree. See AGREEMENT, ASSENT. —*v.t.* grant, bestow; concede. See GIVING. —*n.* AGREEMENT. *Ant.,* DISCORD; withhold, deny.

accordingly, *adv.* hence, so, therefore, thus. See CIRCUMSTANCE.

according to, *adv.* consistent with, in keeping with; based on. See CONFORMITY, EVIDENCE.

according to Hoyle, *adj. & adv.* by the book, *comme il faut,* kosher. See RIGHTNESS, CONFORMITY.

accordion, *n.* concertina, bandonion, squeeze box (*inf.*). See MUSIC.

accost, *v.t.* greet, hail, address. See COURTESY. *Ant.,* scorn.

account, *v.i.* report, relate, narrate. See DESCRIPTION. —*v.t.* attribute. See CAUSE. —*n.* report, recital, narrative, DESCRIPTION, story, tale, history, chronicle, statement; ACCOUNTING. —**on account,** see PAYMENT. —**on account of,** because (see CAUSE, ATTRIBUTION).

accountable, *adj.* liable; responsible; explicable. See CAUSE, ATTRIBUTION. *Ant.,* blameless, innocent.

ACCOUNTING
Keeping of financial records

Nouns—1, *(act of accounting)* accounting, accountance, accountancy, bookkeeping, audit, calculation (see NUMERATION), commercial *or* business arithmetic; cost *or* managerial accounting; horizontal *or* vertical analysis. See MONEY, SALE, PURCHASE.

2, *(accounting tools)* accounts, books, finances, budget, money matters, figures.

3, ledger, journal, daybook, cashbook, petty-cash book, bank book, pass book, checkbook, invoice, balance sheet, general *or* subsidiary ledger, profit-and-loss statement, accounts-payable *or* -receivable ledger, sales ledger, spreadsheet, worksheet; numbered account; statement, invoice, bill, manifest.

4, *(accounting terms)* asset, liability, limited liability; equity, liquidity; credit, debit, deficit; negative *or* positive cash flow; expenditure (see PAYMENT); bill, invoice, statement [of account]; double-entry accounting, rolling *or* continuous budget; [pencil] footing; fixed costs; balance, [adjusted] trial balance, account, A/C, suspense *or* T account; CREDIT, debit (see DEBT); accrual *or* cash basis method, zero base accounting; net worth; calendar *or* fiscal year; reconciliation; bottom line; entry, compound entry; debit card; salaried worker, freelance, independent contractor.

5, accountant, bookkeeper, actuary, certified public accountant, CPA, chartered accountant (*Brit.*); controller, comptroller; auditor, bank examiner; clerk. *Informal,* number cruncher, bean counter. See INQUIRY.

Verbs—**1,** *(do accounting)* keep accounts, keep the books, journalize, enter, log, post [up], book, CREDIT, debit, carry over, balance [accounts *or* the books]; bill, invoice, dun, settle accounts; take stock, take inventory; audit, examine the books; open *or* close an account *or* the books; cost out.

2, *(steal)* falsify *or* doctor accounts; embezzle (see STEALING). *Slang,* cook the books.

Adjectives—accounting, budgetary; in the black *or* red.

Quotations—Accountants are the witch-doctors of the modern world (*Lord Justice Harman*).

---

accouter, *v.t.* outfit, attire, equip. See CLOTHING, PROVISION.

accredit, *v.* authorize, license, certify; believe; attribute. See BELIEF, COMMISSION, ATTRIBUTION.

accretion, *n.* See INCREASE.

accrue, *v.* accumulate, grow; result from, grow out of. See INCREASE, RECEIVING, DEBT, EFFECT. *Ant.,* dissipate, DECREASE.

acculturation, *n.* See CONFORMITY.

accumulate, *v.* amass, gather; aggregate, collect, hoard, bank; pile up. See ACQUISITION, ASSEMBLAGE, STORE. *Ant.,* dissipate, squander.

accurate, *adj.* correct, exact; precise, truthful, on the button *or* nose (*inf.*), to the penny (*inf.*). See TRUTH, RIGHTNESS. *Ant.,* erroneous, false, wrong.

accursed, *adj.* damned, execrable. See BADNESS, IMPRECATION. *Ant.,* blessed.

ACCUSATION
Act of accusing

Nouns—**1,** *(charge)* accusation, charge, incrimination, inculpation; CONDEMNATION, denunciation, invective, implication, imputation, blame, reproach, recrimination; censure. *Informal,* finger-pointing; frame[-up]; trumped-up charge. See DISAPPROBATION.

2, *(legal charge)* LAWSUIT, plaint, complaint, citation, allegation; indictment, arraignment, impeachment, true bill; libel, slander (see DETRACTION).

3, *(one who charges)* accuser, accusant, complainant, plaintiff, complainant; prosecutor, the prosecution, district attorney, attorney general. *Informal,* DA.

4, *(one charged)* accused, defendant, respondent, co-respondent, libelee.

Verbs—**1,** *(make a charge)* accuse, charge; press, prefer, lay *or* bring charges, tax (with), incriminate; allege, impute; inculpate, blame, complain against *or* of, reproach, indict, arraign, impeach, implicate, cite; have something on. *Informal,* throw the book at. See LAWSUIT.

2, *(tell on)* denounce, inform (against), take to task, call to account, lay at one's door, give the lie (to); trump up a charge, bring false charges; tell on, tattle (on); cast the first stone. *Slang,* finger, put the finger on, point the finger (at), rat (on), squawk, redbait, frame.

Adjectives—accusing, accusatory; incriminatory, recriminatory, reproachful; imputative; incriminating, inculpatory.

Phrases—a bad workman blames his tools; it's the poor wot gets the blame; it's not how you win or lose, it's how you place the blame.

Quotations—J'accuse (*Émile Zola*), He that is without sin among you, let him first cast a stone at her (*Bible*).

Antonyms, see APPROBATION, VINDICATION.

---

accustom, *v.* habituate, familiarize, inure. See HABIT.

ace, *n.* expert, adept; particle, iota. See SKILL, LITTLENESS, AVIATION. —*adj.* excellent, first-rate. See SUPERIORITY. —*v.t.* see SUCCESS.

acerbic, *adj.* bitter; harsh, severe. See PUNGENCY, SEVERITY.

ache, *n.* PAIN. —*v.i.* hurt, smart, throb, PAIN; yearn (see DESIRE).

achieve, *v.t.* accomplish, attain, reach. See COMPLETION. *Ant.,* fail.

Achilles' heel, weak point, chink in one's armor. See WEAKNESS.

acid, *adj.* sour, bitter, tart, vinegary; acrimonious, cutting, caustic. See SOURNESS, DISCOURTESY. *Ant.,* sweet, bland; basic.

acid test, litmus test (see EXPERIMENT).

acknowledge, *v.* admit, confess, allow, own up to; ANSWER, receipt. See DISCLOSURE, EVIDENCE, GRATITUDE. *Ant.,* deny, disavow.

acme, *n.* summit, pinnacle (see HEIGHT).

acolyte, *n.* altar boy *or* girl; attendant, assistant; novice. See RELIGION, AUXILIARY, BEGINNING.

acoustic, *n.* See SOUND.

acquaint, *v.t.* inform, notify, tell; familiarize, teach. See INFORMATION, FRIEND, LEARNING.

acquaintance, *n.* familiarity, experience, KNOWLEDGE, ken; FRIEND.

acquiesce, *v.i.* agree, accede, ASSENT, concur, CONSENT. See OBEDIENCE, SUBMISSION.

ACQUISITION
Act of obtaining

Nouns—1, *(something acquired)* acquisition, acquirement, accession, obtainment, procurement; collection, accumulation, amassing, gathering, reaping, gleaning, picking (up); trover. See RECEIVING, POSSESSION, ASSEMBLAGE, STORE, ADDITION.

2, *(something acquired by force)* seizure, confiscation, commandeering, attachment, appropriation, apprehension, expropriation, dispossession; abduction, kidnaping; annexation; STEALING, theft.

3, *(something stolen)* haul, catch; windfall; spoils, plunder, loot, booty, payoff, split. *Informal,* pickings. *Slang,* the take, gravy, velvet.

4, *(one who acquires)* acquirer, obtainer, *etc.;* buyer, purchaser, vendee; inheritor, legatee; good bargainer *or* trader; winner, captor, thief. *Informal,* horsetrader.

5, *(urge to acquire)* acquisitiveness, ambition, hunger; covetousness, avarice; greed, voracity. See DESIRE.

6, *(tool for acquiring)* claw, talon, pincer, tongs, pliers.

Verbs—1, acquire, get, find, gain, obtain, come by, dig up *or* out; secure, win, earn, pull down, realize, receive, take; collect, amass, reap, crop, gather, glean, scare *or* scrape up, scrape together; inherit, come in for, come by honestly; PURCHASE. *Informal,* step into; get hold of, pick up, rake in. *Slang,* clean up, help oneself (to), line one's pockets *or* purse, score, rack up.

2, *(acquire by force)* appropriate, take over, assume, take possession of, commandeer, confiscate, expropriate, arrogate; annex, attach; preempt, usurp; catch, nab, bag, pocket; capture, seize; take away; grasp, clinch, clutch, grip, grab, snatch, seize, cop, snap up, lay hold of, lay one's hands on; beg, borrow, or steal. *Slang,* latch *or* glom on to, hook, snag, collar, corral, drum up, scare *or* scrape up.

Adjectives—acquisitive, avaricious, greedy, grasping, covetous; accessible, obtainable, to be had. *Slang,* on the make, grabby.

Phrases—you cannot get blood from a stone; if you don't speculate, you can't accumulate.

Antonyms, see GIVING, RELINQUISHMENT, LOSS, POSSESSION.

---

acquit, *v.t.* exonerate; discharge, pay. See ACQUITTAL, PAYMENT. *Ant.,* convict.

acquit oneself, *v.* behave; conduct, comport, *or* bear oneself; pay off, settle, square. See CONDUCT, PAYMENT.

ACQUITTAL
Exoneration

Nouns—acquittal, quittance, exculpation, absolution, exoneration, clearing, VINDICA-
TION; discharge, release, dismissal, grace, quietus, reprieve, respite, absolution, remission; amnesty, EXEMPTION. See FORGIVENESS, LIBERATION.

Verbs—acquit, exculpate, exonerate, clear, absolve, vindicate; pardon, grant remission *or*
amnesty, reprieve, discharge, release, [set] free; exempt. *Informal*, whitewash; let off.

Adjectives—acquitted, vindicated, *etc.*; quit, free, clear; in the clear.

Quotations—History will absolve me (*Fidel Castro*).

Antonyms, see CONDEMNATION.

---

acrid, *adj.* pungent, biting, acid; corrosive, caustic. See SOURNESS, PUNGENCY.

acrimony, *n.* bitterness, rancor, acerbity,
asperity, RESENTMENT, DISCOURTESY,
PUNGENCY. *Ant.,* civility; goodwill, amiability.

acrobat, *n.* gymnast, tumbler, contortionist.
See DRAMA, EXERTION, ELASTICITY.

acronym, *n.* acrostic. See SHORTNESS.

acrophobia, *n.* See FEAR.

across, *adv.* crosswise, athwart. —*prep.*
on, over, athwart. See CROSSING.

across-the-board, *adj.* all-inclusive, comprehensive (see INCLUSION).

acrostic, *n.* acronym; double acrostic. See
WORD, SHORTNESS.

act, *n. & v.* See ACTION, DRAMA, CONDUCT,
AFFECTATION, REPRESENTATION, RULE.

acting, *adj.* substitute, representative,
DEPUTY. See SUBSTITUTION.

ACTION
Performance

Nouns—1, *(act of doing)* action, performance, operation, execution, enactment, PRO-
DUCTION; process, procedure, proceeding, transaction; behavior, CONDUCT; work,
EXERTION. See ACTIVITY.

2, *(result of acting)* act, affair, effort, job, deed, business, work; stunt; exploit, feat,
enterprise; transaction, operation, step, move[ment]; LAWSUIT, job action; battle (see
WARFARE, CONTENTION). *Informal*, stunt.

3, *(one who acts)* doer, hack (see AGENT).

Verbs—act, do, execute, perform, function; operate, work, practice, exercise, commit,
perpetrate; raise *or* lift a finger *or* a hand; militate; take care of, bring off, carry out,
put into effect, translate into action; take effect; take action, proceed, go ahead, do
something, lift a finger; progress (see PROGRESSION); labor, toil, drudge, ply; have
many irons in the fire. *Informal*, run with it *or* the ball, put one's money where one's
mouth is, get with the program.

Adjectives—acting, active, operative, in operation, in action, at work, on duty; functional, effective, efficient; hands on; actionable (see LAWSUIT). *Informal,* in harness.

Adverbs—in the act, conspicuously, flagrantly, in flagrante delicto, red-handed.

Phrases — actions speak louder than words; it is better to light one candle than to curse
the darkness; action without thought is like shooting without aim; we do as we are;
we become as we do.

Quotations—Action is eloquence (*Shakespeare*), If it were done when 'tis done, then
'twere well it were done quickly (*Shakespeare*), Action is consolatory (*Joseph Conrad*), I am a verb (*Ulysses S. Grant*).

Antonyms, see INACTIVITY, NEGLECT, REPOSE.

ACTIVITY
State of being active

Nouns—1, *(state of being active)* activity, activeness, business, ENERGY, liveliness, animation; briskness, quickness, alertness; wakefulness, vigil; alacrity, zeal, dash, fervor, eagerness, vivacity, VIGOR, spirit; activism. See ACTION.

2, *(result of activity)* movement, fuss, ado, bustle (see AGITATION); three-ring circus; high gear; industry, diligence, assiduity, assiduousness; activities, comings and goings, goings-on.

3, *(one who acts)* activist, new broom; fan, devotee, addict. *Informal,* hustler, go-getter, ball of fire. *Slang,* live wire; freak, eager beaver.

4, *(that which awakens)* alarm clock; reveille. *Informal,* wake-up call.

Verbs—1, *(act)* be active, busy, *etc.,* have one's hands full, have other fish to fry, have many irons in the fire; bestir oneself, come to life, come alive, get up, go about *or* at, look alive, get into the swing of things, bustle, fuss, stir one's stumps, blow away the cowbwebs; feel one's oats. *Informal,* come alive, stir. *Slang,* get on the stick. See HASTE.

2, *(make active)* activate, actuate, animate; wake [up], awaken, [a]rouse, build a fire under. See ATTENTION.

Adjectives—1, *(in action)* active, busy, astir, at it, in the swim; brisk, alert, spry, smart, quick, spanking; energetic, lively, alive, vivacious, keen, eager; frisky, feisty, forward, spirited; up and doing, quick on the trigger, on the jump, on the go, on the job, on one's toes, in high gear, in full swing, on the fly *or* the job. *Informal,* snappy, psyched up.

2, *(active at work)* working, on duty, at work; in commission, in circulation; in effect, in force; industrious, diligent, assiduous. *Informal,* in harness.

3, awake, up, conscious; wakeful, sleepless, insomniac.

Adverbs—actively, *etc.* See HASTE.

Phrases—a rolling stone gathers no moss; no peace for the wicked.

Quotations—It is wonderful how much may be done if we are always doing (*Thomas Jefferson*), Let us, then, be up and doing (*Longfellow*).

Antonyms, see INACTIVITY, REPOSE.

---

actor, actress, *n.* performer, player; tragedian, comedian, Thespian; playactor; doer, worker. See AGENT, DRAMA.

actual, *adj.* real, veritable, true, genuine; concrete, factual. See EXISTENCE, PRESENT, TRUTH. *Ant.,* fictitious, spurious.

actuary, *n.* clerk, registrar; statistician. See NUMERATION.

actuate, *v.t.* move, induce, compel, persuade; start, get under way. See CAUSE, BEGINNING.

acumen, *n.* discernment, shrewdness, penetration; INTELLIGENCE. *Ant.,* dullness, obtuseness.

acute, *adj.* shrewd, discerning, astute; sharp, poignant, keen, pointed, severe. See INTELLIGENCE, CUNNING, SHARPNESS. *Ant.,* dull, chronic.

ad, *n.* See ADVERTISEMENT.

adage, *n.* proverb, saw, saying, aphorism, motto, MAXIM.

adamant, *adj.* adamantine, hard; inflexible, immovable, firm. See HARDNESS, OBSTINACY. *Ant.,* easygoing; yielding.

adapt, *v.* suit, conform, regulate, fit; adjust, convert, reconcile. See AGREEMENT.

add, *v.* See ADDITION, NUMERATION. *Ant.,* subtract, withdraw.

addendum, *n.* ADDITION; appendix.

adder, *n.* puff adder, VIPER.

addict, *n.* devotee, fan, enthusiast; user, slave (to). *Slang,* head, junkie, freak, mainliner. See HABIT, ACTIVITY.

ADDITION
Process of adding

Nouns—1, *(act of adding)* addition, INCREASE, EXPANSION, annexation, accession; corollary, concomitant (see ACCOMPANIMENT). See SEQUENCE, JUNCTION, AUXILIARY. 2, *(something added)* adjunct; affix, prefix, suffix; appendix, INSERTION, postscript, epilogue, addendum, supplement, attachment, appendage; extension, annex, wing, add-on; rider, codicil; flap, tab, tag; bonus; grace period; bells and whistles; additive. 3, *(mathematics)* plus [sign], addend, sum, total, subtotal; adding machine, calculator, abacus. See NUMERATION, COMPUTERS.

Verbs—add, affix, annex, superimpose, append, subjoin, figure in; tack on; compute, sum, foot, total, tot(e) up. *Informal,* hitch on.

Adjectives—added, *etc.*; additive, cumulative; supplementary, additional, another, further, extra, more; AUXILIARY, ancillary; surplus.

Adverbs—in addition, again, more, plus, extra, besides, also, too, at that, and then some, et cetera, etc., to boot, as well, into the bargain, for good measure, over and above, and so forth, and so on, moreover, furthermore; by the way, by the bye, on the side, in passing. *Informal,* and what not, and what have you, and all that jazz.

Prepositions—apart from, aside from; together with, let alone, not to mention, much less, not to speak of, to say nothing of, as well as.

Conjunctions—and, also, in addition to being.

Antonyms, see DEDUCTION.

---

addle, *v.* confuse, muddle, befuddle. See DISORDER.

address, *v.t.* direct; court; woo; accost, greet, approach, speak to. —*n.* street and number; residence, home; SPEECH, discourse, oration; cleverness, dexterity. See DIRECTION, INDICATION, ABODE, COURTESY, SKILL. *Ant.,* overlook, shun; adroitness.

adduce, *v.t.* present, bring forward, cite, mention. See EVIDENCE.

adept, *adj.* skillful, dexterous, apt; practiced, expert, proficient. —*n.* expert, master. See SKILL. *Ant.,* clumsy; faker.

adequate, *adj.* enough, sufficient; serviceable; satisfactory, ample. See SUFFICIENCY, UTILITY. *Ant.,* inadequate, unfit.

adhere, *v.i.* cling (to), stick; hold closely to. See COHERENCE, DUTY.

adherent, *n.* follower, believer; partisan, disciple. See LEARNING, AUXILIARY.

adhesive, *adj.* sticky, gluey, tenacious. —*n.* adherent; glue, cement, *etc.* See COHERENCE.

ad hoc, *n.* expedient (see EXPEDIENCE). —*adj.* provisional; stopgap, expedient. See EXPEDIENCE, UNPREPAREDNESS.

adieu, *n.* farewell (see DEPARTURE).

ad infinitum, *Lat.,* to infinity; without end. See INFINITY, PERPETUITY, SPACE.

adjacent, *adj.* adjoining, near, close by, next to; touching, bordering, contiguous, neighboring. See CONTACT. *Ant.,* distant, remote, detached.

adjoin, *v.* touch, abut, border, meet, neighbor. See CONTACT.

adjourn, *v.* defer, postpone; discontinue; END. See LATENESS. *Ant.,* convene, prolong.

adjudge, adjudicate, *v.* judge (see JUDGMENT).

adjunct, *n.* ADDITION, appendix, appendage, annex; accessory, extension, postscript; complement, INSERTION; ACCOMPANIMENT.

adjure, *v.t.* charge, bind, command. See REQUEST.

adjust, *v.t.* fix, adapt, true, regulate, straighten; settle, compensate; equalize, rate. See AGREEMENT, EQUALITY.

adjutant, *n.* assistant; aide-de-camp (see AUXILIARY).

ad-lib, *v., informal,* extemporize, improvise. See UNPREPAREDNESS.

ad libitum, *Lat.,* at [one's] pleasure. See WILL.

administer, *v.t.* govern, rule, manage, control; give, dose, dispense. See AUTHORITY, GIVING, APPORTIONMENT, CONDUCT.

administration, *n.* CONDUCT; government,

regime, AUTHORITY; GIVING; APPORTIONMENT.

admirable, *adj.* commendable, exemplary; lovable, likable. See RESPECT, APPROBATION. *Ant.,* repulsive, disreputable.

admire, *v.t.* esteem, idolize, venerate, RESPECT; regard; WONDER, marvel. *Ant.,* despise, dislike.

admission, *n.* confession, DISCLOSURE; entry, admittance; INGRESS; cover [charge], charge, minimum; CONSENT. See INCLUSION. *Ant.,* denial, refusal.

admit, *v.t.* let in; induct, matriculate; concede, acknowledge; receive, allow, 'fess *or* own up (*inf.*). See DISCLOSURE, RECEIVING, PERMISSION. *Ant.,* deny, refuse, repel.

admonition, *n.* reproof (see DISAPPROBATION); caution, WARNING.

ad nauseam, Lat. to the point of nausea; boringly. See WEARINESS.

ado, *n.* bustle, ACTIVITY; fuss, commotion, DISORDER.

adobe, *n.* See ABODE.

adolescence, *n.* YOUTH, minority, juvenility; teens, teenage, nonage; puberty.

adopt, *v.t.* embrace, take to oneself, assume; foster, give a home to, provide a home for, accept as one's own. See CHOICE.

adore, *v.t.* LOVE, WORSHIP, idolize. *Ant.,* hate, condemn.

adorn, *v.t.* ORNAMENT, embellish, deck, garnish, beautify. *Ant.,* mar, deface.

ad rem, Lat. relevant, to the point. See RELATION.

adrift, *adj.* afloat; drifting, loose. See DISJUNCTION, DISPERSION, CHANGEABLENESS.

adroit, *adj.* dexterous, deft, skillful. See SKILL. *Ant.,* clumsy, awkward.

adulate, *v.* flatter (see FLATTERY).

adult, *adj.* grown[-up], full-grown, mature, ripe. —*n.* grown-up, big person; major, senior. See AGE, MALE, FEMALE.

adulterate, *v.t.* mix, water down, weaken, dilute; debase, corrupt. See DETERIORATION, MIXTURE, WEAKNESS. *Ant.,* purify, clarify.

adultery, *n.* infidelity, fornication, licentiousness. See IMPURITY.

adumbrate, *v.t.* foreshadow (see PREDICTION).

ad valorem, Lat. according to value. See RELATION, PRICE.

advance, *v.* progress, go forward, proceed; further, second, AID. —*n.* progress, rise; success, gain; prepayment. See PROGRESSION, DEBT, OFFER. *Ant.,* retard; recede, withdraw.

advantage, *n.* SUPERIORITY, upper hand, leverage, the better (of); gain, profit, benefit, odds, favor, ace in the hole (*inf.*). See CHANCE, SUCCESS. *Ant.,* drawback, handicap.

advent, *n.* arrival; coming. See APPROACH.

adventitious, *adj.* foreign, EXTRINSIC.

adventure, *n.* enterprise, UNDERTAKING; happening, event; risk, hazard, venture. See CHANCE. —*v.* embark upon; dare. See DANGER.

adventurer, *n.* voyager, traveler, wanderer, roamer; gambler, fortune hunter, freelance, soldier of fortune; adventuress (*derog.*). See TRAVEL, CHANCE.

adversary, *n.* opponent, enemy, foe (see OPPOSITION). *Ant.,* ally, FRIEND.

ADVERSITY
Ill fortune

Nouns—1, (*difficulty*) adversity, affliction; bad, ill, adverse, *or* hard luck *or* fortune, Weltschmerz; evil lot; force majeur, frowns of fortune; evil star *or* genius; ups and downs of life, vicissitude; hard case *or* lines; peck *or* sea of troubles, hell upon earth, gall and wormwood; slough of despond; Pandora's box. *Informal,* downside. See EVIL, FAILURE, PAIN, DIFFICULTY.

2, (*hardship*) trouble, hardship, bother, curse, POVERTY, tough sledding, a hard row to hoe; hot seat, thorn in one's side, bête noire; midlife crisis. *Slang,* crunch.

3, (*bad luck*) evil day; time out of joint; hard times, a dog's life; rainy day; gathering clouds, ill wind; visitation, infliction, distress; bitter pill; trial, ordeal. *Slang,* hard knocks, rough going, tough titty, raw deal, bad break.

4, (*accident*) mishap, mischance, misadventure, misfortune; disaster, calamity, fatality, catastrophe; accident, casualty, wreck, collision, crash; cross, reverse, check, contretemps, anomaly, rub; reversal, setback, comedown (see DETERIORATION); losing game; friendly fire; ecocatastrophe, nuclear winter, oil spill. *Slang,* fender-bender, meltdown.

5, *(victim of adversity)* victim, unfortunate; downtrodden, dispossessed, homeless, *etc. Informal,* loser.

Verbs—**1,** go hard *or* ill with, weigh on; fall on evil days; go downhill; go to rack and ruin; go to the dogs, touch *or* hit bottom; fall from high estate; be badly off, have seen better days, have two strikes against one; come to grief. *Slang,* draw a blank; lose one's shirt; take one's lumps; have one's ass in a sling.

2, be unlucky, have bad luck. *Slang,* get the short end of the stick.

3, *(cause adversity)* curse, bring bad luck, cast an evil eye on. *Informal,* jinx, hex.

Adjectives—**1,** *(being cursed)* unfortunate, unhappy; in adverse circumstances, unprosperous, luckless, hapless, out of luck, down on one's luck; in trouble, in a bad way, in an evil plight, in Dutch; under a cloud; bleak, clouded; ill *or* badly off; poor, down in the world, down at heel, hard put [to it], down and out, undone, under the harrow, up against it *or* the wall; underprivileged. *Slang,* on the ropes, in a jam, out on a limb, up a tree, up shit creek [without a paddle], between the Devil and the deep blue sea, between Scylla and Charybdis, between a rock and a hard place, behind the eight ball.

2, unlucky, unblest, ill-fated, ill-starred, star-crossed, born under an evil star; out of luck, down on one's luck.

3, *(causing distress)* adverse, untoward; disastrous, calamitous, ruinous, dire, grievous.

Adverbs—adversely, unfavorably; disastrously, grievously; if worst comes to worst; from bad to worse; out of the frying pan into the fire.

Interjections—tough luck! *Slang,* tough shit! hard cheese!

Phrases—adversity makes strange bedfellows; when the going gets tough, the tough get going; misfortunes never come singly; a dose of adversity is often as needful as a dose of medicine.

Quotations—The whips and scorns of time (*Shakespeare*), Through thick and thin (*Chaucer*), Sweet are the uses of adversity (*Shakespeare*), By trying we can easily learn to endure adversity. Another man's, I mean (*Mark Twain*), These are the times that try men's souls (*Thomas Paine*), Adversity is the first path to truth (*Lord Byron*), Man is born unto trouble, as the sparks fly upward (*Bible*).

Antonyms, see PROSPERITY.

---

advert, *v.i.* refer (to), direct *or* turn ATTENTION (to).

advertisement, *n.* announcement, [public] notice; commercial, [want, classified, personal, *etc.*] ad; advert, advertorial, plug, blurb (*all inf.*); publicity. See PUBLICATION.

ADVICE
Counsel

Nouns—**1,** *(help given)* advice, counsel, suggestion, recommendation; exhortation, expostulation; consultation, counseling, guidance; hint; admonition (see WARNING); sermon; guidance, instruction, pointer, word to the wise, whisper, word in the ear; charge. *Informal,* flea in the ear, two cents' worth, tip.

2, *(one who advises)* adviser, prompter, counselor, Nestor, Polonius, monitor, Dutch uncle; sherpa; mentor (see TEACHING). *Informal,* maven, kibitzer, backseat driver, Monday-morning quarterback.

3, *(something that advises)* guide; consultation, COUNCIL, conference; INFORMATION, NEWS.

Verbs—**1,** *(give advice)* advise, [give] counsel, have a word with; suggest, recommend, prescribe, exhort; instruct, guide, coach; expostulate, dissuade; warn (see WARNING). *Informal,* give one a piece of one's mind, put a flea in one's ear, kibitz.

2, *(consult together)* advise with; consult together; compare notes; hold a council, deliberate, be closeted with, confer.

3, take *or* follow advice, be advised, follow one's lead. *Informal,* go along with, buy into.

Adjectives—1, *(giving advice)* advisory, consultative, consultant; recommendatory, hortative, persuasive, dissuasive, admonitory, cautionary, WARNING.

2, *(worthy of being recommended)* advisable, desirable, commendable.

Phrases—another country heard from; too many cooks spoil the broth; ask advice, but use your common sense; consult with your pillow.

Quotations—Good counselors lack no clients (*Shakespeare*), The smallest current coin (*Ambrose Bierce*), I always pass on good advice . . . It is never of any use to oneself (*Oscar Wilde*), Good but rarely came from good advice (*Lord Byron*).

Antonyms, see DISSUASION.

---

advocate, *v.* favor, plead; recommend, suggest; support. —*n.* patron, supporter; defender; lawyer, attorney. See FRIEND, AUXILIARY, LAWSUIT. *Ant.,* oppose; detractor.

aegis, *n.* protection, sponsorship. See AID.

aerate, *v.t.* AIR; carbonate, charge.

aerial, *adj.* airy, atmospheric; lofty, soaring; graceful, ethereal; visionary. See AIR, HEIGHT, INSUBSTANTIALITY, IMAGINATION. —*n.* rabbit ears (see COMMUNICATION).

aeronautics, *n.* See AVIATION.

aerosol, *n.* spray, atomizer. See VAPOR.

aerospace, *n.* See ASTRONAUTICS, UNIVERSE.

aesthetic, *adj.* artistic, tasteful, beautiful. See BEAUTY, SENSIBILITY.

afar, *adv.* at *or* from a DISTANCE, afar. *Ant.,* near.

affable, *adj.* friendly, sociable, gracious; approachable. See COURTESY. *Ant.,* discontented, sour, impolite.

affair, *n.* occasion, event, happening, OCCURRENCE; BUSINESS; party (see SOCIALITY); amour, love affair, liaison (see LOVE).

affect, *v.t.* INFLUENCE, touch; concern, relate to; move, stir. See RELATION, DISEASE, FEELING, AFFECTATION. —*n.* feeling, emotion. See SENSIBILITY.

AFFECTATION
Artificiality of manner

Nouns—1, *(affected quality)* affectation, affectedness, artificiality, insincerity, histrionics, OSTENTATION; charlatanism, quackery (see DECEPTION); pretense, gloss, veneer, facade, false show *or* front; pose, pretension, airs; false modesty; pedantry, euphuism; preciosity, preciousness; conceit; foppery, dandyism, coxcombry, stiffness, formality; mannerism, character trait, quirk, idiosyncrasy; prudery, prissiness, coquetry, puritanism, sanctimony; posing, posturing; crocodile tears, prunes and prisms. *Informal,* trademark. *Slang,* side; phoniness, put-on. See FALSEHOOD.

2, *(affected person)* fop, coxcomb, dandy, beau, popinjay, blade, sport; attitudinarian; poser, poseur, pretender, hypocrite; faker, sham, pedant, bluestocking, prude, prig, puritan; charlatan, deceiver; whited sepulcher. *Informal,* nice Nelly, Adonis. *Slang,* dude, macaroni; chalker, cookie, frosty; drugstore cowboy; choirboy; straw man; phony, fraud, fake.

Verbs—affect, act, put on *or* give oneself airs, feign, sham; simper, mince; attitudinize, pose, posture, assume *or* strike an attitude, put up *or* on a front; make [out] like; overact, dramatize. *Informal,* fake, playact, camp it up.

Adjectives—affected, pretentious, artificial, insincere, pedantic, stilted, stagy, theatrical, sham, histrionic; unnatural, self-conscious, stiff, starchy, formal, prim, smug, prudish, priggish, puritanical, sanctimonious; foppish, dandified; overmodest; precious, mannered, mincing, namby-pamby; glib, butter wouldn't melt in one's mouth, holier than thou. *Informal,* phony, fake; art[s]y, hinkty, plastic; tight as a drum, goat *or* tick.

Adverbs—affectedly, prudishly, *etc.*; for show *or* effect.

Quotations—Methinks he doth protest too much (*Shakespeare*).

Antonyms, see SIMPLENESS, MODESTY, PROBITY.

affection, *n.* LOVE, regard, esteem, liking, shine (*inf.*). See FEELING, ENDEARMENT. *Ant.,* DISLIKE.

affectionate, *adj.* loving, warmhearted; tender. See LOVE, ENDEARMENT. *Ant.,* neglectful, cold, distant.

affidavit, *n.* deposition, attestation. See EVIDENCE.

affiliate, *v.i.* join, unite. —*n.* associate; branch, subsidiary. See COOPERATION, COMBINATION.

affinity, *n.* liking, ATTRACTION; RELATION, SIMILARITY. *Ant.,* aversion, disparity.

affirm, *v.* assert, declare; confirm, ratify. See AFFIRMATION, ASSENT, APPROBATION. *Ant.,* deny.

AFFIRMATION
Positive assertion

Nouns—1, *(positive statement)* affirmation, statement, allegation, assertion, predication, declaration, profession, proclamation, manifesto, averment. *Informal,* say-so. See INFORMATION, BELIEF.

2, *(legal statement)* asseveration, swearing, oath, affidavit, [sworn] testimony *or* statement, deposition (see EVIDENCE); avouchment, avowal; protestation, profession; ASSENT.

3, *(saying)* observation, expression; saying, dictum, *ipse dixit*. See CERTAINTY.

4, PROMISE, pledge, vow, oath, word, assurance, warrant; oath *or* pledge of allegiance.

Verbs—1, *(state positively)* affirm, assert, say, predicate, declare, state; emphasize, protest, profess; proclaim, submit, maintain, insist, contend, hold; have one's say, declare oneself, nail one's colors to the mast, speak up, give voice *or* utterance (to), speak one's mind; stand up and be counted. *Informal,* put in one's two cents [worth], hammer [away] at.

2, *(claim)* put forth, put forward, express; allege, set forth, hold out, maintain, contend, pronounce. *Informal,* claim.

3, *(make a legal statement)* depose, depone, aver, avow, avouch, asseverate, swear; take one's oath; make an affidavit; kiss the book, vow, stand by, be sworn; vouch, warrant, certify. *Informal,* swear by bell, book, and candle, swear till one is black *or* blue in the face, call heaven to witness, cross one's heart [and hope to die].

4, PROMISE, pledge, vow, warrant.

5, swear [in], administer an oath.

Adjectives—1, affirmative, declaratory, declarative, predicatory, pronunciative, assertive, loud and clear; positive, certain, decided; express, emphatic; unretracted; predicable.

2, deposed, *etc.*; sworn.

Adverbs—affirmatively, in the affirmative, *etc.*; with emphasis, loud and clear, ex cathedra, without fear of contradiction; under oath, on one's honor.

Antonyms, see NEGATION, NULLIFICATION.

affix, *v.t.* fasten, attach; append. See ADDITION, CONNECTION.

afflict, *v.t.* beset, trouble; burden (with). See PAIN, ADVERSITY.

affluent, *adj.* flowing; abundant, plentiful; rich, wealthy. See MONEY, PROSPERITY, FLUIDITY. *Ant.,* destitute, poor.

afford, *v.t.* manage, bear; supply, yield; produce; make available, furnish. See GIVING, PROVISION.

affray, *n.* quarrel, brawl, disturbance. See CONTENTION.

affront, *v. & n.* insult, slight, snub. See DISRESPECT.

aficionado, *n.* enthusiast, devotee. See DESIRE.

afield, *adv.* abroad; off the beaten track. See EXTRINSIC.

afire, aflame, *adj.* See HEAT, FEELING.

afloat, *adj.* floating; in circulation. See PUBLICATION, LEVITY.

aflutter, *adj.* agitated (see AGITATION).

afoot, *adj.* walking, on foot; in progress. See TRAVEL, PROGRESSION.

aforesaid, *adj.* former, aforementioned. See PRECEDENCE.

a fortiori, Lat. all the more. See REASONING.

afoul, *adv.* entangled (see DIFFICULTY).

afraid, *adj.* See FEAR. *Ant.,* fearless.

African American, *adj.* black, colored, Negro, Afro-American. —*n.* black [man or woman], person of color, colored person. See HUMANITY.

aft, *adv.* abaft, astern, rearward. See REAR.

after, *prep.* past, beyond, behind. —*adj.* later, subsequent, following. —*adv.* afterward, subsequently, not now, later. See SEQUENCE, PURSUIT.

aftermath, *n.* results, consequence[s]. See EFFECT.

afternoon, *n.* post meridiem, P.M.; twilight hour. See CHRONOMETRY.

afterthought, *n.* reflection; hindsight. See LATENESS. *Ant.,* forethought.

afterward(s), *adv.* subsequently (see SEQUENCE).

again, *adv.* once more, afresh, anew, repeatedly; twice; encore; in ADDITION. See REPETITION.

against, *prep.* in OPPOSITION to, counter *or* contrary to; dead against, at cross purposes; in exchange for. See CONTACT, SUBSTITUTION, PREPARATION. *Ant.,* for.

agape, *adj.* See OPENING, WONDER.

AGE
Old age

Nouns—1, age, years, OLDNESS; life expectancy, life span; longevity, length of years; gerontology, geriatrics; gerontocracy; ageism.

2, *(maturity)* adulthood, man- *or* womanhood, maturity; legal *or* lawful age, voting, drinking, driving, *etc.* age; prime of life; years of discretion, majority; middle age, the afternoon of life, midlife crisis; change of life, menopause, male menopause, climacteric; seniority, eldership, primogeniture.

3, *(agedness)* old *or* advanced age, senility; senescence; years, anility, gray hairs, climacteric, menopause; declining years, decrepitude, infirmity, feebleness (see DETERIORATION), superannuation; second childhood, dotage; vale of years, decline of life, three-score years and ten; ripe [old] age, silver threads among the gold. See TIME.

4, *(aged person)* adult, grown-up, grown person; old man, elder, doyen, father; old woman, dowager, matron, crone; senior citizen, old-timer, golden ager, patriarch, graybeard, gray eminence, Methuselah, Father Time; veteran; firstling, eldest; sexagenarian, septuagenarian, octogenarian, nonagenarian, centenarian. *Informal,* baby boomer, generation X, postpreppie. *Slang,* fossil, gaffer, geezer, oldster, old rip, sugar daddy, longbeard, harpie.

Verbs—1, age, grow old, decline, senesce, get on [in years]; dodder, shrivel, wizen; live to a ripe old age; be aged, have seen better days, show one's age, have one foot in the grave. *Informal,* be over the hill, have the dwindlies.

2, mature, come of age, grow up, ripen, mellow, temper; come to man's estate, attain *or* reach majority, have cut one's eyeteeth, have sown one's wild oats, settle down.

Adjectives—1, *(being old)* aged, old, elder[ly], senior, senile; aging, graying, senescent; matronly, anile; [along *or* on] in years; ripe, mellow, run to seed, declining, past one's prime; grayheaded, hoary, venerable, gray, timeworn; antiquated (see OLDNESS); decrepit, doddering, wizened, wrinkled, superannuated; of a certain age, no [spring] chicken, over the hill, old as Methuselah, long in the tooth; patriarchal, ancient; advanced in life *or* years; stricken in years; aging, senescent, getting on [in years], long in the tooth, not as young as one used to be; on one's last legs, having one foot in the grave. *Slang,* gaga.

2, *(being mature)* of [full] age, out of one's teens, grown up, mature, full grown, developed, ripe; over age; in one's prime, middle-aged, adult; womanly, matronly; marriageable, nubile (see MARRIAGE); old enough to know better.

Phrases—there's no fool like an old fool; if youth knew, if age could; never send a boy to do a man's job.

Quotations—Life begins at forty (*Walter B. Pitkin*), Midway along the path of our life (*Dante*); Every man desires to live long; but no man would be old (*Jonathan Swift*); Will you still need me, will you still feed me, when I'm sixty-four? (*Lennon/McCartney*), Old age is the most unexpected of all the things that can happen to a man (*Leon Trotsky*), It's the only disease you don't look forward to being cured of (*Welles/Mankiewicz*), It is sobering to consider that when Mozart was my age he had already been dead for a year (*Tom Lehrer*), There's many a good tune played on an old fiddle (*Samuel Butler*).

Antonyms, see YOUTH.

---

ageless, *adj.* perpetual, young at heart. See PERPETUITY, YOUTH.

agelong, *adj.* lengthy, protracted. See DURABILITY.

AGENCY
Means of producing effects

Nouns—**1,** *(act of an agent)* agency, operation; working, POWER, function; office, exercise, play, work; interworking, interaction; causality, causation (see CAUSE); INSTRUMENTALITY, action, MEANS; mediation, medium; METHOD, modus operandi, technique, routine, process.

2, *(one who acts)* AGENT, doer, performer, perpetrator, operator; executor, executrix, administrator, administratrix; practitioner, worker, stager.

3, *(one who produces something)* actor, actress; workman, operative, artisan; craftsman, mechanic; working *or* laboring man *or* woman; hewer of wood and drawer of water, laborer, navvy; handyman, journeyman, hack; tool, beast of burden, drudge; maker, artificer, ARTIST, wright, manufacturer, architect, builder, mason, smith, mechanic, engineer.

Verbs—**1,** *(act)* operate, execute, work; act upon; perform, play, support, sustain, maintain; take effect, quicken, strike.

2, *(put into action)* come *or* bring into operation *or* play, activate; have free play *or* rein; bring to bear upon.

Adjectives—operative, efficient, efficacious, practical, effectual; at work, on foot; acting, doing; in operation, in force, in action, in play; acted upon.

---

agenda, *n.* things to be done, order of the day, schedule, calendar, docket, program, PLAN. See BUSINESS.

AGENT
One who acts for another

Nouns—**1,** *(one who acts for another)* agent, representative, ombudsman, delegate, emissary, instrument, envoy, deputy, proxy, broker, factor, attorney; commissary, commissioner; beadsman *or* -woman; trustee, nominee; salesman, saleswoman (see SALE); middleman, intermediary, go-between, internuncio; power broker; spokesperson, spokesman, spokeswoman, voice; commission agent, auctioneer, one's man of business, [personal] secretary; ambassador[-at-large], ambassadress[-at-large], diplomat, legate, minister [plenipotentiary]; embassy, legation; apostle, messenger; advertising, book, press, publicity, *or* theatrical agent; secret agent (see INQUIRY). *Informal,* connection. *Slang,* bagman, -woman, *or* -person; mouthpiece. See SUBSTITUTION.

2, *(assistant)* lieutenant, henchman; legman; vicar; assistant, right-hand man; man, woman, boy *or* girl Friday; handmaiden, SERVANT, slave; midwife, accoucheur, obstetrician; robot, cat's paw. *Informal,* stooge. See INSTRUMENTALITY.

3, *(act of acting for another)* deputation, assignment; mission, legation, embassy; going-between, mediation; representation, SUBSTITUTION.

Verbs—represent, act on behalf of, act for; substitute for (see SUBSTITUTION); appoint, deputize (see COMMISSION); baby-, house-, dog-(*etc.*)sit; liaise; network.

Adjectives—deputy, representative; plenipotentiary; ministerial, diplomatic, ambassadorial, consular.

Quotations—Taxation without representation is tyranny (*James Otis*), When in trouble, delegate (*James H. Boren*), An ambassador is an honest man sent to lie abroad for the good of his country (*Henry Wotton*), A diplomat . . . is a person who can tell you to go to hell in such a way that you actually look forward to the trip (*Caskie Stinnett*).

---

agent provocateur, *Fr.* professional agitator. See REVOLUTION, VIOLENCE.

agglomerate, *v.* conglomerate (see ASSEMBLAGE). —*n. & adj.* cluster (see DENSITY).

agglutinate, *v.* See COHERENCE.

aggrandize, *v.t.* enlarge, extend (see EXPANSION); exaggerate (see EXAGGERATION). *Ant.,* humble, reduce, minimize.

aggravate, *v.* worsen, intensify, INCREASE; *informal,* irritate, annoy, exacerbate (see RESENTMENT). *Ant.,* alleviate, improve.

aggregate, *n.* total, sum, WHOLE; combination. See QUANTITY, DENSITY.

aggression, *n.* offense, ATTACK, war, invasion; belligerence. See CONTENTION. *Ant.,* PACIFICATION.

aggrieved, *adj.* offended (see RESENTMENT).

aghast, *adj.* awestruck, agape. See FEAR, WONDER.

agile, *adj.* nimble, active, spry; quick, acrobatic, athletic. See ACTIVITY, SKILL. *Ant.,* awkward.

agitate, *v.* foment, instigate, *etc.* trouble; disturb, perturb. See EXCITEMENT, CAUSE, AGITATION.

AGITATION
Violent motion

Nouns—1, *(quality of being agitated)* agitation, stir, tremor, shake, ripple; trepidation, quiver, quaver, dance; flutter. *Informal,* sweat.

2, *(result of agitation)* perturbation, commotion, disquiet, tumult, dither, bustle, fuss, EXCITEMENT, flurry; ebullience; turmoil, hurly-burly, turbulence (see VIOLENCE); demonstration (see REVOLUTION). See DISORDER.

3, *(type of agitation)* spasm, throe, fit, throb[bing], crick, stitch, twinge, palpitation, convulsion, paroxysm; epilepsy (see DISEASE); shaking, shivering, shuddering, *etc.,* St. Vitus' dance, fidgets; delirium tremens (see DRINKING); disturbance, DISORDER; restlessness, jumpiness, nervousness, CHANGEABLENESS; fever, frenzy; ferment, froth, foam, surf, fermentation; ebullition, effervescence; orgasm, climax (see SEX). *Slang,* heebie-jeebies, ants in the pants. See EXCITABILITY.

4, *(agitated person)* bundle of nerves, fussbudget; butterfly. *Slang,* headbanger.

5, *(something that agitates)* agitator, churn, propeller, whirlpool, Jacuzzi; mixer, blender, eggbeater (see MIXTURE).

Verbs—1, *(be agitated)* agitate, shake, tremble, quiver, quaver, quake, shiver, twitch, vellicate, twitter, toss, stagger, bob, reel, sway; wag, wiggle, waggle; wriggle [like an eel]; dance, stumble; throb, pulsate, beat, palpitate, go pit-a-pat; be nervous, flutter, flitter, bustle; fidget, jiggle; ferment, effervesce, fizzle, foam; seethe, boil (over), bubble (up); toss *or* thrash about, toss and turn; shake like an aspen leaf; shake to its foundations. *Informal,* have the jitters, tremble in one's boots, have ants in one's pants. *Slang,* get one's knickers in a twist.

2, *(agitate)* convulse, toss, tumble; flap, brandish, flourish; jiggle, joggle, ruffle, flurry, disturb, fan, stir (up); whip *or* shake up, churn; jounce, bounce.

3, *(bother)* perturb, ruffle, fluster, disturb, rile, startle, shock, give one a turn; pique, infuriate, madden, make one's blood boil, lash into a fury, get on one's nerves, give one fits, give one a hard time, give one gray hair, tie in knots, shake up, throw for a loss.

Adjectives—1, agitated, shaking; jerky, choppy, unsteady; convulsive, spastic; rough, jarring, bumpy, bouncy; orgasmic.

2, perturbed, disturbed, ruffled (see *Verbs,* 3); tremulous; giddy; unquiet, restless, at loose ends, restive, all atwitter, nervous, jittery, jumpy; nervous, jittery, fidgety, jumpy, shaken up; ebullient. *Informal,* antsy, like a monkey on a stick. *Slang,* strung out, all shook up, antsy, squirrelly, in a lather, uptight, aerated, wilding, jacked up, untied, unglued, unraveled, unstuck, unstrung, unwrapped.

Adverbs—agitatedly, shakily, *etc.*; by fits and starts.

Antonyms, see REPOSE.

---

agnostic, *n.* skeptic, doubter (see DOUBT).

Agnus Dei, *Lat.* Lamb of God. See DEITY.

ago, *adv.* since, over, PAST.

agog, *adj.* eager, excited (see EXCITEMENT).

agony, *n.* PAIN, torture; anxiety, anguish; throes of DEATH. *Ant.,* ecstasy.

agree, *v.* yield, CONSENT; ASSENT; coincide, harmonize; conform (see AGREEMENT). *Ant.,* disagree, decline. —agree with, be good for. See HEALTH.

agreeable, *adj.* pleasant, congenial, compatible, harmonious; compliant (see CONSENT). See AGREEMENT, SOCIALITY, PLEASURE. *Ant.,* disagreeable, unpleasant.

AGREEMENT
Concord

Nouns—1, *(quality of agreement)* agreement, accord, accordance, *rapport* (Fr.); unison, harmony, concord, concordance, coincidence, concert; affinity; CONFORMITY, conformance; consonance, consistency, congruity, keeping; congeniality; CORRESPONDENCE, apposition, union. See RIGHTNESS, UNITY.

2, *(state of agreement)* unanimity, common consent, acclamation, chorus; vox populi, public opinion; the silent majority; CONSENT, ASSENT, concurrence, COOPERATION, consensus.

3, *(quality of agreeing)* fitness, aptness, aptitude, applicability, appropriateness, felicity; coaptation, propriety, compatibility; cognation (see RELATION); right person, woman, *or* man in the right place; very thing; decorum, just the thing.

4, *(state of being made to agree)* adaptation, adjustment, accommodation, reconciliation, coordination, regulation, harmonization. See PREPARATION.

5, *(result of agreement)* compact, contract, pact, bargain, meeting of minds, covenant, bond; convention, undertaking; treaty, entente [cordiale], league, alliance; nonagression pact; collective agreement, union *or* wage contract; understanding, bargain; gentlemen's agreement.

6, *(indication of agreement)* signing, signature, handshake; PROMISE; negotiation, execution, enforcement, implementation, observance.

Verbs—1, *(be in agreement)* agree, accord, concur, harmonize, get along, get on; CONSENT, ASSENT; correspond, tally, go with, go together; meet, befit; fall in with, chime in with, fit [right] in, square with, comport with; dovetail, fit like a glove, lend itself to; get together, match, become one; close ranks; see eye to eye, be of one mind, have a meeting of minds, come to an agreement. *Informal,* jibe, check. See SIMILARITY.

2, fit, suit, adapt, tailor, accommodate, reconcile, adjust, tweak; [fine-]tune; harmonize, reconcile; dovetail, square. *Informal,* do the trick, fill the bill.

3, *(make an agreement)* contract, covenant; subcontract, outsource; engage (see PROMISE); stipulate; make *or* come to terms, settle, strike a bargain, come to an understanding; negotiate, bargain, sit down with; sign, shake hands, formalize, strike a bargain; execute, make, carry out, implement, enforce, observe; honor more in the breach than in the observance.

Adjectives—1, *(being in agreement)* agreeing, suiting, in accord, accordant, concordant, consonant, congruous, congruent, correspondent, congenial; harmonious, reconcilable, conformable; in accordance, harmony, *or* keeping with; at one with, of one mind, of one piece; consistent, compatible, proportionate; in phase.

2, *(resulting from agreement)* unanimous, agreed on by all hands, carried [by acclamation]. See ASSENT.

3, *(being suited)* apt, apposite, pat; to the point *or* purpose; happy, felicitous; adapted, apropos, cut out for, in line with, in place, in tune, made-to-order, in character, appropriate, decorous, seasonable, suitable, meet. *Informal,* just what the doctor ordered.

4, contracted, agreed; signed, sealed, and delivered.

Adverbs—1, unanimously, with one voice, with one accord, by common consent, in chorus, to a man, without a dissentient voice; as one man, one and all, on all hands.

2, fittingly, to a T.

3, contractually, according to [the terms of] the agreement *or* contract, as agreed upon.

Prepositions—in agreement with, in line with, in keeping with; together with.

Antonyms, see DISAGREEMENT, DISCORD.

AGRICULTURE
Science of cultivating

Nouns—1, *(art of growing)* agriculture, cultivation, husbandry, farming, tillage, culture; aeroculture, aeroponics, agrobiology, agrology, agronomy, agrostology; gardening, horticulture, floriculture, viniculture, vintage, truck gardening, dry farming, grain farming, extensive *or* intensive cultivation, open-field cultivation, shifting cultivation, slash-and-burn cultivation, terrace cultivation, strip farming, organic farming, monoculture, citriculture; green thumb, growing, raising; aquaculture, fish farming; irrigation (see WATER); arboriculture, forestry, agroforestry, forestation, reforestation, deforestation, lumbering, logging; agroindustry, agribusiness; landscape gardening; georgics, geoponics; permaculture, organic farming; green revolution; agrichemical, fertilizer, manure, muck, side *or* top dressing; smudge; insecticide, pesticide; Future Farmers of America, Four-H; growing season.

2, *(one who grows)* husbandman, horticulturist, gardener, florist, vintager, forester, conservationist; logger, lumberjack; agriculturist, agronomist; gentleman *or* boutique farmer, country squire; dirt farmer; yeoman, farmer, granger, cultivator, tiller of the soil; sharecropper; plowman, reaper, sower; rustic; woodsman; farmworker, farmhand, migrant worker, bracero, campesino, picker, planter, *etc. Informal,* hayseed, hick, rube, peasant, [country] bumpkin, clod[hopper]; white-collar *or* suitcase rancher. See POPULACE.

3, *(place for growing)* farm, grange; field, plot, paddy, swidden; lawn, garden, flower bed; nursery, greenhouse, hothouse, conservatory, potting shed, orangery; bed, border, seed plot, parterre; plantation, ranch, homestead (see ABODE); arboretum, orchard, vineyard, vinery; farmland, grassland; collective farm, cooperative, kibbutz, kolkhoz.

4, *(farm equipment and buildings)* farmhouse, farmstead, grange; farmyard; barn, hovel, lathhouse, granary, grain elevator, hayloft; hayrack; backhoe, baler, binder, colter, combine, crop duster, cultivator, dibble, flail, hoe, harrow, harvester, mattock, mill, pick, pitchfork, plow[share], reaper, rototiller, scythe, sickle, thresher, tiller, tractor, windmill.

5, *(result of growing)* crop, yield, harvest, product, produce; cash crop, field crop; truck; crop rotation, cover crop; subsistence crop; berry crop; legume; cereal, wheat, alfalfa, barley, corn, soybean, *etc.* See VEGETABLE.

6, veterinarian (see DOMESTICATION); school of agriculture. *Informal,* horse doctor. *Slang,* cow college.

7, *(agricultural deities)* fertility god, Persephone, Kore, Dionysus, Demeter, Ceres, Gaea, Pomona, Frey.

Verbs—cultivate, till [the soil], work, prune, fertilize, force; farm, garden; sow, plant, set out, put in, intercrop; reap, harvest, glean, gather, pick, hay, thresh, winnow, bring in the harvest; mow, dress the ground; dibble, hoe, plow, harrow, rake, weed; take root, grow (see VEGETABLE); dust; sharecrop; vernalize.

Adjectives—agricultural, agrarian, farm; arable; predial, rural, rustic, country, georgic; horticultural; organic, geoponic.

Phrases—depressions are farm led and farm fed; we have three crops—corn, freight rates, and interest.

Quotations— All taxes must, at last, fall upon agriculture (*Artaxerxes*), A farm is an irregular patch of nettles bounded by short-term notes (*S. J. Perelman*), Those who labor in the earth are the chosen people of God (*Thomas Jefferson*), The farmers . . . are the founders of human civilization (*Daniel Webster*).

---

aground, *adj.* stranded, grounded. See DIFFICULTY.

ague, *n.* chill. See DISEASE.

ahead, *adv.* before, in advance (of); leading, winning. See PRIORITY, SUPERIORITY, FRONT. *Ant.,* behind.

AID
Give support to

Nouns—1, *(help given)* aid, assistance, help, succor, RELIEF; maintenance, sustenance, provision, upkeep, livelihood, daily bread; support, advance, furtherance, promotion; patronage, auspices, aegis, favor, backing, INFLUENCE; ministration, subministration; accommodation; [helping] hand; self-help; helpfulness. *Informal,* bailout. See BENEVOLENCE, INSTRUMENTALITY, UTILITY.

2, *(one who helps)* helper, assistant, aid, aide; accessory, partisan, supporter, confederate; AGENT; ally, co-worker; supplies, reinforcements, backup; crutch; patron, fairy godmother *or* -father. *Informal,* angel. See AUXILIARY.

Verbs—1, *(provide help)* aid, assist, help [out], be of service, succor, come to the aid of, get behind; lend one's aid, lend oneself to, contribute, subsidize, subscribe to, advocate; reinforce; give *or* lend a [helping] hand, proffer aid, give one a lift, take in tow; oblige, accommodate, encourage.

2, *(help to recover)* relieve, rescue, set on one's legs, pull *or* see through; give new life to, be the making of; push forward, give a lift to, give a leg up, bolster, shore up; promote, further, forward, advance; speed, expedite (see HASTE); support, sustain, uphold, see one through. *Informal,* bail out.

3, *(provide sustenance)* nourish, nurture, foster, cherish, care for; suckle, nurse; feed *or* fan the flames; serve; do service to, administer to.

4, *(assist, support)* second, stand by, stick by, stand *or* stick up for; back [up], abet, take up the cudgels for; espouse [the cause of], advocate, give moral support to, keep in countenance, patronize; finance, subsidize; smile upon, favor, side with, take the part of, play the game of, go to bat for; be of use to, benefit.

5, *(look for help)* turn to, fall back on, enlist the aid of.

Adjectives—aiding, assisting, helping; auxiliary, adjuvant, helpful, instrumental, coadjuvant; ministrant, ancillary, accessory, subsidiary; favorable, well-disposed, benevolent, beneficent; obliging.

Adverbs—helpfully, favorably, beneficially.

Prepositions—with *or* by the aid of, by means of; on *or* in behalf of, in back of, in support of; on account of; for the sake of; on the part of.

Phrases—God helps them that help themselves; it takes two to tango; two heads are better than one.

Antonyms, see HINDRANCE.

---

aide, *n.* assistant; aide-de-camp. See AID, AUXILIARY.

ail, *v.i.* be ill, suffer, fail (in health). See DISEASE, PAIN.

ailment, *n.* DISEASE, illness, malady.

aim, *n.* purpose, INTENTION, goal, end. —*v.* point, direct; aspire to, try for. See DIRECTION.

aimless, *adj.* random, undirected, CHANCE; driftless, idle; wanton. See DISORDER.

air, *n.* atmosphere (see AIR); mien, bearing, APPEARANCE; tune, melody (see MUSIC). —*v.t.* ventilate (see AIR); proclaim, broadcast (see PUBLICATION).

AIR
Earth's atmosphere

Nouns—1, *(atmosphere)* air, atmosphere, ether, ozone, thin air; ventilation, fresh *or* open air; sky, welkin, blue sky; oxygen, nitrogen, hydrogen, *etc.* See VAPOR.

2, *(layers of atmosphere)* troposphere, tropopause, layer, ozone layer, chemosphere, stratosphere, thermosphere, troposphere, [Kennelly-]Heaviside layer, ionosphere, exosphere, magnetosphere, mesosphere, Van Allen *or* radiation belt.

3, *(air passage)* airpipe, air shaft, airway; funnel, vent, tube, flue, chimney, ventilator; nose, nostril, nozzle, blowhole; windpipe, spiracle, larynx, throat; pipe. See PASSAGE.

4, [cross-]ventilation, airing, cooling, air-conditioning; ventilator, air conditioner, heat pump, fan.

5, *(meteorology)* weather, the elements, climate, rise and fall of the barometer; weather map, isobar, isotherm, high *or* low pressure, cold, warm *or* stationary front; aerology, meteorology, climatology; aneroid barometer, baroscope; good, bad, rainy, *etc.* weather. See WATER, WIND.

6, meteorologist, climatologist; weatherman *or* -woman, weather forecaster; weather report *or* forecast; weather bureau *or* station; barometer, weatherglass, hygrometer; weather balloon *or* satellite; weather vane.

Verbs—air, [cross-]ventilate, fan, air-condition; aerate. See WIND, REFRESHMENT.

Adjectives—1, *(of the air)* airy, pneumatic; open-air, *al fresco*; windy (see WIND).

2, *(of the weather)* atmospheric, airy, aerial, aeriform; meteorological, climatic, barometric, isobaric, isothermic.

Adverbs—outdoors, al fresco.

Quotations—This most excellent canopy, the air (*Shakespeare*).

Antonyms, see LAND, WATER.

---

aircraft, *n.* See AVIATION.

airing, *n.* walk, stroll; hearing, consideration, forum. See TRAVEL, PUBLICATION.

airline, *n.* [air] carrier, airways; air shuttle. See AVIATION.

airliner, airplane, airship, *n.* See AVIATION.

air pollution, *n.* smog, effluvium, miasma, mephitis. See ODOR, UNCLEANNESS.

airport, *n.* airfield, landing strip, airstrip. See AVIATION.

airs, *n.pl.* pretension[s], facade. See AFFECTATION, VANITY.

airsick, *adj.* queasy (see DISEASE).

airtight, *adj.* hermetic; flawless. See CLOSURE, STRENGTH.

airy, *adj.* unsubstantial, immaterial; well ventilated, breezy; flimsy, unreal, visionary; sprightly, light, volatile; pretentious. See INSUBSTANTIALITY, AIR, AFFECTATION. *Ant.,* close, heavy.

aisle, *n.* passageway, path, corridor. See OPENING.

ajar, *adj.* open, agape; cracked; discordant. See OPENING, DISCORD.

akimbo, *adj.* crooked, bent (see ANGULARITY).

akin, *adj.* related, kindred, like. See RELATION, SIMILARITY.

alacrity, *n.* promptness, speed; zeal, eagerness. See ACTIVITY, EARLINESS, DESIRE. *Ant.,* apathy, laziness.

alarm, *n.* alarum, WARNING; tocsin; SOS, siren, danger signal, red light *or* flag; condition red; FEAR, unease. —*v.* frighten, panic, scare; shock, horrify; make uneasy; sound the alarm, bell, *or* tocsin; alert, warn; cry wolf. See FEAR. *Ant.,* security, peace.

alarmist, *n.* terrorist, panic- *or* scaremonger. See FEAR.

alas, *interj.* alack! woe is me! (see LAMENTATION).

albeit, *conj.* although, notwithstanding that (see COMPENSATION).

album, *n.* scrapbook, RECORD; looseleaf book; ASSEMBLAGE.

alchemy, *n.* See SORCERY.

alcoholic, *adj.* beery, winy; spirituous. —*n.* dipsomaniac, problem drinker. See DRINKING.

alcove, *n.* recess, niche. See RECEPTACLE, CONCAVITY.

ale, *n.* porter, stout. See DRINKING.

aleatory, *adj.* aleatoric, CHANCE.

alert, *adj.* watchful, on guard, wary; quick, ready. See CARE, ACTIVITY. —*v.* See WARNING. *Ant.,* inattentive, unaware.

al fresco, *Ital.* in the open air; outdoors. See AIR.

alias, *n.* assumed name, pseudonym, nom de plume *or* de guerre; nickname. —*adv.* also known as, aka. See NOMENCLATURE.

alibi, *n., informal,* excuse (see VINDICATION).

alien, *adj.* foreign, strange. —*n.* foreigner, stranger, immigrant. See UNCONFORMITY, EXTERIOR. *Ant.,* alike, native.

alienate, *v.t.* estrange, make hostile; turn off (*inf.*). See DISCORD.

alienist, *n.* psychiatrist. See INTELLECT.

alight, *v.i.* descend, get off, land; dismount; arrive, disembark. See ARRIVAL, DESCENT. —*adj.* glowing, lighted; on fire, burning. See LIGHT, HEAT.

align, *v.* line up, true, range, straighten; regulate; array, take sides. See ARRANGEMENT, STRAIGHTNESS, DIRECTION.

alike, *adj.* analogous, resembling, like; akin. See SIMILARITY. *Ant.,* unlike, different.

aliment, *n.* FOOD, sustenance.

alimony, *n.* maintenance; child support. See PAYMENT, RECEIVING.

alive, *adj.* living (see LIFE); quick-witted, alert, brisk, spry; susceptible. See INTELLIGENCE, ACTIVITY, SENSIBILITY. *Ant.,* dead, lifeless.

all, *n.* See WHOLE, GENERALITY. —**all in,** *informal,* exhausted (see WEARINESS).

all-around, *adj.* complete; versatile. See COMPLETION, SKILL.

allay, *v.t.* lessen; soothe, mitigate, ease; calm. See MODERATION, RELIEF. *Ant.,* agitate, arouse.

allege, *v.* state, assert, affirm; imply; accuse. See ACCUSATION, AFFIRMATION.

allegiance, *n.* loyalty, devotion; DUTY. See OBEDIENCE. *Ant.,* treason, rebellion.

allegory, *n.* parable, fable. See FIGURATIVE.

allergy, *n.* sensitivity, reaction; hay fever, asthma, eczema, *etc.* See SENSIBILITY, DISEASE.

alleviate, *v.* lessen, mitigate; relieve. See MODERATION, RELIEF. *Ant.,* aggravate, intensify.

alley, *n.* PASSAGE, lane, walk. See OPENING, SPORTS.

alliance, *n.* association, federation, league; COMBINATION; treaty, accord; marriage; connection. See COOPERATION, RELATION. *Ant.,* separation, schism.

allocate, *v.t.* allot, assign. See APPORTIONMENT.

allocution, *n.* SPEECH.

allot, *v.* appoint, assign; distribute, parcel out. See APPORTIONMENT.

allow, *v.* grant, permit; concede; tolerate, suffer, let. See DISCLOSURE, CONSENT, PERMISSION. *Ant.,* prohibit, forbid.

allowance, *n.* stipend; DISCOUNT, concession; admission, sanction, PERMISSION. See GIVING, QUALIFICATION.

alloy, *n.* compound, MIXTURE; admixture. See COMPOSITION. —*v.* mix, combine; adulterate. See COMBINATION.

all right, correct; unharmed; yes, very well. See PROBITY, HEALTH, ASSENT.

allude, *v.* refer (see RELATION).

allure, *n.* ATTRACTION, charm. —*v.* tempt, attract, charm, entice. See DESIRE. *Ant.,* repel, deter.

allusion, *n.* reference, suggestion, hint, mention. See INFORMATION, FIGURATIVE.

ally, *n.* FRIEND, confederate, supporter. See AID, AUXILIARY. *Ant.,* enemy, foe.

almanac, *n.* calendar, ephemeris. See CHRONOMETRY, PUBLICATION.

almighty, *adj.* all-powerful, omnipotent. See DEITY, POWER. *Ant.,* powerless, impotent.

almost, *adv.* nearly, not quite, all but, approximately. See NEARNESS.

alms, *n.* charity, dole. See GIVING.

aloft, *adv.* on high, overhead, above, up; in the air; in the rigging. See HEIGHT.

alone, *adj.* apart, solitary, single. —*adv.* individually, solely, singly. See UNITY, SECLUSION. *Ant.,* together; accompanied.

along, *adv.* lengthwise; onward; together (with). See LENGTH, PROGRESSION, ACCOMPANIMENT.

alongside, *adv.* beside, neck-and-neck, abreast, side by side. See SIDE.

aloof, *adj.* distant, unneighborly, reserved, remote; indifferent. See SECLUSION, INDIFFERENCE, AFFECTATION. *Ant.,* open, friendly.

aloud, *adv.* audibly; vociferously, loudly, with full voice. See LOUDNESS, HEARING.

alphabet, *n.* letters; ABCs, crisscross-row. See WRITING, BEGINNING.

already, *adv.* by now, previously. See PRESENT, PART, PRIORITY.

also, *adv.* too, further[more], besides, likewise. See ADDITION, ACCOMPANIMENT.

also-ran, *n.* runner-up, second best; FAILURE. See INFERIORITY.

altar, *n.* communion *or* Lord's table; shrine. See TEMPLE.

alter, *v.* modify, CHANGE.

altercation, *n.* See DISCORD.

alter ego, Lat. another I; intimate friend. See FRIEND.

alternate, *n.* substitute, stand-in, proxy. —*v.* take turns, change, vacillate. See OSCILLATION, INTERCHANGE, DISCONTINUANCE.

alternative, *n.* CHOICE, option; PLAN.

although, *conj.* notwithstanding, albeit, though. See COMPENSATION.

altitude, *n.* HEIGHT, elevation.

altogether, *adv.* entirely, all, collectively, totally. See WHOLE.

altruism, *n.* BENEVOLENCE; selflessness; generosity, LIBERALITY, philanthropy, UNSELFISHNESS. *Ant.,* selfishness.

alumna, alumnus, *n.* graduate, fellow. See SCHOOL.

always, *adv.* at all times, invariably, continually, ever. See GENERALITY, DURABILITY, PERPETUITY. *Ant.,* never.

amain, *adv.* [with] full force *or* speed; hastily. See ENERGY, VELOCITY.

amalgamation, *n.* MIXTURE, blend, COMBINATION; unification, merger, federation, UNITY.

amanuensis, *n.* scribe, secretary. See WRITING.

amass, *v.t.* collect, accumulate; pile *or* heap up, STORE. See ASSEMBLAGE, ACQUISITION. *Ant.,* spend, dissipate.

amateur, *n.* nonprofessional, beginner; dilettante; volunteer. See BEGINNING, TASTE. *Ant.,* professional, connoisseur.

amative, amatory, *adj.* loving, affectionate; amorous, ardent; erotic. See LOVE.

amaze, *v.t.* astonish, astound, SURPRISE.

ambassador, *n.* envoy, emissary; consul; deputy. See AGENT.

ambience, *n.* mood, atmosphere; ENVIRONMENT, FEELING.

ambient, *adj.* surrounding, neighboring. See ENVIRONMENT.

ambiguous, *adj.* vague, undecided, uncertain; obscure, undefined. See DOUBT, LATENCY, OBSCURITY, UNINTELLIGIBILITY. *Ant.,* clear, explicit.

ambit, *n.* compass, boundary, LIMIT.

ambition, *n.* purpose, wish, hope, desire, INTENTION; aspiration, goal, end; resolve; zeal. See DESIRE. *Ant.,* indifference, satisfaction.

ambivalence, *n.* mixed feelings. See DOUBT.

amble, *v.i.* stroll, saunter, shuffle along. See TRAVEL.

ambush, *n.* ambuscade; hiding place, cover, camouflage; pitfall, trap; bushwhacking. —*v.t.* lie in wait for; bushwhack. See CONCEALMENT, ATTACK.

ameliorate, *v.* get better (see IMPROVEMENT). *Ant.,* worsen.

amenable, *adj.* agreeable; pliant, yielding, submissive; liable. See DUTY, CONSENT. *Ant.,* stubborn.

amend, *v.* change; correct, rectify; improve; (*pl.*) recompense (see ATONEMENT). See IMPROVEMENT.

amenities, *n.pl.* See COURTESY.

amiable, *adj.* friendly, agreeable, kindly, pleasant; likable. See COURTESY, BENEVOLENCE, FRIEND. *Ant.,* sour, unfriendly, hostile.

amicable, *adj.* friendly (see FRIEND).

amicus curiae, Lat. a friend of the court. See LAWSUIT.

amid, amidst, *prep.* among, midst, mid. See MIXTURE.

amiss, *adv.* WRONG, ill; badly, improperly. See EVIL.

ammunition, *n.* ammo, bullets, *etc.* See ARMS.

amnesia, *n.* loss of memory (see OBLIVION).

amnesty, *n.* pardon, remission, moratorium. See FORGIVENESS.

amok, amuck, *adv.* in a frenzied *or* berserk manner; running wild. See EXCITABILITY.

among, *prep.* in the middle (of), midst, included in, with. See MIXTURE.

amoral, *adj.* nonmoral, unscrupulous, unprincipled, unethical. See IMPURITY. *Ant.,* moral, principled.

amorous, *adj.* loving, passionate, amative. See LOVE.

amorphous, *adj.* shapeless, formless; heterogenous, vague. See FORMLESSNESS.

amount, *n.* QUANTITY, sum, total, aggregate; DEGREE; PRICE.

amour-propre, Fr. self-esteem. See VANITY, PRIDE.

amphetamine, *n.* See DRUGS.

amphitheater, *n.* gallery, ARENA. See DRAMA.

ample, *adj.* sufficient, copious, plenty; large, expansive, spacious. See GREATNESS, SPACE, SUFFICIENCY. *Ant.,* inadequate, insufficient; cramped.

amplify, *v.t.* enlarge, swell, magnify. See EXPANSION. *Ant.,* summarize, shorten, compress.

amputate, *v.* sever, cut *or* hack off. See DISJUNCTION, DEDUCTION.

amulet, *n.* charm, token, talisman, good-luck piece. See CHANCE, SORCERY.

AMUSEMENT
Pleasurable interest

Nouns—1, amusement, entertainment; diversion, divertissement, distraction; recreation, hobby, avocation, relaxation, pastime, sport; labor of love, PLEASURE; night life; time of one's life.

2, (*something amusing*) fun, frolic, good time(s); laughter (see REJOICING), drollery, tomfoolery, mummery; pleasantry (see WIT). *Informal,* laughs, ball, picnic. See CHEERFULNESS.

3, (*amusing actions*) play, game, gambol, romp, prank, antic, caper, dido, knavery, rascality, roguery, lark, escapade, spree, skylarking; monkeyshine, monkey trick, practical joke. *Informal,* shenanigan.

4, festivity, revelry, merrymaking (see SOCIALITY); fete, festival, gala, revel (see DRINKING), carnival, Mardi Gras, Oktoberfest, brawl, saturnalia, high jinks; banquet, wassail, carouse, carousal; picnic, field day; jubilee (see CELEBRATION). *Slang,* jamboree, blowout.

5, (*location for amusement*) theater, ballroom, music hall, nightclub, honky-tonk, discotheque; circus, big top; park, common(s), arbor, bowling green *or* alley, rink, casino, fairground, fun fair, amusement park, theme park, water park, resort, watering place; midway, boardwalk; playground, gymnasium, playroom. See ARENA, DRAMA.

6, game[s]: **a.** billiards, pool, snooker; pool table, bumper, chalk, crutch, lady's helper (*inf.*), rack; cue ball; carom, English, bank shot, table scratch, pocket. **b.** chess, chessman, piece, pawn, knight, bishop, rook, castle, queen, king; castle, end game, stalemate, check. **c.** backgammon, point, bar, home, inner *or* outer board, checker, blot. **d.** checkers, draughts, queen. **e.** dominoes, bone, muggins, sniff. **f.** cards; playing card, ace, king, queen, jack, knave, joker, two-(*etc.*)spot, deuce, trey; [auction, duplicate, rubber *or* contract] bridge, whist, blackjack, canasta, casino, pinochle, bézique, rummy, cribbage, eights, [draw *or* stud] poker, écarté, euchre, fan tan, five hundred, gin rummy, go fish, hearts, hazard, I doubt it, jass, kalabriás, loo, macao, michigan, napoleon, Oh Hell, old maid, piquet, pitch, samba, sevens, skat, spoil five, stops, triomphe, concentration, solitaire, war, Uno. **g.** gambling; craps, roulette, *etc.* (see CHANCE). **h.** (*indoor games*) Scrabble, Chinese checkers, go, pachisi, Otello, Monopoly, Trivial Pursuit, *etc.*; anagrams, bingo, cat's cradle, darts, jacks, musical chairs, pachinko, post office, skittle, tic-tack-toe. **i.** (*parlor games*) categories, ghosts, charades, geography, animals, *etc.*; spin the bottle. *Slang,* car *or* train surfing; doctors and nurses. **j.** (*electronic games*) Atari, Nintendo, Sega; asteroids, flight simulator, Myst, Pac-Man, Sim City, *etc.* **k.** (*outdoor games*) Frisbee, rollerskating, Rollerblading; hopscotch, jump rope, leapfrog, hide and seek, tug-of-war, ring around the rosie, capture the flag; badminton, croquet, curling, horseshoes, miniature golf, quoits, shuffleboard, trapshooting.

7, fishing, hunting; aquatics, swimming; SPORTS; paintball (see CONTENTION).

8, (*item for amusement*) **a.** toy, plaything, bauble, top; Erector set, Etch-a-Sketch, jack-in-the-box, jigsaw puzzle, yo-yo, pinwheel, Slinky, squirt gun, water pistol, Silly Putty; model train, airplane, *etc.* **b.** doll, Raggedy Ann *or* Andy doll, teddy bear, marionette, puppet, toy *or* tin soldier, action figure; hula hoop; Frisbee, beachball, beanbag; teetotum, knickknack; dollhouse. **c.** merry-go-round, carousel, whirligig, Ferris wheel, roller coaster; jungle gym, rocking horse, teeter-totter, seesaw, slide, swing; water slide; skateboard, sled; bicycle (see VEHICLE). **d.** jacks, blocks, marbles.

9, entertainment industry, show business; Hollywood, Broadway, television, radio, *etc.*

10, master of ceremonies, emcee, MC, entertainment *or* social director, host.

Verbs—**1,** amuse, entertain, divert, distract, recreate, delight, titillate.

2, amuse oneself; play (games, pranks, tricks, *etc.*); sport, disport, toy, revel, drown care; make merry, drive dull care away; frolic, gambol, frisk, romp, caper; sow one's wild oats, have one's fling, live it up, cut up; fool, mess, play, *or* monkey around; take one's pleasure; make holiday, go a-Maying, while away the time, kill time, dally; step out, have fun, have a ball *or* a time, cut a caper, horse around, paint the town [red], let the good times roll, carry on, cut loose, whoop it up, make a night of it, go to town, let one's hair down, blow *or* let off steam, roister. *Slang,* cut up, make whoopee, futz around; dick *or* screw around.

Adjectives—**1,** *(causing amusement)* amusing, entertaining, fun, diverting, recreative; festive; roguish, rompish, frisky, frolicsome, playful [as a kitten], sportive.

2, *(result of amusement)* amused, entertained, diverted, *etc.*

Adverbs—on the town; for fun, for the devil of it, for kicks.

Quotations—Life would be tolerable but for its amusements (*George Lewis*), Suppose entertainment is the Purpose of Life! (*Philip Roth*).

Antonyms, see WEARINESS, PAIN.

---

anachronism, *n.* misdate, prolepsis, anticipation; metachronism, parachronism, prochronism. See TIME, ERROR.

anagram, *n.* acrostic. See WORD.

anal, *adj.* rectal; *informal,* anal retentive, uptight, rigid, [anal-]compulsive. See REAR, BODY, RETENTION, COMPULSION.

analgesic, *adj. & n.* See REMEDY.

analogous, *adj.* like, parallel; related; corresponding, similar. See SIMILARITY, IDENTITY. *Ant.,* dissimilar.

analysis, *n.* breakdown, separation, disintegration; investigation, study; abstract, summary; psychoanalysis. See INQUIRY, DECOMPOSITION, INSANITY. *Ant.,* synthesis.

anarchy, *n.* lawlessness, terrorism, DISORDER, disorganization; nihilism. *Ant.,* ORDER, rule of law.

anathema, *n.* denunciation; curse, execration, IMPRECATION. See DETRACTION.

anatomy, *n.* structure, framework; zootomy; analysis. See FORM, INQUIRY.

ANCESTRY
Series of ancestors

Nouns—**1,** *(family history)* ancestry, paternity, maternity, origins, background, parentage, breeding; house, stem, trunk, branch, tree, roots, stock, stirps, pedigree, lineage, blood, kin, line, family, tribe, sept, race, clan; extended, institutional, *or* nuclear family; spear *or* sword side, distaff *or* spindle side; family tree, genealogy, descent, bloodline, extraction, birth; phenotype; forefathers, patriarchs. See PRECEDENCE, PRIORITY.

2, ancestor, predecessor, forebears, forefathers; grandsire, [great-]grandfather; granddam, [great-]grandmother. *Informal,* gramps, granddad, grandpa, gramma, grandma, granny.

3, [natural, biological, *or* birth] parent, bioparent, begetter, stepparent, adoptive *or* surrogate parent; fatherhood, paternity, father, stepfather, sire, paterfamilias, genitor, progenitor, procreator; motherhood, maternity, mother, stepmother, dam, materfamilias. *Informal,* dad[dy], papa, pa, pop; mom[my], mama, ma; sire, stud[horse], seed horse, top horse (see ANIMAL).

4, *(one who studies family history)* genealogist, archivist, family historian.

5, genetics, eugenics; birth factor, gene, chromosome, genetic code; DNA test, paternity test.

Adjectives—ancestral, family, linear, patriarchal; parental, paternal, fatherly, agnate, maternal, motherly, enate; direct, genealogical, lineal, collateral; hereditary, inherited, genetic, innate.
Phrases—blood is thicker than water; like father [mother], like son [daughter]; honor thy father and mother; the art of being a parent consists of sleeping when the baby isn't looking.
Quotations—The sins of the father are to be laid upon the children (*Shakespeare*), People will not look forward to posterity, who never look backward to their ancestors (*Edmund Burke*), Every man is a quotation from all his ancestors (*Emerson*), There is no king who has not had a slave among his ancestors (*Helen Keller*), Every generation revolts against its fathers and makes friends with its grandfathers (*Lewis Mumford*), You are the bows from which your children are as living arrows sent forth (*Kahlil Gibran*), The family—that dear octopus from whose tentacles we never quite escape (*Dodie Smith*).

Antonyms, see POSTERITY.

---

anchor, *n.* berth, slip, buoy, grapnel, kedge; mainstay, safeguard; anchorman, -woman, *or* -person. —*v.* cast anchor, moor; fix, attach, fasten; hold fast. See NAVIGATION, STABILITY, COMMUNICATION, CONNECTION.

anchorage, *n.* mooring, road[stead], harbor. See SAFETY, LOCATION.

anchorite, *n.* anchoret, recluse, hermit (see ASCETICISM).

ancien régime, *Fr.* the old order. See OLDNESS.

ancient, *adj.* aged, venerable; antique, antiquated; archaic, hoary. See AGE, OLDNESS. *Ant.,* recent, modern, new.

ancillary, *adj. & n.* subordinate, AUXILIARY.

and, *conj.* moreover, also, in addition; plus, to boot, besides. See ADDITION, ACCOMPANIMENT.

andiron, *n.* firedog, grill. See HEAT.

anecdote, *n.* sketch, story, tale, narrative; joke. See DESCRIPTION.

anemia, *n.* bloodlessness. See WEAKNESS.

anesthesia, *n.* See INSENSIBILITY.

anesthetic, *n.* painkiller, novocain. See INSENSIBILITY.

anew, *adv.* again (see REPETITION).

angel, *n.* patron, backer, sponsor, meal ticket (*inf.*), sugar daddy (*inf.*). See ANGEL, MEANS, ENDEARMENT.

ANGEL
Attendant of God

Nouns—1, *(heavenly being)* angel, archangel; celestial being, invisible choir, heavenly host; seraph (*pl.* seraphim), cherub (*pl.* cherubim); ministering spirit, guardian angel. See HEAVEN, GOODNESS, PIETY.
2, Gabriel, Raphael, Uriel, Zadkiel, Machiel, Abdiel, Chamuel; Azrael, angel of death; Madonna.
3, *(study of angels)* angelology; seraphim, cherubim, thrones, dominations *or* dominions, virtues, powers, principalities, archangels, angels.
Verbs—receive one's wings, join the heavenly host.
Adjectives—angelic, seraphic, cherubic, celestial.
Quotations—A wingèd messenger of heaven (*Shakespeare*), How many angels can dance on the head of a pin? (*Anon.*).

Antonyms, see DEMON.

---

anger, *n. & v.* See RESENTMENT. *Ant.,* good nature, jollity.

angle, *n.* corner (see ANGULARITY); aspect, guise, point of view; approach. See APPEARANCE. —*v.i.* fish. See PURSUIT.

angry, *adj.* inflamed, sore (see PAIN). See RESENTMENT. *Ant.,* calm, at peace.

anguish, *n.* agony, anxiety, PAIN.

ANGULARITY
Quality of having angles

Nouns—1, *(quality of having an angle)* angularity, OBLIQUITY; angle, notch, fork, bifurcation; elbow, knee, knuckle, ankle, shoulder, groin, crotch, crutch, crane, fluke; zigzag, switchback; corner, coign, quoin, dovetail, nook; recess, niche, oriel, peak; salient, projection. *Informal,* dogleg. See SHARPNESS, CURVATURE, DEVIATION.

2, *(formation and measurement of angles)* angulation; right, acute, obtuse, *or* oblique angle; angular measurement, elevation, distance, velocity; trigonometry, trig; goniometry; altimeter, clinometer, graphometer, goniometer; theodolite; sextant, quadrant, transit; protractor.

3, *(figure having angles)* triangle, trigon, wedge; rectangle, brick, square, lozenge, diamond; rhomb, rhombus; quadrangle, quadrilateral; parallelogram; quadrature; polygon, pentacle, pentagram, pentagon, hexagon, heptagon, octagon, decagon; cube, block, rhomboid; tetrahedron, octahedron, dodecahedron, icosahedron, polyhedron; prism, pyramid, block, brick; parallelepiped.

4, *(human angularity)* lankiness, boniness, ungainliness (see NARROWNESS).

Verbs—angle, fork, bifurcate; bend, hook, go off on a tangent; zigzag; branch, fork.

Adjectives—angular, crooked; deltoid, triangular, rectangular, square, *etc.* (see *Nouns,* 3); aquiline, sharp, acicular, acuminate, apical, attenuated; cuneal, cuneate; dentiform, spicate; acute, obtuse, oblique; jagged, serrated; falciform, furcated, forked, bifurcate, hastate, sagittate; prismatoid, prismoid; zigzag; knockkneed, akimbo, geniculated; oblique (see OBLIQUITY).

Antonyms, see CURVATURE, STRAIGHTNESS.

---

anile, *adj.* childish, foolish, simple; senile. See AGE.

animadversion, *n.* criticism, reflection. See DISAPPROBATION.

ANIMAL
Any living thing not a plant

Nouns—1, animal, beast, brute, creature, living thing, creeping thing, dumb animal; fauna, animal kingdom; buck, bull, bullock; doe; domestic animal, draft animal; wild animal, game; flesh, flesh and blood; corporeality, carnality; animation, animality; quadruped, biped; zoophyte; protozoan, animalcule. *Informal,* critter, varmint. See DOMESTICATION.

2, *(study of animals)* natural science, zoology, biology, mammalogy, ornithology, herpetology, ichthyology, entomology; animal kingdom, animal life, animalia, fauna; animal morphology, anatomy, zootomy, histology, cytology, embryology, paleontology; zoo-(*etc.*)physics, chemistry, *etc.*; ENVIRONMENT, balance of nature, ecology, bionomics, ethology, teleology, zoography, zoogeography, *etc.*

3, *(one who studies animals)* zoologist, zoographist, naturalist; biologist, bionomist, *etc.*; bird watcher, nature lover.

4, *(vertebrates)* I. *(mammals)* a. monotreme, [duckbill] platypus, anteater, echidna. b. marsupial, bandicoot, bettong, kangaroo, koala, numbat, opossum, potoroo, Tasmanian devil *or* wolf, wallaby, wombat. c. edentate, armadillo, sloth, tatou. d. insectivore, shrew, mole, hedgehog, mole, tenrec. e. dermopteran, lemur; chiropteran, bat, flying fox. f. primate, ape, baboon, monkey, chimpanzee, capuchin, drill, lemur, gibbon, gorilla, Homo sapiens (see HUMANITY), howler, saki, simian, siamang, vervet. g. carnivore, lion, badger, bear, ermine, ferret, hyena, jackal, jaguar(undi), marten, meerkat, mink, mongoose, otter, panda, polar bear, polecat, prairie wolf, puma, raccoon, sable, sea otter, simba, skunk, stoat, weasel, wolverine; feline, leopard, lynx, mountain lion, ounce, panther, tiger, wildcat, ocelot, bobcat, cat (Abyssinian, Angora, Burmese, Himalàyan, Maltese, Manx, Persian, Siamese); canine, fox, wolf, dog (affenpinscher, Afghan hound, Airedale [terrier], malamute, foxhound, pit bull terrier, water spaniel, cattle dog, kelpie, badger dog, Basenji, basset hound, beagle, bearded collie, terrier, sheepdog, coonhound, bloodhound, collie, borzoi, boxer, Briard, griffon, bulldog, bullmastiff, bull terrier, cairn terrier, retriever, chihuahua, sharpei, chow chow, cocker spaniel, corgi, dachshund, Dalmation, deerhound, Doberman pinscher, elkhound, setter, springer spaniel, toy, German shepherd, schnauzer, Great Dane, greyhound, harrier, husky, Jack Russell terrier, keeshond, kelpie, Labrador [retriever], Lhasa apso, malamute, Mexican hairless, miniature, Newfoundland, otterhound, papillon, pariah dog, Pekingese, pointer, poodle, pug, puli, Rottweiler, Saluki, Samoyed, schipperke, Shih Tzu, spitz, St. Bernard, Weimaraner, Welsh corgi, whippet, wirehair), man's best friend. **h.** pinniped, seal, walrus, sea lion. **i.** cetacean, whale, beluga, blackfish, dolphin, cowfish, grampus, humpback [whale], narwhal, orca, porpoise, rorqual, susu. **j.** sirenian, dugong, manatee, sea cow. **k.** proboscid, elephant, mammoth, jumbo, mastodon, pachyderm, tusker. **l.** perissodactyl, ass, burro, donkey, horse, jackass, mule, mustang, onager, pony, Przewalski's horse, quagga, rhinoceros, tapir, tarpan, wild ass, zebra. **m.** hyrax, cony, dassie, klippdach. **n.** tubulidentate, aardvark, ant bear, earth pig. **o.** artiodactyl, addax, alpaca, anoa, antelope, aoudad, argali, deer, babirusa, camel, banteng, sheep, bison, blesbok, boar, buffalo, bull, camelopard, caribou, cattle (see DOMESTICATION), chamois, gazelle, dromedary, eland, elk, gemsbok, giraffe, gnu, goat, hartebeest, hippopotamus, hog, impala, llama, moose, mountain goat, muntjac, musk ox, okapi, oribi, ox, peccary, reindeer, springbok, steenbok, swine, vicuna, wapiti, warthog, water buffalo, wildebeest, yak, zebu. **p.** pangolin, anteater. **q.** rodent, agouti, chipmunk, squirrel, bandicoot, beaver, capybara, chinchilla, coypu, dormouse, gerbil, gopher, groundhog, guinea pig, hamster, jerboa, lemming, marmot, mouse, nutria, paca, prairie dog, rat, suslik, vole, woodchuck. **r.** lagomorph, hare, cony, cottontail, jackrabbit, lapin, leveret, rabbit. **s.** amphibian, anuran, axolotl, bullfrog, frog, eel, eft, salamander, toad, mudpuppy, natterjack, newt, siren, peeper, waterdog. II. *(reptiles)* **a.** dinosaur, archaeopteryx, brachiosaur, brontosaur, ceratopsian, ichthyosaur, mixosaurus, pterodactyl, sauropod, stegosaur, tyrannosaur. **b.** snake, adder, anaconda, asp, blacksnake, boa [constrictor], bullsnake, bushmaster, cobra, copperhead, coralsnake, cottonmouth, daboia, rattlesnake, fer-de-lance, garter snake, hamadryad, harlequin, viper, king snake, krait, mamba, massasauga, milk snake, moccasin, puff adder, python, rat snake, sidewinder, taipan, ticpolonga, urutu, water moccasin, worm snake. **c.** agama, alligator, crocodile, snole, basilisk, blindworm, turtle, caiman, chameleon, terrapin, dragon, lizard, galliwasp, gavial, gecko, Gila monster, tortoise, toad, iguana, matamata, moloch, monitor, mugger, red-ear, skink, slider, slowworm, snapping turtle, stinkpot, swift, tegu, tuatara. *Slang,* cooter. III. See BIRDS. IV. See FISH.

5, *(invertebrates)* I. *(arthropods)* **a.** insect, bee, ant, flea, fly, beetle, butterfly, louse; pismire, red, black, army or carpenter ant, queen, worker, soldier; acarine, aphid, bedbug, black fly, bloodworm, bluebottle, weevil, bookworm, borer, bumblebee, caddisfly, cadelle, caterpillar, tick, moth, centipede, chafer, chigger, chigoe, chinch bug, cicada, cicala, cockroach, conenose, cricket, daddy-longlegs, harvestman, damselfly, deer fly, dermestid, dipteran, dor, dragonfly, drosophila, earwig, elaterid, ephemerid, firefly, gadfly, gnat, grasshopper, greenbug, grub, honeybee, hornet, horntail, housefly, katydid, lacewing, ladybug, [seventeen-year] leech, bloodsucker, locust, longhorn, mayfly, mealworm, medfly, midge, mite, mosquito, podura, praying mantis, punkie, roach, sawfly, sawyer, scarab, silkworm, silverfish, skipjack, skipper, springtail, stink bug, stonefly, termite, thrips, [wood or deer] tick, viceroy, walking stick, wasp, yellow jacket. **b.** arachnid, spider, black widow, scorpion, tabanid, tarantula. **c.** crustacean, barnacle, flea, crab, crawdad, crayfish, krill, lobster, prawn, shrimp, wood louse. II. *(mollusks)* mollusk, echinoderm, sponge, cnidarian, abalone, anemone, bivalve, jellyfish, clam, cockle, conch, coral, cowrie, starfish, cuttlefish, devilfish, squid, hydra, limpet, mussel, nautilus, octopus, oyster, periwinkle, polyp, pompano, Portuguese man-of-war, quahog, sand dollar, sandworm, scallop, sea anemone, sea cucumber, sea slug, sea urchin, shellfish, slug, snail, sponge, whelk. III. *(worms)* worm, angleworm, annelid, cutworm, earthworm, filaria, flatworm, fluke, hookworm, inchworm, larva, leech, nematode, pinworm, planarian, rotifer, roundworm, silkworm, tapeworm, teredo, trematode, tussah, night crawler.

6, *(domestic animals)* livestock; cattle, kine, bird, poultry, fowl, swine; pet; beasts of the field. See DOMESTICATION.

7, *(young animal)* yearling, youngling, calf, colt, filly, whelp, cub (see YOUTH).

8, *(animal parts)* antler, claw, coat, cud, fang, hoof, horn, incisor, mane, maw, snout, tail, muzzle, paw, pelt, pouch, proboscis, tusk, whalebone; litter; bilateral *or* radial symmetry.

9, *(home for animals)* zoological garden, zoo, [wild] animal farm, wildlife conservation center, menagerie, Tiergarten (see ABODE).

Adjectives—**1,** animal, bestial, carnal, corporal, corporeal, physical, fleshly; sensual; human.

2, *(of types of animals)* invertebrate, protozoan, crustacean; vertebrate, mammalian, cetaceous, avian, reptilian, vermicular, piscatory; piscine, molluscous; aquatic, terrestrial; domestic, wild; carnivorous, herbivorous, insectivorous, omnivorous; equine, bovine, canine, feline, lupine, *etc.*

3, *(of animal studies)* zoological, morphological, anthropological, *etc.*

Quotations—A horse! A horse! My kingdom for a horse! *(Shakespeare)*, Animals, whom we have made our slaves, we do not like to consider our equal *(Charles Darwin)*, All animals, except man, know that the principal business of life is to enjoy it *(Samuel Butler)*, I am not over-fond of animals. I am merely astounded by them *(David Attenborough)*, All animals are equal, but some animals are more equal than others *(George Orwell)*, The best thing about animals is that they don't talk much *(Thornton Wilder)*, An animal's eyes have the power to speak a great language *(Martin Buber)*.

Related categories, VEGETABLE, ORGANIC MATTER.

---

animate, *v.* liven, impel; cheer, enliven, enspirit, encourage, inspire. —*adj.* lively; living. See CHEERFULNESS, EXCITEMENT, ACTIVITY, CAUSE, LIFE. *Ant.,* kill, stifle; dead.

animosity, *n.* antipathy, ill will, enmity. See RESENTMENT, DISLIKE. *Ant.,* goodwill.

ankle, *n.* tarsus. See BODY.

annals, *n.pl.* chronicle, archive[s], RECORD.

anneal, *v.t.* temper (see HARDNESS).

annex, *v.* add, attach, affix. See ADDITION, JUNCTION, ACQUISITION.

annihilate, *v.* demolish, destroy; eliminate, exterminate. See DESTRUCTION, NONEXISTENCE.

anniversary, *n.* jubilee (see REGULARITY).

annotate, *v.* comment on, gloss, explain. See INTERPRETATION.

announce, *v.* tell, proclaim, publish, make known; broadcast, report. See INFORMATION, PREDICTION, PUBLICATION.

annoy, *v.* vex, tease, harass, disturb, molest, trouble, bother, irritate, PAIN, peeve (*inf.*). See MALEVOLENCE.

annual, *adj.* yearly, seasonal, anniversary. See REGULARITY. —*n.* yearbook, [annual] report. See RECORD.

annul, *v.t.* cancel, abolish, repeal, rescind, retract, revoke, nullify, quash; dissolve (a marriage); set aside, invalidate. See NULLIFICATION, DIVORCE.

annular, *adj.* ring-shaped (see CIRCULARITY).

anoint, *v.* oil, salve. See RITE.

anomaly, *n.* abnormality, exception (see UNCONFORMITY).

anonymous, *adj.* unnamed, nameless, incognito. See NOMENCLATURE, SECRET.

another, *adj.* different; one more. See DIFFERENCE, ADDITION.

answer, *v.* serve, suit, avail, do; atone (for). See SUFFICIENCY, ATONEMENT, ANSWER.

ANSWER
Response

Nouns—1, answer, response, reply, rescript; acknowledgment; rebuttal, riposte, rejoinder, return, retort; refutation, CONFUTATION; repartee; antiphon; password (see INDICATION); echo, feedback, reverberation (see SOUND); RSVP; answering machine *or* service. *Informal,* comeback, rise. See MUSIC.

2, *(solution to problem)* discovery, DISCLOSURE, solution, explanation, finding, reason; clue (see INDICATION). See INTERPRETATION.

3, answerer, respondent, replier.

Verbs—1, answer, respond, reply; rebut, retort, rejoin; refute, confute; give answer; acknowledge, echo; confute (see CONFUTATION); answer *or* talk back (see INSOLENCE); RSVP.

2, *(solve a problem)* satisfy, resolve, set at rest; find out, determine, solve, explain; figure *or* dope out, work out.

Adjectives—answering, responsive, conclusive; refutative, confutative; antiphonal, echoing.

Adverbs—in reply, in response, in rebuttal.

Phrases—ask a silly question and you get a silly answer; if you're not part of the solution, you're part of the problem; a civil question deserves a civil answer; fools ask questions that wise men cannot answer.

Quotations—One hears only those questions for which one is able to find answers (*Friedrich Nietzsche*), The answer, my friend, is blowin' in the wind (*Bob Dylan*), A soft answer turneth away wrath (*Bible*), What we're saying today is that you're either part of the solution or you're part of the problem (*Eldridge Cleaver*).

Antonyms, see INQUIRY.

---

answerable, *adj.* accountable, liable. See LIABILITY.

antagonism, *n.* animosity, antipathy, enmity; hostility, OPPOSITION. *Ant.,* support, friendship.

ante bellum, Lat. before the war. See PRIORITY.

antecede, *v.t.* go before, precede. See PRIORITY.

antechamber, anteroom, *n.* waiting room, INGRESS; lobby, vestibule, foyer. See RECEPTACLE.

antedate, *v.t.* predate, come before. See PRIORITY. *Ant.,* predate, precede.

antenna, *n.* aerial, rabbit ears, mast, tower. See COMMUNICATION.

anthem, *n.* song, hymn, chorale; national anthem. See MUSIC, WORSHIP.

anthology, *n.* collection, miscellany, garland. See ASSEMBLAGE.

anthropoid, *adj.* humanoid, anthropomorphic. See HUMANITY.

antibiotic, *n.* miracle *or* wonder drug, sulfa drug, antibacterial. See REMEDY.

antic, *n.* caper, escapade, prank, gambol. See AMUSEMENT.

anticipate, *v.* await, expect; precede; forestall; foresee. See PREPARATION, PRIORITY, FUTURITY, EARLINESS. *Ant.,* dread.

anticlimax, *n.* letdown, comedown. See DISAPPOINTMENT.

antidote, *n.* antitoxin, REMEDY.

antipasto, *n.* appetizer, hors d'oeuvres. See FOOD.

antipathy, *n.* DISLIKE; repugnance, aversion. See OPPOSITION. *Ant.,* attraction, liking.

antipodes, *adj.* [opposite] poles, opposites (see OPPOSITION).

antiquary, *n.* archaeologist, historian, student of the PAST.

antiquated, *adj.* antique; outdated, behind the times, outmoded; obsolete. See OLDNESS, AGE. *Ant.,* new, recent.

antique, *n.* relic. See OLDNESS. *Ant.,* new, modern.

antiquity, *n.* old[en] times; the PAST, ancient history; OLDNESS. *Ant.,* modern times, present.

antiseptic, *adj. & n.* germicide, disinfectant. See CLEANNESS.

antisocial, *adj.* cynical, misanthropic. See

MALEVOLENCE. *Ant.*, gregarious, outgoing.

antithesis, *n.* contrast, OPPOSITION. See DIFFERENCE.

anus, *n.* rectum, asshole (*sl.*), bunghole (*sl.*). See REAR, BODY.

anxiety, *n.* concern, CARE; FEAR, mental anguish, PAIN. See EXPECTATION, DOUBT, JEALOUSY. *Ant.*, tranquillity, peace, unconcern.

any, *adj. & pron.* some. See GENERALITY, QUANTITY.

anybody, anyone, *pron.* whoever, no matter who. See GENERALITY.

anyhow, *adv.* anyway; at any rate; nevertheless. See COMPENSATION.

apart, *adv.* separately, alone, independently; away; in pieces. See DISTANCE, DISJUNCTION. *Ant.*, together.

apartment, *n.* flat, suite, rooms, maisonette, tenement, walk-up; condo[minium], co-op. See ABODE, RECEPTACLE.

apathy, *n.* coldness, INDIFFERENCE, unconcern. *Ant.*, care, passion.

ape, *n.* gorilla, anthropoid, simian; imitator, mimic. —*v.* imitate, copy, mimic. See IMITATION.

apéritif, *n.* See DRINKING.

aperture, *n.* OPENING, gap.

apex, *n.* peak, climax. See HEIGHT.

aphorism, *n.* MAXIM, adage, proverb.

aphrodisiac, *n.* [love] philter, love potion, Spanish fly. —*adj.* arousing, venereal. See SEX.

apiece, *adv.* for each, per, for one, respectively, individually. See SPECIALITY.

aplomb, *n.* poise, [self-]assurance. See INEXCITABILITY.

apocalypse, *n.* revelation, prophecy; disaster. See PREDICTION, ADVERSITY.

apology, *n.* excuse, justification, VINDICATION; regret, amends. See ATONEMENT, PENITENCE. *Ant.*, accusation, censure.

apoplexy, *n.* paralysis, stroke (see DISEASE).

apostate, *n.* backslider, renegade, turncoat, deserter, traitor, recreant; double dealer, opportunist. See CHANGEABLENESS, IMPIETY, HETERODOXY, EVILDOER, DISSENT.

a posteriori, *Lat.* from effect to cause. See REASONING.

apostle, *n.* disciple; evangelist. See LEARNING, RELIGION.

apothecary, *n.* pharmacist, druggist. See REMEDY.

apothegm, *n.* saying, MAXIM.

apotheosis, *n.* deification; glorification. See REPUTE, HEAVEN.

appall, *v.t.* horrify, shock; disgust, revolt. See FEAR, PAIN.

apparatus, *n.* machine, machinery; equipment, instruments. See INSTRUMENTALITY, PROVISION.

apparel, *n.* See CLOTHING.

apparent, *adj.* plain, obvious, visible; EVIDENT, manifest, perceptible. See APPEARANCE, VISIBILITY. *Ant.*, unlikely, hidden, secret, obscure.

apparition, *n.* phantom, ghost, specter; dream. See DEMON, IMAGINATION.

appeal, *n.* entreaty, plea, begging, petition; resort; attractiveness, ATTRACTION. See REQUEST, LAWSUIT.

appear, *v.i.* seem (see APPEARANCE); materialize, come into view; be published, hit the stands; testify. See ARRIVAL, PUBLICATION, LAWSUIT.

APPEARANCE
Outward look

Nouns—1, *(what is seen)* sight, show, scene, view; outlook, prospect, vista, angle, perspective, bird's-eye view; scenery, landscape, picture, tableau; display, setting, mise-en-scène. See VISIBILITY.

2, *(visual show)* peep show, magic lantern, phantasmagoria, panorama, diorama, spectacle, pageantry (see OSTENTATION).

3, aspect, phase, seeming, semblance; shape (see FORM); guise, facade, outward show, look, complexion, color, image, mien, air, cast, carriage, port, demeanor; presence, expression, first blush; point of view, light. *Informal*, front, window dressing; spin. See FASHION.

4, *(visible features)* lineament, feature; contour, face, countenance, physiognomy, visage, cast of countenance, figure, profile, cut of one's jib. *Slang*, phiz.

Verbs—seem, look, show; have, take on, *or* assume the appearance *or* semblance of; look like; cut a figure, figure; present to the view.

Adjectives—apparent, seeming, ostensible; on view; evident, manifest, visible. *Informal,* complected.

Adverbs—apparently, ostensibly, seemingly, as it seems, on the face of it, prima facie; at first blush *or* sight; in the eyes of; to the eye.

Phrases—you can't tell a book by its cover; appearances are deceptive; merit in appearance is more often rewarded than merit itself; what you see is what you get; all that glitters is not gold; a carpenter is known by his chips.

Quotations—The world is still deceived with ornament (*Shakespeare*), Your face . . . is as a book where men may read strange matters (*Shakespeare*), You can't expect men not to judge by appearances (*Ellen Glasgow*).

Antonyms, see ABSENCE, DISAPPEARANCE, INVISIBILITY.

---

appease, *v.t.* mollify, pacify, soothe, placate; satisfy, slake. See PACIFICATION, MODERATION, SUFFICIENCY. *Ant.,* antagonize, enrage.

append, *v.t.* add, attach (to), affix. See ADDITION.

appendage, *n.* arm, leg, *etc.;* addendum, ADDITION. See BODY.

appendix, *n.* supplement (see ADDITION).

appetite, *n.* hunger, DESIRE, craving. *Ant.,* aversion, distaste.

appetizer, *n.* relish; hors d'oeuvre, antipasto; dainty. See FOOD, TASTE, PRECEDENCE.

appetizing, *adj.* tempting, tasty, mouthwatering. See TASTE, DESIRE.

applause, *n.* clapping; praise. See APPROBATION.

appliance, *n.* device, machine, implement; attachment, accessory. See INSTRUMENTALITY, REMEDY.

applicable, *adj.* fitting, suitable, appropriate, relevant, pertinent. See UTILITY, AGREEMENT. *Ant.,* irrelevant.

application, *n.* diligence, assiduity; suitability, relevancy; form, blank. See REQUEST, RELATION, ATTENTION, USE.

apply, *v.* put *or* lay on, USE; ask, REQUEST; work, persevere (see RESOLUTION).

appoint, *v.* prescribe, assign, ordain; place, designate, nominate; equip, rig. See COMMISSION, COMMAND.

appointment, *n.* meeting, interview, engagement; office; rendezvous, tryst, date (*inf.*). See BUSINESS, SOCIALITY, COMMISSION.

APPORTIONMENT
Proportional division

Nouns—1, *(act of sharing)* apportionment, allotment, consignment, allocation, assignment, sharing, rationing; appropriation; dispensation, distribution, division, partition, deal; trickle-down. See DISPERSION, PART.

2, *(portion shared)* dividend, portion, contingent, share, interest, lot, measure, dose; dole, meed, pittance; quantum, ration; ratio, percentage, proportion, quota, lion's share, modicum, allowance. *Informal,* jollop, dibs, rake-off, piece of the pie.

Verbs—apportion, admeasure, divide, prorate, budget; distribute, consign, dispense; billet, allot, detail, cast, share, mete; choose up sides; portion, allocate, disburse, ration; dish, hand, give, parcel, *or* dole out, farm out; deal, carve, administer; partition, assign, appropriate, appoint; share and share alike. *Informal,* go halves. *Slang,* divvy (up), deal *or* cut one in. See COOPERATION.

Adjectives—apportioning; respective; proportional, proportionate, commensurate, prorated; divisible.

Adverbs—respectively, pro rata, each to each, severally, individually; per stirpes, per capita, share and share alike. *Informal,* even Stephen. *Slang,* per.

Quotations—From each according to his abilities, and to each according to his needs (*Karl Marx*).

Antonyms, see ACQUISITION.

---

apposite, *adj.* applicable; suitable, well adapted. See AGREEMENT, EXPEDIENCE.

appraise, *v.* evaluate, assess, PRICE. See MEASUREMENT.

appreciable, *adj.* tangible; measurable. See SUBSTANCE.

appreciate, *v.* prize, esteem, value; IN-CREASE [in value]; comprehend, understand; realize worth. See APPROBATION, KNOWLEDGE, MEASUREMENT, GRATITUDE. *Ant.*, DECREASE.

apprehend, *v.* seize, arrest; grasp, see, understand, perceive. See RESTRAINT, KNOWLEDGE.

apprehension, *n.* FEAR, anxiety; arrest, seizure; understanding. See KNOWL-EDGE, RESTRAINT, EXPECTATION.

apprentice, *n.* novice, catechumen, initiate. —*v.* indenture, article, bind over. See LEARNING, SERVILITY.

apprenticeship, *n.* training, probation. See LEARNING.

apprise, *v.t.* inform, give notice, advise. See INFORMATION.

approach, *v.t.* accost, confront, encounter (see CONTACT); draw near, APPROACH. —*n.* access, avenue, INGRESS; bid, OF-FER; fashion, manner, METHOD; nearing, APPROACH. *Ant.*, withdraw, recede.

APPROACH
Motion toward

Nouns—1, approach, nearing, approximation; imminence; CONVERGENCE; advent, AR-RIVAL.

2, *(entrance)* access, entrance, advent; PASSAGE, INGRESS. See NEARNESS.

3, approachability, accessibility, availability, openness.

Verbs—approach, approximate; near, lower, draw near, come *or* step up; come to close quarters; move toward, come at; drift; make up to; gain on, pursue, tread on the heels of; hug the shore; loom ahead, impend, stare one in the face (see DESTINY).

Adjectives—1, approaching, near[ing], approximate; impending, brewing, preparing, forthcoming, oncoming, imminent, destined; on the horizon, on the brink *or* verge of, in the wind; approachable, accessible, *etc.*

2, approachable, accessible, available, open.

Antonyms, see REGRESSION, DISTANCE, AVOIDANCE, RECESSION.

APPROBATION
Approval

Nouns—1, approbation, approval, sanction; esteem, good opinion, favor, countenance; stamp of approval, imprimatur, OK; admiration (see RESPECT); appreciation, popularity, credit; FLATTERY. See ASSENT.

2, *(praise)* commendation, praise, kudos, laudation; good word, compliment; meed, tribute, encomium; eulogy, panegyric; testimonial, [letter of] reference; benediction, blessing, benison.

3, *(audible praise)* applause, plaudit, ovation, clapping [of hands]; acclaim, acclamation, cheer; paean, hosanna; thumbs up; claque. See CONGRATULATION.

4, *(tangible praise)* award, trophy, medal, prize, cup, loving cup, statuette; palm, laurel, garland of bays; crown, wreath, feather in one's cap, honor, decoration; Oscar, Emmy, Edgar, Obie, Tony, Grammy.

5, *(one who commends)* eulogist, encomiast, promoter, flatterer, booster. *Informal,* fan, rooter, plugger.

Verbs—1, approve, OK; think good, much, well, *or* highly of; esteem; value, prize; set great store by, view with favor; do justice to, appreciate; like, favor, take kindly to. *Informal,* hand it to: sign off on.

2, *(give credit to)* stand *or* stick up for; clap *or* pat on the back; endorse, give credit, recommend; commend, praise, laud, compliment, pay a tribute, applaud, cheer, encore; congratulate (see CONGRATULATION); panegyrize, eulogize, cry up, puff, extol, magnify, glorify, exalt, make much of, give credit where credit is due; bless, give a blessing to; have *or* say a good word for; speak well *or* highly of; sing, sound, *or* resound the praises of; damn with faint praise. *Slang,* give a big hand, root for.

3, *(receive praise)* be praised; receive honorable mention; be in [high] favor with; ring with the praises of, gain credit, stand well in the opinion of; pass muster; bring down the house, stop the show; be popular, catch on.

Adjectives—**1,** approving, commendatory, complimentary, benedictory, laudatory, panegyrical, eulogistic, lavish of praise; uncritical, favorable, in favor of, pro.

2, *(worthy of praise)* approved, praised, popular; in good odor; exemplary; in high esteem, respected, riding high, in one's good graces *or* books; in [good] with; good, praiseworthy, laudable, commendable; creditable, unimpeachable; beyond all praise. *Informal,* in one's good books. See GOODNESS.

Adverbs—with credit, well; on approval.

Prepositions—in favor of, pro, for, on the side of.

Interjections—hear, hear! bravo! bravissimo! olé! nice going! so far so good! viva! encore! congratulations!

Antonyms, see DISAPPROBATION.

---

appropriate, *adj.* proper, fit, timely, suitable. See AGREEMENT. —*v.t.* take, seize, confiscate; allot, assign. See STEALING, ACQUISITION, APPORTIONMENT. *Ant.,* inappropriate, unfitting, bequeath.

approve, *v.t.* accept, like, support, recognize, ratify, endorse, OK (*inf.*). See APPROBATION. *Ant.,* reject, refuse.

approximate, *adj.* near, close, rough. See NEARNESS, SIMILARITY, RELATION. *Ant.,* exact, precise.

appurtenance, *n.* privilege, RIGHT; accessory, appendage; (*pl.*) furnishings, apparatus. See ADDITION, PROVISION.

a priori, *Lat.* from cause to effect. See REASONING.

apron, *n.* bib, smock; flap, strip. See CLOTHING, AVIATION.

apropos, *adv.* opportunely, in passing, by the way; in reference to. —*adj.* appropriate, germane, to the purpose. See RELATION. *Ant.,* irrelevant.

apse, *n.* alcove, recess. See CONCAVITY.

apt, *adj.* suitable, appropriate, fitting; quick, clever; likely. See AGREEMENT, SKILL, TENDENCY. *Ant.,* unsuitable, unlikely.

aptitude, *n.* fitness, ability, SKILL; flair, bent, propensity. See TENDENCY.

aquanaut, *n.* diver (see DEPTH).

aquatic, *adj.* watery; oceanic, marine, fresh- *or* salt-water. See WATER.

aquarium, *n.* [fish]tank, vivarium. See RECEPTACLE.

aqueduct, *n.* watercourse, culvert. See PASSAGE.

aquiline, *adj.* beaked, curved, hooked, Roman. See ANGULARITY.

arabesque, *n.* ornament; chinoiserie. See ORNAMENT, MUSIC.

arable, *adj.* tillable, farmable; fertile. See AGRICULTURE.

arbiter, *n.* umpire, arbitrator, judge. See JUDGMENT.

arbitrary, *adj.* despotic, dictatorial; capricious; unreasonable; discretionary, willful. See ILLEGALITY, AUTHORITY, WILL. *Ant.,* planned.

arbitration, *n.* intervention, mediation, settlement (of dispute). See JUDGMENT, COMPROMISE.

arbitrator, *n.* judge, referee, umpire, mediator. See JUDGMENT, COMPROMISE.

arbor, *n.* bower, pergola; shaft. See ABODE, ROTATION.

arboretum, *n.* botanical garden (see AGRICULTURE).

arc, *n. & v.i.* curve (see CIRCULARITY); spark (see ELECTRICITY).

arcade, *n.* corridor (see PASSAGE); penny arcade (see AMUSEMENT).

arcane, *adj.* SECRET.

arch, *n.* curve, arc, vault. See CONVEXITY, CONCAVITY, CURVATURE. —*adj.* CUNNING, roguish; preeminent, chief. See SUPERIORITY.

archaeology, *n.* See PAST.

archaic, *adj.* old, ancient; antiquated, obsolete, outdated; historic. See PAST, OLDNESS. *Ant.,* new, up-to-date.

archer, *n.* bowman. See COMBATANT.

archetype, *n.* model, prototype. See PREP-
ARATION.

architect, *n.* planner, designer, creator. See
AGENCY, ARCHITECTURE.

ARCHITECTURE
Building design

Nouns—**1**, architectural *or* building design, FORM; architectural *or* structural engineering; landscape architecture *or* gardening; architectonics. See BUILDING.

2, *(architectural styles)* **a.** Byzantine, Romanesque, Egyptian, Hellenic, Greco-Roman, Palladian, Greek, Moorish, Norman. **b.** Elizabethan, Queen Anne, Regency, Tudor, perpendicular, Jacobean, baroque; high, decorated, rococo *or* flamboyant Gothic; Renaissance, mannerism, classical, eclectic. **c.** early English, Victorian, churrigueresque, Directoire, Palladian; Colonial, Georgian; Egyptian, Gothic, Greek Revival. **d.** Chicago style, Bauhaus; Art Deco, Moderne *or* Nouveau; neo-Gothic, neoclassical; Prairie; brutalist, postmodern, International.

3, *(classical architectural ornaments)* molding, relief, reticulation, sarcophagus, abacus, capital, dosseret, echinus, crown, caryatid, chapiter, scotia, base, torus, dado, filigree, groin, grotesque, imbrication, fillet, finial, tracery, fluting, architrave, metope, entablature, entasis, extrados, baldacchino; gargoyle; archivolt; corbel, cymatium, acanthus, anthemion, capstone, bezant, boss, foliation, ballflower, trefoil, triglyph, bas-relief; annulet, stringcourse; chigi; egg and dart.

4, *(classical architectural elements)* stereobate; apse, bay, arcade, impost, pier, shaft, pilaster, pillar, intrados, keystone, lintel, quoin, plinth, summer, arch, triumphal arch, springer, voussoir, squinch, skewback, soffit, spandrel, barrel *or* fan vault, facade, gable, atrium, attic, [flying] buttress, canopy, cantilever, cloister, stylobate, colonnade; cupola, pediment, sympanum, predentive, peristyle; cusp, supercilium, cornice, frieze, dentil, corona; lunette; crossette; console; Byzantine, Composite, Corinthian, Doric, Gothic, Ionic, Moorish, Romanesque, *or* Tuscan column, engaged column, telamon; portico, loggia, narthex, transept, nave, spire, steeple, westwork; niche, tabernacle; pantheon, oculus; minaret; pylon, tholos; ziggurat; gopuram, stupa, torii; vomitory.

5, *(construction terms)* modular construction, modular unit, prefab; platform frame, post-and-beam construction; basement, sump, slab, foundation; subfloor; attic; backfill, foundation; fascia; balloon frame; baseboard, dry wall, nonbearing wall, [load-]bearing wall, knee wall, breast wall, retaining wall, sandwich wall, curtain wall, blocking; landing; crawlspace; casement window, double-glazed window, double-hung window; central heating, radiant heating; columniation, fenestration, crenellation; fixture; blueprint, floor plan, maquette, mockup, mechanical drawing, working drawing, drafting, elevation, perspective, section, rise, plat, grade; orientation; water table; dead weight, live load, kip; building codes.

6, architect; urban planner, urbanologist; designer; builder, [sub]contractor.

Verbs—architect, design; build.

Adjectives—architectural.

Quotations—Form ever follows function *(Louis Sullivan),* Architecture in general is frozen music *(Friedrich von Schelling),* Architecture is the art of how to waste space *(Philip Johnson),* Architecture begins where engineering ends *(Walter Gropius),* Architecture is . . . life itself taking form *(Frank Lloyd Wright),* Architecture is inhabited sculpture *(Constantin Brancusi),* In my experience, if you have to keep the lavatory door shut by extending your left leg, it's modern architecture *(Nancy Banks-Smith).*

Related categories, BUILDING, FORM, TEMPLE, ABODE.

archive, *n.* chronicle, annal, RECORD.

archway, *n.* arcade. See PASSAGE.

arctic, *adj.* boreal. See COLD.

ardent, *adj.* warm, passionate, zealous, fervent; glowing, fiery; eager. See FEELING, HEAT, ACTIVITY. *Ant.,* cool, unfeeling.

ardor, *n.* fervor, passion, enthusiasm, élan, zeal; HEAT. See FEELING, VIGOR. *Ant.,* indifference.

arduous, *adj.* onerous, wearisome. See DIFFICULTY, WEARINESS. *Ant.,* easy.

area, *n.* tract, territory; SPACE; expanse; scope. See REGION.

ARENA
Athletic enclosure

Nouns—1, arena, field, theater; [athletic *or* playing] field, terrain, *etc.*; amphitheater, coliseum, Colosseum, stadium, bowl; hippodrome, circus, racecourse *or* -track, turf, cockpit; hall, auditorium; playground, gymnasium, [bull, boxing, *or* wrestling] ring, canvas, mat, rink, lists, tilting ground; gymkhana; stage. *Informal,* gym. See AMUSEMENT, CONTENTION, SPORTS.

2, bailiwick, turf, stamping ground, home territory (see INFLUENCE).

3, theater [of war]; battlefield, battleground, front, field of combat *or* battling field, field of slaughter, Aceldama; combat zone, no-man's-land; theater of operations. See WARFARE.

---

argot, *n.* slang, cant, jargon (see SPEECH).

argument, *n.* debate, dispute; EVIDENCE, case. See REASONING, DISCORD, THOUGHT.

argumentative, *adj.* contentious (see CONTENTION).

aria, *n.* song, air (see MUSIC).

arid, *adj.* dry, parched; jejune, barren; uninteresting. See DRYNESS, WEARINESS, USELESSNESS. *Ant.,* moist, verdant; interesting.

arise, *v.i.* get up, awake; originate, begin. See BEGINNING, ASCENT, EFFECT.

aristocracy, *n.* NOBILITY. See AUTHORITY. *Ant.,* commonalty, plebes.

arithmetic, *n.* mathematics, computation (see NUMERATION).

arm, *n.* limb, member; branch, wing; weapon, strength. See ARMS, POWER, PART. —*v.* equip. See PROVISION.

armistice, *n.* truce, respite, lull, peace. See PACIFICATION.

armoire, *n.* cupboard, wardrobe (see STORE).

armor, *n.* steel plate, mail, shielding. See DEFENSE.

armory, *n.* arsenal. See STORE.

ARMS
Weapons

Nouns—1, arms, weapon[s], weaponry, firearms, armament, engine of war, materiel; hardware; panoply, stand of arms, military establishment; armory, arsenal (see STORE); armor (see DEFENSE). See WARFARE, PROVISION.

2, ammunition, munitions, explosive. *Slang,* hardware. a. ball, bolt, shot, grape [shot], chain shot, pellet, bullet, dumdum bullet, spitzer, cartridge, shell, fragmentation shell, shrapnel. *Informal,* ammo. b. tactical *or* strategic weapon; missile, projectile; grenade, fireball; bomb, antipersonnel bomb, cluster bomb, demolition bomb, dynamite bomb, pipe bomb, ashcan, napalm *or* incendiary bomb, stink bomb, smoke bomb, time bomb, depth charge; radiation enhancement weapon; [thermo]nuclear warhead, atomic bomb, A-bomb, fission bomb, hydrogen bomb, H-bomb, thermonuclear bomb, fusion bomb, neutron bomb, clean bomb, plutonium bomb; blockbuster; torpedo, guided missile, selective ordnance, heat-seeking missile, Nike, Patriot, Exocet, surface-to-air missile, ICBM (intercontinental ballistic missile), rocket, V1, V2; antiballistic *or* antimissile missile, robot bomb; rocket bomb (see PROPULSION); gas bomb; [land *or* ground] mine, claymore, pressure, sonic, *or* castrator mine, fougasse. *Informal,* Molotov cocktail; [mini]nuke; daisy-cutter. *Slang,* pineapple; smart bomb.

3, artillery, gun[s], field *or* siege gun, gunnery, cannon, battery, ordnance, ballistics; piece, fieldpiece, howitzer, mortar, trench gun, stern chaser; siege, coast, *or* field artillery; Big Bertha, Long Tom, French 75, two-pounder, ten-pounder, eight-inch, sixteen-inch, *etc.*; carronade, culverin, basilisk, serpentine, falcon[et], jingle, swivel, petard; antiaircraft, AA, ackack, pompom; bazooka, rocket-launcher, Stinger, missile (see PROPULSION); flamethrower. *Informal,* flak.

4, machine gun, submachine gun, machine pistol, mitrailleuse, assault rifle, pompom, Gatling gun, Maxim gun, Browning machine gun, Bren gun, Thompson *or* Tommy gun, Uzi. *Slang,* chopper, burp gun.

5, small arms; musket[ry], carbine, rifle, shotgun, chokebore, over-and-under, side-by-side, sawed-off shotgun, scattergun, pump-action rifle, bolt- *or* lever-action rifle, recoilless rifle, fowling piece, breechloader, muzzle-loader, chassepot, blunderbuss, jingal, harquebus, arquebus, matchlock, flintlock, petronel, flint-and-steel; .22, .25, .32., .38, .44, .45, .30-30, .30-06, *etc.*; 8-, 12-, 16-gauge, *etc.*; Kentucky long rifle, Springfield, Enfield, Winchester, Lee-Enfield, Garand, *etc.*; pistol, automatic, semiautomatic, derringer, repeater, magazine gun, magnum, revolver, pepperbox, percussion gun, hammerless [revolver], six-shooter, six-gun; stun gun; Colt, Smith and Wesson, Luger, Beretta, *etc.*; BB gun; air rifle *or* gun. *Informal,* Saturday night special. *Slang,* piece, gat, glock, rod, heater, equalizer, iron, roscoe, zip gun, hush-hush, nina, nine, speaker.

6, *(firearm parts)* action, bolt, bore, butt[stock], caliber, chamber, cleaning rod, clip, cock, hammer, cradle, firing pin, sight, gauge, grenade launcher, gunlock, gunpowder, holster, magazine, muzzle, peep sight, percussion lock, pin, pistol grip, propellant, range finder, rear sight, refling, safety, scope, side lock, silencer, tampion, telescopic sight, trunnion.

7, *(mechanical weapon)* armored vehicle, tank; battering ram; bombard; catapult, mangonel, trebuchet, onager, sling[shot] (see PROPULSION).

8, *(swords and knives)* sword, saber, broadsword, backsword, cutlass, curtalax, falchion, scimitar, katana, bilbo, rapier, barong, skean, claymore, creese, spatha, kukri, Toledo; dagger, anlace, dirk, hanger, kirpan, parazonium, poniard, stiletto, stylet, dudgeon, bayonet, misericord, kris, kuttar, puntilla; foil, épée, blade, steel; ax, poleax, battleax, halberd, tomahawk, Lochaber ax; bowie knife, bolo, kukri, pig-sticker, switchblade [knife], barlow, clasp knife, jackknife, yataghan, snickersnee, kard, skean dhu; cold steel. *Slang,* shank, shivhot supper. See SHARPNESS.

9, *(lance)* pike, lance, spear, assegai, atlatl, spontoon, javelin, dart, banderilla, djerrid, pilum, arrow, reed, shaft, bolt, boomerang, harpoon, gaff; ounji stake; fishing spear; blowgun, blowpipe, blowtube.

10, *(club)* club, mace, truncheon, staff, bludgeon, cudgel, bastinado, life preserver, shillelagh, knobkerrie, nulla-nulla, pogamuggan, nunchaku; quarterstaff; battering ram (see IMPULSE); bat, knuckle-duster, brass knuckles *or* knucks; blackjack, sap, billy, nightstick. *Slang,* cosh.

11, archery, bow [and arrow], longbow; crossbow, arbalest, ballista, elastic gun; catapult, sling; bola.

12, warship (see SHIP).

13, *(chemical weapon)* [poison *or* nerve] gas, chemical agent; [nuclear] fallout, anthrax.

14, armsmaker, fletcher; armory, arsenal.

Verbs—arm, equip, PROVISION.

Adjectives—armed, equipped, *etc.*; armed [to the teeth], in arms.

Quotations—This world in arms is not spending money alone. It is spending the sweat of its laborers, the genius of its scientists, the hopes of its children (*Dwight D. Eisenhower*), A bayonet is a weapon with a worker at each end (*Anon.*), The sword is the axis of the world and its power is absolute (*Charles de Gaulle*), The period of debate is closed. Arms, as a last resource, must decide the contest (*Thomas Paine*), Wars may be fought with weapons, but they are won by man (*George S. Patton*).

army, *n.* troops, soldiers, [military] force; host, crowd, throng. See COMBATANT, MULTITUDE.

aroma, *n.* fragrance, smell; quality, characteristic (see SPECIALITY). See ODOR.

around, *adv. & prep.* surrounding, about; near, neighboring. See NEARNESS, ENVIRONMENT.

arouse, *v.* rouse, awaken; stir, excite, stim-

ulate, whet. See EXCITEMENT, ACTIVITY. *Ant.,* calm, put to sleep.

arraign, *v.t.* indict, charge, accuse. See ACCUSATION, LAWSUIT. *Ant.,* discharge, exonerate.

arrange, *v.t.* put in ORDER; settle (see AGREEMENT); PLAN; orchestrate, score (see MUSIC). See ARRANGEMENT. *Ant.,* disturb, scatter, confuse.

ARRANGEMENT
Putting in proper order

Nouns—1, arrangement, plan, PREPARATION, disposition, disposal, distribution, deployment, sorting; configuration, FORM, format, grouping, placement, formation, constitution, assortment, triage; METHOD; allotment (see APPORTIONMENT); taxonomy, organization, classification (see CLASS); register, file (see LIST); echelon; ORDER, array, system; flow chart, Gantt chart, tableau. See SYMMETRY.

2, sorter, filing system; index, table, inventory; organizer; filing clerk.

Verbs—1, arrange, dispose, line up, place, form; put, set, *or* place in order; set out, collate, pack, marshal, range, size, rank, group; dispose of, compartmentalize, pigeonhole, assign places to; assort, sort, prioritize (see PRIORITY); put *or* set to rights, align, line up, put in shape *or* in array, reduce to order, put up; stack. *Informal,* get one's ducks in a row, get one's act *or* head together.

2, classify, alphabetize, file; string together, register (see LIST); graduate (see DEGREE); regulate, systematize, coordinate, organize, straighten up.

Adjectives—arranged, methodical, orderly, tidy, neat, regular, systematic, classified, structured.

Adverbs—methodically, systematically, like clockwork, in apple-pie order.

Antonyms, see DISORDER.

arrant, *adj.* thorough, downright. See COMPLETION, DISREPUTE.

array, *n.* CLOTHING, apparel; host, MULTITUDE; ARRANGEMENT. See ASSEMBLAGE, OSTENTATION, CONTINUITY, ORDER.

arrears, *n.pl.* See DEBT.

arrest, *v.t.* seize, apprehend, capture, nab

(*inf.*), pinch, bust (*both sl.*); stop, halt; retard, suspend. See END, RESTRAINT.

arresting, *adj.* striking, dramatic (see ATTENTION).

arrière-pensée, *Fr.* mental reservation; hidden motive. See CONCEALMENT.

ARRIVAL
Act of reaching a certain point

Nouns—1, arrival, coming, advent; landing, docking, mooring; debarkation, disembarkation, deplaning; homecoming, return, rencounter.

2, (*place of arrival*) home, goal, landing place, destination, journey's end (see END); harbor, haven, port, port of call, station, [air] terminal; terminus, end of the line; attainment (see COMPLETION).

3, (*one who arrives*) newcomer, visitor; Johnny-come-lately; newborn [child].

Verbs—1, arrive, show up; arrive at, get to, come to, reach, attain; come to rest; come up with *or* to; catch up (to); overtake. *Informal,* hit, make it.

2, land, make a landfall, make land, dock, moor; disembark, deplane, detrain, *etc.*

3, (*means of arrival*) light, alight, dismount; land, go ashore, debark, disembark; de-

train, deplane; put in[to], visit, cast anchor, pitch one's tent; sign *or* check in, get to one's journey's end, end up; come *or* get back, come home, return; appear, put in an appearance, come in, drop in, darken one's door. *Slang*, blow in, hit town; make the scene.
Adjectives—arriving, coming; inbound, incoming.
Adverbs—on arrival.
Quotations—It is better to travel hopefully than to arrive (*R. L. Stevenson*).

Antonyms, see DEPARTURE.

---

arrogance, *n.* haughtiness, self-importance; INSOLENCE, presumptuousness. See SEVERITY, VANITY. *Ant.*, modesty, HUMILITY.

arrogate, *v.* usurp, claim, seize; assume, appropriate, take. See ACQUISITION.

arrow, *n.* shaft, bolt; pointer. See ARMS, DIRECTION.

arsenal, *n.* armory, storehouse, supply; resources. See STORE.

arson, *n.* incendiarism, pyromania; *slang*, torch job. See HEAT.

art, *n.* craft, SKILL; CUNNING; science, technics; fine arts (see REPRESENTATION). See BUSINESS.

artery, *n.* vessel, vein, channel. See PASSAGE.

artful, *adj.* crafty, wily. See CUNNING, SKILL. *Ant.*, slow-witted, artless.

article, *n.* item; object, thing; story, piece, essay, report. See SUBSTANCE, INFORMATION, BELIEF, PART, UNITY, GRAMMAR.

articulate, *adj.* jointed, segmented (see JUNCTION); distinct, intelligible; literate, lucid. —*v.* pronounce, enunciate, utter, put in words, verbalize; unite, join. See SPEECH, MEANING. *Ant.*, inarticulate; mumble.

artifact, *n.* relic, manmade product. See PRODUCTION, OLDNESS.

artifice, *n.* trick, stratagem, ruse; device; CUNNING. See DECEPTION. *Ant.*, candor, innocence.

artificial, *adj.* handmade, handcrafted, synthetic; false, sham, fake, deceptive; affected, unnatural. See AFFECTATION, DECEPTION, PRODUCTION, INELEGANCE. *Ant.*, real, genuine.

artillery, *n.* cannon, ordnance. See ARMS.

artisan, *n.* mechanic, craftsman, workman. See AGENCY, SKILL, ARTIST.

ARTIST
Creator or performer

Nouns—1, *(visual creator)* artist, virtuoso, master, maestro, academician; craftsman, artisan; old master. See AGENCY, SKILL.

2, a. painter, limner, drawer, sketcher; colorist; illustrator, portraitist, watercolorist, miniaturist, pointillist, surrealist, genre painter, landscapist, landscape artist, seascapist; engraver, designer, etcher; reetcher, retoucher; cartoonist, caricaturist; copyist, draftsman; commercial *or* graphic artist, advertising artist, layout man; printmaker. See PAINTING, ENGRAVING. b. sculptor, sculptress, carver, chaser, modelist, chiseler, stonecutter; ceramist, potter; glassblower. See SCULPTURE. c. author, writer, novelist (see WRITING); poet (see POETRY). d. dramatist, actor, actress, Thespian, performer, vaudevillian (see DRAMA); dancer, ballerina (see DANCE); musician, composer, arranger, orchestrator, soloist, pianist, *etc.* (see MUSIC). e. architect, builder; landscape architect *or* gardener. See ARCHITECTURE. f. photographer, cameraman, cinematographer. See PHOTOGRAPHY, MOTION PICTURES. g. decorator; interior decorator; window dresser.

Quotations—The artist must be in his work as God is in creation, invisible and all-powerful (*Gustave Flaubert*), The artist is not a special kind of man, but every man is a special kind of artist (*Ananda Coomaraswamy*), Artists are the antennae of the race (*Ezra Pound*), The true artist will let his wife starve, his mother drudge for his living at seventy, sooner than work at anything but his art (*G. B. Shaw*), All men are creative, but few are artists (*Paul Goodman*), Great artists have no country (*Alfred de Musset*).

Antonyms, see UNSKILLFULNESS.

artistic, *adj.* talented, accomplished; cultural; beautiful, esthetic; skillful, masterly. See BEAUTY, TASTE, ELEGANCE.

artless, *adj.* simple; ingenuous, unsophisticated, naive; guileless, innocent. See INNOCENCE. *Ant.*, artful; sophisticated.

ASCENT
Motion upward

Nouns—1, ascent, ascension, mounting, rising, climb, rise, escalade; LEAP; upswing, upsurge, upturn; acclivity, hill; ELEVATION. See OBLIQUITY.

2, *(means of ascent)* flight of steps *or* stairs, stairway, staircase, perron; step, rung, stair, tread, riser, stepping-stone, doorstep, step stool; ladder, accommodation *or* extension ladder, fire escape; incline, ramp, gangway; companionway; elevator, lift, escalator, moving staircase. See OBLIQUITY.

3, mountaineer, [mountain *or* rock] climber, alpinist.

Verbs—ascend, rise, mount, arise, uprise; ride *or* crawl up; spring *or* shoot up; step up; climb, clamber [up], surmount, scale [the heights]; tower, soar, LEAP; gush, fountain; [sky]rocket; take off, become airborne, gain altitude; upturn. *Informal,* shinny.

Adjectives—ascending, rising, scandent, buoyant; in the ascendant; anabatic; upturned, retroussé.

Adverbs—up, upward(s), uphill, upstream; upstairs, abovestairs.

Interjections—excelsior!, onward and upward!; upsy-daisy! alley-oop!

Quotations—All rising to a great place is by a winding stair (*Francis Bacon*).

Antonyms, see DESCENT.

---

ascertain, *v.t.* find, discover, learn; determine, establish, fix; certify, ensure, settle, clinch. See CERTAINTY, DISCLOSURE, LEARNING.

ASCETICISM
Extremism in self-restraint

Nouns—1, asceticism, puritanism, austerity; abstinence, abstemiousness; [self-]mortification, [self-]denial, maceration, sackcloth and ashes, hair shirt, flagellation; penance, fasting, belt-tightening. See ATONEMENT, MODERATION.

2, ascetic, anchoret, anchorite, stylite, troglodyte, hermit, recluse; fakir, dervish; puritan, sabbatarian; flagellant; Franciscan, Trappist, Carmelite.

Verbs—fast, do penance, deny oneself; abstain, eat like a bird; mortify the flesh, flagellate; eat worms; tighten one's belt.

Adjectives—ascetic, austere, puritanical, anchoritic, eremitic; abstinent, abstemious; flagellant.

Quotations—To many total abstinence is easier than perfect moderation (*St. Augustine*).

Antonyms, see PLEASURE, GLUTTONY.

---

ascribe, *v.t.* impute, accredit, attribute (see ATTRIBUTION).

ash, *n.* cinder, ember. See HEAT, REMAINDER.

ashamed, *adj.* abashed, embarrassed, mortified. See REGRET, HUMILITY. *Ant.*, proud.

ashen, *adj.* ashy, pale, bloodless, wan, gray. See COLORLESSNESS.

ashore, *adj.* on land *or* shore. See LAND.

Asian, *adj. & n.* Chinese, Indian, *etc.*; Asiatic, Oriental (*both offen.*). See HUMANITY.

aside, *adv.* apart, aloof, away. See DISTANCE, SIDE. —*n.* parenthesis; [stage] whisper. See SPEECH.

asinine, *adj.* mulish, donkeyish; silly. See FOLLY, ABSURDITY.

ask, *v.* interrogate, question; inquire; invite; REQUEST, demand. See INQUIRY, BARTER.

askance, *adv.* sideways; distrustfully. See SIDE, DOUBT.

askew, *adj.* crooked, awry, lopsided, oblique. See DISTORTION.

aslant, *adj.* slanting, oblique (see OBLIQUITY).

asleep, *adj.* sleeping; dozing; napping; quiescent, dormant; numb; dead (see DEATH). See INACTIVITY, INATTENTION. *Ant.*, awake, alert.

aspect, *n.* look, APPEARANCE, side, view; expression, mien; phase, stage. See LOCATION.

asperity, *n.* harshness, SEVERITY.

asphyxia, *n.* suffocation (see DEATH).

aspire, *v.i.* DESIRE, strive (for).

ass, *n.* donkey, jackass, burro; fool, simpleton; *slang,* buttocks, derriere. See TRANSPORTATION, FOLLY, REAR, BODY.

assail, *v.t.* ATTACK, set upon, assault; criticize. See DISAPPROBATION.

assassin, *n.* killer, slayer, murderer, thug. See KILLING.

assault, *v. & n.* See ATTACK.

assay, *v.t.* test, analyze (see INQUIRY).

ASSEMBLAGE
Persons or things assembled

Nouns—1, *(collection of people)* assemblage, assembly, gathering, meeting, forgathering, convocation, congregation, council, caucus, conclave, congress, diet, convention; symposium, panel; concourse, conflux; muster, levy, posse, posse comitatus, roundup; caravan, convoy; coffee klatsch; pickup band. *Informal,* rat pack. See SOCIALITY, PRESENCE.

2, *(large assemblage)* crowd, throng, rabble, mob, press, crush, horde, body, tribe (see POPULACE); audience (see HEARING); crew, gang, team, knot, squad, band, PARTY; array, bevy, galaxy, constellation; clique, coterie, set; fleet; corps, company, troop; host (see MULTITUDE).

3, *(collection of assorted objects)* compilation, collection, anthology, album, compendium; miscellany, collectanea, assortment, grab-bag, hodgepodge (see MIXTURE); library, treasury, museum, zoo, menagerie (see STORE).

4, *(collection of like objects)* shower, group, cluster, clump, set, batch, lot, pack; battery; bunch, bundle, fascine, bale; wisp, shock, rick, fardel, stack, sheaf, haycock.

5, *(large collection)* accumulation, congeries, heap, pile, drift, aggregate, agglomeration, conglomeration, aggregation, concentration, QUANTITY. See ACQUISITION.

6, *(collection of animals)* a. *(animals)* army, bale, bed, bunch, cete, clowder, colony, drift, drove, flock, gam, gang, herd, host, husk, kennel, knot, labor, leap, nest, pace, pack, pod, pride, sault, school, shoal, shrewdness, skulk, sloth, team, trace, trip, troop. b. *(birds)* bevy, bouquet, charm, confusion, covert, covey, exaltation, flight, flock, gaggle, host, murmuration, muster, parliament, pride, skein, spring, team, watch. c. *(insects)* cloud, hive, plague, swarm.

7, *(one who assembles)* collector, connoisseur, fancier; bill collector, customs agent; miser (see PARSIMONY). *Informal,* pack rat.

8, *(member of a group)* one of the guys *or* girls; groupie. *Slang,* homeboy, banger, mau-mau.

Verbs—1, *(come together)* assemble, be *or* come together, collect, muster; meet, unite, rejoin; cluster, flock, swarm, surge, stream, herd, crowd, throng, associate; congregate, conglomerate, concentrate; rendezvous, resort; come, flock, *or* get together; forgather, huddle.

2, *(bring together)* get *or* bring together, assemble, muster, collect, collocate, call up, gather, convene, convoke, convocate; rake up, dredge; heap, mass; agglomerate, aggregate; bundle, bale, sheaf, collate, compile, take up; package, wrap up, pack; group, concentrate, amass, accumulate; scare up, round up.

Adjectives—assembled, closely packed, massed, serried, crowded, teeming, swarming, populous; cumulative.

Adverbs—en masse, in force, in a crowd.

Phrases—birds of a feather flock together.

Quotations—A crowd is not company (*Francis Bacon*).

Antonyms, see DISPERSION.

assemble, *v.* See ASSEMBLAGE, COMPOSITION, WHOLE.

assembly line, *n.* production line. See PRODUCTION.

ASSENT
Expression of agreement

Nouns—1, *(concurrence)* assent, acquiescence; nod, accord, accordance; concord (see AGREEMENT); unanimity (see UNITY); recognition, concurrence.

2, *(acceptance)* ratification, confirmation, corroboration; [stamp of] approval, acceptance (see APPROBATION); CONSENT, willingness. *Informal,* OK, okay, green light, go-ahead. *Slang,* high five. See PERMISSION, WILL.

3, *(agreeing person)* yes-man, yea-sayer, toady, sycophant, company man; rubber stamp; signator[y], signer, cosigner, endorser; notary [public]. *Slang,* brown-nose, suck, ass-kisser *or* -wipe, boot-lick[er], lickspit[tle].

Verbs—1, *(sign of acceptance)* assent, nod, acquiesce, agree; accept, accede, accord, concur; lend oneself to, CONSENT; go with, go along (with), have no problem with, chime in, jump at, recognize; subscribe (to), say yes; say the word, ditto, amen, *or* aye (to), OK; ratify, validate, approve (see APPROBATION); countersign; corroborate; let ride. *Slang,* give five.

2, *(reach an agreement)* come to an understanding, come to terms, see eye to eye, shake hands on; swim with the stream; be in the fashion, join in the chorus. *Informal,* shake on it.

3, *(be agreed upon)* be ratified, carry, pass, go through.

Adjectives—1, *(in agreement)* assenting, of one accord *or* mind, of the same mind, at one with; agreed; acquiescent, willing; content (with).

2, *(agreed upon)* uncontradicted, unchallenged, unquestioned, uncontroverted; ratified, signed and sealed; signed, sealed and delivered; carried, agreed.

Adverbs—1, yes, yea, aye; true, good, well, very well, well and good; granted; even so, just so, to be sure; truly, exactly, precisely, that's just it, indeed, certainly, of course, indubitably, unquestionably, surely, sure, assuredly, by all [manner of] means, no doubt, doubtless, and no mistake; be it so, so be it, amen; willingly; to a man.

2, *(in an agreeing manner)* affirmatively, in the affirmative.

Interjections—yes sirree! yes sirree Bob! you said a mouthful! you said it! and how! *Informal,* you bet [your ass]! you can say that again! right on! that's about the size of it! so be it!

Quotations—One must know when to blend force with a maneuver, a blow with an agreement (*Leon Trotsky*).

Antonyms, see DISSENT.

---

assert, *v.t.* avow, declare, say, claim, affirm, state. See AFFIRMATION.

assertive, *adj.* positive, dogmatic. See CERTAINTY, INSOLENCE. *Ant.,* shy, meek.

assess, *v.t.* value, appraise, price, estimate; charge, tax. See JUDGMENT, MEASUREMENT, PAYMENT.

assets, *n.pl.* possessions, PROPERTY; capital; resources. See ACCOUNTING. *Ant.,* liabilities.

asshole, *n., slang,* anus; jerk, fool. See BODY, FOLLY, IGNORANCE, BADNESS.

assiduous, *adj.* diligent, attentive. See ACTIVITY. *Ant.,* lazy.

assign, *v.* hand over; allot, distribute; delegate, COMMISSION; appoint, designate;

ascribe (see ATTRIBUTION). See APPORTIONMENT, GIVING, TRANSFER, BUSINESS.

assignation, *n.* rendezvous, tryst (see MEETING).

assimilate, *v.t.* digest, absorb; incorporate, merge (with). See SIMILARITY, IMITATION, LEARNING.

assist, *v.t.* AID, help, second, support; attend (see PRESENCE). *Ant.,* hinder.

assistant, *n.* See AUXILIARY.

associate, *v.* join, fraternize, ally, combine (with); unite, connect, relate, link. See CONNECTION, RELATION. —*n.* FRIEND, comrade; colleague, co-worker, partner. See ACCOMPANIMENT, AUXILIARY, COMBINATION.

association, *n.* club, organization (see PARTY); fraternity; partnership, COMBINATION, league; analogy (see RELATION). See ACCOMPANIMENT, COOPERATION. *Ant.,* disunion, rupture.

assort, *v.t.* arrange, classify; mix. See ARRANGEMENT, MIXTURE.

assuage, *v.t.* lessen (see RELIEF).

assume, *v.t.* suppose, take for granted; put on, affect; appropriate. See SUPPOSITION, AFFECTATION, ACQUISITION.

assurance, *n.* confidence, CERTAINTY, BELIEF; INSOLENCE, boldness; pledge, guarantee, PROMISE. *Ant.,* uncertainty, DOUBT.

astern, *adv.* aft, to the rear, abaft. See REAR.

asteroid, *n.* planetoid (see UNIVERSE).

astir, *adv.* afoot; moving; up and about. See ACTIVITY.

astonish, *v.t.* SURPRISE, amaze, astound.

astray, *adv.* lost, wandering; in ERROR. See DEVIATION.

astride, *adj.* astraddle (see SUPPORT, CROSSING).

astringent, *adj.* binding, styptic; severe (see SEVERITY). See CONTRACTION, PUNGENCY.

astrology, *n.* horoscopy, stargazing. See PREDICTION.

ASTRONAUTICS
Science of space

Nouns—1, *(sciences of space)* astronautics, cosmonautics, space travel *or* flight, manned *or* unmanned flight; space *or* celestial navigation, astrogation, astronavigation; outer- *or* interplanetary space, interplanetary travel; aerospace; aerospace science *or* medicine, exobiology; rocketry. See AVIATION, PROPULSION.

2, rocket, spaceship, spacecraft, booster rocket; command *or* service module, lunar [excursion] module, lunar lander, rover, LEM; [ascent *or* descent] stage; air lock; launch pad; nose cone, heat shield; capsule, cargo bay; space station, space laboratory, Mir, Skylab, Spacelab, spaceport; [communications, weather, observation, *etc.*] satellite; space shuttle, *Challenger, Columbia, Discovery, etc.*; [space] probe, Pioneer, Mariner, Surveyor, Viking, Voyager; Jupiter, Saturn, Titan; Sputnik, Vostok, Gemini, Mercury, Soyuz; mission control; flying saucer, unidentified flying object, UFO. *Informal,* bird.

3, drop-off, capsule; docking; countdown, [number for] go, backout; blastoff, launch, liftoff; separation, blowoff, burnout; escape velocity; payload; injection *or* insertion [into orbit]; launch site, Cape Kennedy, Cape Canaveral, cosmodrome; escape velocity, launch window, reentry corridor; reentry, splashdown; footprint; downlink; liquid *or* solid propellant.

4, free fall, weightlessness; space walk, extravehicular activity, EVA, extravehicular mobility unit; zero gravity; decompression sickness.

5, *(space traveler)* astronaut, cosmonaut, spaceman *or* -woman; space suit; alien. *Slang,* spaghetti suit.

Verbs—launch, blast off; abort; dock; touch down, impact; inject *or* insert into orbit; space-walk.

Adjectives—astronautical, cosmonautical.

Quotations—That's one small step for a man; one giant leap for mankind (*Neil Armstrong*).

---

astronomy, *n.* cosmology, cosmogony. See UNIVERSE.

astute, *adj.* clever, shrewd, CUNNING. See INTELLIGENCE. *Ant.,* slow-witted, obtuse.

asunder, *adv.* apart (see DISJUNCTION, DISTANCE).

asylum, *n.* retreat, refuge, sanctuary, shelter; home, orphanage, sanitarium, sanatorium; mental hospital, psychopathic ward. See SAFETY, INSANITY, ABODE.

asymmetric, asymmetrical, *adj.* uneven, irregular. See DISTORTION, IRREGULARITY.

atavism, *n.* throwback, REVERSION.

atelier, *n.* studio, workshop. See BUSINESS.

atheist, *n.* heretic, unbeliever. See IRRELIGION, HETERODOXY.

athletic, *adj.* sporting, gymnastic, acrobatic; agile, strong. See STRENGTH, AMUSEMENT, EXERTION. *Ant.*, weak, awkward, unskillful.

atlas, *n.* gazetteer (see PLAN).

atmosphere, *n.* AIR, sky, ether, ozone; exosphere; mood, aura, ambience, ENVIRONMENT.

atoll, *n.* [coral] reef. See LAND.

atom, *n.* particle, iota, speck. See LITTLENESS, POWER.

atomize, *v.t.* vaporize; pulverize. See VAPOR, POWDERINESS.

ATONEMENT
Making amends

Nouns—1, *(act of atoning)* atonement, reparation; COMPENSATION, quittance, quits; expiation, redemption, reclamation, propitiation. See PENITENCE, ASCETICISM.

2, *(sign of atonement)* amends, [abject] apology, *mea culpa*, breast-beating; amende honorable, satisfaction, RESTORATION; peace offering, a sop to Cerberus, burnt offering; [self-]sacrifice, sacrificial lamb.

3, *(punishment)* penance, fasting, maceration, mortification, sackcloth and ashes, hair shirt, white sheet, shrift, flagellation, lustration; purgation, purgatory; Day of Atonement, Yom Kippur; Lent.

Verbs—1, *(make amends)* atone (for); expiate; propitiate; make amends, pay for, make good; reclaim, redeem, redress, repair; ransom, purge, shrive; do penance, repent [in sackcloth and ashes] (see PENITENCE); set one's house in order; wipe off old scores, wipe the slate clean; make matters up; pay the penalty; take back, eat one's words, eat humble pie, eat crow; live down. *Informal,* give it up for Lent; pay one's dues.

2, apologize, beg pardon, ask forgiveness, give satisfaction; fall *or* get down on one's knees.

Adjectives—propitiatory, conciliatory, expiatory; sacrificial, piacular; apologetic, repentant.

Phrases—don't make excuses, make good; apology is only egoism wrong side out.

Antonyms, see IMPENITENCE, IMPIETY.

---

atrocity, *n.* enormity; outrage. See MALEVOLENCE, BADNESS.

atrophy, *n.* degeneration, DETERIORATION.

attaché, *n.* diplomat, consul; chargé [d'affaires]; briefcase. See AGENT, RECEPTACLE.

attachment, *n.* ADDITION, adjunct, appendage; legal seizure (see ACQUISITION); affection, LOVE, loyalty, devotion. See JUNCTION. *Ant.*, aversion, antipathy, separation.

attack, *n.* assault, ATTACK; seizure (see DISEASE). —*v.t.* assail, assault, ATTACK; affect, INFLUENCE. *Ant.*, DEFENSE.

ATTACK
Violent assault

Nouns—1, *(human attack)* attack; assault, assault and battery; onset, onslaught, charge; aggression, offense; incursion, inroad, invasion; counterattack, counteroffensive, surgical strike; irruption, outbreak; drive, push, sally, sortie, raid, foray; boarding, escalade; siege, investment, besiegement, beleaguerment; storm[ing]; bombing, strafing, air attack, air raid, preemptive strike, blitz[krieg], bombardment, barrage, cannonade; volley, fusillade, broadside; salvo; raking, crossfire; surprise *or* sneak attack, friendly fire. *Informal,* mugging. See WARFARE, COMBATANT.

2, *(personal attack)* cut, thrust, lunge, pass; kick, punch; stoning. See IMPULSE.

3, *(attacking person)* assailant, aggressor, offender, invader; pusher, go-getter. *Informal,* mugger.

Verbs—1, *(military attack)* attack, assault, charge, assail; counterattack; set *or* fall upon; raid; ambush; make *or* go to war (on *or* against), break a lance with, enter the lists, aggress; assume *or* take the offensive, strike the first blow, throw the first stone; lift a hand *or* draw the sword (against), take up the cudgels; march against *or* upon, invade; take by storm, blitz; harry, show fight.

2, *(personal attack)* strike (at), thrust at, hit, kick, slap, cut, pelt; take a punch, poke, *or* sock at; deal a blow (at), tee off at, lash out, fetch one a blow, fling oneself at *or* upon, lunge at, pounce upon; lace, lay, rip, light, sail, plow, tear, *or* pitch into, launch out against, go at *or* for; bait, slap on the face; make a pass at; bear down upon, close with, come to grips with, come to close quarters, bring to bay; rush, run, fly, *or* have at, ride full tilt against, let fly at, turn on; attack tooth and nail; press hard; run down, strike at the root of; lay about one, run amuck; gang up on *or* against. *Informal,* whale away. *Slang,* kick ass, blaze on; cuff; nuke. See IMPULSE.

3, *(attack with arms)* fire at, shoot at, open up on; pepper, bombard, shell, pour a broadside into; open fire, fire a volley; beset, besiege, beleaguer; lay siege to, invest; sap, mine; storm, board, scale the walls; cut and thrust, bayonet, butt, batter; bomb, strafe, dive-bomb, blitz.

4, *(be attacked)* draw fire, be a sitting duck.

Adjectives—**1,** *(being aggressive)* attacking, aggressive, offensive, pushy; up in arms, on the warpath; forceful, belligerent, combative, warlike.

2, *(being attacked)* under attack *or* fire, under siege.

Adverbs—on the offensive; under attack, under siege.

Interjections—attack! charge! banzai! Geronimo!

Phrases—attack is the best form of defense.

Antonyms, see DEFENSE.

---

attain, *v.t.* achieve, accomplish; reach. See ARRIVAL, SUCCESS. *Ant.,* surrender, fail.

attempt, *n. & v.* try, endeavor, essay; ATTACK. See UNDERTAKING.

attend, *v.* accompany, escort; be present; heed, listen; minister to, serve. See ACCOMPANIMENT, ATTENTION, PRESENCE, REMEDY.

ATTENTION
Direction of the mind toward

Nouns—**1,** attention, mindfulness, intentness, attentiveness, THOUGHT, thoughtfulness, advertence, attention to detail, CARE, special consideration; observance, observation, [special] consideration, heed, notice, look, note, regard; vigil; circumspection, study, scrutiny, inspection (see INQUIRY); fixation, undivided attention. See RESPECT, INFORMATION.

2, *(care)* diligence, application, attention to detail, absorption (of mind), preoccupation (with).

3, calling *or* drawing attention to (see INDICATION); consciousness-raising.

Verbs—**1,** *(pay attention to)* attend (to), observe, look, watch, notice, regard, take notice, mark; give *or* pay [close] attention, have an ear to the ground, prick up the ears, keep the eyes open *or* peeled; be all ears, hang on one's words *or* every word, harken, heed, be attentive, listen, lend *or* give an ear to; hang on the words *or* lips of; trouble one's head about, give a thought to, occupy oneself with; contemplate; look [in]to, see to; turn the mind to, apply oneself to, buckle *or* knuckle down, have an eye to; bear in mind, take into account *or* consideration; keep in sight *or* view, keep one's eye on the ball; have a regard to; take cognizance of, entertain; make *or* take note *or* notice of, note, see about, take under advisement. *Informal,* get with it.

2, *(study)* examine closely *or* intently, consider; inspect, review, take stock of; fix, rivet, *or* devote the mind *or* thoughts on *or* to, zero in on; lose oneself, have eyes only for; go over with a fine-tooth comb. *Informal,* check it out, get a load of.

3, *(attract one's attention)* catch *or* strike the eye; attract attention *or* notice, cut a swath, awaken *or* invite interest; hold the stage, be arresting *or* absorbing; engage, intrigue, excite notice, catch one's ear; be uppermost in one's mind; monopolize, preoccupy, engross, tie up, obsess.

4, *(call attention to)* indicate, bring to one's notice, point out, lay the finger on; bring, direct, call, *or* draw attention to, mention [in passing], touch on; show. *Informal,* put one wise to.

Adjectives—1, *(paying attention)* attentive, mindful, observant, regardful, assiduous; alive *or* awake to; observing, occupied with, engrossed, thoughtful, wrapped up in, absorbed, rapt, all ears *or* eyes; intent (on), open-eyed, on the watch *or* ball, alert, [broad *or* wide] awake, vigilant; watchful, wakeful, Argus-eyed, expectant. *Informal,* laser-eyed, on the ball, on top of; turned on.

2, *(attracting attention)* absorbing, engrossing, eye-catching, catchy, titillating, spell-binding, mesmerizing, hypnotic, arresting; interesting, inviting.

Adverb—attentively, mindfully, devotedly, with undivided attention; in mind.

Interjections—see! look! mark [my words]! lo! behold! hark! mind! observe! lo and behold! attention! ahoy! hear ye, hear ye!; nota bene, N.B., read my lips; this to give notice.

Phrases—the squeaking *or* squeaky wheel gets the grease.

Antonyms, see INATTENTION.

---

attenuate, *v.* weaken; thin out, rarefy. See DECREASE, NARROWNESS, WEAKNESS. *Ant.,* strengthen.

attest, *v.* testify, bear witness, depose, certify, swear, vouch. See EVIDENCE.

attic, *n.* loft, garret. See RECEPTACLE.

attire, *n.* dress, CLOTHING, garb.

attitude, *n.* stand, pose, posture, position. See LOCATION, FORM, CIRCUMSTANCE.

attorney, *n.* lawyer, AGENT. See LAWSUIT.

ATTRACTION
Drawing toward

Nouns—1, *(act of attracting)* attraction, attractiveness; drawing to, pulling toward, adduction, magnetism, gravity, gravitation; affinity. See TRACTION.

2, *(something that attracts)* allurement, seduction, fascination, appeal, enticement, temptation, the world, the flesh, and the devil (see DESIRE); lodestone, lodestar, polestar; [bar *or* horseshoe] magnet, electromagnet, siderite, alnico, magnetic north; lure, glamour, charm, charisma; decoy, bait; femme fatale; center of attraction *or* attention, focus. *Slang,* rainmaker; draw.

Verbs—1, *(attract physically)* attract, lure; draw *or* pull toward; adduct.

2, *(cause desire)* allure, seduce, interest, charm, captivate, fascinate, tempt, entice, lure, lead on; rope in; make one's mouth water. *Slang,* make a play for, hit on, come onto, make, race [off].

Adjectives—1, *(which attracts)* attracting, attrahent, attractive, adducent, adductive; magnetic, magnetized.

2, *(which is attractive)* attractive, charming, alluring, engaging, interesting, winning, prepossessing, captivating, bewitching, fascinating, seductive; mouth-watering; charismatic. See BEAUTY.

Phrases—stolen fruit is sweet.

Quotations—And lead us not into temptation, but deliver us from evil (*Bible*), I can resist everything except temptation (*Oscar Wilde*), There are several good protections against temptations, but the surest is cowardice (*Mark Twain*).

Antonyms, see REPULSION.

ATTRIBUTION
Act of assigning

Nouns—1, *(act of attributing)* attribution, ascription, assignment, reference to; accounting for; imputation, derivation from, credit; explanation, reason, motive (see CAUSE); etiology; INTERPRETATION. See EFFECT.

2, reference, citation, credit, acknowledgment; trademark; by-line.

3, attribute, trait, characteristic, feature, quirk, quality, property. See INDICATION, SPECIALITY.

Verbs—attribute, ascribe, assign, impute, accredit; refer, lay, point, *or* trace to; set *or* put down to; credit with *or* to; ground on; lay at the door of; put words in one's mouth; charge *or* chalk up to; account for, derive from, read into; blame on *or* to, charge with *or* to, fix responsibility *or* blame (see ACCUSATION).

Adjectives—attributed, attributable, imputable, referable, assignable, traceable, ascribably; due to, derivable from, owing to.

Adverbs—1, *(as a result of)* hence, thence, therefore, since, on account of, because, owing *or* due to, consequently; on that account; thanks to, forasmuch as; whence, *propter hoc*; *ergo*; duly.

2, *(determining attribution)* why? wherefore? whence? on what account? *Informal,* how come?

Prepositions—because of, on account of, owing *or* due to; in view of, by virtue of.

Conjunctions—because, since, inasmuch *or* forasmuch as, seeing that, in view of the fact that.

Phrases—give credit where credit is due.

Quotations —The way to get things done is not to mind who gets the credit for doing them (*Benjamin Jowett*), The world is divided into people who do things and people who get the credit. Try, if you can, to belong to the first class. There's far less competition (*Dwight Morrow*).

---

attrition, *n.* abrasion (see DETERIORATION, FRICTION).

au contraire, *Fr.* on the contrary. See OPPOSITION.

au courant, *Fr.* up-to-date; informed. See KNOWLEDGE.

auction, *n.* bidding, vendue, SALE; offering.

audacity, *n.* boldness, COURAGE; impudence; RASHNESS, INSOLENCE. *Ant.,* meekness, forbearance.

audible, *adj.* See HEARING.

audience, *n.* HEARING, interview; onlookers, hearers; assembly. See DRAMA, CONVERSATION.

audit, *v. & n.* See ACCOUNTING.

audition, *n.* hearing, tryout. See EXPERIMENT, HEARING.

auditor, *n.* listener, kibitzer (see HEARING).

auditorium, *n.* hall, meeting place; theater. See DRAMA, AMUSEMENT.

auditory, *adj.* aural, otic; acoustic(al). See HEARING.

au fait, *Fr.* well-informed. See KNOWLEDGE.

augment, *v.* See INCREASE. *Ant.,* DECREASE.

augur, *v.* foretell, prophesy; signify, presage. See PREDICTION.

august, *adj.* noble, exalted, imposing; eminent. See REPUTE. *Ant.,* unimposing.

au naturel, *Fr.* nude. See DIVESTMENT.

au pair, *n. & adj.* nanny, baby-sitter. See SAFETY, CARE.

aura, *n.* atmosphere, air; emanation. See WIND, ENVIRONMENT.

aureole, *n.* halo, nimbus (see LIGHT, CIRCULARITY).

auspice, *n.* omen, token; (*pl.*) patronage, protection, protectorship. See PREDICTION, AID.

auspicious, *adj.* favorable, promising, propitious; fortunate. See HOPE, PREDICTION, OCCASION. *Ant.,* unfavorable, inauspicious.

austere, *adj.* harsh, stern, severe, rigorous; ascetic, simple. See SEVERITY, ASCETICISM. *Ant.* mild, luxurious, comfortable.

authentic, *adj.* genuine, real, authoritative, trustworthy. See TRUTH, AUTHORITY. *Ant.,* fake, spurious, counterfeit.

authenticate, *v.t.* verify, confirm. See EVIDENCE, DEMONSTRATION.

author, *n.* creator, originator; writer, inventor. See PRODUCTION, WRITING, ARTIST, CAUSE.

authoritarian, *adj.* exacting, stringent, dictatorial. See AUTHORITY.

authoritative, *adj.* official, decisive; imperative, peremptory; truthful, reliable; scholarly. See AUTHORITY, CERTAINTY. *Ant.,* doubtful.

authority, *n.* expert, pundit, know-it-all (*inf.*), maven (*inf.*). See SKILL, KNOWLEDGE, AUTHORITY.

AUTHORITY
Right to govern

Nouns—1, *(supremacy)* authority, POWER, right, jurisdiction, title, prerogative; INFLU-ENCE, patronage; prestige (see REPUTE); command, control, rule, sway; dominion, domination, predominance, sovereignty, empire, supremacy; lordship, suzerainty, seigniory; the crown, the sovereign; the state, commonwealth, realm, body politic, polity; the ship of state; divine right, dynasticism, dynasty, regime; popular mandate; black power, gay power. *Informal,* the feds.

2, *(symbols of authority)* mastery, hold, grasp, grip; octopus, fangs, clutches, talons; rod of empire, scepter, throne. See SUPERIORITY.

3, *(offices of authority)* administration, governance, ministration; direction, management, government, conduct, legislation, regulation, guidance; reins [of government]; supervision, superintendence, surveillance, oversight; control, charge; capital, seat [of government]. See LEGALITY.

4, *(types of authority)* government, administration, headquarters; autocracy, autarchy, aristocracy, oligarchy, hierarchy, theocracy, patriarchy, plutocracy, democracy; monarchy, absolute monarchy, kingdom, chiefdom; caliphate, pashalik; pro-consulship, consulship; prefecture, magistracy; directory, triumvirate, *etc.;* absolutism, despotism, tyranny, imperialism, czarism, dictatorship, authoritarianism, fascism, nazism, monolithic government, *Führer Prinzip,* boss rule; communism, Marxism, socialism, dictatorship of the proletariat, syndicalism, collectivism, People's Republic; anarchism, nihilism (see ILLEGALITY); bureaucracy, red tape, officialdom; feudalism, feudality; gerontocracy; meritocracy; gynarchy, gynocracy, matriarchy; autonomy, home rule, representative government, republic, free enterprise (see FREEDOM); constitutional government, constitutional *or* limited monarchy. *Informal,* brass, the man, big brother; petticoat government.

5, *(positions of authority)* directorship, presidency, premiership, senatorship; chair, portfolio; stewardship, proctorship, jurisdiction. *Informal,* driver's seat, saddle.

6, *(positions having authority over countries)* sovereign, ruler, emperor, empress, crowned head, king, queen, prince, princess (see NOBILITY); potentate, liege, suzerain, monarch; czar, tsar, kaiser; boss, dictator, Duce, Führer, despot, tyrant, pharaoh; judge, autocrat; president, vice president, chairperson, the chair, premier, prime *or* first minister; potentate, patriarch, chief, chieftain, sachem, ataman, hetman, caliph, sultan, pasha, emir, sheik; master; gray eminence.

7, *(acts affecting authority)* accession, succession, installation, coronation, crowning.

8, *(those in authority over smaller forces)* master, lord, padrone; employer; superior, DIRECTOR; mayor, majordomo, prefect, regent, chancellor, provost, magistrate, alcalde, burgomaster, seneschal, warden; commandant, commander, captain, skipper, commanding officer; governor, leader, higher-up, apparatchik. *Informal,* Simon Legree; mugwump, big white chief; men in suits. *Slang,* top banana, top dog, [head] honcho, whole cheese *or* show, the man, gaffer; capo, godfather; hammerman, chief cook and bottle washer.

9, *(taking authority from another)* usurpation, assumption, *or* arrogation of authority (see ILLEGALITY); election, delegation, empowerment.

Verbs—1, have *or* wield authority; head, lead, command; dominate, control, boss; dictate, dispose, rule, govern, administer; preside; wear the crown, ascend the throne; have the upper *or* whip hand, wear the pants *or* trousers; rule the roost, throw one's weight around, ride roughshod over; lord it over, bend to one's will, give the law to, lay down the law; have under one's thumb, hold in the hollow *or* palm of one's hand. *Informal,* ride herd.

2, *(run something)* direct, manage, govern, conduct; order, prescribe, cut out work for; head, lead, boss; superintend, supervise, overlook, keep in order, look after, see to, legislate for; administer, ministrate; have care *or* charge of, have *or* take the direction, take over, take charge, pull the strings *or* wires, call the shots *or* the tune; hold office, preside; take, occupy, *or* be in the chair, take over; pull the stroke oar; carry the ball; get a handle on.

3, be under, subject to, *or* in the power of (see SUBJECTION).

4, *(give authority to)* authorize, empower, put in authority (see PERMISSION).

5, usurp, assume, *or* arrogate authority, seize the throne; take charge *or* command, take control, take the helm; be elected *or* appointed; receive the reins of power; take things into one's own hands.

Adjectives—1, *(in position of authority)* ruling, regnant, at the head, in command, dominant, predominant, preponderant, in the ascendant, influential; paramount, supreme (see SUPERIORITY); imperious; authoritative, executive, administrative, clothed with authority, official, ex officio, ex cathedra; imperative, peremptory, overruling, absolute; arbitrary; dictatorial, tyrannical, bossy; regal, sovereign, royal, monarchical, kingly, queenly, imperial, princely; presidential, gubernatorial, mayoral, *etc.*; directing, managing, governing, *etc.*; hegemonic.

2, *(being under authority)* at one's command; in one's power; under one's control.

3, *(of civic authority)* governmental, civic; parapublic.

Adverbs—1, in authority, in charge, at the helm *or* head of, on the throne, in the hand of, in the saddle, on top, in the driver's seat, behind the wheel.

2, *(under one's authority)* at one's pleasure; by a stroke of the pen; imperiously, dictatorially; authoritatively, ex officio, ex cathedra; with a high hand.

Phrases—he who pays the piper calls the tune; might is right; in the country of the blind the one-eyed man is king; better red than dead; a good leader is always a good follower; you can't fight City Hall.

Quotations—Tyranny of the majority *(Tocqueville)*, 'Tis time to fear when tyrants seem to kiss *(Shakespeare)*, Uneasy lies the head that wears a crown *(Shakespeare)*, Power is the great aphrodisiac *(Henry Kissinger)*, Thank heavens we do not get all the government that we are made to pay for *(Milton Friedman)*, Communism is like prohibition, it's a good idea but it won't work *(Will Rogers)*, Capitalism, it is said, is a system wherein man exploits man. And communism—is vice versa *(Daniel Bell)*, Democracy substitutes election by the incompetent many for appointment by the corrupt few *(G. B. Shaw)*, The best government is that which governs least *(John L. O'Sullivan)*, Big Brother is watching you *(George Orwell)*, The art of leadership is saying no, not yes. It is very easy to say yes *(Tony Blair)*, Communism is the corruption of a dream of justice *(Adlai Stevenson)*, The blind lead the blind. It's the democratic way *(Henry Miller)*.

Antonyms, see SUBJECTION, OBEDIENCE, DISORDER, SERVANT.

---

authorization, *n.* PERMISSION.

autocrat, *n.* dictator, czar, despot, monarch. See AUTHORITY.

autograph, *n.* signature; manuscript, holograph. See WRITING.

automatic, *adj.* mechanical; self-operating; instinctive, reflex. See NECESSITY, INTUITION.

automobile, *adj.* self-propelled. See PROPULSION. —*n.* auto, car. See VEHICLE.

autonomy, *n.* self-government; independence. See FREEDOM, AUTHORITY.

autopsy, *n.* postmortem, examination. See INQUIRY.

autumn, *n.* fall, harvest TIME.

AUXILIARY
Giving of support

Nouns—auxiliary, assistant, adjuvant, adjutant, adjunct, help, helper, helpmate, helpmeet, helping hand; colleague, partner, mate, confrère; cooperator, coadjutor, collaborator; ally, confederate, accomplice, accessory, particeps criminis; AID, aide, aide-de-camp; secretary, amanuensis, clerk, associate, right hand [man], man *or* girl

Friday; personal, executive, *or* administrative assistant; handmaid, SERVANT; satellite, adherent; disciple, devotee, votary; acolyte; seconder, backer, upholder, abettor, advocate, partisan, champion, exponent, friend at court; friend in need, guardian angel. *Slang,* shill, batman. See ACCOMPANIMENT.

Verbs—help, AID, assist, second.

Adjectives—auxiliary, helping, helpful, accessory, assistant; subsidiary, subservient; supplementary, reserve, extra.

Antonyms, see HINDRANCE, OPPOSITION.

---

avail, *v.* serve, do, suffice; help, benefit. See SUCCESS, UTILITY. **—avail oneself of,** make USE of, resort to.

available, *adj.* handy, ready, convenient; obtainable; usable. See UTILITY.

avalanche, *n.* snowslide; landslide. See DESCENT, SUCCESS.

avant-garde, *n.* See PRECEDENCE.

avarice, *n.* greed. See DESIRE. *Ant.,* generosity, prodigality.

ave atque vale, Lat. hail and farewell. See DEPARTURE.

Ave Maria, Lat. Hail Mary! See WORSHIP.

avenge, *v.t.* See RETALIATION.

avenue, *n.* thoroughfare, boulevard, artery; MEANS, access. See PASSAGE.

aver, *v.t.* See AFFIRMATION. *Ant.,* deny.

average, *n.* normal, norm, MEAN, standard. *—adj.* MEAN, normal, ordinary. See UNIMPORTANCE, MEDIOCRITY, GENERALITY. *Ant.,* exceptional, extraordinary, outstanding.

averse, *adj.* loath, reluctant; unwilling, opposed. See OPPOSITION, HATE, UNWILLINGNESS, DISLIKE.

avert, *v.t.* keep off, turn aside, ward off; turn away; prevent. See HINDRANCE, DEVIATION.

AVIATION
Science of flight

Nouns—**1,** *(science of flight)* aviation, flight, flying; navigation, aerial navigation; aeronautics, aerodynamics, aerodonetics, aerostatics, avionics, rocketry; aerial navigation, teleran, loran, shoran, instrument flying; airpower, air transportation; commercial *or* private aviation; ballooning, balloonery; skydiving, soaring, [hang] gliding; aerobatics; gliding; air piracy, skyjacking; Civil Aeronautics Board, CAB, Federal Aviation Administration, FAA. See SPORTS.

2, *(commercial flight)* [scheduled, charter, commuter, *or* nonscheduled] airline, major *or* regional carrier, air shuttle, air taxi, air coach, air cargo, air freight; crop duster; nonstop, direct, *or* multistop flight, layover, stopover, red-eye; hub and spoke system; airways; airport, airfield, airdrome, jetport, heliport, flying field; gate, jetway; ground crew; landing field, landing strip, airstrip, taxiway, runway, tarmac; helipad, blast fence; pylon, beacon; control tower, windsock; passenger, no-show, standby, overbooking; checked *or* carry-on baggage, baggage carousel, skycap; hangar; airspace, air lane, skyway, victor airway, flight path, corridor; boarding pass, boarding, deplaning; frequent flyer program.

3, air warfare; air force, RAF, Luftwaffe; formation flying, echelon; bombing, divebombing, pursuit, dogfight; group, wing, flight, squadron; mission, dry run, bombing mission; air cover; formation flying; [de]briefing.

4, aircraft: **a.** lighter-than-air, aerostat; [captive, observation, gas, helium, *or* barrage] balloon; airship, dirigible, Zeppelin, blimp, kite, box kite; parachute. *Informal,* gasbag. **b.** heavier-than-air, airplane, aeroplane, plane, monoplane, biplane, wedgewing, seaplane, hydroplane, amphibian, hydroplane, flying boat; ultralight; glider, sailplane, crate, box, ship, jenny; airliner, transport; pursuit plane, interceptor, fighter, flying fortress, dive bomber, bomber, stealth fighter, tilt-rotor, spy plane, reconnaissance plane, U2; jet plane, turbojet, propjet, pulsejet, JATO (jet-assisted takeoff), RATO (rocket-assisted takeoff), STOL (short takeoff and landing), VTOL (vertical takeoff and landing), SST (supersonic transport); Caravelle, Concorde, Airbus, Lear jet, *etc.*; jumbo jet, wide-body [jet]; autogiro, gyroplane, gyrodyne, rotorcraft, helicopter, whirlybird, Sikorsky, helibus; Hovercraft; ornithopter. *Informal,* kite, chopper. *Slang,* grasshopper.

5, *(parts of aircraft)* airframe, fuselage, monocoque, skin, nose, nose cone, tail, empennage, rudder, fin, stabilizer; cockpit, flight deck, canopy, gondola, nacelle, cabin, ejection seat; belly, hull; balloon, ballonet; engine, engine pod, propeller, airscrew, prop, contraprop; afterburner, throat, inlet; reciprocating, radial, *or* jet engine, fanjet, turbofan, ramjet; rocket; airfoil, wing, leading *or* trailing edge, gull wing, sweptback wing, sweepback, variable-sweep wing, spar, spoiler; cabane, flaperon, aileron, longeron, deceleron, elevon, elevator, stabilator, stabilizer, air brake; stick, Joyce *or* joy stick, control yoke; landing gear, undercarriage, pontoon; console, instrument panel, inertial guidance system, compass, compass card, pelorus, gyrocompass, magnetic compass, altimeter, artificial horizon, artificial *or* automatic pilot, autopilot, Gyropilot, telemetry, tachometer, airspeed indicator, machmeter, drift meter, yaw meter, rate-of-climb indicator, [turn-and-]bank indicator, inclinometer, Earth inductor, terrain clearance indicator, ADF (automatic direction finder), ADI (attitude direction indicator), radar, transponder, LORAN (long range navigation), TACAN (tactical air navigation), PAR (precision approach radar), VOR (very high frequency omni range), air log, ceilometer, climatometer, nephoscope; bomb bay, [inflatable] evacuation slide, safety *or* emergency doors; black box, flight data *or* cockpit voice recorder; overhead rack; radar dome, radome. *Slang,* blue room.

6, *(flying terms)* clearance, takeoff, liftoff; autorotation; zoom, loop, loop the loop, soar, climbout, climb, chandelle, glide; Immelmann turn, barrel roll; sideslip, crabbing, stall, porpoising, buffeting, fishtailing, flutter; cruising altitude; dive, nosedive, volplane, spiral, spin, tailspin, wingover, yaw; buzz, hedgehopping; thrust, lift, drag; airstream, slipstream, jet *or* prop wash, backwash, sideslip, drift; flying circus, barnstorming, stunt flying, lazy eight, loop; formation flying; skywriting; point of no return; vapor trail, contrail; airspeed, ground speed, shock wave; visibility, ceiling, ceiling zero; air pocket, burble, headwind, tailwind, [clear air] turbulence, wind shear; holding pattern, circling; final approach, [instrument] landing, touchdown, three-point landing, straight-in landing, pancake, precision approach; course, heading; airsickness; flight plan; icing; mach number; power loading; pressurization; in-flight refueling, probe and drogue; visual *or* instrument flight rules; ATC, air traffic control.

7, flier, aviator, aeronaut, airman, balloonist, pilot, co-pilot, navigator, bombardier; flight crew, captain, first officer, flight attendant, steward[ess], host[ess]; stunt *or* test pilot; Daedalus, Icarus, Darius Green, Amelia Earhart, Eddie Rickenbacker; air marshal, flying officer; airborne troops, paratroops; passenger (see TRAVEL); air traffic controller. *Informal,* birdman, top gun; hedgehopper; no-show.

8, space travel (see ASTRONAUTICS).

Verbs—aviate, fly, pilot, go by air taxi, take off, take to the air; feather; gain altitude, ascend, climb, zoom; stall, yaw, pitch, roll, bank, dive, cruise, pull out, pull up, soar, glide, porpoise, sideslip; land, set down, descend; stall, flame out, crash-land; stunt, buzz, hedgehop; peel off; nose down, over, *or* up; strafe, dive-bomb; crash, crack up, prang, conk out, bail out; flame out; jettison; barnstorm. *Slang,* skyjack; ditch.

Adjectives—aviation, aeronautic, avionic; airworthy; airsick; flying, airborne, aloft, on the wing, over-the-top; in-flight, onboard, outboard, inboard; supersonic, transonic.

Adverbs—in flight.

Quotations—There are only two emotions in a plane: boredom and terror (*Orson Welles*).

---

avidity, *n.* eagerness, longing, DESIRE; keenness, alarity; avarice, greed, voracity.

avocation, *n.* hobby, sideline. See AMUSEMENT, BUSINESS.

AVOIDANCE
Refraining from

Nouns—1, *(act of avoiding)* avoidance, evasion, default, circumvention, elusion, dodge, sidestep; abstinence, forbearance, refraining (see ASCETICISM); DEPARTURE; ESCAPE, flight; truancy, hooky, French leave (see ABSENCE); subterfuge, quibble, equivocation; CIRCUITY; brush-off. *Informal,* the slip, the go-by, the runaround; tax shelter, blind trust. *Slang,* cop-out. See NEGLECT, UNWILLINGNESS.

2, *(one who avoids)* shirker, slacker, quitter, malingerer, deserter, dodger, truant, fugitive, runaway, absconder, refugee; welsher; abstainer, teetotaler; nonparticipant. *Informal,* goldbrick.

Verbs—1, avoid, shun, sidestep, shirk, circumvent, eschew, refrain (from), not do, let alone, steer clear of, give a wide berth to, fight shy of; pass the buck; abstain, keep aloof, keep one's distance; evade, elude, dodge, lead a merry chase, get around, get by, give the runaround; put off, defer (see LATENESS); set one's face against; shy away from; make way for, give place to; take no part in, have no hand in; hem and haw, fudge, waffle; procrastinate, put off. *Informal,* take the fifth, beg the question; tap-dance. *Slang,* lay off *or* out, fake on; blow off.

2, *(avoid work)* malinger, shirk, slack off; beg off. *Slang,* cop out, fob off, lie down on the job, goof off.

3, *(escape to avoid)* flee, desert, take French leave, abscond; show *or* take to one's heels, beat a retreat, turn tail, run for it, cut and run, steal away, make off, slip off, take off; walk out on, go back on; skip *or* jump bail. *Informal,* shake off; drop out, top out. *Slang,* take it on the lam, clear out.

Adjectives—1, evasive, slippery [as an eel]. *Slang,* Teflon-coated, cagey.

2, avoidable, evadable.

Phrases—once bitten, twice shy.

Quotations—Neurosis is the way of avoiding non-being by avoiding being (*Paul Tillich*).

Antonyms, see PURSUIT.

à votre santé, *Fr.* to your health. See CONGRATULATION.

avouch, *v.t.* vouch for, guarantee; acknowledge. See EVIDENCE.

avow, *v.* declare, confess; assert. See AFFIRMATION, DISCLOSURE. *Ant.,* disclaim, repudiate.

await, *v.* expect, wait for, anticipate, look forward to; impend, lie in store (see DESTINY). See EXPECTATION, LATENESS.

awake, *adj.* alert, heedful, observant, attentive; keen, knowing; informed, astute, watchful, on guard, unsleeping, vigilant. See CARE, KNOWLEDGE, ATTENTION. —*v.* awaken, knock up (*sl.*). See ACTIVITY, EXCITEMENT. *Ant.,* asleep, inattentive.

award, *n.* prize, medal; COMPENSATION; decision, adjudication. See GIVING, JUDGMENT, APPROBATION.

aware, *adj.* cognizant, informed; alert (to). See KNOWLEDGE. *Ant.,* unaware.

away, *adv.* absent, elsewhere, far-off, gone. See DISTANCE, ABSENCE.

awe, *n.* FEAR, dread; WONDER.

awesome, *adj.* impressive, awe-inspiring; *slang,* excellent, splendid. See WONDER, GOODNESS.

awful, *adj.* horrible, dreadful; tremendous. See FEAR, WONDER.

awkward, *adj.* clumsy, ungraceful, ungainly; gauche; embarrassing. See UNSKILLFULNESS, DIFFICULTY. *Ant.,* adroit, dexterous.

awning, *n.* [sun]shade (see COVERING).

awry, *adj.* askance, crooked, askew; out of order; mistaken, amiss, WRONG; cockeyed, screwy (*both sl.*). See OBLIQUITY, DISORDER.

ax, axe, *n.* chopper, hatchet; instrument (see MUSIC). See ARMS, SHARPNESS. — *v., slang,* dismiss (see EJECTION).

axiom, *n.* law, proposition; aphorism, MAXIM.

axis, *n.* shaft, pivot; alliance, coalition. See ROTATION, MIDDLE, COMBINATION.

axle, *n.* shaft, pin. See ROTATION.

azure, *adj.* blue, sky-blue, cerulean. See COLOR.

B

babble, *v.i.* chatter, prattle, gossip; rave, gibber; gurgle. See LOQUACITY, UNMEANINGNESS.

baby, *n.* infant, babe, child, tot, kid (*inf.*); nursling, suckling; offspring. See YOUTH. —*v.t.* pamper. See LENIENCY.

bacchanal, *n.* orgy, debauch. See DRINKING.

bachelor, *n.* celibate, Coelebs; widower, divorcé; licentiate, [post-]graduate. See CELIBACY, SCHOOL. *Ant.,* husband, spouse.

back, *n.* See REAR. —*v.t.* support; AID; promote, fund, finance (see MEANS); stand behind, encourage. —*v.i.* move backward, reverse. See REGRESSION. *Ant.,* FRONT.

backbite, *v.* attack, revile. See DETRACTION.

backbone, *n.* spine, spinal column; COURAGE, RESOLUTION. See SUPPORT.

backfire, *v.i.* boomerang, go awry. See FAILURE, VIOLENCE, RECOIL.

background, *n.* setting, ENVIRONMENT; experience, training; family (see ANCES-TRY). See KNOWLEDGE, DISTANCE, REAR. *Ant.,* foreground.

backlash, *n.* reaction; RECOIL.

backsliding, *n.* recidivism, REGRESSION, lapse; apostasy (see IMPIETY); relapse.

backup, *n.* substitute, alternate. See SUBSTITUTION, AID.

backward, *adj.* retarded, slow, underdeveloped; third-world; delayed, tardy; unwilling, loath, shy. See REAR, UNWILLINGNESS, LATENESS.

backwoods, *adj.* rustic; primitive, uncouth. See VULGARITY.

bad, *adj.* vicious, wicked; defective; hurtful, noxious; unfavorable, unfortunate. See BADNESS, INEXPEDIENCE, IMPERFECTION. *Ant.,* GOOD.

badge, *n.* emblem, sign. See INDICATION.

badger, *v.t.* nag, pester, tease. See DISCONTENT.

badmouth, *v.t., slang* speak ill of, put down, trash, dis. See DISAPPROBATION.

BADNESS
Hurtfulness

Nouns—1, *(quality of being bad)* badness, hurtfulness, virulence, perniciousness, malignancy, malignity; insalubrity; ill *or* bad turn, evil star, ill wind; bane, pest, plaguespot, scourge; pestilence (see DISEASE); skeleton in the closet, thorn in the side *or* in the flesh. *Slang,* bummer, bad hair day, the pits. See EVIL.

2, *(being bad toward others)* ill treatment, molestation, abuse, oppression, persecution, outrage; atrocity, torture. See MALEVOLENCE.

3, *(bad behavior)* misbehavior, mischief, acting out; depravity, vice (see IMPURITY); GUILT; IMPROBITY, knavery.

4, bad influence, bad *or* evil genius. *Informal,* hoodoo, jinx; rotten egg. *Slang,* Jonah.

5, *(bad quality)* IMPERFECTION, defectiveness, poor quality, MEDIOCRITY, INFERIORITY. *Slang,* tackiness, schlock; schlockmeister.

Verbs—1, *(be bad toward)* WRONG, aggrieve, oppress, persecute; trample, tread, *or* put upon, overburden, weigh down, victimize.

2, *(have a bad nature)* be vicious; sin, fall, err, transgress, go astray, forget oneself; misdo, misbehave; trespass, deviate, sow one's wild oats, act up, carry on; horse, fool, monkey, play, *or* mess around. *Informal,* cut up, hack off *or* around.

Adjectives—1, *(having a bad quality)* bad, ill, untoward, as bad as can be, dreadful; horrid, horrible; rank, rotten [at *or* to the core], decayed, decomposed, putrid, tainted. *Slang,* cheesy, punk.

2, *(having bad behavior)* hurtful, harmful, baneful, baleful; detrimental, pernicious; mischievous, full of mischief, mischief-making, full of Old Nick *or* the devil; malefic, malignant, noxious, nocuous, noisome; unlucky, sinister; obnoxious; inauspicious; oppressive, burdensome, onerous; malign, malevolent; virulent, venomous, envenomed, corrosive; poisonous, toxic.

3, *(of bad quality)* mean, paltry; injured, deteriorated, unsatisfactory, exceptionable, indifferent; below par, inferior, imperfect; ill-contrived, ill-conditioned; wretched, abysmal, pitiful, pathetic, sad, grievous, deplorable, lamentable; pitiable; unfortunate (see ADVERSITY). *Slang,* lousy, gnarly, schlocky, hellacious, uncool, lame[-ass], piss-poor *(vulgar).*

4, EVIL, WRONG; depraved, vile, base; flagrant, nefarious; reprehensible, heinous, hateful (see DISAPPROBATION); wicked, sinful. *Informal,* beastly, ungodly.

Adverbs—badly, amiss, awry, WRONG, ill; to one's cost; where the shoe pinches.

Quotations—There is something rotten in the state of Denmark (*Shakespeare*), There's small choice in rotten apples (*Shakespeare*), There is nothing either good or bad, but thinking makes it so (*Shakespeare*).

Antonyms, see GOODNESS, CONDUCT.

---

bad taste, tastelessness, coarseness. See INELEGANCE, VULGARITY.

baffle, *v.* foil, frustrate, balk, block; puzzle, nonplus; muffle. —*n.* obstacle; reflector. See HINDRANCE, DOUBT, SILENCE.

bag, *n.* RECEPTACLE, case, container, pouch, sack. —*v.* trap, capture, take, catch; sag, droop, hang; bulge, protrude, swell. See ACQUISITION, PENDENCY, CONVEXITY.

bagatelle, *n.* trifle, gewgaw, trinket. See UNIMPORTANCE.

baggage, *n.* luggage, impedimenta; trunks, suitcases, valises. See POSSESSION, TRANSPORTATION.

baggy, *adj.* bulging, droopy, shapeless. See FORMLESSNESS. *Ant.,* tight, form-fitting.

bagpipe, *n.* musette, doodlesack, union pipes; chanter. See MUSIC.

bail, *n.* SECURITY, bond, pledge; guarantee, surety. —**bail out,** parachute; get out of; help, aid, bankroll. See AID, ESCAPE.

bailiff, *n.* constable, beagle, bailie; sheriff, marshal, officer. See SAFETY, AGENT.

bailiwick, *n.* district, REGION; area of concern, BUSINESS.

bait, *n.* lure, temptation. —*v.t.* decoy, lure, tempt; tease, torment, badger. See ATTRACTION, MALEVOLENCE, DISCONTENT.

bake, *v.* roast, cook; harden, dry; fire. See HARDNESS, HEAT, FOOD.

balance, *n.* equilibrium, steadiness, stability; surplus, excess, rest, REMAINDER; scales. —*v.* offset, even, square; equalize, level, adjust; equal, match. See EQUALITY, COMPENSATION, SYMMETRY, MEAN, GRAVITY, ACCOUNTING.

balcony, *n.* gallery, loggia, porch, portico; tier, loge, mezzanine, dress circle; peanut gallery, paradise (*both sl.*). See DRAMA, RECEPTACLE.

bald, *adj.* hairless; treeless; bare, unadorned; undisguised. See DIVESTMENT, SIMPLENESS.

balderdash, *n.* nonsense, drivel. See UNMEANINGNESS.

bale, *n.* bundle (see ASSEMBLAGE); sorrow, woe, DEJECTION.

baleful, *adj.* hostile; malignant; hurtful, injurious. See BADNESS.

balk, *v.* rebel; stop, shy; hinder, thwart, foil, frustrate. See HINDRANCE, REFUSAL, DISAPPOINTMENT.

ball, *n.* dance, cotillion; shot, projectile; sphere, globe. See AMUSEMENT, ARMS, ROTUNDITY.

ballad, *n.* song, chantey, spiritual; calypso. See MUSIC, POETRY.

ballast, *n.* counterbalance (see COMPENSATION, GRAVITY).

ballet, *n.* concert *or* classical DANCE, choreography; corps de ballet.

balloon, *n.* aerostat, blimp; free, sounding, kite, pilot, *or* dirigible balloon; fire balloon, montgolfier. See AVIATION. —*v.i.* swell. See CONVEXITY.

ballot, *n.* vote, CHOICE, poll; franchise, voice.

ballroom, *n.* dance hall. See AMUSEMENT.

balm, *n.* balsam, salve; analgesic, sedative, anodyne. See MODERATION, REMEDY, COMPENSATION, ODOR.

balmy, *adj.* fair, mild, halcyon; fragrant;

slang, crazy, eccentric (see INSANITY). See MODERATION, ODOR. *Ant.*, stormy, inclement.

baloney, *n.* nonsense, humbug (see UNMEANINGNESS).

bamboozle, *v.t.* take in, dupe, put something over. See DECEPTION.

ban, *n.* PROHIBITION, restriction, proscription, interdict.

banal, *adj.* common[place], trite. See HABIT.

band, *n.* strip, stripe, FILAMENT; brassard; belt, strap; group, crowd; orchestra, brass *or* military band. See ASSEMBLAGE, MUSIC.

bandage, *n.* tourniquet, dressing; Band-Aid. See REMEDY.

bandit, *n.* highwayman, brigand, outlaw. See STEALING.

bandy, *v.t.* swap, INTERCHANGE.

bandy-legged, *adj.* bowlegged. See DISTORTION.

bane, *n.* poison, venom; curse, mischief; thorn in the side; bale, scourge, nuisance, pest; harm, injury, DESTRUCTION; trouble. See EVIL, BADNESS.

bang, *n.* clap, crash (see LOUDNESS). —*v.* slam, pound, batter; smash, damage. See IMPULSE, DESTRUCTION. —*adv.* See INSTANTANEITY.

bangle, *n.* bracelet, anklet. See ORNAMENT.

banish, *v.t.* exile, dismiss, expel. See EJECTION, PUNISHMENT, EXCLUSION.

bank, *n.* slope, hillside; mound, heap, ridge; tier; beach, shore, shoal; depository, vault. See OBLIQUITY, LAND, STORE. —*v.* tilt, angle, slope; deposit. See EDGE, AVIATION.

banknote, *n.* paper *or* folding MONEY; bill.

bankroll, *n.* cash on hand, resources. *v.t.*, *informal*, back, finance, fund. See MONEY.

bankrupt, *adj.* insolvent, ruined; bereft, indigent, penniless, destitute, broke (*sl.*). —*v.* impoverish; pauperize. See DEBT, POVERTY, FAILURE. *Ant.*, solvent, flush.

banner, *n.* flag, pennant; symbol, badge; headline. See INDICATION.

banquet, *n.* feast, regale, big feed (*inf.*). See FOOD, AMUSEMENT.

banter, *n.* jest, chaff, badinage. See WIT, RIDICULE.

baptize, *v.* sprinkle, immerse, dip; name,

christen; dunk (*inf.*); cleanse. See NOMENCLATURE, RITE.

bar, *n.* barrier, obstacle; barroom (see DRINKING); hurdle; legal profession, court, bench; rod, bolt, rail; measure; stripe. See LAWSUIT, LENGTH. —*v.* forbid; exclude, restrict, reject; lock, bolt, fasten. See EXCLUSION, CLOSURE, PROHIBITION. *Ant.*, admit, permit.

barb, *n.* spike, arrowhead. See SHARPNESS.

barbarian, *n.* foreigner, outsider, alien, savage; ruffian (see EVILDOER). —*adj.* uncivilized, barbarous. See UNCONFORMITY.

barbarism, *n.* solecism; barbarity, savagery, brutality, inhumanity, VIOLENCE; ignorance, rudeness, VULGARITY. See DISCOURTESY, MALEVOLENCE, INELEGANCE.

barbarous, *adj.* uncultured, crude; cruel, brutal. See VULGARITY, INELEGANCE. *Ant.*, civilized, cultivated.

barbecue, *n.* cookout; rotisserie, spit. See FOOD.

barber, *n.* hair stylist, coiffeur, coiffeuse. See BEAUTY.

barbiturate, *n.* See DRUGS.

bare, *adj.* unclothed, naked, nude; uncovered; empty, unfurnished; mere, simple. See DIVESTMENT, SIMPLENESS, ABSENCE. *Ant.*, clothed, covered.

barefaced, *adj.* brazen, shameless, impudent. See INSOLENCE, VISIBILITY.

barely, *adv.* only, just. See NARROWNESS.

barf, *v.i.*, *informal*, throw up (see EJECTION).

bargain, *n.* deal, AGREEMENT, transaction; good buy (see CHEAPNESS). —*v.* negotiate, haggle, BARTER. *Ant.*, white elephant.

barge, *n.* scow (see SHIP).

barge in, *v.i.*, *informal*, crash, bust, *or* burst in. See INGRESS.

bark, *n.* COVERING, rind, skin, shell; yelp, yap, bay (see CRY); barque, brig (see SHIP).

barker, *n.* spieler, pitchman (see SALE).

barn, *n.* stable, mews. See ABODE.

baroque, *adj.* florid, ornate; grotesque. See ORNAMENT, INELEGANCE. *Ant.*, simple, unadorned.

barracks, *n.pl.* caserne, bivouac. See ABODE.

barrage, *n.* ATTACK, bombardment.

barrel, *n.* keg, tun, cask, vat; cylinder, tube. See RECEPTACLE, ROTUNDITY.

barren, *adj.* infertile, unprofitable, unproductive; sterile; stark, bare. See USELESSNESS. *Ant.,* fertile.

barricade, *n.* blockade, stockade; fence, barrier. See DEFENSE, ENCLOSURE, CLOSURE.

barrier, *n.* obstacle, impediment, HINDRANCE. See ENCLOSURE, DEFENSE. *Ant.,* entrance, OPENING.

BARTER
Moneyless exchange of goods

Nouns—1, barter, exchange, truck, INTERCHANGE; marketing, trade, commerce, buying and selling, traffic, BUSINESS, custom, shopping; commercial enterprise, speculation, [stock-]jobbing, brokerage, stockbroking, agiotage; transaction, deal, bargain (see CHEAPNESS); reciprocation; trading, dealing, negotiation; haggling, dickering, free trade, open market; black market; collective bargaining; parallel rate. *Slang,* wheeling and dealing, horse trading. See SALE.

2, *(medium of barter)* trading stamps; trade-in; horse trade. See TRANSFER.

3, *(one who barters)* dealer, trader, merchant, businessman, AGENT. *Slang,* wheeler-dealer.

Verbs—1, barter, exchange, truck, INTERCHANGE; trade, traffic, buy and sell, give and take; carry on, ply, *or* drive a trade; be in business, be in the city; keep a shop; deal in, employ one's capital in. *Slang,* wheel and deal, horse-trade.

2, *(barter with risk)* speculate, give a sprat to catch a herring, buy in the cheapest and sell in the dearest market; rig the market.

3, *(make an agreement to barter)* trade (in), deal *or* have dealings with, transact *or* do business with, open *or* keep an account with, patronize; drive *or* make a bargain, negotiate, bargain, bid for, haggle, palter, dicker; cheapen, beat down; outbid, underbid; ask, charge; strike a bargain, contract, *or* compact. *Informal,* shake on it. See AGREEMENT.

Adjectives—commercial, mercantile, trading; interchangeable, marketable, staple, for sale; wholesale, retail.

Adverbs—across the counter; in *or* on the market.

Phrases—give the Devil his due.

Quotations—Buying and selling is essentially antisocial (*Edward Bellamy*), Here's the rule for bargains: "Do other men, for they would do you" (*Charles Dickens*), Great trade will always be attended with considerable abuses (*Edmund Burke*).

base, *n.* basis, foundation, groundwork, SUPPORT; basement, substructure; headquarters, depot; root; footing, floor; pavement; bottom; bedrock. —*v.* found, establish; predicate; ground, rest, *or* build upon. See CAUSE, ABODE. —*adj.* debased, impure; counterfeit, spurious; low, vile. See DISREPUTE, IMPURITY, BADNESS, SERVILITY, COWARDICE, IMPROBITY. *Ant.,* noble, exalted.

basement, *n.* cellar, vault (see LOWNESS).

bash, *v.t.* strike, batter, beat. —*n.,* informal, wingding, shindig, brawl. See ATTACK, AMUSEMENT.

bashful, *adj.* shy, diffident, timid. See MODESTY. *Ant.,* bold, arrogant.

basic, *adj.* fundamental, essential; alkaline. See INTRINSIC, INORGANIC MATTER.

basin, *n.* bowl, vessel, sink; hollow, valley. See CONCAVITY, RECEPTACLE.

basis, *n.* See BASE.

bask, *v.i.* luxuriate, revel, [take] delight *or* PLEASURE in; prosper, flourish; sunbathe, sun. See PROSPERITY, HEAT.

basket, *n.* hamper, pannier; hoop. See RECEPTACLE.

basket case, *slang,* quadraplegic; driveling idiot, klutz. See IMPOTENCE, USELESSNESS, FOLLY.

bass, *adj.* low, deep[-toned]; bass, [bass-] baritone. —*n.* basso [profundo]. See LOWNESS, MUSIC.

bastard, *n.* illegitimate [child], love child; sham, counterfeit, fraud. —*adj.* illegitimate, natural, misgotten; false, spurious; mongrel, hybrid. See IMPURITY, DECEPTION, POSTERITY.

baste, *v.t.* sew, tack; moisten; beat, thrash, cudgel. See PRODUCTION, ATTACK.

bastion, *n.* fort; rampart, fortification. See DEFENSE.

bat, *n.* cudgel, club, stick, nightstick; brickbat. See ARMS.

batch, *n.* baking; set, series, run, lot, QUANTITY. See ASSEMBLAGE.

bath, *n.* wash(ing); dip, plunge; whirlpool, Jacuzzi; Turkish *or* Swedish bath. See CLEANNESS, WATER.

bathhouse, *n.* cabaña, bathing hut. See RECEPTACLE, CLEANNESS.

bathos, *n.* sentimentality; anticlimax. See FEELING, WIT. *Ant.,* dispassion.

bathroom, *n.* toilet, facilities, head, water closet, WC. See CLEANNESS.

baton, *n.* staff, club, scepter; wand. See ARMS, MUSIC.

batter, *v.* smash, beat, pound. See DESTRUCTION, IMPULSE.

battery, *n.* assault, ATTACK; guns, artillery; array, ASSEMBLAGE; Leyden jar, voltaic cell, accumulator, [wet *or* dry] cell, solar *or* storage battery. See ARMS, STORE, POWER, COMBATANT.

battle, *n.* fight, engagement, combat; contest. See CONTENTION, ACTION, ATTACK.

battle-ax, *n.* broadax (see ARMS); *slang,* shrew, virago. See FEMALE.

battlefield, *n.* battleground. See WARFARE.

battleship, *n.* man-of-war, SHIP of the line, dreadnaught; battle wagon.

batty, *adj., slang,* insane, eccentric. See INSANITY, UNCONFORMITY.

bauble, *n.* trinket (see UNIMPORTANCE).

bawdy, *adj.* coarse, ribald, gross, lewd. See IMPURITY.

bawl, *v.* yell, bellow; CRY, sob.

bawl out, *v.t.* reprimand, reprove. See DISAPPROBATION.

bay, *n.* estuary, bayou, fiord, sound; alcove, niche; inlet; laurel. See WATER, RECEPTACLE, CONCAVITY. **—at bay,** trapped (see PURSUIT).

bayou, *n.* marsh, mouth (see WATER).

bazaar, *n.* market[place], fair; street fair. See BUSINESS.

be, *v.* exist, breathe; occur, take place. See EXISTENCE.

beach, *n.* shore, coast[line]; strand, sands, shingle. **—v.** ground, run aground *or* ashore, strand, hit the beach (*inf.*). See NAVIGATION, LAND.

beachcomber, *n.* beach bum, vagrant (see INACTIVITY).

beacon, *n.* lighthouse, buoy, lightship; beam; signal fire; signal, guide. See INDICATION, LIGHT, WARNING.

bead, *n.* drop; pellet, ball. See ROTUNDITY.

beak, *n.* nose, bill, nib; magistrate (*Brit.*). See CONVEXITY, FRONT.

beaker, *n.* vessel (see RECEPTACLE).

beam, *v.* shine, glow; smile. **—n.** ray, gleam; joist, timber. See LIGHT, SUPPORT.

bean, *n.* See VEGETABLE.

beanery, *n.* eatery, fast-food joint. See FOOD.

bear, *v.* endure, tolerate; suffer; render, yield; hold, sustain; carry, transport, convey. See FEELING, PRODUCTION, SUPPORT, TRANSPORTATION.

bear arms, soldier, serve [one's country]. See COMBATANT.

beard, *n.* whiskers; goatee, vandyke; stubble. See ROUGHNESS, HAIR.

bearded, *adj.* hairy, whiskered, awned, hirsute. See ROUGHNESS, HAIR.

beardless, *adj.* [clean-]shaven, smooth-faced; hairless; youthful. See YOUTH, DIVESTMENT.

bearing, *n.* course, trend; carriage, manner, CONDUCT; MEANING, significance; RELATION. See DIRECTION.

beast, *n.* brute, quadruped; blackguard (see DISCOURTESY). See ANIMAL, TRANSPORTATION.

beastly, *adj.* bestial, brutish; hateful. See MALEVOLENCE. *Ant.,* noble, generous.

beat, *n.* throb, stroke, accent, rhythm; pulse; route. See BUSINESS, REGION. *—v.* throb, pulsate; strike, batter; conquer, defeat. See REGULARITY, IMPULSE, SUPERIORITY, AGITATION.

beatify, *v.* sanctify, hallow, consecrate, bless. See PIETY. *Ant.,* damn.

beatnik, *n.* beat, hipster, Bohemian. See UNCONFORMITY.

beat-up, *adj., slang,* dilapidated, broken-down. See DETERIORATION.

beau, *n.* lover, swain, boyfriend. See LOVE.

beau geste, *Fr.,* fine deed. See COURAGE, AFFECTATION.

beau monde, *Fr.,* fashionable society. See FASHION.

BEAUTY
Quality that arouses pleasure

Nouns—**1**, beauty, the. beautiful; form, ELEGANCE, grace, charm, beauty unadorned; SYMMETRY; loveliness, attractiveness, comeliness, fairness, pulchritude, good looks, body beautiful, shapeliness, hourglass figure; style, polish, gloss (see SMOOTHNESS); bloom, brilliancy, radiance, splendor, gorgeousness, magnificence, glory; delicacy, refinement. *Slang,* curves.

2, *(beautiful person)* **a.** thing of beauty. *Informal,* vision, picture, eyeful, sight for sore eyes. **b.** Venus, Aphrodite, Hebe, the Graces, peri, houri, Helen of Troy; [sex] goddess; witch, enchantress; reigning beauty, beauty queen, Miss *or* Mrs. America, Miss U.S.A., Miss Universe, *etc.*; charmer, belle [of the ball]; poster girl, pinup [girl]. *Informal,* eyeful, picture, dream[boat], stunner, [Georgia] peach, doll, knockout, raving beauty, good-looker, cover *or* pinup girl, sweater girl. *Slang,* looker, cupcake, doll city, dish, dollface, [stone] fox, filly, sex bomb *or* kitten, pigeon, sexpot, quail, wren, barbecue. **c.** Mr. America, Adonis, Narcissus. *Informal,* ladykiller, ladies' man, dreamboat, pistol, beefcake, freak daddy, hunk.

3, *(something that renders beautiful)* **a.** beautification, beautifying; cosmetology; makeover; makeup, cosmetics; foundation, lipstick, lip rouge, nail polish, mascara, eye shadow, eyebrow pencil; mudpack, vanishing cream, *etc.*; vanity case, compact; decoration, adornment, accessory, embellishment, ornamentation (see ORNAMENT); glitz. *Slang,* war paint. **b.** cosmetic surgery, face lift, nose job, tuck. **c.** manicure, pedicure; beautician, cosmetologist, cosmetician, makeup artist; hairdresser, coiffeur, coiffeuse; manicurist, pedicurist; beauty salon *or* parlor. **d.** barber, hair stylist; haircut; barbershop. See HAIR.

Verbs—**1**, beautify; make up, glamorize, do, paint; adorn, embellish (see ORNAMENT); prettify; style. *Slang,* put on one's face, doll *or* gussy up.

2, look good, shine, radiate, glow. *Informal,* look like a million dollars, beggar description.

Adjectives—**1**, *(physically beautiful)* beautiful, beauteous, handsome, attractive, fetching, prepossessing; pretty, lovely, graceful, elegant; delicate, dainty, refined; fair, personable, comely, seemly, bonny, good-looking, eye-filling, eye-catching, cute; photogenic, telegenic, picturesque; well-favored, [well] built, well made, well formed, well proportioned, curvaceous (see ROTUNDITY); proper, shapely; symmetrical, regular, harmonious, sightly. *Informal,* easy on the eyes, sight for sore eyes, cutesy, dishy, nifty, stunning, devastating, breathtaking, long on looks, past gorgeous, [well-]built, hunky. *Slang,* drop-dead, fly, phat, zanzy, killer, against the law.

2, *(producing a feeling of beauty)* brilliant, shining, radiant; splendid, resplendent, dazzling, glowing; glossy, sleek; rich, gorgeous, superb, magnificent, grand, fine, sublime.

3, *(artistically beautiful)* artistic, aesthetic; picturesque, well composed, well grouped; enchanting, attractive, becoming, ornamental; undeformed, undefaced, unspotted; spotless, immaculate; perfect, flawless (see PERFECTION).

4, beautifying, cosmetic; ornamental, decorative.

Adverbs—beautifully, prettily, handsomely, *etc.*

Phrases—beauty is only skin deep; Monday's child is fair of face.

Quotations—The face that launched a thousand ships (*Christopher Marlowe*), Beauty is the gift of God (*Aristotle*), Beauty is in the eye of the beholder (*Margaret Hungerford*), A thing of beauty is a joy forever (*John Keats*), Beauty is truth, truth beauty (*John Keats*), A beautiful woman is a practical poet (*Emerson*), She walks in beauty like the night (*Lord Byron*), A pretty girl is like a melody (*Irving Berlin*).

Antonyms, see UGLINESS.

because, *adv.* by reason of, owing to, on account of. —*conj.* since, for, for the reason that, as. See CAUSE, REASONING.

beckon, *v.* signal, summon; lure, entice. See INDICATION, ATTRACTION.

become, *v.t.* befit, accord with, behoove; turn into, CHANGE [in]to. See DUTY, AGREEMENT.

becoming, *adj.* fit, proper, seemly; attractive, ornamental. See BEAUTY, RIGHTNESS, EXPEDIENCE. *Ant.,* unbecoming, unsuitable.

bed, *n.* couch, cot, resting place; base, foundation; garden. See SUPPORT, AGRICULTURE, LAYER.

bedding, *n.* bedclothes, sheets, linen. See COVERING.

bedlam, *n.* asylum, madhouse; confusion, uproar, turmoil. See INSANITY, DISORDER.

bedraggled, *adj.* unkempt, untidy. See DISORDER.

bedridden, *adj.* laid up, hospitalized. See DISEASE.

bedrock, *n.* basis, foundation; rock bottom. See SUPPORT, LOWNESS.

bedroom, *n.* boudoir, [bed]chamber. See RECEPTACLE.

beef, *n., informal,* muscle, flesh; complaint, grievance. See STRENGTH, LAMENTATION.

beefy, *adj.* brawny, muscular. See STRENGTH. *Ant.,* scrawny.

beeper, *n.* pager, alarm. See WARNING.

beer, *n.* bock, dark, *or* light beer, lager [beer], two-percent beer, hops, malt; ginger beer. See DRINKING.

befit, *v.t.* suit, harmonize with, fit; become, behoove. See AGREEMENT, DUTY. *Ant.,* be unsuitable.

before, *adv.* foremost, ahead; forward; beforehand, sooner, previously, heretofore. See PRIORITY, PRECEDENCE. *Ant.,* after.

befriend, *v.t.* make friends with (see FRIEND). *Ant.,* antagonize.

beg, *v.* implore, beseech; ask alms. See POVERTY, REQUEST.

beget, *v.t.* engender, procreate, generate. See REPRODUCTION.

beggar, *n.* suppliant; pauper, mendicant. See POVERTY, REQUEST, POPULACE.

BEGINNING
Starting point

Nouns—**1**, beginning, commencement, opening, outset, incipience, inception; alpha, initial; installation, inauguration, debut; foundation, reaction, initiation; embarkation, rising of the curtain, kickoff, take-off; outbreak, onset; big bang; initiative, first move, foot *or* toe in the door, running start, foothold; thin end of the wedge; fresh start, new departure, whole new ball game. *Informal,* coming out, square one. *Slang,* git-go. See OLDNESS.

2, *(beginning of growth)* origin, CAUSE, *fons et origo;* source, rise; bud, seed, germ, egg, embryo, nucleus; root, radix, radical, etymon; stem, stock, stirps, trunk, taproot; genesis, birth, nativity; nest, cradle, infancy, womb, nidus, birthplace, hotbed; start, starting point; dawn, morning; first step, openers. *Slang,* jump street. See PRIORITY.

3, *(something that starts)* title page; head, heading, introduction, prelude (see PRECEDENCE); FRONT, forefront, van, vanguard; curtain raiser, appetizer, *etc.*; primum mobile.

4, *(place of entrance)* entrance (see INGRESS); outskirts.

5, *(beginnings of learning)* rudiments, basics; primer, alphabet, ABCs, first principles. *Informal,* nuts and bolts. See PREPARATION, LEARNING.

6, *(one who begins)* beginner, tyro, novice, neophyte, acolyte, freshman, rookie, recruit, cub, learner, amateur, debutant; first-time Charlie, low man on the totem pole (see INFERIORITY). *Informal,* Johnny-come-lately.

7, *(one who initiates)* founder, initiator, creator; aborigine, native.

Verbs—**1**, begin, commence, rise, arise, originate, see the light of day, open its doors, initiate, introduce, inaugurate, set up; install; open, dawn, set in, enter upon; set out, depart, embark on; make one's debut, take up; set about, start out *or* in, get off *or* away, get under way, go ahead, get down to, get going, get to, turn on, trigger, start up, kick off, boot, jump start, kick off, kick-start, initialize, press the button, strike up, set to work, fall to, dig in, make a beginning *or* start; take the first step, get one's feet wet, break ground, break the ice, break cover, cross the Rubicon, open fire; undertake, embark upon, enter upon or into; come on or up. *Informal,* get going, pitch, plunge, or dive in, swing into action; get the show on the road or off the ground, start the ball rolling, fire away; get to first base; get off on the wrong foot.

2, *(be the first event)* usher in, preface; lead off, lead the way, take the lead, start from scratch, take the initiative; inaugurate, swear in; engender (see REPRODUCTION); call to order, head, lay the foundations, prepare, break in, found, CAUSE, set up, set on foot, start the ball rolling, launch, broach; open the door to. *Informal,* head up, ring in.

Adjectives—initial, initiatory, initiative; primary, pristine, maiden; inceptive, introductory, incipient; inaugural; embryonic, rudimentary; primeval, primordial, primitive, aboriginal, natal.

Adverbs—at first blush, glance, or sight, at or in the beginning, [at] first, in the first place, imprimis, first and foremost; in the bud, in its infancy, in the first flush; from the beginning, from [its] birth, from scratch, from the ground up, ab initio. *Informal,* from the word "go," from the get-go, at the drop of a hat. *Slang,* from the git-go.

Phrases—a good beginning makes a good ending; first impressions are the most lasting; the golden rule of life is, make a beginning.

Quotations—Who has begun has half done (*Horace*), The game's afoot! (*Shakespeare*), The distance is nothing; it is only the first step that is difficult (*Mme. Du Deffand*), A journey of a thousand miles must begin with a single step (*Lao-tzu*).

Antonyms, see END.

---

begrudge, *v.t.* envy, covet. See JEALOUSY.

beguile, *v.t.* delude, deceive; amuse, divert. See DECEPTION, PLEASURE.

behalf, *n.* interest, benefit, advantage. See UTILITY.

behave, *v.i.* bear, CONDUCT, or comport oneself, act. *Ant.,* misbehave.

behead, *v.t.* decapitate, decollate. See KILLING, PUNISHMENT.

behind, *adv.* rearward, aft, backward; after, subsequently; slow. —*prep.* in back of, following. See REAR, LATENESS, REGRESSION, SEQUENCE. *Ant.,* ahead.

behold, *v.* see, espy; look at, watch, observe. —*interj.* lo [and behold]! *ecce!* look! voilà! See VISION, ATTENTION.

being, *n.* LIFE, EXISTENCE; person, creature. See SUBSTANCE, HUMANITY.

belabor, *v.t.* harp or dwell on. See REPETITION.

belated, *adj.* See LATENESS.

belch, *v.* eructate; gush, issue. See EJECTION.

BELIEF
Faith

Nouns—1, *(assurance of truth)* belief, credence, credit, assurance, [good] faith, trust, troth, confidence, presumption; dependence on, reliance on. *Informal,* store. *Slang,* stock, gospel. See SUPPOSITION, PIETY, CREDULITY.

2, opinion, persuasion, conviction, CERTAINTY; [matter of] opinion, mind, [point of] view, viewpoint, outlook; impression, notion, idea; vox populi, conventional wisdom; op ed; surmise, conclusion (see JUDGMENT).

3, *(organized belief)* tenet, dogma, principle, article of faith; school, doctrine, articles, canon[s], catechism; declaration or profession of faith, constitution, manifesto, creed, tenets, orthodoxy; cult, ism, weltanschauung. See RELIGION, HETERODOXY.

4, *(believability)* credibility, believability, plausibility, probability.

5, *(one who believes)* [true] believer; devotee, zealot, disciple; fanatic.

Verbs—1, *(trust in)* believe, credit, accredit, give credence to, give the benefit of the doubt, take at face value; take for; consider, esteem (see SUPPOSITION); count, rely, figure, or depend on, pin one's faith on, swear by; take on trust or credit; take for granted or gospel. *Informal,* set store by, bet on, bank on, bet one's bottom dollar on, have the courage of one's convictions; buy, swallow [whole] (see CREDULITY); take stock in, buy into.

2, *(trust in)* confide in, believe in, put one's trust in; take one's word for, take at one's word; give the benefit of the doubt; pin one's hopes on (see HOPE).

3, *(hold a belief)* think, hold, opine, be of the opinion, be persuaded, conceive, fancy, apprehend; have, hold, entertain, hazard, *or* cherish a belief *or* an opinion; feel in one's bones. *Informal,* have a hunch, expect, be afraid.

4, *(inspire belief)* satisfy, persuade, assure, convince, convert, bring [a]round, indoctrinate, teach, bring home to; be convincing, carry conviction; convince oneself, make up one's mind. *Slang,* sell.

Adjectives—1, believing, trusting, unsuspecting; devout; naive; satisfied, confident, unhesitating, convinced, persuaded, secure.

2, believable, credible, trustworthy, worthy, to be depended on, unimpeachable; satisfactory; probable, odds-on; persuasive, impressive, convincing.

3, indubitable, undeniable, indisputable, incontrovertible (see CERTAINTY).

4, convincing, persuasive, inspiring belief *or* trust; authoritative.

5, doctrinal, canonical, dogmatic, of faith.

Adverbs—1, no doubt, on faith, on the strength of, with confidence.

2, in one's opinion *or* judgment, to one's way of thinking, in one's estimation.

Phrases—faith will move mountains; seeing is believing; a believer is a songless bird in a cage.

Quotations—The constant assertion of belief is an indication of fear (*Jiddu Krishnamurti*), Belief must mean something more than desire or hope (*Clarence Darrow*), Hundreds may believe, but each has to believe by himself (*W. H. Auden*), What is it that men cannot be made to believe! (*Thomas Jefferson*), Except ye see signs and wonders, ye will not believe (*Bible*), Why, sometimes I've believed as many as six impossible things before breakfast (*Lewis Carroll*), The great act of faith is when a man decides he is not God (*Oliver Wendell Holmes*), Faith may be defined briefly as an illogical belief in the occurrence of the improbable (*H. L. Mencken*), I submit to you that if a man hasn't discovered something he will die for, he isn't fit to live (*Martin Luther King*).

Antonyms, see DOUBT, CERTAINTY.

---

belittle, *v.t.* run down, disparage, deprecate. See DETRACTION.

bell, *n.* chime, ring; flare. See INDICATION, EXPANSION.

belle, *n.* BEAUTY, fair lady.

belles-lettres, *Fr.* fine literature. See WRITING.

belligerent, *adj.* bellicose, warlike, pugnacious, quarrelsome. See CONTENTION, ATTACK. —*n.* COMBATANT. *Ant.,* peaceful; noncombatant.

bellow, *v.i.* roar, shout, bawl. See CRY.

belly, *n.* stomach, tummy; abdomen; paunch, potbelly; underside; breadbasket, pod, bay window, beer belly, pot, gut, swagbelly *(all inf.)*, corporation *(sl.).* —*v.* bulge, swell, billow. See CONVEXITY, RECEPTACLE, INTERIOR.

belong, *v.i.* form part of; be someone's; relate to. See POSSESSION, RELATION.

beloved, *adj.* See LOVE.

below, *adv.* subordinate, lower, underneath. —*prep.* under, beneath. See INFERIORITY, LOWNESS. *Ant.,* above.

belt, *n.* girdle, band; stripe; zone; circuit. —*v.t.* bind, encircle; gird; whip. See CIRCULARITY, CIRCUMSCRIPTION, IMPULSE.

bench, *n.* seat, settee; court, bar, the judiciary; board. See SUPPORT, LAWSUIT, COUNCIL.

benchmark, *n.* standard, norm (see CONFORMITY, MEASUREMENT).

bend, *n.* curve, turn. —*v.i.* give, yield; curve. —*v.t.* control; shape. See SOFTNESS, AUTHORITY, CURVATURE, OBLIQUITY.

beneath, *adv.* underneath, under, below. —*prep.* under; unworthy of. See LOWNESS, INFERIORITY. *Ant.,* above.

benediction, *n.* See BLESSING. *Ant.,* curse.

benefactor, *n.* See BENEVOLENCE.

beneficent, *adj.* bountiful, generous. See BENEVOLENCE. *Ant.,* miserly, ungenerous.

beneficial, *adj.* useful, helpful, salutary,

advantageous. See GOODNESS, UTILITY. *Ant.*, harmful.

beneficiary, *n.* legatee, donee. See RECEIVING.

benefit, *n.* profit, advantage, gain, good, avail; fund-raiser. —*v.* help, serve, assist; improve. See BENEVOLENCE, UTILITY, AID, REQUEST, GOODNESS, MEANS. *Ant.*, harm, drawback, handicap.

BENEVOLENCE
Kindness

Nouns—1, benevolence, Christian charity, goodwill; God's grace; altruism, philanthropy, unselfishness; good nature, kindness, kindliness, loving-kindness, benignity, brotherly love, charity, humanity, fellow-feeling, sympathy, goodness of heart, heart of gold, open heart, bonhomie, kindheartedness; amiability, milk of human kindness, tenderness, LOVE, friendship; consideration, mercy (see PITY).

2, generosity, LIBERALITY, bounty, almsgiving; good works, beneficence, act of kindness, good turn, the shirt off one's back; good offices, labor of love; public service, social science, sociology.

3, philanthropist, benefactor, good Samaritan, Robin Hood, ministering angel; good citizen; sympathizer, altruist, humanitarian; welfare, social, *or* case worker; charity; Salvation Army, Good-Will Industries, Red Cross, *etc. Informal,* do-gooder. See GIVING, GOODNESS.

Verbs—bear goodwill, mean well by, wish well, take an interest in, sympathize with, feel for; have one's heart in the right place; do as you would be done by, do unto others [as you would have others do unto you]; meet halfway; treat well, give comfort, do a good turn, benefit, render a service, open one's heart, be of use; give of oneself; AID, philanthropize; heap coals of fire on a person's head.

Adjectives—1, benevolent, benign, kindly, well-meaning; amiable, good-natured, cordial, obliging, courteous (see COURTESY); gracious, unselfish, magnanimous; considerate, sympathetic, tender, warmhearted, kindhearted; charitable, liberal, generous, beneficent, altruistic, humane, bounteous, bountiful; public-spirited; well-intentioned, well-meaning, well-meant.

2, fatherly, motherly, brotherly, sisterly; paternal, maternal, fraternal; Christian, Christ-like.

Adverbs—benevolently, charitably, with good *or* the best intentions; with all one's heart, with [a] good will; liberally, generously.

Phrases—charity begins at home; handsome is as handsome does; all that is not given is lost; charity begins at home; the roots of charity are always green.

Quotations—Cast thy bread upon the waters (*Bible*), It is more blessed to give than to receive (*Bible*), We do not quite forgive a giver (*Emerson*), I have always depended on the kindness of strangers (*Tennessee Williams*), The living need charity more than the dead (*George Arnold*), Kind hearts are more than coronets (*Lord Tennyson*).

Antonyms, see MALEVOLENCE.

---

benign, *adj.* benignant, gracious; favorable. See HEALTH, BENEVOLENCE. *Ant.*, sinister, harmful.

bent, *n.* curved, crooked; TENDENCY, inclination, nature, propensity. See CURVATURE, DESIRE. *Ant.*, straight.

bequest, *n.* legacy. See GIVING, RECEIVING, TRANSFER.

berate, *v.t.* rebuke, scold, vilify. See DISAPPROBATION.

bereft, *adj.* bereaved, deprived of. See LOSS.

berserk, *adj.* amuck, frenzied, frantic. See EXCITEMENT. *Ant.*, calm.

berth, *n.* bunk, compartment; couchette; dock, slip; position, office; lodging. See BUSINESS, SUPPORT, ABODE.

beseech, *v.t.* beg, implore. See REQUEST.

beset, *v.t.* besiege, ATTACK, invest; stud (see ORNAMENT).

beside, *prep.* by, near, alongside, abreast. See NEARNESS, SIDE.

besides, *adv.* also, further, moreover. See ADDITION.

besiege, *v.t.* beset, surround, beleaguer, invest; plague, pester. See ATTACK.

besmirch, *v.t.* soil, sully, defile, blacken. See UNCLEANNESS, DISREPUTE.

best, *adj.* choice, unequaled, unparalleled. See GOODNESS, PERFECTION. —*v.t.* defeat, surpass. See SUPERIORITY.

bestial, *adj.* beastlike, brutal, brutish, ANIMAL. See VIOLENCE.

bestow, *v.t.* donate, present, confer, bequeath. See GIVING.

bet, *v.* wager, stake, gamble, play, lay odds. See CHANCE, IMPROBITY.

bête noire, *Fr.* object of dislike *or* dread. See HATE.

betray, *v.* play false; divulge, reveal. See INFORMATION, IMPROBITY, DISCLOSURE.

betrothal, *n.* engagement. See MARRIAGE, PROMISE.

better, *v.t.* mend, correct, relieve. See IMPROVEMENT, SUPERIORITY.

bettor, *n.* gambler, punter. See CHANCE.

BETWEEN
In the space separating two things

Nouns—1, *(act of lying between)* interjacence, intervenience, interlocation, interpenetration; interjection, interpolation, interlineation, interspersion, intercalation; interlocution, *obiter dictum,* intervention, interference, interposition, intrusion, obtrusion, insinuation, INSERTION.

2, *(something interposed)* buffer [state]; parenthesis, episode; flyleaf; embolism; partition, septum, diaphragm, midriff; property line, dividing line, Mason-Dixon line; party wall, bulkhead; panel, halfway house; interim. See MIDDLE, TIME.

3, *(person)* intermediary, go-between, middleman, medium (see AGENT); intruder, interloper, trespasser, meddler; kibitzer. *Slang,* buttinsky, chiseler, gate-crasher.

Verbs—1, intervene, come between, step in, slide in, interpenetrate; interfere, put an oar in, thrust one's nose in, cut in; intrude, obtrude; have a finger in the pie. *Informal,* liaise. *Slang,* butt in, horn in, barge in, muscle in; tamper with, fuck with. See HINDRANCE.

2, put between, introduce, insinuate, import; interpose, interject, intercalate, interpolate, interline, interleave, intersperse, interweave, interlard, insert, sandwich; divide, partition, separate, fence *or* screen off; throw, let, wedge, edge, drag, worm, run, *or* work in; dovetail, splice, mortise (see JUNCTION).

Adjectives—1, interjacent, intervenient, intervening, intermediate, intermediary, intercalary, interstitial, intramural; embolismal; parenthetical, episodic; mediterranean; intrusive, interfering, meddlesome, officious, obtrusive.

2, divided, partitioned, separated, fenced *or* screened off.

Adverbs—between, betwixt; among[st], amid[st], in the thick (of), in the middle; betwixt and between; parenthetically, *obiter dictum.*

Quotations—Something there is that doesn't love a wall (*Robert Frost*), There's a front seat and a back seat, and a window in between (*Billy Wilder*).

Antonyms, see EXTERIOR, END, SIDE.

bevel, *v.* slant, slope. See OBLIQUITY.

beverage, *n.* liquor, drink, potable. See DRINKING.

bevy, *n.* flock (see ASSEMBLAGE).

beware, *v.* take care, be on guard; avoid, shun. See WARNING.

bewilder, *v.t.* puzzle, confuse, perplex; daze. See DOUBT, WONDER.

bewitch, *v.t.* fascinate, charm; enchant. See SORCERY, PLEASURE.

beyond, *adv.* farther, yonder. —*prep.* over; past. See DISTANCE, SUPERIORITY.

bias, *n.* prejudice, partiality; bent, inclination; slope, diagonal. —*v.t.* INFLUENCE, sway, prejudice. See OBLIQUITY, TENDENCY, INJUSTICE.

Bible, *n.* See SACRED WRITINGS.

bicker, *v.i.* quarrel, wrangle, dispute; flicker, flutter; gurgle, ripple. See DISCORD, AGITATION. *Ant.,* agree.

bicycle, *n.* tandem, two-wheeler, bike (*inf.*). See VEHICLE.

bid, *n.* OFFER; effort, try (see UNDERTAK-

ING); invitation. —*v.* COMMAND, enjoin; invite, REQUEST.

bier, *n.* litter, catafalque. See INTERMENT.

big, *adj.* large, bulky, huge; mountainous, enormous; massive, impressive; important, weighty. See GREATNESS, SIZE. *Ant.*, small.

bigot, *n.* dogmatist, zealot; racist. See CERTAINTY, HETERODOXY, INJUSTICE.

big shot, *informal* leader, boss, bigwig (*inf.*). See AUTHORITY, IMPORTANCE.

bikini, *n.* two-piece [bathing suit], tonga. See CLOTHING.

bilateral, *adj.* two-sided, symmetrical. See SIDE, SYMMETRY.

bile, *n.* gastric juice; rancor, acrimony. See RESENTMENT, EXCRETION.

bilge, *n.* bulge; slops; sewer, cesspool; *slang,* buncombe, nonsense, obscenity. See UNCLEANNESS, UNMEANINGNESS.

bilk, *v.t.* defraud, swindle. See STEALING.

bill, *n.* score, reckoning; invoice, statement, dun; account, charges; [bank]note, greenback; beak. See ACCOUNTING, MONEY, PRICE, LEGALITY, CONVEXITY.

billboard, *n.* bulletin *or* message board. See PUBLICATION.

billet-doux, *Fr.* love letter. See COMMUNICATION, ENDEARMENT.

billfold, *n.* wallet. See STORE.

bill of fare, *n.* menu, *carte.* See FOOD.

billow, *v.i.* surge, swell. —*n.* undulation, wave. See WATER, CONVEXITY.

bin, *n.* compartment, crib, bunker. See RECEPTACLE.

bind, *v.t.* restrain, secure, fasten; obligate. See RESTRAINT, DUTY, COMPULSION, JUNCTION.

binder, *n.* album, folder (see COVERING).

binge, *n.,* *slang,* spree (see DRINKING.)

bingo, *n.* lotto, beano. See AMUSEMENT.

biography, *n.* life story, history, memoirs. See DESCRIPTION.

biology, *n.* life science, botany, zoology, naturalism. See EXISTENCE.

BIRDS
Flying animals

Nouns—1, fowl; songbird, warbler; bird of prey; cock, hen; nestling, fledgling. See ANIMAL.

2, *(land birds)* I. *(passerine)* a. songbird, oscine, warbler, oriole, swallow, blackbird, blackcap, bluebill, bluebird, blue jay, bobolink, thrasher, thrush, bullfinch, bunting, canary, cardinal, catbird, waxwing, chaffinch, chewink, chat, chickadee, corbie, cotinga, cowbird, creeper, crossbill, crow, drongo, finch, goldfinch, grackle, grosbeak, honeycreeper, martin, jackdaw, jay, junco, kingbird, lark, linnet, magpie, mavis, meadowlark, merle, mockingbird, myna, nutcracker, nuthatch, ortolan, ouzel, pipit, raven, redwing, robin, redwinged blackbird, rook, tanager, shama, shrike, siskin, snowbird, solitaire, sparrow, starling, sunbird, titmouse, towhee, vireo, weaver, wren, whydah. b. suboscine, antbird, bellbird, broadbill, flycatcher, lyrebird, manakin, ovenbird, pewee, phoebe, pitta, woodcreeper. c. ani, barbet, bird of paradise, grouse, quail, turkey, budgerigar, bustard, capercaillie, cassowary, chicken (see DOMESTICATION), swift, cockatiel, cockatoo, crane, cuckoo, curassow, culver, dodo, dove, egret, emu, erne, flicker, frogmouth, goatsucker, grouse, guan, guinea fowl, hoopoe, hornbill, hummingbird, woodpecker, jacamar, kea, killdeer, kiwi, kookaburra, lapwing, lorikeet, lory, lovebird, macaw, marabou, moa, moundbird, nightingale, ostrich, parakeet, parrot, partridge, carrier *or* homing pigeon, plover, potoo, ptarmigan, quetzal, rhea, roadrunner, rosella, sapsucker, secretary bird, seriema, snipe, stork, tinamou, toucan, trogon, trumpeter, turtledove, whippoorwill, whistler, woodcock, wryneck. *Slang,* gospel bird. d. bird of prey, raptor, eagle, buzzard, condor, falcon, goshawk, gyrfalcon, harrier, hawk, hoot owl, kestrel, kite, merlin, owl, vulture.

3, *(seabirds)* a. waterfowl, albatross, auk(let), kingfisher, booby, brant, Canada goose, coot, duck, cormorant, dabchick, darter, diver, dovekie, erne, frigate bird, fulmar, gallinule, gannet, goose, grebe, guillemot, gull, honker, jaeger, kittiwake, loon, mallard, merganser, mew, murre, notornis, osprey, pelican, penguin, petrel, pintail, razorbill, scaup, scoter, sheldrake, skua, stormy petrel, swan, teal, tern, widgeon. **b.** wading bird, wader, shorebird, avocet, bittern, crane, crake, curlew, egret, flamingo, godwit, gull, hammerhead, heron, ibis, jacana, knot, limpkin, marabou, heron, oystercatcher, plover, rail, sanderling, sandpiper, shoebill, skimmer, snipe, stilt, stint, stork, turnstone.

4, *(bird home)* nest, birdhouse.

5, *(terms)* axilla, beak, bill, brood, claw, clutch, comb, covert, crest, feather, mandibles, [eclipse *or* nuptial] plumage, pileum, quill, wattle, wing.

6, *(young bird)* chick, fledgling (see YOUTH).

7, birdwatcher, birder.

Verbs—go birdwatching, birdwatch.

Adjectives—birdlike, avian; passerine, oscine, suboscine, corvine; nesting.

Phrases—a mockingbird has no voice of his own.

Quotations—A robin red breast in a cage puts all Heaven in a rage (*William Blake*), From the troubles of the world I turn to ducks, beautiful comical things (*F. W. Harvey*), Blackbirds are the cellos of the deep farms (*R. L. Stevenson*), A hen is only an egg's way of making another egg (*Samuel Butler*), Cheerfulness is proper to the cock (*Leonardo da Vinci*).

---

birth, *n.* origin, creation; genesis, inception; childbirth, parturition. See REPRODUCTION. *Ant.,* DEATH.

birth control, contraception, prophylasis (see HINDRANCE).

birthplace, *n.* native land or country, father- *or* motherland, homeland. See REGION.

biscuit, *n.* cracker, hardtack, cookie; bun, cake. See FOOD.

bisect, *v.* bifurcate, halve. See DISJUNCTION, NUMERATION.

bisexual, *adj.* ambisexual, AC/DC, bi (*inf.*). See SEX.

bishop, *n.* prelate, lawn sleeves; overseer; episcopacy. See CLERGY.

bistro, *n.* café, bar (see FOOD).

bit, *n.* scrap, mite; slice, piece; tool, drill; curb; *informal,* routine. See PART, LITTLENESS, SPECIALITY.

bitch, *n.* she-dog; *slang,* complaint; shrew, vixen; tough job, chore. —*v.i., slang* complain, protest, object. See ANIMAL, LAMENTATION, DIFFICULTY.

bite, *n.* morsel, scrap; nip. —*v.* cut; snap, snip; corrode; sting. See FOOD, LITTLENESS, PUNGENCY.

biting, *adj.* sharp, piercing, keen; pungent, acrid; forceful, telling. See VIGOR, PUNGENCY, COLD.

bitter, *adj.* stinging, cutting; spiteful; rigorous; acrid, unpalatable. See MALEVOLENCE, RESENTMENT, PUNGENCY, COLD.

bivouac, *n.* barracks (see ABODE).

bizarre, *adj.* grotesque, odd. See UNCONFORMITY.

blab, blabber, *v.i.* babble, chatter; tattle, gossip. See LOQUACITY, DISCLOSURE.

black, *n.* darkness, midnight, Stygian hue; Negro, African American. —*v.t.* shine, polish (shoes). See COLOR, DARKNESS. *Ant.,* white.

blackball, *v.* exclude, ostracize, reject, boycott. See EXCLUSION.

blackboard, *n.* slate, chalkboard. See WRITING.

blacken, *v.t.* besmirch; smudge; malign, slander. See COLOR, DETRACTION.

blackguard, *n.* rascal, villain; scoundrel. See EVILDOER.

blackjack, *n.* cudgel, cosh. See ARMS.

blacklist, *v.* ostracize, exclude (see EXCLUSION).

black magic, demonism, Satanism, the black art. See DEMON.

blackmail, *n.* extortion, hush money, protection, shakedown (*sl.*). See STEALING, PAYMENT, THREAT.

black-market, *adj.* contraband, bootleg, illegal. See ILLEGALITY.

blackout, *n.* brownout, power outage *or* failure; faint, unconsciousness; memory loss. See POWER, INSENSIBILITY, OBLIVION.

bladder, *n.* sac, vesicle, blister. See RECEPTACLE.

blade, *n.* cutter, edge; sword; knife; leaf

(of grass); dandy, sport. See SHARPNESS, IMPURITY, AFFECTATION.

blahs, *n.,* *slang,* listlessness, blues, doldrums. See WEARINESS. *Ant.,* exhilaration.

blame, *n.* criticism, censure; culpability, GUILT. —*v.t.* charge, reproach, condemn. See ACCUSATION, DISAPPROBATION, WRONG.

blanch, *v.* whiten; scald. See COLORLESSNESS, FOOD.

bland, *adj.* suave; affable, gracious; mild, unflavored. See COURTESY, INSIPIDITY. *Ant.,* tasty, spicy; harsh.

blandish, *v.t.* coax, cajole. See FLATTERY.

blank, *adj.* empty, unfilled; vacant, vacuous, expressionless; unloaded. See NONEXISTENCE, INSUBSTANTIALITY, ABSENCE, FORMLESSNESS.

blanket, *n.* See COVERING. —*adj.* widespread, comprehensive. See GENERALITY.

blare, *n.* blast, fanfare. See LOUDNESS.

blasé, *adj.* bored (see WEARINESS).

blasphemy, *n.* irreverence, profanity; heresy. See IMPIETY. *Ant.,* PIETY.

blast, *n.* explosion; discharge; gust; harangue (see SPEECH). —*v.t.* destroy, shatter, ruin; explode. See VIOLENCE, DESTRUCTION.

blast off, take off, launch, lift off. See ASTRONAUTICS, BEGINNING.

blatant, *adj.* noisy, obtrusive. See LOUDNESS, OSTENTATION. *Ant.,* hidden.

blaze, *n.* fire, flame; mark, spot. See HEAT, INDICATION.

blazon, *v.* proclaim, advertise; embellish, decorate. See PUBLICATION, ORNAMENT.

bleach, *v.t.* whiten, blanch, lighten. See COLORLESSNESS.

bleachers, *n.pl.* grandstand, gallery. See SUPPORT.

bleak, *adj.* raw, desolate, unsheltered; COLD; discouraging, inauspicious. See ADVERSITY. *Ant.,* bright, cheerful.

blear, *adj.* blurred; bloodshot. See VISION, DIMNESS.

bleed, *v.* flow, hemorrhage; let blood; overcharge, fleece, soak (*sl.*), skin (*sl.*); suffer. See PAIN, STEALING, FLUIDITY.

blemish, *n.* flaw, defect, IMPERFECTION; spot, taint, mark; smear, smudge. —*v.* disfigure, mar; bruise, rot; stain, spot; injure, hurt; sully, disgrace, tarnish. See UNCLEANNESS, UGLINESS, DETERIORATION, DISREPUTE.

blend, *n.* COMBINATION, MIXTURE; crossbreed. —*v.* merge, amalgamate.

bless, *v.t.* hallow, consecrate; praise; thank. See DEITY, PIETY, APPROBATION.

blessing, *n.* benediction, commendation; godsend, boon. See APPROBATION, GOODNESS, PROSPERITY.

blight, *n.* decay, rot; rust, smut. —*v.t.* stunt, rot, impair, corrupt; thwart, foil. See DETERIORATION, HINDRANCE, DESTRUCTION.

blimp, *n.* dirigible (see AVIATION).

blind, *n.* ambush, screen; shade, shutter; DECEPTION, ruse, subterfuge. —*adj.* sightless; shortsighted; unperceptive. See BLINDNESS, INATTENTION, CONCEALMENT.

blindfold, *n.* blinders. See DIMNESS, DECEPTION.

BLINDNESS
Lack of sight

Nouns—1, blindness, sightlessness, anopsia, cecity; total *or* legal blindness, binocular deprivation; blind spot; amaurosis; cataract; dimsightedness (see VISION); benightedness; night *or* day blindness, snow blindness, *etc.*; color blindness, achromatopsia, dichromatism; darkness; blinding, blindfolding.

2, *(tools for the blind)* Braille, Moon's type, New York point, American Braille; Seeing Eye *or* guide dog, [white] cane; talking book.

3, the blind; blind man; mole, bat.

Verbs—1, be blind, not see; lose sight; grope in the dark, feel one's way; wear blinkers; shut one's eyes to, be blind to.

2, *(make blind)* blind, darken, benight, put *or* gouge one's eyes out; blindfold, hoodwink, throw dust into one's eyes, dazzle; screen, hide (see CONCEALMENT).

Adjectives—1, blind, eyeless, sightless, unseeing; dark, stone-blind; visually impaired, challenged, *or* handicapped; undiscerning, unperceiving; blind as a bat, a mole, *or* an owl, amaurotic, dimsighted, colorblind, snowblind; blindfolded.

2, blinding, dazzling.

Adverbs—blindly, sightlessly, gropingly; blindfold; darkly.

Phrases—When the blind lead the blind, both shall fall into the ditch; there's none so blind as those who will not see.

Antonyms, see VISION.

---

blink, *v.* wink; flash, twinkle; glimmer; disregard, ignore. See VISION, NEGLECT.

bliss, *n.* happiness, ecstasy, rapture, PLEASURE.

blister, *n.* vesicle; bubble, sac. See RECEPTACLE.

blithe, *adj.* gay, lighthearted, merry. See CHEERFULNESS.

blithering, *adj.* babbling, driveling. See FOLLY.

blitz, blitzkrieg, *n.* See ATTACK.

blizzard, *n.* snowstorm, whiteout. See WIND, COLD.

bloat, *v.* distend, swell, puff up. See CONVEXITY.

blob, *n.* drop, bubble, lump. See ROTUNDITY.

bloc, *n.* PARTY, faction, ring; union, alliance, coalition. See COOPERATION.

block, *n.* HINDRANCE, blockage, obstruction; row, street, square (see ABODE); mass, lump, cube (see DENSITY). —*v.t.* impede, check, stop, bar; thwart, foil. See CLOSURE, IDENTITY.

blockade, *n.* barrier, stoppage; embargo, siege. —*v.t.* obstruct, bar, barricade. See CLOSURE, HINDRANCE.

blond, *adj.* light-colored, fair-skinned; light-haired, yellow, flaxen, platinum. See COLORLESSNESS, COLOR.

blood, *n.* serum, essence; sap; gore; kindred; lineage, heritage. See RELATION, FLUIDITY, ANCESTRY, CLASS.

bloodless, *adj.* anemic; pale; unfeeling, cold; peaceful; cowardly. See COLORLESSNESS, COWARDICE, INSENSIBILITY.

bloodletting, *n.* phlebotomy, venesection; bloodshed. See REMEDY, KILLING.

bloodshed, *n.* KILLING, slaughter.

bloodsucker, *n.* leech, parasite; tick, mosquito, *etc.;* extortionist. See ANIMAL, ACQUISITION.

bloodthirsty, *adj.* murderous, sanguinary. See KILLING, MALEVOLENCE.

bloody, *adj.* gory, sanguinary, bleeding; red. See KILLING.

bloom, *n.* blossom, flower; glow; flowering. —*v.i.* blossom; mature; glow, flourish, thrive. See HEALTH, PROSPERITY, VEGETABLE. *Ant.,* fade.

blooper, *n.* blunder, ERROR.

blossom, *v.* flower, bloom; develop, flourish. See VEGETABLE, PROSPERITY. *Ant.,* fade.

blot, *v.* stain, blemish, spot; sully. —*n.* spot, smear, blemish. See DISREPUTE, UNCLEANNESS, GUILT.

blotch, *n.* spot, blot (see UNCLEANNESS).

blow, *n.* knock, stroke, hit; DISAPPOINTMENT; blast, WIND, breeze, gale. See IMPULSE, SURPRISE. —*v.* brag; gasp, pant, puff; SOUND; storm, breeze, whiff, waft; *slang,* miss, squander. See FAILURE, WASTE.

blowup, *n.* explosion; outburst; enlargement. See EXPANSION, VIOLENCE.

blowzy, *adj.* disheveled, untidy, unkempt; ruddy. See UNCLEANNESS, DISORDER.

blubber, *v.i.* weep, sob (see DEJECTION).

bludgeon, *n.* club. —*v.t.* coerce, bully; club. See COMPULSION, ATTACK.

blue, *adj.* azure, indigo, sapphire (see COLOR); delft; severe, puritanical; sad, dejected, depressed, dispirited, downhearted; risqué, profane. See IMPURITY, DEJECTION. *Ant.,* happy.

blue jeans, jeans, dungarees. See CLOTHING.

blueprint, *n.* PLAN, design, scheme.

blues, *n.* melancholy, despondency. See DEJECTION.

bluff, *n.* cliff, bank, headland; hoax. —*v.* mislead; brag; intimidate. See BOASTING, DECEPTION, VERTICAL. —*adj.* frank, abrupt. See DISCOURTESY.

blunder, *n.* slip, botch, mess; solecism. —*v.i.* botch, fail, err; bungle, flounder. See ERROR, UNSKILLFULNESS.

blunt, *v.t.* dull, deaden, numb; moderate.
—*adj.* dull; direct; brusque; undiplo-
matic, forthright. See BLUNTNESS, DIS-
COURTESY, INSENSIBILITY, MODERATION.

BLUNTNESS
Lack of sharpness
Nouns—bluntness, dullness; obtundity; obtuseness.
Verbs—blunt, full, take off the edge *or* point of, obtund.
Adjectives—blunt, dull, edgeless, obtundent, unpointed, unsharpened; obtuse.
Antonyms, see SHARPNESS.

---

blur, *v.* blot, smear; obscure, dim; swim,
be indistinct. See DIMNESS, OBSCURITY,
UNCLEANNESS.

blurt, *v.t.* blab (see DISCLOSURE).

blush, *v.i.* COLOR, flush, glow; redden (see
MODESTY). See FEELING.

bluster, *n.* bravado; braggadocio, BOAST-
ING; bullying, hectoring; front. —*v.i.*
swagger; play the bully, hector, vapor;
roar (see LOUDNESS). See INSOLENCE,
THREAT.

board, *n.* COUNCIL, cabinet, panel, committee, directorate; plank; cardboard;
provisions, fare. —*v.* lodge, feed; embark (see DEPARTURE). See FOOD, AT-
TACK, LAYER.

boardinghouse, *n.* rooming *or* lodging
house (see ABODE).

BOASTING
Bragging speech
Nouns—1, boasting, boast, vaunt[ing], puff, fanfaronade, bluster, gasconade, braggadocio, bravado, swagger, exultation, jactation; gloating, exultation; buncombe (see
ABSURDITY); bounce (*Brit.*); rodomontade, bombast, bluff, tall talk, magniloquence,
grandiloquence, heroics, chauvinism; EXAGGERATION, much cry and little wool.
Slang, [hot] dog, side, bunk, hot air, big *or* fancy talk, front, bullshit, fish story. See
VANITY, REJOICING, OSTENTATION.
2, boaster, braggart, Gascon, pretender, soi-disant, blusterer. *Slang,* blowhard, windbag, loudmouth, drugstore cowboy, knocker. See EVIDENCE, INSOLENCE.
Verbs—boast, make a boast of, brag, vaunt, puff, swagger, roister; preen *or* plume oneself; bluster, bluff; exult, gloat, crow over, neigh, throw up one's cap; flatter oneself,
pat oneself on the back; gloat, exult, crow. *Informal,* talk big, show off, blow *or* toot
one's own horn. *Slang,* give oneself airs, put on the side *or* dog, put up a big front,
profile, cack, gam; lay it on thick, bullshit.
Adjectives—boastful, magniloquent, soi-disant; vainglorious, bombastic, pompous,
chauvinist, extravagant, high-flown, ostentatious, heroic, grandiose; exultant; in
high feather, flushed with victory, cock-a-hoop, on stilts, inflated, pretentious; gloating, exultant, crowing. *Slang,* all piss and wind, all mouth and trousers.
Adverbs—boastfully, bombastically, *etc.*
Phrases—big boast, small roast.
Quotations—It ain't braggin' if you can do it (*Dizzy Dean*), Anything you can do, I can
do better (*Irving Berlin*), He was like the cock who thought the sun had risen to hear
him crow (*T. S. Eliot*).
Antonyms, see MODESTY.

---

boat, *n.* See SHIP.

bob, *v.t.* dock, cut, curtail. —*v.i.* jerk,
LEAP, float; nod, bow, curtsy. —*n.*
weight, float; bobsled; shilling. See AGI-
TATION, OSCILLATION, SHORTNESS.

bobble, *v.* fumble; bob, jerk. See ERROR,
OSCILLATION.

bode, *v.* forbode, threaten (see THREAT).

bodily, *adj.* corporeal, physical, material.
—*adv.* wholly, entire. See WHOLE, SUB-
STANCE.

body, *n.* torso (see BODY); solid, mass;
group, ASSEMBLAGE; SUBSTANCE, bulk;
main part. See WHOLE, PARTY.

BODY
Physical structure

Nouns—1, body, anatomy, torso; carcass, cadaver, corpse, remains (see DEATH); [basal] metabolism, anabolism, assimilation, catabolism; breathing (see AIR); digestion, ingestion, absorption.

2, frame, skeleton; skull, cranium; sphenoid, temporal, parietal, *or* occipital bone, mandible, frontal, maxilla, mastoid, zygomatic, nasal, *or* cheek bone, orbit, clavicle, manubrium, sternum, breastbone, rib, gladiolus, carpus, metacarpus, radius, ulna, humerus, scapula, shoulder blade, backbone, [lumbar, thoracic, *or* sacral] vertebra, coccyx, tailbone, coxa, ilium, sacrum, sacroiliac, ischium, acetabulum, femur, fibula, patella, tibia, shinbone, pubis, kneebone, calcaneus, tarsus, metatarsus, phalanges; [ball-and-socket, gliding, *or* hinge] joint; spinal *or* vertebral column; boss, cartilage, ligament, marrow, torus, tendon.

3, skin, epidermis, dermis; integumentary system, membrane; nail; endo- *or* entoderm, mesoderm, blastoderm, ectoderm, *etc.*; epithelium, fascia.

4, musculature, muscles; biceps, triceps, quadriceps, rectus abdominis *or* femoris, rotator cuff, fascia lata; sternocleidomastoid, deltoid, flexor, extensor, pectoral, abdominal, erector, trapezius, latissimus dorsi, oblique, sartorius, gluteus, hamstring, gastrocnemius, *or* soleus muscle. *Slang,* pecs, hams, glutes, quads, lats.

5, a. [central, peripheral, *or* autonomic] nervous system, spinal cord. b. [brachial, cervical, coccygeal, digital, femoral, intercostal, lumbar, mandibular, maxillary, median, ophthalmic, peroneal, radial, sacral, sciatic, thoracic, tibial, *or* ulnar] nerve, neuron, axon, dendrite, ganglion, synapse, myelin; sensory receptor. c. brain, encephalon, gray matter, neocortex, [occipital, temporal, *or* parietal] lobe, ventricle, thalamus, cerebellum, cerebrum, medulla, meninges, cerebral cortex, cerebral hemisphere, frontal lobe, right *or* left brain, cortex, pallium, limbic system, pons.

6, a. head, skull, face, cranial cavity, eye socket; ear (see HEARING); eye (see VISION). *Slang,* coconut, bean, noodle, gourd, noggin; puss, kisser, mug. b. pate, scalp; HAIR. c. forehead, brow. d. cheek; jaw, mandible; mouth, oral *or* buccal cavity, lip, soft *or* hard palate, taste bud, tongue. e. tooth, tusk, fang, alveolus, cuspid, bicuspid, canine, dogtooth, eyetooth, enamel, molar, grinder, incisor, foretooth, wisdom tooth, milk, baby, *or* permanent tooth. f. nose, proboscis, nostril, nares. *Slang,* schnozz, snout, snoot, beak, muzzle. g. neck, septum, temple, throat, esophagus, windpipe, Adam's apple; larynx, voicebox (see SPEECH).

7, a. trunk, torso. b. chest, rib, breastbone, sternum, collarbone, clavicle, shoulder [blade], thoracic, pleural, *or* pericardial cavity. c. breast, bosom, nipple, teat. *Slang,* babaloos, bags, balloons, bazongas, bazonkers, bazooms, boobs, knockers, headlamps *or* -lights, ju-jubes, melons, tatas, titties, maracas, hooters, bumpers, paps, first base; tits, [rasp]berries. d. abdomen, midriff, belly, abdominal cavity, [vermiform] appendix, navel, umbilicus, solar plexus. *Informal,* belly button; paunch, love handles, tummy, pot[belly]. *Slang,* breadbasket, corporation, spare tire. e. back, backbone, spine, spinal column, coccyx. f. buttocks, hipbone, ilium, ischium, loin, pelvis, pelvic cavity, sacrum; crotch, groin, perineum, pubis. *Informal,* derriere, posterior, rear [end], rump. *Slang,* ass, behind, bum, buns, butt, duff, fanny, heinie, keister, tokus, tush, biscuits.

8, limb, extremity; arm, forearm, upper arm, armpit, underarm, axilla, biceps, triceps, ulna, elbow, funny bone; leg, femur, fibula, ankle, tarsus, calf, shin[bone], tibia, thigh, thighbone, femur, hamstring, shank; wrist, carpus; hand, fist, [annulary, ring, middle, *or* little] finger, thumb, digit, knuckle, cuticle; foot, toe, big *or* little toe, ball, sole, heel, instep; hip, haunch. *Slang,* duke, mitt, paw, [meat]hook; wing, fin, flapper; wheel, pin, gam, stick, stump; tootsy, dog, pup, hoof.

9, a. [vital] organs, viscera, bowel, chitterlings, innards, tripe. b. heart, heartbeat, aorta, [carotid, coronary, or pulmonary] artery, auricle, cardiac muscle; diastole, systole. *Slang,* pump, ticker. c. respiratory system; lung, pleural cavity, pleura, bronchiole, bronchus, alveolus; diaphragm, windpipe, trachea; bronchial tube; respiration, inhalation, inspiration, exhalation, expiration. See AIR. d. glandular system; gallbladder, kidney, liver, ovary, pancreas, testis, thymus, gonad; [adrenal, endocrine, exocrine, lacrimal, mammary, parathyroid, parotid, pituitary, prostate, salivary, sebaceous, sublingual, submaxillary, suprarenal, sweat, or thyroid] gland, eccrine, holocrine, or merocrine glandadrenalin, *etc.* (see EXCRETION). e. digestive system, stomach, alimentary canal, ascending or descending colon, [large or small] intestine, duodenum, gut, ileum, jejunum, gastrointestinal tract, pylorus, sygmoid flexure; gastric juice, saliva, bile; villus, peristalsis. *Slang,* kishkes. f. anus, rectum, sphincter, [urinary] bladder, ureter, urethra, bowel; urine, feces (see EXCRETION). *Slang,* where the sun don't shine, ass, asshole, arse, backdoor, bunghole, glory hole, A-hole, tailpipe, round-eye.

10, vascular, circulatory, portal, or lymphalic system; blood, bloodstream, blood vessel, vein, capillary; red or white blood cell, corpuscle, erythrocyte, lymphocyte, leukocyte, phagocyte, cytoplasm, phagocyte, hemoglobin, lymph, plasma, serum, platelet, thrombocyte; clot, fibrin, thrombin.

11, a. reproductive system; genitals, genital organs, genitalia, private parts, privates, vitals; pubic region, crotch; glans; gamete; smegma, pubic hair. *Slang,* down there, yinyang; jingjang; short hairs, beard. b. vulva, vagina, pudendum, clitoris, labia [majora or minora], mons veneris; cervix, uterus, womb, fallopian tube; ovum. *Slang,* beard, beaver, box, bush, cassava, cat, cherry, [bearded] clam, cony, cooch, cooze, crack, crease, cunt, dead-end street, down, fern, fuckhole, fur, gash, hair pie, honeypot, it, jelly roll, monosyllable, muff, nooky, passage, penocha, pink, poontang, pussy, quim, sex, slit, snatch, thatch, twat, Venus mound, Venus flytrap, yoni; clit, man in the boat. c. penis, phallus, apparatus, lingam, member, [male] organ; testicle, testis, [sex or interstitial] gland, scrotum; vas dererens, epididymis; foreskin; erection, priapism, tumescence, virile member; spermatozoan. *Informal,* equipment, crotch, crown jewels, loins, dingaling. *Slang,* bicho, bingy, blacksnake, bone[r], cock, dick, dink, dong, dork, [one-holed] flute, jigger, Johnnie, johnson, joint, love muscle, meat, middle leg, pecker, peter, prick, prong, putz, rail, rod, root, sausage, schlong, schwanz, tool, trouser snake, whang, wick, wiener, wieny, wing-wang, wong; hard-on, boner, rail; balls, ballocks, basket, cojones, crown or family jewels, nuts, rocks, mountain oysters, prunes; cod, purse, sack, tool bag; lace curtain. See SEX.

Adjectives—bodily, skeletal, bony, spinal, muscular; cutaneous, epidermal, hypodermic, dermal, cortical, membranous; neural, cerebral; digestive, abdominal, ventral, gastric, metabolic, anabolic, catabolic; respiratory, nasal, rhinal, bronchial, tracheal; pulmonary; circulatory, vascular, capillary, arterial, hematic; lachrymal; genital, vulvar, vaginal, clitoral, cervical, ovarian, uterine, phallic, penile, testicular, seminal.

Quotations—Your body is the temple of the Holy Ghost (*Bible*), I give thanks unto thee, for I am fearfully and wonderfully made (*Bible*), O, that this too too sullied flesh would melt, thaw and resolve itself into a dew (*Shakespeare*), If anything is sacred, the human body is sacred (*Walt Whitman*), I sing the body electric (*Walt Whitman*), The human body is an instrument for the production of art in the human soul (*Alfred North Whitehead*), The body says what words cannot (*Martha Graham*).

Antonyms, see INTELLECT.

---

bodyguard, *n.* [armed] escort, retinue. See DEFENSE, ACCOMPANIMENT.

bog, *n.* swamp, morass, quagmire, marsh, fen. See WATER.

boggle, *v.t.* amaze, astound. See SURPRISE.

bogus, *adj.* fake, counterfeit, spurious. See DECEPTION.

bogy, bogie, *n.* hobgoblin, gremlin. See DEMON.

Bohemian, *n. & adj.* hippie, beatnik. See UNCONFORMITY.

boil, *n.* sore, suppuration. See CONVEXITY. —*v.* bubble, seethe; scald; cook; fume, rage. See DISEASE, HEAT, VIOLENCE, AGITATION, EXCITABILITY, FOOD.

boisterous, *adj.* noisy, clamorous, vociferous; unrestrained, rambunctious, riotous, stormy, uproarious. See EXCITEMENT, VIOLENCE, LOUDNESS. *Ant.,* quiet, serene.

bold, *adj.* daring, audacious, forward; intrepid, brave; impudent. See COURAGE, INSOLENCE, DEFIANCE, VIGOR. *Ant.,* timid.

bollix up, *informal,* frustrate, defeat; baffle; botch. See HINDRANCE, ERROR.

bolt, *n.* lock, latch, bar; thunderbolt, stroke, flash. See CLOSURE, LIGHT. —*v.* dash, run [away]; winnow, sift; gobble, gulp. See ESCAPE, GLUTTONY, VELOCITY, FOOD.

bomb, *n.* [bomb]shell; *slang,* flop (see FAILURE). See ARMS.

bombard, *v.* ATTACK.

bombast, *n.* BOASTING, braggadocio, grandiloquence, EXAGGERATION.

bona fide, *Lat.* real, genuine, authentic. See TRUTH.

bonanza, *n.* [gold] mine, mother lode (see MONEY, STORE).

bond, *n.* union, CONNECTION, tie; accord, sympathy; guaranty, pledge; shackle. See RELATION, SECURITY, CONNECTION, RESTRAINT.

bondage, *n.* slavery, serfdom, SUBJECTION; helotry, peonage. *Ant.,* FREEDOM.

bone, *n.* whalebone, ivory, *etc.* See DENSITY, BODY.

boner, *n., informal,* blunder, ERROR.

bon mot, *Fr.* witty saying. See WIT.

bonnet, *n.* cap, cowl; hood. See COVERING.

bon ton, *Fr.* good manners *or* breeding. See COURTESY, FASHION.

bonus, *n.* premium, extra, dividend. See GIVING, ADDITION, PAYMENT.

bon vivant, *Fr.* epicure; good companion. See GLUTTONY, SOCIALITY.

bon voyage, *Fr.* happy trip; farewell. See DEPARTURE.

bony, *adj.* skeletal, stiff; osseous; lank, lean. See HARDNESS, NARROWNESS.

booby, *n.* dunce, boob (see FOLLY).

book, *n.* volume, tome (see BOOK); collection; RECORD, script, libretto. See ASSEMBLAGE, WRITING. —*v.t.* RECORD, enter; reserve, schedule, engage, program; charge. See LIST, ACCUSATION. —**by the book,** *informal,* properly, according to RULE. —**throw the book at,** *informal,* punish, chide. See PUNISHMENT, SEVERITY.

BOOK
Written or printed volume

Nouns—1, book, volume, folio, tome, opus; novel; tract, brochure; libretto; handbook, codex, manual, textbook, schoolbook, primer, hornbook, pamphlet, chapbook, broadside, booklet, circular; edition, pocket edition, bibelot, production; bestiary; reference book, encyclopedia, dictionary, lexicon, glossary, thesaurus; anthology; gazetteer, almanac, digest, compilation, variorum, compendium, commonplace book, abridgment, concordance, chrestomathy. See PUBLICATION, WRITING, DISSERTATION.

2, printed book, hardbound *or* hardcover book, softcover *or* softbound book, paperback, pocket book; quarto, octavo, imperial, super, royal, medium, crown.

3, makeup, front *or* back matter, title page, table of contents, index, bibliography, errata; colophon; dedication, inscription; foreword, backword, preface; flyleaf, endpaper, signature, folio, page; chapter, section, part, passage; [book]binding, cover, spine, [book *or* dust] jacket; river of white.

4, bookstore, bookshop, bookstall, information [resource] center, on-line bookstore, Amazon.com; [circulating, lending, *or* research] library, bookmobile, Library of Congress; book club; bookcase, bookshelf, bookmark, bookrest, book end.

5, [avid] reader, booklover, bibliophile, bibliomane; librarian, information [retrieval] specialist, cataloger.

Adjectives—bibliographic[al], bibliological.

Phrases—a book is like a garden carried in the pocket.

Quotations—A good book is the precious life-blood of a master spirit (*John Milton*), I hate books; they only teach us to talk about things we know nothing about (*Jean-Jacques Rousseau*), A good book is the best of friends (*Martin Tupper*), Books make sense of life. The only problem is that the lives they make sense of are other people's lives, never your own (*Julian Barnes*), There is no such thing as a moral or an immoral book. Books are well written, or badly written (*Oscar Wilde*), A library is thought in cold storage (*Lord Samuel*), Choose an author as you choose a friend (*Lord Roscommon*), Reading is to the mind what exercise is to the body (*Richard Steele*).

---

bookish, *adj.* studious; formal. See LEARNING.

bookkeeping, *n.* See ACCOUNTING.

bookmaker, *n.* gambler, bookie (*sl.*). See CHANCE.

bookworm, *n.* scholar, pedant, grind (*inf.*); bibliophile. See KNOWLEDGE.

boom, *v.* push, boost, plug; flourish; thunder, drum, rumble (see LOUDNESS). —*n.* beam, spar, jib; PROSPERITY. See PUBLICATION, SHIP.

boomerang, *v.i.* RECOIL, rebound, backfire.

boon, *n.* benefit; favor. See ACQUISITION, REQUEST.

boondocks, *n., slang,* wilderness. See REGION.

boorish, *adj.* ill-mannered, vulgar, rude; rustic, clownish. See VULGARITY, DISCOURTESY.

boost, *n.* AID, help, endorsement; lift, hoist. —*v.i.* assist, promote, recommend; lift, hoist. —*v.t., slang,* steal, shoplift. See APPROBATION, ELEVATION, STEALING.

boot, *n.* footwear, shoe; Hessian boot; blucher, hip *or* jack boot; seven-league boot; brogan, buskin, chukka. See CLOTHING. —*v.t., slang,* kick out, dismiss, give the boot. See EJECTION. —**to boot,** in ADDITION.

booth, *n.* hut; compartment, stall. See RECEPTACLE, ABODE.

booty, *n.* spoil, plunder, prize, loot; graft, swag, boodle; pork barrel, pickings; pillage, blackmail; prey. See ACQUISITION.

border, *n.* EDGE, LIMIT, margin, rim; frontier, boundary; trim (see ORNAMENT). See NEARNESS, CONTACT, AGRICULTURE. *Ant.,* center.

bore, *n.* diameter, caliber; nuisance. —*v.* drill, pierce; tire, weary, annoy. See BREADTH, WEARINESS, OPENING. *Ant.,* amuse.

born-again, *adj.* saved, reborn, redeemed. See RESTORATION, RELIGION.

borough, *n.* See REGION.

BORROWING
Obtaining temporary possession of

Nouns—1, borrowing; mortgaging, financing, raising money; pawning, pledging, hypothecation. *Slang,* hitting up. See ACQUISITION.

2, appropriation, use, taking, adoption; IMITATION, plagiarism, pirating, copying, STEALING.

3, borrower, mortgagor; defaulter; credit card, line of credit, charge account; mortgage, note, chit, account. See DEBT, SECURITY.

Verbs—1, take, receive (as a loan); float a loan, raise money. *Slang,* hit up, touch, put the bite on; get on tick.

2, appropriate, adopt, imitate, make use of; plagiarize, copy from. See STEALING.

Adjective—borrowed; pledged, financed, raised; appropriated, plagiarized, pirated, copied, stolen. *Slang,* on tick, on the cuff, on the slate.

Phrases—the early man never borrows from the late man; he that goes a-borrowing, goes a-sorrowing.

Quotations—Neither a borrower, nor a lender be (*Shakespeare*), Credit is the lifeblood of business (*Herbert Hoover*), I owe my soul to the company store (*Merle Travis*).

Antonyms, see GIVING, DEBT.

---

bosh, *n.* nothing; nonsense, bunk. See AB-
SURDITY.

bosom, *n.* breast, bust; heart (see FEEL-
ING). See CONVEXITY. —*adj.* intimate,
close, confidential. See FRIEND.

boss, *n.* knob, stud; manager, supervisor.
See CONVEXITY, AUTHORITY. —*v.* over-
see, direct; bully, domineer. See AU-
THORITY, FEAR.

botany, *n.* See VEGETABLE.

botch, *v.* bungle, blunder, butcher; mar,
spoil; mismanage. See UNSKILLFULNESS.

both, *pron.* the two, twain, pair. —*adj.*
dually, equally, as well as, together. See
EQUALITY, ACCOMPANIMENT.

bother, *n.* nuisance, annoyance; trouble;
perplexity, worry. —*v.t.* irritate, pester,
worry. See PAIN, ADVERSITY, DISCON-
TENT.

bottle, *n.* carafe, decanter; carboy; flacon,
phial; canteen. See RECEPTACLE.

bottleneck, *n.* obstruction (see CLOSURE).

bottom, *n.* base, foot, sole; foundation;
buttocks. See SUPPORT, LOWNESS, REAR.
—*v.* fathom; run aground. See DEPTH.
Ant., top, surface.

bottomless, *adj.* unfathomable. See
DEPTH, INFINITY.

bottom line, *n.* essence, main point, score.
See SUBSTANCE.

boudoir, *n.* bedroom, sitting room. See
RECEPTACLE.

bough, *n.* limb, branch. See PART.

boulder, *n.* See LAND.

boulevard, *n.* avenue, promenade. See
PASSAGE.

bounce, *v.* rebound, RECOIL; LEAP; *slang,*
eject (see EJECTION).

bound, *v.* LIMIT, confine, delimit, demarcate; LEAP, spring, vault. See CERTAINTY,
DUTY.

boundary, *n.* LIMIT, border, confines. See
EDGE.

boundless, *adj.* infinite, endless, limitless,
illimitable. See INFINITY, SPACE.

bounty, *n.* grant, subsidy; premium; generosity, munificence. See PAYMENT, LIB-
ERALITY. *Ant.,* miserliness.

bouquet, *n.* fragrance, perfume, aroma;
corsage, boutonniere, nosegay, garland.
See ORNAMENT, ODOR.

bourgeois, *adj.* middle-class; conservative.
See MEDIOCRITY.

bout, *n.* contest, match; turn, round; prize-
fight. See CONTENTION, REGULARITY.

boutique, *n.* specialty store, shop[pe]. See
BUSINESS.

bow, *n.* obeisance, curtsy, kowtow, salaam;
FRONT, prow. —*v.i.* nod, incline, bend;
yield, concede; [make one's] debut. See
COURTESY, RESPECT, SUBMISSION, BE-
GINNING.

bow, *n.* curve, arc, crescent; bowknot;
crossbow. See CURVATURE, ARMS.

bowels, *n.pl.* intestines, guts, viscera, innards; depths, recesses. See INTERIOR,
DEPTH.

bower, *n.* arbor, grotto. See RECEPTACLE.

bowl, *n.* basin, vessel, dish; cup, breaker;
ARENA. See RECEPTACLE, CONCAVITY.

bowling, *n.* tenpins, duckpins, candlepins;
ninepines, skittles; lawn bowling, bowls.
See AMUSEMENT.

box, *n.* chest, case, carton, container; coffin. See RECEPTACLE. —*v.* fight, spar,
come to blows. See CONTENTION.

boxer, *n.* pugilist, prizefighter. See CON-
TENTION.

boy, *n.* lad, YOUTH.

boycott, *v.t.* shun; blackball. See RESIS-
TANCE.

brace, *v.t.* invigorate, stimulate; SUPPORT,
prop, strengthen. See REFRESHMENT.
—*n.* bracket, stay, girder; bit, stock; pair.
See STRENGTH, NUMERATION, POWER.

bracelet, *n.* armlet, wristlet, bangle; handcuffs, manacles. See ORNAMENT, RE-
STRAINT, CIRCULARITY.

bracket, *n.* brace; shelf. —*v.t.* link, tie,
parenthesize. See SUPPORT, CONNECTION.

brag, *v.i.* See BOASTING.

braid, *n.* trim, ribbon. —*v.t.* intertwine,
interweave, plait. See CROSSING, ORNA-
MENT, TEXTURE.

brain, *n.* cerebrum, cerebellum; mentality,
INTELLECT, intelligence, mind; gray matter. —*v.t.* See KILLING.

brainchild, *n.* creation (see IMAGINATION).

brainstorm, *n.* inspiration (see IMAGINA-
TION).

brainwash, *v.t.* [counter]indoctrinate, misinform. See DECEPTION, FALSEHOOD.

brake, *v.* retard, check, curb; slow down,
stop. See SLOWNESS, RESTRAINT. *Ant.,*
accelerator.

bramble, *n.* brier, nettle. See SHARPNESS.

branch, *n.* member, arm, bough, limb, ramification; shoot, offshoot; PART. See ANCESTRY. —*v.i.* fork, divide, bifurcate; radiate, diverge. See DISJUNCTION.

brand, *n.* kind, sort, stamp; stigma, stain; mark, identification, trademark; ember; branding iron; torch. See DISREPUTE, HEAT, INDICATION, FUEL.

brandish, *v.t.* flourish, wave, make a show of, flaunt, display. See AGITATION, OSTENTATION.

brash, *adj.* reckless, impetuous; impudent. See RASHNESS, IMPUDENCE.

brass, *n., informal,* assurance, IMPUDENCE; top brass. See AUTHORITY.

brat, *n.* pest, enfant terrible, monster. See DISOBEDIENCE, YOUTH.

bravado, *n.* See BOASTING, INSOLENCE.

brave, *adj.* courageous, valiant. —*v.t.* face, defy. See COURAGE, DEFIANCE. —*n.* buck, redskin (*derog.*).

bravura, *n.* daring, COURAGE.

brawl, *n.* fight, free-for-all; revel. See CONTENTION, AMUSEMENT.

brawn, *n.* STRENGTH, muscle.

brazen, *adj.* shameless, impudent. See IMPUDENCE, COURAGE.

breach, *n.* split, rift, schism; dissension, DISCORD; hole, chasm, OPENING; violation, infringement. See ILLEGALITY, INTERVAL.

bread, *n.* staff of life; white, rye, pumpernickel, sourdough, whole wheat, *etc.* bread; *slang,* MONEY.

BREADTH
Measure from side to side

Nouns—breadth, width, broadness, scope, extent, latitude, amplitude, spaciousness, expanse, beam; diameter, bore, caliber, radius; thickness, bulk, corpulence (see SIZE). See EXPANSION, SPACE, GENERALITY, LIBERALITY.

Verbs—broaden, widen, amplify, extend, enlarge, expand; thicken, fatten.

Adjectives—broad, wide, ample, extended; thick; broad-beamed; outspread, outstretched; vast, spacious, roomy; comprehensive, extensive.

Antonyms, see NARROWNESS.

---

breadwinner, *n.* wage earner (see ACQUISITION).

break, *n.* interruption, disconnection; breach, fracture, fissure, crack; pause; boon, advantage. —*v.* crack, fracture, shatter; tame, subdue; CHANGE; train; surpass; violate, infringe. See BRITTLENESS, DOMESTICATION, DISCONTINUANCE, DESTRUCTION. *Ant.,* mend, repair.

breakdown, *n.* collapse, FAILURE; [nervous] prostration, crack-up. See INSANITY.

breakneck, *adj.* hazardous (see RASHNESS).

breakthrough, *n.* discovery, development; penetration. See DISCLOSURE, ATTACK.

breakup, *n.* ruin, disintegration. See DECOMPOSITION, DESTRUCTION. *Ant.,* synthesis, composition.

breakwater, *n.* mole, sea wall, jetty. See HINDRANCE.

breast, *n.* bosom, bust, mama; spirit. See CONVEXITY, FEELING, BODY. —*v.* face, brave. See OPPOSITION.

breath, *n.* respiration, inhalation, exhalation; breeze. See LIFE, WIND.

breather, *n.* pause, moment of REPOSE.

breathless, *adj.* puffing, panting, short-winded, out of breath *or* wind; excited, overcome. See WONDER, WEARINESS, FEELING.

breathtaking, *adj.* See SURPRISE.

breeches, *n.pl.* knickers, knickerbockers; trousers, pantaloons. See CLOTHING.

breed, *v.* create, multiply; generate, produce. —*n.* strain, race, stock. See RELATION, CLASS, REPRODUCTION.

breeding, *n.* background; culture, gentility, lineage. See COURTESY, ANCESTRY, FASHION.

breeze, *n.* zephyr, breath [of air]. See WIND.

brevity, *n.* concision, briefness, SHORTNESS, TRANSIENTNESS.

brew, *v.* stew, cook, steep, simmer; ferment, distill; scheme, foment, PLAN. —*n.* beer, ale; soup, stew; MIXTURE. See FOOD, DRINKING.

bribe, *n.* graft, bait; grease, payola, fix, hush money (*all sl.*). —*v.t.* overtip; suborn, tempt, corrupt, grease [the palm]. See OFFER, PURCHASE.

bric-a-brac, *n.* knickknacks, curios. See ORNAMENT.

brick, *n.* block; adobe, clay; loaf, lump, bar, briquet[te]. See MATERIALS, DENSITY.

bridal, *adj.* nuptial, connubial. See MARRIAGE.

bridge, *n.* span, trestle, viaduct, causeway; auction *or* contract bridge, whist (see AMUSEMENT). —*v.t.* connect, span, link, cross. See CONNECTION, CROSSING.

bridle, *v.* curb, check; harness; bristle. See RESTRAINT, RESENTMENT.

brief, *adj.* short, succinct, terse; quick, fleeting. —*n.* summary, argument. —*v.t.* instruct. See INFORMATION, LAWSUIT, SHORTNESS.

briefcase, *n.* valise, portfolio. See RECEPTACLE.

brier, *n.* bramble, nettle (see SHARPNESS).

brigand, *n.* bandit, thug, highwayman, robber, pirate. See STEALING.

bright, *adj.* brilliant, shining, glistening; luminous; clever, intelligent; gay, flashing, sparkling. See COLOR, INTELLIGENCE, LIGHT. *Ant.*, dark, dim; stupid; clouded, dismal.

brilliant, *adj.* resplendent, radiant; luminous, sparkling, bright; intelligent, clever, quick-witted. See BEAUTY, INTELLIGENCE, LIGHT. *Ant.*, dull.

brim, *n.* EDGE, rim, brink.

brindled, *adj.* particolored, banded, tabby. See VARIEGATION.

bring, *v.t.* fetch, carry, convey, conduct; command (a price); CAUSE, occasion. See TRANSPORTATION. *Ant.*, leave.

brink, *n.* EDGE, brim, rim, bluff; verge, turning point.

brisk, *adj.* alert, quick, lively, animated, sprightly; cool, sharp. See ACTIVITY, COLD, REFRESHMENT. *Ant.*, languid.

bristle, *n.* hair, stubble. —*v.i.* stand, stick up; stiffen. See SHARPNESS, RESENTMENT, ROUGHNESS.

BRITTLENESS
Fragility

Nouns—1, brittleness, fragility, friability, breakability, frangibility, frailty; crispness, delicacy, crumbliness; vulnerability. See POWDERINESS, WEAKNESS.

2, *(something brittle)* glass, porcelain, *etc.*; eggshell, shortbread; house of cards.

Verbs—break, crack, snap, split, shiver, splinter, shatter, fracture; bust, fall to pieces, break up, disintegrate, fragment; crisp.

Adjectives—brittle, frangible, friable, fragile, breakable, frail, gimcrack, shivery, splintery; splitting; eggshell, delicate; crisp, crumbly, short, brittle as glass, glassy, vitreous.

Antonyms, see COHERENCE.

---

broach, *v.t.* launch, introduce; tap, open. See BEGINNING, OPENING.

broad, *adj.* wide; widespread, extensive; marked (as an accent); sweeping, comprehensive; liberal, tolerant. See BREADTH, LIBERALITY, GENERALITY, IMPURITY. *Ant.*, narrow.

broadcast, *v.* scatter, distribute, disseminate; spread, transmit, publish. —*n.* program, show, telecast. See DISPERSION, COMMUNICATION, PUBLICATION, DISCLOSURE.

broadminded, *adj.* liberal, unbiased. See LIBERALITY.

brochure, *n.* pamphlet, booklet, leaflet; tract, treatise; literature. See PUBLICATION.

brogue, *n.* accent, twang, burr. See SPEECH.

broil, *v.* cook, grill, charbroil; fret, stew. See HEAT, RESENTMENT. —*n.* brawl, riot. See CONTENTION.

broke, *adj.* penniless, flat broke. See DEBT, POVERTY. *Ant.*, rich, wealthy.

broken, broken-down, *adj.* See BREAK, BREAKDOWN.

brokenhearted, *adj.* crushed, stricken, heartbroken. See DISAPPOINTMENT.

broker, *n.* AGENT, jobber, middleman, factor; pawnbroker, stockbroker.

brooch, *n.* [stick]pin (see ORNAMENT).

brood, *n.* hatch, progeny. See POSTERITY. —*v.i.* ponder, mope, meditate, ruminate; sit (on eggs). See THOUGHT.

brook, *n.* stream, creek, rivulet, run. See WATER.

broom, *n.* brush, besom, whisk. See CLEANNESS.

broth, *n.* stock, bouillon, consommé; decoction, potion, elixir. See FOOD, REMEDY.

brothel, *n.* bawdy house, house of ill repute. See IMPURITY.

brother, *n.* friar, frère, Frater; cadet; kinsman, sibling; fellow, colleague, associate; soul brother. See CLERGY, FRIEND.

brotherhood, *n.* kinship, family; association, fraternity, fellowship. See PARTY, FRIEND, SOCIALITY.

brow, *n.* forehead; summit, crest. See FRONT, HEIGHT, EDGE.

browbeat, *v.t.* bully (see FEAR).

brown, *v.t.* toast, braise, singe; sunburn, tan, bronze. See COLOR, HEAT.

brown-nose, *v.t.* toady, grovel (see SERVILITY).

browse, *v.* graze, feed, nibble, pasture. See FOOD, INQUIRY.

bruise, *n.* contusion, black-and-blue spot; mouse, black eye, shiner. —*v.t.* batter, contuse; crush. See IMPULSE.

brunet, brunette, *adj.* dark, dark-haired, dark-complexioned; brown, swarthy. See DARKNESS.

brunt, *n.* shock, burden (see IMPULSE).

brush, *n.* thicket, scrub, shrubbery; broom. —*v.* sweep; graze. See CLEANNESS, ROUGHNESS, TOUCH, PAINTING, CONTENTION.

brusque, *adj.* gruff, curt, abrupt. See DISCOURTESY. *Ant.* courteous.

brutal, *adj.* cruel, inhuman; crude, coarse. See MALEVOLENCE, DISCOURTESY. *Ant.*, gentle, kind.

brutalize, *v.t.* See DETERIORATION.

brute, *n.* beast, ANIMAL; ruffian, scoundrel, bull. See EVILDOER.

bubble, *n.* globule, blob. See ROTUNDITY, DECEPTION. —*v.i.* effervesce, boil, gurgle. See AGITATION, TRANSIENTNESS, WATER.

buccaneer, *n.* pirate (see ILLEGALITY).

buck, *v.* strive (against), take on, fight. See OPPOSITION.

bucket, *n.* pail, tub; scoop. See RECEPTACLE.

buckle, *n.* clasp, fastening. —*v.* bend, twist, crumple; collapse. See CONNECTION, CONVOLUTION, FAILURE.

bucolic, *adj.* rustic, rural; pastoral. See REGION, POETRY.

bud, *v.i.* sprout, shoot; germinate; burgeon; mature. See BEGINNING, EXPANSION.

buddy, *n.*, *informal*, comrade, pal, chum, FRIEND.

budge, *v.* move, stir, shift; alter, change, INFLUENCE. See MOTION.

budget, *n.* APPORTIONMENT, allowance; [estimate of] expenses. See ACCOUNTING, PLAN.

buff, *v.* polish (see SMOOTHNESS, FRICTION). —*n.* See COLOR.

buffer, *n.* fender, bumper; polisher. See SAFETY, HINDRANCE, SMOOTHNESS.

buffet, *v.t.* beat, slap; pelt. —*n.* slap, stroke, blow. See IMPULSE.

buffet, *n.* sideboard, cupboard, cabinet; refreshments, smorgasbord; counter. See RECEPTACLE, FOOD.

buffoon, *n.* fool, clown, jester; comedian, mountebank. See DRAMA, WIT.

bug, *n.* insect, arthropod, mite, nit, bedbug; vermin; *slang*, [wire]tap; flaw, defect, fault, IMPERFECTION; enthusiast (see ACTIVITY). See ANIMAL, LITTLENESS. —*v.*, *slang*, [wire] tap; pester, annoy, bother. See DISCONTENT, INQUIRY.

bugbear, *n.* bogy, bugaboo. See FEAR.

buggy, *n.* carriage; jalopy (see VEHICLE).

build, *v.t.* construct, make, fashion; erect; found. See FORM, PRODUCTION. —*n.* physique, body. See BUILDING. *Ant.*, demolish, raze.

BUILDING
Architectural structure

Nouns—1, edifice, structure, construction. See FORM, PRODUCTION, ARCHITECTURE. 2, house, home, ABODE.

3, *(types of buildings)* A-frame, prefab, Quonset hut, ranch house, saltbox, split-level; acropolis, basilica; balok, bower, cabin, Cape Cod, cottage, izba, jacal, log cabin, Nissen hut, outbuilding, outhouse (see CLEANNESS), shack, shanty, shebang; barracks, dormitory, apartment, boardinghouse (see ABODE); house, loft, maisonette, semidetached, tenement, town house, duplex, triplex; fixer-upper, handyman's special; carriage house, garage, hangar; high-rise, skyscraper; low-rise; conservatory, greenhouse; blockhouse, bunker; mall, market, plant, rialto, shop, stall, stand, supermarket, tavern, terminal, warehouse, washhouse; pyramid, tholos; pagoda, stupa, yurt; ARENA; bathhouse, cabaña, chalet, gazebo, kiosk, resort; booth, crib, lean-to, shed, woodshed; tent, pavilion; TEMPLE; tower, barbican, belfry, bell tower, campanile, donjon, flèche, lou, obelisk, observation tower, spire, turret, ziggurat.

4, *(building parts and materials)* **a.** arch, keystone, quoin. **b.** beam, berm, boom, box beam, built-up beam, bulwark, chord, collar beam, common rafter, cripple, cross bridging, crossbar, crossbeam, crosstie, flitch, girder, H-beam, haunch, headpost, hip rafter, I-beam, jack rafter, joist, keystone joist, king post, ridge beam, ridgepole, scantling, stanchion, stud, tail, tie beam, timber, trave, trimmer, truss beam, valley rafter, wale bracket. **c.** board, batten, crib, lath, lattice, panel, shim, slat, strake, plank. **d.** column, pier, baseplate, piloti, pole. **e.** door, [door] frame, [door] jamb, reveal, head, latch, lintel, rail, sill, sill plate, stile, stop, strike plate, threshold, transom. **f.** floor, floor joist, floorboard, sleeper, subfloor, underlayment. **g.** foundation, bearing pile, caisson, footing, girder pocket, soleplate, sump. **h.** [dovetail, lap, expansion, foliated, *or* knuckle] joint, beam pocket, chamfer, framing, bondstone, gain, gusset, joggle, mortise, notch, rabbet, scab, tenon, tongue-and-groove joint. **i.** cornice, molding, fascia, frieze, trim. **j.** [barrack, butterfly, flat, gambrel, helm, hip-and-valley, hipped, jerkinhead, mansard, monopitch, pantile, pitched, pyramid, rainbow, sawtooth, shingle, skirt, slate, *or* thatched] roof, roofing, angle rafter, awning, counterflashing, gutter, leader, plancier, purlin, rake, roof plate, gable, chimney, crest, cullis, dome, geodesic dome, lean-to, gutter, scupper, cupola, chimney pot, cowl, eave, dormer, sheathing, soffit, valley. **k.** stair, staircase, platform, baluster, landing, newel, nosing, rise(r), run, stringer, tread. **l.** support, anta, bailey, brace, bracket, bridging, building block, buttress, cantilever, ceiling joist, cleat, crutch, frame, grate, header, jack, lally column, ledger, lookout, pilaster, pile, plate, post, rafter, ribbon, sandwich panel, shoring, skid, spar, standard, steel framing, strut, tierod, truss, W-beam, waler. **m.** [bearing, load-bearing, perpend, Trombe, retaining, nonbearing, dead, curtain, exterior, *or* interior] wall, baseboard, baseshoe, louver, bulkhead, fire wall, firestop, furring, gable end, partition, siding, clapboard, clerestory, coping, cornerstone, template, top plate, wall section. **n.** window, bay window, oriel, bow *or* compass window, bull's-eye window, œil de bœuf, Diocletian *or* Palladian window, dormer, double- *or* single-hung window, French window, picture window, porthole, quarrel, Judas hole, lancet window, rose window, roundel, skylight, storm window, transom, embrasure, jamb, sconcheon, fanlight, casement, mullion, muntin, sash, stool, windowpane. **o.** turret, bartizan, bastion, battlement, crenel, crenelation, merlon.

5, building trades; builder, contractor, designer, architect (see ARCHITECTURE); bricklayer, cabinetmaker, carpenter, construction worker, electrician, engineer, glazier, interior decorator, mason, painter, paperhanger, plasterer, plumber, rigger, roofer, stonemason, tilesetter, woodworker.

Verbs—build, construct, erect, put up, raise, frame.

Quotations—Houses are built to live in and not to look on (*Francis Bacon*), Light (God's eldest daughter) is a principal beauty in building (*Thomas Fuller*), When we build, let us think that we build for ever (*John Ruskin*), A house is a machine for living in (*Le Corbusier*), The most beautiful house in the world is the one that you build for yourself (*Witold Rybczynski*).

---

bulb, *n.* knob, globe; tuber, corm; lamp. See CONVEXITY, VEGETABLE, LIGHT, ROTUNDITY.

bulge, *v.* swell, protrude, bag. See CONVEXITY.

bulk, *n.* SIZE, QUANTITY, measure, amount, volume; mass, expanse; body; generality, majority.

bulldoze, *v.t.* coerce, bully; frighten. See COMPULSION, FEAR.

bullet, *n.* missile, shot, ball, lead, slug; buckshot, BB shot. See ARMS.

bulletin, *n.* report, statement, INFORMATION, flash (*inf.*). See COMMUNICATION, NEWS.

bullfighter, *n.* matador; picador, banderillo; toreador. See AMUSEMENT.

bull's-eye, *n.* target, black. See MIDDLE.

bullshit, *n., slang,* nonsense (see ABSURDITY).

bully, *n.* hector, brawler; plug-ugly; tyrant. —*v.t.* intimidate, browbeat, hector, bulldoze. See EVILDOER, INSOLENCE, THREAT.

bulwark, *n.* fortification, rampart; safeguard; barrier, parapet. See DEFENSE.

bum, *n., slang,* beggar, loafer. See INACTIVITY.

bump, *v.* collide, knock, strike, hit. See IMPULSE.

bumpkin, *n.* yokel (see UNSKILLFULNESS).

bump off, *v.t. slang,* kill (see KILLING).

bun, *n.* roll, sweet roll, Danish [pastry], hot-cross bun; knot, chignon. See FOOD, ROUGHNESS.

bunch, *n.* crowd, group; cluster, bundle. See CONVEXITY, ASSEMBLAGE.

bundle, *n.* package, parcel, packet; bunch, bale; *informal,* riches, wealth. See ASSEMBLAGE, MONEY.

bung, *n.* stopper, cork, plug. See CLOSURE.

bungalow, *n.* cottage, cabin (see BUILDING).

bungle, *v.* spoil; botch; blunder, goof. See UNSKILLFULNESS.

bunk, *n.* bed, berth, cot; *informal,* applesauce, nonsense, buncombe, claptrap, humbug, bosh. See SUPPORT, ABSURDITY.

bunker, *n.* blockhouse, shelter; bastion. See SAFETY.

bunting, *n.* banner, streamer (see INDICATION).

buoy, *n.* float; marker; bellbuoy, lifebuoy. See NAVIGATION, INDICATION.

buoyant, *adj.* light, floating; resilient, springy; confident, sanguine. See ASCENT, HOPE, CHEERFULNESS, ELASTICITY. *Ant.,* heavy.

burden, *n.* HINDRANCE; load, weight, encumbrance; charge; refrain. See GRAVITY, REPETITION.

bureau, *n.* department, office; chest, dresser; secretary, desk; division, branch, section, AGENCY. See RECEPTACLE.

bureaucracy, *n.* officialism; officiousness; red tape. See AUTHORITY.

burgeon, *n.* bud, sprout. See VEGETABLE, EXPANSION.

burglar, *n.* housebreaker, second-story man. See STEALING.

burial, *n.* INTERMENT.

burlesque, *n.* farce, parody; comedy, buffoonery. —*v.t.* satirize, parody, mimic, caricature. See IMITATION, RIDICULE, DRAMA.

burly, *adj.* stout, brawny (see STRENGTH).

burn, *v.* oxidize, consume; blaze, flame; fire; sear, char, scorch; destroy. See HEAT, DESIRE, EXCITABILITY.

burnish, *v.t.* polish (see LIGHT, SMOOTHNESS).

burp, *v.i., informal,* eructate, belch. See EJECTION.

burrow, *n.* hole, tunnel, excavation, foxhole. —*v.* dig, mine. See CONCAVITY.

bursary, *n.* treasury; scholarship. See STORE, MEANS.

burst, *v.* rupture, break, rend, bust (*sl.*); explode, shatter. See VIOLENCE, DISJUNCTION.

bury, *v.t.* inter, inhume, immure; cover, sink. See INTERMENT, DEPTH, CONCEALMENT. *Ant.,* exhume.

bus, *n.* omnibus, motorbus, coach, jitney, trolley [bus]. See VEHICLE.

bush, *n.* shrub, clump, thicket, hedge; scrub; wilderness. See VEGETABLE, USELESSNESS.

bushy, *adj.* hairy, shaggy, dense, bushlike. See ROUGHNESS.

BUSINESS
Commercial enterprise

Nouns—1, business, occupation, employment, pursuit; venture (see UNDERTAKING); task, work, job, chore, errand, commission, charge, care, assignment; busy work; racket. *Slang,* bag.

2, *(area of one's business)* province, function, bailiwick, lookout, department, station, capacity, sphere, orb, field, line, DUTY; affair, concern, matter, case; walk [of life]; beat, round, range, routine; career, vocation, calling, profession; art, craft, handicraft; trade, commerce, industry, cottage industry; enterprise zone.

3, occupation, place, post, function, capacity, position, office, incumbency, living; situation, berth, employ; service; appointment, engagement; line of business *or* work, calling, vocation, profession, practice, trade, career; avocation (see AMUSEMENT). *Slang*, gig. See ACTIVITY, EXERTION.

4, market, marketplace, mart, agora, fair, bazaar; industrial park; store, shop, stall, booth, workshop; office, bureau; [stock] exchange, curb, bourse, rialto, pit, Wall Street, the street; bank; [sunrise *or* sunset] industry, big business, firm, concern, establishment, house, sole proprietorship, company, concern, limited company, start-up company, growth company, holding company, blind trust, conglomerate, [closed, alien, collapsible, multinational, privately held, public, public service, *or* nonprofit] corporation, conglomerate, consortium, [co-]partnership, cottage industry; foundation, nonprofit trust, institution; concession; facility, franchise; dot.com.

5, *(business terms)* charter, articles of incorporation; annual report, prospectus; board of directors, interlocking directorates; annual meeting, proxy fight; corporate veil; home office; pension fund; diversification, merger, takeover, divestiture, spin-off, dissolution, liquidation, golden parachute; capitalization, budgeting, cash flow, market share, bottom line (see ACCOUNTING).

6, management, middle management; businessperson, -man, *or* -woman, captain of industry, robber baron, organization man, entrepreneur, intrapreneur, industrialist, tycoon, magnate, mogul; nabob; small-business man; owner, [silent] partner, director, CEO, chief executive officer, president, superintendent, comptroller, treasurer; manager, foreman, supervisor, overseer; merchant, tradesman, store- *or* shopkeeper, dealer, monger, retailer, dealership; wholesaler, distributor[ship], concession; banker, broker, middleman, buyer, seller, sales AGENT; bear, bull; financier, speculator; man in the gray flannel suit; white-collar worker; auctioneer. *Informal,* movers and shakers, player, number cruncher; the butcher, the baker, the candlestick maker. *Slang,* suit, rainmaker. See SALE, PURCHASE, PROVISION, DIRECTOR.

7, employment agency, headhunter. *Slang,* bodyshop.

Verbs—1, busy *or* occupy oneself with; undertake, attempt, turn one's hand to; do, carry on, *or* transact business, keep a shop, ply one's trade; talk shop *or* turkey; play the market. *Informal,* hang out one's shingle. See ACTIVITY, EXERTION.

2, *(have as one's business)* serve *or* act as, do duty as, discharge the duties of, hold office, fill *or* hold [down] a situation; be engaged in, concern oneself with, have in hand; have on one's hands, bear the burden, have one's hands full. *Informal,* hold down a job, be into (something).

3, incorporate, go public.

Adjectives—businesslike, orderly, thorough, methodical, efficient, systematic, workaday; professional, vocational; official, functional; authoritative; busy, in hand, afoot; on foot, on the fire; going on, acting; commercial, entrepreneurial.

Phrases—business before pleasure; business goes where it is invited and stays where it is well treated; business is like a car: it will not run by itself except downhill.

Quotations—We used to build civilizations. Now we build shopping malls (*Bill Bryson*), No nation was ever ruined by trade (*Benjamin Franklin*), Corporations have no souls, but they can love each other (*Henry Demarest Lloyd*), The chief business of the American people is business (*Calvin Coolidge*).

Antonyms, see INACTIVITY, REPOSE.

---

bust, *n.* bosom, breast; statuette; *informal,* FAILURE; *informal,* spree, fling. See CONVEXITY, REPRESENTATION, AMUSEMENT. —*v.i.* , *informal,* burst (see BRITTLENESS). —*v.t.*, *slang,* arrest (see RESTRAINT).

bustle, *n.* stir, rustle, fluster, flurry, ado. See ACTIVITY, AGITATION, HASTE.

busy, *adj.* occupied, engaged, engrossed; employed; meddlesome. See ACTIVITY, BUSINESS.

busybody, *n.* meddler, snooper, gossip, talebearer, kibitzer. See CURIOSITY.

but, *conj.* still, yet, however. —*prep.* except, save, saving, excepting. See COMPENSATION, UNCONFORMITY.

butch, *adj., slang,* mannish, lesbian. See FEMALE.

butcher, *v.t.* slaughter, kill; bungle, spoil. See KILLING, UNSKILLFULNESS, FOOD.

butler, *n.* steward, maître d'hôtel. See SERVANT.

butt, *n.* target, goat, laughingstock; handle. See RIDICULE, END. —*v.* abut; collide, strike. See IMPULSE, CONTACT.

butte, *n.* hill (see HEIGHT).

buttocks, *n.* rump, seat, hindquarters, breech, ass (*sl.*). See REAR.

button, *n.* fastener; disk, boss; badge, emblem; pushbutton. —*v.* fasten, loop, close. See CLOSURE, JUNCTION, CONNECTION, INDICATION, INSTRUMENTALITY.

buttress, *n.* flying buttress; SUPPORT; prop, brace. See DEFENSE.

buxom, *adj.* plump, healthy; shapely, [well-]built. See FORM.

buy, *v.* procure, PURCHASE. *Ant.,* sell.

buzz, *v.* drone, hum, whirr; whisper, gossip; *informal,* bustle, fuss, hurry; *informal,* telephone, ring up. —*n.* hum, whirr, *etc.; informal,* [telephone] call, ring. See SOUND, EXCITEMENT.

by, *adv. & prep.* beside, alongside; past, beyond; no later than; through. See INSTRUMENTALITY, CAUSE, SIDE.

bygone, *adj.* former, PAST; antiquated, obsolete. See OBLIVION.

bypass, *n.* detour, roundabout. See CIRCUITY, DEVIATION.

by-product, *n.* EFFECT, result; spinoff, offshoot; residue.

bystander, *n.* spectator, onlooker. See PRESENCE.

byway, *n.* lane, byroad. See PASSAGE.

byword, *n.* proverb; motto, slogan; shibboleth, password. See MAXIM, INDICATION, NOMENCLATURE.

Byzantine, *adj.* elaborate, ornate; scheming, manipulative. See PLAN, ORNAMENT.

C

cab, *n.* taxi[cab], hack[ney], hansom; cockpit. See VEHICLE, RECEPTACLE.

cabal, *n.* junto, conspiracy; plot. See PLAN, CONCEALMENT.

cabalistic, *adj.* occult, arcane. See SECRET.

cabaña, *n.* bathhouse (see BUILDING).

cabaret, *n.* nightclub, bistro, night spot. See FOOD, DRINKING.

cabin, *n.* shack, shed, shanty, lodge, hut, cottage; stateroom, cockpit. See RECEPTACLE, ABODE.

cabinet, *n.* room, boudoir, chamber, closet; étagère, case; repository; ministry, board, COUNCIL. See RECEPTACLE.

cable, *n.* rope, line, cord; cablegram. See FILAMENT, COMMUNICATION.

cache, *n.* hiding place, stash; [memory] buffer. See CONCEALMENT, COMPUTERS.

cachet, *n.* seal, stamp; prestige; feature. See INDICATION, SPECIALITY.

cackle, *n. & v.i.* chatter, prattle; giggle. See SPEECH, AMUSEMENT.

cad, *n.* scoundrel, bounder, churl. See EVILDOER, DISCOURTESY.

cadaver, *n.* body (see DEATH).

cadence, *n.* rhythm, beat, pulse, meter. See MUSIC, TIME.

cadet, *n.* recruit (see COMBATANT).

café, *n.* coffeehouse; saloon, bar; cabaret, bistro. See FOOD.

cafeteria, *n.* restaurant, Automat. See FOOD.

cage, *n.* ENCLOSURE, bars; aviary, pen. — *v.t.* restrain, imprison, incarcerate, pen. See RESTRAINT. *Ant.,* set free, release.

cagey, *adj., informal,* wary, shrewd. See CAUTION.

cajole, *v.* flatter, wheedle, inveigle; beguile, blandish; coax. See FLATTERY, DECEPTION.

cake, *v.i.* harden; consolidate, cohere; thicken, congeal, condense. See COHERENCE. — *n.* mass, brick, block, floe; torte. See DENSITY, FOOD.

calamity, *n.* catastrophe, disaster. See ADVERSITY, EVIL. *Ant.,* blessing, benefit.

calculate, *v.* compute, reckon; count, appraise; estimate; *informal,* consider, deem, figure. See NUMERATION, EXPECTATION, PLAN.

calculating, *adj.* scheming, crafty, designing, CUNNING. See PLAN.

calendar, *n.* almanac; diary, journal, log; register, schedule; docket. See CHRONOMETRY.

calf, *n.* dogie, weaner. See YOUTH.

caliber, *n.* gauge, bore; quality; ability, capability. See SIZE, BREADTH, INTELLIGENCE, DEGREE.

calibrate, *v.t.* graduate; rectify. See MEASUREMENT.

calisthenics, *n.* gymnastics, workout, exercise. See EXERTION.

call, *v.* CRY, shout, yell; summon, bid; convoke, muster; choose, appoint, elect; name, designate; visit, interview. —*n.* summons, demand; shout, yell; signal; impulse, urge; visit. See CHOICE, ASSEMBLAGE, COMMAND, NOMENCLATURE, SOCIALITY.

call girl, prostitute, escort. See IMPURITY.

calligraphy, *n.* hand[writing], script, good penmanship. See WRITING.

calling, *n.* vocation, profession; occupation, trade, BUSINESS; DUTY.

callous, *adj.* horny, tough; unfeeling, insensitive, hardened. See HARDNESS, INSENSIBILITY. *Ant.,* compassionate.

callow, *adj.* featherless, unfledged; immature, inexperienced. See YOUTH. *Ant.,* mature, experienced.

calm, *adj.* placid, serene, unruffled, cool, composed, undisturbed; phlegmatic, sedate; tranquil, still, motionless, halcyon; peaceful, pacific. —*v.t.* still, pacify. See REPOSE, PACIFICATION, DISSUASION, INEXCITABILITY. *Ant.,* agitated, excited, angry, passionate.

calumny, *n.* slander (see DETRACTION).

camaraderie, *n.* comradeship, fellowship. See FRIEND.

camera, *n.* See OPTICAL INSTRUMENTS.

camouflage, *v.t.* disguise, conceal. —*n.* disguise, mask; pretense. See CONCEALMENT.

camp, *n.* encampment, bivouac, cantonment; group, clique. See ABODE, PARTY.

campaign, *n.* operations; PLAN. —*v.i.* canvass, electioneer; fight, war. See WARFARE, CONDUCT.

camp follower, prostitute; observer, follower, hanger-on. See IMPURITY, ATTENTION.

campus, *n.* grounds, quad[rangle]. See SCHOOL.

can, *n.* tin, container; *slang,* jail; *slang,* toilet. See RECEPTACLE, PRISON, CLEANNESS.

canal, *n.* channel, waterway; ditch, culvert, conduit. See PASSAGE.

cancel, *v.t.* delete; offset, neutralize; void, annul; postmark. See NULLIFICATION, COMPENSATION, INDICATION, NONPAYMENT.

cancer, *n.* carcinoma, sarcoma, malignancy. See DISEASE.

candid, *adj.* frank, straightforward; outspoken, blunt. See TRUTH.

candidate, *n.* nominee, officeseeker; applicant, aspirant; probationer. See DESIRE, CHOICE.

candle, *n.* taper, wax, cierge. See LIGHT.

candor, *n.* honesty, sincerity, frankness; simplicity, naiveté, INNOCENCE. See TRUTH.

candy, *n.* confection, sweet, bonbon, kiss. See SWEETNESS.

cane, *n.* switch, stick, rod, birch; walking *or* swagger stick; canebrake. —*v.* thrash, flog, switch, beat. See PUNISHMENT, SUPPORT.

canine, *n.* dog, wolf, fox. See ANIMAL, BODY.

canister, *n.* caddy, container. See RECEPTACLE.

cannibal, *n.* man-eater, savage, anthropophagus. See EVILDOER.

cannon, *n.* gun, field gun *or* piece; artillery, ordnance, battery. See ARMS.

canny, *adj.* wary, sagacious. See CUNNING. *Ant.,* unwise, imprudent.

canoe, *n.* dugout, kayak, bungo, pirogue. See SHIP.

canon, *n.* decree, code, law; principle; criterion; round, catch; œuvre, corpus. See CLERGY, MUSIC, RELIGION, RULE, BELIEF, RITE, WRITING.

canopy, *n.* awning, tester; vault, sky; pavilion, cope; howdah. See COVERING.

cant, *n.* pretense, hypocrisy, insincerity; tilt, OBLIQUITY; argot, lingo, jargon. See IMPIETY, FALSEHOOD, CONCEALMENT, SPEECH.

cantankerous, *adj.* cross, ill-natured. See IRASCIBILITY. *Ant.,* pleasant, goodnatured.

canteen, *n.* flask, waterbag; commissary. See RECEPTACLE, STORE, FOOD.

cantilever, *n.* projection, overhang (see ARCHITECTURE).

canton, *n.* district, subdivision (see REGION).

cantus firmus, *Lat.* fixed melody; chant, musical theme. See MUSIC.

canvas, *n.* sail, tarpaulin, tent; circus; PAINTING. See COVERING, SHIP.

canvass, *v.t.* examine, sift, discuss; solicit, campaign, poll, survey. See INQUIRY, REQUEST.

canyon, *n.* ravine, defile, gorge, gulch, chasm. See INTERVAL.

cap, *n.* skullcap, tam-o'-shanter, beret, beanie, kepi, glengarry; acme, top; climax; bottlecap. —*v.* cover; outdo, excel; complete, climax. See COVERING, CLOTHING, SUPERIORITY, SPACE, COMPLETION.

capable, *adj.* able, competent, proficient; susceptible. See SKILL, POWER. *Ant.,* incapable, incompetent.

capacity, *n.* content, volume; aptitude, faculty, ability. See SIZE, INTELLIGENCE, POWER, BUSINESS. *Ant.,* incapacity, incompetence.

cape, *n.* mantle, cloak, tippet, fichu, pelerine, bertha; shawl; headland, promontory, point, tongue, peninsula. See CLOTHING, CONVEXITY.

caper, *v.i.* LEAP; cavort, gambol, frisk, frolic, prance, skip. —*n.* LEAP, capriole; prank, antic, trick. See AMUSEMENT.

capital, *adj.* excellent, paramount, firstrate, first-class, unequaled; important, primary, principal; metropolitan; uppercase. See GOODNESS, HEIGHT, PUNISHMENT. —*n.* metropolis, seat; funds, assets, resources. See MONEY, IMPORTANCE, MEANS.

capitalism, *n.* free enterprise (see ECONOMY, AUTHORITY).

capitalize, *v.* finance, fund, subsidize; turn to advantage. See PAYMENT, SUCCESS.

capitol, *n.* statehouse. See COUNCIL.

capitulate, *v.i.* surrender. See SUBMISSION.

caprice, *n.* fancy, humor (see CHANGE-ABLENESS).

capsize, *v.* overturn, upset, turn turtle, turn *or* tip over. See INVERSION.

capsule, *n.* pill (see REMEDY).

captain, *n.* commander, skipper; leader; chief, headman. See AUTHORITY.

caption, *n.* title, subtitle, headline, heading, subhead, legend. See INDICATION.

captious, *adj.* caviling, carping, hairsplitting, faultfinding, hypercritical. See DISAPPROBATION.

captivate, *v.t.* charm, fascinate, enchant, enamor; enthrall; bewitch. See PLEASURE, ATTRACTION. *Ant.,* offend, displease.

captive, *n.* prisoner (see PRISON, RESTRAINT).

capture, *v.t.* seize, apprehend, arrest; grab; bag, snare, trap, nab *(inf.),* collar *(sl.).* See RESTRAINT. *Ant.,* release.

car, *n.* See VEHICLE.

carafe, *n.* decanter (see RECEPTACLE).

caravan, *n.* procession, motorcade; van. See TRAVEL, VEHICLE.

carbohydrate, *n.* sugar, starch (see ORGANIC MATTER).

carbonated, *adj.* bubbly, effervescent, fizzy, sparkling. See AIR. *Ant.,* flat.

carbuncle, *n.* boil, wen (see CONVEXITY).

carcass, *n.* corpse, remains, shell, hull. See REMAINDER, DEATH.

carcinogenic, *adj.* cancerous, malignant. See DISEASE.

card, *n.* tarot, playing card; visiting *or* calling card; *informal,* character, oddball. See INDICATION, UNCONFORMITY.

cardinal, *adj.* principal, leading, fundamental. See IMPORTANCE, CLERGY. *Ant.,* minor, lesser.

care, *v.i.* like, have affection (for). See CARE, PITY, FEELING.

CARE
Solicitude

Nouns—1, *(concern)* care, concern, consideration, solicitude, anxiety, heed, heedfulness; conscientiousness, watchfulness, vigilance, surveillance, eyes of Argus; watch, vigil, lookout, weather eye, watch and ward; childcare, healthcare, etc. See SAFETY.

2, alertness, ATTENTION, charge; precaution, prudence, circumspection, CAUTION.

3, *(care for order)* tidiness, orderliness, cleanliness; accuracy, exactness, minuteness, attention to detail, meticulousness, rigor.

Verbs—1, care [about], heed, consider, pay heed to, be concerned, pay ATTENTION to.

2, be careful, take care, have a care, deliberate, take pains, be cautious, take precautions; pay attention to, take care of, look *or* see to, look *or* see after, keep an eye on; double-check; keep in sight *or* view, mind; mind one's business; keep tabs on.

3, *(be attentive)* have all one's wits about one; watch for, expect (see EXPECTATION); mind one's Ps and Qs, weigh one's words, put one's best foot forward, speak by the card, pick one's steps.

4, *(pay attention)* observe, heed; do one's duty; make good, keep one's word *or* promise.

5, *(be careful)* keep watch, be on one's guard, be on the lookout, keep one's eyes open, be vigilant; stop, look, and listen (see CAUTION). *Informal,* keep one's eyes peeled.

6, care for, nurture, tend, look after, take care of. See SAFETY.

Adjectives—1, *(showing care)* careful, regardful, heedful; particular, painstaking, prudent, cautious, discreet; considerate, thoughtful, solicitous; deliberative, provident, prepared.

2, *(showing attention to detail)* accurate, exact, deliberate, studied; fastidious, dainty, meticulous, conscientious. *Slang,* goosey.

Adverbs—carefully, meticulously, *etc.;* with care, gingerly; in detail, with attention to detail.

Phrases—care killed the cat; if you can't be good, be careful.

Quotations—One cannot weep for the entire world (*Jean Anouilh*), Thus conscience doth make cowards of us all (*Shakespeare*), Wisely and slow. They stumble that run fast (*Shakespeare*), Teach us to care and not to care (*George Eliot*), Sleep that knits up the ravelled sleeve of care (*Shakespeare*), Care and diligence bring luck (*Thomas Fuller*).

Antonyms, see NEGLECT.

---

careen, *v.* sway, lean; career, speed. See OBLIQUITY, VELOCITY.

career, *n.* profession, calling, lifework; history. See BUSINESS. —*v.* race, dash. See VELOCITY.

careless, *adj.* carefree, nonchalant; casual, offhand; negligent, slack, slovenly; reckless, rash, indiscreet. See INDIFFERENCE, NEGLECT, INATTENTION, RASHNESS. *Ant.,* careful, attentive.

caress, *v.t. & n.* fondle, pet, stroke. See ENDEARMENT.

caretaker, *n.* guardian, custodian; janitor. See SAFETY, CLEANNESS.

careworn, *adj.* worried, anxious. See FEAR.

cargo, *n.* freight, lading, shipment, load. See TRANSPORTATION.

caricature, *n.* burlesque, travesty; sketch. —*v.t.* satirize, take off, distort. See RIDICULE, IMITATION, EXAGGERATION.

caring, *adj.* mindful, attentive, sympathetic. See PITY, FEELING. *Ant.,* indifferent, uncaring.

carnage, *n.* massacre, slaughter; shambles, butchery. See KILLING.

carnal, *adj.* bodily, fleshly; worldly, sensual. See ANIMAL, IRRELIGION, INTEMPERANCE.

carnival, *n.* festival, fete, gala; masquerade, bacchanal; revelry; jamboree. See AMUSEMENT.

carnivorous, *adj.* flesh-eating; predatory, predaceous. See FOOD, ANIMAL. *Ant.,* herbivorous.

carol, *n.* noël. See MUSIC.

carom, *n.* cannon; rebound. See RECOIL.

carouse, *v.i.* feast, revel; debauch, drink. See DRINKING.

carousel, *n.* merry-go-round, whirligig (see ROTATION).

carp, *v.i.* find fault, nitpick, cavil. See DISAPPROBATION.

carpe diem, *Lat.* make use of the [present] day. See ACTIVITY.

carpenter, *n.* cabinetmaker, woodworker, joiner. See PRODUCTION.

carpet, *n.* rug, drugget; wall-to-wall, broadloom, Oriental, *etc.* See COVERING.

carriage, *n.* bearing, mien, behavior, CONDUCT, front; wagon, cart, stage[coach], coach, equipage. See APPEARANCE, VEHICLE, TRANSPORTATION.

carrion, *n.* flesh, carcass, remains. See DECOMPOSITION.

carry, *v.t.* uphold, SUPPORT; transport, convey, bear; adopt; [have *or* keep in] stock. See TRANSPORTATION, STORE, ASSENT.

carry on, continue; misbehave, act up; emote. See CONTINUITY, BADNESS.

cart, *n.* tumbrel, tumbril; pushcart, dogcart; gocart. See TRANSPORTATION, VEHICLE.

carte blanche, *Fr.* unlimited authority. See PERMISSION.

cartel, *n.* syndicate (see PARTY).

carton, *n.* box (see RECEPTACLE).

cartoon, *n.* sketch, drawing; caricature; comic strip, comics, funnies, funny papers. See PAINTING, RIDICULE.

cartridge, *n.* shell; case, cassette. See ARMS, ENCLOSURE.

carve, *v.i.* cut, slice; shape, fashion; chisel, engrave, SCULPTURE. See DISJUNCTION, FORM, ENGRAVING.

cascade, *n.* waterfall (see WATER).

case, *n.* instance, situation, plight; sheath, scabbard, holster; portfolio; suit, action, litigation; argument, proposition; box, container, carton, casket, cabinet; bag, suitcase, handbag, grip, valise. See BUSINESS, COVERING, LAWSUIT, RECEPTACLE, CIRCUMSTANCE.

cash, *n.* MONEY, specie, ready money, hard cash, currency, brass (*sl.*), dust (*sl.*).

cashier, *n.* teller, clerk. See SALE. —*v.t.* fire, dismiss. See EJECTION.

casing, *n.* shell (see COVERING).

cask, *n.* barrel, hogshead, keg, butt. See RECEPTACLE.

casket, *n.* coffin; reliquary, chest, box. See RECEPTACLE.

cassette, *n.* case, [video]tape. See RECEPTACLE.

cast, *v.t.* throw, toss, heave, hurl, sling, fling; shed; mold; plan, compute. See

EJECTION, FORM, PROPULSION. —*n.* APPEARANCE, aspect, air; company, actors, dramatis personae; casting, COPY, mold, sculpture. See DRAMA, COLOR.

castaway, *n.*, castoff, pariah (see EJECTION, ABANDONMENT).

caste, *n.* CLASS, rank.

caster, *n.* cruet, sifter; wheel; swivel. See RECEPTACLE, CIRCULARITY.

castigate, *v.t.* criticize; correct, punish. See DISAPPROBATION, PUNISHMENT.

castle, *n.* fort[ress], stronghold; donjon, keep; rook. See DEFENSE, ABODE.

castrate, *v.t.* emasculate, unman; geld. See IMPOTENCE.

casual, *adj.* accidental, CHANCE; careless, cursory; irregular, occasional; informal; happy-go-lucky. See NEGLECT, IRREGULARITY.

casualty, *n.* accident; disaster, calamity. See ADVERSITY, EVIL, OCCURRENCE.

casus belli, *Lat.* provocation, last straw. See CONTENTION.

cat, *n.* feline, puss[y], tomcat, tabby, grimalkin, alley cat, mouser, kitten; lion, tiger, leopard, cougar, catamount, lynx, cheetah, liger, *etc.* See ANIMAL.

cataclysm, *n.* upheaval, disaster. See VIOLENCE, DESTRUCTION.

catacombs, *n.* charnel house; vaults, tombs. See INTERMENT.

catalog, *n.* LIST, index, register.

cataract, *n.* waterfall, downspout (see WATER).

catastrophe, *n.* calamity, disaster, upheaval, cataclysm, paroxysm. See ADVERSITY, DESTRUCTION, EVIL.

catcall, *n.* boo, hiss. See DISAPPROBATION.

catch, *v.t.* take, seize; overtake; land, net, hook; surprise, detect; snare, trap; capture, arrest, apprehend, nab (*inf.*); snatch. See RESTRAINT, DECEPTION, DIFFICULTY, HINDRANCE.

catching, *adj.* infectious (see TRANSFER).

catchy, *adj.* attractive, melodious, memorable. See ATTENTION.

categorical, *adj.* unconditional, explicit; taxonomic. See CLASS, MEANING.

category, *n.* CLASS; status, place; pigeonhole.

cater, *v.i.* purvey (see PROVISION); indulge, humor. See PLEASURE.

cathartic, *adj.* laxative, physic, purgative, aperient, purifying. See REMEDY, CLEANNESS.

cathedral, *n.* cathedral church, duomo. See TEMPLE.

catholic, *adj.* tolerant, liberal; universal, general. See GENERALITY, LIBERALITY, RELIGION.

cattle, *n.* livestock; kine, cows, bulls, steers. See ANIMAL, DOMESTICATION.

catty, *adj.* malicious, cattish, spiteful, bitchy (*inf.*). See MALEVOLENCE.

caucus, *n.* meeting, smoky *or* smoke-filled room. See ASSEMBLAGE.

cause, *n.* source (see CAUSE); subject, basis; case; doctrine, view. See THOUGHT, BELIEF.

CAUSE
That which produces an effect

Nouns—1, cause, origin, source, wellspring, principle, element; leaven; groundwork, base, basis, foundation (see BEGINNING); pivot, hinge, key; straw that breaks the camel's back. *Informal,* trigger, gremlin.

2, (*principle of cause*) causality, causation, origination; ground[s], reason [why]; motive, ax to grind; why and wherefore, rationale, occasion, derivation, root, determinant; etiology; ripple effect, butterfly effect. See ATTRIBUTION.

3, (*types of causality*) weight, sway, leverage (see INFLUENCE); motive, impetus, impulse, consideration, motivation; temptation, enticement (see ATTRACTION); inspiration, exhortation, persuasion; goad, spur.

4, (*one who causes*) occasioner, prime mover, author, creator, producer; progenitor, parent, mother, father (see ANCESTRY); mainspring, agent (see AGENCY); instigator, rabblerouser.

Verbs—1, cause, be the cause of, originate, give rise to, occasion, bring, sow the seeds of, engender, [en]kindle; bring to pass, effectuate, bring about; produce, create, give birth to, generate; set up, set afloat, set on foot, found, broach, carry through, bring on, institute, lay the foundation of (see BEGINNING); lie at the root of. *Informal,* trigger.

2, (*cause to happen*) procure, induce; draw down, open the door to, let; evoke, entail, elicit, provoke; conduce to, contribute; have a hand in, have a finger in the pie; determine, decide, turn or tip the scale or balance.

3, (*be caused by*) have a common origin, derive from (see EFFECT).

4, (*cause someone to do something*) move, prompt, motivate, put up to; sway, persuade, talk into, bear upon, prevail upon, twist one's arm; inspire, inspirit, stimulate, rouse, animate, incite, stir or whip up; set or touch off, precipitate, instigate (see ACTIVITY); urge, exhort, spur, goad, egg on.

Adjectives—causal, causative, etiological, efficient, original; primary, primitive, primordial; aboriginal; radical; seminal, generative, germinal; at the bottom of, [in] back of; basic, fundamental, crucial; proactive.

Adverbs—because, by reason of, on account of, due to; since, for as much as, inasmuch as, what with, in consideration of, in view of, in [the] light of, therefore; by, per, in or by virtue of; now that.

Phrases—the end justifies the means; as you sow, so shall you reap.

Quotations—The why is plain as way to parish church (*Shakespeare*), There is occasions and causes why and wherefore in all things (*Shakespeare*), Most of the great results of history are brought about by discreditable means (*Emerson*), A man always has two reasons for what he does—a good one and the real one (*J. P. Morgan*), What is found in the effect is already in the cause (*Henri Bergson*).

Antonyms, see EFFECT.

---

cause célèbre, (*Fr.*) controversy. See DISCORD.

causeway, *n.* highway (see PASSAGE).

caustic, *adj.* corrosive, burning; mordant, sarcastic, satirical, biting, acrimonious; severe. See DISCOURTESY, RESENTMENT, DETRACTION, FEELING.

CAUTION
Wariness

Nouns—**1**, caution, cautiousness, discretion, prudence, heed, circumspection, calculation; coolness, deliberation, forethought, foresight; vigilance, CARE; WARNING.

2, (*cautious attitude*) coolness, self-possession, presence of mind, sangfroid; worldly wisdom, Fabian policy.

3, insurance; provision, precaution(s), steps; safety net, pressure or safety valve; preventive measure(s).

Verbs—**1**, be cautious, take care, take heed, have a care, watch it, look sharp, watch or look out, keep an eye out; mind, be on one's guard, keep watch, watch one's step, keep one's eyes open or peeled, sleep with one eye open, be on one's toes; watch one's step, walk on eggshells or thin ice, make assurance doubly sure, think twice, look before one leaps, count the cost, look to the main chance, feel one's way, see how the land lies, wait to see how the cat jumps; bridle one's tongue; let well enough alone, keep out of harm's way; keep at a respectful distance; *timeo Danaos, festina lente; cave canem; caveat emptor;* stop, look, and listen.

2, take precautions, make provisions, take steps, guard against; look before one leaps, be on the safe side; lie low, keep a low profile; hedge [one's bets], take out insurance. *Informal,* play safe.

Adjectives—cautious, prudent, wary; alert, guarded, on one's guard, on the qui vive, on the alert, on watch, on the lookout; awake, broad awake, vigilant; watchful, wakeful, Argus-eyed, wide-awake, expectant; noncommittal; gingerly. *Slang,* goosey.

Adverbs—cautiously, prudently, warily; askance, with care or caution.

Interjections—take care! be careful! have a care! watch out! watch it! look out!

Phrases—if it ain't broke, don't fix it; don't put all your eggs in one basket; caution is the parent of safety; he who fights and runs away may live to fight another day; look before you leap; don't count your chickens before they are hatched; slow and steady wins the race.

Quotations—The cautious seldom err (*Confucius*), The better part of valor is discretion (*Shakespeare*), Prudence is a rich, ugly, old maid courted by Incapacity (*William Blake*), Tar-baby ain't sayin' nuthin', en Brer Fox, he lay low (*Joel Chandler Harris*).
Antonyms, see RASHNESS.

---

cavalcade, *n.* procession, caravan. See CONTINUITY, TRAVEL.

cavalier, *n.* horseman, knight; escort. See ACCOMPANIMENT, TRAVEL. —*adj.* haughty, disdainful. See CONTEMPT, DISCOURTESY.

cavalry, *n.* horse soldiers, horsemen, dragoons, hussars; armored *or* mechanized cavalry. See COMBATANT.

cave, cavern, *n.* recess, grotto; lair, burrow, den. See CONCAVITY, ABODE.

caveat emptor, Lat. let the buyer beware. See CAUTION.

cave canem, Lat. beware the dog. See CAUTION.

cavernous, *adj.* hollow, gaping. See CONCAVITY.

cavil, *v.i.* carp, find fault, take exception; be captious, quibble. See DISAPPROBATION, DISSENT.

cavity, *n.* hole, excavation, hollow, pit; OPENING, depression, pocket, dent. See CONCAVITY.

cavort, *v.i.* caper. See AMUSEMENT.

cease, *v.* stop, desist, discontinue, END. See DISCONTINUANCE. *Ant.,* start.

cease-fire, *n.* truce (see PACIFICATION).

ceaseless, *adj.* continual, incessant (see CONTINUITY). *Ant.,* discontinuous.

cede, *v.t.* yield, relinquish; grant, assign, TRANSFER; surrender, hand over. See RELINQUISH, SUBMISSION.

ceiling, *n.* roof, cupola, vault, canopy; maximum, LIMIT. See COVERING.

celebrated, *adj.* famous, noteworthy, eminent. See REPUTE.

CELEBRATION
Commemoration

Nouns—1, celebration, solemnization, jubilee, commemoration; ovation, paean (see APPROBATION); triumph, jubilation; RITE. See REJOICING, OSTENTATION, AMUSEMENT.

2, *(sign of celebration)* bonfire, salute, salvo; flourish [of trumpets], fanfare, colors flying, illuminations, fireworks; trophy, triumphal arch; Christmas tree, Hanukkah bush, etc.

3, *(celebratory event)* fete, festival, festivity, gala, gala occasion, holiday (see REGULARITY); parade, callithump; party, love-in; harvest home; red-letter day; thanksgiving; inauguration, coronation, *etc.* (see REPUTE). *Slang,* jamboree, punch.

Verbs—1, celebrate, keep, signalize, honor, do honor to, commemorate, solemnize, memorialize, hallow, observe, mark.

2, *(have a celebration)* pledge, drink to, toast; rejoice, make merry, kill the fatted calf, hold jubilee, jubilate, kick up one's heels. See REJOICING.

Adjectives—celebrated, famous (see REPUTE); celebratory, commemorative; festive, gala.

Adverbs—in memory of, in honor of, to the greater glory of.

Quotations—The secret anniversaries of the heart (*Longfellow*), Tomorrow 'ill be the happiest time of all (*Lord Tennyson*).

Antonyms, see INDIFFERENCE, LAMENTATION.

---

celebrity, *n.* star, notable, lion, [big] name; eminence, fame, renown. See REPUTE. *Ant.,* nobody; dishonor.

celestial, *adj.* heavenly, divine, holy; unearthly, supernal; empyreal. See DEITY, HEAVEN, UNIVERSE, ANGEL.

CELIBACY
Unmarried state

Nouns—1, celibacy, singleness, single blessedness; bachelorhood, bachelorship, spinsterhood, maidenhood; misogamy, misogyny; virginity, pucelage, maidenhood; chastity, continence, sexual abstinence. *Slang*, light housekeeping. See ASCETICISM.

2, *(celibate person)* bachelor, Coelebs, agamist, misogamist, misogynist, monk, priest, lone wolf; spinster; maid, maiden, virgin, femme sole, old maid. *Informal*, single, the answer to a maiden's prayer.

3, bachelor apartment. *Slang*, repent pad.

Verbs—be unmarried, live alone; take the vow, save oneself.

Adjectives—celibate, monastic, abstinent; unmarried, unwed[ded], wifeless, spouseless; bachelorly, spinsterly, maidenly; single, lone; maiden, virgin, chaste.

Quotations—A young man married is a man that's marred (*Shakespeare*), Marriage has many pains, but celibacy has no pleasures (*Samuel Johnson*), A single man . . . is an incomplete animal. He resembles the odd half of a pair of scissors (*Benjamin Franklin*), Chastity—the most unnatural of all the sexual perversions (*Aldous Huxley*).

Antonyms, see MARRIAGE.

---

cell, *n.* protoplasm; cage, jail; compartment, room, vault; dry *or* wet cell, battery. See ORGANIC MATTER, PRISON, ABODE.

cellar, *n.* basement, subcellar; vault, shelter; wine, cyclone, *etc.* See RECEPTACLE, LOWNESS.

cement, *n.* mortar, concrete, grout, Portland cement; adhesive, glue, mucilage, paste. See CONNECTION, COHERENCE, UNITY.

cemetery, *n.* graveyard, necropolis, burial ground *or* mound. See INTERMENT.

censor, *n.* reviewer, critic; faultfinder; watchdog. —*v.t.* expurgate, delete; cut, edit; suppress, muzzle, silence. See DEDUCTION, SECRET.

censorious, *adj.* critical, faultfinding, condemnatory. See DISAPPROBATION.

censure, *v.t.* upbraid, chide, reprove; criticize, blame; hit, knock, pan *(all sl.)*. —*n.* reproof, blame, criticism, disapproval. See DISAPPROBATION, CONDEMNATION.

census, *n.* enumeration, count. See NUMERATION.

center, *n.* See MIDDLE.

centrist, *adj.* moderate, midde-of-the-road. See PERMANENCE.

ceramics, *n.pl.* pottery, clay working; SCULPTURE; crockery, earthenware, china, porcelain, ironstone, faience, stoneware; enamel, cloisonné; brick, terra-cotta, adobe, glass. See MATERIALS.

cereal, *n.* grain, seed, corn; porridge, gruel, pabulum. See FOOD.

cerebral, *adj.* mental, intellectual; phrenic. See THOUGHT.

ceremony, *n.* ritual, formality, punctilio, protocol; form, observance, RITE, sacrament, function. See OSTENTATION.

certain, *adj.* some; specified. See QUANTITY, SPECIALITY, CERTAINTY.

CERTAINTY
Confidence in being right

Nouns—1, certainty, certitude, confidence, sureness, conviction, surety, assurance, faith; dead *or* moral certainty; positiveness, assuredness; self-confidence, -reliance, *or* assurance; dogmatism, absolutism, pontification; undeniability, irrefutability, infallibility, reliability; NECESSITY. See TRUTH, BELIEF.

2, confirmation, certification, verification, corroboration (see EVIDENCE).

3, *(one who is certain)* dogmatist, doctrinaire, bigot, opinionist, Sir Oracle.

4, *(something certain)* [proven] fact, matter of fact; AFFIRMATION; fait accompli; ipse dixit; guarantee. *Informal,* shoo-in, sure thing, [lead-pipe] cinch, open-and-shut case.

Verbs—1, be certain, stand to reason, admit of no doubt, go without saying; render certain, ensure, insure, assure, clinch, make sure; determine, ascertain, decide, settle; fix, button, *or* nail down; set at rest, make assurance *or* doubly sure; convince, persuade.

2, be confident, know for certain, have no doubt; go without saying. *Informal,* bet [the ranch, *etc.*] on.

3, *(act out of certainty)* dogmatize, pontificate, lay down the law, make no bones about; bet one's bottom dollar, one's life, *or* one's boots; know like a book *or* like the back of one's hand; know [for certain].

4, make certain *or* sure, establish, determine; confirm, certify, verify, corroborate, [double-]check.

Adjectives—**1,** certain, sure, assured; solid, well-founded; unqualified, absolute, positive, determinate, definite, clear, unequivocal, categorical, unmistakable, cut-and-dried, black-and-white, decisive, decided, on ice, sewed up, ascertained, known, proven. *Informal,* sure as fate, sure as death and taxes, sure as shooting, open-and-shut, sure as God made little green apples. *Slang,* on ice, in the bag, clinched, cinched.

2, inevitable, unavoidable; utter; unchangeable; to be depended on, trustworthy, reliable; bound.

3, *(factual)* unimpeachable, undeniable, unquestionable, indisputable, incontestable, incontrovertible, indubitable; irrefutable, conclusive, without power of appeal; beyond a doubt, without question, beyond a shadow of a doubt; past dispute, beyond [all] question; undoubted, doubtless; clear as day, crystal-clear, evident.

4, *(expressing certainty)* assertive, dogmatic; opinionated, bigoted, doctrinaire; authoritative, authentic, official, magisterial, ex cathedra (see AUTHORITY); unerring, infallible; straight from the horse's mouth.

Adverbs—certainly, for certain, for sure, certes, sure, no doubt, doubtless, by all odds; and no mistake, sure enough, to be sure, of course, as a matter of course; at any rate, at all events; without fail, come what may *or* will, sink or swim, rain or shine; sight unseen; truly (see TRUTH), no question, as sure as eggs is eggs.

Phrases—that's for sure; that goes without saying; nothing is certain but death and taxes.

Quotations—My mind is not a bed to be made and remade (*James Agate*), Human beings are perhaps never more frightening than when they are convinced beyond doubt that they are right (*Laurens van der Post*), *The Power of Positive Thinking* (*Norman Vincent Peale*).

Antonyms, see DOUBT, QUALIFICATION.

---

certificate, *n.* certification, warrant, diploma; testimonial; policy, debenture, stock. See EVIDENCE, SECURITY, RECORD.

certify, *v.* attest (see AFFIRMATION, EVIDENCE).

cessation, *n.* See END.

chacun à son goût, Fr. each to his own taste. See JUDGMENT.

chafe, *v.t.* abrade, wear, rub; vex, anger, annoy, eat. See FRICTION, RESENTMENT, PAIN, DISCONTENT.

chaff, *n.* husks; banter, jesting, raillery. See REMAINDER, RIDICULE.

chagrin, *n.* mortification, vexation. See DEJECTION, DISAPPOINTMENT.

chain, *n.* series, progression, course, row, string; bond, fetter. See CONTINUITY, CONNECTION, RESTRAINT.

chair, *n.* chairperson, -man, *or* -woman, convenor, coordinator, moderator, speaker, master of ceremonies, MC, emcee, toastmaster, roastmaster (*sl.*); seat (see SUPPORT); professorship, judgeship, fellowship. See DIRECTOR.

chalk up, score, earn; write. See CREDIT, WRITING.

challenge, *v.* query, question; controvert, dispute; dare, defy, stump. —*n.* exception; invitation, dare. See DEFIANCE, DOUBT.

chamber, *n.* room, bedroom; cavity, cell; hall; legislature, assembly. See RECEPTACLE, CONCAVITY, COUNCIL.

chameleon, *n.* turncoat, renegade, Proteus. See ANIMAL, CHANGEABLENESS, VARIEGATION.

champion, *n.* defender, protector, squire, knight; backer, supporter; conqueror, victor, winner, champ. —*v.t.* defend, protect; support. See DEFENSE, SUCCESS, AUXILIARY, SUPERIORITY.

CHANCE
Fortuity

Nouns—1, chance, accident, lot; fate, kismet, karma (see DESTINY); Lady Luck, [Dame] Fortune; luck, fortune, hap, hazard; contingency, adventure, fortuity; randomness, indetermination, indeterminacy, stochastics, pot luck. *Informal,* wheel of fortune, fickle finger of fate. *Slang,* tough luck.

2, speculation, venture, gamble, risk taking; random shot, guessing game, blind bargain, shot *or* leap in the dark, pig in a poke; flip of a coin, turn of the cards, throw of the dice; calculated risk; long shot, dark horse; fluke; pot luck; enterprise zone. *Slang,* the way the ball bounces, the way the cookie crumbles, crapshoot. See DANGER, RASHNESS, OCCASION, OPPORTUNITY, GAMBLING.

3, *(chance of happening)* probability, POSSIBILITY, expectancy (see EXPECTATION); toss-up, even chance, fifty-fifty; odds, odds-on, edge, advantage, spread, sporting chance, best bet; poor chance *or* prospect, unlikelihood, outside chance, ghost of a chance (see IMPROBABILITY); IMPOSSIBILITY; theory of probabilities, theory of games, law of averages. *Informal,* sure thing; even break; long shot, fluke, fighting chance.

4, *(lucky item)* good-luck piece, talisman, four-leaf clover, rabbit's foot; lucky number. *Slang,* hand, toby.

Verbs—1, chance, befall, hap, turn up; fall to one's lot, be one's fate; happen, hit *or* light upon, run into *or* across, stumble on. *Informal,* pop up.

2, *(take a chance)* chance [it], gamble, risk, venture, speculate; try one's luck, tempt fortune, take a chance, trust to chance; draw lots, toss a coin; shoot the works, go for broke; game, [set at] hazard, stake, bet, wager, fade, play (for); go out on a limb, lay on the line. *Informal,* put one's ass on the line.

3, be possible *or* probable; have *or* stand a chance; bid fair, seem likely; expect, think likely, dare say, flatter oneself; not stand a chance *or* a prayer, be out of the running. *Informal,* have a shot; not stand a snowball's chance in hell.

Adjectives—1, chance, random, accidental, adventitious, casual, fortuitous, contingent, eventual, causeless, indeterminate, uncontrollable; indiscriminate; hit-or-miss, catch-as-catch-can; aleatory, aleatoric; lucky.

2, unintentional, involuntary, undirected, aimless, purposeless, undirected, haphazard, unpremeditated, unwitting, inadvertent.

3, probable, possible, likely, in the cards; improbable, impossible, unlikely.

4, at stake *or* risk, on the line; out on a limb.

Adverbs—1, by chance, casually, at random, haphazard; incidentally, en passant, by the way; as luck would have it.

2, possibly, probably, likely; perhaps, perchance, peradventure; maybe, mayhap, haply (see DOUBT); God willing, Deo volente, D.V., wind and weather permitting. *Informal,* like as not, dollars to doughnuts, on the off chance.

Phrases—accidents will happen; Moses took a chance; in the lap of the gods; nothing ventured nothing gained; good luck beats early rising; never look a gift horse in the mouth.

Quotations—As good luck would have it (*Shakespeare*), The slings and arrows of outrageous fortune (*Shakespeare*), The only sure thing about luck is that it will change (*Bret Harte*), Luck is what happens when preparation meets opportunity (*Darrell Royal*).

Antonyms, see NECESSITY, IMPROBABILITY, CERTAINTY.

---

chancellor, *n.* minister; judge. See AUTHORITY, LAWSUIT.

chandelier, *n.* candelabra, electrolier, luster. See PENDENCY, LIGHT.

CHANGE
Alteration

Nouns—1, change, alteration, mutation, permutation, variation, modification, modulation, innovation, metastasis; transition; menopause; deviation, flux, turn; shift; diversion, break; reform, revision, REVOLUTION; change for the better, IMPROVEMENT, innovation, breath of fresh air; change for the worse, degeneration, DETERIORATION; radicalism, revisionism; New Deal, New Frontier, *etc.*; reorganization, shake-up, *perestroika*; vicissitude; watershed, groundswell. *Informal,* megatrend, new take. See CHANGEABLENESS.

2, transformation, transfiguration; makeover; evolution, metamorphosis; transmutation; transubstantiation; metagenesis, transanimation, transmigration, metempsychosis; metabolism, catabolism; alternative. *Informal,* quantum leap, flip-flop.

3, *(change from one type to another)* conversion; technical adjustment *or* correction; alchemy; REVOLUTION, sea change, reversal; transposition; new wine in old bottles; sex change *or* reassignment; transference, TRANSFER; CHANGEABLENESS, tergiversation. See DIFFERENCE, INTERCHANGE.

4, *(something causing or undergoing change)* progressive, reformer, revisionist, socialist, communist, revolutionary, radical; innovator, transformer, modifier; leaven, yeast; convert.

Verbs—1, change, alter, vary, wax and wane; temper, modulate, tamper with; turn, shift, veer, tack, swerve; [do an] about-face; change one's tune, whistle *or* sing a different tune, dance to another tune, reconsider, work a change, modify. *Informal,* tweak, revamp, flip-flop.

2, transform, translate, transfigure, transmute, transume, make over; metamorphose, ring the changes; metabolize; convert, innovate, revolutionize, introduce new blood, shuffle the cards; influence, turn the scale *or* the tide; shift the scene, turn over a new leaf; recast, remodel, revamp; reverse, overturn, upset; transpose; reform, reorganize; come round; change horses in midstream; take a turn for the better *or* worse.

3, be changed, be converted (into), turn into, become, evolve, come to; grow, mature, mellow, ripen; resolve into; inflect; assume the form, *etc.* of; improve, better; worsen.

Adjectives—1, changed, altered; newfangled, novel (see NEWNESS); changeable, variable; transitional, divergent; modifiable.

2, progressive, innovative; metabolic, catabolic, anabolic; catalytic.

3, reform, revisionary, revolutionary, radical, unconservative, leftish, communist[ic], socialist[ic], pink[ish], red. *Slang,* commie, pinko.

Phrases—the leopard does not change his spots; new brooms sweep clean.

Quotations—For the times they are a-changin' (*Bob Dylan*), Nothing is permanent but change (*Heraclitus*), The more things change, the more they remain the same (*Alphonse Karr*), Variety's the very spice of life (*William Cowper*), The wind of change is blowing through this continent (*Harold Macmillan*), And now for something completely different (*Monty Python*), The old order changeth, yielding place to the new (*Lord Tennyson*).

Antonyms, see STABILITY, PERMANENCE, REVERSION.

CHANGEABLENESS
Variability

Nouns —1, changeableness, alterability; mutability, variability; inconstancy, fickleness; inconsistency; versatility; instability, vacillation, irresolution; eccentricity, flightiness, moodiness; fluctuation, fluidity, alternation (see OSCILLATION); restlessness, unrest; AGITATION; iridescence. See IRREGULARITY, DOUBT.

2, *(something changeable)* moon, Proteus, Cheshire cat, chameleon, quicksilver, mercury, shifting sands, weathervane, kaleidoscope, harlequin, Cynthia of the minute,

April showers, phases of the moon; wheel of fortune, musical chairs; flibbertigibbet; double-dealer, tergiversator; fair-weather friend. See TRANSIENTNESS.

3, caprice, whimsy, vagary, notion, coquetry, fad; capriciousness.

Verbs—fluctuate, flitter, shuffle, vacillate, turn and turn about, ring the changes; sway or shift to and fro; change one's mind, play fast and loose, play the field; change horses in midstream, play musical chairs; blow hot and cold, oscillate; have as many phases as the moon, chop and change. See CHANGE.

Adjectives—changeable, changeful; changing; alterable, mutable, movable, variable; kaleidoscopic, ever-changing, protean; versatile; inconstant, unsteady, unstable, unfixed, unsettled, adrift; fluctuating, restless, agitated; erratic, fickle, shifty; irresolute, capricious, whimsical; volatile, desultory, mercurial; touch-and-go; fitful, roving, wayward; alternating; transient; iridescent, chatoyant; blowing hot and cold; convertible, modifiable.

Adverbs—seesaw; off and on; off again, on again; back and forth.

Phrases—a rolling stone gathers no moss; there is nothing constant but inconstance.

Quotations—Fickle and changeable always is woman (*Virgil*).

Antonyms, see STABILITY.

---

changeless, *adj.* unchanging. See STABILITY.

changeling, *n.* See SUBSTITUTION.

channel, *n.* duct, conduit, PASSAGE; wavelength, band; artery, vein, blood vessel. —*v.* FURROW, groove.

chant, *n.* Gregorian, Roman, *or* Anglican chant; plainsong *or* -chant; intonation, incantation; psalm, canticle, requiem. See MUSIC, RITE.

chaos, *n.* DISORDER, confusion, jumble, disorganization; abyss, void. See FORMLESSNESS. *Ant.,* ORDER.

chapel, *n.* oratory (see TEMPLE).

chaperon, *n.* attendant, escort; matron, monitor. See SAFETY, ACCOMPANIMENT.

chaplain, *n.* padre, sky pilot (*sl.*). See CLERGY.

chapter, *n.* division, section, PART, verse, canto; branch, lodge, post, corps. See COUNCIL.

char, *v.t.* burn, singe, scorch, sear, carbonize. See HEAT.

character, *n.* kind, CLASS; nature, disposition, temperament, personality; part, role; sign, brand, stamp; figure, letter, hieroglyphic, ideograph, pictograph; *informal,* personage, eccentric, crank, original. See WRITING, SPECIALITY, INTRINSIC, IDENTITY, DRAMA.

characteristic, *adj.* distinctive, typical, peculiar. —*n.* quality, trait, mark, lineament, feature, peculiarity, attribute, distinction. See INDICATION, SPECIALITY, ATTRIBUTION, INTRINSIC.

charade, *n.* pantomime (see DRAMA).

charge, *v.* COMMAND, exhort, instruct; assess, tax; set a price; burden; debit; strike, ATTACK; fill, load, prepare; accuse, blame. —*n.* ACCUSATION, allegation, impeachment, indictment; COMMAND, order, mandate, requirement; onset, onslaught, ATTACK; PRICE, expense, tax, burden, LIABILITY, encumbrance, assessment, rate, debit; supervision, custody, ward, trust, CARE; load, blast. See ADVICE, DEBT, PAYMENT, COMMISSION.

chariot, *n.* carriage, phaeton (see VEHICLE).

charisma, *n.* glamour, magnetism. See SPECIALITY, ATTRACTION.

charitable, *adj.* generous, liberal, kindly, Christian, forgiving; altruistic, eleemosynary. See BENEVOLENCE, LIBERALITY, PITY. *Ant.,* ungenerous.

charlatan, *n.* quack, pretender, fraud, mountebank. See DECEPTION, FALSEHOOD.

charm, *v.t.* fascinate, hypnotize, enamor, bewitch, enchant, disarm, captivate, attract; soothe, calm, allay. —*n.* attractiveness, personality, captivation, fascination; amulet, talisman, good-luck piece; incantation, spell, magic. See LOVE, PLEASURE, SORCERY, ATTRACTION, BEAUTY. *Ant.,* repel, offend.

chart, *n. & v.* map, PLAN; graph. See INFORMATION, RECORD.

charter, *n.* grant, sanction, license, franchise; constitution. —*v.* establish, license, empower; rent, lease, hire, let, book. See PERMISSION, COMMISSION, LEGALITY, SECURITY.

chase, *v.t.* pursue, follow, hunt; dispel, put to flight, rout, repel; tool, engrave. See PURSUIT, ORNAMENTATION.

chasm, *n.* canyon, crevasse, rift, fissure, cleft; abyss. See INTERVAL.

chassis, *n.* frame, skeleton; See FORM.

chaste, *adj.* virtuous, pure, undefiled, clean, innocent; simple, classic, severe. See INNOCENCE, SIMPLENESS, ELEGANCE, CELIBACY, CLEANNESS. *Ant.,* libidinous, wanton.

chastise, *v.t.* chasten, castigate, discipline. See PUNISHMENT.

château, *n.* castle, villa (see ABODE).

chat, *n.* & *v.* See CONVERSATION.

chattel, *n.* PROPERTY; vassal, subject. See SERVILITY.

chatter, *n.* prattle, talk, gabble, gibberish, patter, gossip. See LOQUACITY, SPEECH.

chauffeur, *n.* driver. See TRANSPORTATION.

chauvinist, *n.* nationalist, patriot; jingo, warmonger; macho, [male] chauvinist pig (*both sl.*). See WARFARE, BOASTING.

CHEAPNESS
Low price

Nouns—1, cheapness, inexpensiveness, cut rates, low, budget, *or* reduced price; SALE, discount, depreciation, price war, going-out-of-business sale; drug on the market; loss leader; buyer's market; cutthroat competition; cheapening (see REDUCTION). *Informal,* steal.

2, *(low value)* triviality, paltriness, insignificance; trashiness, worthlessness. *Slang,* chicken feed. See UNIMPORTANCE.

3, *(no cost)* gratuity (see NONPAYMENT). *Slang,* freebee, comp.

4, *(low-priced store)* bargain basement, dime store, five-and-dime, five-and-ten; warehouse *or* price club; outlet store *or* mall.

5, bargain, good buy, loss leader, markdown, bargain, pig in a poke; irregulars, seconds. *Slang,* schlock, tawdry.

6, miser, cheapskate (see PARSIMONY). *Slang,* schlockmeister.

Verbs—1, be cheap, cost little; come down in price, be marked down; get *or* buy for a song; buy at a bargain, buy dirt cheap *or* at wholesale; get one's money's worth; cut (competitor's) throat. *Informal,* beat down. *Slang,* prostitute. See ECONOMY.

2, cheapen, mark down, depreciate, undervalue, underprice, discount; cut prices; deflate; come down in price.

Adjectives—1, *(low-priced)* cheap, underpriced, modest, affordable, low-priced; moderate, reasonable, inexpensive; worth the money, economical, cheap at the price, dirt-cheap; reduced, cut-rate, half-price, marked down, bargain-basement; depreciated, unsalable; shoddy, shabby. *Slang,* schlocky.

2, *(of low value)* trivial, paltry, insignificant; trashy, worthless. *Slang,* doodly-squat, ticky-tacky.

3, *(having no cost)* gratuitous, gratis, free, for nothing, without charge, untaxed; scot-free, free of cost, complimentary; honorary. *Informal,* on the house, dime a dozen; five-and-ten, nickel-and-dime.

Adverbs—cheaply, inexpensively; for a song, at cost [price], at a reduction, at wholesale, at a bargain, at a sacrifice; below cost.

Phrases—the best things in life are free; if you pay peanuts, you get monkeys; why buy a cow when milk is so cheap; a sprat to catch a mackerel.

Quotations—Pile it high, sell it cheap (*Jack Cohen*), Two can live cheaper than one (*Ring Lardner*).

Antonyms, see DEARNESS.

---

cheat, *v.* deceive, defraud (see DECEPTION).

check, *v.t.* control, test, verify, tally, count;

restrain, repress, halt, stop, arrest, impede, interrupt, curb; stunt. —*n.* draft, money order; interruption, rebuff; setback, reverse, stop, RESTRAINT; supervision, control, tab; checkup; drag, block, brake; plaid, tartan, checkerboard; ticket, token, bill, stub; counter, chip. See ADVERSITY, HINDRANCE, MONEY, VARIEGATION, EXPERIMENT. —check in, register (see RECORD). —check out, depart (see DEPARTURE); *slang*, die (see DEATH).

checkered, *adj.* varied, irregular; colorful; checked, plaid. See VARIEGATION, IRREGULARITY.

cheek, *n.* jowl; INSOLENCE, impertinence, sauce, impudence, effrontery, face, brass (*inf.*); nerve, gall, sass (*all sl.*). See SIDE.

CHEERFULNESS
Good humor

Nouns—1, cheerfulness, geniality, gaiety, sunniness, good nature; cheer, good humor, high spirits, animal spirits; glee, light heart; optimism (see HOPE). *Slang*, joygerm fever. See PLEASURE.

2, liveliness, vivacity, animation, exuberance, spirit. *Informal*, zip. See ACTIVITY.

3, mirth, merriment, hilarity, exhilaration; joviality, jollity, levity; jocularity (see WIT); playfulness, laughter, merrymaking, fun, AMUSEMENT. See REJOICING.

4, contentment, contentedness; happiness, peace of mind (see CONTENT).

Verbs—1, be cheerful, have the mind at ease, put a good face upon, keep up one's spirits; be of good cheer, see the bright side; cheer up, brighten up, light up, bear up; take heart, cast away care, drive dull care away, perk up, snap out of it; tread on air; rejoice, carol, chirrup, chirp; frisk, lilt. *Slang*, feel one's oats, kick up one's heels.

2, cheer [up], enliven, elate, exhilarate, gladden, hearten, inspirit, animate, raise the spirits, buck up, inspire; encourage, refresh. *Slang*, jazz up, give a shot in the arm.

Adjectives—1, cheerful, genial, happy, glad, cheery, of good cheer, good-natured, smiling, sunny, blithe; in good spirits, high-spirited, happy as the day is long, happy as a clam, gay [as a lark]; light, lightsome, lighthearted; buoyant, free and easy, airy, jaunty. *Informal*, high.

2, lively, sprightly, spirited, animated, vivacious; sparkling, full of play, full of spirit, all alive.

3, merry as a cricket *or* grig, joyous, joyful, jocund, jovial, jolly, blithesome, gleeful, hilarious; playful [as a kitten], tricksy; mirth-loving, laughter-loving, mirthful, rollicking; elated, jubilant, REJOICING; cock-a-hoop; cheering, inspiriting, exhilarating; pleasing.

Adverbs—cheerfully, cheerily, with relish, with zest; in fine fettle, in high spirits *or* feather; [sitting] on top of the world, flying *or* riding high, in [the] seventh heaven, on cloud nine.

Phrases—happiness is what you make of it.

Quotations—The joyfulness of a man prolongeth his days (*Bible*), As cheerful as the day is long (*Shakespeare*), Happiness is no laughing matter (*Richard Whately*), Ask yourself whether you are happy, and you cease to be so (*John Stuart Mill*), Happiness is not an ideal of reason but of imagination (*Immanuel Kant*).

Antonyms, see DEJECTION.

---

cheerless, *adj.* See DEJECTION. *Ant.*, cheerful.

cheesy, *adj.*, *informal*, shoddy, second-rate. See INFERIORITY.

chef, *n.* [head] cook (see FOOD).

chef d'oeuvre, *Fr.* masterpiece. See SKILL, GOODNESS, PRODUCTION.

chemical, *n.* See INORGANIC MATTER.

cherish, *v.t.* nurture, nourish, foster, protect, nurse; entertain, harbor, cling to; prize, treasure, hold dear, revere. See LOVE, AID, ENDEARMENT. *Ant.*, abandon.

cherub, *n.* cupid, amor; child, moppet, urchin; infant. See ANGEL, YOUTH.

che sarà, sarà, *Ital.* what will be, will be. See CERTAINTY, NECESSITY.

chest, *n.* case, box, casket; coffer; cabinet, commode, locker, bureau; thorax, breast. See RECEPTACLE, CONVEXITY.

chestnut, *n., slang,* cliché, commonplace, platitude (see MAXIM).

chew, *v.* masticate, gnaw, grind, champ. See FOOD.

chic, *n. & adj.* stylish (see FASHION).

chicanery, *n.* trickery (see DECEPTION, CUNNING).

chicken, *n.* fowl, cock, hen, pullet; fryer, broiler, capon; *slang,* coward (see COWARDICE). See BIRDS, FOOD.

chide, *v.* scold, lecture, reprove. See DISAPPROBATION.

chief, *n.* chieftain, leader, president; captain, commander, general; superior, foreman, overseer; elder. See AUTHORITY. —*adj.* principal, foremost, leading, supreme. See IMPORTANCE.

chiefly, *adv.* mainly, mostly, primarily. See IMPORTANCE.

child, *n.* See YOUTH.

childbirth, *n.* delivery, parturition, labor pains; natural childbirth, Lamaze, *etc.* method. See REPRODUCTION.

childhood, *n.* infancy, YOUTH.

childish, *adj.* infantile, puerile, juvenile, youthful, babyish; brattish; senile, simpleminded, weak, silly; credulous, naive, trustful. See CREDULITY, YOUTH. *Ant.,* mature, wise.

child's play, simple (see FACILITY).

chill, *n.* shivering, shakes, ague; chilliness; frost. See COLD. —*v.* ice, frost; discourage, dispirit. See DISSUASION.

chime, *n.* [tubular] bell; doorbell. See MUSIC.

chime in, *v.i.* See ASSENT.

chimera, *n.* fancy, fantasy; monster; vain HOPE. See IMAGINATION, MYTHICAL DEITIES, NONEXISTENCE.

chimney, *n.* smokestack, spout, flue; vent. See OPENING.

china, *n.* chinaware, dishes, crockery; stoneware. See RECEPTACLE.

chink, *n.* crack, rift, fissure, cleft; soft spot. See BRITTLENESS, WEAKNESS.

chintzy, *adj., informal.* See CHEAPNESS.

chip, *n.* piece, splinter, fragment, flake; counter, check. See PART, MONEY. —*v.t.* break, split. See DISJUNCTION.

chipper, *adj., informal,* lively, gay. See CHEERFULNESS, ACTIVITY.

chirp, *v.i.* chirrup, cheep, peep, crick, stridulate. See CRY.

chisel, *v.* trim, pare, sculpt, carve; *slang,* swindle, cheat. See DECEPTION, SCULPTURE, FORM.

chivalrous, *adj.* knightly, gallant, noble, courteous, brave. See COURTESY, COURAGE, UNSELFISHNESS.

CHOICE
Act of choosing

Nouns—1, choice, option, selection, determination, pick, discretion; preference, predilection, fancy, penchant; choosiness, discrimination; volition, DESIRE; adoption, JUDGMENT; triage; alternative, lesser of two evils; dilemma, catch-22, no choice, Hobson's choice (see DIFFICULTY). *Informal,* druthers, one's cup of tea. See EXCLUSION, FREEDOM.

2, a. election, poll, ballot, vote, straw vote; secret ballot; voice, suffrage; plebiscite, referendum; proxy, absentee vote; voice *or* hand vote, show of hands; write-in [vote]; vox populi; electioneering; voting; [split *or* straight] ticket; franchise; exit poll. *Informal,* counting noses. b. voter, balloter, elector; suffragist; electorate, constituency. c. appointment, nomination, designation.

3, chosen one, elect, elite, pick of the crop, favorite, favorite son; first choice, pick of the litter; lame duck. *Slang,* fave.

Verbs—1, choose, elect, opt, fix upon; determine, make up one's mind (see RESOLUTION); exercise one's option, do as one pleases; adopt, take up, embrace, espouse; take sides. *Informal,* shop around, choose up sides, have one's druthers.

2, [cast a] vote, ballot; poll, canvass; hold up one's hand, stand up and be counted; thumbs up *or* down; nominate, appoint, designate.

3, select, pick, designate, call, pick and choose, handpick; nominate, put up; pick over; pick *or* single out, cull, glean, winnow, sift; pick up, pitch upon; pick one's way; indulge one's fancy; set apart, mark out for; prefer, have rather, have as lief; DESIRE; take a decisive step, commit oneself to a course, throw one's hat in the ring, stand for;

cross the Rubicon; cast in one's lot with (see COOPERATION); take for better or for worse.

Adjectives—1, elective, optional, discretionary, voluntary; selective, preferential, discriminating; either; eclectic; chosen; choice (see GOOD); on approval; on the bandwagon; pro-choice, pro-abortion. *Informal,* choosy.

2, preferable, to be preferred; acceptable, worthy to be chosen.

3, chosen, selected, designated, handpicked; adopted, ratified, carried; elected, nominated, appointed, named.

Adverbs—optionally, at pleasure, at will, at one's discretion; at the option of; whether or not; if anything; once and for all; for one's money; by choice, by preference; rather, sooner, before.

Conjunctions—either . . . or, and/or.

Phrases—one man's meat is another man's poison; no accounting for taste; different strokes for different folks; you pays your money and you takes your chances; when in doubt do nothing; the obvious choice is usually a quick regret; a straw vote only shows which way the hot air blows; vote early and vote often.

Quotations—For many are called, but few are chosen (*Bible*), We few, we happy few, we band of brothers (*Shakespeare*), You say potato, I say potahto (*George Gershwin*), The die is cast (*Julius Caesar*), Two roads diverged in a wood, and I—I took the one less travelled by, and that has made all the difference (*Robert Frost*).

Antonyms, see NECESSITY, REJECTION, WILL.

---

choir, *n.* See CHORUS.

choke, *v.* strangle, suffocate, garrote; stifle, obstruct, clog, jam, plug. See CLOSURE, KILLING.

choose, *v.* See CHOICE.

choosy, *adj., informal,* fussy, finicky. See TASTE.

chop, *v.* cut, mince; cleave, lop, hack, hew; strike. See DISJUNCTION.

choppy, *adj.* rough, jerky. See AGITATION. *Ant.,* smooth.

chord, *n.* cord; harmony; triad, arpeggio. See MUSIC, FILAMENT.

chore, *n.* job, task, assignment; (*pl.*) housework, rounds. See BUSINESS, WEARINESS.

chorus, *n.* choir, singers, choristers; chorus line, dancers; refrain, burden. See MUSIC, CRY.

chow, *n., informal,* grub (see FOOD).

christen, *v.t.* baptize, sponsor, name; initiate. See NOMENCLATURE, RITE.

Christian, *n.* believer, gentile. See RELIGION, PIETY.

Christmas, *n.* yule, Noël. See TIME.

chronic, *adj.* continuing, persistent, constant; inveterate, rooted. See CONTINUITY, HABIT. *Ant.,* acute.

chronicle, *n.* history, annals, RECORD. See CHRONOMETRY, DESCRIPTION.

chronological, *adj.* dated, sequential, in SEQUENCE. See CHRONOMETRY.

CHRONOMETRY
Science of time

Nouns—1, (*science of time*) chronometry, horometry, chronology, horology; dating, carbon-14 dating; date; epoch, period, era; times.

2, (*measure of time*) a. calendar, almanac; date; aeon, epoch, period; [bi]millennium, chiliad, century, turn of the century, decade, twelvemonth, year, leap year, month (January, February, *etc.*), week, fortnight; lustrum, indiction, olympiad; day (Sunday, Monday, *etc.*), sidereal day. *Informal,* blue moon, coon's age, donkey's years; hitch; set of seven brights. b. picosecond, nanosecond, millisecond, split second, second, minute, quarter hour, half hour, hour; sunrise, morning, evening, noon, midday, afternoon, twilight, sunset, night, midnight. *Slang,* can to can't, two camels. c. season, spring, summer, fall, autumn, winter; term, semester, trimester, quarter. d. geologic[al] time; eras: Cenozoic, Mesozoic, Paleozoic, Precambian; periods: Quaternary, Tertiary, Cretaceous, Jurassic, Triassic, Permian, Pennsylvanian, Mississippian, Carboniferous, Devonian, Silurian, Ordovician, Cambrian, Proterozoic, Archeozoic;

epochs: recent, pleistocene, pliocene, miocene, oligocene, eocene, paleocene. **e.** fiscal, calendar, *or* historical year. **f.** standard *or* daylight time, Atlantic, Eastern, Central, Mountain, Pacific, *or* Alaska time, Greenwich mean time; International Date Line, time zone. **g.** timetable, schedule; time chart, time line; diary, journal, chronicle, register (see LIST).

3, *(measurer of time)* timekeeper, timepiece; clock, watch, digital *or* analog watch, Big Ben; self-winding, quartz, *or* electric clock *or* watch; chronometer, chronoscope, stopwatch, timer, chronograph; [taxi]meter; repeater; clock radio; dial, sundial, gnomon, pendulum, hourglass, water glass, clepsydra; time signal; movement, watchworks. *Informal,* ticker. See TIME.

Verbs—fix *or* mark the time; punch the clock, punch in *or* out, clock in *or* out; date, register, chronicle, predate, postdate, backdate, antedate; keep, measure, beat, *or* mark time; bear a date, date-stamp; time; elapse.

Adjectives—**1,** chronometrical, chronological, chronoscopic, chronographical.

2, hourly, diurnal, daily, weekly, fortnightly, monthly, menstrual, yearly, annual, biennial, centennial, millenary, bicentennial, bimillenary; morning, matutinal, antemeridian; evening, vesper, crepuscular; nocturnal, nightly; vernal, estival, autumnal, wintry, brumal; around-the-clock, 24/7[/365]; nine-to-five; overnight.

Adverbs—on the hour, minute, *etc.;* o'clock.

Phrases—each hour injures, the last one slays.

Quotations—Every instant of time is a pinprick of eternity (*Aurelius*), I must govern the clock, not be governed by it (*Golda Meir*), Everything is a matter of chronology (*Marcel Proust*).

---

chubby, *adj.* plump, stout, obese; overweight. See SIZE. *Ant.,* slim, emaciated.

chuck, *v.t.* toss, throw; discard. See EJECTION, PROPULSION.

chuckle, *v. & n.* chortle, cluck, snicker, cackle. See REJOICING.

chum, *n.* pal, buddy (see FRIEND).

chump, *n., informal,* blockhead; sucker, sap. See CREDULITY, IGNORANCE. *Ant.,* nobody's fool.

chunk, *n.* lump, hunk. See PART.

chunky, *adj.* stocky, thickset. See SHORTNESS. *Ant.,* slim, lanky.

church, *n.* WORSHIP, service; ministry; denomination; Christendom, Holy Church; chapel, cathedral, synagogue, TEMPLE. See RELIGION.

churl, *n.* villein, ceorl; peasant, rustic, yokel; boor, varlet, knave. See DISCOURTESY, POPULACE. *Ant.,* gentleman.

churlish, *adj.* rude, surly (see DISCOURTESY). *Ant.,* polite, courteous.

churn, *v.* agitate, whip; seethe, boil. See AGITATION.

chute, *n.* fall, DESCENT; rapids; white water; shoot, slide, trough, hopper. See WATER, PASSAGE.

chutzpah, *n., informal,* effrontery, IMPUDENCE.

cigar, *n.* cheroot, stogie; panatela, perfecto, corona, belvedere; cigarillo; Havana. See PUNGENCY.

cigarette, *n.* smoke; regular, king-size, long[-size], plain, oval, cork-tip, filter-tip, 100s; butt; coffin nail, cig, fag, gasper, tube, weed, reefer (*all sl.*). See PUNGENCY.

cinch, *n.* girth; *informal,* certitude, sure thing. See FACILITY, CIRCULARITY. *Ant.,* bear.

cinder, *n.* slag, ash[es]; brand, ember, coal; lava. See REMAINDER, HEAT, FUEL.

cinema, *n.* movies, film. See DRAMA.

cipher, *n.* naught, zero; nonentity; cryptogram, codes, cryptology; monogram, device. See CONCEALMENT, INSUBSTANTIALITY, NUMERATION.

circa, *prep.* [on or] about (see NEARNESS).

circle, *v.* encircle, ring, girdle; circumnavigate; circumscribe, compass. —*n.* circumference; CIRCUIT; ring, circlet; disk; set, clique. See PARTY, CIRCULARITY, CIRCUMSCRIPTION.

CIRCUIT
Closed continuous path

Nouns—circuit, circumference, circle, compass; itinerary, excursion; cycle, loop, lap; perimeter, round, contour, outline; turn, curvet; circumnavigation, circumambulation; route, orbit, rounds; period, *etc.*; circulation, CIRCULARITY. See TRAVEL.

Verbs—circuit, circle, round; circumnavigate, circumambulate, make the tour of, girdle, go the round, make the rounds of; put a girdle around the earth, orbit; go round the horn; make a round trip, go round in circles.

Adjectives—circumnavigatory, circumambulatory; excursionary.

Quotations—Put a girdle round about the earth (*Shakespeare*).

Antonyms, see STRAIGHTNESS, DIRECTION.

CIRCUITY
Indirectness

Nouns—circuity, circuitousness, circuition, circumvention, circumlocution, indirectness; bypass, roundabout way, ambages, detour, loop, winding, zigzag, DEVIATION. See AVOIDANCE, CONVOLUTION.

Verbs—bypass, circumvent; go roundabout, go out of one's way; detour, meander; beat around *or* about the bush; veer, tack, twist.

Adjectives—circuitous, indirect, roundabout; zigzag, deviating, wandering, circumlocutory; devious.

Adverbs—circuitously, indirectly, deviously, zigzag.

Antonyms, see DIRECTION.

CIRCULARITY
Circular shape

Nouns—1, circularity, roundness; sphericity, ROTUNDITY.

2, circle, circlet, circumference, ring, areola, hoop, annulus, annulet, bracelet, armlet, ringlet; eye, grommet, loop; wheel, round, rundle, trolley; orb, ball, sphere, globe (see ROTUNDITY); orbit (see CIRCUIT); zone, belt, cordon, band (see CIRCUMSCRIPTION); wreath, garland; crown, corona, halo; coronet, diadem; chaplet, snood, necklace, collar, noose, lasso; napkin ring; meridian, equator, parallel, tropic, great circle. *Slang,* cock ring.

3, *(rounded shape)* ellipse, oval, ovoid, ellipsoid, spheroid, cycloid; epicycloid, epicycle; hemisphere, semicircle, arc; quadrant, sextant, sector, segment.

Verbs—circle, surround; enclose, encompass; rotate, revolve (see ROTATION).

Adjectives—circular, round, rounded, annular, coronary; oval, ovate; elliptical, egg-shaped; rotund, spherical (see ROTUNDITY).

Phrases—the nature of God is a circle of which the centre is everywhere and the circumference is nowhere.

Antonyms, see ANGULARITY.

---

circulate, *v.* pass, go about, change hands, mix, move; spread, publish, diffuse, disseminate, propagate. See MONEY, PUBLICATION, ROTATION.

circumference, *n.* perimeter, boundary, compass. See CIRCUIT, ENVIRONMENT.

circumlocution, *n.* paraphrase, periphrasis, indirection. See AVOIDANCE, DIFFUSENESS.

CIRCUMSCRIPTION
Limitation

Nouns—1, circumscription, circumjacence; limitation, ENCLOSURE; confinement, RE-STRAINT; bound, LIMIT, boundary. See CIRCUIT.

2, *(circumscribing object)* zone, belt, cordon, band; sash, girdle, cestus, cincture, baldric, fillet.

Verbs—circumscribe, LIMIT, bound, confine, enclose; [en]circle, girth, gird, surround, compass about, close in, immure; imprison, restrict, restrain; wall in, fence in, hem in, hedge round; picket, pen, corral, enkraal; enclose, embrace, wrap *or* tie up; besiege (see ATTACK).

Adjectives—circumscribed, begirt, lapped, buried *or* immersed in; hemmed in, pent in *or* up, mewed up; immured, imprisoned; landlocked, seagirt.

Adverbs—out of bounds.

Antonyms, see FREEDOM, SPACE.

circumspect, *adj.* careful, discreet. See CARE.

CIRCUMSTANCE
Concomitant condition

Nouns—1, circumstance, situation, condition, case, phase, position, posture, attitude, place, ENVIRONMENT; footing, standing, status, state; OCCASION, eventuality, juncture, conjuncture; contingency; event; quandary, dilemma, predicament (see DIFFICULTY); emergency; exigency, crisis, pinch, pass, push; turning point; bearings, lay of the land, how the land lies.

2, OCCURRENCE, incident, instance; particular, regard, detail, aspect, fact, point, thing, trifle; happening, phenomenon.

3, circumstantiation, particularization, itemization; analysis. See INQUIRY.

Verbs—1, circumstantiate, itemize, detail, spell out, particularize, enter into particulars, quote chapter and verse.

2, occur; undergo, fall to the lot of, be one's lot; find oneself; shape up.

Adjectives—1, circumstantial, given, conditional, provisional (see QUALIFICATION); contingent, incidental; adventitious, EXTRINSIC; occasional.

2, itemized, detailed, particular, specific, exact.

Adverbs—1, in *or* under the circumstances, thus, in such wise, accordingly; therefore, consequently, that *or* such being the case, that being so, since, seeing that, so, then; conditionally, provided, if, in case; if so, in the event of; so *or* as long as; in such a contingency *or* case; occasionally; provisionally, unless, except, without (see QUALIFICATION); according to the circumstances, according as, as the case may be, as the wind blows. *Informal,* thusly.

2, eventually, in the [natural] course [of things]; as things go.

Phrases—one man's loss is another man's gain.

Quotations—The time is out of joint (*Shakespeare*), Anyone who isn't confused doesn't really understand the situation (*Edward R. Murrow*).

Antonyms, see NONEXISTENCE.

circumstantiate, *v.t.* prove, document (see EVIDENCE).

circumvent, *v.t.* evade; outwit. See DECEPTION, AVOIDANCE.

circus, *n.* ring, ARENA; carnival, menagerie; sideshow, midway, the big top, greatest show on earth; travesty. See AMUSEMENT, DRAMA.

cistern, *n.* tank, reservoir; rain barrel. See STORE, RECEPTACLE.

citadel, *n.* fortress. See DEFENSE.

cite, *v.t.* mention, bring forward, quote;

arraign, summon; commend. See EVI-
DENCE, DEMONSTRATION, REPUTE.

citizen, *n.* resident, INHABITANT; civilian,
native.

city, *n.* town, municipality; capital, metropolis, megalopolis, cosmopolis; city-
state, burg (*inf.*), big town (*inf.*). See
ABODE.

civic, *adj.* governmental; public-spirited.
See AUTHORITY.

civil, *adj.* courteous, mannerly, polite;
civic, secular, lay. See COURTESY, AU-
THORITY. *Ant.*, rude, ill-mannered.

civilization, *n.* culture, society. See HU-
MANITY, SOCIALITY.

civilize, *v.t.* educate, cultivate, refine; reclaim, enlighten. See IMPROVEMENT,
COURTESY, FASHION.

civil servant, *n.* functionary, official, apparatchik. See AUTHORITY.

claim, *v.t.* ask, demand, requisition, require; lay claim to; *informal,* contend,
allege, assert. —*n.* demand, requisition,
requirement, prerogative; lien, hold;
plea, counterclaim; title. See AFFIRMA-
TION, COMMAND, LAWSUIT, POSSES-
SION, RIGHTNESS, JUSTICE.

claimant, *n.* pretender, pleader, claimer,
heir. See REQUEST.

clairvoyance, *n.* second sight, foreknowledge; fortune-telling, divination; insight. See INTUITION, PREDICTION.

clamber, *v.i.* scramble, crawl, shin up. See
ASCENT.

clammy, *adj.* moist, damp, sweaty. See
MOISTURE.

clamor, *n.* outcry, hullabaloo, uproar,
racket, tumult, din. See CRY, LOUD-
NESS, DISAPPROBATION.

clamp, *n.* grip, vise; fastener, clasp. See RE-
TENTION.

clan, *n.* family, tribe, sept; brotherhood,
association; breed, caste; clique. See
ANCESTRY, PARTY, CLASS.

clandestine, *adj.* SECRET, furtive, sly, undercover; veiled; illicit, fraudulent. See
CONCEALMENT. *Ant.,* open, aboveboard.

clang, *v.i.* peal, toll, ring. See LOUDNESS.

clap, *v.* applaud, acclaim; strike, slap,
bang, slam; impose, put; *slang,* gonorrhea. See APPROBATION, IMPULSE, DIS-
EASE.

claptrap, *n.* nonsense (see UNMEANING-
NESS).

clarify, *v.t.* filter, refine, purify; render; explain, elucidate, throw light on, clear
up. See PURITY, INTERPRETATION. *Ant.,*
cloud, obfuscate, confuse.

clarity, *n.* clearness, TRANSPARENCY. See
MEANING. *Ant.,* obscurity, opacity.

clash, *v.* collide, conflict; disagree, dispute,
differ, contend. —*n.* collision, impact,
concussion, conflict, DISAGREEMENT.
See IMPULSE, CONTENTION, DISCORD.

clasp, *v.t.* hug, embrace, enfold; fasten,
hook, buckle; clutch, hold. See COHER-
ENCE, ENDEARMENT, CONNECTION.

CLASS
Rank

Nouns—**1**, class, division, category, head, section; department, province, domain (see
PART); [sub]kingdom, [super- *or* sub-]phylum, division, [super- *or* sub-]class, order,
[super]family, genus, species, variety; biotype, genotype; race, tribe, sept, clan; breed;
type, sect, set, genre; coterie, clique (see PARTY); estate; assortment; feather, stripe,
blood, ilk, kidney, the likes of; suit; gender, sex, kin; kind, sort, manner, description,
denomination, designation (see NOMENCLATURE); character, stamp.

2, (*act of classifying*) classification, classing, categorization, pigeonholing, sorting,
grouping; ranking, grading; taxonomy; organization, ARRANGEMENT, ORDER.

3, hierarchy, power structure, pecking order; chain of command; rank, standing, status, station, condition, [social] level, caste; rating, quality; grade point; class warfare
or struggle. See DEGREE.

Verbs—class, classify, sort, screen, pigeonhole; rank, rate, organize, arrange, catalog[ue],
categorize; grade, rank; characterize, type, put *or* set down.

Adjectives—**1**, classified, specified; systematic, ordered, organized; sorted, pigeonholed;
graded, ranked, hierarchic.

2, categorical, taxonomic; differential, particular, defining.

Quotations—What have kings that privates have not too, save ceremony? (*Shakespeare*), The rich man in his castle, the poor man at his gate (*Cecil Francis Alexander*).

Antonyms, see WHOLE.

---

classic, *adj.* standard; chaste, simple. See SIMPLENESS, ELEGANCE.

classification, *n.* grouping, category, allocation; ARRANGEMENT, systematization, taxonomy, ORDER. See CLASS, SECRET.

classy, *adj.*, *slang*, modish, chic. See FASHION. *Ant.*, crude, vulgar.

clatter, *n.* rattle, racket, din. See LOUDNESS.

clause, *n.* article, paragraph, section; proviso, condition, stipulation. See QUALIFICATION, PART.

claw, *n.* talon, nail, hook; pincer, nipper. See ACQUISITION.

clay, *n.* earth, potter's clay, kaolin; mud, loam; flesh. See LAND, SUBSTANCE.

CLEANNESS
Freedom from dirt

Nouns—1, cleanness, cleanliness, PURITY, spotlessness; purification, circumcision; purgation, lustration, ablution; cleansing, wash[ing], lavation; laundering, dry cleaning; sanitation, disinfection, hygiene, bathing; fumigation; irrigation, lavage; delousing; drainage, sewerage, plumbing. See SIMPLENESS, IMPROVEMENT.

2, cleaning, cleansing, washing; purging, purifying. *Slang*, bubble dancing.

3, (*place for cleaning*) bath, shower [bath], sponge bath; lavatory, lavabo, bathhouse, public bath, swimming pool, Turkish *or* steam bath, Swedish *or* Finnish bath, sauna, hot tub, Jacuzzi; bathhouse, baths; laundry, washhouse, coin[-operated] laundry, Laundromat, car wash; [kitchen] sink, washroom, washstand, washbasin, toilet, commode, necessary, bathroom, rest room, ladies' *or* gentlemen's room, outhouse; toilet paper *or* tissue, bathroom tissue *or* roll. *Informal*, W.C., water closet, little boy's *or* girl's room, comfort station, bog, [public] convenience, indoor plumbing, poet's corner, powder room; T.P. *Slang*, head, john, loo, hopper, jakes, jane, pisser, shitter, throne [room], ajax, altar room, marble palace, domus, chamber of commerce, crock, daisy, growler; ass-wipe.

4, (*cleaning object*) a. brush, broom, besom; mop, hose, sponge, swab; carpet sweeper, dustpan, dust mop, vacuum cleaner; dishpan; automatic dishwasher, washing machine, washer, washtub; duster, dustcloth; washcloth, washrag; towel, napkin. *Slang*, pooper-scooper. b. soap, shampoo; detergent, scouring powder, cleanser, disinfectant; cold *or* cleansing cream; mouthwash, toothpaste, dentifrice, tooth powder; purgative, cathartic; filter.

5, (*cleaning person*) washerwoman *or* -man, launderer, laundryman *or* -woman, laundress; charwoman, maid, day-worker; houseman; sanitation *or* garbage man, garbologist; janitor, cleaning man *or* woman, street-sweeper *or* -cleaner, chimney sweep[er]. *Informal*, whitewing, kitchen mechanic.

Verbs—1, (*make clean*) clean [up], cleanse, do up; keep *or* clean house; rinse, flush, irrigate; dry-clean; wipe, mop, sponge, scour, rub, swab, scrub; dust, brush up; sweep [up], vacuum; sandblast; wash, bathe, shower; lave, launder, dry-clean; purify, expurgate, lustrate, clarify, refine; filter, filtrate; drain, strain, percolate, lixiviate, leach; elutriate.

2, sanitize, disinfect, decontaminate, freshen, purge, sterilize, fumigate, delouse, deodorize.

3, sift, winnow, weed; groom, comb, rake, brush, sweep, card; sieve.

Adjectives—1, clean, cleanly, sanitary; pure, chaste, immaculate; spotless, stainless; without a stain, unstained, unspotted, unsoiled, unsullied, untainted, unadulterated, uninfected, sterile; sweet; neat, spruce, tidy, trim; bright as a new penny; snowy, snow-white, white; spic and span, clean as a whistle. *Informal*, squeaky-clean.

2, sanitary, sterile, antiseptic, disinfected, hygienic; sterilized, pasteurized.

3, *(that can be cleaned)* [hand *or* machine] washable, cleanable, wash and wear, drip-dry, permanent *or* durable press.

Phrases—if every man would sweep his own doorstep, the city would soon be clean.

Quotations—Cleanliness is indeed next to godliness (*John Wesley*), While we spend energy and imagination on new ways of cleaning the floors of our houses, the Japanese solve the problem by not dirtying them in the first place (*Bernard Rudofsky*).

Antonyms, see UNCLEANNESS.

---

clean up, *informal*, make money, rake it in (see MONEY).

clear, *adj.* clear-cut, plain, sharp, understandable; fair, unclouded, cloudless, fine; open, evident; lucid, pellucid, transparent, limpid; liquid, pure, silvery; innocent. —*v.* clarify; extricate, free; realize; make; acquit, exonerate, absolve. See CERTAINTY, TRANSPARENCY, ACQUITTAL, VISION, PAYMENT. *Ant.,* opaque, obscure. —**clear up**, explain, resolve. See ANSWER. —**clear out**, go, decamp (see DEPARTURE).

clearance, *n.* margin, room; authorization. See SPACE, PERMISSION.

clear-cut, *adj.* distinct, obvious. See CERTAINTY. *Ant.,* in doubt.

clearing, *n.* OPENING, break.

cleave, *v.* stick, hold fast, adhere, cling; sever, shear, split, rive, rend, divide. See COHERENCE, DISJUNCTION.

cleft, *n.* split, rift, fissure, crack, crevice. See INTERVAL.

clemency, *n.* mildness, mercy, LENIENCY. *Ant.,* SEVERITY.

clench, *v.t.* grip, clutch (see RETENTION).

CLERGY
Religious personnel

Nouns—**1**, *(body of clergy)* clergy, ministry, priesthood, rabbinate, abbacy, ulema, imamate; the cloth, Roman collar. See RELIGION, WORSHIP.

2, *(member of the clergy)* clergyman *or* -woman, cleric, divine, ecclesiastic, churchman *or* -woman, priest, celebrant, minister, preacher, dominie, pastor, parson, man of the cloth, leader of the flock, shepherd, precentor, predicant; father, father in Christ; padre, curate, abbé, curé; patriarch; reverend; confessor; dewal; lama; magi. *Slang,* Bible-pounder *or* -thumper, devil-catcher, divine, fire insurance agent, gospel-shouter, Jesus-screamer; sky pilot.

3, *(governing clergy)* Pope, pontiff, cardinal, eminence, reverence, primate, metropolitan, archbishop, bishop, prelate, diocesan, suffragan, archpriest, provost; patriarch, eparch, exarch, metropolitan; high priest, rabbi, mohel; caliph, imam, muezzin; dean, subdean, archdeacon, deacon, subdeacon, prebendary, canon, rector, parson, vicar, chaplain, curate; preacher, reader, lecturer; missionary, propagandist, Salvationist, revivalist, gospel singer *or* preacher, evangelist; almoner, verger, beadle, sexton, sacristan; Brahman, pundit, guru, bashara; ayatollah; druid[ess], hierophant; Dalai Lama.

4, **a.** *(male member of an order)* cenobite, anchorite, eremite, conventual, abbot, abbé, prior, monk, friar, brother, mendicant, manciple; bhikshu, bonze, fakir, sannyasi; hegumen; lay brother, pilgrim. **b.** *(female member of an order)* abbess, prioress, canoness; mother superior, nun, sister, novice, postulant. **c.** *(orders)* Jesuits, Franciscans, Gray Friars, Friars minor, Minorites; Capuchins, Dominicans, Black Friars; Carmelites, White Friars; Augustinians, Austin Friars; Carthusians, Benedictines, Cistercians, Trappists, Cluniacs, Maturines; Templars, Hospitallers.

5, holy orders, ordination, consecration, induction; clericalism, theocracy, hierarchy, ecclesiology; monasticism, monkhood, ASCETICISM, cloistered life; papacy, pontificate; prelacy; benefit of clergy.

6, *(clerical clothing and equipment)* vestments, canonicals; cloth; habit; robe, gown, frock, surplice, alb, rochet, cassock, soutane, dalmatic, Geneva gown, scapular[y], cope, scarf, amice, chasuble, stole, maniple, mozzetta, pallium; fanon; cincture; tonsure, cowl, coif, hood; clerical collar; calotte; bands; pontificals, pall; miter, tiara, triple crown; cardinal's or red hat, biretta; kamelaukion; shovel hat, zucchetto; crozier, pastoral staff; thurible.

7, *(council of clergy)* consistory, synod, council, Sanhedrin; college.

Verbs—call, ordain, consecrate, induct; take orders or vows, take the veil.

Adjectives—ordained, in holy orders, called to the ministry; clerical, priestly, ecclesiastical, pastoral, ministerial; episcopal, hierarchical; pontifical, papal.

Quotations—I look upon all the world as my parish *(John Wesley)*, In all ages of the world, priests have been enemies of liberty *(David Hume)*, The world would be poorer without the antics of clergymen *(V. S. Pritchett)*, Priests and conjurors are of the same trade *(Thomas Paine)*, Did man e'er live saw priest or woman yet forgive? *(James Russell Lowell)*, As the French say, there are three sexes—men, women, and clergymen *(Sydney Smith)*.

Antonyms, see LAITY.

---

clerk, *n.* salesperson, -man, or -woman; registrar, scribe, secretary; copyist, writer. See WRITING, ACCOUNTING, AUXILIARY.

clever, *adj.* adroit, skillful; talented, adept, gifted; smart, cute. See SKILL, CUNNING. *Ant.,* dull, witless.

cliché, *n.* stereotype, plate, cut (see PRINTING); truism, commonplace, platitude; banality, triviality, bromide *(inf.)*. See MAXIM.

click, *v.,* *informal,* fall into place, jibe; go over, succeed, make the grade. See SUCCESS.

client, *n.* customer, buyer, patron. See PURCHASE.

cliff, *n.* precipice, palisade, crag, bluff, steep. See HEIGHT, VERTICAL.

climate, *n.* weather; temperature, rainfall, precipitation, *etc.*; REGION. See AIR.

climax, *n.* acme, zenith, summit, pinnacle; turning point, culmination; orgasm. See HEIGHT.

climb, *v.* mount, scale, ascend, rise, go up; succeed; clamber, scramble, shin[ny]. See ASCENT, DESCENT.

clinch, *v.t.* confirm; fasten, secure, rivet, clamp; clench, grapple; seize, grasp. —*v.i.,* *informal,* embrace. See COMPLETION, JUNCTION, CERTAINTY, ACQUISITION, RETENTION.

cling, *v.i.* stick, hold, cleave, adhere; grasp, hold on to, hug. See COHERENCE, LOVE.

clinic, *n.* dispensary, hospital, polyclinic, ward; workshop, seminar. See REMEDY, SCHOOL.

clip, *v.t.* cut, snip, scissor, trim, shorten; prune, mow; dock; *slang,* gyp, fleece. See SHORTNESS, DECEPTION.

clique, *n.* set, circle, group, coterie. See PARTY, ASSEMBLAGE, EXCLUSION.

cloak, *n.* cape, wrap, mantle, robe, burnoose, domino; shield, disguise. See CLOTHING, CONCEALMENT.

clobber, *v.t.,* *slang,* pummel, punish; defeat. See IMPULSE, SUCCESS.

clock, *n.* timepiece, chronometer (see CHRONOMETRY).

clod, *n.* chunk, lump; clodhopper, dolt, lout, oaf. See DENSITY, IGNORANCE.

clog, *v.t.* obstruct, block, congest, choke; hamper, encumber, jam, impede, restrain. See HINDRANCE, CLOSURE.

cloister, *n.* abbey, priory, convent, hermitage, monastery; retreat, sanctuary; arcade, colonnade. See SECLUSION, ABODE, TEMPLE.

clone, *n. & v.* COPY.

close, *adj.* compact, dense, firm; stifling, oppressive, muggy, stale, stuffy; stingy, tight-fisted, niggardly; taut; confining, constrictive; near, intimate; secretive, reticent, reserved; approximate. See DENSITY, HEAT, JUNCTION, NEARNESS, PARSIMONY, NARROWNESS, TACITURNITY. —*v. & n.* See CLOSURE, END, CONTENTION. *Ant.,* distant; loose; open.

close call, *informal,* close shave, near miss, narrow escape, squeaker (see NEARNESS).

close-knit, *adj.* attached, intimate. See NEARNESS.

close-out, *n.* SALE.

closet, *n.* cupboard, locker, wardrobe, clothespress. See RECEPTACLE, STORE. —*v.t.* shut in, enclose. See ENCLOSURE.

close-up, *n.* See NEARNESS.

CLOSURE
Act of closing

Nouns—1, closure, occlusion; blockade, obstruction; shutting up; constipation, bottleneck; embolism; blind alley, dead end, stone wall, cul-de-sac; obstacle, block, impediment. See HINDRANCE, RESTRAINT.

2, imperforation, imperviousness, impermeability.

3, *(something that closes)* stopper, plug, seal[er] valve, cork, bung, stopple, tamp[on]; stopcock, valve, spigot, tap, faucet, spile; spike, ramrod, wad[ding], stuffing, pad[ding]; barrier, tourniquet; latch, bolt, lock. See COVERING.

Verbs—1, close, occlude, plug, choke up; lid, cork; button [up]; stop, shut, *or* dam up, fill in; block, blockade, clog, obstruct, congest; hinder; fasten, bar, bolt, barricade, latch, lock, stop, seal, plumb; fence in (see ENCLOSURE); choke, strangle, throttle; shut the door (on); confine, restrain (see RESTRAINT).

2, close *or* shut up *or* down, close up shop, go out of business. *Informal,* fold. See END.

Adjectives—closed, shut, unopened, hermetic; unpierced, imporous, imperforate, impervious, impermeable; impenetrable, impassable; untrodden; unventilated; airtight, watertight, waterproof; vacuum-packed, hermetically sealed; tight, snug.

Antonyms, see OPENING.

---

clot, *n.* lump, clump, blob, dollop. —*v.* coagulate, thicken; clabber, curdle. See DENSITY.

cloth, *n.* material, stuff, fabric, textile; fiber, synthetic; [dry, bolt, *or* piece] goods, remnant; napkin, dust cloth, *etc.* See MATERIALS.

CLOTHING
Wearing apparel

Nouns—1, clothing, clothes, apparel, wear, dress, attire, array, raiment, garments, garb, costume, outfit, habiliment, habit, rig, ensemble, caparison, drapery, toilette, fig, wardrobe, garmenture *(archaic)*, vesture *(archaic)*; wedding clothes, trousseau; FASHION, ready-made clothes, store-bought clothes; millinery, hosiery, headwear, footwear, underwear, outerwear; equipment, accouterments, trappings, gear, trim; uniform, dress uniform, fatigues, mufti; activewear, sportswear, beachwear, playclothes, outerwear; hand-me-downs, secondhand clothes, rags, tatters; frippery; evening dress, finery, formals, full fig, regalia, Sunday best; civilian clothes; unisex clothing; vestments (see CLERGY); armor (see DEFENSE). *Informal,* get-up, civvies, toggery, togs, duds, threads, bib and tucker, glad rags. *Slang,* schmatte.

2, *(accessories)* a. accessory; whim-wham; armlet, band, cordon, pompom; epaulet, shoulder knot; sporran; bow, comb; netsuke; boutonniere, wreath; jewelry (see ORNAMENT). b. ascot, fichu, foulard, neckerchief, kerchief, bandanna, comforter, shawl, stock, stole, tallith, tippet; bertha collar, golilla, guimpe, jabot, priest's, Roman, *or* clerical collar, Geneva bands, rabato, dickey, ruff; dog collar; boa; [neck]tie, bolo *or* string tie, clip-on [tie], cravat, four-in-hand, Windsor tie, [old] school tie. c. glove, mitten, mousquetaire; muff; baseball, boxing, hockey, *etc.* glove, cestus, cesta. d. belt, baldric, bandolier, bellyband, ceinture, cestus, cincture, cummerbund, fascia, hamaki, obi, sash, surcingle, waistband; money belt.

3, *(men's clothing)* a. suit, business, dress *or* leisure suit, two-piece *or* doublebreasted suit, Dillinger *or* gangster front, three-piece suit, gray flannel suit, seersucker suit, sport suit, town-and-country suit, tropical suit, zoot suit; evening clothes, formal wear *or* attire, tails, spiketail *or* swallow-tailed coat, tuxedo [jacket], dinner coat *or* jacket, formal, black *or* white tie, frock coat, Prince Albert, morning coat; undress, full dress, [dress] blues, fatigues, regimentals; bodysuit; cap and gown; sack suit. *Slang,* soup-and-fish. b. lounge coat, smoking jacket; coat, jacket, blazer, doublet, reefer, sack coat, pourpoint, cardigan, Eton jacket, Mao *or* Nehru jacket, maxicoat, sport coat, business suit, swagger coat, mess *or* monkey jacket, flyaway jacket, jerkin, justaucorps, kirtle; bomber *or* pilot jacket, shell jacket, box coat, bush jacket, safari jacket, guernsey, hacking jacket, shooting jacket; caftan; cutaway, frock coat, Prince Albert; boubou. **c.** overcoat, topcoat, long coat, windbreaker, surcoat, greatcoat, dread- *or* fearnought, loden [coat], macfarlane, duffle, duster, covert coat, Mackinaw, chesterfield, gaberdine, lumberjacket, capote, parka, balmacaan, petersham, poncho, ruana, serape, shador, shearling, raglan, rebozo, redingote, anorak, Inverness, ulster, pea-jacket, watch coat, peacoat, car coat; raincoat, cagoule, slicker, oilskin, sou'wester, mackintosh, topsider, Aquascutum, Burberry; burnoose, caftan, haik, himation, djellabah, jubbah; cape[let], cloak, tabard, talma, tippet, roguelaure, paletot, kaross, kibr, manta, manteau, matelet, mantle, cowl, chlamys, domino. *Informal,* tux, [best] bib and tucker, Sunday best, claw hammer; benjamin. *Slang,* glad rags, soup-and-fish, boolhipper. **d.** shirt, sportshirt, bush shirt, camp shirt, dashiki, Hawaiian shirt, Pendleton, hickory shirt; dress *or* evening shirt, long- *or* short-sleeved shirt, polo *or* rugby shirt, Russian blouse; jupon; hair shirt (see PENITENCE); sweater, cardigan, crewneck, pullover, turtleneck, V-neck, vest, blouse, tunic, waistcoat. **e.** trousers, [long *or* short] pants, gabardines, Capri pants, breeches, britches, slacks, moleskins, overalls, pegleg trousers, plus fours, Oxford bags, pantaloons, Levi's, overalls, dungarees, [blue] jeans, chinos, ducks, corduroys, cords, kerseys, knee breeches, trunk hose, buckskins, jodhpurs, riding breeches; waders; shorts, Bermuda shorts, cut-offs, lederhosen; swimwear, bathing suit, swimsuit, [swim] trunks, wetsuit; gym pants *or* suit, track suit, jogging suit, muscle shirt, sweatpants, sweats, sweat suit; kilt, filibeg, trews; dhoti. *Slang,* high-waters, barn *or* garage door, galligaskins. **f.** underwear, underclothes, undergarments, linen, unmentionables, chuddies; underpants, [under]shorts, briefs, jockey shorts, boxer shorts, drawers, long johns *or* underwear, thermals, woolens, union suit, BVDs; [athletic] supporter, jockstrap, G-string, codpiece, cup; breechcloth, loincloth; T-shirt, undershirt, tank top, singlet, undervest, union vest. *Informal,* baggies; briefs, drawers, skivvies. **g.** dressing gown, smoking jacket; nightclothes, pajamas, PJs, nightshirt. **h.** footwear, [dress *or* casual] shoe, patent-leather shoe, lounger, blucher, brogan, stogy, brogue, romeo, wingtip, oxford, [white] buck, bulldog shoe, monk shoe, buskin, veltschoen, kiltie, clodhopper, patten, clog, klomp, geta, espadrille, rope-sole shoe; boot, riding boot, hobnail boot, mukluk, square- *or* steel-toed boot; walking shoe, desert boot, wafflestomper, seaboot, ski boot; dancing shoe, jazz shoe; slipper, everett, scuff; loafer, moccasin, slip-on [shoe], larrigan, docksider, duck, sandal, huarache, Roman sandal, flip-flop, zori; overshoes, galoshes, rubbers, gumshoe, plimsoll; athletic shoe, running *or* track shoe, sneaker, gym shoe, cleat; golf, basketball, tennis, *etc.* shoe; combat boot, jackboot, paratrooper boot, wader, pac; gaiter, spatterdashes, spats, garters, chaps, leggings, puttees, putts, galligaskins, gamashes, gambados; aglet, arch, breasting, captoe, collar, counter, creeper, cuff, eyelet, facing, heel, hook, insole, lift, [out]sole, platform, shank, toe box, tongue, upper, vamp, welt, shoelace; shoehorn, bootjack; shoetree. **i.** hat, headgear; tophat, silk hat, opera hat, topper; gibus, derby, billycock, pot hat, Homburg, fedora, porkpie, stingy brim, bowler, plug hat, felt hat, slouch hat, snap brim, wide-awake, crush hat, crusher, glengarry, havelock; hard hat; deerstalker, montero; straw, Panama, *or* beaver hat, skimmer, leghorn, kelly, Tyrolean hat, Watteau hat; cowboy hat, ten-gallon hat, Stetson; cap, billed hat, nightcap, sailor, watch cap, tam-o'-shanter, beret, biretta, bluebonnet, boater, stocking cap, beanie, dink, skullcap, yarmulke; peaked hat, balmoral, sombrero, jipijapa, shako, forage cap, cocked hat, fore-and-after, sugarloaf, terai, bearskin, coonskin, castor, bicorne, three-cornered hat, tricorne, service cap, busby, chaperon, chéchia, petasus, Phrygian cap, astrakhan, kossuth hat, tarboosh, kepi, fez, bangkok, coolie hat, calpac; helmet (see DEFENSE); fool's *or* jester's cap, coxcomb, monkey cap; liberty cap, campaign hat, overseas *or* garrison cap; baseball cap, football helmet, crash helmet, pith helmet, sun helmet, topee; dunce cap; mortarboard; capuche; rumal; headdress, aigrette, crown, pschent, turban; puggaree, earmuffs. *Informal,* stovepipe, tam. *Slang,* lid, scraper. j. collar; scarf, muffler; sash; tie, necktie, cravat, Ascot, bow tie, four-in-hand. k. sock, hose, argyles, lisle hose; athletic *or* varsity sock, sweat sock, crew sock, tube sock; work sock.

4, *(women's clothing)* **a.** dress, gown, evening gown, float, formal, Beardsley gown, tea dress; frock, housedress, cheongsam, coat dress, cocktail dress, pant dress, wrap-around, granny dress, cotehardie, crinoline, jumper, pinafore, lavalava, sari, sarong, sheath, tent dress, tube dress, shift, shirtdress, slit dress, sundress; bridal dress *or* gown; suit, tailormade, basque, bolero, dolman; jumpsuit, pantsuit, slack suit, pant dress, body suit *or* stocking; kimono, kirtle, pelisse, mantua. **b.** capuchin, cardinal, shrug, bertha, pelerine, Newmarket, joseph, topper; fur coat; peplos. **c.** blouse, blouson, sacque, sark, shell, shirtwaist, tank top, body shirt, camise, jupe, garibaldi, bustier, halter, bodice, liberty bodice, basque, middy blouse, slipover, pullover, shirtwaist, tunic; sweater, cardigan, cashmere, bulky; shawl, stole, mantle. **d.** skirt, jumper, hoopskirt, bouffant skirt, peplum, crinoline, dirndl, grass *or* hula skirt, harem skirt, wrapskirt, hobble skirt, pollera, hoop skirt, gymslip, maxi-, midi-, mini-, *or* microminiskirt, tutu; bloomers, capris, clam diggers, culottes, hiphuggers, hot pants, short shorts, knickerbockers, knickers, pedal pushers, matador *or* toreador pants, spandex pants, stretch pants; bathing suit, bikini, monokini, one-piece, string bikini, thong, tonga, tank suit *or* top; bodywear, body stocking, leotard, unitard, tights, maillot. **e.** lounging clothes *or* robe, dressing gown *or* jacket, *robe de chambre,* morning dress, housecoat, brunch coat, boudoir dress, smock, apron, dishabille, negligee, peignoir, camisole, cover-up, robe; tea gown, kimono, yukata, sari, at home; bathrobe; coat, jacket, shortie. **f.** foundation garment, underwear, undies, step-ins; woolies, panties, underpants, undies, tap pants, pettipants, drawers, pantalets, bikini, scanties, G-string, step-ins, knickers, bloomers, underall, crotchless panties, cutty sark; lingerie, slip, underskirt, half-slip, teddy, petticoat, wyliecoat, crinoline, camisole, chemise, shimmy, smock, chemisette, shift, body stocking, bustle, tournure, farthingale; support garment, corset, girdle, truss, panty girdle, stays, corselet, foundation, bodice, pannier; garter *or* suspender belt, garters; brassiere, [padded, push-up, uplift, *or* underwire] bra, WonderBra, bandeau, peek-a-boo, pasties, cheaters; chastity belt. *Informal,* falsies; birdcage, bishop, tournure. *Slang,* merry widow, back staircase, tit-bag; gay deceivers. **g.** nightclothes, nightdress, nightgown, nightshirt, bed *or* sleeping gown, bed jacket, pajamas, baby doll. *Informal,* nightie, nether garments. **h.** footwear, shoe, pump, step-in, spectator pump, button shoe, buskin, chopine, d'orsay, Oxford, saddle oxford *or* shoe, sabot, wedgie, casuals, flats, penny loafer, [high] heels, high-topped shoe, sandal, thong, gillie, mules, walking shoe, athletic shoe, sneaker; slipper, babouche, Faust slipper, pantoufle; boot, half-boot, hiking boot, hip *or* thigh boot, top boot, Wellington boot, chukka, bootee, bootie, balmoral; ballet slipper, toe shoe; platform, spike, *or* stiletto heel. **i.** millinery; hat, breton, commode, toque, picture hat, pillbox, pinner, pixie, bonnet, mobcap, poke bonnet, sunbonnet, sun hat, postillion, juliet cap, mutch, capote, flowerpot, calash, sundown, cloche, Dutch cap, chapeau, hood, veil, caul, cowl, coif, snood, babushka, balaclava, wimple, yashmak; bandanna, bandeau, fanchon, fascinator, fillet, hennin, kaffiyeh, lappet, mantilla, pelage, cornet, diadem; bathing cap, hair net; nightcap. **j.** hose, hosiery, sock, stockings, nylons, woolens, silk stocking, sheer stocking, dress sheer, fishnet *or* mesh stocking, support hose, garter stocking, knee-high, -hose, *or* -sock, halfhose, boothose; leg warmer; slouch sock, bobby socks; footlet, anklet. *Informal,* sheers.

5, *(children's clothing)* layette; baby clothes, infantwear; rompers, creeper, sleeper, gertrude; diaper, clout, hippany, napkin, nappy, britchings; bootee; biggin, nightcap. *Informal,* jammies.

6, garment industry; clothier, haberdasher, furrier, hosier, outfitter; tailor, sartor, clothier, dressmaker, seamstress, modiste, couturière; bootmaker, booter, shoemaker; couturier, furrier, cloakmaker; milliner, hatter. *Informal,* rag trade.

Verbs—1, clothe, dress, attire, garb, costume, gown, do up, drape, deck; dress up; wrap *or* bundle up; invest; outfit, accouter, equip, rig out, fit out; tailor; overdress, underdress; cross-dress. *Informal,* tog, spruce up, doll up, deck out, put on the dog.

2, don, put on, wear, have on. *Informal,* sport.

Adjectives—clothed, costumed, attired, dressed, clad. *Informal,* dressed [up] to the nines, in one's glad rags.

Phrases—clothes make the man.

Quotations—Brevity is the soul of lingerie (*Dorothy Parker*), All dressed up, with nowhere to go (*William Allen White*), You should never have your best trousers on when you go out to fight for freedom and truth (*Henrik Ibsen*), Her frocks are built in Paris, but she wears them with a strong English accent (*Saki*), She wears her clothes as if they were thrown on her with a pitchfork (*Jonathan Swift*), Haute couture should be fun, foolish, and almost unwearable (*Christian Lacroix*).

Antonyms, see DIVESTMENT.

---

cloud, *n.* haze (see CLOUDINESS, OBSCURITY); flight (see ASSEMBLAGE).

cloudburst, *n.* downpour, deluge, spate, thundershower. See WATER.

CLOUDINESS
Presence of suspended water

Nouns—1, cloudiness, haziness, nebulosity, cloud cover, overcast; shade; nephology. See DARKNESS, OBSCURITY.

2, cloud, cloud bank; cumulus, woolpack, altocumulus, cirrus, cirrocumulus, stratus, cirrostratus, cumulocirrus, -nimbus, *or* -stratus, nimbus, nimbostratus, stratus, stratocumulus; scud, raincloud, thundercloud, thunderhead; rack.

3, fog, mist, VAPOR, haze, haziness, veil; murk, murkiness; smog. *Informal,* [pea] soup, smaze. See DIMNESS.

Verbs—cloud, cloud over, shadow, obscure, overcast, shade, fog, mist, haze.

Adjectives—cloudy, clouded, overcast, murky, misty, foggy, hazy, dirty, turbid, muggy, so thick you can cut it with a knife; threatening, lowering; nubilous, cumulus, stratiform; cloud-capped; billowing; shady, gray, umbrageous; obfuscated; opaque; nephological.

Phrases—Every cloud has a silver lining.

Quotations—The fog comes on little cat feet (*Carl Sandburg*), The yellow fog that rubs its back upon the window-panes (*George Eliot*).

Antonyms, see LIGHT.

---

clout, *n.* belt, swat, whack; *slang,* INFLUENCE, pull, impact. See IMPULSE.

cloverleaf, *n.* interchange (see PASSAGE.)

clown, *n.* buffoon, comic, comedian, jester; boor, rustic (see POPULACE). See DRAMA, WIT.

cloy, *v.* glut, satiate, surfeit, sate; pall, bore. See SUFFICIENCY, WEARINESS.

club, *n.* cudgel, stick, bat, bludgeon; society, fraternity, sorority, association; nightclub; trefoil. See ARMS, ASSEMBLAGE, ABODE, SOCIALITY, PARTY.

clubfoot, *n.* splayfoot, Dutch-foot, taliped, talipes. See DISTORTION.

clue, *n.* suggestion, intimation, hint, key,

guide. See ANSWER, INDICATION, DISCLOSURE.

clueless, *adj., slang,* ignorant, out of it (see IGNORANCE). *Ant.,* with it.

clump, *n.* cluster, bunch, patch, thicket, grove; lump. See ASSEMBLAGE, DENSITY.

clumsy, *adj.* awkward, lumbering; bungling, bumbling, left-handed; cumbersome, unwieldy. See UNSKILLFULNESS, GRAVITY, UGLINESS. *Ant.,* adroit, facile.

clunk, *n. & v.i.* thud, thump (see SOUND).

cluster, *n.* bunch, clump, group. See ASSEMBLAGE.

clutch, *v.t.* hold fast, grip, cling to, clench; snatch, seize, grasp, grab, collar; clasp, squeeze, embrace. See ACQUISITION, RETENTION.

clutter, *n.* DISORDER, mess, jumble; litter, debris.

coach, *v.t.* teach, help, tutor, train. —*n.* trainer, director, teacher; stage[coach], bus, omnibus, car, carriage, Pullman. See TEACHING, VEHICLE.

coagulate, *v.* clot, clabber, thicken, curdle; set, congeal. See DENSITY, COHERENCE.

coal, *n.* ember, cinder; charcoal, briquette (see FUEL). See HEAT.

coalesce, *v.* unite, consolidate. See COMBINATION.

coalition, *n.* union, alliance, league, axis; merger, bloc. See PARTY, COMBINATION.

coarse, *adj.* rough, harsh-textured, coarse-grained; uncouth, rude, crude, crass, vulgar, gross, unrefined; broad, bawdy, ribald. See ROUGHNESS, DISCOURTESY, IMPURITY, TEXTURE. *Ant.,* smooth, delicate, refined.

coast, *n.* shore, tideland, shoreline, waterfront, seacoast, beach. See LAND. —*v.i.* slide, glide; take it easy, go with the flow. See SMOOTHNESS, IDLENESS.

coat, *v.t.* cover, crust; plaster, paint, varnish, glaze; plate; protect. —*n.* jacket, overcoat, ulster, sack, cutaway, tunic; coating; tegument, shell, envelope, skin, peel, rind, surface, cover. See CLOTHING, COVERING, LAYER.

coax, *v.* cajole, inveigle, wheedle, persuade. See FLATTERY.

cocaine, *n.* See DRUGS.

cock, *n.* rooster, chanticleer. See MALE, BODY. —*v.t.* prime, set. See PREPARATION.

cockeyed, *adj.* cross-eyed, strabismic; *slang,* drunk (see DRINKING), twisted. See VISION, DISTORTION.

cocksure, *adj.* [self-]confident, sure of oneself. See CERTAINTY. *Ant.,* insecure, timid.

cocktail, *n.* mixed drink; martini, old-fashioned, daiquiri, *etc.;* salad, appetizer. See FOOD, DRINKING.

cocky, *adj.* conceited (see VANITY). *Ant.,* timid, humble.

coddle, *v.t.* humor, pamper. See LENIENCY.

code, *n.* cipher, secret writing, cryptogram; law, canon, principle, codex, constitution, system, standard, RULE. See CONCEALMENT, LEGALITY, INTERPRETATION.

codify, *v.t.* classify, systematize, standardize. See CLASS, CONFORMITY, ARRANGEMENT.

coerce, *v.t.* compel, force, make. See COMPULSION.

coexist, *v.i.* coincide, live and let live, tolerate. See SYNCHRONISM, COOPERATION.

coffee, *n.* mocha, espresso, cappuccino; Sanka; percolated, drip, instant, freeze-dried, *etc.* coffee, java (*sl.*), mud (*sl.*). See DRINKING.

coffer, *n.* chest, strong box, vault; (*pl.*) treasury. See RECEPTACLE.

coffin, *n.* casket, pine box, sarcophagus. See INTERMENT.

cogent, *adj.* potent, forceful, convincing, persuasive, weighty, compelling. See POWER, VIGOR.

cogitate, *v.* reflect, think, muse, ponder, mull, consider, meditate; PLAN, think up. See THOUGHT.

cognizant, *adj.* sensible, aware, conscious. See KNOWLEDGE.

cohabit, *v.i.* live *or* sleep together; live in sin, shack up (*sl.*). See ACCOMPANIMENT, MARRIAGE.

COHERENCE
Sticking together

Nouns—1, coherence, adherence, adhesion, cohesion, adhesiveness; concretion, accretion; conglutination, coagulation, agglutination; set, gel, jell, jelly, cementation; sticking, soldering. TENACITY, stickiness, viscosity; inseparability; conglomerate, concrete. See DENSITY, UNITY, JUNCTION.

2, (*sticky substance*) adhesive; astringent, binder, birdlime, cement, court plaster, paste, gum, glue, gutta-percha, gypsum, isinglass, epoxy, Portland cement, lute, mastic, mucilage, size; jelly, gelatin, starch, gluten, albumen; mire, mud, slush, ooze; syrup, molasses. See CONNECTION.

3, (*something that sticks*) leech, limpet, remora, barnacle; burr, bramble, prickle, thorn, briar; sticker, decalcomania, decal.

Verbs—1, (*stick to something*) cohere, adhere, stick, cling, cleave; hold, take hold of, hold fast, close with, clasp; grow together, hang together; twine around; stick like a leech; stick close; cling like ivy, cling like a burr. *Slang,* cling like shit to a shovel.

2, *(become sticky)* glue; agglutinate, conglutinate; cement, lute, paste, gum; solder, weld; cake, solidify, gel, jell, jelly, set.

Adjectives—1, cohesive, adhesive, adhering, tenacious, sticky; united, unseparated, sessile, inseparable, indivisible, inextricable, unbreakable, shatterproof, infrangible; compact, dense, solid, thick.

2, *(of a sticky nature)* mucilaginous, gelatinous, glutinous, gluey; viscid, viscous, semiliquid; mucid, mucous, tacky; deliquescent, emulsive.

Antonyms, see DISJUNCTION.

---

coherent, *adj.* consistent, lucid. See MEANING. *Ant.,* incoherent.

cohort, *n.* band, company. See ASSEMBLAGE.

coiffure, *n.* hairdo, headdress. See BEAUTY.

coil, *n.* spiral, curl, roll, winding, circle, CONVOLUTION.

coin, *v.t.* mint, strike, stamp; invent, originate. See IMAGINATION, FORM. —*n.* MONEY, specie, currency, change, piece; gold, silver, copper, nickel, dime, cent, *etc.;* tin, brass (*both inf.*).

coincidence, *n.* concurrence, conjunction, concomitance, correspondence, AGREEMENT. See IDENTITY, SYNCHRONISM.

colander, *n.* strainer, sieve, sifter, riddle. See OPENING.

coitus, *n.* sexual intercourse, copulation (see SEX).

cold, *n.* iciness; ailment, flu. —*adj.* chilling (see COLD); unheated; unresponsive, indifferent, unenthusiastic. See COLD, DISEASE, INSENSIBILITY.

COLD
Condition of low temperature

Nouns—1, cold, coldness, frigidity, severity, iciness, winter, cold wave *or* snap, nip; Alaska, Siberia, Arctic, Antarctic, polar regions, tundra.

2, *(something cold)* ice, snow, red snow, snowflake, snow flurry, snowfall, snowstorm, blizzard; snowdrift, snowfield, snowpack, snowslide, whiteout; sleet, freezing rain; hail, hailstone (pea, marble, golf ball, hen's egg, tennis ball, grapefruit, football), rime, frost, hoar[frost], ice fog, pogonip; black ice, verglas; icicle, iceberg, snowberg, [ice] floe, ice field, ice cap, serac, nieve, glacier, growler.

3, *(result of cold)* chilliness, chill, coolness; shivering, gooseflesh *or* -pimples, rigor, horripilation, chattering of teeth; frostbite, chilblains, kibe; frost heave. *Informal,* goose bumps.

4, refrigeration, cooling, quick *or* deep freezing; air-conditioning; hypothermia; refrigerator, icebox, Frigidaire, cooler, ice tray; ice cube *or* block, dry ice; refrigerant, ammonia, Freon; freezer, ice-cream machine *or* freezer, deep-freeze, cold storage, [frozen-food] locker, icehouse; refrigerant, coolant, Freon, ice cube, shivered *or* crushed ice; dry ice, liquid nitrogen, oxygen, *etc.*

Verbs—1, be cold, shiver, quake, shake, tremble, shudder, quiver (see AGITATION); perish with cold. *Informal,* have goose pimples *or* bumps. *Slang,* freeze one's balls off.

2, cool, refrigerate, chill, ice, freeze, congeal, quick-freeze, freeze-dry, super-cool; air-condition, ventilate, water- *or* air-cool; snow, hail, sleet; freeze over, snow in, snow under (see COVERING).

Adjectives—cold, cool; chill[y]; gelid, frigid, frozen, algid; brisk, crisp, fresh, keen, bleak, raw, bitter, biting, cutting, nipping, piercing, pinching; icy, glacial, frosty, freezing, wintry, boreal, arctic, subzero, Siberian, polar; icebound, snowbound; snowy, snow-covered, snow-capped; shivering, frostbitten, frost-nipped; stone cold, cold as marble *or* charity; blue with cold; quick-frozen, freeze-dried; refrigerated, cooled, air- *or* water-cooled, iced, super-cooled; cryogenic. *Slang,* cold as hell, cold as a witch's tit.

Adverbs—under refrigeration, on ice.

Phrases—cold hands, warm heart.

Quotations—In the bleak mid-winter frosty wind made moan (*Christina Rossetti*), Winter is icumen in, lhude sing Goddamm (*Ezra Pound*).

Antonyms, see HEAT.

---

cold-blooded, *adj.* merciless, unfeeling, cruel, ruthless, heartless. See MALEVOLENCE.

cold shoulder, *n. & v.t.* rebuff, snub (see DISCOURTESY).

cold turkey, *slang,* withdrawal, detoxification (see DRUGS).

colic, *n.* indigestion; bellyache, stomachache; gripe. See DISEASE, PAIN.

coliseum, *n.* See ARENA.

collaborate, *v.i.* cooperate, pull together, pitch in; fraternize. See COOPERATION, IMPROBITY.

collage, *n.* montage. See REPRESENTATION.

collapse, *v.i.* break down, fail; cave *or* fall in. —*n.* prostration, dejection, breakdown, exhaustion; downfall, ruin; cave-in. See FAILURE, IMPOTENCE, CONTRACTION, DETERIORATION, INSANITY.

collar, *n.* neckband, neckwear; necklace; gorget, bertha, dicky; harness. See CLOTHING, CIRCULARITY. —*v.t., slang,* nab, arrest, catch. See RESTRAINT.

collate, *v.t.* assemble, gather, compile. See ASSEMBLAGE, ARRANGEMENT.

colleague, *n.* associate, partner; co-worker, confrère. See FRIEND, ACCOMPANIMENT, AUXILIARY.

collect, *v.* gather, collate, assemble, amass, compile; throng, congregate, flock; scrape *or* round up, garner, accumulate, save. See ASSEMBLAGE, ACQUISITION. *Ant.,* disperse, scatter.

collective, *adj.* combined, aggregate; general. See GENERALITY.

college, *n.* SCHOOL, academy, university, seminary, institute; junior college; finishing *or* preparatory school; association, guild. See PARTY.

collegial, *adj.* collegiate; friendly, comradely. See SCHOOL, FRIEND.

collide, *v.i.* bump, crash, clash, conflict; interfere, impinge. See IMPULSE.

collision, *n.* impact, concussion; smashup, crash, fender-bender (*inf.*); clash, opposition, interference; conflict, engagement. See CONTENTION, IMPULSE.

colloquial, *adj.* idiomatic, informal, conversational, vernacular; chatty. See CONVERSATION, FIGURATIVE.

collusion, *n.* conspiracy, scheme, intrigue, cabal; conniving, DECEPTION; logrolling, price-fixing, hookup (*inf.*), cahoots (*inf.*). See PLAN, COOPERATION.

cologne, *n.* toilet, bay, *or* lavender water, eau de cologne. See ODOR.

colonize, *v.t.* settle, establish, found, populate. See LOCATION, ABODE.

colony, *n.* settlement, community; territory; swarm, hive. See ASSEMBLAGE, INHABITANT.

COLOR
Rainbow hue

Nouns—1, color, hue, tint, tinge, shade, dye, complexion, tincture, cast, coloration, glow, flush; tone, key; color organ; Technicolor.

2, pure, primary, positive, *or* complementary color; three primaries; spectrum, chromatic dispersion; secondary color, tertiary color; coloring, pigmentation, perspective, value; brilliance, saturation; light, dark, medium; chromatics; spectrum analysis, prism, spectroscope, VIBGYOR (the spectrum: violet, indigo, blue, green, yellow, orange, red); rainbow, kaleidoscope. See VARIEGATION.

3, pigment, stain (see PAINTING); dye[stuff].

4, a. black, blueblack, carbon, charcoal, coal, crow, ebony, India ink, ink, jet, lampblack, pitch, raven, sable, sloe-black, soot. b. [baby, calamine, cobalt, Copenhagen, Delft, Dresden, ice, midnight, Napoleon, navy, peacock, powder, royal, Prussian, sea, sky, steel, Venetian, *or* Wedgwood] blue, aquamarine, azure, blueberry, bluebonnet, cerulean, cobalt, copen, cornflower, cyan, delft, gentian, huckleberry, hydrangea, indigo, indrathene, jouvence, lapis lazuli, lucerne, lupine, marine, milori, sapphire, smalt, teal, turquoise, ultramarine, wisteria, woad, zaffer. c. brown; burnt almond, sienna, ocher, *or* umber; acorn, anthracene, auburn, baize, bay, beige, biscuit, brick, brindle, bronze, buff, burgundy, butternut, café au lait, camel, caramel, chestnut, chocolate, cinnamon, cocoa, coffee, copper, doeskin, drab, dun, ecru, fallow, fawn, fox, hazel, istre, khaki, mahogany, manila, maple sugar, mocha, negro, nougat, nutria, ocher, pongee, putty, raffia, raw sienna, russet, rust, sandalwood, sepia, sienna, sorrel, tan, tanaura, tawny, toast, umber, Vandyke brown, walnut. **d.** gray, dun, flint, granite, greige, henna, liver, merle, moleskin, mushroom, neutral, nutmeg, obsidian, oxblood, pelican, piccolopasso, plumbago, roan, russet, salt-and-pepper, sand, sedge, sepia, silver, slate, smoke, sorrel, taupe, terra-cotta, titian. **e.** [Brunswick, cadmium, chrome, emerald, forest, kelly, Kendal, Paris, Lincoln, Niagara, *or* Nile] green, absinthe, aqua, avocado, bay, beryl, bice, brewster, celadon, chartreuse, clair de lune, corbeau, cucumber, cypress, drake, fir green, flagstone, grass, gunpowder, holly, jade, leaf, lime, lizard, loden, lotus, malachite, marine, mint, moss, myrtle, olive, parrot, patina, pea green, pistachio, reseda, sea green, serpentine, shamrock, spruce, teal, terre verte, tourmaline, turquoise, verdancy, verdigris, vert, viridian, yew. **f.** orange, apricot, cadmium, carotene, carrot, chrome, copper, helianthin, hyacinth, mandarin, marigold, mikado, ocher, pumpkin, realgar, Spanish ocher, tangerine. **g.** purple, amaranth, amethyst, Argyle, aubergine, bokhara, campanula, clematis, dahlia, damson, fuchsia, grape, gridelin, heliotrope, hyacinth, lavender, lilac, magenta, mauve, monsignor, mulberry, orchid, pansy, periwinkle, phlox, plum, prune, puce, raisin, raspberry, rubine, solferino, tulip, violet[ta]. **h.** [Castilian, Chinese, fire-engine, iron, Persian, Prussian, *or* Venetian] red, alpenglow, annatto, beet, begonia, blood, blush, bois de rose, Bordeaux, bougainvillea, brick, cameo, cardinal, carioca, carmine, carnation, carnelian, cerise, cherry, cinnabar, claret, cochineal, coral, cranberry, crimson, crimson lake, damask, fiesta, flamingo, garnet, geranium, grenadine, gules, hot pink, incarnadine, jockey, lake, lobster, madder, maroon, melon, moonlight, murrey, nymph, ombre, paprika, peach, pink, ponceau, poppy, puce, red lead, rhodamine, rose, rose madder, rouge, ruby, rust, salmon, scarlet, shocking pink, stammel, strawberry, tea rose, vermilion, wild cherry, wine. **i.** white, alabaster, argent, chalk, columbine, eggshell, flake, ivory, milk, milkiness, nacre, oyster, snow, zinc white. **j.** [cadmium, barium, chrome, Cassel, Indian, *or* Naples] yellow, amber, auramine, aureolin, banana, beige, blond, brass, brazilin, buff, butter, calendula, canary, chalcedony, chamois, champagne, chartreuse, citron, corn, cream, crocus, dandelion, ecru, flax, gamboge, gold, goldenrod, honey, jonquil, lemon, linen, maize, mustard, orpiment, palomino, pear, primrose, purree, quince, reed, saffron, safranine, sallow, sand, snapdragon, straw, sulphur, sunflower, wheaten, yellow ocher, yolk.

5, brunet, red- *or* towhead, [natural, bleached, strawberry, platinum, *or* peroxide] blond, raven-hair.

6, VARIEGATION, iridescence, play of colors; chameleon.

Verbs—color, colorize, dye, tinge, stain, tint, shade, paint, wash, gild; illuminate, emblazon; bedizen, imbue; suffuse; blush, change color (see MODESTY). See PAINTING.

Adjectives—**1,** colored, colorific, chromatic, prismatic; full-colored, high-colored, Day-Glo; double-dyed; polychromatic; bright, brilliant, vivid, intense, deep; fresh, unfaded; rich, gorgeous, gay; soft-colored, pastel.

2, colorful, gaudy, florid, garish, showy, flaunting, flamboyant, flashy; raw, crude; glaring, flaring; discordant, harsh, clashing, inharmonious; mellow, harmonious, pearly, sweet, delicate, tender, refined; off-color.

3, (See also *Nouns,* 4) **a.** inky, coal-black, jet-black, pitchy, sooty. **b.** cerulean. **c.** coppery, brunet[te], fulvous. **d.** steel-gray, French-gray, ashen, silvery, dove-gray, slaty, drab, mousy, battleship, cinereous. **e.** pea-green, sea-green, bottle-green. **f.** flame-colored. **g.** plum-colored. **h.** ruby-red, blood-red, beet-red, brick-red, rosy, roseate. **i.** snowy, milky, chalky, creamy, pearly, off-white, oyster-white. **j.** golden, sallow, cream-colored, xanthic, xanthous.

4, variegated (see VARIEGATION).

Quotations—Life is Color and Warmth and Light *(Julian Grenfell)*, With color one obtains an energy that seems to stem from witchcraft *(Henri Matisse)*, I try to apply colors like words that shape poems, like notes that shape music *(Joan Miró)*.

Antonyms, see COLORLESSNESS.

---

colored, *adj.* Negro, black, dark-skinned; biased, deceptive. See HUMANITY, DECEPTION.

colorful, *adj.* picturesque, vivid; dramatic. See COLOR, VARIEGATION, DRAMA. *Ant.,* monochromatic, pallid, dull.

COLORLESSNESS
Absence of color

Nouns—1, colorlessness, achromatism; decoloration, discoloration; pallor, pallidity; paleness, etiolation; neutral tint, monochrome, black-and-white; fading, dimming; bleaching. See WEAKNESS, DIMNESS.

2, bleach, whitener, decolorizer.

Verbs—lose color, fade, turn pale, pale, change color; decolorize, discolor, bleach, whiten, achromatize, blanch, etiolate, wash *or* tone down.

Adjectives—colorless, uncolored, achromatic, aplanatic, hueless, pale, pallid; pale-faced; faint, dull, muddy, leaden, gray, dun, wan, sallow, dead, dingy, ashy, ashen, pasty, lurid, ghastly, bloodless, deathly, ghostly, cadaverous, glassy, lackluster; blond, ash-blond, platinum-blond, fair; white; pale as death, pale as a ghost; white as a sheet; bleached.

Antonyms, see COLOR, VARIEGATION.

---

colossus, *n.* giant, titan, monster, prodigy. See SIZE.

colt, *n.* foal. See YOUTH, ANIMAL.

column, *n.* pillar, shaft; formation (of troops, figures, *etc.*); article, byline. See CONTINUITY, ROTUNDITY, SUPPORT, COMBATANT, NEWS, HEIGHT.

coma, *n.* unconsciousness; stupor, torpor. See INSENSIBILITY, INACTIVITY.

comb, *v.t.* scrape; card; dress, tease, back-comb; search. See CLEANNESS, INQUIRY.

combat, *n.* conflict, WARFARE; battle, close combat. —*v.t.* fight, oppose. See CONTENTION.

COMBATANT
Fighter

Nouns—1, *(one who fights)* combatant, disputant, litigant, belligerent; fighter, assailant; swashbuckler, fire-eater, duel[l]ist, bully; fighting-man, prizefighter, pugilist, boxer, bruiser, gladiator, wrestler, bullfighter; street fighter; swordsman; noncombatant, civilian. *Informal,* scrapper, goon, palooka, jodie.

2, levy, draft; conscript, recruit, cadet, draftee, selectee, enlistee.

3, warrior, soldier, man-at-arms; campaigner, veteran; military man, GI, doughboy, Tommy Atkins, poilu; armed force, troops, soldiery, forces, the army, standing army, regulars, militia, volunteers, auxiliaries, reserves, national guard, beefeater; guards, guardsman.

4, *(irregular fighter)* janizary, myrmidon, spahi, Cossack; irregular, mercenary, freelance, soldier of fortune; guerrilla, bushfighter, partisan, resistance fighter; commando.

5, *(types of soldiers)* private, rank and file, trooper, legionnaire, legionary, cannon fodder; officer, commander, subaltern, ensign, standard bearer; sentry; archer, [long]bowman; spearman, pikeman; halberdier, lancer; musketeer, rifleman, sharpshooter, sniper, skirmisher, commando, ranger, shock *or* elite troops, Special Forces, Green Berets; grenadier, fusileer; horse, *or* foot-soldier; infantry[man], artillery[man], cavalry[man], horse, carabiniere; military police, MP, shore patrol; tanks, panzer, armor (see ARMS); paratrooper, paramarine; patrol leader, point man; Uhlan, dragoon, hussar; cuirassier; gunner, cannoneer, bombardier; sapper, miner, engineer, Seabee;

light infantry, rifles, chasseur, Zouave, camel corps, cameleers; frogman; chaplain (see CLERGY); medic (see REMEDY). *Informal,* sky pilot. *Slang,* sawbones.

6, *(military ranks)* army, air force, navy, marine corps, SEALS, special forces. **a.** Joint Chiefs of Staff, chief of staff, general of the army, five-star general, [field] marshal, [four-star] general, three-star *or* lieutenant general, two-star *or* major general, one-star *or* brigadier general, colonel, major, captain, lieutenant, [non]commissioned officer, [chief] warrant officer, sergeant major, first sergeant, [chief] master sergeant, sergeant first class, specialist, gunnery *or* technical sergeant, staff sergeant, drill sergeant, corporal, lance corporal, private first class, PFC, airman first class, [buck] private, airman, [raw] recruit, draftee, call-up, enlistee, inductee, enlisted man *or* woman, cadet. *Informal,* sarge, doughboy, dogface, flyboy, lifer, war-horse. *Slang,* shavetail, yardbird, galoot, lobster, batman, ninety-day wonder, pogue. **b.** *(navy)* chief of naval operations, [fleet, vice, *or* rear] admiral, commodore, captain, [lieutenant] commander, lieutenant [junior grade], ensign, chief warrant officer, [master *or* senior chief] petty officer, yeoman, quartermaster, seaman, seaman apprentice *or* recruit, midshipman. *Informal,* middie. *Slang,* gob, jarhead, squid, grunt, leatherneck, swabby. **c.** field grade officer. **d.** *(historical or foreign)* centurion, chasseur, condottiere, dragoon, evzone, fedayee, fusilier, ghazi, hoplite, hussar, janissary, kamikaze, kern, legionnaire, Minuteman, pandour, sepoy, spahi, storm trooper, Spetznaz, sutler, uhlan, vexillary, Zouave, redcoat, askari.

7, *(force of soldiers)* army, host; division, column, wing, tactical unit, detachment, patrol, garrison, brigade, regiment, corps, battalion, squadron, escadrille, company, platoon, battery, squad; guard, legion, phalanx, cohort; troops; militia, National Guard; reserves, auxiliaries.

8, *(navy)* marine, navy, naval forces; fleet, flotilla, armada, squadron; man-of-war (see SHIP); sailor, seaman (see NAVIGATION). *Slang,* leatherneck.

9, *(airborne soldiers)* air force, air arm, Luftwaffe, RAF (see AVIATION).

10, militarist, chauvinist, jingo[ist], warmonger. *Informal,* hawk.

Phrases—he who lives by the sword dies by the sword; old soldiers never die, they just fade away; your soul may belong to God, but your ass belongs to the army.

Quotations—Into the valley of Death rode the six hundred (*Lord Tennyson*), Every citizen should be a soldier (*Thomas Jefferson*), A soldier has a hard life, and but little consideration (*Robert E. Lee*), All a soldier needs to know is how to shoot and salute (*Gen. John Pershing*), Look at an infantryman's eyes, and you can tell how much war he has seen (*Bill Mauldin*).

Antonyms, see PACIFICATION.

---

combative, *adj.* pugnacious, aggressive. See ATTACK, CONTENTION.

combat fatigue, shell shock, war neurosis, trauma. See DISEASE.

COMBINATION
Coming together

Nouns—**1,** *(combination of things)* combination, composite, synthesis, MIXTURE; JUNCTION, union, unification; incorporation, merger, amalgamation, embodiment, coalescence, crasis, fusion, blending, absorption, centralization; compound, amalgam, composition, alloy; resultant; impregnation. *Slang,* combo. See UNITY.

2, *(combination of people)* coalition, alliance, syndicate, consortium, federation, affiliation, association. See COOPERATION, PARTY.

Verbs—combine, unite, incorporate, amalgamate, affiliate, compound, embody, absorb, reembody, blend, merge, fuse, melt into one, consolidate, coalesce, centralize; put *or* lump together; cement a union, marry; federate, associate, syndicate, fraternize; gang up, throw *or* go in with, join up with. *Slang,* get into bed with.

Adjectives—combined, affiliated, allied, united; combinatorial; impregnated with, ingrained. *Informal,* in cahoots.

Phrases—don't put all your eggs in one basket; it takes two to tango; two heads are better than one; united we stand, divided we fall.
Quotations—All for one, one for all (*Dumas*).
Antonyms, see DECOMPOSITION, DISJUNCTION.

---

combustible, *adj.* inflammable, burnable, flammable. See FUEL. *Ant.,* nonflammable, fireproof.

come, *v.i.* arrive, reach; APPROACH, move toward, near; befall, happen, occur. See ARRIVAL, OCCURRENCE. *Ant.,* leave, depart.

come across, *v.i.* encounter; *informal,* pay up; tell the truth. See CONTACT, CHANCE, TRUTH, PAYMENT.

comeback, *n., informal,* recovery, revival, RESTORATION, return; retort, rejoinder. See ANSWER.

comedian, comedienne, *n.* See WIT.

comedown, *n.* DESCENT, decline; setback, reverse; DISAPPOINTMENT, letdown. See HUMILITY.

comedy, *n.* satire, parody, burlesque, travesty; comedy of errors; tragicomedy; humor, WIT, AMUSEMENT. See DRAMA.

comely, *adj.* attractive, good-looking, handsome, fair, pleasing. See BEAUTY.

come off, *v.i.* succeed (see SUCCESS).

come-on, *n., slang,* lure, gimmick. See DECEPTION.

come to, *v.i.* revive, awaken (see RESTORATION).

comeuppance, *n., slang,* reward, [just] deserts. See RETALIATION.

comfort, *n.* luxury; ease, coziness; enjoyment, satisfaction; solace, consolation; cheer, air. See PLEASURE, RELIEF, CONTENT.

comfortable, *adj.* content[ed], at ease; *informal,* well off, fixed. See CONTENT, PROSPERITY. *Ant.,* uncomfortable, wretched; poor.

comforter, *n.* quilt, bedspread. See COVERING.

comic, *adj.* comical, funny, hilarious, laughable, sidesplitting, clownish, ludicrous, droll, slapstick, farcical. —*n.* comedian, stand-up comic. See ABSURDITY, WIT.

comics, *n.pl.* comic strip *or* book; *informal,* funnies. See BOOK.

COMMAND
Order of authority

Nouns—**1,** command, commandment, order, ordinance, fiat, bidding, dictum, behest, call, beck, nod; direction, injunction, charge; instructions. *Informal,* say-so. See AUTHORITY, RULE.

2, *(request for something)* demand, exaction, imposition, requisition, claim, ultimatum, terms, requirement, directive.

3, *(command to do something)* dictation, dictate, mandate; caveat, decree, rescript, precept; bull, edict, prescription, brevet, ukase, mittimus, mandamus, summons, subpoena, nisi prius, citation, court order; word of command; bugle *or* trumpet call, beat of drum, tattoo; order of the day.

4, *(person giving a command)* commander, commandant, captain, commanding officer, skipper, commodore; chief, headman, chieftain, leader; process server. See DIRECTOR, COMBATANT.

Verbs—command, order, decree, ordain, dictate, direct, give orders; prescribe, set, appoint, mark out; set *or* impose a task; set to work; bid, enjoin, charge, call upon, instruct; require, exact, impose, tax, task; demand, insist on, compel (see COMPULSION); claim, lay claim to, reclaim; cite, summon; call *or* send for, subpoena, beckon; make a requisition, decree, *or* order, issue a command; give the word *or* signal; call to order; lay down the law; assume command (see AUTHORITY); remand.

Adjectives—**1,** commanded, mandatory, compulsory, mandated, prescriptive, obligatory; required, imposed; absolute, carved in stone, decisive, final, irrevocable.

2, commanding, peremptory, authoritative, in command (see AUTHORITY); demanding, exacting, insistent.

Adverbs—in demand, at *or* on sight, on call, to order, by command.

Phrases—he that cannot obey cannot command.

Quotations—It is sad to remember that when anyone has fairly mastered the art of command, the necessity for that art usually expires (*Gen. George S. Patton*).
Antonyms, see OBEDIENCE.

---

commandeer, *v.t.* confiscate, usurp, appropriate, seize. See ACQUISITION.

commanding, *adj.* imperative, imperious; panoramic, inclusive; impressive. See AUTHORITY, INCLUSION.

commando, *n.* ranger, raider, guerrilla, saboteur. See COMBATANT.

comme ci, comme ça, Fr., so-so. See MEDIOCRITY.

comme il faut, Fr., as is required; as it should be. See TASTE, FASHION.

commemorate, *v.t.* celebrate, solemnize, observe, keep, memorialize. See RECORD, CELEBRATION, MEMORY.

commence, *v.* See BEGINNING.

commencement, *n.* BEGINNING; graduation; exercises.

commend, *v.t.* praise, applaud, cite, acclaim, approve, compliment; recommend; entrust. See APPROBATION, COMMISSION.

commensurate, *adj.* comparable, analogous (see SIMILARITY).

comment, *n.* observation, remark, note, reflection, criticism, annotation; aside, opinion; talk, gossip. See INTERPRETATION, CONVERSATION.

commentator, *n.* reviewer, critic, editor, news analyst, newscaster. See INTERPRETATION, INFORMATION.

commerce, *n.* BUSINESS, trade, BARTER; CONVERSATION; SEX.

commercial, *adj.* mercantile, trade; salable. See BARTER, SALE. —*n.* ad[vertisement], spot [announcement], infomercial (*inf.*). See PUBLICATION.

commiserate, *v.t.* PITY, condole.

commissary, *n.* commissar; store, canteen, Post Exchange, PX. See PROVISION, SALE.

COMMISSION
Body of persons with an assignment

Nouns—1, commission, delegation; consignment, assignment; deputation, legation, mission, embassy; committee (see COUNCIL); agency, power of attorney; task, errand, charge, mandate; diploma; permit (see PERMISSION).

2, (*act of appointing*) appointment, nomination, assignment, charter; ordination, installation, induction, investiture, coronation, enthronement; engagement, hiring, appointment; recruitment, conscription, enlistment.

3, (*person appointed*) deputy, proxy, AGENT; commissionaire, errand-boy; diplomat.

4, (*member of a commission*) commissioner, commissar; minister, mayor, warden, councilor.

5, rental, lease, hire, charter.

Verbs—commission, delegate, depute; consign, assign; charge, entrust, commit, commend; authorize, empower, permit; put in commission, accredit; engage, hire, employ; appoint, name, nominate; ordain, install, induct, invest, crown; sign up, take on; rent, hire out; lease; demise.

Adjectives—commissioned, delegated, assigned, *etc.;* paid; rented, leased, chartered; sent to committee.

Adverbs—for, instead of, in place of, in lieu of, as proxy for; for hire, lease, *or* rent, to let.

Quotations—Every time I make an appointment, I create a hundred malcontents and one ingrate (*Louis XIV*).
Antonyms, see NULLIFICATION.

---

commit, *v.t.* perpetrate, perform, do; refer, consign, entrust; confide, commend; take into custody, confine. See ACTION, COMMISSION, LAWSUIT, PROMISE.

commitment, *n.* commission; committal, PROMISE, pledge; involvement.

committee, *n.* See COUNCIL, COMMISSION.

commodious, *adj.* spacious, capacious,

ample, roomy. See SPACE. *Ant.,* cramped, tight.

commodity, *n.* article, product; goods, wares. See SALE.

common, *adj.* ordinary, standard, usual, conventional; joint, shared; prevalent, general, universal, popular, customary, vulgar, ill-bred, plebeian, coarse. See CONFORMITY, HABIT, GENERALITY, POPULACE.

commoner, *n.* gentleman, freeman, yeoman, tradesman, bourgeois; plebeian; citizen, subject. See POPULACE. *Ant.,* aristocrat, noble.

commonplace, *adj.* ordinary, usual, everyday; prosy, monotonous, stale, te-

dious, hackneyed, threadbare, trite, banal. See HABIT. *Ant.,* unusual, special.

common sense, logic, reason (see INTELLIGENCE, JUDGMENT).

commonwealth, *n.* state, community, body politic, government. See AUTHORITY.

commotion, *n.* stir, fuss, ferment, hurlyburly, ado; turmoil, AGITATION, tumult, DISORDER, disturbance, unrest, EXCITEMENT, turbulence.

communal, *adj.* public, common. See HUMANITY.

commune, *v.i.* communicate, converse. See CONVERSATION. —*n.* community; collective, mir, kolkhoz, kibbutz. See ABODE.

COMMUNICATION
Act of communicating ideas

Nouns—1, communication, intercourse, CONVERSATION, SPEECH, WRITING, CORRESPONDENCE; message, tidings, NEWS (see INFORMATION).

2, communicator, messenger, nuncio; herald, crier, trumpeter, bellman, courier, runner; postman, letter carrier; Mercury, Iris, Ariel; operator (radio, telephone, switchboard, *etc.*). See TRANSPORTATION.

3, the media, radio, television, cable, wireless, telephone, radiotelephony, telegraphy, *etc.*; broadcast, cablecast, simulcast; newspapers, press, fourth estate; magazines, reviews, journals; tabloid TV, shock radio; public-address system; switchboard; press box. See PUBLICATION.

4, **a.** radio; band, AM, FM, citizens band, CB, shortwave, wireless; crystal, capsule, car, *or* pocket radio, radio pill, Walkman, ghetto blaster, boom box, clock radio; transmitter, station, channel; multiplex. **b.** [broadcast, satellite, cable, network, *or* high-definition] television, UHF, VHF, HDTV, CATV, small screen; video, videocassette, videodisk, videotape, VHS, Beta, videotape recorder, VTR; minicam, steadicam, mobile camera *or* unit, portapak; TelePrompTer; teletext, videotext; test pattern; monitor. *Slang,* idiot box. **c.** telephone, receiver, transmitter, mouthpiece; extension; wall *or* desk telephone, speakerphone; dial *or* [Touch-]Tone dialing; beeper, pager; pay [tele]phone, call box; mobile, portable *or* cordless telephone, cellular telephone, airtime, home area, roaming area; call waiting, call forwarding, caller ID, *etc.*; telephone number, area code, telephone book, [un]listed number; station-to-station *or* person-to-person call, conference call, collect call, calling card call; answering machine, voicemail; telemarketing; telephone line, private, trunk, *or* party line, hot line; wide-area telecommunications service, WATS; integrated services digital network, ISDN; DSL. *Informal,* tinkle, the horn, jingle, boody call. **d.** facsimile, fax, telefax; Wirephoto; telegram, wire, telex; cable[gram]; day *or* night letter; Internet mail, electronic mail, e-mail (see COMPUTERS). **e.** parallel *or* serial communication, data transmission; modem, acoustic coupler; bawd, bandwidth, full *or* half duplex, packet switching; communications protocol, X-, Y-, *or* Z-modem, fax modem, Kermit; bulletin board system, BBS, bulletin board; network, local-area network, LAN, wide-area network, WAN, neural network, intranet, client, [file] server, firewall; information superhighway, Internet, Bitnet, Usenet, Infobahn, World Wide Web, WWW, cyberspace, Web page *or* site, domain, host name, HTML, HTTP, address, uniform resource locator, URL, site, home page, avatar, meme, e-zine, thread, emoticon, 'bot, chat, Internet relay chat, IRC, handle, mailing list, newsgroup; Java; Web browser, Mosaic, Netscape, Internet Explorer; service provider, gate, portal; archie, gopher, veronica, jughead, WAIS; listserv, [anonymous] FTP (file transfer protocol), TCP/IP, telnet; electronic mail, e-mail, mailbox, spam[ming], crossposting, junk mail, spoiler; on-line help, technical support; bandwidth. *Informal,* sysop.

5, communiqué, bulletin; wire *or* press service, syndicate; telegram, cable, wire, night *or* day letter; carrier pigeon; heliograph, wigwag, semaphore, signal; news flash, press release. See NEWS.

6, [mental] telepathy, thought transference, telekinesis, extrasensory perception, ESP; spiritualism, spirit rapping.

7, *(types of antennas)* aerial, antenna; dipole, parabolic, *etc.* antenna; community antenna, CATV; rabbit ears.

8, intercourse, CONVERSATION, exchange of talk *or* ideas. See SPEECH.

9, newsman, talking head (see NEWS); publisher; correspondent, pen pal; medium, spiritualist; messenger (see AGENT); couch potato; football, golf, *etc.* widow.

10, communicativeness, openness, accessibility, sociability.

Verbs—1, communicate, send messages, broadcast, publish, write, preach, disseminate news *or* information; radio, telegraph, [tele]fax, e-mail, telex, wire, cable; call [up], ring up, phone, give a ring *or* buzz, telephone; signal; sign on *or* off.

2, correspond (with) (see CORRESPONDENCE); intercommunicate; keep track (of), keep in touch, touch base with.

Adjectives—communicative, talkative; outgoing, extrovert; correspondent, corresponding, epistolary, postal; multimedia; on the air; cable-ready.

Quotations—Because television can make so much money doing its worst, it often cannot afford to do its best (*Fred W. Friendly*), The medium is the message (*Marshall McLuhan*), The more we elaborate our means of communication, the less we communicate (*J. B. Priestley*), What we've got here is failure to communicate (*Frank R. Pierson*), Television contracts the imagination and radio expands it (*Terry Wogan*).

Antonyms, see CONCEALMENT, SILENCE.

---

communion, *n.* talk, CONVERSATION, intercourse, communication; concord, unity; sympathy; mass, Lord's Supper, [Holy] Sacrament, Eucharist. See RITE, SOCIALITY, PARTY.

communiqué, *n.* bulletin (see NEWS).

communist, *n.* communalist, leftist, Red, fellow traveler, [parlor] pink. See CHANGE.

community, *n.* neighborhood, district, commonwealth; body, group; partnership, society. See PARTY, SOCIALITY, REGION.

commute, *v.* See INTERCHANGE, TRAVEL.

compact, *n.* contract, covenant; subcompact, mini; makeup *or* vanity case. See AGREEMENT, VEHICLE, BEAUTY. —*adj.* solid, dense, concentrated; concise. See DENSITY, SHORTNESS.

companion, *n.* associate, colleague; pal, chum, comrade; shadow; escort; accomplice. See ACCOMPANIMENT, FRIEND.

company, *n.* companionship, fellowship; association, corporation, partnership, firm; cast, troupe; group, assembly; troop, platoon, squad; society; gang; crowd, party (*both inf.*). See ACCOMPANIMENT, ASSEMBLAGE, DRAMA, COMBATANT, BUSINESS, SOCIALITY.

COMPARISON
Representation as similar

Nouns—1, comparison, matching, examining side by side, holding up to comparison; cross-check, verification; analogy, parallel; contrast, OPPOSITION; RELATION.

2, comparability, SIMILARITY.

Verbs—1, compare, liken, examine *or* place side by side; draw *or* make a comparison *or* parallel, collate, parallel, relate, test, verify, cross-check, weigh; confront, contrast, set against one another; compare notes.

2, be comparable, be worthy of comparison, resemble each other, match; measure up to. *Informal,* stack up with.

Adjectives—1, comparative, relative.

2, comparable, commensurate, analogous; similar.

Adverbs—comparatively, relatively; on the one *or* the other hand; pound for pound, etc.

Prepositions—compared to *or* with, taken with, by comparison with, than.

Quotations—Comparisons are odious (*John Fortescue*).

Antonyms, see DIFFERENCE

---

compartment, *n.* section, chamber, bin, cell. See RECEPTACLE. —*v.t.* compartmentalize, sort, classify. See CLASS.

compass, *v.* encompass, bound, surround, define, encircle; beset, besiege; reach, accomplish, effect. —*n.* bounds, extent, scope, area, circumference, range; gamut; needle (*naut.*). See DIRECTION, LIMIT, CIRCUIT, ENVIRONMENT, SPACE, CIRCUMSCRIPTION.

compassion, *n.* sympathy, tenderness, kindness, mercy, condolence; PITY, ruth, commiseration, heart. *Ant.,* cruelty.

compatible, *adj.* harmonious, well-matched, suitable, congruous; consistent; congenial. See AGREEMENT. *Ant.,* incompatible, ill-suited.

compatriot, *n.* countryman; *informal,* colleague. See FRIEND, INHABITANT.

compel, *v.t.* See COMPULSION.

compendium, *n.* abstract, précis, epitome, summary, digest, synopsis; compilation, anthology. See ASSEMBLAGE, SHORTNESS.

COMPENSATION
Equalizing payment

Nouns—1, *(act of compensating)* compensation, satisfaction, indemnification, indemnity; COMPROMISE; counteraction, [equal and opposite] reaction; measure for measure; RETALIATION, backlash, redress; equalization (see EQUALITY); robbing Peter to pay Paul, an eye for an eye [and a tooth for a tooth]; offset, counterpoise, counterbalance, ballast, equipoise.

2, *(compensatory response)* equivalent, quid pro quo, consideration; fee, recompense (see PAYMENT); reward, award; due; amends, ATONEMENT; reparation, requital, redress, damages, balm.

Verbs—make compensation, compensate, indemnify; counteract, countervail, counterpoise, balance, counterbalance, set off, offset, cancel [out]; outbalance, overbalance; hedge, make up for, cover, fill up, make good; recoup, square oneself, redeem, atone. *Informal,* lean over backward.

Adjectives—compensating, compensatory; counteracting, countervailing, offsetting, etc.; retaliatory; equivalent, equal.

Adverbs—in return, in consideration; but, however, yet, still, notwithstanding, despite, in spite of, in the face of, in any case *or* event; nevertheless, anyhow; although, though; albeit; at all events, at any rate; be that as it may, just *or* all the same, for all that, even so, on the other hand, at the same time, at least, at [the] most; at that, however, that may be; after all, after all is said and done; duly; taking one thing with another; come hell or high water, come what may.

Quotation—No rose without a thorn (*John Ray*).

Antonyms, see LOSS.

---

compete, *v.i.* vie, contend, rival. See CONTENTION.

competence, *n.* capability, capacity, ability, efficiency, proficiency; MEANS, resources, income, SUFFICIENCY. See SKILL. *Ant.,* incompetence, inadequacy.

competition, *n.* See CONTENTION.

compile, *v.t.* collect, arrange; edit, write, make. See ASSEMBLAGE.

complacent, *adj.* CONTENT, pleased; self-satisfied, smug; apathetic, blasé, indifferent. See INDIFFERENCE, VANITY. *Ant.,* insecurity, concern.

complaint, *n.* ACCUSATION, charge; DISEASE, ailment, sickness, indisposition, disorder; lament, grievance (see LAMENTATION).

complement, *n.* rest, extra, counterpart, opposite; personnel, staff. —*v.t.* complete, realize, fulfill, fill *or* round out; balance, offset, neutralize. See COMPLETION, PART.

COMPLETION
Finishing of an action

Nouns—1, completion; accomplishment, achievement, fulfillment, realization, fruition; execution, performance; dispatch; consummation, culmination; finish, close, END; terminus (see ARRIVAL); issue, outcome (see EFFECT); final, crowning, *or* finishing touch, epilogue, coup de grâce; fait accompli; feat; missing link, makeweight; PERFECTION; elaboration; exhaustion. *Informal,* windup, capper, icing on the cake. See PRODUCTION, SUCCESS.

2, completeness, totality, alpha and omega (see WHOLE).

3, *(state of being complete)* fullness, impletion, repletion, saturation, high water; fill, load, bumper, brimmer; bellyful. *Informal,* full house, the works, the business, whole nine yards. See SUFFICIENCY.

Verbs—1, complete, effect; accomplish, achieve, compass, consummate, go through with; bring to maturity; bring to perfection, perfect, elaborate.

2, do, execute, make, follow out; go *or* get through, knock *or* pull off; bring about *or* off, bring to pass, dispatch, polish off, make short work of, dispose of, mop up, set at rest; perform, discharge, fulfill, realize; put through, put in practice, carry out, make good, be as good as one's word; drive home, do thoroughly, not do by halves, go the whole hog, shoot the works, do up brown, do to a turn, go all out, go to any length; see out *or* through, touch all the bases; round out, complement; be in at the death, carry through, play out, exhaust; do the job, fill the bill, turn the trick; deliver.

3, conclude, finish, close, END, wrap up; clinch, seal, set the seal on, put the seal to; cross the wire; give the final touch to, put the last hand to; crown (see SUPERIORITY).

4, ripen, mature, culminate; run its course, run one's race, reach the goal, arrive; get in the harvest.

5, fill, charge, load; fill *or* piece out, replenish, eke out; fill up, saturate. See SUFFICIENCY.

Adjectives—1, complete, perfect, consummate, full-fledged; diametric[al]; entire, WHOLE; thorough, plenary; solid, undivided, with all its parts; exhaustive, sweeping, encyclopedic, thoroughgoing, out-and-out, utter, arrant, radical; crowning, final; abundant, sufficient. *Slang,* maxed out, ass out, fucking, way-out.

2, completing, supplemental, supplementary, complementary.

3, ripe, mature, fully *or* full-grown.

Adverbs—completely, altogether, outright, downright, wholly, soundly, totally, in toto, quite, from soup to nuts; hook, line, and sinker; thoroughly, conclusively, finally; effectually, for good and all, nicely, fully, all of, in all respects, in every respect; through and through, out and out, leaving no stone unturned, all told, to all intents and purposes; utterly, to the utmost, all out, all hollow, stark; heart and soul, root and branch, down to the ground; head over heels; lock, stock, and barrel; inside out; bag and baggage; to the top of one's bent, to the limit, as far as possible; throughout, from first to last, from beginning to end, from A to Z, from hell to breakfast, from end to end, from one end to the other, from head to foot, cap-a-pie, from top to toe, from top to bottom, from the ground up, backward and forward, fore and aft, every whit, every inch, to the nines; up to the brim, up to the ears; with a vengeance, to a fare-thee-well, for fair, but good, all the way, down the line, to the full, to the hilt; to the bone; to the bitter end. *Slang,* to the max.

Phrases—in for a penny, in for a pound; one might as well be hanged for a sheep as a lamb.

Quotations—Give us the tools and we will finish the job (*Winston Churchill*), There must be a beginning of any great matter, but the continuing unto the end until it be thoroughly finished yields the true glory (*Francis Drake*).

Antonyms, see INCOMPLETENESS.

complex, *adj.* intricate, manifold, complicated, involved, knotty. —*n.* tangle, knot, maze; *informal,* obsession, fixation; inferiority, persecution, Oedipus, *etc.* complex. See DISORDER, INSANITY, INTELLECT.

complexion, *n.* hue, COLOR, tinge, tint; skin texture; aspect, APPEARANCE.

compliant, *adj.* obedient, submissive. See OBEDIENCE, SUBMISSION, CONFORMITY.

complicate, *v.t.* involve, embarrass, confuse; perplex; aggravate, compound. See DISORDER, DIFFICULTY.

complicity, *n.* guilt by association; collusion, participation, connivance, conspiracy. See COOPERATION.

compliment, *v.t.* praise, flatter, commend, congratulate. See APPROBATION, CONGRATULATION, COURTESY.

complimentary, *adj.* commendatory; courteous, polite; [con]gratulatory, laudatory, favorable; free, gratis, on the house. See APPROBATION, CHEAPNESS, CONGRATULATION.

comply, *v.t.* CONSENT, conform, yield, submit, obey. See OBEDIENCE, CONFORMITY, SUBMISSION.

component, *n.* PART, element, factor, constituent, ingredient; makings, fixings; link, feature, member.

comport, *v.* behave *or* CONDUCT oneself; suit, fit (see AGREEMENT).

compose, *v.* form (see COMPOSITION); settle, adjust; create, formulate; calm, quiet, relax. See INEXCITABILITY, MUSIC, WRITING.

composed, *adj.* cool, unruffled, collected, self-possessed; calm, tranquil. See INEXCITABILITY.

composer, *n.* See ARTIST.

COMPOSITION
Formation by putting parts together

Nouns—1, (*act or result of composing*) composition, constitution, construction, formation, composite; incorporation, embodiment; COMBINATION, setup; INCLUSION. See MIXTURE, JUNCTION.

2, (*things that make up*) component, ingredient, contents, makeup, constituent parts, makings, fixings; factor, element, feature; capacity, volume; cargo, freight, load[ing]; cupful, basketful, bottleful, *etc.*; stuffing, packing, filling, wadding. See PART.

Verbs—1, be composed of, be made of, be formed of; consist of, be resolved into; include, hold (see INCLUSION).

2, (*form by putting parts together*) compose, compound, constitute, form, make, put together, assemble, make up, synthesize, combine, mix; enter into the composition of, be a component, figure in, have a part in.

Adjectives—composite; composing, constituting, *etc.*; constituent, component, integral, formative; composed *or* made of, comprising, containing, incorporating.

Antonyms, see DECOMPOSITION, INSUBSTANTIALITY.

compos mentis, *Lat.* sane. See SANITY.

compost, *n.* fertilizer, manure, humus (see AGRICULTURE).

composure, *n.* placidity, serenity, self-possession, calmness. See REPOSE, INEXCITABILITY. *Ant.,* AGITATION.

compound, *v.t.* combine, compose, concoct, amalgamate, mix; join, unite. —*n.* MIXTURE; enclave, ENCLOSURE. See JUNCTION, COMBINATION, COMPOSITION.

comprehend, *v.t.* comprise, embrace, include; grasp, apprehend, conceive, understand, see, know. See KNOWLEDGE, INCLUSION, INTELLIGENCE.

comprehensive, *adj.* full, inclusive, all-embracing. See GENERALITY, BREADTH, INCLUSION.

compress, *v.t.* reduce, digest, abridge, consolidate, condense; crowd, squeeze, contract. See DENSITY, CONTRACTION. —*n.* pad, dressing. See REMEDY.

comprise, *v.t.* consist of, involve, embrace, cover, embody; include, comprehend, contain. See INCLUSION.

COMPROMISE
Settlement of differences by mutual concession

Nouns—1, compromise; mediation, arbitration, negotiation, give-and-take, bargaining. 2, settlement, concession, appeasement, COMPENSATION; terms, bargain, understanding; middle ground, midcourse. *Informal,* deal, horsetrading. See PACIFICATION. 3, *(one arranging compromise)* arbitrator, mediator, middleman, negotiator.

Verbs—1, compromise, take the mean, split the difference, strike a balance *or* a happy medium; meet one *or* go halfway, go fifty-fifty, give and take; come to terms, settle out of court; submit to arbitration; patch up, bridge over, arrange; adjust differences; agree; make the best of, make a virtue of necessity; take the will for the deed; bend over backward.

2, *(arrange a compromise)* mediate, arbitrate, intercede; negotiate, bargain; reconcile, iron out; plea-bargain.

Adjectives—conciliatory, diplomatic, give-and-take; mediatory, mediating, intermediary, intercessory.

Phrases—you can't win them all; half a loaf is better than one; make sure you leave some fat for the other side.

Quotations—A compromise in the sense that being bitten in half by a shark is a compromise with being swallowed whole (*P. J. O'Rourke*), An agreement between two men to do what both agree is wrong (*Lord Cecil*), He never wants but what's right and fair; only when you come to settle what's right and fair, it's everything that he wants and nothing that you want. And that's his idea of a compromise (*Thomas Hughes*).

Antonyms, see OBSTINACY, RESOLUTION.

COMPULSION
Coercion

Nouns—compulsion, coercion, coaction, constraint, duress, obligation; enforcement, pressure; [physical, brute, *or* main] force; the sword, martial law, strong arm [of the law]; draft, conscription; RESTRAINT; requirement, NECESSITY, force majeure; Hobson's choice. *Informal,* arm-twisting, strong-arm tactics. See SEVERITY.

Verbs—compel, force, make, drive, coerce, constrain, enforce, necessitate, oblige; force one's hand, impose on, twist one's arm; force upon, press; cram, ram, thrust, *or* force down the throat; make a point of, insist upon, take no denial; put down; require, exact, tax, put in force, put teeth in; restrain, hold down; draft, conscript, impress, shanghai. *Informal,* twist one's arm, cram down one's throat, pressure, put on the heat, pull rank. *Slang,* mind-fuck.

Adjectives—compulsory, compelling; coercive, coactive; obligatory, stringent, peremptory; forcible, not to be trifled with; irresistible; compulsive.

Adverbs—compulsorily, by force, by force of arms; on *or* under compulsion, perforce; at sword's point, forcibly, under duress; under protest, in spite of; against one's will; under press of; de rigueur, willy-nilly.

Phrases—you can take a horse to water, but you can't make him drink.

Quotations—Force without wisdom falls of its own weight (*Horace*).

Antonyms, see FREEDOM.

compunction, *n.* regret, remorse; scruple, twinge. See PENITENCE, DOUBT.

compute, *v.* figure, calculate, reckon. See NUMERATION.

COMPUTERS
Electronic data processors

Nouns—1, computer, analog *or* digital computer, CISC *or* RISC computer, workstation, supercomputer, mainframe, minicomputer, microcomputer, personal computer, PC, Macintosh, IBM-compatible, Amiga, clone; 286, 386, 486, Pentium, PowerPC, G3, *or* G4 processor; personal computer, desktop computer, portable, laptop, notebook, *or* palmtop [computer]; peripheral; digitizer; binary system; computerese, computer literacy; computer science, cybernation, electronic *or* desktop publishing, DTP, digital imaging; multitasking, multiprogramming, serial *or* parallel processing, timesharing; configuration; computer graphics, line drawing; multimedia; pixel; telecommuting, paperless office; hacking, cybercrime; Silicon Valley. *Slang,* confuser, 'puter.

2, *(computer science)* informatics, computerization, automated data processing, ADP; artificial intelligence, AI; computing, batch processing; hierarchical system *or* menu; computer-aided design, CAD; electronic mail, e-mail, first in first out, FIFO; last in first out, LIFO; garbage in garbage out, GIGO; management information system, MIS. *Slang,* glitch.

3, *(terms)* access code, password; batch file; clock speed; access time, response time, cycle time, downtime, real time, execution time, rollover, throughput, seek time; background operation; interface; graphic user interface, GUI, shell, icon, window, toolbar, Windows; WYSIWYG, what you see is what you get; bomb, crash; cursor, prompt; readout; data file; computer graphics, crosshair, line *or* halftone art; virtual reality; backup; universal product code, UPC, bar code, optical reader wand; baud, parity; cold *or* warm boot; [virtual] storage, swapping, tape *or* disk memory, [non]volatile memory; data entry, input, output; decryption, encryption; default; delimiter; hit; housekeeping; [conventional, expanded, extended, random access, cache, *or* read-only] memory, RAM, ROM, bubble memory, flash memory, memory bank; clipboard; [bad] sector, track, cluster, cylinder, file allocation table, FAT, interleave, partition.

4, electronic communications (see COMMUNICATION).

5, *(programming)* a. bit, byte, nibble, chunk; kilobyte, megabyte, gigabyte, terabyte; [source, object, *or* executable] code, operation code, algorithm, parameter, recursion; assembler, compiler, interpreter; parity bit, binary coded decimal, BCD; bit vector, bitmap, Bézier curve; object-oriented graphics *or* programming; object linking and embedding, OLE; character; Boolean variable, floating point, fractal; file name, extension; bootstrap, branch; bug, patch; handshaking; command; directory tree, [parent, root, child, *or* sub]directory, folder, file; HTTP, hypertext, hypermedia, [hyper]link; benchmark [program]; BIOS; operating system, OS, DOS, disk operating system, MSDOS; memory management; interrupt, job, instruction, jump, loop, push, poke, nesting, default; radio *or* option button; sentinel, tag; mnemonic; string, delimiter; [pop-up *or* pull-down] menu, directory; virus, worm, Trojan horse; error message. *Informal,* bells and whistles. *Slang,* kludge, gulp. b. low-level language, machine language, assembly language; high-level, object-oriented, *or* structured language, Ada, Algol, AppleDOS, BASIC, Pascal, C, C++, Cobol, CP/M, Fortran, FORTH, HTML, Java[script], Linux, Lisp, Logo, Prolog, SNOBOL, Unix; structured query language, SQL; job control language, JCL; graphics interchange format, GIF, joint photographic experts group, JPEG, tagged image file format, TIFF, motion picture experts group, MPEG; page description language, PDL, PostScript.

6, *(hardware)* a. [micro]chip, integrated circuit, IC, large scale integration, LSI, very large scale integration, VLSI, biochip, open architecture. b. central processing unit, CPU, processor, [math, graphics, *etc.*] coprocessor, accumulator, arithmetic logic unit, ALU, motherboard, backplane, logic board, buffer, card, accelerator board *or* card; firmware; clock; expansion slot, data bus, channel, card, chad; parallel *or* serial port, COM *or* LPT port, small computer system interface, SCSI, universal serial bus, USB; footprint. **c.** modem (see COMMUNICATION). **d.** *(input)* optical character recognition, OCR; keypunch; keystroke, [QWERTY *or* Dvorak] keyboard, ASCII, [alt, control, enter, line feed, escape, reset, return, arrow, *or* function] key; keypad, graphics tablet, mouse, click, trackball, light pen, stylus, pointer, joystick, voice recognition *or* synthesis; [optical image *or* flatbed] scanner. **e.** *(output)* [laser, inkjet, thermal, thimble, impact, letter-quality, draft, daisy wheel, line, page, *or* dot-matrix] printer, plotter, bidirectional printing, boustrophedon, landscape *or* portrait printing, print spooling, carriage, fanfold paper, printout, anti-aliasing, jaggies, [Encapsulated] PostScript, [scalable *or* bit-mapped] font, screen *or* printer font, soft *or* downloadable font, PostScript, TrueType; video monitor, video display terminal, cathode ray tube, CRT, active *or* passive display, pixel, sprite, LED *or* light-emitting diode display, LCD *or* liquid crystal display, [gas] plasma display; ANSI, CGA, EGA, VGA, SVGA; dots per inch, DPI, dithering. **f.** CD-ROM drive, magneto-optical drive, disk drive, hard *or* fixed disk, floppy disk, diskette, index hole, read/write head; Syquest cartridge; ZIP disk, Bernoulli *or* Winchester drive, holographic storage; physical *or* logical drive.

7, *(marketing)* bundling; end user.

8, *(software)* software, shareware, freeware, groupware; productivity, recreational, instructional, *or* utility program, application, applet; macro; platform; bundled sortware; relational, free-form, *or* flat-file database, database management system, DBMS; word processor, text editor; spreadsheet; draw, paint, *or* illustration program, clip art; emulator; utility; control panel, extension, desk accessory, DA; memory-resident program, terminate-and-stay-resident program, TSR; driver; screen saver; spell check. *Slang,* vaporware, bloatware.

9, computer scientist, computer engineer; power user; programmer; computer nerd, hacker, cyberthief. *Slang,* geek, propeller-head, net potato, lamer, computer widow.

Verbs—computerize, digitize, rasterize; crunch; debug; import, export; load, upload, download, dump, read, write, write-protect; execute, launch, fetch, close, exit, terminate; format, configure; retrofit, reprogram; flame; navigate *or* surf [the Web], point-and-click; abort; boot, reboot; capture; clear, erase, delete, undelete, undo, overwrite, restore, override, refresh; save, close, archive, copy; get, put; compress, zip, unzip; upgrade; drag; crash, hang, bomb, lock up; park; log on, out, *or* off; hack into; power down *or* up. *Informal,* zap.

Adjectives—alphanumeric; dedicated; up, down; fuzzy; user-friendly; computer literate; interactive; octal, hexadecimal, binary; off- *or* on-line, on-screen, plug-and-play, drag-and-drop; case-sensitive; memory resident; menu-driven; backward compatible.

Phrases—to err is human, but to really foul things up requires a computer.

Quotations—A modern computer hovers between the obsolescent and the nonexistent (*Sydney Brenner*), The Puritan work of an eyeless computer (*John Betjeman*).

Related categories, NUMERATION.

---

comrade, *n.* FRIEND, companion, mate, fellow, associate; communist. See ACCOMPANIMENT.

con, *v.t.* steer, pilot (see DIRECTION). —*v. & n., slang,* swindle (see DECEPTION).

concatenate, *v.t.* link (see CONTINUITY, CONNECTION).

CONCAVITY
Shape like the inside of a sphere *or* circle

Nouns—1, concavity, depression, dip, hollow, indentation, cavity, hole, dent, dint, dimple, follicle, pit, sinus alveolus; excavation, crater, pocket; trough, FURROW, burrow; cup, basin, bowl (see RECEPTACLE); intaglio (see SCULPTURE); coil; socket. See DEPTH, INTERIOR.

2, *(concave thing)* valley, vale, dale, dell, dingle, bottom, blade, gully, cave, cavern, cove; pothole, sinkhole, crater; armpit; grotto, grot; alcove; cul-de-sac; arch, bay, *etc.*

3, *(machine to make concave)* excavator, sapper, miner, digger, [steam] shovel, spade, *etc.* (see RECEPTACLE).

Verbs—cave in, depress, hollow, scoop [out], gouge, indent, dent, dint; excavate, mine, sap, undermine, burrow, tunnel; stave in.

Adjectives—concave, depressed, hollow, pitted, stove in; retiring; retreating, cavernous; cellular, porous; spongy, honeycombed, alveolar; infundibular, funnel-shaped, cupular; bell-shaped, campaniform; capsular, vaulted, arched.

Antonyms, see CONVEXITY.

CONCEALMENT
Keeping secret

Nouns—1, concealment; hiding[-place]; curtain, screen, blind; smokescreen, ambush, camouflage; hideaway, hideout, *sanctum sanctorum,* safe house; secret passage *or* exit, back *or* side door, escape hatch; trench, foxhole, *etc.;* disguise, costume, mask, domino, masquerade, shroud, curtain, cloak, smokescreen, veil; invisible ink; incognito, pseudonym; cryptography, steganography, cipher, code; hidden agenda; ace up one's sleeve. *Slang,* camo. See INVISIBILITY.

2, *(concealed act)* stealth, stealthiness; slyness, CUNNING; privacy, SECLUSION; secrecy, secretness (see SECRET); hide-and-seek, peek-a-boo.

3, *(concealing behavior)* reticence, silence, TACITURNITY; arrière pensée, suppression, circumlocution (see AVOIDANCE); evasion, equivocation, white lie, misprision (see DECEPTION); cover-up, hush-up, conspiracy of silence; underhand dealing; closeness, secretiveness, mystery; LATENCY; stowaway; jargon, cant, officialese, shop talk, gobbledygook, double-talk, subtext. *Informal,* poker face.

4, *(one who operates concealed)* operative, sleuth, private investigator, undercover agent, secret agent, spy, mole, plainclothesman. *Slang,* plumber, spook.

Verbs—1, *(hide physically)* conceal, hide, secrete, put out of sight, stow; launder; lock up, bottle up; cover, screen, cloak, veil, shroud; draw the veil *or* curtain, curtain, shade, eclipse, becloud, mask, camouflage, disguise; dissemble (see DECEPTION); ensconce, muffle. *Slang,* stash, plant. See COVERING.

2, *(withhold information)* keep from, keep to oneself, keep dark, bury, sink, suppress, keep out of sight, keep in the background; stifle, hush up, gloss over, black out, cover up, smother, withhold, stonewall, bleep, blip, reserve; keep a secret, keep one's own counsel, hold one's tongue; not let the right hand know what the left is doing; hide one's light under a bushel.

3, be concealed *or* hidden; hide oneself, cover one's tracks, lie in ambush, lie in wait, lie low, lurk, sneak, skulk, slink, prowl; lay for; bury one's head in the sand; play hide-and-seek; take to the woods; hide in holes and corners.

Adjectives—1, concealed, hidden; behind the scenes; up one's sleeve; SECRET, recondite, arcane, Masonic, mystic; cabalistic, cryptic; privy, clandestine, sub rosa.

2, undercover, in ambush, in hiding, in disguise; in the dark; clouded, invisible; buried, underground, perdu; secluded (see SECLUSION); undisclosed, untold; cloak-and-dagger; covert, mysterious, unintelligible (see UNINTELLIGIBILITY); confidential, classified, top *or* most secret; latent.

3, furtive, stealthy; skulking, surreptitious, underhand, hole and corner; sly, CUN-
NING; secretive, evasive; reserved, reticent, uncommunicative, buttoned up, taciturn.
Adverbs—secretly, in secret, privately, in private; in the dark; behind closed doors, in
closed session, hugger-mugger; under the rose, the counter, *or* the table; sub rosa, in
the background, aside, on the sly, with bated breath, sotto voce, in a whisper; under
cover *or* wraps; in [strict] confidence; confidentially, off the record, between ourselves, between you and me, entre nous, in camera; underhand, by stealth, like a thief
in the night, stealthily; behind the scenes, behind one's back; incognito.
Phrases—still waters run deep; expletive deleted.
Quotations—Sometimes you need to conceal a fact with words (*Machiavelli*).

Antonyms, see DISCLOSURE.

---

concede, *v.t.* CONSENT, yield, give in, allow; accede; grant, admit, acknowl-
edge, confess; cede, give up, surrender.
See RELINQUISHMENT, DISCLOSURE,
GIVING, PERMISSION, COMPROMISE.

conceit, *n.* VANITY, PRIDE, egotism, self-
esteem; epigram, bon mot, quip; whim,
fantasy, fancy, caprice, notion, quirk.
See WIT, IMAGINATION, FIGURATIVE.

conceivable, *adj.* plausible, believable;
knowable. See BELIEF, KNOWLEDGE,
IMAGINATION.

conceive, *v.* devise, frame, imagine, visualize, fancy; grasp, realize, take in, understand; become pregnant, get in a family
way (*inf.*). See IMAGINATION, KNOWL-
EDGE, REPRODUCTION.

concentrate, *v.* distill, condense, consolidate; intensify, fix, aim, focus; converge,
center, localize; collect, assemble, gather.
See ASSEMBLAGE, CONVERGENCE.

concentration camp, see PRISON.

concentric, *adj.* See MIDDLE.

concept, *n.* conception, conceit,
THOUGHT; INTERPRETATION.

conception, *n.* idea, notion; pregnancy,
fertilization; BEGINNING. See IMAGINA-
TION, REPRODUCTION.

concern, *v.t.* regard, affect, relate, refer to,
pertain to, have to do with, bear upon,
belong to, treat of; interest; disturb,
trouble. —*n.* matter, affair; CARE, anxiety, worry, solicitude, regard; significance, import, interest; firm, BUSINESS.
See RELATION, IMPORTANCE, DOUBT.

concert, *n.* recital, program, serenade,
musicale; COOPERATION, AGREEMENT,
harmony, accord; conspiracy. See MU-
SIC, UNITY.

concession, *n.* COMPROMISE; grant, franchise (see BUSINESS).

conciliate, *v.t.* reconcile; pacify, appease,
placate, mollify, propitiate; win, curry
favor. See CONTENT, FORGIVENESS,
PACIFICATION.

concise, *adj.* succinct, short, brief, terse,
laconic, epigrammatic, summary, com-
pact. See SHORTNESS.

conclave, *n.* assembly (see ASSEMBLAGE).

conclude, *v.* END, close, finish, wind up,
terminate; infer, deduce; arrange, settle;
resolve, judge, determine. See RESOLU-
TION, JUDGMENT.

conclusive, *adj.* decisive. See CERTAINTY,
DEMONSTRATION.

concoct, *v.t.* prepare, invent, devise, contrive; brew; mix, cook; PLAN, make up,
hatch. See PREPARATION, FALSEHOOD.

concomitant, *adj.* attending, accompanying (see ACCOMPANIMENT).

concord, *n.* accord, harmony, AGREEMENT,
ASSENT; sympathy, rapport, congruous-
ness, congruence; concurrence; union,
UNITY; peace; alliance, league, compact;
treaty, entente, understanding.

concourse, *n.* throng, crowd; arcade,
square. See ASSEMBLAGE, PASSAGE.

concrete, *adj.* actual, real, tangible, solid;
specific, definite, exact, particular. See
SUBSTANCE, HARDNESS, COHERENCE,
SPECIALITY. —*n.* See CEMENT.

concubine, *n.* hetaera; mistress, paramour,
kept woman; wench, harem girl, odal-
isque; demimondaine, courtesan, prostitute. See IMPURITY.

concur, *v.i.* agree, ASSENT, harmonize, jibe
(*inf.*); coincide; see eye to eye (with),
pull together, parallel; acquiesce. See
AGREEMENT, SYNCHRONISM, COOPERA-
TION, UNITY.

concussion, *n.* shock, blow, impact. See
IMPULSE, PAIN.

CONDEMNATION
Censure

Nouns—condemnation, conviction, proscription, damnation, doom; death warrant, death sentence *or* penalty, capital punishment; attainder, attainture, attaintment; denunciation, commination; DISAPPROBATION, disapproval, censure. See ACCUSATION, JUDGMENT, IMPRECATION.

Verbs—condemn, convict, find guilty, damn, doom, sign the death warrant, sentence to death; sentence, pass sentence on, send up; attaint, proscribe, sequestrate; disapprove, censure, denounce, blame.

Adjectives—condemnatory, damnatory; denunciatory; censorious; condemned, damned, convicted; self-convicted.

Quotations—He that is without sin among you, let him first cast a stone at her (*Bible*), Society needs to condemn a little more and understand a little less (*John Major*).

Antonyms, see ACQUITTAL.

---

condense, *v.* abridge, digest, abbreviate, shorten, cut, epitomize; compress, compact, thicken, concentrate, distill. See DENSITY, SHORTNESS, CONTRACTION, LIQUEFACTION.

condescend, *v.i.* stoop, deign, descend, vouchsafe. See HUMILITY, PRIDE.

condiment, *n.* seasoning, sauce, spice, relish, chutney; herb, caraway; salt, pepper, cayenne, mustard, curry, onion, garlic, pickle, catsup, vinegar, mayonnaise, olive oil, salad dressing. See TASTE, FOOD, PUNGENCY.

condition, *n.* fitness; state, birth, rank, place, estate, station, CLASS; demand, QUALIFICATION, proviso; plight, situation, status, position, pass, case, circumstances. See REPUTE, CIRCUMSTANCE.

condolence, *n.* LAMENTATION, sympathy, PITY, consolation, commiseration.

condom, *n.* prophylactic, contraceptive, rubber (*inf.*), sheath (*inf.*). See HINDRANCE.

condominium, *n.* cooperative [apartment house], co-op. See ABODE.

condone, *v.t.* See FORGIVENESS.

conduce, *v.i.* lead, tend, contribute. See TENDENCY, CAUSE, UTILITY.

conduct, *v.* escort, guide; manage, carry on, transact; convey, transmit; lead. See DIRECTION, BUSINESS, MUSIC.

CONDUCT
Deportment

Nouns—1, *(act in business)* conduct, dealing, transaction, ACTION, business; tactics, game plan, policy; generalship, statesmanship, seamanship; strategy, strategics; PLAN, program, execution, manipulation, treatment, campaign; husbandry, housekeeping, stewardship; ménage, regime; management, government, direction (see AUTHORITY); praxeology. See ACTIVITY, HABIT.

2, *(personal acts)* behavior, deportment, comportment; carriage, demeanor, mien, bearing, manner; line of conduct, course of action; role, process, ways, practice, procedure, modus operandi, modus vivendi, behavior trait, METHOD; conduct unbecoming. *Informal,* goings-on. *Slang,* shtick, behavishness. See COURTESY.

Verbs—1, *(carry on)* conduct, transact, execute, administer, deal with, have to do with; treat, handle, manipulate; play someone for; take steps, take measures; dispatch; proceed with, discharge; carry on *or* through, put into practice; direct, officiate.

2, *(act)* conduct, behave, comport, deport, demean, carry *or* acquit oneself; do by; act one's age; give a good account of oneself, mind one's Ps and Qs; run a race, lead a life, play a game; take *or* adopt a course; steer *or* shape one's course, play one's part *or* cards; shift for oneself, paddle one's own canoe. *Slang,* straighten up and fly right.

Adjectives—strategical, tactical, businesslike, practical, executive; behavioral, behaviorist.

Adverbs—on one's good *or* best behavior.

Phrases—good behavior is the last refuge of mediocrity; when in Rome, do as the Romans do.

Quotations—Conduct is three-fourths of our life and its largest concern (*Matthew Arnold*), He combines the manners of a Marquis with the morals of a Methodist (*W. S. Gilbert*).

Antonyms, see BADNESS, NEGLECT.

---

conductor, *n.* guide, escort, DIRECTOR; manager, operator, supervisor; guard; drum major, leader, maestro, choirmaster, time beater (*inf.*); transmitter, conveyor. See TRANSPORTATION, MUSIC.

conduit, *n.* channel, duct, PASSAGE.

cone-shaped, *adj.* conic[al], conoid[al]; coniferous, pyramidal. See SHARPNESS, ROTUNDITY.

confection, *n.* sweet, candy, bonbon. See SWEETNESS, CLOTHING.

confederacy, *n.* confederation, league, federation, union, alliance; compact, combine. See PARTY.

confederate, *n.* aide, ally; accomplice; companion, associate. See AID, AUXILIARY, COOPERATION.

confer, *v.* converse, discuss, consult, debate, deliberate, talk, parley, palaver; give, grant, bestow. See ADVICE, CONVERSATION, GIVING.

confess, *v.* acknowledge, avow, own, admit; disclose, tell, reveal, unbosom, unburden, divulge. See DISCLOSURE, PENITENCE, RITE.

confidant, confidante, *n.* FRIEND, intimate.

confide, *v.* trust, believe in, rely on; entrust, commit; tell, divulge, unbosom, unburden. See BELIEF, DISCLOSURE. *Ant.,* mistrust.

confidence, *n.* assurance, CERTAINTY, positiveness; spirit, boldness, self-reliance; communication; privacy, SECRET; faith, trust. See BELIEF, COURAGE, HOPE. *Ant.,* DOUBT, UNCERTAINTY.

confidential, *adj.* SECRET, private; intimate. See CONCEALMENT. *Ant.,* public, open.

configuration, *n.* FORM, shape, figure, contour; grouping, ARRANGEMENT.

confine, *v.t.* imprison, incarcerate, immure, jail, detain; cage, pen; restrict, bound, LIMIT. See CIRCUMSCRIPTION, ENCLOSURE, RESTRAINT.

confinement, *n.* childbirth, childbed; imprisonment, incarceration, captivity, custody, detention; CIRCUMSCRIPTION, limitation, restriction. See RESTRAINT, REPRODUCTION.

confirm, *v.t.* establish, strengthen; ratify, validate, approve, endorse; verify, substantiate, prove, corroborate. See ASSENT, STRENGTH, EVIDENCE, DEMONSTRATION. *Ant.,* cancel, contradict.

confiscate, *v.t.* take, seize, commandeer, appropriate. See ACQUISITION, CONDEMNATION.

conflagration, *n.* fire, flame (see HEAT).

conflict, *n.* battle, combat, strife, fight, encounter, clash, collision, struggle; discord, antagonism, dissension, hostility. See CONTENTION, DISAGREEMENT.

CONFORMITY
Accordance

Nouns—1, *(following a model)* conformity, conformance; conventionality, HABIT, custom, formality; AGREEMENT, compliance; uniformity, orthodoxy, homeostasis; acculturation, enculturation.

2, *(model)* object lesson, example, instance, specimen, sample, swatch; run of the mill *or* mine, RULE, exemplification, case in point; pattern, prototype; mainstream, norm; master, master copy; benchmark, paradigm; role model; Procrustean bed; Main Street. See FASHION.

3, *(one who conforms)* conformist, conventionalist, formalist; stickler; bookman; bourgeois; sheep, parrot; organization *or* yes-man; in-group.

Verbs—1, *(follow a model)* conform, follow suit, be regular, run true to form; follow, go by, *or* observe the rules, go by the book; comply with, chime in with, fall in with;

be guided by; follow the fashion *or* crowd, lend oneself to; assimilate, pass muster, come up to scratch, shape up; toe the mark *or* line, walk the chalk, play the game, not rock the boat, not make waves, do as others do, in Rome do as the Romans do; go *or* swim with the stream *or* current, keep in step.

2, *(be a model)* exemplify, be a model for, set the pace *or* fashion; stand on ceremony.

Adjectives—conformable; conforming, regular (see REGULARITY); well-regulated, orderly; conventional, customary, ordinary, common, habitual, politically correct, P.C.; usual; typical, normal, nominal, formal, par for the course, all in a day's work; exemplary; canonical, orthodox, uniform (see RULE). *Informal,* ticky-tacky.

Adverbs—conformably, by rule; agreeably to; in conformity with, in accordance with, in keeping with, in step; according to, consistent with, as usual; of course, as a matter of course; pro forma, for form's sake, by the book, according to rule, according to Hoyle; to scale; for example, for instance, for one [thing].

Phrases—do as I say, not as I do; what everybody says must be true.

Quotations—A foolish consistency is the hobgoblin of little minds (*Emerson*), Imitation lies at the root of most human actions (*Anatole France*).

Antonyms, see UNCONFORMITY.

---

confound, *v.t.* confuse, bewilder, perplex, nonplus, dumbfound, dismay, mix up, puzzle; rout, overcome, overthrow. See SURPRISE, SUCCESS.

confrere, *n.* colleague, associate, FRIEND. See AUXILIARY.

confront, *v.t.* face, oppose; resist, brave. See OPPOSITION, COURAGE.

confuse, *v.t.* perplex, confound, disconcert; embroil, muddle; abash, embarrass. See DISORDER, HUMILITY, UNINTELLIGIBILITY.

CONFUTATION
Proving false

Nouns—confutation, refutation, disproof, rebuttal, ANSWER; reductio ad absurdum; conclusive *or* knockdown argument. *Informal,* clincher, squelcher, crusher. See NULLIFICATION, NEGATION.

Verbs—confute, refute, disprove, show up, show the fallacy of, rebut, defeat; demolish, destroy, tear down, blow sky high; overwhelm, overthrow, overturn, squash, squelch; scatter to the winds, explode; put *or* reduce to silence, shut up; clinch an argument; not leave a leg to stand on, cut the ground from under one's feet.

Adjectives—confuting, confuted, confutative, negative (see NEGATION); refuted, refutable; condemned on one's own showing, condemned out of one's own mouth.

Antonyms, see DEMONSTRATION, EVIDENCE.

---

congeal, *v.* solidify, harden, fix, gel, jell, set, coagulate, stiffen, thicken; freeze; condense. See DENSITY, HARDNESS.

congenial, *adj.* compatible, agreeable, pleasing, sympathetic, kindred, harmonious. See AGREEMENT. *Ant.,* disagreeable.

congenital, *adj.* native, innate (see INTRINSIC).

congest, *v.t.* overfill, clog, block; plug, stop, *or* stuff up; [over]crowd, jam, choke, cram; constipate. See CLOSURE.

conglomerate, *adj.* gathered, assembled. See ASSEMBLAGE. —*n.* concrete (see COHERENCE); diversified company (see BUSINESS).

CONGRATULATION
Felicitation

Nouns—congratulation[s], gratulation, felicitation; salute; compliments [of the season], *etc.*; pat *or* slap on the back, best wishes; toast. *Slang,* high *or* slapping five. See AP-PROBATION, FLATTERY.

Verbs—congratulate, gratulate, felicitate, wish one joy; compliment, tender *or* offer one's congratulations, wish many happy returns of the day; pat on the back, shake one's hand; take a bow. See REJOICING.

Adjectives—congratulatory, complimentary, flattering.

Interjections—congratulations! well done! way to go! bravo! *Informal,* right on!

Antonyms, see REGRET, DISAPPROBATION.

---

congregation, *n.* ASSEMBLAGE, assembly, gathering, collection, meeting, aggregation; church, parish, flock, fold, brethren. See RELIGION.

congress, *n.* assembly, legislature, parliament; meeting, convention; intercourse. See ASSEMBLAGE, COUNCIL, CONVERSATION.

conjecture, *n.* SUPPOSITION, hypothesis, extrapolation, speculation, guess; inference, surmise.

conjugal, *adj.* connubial (see MARRIAGE).

conjugate, *adj.* yoked, united, mated, coupled; related, paronymous, coderived. See JUNCTION.

conjure, *v.* cast spells, enchant; invoke, summon up; beseech, implore, beg. See SORCERY, REQUEST.

con man, *informal,* hustler, shark, flim-flam man. See STEALING, DECEPTION.

CONNECTION
Physical link

Nouns—1, connection, bond, tie, link, concatenation; connective, interconnection; daisy chain; nexus, neck, isthmus; nape; bridge, tunnel, causeway, viaduct, *etc.* See CONTACT, JUNCTION.

2, a. ligature, ligament; chain, sinew, tendon, umbilical cord. b. strap; fastening, clasp, buckle, button, snap, hook [and eye], zipper, Velcro fastener. c. lacing, latch, anchor, moorings, guy rope, hawser, grappling iron, painter; leash. d. knot, slipknot, running knot, bowknot, surgeon's knot, square knot, granny knot, *etc.* e. bracket, brace, clevis; hinge, hasp, shackle, wye; brace, clamp, clip, alligator clip.

3, *(knots)* anchor, barrel, becket, blood, bow, builder's, diamond, double, flat, granny, lanyard, loop, lubber's, manrope, mesh, nail, netting, open hand, overhand, prolonge, reef, rope-yarn, running, Shelby, shroud, single, slide, square, stevedore's, stopper, surgeon's, thumb, truelove, turle, wall, weaver's, *or* [half-]Windsor knot; [Blackwall, clove, half, harness, Magnus, marlinespike, marling, midshipman's, rolling, stunner, timber, *or* weaver's] hitch; [becket, carrick, fisherman's, heaving-line, reeving-line, sheet, *or* tack] bend; bight, bowline, cat's-paw, clinch, crown, cuckold's neck, figure of eight, half-knot, inside clinch, lash, loop, noose, ring *or* round seizing, running bowline, sailor's breastplate, sheepshank, slipknot, splice, turn.

4, [boat, box, brass, common, cut, finishing, roofing, screw, tree, *or* wire] nail, brad, butterfly hook, spike, [Allen, drive, drywall, flat- *or* roundhead, lag, machine, panhead, *or* Phillips] screw, setscrew, spike, staple, anchor, [anchor, chain, expansion, drift, extension, eye, hanger, machine, ring, toggle, *or* wing] bolt, [cotter] pin, staple, tack, thumbtack; rivet.

5, *(adhering link)* adhesive, Scotch, double-stick, Magic, duct, electrical, gaffer's, *or* masking tape; cement, glue, paste, mucilage, gum (see COHERENCE); mortar, stucco, putty, lime, plaster, solder.

6, screwdriver, screw gun, nailer, riveter, impact driver, plate joiner, stapler, staple gun, glue gun. See INSTRUMENTALITY.

Verbs—1, connect, link, join; tie in, plug in, hook up; associate, relate. See JUNCTION, RELATION.

2, attach, affix, fasten, bind, secure; blend, merge, fuse; tie, sew, stitch, tack, knit, button, hitch, knot, lash, truss, bandage, braid, splice, gird, tether, moor, picket, harness, chain; fetter, lock, latch, leash, couple, link, yoke, bracket, span, marry, wed.

3, pin, nail, bolt, clasp, clamp, clinch, screw, rivet, solder, weld, mortise, miter, dovetail, graft, entwine; interlace, entangle, intertwine.

Adjectives—firm, fast, tight, taut, secure, set, inseparable, indissoluble; mixed up.

Antonyms, see DISJUNCTION.

---

connivance, *n.* COOPERATION, collusion, complicity; PERMISSION, sufferance.

connoisseur, *n.* critic, gourmet, epicure, adept. See TASTE.

connotation, *n.* implication, suggestion, association, MEANING.

connubial, *adj.* conjugal, marital. See MARRIAGE.

conquer, *v.t.* overcome, overthrow, vanquish, subdue, subjugate. See SUCCESS.

conquest, *n.* victory (see SUCCESS). *Ant.,* defeat.

consanguinity, *n.* See RELATION.

conscience, *n.* See PROBITY.

conscientious, *adj.* faithful, honorable, upright, trusty, scrupulous, meticulous; religious; thorough, particular, careful, painstaking. See PROBITY, CARE, DUTY. *Ant.,* negligent, indifferent.

conscionable, *adj.* conscientious (see SUCCESS).

conscious, *adj.* sensible, cognizant, percipient, understanding; awake, aware, sentient. See INTELLECT, KNOWLEDGE, SENSIBILITY. *Ant.,* unconscious, insensible.

conscription, *n.* enlistment, draft, impressment. See COMPULSION, WARFARE.

consecrate, *v.t.* bless, sanctify, hallow; seal, dedicate, devote. See PIETY, REPUTE, CLERGY.

consecutive, *adj.* See CONTINUITY, SEQUENCE. *Ant.,* broken, intermittent.

consensus, *n.* concord, ASSENT, AGREEMENT; general *or* popular opinion, common belief; poll[ing], sampling; silent majority.

CONSENT
Voluntary compliance

Nouns—consent, ASSENT, acquiescence; approval, APPROBATION; compliance, AGREEMENT, concession; yielding, accession, allowance, acceptance; ratification, confirmation; permit, PERMISSION, PROMISE.

Verbs—consent, ASSENT, yield, allow, concede, grant, deign; come over, come [a]round; give in, give consent, comply with, acquiesce, agree to, fall in with, accede, accept, embrace an offer, close with, take at one's word, have no objection; satisfy, meet one's wishes, come to terms; turn a willing ear (see WILL); jump at; deign, vouchsafe.

Adjectives—consenting, acquiescent, compliant, willing, easy, docile, amenable, agreeable; permissible; agreed; unconditional.

Adverbs—yes, willingly, by all means, of course, if you please, as you please.

Interjections—be it so! amen! so be it! well and good!

Phrases—silence means consent.

Antonyms, see REFUSAL.

---

consequence, *n.* EFFECT, end, result, sequel, outcome, product, fruit; import, account, concern, interest, significance, matter, moment; notability, esteem, greatness, value, prominence; self-importance, arrogance, pomposity. See IMPORTANCE. *Ant.,* cause.

consequential, *adj.* consequent, sequen-

tial; inferable, deducible; indirect, resultant, resulting; important, of consequence. See EFFECT, IMPORTANCE, CIRCUMSTANCE. *Ant.,* unimportant.

consequently, *adv.* therefore (see CIRCUMSTANCE).

conservation, *n.* maintenance, protection, keeping, PRESERVATION. See STORE.

conservative, *adj.* unprogressive; moderate; protective; unchanging, stable; reactionary, mossback, diehard, Tory. See PERMANENCE. *Ant.*, liberal, radical.

conservatory, *n.* greenhouse, nursery; SCHOOL, academy. See AGRICULTURE.

conserve, *v.t.* See STORE, PRESERVATION.

consider, *v.* deliberate, ponder, brood, contemplate, meditate, ruminate, reflect; speculate, turn, revolve, weigh, muse; believe, judge, deem; regard, take into account, heed, mark, notice, mind; entertain; esteem. See ATTENTION, THOUGHT, RESPECT, JUDGMENT, BELIEF.

considerable, *adj.* large, sizable, substantial, important, big; tolerable, fair, respectable; material, noteworthy, weighty. See GREATNESS, SIZE.

considerate, *adj.* thoughtful, kind, humane, sympathetic. See CARE, BENEVOLENCE. *Ant.*, inconsiderate, unfeeling.

consideration, *n.* THOUGHT, deliberation, contemplation, reflection, rumination; CARE, regard; esteem, deference; ATTENTION, notice; IMPORTANCE, consequence; motive, reason, ground, basis; gratuity, fee, COMPENSATION. See BENEVOLENCE, RESPECT, CAUSE, QUALIFICATION.

consign, *v.t.* deliver, commit, assign, delegate; remit, remand; send, dispatch, ship, condemn. See TRANSFER, COMMISSION, APPORTIONMENT.

consignee, *n.* committee; functionary, curator, treasurer; AGENT, factor, bailiff, clerk, proctor, underwriter, factotum, DIRECTOR; negotiator, go-between; middleman; employee; SERVANT, caretaker.

consignment, *n.* goods, shipment; delivery, consignation, commitment; allotment, assignment. See APPORTIONMENT, COMMISSION, TRANSFER.

consist, *v.i.* lie, reside, inhere; include, comprise. See EXISTENCE, COMPOSITION.

consistency, *n.* solidity, DENSITY; harmony, correspondence. See AGREEMENT, REGULARITY.

consistent, *adj.* accordant, coherent, uniform, congruous, compatible, consonant, harmonious; reconcilable; homogeneous, regular. See AGREEMENT, UNITY, REGULARITY.

consolation, *n.* condolence, solace, sympathy; assuagement, sop; encouragement. See RELIEF.

console, *v.t.* See RELIEF. —*n.* SUPPORT, bracket; cabinet, floor model. See RECEPTACLE.

consolidate, *v.t.* unite, join, combine, federate, syndicate, merge, pool, fuse, incorporate; compress, solidify, strengthen. See COMBINATION, DENSITY, UNITY.

consonance, *n.* AGREEMENT, harmony; UNITY, accordance, concord.

consort, *n.* spouse, husband, wife. See ACCOMPANIMENT. —*v.* associate, fraternize. See SOCIALITY.

consortium, *n.* cartel, syndicate; meeting, colloquium. See COMBINATION, CONVERSATION.

conspectus, *n.* compendium, epitome. See SHORTNESS.

conspicuous, *adj.* prominent, notable, eminent, outstanding; signal, striking, salient, noticeable, obvious, marked; glaring, obtrusive, notorious, flagrant. See REPUTE, VISIBILITY. *Ant.*, inconspicuous, hidden.

conspire, *v.i.* plot, intrigue, collude, scheme; concur, combine. See PLAN, COOPERATION.

constant, *adj.* staunch, steadfast, loyal; fast, firm, unwavering, unchanging, unswerving, unflagging; permanent, abiding, enduring; steady, stable; regular, even; continual, incessant. See PROBITY, STABILITY, FREQUENCY, PERPETUITY, TENACITY, PERMANENCE, CONTINUITY, REGULARITY.

constellation, *n.* cluster, asterism; sign of the zodiac; ASSEMBLAGE, confluence, gathering. See UNIVERSE.

consternation, *n.* dismay, FEAR.

constipate, *v.t.* clog, stop up (see CLOSURE, DENSITY).

constituency, *n.* constituents, following; clientele; electorate, voters; district, ward. See CHOICE.

constituent, *adj.* integral, formative; elective, appointive, electoral. —*n.* component, PART; voter, supporter, elector (see CHOICE).

constitute, *v.t.* form, be, make, frame, compose; total; set up, establish, found; appoint. See COMPOSITION, PRODUCTION.

constitution, *n.* nature, makeup, temperament, physique, disposition; structure, construction; state, condition; bylaws, code, charter; designation, settlement;

creation, foundation. See COMPOSITION, LEGALITY, INTRINSIC.

constraint, *n.* pressure, force, stress; RESTRAINT, confinement, repression; reserve, embarrassment, stiffness; COMPULSION, coercion, NECESSITY, duress. See MODESTY.

constrict, *v.t.* hamper, limit, contract, bind, cramp, squeeze, compress; choke, strangle, strangulate. See CONTRACTION.

construction, *n.* building, fabrication, COMPOSITION; formation, structure, erection; conformation; creation; explanation, INTERPRETATION. See FORM, PRODUCTION.

consul, *n.* emissary, resident. See AGENT.

consult, *v.* confer, refer (to). See ADVICE, CONVERSATION.

consume, *v.t.* destroy, demolish, annihilate; burn, decompose, corrode; devour, swallow, eat, drink; exhaust, drain, use up, expend. See DESTRUCTION, USE, WASTE.

consumer, *n.* customer, purchaser, user. See PURCHASE, USE.

consummate, *adj.* complete, perfect, finished, absolute. —*v.t.* complete, achieve, accomplish; perfect. See COMPLETION, PERFECTION.

consumption, *n.* DESTRUCTION, USE, burning; tuberculosis. See DISEASE, WASTE.

contact, *n.* intermediary, middleman (see AGENT). —*v., informal,* get in touch (with). See CONTACT.

CONTACT
Touching of two things

Nouns—contact, contiguity, abutment, TOUCH, CONNECTION; osculation; meeting, encounter, border[land], frontier, tangent. See NEARNESS.

Verbs—be in contact, be contiguous, join, adjoin, abut; butt; TOUCH, meet, encounter, run *or* bump into, meet up with, come *or* chance upon, happen on, run *or* come across, fall on; osculate, come in contact, march with, rub elbows *or* shoulders, keep in touch, hobnob. See JUNCTION.

Adjectives—in contact, contiguous, adjacent, touching; bordering, neighboring; conterminous, end to end, osculatory; tangent, tangential; hand to hand; close to, in touch with, shoulder to shoulder, cheek by jowl.

Prepositions—against, upon.

Quotations—Ships that pass in the night, and speak each other in passing (*Longfellow*).

Antonyms, see INTERVAL, DISTANCE.

contagion, *n.* infection; epidemic, pestilence, virus; TRANSFER, transmission. See DISEASE.

contagious, *adj.* catching, infectious, epidemic, communicable, transmittable, pestilential, noxious, contaminative. See TRANSFER, DISEASE.

contain, *v.t.* include, comprise, incorporate, embrace, embody, comprehend, hold; restrain, check. See INCLUSION, RESTRAINT.

container, *n.* vessel, RECEPTACLE.

contaminate, *v.t.* corrupt, infect, taint,

pollute, soil; defile, sully, befoul, stain, dirty; debauch, deprave, degrade. See DETERIORATION, UNCLEANNESS. *Ant.,* purify.

contemplate, *v.* consider, meditate, ponder, muse, reflect; view, behold; propose, purpose, PLAN, mean, aim, intend, design. See THOUGHT, VISION, EXPECTATION, INTENTION, LEARNING.

contemporary, *adj.* simultaneous; coexistent, contemporaneous, coeval, synchronous, coincident, concomitant. See TIME, SYNCHRONISM.

CONTEMPT
Feeling of disdain

Nouns—1, contempt, contemptuousness, disdain, scorn, despisal, contumely; DETRAC-TION, DISAPPROBATION; derision, DISRESPECT; DEFIANCE; arrogance (see INSO-LENCE); RIDICULE, mockery; hoot, catcall.

2, slight, cold shoulder, snub, rebuff; sneer, dismissal. *Informal,* dig, cut. *Slang,* slam. See REPULSION.

Verbs—1, *(feel contempt)* be contemptuous of, despise, contemn, scorn, disdain, feel contempt for; disregard, slight; not mind, pass by, look down upon; hold cheap, hold in contempt, think nothing of, think small beer of; underestimate; take no account of, care nothing for, set no store by, not care a straw, set at naught.

2, *(show contempt)* laugh up one's sleeve, snap one's fingers at, shrug one's shoulders; snub, turn up one's nose at, pooh-pooh, damn with faint praise; sneeze at, sneer at; curl one's lip, toss one's head, look down one's nose at; draw oneself up; laugh at *or* off, brush off; be disrespectful, point the finger of scorn, hold up to scorn, laugh to scorn; scout, hoot, flout, hiss, scoff at, jeer, revile, taunt (see RIDICULE); turn one's back, turn a cold shoulder, leave in the lurch *or* out in the cold; trample upon *or* un-derfoot, spurn, kick, fling to the winds. *Informal,* cut. *Slang,* diss, dump on, cut dead, frost, kiss off. See AVOIDANCE.

Adjectives—1, *(showing contempt)* contemptuous, disdainful, scornful; withering, con-tumelious, supercilious, cynical, haughty, cavalier; derisive.

2, *(deserving contempt)* contemptible, despicable; pitiable, pitiful; unimportant, de-spised, downtrodden; unenvied.

Adverbs—contemptuously, arrogantly, insolently, *etc.*

Interjections—bah! pooh! pshaw! tut! fiddle-de-dee!; away with! *Slang,* in your hat! come off it!

Phrases—familiarity breeds contempt.

Quotations—Who can refute a sneer? (*William Paley*), Silence is the most perfect ex-pression of scorn (*G. B. Shaw*).

Antonyms, see APPROBATION, RESPECT.

---

contend, *v.i.* struggle (see CONTENTION); dispute, debate (see DISCORD); main-tain, assert, argue, hold, allege. See AF-FIRMATION.

CONTENT
Satisfaction

Nouns—content, contentment, contentedness; complacency, satisfaction, ease, peace of mind, clear conscience; serenity, euphoria; CHEERFULNESS; gratification; comfort, well-being, life of Riley, bed of roses; self-content, self-satisfaction, complacency. *Slang,* fat city. See PLEASURE, RELIEF.

Verbs—1, *(be content)* rest satisfied, let well enough alone, feel *or* make oneself at home, hug oneself, take in good part; take heart, take comfort, breathe easily *or* freely; rest on one's laurels. *Informal,* have nothing to complain about; go with the flow.

2, *(make content)* tranquilize, set at rest *or* ease, comfort, set one's heart *or* mind at ease *or* rest; speak peace; content, satisfy, gratify, please, soothe, assuage, mollify. See PACIFICATION.

Adjectives—1, content[ed], satisfied, at [one's] ease, at rest, serene, at home, in clover, on cloud nine; with the mind at ease, *sans souci,* easygoing, not particular; compla-cent, imperturbable; unrepining; resigned, patient, cheerful; unafflicted, unvexed, un-molested, unplagued; snug, comfortable [as an old shoe], in one's element. *Informal,* mellow, laid-back; in like Flynn.

2, *(causing content)* satisfactory, tolerable, adequate, bearable, acceptable, desirable.

Adverbs—contentedly, to one's heart's content; all for the best.

Interjections—very well! so much the better! well and good!; that will do!

Quotations—An elegant sufficiency, content, retirement, rural quiet, friendship, books (*James Thomson*), To be contented—that's for cows (*Coco Chanel*), A jug of wine, a loaf of bread—and Thou beside me singing in the wilderness—Oh, wilderness were paradise enow! (*Edward Fitzgerald*), This is the last of earth! I am content (*J. Q. Adams*).

Antonyms, see DISCONTENT, PENITENCE.

CONTENTION
Act of contending

Nouns—1, *(act of contending)* contention, strife, contest, contestation, altercation, infighting; struggle; belligerency, pugnacity, combativeness (see IRASCIBILITY); competition, rivalry; litigation (see LAWSUIT); OPPOSITION; bone of contention.

2, *(verbal contention)* controversy, polemics (see DISCORD, REASONING). *Slang,* busting.

3, *(group contention)* battle, conflict, face-off, skirmish, dogfight, row, mixup; encounter, rencontre, rencounter; collision, affair, brush, fight; battle royal, pitched battle, *casus belli,* WARFARE; combat, action, engagement, joust, tournament; tilt[ing], tourney, list; death struggle, Armageddon; fracas, clash of arms; tussle, scuffle, brawl, fray; street fight; melée, scrimmage, bush-fighting; naval engagement, sea fight. *Informal,* set-to, free-for-all. *Slang,* shindy, scrap, run-in, hassle, dingdong, rumble, fist junction, gin. See OPPOSITION.

4, *(one on one contention)* duel, single combat, monomachy; feud, vendetta; satisfaction, passage of arms, affair of honor.

5, SPORTS, games of skill, gymkhana, Olympics, round robin, tug-of-war; match, race, relay race, foot race, dash, hurdles, Iditarod; athletics, gymnastics, *etc.*

6, life-or-death struggle, all-out *or* total war, fight to the death, last-ditch effort.

7, contender, contestant, competitor, competer, entry; militant; soldier (see COMBATANT).

Verbs—1, contend, contest, oppose, strive, struggle, fight, combat, battle, engage, skirmish; make something of; contend, grapple, *or* close with; try conclusions with, have a brush with, join issue, start something, come to blows, fall to, be at loggerheads, set to, come to scratch, meet hand to hand.

2, wrangle, scramble, wrestle, spar, exchange blows *or* fisticuffs, square off, pitch into, tussle, scuffle, tilt, box, stave, fence, encounter, take on, lay *or* light into, fall foul of, cross *or* measure swords, lock horns with; take up cudgels, the glove, *or* the gauntlet, enter the lists, couch one's lance; shoot it out; give satisfaction; lay about one, break the peace, lift one's hand against. *Informal,* pitch into. *Slang,* [put up a] scrap, rumble.

3, compete, cope, vie, *or* race with; contend for, run a race. *Slang,* drag. See SPORTS.

Adjectives—contending, at loggerheads, at cross purposes, at war, at swords' points, at issue; competitive, rival, cutthroat; belligerent; contentious, combative, bellicose, unpeaceful, on the warpath; warlike (see WARFARE); quarrelsome, pugnacious; pugilistic, fistic.

Phrases—it takes two to make a quarrel.

Quotations—There is no good in arguing with the inevitable (*James Russell Lowell*), Making noise is an effective means of opposition (*Joseph Goebbels*).

Antonyms, see PACIFICATION.

---

contents, *n.* See COMPOSITION.
contest, *v.t.* See CONTENTION.
contestant, *n.* contender, competitor, competer, *etc.* (see CONTENTION).

context, *n.* setting, background, position, situation. See ENVIRONMENT.
contiguity, *n.* juxtaposition, abutment, union, meeting. See CONTACT.

continence, *n.* self-restraint (see MODERA-
TION). *Ant.,* incontinence.

continental, *adj.* mainland (see LAND);
cosmopolitan, sophisticated, worldly,
urbane; charming. See FASHION, COUR-
TESY.

contingency, *n.* CHANCE, POSSIBILITY,
likelihood, accident, casualty, prospect;
situation, predicament, case. See CIR-
CUMSTANCE, LIABILITY, EXPECTATION.

contingent, *adj.* possible; provisional, conditional, provisory, dependent; incidental,
accidental, casual. See CHANCE, LIABIL-
ITY, CIRCUMSTANCE, QUALIFICATION.

continual, *adj.* constant; repeated, frequent. See FREQUENCY, CONTINUITY.
Ant., intermittent.

continuance, *n.* CONTINUITY; persistence,
perseverance, endurance; postponement, extension, prolongation. See
LATENESS.

continue, *v.* persist; keep, go, carry, run,
or hold on; maintain, keep up, sustain,
uphold; prolong, remain, last, endure,
withstand; protract, persevere, be permanent, stay, stick, abide; resume. See
DURABILITY, CONTINUITY. *Ant.,* stop,
cease.

CONTINUITY
Unbroken sequence

Nouns—1, continuity, continuum, SEQUENCE; round, suite, progression, series, train,
[daisy] chain; continuance, continuation, PERPETUITY; concatenation, scale. See FRE-
QUENCY, INFINITY, DURABILITY.

2, course; procession, column; retinue, caravan, cortege, cavalcade, rank and file, line
of battle, array; running fire; pedigree, genealogy (see ANCESTRY, POSTERITY); rank,
file, line, row, range, string, thread, suite; Möbius strip, endless belt, conveyor belt;
colonnade; radiothon, telethon, marathon.

Verbs—1, continue, follow in a series, form a series; fall in; arrange in a series, string together, thread, graduate; tabulate, list, file.

2, *(continue doing)* keep at, on, *or* up, carry on *or* over, keep the ball rolling, stick
with, go on. *Slang,* keep on trucking, fish or cut bait.

Adjectives—continuous, continued; consecutive, progressive, serial, unbroken, linear;
in a line, row, *or* column; uninterrupted, unintermitting, unremitting, endless, incessant, unceasing, ceaseless; perennial, evergreen; constant, chronic, continual, repeated, persistent, repeating, persisting; year-round; wall-to-wall, back-to-back.

Adverbs—continuously, *etc.*; seriatim; running, step by step, at a stretch; all along, all
the time *or* while, [a]round the clock, at every turn, day and night, 24/7; serially, seriatim, in a line; wall-to-wall, back-to-back, one after the other.

Antonyms, see DISCONTINUANCE.

---

contortion, *n.* DISTORTION, twist, dislocation, deformity; grimace. See CONVO-
LUTION.

contour, *n.* outline, profile, shape, FORM,
conformation, figure. See APPEARANCE,
CIRCUIT.

contraband, *adj.* forbidden, banned, prohibited; smuggled. See PROHIBITION,
ILLEGALITY. *Ant.,* legal.

contraception, *n.* birth control, Planned
Parenthood; rhythm method, condom,
intrauterine device, IUD, diaphragm,
the pill; zero population growth. See
HINDRANCE.

contraceptive, *adj.* See HINDRANCE.

contract, *n.* compact, AGREEMENT, PROM-
ISE, bargain, covenant, stipulation,
convention.

CONTRACTION
Shrinking

Nouns—1, *(becoming smaller)* contraction, reduction, diminution; DECREASE; shrinking,
shriveling, atrophy, astringency; emaciation, attenuation, consumption, tabescence;
abbreviation. See LITTLENESS, NARROWNESS.

2, *(becoming more compact)* condensation, compression, compactness; squeezing, choking, strangulation (see CLOSURE); cramp, seizure; contractility, compressibility. See DENSITY.

Verbs—1, (become smaller) contract, become small[er]; DECREASE, shrink, narrow, shrivel, collapse, lose flesh, reduce, deflate; decay, deteriorate (see DETERIORATION). *2, (become narrower)* diminish, draw in, narrow; constrict, constringe, astringe; condense, compress, squeeze, cramp, crimp, crush, crumple up, purse *or* pucker up; wind up, tighten, pinch, strangle; stunt, dwarf; empty; waste away; pare, attenuate, shorten (see SHORTNESS).

Adjectives—contracting, contractive, contractile; tabescent; styptic, astringent; shrunk, strangulated, wizened, stunted; compact.

Antonyms, see EXPANSION.

---

contractor, *n.* builder, architect, padrone; entrepreneur. See PRODUCTION, UNDERTAKING, BUILDING.

contradict, *v.t.* gainsay, deny, belie, controvert, refute, disprove, overthrow; dispute, DISSENT. See NEGATION. *Ant.,* confirm, accept.

contraption, *n., informal,* gadget, contrivance (see INSTRUMENTALITY).

contrariety, *n.* OPPOSITION, OBSTINACY; antagonism, DISAGREEMENT, DISOBEDIENCE.

contrary, *adj.* opposed, opposite, counter, conflicting, contradictory; unfavorable, adverse; captious, willful, perverse; hostile, antagonistic. See OPPOSITION, NEGATION, OBSTINACY. *Ant.,* favorable; obliging.

contrast, *n.* DIFFERENCE, opposition, foil, dissimilarity, unlikeness, disparity. *Ant.,* compare, SIMILARITY.

contravene, *v.t.* violate, infringe upon; oppose, contradict, conflict with, defy. See OPPOSITION, NEGATION, ILLEGALITY.

contretemps, *n.* embarrassment; mischance, mishap. See DIFFICULTY.

contribute, *v.* give, subscribe, donate; help, AID, assist; conduce, advance, tend, serve, redound, go. See GIVING, CAUSE.

contributor, *n.* giver, subscriber, donor; author, correspondent, editor, columnist, reviewer, stringer; helper. See PUBLICATION, GIVING.

contrite, *adj.* penitent, sorry (see PENITENCE). *Ant.,* unrepentant, obdurate.

contrivance, *n.* device, invention, construction, machine, apparatus, contraption *(inf.)*; PLAN, scheme, trick, stratagem. See INSTRUMENTALITY, CUNNING.

control, *v.t.* command, dominate, govern, rule, regulate, direct, master; restrain, subdue, modify, check; test, verify. —*n.*

COMMAND, mastery, domination, sway, upper hand, POWER, regimentation, government, direction, management, dominion; RESTRAINT, ceiling, regulation. See AUTHORITY, EVIDENCE.

controversy, *n.* contention, dispute, argument, DISCORD, discussion, debate, quarrel, wrangle, altercation.

controvert, *v.t.* deny, contradict, contravene, traverse *(legal)*, impugn, refute, confute, oppose, argue against, dispute, counter, debate. See NEGATION. *Ant.,* confirm, support.

contumacy, *n.* rebelliousness, DISOBEDIENCE.

contumely, *n.* insult, abuse. See CONTEMPT, DISAPPROBATION, DISRESPECT.

contusion, *n.* bruise, black-and-blue [mark]. See DISEASE.

conundrum, *n.* riddle, enigma, puzzle. See SECRET.

convalesce, *v.i.* recover, recuperate, rally, revive, improve. See HEALTH, RESTORATION.

convene, *v.* assemble, gather, collect, congregate, meet, convoke. See ASSEMBLAGE.

convenience, *n.* accessibility, handiness, availability, suitability; advantage, accommodation, comfort, opportunity, ease. See UTILITY, EXPEDIENCE. *Ant.,* inconvenience, unsuitability.

convent, *n.* cloister, nunnery. See TEMPLE.

convention, *n.* assembly, gathering, congregation, congress, meeting, caucus, COUNCIL; convocation; RULE, custom, usage, formality, practice; propriety, conventionality. See FASHION, ASSEMBLAGE, CONFORMITY.

conventional, *adj.* customary, accepted, orthodox, approved, habitual, usual; formal. See CONFORMITY, HABIT. *Ant.,* unconventional, foreign.

CONVERGENCE
Inclination toward each other

Nouns—convergence, confluence, conflux, concourse; centralization, concentration, corradiation; collision course; bottleneck, funnel; appulse, meeting; focus, focal point, asymptote. See APPROACH, ASSEMBLAGE, NEARNESS, MIDDLE, CROSSING.

Verbs—converge, come together, unite; meet, close with, close in upon; centralize, center round, center in; enter in; pour in; concentrate, bring into focus; home in (on); crowd, press.

Adjectives—convergent, confluent, concurrent; centripetal; asymptotic.
Antonyms, see DEVIATION.

conversant, *adj.* acquainted, [well-]informed; skilled, versed, practiced, proficient. See KNOWLEDGE, SKILL.

CONVERSATION
Social talk

Nouns—1, conversation, interlocution, intercourse; collocution, colloquy, converse, discussion, talkfest; confabulation; talk, discourse, social intercourse; oral communication, communion, commerce; dialogue, duologue; feast of reason. *Informal,* confab. *Slang,* bull session *or* fest, he-said-she-said, gabfest, rap session, facemail.

2, *(inconsequential talk)* chat, chitchat, causerie, tête-à-tête; small talk, table talk, idle talk; comment, gossip, pillow talk (see INFORMATION); tittle-tattle, prattle (see LOQUACITY); on dit; talk of the town; glittering generalities. *Slang,* schmooze.

3, *(formal discussion group)* conference, consortium, parley, palaver, consultation; interview, audience, press conference, audition, pourparler; conversazione; congress, COUNCIL; debate, logomachy, war of words; panel discussion, symposium, colloquium, forum; teleconference, conference call. *Informal,* powwow, huddle, sit-down.

4, *(one who converses)* interlocutor, conversationalist, colloquist, dialogist, talker, spokesman, interpreter; Paul Pry; chatterer (see LOQUACITY).

Verbs—1, *(talk in a conversation)* converse, talk together, discuss; confabulate; hold a conversation, carry on *or* engage in a conversation, make conversation; put in a word; shine in conversation; bandy words, parley, palaver, chat, gossip; fence *or* spar with; compare notes. *Informal,* go into a huddle, rap. *Informal,* talk nineteen to the dozen. *Slang,* visit, coze, chew the fat *or* the rag; shoot, fan, *or* bat the breeze, let one's hair down. See SOCIALITY.

2, *(converse with)* discourse, confer, consult, advise, confer, *or* commune with; hold converse, hold a conference; interview; talk it over, hash out, go into; be closeted with, talk in private. *Informal,* touch base with.

Adjectives—conversing, talking; interlocutory; conversational, conversationable, discursive, chatty, sociable; colloquial.

Adverbs—conversationally, colloquially.

Quotations—Teas, where small talk dies in agonies (*Percy Bysshe Shelley*), I cannot hold with those who wish to put down the insignificant chatter of the world (*Anthony Trollope*), "The time has come," the Walrus said, "To talk of many things . . ." (*Lewis Carroll*), Most English talk is a quadrille in a sentry-box (*Henry James*).

converse, *adj.* transposed, reversed, turned about; reciprocal; other, opposite, contrary. See OPPOSITION. —*n.* reverse, contrary, opposite; counterpart, reciprocal; vice versa. —*v.* See CONVERSATION.

conversion, *n.* reduction, CHANGE; retooling, changeover, adaptation; transmogrification; alchemy; RESOLUTION, assimilation; reformation; sex change.

convert, *v.t.* CHANGE, make over; retool, adapt; reorganize, remodel, regenerate;

reduce, transmute, transform, transmo-
grify, render; exchange. —*n.* neophyte,

disciple; renegade, apostate; transsexual. See CHANGEABILITY. *Ant.,* retain.

CONVEXITY
Curved like the outside surface of a sphere or circle

Nouns—1, *(shape)* convexity, prominence, projection, swell[ing], bulge, protuberance, protrusion, growth, lump; stud. See ROTUNDITY.

2, *(convex object)* excrescence, tumescence, outgrowth, tumor, tubercle, tuberosity; hump, hunch, bunch; tooth, knob, elbow; bulb, node, nodule; tongue; pimple, wen, weal, postule, sarcoma, carbuncle, corn, wart, furuncle, polyp, fungus, blister, boil, proud flesh (see DISEASE); papilla; breast, bosom, nipple, teat, mammilla; nose, proboscis, beak, snout; belly; withers, humpback; shoulder, lip; [speed] bump. *Informal,* pot, zit, burble, goober, sleeping policeman. *Slang,* corporation. See BODY.

3, *(landmass having convex shape)* hill, HEIGHT, cape, promontory, headland; peninsula, neck, isthmus, point of land; reef; mole, jetty, ledge, spur.

4, *(convex arthitectural feature)* cupola, dome, vault, arch, extrados, balcony, eaves; pilaster; boss; relief, bas-relief, cameo.

Verbs—project, bulge, protrude, pout, bunch; billow; jut, stand, stick, *or* poke out; start up, shoot up *or* out; arch, vault; swell, bag, bloat, intumesce, hang over, bend over; beetle; raise, emboss, chase.

Adjectives—convex, prominent, protuberant; projecting; bossed; nodular, bunchy; clavate; mammiform, papulous; hemispheric, bulbous; bowed, parched; bold; bellied; tuberous, tuberculous; humpbacked, gibbous; tumid, tumorous; cornute, odontoid; lentiform, lenticular; salient, in relief, raised, repoussé; bloated.

Antonyms, see CONCAVITY.

---

convey, *v.t.* bear, carry, transport; transmit, impart, communicate; TRANSFER, grant, cede, will. See INFORMATION, TRANSPORTATION.

conveyance, *n.* VEHICLE; TRANSFER, assignment, sale, legacy, disposal; transmission, communication. See INFORMATION.

convict, *v.t.* condemn, find guilty, doom. See CONDEMNATION, JUDGMENT. —*n.* criminal, felon, jailbird, prisoner, captive. See PRISON. *Ant.,* acquit.

conviction, *n.* BELIEF, persuasion, faith, opinion, view; CONDEMNATION, sentence, penalty.

convince, *v.t.* persuade, satisfy. See BELIEF.

conviviality, *n.* SOCIALITY, sociability, festivity, gaiety, joviality.

convoke, *v.t.* convene, assemble, summon, call, collect, gather. See ASSEMBLAGE.

convoluted, *adj.* complicated (see DIFFICULTY); twisting, tortuous. See CONVOLUTION.

CONVOLUTION
Shape like a coil

Nouns—1, convolution, winding; involution, circumvolution; wave, undulation, tortuosity, anfractuosity; intricacy; sinuosity, sinuation; meandering, circuit; twist, twirl, windings and turnings; ambages; torsion; reticulation (see CROSSING). *Informal,* [body] English. See CIRCUITY, ROTATION.

2, *(coiled shape)* coil, roll, curl, curlicue, buckle, spiral, helix, corkscrew, worm, volute, tendril; skein; scallop, escalop; serpent, eel; maze, labyrinth; ringlet, curl, braid.

3, [hair] curler, curling iron.

Verbs—convolve, be convoluted, wind, twine, turn and twist, twirl; wave, undulate, meander; entwine, twist, coil, roll; wrinkle, curl [up], crisp, friz[z], frizzle; crimp, scallop; wring, intort, contort.

Adjectives—convoluted; winding, twisting, tortile, tortuous; wavy; undulatory; circling, snaky, snakelike, serpentine; anguilliform, vermiform, vermicular; mazy, sinuous, involute, flexuous, sigmoidal; spiral, coiled, helical, turbinated; involved, intricate, complicated, perplexed (see DISORDER); labyrinthine.

Adverbs—convolutely, in and out, round and round.

Antonyms, see DIRECTION.

---

convoy, *v.t.* accompany, escort, conduct; guard, support. See ACCOMPANIMENT. —*n.* escort, [body]guard, safe-conduct; caravan. See ACCOMPANIMENT, ASSEMBLAGE, SAFETY.

convulse, *v.t.* agitate, shake, disturb, trouble, excite, stir; rend, wring, hurt. See AGITATION, PAIN, REVOLUTION, VIOLENCE.

cook, *v.t.* prepare, concoct, fix; make; roast, broil, boil, fry, *etc.; informal,* doctor; *slang,* ruin, spoil. See FOOD, HEAT, DETERIORATION, FALSEHOOD.

cooking, *n.* cookery, cuisine; culinary art. See PREPARATION, FOOD.

cookie, *n.* wafer, biscuit; shortbread, sugar cookie, gingersnap, *etc.* See FOOD.

cookout, *n.* barbecue, picnic. See FOOD.

cool, *v.* chill, refrigerate, ice, freeze, harden; calm, allay. See DISSUASION, REFRESHMENT. —*adj.* COLD, chilly, frigid; inexcitable, self-controlled, calm, deliberate, composed; indifferent, unemotional, self-possessed; easygoing, placid; unfriendly, distant, lukewarm; *slang,* great, fine. See COLD, MODERATION, INEXCITABILITY, MALEVOLENCE, GOODNESS. —**cool off,** *informal,* relax, take it easy; compose oneself, calm down. See INEXCITABILITY.

COOPERATION
Working toward a common goal

Nouns—1, *(act of cooperating)* cooperation, coadjuvancy, coadjutancy; coagency, coefficiency, concert, concurrence, participation, collaboration, coexistence; bipartisanship; cogeneration; COMBINATION, collusion, complicity, conspiracy, connivance, fraternization; teamwork, solidarity; symbiosis. *Informal,* old boy network.

2, *(cooperative group)* association, alliance, colleagueship, [co]partnership; confederation, affiliation, coalition, bloc, fusion (see COMBINATION); cooperative, co-op, commune; logrolling, give-and-take; common ground, unanimity (see ASSENT); esprit de corps, party *or* team spirit; clanship, partisanship. See PARTY, AGREEMENT.

Verbs—1, cooperate, coexist; concur; conspire, collaborate, collude, connive, fraternize, concert, lay heads together, get together; confederate, affiliate, be in league with; unite one's efforts; keep, pull, club, hang, hold, league, *or* band together; be banded together, stand shoulder to shoulder, be in the same boat, act in concert, put one's heads together, pool resources, line up, gang up, join forces, understand one another, get along, hunt in couples; split the difference (see COMPROMISE). *Informal,* play ball, team *or* hook up.

2, *(cooperate with)* side with, go *or* play along with, sign up, go hand in hand with, join hands with, make common cause with, chime in, pitch in, go along for the ride, unite *or* join with, mix oneself up with, pull one's weight, hold up one's end, take part in, cast in one's lot with, enter into partnership with, throw in with, line up with; go around with, hang *or* stick together; play politics. *Informal,* throw in with. *Slang,* play footsie with, get into bed with.

3, be a party to, be in on, lend oneself to, participate, have *or* keep a hand in, have a finger in the pie, take part in, chip in; second, AID.

Adjectives—cooperating, in cooperation *or* league; coadjuvant, coadjutant; cooperative, coefficient, collegial; participatory, partaking; favorable to; unopposed. *Informal,* in cahoots with.

Adverbs—cooperatively; as one man, together, unanimously, shoulder to shoulder, side by side, hand in hand, hand in glove, in common, share and share alike, pro rata.

Prepositions—with, in cooperation with, in league with.

Phrases—politics make strange bedfellows; four eyes see better than two; a chain is no stronger than its weakest link; united we stand, divided we fall.

Quotations—Government and cooperation are in all things the laws of life (*John Ruskin*).

Antonyms, see OPPOSITION.

coordinate, *v.t.* equalize, adapt, harmonize, synchronize, adjust; organize. See ARRANGEMENT.

cop, *v.* seize, grap, take; steal, filch, pilfer; win, capture. See ACQUISITION, STEALING. —*n.*, *slang,* policeman (see SAFETY).

cope, *v.i.* contend, strive, deal with; face; manage, handle. See CONTENTION.

copious, *adj.* abundant, plentiful, ample, overflowing; wordy, profuse, diffuse, prolix. See SUFFICIENCY. *Ant.,* meager, scanty.

cop out, *v.i. slang,* renege, back out (see AVOIDANCE).

copulate, *v.i.* unite, join, couple; mate; have coitus *or* sex; cohabit, breed, fornicate, make love, live together, have relations. See MARRIAGE, JUNCTION.

COPY
Reproduction

Nouns—1, copy, facsimile, counterpart, effigy, form, semblance, cast[ing], ecotype, fake; IMITATION; model, study, portrait (see REPRESENTATION); tracing; duplicate; photocopy, instant copy, Ditto, Ozalid, Xerox, Photostat, hectograph, mimeograph; transcript[ion], apograph; reflex, reflection, mirror; replica, clone; shadow, echo; chip off the old block; print, reprint, reproduction, second edition; REPETITION, apograph, fair copy. *Informal,* carbon [copy]. *Slang,* dupe, spit and image, dead ringer, knockoff. See PRINTING, WRITING, IDENTITY, SIMILARITY.

2, copying, duplication, reproduction; reverse engineering; photocopying, xerography, mimeography, hectography.

3, parody, caricature (see RIDICULE); paraphrase, IMITATION; counterfeit, forgery (see DECEPTION). *Slang,* phony, fake.

4, *(person or machine that copies)* copyist, transcriber; telecopier, photocopier, Xerox, [tele]fax, scanner, *etc.*; scribe, plagiarist; ape, parrot (see IMITATION).

Verbs—copy, duplicate, imitate, reproduce, trace, transcribe; Xerox, photocopy, Photostat, facsimile, fax, hectograph, ditto; trace; plagiarize, crib; parody, mimic, forge, counterfeit; echo; reprint; clone. *Informal,* fake. *Slang,* knock off.

Adjectives—faithful; lifelike, similar (see SIMILARITY).

Antonyms, see IDENTITY, DIFFERENCE.

---

coquette, *n.* flirt. See ENDEARMENT.

cord, *n.* string, rope, band, bond, twine; tendon; cable. See FILAMENT, CONNECTION.

cordial, *adj.* sincere, heartfelt; hearty, genial, friendly, amicable, kindly. See COURTESY, FEELING. —*n.* liqueur (see DRINKING).

core, *n.* center, interim, heart, nucleus, kernel, pith; nut, nub, SUBSTANCE, gist. See MIDDLE, IMPORTANCE, INTRINSIC.

cork, *n.* stopper, plug, bung; float, bob. —*v.t.* stop, plug, bung, seal. See CLOSURE, MATERIALS.

corkscrew, *n.* bottle opener (see OPENING). —*adj.* twisted, tortuous. See CONVOLUTION.

corner, *n.* angle; nook, niche; control, monopoly; predicament; tight spot. See ANGULARITY, POSSESSION, DIFFICULTY. —cut corners, economize, save money; take a shortcut. See ECONOMY, SHORTNESS.

cornerstone, *n.* keystone, salient point. See IMPORTANCE, BUILDING.

cornucopia, *n.* horn of plenty *or* of Amalthea. See SUFFICIENCY.

corny, *adj., slang,* sentimental, mushy, sticky; old-fashioned, stale, musty, banal, sticky. See SENSIBILITY.

corollary, *n.* adjunct, offshoot. See JUDGMENT, ACCOMPANIMENT.

corona, *n.* halo, crown, aureola. See LIGHT.

coronary, *adj.* coronal, crownlike, ringlike, round, circular. See CIRCULARITY. —*n.* [coronary] thrombosis, heart attack, apoplexy, paralysis, stroke. See DISEASE.

coronation, *n.* crowning, investment. See COMMISSION.

corporation, *n.* association, syndicate, company, society, partnership, merger, trust. See PARTY, BUSINESS.

corporeal, *adj.* bodily, material. See BODY, SUBSTANCE. *Ant.,* spiritual, intangible.

corps, *n.* body, company, outfit, branch, service. See ASSEMBLAGE, COMBATANT.

corpse, *n.* cadaver (see DEATH).

corpulence, *n.* fatness, fleshiness, obesity, plumpness, portliness, bulk. See SIZE, ROTUNDITY. *Ant.*, emaciation, thinness.

corpus delicti, *Lat.* facts, EVIDENCE.

corral, *n.* pen, yard. —*v.t.* pen up; seize, collect. See ENCLOSURE, ACQUISITION.

correct, *v.t.* improve, rectify, [set] right, remedy, repair, amend, reform, better; edit, mark; reprove, punish, chastise, discipline; counteract, neutralize. See IMPROVEMENT, PUNISHMENT. —*adj.* right, regular, true, strict, accurate, exact, precise, perfect; proper, comme il faut, right on (*sl.*). See RIGHTNESS, ELEGANCE.

correlation, *n.* correlativity; reciprocation, reciprocity; mutuality; interrelation, correspondence; analogy, likeness. See RELATION.

CORRESPONDENCE
Communication by letter, *etc.*

Nouns—1, correspondence, communication by letter, postcard, *etc.*, letter writing; personal *or* business correspondence; mail-order selling (see SALE).

2, a. letter, epistle, note; billet, billet doux, love letter; aerogram; [picture] postcard; poison-pen letter, fan letter, Dear John letter, round robin, bread-and-butter letter; missive, favor; dispatch, these presents; rescript (see ANSWER); cover letter, form letter, circular, newsletter (see PUBLICATION); open letter; round robin, chain *or* circular letter; first-, second-(*etc.*)class mail; drop letter, express mail, post, mail, air mail, special delivery *or* handling, priority mail, *etc.*; letter of resignation; letter of CREDIT. *Informal*, snail mail. b. letterhead, inside address, salutation, letter body, complimentary close, address, destination, enclosure, attachment, P.S., P.P.S.

3, a. mail, post, postal service; post office, post office box, P.O. box, general post office, GPO; mailbox, postbox, letter box; mail drop; mail bag; postage, stamp, postmark, postage meter; mail carrier, mailman, mailwoman; ZIP code, ZIP + 4, postal code; Express Mail, Priority Post, Federal Express, FedEx, United Postal Service, UPS, *etc.*; Pony Express, stage coach; poste restante. b. electronic mail, e-mail; mail server; Eudora, Outlook Express. See COMPUTERS.

4, correspondent, letter writer; pen pal.

Verbs—correspond, write; write to, send *or* post a letter to, keep up a correspondence (with); write back, acknowledge, ANSWER, reply, RSVP; mail, send, post. *Informal*, drop a line.

Adjectives—postal; epistolary; mail-order.

Adverbs—by mail, by letter.

Phrases—RSVP.

Quotations—Sir, more than kisses, letters mingle souls (*John Donne*), Correspondences are like small-clothes before the invention of suspenders; it is impossible to keep them up (*Sydney Smith*).

---

corridor, *n.* hall, hallway, gallery, arcade, PASSAGE; skyway, airway, route.

corrigible, *adj.* amendable, rectifiable; amenable, tractable, docile. See IMPROVEMENT. *Ant.*, incorrigible, inveterate.

corroborate, *v.t.* confirm (see EVIDENCE, ASSENT, DEMONSTRATION). *Ant.*, contradict.

corrode, *v.* consume, gnaw, rust, decay, wear; eat, etch. See DETERIORATION.

corrugate, *v.t.* FURROW, wrinkle, groove. See ROUGHNESS.

corrupt, *v.t.* demoralize, vitiate, deprave, defile, degrade, debase, debauch; bribe, pervert; contaminate, spoil, taint. —*adj.* wicked, demoralized, immoral, impure, dissolute, depraved, profligate, base; vicious; rotten, infected, tainted, spoiled. See IMPROBITY, UNCLEANNESS, EVIL, DECOMPOSITION, DETERIORATION, WRONG. *Ant.*, pure, clean; cleanse, purify.

corsage, *n.* bouquet, boutonniere. See ORNAMENT.

corset, *n.* girdle, foundation [garment]. See CLOTHING.

cortege, *n.* procession; retinue. See CONTINUITY, ACCOMPANIMENT.

cosmetic, *adj.* beautifying, adorning, decorative. —*n.* preparation, makeup; war paint, face, mask (*all sl.*). See BEAUTY.

cosmic, *adj.* universal, galactic, heavenly; vast, grandiose; harmonious, orderly. See UNIVERSE, ORDER.

cosmopolitan, *adj.* sophisticated, urbane, worldly[-wise], polished; informed, tolerant. See KNOWLEDGE, COURTESY, ABODE.

cost, *n.* PRICE, charge, expense; expenditure, outlay, disbursement, PAYMENT.

costly, *adj.* expensive, high-priced, dear, precious, valuable; extravagant; gorgeous, sumptuous. See DEARNESS. *Ant.,* cheap.

costume, *n.* CLOTHING; fancy dress, uniform; outfit, rig. See CONCEALMENT.

cot, *n.* bed, pallet, couch, roll-away [bed]. See SUPPORT.

coterie, *n.* set, clique. See PARTY.

cotillion, *n.* german; ball, square dance. See AMUSEMENT.

cottage, *n.* bungalow (see ABODE).

couch, *n.* bed, cot, pallet; lounge, divan, settee, convertible, davenport, chaise longue. See SUPPORT, LAYER, HORIZONTAL. —*v.t.* express, frame (see MEANING).

cough, *n.* hack, racking cough. See DISEASE.

COUNCIL
Deliberative assembly

Nouns—1, council, committee, subcommittee, panel, advisory council, brain trust, comitia, chamber, board, bench, directory, chapter, syndicate, junta, camarilla, cabal, clique; cabinet, privy council, troika; council of war; senate, upper house, house of representatives, lower house; parliament, chamber of deputies, legislature, congress, diet, divan; county council, city council; court, forum, tribunal, court of appeal[s]; consistory; diocesan, plenary, *or* ecumenical council; Council of Trent *or* Nicaea, Vatican Council, Lateran Council; vestry; grievance committee; council fire. *Informal,* brain trust.

2, convention, assembly (see ASSEMBLAGE).

3, *(member of a committee)* statesman, senator, congressman, representative, member of parliament, M.P., council member, councilperson, councilor, councilman *or* -woman, assemblyman, legislator; majority leader, minority whip *or* leader; conventioneer; jurist, judge, justice.

Verbs—sit, assemble; sit on; deliberate, debate; serve, attend, hold court.

Adjectives—conciliar; consultative, consultatory, consultory; bicameral, unicameral.

Adverbs—in council, committee, session, executive session, conference, *etc.*

Phrases—a committee is a group of the unwilling, chosen from the unfit, to do the unnecessary.

Quotations—Committee—a group of men who individually can do nothing but as a group decide that nothing can be done (*Fred Allen*), A camel is a horse designed by a committee (*Alec Issigonis*), A cul-de-sac down which ideas are lured, and then quietly strangled (*Sir Barnett Cocks*).

---

counsel, *v.t. & n.* See ADVICE.

count, *v.* enumerate, tell, score, figure, account; matter, reckon; deem, consider, estimate. See JUDGMENT, NUMERATION, NOBILITY.

countenance, *n.* face, features, visage, physiognomy, mug (*sl.*); expression, complexion, aspect; approval, sanction, acceptance, favor, patronage. —*v.t.* AID, encourage; tolerate. See APPEARANCE, APPROBATION, FRONT.

counter, *adj.* opposing, opposite, contrary, counterclockwise, cross, against.

—*v.t.* oppose; contradict; retaliate. See OPPOSITION, RETALIATION.

counteract, *v.t.* check, thwart, nullify, negate, frustrate; counterbalance, offset; contravail, neutralize, render harmless. See OPPOSITION, COMPENSATION.

counterattack, *n.* reprisal, RETALIATION.

counterfeit, *adj.* false, sham, fake, forged, bogus, bastard, spurious, phony (*inf.*). —*n.* forgery, fake, slug, sham, brummagem, dummy, pretense, phony (*inf.*). See DECEPTION, IMITATION, COPY.

countermand, *v.t.* revoke, overrule. See NULLIFICATION.

counterpane, *n.* bedspread, coverlet. See COVERING.

counterpart, *n.* COPY, duplicate, double, facsimile, replica; likeness, image, similitude, match, parallel, twin, mate; complement. See SIMILARITY.

counterpoise, *n.* balance, equilibrium, equipoise; counterweight. See COMPENSATION.

counterproductive, *adj.* impractical, self-defeating, ill-advised. See IMPOTENCE, USELESSNESS.

countersign, *n.* password, shibboleth, watchword. See INDICATION.

countless, *adj.* innumerable, infinite, numberless, uncountable, incalculable, illimitable. See MULTITUDE, INFINITY. *Ant.,* finite.

country, *n.* land, REGION, tract, district, territory; countryside, plain, fields, the sticks (*inf.*); state, people, fatherland, home, nation; power.

countryman, *n.* national, citizen, compatriot; rustic, farmer, hayseed (*inf.*), rube (*sl.*), hick (*sl.*). See FRIEND, POPULACE.

coup, *n.* stroke, master stroke. See IMPULSE, SKILL, CUNNING.

coup de grâce, *Fr.* finishing blow, mercy killing. See KILLING, COMPLETION, PITY.

coup de maître, *Fr.* master stroke. See SKILL, SUCCESS.

coup d'état, *Fr.* political stroke, coup. See REVOLUTION.

coup d'œil, *Fr.* glance. See VISION.

couple, *v.t.* join, tie, link; yoke, unite, pair; marry. See JUNCTION, MARRIAGE.

coupon, *n.* certificate, ticket, slip; premium *or* trading stamp. See INDICATION, RECORD.

COURAGE
Lack of fear

Nouns—1, courage, bravery, valor; boldness, strength; daring, gallantry, heroism, intrepidity; DEFIANCE, audacity; RASHNESS, brinkmanship; confidence, self-reliance; chivalry, prowess, derring-do; RESOLUTION.

2, manliness, manhood; nerve, pluck, backbone, grit, mettle, game; fearlessness, foolhardiness; heart, heart of grace; hardihood, fortitude; heart of oak. *Informal,* spunk, sand, what it takes; shot in the arm. *Slang,* guts, crust, moxie, hair, balls, cojones.

3, *(act of courage)* exploit, feat, enterprise, [heroic] deed *or* act; bold stroke.

4, *(courageous person)* man *or* woman of courage *or* mettle; hero[ine], demigod-[dess]; lion, tiger, panther, bulldog; fire-eater; David, Hector, knight in shining armor.

Verbs—1, be courageous, dare, venture, make bold, brave, beard, defy, face up to, face, meet, stand up to; put a bold face upon, show fight, brave it out; go through fire and water, run the gantlet; bell the cat, take the bull by the horns, beard the lion in his den. *Informal,* face the music, put one's life on the line.

2, *(summon one's courage)* take muster; summon up, screw up, *or* pluck up courage; get up the nerve, nerve *or* steel oneself, take heart, keep one's chin up, keep a stiff upper lip; hold up one's head, screw one's courage to the sticking place, whistle in the dark; come up to scratch, stand to one's guns, stand against; bear up (against). *Slang,* stand the gaff, keep a stiff upper lip, hang tough, keep one's chin *or* pecker up.

3, give *or* inspire courage, hearten, reassure, encourage, nerve, put upon one's mettle, rally, raise a rallying cry; make a man of. See CHEERFULNESS.

Adjectives—1, courageous, brave; valiant, valorous; gallant, intrepid; mettlesome, plucky, gritty, bold as brass; manly, manful; resolute; stout, hardy, stout-hearted; iron-hearted, lion-hearted; enterprising, adventurous, venturous, venturesome; dashing, chivalrous; soldierly, warlike, heroic; strong-minded, hardy, doughty; firm, determined, dogged, indomitable, persevering. *Slang,* gutsy, ballsy; pot-valiant.

2, *(fearless)* bold, bold-spirited, daring, audacious, game; fearless, dauntless, undaunted, unappalled, undismayed, unawed, unabashed, unalarmed, unflinching, unshrinking, unblenching, unapprehensive; confident, self-reliant; bold as a lion, cool as a cucumber.

Adverbs—courageously, bravely, gallantly, boldly, heroically, intrepidly, *etc.;* like a man, like a Trojan.

Phrases—faint heart never won fair lady; fools rush in where angels fear to tread.

Quotations—Fortune sides with him who dares (*Virgil*), Courage mounteth with occasion (*Shakespeare*), No man is a hero to his valet (*Mme. Cornuel*), See, the conquering hero comes! Sound the trumpets, beat the drums! (*Thomas Morell*), Every hero becomes a bore at last (*Emerson*), Heroing is one of the shortest-lived professions there is (*Will Rogers*), Show me a hero and I will write you a tragedy (*F. Scott Fitzgerald*), One man with courage makes a majority (*Andrew Jackson*), Until the day of his death, no man can be sure of his courage (*Jean Anouilh*).

Antonyms, see COWARDICE, MODESTY, FEAR.

---

courier, *n.* messenger, runner. See COMMUNICATION.

course, *n.* channel, PASSAGE; march, progression; mode, METHOD; curriculum (see LEARNING); CIRCUIT. —*v.i.* run, flow (see FLUIDITY).

court, *v.t.* solicit, invite; curry favor, cultivate, cajole, praise; woo, sue, make love to. *Informal,* spark. —*n.* ENCLOSURE, [court]yard, quadrangle, patio; tribunal, bench, bar, jurisdiction, session; courtship, addresses, attention; palace, hall; retinue, following, train. See ENDEARMENT, ENCLOSURE, FASHION, FLATTERY, LAWSUIT, SERVANT, ABODE, COUNCIL, JUDGMENT.

courteous, *adj.* See COURTESY.

courtesan, *n.* harlot, prostitute. See IMPURITY.

COURTESY
Politeness

Nouns—1, courtesy, courteousness; RESPECT; good manners, behavior, *or* breeding; manners, politeness, urbanity, comity, gentility, breeding, cultivation, polish, grace, civility, culture, civilization, social graces; tact, diplomacy; amenity, suavity; good *or* easy temper, good humor, amiability, gentleness, soft tongue; HUMILITY, affability, gallantry, chivalry, bushido; hospitality, cordiality. See SOCIALITY, BENEVOLENCE.

2, *(act of courtesy)* compliment; fair, soft, *or* sweet words, honeyed phrases; greeting, salutation, reception, presentation, introduction, mark of recognition, nod, recognition; welcome, respects, devoir, welcome mat; valediction, farewell, good-bye; regards, remembrances; kind regards *or* remembrances.

3, *(act of respect)* obeisance, reverence, bow, curtsy, salaam; kneeling, genuflection (see WORSHIP); salute, handshake, grip of the hand, embrace, hug, squeeze; accolade. *Informal,* high sign, glad hand.

4, guest, invitee, visitor; host[ess], greeter.

Verbs—1, be courteous, show courtesy, keep a civil tongue in one's head; receive, do the honors, usher, greet, hail, bid welcome, accost, welcome [with open arms]; entertain, host; shake hands; hold out, press, *or* squeeze the hand; roll out the red carpet; bid Godspeed, see off; speed the parting guest. *Informal,* have one's latch string out.

2, *(show courtesy)* embrace, kiss hands, kiss on the cheek; drink to, pledge, hob and nob; move to, nod to; smile upon; touch *or* take off the hat, doff the cap, uncover, cap; present arms, salute; make way for, bow, make one's bow; curtsy, bob [a curtsy], kneel, bend the knee, prostrate oneself.

3, visit, wait upon, present oneself, pay one's respects, pay a visit (see SOCIALITY); pass the time of day; dance attendance on (see SERVILITY); pay attentions to, do homage to (see RESPECT).

4, *(show good manners)* mind one's Ps and Qs, behave oneself, be all things to all men, conciliate, speak one fair, take in good part; look as if butter would not melt in one's mouth; mind one's manners.

5, *(make more courteous)* polish, cultivate, civilize, humanize.

Adjectives—courteous, polite, civil, mannerly, urbane, continental, cosmopolitan; well-behaved, well-mannered, well-bred, well brought up, gentlemanly, courtly, gallant, chivalrous; good-mannered, polished, civilized, cultivated, refined (see TASTE); fine-spoken, fair-spoken, soft-spoken; honey-mouthed *or* -tongued; mealy-mouthed; obliging, conciliatory, on one's good behavior, ingratiating, winning; genteel; gentle, mild; good-humored, cordial, gracious, affable, amiable, familiar, suave; neighborly; hospitable, cordial.

Adverbs—courteously; with a good grace, with open *or* outstretched arms.

Interjections—greetings! salutations! good morning, afternoon, *or* evening; how do you do! *Informal,* howdy! how's tricks? long time no see!

Phrases—a civil question deserves a civil answer; civility costs nothing; one can catch more flies with honey than with vinegar.

Quotations—To jaw-jaw is always better than to war-war (*Winston Churchill*), My father used to say, "Superior people never make long visits" (*Marianne Moore*), Charm is a way of getting the answer yes without ever having asked a clear question (*Albert Camus*).

Antonyms, see DISCOURTESY.

---

courtier, *n.* flatterer, sycophant. See FLATTERY, SERVILITY.

courtly, *adj.* elegant, refined. See ELEGANCE, COURTESY.

courtship, *n.* flirtation, wooing. See ENDEARMENT.

courtyard, *n.* court, square (see ENCLOSURE).

couturier, *n* dressmaker, designer. See CLOTHING.

cove, *n.* inlet, bay, lagoon; nook. See CONCAVITY, WATER.

covenant, *v.* contract, agree, undertake, stipulate, engage, bargain, PROMISE. —*n.* AGREEMENT, contract, bargain, pact, PROMISE, SECURITY.

COVERING
Something placed over another

Nouns—1, covering, cover; superposition, superimposition; packaging; eclipse.

2, roof, ceiling, canopy, awning, tent, pavilion, marquee; umbrella, parasol, sunshade; veil, shade, visor; hood, dome (see CONVEXITY); shelter, shield, DEFENSE; cover, lid, pop- *or* screw-top; CLOTHING. See CONCEALMENT, BUILDING.

3, bedclothes, bedding, coverlet, bedspread, comforter, duvet, quilt; counterpane, sheet, blanket, pillowcase; flooring, floor covering, linoleum, tiling; rug, carpet, tapestry, drugget; upholstery, drapery; tarpaulin, canvas; pavement, macadam, asphalt, blacktop, tar.

4, housing; plating, coating, layer; bandage, wrapper, wrapping, gift-wrap, plastic wrap, waxed paper, aluminum *or* tin foil.

5, peel, crust, bark, rind, cortex, hull, husk, carapace, shell, nutshell, coat, jacket; capsule, house; scab; sheath, sheathing, sleeve; pod; casing, case; envelope, vesicle.

6, (*coating layer*) overlay, film; veneer, facing; pavement; scale, LAYER; coating, paint (see PAINTING); masking tape; varnish; incrustation, ground; whitewash, plaster, stucco, compo; siding; lining; cerement.

7, (*animal covering*) integument; skin, pellicle, fleece, feathers, fell, fur, hide; pelt, peltry; cuticle; epidermis.

Verbs—cover, mask; superpose, superimpose; overlay, overspread; drape; wrap, encase, do up, package; face, case, veneer, pave, paper; tip, cap; carpet, floor; pave, [re]surface, macadamize; upholster, drape; coat, paint, varnish, incrust, stucco, dab, plaster, tar; wash; besmear, smear; bedaub, daub; anoint, do over; veil; glaze, gild, plate, japan, lacquer, enamel, whitewash; overlie, overarch, overlap, overhang; conceal; insulate.

Adjectives—1, covering; cutaneous, dermal, epidermal, cortical, cuticular, tegumentary, skinlike, skinny, scaly, squamous.

2, covered, imbricated; gold-, silver-, armor-(*etc.*)plated, ironclad; upholstered; overlapping, overlying, superimposed; under cover (see CONCEALMENT).

Prepositions—on, upon, over, above.

Antonyms, see DIVESTMENT.

---

coverage, *n.* protection; market, readership, viewership, *etc.* See SECURITY, PUBLICATION.

covert, *adj.* SECRET, hidden, sheltered. See CONCEALMENT.

cover-up, *n.* whitewash, censorship, veil (see CONCEALMENT).

covet, *v.t.* DESIRE, long for, crave, want, envy. See JEALOUSY.

covey, *n.* flock, brood, bevy. See ASSEMBLAGE.

cow, *n.* bovine, calf, heifer; (*pl.*) kine, cattle. See ANIMAL. —*v.t.* intimidate, frighten. See FEAR.

COWARDICE
Shrinking from pain or danger

Nouns—**1**, cowardice, cowardliness, pusillanimity, poltroonery, baseness; dastardliness; abject fear, funk; Dutch courage; FEAR, white feather, faint heart, timidity. *Informal*, cold feet, yellow streak. See WEAKNESS.

2, coward, poltroon, dastard, sneak, craven, recreant, scaredy- *or* fraidy-cat; milksop, whiteliver, mama's boy, sissy, rabbit; runagate, runaway. *Informal*, weak sister, wimp, milquetoast, pansy, pantywaist. *Slang*, chicken-heart, chicken[-liver], chickenshit, candy-ass, ring-tail, yellow-dog, lily- *or* yellow-liver.

Verbs—be cowardly, be a coward; cower, skulk, sneak; quail, flinch, shy, fight shy, slink, turn tail; lose one's nerve, run away (see AVOIDANCE); show the white feather; be psyched out. *Informal*, have cold feet. *Slang*, chicken out.

Adjectives—coward[ly], fearful, shy; poor-spirited, spiritless, soft, effeminate; weakminded; weak-, faint-, chicken-, lily-, *or* pigeon-hearted, lily- *or* white-livered; pusillanimous, spineless, bloodless; unable to say "Boo" to a goose, afraid of one's shadow; dastard[ly]; base, craven, sneaking, recreant; unwarlike, unsoldierlike, unmanned, unmanly; frightened, afraid (see FEAR). *Informal*, yellow[-bellied]. *Slang*, chicken[-livered], chicken-shit.

Phrases—a bully is always a coward.

Quotations—Thus conscience doth make cowards of us all (*Shakespeare*), Cowards die many times before their deaths (*Shakespeare*).

Antonyms, see COURAGE.

---

cowboy, *n.* cowherd, cowman, cowgirl, cowpoke; cattleman *or* -woman, cowpuncher, cowhand, buckaroo; wrangler, broncobuster; trail boss, top hand; vaquero, gaucho, ranchero, pard[ner] (*sl.*). See DOMESTICATION.

cower, *v.i.* cringe, shrink, crouch, quail; fawn, grovel. See COWARDICE, SERVILITY, FEAR, RECOIL.

co-worker, *n.* associate, confrere, colleague. See AGENT.

coy, *adj.* bashful, reserved; chary; shrinking, shy, demure, retiring; coquettish. See MODESTY. *Ant.*, forward, bold.

cozy, *adj.* snug, comfortable, homey, gemütlich; warm, plush. See PLEASURE, SOCIALITY.

crabbed, *adj.* crabby, ill-tempered, irascible, surly, growly, cross, peevish; cramped, illegible, squeezed. See IRASCIBILITY, UNINTELLIGIBILITY.

crack, *v.t.* pop, rend, explode, bang; crackle; break, split, burst, cleave, fracture, crush; *informal*, fail, bust, break down. —*n.* snap, break, fracture; crevice, crackle, craze, chink, flaw, cleft, rift, rent, fissure; slit, rut, groove, seam; pop, crash, clap; *slang*, attempt, try; *slang*, gibe (see WIT); *slang*, cocaine (see DRUGS). See INTERVAL, DISJUNCTION, LOUDNESS, BRITTLENESS, FURROW, UNDERTAKING. —*adj.*, *informal*, expert (see SKILL).

crackpot, *n.*, *slang*, eccentric, screwball. See UNCONFORMITY.

cradle, *n.* crib; origin[s], infancy. See BE-
GINNING, SUPPORT.

craft, *n.* SKILL, expertise; art, handicraft;
trade; vessel, SHIP, boat; CUNNING, art-
fulness, deceit, trickery. See BUSINESS.

craftsman, *n.* artisan, craftsperson. See
ARTIST, AGENCY.

crafty, *adj.* guileful, CUNNING.

crag, *n.* rock, boulder. See LAND.

cram, *v.* crowd, stuff, press, force, jam,
pack, choke; satiate, surfeit, gormandize, gorge, guzzle; study, burn the midnight oil. See CLOSURE, GLUTTONY,
LEARNING.

cramp, *v.t.* restrict, hamper, handicap;
compress, confine; fasten; cripple, paralyze, incapacitate. —*n.* seizure, spasm,
charley horse (*inf.*). See HINDRANCE, IM-
POTENCE, PAIN, CONTRACTION.

crane, *n.* heron; derrick. See ELEVATION,
ANGULARITY. —*v.* stretch, rubberneck.
See VISION.

crank, *n.* handle, winder, key; quirk; eccentric, oddball, fanatic, grouch (*inf.*),
crab, crackpot (*sl.*), screwball (*sl.*), nut
(*sl.*). —*v.* crank up, start; wind, turn,
twist. See UNCONFORMITY, ROTATION,
ELEVATION.

cranky, *adj.* irritable (see IRASCIBILITY).
Ant., amiable, good-natured.

cranny, *n.* crevice, crack. See INTERVAL.

crash, *n.* collision, shock, smash, shatter-
ing; FAILURE, collapse, downfall; burst,
blast. See DESTRUCTION, IMPULSE,
LOUDNESS.

crass, *adj.* coarse, crude, gross, unrefined,
raw; obtuse, dense, stupid. See VULGAR-
ITY, IGNORANCE. *Ant.,* sensitive, refined.

crate, *v.* pack, box, encase. —*n.* box, shipping case. See RECEPTACLE.

crater, *n.* volcano; hole, OPENING, depression, pit, mouth. See CONCAVITY.

crave, *v.t.* DESIRE, long *or* yearn for; ask,
beg, seek, solicit, supplicate, beseech,
pray, petition; need, require. See NECES-
SITY, REQUEST.

craven, *adj. & n.* See COWARDICE.

craving, *n.* DESIRE.

crawl, *v.i.* creep, lag, drag; cringe, fawn,
cower, grovel. See SERVILITY, SLOW-
NESS, LOWNESS.

crayon, *n.* grease *or* wax pencil, pastel,
chalk. See PAINTING.

craze, *v.t.* derange, unbalance, madden,
unsettle. See INSANITY. —*n.* fad, rage.
See FASHION.

crazy, *adj.* insane (see INSANITY). *Ant.,*
sane.

creak, *v.i.* squeak, stridulate. See LOUD-
NESS.

cream, *n.* crème, top milk, rich milk; best,
flower, pick, elite; gist, kernel; paste, lotion. See GOODNESS, FLUIDITY, IMPOR-
TANCE.

creamy, *adj.* smooth, velvety (see
SMOOTHNESS). *Ant.,* grainy.

crease, *n.* FOLD, pleat; bend; mark, wrinkle, FURROW; scrape, wound, cut. —*v.*
mark, FOLD, pleat, FURROW, wrinkle,
wound.

create, *v.t.* CAUSE, make, form, bring into
being, EFFECT, fashion, originate, occasion; produce, procreate, propagate,
breed; devise, design, conceive, invent,
construct; bring to pass; imagine, visualize, envisage. See PRODUCTION, IMAG-
INATION.

creator, *n.* God, Supreme Being; author,
maker, fashioner, originator, producer,
inventor, designer. See CAUSE, PRODUC-
TION, DEITY.

creature, *n.* ANIMAL, beast; creation, being, thing; human being, individual,
mortal; SERVANT, instrument, slave,
tool, dependent; critter (*dial.*). See SUB-
STANCE.

credence, *n.* BELIEF.

credentials, *n.pl.* papers, documents,
dossier; voucher, pass, passport, license; diploma, *etc.* See INDICATION.

credible, *adj.* believable (see BELIEF).

credit, *n.* faith, BELIEF; credibility, trust;
CREDIT, borrowing power. —*v.t.* believe, trust; credit. See ACCOUNTING.

CREDIT
Borrowing power

Nouns—1, credit, trust, score, tally, account, tab; loan (see DEBT); credit instrument, instrument of credit, letter of credit, line of credit, draft, paper credit, floating capital, certificate of deposit, CD; charge account, installment plan, layaway, revolving credit; credit rating, credit bureau; credit union; credit *or* debit card, bank card, gold *or* platinum card, smart card. *Informal,* tick. See ACCOUNTING.

2, creditor, lender, lessor, mortgagee, funder, mortgage broker *or* holder; bill collector.

Verbs—credit, charge; keep an account with, run up an account with, buy on the installment plan; entrust, accredit; place to one's credit *or* account; give *or* take credit. *Slang,* fly a kite, go on tick, go in[to] hock for, rack up.

Adjectives—crediting, credited; accredited; to the account *or* credit of.

Adverbs—on credit, on deposit; on account, in installments; on time. *Informal,* on tick. *Slang,* on the cuff.

Antonyms, see DEBT.

---

creditable, *adj.* praiseworthy, honorable. See VIRTUE, RESPECT.

creditor, *n.* lender (see CREDIT).

credo, *n.* creed, credenda. See BELIEF.

CREDULITY
Willingness to believe

Nouns—1, credulity, credulousness, gullibility, ingenuousness, naiveté; self-delusion, self-deception; superstition; one's blind side; blind faith. See BELIEF.

2, superstition, old wives' tale, popular belief; urban myth.

3, dupe, gull, April fool. *Informal,* sucker, fruit, pigeon, schlemiel, tool, woodcock, zib, jay, [Joe] Schmo, [easy] mark, sap, schnook, patsy, pushover.

Verbs—1, be credulous; fall for, take on trust *or* faith, take for granted, take for gospel; run away with a notion *or* idea, jump *or* rush to a conclusion; take the shadow for the substance; catch at straws; bite, take the bait, buy a pup, accept a wooden nickel. *Informal,* swallow [whole], gulp down, eat *or* lap up, swallow hook, line and sinker, go for, buy [into].

2, be superstitious, take on faith; knock on wood, cross oneself, keep one's fingers crossed.

3, *(take advantage of one's credulity)* impose upon, dupe, gull, delude, deceive (see DECEPTION). *Slang,* vic.

Adjectives—credulous, gullible, ingenuous; easily deceived, unsuspecting, simple, green, soft, childish, silly, stupid; overcredulous, overconfident; superstitious.

Quotations—They'll take a suggestion as a cat laps milk (*Shakespeare*), Superstition is the religion of feeble minds (*Edmund Burke*), There's a sucker born every minute (*Joseph Bessimer*).

Antonyms, see INCREDULITY.

---

creed, *n.* credo, BELIEF, tenet, doctrine, persuasion, dogma, faith; sect, denomination. See RELIGION.

creek, *n.* stream, brook. See WATER.

creep, *v.i.* crawl, worm, grovel. See SLOWNESS.

creepy, *adj.* spooky, weird. See FEAR, UNCONFORMITY.

cremation, *n.* burning, incineration, suttee. See HEAT, INTERMENT.

crème de la crème, *Fr.* the cream of the cream; the very best. See SUPERIORITY.

crescent, *adj.* crescent-shaped, lunate, moon-shaped, luniform. See CURVATURE.

crest, *n.* crown, tuft, topknot, comb, plume; summit, peak, ridge, tip, HEIGHT, top;

seal, device; culmination, climax. See PERFECTION.

crestfallen, *adj.* abashed, dejected. See DEJECTION.

crevice, *n.* cleft, split, fissure, break, breach, opening, DISJUNCTION, hole, slit, chink; nook, cranny, space, INTERVAL, cavity; crevasse.

crew, *n.* force, gang, band, set, squad; ASSEMBLAGE, company; sailors. See INHABITANT, PARTY.

crib, *n.* manger, trough, box, stall, bin; cot, bed, cradle; translation, key; *informal,* pony, trot. See RECEPTACLE, SUPPORT, STEALING.

crick, *n.* spasm; *dial.* creek. See PAIN, WATER.

cricket, *n.* See SPORTS, ANIMAL. —*adj., informal,* fair[play], kosher (*sl.*). See JUSTICE.

crime, *n.* offense, WRONG; misdemeanor, felony, outrage; transgression, sin, evil, wrongdoing; ILLEGALITY, lawbreaking.

criminal, *n.* offender, malefactor, felon, sinner, culprit, convict. See ILLEGALITY, EVILDOER. —*adj.* illegal, unlawful, felonious.

crimp, *v.t.* wave, curl, crinkle, wrinkle, ripple; gather, bunch, pinch, tighten, FOLD, pleat, plait. —*n.* curl; notch. See CONVOLUTION, FURROW.

cringe, *v.i.* cower, stoop, flinch, wince, crouch, shrink; fawn, truckle, crawl, grovel; sneak. See RECOIL, FEAR, SERVILITY.

crinkle, *v.* wrinkle, roughen, crease, crumple, rumple, ripple, FOLD, crimp, corrugate. —*n.* wrinkle, crease. See FURROW.

cripple, *v.t.* disable, incapacitate, unfit; lame, paralyze, maim; hurt, enfeeble, cramp. See IMPOTENCE, HINDRANCE, WEAKNESS.

crisis, *n.* turning point, juncture; exigency, emergency, extremity, pinch, trial, crux, crunch, climax. See CIRCUMSTANCE, DIFFICULTY, OCCASION.

crisp, *adj.* brittle, curly, blunt, friable; short, crunchy, crumbly; pithy, terse; COLD, stiff; firm, fresh; bracing. See BRITTLENESS, NEWNESS, SHORTNESS. *Ant.,* soggy, soft.

crisscross, *adj. & n.* See CROSSING.

criterion, *n.* standard, model, rule, test, measure, norm, touchstone. See MEASUREMENT.

critic, *n.* judge, connoisseur, expert, reviewer, commentator; censor, censurer. See DETRACTION, TASTE.

critical, *adj.* exacting, captious, censorious, faultfinding, disparaging; judicious, accurate, analytical; decisive; urgent, crucial; dangerous, risky. See DISAPPROBATION, IMPORTANCE, DETRACTION.

criticize, *v.t.* judge, censure, excoriate, blame, reprove, flay; examine, dissect, analyze, review; nitpick; roast, pan, badmouth (*all sl.*). See DISAPPROBATION, DETRACTION, JUDGMENT.

critique, *n.* review, criticism. See JUDGMENT.

crockery, *n.* pottery, earthenware, ceramics. See MATERIALS.

crone, *n.* hag, witch. See FEMALE.

crony, *n.* chum, pal, FRIEND.

crook, *n.* bend, curve, hook; thief, robber. See CURVATURE, ILLEGALITY, STEALING, EVILDOER.

crooked, *adj.* bent, curved, angular, sinuous, winding, askew, zigzag, twisted, warped; false, dishonest, fraudulent, deceptive, sneaking; oblique, aslant, distorted, awry. See IMPROBITY, DISTORTION.

croon, *v.* sing, serenade. See MUSIC.

crop, *n.* craw, gorge; whip; harvest, yield, fruit, product. See EFFECT, PUNISHMENT, AGRICULTURE.

cross, *n.* rood, crucifix; crosspiece, cross mark, X, ex; gibbet; burden, trial, trouble, ADVERSITY, affliction; hybrid, MIXTURE, crossbreed; half-caste, half-breed; (*cap.*) Christianity, the Church, Gospel. —*v.* cross-breed, cross-pollinate, mix; traverse, go across, ford; mark out, cancel, strike out; pass over, lie across *or* athwart; bar, line, crosshatch; circumvent, thwart, frustrate, foil, oppose, hinder, obstruct. See CROSSING, NULLIFICATION, OPPOSITION, TRAVEL. —*adj.* opposite, converse; peevish (see IRASCIBILITY).

cross-examine, *v.t.* See INQUIRY.

CROSSING
Intersection

Nouns—1, crossing, intersection, interchange, crossroad[s], roundabout (*Brit.*), crosswalk, grade crossing; under- *or* overpass, bridge, tunnel; overflight. See JUNCTION, CONNECTION.

2, *(crossing pattern)* crisscross; textile, fabric; decussation, transversion; intertexture, reticulation, network, net, plexus, web, mesh, twill, tissue, lace; warp, woof; wicker; mat[ting]; cross, X, crucifix, rood; swastika, fylfot; crossbones; plait, trellis, wattle, lattice, grate, grating, grill[e], grid[iron], tracery, fretwork, reticle (see ORNAMENT); braid, cat's cradle, knot; entanglement (see DISORDER). See CONVOLUTION, OBLIQUITY, TEXTURE.

3, crosstree, crosspiece, crossbar, transept.

Verbs—cross, go over, intersect, crisscross, interlace, intertwine, intertwist, interweave, interlink; decussate; twine, entwine, weave, inweave, reticulate, twist, wreathe; mat, plait, braid, twill; tangle, entangle, ravel; net, knot; raddle (*dial.*).

Adjectives—crossing, crossed, crisscross, antiparallel; matted, transverse; cross [-shaped], cruciate, cruciform, crucial, decussate; retiform, reticular, reticulate[d]; areolar, cancellated, grated, barred, streaked; textile.

Adverbs—across, athwart, transversely; crosswise, obliquely, sidewise; against the grain.

Antonyms, see SIMILARITY.

---

crossroads, *n.* intersection (see CROSSING); turning point, critical juncture. See CHOICE, IMPORTANCE.

cross section, *n.* [random] sample. See INQUIRY.

crotch, *n.* fork, divergence, branch, corner; groin, inguinal region, inguen; genitals, genitalia. See ANGULARITY.

crotchety, *adj.* eccentric, cranky. See DISCOURTESY.

crouch, *v.i.* bend, squat, stoop; cower, cringe. See DEPRESSION, SERVILITY, FEAR.

crow, *v.* caw; brag, boast, gloat. See BOASTING, CRY. —*n.* raven, blackbird.

crowd, *n.* gathering, concourse, horde, press, mass, gang, mob, MULTITUDE; host, herd, swarm, rout, crush, throng; *informal,* set, coterie, clique; POPULACE, rabble, hoi polloi. See ASSEMBLAGE.

crown, *v.t.* coronate, wreathe, enthrone, adorn, invest, install; top, cap, head, crest; complete, perfect, round out, finish. See COMPLETION, IMPULSE, HEIGHT. —*n.* chaplet, circlet, diadem, coronet, aureole; laurel, wreath, garland, reward, prize; pate, crest, top. See CIRCULARITY, APPROBATION.

crucial, *adj.* decisive, determining, final; urgent, critical, supreme; trying, severe; cruciform. See IMPORTANCE, CROSSING. *Ant.,* unimportant.

crucifix, *n.* cross (see CROSSING).

crucify, *v.t.* See KILLING.

crude, *adj.* rough, raw, unfinished, imperfect, plain, unwrought, unrefined, incomplete; unprepared, sketchy; coarse, crass, rude, tasteless, gross, immature, vulgar, uncouth. See INELEGANCE, IMPERFECTION, UNPREPAREDNESS, VULGARITY.

cruel, *adj.* coldblooded, harsh, pitiless. See MALEVOLENCE, SEVERITY.

cruise, *n.* voyage, journey, *etc.;* sail; ride, flight. —*v.i.* voyage, sail, yacht, steam; soar, coast; wander, rove, roam, meander, range, hunt. See TRAVEL, NAVIGATION, AVIATION.

crumb, *n.* bit, fragment, scrap, mite, morsel, jot, ort; leaving, leftover. See PART, LITTLENESS, REMAINDER, POWDERINESS.

crumble, *v.i.* disintegrate, break up, fall to pieces; decay, degenerate. See DESTRUCTION, DETERIORATION, POWDERINESS, WEAKNESS.

crummy, *adj.* inferior, shabby (see INFERIORITY, BADNESS). *Ant.,* excellent.

crumple, *v.t.* rumple, wrinkle; *informal,* collapse. See FOLD, CONTRACTION, DESTRUCTION.

crunch, *v.* chew, crush, grind. See FOOD, POWDERINESS. —*n.* DIFFICULTY, pickle, crisis, moment of truth.

crusade, *n.* Holy War, jihad; campaign, cause, drive. See WARFARE.

crush, *v.t.* press, mash, squash, squeeze, bruise; overcome, conquer, vanquish, subdue, quell, overwhelm, suppress, blot out; shame, disconcert. See CONTRACTION, DESTRUCTION, POWDERI-NESS, HUMILITY. —*n.* press, pressure; crowd; *slang,* infatuation, thing. See ASSEMBLAGE, LOVE.

crust, *n.* cake, coating, rind, shell, hull, incrustation; *slang,* nerve (see COURAGE). See COVERING.

crutch, *n.* staff, walking stick; SUPPORT; crotch (see ANGULARITY).

crux, *n.* gist, key; crisis. See IMPORTANCE, DIFFICULTY.

CRY
Loud call

Nouns—1, cry, shout, call (see *Verbs*); vociferation, exclamation, outcry, hullabaloo, chorus, clamor, hue and cry; Bronx cheer; plaint (see LAMENTATION); stentor (see LOUDNESS); bark, ululation. See SPEECH, SOUND.

2, crier, street vendor, hawker (see SALE), barker, herald.

Verbs—cry, roar, shout, bawl, bellow, halloo, halloa, whoop, yell, howl, give a cry, scream, screech, shriek, squeak, squeal, squall; whine, pule; pipe; bark, bay, bell, bellow, blat, bleat, boo, boom, bray, call, caw, cheep, chirp, chitter, clack, cluck, coo, cough, crack, croak, crow, gargle, gasp, gibber, giggle, gobble, grunt, gulp, gurgle, hawk, hem, hiss, huff, hum, lisp, mew, mewl, moo, neigh, oink, peep, puff, purr, quack, roll, scat, snap, sniffle, snuffle, squall, squawk, titter, twitter, ululate, wail, wheeze, whinny, yap, yelp, yip, yodel, yowl, zing; weep (see LAMENTATION); cheer, hoot, shrill; snore, snort; vociferate, ejaculate; cry, call, *or* sing out, raise *or* lift up the voice, exclaim; strain the throat, voice, *or* lungs, rend the air, thunder, shout at the top of one's voice *or* lungs.

Adjectives—crying, clamant, clamorous; vociferous; stentorian (see LOUDNESS).

Antonyms, see SILENCE.

---

crypt, *n.* vault, tomb. See INTERMENT, TEMPLE.

cryptic, *adj.* hidden, SECRET, occult. See CONCEALMENT.

cryptograph, *n.* cipher, cryptogram, code. See CONCEALMENT.

crystal, *adj.* lucid, pellucid, crystalline, clear. See TRANSPARENCY.

crystallize, *v.i.* take form *or* shape, come together (see FORM).

cub, *n.* offspring, whelp, youngster, pup[py]; novice. See ANIMAL, YOUTH, BEGINNING.

cubbyhole, *n.* cubby, nook, compartment. See RECEPTACLE.

cube, *n.* solid, square, die; hexahedron. See ANGULARITY, NUMERATION. —*v.i.* dice, chop. See DISJUNCTION.

cubicle, *n.* carrel, compartment (see RECEPTACLE).

cuddle, *v.* snuggle, nestle, curl up, huddle; clasp, fondle. See ENDEARMENT.

cudgel, *n.* club, bludgeon, staff, shillelagh, stick. See ARMS.

cue, *n.* hint, clue, intimation; catchword, signal, password; cuestick. See INDICATION, INFORMATION, MEMORY.

cuisine, *n.* kitchen; cookery. See FOOD.

cul-de-sac, *n.* blind alley, dead end. See PASSAGE.

cull, *v.t.* select (see CHOICE).

culminate, *v.* crown; come to a head; conclude, finish. See COMPLETION, HEIGHT.

culpable, *adj.* guilty (see GUILT). *Ant.,* innocent.

culprit, *n.* offender, malefactor, wrongdoer, EVILDOER. See GUILT.

cult, *n.* cultus, sect, RELIGION, denomination; WORSHIP, devotion; school [of thought], BELIEF; mystique, fad, craze, vogue.

cultivate, *v.t.* farm, till, work, grow, develop; civilize, refine; pursue, court; foster, advance, cherish. See AGRICULTURE, IMPROVEMENT.

cultivation, *n.* farming, tillage, husbandry, AGRICULTURE; elevation, civilization, refinement, breeding; learning, education; pursuit. See IMPROVEMENT, COURTESY.

culture, *n.* cultivation, tillage; development, education, learning; enlightenment; refinement, breeding, polish; civilization. See AGRICULTURE, COURTESY, IMPROVEMENT, KNOWLEDGE.

culvert, *n.* CONDUIT, drain.

cumbersome, *adj.* cumbrous, unwieldy, clumsy, burdensome, ponderous, oppressive. See HINDRANCE.

cum laude, *Lat.* with praise. See APPROBATION, SUPERIORITY.

cumulative, *adj.* additional (see ADDITION).

CUNNING
Craftiness

Nouns—1, cunning, craft, craftiness, canniness, WIT; gumption; slyness, artifice, art; subtlety, finesse, maneuvering; diplomacy, Machiavellianism, politics; resourcefulness; Jesuitry; gamesmanship, oneupmanship. *Informal,* foxiness, caginess. See SKILL, INTELLIGENCE.

2, *(deceptive cunning)* chicane, chicanery, knavery, guile; fine Italian hand. *Informal,* finagling. See DECEPTION, IMPROBITY.

3, *(cunning act)* art, artifice; device, machination, plot, PLAN, maneuver, coup, stratagem, contrivance, feint, gambit, dodge, artful dodge, wile, trick; trickery, DECEPTION; ruse, side-blow, shift, go by, subterfuge; tour de force, tricks of the trade. *Informal,* gimmick[ry], shuttle diplomacy.

4, schemer, intriguer, strategist, tactician; diplomat, politician, power broker, kingmaker; Machiavelli; slyboots, knave, fox, Renard, horse trader. *Informal,* sly dog, slicker, grafter, Philadelphia lawyer.

Verbs—be cunning, contrive, machinate, PLAN, live by one's wits; chicane (see DECEPTION); play both ends against the middle; maneuver, scheme, finagle, play a deep game, play tricks (with); be too much for, get the better of, outsmart, outmaneuver, outwit, outfox. *Slang,* ace out, sandbag.

Adjectives—cunning, crafty, clever, calculating, artful; skillful (see SKILL); subtle, feline, vulpine; roguish; cunning as *or* crazy like a fox, cunning as the serpent; deep[-laid]; arch, designing, scheming, contriving; strategic, diplomatic, politic, Machiavellian, artificial, tricky, shifty, wily, sly (see DECEPTION); shrewd, acute; sharp [as a needle]; canny, astute, knowing, up to snuff, too clever by half. *Slang,* fly.

Adverbs—cunningly, slyly, cannily, cleverly, foxily, on the sly. *Slang,* cagily.

Phrases—in politics a man must learn to rise above principle.

Quotations—Politics is the art of the possible (*Otto von Bismarck*), Politics is perhaps the only profession for which no preparation is thought necessary (*R. L. Stevenson*), Politics is war without bloodshed (*Mao Zedong*), Politics are too serious a matter to be left to the politicians (*Charles de Gaulle*), To make a living, craftiness is better than learnedness (*Beaumarchais*).

Antonyms, see UNSKILLFULNESS.

cup, *n.* mug, tankard, chalice, goblet; [Holy] Grail; excavation, hollow, crater. See RECEPTACLE, CONCAVITY, APPROBATION.

cupboard, *n.* closet, storeroom; buffet, locker, press; pantry. See RECEPTACLE.

cupola, *n.* vault, dome. See CONVEXITY.

cur, *n.* mutt, dog (see ANIMAL); cad, heel, coward. See EVILDOER.

curate, *n.* See CLERGY.

curator, *n.* librarian; custodian, overseer; guardian. See SAFETY, DIRECTOR.

curb, *v.t.* restrain, subdue, control, check, repress; guide, manage; slacken, retard. —*n.* RESTRAINT, check, control; curb market; curbstone. See HINDRANCE.

curdle, *v.* clabber; curd, clot, thicken, coagulate, congeal, lump; separate; spoil, turn, sour. See DENSITY, DETERIORATION, SOURNESS.

cure, *v.t.* heal, restore, relieve; preserve, dry, smoke, tan, pickle. See REMEDY, PRESERVATION.

curfew, *n.* bedtime, vespers; siren, tocsin, whistle. See INDICATION.

curio, *n.* bric-a-brac, knickknack, objet d'art, ORNAMENT, whatnot, antique, gewgaw, gimcrack.

CURIOSITY
Eagerness to learn

Nouns—1, curiosity, curiousness; interest, thirst for knowledge; inquiring mind; inquisitiveness; meddling, nosiness; sightseeing; voyeurism; morbid curiosity, prurience. See INFORMATION.

2, sightseer; questioner (see INQUIRY); gossip, busybody, quidnunc; peeping Tom, voyeur, Paul Pry; eavesdropper; bush telegraph. *Informal,* snooper, nosy Parker. *Slang,* rubberneck, keek.

Verbs—be curious, take an interest in; stare, prick up the ears; sightsee, see sights; peep, eavesdrop; gossip; meddle. *Informal,* snoop. *Slang,* rubberneck, dish the dirt, bug, stick one's nose into.

Adjectives—curious, inquisitiveness, burning with curiosity, overcurious, curious as a cat; inquiring (see INQUIRY); prying, nosy, prurient, voyeuristic; meddlesome; inquisitorial.

Phrases—curiosity killed the cat.

Quotations—Curiosity is the thirst of the soul (*Samuel Johnson*), The public have an insatiable curiosity to know everything, except what's worth knowing (*Oscar Wilde*).

Antonyms, see INDIFFERENCE.

curl, *v.* roll, wave, ripple, spiral, twist, coil. See CONVOLUTION, CURVATURE.

curlicue, *n.* curl, twist. See CONVOLUTION.

currency, *n.* MONEY, coin, specie; publicity, circulation; topicality, timeliness. See PUBLICATION, NEWNESS.

current, *adj.* common, prevalent, PRESENT, in vogue, prevailing; accepted, abroad, rife; existing, circulating, rumored. See PUBLICATION, GENERALITY, NEWS. —*n.* stream, flow; movement, tendency; draft. See WIND, WATER, DIRECTION, COURSE. *Ant.,* passé, out of date.

curry, *v.t.* groom, tend; dress. See PREPARATION.

curse, *v.* execrate, damn, swear, denounce; blaspheme. —*n.* malediction, IMPRECA-TION, execration, anathema; bane, plague. See EVIL, ADVERSITY.

cursory, *adj.* hasty, superficial. See HASTE.

curt, *adj.* short, concise, brief, succinct; snappish, tart, rude, brusque, bluff, blunt, abrupt. See SHORTNESS, DISCOURTESY.

curtail, *v.t.* shorten, clip, cut, abbreviate; abate, diminish, reduce, lessen, abridge; deprive. See SHORTNESS, DECREASE, DISCONTINUANCE.

curtain, *n.* screen, veil, valance, drapery, portiere, hanging, blind, shade. See CONCEALMENT.

curtsy, *n.* bow, reverence. See COURTESY.

curvaceous, *adj., informal,* buxom, voluptuous. See BEAUTY.

CURVATURE
Curving

Nouns—1, curvature, curving, curvity, curvation; incurvity, incurvation; flexure, crook, hook, bend[ing]; deflection, inflection; arcuation, devexity, turn; recurvity, recurvation; ROTUNDITY; curl[ing], sinuosity (see CONVOLUTION). See CIRCULARITY, CONVEXITY, CONCAVITY, FOLD.

2, curve, arc, arch, vault, bow, bend, hairpin turn, S-curve, U-turn; crescent, half moon, semicircle, horseshoe, lunule, miniscus, scythe, crane-neck, parabola, hyperbola; catenary, festoon, swag; conchoid, cardioid, caustic; Bézier curve; tracery (see ORNAMENT).

Verbs—1, (*have curvature*) be curved, sweep, swag, sag; turn, incurve.

2, (*move in a curve*) curve, bend, incurve, incurvate, double up; deflect, inflect; crook; turn, round, arch, arch over, bow, curl, recurve.

Adjectives—curved, curviform, curvilineal, curvilinear; recurved, recurvate; bowed, bent, vaulted, arched, arcuate, hooked; convex, concave; falciform, falcated; semicircular, crescentic; liniform, lunilar; semilunar; conchoidal; cordiform, cordated; heart, bell-, pear-, *or* fig-shaped; cardioid; hook-shaped, crescent[-shaped]; kidney-shaped, reniform; lens-shaped, lentiform, lenticular; arcuate[d]; bowlegged (see DISTORTION). *Informal,* curvaceous.

Antonyms, see STRAIGHTNESS, ANGULARITY.

---

cushion, *n.* pillow, bolster; ottoman. hassock; fender, bumper, *etc.*; buffer. —*v.t.* pad, soften, ease, absorb; protect, buffer, come between; soften the blow, let down easy. See SUPPORT, SOFTNESS, RELIEF.

custody, *n.* care, [safe]keeping, charge, protection; imprisonment, bondage. See SAFETY, RESTRAINT, RETENTION.

custom, *n.* practice, use, usage, wont, FASHION, precedent, RULE; HABIT, mores, convention; patronage, support, trade; (*pl.*) [import] duties. See CONFORMITY, PRICE, REGULARITY, PLAN.

customary, *adj.* usual, normal, standard, wonted. See HABIT.

customer, *n.* buyer (see PURCHASE).

cut, *v.t.* incise, carve, dissect, slice, shave, trim, shape; separate, divide, split, sever; abridge, shorten, diminish, reduce, curtail; hurt, sting, wound, snub, ignore; reap, gather. See DISJUNCTION, SHORTNESS, WEAKNESS, NEGLECT, DISCOURTESY, PAIN. —*n.* style, manner; woodcut (see ENGRAVING). See FORM.

cutback, *n.* reduction; retrenchment. See DECREASE, ECONOMY.

cute, *adj.* attractive, pretty; coy, cutesy (*inf.*). See BEAUTY.

cut-rate, *adj.* cheap, reduced. See CHEAPNESS.

cutthroat, *n.* murderer, thug. See KILLING. —*adj.* relentless. See SEVERITY, CONTENTION.

cutting, *adj.* sharp, incisive, keen-edged; biting, stinging, acrimonious, sarcastic, caustic, tart; bitter, raw, nippy. See DISAPPROBATION, SHARPNESS, COLD, RIDICULE.

cutting edge, *n.* forefront, avant garde, lead. See PRIORITY, PRECEDENCE.

cycle, *n.* period, age, epoch; circle, round; bicycle, velocipede, tricycle; motorcycle. See REGULARITY, CIRCUIT, VEHICLE.

cyclone, *n.* tornado, twister, gale, hurricane; vortex. See VIOLENCE.

cylinder, *n.* barrel, tube, roller, *etc.* See ROTUNDITY.

cynic, *n.* misanthrope, pessimist; philosopher. See THOUGHT, MALEVOLENCE.

cynical, *adj.* misanthropic, sneering, satirical, pessimistic, distrustful, sarcastic, cutting, disdainful, contemptuous, censorious; surly, snarling, captious. See CONTEMPT, DISAPPROBATION, MALEVOLENCE. *Ant.,* optimistic, positive.

czar, *n.* tsar, emperor, caesar, kaiser, king, czar of all the Russias; despot. See AUTHORITY.

D

dab, *n.* spot, pinch, bit. See LITTLENESS.
—*v.* pat, tap. See IMPULSE.

dabble, *v.* splash, spatter; patter, trifle,
fritter away. See WATER, INACTIVITY.

daffy, *adj., informal,* daft, crazy, silly. See
FOLLY, INSANITY.

dagger, *n.* dirk, stiletto, poniard, knife,
bodkin. See ARMS.

daily, *adj.* everyday, diurnal, quotidian; once
a day. See FREQUENCY, REGULARITY.

dainty, *adj.* delicate, exquisite; fastidious,
neat; delicious. See BEAUTY, TASTE,
CARE, FOOD.

dais, *n.* platform, stage. See SUPPORT.

daisy chain, *n.* series, set (see CONTINUITY).

dally, *v.i.* delay, prolong, idle; trifle, flirt,
philander. See AMUSEMENT, LATENESS.

dam, *n.* dike, seawall, levee, breakwater,
embankment, floodgate. —*v.t.* embank,
sandbag; clog, plug, stop up, jam. See
ENCLOSURE, HINDRANCE, CLOSURE.

damage, *v.t.* harm, injure, mar, impair.
—*n.* DETERIORATION, harm, injury;
(*pl.*), amends, recompense (see COM-
PENSATION). See WEAKNESS, WRONG.

damn, *v.t.* See CONDEMNATION, DISAPPRO-
BATION, IMPRECATION. *Ant.,* bless,
praise.

damp, *adj.* dank, humid, moist. —*v.t.*
dampen, dispirit, deaden; smother,
muffle, subdue; wet, moisten. See SI-
LENCE, MODERATION, DEJECTION, DIS-
SUASION, MOISTURE.

DANCE
Motion to music

Nouns—1, dance, dancing; ball, formal, tea dance, *thé dansant,* cotillion, promenade, dinner-dance; masquerade, masked ball, *bal masqué,* fancy-dress ball. *Informal,* drag, hop, prom, mixer. *Slang,* trucking. See AGITATION, AMUSEMENT, LEAP, OSCIL-LATION.

2, a. modern dance, interpretive dance, modern ballet; percussive movement. b. (*world dances*) clog; fandango, malaguena, zapateado, paso doble, flamenco, ale-grias, folklorico, bolero, bossa nova, samba, carioca, habanera; ballo, cachucha; belly dance; bergamasca, tarantella; bugaku, nihon buyo; cancan, caramagnole, farandole, tambourin; czardas; djanger, haka; hora; hula; kathak[ali], Bharat Natya; kebiyar, legong, manipuri; limbo; khon. c. court dance, basse danse, bourrée, canary, cotillion, courante, galliard, galop, gavotte, minuet, passacaglia, pavane, polonaise, saltarello, saraband. d. folk *or* popular dance; slam dancing, dirty dancing, disco dancing, break dancing, hip-hop; barn dance, breakdown, chica, contredanse, coun-try dance, écossaise, [highland] fling, gopak, hoedown, square dance, do-si-do, sashay, set, hornpipe, jota, juba, kazatsky, kolo, ländler, mazurka, Mexican hat dance, morris dance, morisco, ox dance, polka, quadrille, reel, rigadoon, round dance, salsa, schottische, sequidilla, siciliano, Sir Roger de Coverley, skirt dance, slow dance, step dancing, strathspey, tarantella, trepak, villanella, Virginia reel. e. ballroom dance, social dancing; begine, bocane, cha-cha, Charleston, conga, fox trot, gigue, jig, joropo, lambada, Lambeth walk, mambo, maxixe, merengue, one-step, peabody, rumba, samba, tango, [Texas] two-step, waltz, Washington Post. f. jazz dance, jazz tap, ball-change, bamboula, black bottom, [black] boogaloo, bomber-shay, bop, [buck-and-]wing, bunny hug, buzzard lope, cakewalk, camel walk, circus [love], cootie crawl, eagle rock, flapping eagle, grizzly bear, hand jive, huckabuck, jam back, jitterbug, jive, lambada, lindy, locomotion, mashed potatoes, mooch, pas-mala, possum-la, pull-back, sand, sconch, shag [and stomp], shimmy, shuffle, soft shoe, stomp, Susie-Q, swing, tap dance, toddle, turkey trot, walking the dog. *Slang,* electric boogie, uprock. **g.** rock dance, achy-breaky, acid house, alligator, bedrock, bird, birdland, boogaloo, break dancing, bump, cabbage patch, camel walk, continental walk, dirty dancing, disco, dive, dog, Egyptian, electric slide, file dance, fly, freak, freddie, frug, funky chicken *or* pigeon, guess, handjive, hitchhike, hop, hully gully, hustle, jerk, line dance, locomotion, macarena, mashed potato, monkey, moonwalk, moshing, nasty, night fever, pogo, pony, popcorn, rocking chair, roller coaster, running man, salsa, shake, shuffle, skate, slam dance, slauson, slog, smurf, snake, stroll, sway, swim, tush push, twine, twist, vogue, walk, watermelon crawl, watusi. **h.** erotic *or* exotic dance, striptease, fan dance, cooch, hootchy-kootchy, nautch dance. **i.** ritual dance, ghost dance, rain dance, snake dance, sword dance, war dance. **j.** Dancercize.

3, a. ballet, classical dance. **b.** ballet d'action, divertissement, entr'acte; adagio, allegro, [grand] pas de deux, entrée, coda, toe dance, character dance, solo [dance], pas seul, variation. **c.** choreography, terpsichore; Labanotation; French *or* Russian school, Cecchetti method. **d.** elevation, extension, partnering, placement. **e.** allongé, arabesque, assemblé, attitude, balance, ballon[né], [grand *or* petit] battement, batterie, cabriole, bourrée, brisé, cambré, chaîné, changement de pied, chassé, ciseaux, combination, enchaînement, figure, contretemps, coupé, croisé, dégagé, [grand] plié, demi-plié, pointe, demi-pointe, developpé, échappé, emboîtés, entrechat, épaulement, failli, fish dive, fondu, fouetté, frappé, glissade, grand jeté, pas [de basque, bourrée, chat, *or* cheval], passé, petit tour, piqué, pirouette, port de bras, posé tour, promenade, relevé, révérence, rond de jamb, royalement, saut de basque *or* de chat, sisonne, soubresant, sour-sour, stulchak, temps, temps de flèche, temps levé *or* lié, tour [en l'air *or* jeté], turnout, vole. **f.** [first, second, *etc.*] position, closed *or* open position, écarté, effacé, sur le coup de pied. **g.** dance studio, barre; pointe shoes, tutu.

4, dancer, terpsichorean, ballet dancer, danceur [noble], premier danseur, [première] danceuse, [prima] ballerina, coryphée, principal, figurant[e]; corps de ballet; chorus girl, boy *or* man, chorine; geisha, nautch girl; hula dancer; choreographer, régisseur, répétiteur; balletomane; Terpsichore; go-go dancer, exotic [dancer], topless dancer, burlesque dancer, variety dancer. *Slang,* hoofer, taxi dancer; stripper, coffee-grinder; jitterdoll *or* -jane, rugcutter.

5, dance hall, ballroom; discotheque. *Slang,* glad pads.

Verbs—dance, glide, jug, flutter; jazz dance, tap dance, *etc.*; choreograph. *Informal,* trip the light fantastic, cut the rug, hoof.

Adjectives—**1,** terpsichorean, balletic; choreographic.

2, en arrière, en avant, en dedans, en dehors, en face, en l'air, en seconde, par terre, penché, tendu.

Quotations—A perpendicular expression of a horizontal desire (*G. B. Shaw*), Dance is the hidden language of the soul (*Martha Graham*).

Related categories, see MUSIC.

---

dander, *n.* dandruff, scurf; *informal,* temper, ANGER. See RESENTMENT, POWDERINESS.

dandy, *n.* beau, coxcomb, dude, fop, macaroni. See AFFECTION. —*adj.* fine, excellent. See GOODNESS.

DANGER
Exposure to injury

Nouns—**1,** danger, peril, jeopardy, risk, hazard, THREAT, adventure, insecurity, precariousness, slipperiness; Russian roulette (see CHANCE).

2, *(vulnerability to danger)* exposure, vulnerability; vulnerable point, Achilles' heel, glass jaw.

3, *(dangerous situation)* forlorn hope, dangerous course, leap in the dark (see RASH-NESS), road to ruin; hairbreadth escape; cause for alarm, breakers ahead, storm brewing, gathering clouds, a lion in the way, lion's mouth; valley of the shadow of death; house of cards, hornet's nest, powder keg, time bomb; China syndrome; apprehension (see WARNING). *Slang,* killer litter, loose cannon.

4, pitfall; [booby] trap, snare, trip wire; quicksand, undertow; snake in the grass, sword of Damocles; whirlpool, maelstrom, ambush, *etc.;* clay pigeon.

Verbs—**1,** be in danger; be exposed to danger, run into *or* encounter danger; run a risk, lay oneself open to (see LIABILITY); lean on a broken reed, feel the ground sliding *or* slipping from under one; have to run for it; have the odds against one; sit, sleep, *or* stand on a volcano, hang by a thread, totter [on the brink], sit on a barrel of gunpowder, sit on a powderkeg, sit on dynamite, live in a glass house.

2, *(place in danger)* endanger; bring, place, *or* put in danger, expose to danger, imperil, jeopardize, compromise, throw to the wolves.

3, *(take chances)* adventure, play with fire, tempt fate, take a chance, take one's life in one's hands, skate on thin ice, risk one's neck, bell the cat, dice with death, ride for a fall; run the gauntlet, go through the mill, go through hell and high water; dare (see COURAGE); engage in a forlorn hope, sail too near the wind (see RASHNESS). *Slang,* chase the dragon. See CHANCE, DEFIANCE.

4, be dangerous, bear watching.

Adjectives—**1,** dangerous, hazardous, perilous, parlous, fateful; at stake, in question; precarious, ticklish, slippery, fraught with danger; built on sand, hanging *or* trembling in the balance, touch and go; threatening (see WARNING); explosive. *Slang,* hairy.

2, in danger, endangered, unsafe, unprotected, insecure; defenseless, unshielded, vulnerable, pregnable, exposed, open (to); at bay, on the rocks; hanging by a thread, between life and death, between Scylla and Charybdis, between two fires, between the Devil and the deep blue sea; on the edge, in deep [water], out on a limb, on the brink *or* verge of a precipice, in the lion's den, on slippery ground, on thin ice, under fire, not out of the woods; with one's back to the wall, on the spot; unprepared, off one's guard; helpless, in a bad way, in the last extremity.

Adverbs—dangerously, hazardously, *etc.*

Phrases—if you play with fire, you get burned; the female of the species is more dangerous than the male.

Quotations—In skating over thin ice, our safety is in our speed (*Emerson*).

Antonyms, see SAFETY.

---

dangle, *v.i.* hang, suspend; swing. See PENDENCY.

dank, *adj.* humid, moist. See MOISTURE. *Ant.,* dry.

danse macabre, *Fr.* dance of DEATH.

dapper, *adj.* neat, trim; diminutive. See FASHION, LITTLENESS. *Ant.,* dowdy, seedy.

dare, *v.t.* face, defy, challenge, brave; venture upon *or* into. See DEFIANCE, COURAGE, RASHNESS.

daredevil, *adj.* rash, reckless. See RASHNESS.

daring, *adj.* audacious, adventurous. —*n.* recklessness, intrepidity, bravado. See COURAGE, RASHNESS. *Ant.,* timidity.

DARKNESS
Absence of light

Nouns—**1,** darkness, dark; blackness, OBSCURITY, gloom, murk; dusk (see DIMNESS); CLOUDINESS; shade, shadow, umbra, penumbra; skiagraphy; shading; swarthiness.

2, *(total darkness)* Cimmerian darkness, Stygian darkness, pitch-blackness, night, midnight, dead of night, witching hour, dark of the moon, watches of the night; late black.

3, *(gradual darkening)* obscuration, adumbration, obfuscation; extinction, extinguishment, [solar, lunar, total, *or* partial] eclipse; blackout, brownout, dimout; darkroom, camera obscura.

Verbs—darken, bedarken, obscure, shade; black out; dim; overcast, overshadow (see CLOUDINESS); eclipse; obfuscate, adumbrate, cast into the shade *or* shadow; cast, throw, *or* spread a shadow; put, blow, *or* snuff out, extinguish, douse; turn out *or* off, switch off, extinguish.

Adjectives—dark, darksome, darkling, darkened; obscure, tenebrous, somber, pitch dark, pitchy, Cimmerian, Stygian; black (see COLOR); sunless, moonless, lightless; dusky; unilluminated; nocturnal; lurid, gloomy, murky, shady, umbrageous; dark as pitch *or* as a pit.

Adverbs—darkly, in the dark, in the shade, in the dead of night.

Quotations—Night hath a thousand eyes (*John Lyly*).

Antonyms, see LIGHT.

---

dark horse, outside chance, long shot. See IMPROBABILITY. *Ant.,* sure thing.

darling, *n.* sweetheart, dearest, dear one, angel, treasure; hero, pet, idol, fair-haired boy. —*adj.* beloved, favorite; charming, winsome, adorable, cute. See ENDEARMENT.

darn, *v.t.* repair, patch [up], mend. See RESTORATION.

dart, *v.* hurl, cast, throw; spring, rush; dartle. —*n.* spear, javelin, arrow; dash; seam. See ARMS, VELOCITY, HASTE, PROPULSION.

dash, *v.* shatter, smash; frustrate, dishearten; hurl, cast; dart. See DESTRUCTION, DEJECTION, HASTE, PROPULSION. —*n.* élan, spirit; spurt, soupçon, trace. See ACTIVITY, VELOCITY, LITTLENESS, ENERGY, OSTENTATION.

dashing, *adj.* high-spirited, gay; showy, stylish. See FASHION.

data, *n.pl.* facts, EVIDENCE, INFORMATION.

date, *n.* day, TIME, moment; age, era, epoch; *informal,* rendezvous, tryst; escort, suitor, steady, blind date. —*v.* place [in time], begin, start; outmode, age; *informal,* court, escort, take out, show the town *or* a good time, go [out] with, go steady. See SOCIALITY, CHRONOMETRY, OLDNESS.

dated, *adj.* out-of-date, outmoded (see PAST, OLDNESS). *Ant.,* up-to-date.

daub, *v.* smear, spread. See COVERING.

daunt, *v.t.* intimidate, cow, dismay, discourage. See FEAR, DEJECTION.

dawdle, *v.i.* idle, loiter, loaf, waste *or* kill time, goldbrick, (*inf.*), goofoff (*sl.*). See INACTIVITY, SLOWNESS.

dawn, *n.* BEGINNING, origin, inception. See DIMNESS. *Ant.,* dusk.

day, *n.* daytime, LIGHT; dawn, daybreak; around the clock; era, period. See TIME.

daybreak, *n.* dawn, sunrise. See EARLINESS.

daydream, *n.* reverie, castle in the air, fancy. See HOPE, IMAGINATION, INATTENTION.

daze, *v.t.* confuse, dazzle, bewilder, awe; stun, shock, stupefy. See SURPRISE, INSENSIBILITY.

dazzle, *v.t.* blind; impress, overpower; dumbfound, bewilder. See RESPECT, SURPRISE, VISION.

deactivate, *v.t.* demobilize, decommission. See LIBERATION.

dead, *adj.* deceased, perished, defunct; lifeless, inanimate; obsolete, extinct. See DEATH, NONEXISTENCE, INSENSIBILITY. *Ant.,* alive, living.

deadbeat, *n., slang,* sponger. See DEBT, NONPAYMENT.

deaden, *v.t.* benumb; muffle; damp. See INSENSIBILITY, IMPOTENCE, SILENCE.

dead end, *n.* impasse, cul-de-sac. See PASSAGE, DIFFICULTY.

deadline, *n.* time LIMIT.

deadlock, *n.* impasse, bottleneck, stalemate; standoff, tie, draw, even match; hung jury. See EQUALITY, DIFFICULTY.

deadly, *adj.* lethal, fatal; malignant; *informal,* dull. See KILLING, DISEASE, WEARINESS.

deadpan, *adj., slang,* expressionless. See UNMEANINGNESS.

deaf, *adj.* unpersuaded, insensitive; inattentive, oblivious. See INATTENTION, DEAFNESS.

deafening, *adj.* earsplitting (see LOUDNESS).

DEAFNESS
Lack of ability to hear

Nouns—1, deafness, hardness of hearing, hearing impairment, hearing loss, loss of hearing, surdity; deaf-mutism.

2, *(communication with deaf)* lip-reading, deaf-and-dumb alphabet, dactylology, manual alphabet, hand signals, signing; closed *or* open captions.

3, *(deaf person)* deaf-mute, lip reader, deaf-and-dumb person.

Verbs—1, be deaf, go deaf, suffer hearing impairment.

2, deafen, stun, split the ears; fall on deaf ears. See LOUDNESS.

Adjectives—1, deaf, earless, surd; hard *or* dull of hearing, hearing-impaired, unhearing; deaf-mute, deaf-and-dumb; stone-deaf, deafened, deaf as a post *or* an adder; tone-deaf.

2, closed-captioned.

Antonyms, see HEARING.

---

deal, *v.t.* apportion, allocate, allot, distribute; BARTER; inflict; give, bestow, dole. See APPORTIONMENT, GIVING.

dealer, *n.* merchant, tradesman (see SALE).

dear, *adj.* expensive (see DEARNESS); precious, beloved, cherished, darling. —*n.* darling, beloved, love, dearie, honey, sweetheart. See LOVE, ENDEARMENT. *Ant.,* cheap, despised.

DEARNESS
High cost

Nouns—1, dearness, costliness, high, stiff, *or* famine price, pretty penny; overcharge, price gouging; extravagance, exorbitance; heavy pull upon the purse, an arm and a leg; sellers' market; inflation (see INCREASE). *Informal,* big ticket. *Slang,* highway robbery, scalping.

2, big-ticket item.

Verbs—1, be dear, cost much, cost a pretty penny; rise in price, look up; overcharge, overprice, gouge, scalp, jack up [the price]; soak, bleed [white], fleece, extort (see STEALING). *Slang,* stick, clip, soak, skin, take [to the cleaners].

2, pay too much; pay through the nose, pay dear, give *or* pay an arm and a leg.

Adjectives—dear, high, high-price[d]; of great price, expensive, costly, precious, dear bought; overpriced, unreasonable, excessive, extravagant, exorbitant, extortionate; at a premium, not to be had for love *or* money, beyond *or* above price; priceless, of priceless value, invaluable; worth its weight in gold, more precious than rubies, more precious than life itself. *Informal,* pricy, too rich for one's blood, out of sight.

Adverbs—dear, dearly; at great cost *or* expense, at a premium.

Quotations—If you have to ask the price, you can't afford it (*J. P. Morgan*), Those things are dearest to us because they have cost us most (*Montaigne*), Money often costs too much (*Emerson*), Never buy what you do not want, because it is cheap; it will be dear to you (*Thomas Jefferson*).

Antonyms, see CHEAPNESS.

---

dearth, *n.* scarcity, lack, shortage. See INSUFFICIENCY. *Ant.,* abundance.

DEATH
Absence of life

Nouns—1, death, expiration, decease, demise, the grave, the narrow bed, one's latter end; END, cessation; loss, extinction, *or* ebb of life, mortality experience; dissolution, departure, passing on *or* away; release, [eternal *or* final] rest, quietus, fall; stillbirth; thanatology; mortality; morbidity; loss, bereavement; death instinct, thanatos; death rate, death toll; death's head; memento mori; necrophilia; skull and crossbones; megadeath. *Slang*, back-gate parole, cold storage, last roundup.

2, *(surroundings of death)* death warrant, death watch, death rattle, deathbed; stroke, agonies, *or* shades of death; valley of the shadow of death, jaws, gates, *or* hand of death, great divide; last breath, last gasp, last agonies; dying day *or* breath; swan song; rigor mortis; Stygian shore; last will [and testament], living will, no-code; autopsy, coroner's inquest. *Slang*, curtains, last roundup.

3, *(mythology of death)* Death, king of terrors, King of Death; Grim Reaper, Angel of Death, Azrael; mortality, doom; the great leveler; pale rider; river Styx, river of death.

4, *(cause of death)* natural, sudden, *or* violent death, untimely end, drowning, watery grave; suffocation, asphyxia; Black Death, plague, DISEASE, fatality; death blow, asphyxiation, choking, overdose, OD, old age, pestilence, smothering, starvation, suffocation; brain death, euthanasia; beheading, suicide (see KILLING); kiss of death; demographic fatigue; no mayday, do not resuscitate, DNR.

5, *(records of death)* necrology, bills of mortality; obituary, obit; death song (see LAMENTATION). *Informal,* obit.

6, casualty, fatality; corpse, body, cadaver, carcass; [mortal] remains; [dry] bones, skeleton, relics; dust, ashes, earth, clay; mummy, fossil, carrion, food for worms *or* fishes; tenement of clay, this mortal coil; the deceased, the decedent, the [dear] departed; zombie; shade, ghost; widow[er]; dead duck; road kill. *Informal,* goner. *Slang,* stiff, crowbait, cold meat, landowner, road pizza, flatliner, gork.

7, death house; hospice, palliative care unit.

Verbs—1, die [off], expire, perish, go, depart; drown, smother; suffocate; meet one's death *or* end; pass away, be taken, yield *or* resign one's breath, resign one's being *or* life, end one's days *or* life, breathe one's last, cease to live *or* breathe, depart this life, leave this world, go the way of all flesh, join the great majority, meet one's maker, go to a better world; be no more; lose, lay down, relinquish, *or* surrender one's life; die for one's country; sink into the grave, close one's eyes, fall dead, drop [down] dead, succumb; break one's neck, give up *or* yield the ghost; die in harness; walk the plank; die with one's boots on *or* in one's boots, die a violent death; predecease. *Informal,* bite the dust, cash in [one's chips], flatline, go to the last roundup, pass over Jordan, join the choir invisible, jump the last hurdle. *Slang*, kick in *or* off, kick the bucket, go belly-up, check out, croak, pop off, take a ride, sign off, turn up one's toes, buy the farm, beam up, cross the great divide, code out, go south *or* west.

2, put to death (see KILLING); pay the debt to nature, shuffle off this mortal coil, take one's last sleep, go the way of all flesh; come, turn, *or* return to dust, cross the Styx, go to one's long account *or* one's last home, go west, go to Davy Jones's locker, cross the bar; receive one's death warrant, make one's will, die a natural death, go out like a candle; come to an untimely end; catch one's death.

3, be on the brink of death, have one foot in the grave, not be long for this world, turn one's face to the wall.

4, bereave, widow, orphan; leave behind.

Adjectives—1, dead, lifeless; deceased, demised, departed, defunct; late, gone, no more; asleep; dead on arrival, DOA; brain-dead; at peace, at rest; exanimate, inanimate; out of the world, taken off, released, departed this life, dead and gone, launched into eternity, gathered to one's fathers, numbered with the dead; stillborn, extinct; beyond the veil. *Informal,* dead as a doornail, stone dead, stiff, pushing up the daisies, six feet under, done in. *Slang,* eighty-sixed, iced, on ice, ten toes up.

2, fatal, deadly (see KILLING).

3, *(in the process of dying)* dying, moribund, in extremis, amort *(archaic),* in the jaws of death; mortally ill *or* wounded; going [off], on one's deathbed; at the point of death, at death's door, at the last gasp, done for, on one's last legs, on the spot; with one foot in the grave, *in articulo mortis,* as good as dead, done for; perimortem, post-mortem.

Phrases—let the dead bury the dead; dead men tell no tales; death is the great leveler; you can only die once; the sands of life are running out.

Quotations—Dust thou art, and unto dust shalt thou return *(Bible),* O death, where is thy sting? O grave, where is thy victory? *(Bible),* And I looked, and behold a pale horse, and his name that sat on him was Death *(Bible),* Nothing in his life became him like the leaving it *(Shakespeare),* A great reckoning in a little room *(Shakespeare),* All that lives must die, passing through nature to eternity *(Shakespeare),* Let's talk of graves, of worms, and epitaphs *(Shakespeare),* The undiscovered country, from whose bourn no traveler returns *(Shakespeare),* Never send to know for whom the bell tolls; it tolls for thee *(John Donne),* Death must be distinguished from dying, with which it is often confused *(Sydney Smith),* Dying is an art, like everything else *(Sylvia Plath).*

Antonyms, see LIFE.

---

deathless, *adj.* immortal, lasting. See PERPETUITY. *Ant.,* mortal.

debacle, *n.* FAILURE; stampede, panic. See REVOLUTION, DESTRUCTION.

debar, *v.t.* exclude, shut out. See EXCLUSION, PROHIBITION.

debasement, *n.* abasement, debauchery, corruption, degradation, DISREPUTE; adulteration, impairment, impurity. See WEAKNESS, DETERIORATION.

debate, *n.* argument, dispute, controversy; forum, panel discussion; war of words.

—*v.* argue, discuss, dispute; bandy words, take sides, lock horns, contend; reflect, consider. See CONVERSATION, REASONING.

debauch, *v.* corrupt, ruin. See IMPURITY.

debilitate, *v.t.* See WEAKNESS.

debit, *n. & v.* See DEBT.

debonair, *adj.* courteous; gay, affable. See CHEERFULNESS.

debrief, *v.t.* interrogate (see INQUIRY).

debris, *n.* rubbish, rubble, detritus, wreckage, ruins, trash. See REMAINDER, PART.

DEBT
State of owing money

Nouns—1, debt, indebtedness, obligation, LIABILITY, debit, score; charge, charge account; arrears, deferred payment, accounts receivable; deficit, default; insolvency, nonpayment, bankruptcy; bad debt, bills, nonperforming asset; national *or* public deficit; interest, usury; floating debt *or* capital. *Informal,* megadebt. See BORROWING, ACCOUNTING, INSUFFICIENCY, FAILURE, POVERTY, NONPAYMENT.

2, debtor, debitor; defaulter. *Slang,* deadbeat.

3, lending, loan, [cash] advance, accommodation; encumbrance.

4, interest, usury; interest rate, points, prime rate, bank rate; simple *or* compound interest.

5, lender, banker, mortgagee, pawnbroker, pawnshop.

Verbs—1, be in debt, owe; incur *or* contract a debt; run up a bill *or* a score, run a tab, run up an account; borrow (see BORROWING); run *or* get into debt; accrue debts; outrun the constable; answer for, go bail for, bail out. *Informal,* run a tab, go on tick. *Slang,* touch, go broke.

2, lend, advance, finance, accommodate (with), loan, encumber; mortgage, hypothecate, pledge, pawn, borrow from Peter to pay Paul. *Informal,* hock.

3, *(refuse to honor a debt)* repudiate, stop payment, dishonor; charge *or* write off. See NONPAYMENT.

Adjectives—**1,** indebted, liable, chargeable, answerable for, in debt, in embarrassed circumstances, in difficulties, encumbered, involved, plunged *or* deep in debt, short, up against it, in the red, in the hole, fast tied up; bankrupt, insolvent; minus, out of pocket. *Informal,* in hock. *Slang,* broke, on the cuff, in hock, head over heels in debt.
2, unpaid; unrequited, unrewarded; owing, due, past due, in arrears, outstanding; delinquent.

Phrases—lend your money and lose your friend.

Quotations—Home life ceases to be free and beautiful as soon as it is founded on borrowing and debt (*Henrik Ibsen*), He that dies pays all debts (*Shakespeare*).

Antonyms, see PAYMENT, CREDIT.

---

debunk, *v.t.* disabuse, set straight (see RIGHTNESS).

debut, *n.* See BEGINNING.

decadent, *adj.* ruined, fallen; depraved, debauched, dissolute; sentimental, nostalgic; blasé, cynical. See DETERIORATION, IMPURITY.

decamp, *v.i.* break camp, depart (see DEPARTURE).

decapitate, *v.t.* behead, chop off one's head. See KILLING.

decay, *n.* DECOMPOSITION, DETERIORATION, disintegration, dilapidation, putrefaction, rot, caries. —*v.i.* rot, putrefy, mortify; disintegrate. See OLDNESS, UNCLEANNESS.

decease, *n. & v.* See DEATH.

deceit, *n.* fraud, artifice, cheating. See DECEPTION.

decent, *adj.* decorous, chaste, pure in heart; acceptable, reasonable, tolerable; virtuous, modest, respectable. See PROBITY, REPUTE, MODESTY. *Ant.,* gross, indecent, unseemly.

DECEPTION
Misrepresentation

Nouns—**1,** *(act of deceiving)* deception, deceptiveness; falseness, FALSEHOOD, untruth; imposition, imposture, misinformation, disinformation; fraud, fraudulence, deceit, deceitfulness, speciousness, guile, bluff; bad *or* rubber check, bad paper; knavery (see CUNNING). See ERROR.

2, *(something deceptive)* delusion, illusion, gullery; juggling, jugglery; sleight of hand, legerdemain, prestidigitation, magic (see SORCERY); trickery, chicanery; cozenage, circumvention, collusion; treachery (see IMPROBITY); practical joke, trick, hoax, cheat, blind, feint, plant; bubble (see IMAGINATION); fetch, catch, juggle, reach, hocus, hokey-pokey, fake, hanky-panky, blarney; weasel words; fine print; thimblerig, card-sharping, artful dodge, swindle, racket, shell game; stratagem, artifice. *Slang,* sell, spoof, con *or* badger game, [flim]flam, gyp, scam, sting, dipsy-doodle, fast one, head trip, jay, snow job, gig, honey-fuggle.

3, *(deception meant to entrap)* snare, trap, springe, gin, decoy, come-on; bait, decoy duck, baited trap (see ATTRACTION); mousetrap, beartrap, steel trap, mantrap; cobweb, net, toils; trapdoor, sliding panel, false bottom; spring-net, spring-gun, masked battery; booby trap. *Slang,* clip joint.

4, *(something meant to fool one)* mockery, IMITATION, counterfeit, sham, make-believe, forgery, fraud, fake, lie; hollow mockery; whited sepulcher; tinsel, paste, false *or* counterfeit jewelry, glass; man of straw; ormolu; jerrybuilding; mirage; wooden nutmeg, German silver; Britannia metal, Potemkin village. *Informal,* phony. *Slang,* gold brick.

5, *(one who deceives)* deceiver, trickster, sharper, swindler, liar, snake [in the grass]; humbug, charlatan, quack, mountebank, fast talker; impostor, fraud, fake[r], sham, hoax[er], cheat; pretender, Judas; wolf in sheep's clothing, cheat; magician, conjuror; dodger, swindler, *etc. Slang,* con man, fourflusher, ringer, hoser, shyster, deadbeat, yaffner, cunt teaser, flimp, shicer, chiaus. See STEALING, IMPROBITY.

6, *(one deceived)* dupe, gull, victim, monkey. *Informal,* con artist, sucker, chump. *Slang,* pigeon, joe, mark, quack, tool, schlemiel, sap, easy touch. See CREDULITY.

Verbs—1, deceive, take in; defraud, cheat, jockey, cozen, fleece, nab, play one false, do in, bilk, bite, pluck, swindle, hustle, victimize, gull, hoax, dupe, take, rope in; stuff the ballot box; abuse, mystify, blind one's eyes; kid; blindfold, hoodwink, take for a ride; throw dust into the eyes; impose, practice, play, put, palm, *or* foist upon; snatch a verdict; palm off; circumvent, overreach, outreach, outwit, outmaneuver, finagle, get around, cross up; steal a march upon, give the go-by, leave in the lurch. *Informal,* gouge, slip one over on, diddle. *Slang,* clip, give the runaround, chisel, con, do a number on, jive, murphy, stiff, take to the cleaners, cuckold, fuck [over], hump, jape, pimp someone over, pull someone's dick, screw, scrog, trim, yentz.

2, *(entrap)* set *or* lay a trap, lay a snare for; bait the hook, spread the toils, decoy, lure, beguile, delude, inveigle, suck in; hook, trick, entrap, ensnare, throw a curve, trip up; nick, springe; catch in a trap; hocus, practice on one's credulity, fool, befool, pull the wool over one's eyes, pull one's leg; humbug, bamboozle, flimflam, bilk, put one *or* something over (on), hand a person a lemon, lead up the garden path, work the rabbit's foot on, take for a sleigh ride; stuff up, sell; play a trick upon; play a practical joke upon; send on a fool's errand, make a game of, make a fool of, make an April fool of, make an ass of; come over, dissemble, lie (see FALSEHOOD); misinform, brainwash, mislead (see ERROR); throw off the scent; betray. *Slang,* fourflush, finesse, sandbag, fake on.

3, *(act to deceive)* load the dice, stack the cards *or* deck; live by one's wits, play at hide-and-seek, play possum, play the fox; obtain money under false pretenses (see STEALING); conjure, juggle, practice chicanery; pass, palm, foist, *or* fob off.

Adjectives—1, deceived, caught; hoist with one's own petard. *Slang,* shot through the grease.

2, deceiving, guileful, CUNNING, deceptive, deceitful, devious, delusive, delusory, colored; illusive, illusory; elusive, insidious; untrue (see FALSEHOOD); mock, sham, make-believe, counterfeit, pseudo, spurious, so-called, pretended, feigned, trumped up, bogus, fraudulent, tricky, factitious, artificial, bastard, fake; surreptitious, underhand[ed], illegitimate, contraband, adulterated, sophisticated; unsound, rotten at the core; disguised, meretricious; tinsel, pinchbeck; catchpenny; brummagem; simulated, plated. *Informal,* doctored, phony. *Slang,* jive-ass, full of shit.

Adverbs—deceptively, *etc.;* under false colors, under cover of; behind one's back, cunningly; slyly; on the sly.

Phrases—deceit is a lie that wears a smile; all done with mirrors; all that glitters is not gold; never give a sucker an even break.

Quotations—O what a tangled web we weave, when first we practice to deceive! (*Sir Walter Scott*), You may fool all the people some of the time; you can even fool some of the people all the time; but you can't fool all of the people all the time (*Abraham Lincoln*), The Devil can cite the Scripture for his purpose (*Shakespeare*), The world is still deceived with ornament (*Shakespeare*).

Antonyms, see PROBITY, TRUTH.

---

decide, *v.* determine, elect, choose, settle, fix; make up one's mind; arbitrate. See RESOLUTION, CHOICE, CERTAINTY, CAUSE. *Ant.,* vacillate, straddle the fence.

decimate, *v.* destroy, wipe out. See KILLING, DESTRUCTION.

decipher, *v.t.* make out, decode; translate, interpret. See INTERPRETATION.

decision, *n.* firmness, RESOLUTION; JUDGMENT, determination; verdict, finding. See LAWSUIT.

decisive, *adj.* final, conclusive, resolute.

See RESOLUTION, CERTAINTY. *Ant.,* indecisive, vacillating.

deck, *n.* floor, platform, flooring; quarterdeck, forecastle, fo'c'sle; after, boat, flight, *etc.* deck; pack [of cards]. —*v.t.* deck out, bedeck, ORNAMENT, array, adorn, decorate; *slang,* knock down (see IMPULSE). See COVERING, SHIP.

declaim, *v.i.* recite, harangue, rant. See SPEECH.

declaration, *n.* AFFIRMATION, proclamation, statement, assertion, avowal. See SPEECH, EVIDENCE.

decline, *n.* droop, slant, slope; decadence, wasting, aging, DETERIORATION. —*v.* worsen, slump; refuse, turn down (an offer). See OLDNESS, AGE, REFUSAL, DESCENT, WEAKNESS, RECESSION.

DECOMPOSITION
Decay

Nouns—decomposition, disintegration, decay, corruption (see UNCLEANNESS); analysis, dissection, resolution, dissolution, breakup; fragmentation, crumbling, SEPARATION; wasting away; catalysis, hydrolysis, dialysis, electrolysis; DISPERSION; DISJUNCTION.

Verbs—decompose, decompound, disintegrate; corrupt; analyze, dissolve; resolve, separate into its elements; catalyze, hydrolyze, dialyze, electrolyze; dissect, break up *or* down; disperse; unravel, unroll; crumble into dust, fall to pieces; waste away.

Adjectives—decomposed, corrupt, decayed; analytical, catalytic, hydrolytic, dialytic, electrolytic.

Antonyms, see COMPOSITION.

---

decor, *n.* decoration. See ORNAMENT.

decoration, *n.* ORNAMENT, garnishment, trimming; trophy, ribbon, *etc.* (see APPROBATION).

decorum, *n.* decency; protocol. See AGREEMENT, FASHION.

decoy, *v.t.* entice, lure, entrap. See ATTRACTION, DECEPTION.

DECREASE
Diminution

Nouns—1, *(decrease in amount)* decrease, diminution; lessening, subtraction (see DEDUCTION); reduction, abatement; shrinking, CONTRACTION, extenuation; cut back, discount. See SHORTNESS.

2, *(decrease in intensity)* subsidence, wane, ebb, decline; scaling down, deescalation; downsizing; decrement, reflux, depreciation, deflation; deceleration, slowdown; DETERIORATION; mitigation (see MODERATION). *Informal,* letup.

Verbs—1, decrease, diminish, lessen, shrink; drop, fall, *or* tail off; fall away, wane, ebb; descend, subside, let up; melt, die, *or* fade away; retire into the shade, fall to a low ebb, die down; run low, out, dry, *or* short, wear away; dwindle, slacken, peter out.

2, abate, bate; discount, depreciate, lower; attenuate, extenuate, mitigate, moderate; cut to the bone; cut back, down, *or* into; curtail, reduce; step, turn, *or* scale down, roll back, take in; demote, downgrade; downscale, downsize.

Adjectives—unincreased, decreased, decreasing, short, diminishing, waning, wasting away, wearing out, reduced, lessening, ebbing, dwindling, petering out, fading, disappearing, vanishing, falling off; dwarfish.

Adverbs—on the wane, on the decrease, smaller and smaller, less and less.

Antonyms, see INCREASE.

---

decree, *n.* COMMAND, edict, ordinance, law, fiat; JUDGMENT. See LEGALITY.

decrement, *n.* reduction, loss (see DECREASE).

decrepit, *adj.* dilapidated, broken-down;

shaky; doddering, senile, on one's last legs (*inf.*), ready for the scrap heap (*inf.*). See DETERIORATION, DISEASE, WEAKNESS.

decry, *v.* blame, censure. See DISAPPROBATION.

dedicate, *v.t.* devote, consecrate; inscribe. See USE, REPUTE.

deduce, *v.* infer, conclude, derive; reason, reckon, assume, opine, think, believe. See REASONING.

DEDUCTION
Subtraction

Nouns—1, deduction, removal, excision; subtraction, subtrahend, minuend; minus, minus sign, subtrahend, minuend; REMAINDER, difference; abstraction, abbreviation, curtailment (see SHORTNESS); reduction (see DECREASE); depreciation, detraction; retrenchment; amputation, truncation; castration, spaying.

2, (*amount deducted*) decrement, discount, rebate.

3, censorship, expurgation, bowdlerization; castration, circumcision; excision, deletion, editing; editor, censor.

Verbs—1, deduct, subduct, subtract, take away; remove, excise, cut out, rub off, wipe out, rule out; abstract, abbreviate, curtail; reduce; retrench; amputate, dock, truncate; deduce, discount; abate, rebate, write off; pare, shave, prune; refine; castrate, spay.

2, censor, expurgate, bowdlerize, cut, edit; castrate, circumcise; excise, delete, edit; abridge (see SHORTNESS). *Informal*, bleep [out].

Adjectives—deducted, deductive, deducible, subtractive; sawed off; censorial, expurgative.

Prepositions—minus, diminished by, less; without, except, barring, excluding.

Antonyms, see ADDITION.

---

deed, *n.* act, ACTION, feat, achievement, exploit; conveyance, TRANSFER. See COURAGE, RECORD.

deem, *v.* consider, judge, regard; assess; calculate, reckon (*both inf.*). See JUDGMENT.

deemphasize, *v.t.* belittle, trivialize, minimize, downplay (see DETRACTION).

deep, *adj. & n.* DEPTH, CUNNING.

deep-seated, *adj.* established, inveterate, rooted. See HABIT.

deface, *v.t.* mar, disfigure, mutilate, blemish; maim, mangle, scar. See DETERIORATION, FORMLESSNESS.

de facto, *Lat.* in fact; actual; realistically. See EXISTENCE, TRUTH.

defame, *v.t.* traduce, vilify, revile, calumniate, asperse, abuse, malign, slander. See DISREPUTE, DETRACTION. *Ant.*, praise, extol.

default, *n.* omission, breach, NEGLECT; NONPAYMENT, delinquency, arrears; AVOIDANCE, nonappearance. See DEBT. —*v.* back out, NEGLECT, disregard; not pay, renege (*inf.*), welsh (*inf.*); absent oneself, be missing.

defeat, *v.t.* thwart, frustrate, foil, outwit; rout, conquer, overcome, beat, vanquish, subdue, lick (*inf.*). —*n.* frustration, setback, loss, rout, vanquishment. See FAILURE, SUCCESS, CONFUTATION. *Ant.*, surrender, resign.

defect, *n.* blemish, fault, flaw, IMPERFECTION; deficiency, lack, INCOMPLETENESS. —*v.i.* desert, flee, abandon. See RELINQUISHMENT, ESCAPE.

defend, *v.t.* support, prove; vindicate. See EVIDENCE, DEFENSE.

defendant, *n.* accused, suspect, [co]respondent. See LAWSUIT, ACCUSATION.

DEFENSE
Resistance against assault

Nouns—1, defense, protection, guard, ward; shielding, PRESERVATION, guardianship; self-defense, self-preservation; deterrent; defense *or* escape mechanism; resistance; safeguard (see SAFETY).

2, shelter, fortification; bulwark; foss[e], moat, entrenchment; foxhole; dike, parapet, embankment, mound, mole, bank; earthwork; fieldwork; fence, wall, dead wall; paling, sunk fence, haha, palisade (see ENCLOSURE), barrier, barricade; portcullis, *chevaux de frise*, abatis; battlement, rampart, scarp; glacis, casemate, buttress, abutment; breastwork, curtain, bastion, redan, ravelin; redoubt; lines, loophole, machicolation; barrage balloon, radar screen, civil defense, DEW (distant early warning) line, EBS (emergency broadcast system).

3, *(defensive building)* hold, stronghold, fastness; sanctuary, refuge (see SAFETY); keep, dungeon, fortress, citadel, castle; tower, tower of strength; fort, blockhouse; air-raid shelter.

4, *(defensive clothing)* armor, [chain] mail, coat of mail, lame, plate, surcoat; shield, buckler, aegis; gorget, ailette, brassard, pallette, epaulière, pauldron, vambrace, cubitiere, gauntlet, plastron, breastplate, cuirass, skirt of tasses, fauld, habergeon, mail, hauberk, kneepiece, poleyn, tuille, cuisse, greave, jambeau, lorication, backplate, footpiece, solleret; [steel] helmet, basinet, burgonet, heaume, siege cap, casque, sallet, tin hat, cask, shako, bearskin, beaver, visor; weapon (see ARMS).

5, *(one who defends)* defender, protector, guardian, guard, bodyguard, champion, knight [errant]; garrison, patrol, watch, national guard (see COMBATANT); sentinel, sentry, lookout; keeper, watchman; watchdog. See SAFETY.

Verbs—defend, go to bat for, stick up for, take up the cudgels for; forfend, fend off; shield, screen, fence round (see CIRCUMSCRIPTION); entrench, dig in; guard (see SAFETY); guard against; take care of, bear harmless; keep, ward, stave, fight, *or* beat off, parry; put to flight; hold *or* keep at bay, keep at arm's length; stand *or* set on the defensive; man the barricades, hold the fort; show fight; maintain *or* stand one's ground; stand by, hold a brief for; hold one's own, defend oneself; bear the brunt; fall back upon, hold. *Slang,* stonewall, cover one's ass.

Adjectives—1, defending, defensive; protective, preservative; self-protective, self-defensive.
  2, fortified, armored, armed, armed at all points, armed to the teeth; embattled; panoplied, iron-plated, ironclad; loopholed, castellated, machiocolated, casemated; defended, invulnerable, impervious, proof (against).
  3, defensible, protectable.

Adverbs—defensively; on the defense *or* defensive; in defense; at bay.

Phrases—attack is the best form of defense.

Antonyms, see attack.

---

defenseless, *adj.* helpless, exposed, unprotected, open, bare, vulnerable. See WEAKNESS, DANGER.

defensible, *adj.* justifiable, tenable, warrantable. See EVIDENCE. *Ant.,* indefensible, weak.

defer, *v.* delay, suspend, postpone, stay, procrastinate; submit, yield, give in, abide by, RESPECT. See LATENESS, SUBMISSION.

DEFIANCE
Challenge to fight

Nouns—defiance, dare, challenge, THREAT; provocation; war cry, war whoop; rebellion (see DISOBEDIENCE); INSOLENCE; contempt, disdain; audacity, daring; fighting words, gauntlet; chip on one's shoulder. *Informal,* cheek[iness], brass[iness], sauciness. See RASHNESS, OPPOSITION.

Verbs—defy, dare, double-dare, beard, brave (see COURAGE); bid defiance to, set at naught, set at defiance, provoke; hurl defiance at; face down, fly in the face of, brazen it out, kick against the pricks, nail one's colors to the mast; dance the war dance; snap one's fingers at, bite the thumb, thumb one's nose at, laugh to scorn; disobey; show fight, show one's teeth, show a bold front, call a bluff; look big, stand akimbo; double *or* shake the fist, threaten (see THREAT); throw in the teeth; throw down *or* pick up the gauntlet, gage, *or* glove; stick to one's guns; challenge, call out; toss one's hat in the ring.

Adjectives—defiant; defying, daring; with arms akimbo; insolent, contemptuous, bold, rebellious. *Informal,* brassy, saucy, cheeky.

Adverbs—defiantly, in defiance, in the teeth of; under one's very nose.
Phrases—you can lead a horse to water, but you can't make him drink.

Antonyms, see OBEDIENCE, FEAR.

deficient, *adj.* lacking, wanting, inadequate, insufficient, imperfect, incomplete. See INFERIORITY, IMPERFECTION, INSUFFICIENCY. *Ant.,* adequate, ample.

deficit, *n.* shortfall (see DEBT). *Ant.,* surplus.

defile, *v.t.* dirty, [be]foul, tarnish, blacken; corrupt, debauch, contaminate; dishonor, debase, sully, drag in the dust, give a bad name. See UNCLEANNESS, IMPURITY, DISREPUTE. —*n.* ravine, gorge, passage. See INTERVAL.

define, *v.t.* explain, interpret; prescribe; describe, circumscribe, LIMIT, demarcate. See INTERPRETATION.

definite, *adj.* exact, explicit, plain, limited, precise, unequivocal. See SPECIALITY, LIMIT, CERTAINTY, TRUTH. *Ant.,* indefinite, vague.

definitive, *adj.* conclusive, fixed, final. See CERTAINTY, END. *Ant.,* provisional.

deflate, *v.t.* exhaust, empty; reduce, humble, lower. See HUMILITY, CONTRACTION. *Ant.,* inflate.

deflect, *v.* bend, curve, twist; deviate, avert, swing, sidetrack. See DEVIATION, CURVATURE.

deflower, *v.t.* ravish, despoil. See IMPURITY.

deformity, *n.* malformation, disfigurement, DISTORTION, UGLINESS, IMPERFECTION, FORMLESSNESS.

defraud, *v.t.* swindle, cheat, dupe, fleece. See STEALING, DECEPTION.

defray, *v.* reimburse (see PAYMENT).

deft, *adj.* dextrous, skillful. See SKILL. *Ant.,* inept, awkward.

defy, *v.t.* See DEFIANCE.

degeneracy, *n.* DETERIORATION, demoralization; viciousness, depravity, turpitude, vice.

degrade, *v.* humiliate, shame, debase, demean; degenerate. See DETERIORATION, DISREPUTE. *Ant.,* elevate, honor.

DEGREE
Step in a series

Nouns—degree, grade, extent, measure, amount, ratio, standard, height, pitch; reach, amplitude, range, scope, caliber; gradation, graduation, shade; echelon; station, estate, status, rank, hole, notch; standing (see CLASS); rate; point, mark (see INDICATION); intensity; proportion. See MEASUREMENT, QUANTITY.

Verbs—compare; calibrate; rank, SIZE, graduate, grade, shade off.

Adjectives—comparative, relative; gradual, shading off.

Adverbs—by degrees, gradually, step by step, bit by bit, little by little, inch by inch, drop by drop; by inches, by slow degrees; in some degree, in some measure; so *or* as far as; to some extent, to a degree, rather; in the least, at all. *Informal,* kind of, sort of.

dehydrate, *v.* dry [out], dessicate, evaporate. See DRYNESS, PRESERVATION.

deify, *v.t.* worship, exalt, apotheosize (see IDOLATRY).

deign, *v.* condescend, lower oneself, stoop; vouchsafe, CONSENT. See HUMILITY.

Dei gratia, Lat. by the grace of God. See JUSTICE.

DEITY
Divine nature

Nouns—1, *(nature of God)* Deity, Divinity; Godhead, Godship; Omnipotence, Providence; *anima mundi.*

2, *(God's names)* **a.** God, Lord; Jehovah, Yahweh, Jah, JHVH, Tetragrammaton, Adonai, Elohim, Shaddai, S[h]iva; Supreme Being, First Cause; Author *or* Creator of all things, Maker; the Infinite, the Eternal; the All-powerful, -wise, -merciful, -knowing, *or* -holy; Allah; God of Abraham, *etc.*; Ancient of Days, First Cause, Great Spirit, Lord of Hosts, Lord of Sabaoth, the Lord God, King of Heaven; Divine Mind. **b.** olorum; Ahura Mazda, Ormazd; Allah, Brahma, Buddha, deva, Great Mother, Indra, kami, Krishna, Mahdi, Rama, Sat Guru, Tathagata, Trimurti, Vishnu, Yama.

3, *(attributes)* infinite power, omnipotence; infinite wisdom, omniscience; goodness, justice, truth, mercy; omnipresence; unity, immutability, holiness, glory, majesty, sovereignty, infinity, eternity; redemption, salvation.

4, The Trinity, Holy Trinity, *or* Trinity in Unity: **a.** God the Father, Maker, Creator, *or* Preserver; creation, preservation, divine government; theocracy, thearchy; Providence, ways *or* dispensation of Providence. **b.** God the Son, Jesus, Christ, the Messiah, Anointed, Savior, Redeemer; the Son of God, Man, *or* David; the Lamb of God, the Word [Incarnate]; Emmanuel, Immanuel; the King of Kings and King of Glory, Prince of Peace, Good Shepherd, Light of the World, the Incarnation; salvation, redemption, atonement, propitiation, mediation, intercession, judgment. **c.** God the Holy Ghost, the Holy Spirit, Paraclete; inspiration, unction, regeneration, sanctification, consolation. **d.** special providence, Deus ex machina; avatar.

5, joss. See MYTHICAL DEITIES.

Verbs—1, create, uphold, preserve, govern, atone, redeem, save, propitiate, predestinate, elect, call, ordain, bless, justify, sanctify, glorify.

2, deify (see IDOLATRY, REPUTE).

Adjectives—godly, divine; almighty, holy, hallowed, sacred, divine, heavenly, celestial, sacrosanct, superhuman, supernatural; omnipotent, almighty, omnipresent, ubiquitous, omniscient; ghostly, spiritual, hyperphysical, unearthly; theistic, theocratic; anointed; three-in-one, triune.

Adverbs—divinely, by divine right; with the help of God.

Phrases—God helps them that helps themselves; The nature of God is a circle of which the center is everywhere and the circumference is nowhere; God is not dead but alive and well and working on a much less ambitious project.

Quotations—With God all things are possible (*Bible*), He that loveth not knoweth not God; for God is love (*Bible*), If God did not exist, it would be necessary to invent him (*Voltaire*), If God made us in His image, we have certainly returned the compliment (*Voltaire*), God is subtle, but he is not malicious (*Albert Einstein*), God is that, the greater than which cannot be conceived (*St. Anselm*), He was a wise man who invented God (*Plato*), Man proposes, God disposes (*Thomas à Kempis*).

Antonyms, see HUMANITY, DEMON.

---

déjà vu, Fr. familiarity. See IMAGINATION, MEMORY.

DEJECTION
Sadness

Nouns—1, dejection, dejectedness, depression; lowness *or* depression of spirits; weight *or* damp on the spirits; low, bad, drooping, *or* depressed spirits; sinking heart, heaviness of heart; heaviness, gloom; weariness, disgust of life; homesickness; melancholy, sadness, melancholia, doldrums, vapors, megrims, spleen, mal de siècle; blue Monday; horrors, hypochondria, pessimism; despondency, dismay, slough of despond; disconsolation, DISCONTENT; hope deferred, blank despondency; Weltschmerz. See DISAPPOINTMENT, PAIN.

2, grief, chagrin, sorrow, heartache, heavy heart, prostration, blues, dumps; broken heart; despair; gravity, solemnity; straight, long, *or* grave face; death's-head at the feast. *Informal,* blue devils, mulligrubs.

3, *(dejected person)* hypochondriac, pessimist; mope, killjoy, spoilsport, wet blanket, party pooper. *Informal,* grinch. *Slang,* sourpuss, wet blanket, crepe hanger. See HOPELESSNESS.

Verbs—1, be dejected, grieve, mourn, lament (see LAMENTATION); take on, give way, lose heart, despond, languish, flag, droop, sink, lower, look downcast, frown, pout, hang down the head, pull, draw, wear, *or* make a long face, laugh on the wrong side of the mouth, grin a ghastly smile, look blue; lay *or* take to heart; mope, brood (over), fret, sulk, pine, repine, despair, dismay.

2, *(cause dejection)* deject, depress, discourage, dishearten, demoralize, daunt, dispirit, damp[en], dash, cast *or* knock down; unman, prostrate, break one's heart, cast a gloom *or* shade on, cast a pall upon, sadden; damp, dash, *or* wither one's hopes; weigh *or* lie heavy on the mind; prey on the mind; depress the spirits. *Informal,* hit one like a ton of bricks.

Adjectives—**1,** dejected, cheerless, joyless, spiritless; uncheerful, unlively, unhappy, sad, triste, gray, melancholy; oppressed with *or* a prey to melancholy; downcast, downhearted; down in the mouth, down on one's luck; heavy, heavy-heart; [down] in the dumps, in the sulks, in the doldrums; in bad humor, sullen, mumpish, dumpish; mopish, moping, moody, blue, glum, sulky, discontented, out of sorts, out of humor, out of spirits; ill at ease, low-spirited, in low spirits; weary, discouraged, disheartened; bearish; despondent, chapfallen, crestfallen.

2, sad, pensive, tristful, doleful, woebegone, tearful, lachrymose, in tears, melancholic, hypochondriacal, bilious, jaundiced, atrabilious, saturnine, splenetic; lackadaisical; grave, sober [as a judge], solemn, grim, grim-faced, grim-visaged, rueful, long-faced.

3, *(dejected past consoling)* disconsolate, inconsolable, forlorn, comfortless, desolate; sick at heart, soul-sick, heartsick, in despair, lost; overcome, broken down, borne *or* bowed down; heart-stricken, cut up, dashed, sunk; unnerved, unmanned; downfallen, downtrodden; heartbroken, brokenhearted; careworn.

Adverbs—dejectedly, with a long face, with tears in one's eyes; sadly, *etc.*

Phrases—misery loves company; Wednesday's child is full of woe; laugh and the world laughs with you, weep and you weep alone.

Quotations—Everywhere I see bliss, from which I alone am irrevocably excluded (*Mary Shelley*), There is no greater pain than to remember a happy time when one is in misery (*Dante*), When sorrows come, they come not as single spies, but in battalions (*Shakespeare*), I tell you, hopeless grief is passionless (*Elizabeth Browning*), Sorrow is tranquillity remembered in emotion (*Dorothy Parker*), Suffering is the sole origin of consciousness (*Fyodor Dostoyevsky*), The flesh is sad, alas, and I've read all the books (*Stéphane Mallarmé*), Happiness is beneficial for the body, but it is grief that develops the powers of the mind (*Marcel Proust*).

Antonyms, see CHEERFULNESS.

---

de jure, *Lat.* by right; lawfully. See LEGALITY.

delay, *v.* put off, retard, defer, postpone; linger, dally, loiter, procrastinate.—*n.* postponement, stay; procrastination. See LATENESS, SLOWNESS, HINDRANCE, DURABILITY. *Ant.,* hasten.

delectable, *adj.* delightful, delicious, exquisite. See PLEASURE.

delegate, *n.* deputy, envoy, emissary, AGENT. —*v.t.* COMMISSION, entrust, depute, empower. See SUBSTITUTION.

delete, *v.t.* erase, cancel, expunge, take out, cross out, excise, dele. See NULLIFICATION, DEDUCTION.

deleterious, *adj.* injurious. See WRONG, INEXPEDIENCE.

deliberate, *adj.* intentional, studied; cool, careful, thoughtful, unhurried, See CARE, SLOWNESS. —*v.i.* ponder, consider, think, weigh. See THOUGHT, ADVICE, CAUTION, PLAN. *Ant.,* hasty, rash; pass over.

delicacy, *n.* sensitiveness, tact, nicety; frailty, daintiness, exactness; tidbit, dainty; discrimination, TASTE, fastidiousness. See BEAUTY, FOOD, SKILL, PLEASURE, BRITTLENESS.

delicious, *adj.* delectable, delightful, luscious, toothsome, palatable, savory. See TASTE. *Ant.,* tasteless, bad tasting, unpleasant.

delight, *n.* joy, rapture. —*v.* please, thrill. See PLEASURE. *Ant.,* dismay.

delightful, *adj.* pleasing, enjoyable, charming, attractive, alluring. See PLEASURE, BEAUTY. *Ant.,* disagreeable.

delineate, *v.t.* sketch, draw, limn, portray, outline, depict, describe. See PLAN, REPRESENTATION.

delinquent, *adj.* neglectful, negligent, defaulting, undutiful; culpable. —*n.* defaulter; transgressor, troublemaker, lawbreaker; juvenile delinquent, J.D. See DEBT, EVILDOER, GUILT, ILLEGALITY, NEGLECT.

delirious, *adj.* mad, raving, wandering, unbalanced, frenzied. See INSANITY, FEELING.

deliver, *v.* discharge, give forth, emit, deal; [set] free, liberate, release, emancipate; save, rescue, redeem; convey, carry to; rid; grant, cede, surrender; pronounce, speak, utter; give birth (to), produce; *informal,* make good. See GIVING, SPEECH, LIBERATION, TRANSPORTATION, RELIEF.

delivery, *n.* surrender; conveyance; childbirth, parturition; rescue, ESCAPE, salvation, redemption (see LIBERATION); address (see SPEECH).

delude, *v.t.* See DECEPTION.

deluge, *n.* flood, inundation; downpour, spate; plethora. See SUFFICIENCY, WATER.

delusion, *n.* DECEPTION; illusion, fantasy, misconception, hallucination. See ERROR.

de luxe, *adj.* elegant, sumptuous, luxurious. See OSTENTATION.

delve, *v.i.* research, dig. See INQUIRY.

demagogue, *n.* instigator, agitator, rabble-rouser. See CAUSE.

demand, *v.t.* require, charge; levy, exact, order, call for, claim, requisition. See COMMAND, NECESSITY. —*n.* requirement, requisition; ultimatum; market; COMMAND. See PRICE, JUSTICE.

demanding, *adj.* arduous, difficult; insistent, exacting. See DIFFICULTY, COMMAND. *Ant.,* lax, permissive.

demarcation, *n.* boundary (see LIMIT).

demean, *v.t.* debase, lower. See HUMILITY.

demeanor, *n.* behavior, bearing. See CONDUCT, APPEARANCE.

demented, *adj.* deranged, crazed. See INSANITY. *Ant.,* sane.

demerit, *n.* black mark, minus, fault; defect, failing. See ERROR, DISAPPROBATION. *Ant.,* [gold] star, credit.

demise, *n.* DEATH; TRANSFER.

demobilize, *v.* discharge, muster out, send home; disarm, demilitarize; disband, scatter. See LIBERATION, DISJUNCTION. *Ant.,* mobilize, conscript.

democratic, *adj.* unsnobbish; popular. See AUTHORITY.

demolish, *v.t.* raze, level, ruin, wreck, destroy, wipe out. See DESTRUCTION, CONFUTATION.

DEMON
Evil spirit

Nouns—1, demon, demonry, demonology; evil genius, fiend, familiar, devil; bad spirit, unclean spirit; cacodemon, incubus, succubus; Frankenstein's monster; Ahriman; fury, harpy. *Informal,* things that go bump in the night. See MYTHICAL DEITIES, FEAR, IDOLATRY.

2, *(incarnation of Evil)* the Devil, Lucifer, Mephistopheles, Belial; Beelzebub, Asmodeus, Apollyon, Avernus, Nicholas; the tempter, EVIL, the evil one, the evil spirit, the Prince of Darkness, fallen angel, the cloven hoof, Lord of the Flies; Pluto, god of the underworld; the foul fiend, the archfiend; the Devil incarnate; the serpent, 666 (Revelations or Apocalypse 13:18). *Slang,* the deuce, the dickens, old Nick, Sam Hill, old Scratch, old Harry, dibble, Dad.

3, *(mischievous demons)* vampire, ghoul; ogre, ogress; gnome, affreet, genie, imp, kobold, fairy, brownie, pixy, elf, gremlin, dwarf, urchin, Puck, leprechaun, troll, sprite, bad fairy, nix, will-o'-the-wisp, poltergeist, basilisk, cacodemon, dhoul, diablotin, gogmagog, lamia, spoorn, succuba, succubus, troll; werewolf, lycanthrope.

4, *(spirit of the dead)* ghost, specter, apparition, spirit, shade, shadow, vision, hobgoblin; bugaboo, bugbear, bogey; dybbuk, revenant; specter, spook, wraith; zombie; banshee; evil eye; mawkin, nightmare. *Informal,* haint. See HELL.

5, *(benign spirits)* mermaid, merman, merfolk; siren; satyr, faun; changeling, elf-child.

Verbs—possess, obsess, bewitch, demonize.

Adjectives—demonic, demoniacal; supernatural, weird, uncanny, unearthly, spectral; ghostly, ghostlike; elfin, elflike; fiendish, fiendlike; impish, haunted; satanic, Mephistophelian; diabolic[al], devilish; infernal, hellish, hell-born, Plutonic.

Phrases—where God builds a church, the Devil will build a chapel.

Quotations—The prince of darkness is a gentleman (*Shakespeare*).

Antonyms, see ANGEL.

---

demonstrate, *v.* prove (see DEMONSTRATION); protest, rally, march, sit-in, strike, boycott, picket. See DISSENT.

DEMONSTRATION
Act of proving

Nouns—demonstration, substantiation, proof, probation, verification, authentication; confirmation, corroboration, EVIDENCE; conclusiveness; test (see EXPERIMENT); argument (see REASONING). See DEMONSTRATION.

Verbs—1, demonstrate, prove, confirm, substantiate, uphold, corroborate, establish; make good, show, bring home; evince, verify; settle the question; make out, make out a case; go to show *or* prove; prove one's point, have the best of the argument, beg the question.

2, *(be demonstrable)* follow, stand to reason; hold good, hold water (see TRUTH).

Adjectives—1, demonstrating, demonstrative, probative, unanswerable, convincing, conclusive; apodictic, irresistible, irrefutable, irrefragable; categorical, decisive, crucial; demonstrated, proven; unanswered, unrefuted; evident.

2, demonstrable, deducible, consequential, inferential, following, valid.

Adverbs—of course, in consequence, consequently, as a matter of course, quod erat demonstrandum, QED.

Antonyms, see CONFUTATION.

---

demoralize, *v.t.* disconcert, dishearten; disorganize, confuse; corrupt, deprave. See IMPOTENCE, DEJECTION, IMPROBITY. *Ant.,* boost, encourage.

demote, *v.t.* downgrade, reduce, degrade, bust (*sl.*). See PUNISHMENT, DECREASE. *Ant.,* promote.

demotic, *adj.* common, popular; enchorial. See POPULACE, LANGUAGE.

demur, *v.i.* take exception, hesitate, object, scruple.—*n.* objection; irresolution, delay. See DOUBT, DISSENT, UNWILLINGNESS.

demure, *adj.* sedate, staid; modest, diffident, prim, coy. See INEXCITABILITY, MODESTY. *Ant.,* brazen, impudent.

den, *n.* lair, cavern; sanctum, study; dive, haunt, hangout. See ABODE, RECEPTACLE, PRISON.

denial, *n.* NEGATION, repudiation, REFUSAL, contradiction; abnegation, temperance;

disown, renounce. See ASCETICISM. *Ant.,* admission, confession.

denigrate, *v.t.* blacken, defame. See DETRACTION.

denizen, *n.* dweller, INHABITANT.

denomination, *n.* NOMENCLATURE, name, title; CLASS, SCHOOL, PARTY, kind, sect, persuasion. See HETERODOXY.

denote, *v.t.* designate, signify, indicate, express, mean, specify. See EVIDENCE, MEANING, INDICATION.

denouement, *n.* resolution, solution, END, outcome, EFFECT. See DISCLOSURE.

denounce, *v.t.* stigmatize, condemn, decry, censure; arraign, charge, accuse; curse, rail at. See ACCUSATION, CONDEMNATION.

de novo, Lat. from the BEGINNING.

dense, *adj.* compact (see DENSITY); stupid, dull (see IGNORANCE).

DENSITY
Compactness

Nouns—1, density, denseness, solidity, solidness; impenetrability, impermeability; incompressibility; imporosity; cohesion (see COHERENCE); constipation; consistency, spissitude; specific gravity.

2, *(act of becoming dense)* condensation, solidification, consolidation, concretion, coagulation, petrifaction; crystallization, precipitation; thickening, jelling, curdling, setting; indissolubility, infrangibility. See HARDNESS.

3, *(dense matter)* solid, mass, block, knot, lump; concrete, conglomerate; precipitate; cake, brick, clot, coagulant; stone, curd; gob, clump; bone, gristle, cartilage.

4, densitometer, hydrometer.

Verbs—solidify, concrete, set, take a set, consolidate, congeal, coagulate; curd, curdle; fix, clot, cake, precipitate, deposit; cohere, crystallize; petrify, harden; condense, thicken, inspissate; compress, constipate; compact, jell, jellify; precipitate, sediment.

Adjectives—dense, solid, solidified, coherent, cohesive (see COHERENCE); compact, close, serried, firm, thickset; massive, lumpish; impenetrable, impermeable, imporous; incompressible; constipated; concrete, knotted, knotty; crystalline; thick, stuffy; undissolved, unmelted, unliquefied, unthawed; indivisible, indissolvable, indissoluble, infusible.

Adverbs—densely, thick[ly], compactly.

Antonyms, see RARITY, VAPOR.

---

dent, *n.* indentation, depression, hollow, dimple. —*v.t.* indent, buckle, mar. See CONCAVITY.

denunciation, *n.* ACCUSATION; DISAPPROBATION, censure, CONDEMNATION, arraignment; malediction, IMPRECATION, diatribe, anathema; THREAT.

deny, *v.t.* contradict, negate; refuse, withhold; DOUBT, reject; oppose, protest; renounce, doom. See NEGATION, REFUSAL, REJECTION. *Ant.,* acknowledge, admit.

deodorant, *n.* antiperspirant, [air] freshener; cream, spray, *or* roll-on deodorant. See ODOR.

Deo gratias, *Lat.* thank God. See GRATITUDE.

Deo volente, *Lat.* God willing. See CHANCE, POSSIBILITY.

department, *n.* PART, section, division; service, agency, bureau; sphere, domain, jurisdiction, BUSINESS, concern; REGION.

DEPARTURE
Moving away from

Nouns—1, departure, leaving, parting, decampment; DISAPPEARANCE; retreat, embarkation; outset, start; removal, exit, EGRESS, exodus, hejira, evacuation; flight (see ESCAPE); RECESSION.

2, *(departing gift)* leavetaking, valediction, adieu, farewell, good-bye, word of parting, send-off; stirrup-cup, gold watch, *etc.*

3, *(point of departure)* starting point, gate, *or* post; jumping-off point, point *or* place of departure *or* embarkation; port of embarkation.

Verbs—1, depart; go [away]; take one's departure, set out, set off, march off, put off, start off, be off, move off, get off, pack off, go off, take oneself off; start, issue, march out, debouch; go forth, sally [forth], set forth *or* forward; break camp, pull up stakes; be gone, shake the dust off one's feet. *Slang,* toddle *or* mosey along, bolt, bug out, cheese it, fade, flake out, leg it, take a powder, wing it, piss off, bag someone's ass.

2, leave, quit, vacate, evacuate, abandon (see RELINQUISHMENT), go off the stage, make one's exit; retire, retreat, withdraw, remove, check *or* sign out; go one's way, go along, head out, go from home; show *or* take to one's heels, beat a retreat, make oneself scarce, run for it, cut and run, steal away, slip *or* take off; take flight, take wing;

spring, fly, flit, wing one's way, fly away, embark; go on board, go aboard; set sail, put to sea, go to sea, sail, push off; take ship, get under way, weigh anchor, strike tents, decamp, clear out, bow out; take leave, excuse oneself; see off, say *or* bid good-bye, disappear, take French leave; elope, bolt, abscond, run away, make off, shove off, vamoose; avoid (see AVOIDANCE); light *or* skip out. *Slang,* skedaddle, skiddoo, break wide, butt out, head for the hills, take it on the lam, beat it, blow, lam, get in the wind, make oneself scarce, make tracks, go fly a kite, hit the road, strike out; bag, barrel, cut, drag, haul, *or* shag ass.

3, check *or* sign out. *Informal,* punch *or* clock out.

Adjectives—departing, leaving; valedictory; outward bound; outgoing, retiring.

Adverbs—whence, hence, thence; with a foot in the stirrup; on the wing, on the move.

Interjections—farewell! adieu! good-bye! bye-bye! till we meet again! God be with you! Godspeed! fare you well!; adieu! adios! au revoir! arrivederci! ciao! auf Wiedersehen! aloha! ave! shalom! sayonara! pax vobiscum! see you [later]! so long! cheerio! have a nice day!

Phrases—the best of friends must part.

Quotations—Parting is such sweet sorrow that I shall say good night till it be morrow (*Shakespeare*), In every parting there is an image of death (*George Eliot*), Parting is all we know of heaven, and all we need of hell (*Emily Dickinson*), All farewells should be sudden (*Lord Byron*).

Antonyms, see ARRIVAL.

---

depend, *v.i.* rely, trust; dangle, hang; be contingent, rest. See BELIEF, PENDENCY, EFFECT, SUBJECTION.

dependable, *adj.* reliable, trustworthy; faithful, steadfast. See CERTAINTY, PROBITY. *Ant.,* unreliable.

dependency, *n.* dependence, reliance; appurtenance; territory, colony. See BELIEF, POSSESSION.

depict, *v.t.* delineate, picture, limn, portray. See REPRESENTATION.

deplete, *v.* exhaust (see INSUFFICIENCY).

deplorable, *adj.* lamentable, sad, regrettable, disastrous. See BADNESS, PAIN, REGRET.

deploy, *v.* send, spread, *or* fan out; distribute, locate. See EXPANSION.

deport, *v.t.* conduct (oneself), behave; expel, send away, banish, exile, expatriate. See EJECTION, TRANSFER, CONDUCT.

depose, *v.* swear, affirm, testify; dethrone, uncrown, unseat, oust, disbar. See NULLIFICATION, EVIDENCE.

deposit, *n.* precipitate, sediment, dregs, lees; vein; pledge, PAYMENT, SECURITY. See REMAINDER.

deposition, *n.* affidavit, testimony, AFFIRMATION; dethronement, deposal. See EVIDENCE, NULLIFICATION.

depository, *n.* storehouse, warehouse, depot, vault, bank, treasury. See STORE.

depot, *n.* warehouse, depository; station. See STORE, LOCATION.

depravity, *n.* degeneracy, corruption, turpitude, degradation, perversion. See BADNESS, DETERIORATION, IMPURITY.

deprecate, *v.t.* protest, regret, disfavor, disapprove; expostulate, inveigh, *or* remonstrate (against). See DISAPPROBATION, DISSUASION.

depreciate, *v.* disparage, derogate, discredit, belittle, cheapen, slump, fall, rundown (*inf.*), knock (*sl.*); See DETRACTION, CHEAPNESS, DECREASE.

depression, *n.* RECESSION, slowdown.

DEPRESSION
Pressing downward

Noun—1, depression, lowering; dip (see CONCAVITY); abasement, debasement; reduction.

2, overthrow, overset, overturn; upset; prostration, subversion, precipitation.

3, (*lowering*) bow; curtsy; genuflection, kowtow, obeisance. See RESPECT.

Verbs—1, depress, lower; let *or* take down, take down a peg; cast; let drop *or* fall; sink, debase, bring low, abase, reduce, pitch, precipitate; dent (see CONCAVITY).

2, *(press down)* overthrow, overturn, overset; upset, subvert, prostrate, level, fell; cast, take, throw, fling, dash, pull, cut, *or* knock down, lay out; raze [to the ground]; trample in the dust; pull about one's ears.

3, *(lower oneself)* sit [down]; couch, crouch, squat, stoop, bend, bow; courtesy, curtsey; bob, duck, dip, kneel; bend, bow the head, bend the knee; slouch; bow down; cower.

Adjectives—depressed; at a low ebb; prostrate, overthrown; downcast.

Antonyms, see ELEVATION.

---

deprive, *v.t.* dispossess, divest, denude, bereave, strip; despoil, usurp; take [away] from; withhold. See LOSS, STEALING, INSUFFICIENCY.

de profundis, *Lat.* out of the depths. See PENITENCE, WORSHIP.

DEPTH
Deepness

Nouns—**1,** depth; deepness, profundity; deepening, lowering (see DEPRESSION). See LOWNESS.

2, depression, CONCAVITY; shaft, well; bowels of the earth, bottomless pit; HELL; valley; abyss, chasm (see INTERVAL); deep sea, deeps, depths, ocean bottom, Davy Jones's locker; deep space; soundings; submersion; draft.

3, plummet, plumb line, sound, probe, sounding rod *or* line; lead.

Verbs—**1,** deepen; submerge, bury, sink, plunge; dig, excavate.

2, sound, have the lead, take soundings, plumb, mark the twain.

Adjectives—deep, deep-seated, profound; sunk, buried; submerged, subaqueous, submarine, subterranean, underground; bottomless, soundless, fathomless; unfathomed, unfathomable; abysmal; abyssal; deep as a well, yawning; knee-deep, ankle-deep, *etc.*; deep-sea *or* -water.

Adverbs—beyond one's depth, out of one's depth; over head and ears, up to one's elbows.

Phrases—still waters run deep.

Quotations—Out of the depths have I cried unto thee, O Lord (*Bible*), They that go down to the sea in ships, that do business in great waters; these see the works of the Lord, and his wonders in the deep (*Bible*).

Antonyms, see SHALLOWNESS, HEIGHT.

---

deputy, *n.* AGENT, representative, delegate; substitute, proxy; envoy; factor; deputy sheriff. See SUBSTITUTION, COMMISSION.

derangement, *n.* craziness (see INSANITY); disturbance, upset, imbalance; confusion, turmoil, DISORDER; disconcertment, discomfiture, discomposure. See DISEASE.

derelict, *n.* wreck, hull; outcast; slacker, drifter, beachcomber, castaway. —*adj.* castaway, wrecked, stranded, abandoned, deserted, forsaken; delinquent, negligent, neglectful, remiss. See NEGLECT, RELINQUISHMENT.

de rigueur, *Fr.* obligatory. See COMPULSION, FASHION, TASTE.

derisive, *adj.* derisory, mocking, sarcastic, contemptuous, supercilious, disdainful. See RIDICULE, DISRESPECT, CONTEMPT, DETRACTION.

derive, *v.* get, obtain; deduce, originate, arise; infer. See RECEIVING, CAUSE, REASONING, ATTRIBUTION, EXTRACTION.

dernier cri, *Fr.* the last word; modern, cutting edge. See NEWNESS, FASHION.

derogatory, *adj.* depreciative, disparaging, defamatory, humiliating. See DISREPUTE, DETRACTION.

derrick, *n.* crane; [oil] rig. See ELEVATION, HEIGHT.

descant, *n.* variation; counterpoint. See MUSIC. —*v.i.* discourse, comment. See DIFFUSENESS.

descend, *v.i.* go down (see DESCENT); lower or debase oneself (see DISREPUTE). —descend [up]on, ATTACK.

descendant, *n.* See POSTERITY.

DESCENT
Motion downward

Nouns—1, descent, descension (*rare*), declension, declination, inclination, fall; falling, drop, subsidence, lapse; comedown.

2, downfall, tumble, slip, cropper, stumble, nosedive, crash dive; parachute jump; vertical insertion; declivity, incline, dip, hill (see OBLIQUITY); avalanche, snowslide, mudslide, debacle, landslip, landslide, chute; fall, pratfall, plunge. *Informal,* spill, flop.

3, speleology; speleologist.

Verbs—1, (*fall*) descend; go, drop, *or* come down, fall, dive, gravitate, drop, slip, slide, settle, subside, lapse, decline, set, sink, plummet; swoop, fall prostrate, precipitate oneself, come a cropper; let fall; tumble, stumble, flop, topple, take a spill *or* header; topple *or* tumble down *or* over, plump down; parachute, skydive. *Informal,* come down a peg.

2, (*climb down*) dismount, climb down, alight, light, get off *or* down; rappel.

Adjectives—descending, descendent; decurrent, decursive; deciduous; downhill; nodding to its fall.

Adverbs—down, downhill, downward, downstream, downstairs.

Phrases—what goes up must come down; go down like the *Titanic.*

Antonyms, see ASCENT, LEAP.

DESCRIPTION
Act of representation

Nouns—1, description, account, exposé (see DISCLOSURE); specification, particulars; summary (see SHORTNESS); guidebook (see INFORMATION); delineation, REPRESENTATION, sketch, portrait; bitmap; minute, detailed, circumstantial, *or* graphic account; narration, recital, rehearsal, relation, recitation. See LIST, NEWS.

2, history, oral *or* written history; biography, autobiography; necrology, obituary; narrative, memoir, curriculum vitae; annals, chronicle, legend, story, tale, yarn, anecdote, historiette; personal narrative, journal, life, adventures, fortunes, experiences, confessions; work of fiction, novel, novelette, novella, romance, love story; detective story, thriller; fairy tale, nursery tale; fable, parable, apologue. *Informal,* traveler's tale, shaggy-dog story, cock-and-bull story, a whole Megillah, herstory. *Slang,* whodunit.

3, narrator, relator, historian, recorder, biographer, fabulist, novelist; raconteur, anecdotist, storyteller. See WRITING.

Verbs—describe, narrate, relate, recite, recount; set forth, draw a picture, limn, picture; portray, represent, characterize, particularize; sum up, run over, recapitulate, rehearse, fight one's battles over again; unfold, tell, give *or* render an account of, write up, [make a] report, draw up a statement; enter into details *or* particulars, specify.

Adjectives—descriptive, graphic, narrative, well-drawn; historical, epic, suggestive, traditional; fabulous, legendary; picaresque, anecdotal, expository, storied; biographical, autobiographical; fictional, fictitious; true-to-life, lifelike.

Phrases—fact is stranger than fiction.

Quotations—A novel is a mirror which passes over a highway (*Stendhal*), Literature is a luxury; fiction is a necessity (*G. K. Chesterton*), A beginning, a muddle, and an end (*Philip Larkin*).

Antonyms, see DISTORTION.

desecrate, *v.t.* profane. See DISRESPECT. *Ant.*, venerate.

desert, *n.* waste, wilderness, solitude. See USELESSNESS, SECLUSION.

desert, *v.* leave, forsake, abandon; secede, run away; leave in the lurch, be faithless, ditch (*sl.*). See AVOIDANCE, RELINQUISHMENT. —*n.* reward, due, merit. See JUSTICE.

deserve, *v.t.* merit, be worthy of, be entitled to. See JUSTICE.

desiccate, *v.* dry up, wither; dehydrate. See DRYNESS. *Ant.*, moisten, water.

design, *n.* PLAN, INTENTION, scheme, project; REPRESENTATION, drawing, diagram, pattern; decoration; purpose, METHOD. —*v.t.* PLAN, intend; draw, sketch. See PAINTING.

designate, *v.t.* name, specify, indicate, point out; appoint. See NOMENCLATURE, CHOICE, INDICATION.

designing, *adj.* artful, CUNNING.

DESIRE
Craving

Nouns—1, desire, wish, fancy, fantasy; want, need (see NECESSITY).

2, desirability, appeal, magnetism, ATTRACTION.

3, inclination, mind, devices, animus, partiality, penchant, predilection; weakness, proclivity (see TENDENCY); willingness; liking, LOVE, fondness, relish; CHOICE. *Informal,* yen. See INTENTION, WILL.

4, longing, hankering, avidity, longing *or* wistful eye; solicitude, yearning, coveting, envy; aspiration, [vaulting] ambition, fire in the belly; alacrity, eagerness, impatience, overanxiety; HOPE.

5, *(hunger)* [sharp] appetite, keenness, hunger, torment of Tantalus, ravenousness, voracity, GLUTTONY; thirst, thirstiness; itch[ing]. *Informal,* sweet tooth, the munchies.

6, avarice, greed[iness], itching palm, covetousness, acquisitiveness, grasping, craving, rapacity, passion, rage, furor, mania, dipsomania, kleptomania; prurience, cacoëthes, cupidity, lust, concupiscence, ardor, carnality, desires of the flesh. *Slang,* horniness, itch, the hots, nasties, blue balls, jungle fever, flame. See SEX.

7, desirer, lover (see LOVE), votary, devotee, fiend, aspirant, social climber, solicitant, candidate; lecher. *Informal,* fan. *Slang,* breadhead, wannabe, eager beaver, knocker, mink.

8, *(something desired)* desideratum, want, requirement; heart's desire, consummation devoutly to be wished; height of one's ambition, whim[sy].

Verbs—1, desire, wish (for); be desirous, have a longing; HOPE; care for, like, list (*archaic*), take to, take kindly to, cling to, take a fancy to, fancy; prefer, choose (see CHOICE); have an eye *or* mind to; have a fancy for, set one's eyes upon; take into one's head, have at heart, be bent upon; set one's cap for, set one's sights, have one's eye on, set one's heart *or* mind upon, covet, envy, want, miss, need, feel the want of, feel like; would fain have *or* do; would be glad of. *Informal,* give one's right arm for, kill for. *Slang,* have the hots for.

2, be hungry, have a good appetite; hunger, thirst, crave, lust, itch, *or* hanker after, make a play for; die for; burn to, have one's fingers itch to; desiderate; sigh, cry, gasp, pine, pant, languish, yearn, *or* long for; be on thorns for, hope for; aspire after; champ at the bit; catch at, grasp at, jump at; fish for, whistle for.

3, be greedy, have eyes bigger than one's belly, make a pig of oneself.

4, *(provoke desire)* cause, create, excite, *or* provoke desire, whet the appetite; appetize, titillate, take one's fancy, tempt; hold out temptation, tantalize, make one's mouth water.

Adjectives—1, desirous, desiring, inclined, fain, wishful, optative.

2, craving, hungry, sharp-set, peckish, ravening, with an empty stomach, pinched with hunger, famished; hungry as a hunter, horse, *or* churchmouse; thirsty, athirst, parched with thirst, dry; greedy [as a hog], piggish; overeager; voracious, omnivorous, ravenous, openmouthed, covetous, avaricious, rapacious, grasping, extortionate, exacting, sordid, insatiable, insatiate; unquenchable, quenchless; unsatisfied, unsated, unslaked.

3, eager, avid, keen; burning, fervent, impatient; set, bent, *or* intent on, mad after, rabid, dying for, bad off for, devoured by desire; aspiring, ambitious, vaulting, sky-aspiring. *Slang,* horny, hard up, hot to trot, queer for, rooty.

4, desirable; desired, sought after, in demand; pleasing (see PLEASURE); appetizing, tantalizing, seductive.

Adverbs—desirously, wistfully, fain, would that, if only; solicitously, yearningly, fondly, ambitiously, *etc.;* with bells on.

Phrases—you cannot have your cake and eat it too; there is always room at the top; the more you get the more you want.

Quotations—Ah, but a man's reach should exceed his grasp, or what's a heaven for? (*Robert Browning*), There is enough in the world for everyone's need, but not enough for everyone's greed (*Frank Buchman*), If all the rich people in the world divided up their money among themselves there wouldn't be enough to go round (*Christina Stead*), Hitch your wagon to a star (*Emerson*), Vaulting ambition, which o'erleaps itself and falls on the other (*Shakespeare*).

Antonyms, see HATE, SUFFICIENCY, INDIFFERENCE.

---

desist, *v.i.* stop, cease, abstain, quit, forbear. See END, DISCONTINUANCE.

desk, *n.* escritoire, secretary, lectern, counter; bureau. See RECEPTACLE.

desolate, *adj.* bleak, barren, inhospitable, unpeopled; lonely, abandoned, forlorn; comfortless, miserable. See ABSENCE, SECLUSION, DEJECTION. —*v.t.* waste, depopulate, devastate. See DESTRUCTION.

despair, *n.* HOPELESSNESS, sadness, DEJECTION, despondency, discouragement. *Ant.,* HOPE.

despatch, *n.* See DISPATCH.

desperado, *n.* bravo, outlaw, cutthroat, ruffian, thug. See RASHNESS, EVILDOER.

desperate, *adj.* hopeless, incurable; reckless, rash, foolhardy; furious, heroic. See RASHNESS, HOPELESSNESS.

despicable, *adj.* detestable, hateful, contemptible. See HATE, CONTEMPT. *Ant.,* admirable.

despise, *v.t.* scorn, disdain, hold in CONTEMPT, HATE. *Ant.,* LOVE.

despite, *prep.* in spite of, regardless of, notwithstanding; contrary to [expectations], in the teeth *or* face of. See OPPOSITION, COMPENSATION.

despoil, *v.t.* pillage, plunder. See STEALING.

despondent, *adj.* downcast, melancholy, depressed, dejected, disconsolate, wretched; discouraged, dispirited, prostrate, down in the mouth (*inf.*). See DEJECTION, HOPELESSNESS.

despotism, *n.* dictatorship, autocracy, tyranny, oppression. See SEVERITY, AUTHORITY, ILLEGALITY.

dessert, *n.* sweet, savory, confection, treat, trifle. See SWEETNESS, FOOD.

destination, *n.* goal, terminus, port; DESTINY, END, objective. See INTENTION.

DESTINY
Fate

Nouns—1, destiny, future state, next world, world to come (see FUTURITY).

2, fate, kismet, God's will, act of God, the will of God *or* Allah; Karma; doom, determinism, fatalism, predestination, predetermination, NECESSITY, inevitability; luck, star, lot, fortune, destination; a cross to bear, a row to hoe; wheel of fortune, spin *or* turn of the wheel, fall of the dice *or* cards, the way the cookie crumbles, fickle [finger of] fortune; the mills of the gods; hour of destiny.

3, the Fates, Parcae, weird sisters, Clotho, Lachesis, Atropos; Lady Fortune.

4, fatalist, predestinarian, Calvinist.

Verbs—1, *(lie in the future)* impend, hang *or* lie over, loom, approach, stare one in the face.

2, *(intend for the future)* ordain, foreordain, preordain; [pre]destine, doom, have *or* lie in store.

Adjectives—1, destined, impending, fated, about to be *or* happen, coming, in store, to come, instant, at hand, near; near *or* close at hand; overhanging, hanging over one's head, imminent, fateful; in the wind, in the cards, in the lap of the gods, in the offing, in reserve; in prospect, expected (see EXPECTATION), looming in the distance *or* future *or* on the horizon; inevitable.

2, fatalistic, determinalist, deterministic.

Adverbs—1, in time, in the long run; all in good time; eventually, whatever may happen, as chance *or* luck would have it.

2, fatally, fatalistically, imminently, *etc.*; in the hands of fate, in the lap of the gods, in God's hands; out of luck, in luck; by chance.

Phrases—fate can be taken by the horns, like a goat, and pushed in the right direction; man proposes, God disposes; what goes up must come down; it is written; what must be must be; *che sarà sarà*; *c'est la vie*; *c'est la guerre*.

Quotations—There's a divinity that shapes our ends (*Shakespeare*), Our manifest destiny is to overspread the continent allotted by Providence for the free development of our yearly multiplying millions (*John O'Sullivan*), This generation of Americans has a rendezvous with destiny (*F. D. Roosevelt*), The destiny of countries depends on the way they feed themselves (*Anthelme Brillat-Savarin*), The destiny of the colored America . . . is the destiny of America (*Frederick Douglass*), I am obliged to state it: for the black man there is only one destiny. And it is white (*Frantz Fanon*), [Destiny is] a tyrant's authority for crime and a fool's excuse for failure (*Ambrose Bierce*).

Antonyms, see CHANCE, CHOICE, WILL.

---

destitute, *adj.* wanting, lacking; stripped, bereft, penniless, poverty- stricken, down-and-out (*sl.*). See INSUFFICIENCY, POVERTY. *Ant.*, affluent.

DESTRUCTION
Act of destroying

Nouns—1, destruction, waste, dissolution, break[ing] up; disruption; consumption; disorganization. See LOSS.

2, *(fact of destruction)* fall, downfall, ruin, perdition, crash, smash, havoc, debacle, breakup; desolation, bouleversement, wreck, shipwreck, catastrophe, cataclysm; extinction, annihilation; destruction of life (see KILLING); obliteration; knock-down blow; [crack of] doom.

3, *(act of destruction)* destroying, demolition, demolishment; overthrow, subversion, REVOLUTION, sabotage; vandalism; abolition; NULLIFICATION; sacrifice, ravage, devastation, incendiarism, extirpation, extermination, eradication; mayhem; road to ruin; dilapidation (see DETERIORATION).

4, *(agent of destruction)* destroyer, exterminator; nihilist; bane, blight, moth, locust; executioner.

Verbs—1, *(nullify)* destroy, do *or* make away with, exterminate, kill off; nullify, annul (see NULLIFICATION); obliterate, eradicate, stamp *or* wipe out; sacrifice, demolish, dismantle (see USEFULNESS); tear up *or* down; overturn, overthrow, overwhelm; disrupt, upset, subvert, put an end to; seal the doom of; break up, cut up; break, cut, pull, mow, *or* beat down; cut short, take off, blot out; dispel, consume, burn out *or* up; disorganize, play *or* raise havoc with. *Slang*, total.

2, be destroyed, perish, fall [to the ground]; tumble, topple (see DESCENT); go *or* fall to pieces, break up, crack up, crumble to dust; go to smash, pot, *or* wreck, go to the dogs *or* wall, go to wrack and ruin; go by the board, go all to smash; be all up *or* over with; cook one's goose; totter to its fall; [self-]destruct.

3, *(break up)* smash, dash, quell, squash, squelch, crumple up, shatter, shiver (see BRITTLENESS); tear, cut, crush, pull, *or* pick to pieces; nip [in the bud]; ruin; strike out; throw *or* knock down, lay low; fell, sink, swamp, scuttle, wreck, shipwreck, engulf, submerge; lay in ashes *or* ruins; sweep away, eradicate, erase, expunge; raze, level. *Slang,* trash.

4, *(destroy violently)* deal destruction, lay waste, ravage; gut; swallow up, devour, desolate, devastate, sap, mine, blast, bang up; sabotage; extinguish, quench; annihilate; snuff, put, *or* stamp out; trample under foot; make short work of, make a clean sweep of, make mincemeat of; cut up root and branch; fling *or* scatter to the winds, throw overboard; strike at the root of, sap the foundations of, spring a mine, blow up.

Adjectives—1, destroyed; disrupted; perishing, trembling; nodding *or* tottering to its fall; in course of destruction; done for; extinct. *Informal,* kaput. *Slang,* down the tubes *or* chute, fucked.

2, destructive, subversive, ruinous, incendiary, deletory; destroying, suicidal; deadly (see KILLING).

Phrases—the road to ruin is always kept in good repair.

Quotations—All men that are ruined are ruined on the side of their natural propensities (*Edmund Burke*), Let everyone witness how many different cards fortune has up her sleeve when she wants to ruin a man (*Benvenuto Cellini*).

Antonyms, see PRODUCTION.

---

desultory, *adj.* aimless, fitful, rambling, unmethodical, erratic. See DISORDER, IRREGULARITY, DEVIATION, DIFFUSENESS, DISCONTINUANCE. *Ant.,* stable, constant.

detach, *v.t.* separate, disconnect, remove, unfix, unfasten. See DISJUNCTION. *Ant.,* attach.

detached, *adj.* separate, independent; aloof, preoccupied. See DISJUNCTION, INATTENTION. *Ant.,* attached, attentive.

detachment, *n.* separation, isolation, DISJUNCTION; preoccupation, aloofness, abstraction; PART; detail. See INATTENTION, COMBATANT. *Ant.,* interest, concern, attachment.

detail, *n.* PART, unit, item; particular, trifle; detachment. —*v.t.* particularize, itemize, enumerate; appoint, assign. See SPECIALITY, APPORTIONMENT, ORNAMENT, UNITY, UNIMPORTANCE. *Ant.,* WHOLE.

detain, *v.t.* delay, check, hold back; hold in custody; keep, retain. See HINDRANCE, RESTRAINT.

detect, *v.t.* discover, find out, perceive, espy, ferret out. See LEARNING, KNOWLEDGE, DISCLOSURE.

detective, *n.* investigator, agent; policeman, plainclothesman, operative, shadow, undercover man; house detective, floorwalker; private investigator, private eye; Sherlock Holmes; sleuth[hound] (*inf.*); gumshoe, shamus, house dick, fed (*all sl.*). See INQUIRY.

detent, *n.* catch, pawl. See HINDRANCE.

détente, *n.* truce, relaxation (of international relations). See PACIFICATION.

deter, *v.t.* restrain, hinder, discourage, give pause. See HINDRANCE, FEAR. *Ant.,* encourage, foster.

detergent, *adj.* detersive, clean[s]ing, washing; solvent, saponaceous. —*n.* clean[s]er, soap, wetting agent, solvent. See CLEANNESS.

DETERIORATION
Growing worse

Nouns—1, deterioration, debasement; wane, ebb (see DECREASE); decline, declension; relapse, backsliding (see REGRESSION); RECESSION; rust belt.

2, *(moral deterioration)* degeneracy, degeneration, degenerateness, degradation; comedown; depravation; depravity, perversion, retrogression, anomie, labefaction; decadence; rake's progress. See UNCLEANNESS, OLDNESS.

3, *(act of causing deterioration)* impairment, injury, damage, detriment; vitiation; discoloration, oxidation; disrepair; debasement; poisoning, pollution, contamination, corruption; adulteration, alloy. See WEAKNESS.

4, *(gradual worsening)* decay, DECOMPOSITION, dilapidation, decrepitude, ravages of time, wear and tear; corrosion, erosion; moldiness, rottenness; moth and rust, dry rot, mildew, blight; atrophy, attrition, DESTRUCTION. See POWDERINESS.

Verbs—1, deteriorate, degenerate; have seen better days, fall off; wane, ebb (see DECREASE); retrograde (see REGRESSION); decline, go down, sink, go downhill, go from bad to worse, go into a tailspin *or* nosedive, take a turn for the worse, go down in the world, go to the dogs, go to wrack and ruin; jump out of the frying pan into the fire; go *or* run to seed, run down, lapse, be the worse for; break down; spring a leak, crack; shrivel (see CONTRACTION); fade, wilt, go off, wither, molder, rot, decay, go bad; lose ground; cave in; rust, crumble, collapse, go to pieces, totter [to its fall]; perish (see DEATH). *Informal,* go to pot, go to hell in a handbasket.

2, weaken (see IMPOTENCE); taint, infect, contaminate, poison, envenom, canker, corrupt, pollute, vitiate, debase, denaturalize; debauch, defile (see IMPURITY); play havoc with; deprave, degrade; pervert, prostitute, discolor, alloy, adulterate, tamper with, gum up; do a job on; fester; curdle; blight, corrode, erode; wear away *or* out, fray; eat [away *or* out], gnaw [at the root of]; sap, mine, undermine, sap the foundations of, destroy (see DESTRUCTION); upset the applecart.

3, injure, impair, damage, harm, hurt, scathe, spoil, mar, dilapidate; mangle, mutilate, disfigure, blemish, deface. *Informal,* cook.

Adjectives—1, deteriorated, altered [for the worse]; injured, sprung; withering, spoiling, on the wane, on the decline; degenerate, effete; depraved; worse, the worse for; in disrepair; out of order, kilter, commission, *or* whack, out of repair *or* tune, ramshackle, on the blink; adulterated, base; imperfect (see IMPERFECTION); the worse for wear; battered, weathered, weatherbeaten; stale; dilapidated, ragged, frayed, faded, wilted, shabby, threadbare; seedy, grungy, run-down; worn [to a thread *or* to a shadow], worn to rags; reduced to a skeleton; at a low ebb, in a bad way, on one's last legs, down on one's luck; undermined; deteriorative, ruinous, deleterious (see BADNESS). *Informal,* tacky, low-rent. *Slang,* grotty.

2, decayed, moth-eaten, worm-eaten; mildewed, rusty, moldy, spotted, timeworn, moss-grown; discolored; wasted, crumbling, moldering, rotten, cankered, blighted, tainted; decadent, decrepit; broken down; done for, done up; worn out, used up.

Adverbs—for the worse; out of the frying pan into the fire; if worse comes to worst.

Quotations—Everything is good when it leaves the Creator's hands; everything degenerates in the hands of man *(Jean-Jacques Rousseau).*

Antonyms, see IMPROVEMENT.

---

determinate, *adj.* fixed, definite. See CERTAINTY. *Ant.,* indeterminate.

determination, *n.* RESOLUTION, WILL, firmness; JUDGMENT; MEASUREMENT.

determine, *v.t.* decide, resolve; END, settle, ANSWER; delimit, define, bound; find out, ascertain; specify, restrict, differentiate. See RESOLUTION, LEARNING, CERTAINTY, CHOICE.

determined, *adj.* resolute, decisive. See RESOLUTION.

deterrent, *adj.* preventive, retardative, prohibitive, defensive. —*n.* preventa-tive, RESTRAINT; obstacle, HINDRANCE, stumbling block. See DISSUASION.

detest, *v.t.* HATE, abhor, despise, abominate. *Ant.,* LOVE.

dethrone, *v.t.* depose; oust. See NULLIFICATION. *Ant.,* enthrone.

detonate, *v.* set, touch, *or* let off; discharge, explode, blow up, shoot [off], fire; go off. See LOUDNESS, VIOLENCE.

detonator, *n.* [fuse] cap, squib, powder, primer. See VIOLENCE.

detour, *n.* DEVIATION, digression, excursion; byway, bypass.

DETRACTION
Disparagement

Nouns—1, detraction, derogation, disparagement, dispraise, depreciation, disvaluation, vilification, obloquy, scurrility, scandal, defamation, aspersion, traducement, slander, calumny, evil-speaking, backbiting, vituperation; underestimation; libel; lampoon, derision (see RIDICULE); criticism, invective. *Informal,* bringdown, headhunting. See DISAPPROBATION, DISRESPECT, IMPRECATION.

2, detractor, derogator, *etc.* (see *Verbs*); cynic, critic; hatchetman; muckraker, mudslinger; satirist.

Verbs—detract, derogate, decry, depreciate, discount, disparage, denigrate, downplay; underestimate, belittle, cut down to size, put in one's place, minimize, run down, cry down, sneer at (see CONTEMPT); deride, RIDICULE; criticize, pull *or* pick to pieces, pick apart, pick holes in, asperse, cast aspersions, blow upon, bespatter, blacken, run *or* tear down, take down a peg; vilify, revile, give a dog a bad name, sell short, malign, backbite, libel, lampoon; vituperate, traduce, slander, defame, calumniate, bear false witness against; stab in the back; speak ill of, call names, anathematize, dip the pen in gall, view in a bad light. *Slang,* bad-mouth, low-rate, dump on, eat out, diss, dirty-mouth, put down.

Adjectives—detracting, detractory, derogatory, defamatory, disparaging, libelous; caustic, critical, scurrilous; abusive; slanderous, calumnious, calumniatory, sarcastic, satirical, cynical.

Quotations—Animals are such agreeable friends—they ask no questions, they pass no criticisms (*George Eliot*).

Antonyms, see APPROBATION, EXAGGERATION, FLATTERY.

---

detriment, *n.* harm, injury, DETERIORATION; LOSS, liability; discredit, prejudice, disgrace; obstacle, impediment. See DISREPUTE, BADNESS.

de trop, Fr. too much. See SUFFICIENCY.

deus ex machina, Lat. device, gimmick. See PLAN, SORCERY.

devaluate, devalue, *v.* See CHEAPNESS.

devastate, *v.t.* [lay] waste, ravage, desolate, pillage; ruin, raze, destroy, demolish; *informal,* disappoint, crush. See DESTRUCTION, DISAPPOINTMENT.

develop, *v.* evolve, unfold, mature, grow; bring about, cultivate, produce, amplify; elaborate, train, improve. See INCREASE, TEACHING, IMPROVEMENT, EXPANSION.

development, *n.* outgrowth, consequence; growth, EXPANSION; CHANGE, evolution; [building] project, housing development. See INCREASE, EFFECT, IMPROVEMENT, ABODE.

deviant, *adj.* perverted, aberrant. —*n.* pervert; sodomite, pederast, *etc.* See UNCONFORMITY, IMPURITY.

DEVIATION
Turning away

Nouns—deviation; swerving, warp, refraction; deflection, declination; diversion, divergence, digression, excursion, departure from, aberration; zigzag; siding; detour, bypass, byroad, circuit; wandering; sidling, knight's move. See CIRCUITY, AVOIDANCE, OBLIQUITY, IRREGULARITY.

Verbs—1, deviate, alter one's course, turn off; depart from, turn, bend, curve (see CURVATURE); swerve, heel, bear off, deflect, head off, divert [from its course], distract; put on a new scent, shift, shunt, draw aside, warp.

2, stray, straggle; sidle, diverge, part, separate; jump the track; digress, divagate, wander, wind, twist, meander, roam, zigzag, veer, tack, fishtail; come round; turn aside, avert, turn a corner, turn away from; wheel, steer clear of; ramble, rove, drift; go astray, go adrift; yaw, dodge, step aside; ease off, make way for, shy; fly off at a tangent; glance off; wheel *or* face about; turn to the right about; go out of one's way, lose one's way *or* bearings.

Adjectives—deviating, deviative, aberrant, errant, roundabout; excursive, discursive; devious, desultory, rambling; stray, erratic, undirected, divergent, radial, forked, centrifugal; circuitous, indirect, zigzag; crablike; off center; off one's beat, off the beaten track.
Adverbs—astray from, round about, wide of the mark; to the right about, all manner of ways; circuitously; obliquely, sidling.
Antonyms, see DIRECTION, CONVERGENCE.

---

device, *n.* scheme, trick, stratagem, ruse, expedient; badge, emblem, motto; mechanism, contrivance, instrument, invention, gadget; (*pl.*) inclination, pleasure. See INSTRUMENTALITY, PLAN; DESIRE, CUNNING.

devil, *n.* DEMON; wretch, unfortunate (see EVILDOER). —*v.t., informal,* bother, torment. See DISCONTENT.

devilish, *adj.* diabolical, fiendish; extreme. See DEMON, GREATNESS.

devil-may-care, *adj.* reckless, casual. See RASHNESS. *Ant.,* cautious.

devious, *adj.* See DEVIATION, CIRCUITY, DECEPTION.

devise, *v.t.* bequeath, will; produce, invent, fashion, concoct. See GIVING, IMAGINATION, PLAN, TRANSFER.

devoid, *adj.* lacking, without, destitute, empty. See ABSENCE, INSUFFICIENCY. *Ant.,* replete.

devote, *v.t.* give to, employ at; destine, dedicate, consecrate. See UNDERTAKING, ATTENTION, USE, RESOLUTION, WORSHIP.

devotee, *n.* enthusiast, zealot, fanatic, votary, follower, disciple, fan (*inf.*), addict (*inf.*). See DESIRE, PIETY, AUXILIARY.

devotion, *n.* dedication; PIETY, godliness; affection, LOVE; (*pl.*) prayers, WORSHIP.

devour, *v.t.* eat, wolf [down]; consume, destroy. See FOOD, GLUTTONY, DESTRUCTION, USE.

devout, *adj.* pious, reverent, religious, godly, worshiping, fervent, sincere. See PIETY, FEELING. *Ant.,* impious.

dew, *n.* dewdrops, night damp. See MOISTURE.

dexterous, *adj.* skillful (see SKILL, FACILITY). *Ant.,* awkward.

diabolic, *adj.* devilish, demoniac, wicked, impious, malevolent. See DEMON, BADNESS, MALEVOLENCE. *Ant.,* angelic.

diadem, *n.* crown, tiara. See CIRCULARITY, ORNAMENT.

diagnosis, *n.* diagnostics; analysis, examination, explanation; symptomatology, semiology; conclusion, finding. See INTERPRETATION, IDENTITY.

diagonal, *adj.* aslant, oblique; catty-corner; inclined; tilted, pitched. See OBLIQUITY.

diagram, *n.* PLAN, sketch, chart, blueprint, map. —*v.t.* draw, outline, layout. See FORM.

dial, *n.* face, indicator, gauge; disk. See INDICATION, COMMUNICATION, MEASUREMENT.

dialect, *n.* language, tongue; vernacular, idiom, argot, patois, jargon, cant. See SPEECH.

dialogue, *n.* CONVERSATION; part, speeches, lines, script. See DRAMA.

diameter, *n.* BREADTH, thickness, width, caliber, bore. See LENGTH.

diametrical, *adj.* absolute, complete. See COMPLETION.

diamond, *n.* gem[stone], jewel, sparkler, ice (*sl.*); engagement ring; parallelogram, lozenge, rhomb[oid], rhombus; check. See ORNAMENT, ANGULARITY, GOODNESS.

diaper, *n.* breech cloth, napkin. See CLOTHING.

diaphragm, *n.* midriff; pessary. See BETWEEN.

diarrhea, *n.* dysentery, Montezuma's revenge, trots (*sl.*), runs (*sl.*). See DISEASE, EXCRETION.

diary, *n.* journal, log, chronicle; memoirs. See WRITING, RECORD.

diatribe, *n.* denunciation (see DISAPPROBATION).

dice, *n.pl., slang,* cubes, ivories; cheaters, doctors. —*v.t.* cube, cut up. See DISJUNCTION.

dicey, *adj., slang,* risky, chancy (see CHANCE, DANGER).

dicker, *v.i.* bargain, negotiate, haggle; trade, BARTER.

dictate, *v.t.* enjoin, COMMAND; draw up, say for transcription; domineer, browbeat. See INSOLENCE.

dictatorial, *adj.* dogmatic, opinionated, despotic, arbitrary. See SEVERITY, INSOLENCE, AUTHORITY.

diction, *n.* expression; enunciation. See SPEECH.

dictionary, *n.* wordbook, lexicon, vocabulary. See PUBLICATION.

dictum (*pl.* dicta), *n.* saying, MAXIM; decision, judgment; pronouncement. See AFFIRMATION.

die, *v.i.* perish (see DEATH). —*n.* mold, matrix, punch, thread-cutter, prototype, perforator; cube, *etc.* See FORM, ENGRAVING.

diehard, *adj.* stubborn, obstinate; inflexible, dogmatic. —*n.* reactionary, conservative; fanatic, bigot. See PERMANENCE, STABILITY, OBSTINACY.

Dies Irae, *Lat.* day of wrath; JUDGMENT day.

diet, *n.* parliament, congress; food, aliment, edibles, intake, victuals; regimen. See FOOD, REMEDY, ASSEMBLAGE, COUNCIL.

DIFFERENCE
Dissimilarity

Nouns—1, difference, differentness, unlikeness, variance, variation, variety; diversity, dissimilarity, multiformity; divergence, dissimilitude; odds, incompatibility (see DISAGREEMENT); uniqueness, novelty (see UNCONFORMITY); DEVIATION; disparity, INEQUALITY, differential, margin; distinction, contradistinction; analysis, hairsplitting; nice, fine, delicate, *or* subtle distinction; generation gap; ableism, ageism; incongruence, shade of difference, nuance; discordance, discrimination, differentiation; antithesis, contrast; culture shock; moods and tenses.

2, different thing, far cry, horse of a different *or* another color, different story, something else again, quite another thing, tertium quid; this, that, and the other; no such thing; grab bag; gender bias, gender gap, genderism, glass ceiling; deviate, deviant. *Informal,* something completely different. See CHANGE.

Verbs—be different, differ, vary, mismatch, contrast, compare; diverge, deviate, branch out, disagree with; ring the changes; differentiate; draw a line, tell apart, particularize; specialize (see SPECIALITY); diversify; vary, CHANGE; discriminate, distinguish, set off, separate the men from the boys; analyze; split hairs.

Adjectives—differing, different, distinct, diverse, disparate, heterogeneous, eclectic, all manner of; distinguishable, varied, modified; diversified, various, divers, all manner of; variform; daedal; incongruous, incompatible; distinctive, characteristic; discriminative; other, another, not the same; unequal, unmatched; separate but equal; widely apart, dissimilar, poles apart.

Adverbs—differently; otherwise, else; alongside of; on the one *or* other side, on the other hand.

Phrases—every fool is different; one man's meat is another man's poison; every land has its own law.

Quotations—Variety is the spice of life, that gives it all its flavor (*William Cowper*), It were not best that we should all think alike; it is difference of opinion that makes horse races (*Mark Twain*), The difference between burlesque and the newspapers is that the former never pretended to be performing a public service by exposure (*I. F. Stone*), It makes a difference whose ox is gored (*Martin Luther*), There is very little difference between one man and another; but what little there is, is very important (*William James*), If you aren't doing something different, you aren't doing anything at all (*Neil Cargile*).

Antonyms, see IDENTITY, SIMILARITY.

---

differentiate, *v.t.* isolate, particularize, set off *or* apart; discriminate, distinguish, alter, CHANGE. See DIFFERENCE, SPECIALITY.

DIFFICULTY
That which is hard to overcome

Nouns—1, difficulty, hardness, impracticability, hard work, uphill work, hurdle; hard task, Herculean task, large order, hard row to hoe; task of Sisyphus, Sisyphean labor; tough job; hard way.

2, *(difficult decision)* dilemma, horns of a dilemma, predicament; embarrassment, contretemps; perplexity, entanglement; growing pains; awkwardness, Gordian knot, maze; coil (see CONVOLUTION); nice *or* delicate point; vexed question, poser, enigma, puzzle, riddle, paradox, catch-22, knotty point, snag; hard nut to crack; bone to pick. See INQUIRY, SECRET.

3, *(difficult situation)* quandary, strait, pinch, [pretty] pass, plight, critical situation, crisis; trial, rub, crux, emergency, exigency; quagmire, hot water, hornet's nest; sea of troubles, deep water; pretty kettle of fish, fat is in the fire, the devil to pay, can of worms, where the shoe pinches; imbroglio, mess, impasse, deadlock, moment of truth, point of no return; gridlock; final straw; scrape, cul-de-sac, hitch, catch; stumbling block, HINDRANCE. *Informal,* pickle, stew, fix, hole, crunch, little red wagon. *Slang,* jam, bad hair day, hambone, hump, wanker. See ADVERSITY.

Verbs—1, be difficult, go against the grain, try one's patience, put one out; put to one's wits' end; go hard with, be on one's back; try one; pose, perplex, distress, bother, take aback, nonplus, bring to a deadlock; be impossible.

2, meet with difficulties, labor under difficulties *or* a disadvantage; be in difficulty, run afoul of; fish in troubled waters, buffet the waves, swim against the stream *or* tide; have much ado with, have a hard time of it, eke out; bear the brunt, carry *or* bear one's cross; grope in the dark, lose one's way; be in a corner. *Slang,* milk a duck.

3, get into difficulties, get into a scrape, burn one's fingers, take it on the chin; stir up a hornet's nest, bring a hornet's nest about one's ears, put one's foot in it, paint oneself into a corner; ask for *or* borrow trouble; flounder, boggle, struggle; not know which way to turn (see DOUBT); stick at, stick in the mud, stick fast; come to a standstill. *Slang,* get all balled up, have one's ass in a crack *or* sling.

4, *(make difficult for)* encumber, embarrass, ravel, entangle, complicate, involve; put a spoke in the wheel, put through the mill, hinder (see HINDRANCE); play the devil *or* hob with; stump; tree.

Adjectives—1, difficult, not easy, hard, tough, troublesome, toilsome, irksome; laborious (see EXERTION); onerous, arduous, demanding, Herculean, formidable; sooner *or* easier said than done; difficult *or* hard to deal with; ill-conditioned. *Slang,* hairy.

2, awkward, unmanageable; intractable, stubborn, obstinate (see OBSTINACY).

3, knotted, knotty; pathless, trackless, labyrinthine, convoluted (see CONVOLUTION); intricate, complicated, tangled, afoul; impracticable, desperate, hopeless (see HOPELESSNESS); embarrassing, perplexing, uncertain (see DOUBT).

4, at the end of one's rope *or* tether, at one's wits' end, at a standstill; at sea, nonplused; stranded, aground, stuck fast; up a tree, out on a limb, at bay, driven into a corner, driven from pillar to post, driven to extremity, driven to the wall, on the ropes *or* rocks; in a bind, hole, box, *or* spot, up against it *or* the wall; out of one's depth, in deep, thrown out. *Slang,* behind the eight ball, in the soup, up the creek [without a paddle], jacked up.

Adverbs—with difficulty, with much ado; hardly, uphill; against the stream *or* grain; coming and going; in the teeth of, in a pinch; at long odds; when push comes to shove, when the chips are down.

Phrases—the difficult is done at once, the impossible takes a little longer; *per ardua ad astra.*

Quotations—We're eyeball to eyeball, and I think the other fellow just blinked (*Dean Rusk*), What we're saying today is that you're either part of the solution or you're part of the problem (*Eldridge Cleaver*), Problems are only opportunities in work clothes (*Henry J. Kaiser*), When written in Chinese the word *crisis* is composed of two characters. One represents danger and the other represents opportunity (*J. F. Kennedy*), Whatever women do, they must do it twice as well as men to be thought half as good. Luckily, this is not difficult (*Charlotte Whitton*).

Antonyms, see FACILITY.

---

diffident, *adj.* shy, timid; restrained. See HUMILITY, MODESTY.

diffuse, *v.* scatter, disperse. —*adj.* dispersed; verbose. See DISPERSION, DIFFUSENESS.

DIFFUSENESS
Verbosity

Nouns—diffuseness, expatiation, enlargement, expansion, development, dilation, dilating; verbosity, LOQUACITY; peroration, REPETITION; pleonasm, exuberance, redundance, thrice-told tale; prolixity, circumlocution; penny-a-lining; richness.

Verbs—be diffuse, be loquacious, run on, descant, expatiate, enlarge, dilate, expand; harp upon, repeat, iterate, dwell upon, insist upon; digress, divagate, maunder, ramble, beat about the bush, perorate, enlarge *or* expand [up]on, flesh out, verbalize.

Adjectives—diffuse, profuse, wordy, verbose, prolix; copious, exuberant, pleonastic, longwinded, desultory, long-drawn-out, spun out, protracted; prolix; maundering, digressive, discursive, rambling, episodic; circumlocutory, periphrastic, roundabout; flatulent, frothy. *Informal*, windy.

Adverbs—diffusely, redundantly, *etc.*, at large, in extenso, at length, ad nauseam.

Antonyms, see TACITURNITY.

---

dig, *v.* shovel, spade, excavate, grub, delve; labor, speed; unearth; *slang*, enjoy (see PLEASURE). See CONCAVITY, EXERTION.

digest, *v.t.* transform; absorb, assimilate; ruminate, ponder, weigh; shorten, abridge, condense. See THOUGHT, SHORTNESS, FOOD. —*n.* list, catalog; abstract, condensation, compendium. See WRITING.

digit, *n.* member, finger, toe; dewclaw; figure, numeral, cipher, NUMBER.

dignify, *v.t.* ennoble, exalt, distinguish. See REPUTE. *Ant.,* degrade, disgrace.

dignitary, *n.* official, officer. See IMPORTANCE.

dignity, *n.* REPUTE; nobility, eminence; PRIDE, stateliness, decorum; greatness, station, honor.

digress, *v.i.* diverge, ramble, deviate, wander. See DEVIATION, LOQUACITY, DIFFUSENESS.

dike, *n.* embankment, levee; ditch. See ENCLOSURE, DEFENSE.

dilapidated, *adj.* decayed, disintegrating, crumbling, tumbledown, ramshackle. See DETERIORATION.

dilate, *v.* expatiate, descant; stretch, distend, enlarge. See INCREASE, EXPANSION, DIFFUSENESS.

dilatory, *adj.* delaying, procrastinating. See LATENESS. *Ant.,* timely, prompt.

dilemma, *n.* predicament, perplexity, quandary. See DOUBT, DIFFICULTY.

dilettante, *n.* amateur, enthusiast; dabbler, poetaster; lightweight, poseur, pretender, faker. See TASTE, IGNORANCE. *Ant.,* professional.

diligence, *n.* application, industry, assiduity, ACTIVITY; stagecoach (see VEHICLE). See ATTENTION. *Ant.,* laziness, disregard.

diluted, *adj.* thin, weak, watery. See WATER, WEAKNESS. *Ant.,* full strength.

dimension, *n.* amplitude, area, extent, measurement, SIZE, LENGTH.

diminish, *v.* lessen, reduce, shrink, abridge; wane, dwindle, peter out, DECREASE. See LITTLENESS, CONTRACTION. *Ant.,* INCREASE.

diminutive, *adj.* small, little, tiny, wee. See LITTLENESS.

DIMNESS
Shadowiness

Nouns—dimness, OBSCURITY, shadow, shade; DARKNESS, opacity; partial darkness, partial shadow, partial eclipse; CLOUDINESS; dusk, gloaming, twilight, evening, shades of evening; moonlight, moonbeam, moonshine, starlight, candlelight, firelight; paleness, half-light, faintness, nebulosity, glimmer[ing], aurora, daybreak, dawn. See COLORLESSNESS, INVISIBILITY.

Verbs—be *or* grow dim; flicker, twinkle, glimmer (see LIGHT); loom; fade, pale; dim, bedim, obscure, blur, cloud, mist; fog, befog; shadow, overshadow.

Adjectives—dim, dull, lackluster, dingy, darkish, dark; obscure, indistinct, faint, shadowed; cloudy, misty, blear, opaque; nebulous, nebular; looming; pale, colorless.

Antonyms, see LIGHT.

dimple, *n.* hollow, dent. See CONCAVITY.

dimsighted, *adj.* nearsighted (see VISION).

dimwit, *n., slang,* dunce (see IGNORANCE).

din, *n.* noise, clamor (see LOUDNESS); DISCORD, cacophony.

diner, *n.* dining car, luncheonette, lunchroom, eatery (*inf.*). See FOOD.

dingy, *adj.* discolored, grimy, dirty, tarnished. See DIMNESS, COLORLESSNESS, UNCLEANNESS.

dinner, *n.* supper, buffet, TV *or* frozen dinner; banquet. See FOOD.

dinosaur, *n.* brontosaurus, *etc.* (see ANIMAL); old dog, relic, fossil. See OLDNESS.

diocese, *n.* district, REGION.

dip, *n.* plunge, dive; declivity, slope; hollow, depression; swim. —*v.t.* immerse, plunge; scoop; sink. See OBLIQUITY, WATER, CONCAVITY. *Ant.,* rise, incline, emerge.

diploma, *n.* certification, COMMISSION,

franchise; degree, sheepskin (*inf.*). See EVIDENCE.

diplomacy, *n.* statesmanship, statecraft, negotiation; shuttle diplomacy; finesse, tact, savoir-faire; SKILL, CUNNING, shrewdness, strategy. See COURTESY.

diplomat, *n.* envoy, ambassador; statesman; foreign-service officer. See CUNNING, COMPROMISE, AGENT.

dipper, *n.* scoop, ladle. See RECEPTACLE.

dire, *adj.* appalling, calamitous, fateful, dreadful, ominous; deplorable. See FEAR, ADVERSITY.

direct, *v.t.* guide, lead; regulate, govern, CONDUCT, head, manage, supervise, boss, rule; aim, point; order, COMMAND, prescribe, bid, instruct, teach, coach, prompt; show *or* lead the way; address. See AUTHORITY. —*adj.* straight, undeviating (see DIRECTION); blunt (see DISCOURTESY).

DIRECTION
Pointing toward

Nouns—1, direction, bearing, course, set; drift, tenor, orientation, TENDENCY; incidence; tack, aim, line of fire; collimation. See STRAIGHTNESS.

2, point of the compass, cardinal points: north, northward, northeast, northwest; east, eastward, orient, sunrise; south, southward, southeast, southwest; west, westward, occident, sunset; rhumb, azimuth, vector, line of collimation; arrow.

3, line, path, course, road, range, quarter, line of march; alignment. See MOTION, TRAVEL.

4, (*device for changing direction*) helm, rudder, joystick; needle, compass; guiding star, loadstar, lodestar, polestar, North Star, Polaris; cynosure; crosshair, joystick.

5, (*one who steers*) director, guide, cicerone, pilot, helmsman, steersman; driver, Jehu, charioteer.

Verbs—1, direct, tend, incline; take aim, point toward, face, aim at, draw a bead on, zero in on, level at, set one's sights on; go toward, set out for, head for, make [a beeline] for, steer toward; keep *or* hold a course; be bound for, bend one's steps toward; direct, steer, bend, *or* shape one's course; go straight [to the point].

2, ascertain one's direction, orient, get one's bearings, see which way the wind blows; box the compass; follow one's nose; lock on.

3, lead *or* show the way, take the lead, lead on; guide, steer, pilot; take the helm; take, hold, have, *or* handle the reins.

4, direct oneself toward, head, steer, go, *or* make for, make one's course for, strike out for, make a beeline for.

Adjectives—1, direct, straight, undeviating, unswerving, straightforward; directed *or* pointing toward, bound for. *Informal,* every which way.

2, northern, boreal; southern, austral; eastern, oriental; western, occidental; northeastern, northwestern, southeastern, southwestern.

3, directional; north-, south-, east-, *or* westbound.

Adverbs—1, directly, directionally, straight, northward, northerly, *etc.*; hither, thither, whither; straight as an arrow, as the crow flies, point-blank, head-on, in a line with; full tilt at; before the wind, windward, leeward; in all directions, hither and thither; here and there, everywhere, far and near; in all manner of ways, every which way.

2, north, northward[s], northerly; south, southward[s], southerly; east, eastward[s], easterly; west, westward[s], westerly; northeast, northwest, southeast, southwest, *etc.*

3, clockwise, counterclockwise, widdershins.

Prepositions—through, via, by [the] way of; toward.

Quotations—Go West, young man, and grow up with the country (*Greeley*), But, soft! What light through yonder window breaks? It is the east, and Juliet is the sun (*Shakespeare*), The mysterious East, perfumed like a flower, silent like death, dark like a grave (*Joseph Conrad*), Oh, East is East, and West is West, and never the twain shall meet (*Rudyard Kipling*), The spirit of the West, the modern spirit, is a Greek discovery (*Edith Hamilton*).

Antonyms, see DEVIATION.

---

directive, *n.* instruction. See COMMAND.

directly, *adv.* straightway, immediately, instantly, promptly; bluntly, flatly, unequivocally; expressly; straight. See INSTANTANEITY, DIRECTION.

DIRECTOR
One who directs

Nouns—1, director, manager, governor, rector, comptroller, controller; superintendent, supervisor; executive director; overseer, foreman, overlooker; inspector, visitor, ranger, surveyor, aedile, moderator, monitor, taskmaster; employer; master, [born] leader, ringleader, demagogue, conductor, precentor, bellwether, agitator, boss. *Informal,* straw boss.

2, management; head, executive, president, chief executive officer (CEO), chief financial officer (CFO), chief operating officer (COO); chairman, -woman, *or* -person, chairman of the board, speaker, chair; captain, superior; mayor; vice president, prime minister, premier, officer, functionary, minister, official, bureaucrat; officeholder; statesman, strategist, legislator, lawgiver, politician; Minos, Draco; arbiter, judge (see JUDGMENT); board, COUNCIL; secretary of state. *Informal,* prexy.

3, *(assistant to director)* vicar, deputy, steward, factor; AGENT, bailiff, middleman; factotum, majordomo, seneschal, housekeeper; shepherd; croupier; proctor, procurator.

4, guide, pilot, shepherd, conductor, cicerone; tour guide *or* director; guidebook. See INFORMATION, DIRECTION.

---

directory, *n.* index, guide; COUNCIL. See DIRECTION.

dirge, *n.* requiem, threnody, funeral hymn, elegy. See LAMENTATION.

dirigible, *n.* airship, blimp. See AVIATION.

dirt, *n.* earth, soil; dust, mud, *etc.*; gossip. See LAND, UNCLEANNESS, INFORMATION.

dirty, *adj.* unclean, filthy, soiled, foul;

murky, miry, stormy; vile, sordid, mean; pornographic; dishonest. See UNCLEANNESS, DIMNESS, IMPURITY, CLOUDINESS.

disable, *v.t.* incapacitate, cripple, damage, unfit, maim. See IMPOTENCE.

disadvantage, *n.* drawback, check, HINDRANCE. See EVIL.

disadvantaged, *adj.* underprivileged, handicapped, disabled. See HINDRANCE.

DISAGREEMENT
Act of disagreeing

Nouns—1, disagreement, DISCORD, discordance; dissonance, dissidence, discrepancy; UNCONFORMITY, incongruity, incongruence; discongruity, misalliance; jarring; DISSENT, dissension, conflict; OPPOSITION; disunity.

2, mismatch, misjoining, disproportion, disproportionateness, variance, divergence; repugnance. See DIFFERENCE.

3, unfitness, inaptitude, impropriety; inapplicability; inconsistency, irrelevancy, irrelation.

4, nonconformist, misfit, fish out of water (see UNCONFORMITY).

Verbs—disagree, vary; clash, jar, contend (see CONTENTION); diverge; come amiss; not concern, mismatch.

Adjectives—1, disagreeing, discordant, discrepant, incongruous; repugnant, incompatible, irreconcilable, inconsistent with; unconformable; disproportionate, unharmonious, unconsonant; divergent.

2, inapt, unapt, inappropriate, improper; impertinent; unsuited, unsuitable; inapplicable, beside the point or question, neither here nor there; unfit[ting], unbefitting, unbecoming; ill-timed, unseasonable, mal à propos, inadmissible; inapposite, irrelevant; uncongenial; ill-assorted, mismatched, misjoined, misplaced; unaccommodating; irreducible, uncommensurable; out of character, keeping, proportion, line, joint, tune, place, or season; out of its element; at odds or variance with, out of whack.

Adverbs—in disagreement; discordantly.

Quotations—If a man does not keep pace with his companions, perhaps it is because he hears a different drummer (*Henry Thoreau*).

Antonyms, see AGREEMENT, RELATION.

DISAPPEARANCE
Vanishing

Nouns—disappearance, evanescence; eclipse (see CONCEALMENT); occultation; exit, DEPARTURE; vanishing point; dissolving views. See INSUBSTANTIALITY, NONEXISTENCE.

Verbs—disappear, vanish, dissolve, evanesce, fade, melt away, pass, go; be gone; leave no trace, evaporate; undergo an eclipse; retire from sight; lose sight of; depart (see DEPARTURE); dry up, go up in smoke, fade into thin air, dissolve, melt away, go down the drain, pass or go by the board; make away with.

Adjectives—disappearing, vanishing, evanescent; missing, lost; lost to sight or view; gone [with the wind]. *Slang,* cold.

Antonyms, see APPEARANCE.

DISAPPOINTMENT
Failure to fulfill expectations

Nouns—1, disappointment, sad or bitter disappointment, chagrin, frustration, letdown, comedown; blighted hope, balk, blow, bitter pill, cold comfort; slip 'twixt cup and lip, trick of fortune, false or vain expectation, forlorn hope; MISJUDGMENT, miscalculation; mirage, fool's paradise; dust and ashes, false dawn, famous last words; disillusion[ment]. *Informal,* body blow. See FAILURE, DISCONTENT, REGRET, HOPELESSNESS.

2, jilter. *Slang,* broad-jumper.

Verbs—1, be disappointed, not realize one's hopes, have one's heart sink; look blue; find to one's cost; laugh on the wrong side of one's mouth.

2, disappoint, balk, jilt, bilk; play one false, play one a trick; dash the cup from the lips, cut the ground from under; disillusion, devastate, let down, turn to ashes in one's mouth; dissatisfy (see DISCONTENT). *Slang*, do a number on.

Adjectives—disappointed, disconcerted; out of one's reckoning; crushed, dashed, *etc.*; disappointing. *Slang*, underwhelmed.

Adverbs—disappointingly, not up to par.

Phrases—blessed is he who expects nothing, for he shall never be disappointed; hell hath no fury like a woman scorned.

Quotations—It is folly to expect men to do all that they may reasonably be expected to do (*Richard Whately*).

Antonyms, see EXPECTATION, SUCCESS.

DISAPPROBATION
Condemnation

Nouns—1, disapprobation, disapproval; DISLIKE.

2, *(lack of approval)* discommendation, demerit; blame, DETRACTION, CONDEMNATION.

3, *(criticism)* animadversion, reflection, stricture, objection, exception, criticism; hypercriticism, picking; sardonic grin *or* laugh; left-handed compliment; sneer, derision (see CONTEMPT); taunt, DISRESPECT. *Slang*, knock, slam, king's elevator, royal shaft.

4, *(petty criticism)* cavil, carping, censure, censoriousness; reprehension, remonstrance, expostulation, reproof, reprobation, reproach; chiding, upbraiding, rebuke, reprimand, castigation, lecture, scolding, trimming, dressing down (see *Verbs*, 3), rating, what-for, calling down; setdown, rap on the knuckles; frown, scowl, black look, evil eye; tirade, tongue-lashing, blowup. *Informal*, talking-to, static. *Slang*, rib-roast.

5, *(verbal disapprovation)* abuse, vituperation, objurgation, contumely; hard, bitter, *or* cutting words, dirty look; clamor, outcry, hue and cry; hiss[ing], catcall. *Slang*, Bronx cheer.

6, critic, armchair critic, Monday-morning quarterback.

Verbs—1, disapprove; DISLIKE; object to, take exception to; be scandalized at, think ill of, take a dim view of, view with disfavor *or* with jaundiced eyes.

2, *(show disapproval)* frown upon, scowl, look grave, knot one's brows, shake one's head, shrug one's shoulders; turn up one's nose (see CONTEMPT); look askance, make a wry face at; set one's face against.

3, *(chide)* discommend, speak ill of, not speak well of, denounce, damn, condemn; blame, lay blame upon, censure, reproach, pass censure on, reprobate, impugn; remonstrate, expostulate, recriminate, call to account; reprehend, chide, take to task, reprove, lecture, read the riot act, tell a thing or two, give a piece of one's mind; call on the carpet, chew out, get after, get on one's case, pick on, bring to book, rebuke, bawl out, reprimand, chastise, castigate, lash, rap one's knuckles, trounce, jump all over, come down hard on, trim, tongue-lash, flay, call *or* dress down, tell off, rip into, haul *or* rake over the coals, do a hatchet job on, rap, give what-for, pin one's ears back, dip one's pen in gall; sail, tear, lay, *or* light into. *Informal*, lace into, skin alive. *Slang*, knock, roast, jaw, ride down to the ground, chew one's ass out.

4, *(reprove)* exprobate, look daggers, vituperate, sound off, dish it out; abuse, scold, rate, objurgate, upbraid, rail (at), bark at; rave, fulminate, exclaim, protest, inveigh, declaim, cry out, *or* raise one's voice against; decry, run down; clamor, hiss, hoot, mob; draw up *or* sign a round robin; animadvert upon, reflect upon; cast reflection *or* a slur upon, damn with faint praise.

5, criticize, find fault with, give a hard time, jump down one's throat, cut up; be on one's back, pick on, draw a bead on; pull *or* pick to pieces; take exception; cavil, carp at; be censorious, pick holes, make a fuss about, kick against. *Slang*, diss, cut, dog, bust, blow away, dump on, hike, jam, talk trash. See DETRACTION, CONTEMPT, DISRESPECT.

6, incur disapprobation, incur blame, scandalize, shock, revolt; get a bad name, forfeit one's good name, get the eye, be on one's bad side; be under a cloud (see DISRE-

PUTE); bring a hornet's nest about one's ears; be in one's bad books; take blame, stand corrected; catch it or get it in the neck; have to answer for.

Adjectives—1, disapprobatory, disapproving, scandalized; disparaging, condemnatory, damnatory, denunciatory, reproachful, abusive, objurgatory, clamorous, vituperative; defamatory (see DETRACTION); satirical, sardonic, cynical; censorious, critical, faultfinding, captious, carping, hypercritical, catty; sparing or grudging of praise. 2, disapproved, in bad odor, unapproved, in one's bad graces, in one's black book[s], unblest, in bad; at a discount, exploded; weighed in the balance and found wanting; blameworthy, reprehensible, to blame, worthy of blame; answerable, uncommendable, objectionable, exceptionable, not to be thought of, beyond the pale; bad, vicious (see IMPROBITY). *Slang*, in the doghouse.

Adverbs—with a wry face; reproachfully, *etc.*

Interjections—thumbs down! it won't do [at all]! it will never do!; God forbid! Heaven forbid!; away with!; shame! for shame!

Phrases—criticism is something you can avoid by saying nothing, doing nothing, and being nothing; never speak ill of the dead; those who live in glass houses shouldn't throw stones.

Quotations—She ran the whole gamut of emotions from A to B (*Dorothy Parker*), I disapprove of what you say, but I will defend to the death your right to say it (*Voltaire*), The lot of critics is to be remembered by what they failed to understand (*Marianne Moore*), Parodies and caricatures are the most penetrating of criticisms (*Aldous Huxley*), A critic is a bundle of biases held loosely together by a sense of taste (*Whitney Balliett*), A critic is a man who knows the way but can't drive the car (*Kenneth Tynan*), Art made tongue-tied by authority (*Shakespeare*).

Antonyms, see APPROBATION.

---

disarm, v. demilitarize (see PACIFICATION); pull one's teeth; pacify, appease, charm. See IMPOTENCE, LOVE. *Ant.*, arm.

disarray, n. confusion, DISORDER.

disaster, n. calamity, cataclysm, misfortune, catastrophe, tragedy. See ADVERSITY, EVIL.

disband, v. break up, dismiss, dissolve. See DISJUNCTION, DISPERSION.

disbelief, n., **disbelieve**, v.t. See DOUBT, IRRELIGION.

disburse, v.t. pay out, spend, expend, lay out; allot, apportion. See PAYMENT, APPORTIONMENT.

discard, v.t. cast off, reject, abandon, repudiate, throw aside. See NULLIFICATION, EJECTION, DISUSE, RELINQUISHMENT.

discern, v.t. espy; discover, perceive, distinguish, detect, discriminate. See VISION, VISIBILITY, INTELLIGENCE, DIFFERENCE.

discharge, v.t. dismiss, deselect, retire; expel, emit; shoot, fire; perform, do; settle, pay; unload; free, acquit. See LIBERATION, CONDUCT, PAYMENT, ACQUITTAL, COMPLETION, EJECTION, EXCRETION, EXEMPTION.

disciple, n. follower, devotee, adherent, pupil. See LEARNING, AUXILIARY.

discipline, n. training, regimen, drill, practice; OBEDIENCE, RESTRAINT, control, repression; PUNISHMENT, correction; course of study. See TEACHING, BUSINESS, ORDER.

disclaim, v.t. disavow, deny, repudiate; disown, renounce. See NULLIFICATION, NEGATION.

DISCLOSURE
Bringing to light

Nouns—1, disclosure, divulgence, unveiling, revealing, revealment, revelation; exposition, exposure, expose; whole truth; telling (see INFORMATION); acknowledgment, admission, concession; exposé; avowal; confession, shrift; denouement, manifestation, PUBLICATION; clue, hint, intimation. See VISIBILITY, PENITENCE, TRUTH.

2, discovery, detection, ascertainment, find[ing], unearthing; ANSWER; first sight or glimpse; disinterment, exhumation.

3, observation area. *Informal*, fish tank.

4, investigative reporter; exhibitionist; burlesque, peep show. *Slang,* whistleblower, flasher, dangler.

Verbs—1, disclose, uncover, discover, detect, find, unmask, expose; lift *or* raise the veil *or* curtain; reveal, unveil, unfold, unseal, break the seal; lay open *or* bare, show up, bring to light, let into the secret; tell, inform (see INFORMATION); breathe, utter, blab, divulge, give away, let out, let fall, let drop, let slip, come out with, let the cat out of the bag, blow the lid off; betray; air *or* wash one's dirty linen in public; bruit abroad, broadcast; tell tales [out of school]; come out with, give vent *or* utterance to, blurt out, spill the beans, open the lips, vent, wash one's [dirty] linen in public; hint, intimate, whisper about; speak out, make manifest *or* public; exhume, disinter. *Slang,* peach, squeal, fink; spill the beans, give the show away.

2, acknowledge, allow, concede, admit, own [up], let on, confess, speak up *or* out, avow, shoot off one's mouth; turn inside out, make a clean breast, declare oneself, give oneself away, open up, show one's hand *or* cards, let it all hang out, unburden oneself *or* one's mind, open *or* lay bare one's mind, unbosom oneself, confide (in), let one's hair down, show one's [true] colors; get off one's chest; say *or* speak the truth; turn king's, queen's, *or* state's evidence. *Informal,* come clean, sing. *Slang,* spill one's guts, come out; flash, moon.

3, be disclosed, transpire, come to light, come out [in the wash]; come in sight (see APPEARANCE); become known, escape the lips; come *or* leak out, crop up; show its face *or* colors; break through the clouds, flash on the mind. *Slang,* be caught with one's pants down.

4, *(learn by research)* discover, spot; solve, unravel, smell *or* nose out, see through. *Slang,* dope out. See LEARNING, INQUIRY.

Adjectives—disclosed, expository, revelatory, *etc.*

Phrases—never tell tales out of school; one does not wash one's dirty linen in public.

Quotations—I will wear my heart upon my sleeve (*Shakespeare*).

Antonyms, see CONCEALMENT.

---

discolor, v. stain; fade. See DETERIORATION, COLORLESSNESS.

discomfit, *v.t.* embarrass, disconcert; frustrate; confuse. See HINDRANCE, SUCCESS.

discomfort, *n.* uneasiness, distress, annoyance, embarrassment; PAIN, soreness. *Ant.,* comfort, ease.

disconcert, *v.t.* upset, discompose, embarrass; perplex, confuse; frustrate, thwart. See HINDRANCE, PAIN, DISCONTENT.

disconnect, *v.t.* detach, unplug. See DISJUNCTION. *Ant.,* connect.

disconsolate, *adj.* inconsolable, comfortless, hopeless; melancholy, forlorn, sad. See DEJECTION.

DISCONTENT
Want of satisfaction

Nouns—1, discontent, discontentment, displeasure; dissatisfaction, RESENTMENT; inquietude, vexation, soreness, heartburning (see DEJECTION); querulousness (see LAMENTATION); dissidence, DISSENT; hypercriticism; petulance. *Informal,* gripe. *Slang,* the blahs, attitude.

2, *(cause of discontent)* fly in the ointment, sour grapes, thorn in the flesh *or* in one's side (see DISAPPOINTMENT); harassment.

3, *(discontent person)* malcontent, grumbler, growler, croaker, fussbudget. *Informal,* grouch, griper, crab. *Slang,* grouser, kvetch, sorehead, sourpuss.

Verbs—1, be discontented *or* dissatisfied; quarrel with one's bread and butter; repine, REGRET; take on, take to heart; shrug the shoulders, make a wry face, pull a long face, knot one's brows, look blue *or* black, look blank, look glum; cut off one's nose to spite one's face; take in bad part, take ill; fret, chafe, grumble, croak; lament (see LAMENTATION). *Informal,* gripe, beef. *Slang,* grouse, kvetch, make a stink, rattle beads, ride the rag, have an attitude.

2, cause discontent, displease, dissatisfy, not sit right with; be a pain in the neck, vex, disappoint, chagrin, distress, exercise, afflict, annoy, ail, bother, badger, pester, lacerate, besiege, disconcert, harass, molest, nettle, heckle, persecute, get under one's skin, stick in one's craw *or* crop, put one's nose out of joint, rub the wrong way, jangle. *Informal*, bug, put off, devil, mess with.

Adjectives—1, discontented, dissatisfied, disgruntled, ill at ease, unsatisfied, ungratified; dissident, dissenting, malcontent (see DISSENT); exigent, exacting, hypercritical; repining, regretful; down in the mouth, morose, dejected (see DEJECTION); in high dudgeon, in the dumps, in bad humor, glum, sulky, sullen, querulous; sour[ed], out of humor *or* temper, grumpy. *Informal*, sore, grouchy. *Slang*, crabby.

2, disappointing, unsatisfactory; pesky, annoying; ungrateful.

Quotations—We loathe our manna, and we long for quails (*John Dryden*), In pale contented sort of discontent (*John Keats*), Content is disillusioning to behold: what is there to be content about? (*Virginia Woolf*), Discontent is the want of self-reliance: it is infirmity of will (*Emerson*).

Antonyms, see CHEERFULNESS, PLEASURE, CONTENT.

DISCONTINUANCE
Lack of continued connection

Nouns—discontinuance, discontinuity; disruption; DISJUNCTION, disconnection, interruption, letup, break, gap, INTERVAL, caesura; broken thread; intermission, half-time. *Slang*, pit stop. See DISUSE, IRREGULARITY, RELINQUISHMENT.

Verbs—1, be discontinuous, alternate, intermit. See IRREGULARITY.

2, *(make discontinuous)* discontinue, call off, pause, disrupt, interrupt, break into, hang up, cut short, break off, lay off; stop, cease, desist, give over, knock off, call it a day *or* quits, grind to a halt; draw *or* pull up, intervene, break in upon; interpose (see BETWEEN); break the thread; drop out; disconnect, disjoin, dislocate; cut, shut, *or* turn off, curtail, close *or* shut down, shut up shop, suspend, have done with, quit, throw in the sponge, give up the argument (see RESIGNATION). See END.

Adjectives—discontinuous, discrete, unsuccessive, broken, interrupted, disconnected, unconnected; parenthetical, episodic, fitful, irregular (see IRREGULARITY); spasmodic, desultory, intermitting, intermittent; alternate, recurrent, periodic; few and far between; abrupt. *Informal*, herky-jerky.

Adverbs—discontinuously, sporadically, at intervals; by snatches, by fits and starts, fitfully; so much for.

Antonyms, see CONTINUITY.

DISCORD
Want of agreement

Nouns—1, discord, discordance, disaccord, dissidence, DISAGREEMENT, dissonance; friction, incompatibility; variance, DIFFERENCE, dissension, DISSENT; misunderstanding, cross purposes, odds; division, rupture, disrupture, DISORDER, house divided against itself; breach.

2, *(verbal discord)* quarrel, falling-out, dispute, debate, argument, discussion, controversy, squabble, tiff, altercation, hassle, [high] words, wrangling, bicker, flap, spat, jangle, cross questions and crooked answers, war of words; polemics (see REASONING).

3, *(physical discord)* strife, WARFARE, open rupture, declaration of war; jar[ring], clash, imbroglio, crossfire, *etc.* (see CONTENTION).

4, *(subject of dispute)* ground of quarrel, battleground, disputed point; bone of contention, bone *or* crow to pick; apple of discord, casus belli; question at issue, vexed question. *Informal*, hot potato. See INQUIRY.

5, *(sonic discord)* dissonance, cacophony, caterwauling; false *or* sour note; harshness, stridency, din; babel. *Informal,* clinker, clam. See MUSIC.

Verbs—**1,** be discordant, disagree; clash, jar, jangle; misunderstand, differ, DISSENT; have a bone to pick with.

2, fall out, quarrel, dispute, litigate, squabble, wrangle, bicker, have words (with), have it out, set to, fall foul of; break, part company (with); declare war; try conclusions, join an issue, pick a quarrel, sow dissension; embroil, widen the breach; set at odds, pit against.

Adjectives—**1,** discordant; disagreeing, out of tune, ajar, on bad terms; dissenting, unreconciled, unpacified, unpacific; quarrelsome, unpacific; controversial, polemic, disputatious, factious; litigious, litigant; pettifogging; at odds, at loggerheads, at variance, at issue, at cross purposes, at sixes and sevens, up in arms, in hot water, embroiled; torn, disunited, divisive, disruptive.

2, discordant, dissonant, out of tune, off-key; tuneless, unmusical, unmelodious, unharmonious, harsh, cacophonous.

Antonyms, see AGREEMENT.

---

discotheque, *n.* disco, nightclub. See AMUSEMENT.

discount, *v.t.* rebate, allow, reduce; deduct, lessen, diminish; mark down, lower (the price); disregard, ignore; belittle. —*n.* allowance, qualification; markdown, rebate, refund, deduction; percentage. See DECREASE, CHEAPNESS, DETRACTION, DEDUCTION, SALE. *Ant.,* mark up.

discountenance, *v.t.* disconcert, abash; disapprove of. See HINDRANCE, DISAPPROBATION.

discourage, *v.t.* depress, dishearten, dismay; dissuade, deter. See DEJECTION, DISSUASION, FEAR. *Ant.,* encourage, persuade.

discourse, *v.i.* converse, talk, discuss; declaim, hold forth, dissertate. See CONVERSATION, SPEECH.

DISCOURTESY
Ill manners

Nouns—**1,** discourtesy, discourteousness; ill-breeding; rudeness, ill *or* bad manners. *Slang,* boardinghouse reach.

2, *(discourteous behavior)* uncourteousness, inurbanity; illiberality, incivility, DISRESPECT; offense, insult, INSOLENCE, impudence; barbarism, barbarity, brutality, misbehavior, blackguardism, conduct unbecoming (a gentleman, lady, *etc.*), VULGARITY; churlishness, sullenness, IRASCIBILITY; tartness, acrimony, acerbity, the rough side of one's tongue. *Slang,* attitude.

3, *(discourteous look)* scowl, black look, frown; short answer, rebuff, slap in the face, cold shoulder; hard words, contumely; unparliamentary language *or* behavior.

4, *(discourteous person)* bear, brute, boor, churl, cad, heel, blackguard, saucebox, beast; frump; bull in a china shop; cold fish. *Informal,* crosspatch. *Slang,* sleazeball, slimeball *or* -bucket.

Verbs—**1,** be discourteous, be rude; speak out of turn; insult, cut, treat with discourtesy; take a name in vain; make bold *or* free with, take a liberty; stare out of countenance; ogle, point at, put to the blush; turn one's back upon, turn on one's heel, give the cold shoulder, cold-shoulder; keep at a distance *or* at arm's length; look coldly upon; show the door to, give the brush-off, brush off; answer back, send away with a flea in the ear, add insult to injury; lose one's temper; sulk, frown, scowl, glower, pout; snap, snarl, growl. *Informal,* do the dozens, diss, flip the bird.

2, *(result of discourtesy)* wear out one's welcome, get the brush-off.

Adjectives—**1,** discourteous, uncourteous; uncourtly; ill-bred, ill-mannered, disrespectful, ill-behaved, unmannerly, impolite; unpolished, uncivilized, ungentlemanly; unladylike; blackguard; vulgar, indecorous; foul-mouthed, abusive, uncivil, ungracious, unceremonious, cool; pert, forward, direct, obtrusive, impudent, rude, coarse, curt, saucy; precocious. *Informal,* bearish. *Slang,* fresh, sassy, snippy, high-hat, badass, corroded, dorky.

2, repulsive, unaccommodating, unneighborly, ungentle, ungainly; rough, bluff, blunt, gruff, churlish, nasty, boorish, bearish; brutal, brusque, snarling, harsh, cavalier, tart, crabbed, sharp, short, trenchant, sarcastic, biting, caustic, virulent, bitter, acrimonious, venomous, contumelious; distasteful; perverse; dour, sullen, peevish, irascible.

Adverbs—with a bad grace.

Quotations—An injury is much sooner forgotten than an insult (*Lord Chesterfield*), Sarcasm is the greatest weapon of the smallest mind (*Alan Ayckbourn*).

Antonyms, see COURTESY.

---

discover, *v.t.* uncover, reveal, disclose, manifest; find, espy, descry; detect, unearth; realize. See DISCLOSURE, VISION, KNOWLEDGE, LEARNING.

discovery, *n.* revelation, DISCLOSURE; detection, first sight *or* glimpse; unearthing; find[ing]; invention, innovation. See NEWNESS, ANSWER.

discredit, *v.t.* disparage, stigmatize, shame; doubt, disbelieve, impeach. See DISREPUTE, DOUBT. *Ant.,* prove, rehabilitate.

discreet, *adj.* prudent, judicious, careful, tactful, cautious. See CAUTION, CARE. *Ant.,* indiscreet, incautious.

discrepancy, *n.* inconsistency, DISAGREEMENT.

discrete, *adj.* separate, distinct; discontinuous. See DISJUNCTION, DISCONTINUANCE.

discretion, *n.* JUDGMENT; tact, finesse, TASTE. See CAUTION, WILL.

discrimination, *n.* differentiation, DIFFERENCE, distinction; TASTE, JUDGMENT, insight, critical perception, discernment; bias, prejudice, EXCLUSION. See ELEGANCE, INTELLIGENCE.

discursive, *adj.* wandering, rambling, desultory, digressive. See DEVIATION.

discuss, *v.t.* talk over, debate, canvass, argue; analyze, explain. See REASONING, CONVERSATION.

disdain, *n.* scorn, CONTEMPT; arrogance, hauteur. See INATTENTION, INDIFFERENCE.

DISEASE
Condition of ill health

Nouns—1, disease, illness, sickness, ailment, ailing; morbidity, infirmity, ailment, indisposition; complaint, disorder, malady; functional disorder.

2, condition, affliction, disorder, syndrome; pre-existing condition; environmental *or* ecological illness, toxic tort, sick- *or* tight-building syndrome; delicacy, loss of health, invalidism, cachexia, atrophy, marasmus; dehydration; addiction, dependence, alcoholism (see DRINKING, DRUGS); edema, dropsy; enuresis, bedwetting, incontinence; irritable bowel syndrome, spastic colon; brain damage; paresis; [nervous, heat, *etc.*] prostration; nausea; acidosis, alkalosis; carpal tunnel syndrome, writer's cramp; housemaid's knee; coronary; cough; combat fatigue; simulator sickness, barfogenesis; fibrosis; malnutrition; infection, plague; balding, alopecia; colic; shock; motion sickness, carsickness, seasickness, mal de mer, airsickness, jet lag, altitude sickness *or* discomfort, aeroembolism, decompression sickness, bends, caisson disease; amblyopia (see BLINDNESS); amnesia (see OBLIVION); dysentery, diarrhea; diaper rash; hemorrhoids, piles; anorexia nervosa, binge-purge syndrome, bulimia; malnutrition, pica; obesity; menorrhagia, menstrual bleeding; anoxia; goiter; hangnail, ingrown toenail; astigmatism (see VISION); paralysis, diplegia, sclerosis; allergy, allergic reaction, atopy, hay fever; vertigo; heat exhaustion *or* prostration, heatstroke, sunstroke; distemper; priapism; psilosis, sprue; visitation, attack, seizure, stroke; backache, lumbago, sciatica, sponsylosis; fit, cramp, convulsion; tendonitis, tennis elbow, surfer's knee; varicose veins; decay (see DETERIORATION). *Slang,* grapes.

3, a. symptom, sign; tumescence, detumescence; toxemia, toxicosis, [lead, mercury, *etc.*] poisoning; putrescence (see ODOR); neuralgia, nephralgia (see PAIN); bruit, crepitus; adhesion, ankylosis; anesthesia. **b.** tumor, growth, fibroma, fibrosarcoma, lymphoma, teratoma, hematoma, neoplasm, polyp; ecchymosis, black-and-blue mark, bruise, lividity, contusion; callus, bunion, corn, plantar wart, clubbing; eruption, rash, efflorescence, papule, hives, urticaria, breaking out, inflammation, swelling; sore, lesion, tubercle, ulcer, chancre, abscess, bubo, cyst, wen, furuncle, boil, cold sore, blister, vesicle, growth, bedsore, granuloma; pimple, blackhead, pustule, comedo, pock; swelling, carbuncle, rot, canker, cancrum, mortification, corruption, gangrene; acne, rosacea, seborrhea; wart, verruca; lentigo, liver spot, mole; scar, cicatrix, scab; gallstone, kidney stone, calculus, concretion; flush, mottling; jaundice; dandruff, scurf; chapping. *Slang,* zit, goober, Irish button, poulain. **c.** hemolysis, high *or* low blood pressure, hypertension, hemorrhage, hyper- *or* hypoglycemia, ischemia; necrosis; hyperplasia; hyper- *or* hypothermia; fever, pyrexia, chills, shivers, tremor, dizziness, malaise; goose bumps *or* flesh, horripilation; itching, pruritus; poliosis; hydrocephalus; perspiration, sweating, diaphoresis. **d.** indigestion, dyspepsia, heartburn, pyrosis, colic, constipation, irregularity, dyspepsia, indigestion, stomachache, diarrhea, runs; bad breath, halitosis; belch, breaking of wind, flatulence, flatus, gas, turista; uremia, albuminaria; vomiting, regurgitation, emesis. *Informal,* burp, collywobbles, mulligrubs, gullion, runs, movies. *Slang,* fart, backdoor trots, Delhi belly, Montezuma's revenge. **e.** angina, chest pain, arrhythmia, bradycardia, tachycardia, cardiac arrest, fibrillation, heart murmur, palpitation. **f.** headache, cephalalgia, migraine; insomnia, sleeplessness; anxiety, hysteria, mania, illusion, confusion, incoherence, toxic shock syndrome, Munich syndrome, Gulf War syndrome. **g.** apnea, asthma, asphyxiation, breathlessness, tachypnea, dyspnea, bronchospasm, crepitation, rale, hiccup, stridor; choking; caries, cavity; nosebleed, epistaxis; earache, otalgia; toothache; cyanosis, tinnitus. **h.** ataxia, atony, atrophy, attrition, emaciation, underweight, enervation, exhaustion, fatigue, prostration, torpor, neurasthenia; cachexia, collapse, blackout, fainting, syncope; unconsciousness, coma; senescence, senility (see AGE); [morbid] obesity, overweight; convulsion, paroxysm, spasm, stitch, cramp, crick, eclampsia, tetany, tic, economy class syndrome. **i.** cough, tussis, sneeze, catarrh, blennorrhagia, empyema, suppuration, phlegm, sputum, rheum, mucus, postnasal drip.

4, mental illness, catalepsy, catatonia, delirium, breakdown, debility (see INSANITY).

5, *(diseases)* **a.** *(immune system)* autoimmune disease, acquired immune deficiency syndrome, AIDS. **b.** *(diseases of blood)* Addison's disease, agranulocytosis, anemia, arteriosclerosis, atheroma, atherosclerosis, blood poisoning, septicemia, toxemia, bacteremia, hypoglycemia, leukemia, phlebitis, puerperal fever, childbed fever, sickle cell anemia, sleeping sickness, encephalitis, hemophilia, nephrosis, Raynaud's disease, thalassemia, thrombocytosis, thromboembolism, thrombosis. **c.** *(glandular disease)* adenitis, adenocarcinoma, bilirubinemia, nephritis, kidney disease, Bright's disease, cat-scratch disease, cyrrhosis, Cushing's disease, cystic fibrosis, elephantiasis, Epstein-Barr syndrome, mononucleosis, glandular fever, filariasis, Graves' disease, hepatitis, Hodgkin's disease, hyper- *or* hypothyroidism, mastitis, prostatitis, reticulosis, scrofula, tularemia. *Informal,* kissing disease. **d.** *(infectious diseases)* malaria, ague, blackwater fever, blastomycosis, botulism, amebiasis, amebic dysentery, [bubonic] plague, black death, Ebola virus, brucellosis, chickenpox, varicella, childbed fever, cholera, cowpox, dengue, diabetes [mellitus *or* insipidus], diphtheria, frambesia, yaws, rubella, roseola, German measles, leprosy, Hansen's disease, Lassa fever, mumps, paratyphoid fever, Q fever, smallpox, variola, strep throat, typhoid fever, typhus, yellow fever, athlete's foot, tinea. **e.** *(brain disorders)* Alzheimer's disease, stroke, apoplexy, cerebrospinal fever, spotter fever, encephalitis, epilepsy, Huntington's chorea, meningitis, relapsing fever, Rocky Mountain spotted fever. **f.** *(respiratory disease)* anthrax, asbestosis, black *or* miner's lung, pneumonoconiosis, brown lung, byssinosis, [common] cold, consumption, emphysema, influenza, flu, grippe, legionnaires' disease, mesothelioma, pleurisy, pneumonia, old man's friend, rheumatic fever, sandfly fever, silicosis, trench mouth, tuberculosis, pneumonitis. **g.**

(gastrointestinal disease) appendicitis, cellulitis, colitis, Crohn's disease, diverticulitis, dysentery, enteritis, gastric ulcer, gastritis, gastroenteritis, hookworm, ileitis, kala-azar, peptic ulcer, peritonitis, schistosomiasis, snail fever, celiac disease, fluxes. **h.** *(bones and joints)* arthritis, gout, myeloma, osteoarthritis, osteomyelitis, osteoporosis, podagra, rheumatoid arthritis, rheumatism. **i.** *(heart disease)* cardiovascular disease, endocarditis, cardiac arrest, cardiac stenosis, cardiomyopathy, arrhythmia, carditis, congestive heart failure, coronory heart disease, heart attack, coronary *or* myocardial infarction, coronary occlusion *or* thrombosis, endocarditis, pericarditis, rheumatic heart disease, Barlow's syndrome. **j.** *(cancer)* cancer, carcinoma, Kaposi's sarcoma, lung cancer, breast cancer, colon cancer, melanoma. **k.** *(nutritional disorder)* beriberi, food poisoning, botulism, kwashiorkor, pellagra, rickets, salmonella poisoning, scurvy, hepatitis. **l.** *(eye disease)* blepharitis, conjunctivitis, trachoma, pinkeye, glaucoma, keratitis, sty, cataract. **m.** *(fungal disease)* candidiasis, thrush, mycosis. **n.** *(skin disease)* dermatitis, eczema, carbuncle, dracontiasis, erysipelas, herpes [simplex *or* zoster], icthyosis, impetigo, lupus, miliaria, prickly heat, scabies, scleroderma, psoriasis. *Slang,* crotch-rot, creeping crud, jock itch, dhobie itch. **o.** *(tooth or gum disease)* caries, periodontal disease, pyorrhea. **p.** *(genital and urinary disease)* urethritis, vaginitis, cervicitis; venereal disease, VD, sexually transmitted disease, STD, chlamydia, gonorrhea, crab louse, cystitis, genital herpes, orchitis, syphilis, specific stomach, tabes dorsalis, *Informal,* social disease, dose. *Slang,* clap, crud, load, blue balls, French disease, old Joe, gentleman's complaint. See SEX. **q.** *(nervous disorders)* chorea, St. Vitus's dance, chronic fatigue syndrome, epilepsy, grand *or* petit mal, rabies, hydrophobia, polio[myelitis], infantile paralysis, tetanus, lockjaw, Lou Gehrig's disease, Lyme disease, multiple sclerosis, MS, neuritis, neuropathy, Parkinson's disease, parkinsonism, radiation sickness, herpes zoster, shingles, Tourette's syndrome, narcolepsy. **r.** *(tissue disease)* collagen disease, lupus, rheumatic fever, rheumatoid arthritis, sclerodoma, coryza, gingivitis, glioma, laryngitis, whooping cough, pertussis, pharyngitis, quinsy, sinusitis, tonsilitis. **s.** *(diseases of children)* crib death, sudden infant death syndrome, SIDS, Tay-Sachs disease, croup, Reye's syndrome, scarlet fever, scarlatina. **t.** *(ear disease)* Ménière's syndrome, otitis, otosclerosis, adenoma. **u.** *(muscular disease)* muscular dystrophy, myasthenia gravis, rheumatism, bursitis. **v.** *(infestations)* pediculosis, tapeworm, hookworm, trichinosis, ringworm. *Slang,* crabs.
6, invalid, patient, case, shut-in; inpatient, outpatient; terminal patient; cripple, handicapped person, amputee, paralytic; leper, consumptive, epileptic. *Slang,* gimp, gork.
7, *(study of illness)* pathology, etiology, therapeutics, diagnosis, prognosis, epidemiology.
8, *(disease-causing situation)* insalubrity, insalubriousness, unhealthiness; taint, pollution, infection, contagion, septicity, toxicity, epidemic, endemic; plague, pestilence, pox, scourge; allergen, carcinogen, toxin; carrier; fungus; pathogen, germ, microbe, microorganism, ameba, bacterium, virus, staphylococcus, streptobacillus, streptococcus, arbovirus, saprophyte; vector, parasite, infestation, rickettsia[e].
Verbs—**1,** be ill, ail, run a temperature; suffer, labor under, be affected *or* afflicted with; complain of; droop, flag, languish, halt; sicken, peak, pine; keep [to] one's bed; feign sickness, malinger; catch, pick up, contract, *or* come down with (a disease), fall *or* take sick *or* ill, catch one's death of. *Informal,* feel bad *or* awful.
2, disease, sicken, indispose, derange, attack; lay up; fester; infect, contaminate; poison; infest.
Adjectives—**1,** diseased, ailing, ill (of), taken ill, seized with; indisposed, unwell, sick, feverish, flushed, febrile, squeamish, queasy, poorly, seedy, under the weather; laid up, confined, bedridden, invalided, in the hospital, on the sick list, in sick bay (*naut.*); ambulatory; out of health *or* sorts; valetudinary; emergent, urgent, routine. *Informal,* off one's feed, green around the gills.
2, unsound, unhealthy; sickly, rheumy, phthisic, scorbutic, tubercular, an[a]emic, cadaverous, delicate, infirm, drooping, flagging, lame, palsied, paralytic, dyspeptic, weak (see IMPOTENCE); crippled, halt, halting; decrepit; decayed, deteriorated; incurable,

terminal, moribund (see DEATH); in declining health; in a bad way, in danger, prostrate. See WEAKNESS.

3, pathogenic, insalubrious, unhealthful, morbid, gangrenous, tainted, vitiated, contaminated, poisoned, poisonous, venomous; noxious, toxic, septic, virulent, malignant; harmful, unsanitary.

4, degenerative, progressive; irreversible; life-threatening, [non]fatal; congenital, genetic; iatrogenic, idiopathic; psychomotor, psychosomatic; infectious, communicable, contagious, endemic, pandemic, epidemic (see TRANSFER).

Phrases—feed a cold and starve a fever; illness tells us what we are.

Quotations—Illness is the night-side of life (*Susan Sontag*), I now begin a journey that will lead me into the sunset of my life (*Ronald Reagan*), The thousand natural shocks that flesh is heir to (*Shakespeare*), Illness is not something a person *has*. It's another way of being (*Jonathan Miller*), Ask not what disease the person has, but rather what person the disease has (*Oliver Sacks*).

Antonyms, see HEALTH.

---

disembark, *v.i.* land; deplane, detrain, *etc.* See ARRIVAL. *Ant.,* embark, board.

disenchant, *v.* See DISILLUSION.

disengage, *v.t.* cut loose, [set] free, release. See LIBERATION, DISJUNCTION.

disentangle, *n.* extricate, [set] free; untangle, unsnarl; organize; comb, card. See DISJUNCTION, LIBERATION, FREEDOM.

disfavor, *n.* displeasure, disesteem. See DISRESPECT. *Ant.,* favor.

disfigure, *v.t.* deface, mar, mutilate, blemish. See DETERIORATION, DISTORTION, FORMLESSNESS, UGLINESS.

disgorge, *v.t.* vomit (see EJECTION).

disgrace, *v.t.* degrade, abase, dishonor, humiliate; shame, discredit. See DISREPUTE, HUMILITY. *Ant.,* honor.

disgruntled, *adj.* cross (see IRASCIBILITY).

disguise, *n.* camouflage, makeup, dissimulation, CONCEALMENT, mask.

disgust, *v.t.* nauseate, sicken, revolt, repel, offend. —*n.* aversion, nausea, loathing, abhorrence. See PAIN, DISLIKE.

dish, *n.* plate, saucer, *etc.*; serving; recipe; (*pl.*) tableware. See RECEPTACLE, FOOD.

dishearten, *v.t.* discourage, dispirit. See DEJECTION. *Ant.,* encourage, cheer.

dishevel, *v.t.* muss, tousle. See DISORDER.

dishonest, *adj.* false, untrustworthy, deceitful, cheating, fraudulent, crooked. See FALSEHOOD, IMPROBITY.

dishonor, *n.* treachery, infamy, perfidy; infidelity, adultery; disgrace. —*v.t.* disgrace, shame; default (on) (see NONPAYMENT). See DISRESPECT, DISREPUTE, IMPROBITY, WRONG.

disillusion, *n.* disillusionment, disenchantment, revelation; DISAPPOINTMENT, cynicism. —*v.t.* disenchant, disabuse, remove the scales from one's eyes, enlighten; disappoint, puncture one's balloon, pour cold water on, deflate, bring down to earth, debunk (*inf.*). See DISCLOSURE.

disincline, *v.t.* dissuade, indispose, discourage. See DISLIKE, DISSUASION.

disinfect, *v.t.* sterilize, sanitize, purify, fumigate. See CLEANNESS.

disinfectant, *n.* antiseptic, germicide. See CLEANNESS, REMEDY.

disinherit, *v.t.* disown, cut off, deprive. See NULLIFICATION.

disintegrate, *v.* break up, separate, decompose; decay, crumble, dissolve, fall apart. See DISJUNCTION, DECOMPOSITION.

disinter, *v.t.* dig up, unearth. See INTERMENT, DISCLOSURE. *Ant.,* bury.

DISJUNCTION
Act or state of separation

Nouns—1, disjunction, disconnection, disunity, disunion, disassociation, disengagement; isolation, separateness, DISPERSION.

2, fissure, rent, crevice, gash (see INTERVAL).

3, separation, parting, detachment, segregation; DIVORCE; caesura, division, schism, subdivision, break, fracture, rupture; dismemberment, disintegration; dislocation, luxation (see DISPLACEMENT); severance, disseverance; disassembly, taking apart, dismantlement; scission, rescission, abscission; section, resection, cleavage; median [strip]; breakaway; surgery (see REMEDY); dissection; DECOMPOSITION.

4, discontinuity, interruption (see DISCONTINUANCE).

5, sieve, separator; analyzer; centrifuge; slicer, cutter.

Verbs—1, be disjoined, come off, fall off, fall to pieces; peel off; get loose; branch [off], bisect, fork.

2, disjoin, disconnect, disengage, disunite, dissociate, DIVORCE, PART, detach, separate, cut loose *or* off, filter out, break off, segregate; set *or* keep apart; isolate; estrange, cut adrift, cast off *or* loose; loose[n], unloose, undo, unbind, unchain, untangle, disentangle; set free, demobilize, liberate (see LIBERATION).

3, sunder, divide, subdivide, sever, dissever, cut, saw, chop, cube, dice, mince, cleave, rive, rend, split, splinter, chip, crack, snap, break, tear, rip, burst; rend asunder, wrench, rupture, shatter, shiver; hack, hew, slash; amputate. *Informal,* smash to smithereens.

4, cut up, carve, gash, dissect, anatomize; cut, take, pull, *or* pick to pieces; disintegrate, dismember, disbranch, disband, disperse, displace, dislocate, disjoint, luxate; take *or* tear down; break up; apportion (see APPORTIONMENT).

Adjectives—disjoined, discontinuous, multipartite, inarticulate, disjunctive; isolated, separate, disparate, discrete, apart, asunder, far between, loose, free; detached, unattached, unannexed, unassociated, distinct; adrift, straggling, unconnected; scissile, divisible; several.

Adverbs—disjunctively, separately; one by one, severally, apart; adrift, asunder, in two, in twain; in the abstract, abstractedly.

Antonyms, see JUNCTION, COHERENCE.

---

disk, *n.* plate, record, discus; face; floppy *or* fixed disk; wafer; wheel. See CIRCU- LARITY, FRONT, LAYER. —*v.* plow, harrow. See AGRICULTURE, PREPARATION.

DISLIKE
Fixed aversion

Nouns—1, dislike, distaste, disinclination; reluctance; backwardness (see UNWILLINGNESS); repugnance, disgust, nausea, loathing; antipathy, aversion, enmity, HATE, animosity, no love lost; phobia (see FEAR).

2, unpopularity, lack of favor.

3, persona non grata; not one's cup of tea. *Slang,* geek, scumbag, hairbag, jerkoff, sleazeball, slimeball.

Verbs—1, dislike, mislike; mind, object to (see DISAPPROBATION); not care for; have, conceive, entertain, *or* take a dislike to; have no taste for, have no use for, have no stomach for; shun, avoid (see AVOIDANCE); shudder at, turn up the nose at, look askance at; abhor, HATE.

2, cause *or* excite dislike; disincline, repel, sicken, leave a bitter taste in the mouth; make sick; turn one's stomach, nauseate, disgust, go against the grain; stick in the throat; make one's blood run cold; pall. *Slang,* turn off, gross out.

Adjectives—1, disliking, averse, loath; shy of, sick of, disinclined. *Informal,* allergic.

2, disliked, uncared for, unpopular, out of favor.

3, unlikable, repulsive, repugnant, repellent; abhorrent, insufferable, fulsome, nauseous, sickening, disgusting, disagreeable.

Phrases—one man's meat is another man's poison; not one's cup of tea. *Slang,* gag me with a spoon.

Quotations—Violent antipathies are always suspicious, and betray a secret affinity (*William Hazlitt*), Tiggers don't like honey (*A. A. Milne*), Do not unto others as you would that they should do unto you. Their tastes may not be the same (*G. B. Shaw*), Take care to get what you like or you will be forced to like what you get (*G. B. Shaw*).

Antonyms, see APPROBATION, LOVE.

dislocate, *v.t.* displace; disarrange; disjoin, disarticulate. See DISJUNCTION, DISCONTINUANCE.

dislodge, *v.t.* displace, topple; expel, evict, drive out. See EJECTION, DISPLACEMENT.

disloyal, *adj.* unfaithful, false; untrue, inconstant. See IMPROBITY. *Ant.,* loyal, faithful.

dismal, *adj.* cheerless, depressing, gloomy; doleful, somber, funereal. See DEJECTION. *Ant.,* joyous, delightful.

dismantle, *v.t.* take apart; raze, demolish; disrobe, undress. See DIVESTMENT, USELESSNESS, DISUSE.

dismay, *n.* consternation, terror; discouragement. —*v.t.* appall; discourage. See FEAR, DEJECTION.

dismember, *v.t.* disjoint, disarticulate, dissect, tear limb from limb, cut to pieces. See DISJUNCTION.

dismiss, *v.t.* send away; discharge, liberate, disband; cancel (*law*). See NULLIFICATION, EJECTION, LIBERATION.

dismount, *v.t.* take apart, dismantle. See DISJUNCTION. —*v.i.* get off, climb down. See ARRIVAL, DESCENT.

DISOBEDIENCE
Refusal to obey

Nouns—1, disobedience, insubordination, contumacy; infraction, infringement; naughtiness; violation, noncompliance; recusancy; nonobservance. *Slang,* behavishness, orneriness. See UNCONFORMITY.

2, revolt, rebellion, outbreak, breakaway; rising, uprising (see REVOLUTION); insurrection; civil disobedience, nonviolence, sit-down strike, sit-in, sickout; [wildcat] strike, job action, RESISTANCE; DEFIANCE; mutiny, mutinousness, mutineering; sedition, lese majesty. *Informal,* walkout, blue flu. See ILLEGALITY.

3, insurgent, mutineer, rebel, revolter, rioter, insurgent, seceder, runagate, brat, brawler.

Verbs—disobey, violate, infringe; defy; riot, run riot, run amuck, fly in the face of; take the law into one's own hands; kick over the traces; strike, resist (see OPPOSITION); revolt, secede; mutiny, rebel; turn restive, champ at the bit, strain at the leash, step out of line. *Informal,* walk out.

Adjectives—disobedient, uncomplying, uncompliant, unsubmissive, naughty, out of line, unruly, restive, ungovernable, insubordinate, refractory, contumacious, recalcitrant; resisting (see OPPOSITION); lawless, mutinous, seditious, insurgent, riotous, rebellious, defiant. *Slang,* behavish, ornety.

Quotations—Every generation revolts against its fathers and makes friends with its grandfathers (*Lewis Mumford*).

Antonyms, see OBEDIENCE.

DISORDER
Lack of order

Nouns—1, disorder, derangement; irregularity; misrule, anarchy, anarchism; untidiness, disunion; disquiet, DISCORD; confusion, confusedness; disarray, jumble, huddle, litter, mess, mishmash, muddle (see MIXTURE); disorganization, dishevelment; laxity; imbroglio, chaos, havoc, ado, clutter, muss, medley, commotion. *Slang,* just-raped look. See VIOLENCE, FORMLESSNESS.

2, complexity, complexness, complication, implication; intricacy, intrication; perplexity; network (see CROSSING), maze, labyrinth; wilderness, jungle, involution, entanglement; coil, CONVOLUTION, tangled skein, [Gordian] knot, wheels within wheels. See UNINTELLIGIBILITY.

3, turmoil, ferment, AGITATION, row, disturbance, tumult, uproar, riot, pandemonium, bedlam, scramble, fracas, embroilment, melee, rough and tumble; whirlwind, *sauve qui peut*; Babel, Saturnalia, Donnybrook Fair; confusion twice confounded. *Informal,* all hell let loose, a pretty kettle of fish. *Slang,* dog's breakfast.

Verbs—1, be disorderly; kick up a fuss *or* a row *or* dust, raise the roof, raise Cain *or* the devil, stir up a hornets' nest.

2, throw into disorder or confusion, put out of order, derange, ravel, ruffle, rumple, mess, mix up, muss, dishevel; complicate, [en]tangle; disorganize, disorder, disrupt; rock the boat, upset the apple cart. *Informal,* put the cat among the pigeons. *Slang,* foul up, roust.

3, perplex, confound, distract, disconcert, flurry, addle, fluster, bewilder; mix, embroil, muddle, disarrange, misplace. *Slang,* snow out, mind-fuck.

Adjectives—1, disorderly, orderless, out of order, out of place, irregular, desultory; unmethodical, unsymmetric, unsystematic; untidy, slovenly, mussy, messy, sloppy, like something the cat brought or dragged in; dislocated; promiscuous, indiscriminate; chaotic; anarchical, unarranged, disarranged, confused, deranged, mixed-up, topsy-turvy, helter-skelter, harum-scarum; aimless, shapeless; awry, haywire, disjointed, out of order, out of joint; all over the place, rough-and-tumble. *Informal,* out of kilter or whack, at sixes and sevens, [all] at sea, untogether. *Slang,* balled or fouled up, raggedy-ass, out to lunch, spaced out.

2, complex, intricate, complicated, perplexed, involved, labyrinthine, entangled, knotted, tangled, inextricable; tumultuous, riotous. *Slang,* screwed, fouled, or fucked up, ass-backward.

Adverbs—irregularly, by fits and starts; pell-mell, in a ferment, at sixes and sevens, at cross purposes; upside down, higgledy-piggledy, harum-scarum, willy-nilly, any or every which way.

Quotations—Confusion worse confounded (*Milton*), Chaos often breeds life, when order breeds habit (*Henry Adams*), There are some enterprises in which a careful disorderliness is the true method (*Melville*), A large army is always disorderly (*Euripides*), Democracy . . . is a charming form of government, full of variety and disorder. It dispenses a sort of equality to equals and unequals alike (*Plato*), A sweet disorder in the dress kindles in clothes a wantonness (*Robert Herrick*).

Antonyms, see ORDER, SIMPLENESS, ARRANGEMENT.

---

disorganize, *v.t.* upset, disrupt, DISORDER, derange. See DESTRUCTION. *Ant.,* organize, arrange.

disorient, *v.t.* confuse, bewilder (see DISORDER).

disown, *v.t.* disinherit; disclaim, repudiate, deny, disavow. See NEGATION, NULLIFICATION.

disparage, *v.t.* depreciate, discredit, belittle, decry, run down; asperse, traduce. See DETRACTION, DISAPPROBATION, DISRESPECT.

disparity, *n.* INEQUALITY, unbalance.

dispatch, *v.t.* send; expedite; kill; accomplish. —*n.* message, telegram; promptness, expedition, HASTE, speed; consummation, KILLING. See COMPLETION, NEWS, CONDUCT, EARLINESS.

dispel, *v.t.* scatter, dissipate, disperse, dissolve. See DESTRUCTION, DISPERSION.

dispensable, *adj.* redundant, needless, unnecessary. See REPETITION.

dispense, *v.t.* distribute, apportion; administer; excuse, exempt. See GIVING, APPORTIONMENT, EXEMPTION.

DISPERSION
Scattering

Nouns—dispersion, diffuseness; DISJUNCTION, scattering, dissemination, diffusion, dissipation, distribution, APPORTIONMENT, spread, disbanding, diaspora, DECOMPOSITION; irradiation; decentralization. See WASTE.

Verbs—disperse, scatter, stud, sow, distribute, broadcast, disseminate, diffuse, shed, spread, overspread; dispel, disband, apportion; blow off, let out, dispel, cast forth, strew, sprinkle; intersperse; cast adrift, scatter to the winds, dissipate; irradiate; spread like wildfire; decentralize.

Adjectives—dispersed, diffuse, disseminated, broadcast, widespread; epidemic (see GENERALITY); adrift, stray; streaming; dispersive, distributive. *Informal,* all over the place or lot.

Adverbs—here and there, in spots; all over, everywhere, to the four corners or winds.

Quotations—He hath scattered the proud in the imagination of their hearts (*Bible*).
Antonyms, see ASSEMBLAGE.

dispirit, *v.t.* discourage, dishearten. See
DEJECTION.

DISPLACEMENT
Removal from the usual place

Nouns—1, displacement, misplacement, dislocation (see DISJUNCTION); transposition; EJECTION, dislodgment, exile; removal (see TRANSPORTATION); fish out of water; dispossession, disestablishment; migration. *Slang*, golden exile, outplacement.

2, displaced person, DP; displaced homemaker; expatriate, refugee, evacuee boat person; Ishmael, outcast, Wandering Jew, man without a country, Burakumin; exile, émigré, emigrant; lost generation; homeless person. See EXCLUSION.

Verbs—displace, dislocate, displant, dislodge, disestablish; dispossess; exile, seclude, transpose; set aside, move, remove; take away *or* off; unload, empty (see EJECTION); TRANSFER, cart off *or* away; dispel; disarrange, DISORDER; vacate, depart (see DEPARTURE). *Slang*, bump.

Adjectives—displaced, misplaced, dislocated, unplaced, unhoused, unharbored, unestablished, unsettled; dispossessed, homeless; out of place; out of its element. *Informal*, like a fish out of water.

Quotations—Arms and the man I sing, the first who came, compelled by fate, an exile out of Troy, to Italy and the Lavinian coast (*Virgil*).
Antonyms, see LOCATION.

display, *n.* show, exhibition; pomp, OSTENTATION. —*v.t.* show, manifest, exhibit, disclose; flaunt, show off. See EVIDENCE, APPEARANCE.

displease, *v.* offend, vex, annoy, irritate, disturb. See PAIN, DISCONTENT, RESENTMENT. *Ant.*, please, satisfy.

dispose, *v.t.* arrange; regulate, adjust; incline. See AUTHORITY, ARRANGEMENT, TENDENCY.

disposed, *adj.* tending, inclined, prone, bent (upon), fain. See WILL.

disposition, *n.* ARRANGEMENT, classification, disposal, distribution, state; temperament, temper, nature, spirit; inclination, TENDENCY, propensity. See SALE.

dispossess, *v.t.* evict, dislodge; confiscate, usurp. See DISPLACEMENT, ACQUISITION.

disprove, *v.t.* refute, confute, explode, defeat. See NEGATION, CONFUTATION. *Ant.*, prove, demonstrate.

dispute, *v.* contradict, controvert, DOUBT, contest, question; argue, debate, quarrel, bicker, wrangle. —*n.* disputation, debate, argument, disagreement. See DISCORD, NEGATION, REASONING.

disqualify, *v.t.* disable, unfit, incapacitate, disfranchise. See IMPOTENCE.

disquiet, *n.* disquietude, AGITATION, uneasiness, anxiety, unrest; commotion. See DISORDER, FEAR, EXCITABILITY.

disregard, *v.t.* ignore, NEGLECT, overlook; disobey, defy; underestimate. See DISRESPECT, CONTEMPT.

disrepair, *n.* impairment, dilapidation. See DETERIORATION.

DISREPUTE
Want of good reputation

Nouns—1, disrepute, disreputableness, discredit, ill repute, bad name, bad odor, ill favor; DISAPPROBATION; ingloriousness, derogation, debasement; degradation, obloquy, ignominy; dishonor, disgrace, DISRESPECT; detriment, shame, humiliation; notoriety, scandal, baseness, vileness, infamy, opprobrium. See HUMILITY.

2, (*shame*) tarnish, taint, defilement, stigma, stain, blemish, blot, spot, brand, reproach, imputation, slur; badge of infamy, blot on one's escutcheon, egg on one's face; bend *or* bar sinister. *Slang*, black eye, dirty shame.

3, disreputable person, scoundrel, reprobate, miscreant, scapegrace, degenerate; stigmatized house..*Slang,* lowlife. See EVILDOER, BADNESS, IMPROBITY, IMPURITY.

Verbs—1, be in disrepute, be discredited, incur disgrace, lose face, fall from grace, have a bad name, have one's name be mud; disgrace oneself, soil *or* dirty one's hands, stoop, foul one's own nest, look foolish, cut a sorry figure, slink away; draw fire. *Slang,* be in the doghouse, rally.

2, shame, disgrace, put to shame, dishonor, defame, reflect dishonor upon; be a reproach to, derogate from; stigmatize, blemish, tarnish, stain, blot, sully, taint; discredit, degrade, debase, defile; impute shame to, brand, post, vilify, defame, slur, give a bad name; not be caught dead.

Adjectives—1, disreputable, shameful, disgraceful, discreditable, despicable, heinous, questionable; unbecoming, unworthy; derogatory, degrading, humiliating, ignoble, infra dignitatem, undecorous; scandalous, infamous, too bad, deplorable, unmentionable; arrant, shocking, outrageous, notorious; ignominious, scrubby, dirty, abject, vile, beggarly, pitiful, low, mean, knavish, shabby, base, dishonorable (see IMPROBITY). *Slang,* scuzzy.

2, in disrepute, at a discount, under a cloud, out of favor, down in the world, down at heel; stigmatized, discredited, disgraced; inglorious, nameless, unhonored, unglorified.

Phrases—throw enough dirt and some will stick; no smoke without fire; he that has an ill name is half hanged.

Quotations—I'm the girl who lost her reputation and never missed it (*Mae West*), You can't shame or humiliate modern celebrities. What used to be called shame and humiliation is now called publicity (*P. J. O'Rourke*), At ev'ry word a reputation dies (*Alexander Pope*), O! I have lost my reputation. I have lost the immortal part of myself, and what remains is bestial (*Shakespeare*), He was a fiddler, and consequently a rogue (*Jonathan Swift*).

Antonyms, see REPUTE.

DISRESPECT
Lack of respect

Nouns—1, disrespect, disesteem, disregard, disestimation, disfavor, DISREPUTE, disparagement (see DISAPPROBATION); DETRACTION; irreverence; slight, superciliousness, CONTEMPT; contumely, affront, dishonor, insult, snub, indignity, outrage, DISCOURTESY; practical joking, left-handed compliment, scurrility, scoffing, derision; mockery, RIDICULE, sarcasm. *Informal,* brickbat. *Slang,* cracking, dissing, static, dig, put-down, slam.

2, (*sign of disrespect*) hiss, hoot, gibe, flout, jeer, slap in the face. *Slang,* razzberry.

Verbs—1, hold in disrespect, despise; disregard, slight, trifle with, set at naught, pass by, push aside, turn one's back upon, laugh up one's sleeve; spurn, scorn.

2, be disrespectful, be discourteous, treat with disrespect, set down, dishonor, desecrate; insult, affront, outrage; speak slightingly of; disparage; call names, drag through the mud, point at, indulge in personalities, bite the thumb; burn *or* hang in effigy. *Slang,* diss, snipe, bad-mouth, trash, dump on, roast, slam.

3, deride, scoff, sneer, RIDICULE, gibe, mock, jeer (see CONTEMPT); make game of, make a fool of, play a practical joke, lead one a dance; scout, hiss, hoot, mob. *Informal,* razz. *Slang,* give the razz[berry].

Adjectives—disrespectful, irreverent, disparaging; insulting, supercilious; rude, derisive, sarcastic; scurrilous, contumelious; unrespected, unenvied, unsaluted, unregarded, disregarded.

Quotations—When you call me that, *smile!* (*Owen Wister*), As a matter of fact, we both are [offensive], and the only difference is that I am trying to be, and you can't help it (*F. E. Smith*), I regard you with an indifference closely bordering on aversion (*R. L. Stevenson*).

Antonyms, see RESPECT.

disrobe, *v.* undress (see DIVESTMENT). *Ant.*, dress.

disrupt, *v.* disorganize, disturb, upset; turn inside out *or* upside down; mess up, play havoc with; separate. See DESTRUCTION, DISCONTINUANCE, DISORDER.

diss, *v.t., slang,* show disrespect for (see CONTEMPT).

dissatisfy, *v.t.* DISCONTENT, displease, disappoint; vex, annoy, anger.

dissect, *v.t.* cut up, anatomize; examine, analyze. See DISJUNCTION, INQUIRY, DECOMPOSITION.

dissemble, *v.* pretend, feign, dissimulate; camouflage, conceal. See CONCEALMENT, FALSEHOOD.

disseminate, *v.* distribute, sow (see DISPERSION).

DISSENT
Difference of opinion

Nouns—1, dissent, dissension, dissidence, DISCORD, discordance, DISAGREEMENT, nonagreement; difference *or* diversity of opinion; UNCONFORMITY; protestantism, recusancy, schism; secession (see RELINQUISHMENT); apostasy; caviling, protest, hue and cry, objection, demur, exception; contradiction (see NEGATION). See HETERODOXY, OPPOSITION.

2, demonstration, rally, sit-in, march, protest.

3, dissentient, dissenter; recusant, schismatic, nonconformist; protestant, sectarian.

Verbs—1, dissent, demur; call in question, differ, beg to differ, take issue, disagree, take exception, contradict (see NEGATION); say no, refuse assent, refuse to admit; cavil, object, quibble, split hairs, protest, raise one's voice against, take issue; repudiate; shake the head, shrug the shoulders; secede (see RELINQUISHMENT). *Slang,* kick, raise a stink, bitch, beef, yell bloody murder.

2, demonstrate, rally, hold a sit-in, march, protest.

Adjectives—dissenting, dissident, dissentient; negative (see NEGATION), unconsenting, noncontent; protestant, recusant; unconvinced, unconverted; sectarian, denominational, schismatic; unavowed, unacknowledged; out of the question; discontented (see DISCONTENT); unwilling.

Adverbs—dissentingly, at variance, at issue with; under protest.

Interjections—God forbid! not for the world! by no means! not on your life! no sir[r]ee! not by a long shot!; pardon me!

Quotations—We must not confuse dissent with disloyalty (*Edward R. Murrow*), If our democracy is to flourish, it must have criticism; if our government is to function, it must have dissent (*Henry Steele Commager*), I will have no laws. I will acknowledge none. I protest against every law which an authority calling itself necessary imposes upon my free will (*Pierre-Joseph Proudhon*).

Antonyms, see ASSENT.

DISSERTATION
Formal discourse

Nouns—1, dissertation, essay, thesis, term paper, theme; research paper, monograph, treatment; lecture, sermon, homily, tract; discussion, disquisition; treatise, discourse, screed, diatribe; exposition, study, critique (see INTERPRETATION). See REASONING, PUBLICATION, WRITING.

2, essayist, writer, author, expositor.

Verbs—dissertate, dissert, discourse, discuss, treat, handle.

Adjectives—dissertational, discoursive, monographic, homiletic, expository.

Quotations—Most philosophical treatises show the human cerebrum loaded far beyond its Plimsoll mark (*H. L. Mencken*).

disservice, *n.* disfavor, wrong, INJUSTICE. See EVIL. *Ant.,* favor.

dissidence, *n.* DISAGREEMENT, DISSENT, DISCORD, DISCONTENT.

dissimilarity, *n.* See DIFFERENCE.

dissimulate, *v.* disguise, feign; dissemble. See FALSEHOOD.

dissipate, *v.t.* scatter, dispel, diffuse; WASTE, squander. See USE, DISPERSION, IMPURITY.

dissipated, *adj.* dissolute, profligate, de-

bauched, licentious; dispersed (see DISPERSION). See INTEMPERANCE, IMPURITY.

dissolute, *adj.* vicious, dissipated. See INTEMPERANCE, IMPURITY.

dissolve, *v.* liquefy, break up, end; melt, vanish, evaporate, fade, disintegrate. See DECOMPOSITION, DISAPPEARANCE.

dissonance, *n.* DISCORD, cacophony, inharmoniousness; DISAGREEMENT, dissension. *Ant.,* harmony, concord.

DISSUASION
Act of changing one's intention

Nouns—dissuasion, determent, deterrent, dehortation, expostulation, remonstrance, admonition, WARNING; deprecation; discouragement, damper, cold water, wet blanket; RESTRAINT, curb; ADVICE.

Verbs—dissuade, dehort, cry out against, remonstrate, expostulate, warn; advise; disincline, indispose, discourage, talk out of, deter; hold *or* keep back, restrain; repel, turn aside, put off; wean from; act as a drag, hinder; throw cold water on, quench, damp, cool, chill, calm; deprecate.

Adjectives—dissuading, dissuasive; dehortatory, expostulatory; monitory; offputting.

Antonyms, see INFLUENCE, CAUSE.

DISTANCE
Measure of interval

Nouns—1, distance, remoteness, farness, long way; offing, background; perspective, parallax; reach, span, stride; MEASUREMENT; separation, DISJUNCTION; interstellar *or* intergalactic space. *Informal,* a far piece, a ways. See LENGTH, BREADTH.

2, *(distant place)* offing; outpost, outskirt; horizon; aphelion; foreign parts, ultima Thule, ne plus ultra, ends of the earth, world's end, antipodes, interstellar space; long haul *or* pull; long range, giant's stride; middle of nowhere, back of beyond. *Informal,* godforsaken place, boondocks.

Verbs—be distant; extend, reach, spread, *or* stretch to; range; remain at a distance, keep one's distance, distance oneself, stand off; keep *or* stand away *or* out of the way of, keep off, stand aloof, sit back, steer *or* stand clear of. See DISCOURTESY.

Adjectives—distant, remote; telescopic; far off, faraway; wide of; stretching to; yon[der]; ulterior, transmarine, overseas, transpontine, transatlantic, transpacific, transalpine; tramontane, ultramontane, ultramundane; hyperborean, antipodean; inaccessible, out of the way, unapproachable; unapproached, incontiguous. *Informal,* god-forsaken.

Adverbs—far off, far away, afar, off, away, a long way off; wide *or* clear of; out-of-the-way, far-out, out of reach; abroad, overseas, yonder, farther, further, beyond; far and wide, over the hills and far away; from pole to pole, to the ends of the earth, all over, out of this world; aside, out of hearing; nobody knows where; wide of the mark, a far cry from, not nearly, [wide] apart, [wide] asunder; at arm's length. *Slang,* to hell and gone, back of beyond.

Phrases—a miss is as good as a mile; Thursday's child has far to go; distance lends enchantment to the view.

Quotations—The distance is nothing. It's only the first step that's important (*Marquise du Deffand*), In what distant deeps or skies burnt the fire of thine eyes (*William Blake*), All places are distant from heaven alike (*Robert Burton*).

Antonyms, see NEARNESS.

---

distaste, *n.* aversion, DISLIKE.

distasteful, *adj.* unpalatable, unappetizing, unattractive, unpleasant, uninviting, disagreeable, offensive. See SOURNESS, DISCOURTESY. *Ant.,* pleasant, appetizing.

distend, *v.* stretch, expand, dilate, inflate, swell. See EXPANSION.

distill, *v.* extract, express, concentrate; drip, trickle, evaporate; purify. See PURITY, EXTRACTION, VAPOR.

distinct, *adj.* separate, unattached, discrete; definite, different, explicit; sharp, unmistakable, clear, well-defined. See DISJUNCTION, DIFFERENCE, VISIBILITY. *Ant.,* indistinct, obscure.

distinction, *n.* DIFFERENCE, separateness, variation; discrimination; dignity, refinement, elegance; eminence, importance, REPUTE. See TASTE, FASHION, SPECIALITY.

distinctive, *adj.* distinguishing, characteristic. See SPECIALITY, DIFFERENCE.

distinguish, *v.t.* differentiate, characterize; separate, discriminate; discern, pick out; honor. See DIFFERENCE, TASTE, VISION.

distinguished, *adj.* notable, renowned, celebrated, eminent. See REPUTE. *Ant.,* obscure, unknown.

DISTORTION
Twisting out of shape

Nouns—1, distortion, contortion; twist, torque, torsion; crookedness, OBLIQUITY; grimace, pout; asymmetry, anamorphosis.

2, disability, crippling, debility, handicap, defect; deformity, malformation, mutation, mutilation, disfigurement, abnormality, congenital *or* birth defect; birthmark, nevus; BLINDNESS, color blindness, daltonism; dwarfism, cretinism, achondroplasia; acromegaly, gigantism; albinism; amputation; anencephaly; talipes, clubfoot, clawfoot, hammertoe, pigeon toes, clawhand; bowleg, knock-knee, lameness; bucktooth, gap-tooth, malocclusion, cleft palate, deviated septum, harelip; heart defect; cauliflower ear; crossed eyes, goggle-eyes, bug-eyes, strabismus, diplopia, double VISION; Down's syndrome, mongolism; elephant man's disease, neurofibromatosis, humpback, kyphosis; curvature of the spine, scoliosis, lordosis, swayback, kyphosis, spina bifida; cerebral palsy; [central *or* conductive] hearing loss. See UGLINESS.

3, contortionist; freak [of nature], monster, monstrosity; elephant man.

4, perversion, misinterpretation, misconstruction; misrepresentation, FALSEHOOD, EXAGGERATION.

Verbs—1, distort, contort, twist, warp, crook, wrest, writhe, deform, misshape, mutilate, disfigure, deface, gnarl, knot; make a face, pout, grimace. *Slang,* mug.

2, pervert, misinterpret, misconstrue; misquote, misrepresent, twist, garble; color, bias, slant, put a false spin on, put words in one's mouth.

Adjectives—distorted, contorted, out of shape, irregular, unsymmetrical, awry, wry, askew, crooked, cockeyed; asymmetrical; not true, not straight; on one side, one-sided, deformed, misshapen, misproportioned, ill-proportioned, ill-made; monstrous, grotesque, gnarled, hump- *or* hunchbacked; bandy[legged], bowlegged; knock-kneed; taliped, splay-footed, clubfooted; cross-eyed, goggle-eyed, bug-eyed, round-shouldered; snub-nosed; stumpy, gaunt, thin, *etc.;* bloated. *Slang,* cockeyed.

Adverbs—distortedly, crookedly, *etc.*

Quotations—Get your facts first, and then you can distort them as much as you please (*Mark Twain*).

Antonyms, see SYMMETRY, INTERPRETATION, REPRESENTATION.

---

distract, *v.t.* divert, turn aside; confuse, bewilder; derange, madden; entertain, amuse. See DEVIATION, AMUSEMENT, INSANITY.

distracted, distraught, *adj.* agitated, frenzied, frantic; bewildered. See EXCITEMENT, INSANITY, INATTENTION.

distress, *n.* discomfort, PAIN; trouble, affliction, trial, privation, harassment, grief, anxiety; calamity, ADVERSITY. See POVERTY, DIFFICULTY.

distribute, *v.t.* allot, parcel, apportion; disperse, scatter; divide, classify. See APPORTIONMENT, ARRANGEMENT, DISPERSION.

district, *n.* REGION, province, ward, quarter, section, tract, bailiwick.

distrust, *n.* DOUBT, suspicion, disbelief. — *v.t.* suspect, disbelieve, mistrust, FEAR. See JEALOUSY. *Ant.,* trust.

disturb, *v.t.* worry, agitate, disquiet, trouble; disarrange, confuse; interrupt, unsettle. See AGITATION, DISORDER. *Ant.,* calm, soothe.

disturbance, *n.* confusion, tumult, riot, DISORDER; commotion, AGITATION, perturbation.

disturbed, *adj.* unbalanced, touched. See INSANITY.

DISUSE
Lack of use

Nouns—1, disuse, forbearance, abstinence; obsoleteness, [planned] obsolescence; RELINQUISHMENT; cessation, DISCONTINUANCE; abandonment; castaway, throwaway, reject. *Informal,* cold storage. See REJECTION.

2, *(lack of practice)* desuetude, disusage, want of habit *or* practice, unaccustomedness, newness to; nonprevalence.

Verbs—1, disuse, not use; do without, dispense with, let alone, not touch, forbear, abstain, spare, waive, neglect; keep back, reserve.

2, *(store)* lay up *or* by, lay on the shelf, shelve; set, put, *or* lay aside; obsolesce, be superseded (see SUBSTITUTION); taper off.

3, discard, abandon, throw aside *or* away, toss *or* throw out, relinquish; make away with, cast overboard, cast to the winds, jettison; dismantle, *etc. Informal,* scrap, junk, deep-six.

4, be unaccustomed to, break *or* wean oneself of a habit.

Adjectives—1, disused, not used, unemployed, unapplied, undisposed of, unspent, unexercised, untouched, untrodden, unessayed, ungathered, unculled; uncalled for, not required; run-down, obsolete, obsolescent.

2, unused, unseasoned; new, green; unhackneyed. See OLDNESS.

Phrases—rights are lost by disuse.

Quotations—Iron rusts from disuse, stagnant water loses its purity and in cold weather becomes frozen; even so does inaction sap the vigors of the mind (*Leonardo da Vinci*).

Antonyms, see HABIT, USE.

---

ditch, *n.* channel, trench, gully, canal, moat, watercourse. See FURROW. —*v.t., slang,* cast off. See RELINQUISHMENT.

dither, *n.* fluster, commotion, twitter, flurry, confusion. See AGITATION, EXCITEMENT.

ditsy, *adj., informal,* frivolous, eccentric, flighty (see FOLLY).

ditto, *adv.* as before, again, likewise; in the same way. See COPY.

ditty, *n.* song (see MUSIC).

diva, *n.* prima donna (see MUSIC).

divagate, *v.i.* stray, digress. See DEVIATION, DIFFUSENESS.

divan, *n.* sofa, couch; COUNCIL. See SUPPORT.

dive, *n.* plunge, dip, swoop; nosedive, power dive, *slang,* honky-tonk. See DESCENT, DRINKING.

diverge, *v.i.* separate, branch off, fork; sunder; divaricate, deviate; differ, vary, disagree; veer, swerve; detach; go off at a tangent; radiate. See DIFFERENCE, DEVIATION, DISAGREEMENT.

divergence, *n.* DIFFERENCE; DEVIATION; dispersion; fork[ing], branching off; ramification, variation; DISAGREEMENT; divergency.

diverse, *adj.* unlike, varied. See DIFFERENCE.

diversify, *v.* vary; variegate. See DIFFERENCE, VARIEGATION.

diversion, *n.* AMUSEMENT, entertainment, divertisement, pastime, recreation, sport; variation, change, DEVIATION. See REFRESHMENT.

diversity, *n.* DIFFERENCE, dissimilarity, variation, variety. See VARIEGATION.

divert, *v.t.* amuse, beguile, entertain; distract, turn aside. See AMUSEMENT, DEVIATION.

DIVESTMENT
Stripping of covering

Nouns—1, divestment, divestiture; taking off, disrobing, undressing; [de]nudation; decortication, hair removal, depilation, excoriation, desquamation; molting, ecdysis; exfoliation. *Slang,* strip tease, flashing.

2, [full frontal] nudity, bareness, undress, dishabille, the nude, the buff, the raw; calvities, baldness, hairlessness; indecent exposure, exhibitionism. *Informal,* the altogether, birthday suit. *Slang,* cheesecake.

3, bald person; naturist, nudist; striptease, burlesque. *Informal,* skinhead. *Slang,* chrome-dome; raw meat; stripper, coffee-grinder.

Verbs—1, divest; uncover, denude, bare; strip, undress, disrobe, uncoif; dismantle; get, put, *or* take off; doff, cast, *or* slough off; shed; take off one's hands. *Slang,* peel, streak, husk, wear a smile, Adam-and-Eve it, not have a stitch on.

2, peel, pare, shell, decorticate, excoriate, skin, scale; scalp, shave, shear; flay; expose, lay open; exfoliate, molt; cast the skin.

Adjectives—divested, denuded, bare, naked, shorn, nude, in a state of nature, in one's birthday suit, with nothing on, stark naked, in the buff, [in the] raw; undressed, undraped, exposed, in dishabille; threadbare, out at elbows, ragged; bald[-headed], balding, bald as an egg, a coot, *or* a billiard ball; bare as the back of one's hand; barefoot; leafless, napless, hairless, beardless, clean-shaven. *Informal,* in the altogether. *Slang,* laid to the [natural] bone, au naturel, wearing nothing but a smile, naked as a jaybird, naked as the day one was born.

Phrases—clothing optional.

Quotations—Naked came I out of my mother's womb, and naked shall I return thither (*Bible*), Had I but served my God with half the zeal I served my king, he would not in mine age have left me naked to mine enemies (*Shakespeare*), To go naked is the best disguise (*William Congreve*).

Antonyms, see CLOTHING, COVERING.

---

divide, *v.* separate; partition, allot, assign; split [up], part; distribute, share; divvy (*sl.*). See APPORTIONMENT, DISJUNCTION.

dividend, *n.* share, part, portion; interest, bonus, plum. See APPORTIONMENT, PAYMENT.

divination, *n.* PREDICTION, prophecy, augury, guess; SORCERY.

divine, *adj.* godlike, superhuman; celestial, heavenly; holy, spiritual; religious. See DEITY, RELIGION, GOODNESS.

division, *n.* severance, separation, disunion, DISCORD, DISJUNCTION, schism; APPORTIONMENT, partitionment; PART, section; unit, group. See CLASS, COMBATANT.

DIVORCE
Dissolution of marriage

Nouns—1, divorce, divorcement, [legal *or* trial] separation, dissolution, annulment, parting of the ways, breakup, split-up; contested *or* uncontested divorce, no-fault divorce, Enoch Arden divorce; marriage counseling; conflict-habituated marriage; binuclear family, broken home; digamy. *Slang,* matchruptcy, holy deadlock. See DISJUNCTION.

2, alimony, palimony, child support; nonsupport; visiting privilege.

3, (*grounds for divorce*) adultery, affair, bigamy, incompatibility, [mental] cruelty, spousal abuse, estrangement, infidelity, inconstancy.

4, divorcé[e]; grass widow[er]; cuckold, bluebeard.

Verbs—divorce, get a divorce *or* an annulment, sue for divorce; separate, break up, split [up]. *Informal,* go to Reno, call it quits, get unhitched, cut loose, untie the knot. *Slang,* dewife, ratfuck.

Adjectives—divorced, separated, split, newly single. *Informal,* unhitched, in circulation; on the rocks.
Phrases—hell hath no fury like a woman scorned.
Quotations—The divorce will be gayer than the wedding (*Colette*), Love, the quest; marriage, the conquest; divorce, the inquest (*Helen Rowland*).

Antonyms, see MARRIAGE.

---

divulge, *v.t.* disclose, reveal, let slip, tell. See DISCLOSURE. *Ant.,* conceal.

dizzy, *adj.* giddy, light-headed; *slang,* silly, mixed-up, flighty. See INSANITY.

do, *v.t.* perform, achieve, contrive, manage; solve, finish, work out; serve, render; *informal,* swindle, defraud. See ACTION, COMPLETION, PRODUCTION.

docile, *adj.* gentle, tractable, teachable, submissive. See CONSENT, SUBMISSION.

dock, *n.* dockage, mooring; berth, wharf, pier, slip, quay; anchorage, marina, boat *or* ship's basin; drydock, jetty; harbor, haven, prisoner's dock, witness stand. See ABODE. —*v.* cut, trim, curtail, reduce, deduct; fine, penalize. See SHORTNESS, PUNISHMENT, DEDUCTION.

docket, *n.* calendar, agenda, register; label. See RECORD, INDICATION.

doctor, *n.* physician, surgeon; learned man, sage. See REMEDY.

doctrinaire, *adj.* theoretical; dogmatic. See CERTAINTY.

doctrine, *n.* creed, theory, dogma, tenet, principle. See BELIEF.

document, *n.* instrument, writing, documentation, RECORD, EVIDENCE.

dodder, *v.i.* tremble, totter, shake. See WEAKNESS.

dodge, *v.* elude, evade, escape, avoid, duck. See DEVIATION, AVOIDANCE, CUNNING.

doer, *n.* See AGENT.

doff, *v.t.* take off (see DIVESTMENT).

dog, *n.* canine, cur, whelp; pup[py], tyke, bitch, slut; doggy (*inf.*); pooch, mutt (*both sl.*). See ANIMAL.

dogged, *adj.* obstinate, persistent. See OBSTINACY.

doggerel, *adj.* inelegant, crude; burlesque.

See INELEGANCE. —*n.* poetastery, macaronics. See POETRY.

dogma, *n.* doctrine, tenet, precept. See BELIEF.

dogmatic, *adj.* dictatorial, imperious, arrogant, peremptory, positive, opinionated. See CERTAINTY, MISJUDGMENT, SEVERITY, RELIGION.

dolce far niente, Ital. idleness. See INACTIVITY.

doldrums, *n.pl.* lull, calm; depression, despondency, DEJECTION; blues, dumps.

dole, *n.* alms, pittance, handout. See INSUFFICIENCY, GIVING.

doleful, *adj.* sorrowful, sad. See DEJECTION.

doll, *n.* dolly; kewpie doll, Barbie [doll]; puppet, Muppet, marionette, figurine; voodoo; *slang,* babe, baby[doll], sweetheart. See AMUSEMENT, BEAUTY.

dollar, *n.* single, one; buck, bean, iron man, simoleon, cartwheel (*all sl.*). See MONEY.

dolly, *n.* doll; hand truck. See AMUSEMENT, TRANSPORTATION.

dolorous, *adj.* mournful (see DEJECTION).

dolphin, *n.* porpoise, sea hog *or* pig, cetacean. See ANIMAL.

dolt, *n.* dunce (see IGNORANCE).

domain, *n.* realm, dominion, territory; REGION, land, sphere [of action]; estate (see ABODE).

dome, *n.* vault, cupola. See COVERING, CONVEXITY.

domestic, *adj.* household, homely; family, home; internal; native, homegrown, home-bred; tame. See SECLUSION, DOMESTICATION, INHABITANT. —*n.* SERVANT.

DOMESTICATION
Animal husbandry

Nouns—1, domestication, taming; animal husbandry; cattle raising, dairy farming, ranching, stock breeding, horse training; transhumance; veterinarianism, veterinary medicine; browsing, grazing; cattle drive; fodder, forage, hay, oats, corn, straw; pasturage.

2, domestic animals: **a.** livestock, beef, cattle, Aberdeen Angus, Alderney, Guernsey, Hereford, Holstein, Jersey, Longhorn, Shorthorn, *etc.;* hog, swine, pig, shoat, suckling pig; horse, colt, pony, filly, mare, bronco, mustang, cutting *or* stock horse, stallion, stud horse, gelding; saddle, draft, *or* workhorse; sheep. **b.** poultry, [domestic] fowl, chicken, bantam, brahma, Cornish, leghorn, plymouth rock, Rhode Island, *etc.;* rooster, cock, hen, fryer, roaster, stewing chicken; goose; duck, duckling; turkey, gobbler, tom *or* hen turkey. **c.** pet, animal companion; cat, dog, rabbit. See ANIMAL.

3, *(place for keeping animals)* menagerie, zoo, aquarium; stable, barn (see ABODE); corral, ranch, cote, feedlot, hutch, stockyard; dairy, creamery; fishpond, hatchery.

4, *(animal keeper)* husbandman, stockman, breeder, keeper, dairy farmer, rancher; groom, stableman; cowboy, cowgirl, cowherd, herder, hardsman, cowman, cowpoke, cattleman, cowpuncher, cowhand, buckaroo; wrangler, trail boss, top hand; vaquero, gaucho, ranchero, broncobuster; shepherd, sheepherder, herdsman; swineherd; apiarist, beekeeper; handler, trainer. *Slang,* pard[ner].

5, *(animal doctor)* veterinary, veterinarian, vet, horse doctor.

Verbs—domesticate, tame, breed, rear, train, break, ride herd, feed, water, milk, shear, rub down; round up, corral, housebreak; free-range.

Adjectives—domesticated, domestic, tame, gentle, broken; housebroken, trained.

Antonyms, see VIOLENCE.

---

domicile, *n.* See ABODE.

dominate, *v.t.* govern, control; domineer, overbear, tyrannize; predominate, stand out. See AUTHORITY, SUPREMACY.

domineer, *v.i.* tyrannize, overbear, bully. See INSOLENCE, SEVERITY.

dominion, *n.* power, AUTHORITY; domain, state, territory. See REGION, POSSESSION.

domino, *n.* bone; cloak, half-mask. See CONCEALMENT.

don, *v.t.* assume, put on. See CLOTHING. *Ant.,* doff.

donation, *n.* contribution, gift, present, benefaction, grant. See GIVING, LIBERALITY.

donkey, *n.* ass, jackass, burro; blockhead, fool. See ANIMAL, FOLLY.

donnybrook, *n.* dispute, brawl (see DISCORD).

do-nothing, *n.* fence-sitter, [time-]waster, drone, idler. See INACTIVITY.

doodle, *n., slang,* scribble, sketch. See PAINTING.

doohickey, *n.* gadget (see INSTRUMENTALITY).

doom, *n.* DESTINY, lot, fate, fortune; JUDGMENT, damnation, CONDEMNATION; DESTRUCTION, DEATH. See NECESSITY.

door, *n.* doorway, gate, portal, entrance, exit; barrier; inlet, outlet, path. See OPENING, INGRESS, EGRESS.

doorkeeper, *n.* doorman, porter, gatekeeper, concierge, sentry, access controller. See SAFETY.

dope, *n.* hint, INFORMATION; *informal,* drug, stimulant; *slang,* dunce. See REMEDY, IGNORANCE, DRUGS.

dormant, *adj.* torpid; quiescent. See LATENCY, INACTIVITY. *Ant.,* active.

dormitory, *n.* quarters, hostel, bunks, dorm (*inf.*). See ABODE.

dose, *n.* dosage, measure, portion; mouthful, *etc.; slang,* venereal disease. See REMEDY, APPORTIONMENT, PART, DISEASE.

dossier, *n.* file, folder, papers, documents, RECORD.

dot, *n.* spot, speck, point; jot, whit, iota; dowry. See LITTLENESS, POSSESSION.

dotage, *n.* senility, feebleness; fondness. See AGE, ENDEARMENT.

dote, *v.i.* like, be fond of; worship, adore, be infatuated (with). See LOVE.

double, *adj.* twofold, duplicate, duplex, dual. —*v.t.* duplicate, increase, twofold; FOLD. —*n.* duplication; twin, counterpart; understudy, stand-in. See COPY, SIMILARITY, SUBSTITUTION. —**on the double,** quickly (see HASTE).

double-cross, *v.t., slang,* betray. —*n.* betrayal. See IMPROBITY.

double-dealing, *adj. & n.* treachery. See FALSEHOOD.

double meaning, equivocation, double entendre, ambiguity. See VULGARITY, WIT.

double-talk, *n.* gibberish, jargon, nonsense, cant. See ABSURDITY.

DOUBT
Indecision

Nouns—1, doubt, dubiousness, dubiety; unbelief, skepticism, pyrrhonism, disbelief; agnosticism, IRRELIGION; incredulity, discredit; credibility gap, image spill. See IMPROBABILITY, DEJECTION.

2, JEALOUSY, suspicion, distrust, anxiety, concern.

3, uncertainty, uncertainness, incertitude; hesitation, hesitancy, suspense; perplexity, irresolution, indecision; demur, scruple, qualm, misgiving, [serious] reservations; dilemma, quandary, anybody's guess; bewilderment, vacillation, CHANGEABLENESS; vagueness, OBSCURITY; riskiness, precariousness, insecurity. *Informal,* dark horse, cliffhanger, twilight zone.

4, doubter, unbeliever, skeptic, pyrrhonist, agnostic, doubting Thomas, man from Missouri.

Verbs—1, doubt, be doubtful, disbelieve, discredit; misbelieve; refuse to admit *or* believe, doubt the truth of, be skeptical, not believe one's ears *or* eyes, distrust, mistrust, suspect, have doubts, harbor suspicions, have one's doubts, have cold feet; take with a grain of salt; be from Missouri. *Slang,* not buy, set no store by.

2, *(hesitate because of doubt)* demur, stick at, pause, hesitate, think twice, falter, scruple. *Slang,* smell a rat.

3, cast doubt upon, raise a question, give pause, bring *or* call in question; question, challenge, dispute, deny, cause *or* raise a doubt *or* suspicion; leave hanging [in the air].

4, *(be of doubtful truth)* be unbelievable, fill with doubt, startle, stagger; shake *or* stagger one's faith *or* belief.

5, be uncertain, wonder whether, waver, hover, seesaw, teeter, hem and haw, sit on the fence; not know which way to turn *or* jump; hang by a thread *or* a hair, hang in the balance.

6, *(cause to doubt)* confuse, bewilder, baffle, stump. *Slang,* kerflummox.

Adjectives—1, doubting, unbelieving, incredulous, skeptical; uncertain, irresolute; distrustful, suspicious, *or* shy of; heretical, faithless; dubious, scrupulous.

2, doubtful, disputable, debatable, controversial, questionable, moot, problematical, suspect, under a cloud, unsettled, undecided, in midair, up in the air; open to suspicion *or* doubt; farfetched; staggering, fabulous, hard to believe, unbelievable, incredible, not to be believed, inconceivable, fishy; ambiguous; fallible; undemonstrable; controvertible. *Slang,* hinky, iffy, tall.

Adverbs—with a grain of salt, with reservations, maybe; betwixt and between.

Phrases—tell it to the marines!, councils of war never fight, between two stools one falls to the ground, he who hesitates is lost; when in doubt, do nothing.

Quotations—The fool hath said in his heart: There is no God (*Bible*), Except ye see signs and wonders, ye will not believe (*Bible*), The trouble with the world is that the stupid are cocksure and the intelligent are full of doubt (*Bertrand Russell*), I am too much of a skeptic to deny the possibility of anything (*Aldous Huxley*), I'll give you a definite maybe (*Samuel Goldwyn*), To philosophize is to doubt (*Montaigne*), There are no atheists in the foxholes (*W. T. Cummings*).

Antonyms, see BELIEF, CERTAINTY, RESOLUTION.

---

doubtless, *adv.* unquestionably (see CERTAINTY).

doughnut, *n.* cruller, beignet, fried cake, dunker (*sl.*), tire (*sl.*). See FOOD.

doughty, *adj.* redoubtable, fearless, strong, brave, bold, gallant, daring, spunky. See COURAGE.

dour, *adj.* sour, sullen; harsh, hard. See SEVERITY, DISCOURTESY.

douse, *v.* soak, drench, souse; put out, extinguish. See WATER, DARKNESS.

dovetail, *v.* match, interlock, fit. See AGREEMENT.

dowager, *n.* widow; matron, grande

dame, beldam; battle-ax (*sl.*). See FE-MALE.

dowdy, *adj.* frumpy, frowsy, down-at-the-heels; inelegant, old-fashioned. See IN-ELEGANCE, VULGARITY.

dower, *n.* See DOWRY.

down, *adv.* downward; under, beneath, below. See LOWNESS, DESCENT. *Ant.,* up, above.

down-and-out, *adj.* needy, destitute, poor, on the skids. See POVERTY. *Ant.,* well-off, on easy street.

downcast, *adj.* downhearted, dejected, modest, bashful. See HUMILITY, DEJEC-TION. *Ant.,* upbeat, happy.

downfall, *n.* drop, comedown, disgrace, demotion; overthrow, defeat; collapse, crash. See DESCENT, FAILURE, DESTRUC-TION. *Ant.,* rise, SUCCESS.

downgrade, *v.t.* demote (see DECREASE). —*n.* See OBLIQUITY. *Ant.,* promote.

downhearted, *adj.* dejected, discouraged, downcast, sad. See DEJECTION. *Ant.,* happy, cheerful.

downplay, *v.t.* belittle (see DETRACTION).

downpour, *n.* cloudburst, deluge. See WA-TER.

downright, *adv.* plainly, bluntly; extremely; thoroughly, completely. —*adj.* unqualified, frank, absolute; direct, plain, blunt; complete, utter, absolute. See COMPLETION.

downtime, *n.* stoppage, delay (see HIN-DRANCE).

down-to-earth, *adj.* sensible, practical. See SIMPLENESS, POSSIBILITY.

downtrodden, *adj.* oppressed, subjugated; in the dust *or* mire, treated like dirt; underprivileged. See SUBJECTION.

downturn, *n.* drop, slump (see DETERIO-RATION). *Ant.,* upturn, improvement.

downward, *adj.* & *adv.* See DESCENT. *Ant.,* upward.

downy, *adj.* fluffy, feathery, fleecy, flocculent, soft. See SOFTNESS.

dowry, *n.* dower, dot; inheritance. See POSSESSION.

doze, *n.* & *v.i.* snooze, nap, drowse. See REPOSE.

drab, *adj.* grayish, brownish, dun; monotonous, dull, humdrum, uninteresting. See WEARINESS, COLOR. *Ant.,* colorful, bright.

draft, *n.* sketch, outline; breeze, air current, WIND; drink, dram; conscription, levy; load, pull, displacement; check, bill of exchange, demand note. See DRINKING, MONEY, CREDIT, DEPTH. —*v.t.* outline; draw, sketch, formulate; conscript, enlist, impress. See COMPUL-SION, PLAN, TRACTION, WRITING.

draftee, *n.* recruit, inductee, conscript; rookie (*sl.*). See COMBATANT. *Ant.,* enlistee, volunteer.

draftsman, *n.* delineator; ARTIST, drafter.

drag, *v.* draw, pull, tow, tug, haul; protract, draw out; lag, dawdle, inch along. *Slang,* race. See SLOWNESS, TRACTION, LATENESS. —**in drag,** cross-dressed (see CLOTHING).

drain, *v.* draw off, empty, exhaust, leak, drip, dry up. —*n.* outlet, spout, sewer, ditch, gutter. See WATER, USE, DRYNESS, EGRESS, WASTE, CLEANNESS.

dram, *n.* draft, drink. See DRINKING, MEASUREMENT.

DRAMA
Theater

Nouns—1, drama; the drama, the stage, the theater, legitimate theater, street theater; show business, theatricals, theatrics, performance art; theater of the absurd, the mind, cruelty, involvement, protest, *etc.*; closet drama; *son et lumière*; dramaturgy, stagecraft, histrionics, sock and buskin; commedia dell'arte; Muse of Tragedy, Melpomene; Muse of Comedy, Thalia; Thespis; puppetry, Punch and Judy; classical theater, ancient tragedy, cothurnus; bunraku, Noh, Kabuki. *Slang,* legit.

2, *(dramatic staged work)* play, playlet, drama, stage play, piece, vehicle, tragedy, [high *or* low] comedy, black comedy, tragicomedy; opera, operetta, musical comedy, review, revue, road show, vaudeville, variety, burlesque, minstrel show, shadow play, improv[isation], farce, Grand Guignol, divertissement, skit, playlet, extravaganza, harlequinade, pantomime, opéra bouffe, ballet, spectacle, masque, melodrama, monologue, duologue, dialogue; trilogy, tetralogy, *etc.*; charade; mystery, morality, chronicle, or miracle play; agitprop, guerrilla theater; television or radio drama, soap opera, daytime drama, Theater of the Air; puppet show; audition (see EXPERIMENT); libretto; epitasis, protasis, catastasis, catharsis. *Slang,* diaper drama or play, oater; docutainment, infotainment.

3, *(section of a dramatic work)* act, scene, tableau; introduction, prologue, curtain raiser; turn, number; entr'acte, intermission, intermezzo, interlude, half-time; epilogue, afterpiece; curtain; curtain call, encore.

4, a. performance, REPRESENTATION, mise en scène, stagery, stagecraft; acting, impersonation; stage business, slapstick, buffoonery; showmanship; part, role, character, cast, dramatis personae, road company; repertory, repertoire; [out-of-town] tryout; summer theater, amateur theatricals, [summer] stock; theater in the round, open-air theater, arena theater, odeum, showboat. *Informal,* gag. *Slang,* ham acting. **b.** rehearsal, dress rehearsal, [cold] reading, walk-through, run-through, tech[nical] rehearsal.

5, *(motion picture)* motion or moving picture, film, cinema, talking picture, silver screen; photoplay, screenplay. *Informal,* movie [show], talkie. *Slang,* flickers.

6, *(theatrical performance)* **a.** theater, house; legitimate theater, playhouse, opera house, music hall, movie theater, off- or off-off-Broadway theater; amphitheater, circus, hippodrome; puppet or marionette theater. See ARENA. **b.** auditorium, front of house, stalls, boxes, orchestra, balcony, loges, gallery, peanut gallery; greenroom; festival seating. **c.** stage, proscenium, apron, forestage; the scene, the boards; trap; wings, flies; up- or downstage, stage right or left; float, light, spotlight, footlight; orchestra pit, dressing room, quick-change room; stage door; scenery, flat, [back]drop, screen, scrim, cyclorama, side-scene; transformation scene, curtain; periaktoi. **d.** makeup, greasepaint; theatrical costume; properties, props; stage direction, blocking, staging.

7, *(people of the theater)* **a.** cast; actor, actress, player, stage player, performer, trouper, vaudevillian, Thespian; showman; star, hero, headliner, matinee idol; protagonist, leading man or woman; comedian, tragedian, villain, heavy; ingenue, soubrette; foil, straight man; pantomimist, mummer, masker, clown, harlequin, buffo, buffoon, farceur, Pantaloon, Columbine; Punch, Punchinello; tumbler, juggler, acrobat; contortionist. *Informal,* stooge. *Slang,* ham [actor], juvie; talking head, media whore. **b.** supporting cast, super[numerary], extra spear carrier, bit player. **c.** librettist, scenario writer, dramatic author; playwriter, playwright; dramatist; dramaturg. **d.** [stage] director; producer, impresario; prompter; stage manager; set, costume, *etc.* designer; stagehand. *Slang,* grip, gaffer. **e.** audience, public, theatergoer, spectator. **f.** booker, booking agent, talent coordinator.

Verbs—act, play, perform; mount, put on the stage; impersonate (see REPRESENTATION); mimic, IMITATE, enact; play or act [out] a part; rehearse; tread the boards, barnstorm; hold the stage; blow or fluff one's lines; star, figure in; overact, upstage, steal the show; adapt for the stage, dramatize; ring down or up the curtain; paper the house. *Slang,* ham [it up], mug, chew the scenery.

Adjectives—dramatic, theatrical, scenic, histrionic, comic, tragic, farcical, tragicomic, melodramatic, colorful, operatic; first- or second-run; stagy.

Adverbs—on the stage or boards; before the footlights.

Interjections—break a leg! *[in] bocca al' lupo! (crepi lupo!);* bravo! bis!

Quotations—Acting is merely the art of keeping a large group of people from coughing (*Sir Ralph Richardson*), Just say the lines and don't trip over the furniture (*Noel Coward*), Acting is a masochistic form of exhibitionism (*Laurence Olivier*), The play's the thing wherein I'll catch the conscience of the king (*Shakespeare*), There still remains, to mortify a wit, the many-headed monster of the pit (*Alexander Pope*), We should show life neither as it is nor as it ought to be, but as we see it in our dreams (*Anton Chekhov*), There's no business like show business (*Irving Berlin*), I go to the theatre to be entertained, I want to be taken out of myself (*Alan Bennett*), Drama is action, sir, action and not confounded philosophy (*Luigi Pirandello*), Acting is an empty and useless profession (*Marlon Brando*).

---

dramatis personae, *Lat.* cast [of characters]. See DRAMA.

drape, *n.* drapery, curtain, tapestry; hang, fall, look. .—*v.t.* hang (curtains, *etc.*); shape, cut; dress, clothe, caparison; swathe, shroud, veil. See PENDENCY, CLOTHING.

drastic, *adj.* radical, extreme, stringent, severe; rash, impulsive. See SEVERITY.

draw, *v.t.* haul, drag, pull, tub, extract; attract, allure; depict, sketch; draft; win, receive; displace; inhale; elicit, get; disembowel, eviscerate. See ATTRACTION, PAINTING, TRACTION. —*n.* tie. See EQUALITY. —**draw back,** retreat, cower (see FEAR, ESCAPE).

drawback, *n.* HINDRANCE, handicap, clog, encumbrance, restraint; objection, disadvantage. See EVIL. *Ant.,* advantage, benefit.

drawing, *n.* picture, sketch, plan; delineation. See PAINTING. —**drawing card,** draw, ATTRACTION.

drawl, *n.* brogue, burr (see SPEECH).

dread, *v.t. & n.* See FEAR. *Ant.,* welcome.

dreadful, *adj.* fearful, dire, frightful, shocking, horrible; awful, bad. See FEAR, BADNESS.

dream, *n.* vision, reverie, fantasy, fancy; daydream, chimera, nightmare; delusion, hallucination. See IMAGINATION, INSUBSTANTIALITY.

dreamy, *adj.* vague, fanciful; peaceful; *informal,* delightful, wonderful. See INSUBSTANTIALITY, CONTENT, GOODNESS.

dreary, *adj.* drear, cheerless, gloomy, somber; depressing, lonely, wearisome, tedious. See DEJECTION, WEARINESS. *Ant.,* bright, cheerful.

dredge, *v.* clear, dig up (see CONCAVITY, INQUIRY).

dregs, *n.* residue, sediment, silt, lees, grounds, heeltaps; scum, riffraff, offscourings. See REMAINDER, POPULACE, UNCLEANNESS. *Ant.,* cream.

drench, *v.t.* douse, souse, soak, wet, saturate. See WATER, MOISTURE.

dress, *v.* clothe, attire, array; scold, reprove, berate, whip; adorn, garnish, decorate; align, equalize; prepare, bandage. See CLOTHING, DISAPPROBATION, ORNAMENT, REMEDY. —*n.* CLOTHING, costume, vesture, garb, raiment, apparel, habit; frock, gown. *Ant.,* undress.

dresser, *n.* bureau, chest [of drawers], vanity [table], dressing table. See RECEPTACLE.

dressing, *n.* decoration, ORNAMENT; sauce, seasoning, condiment; stuffing; garnish; bandage, application. See FOOD, REMEDY.

dressmaker, *n.* seamstress; stylist, fashion designer, modiste, couturier, couturière. See CLOTHING.

dressy, *adj.* stylish, fashionable, smart, chic; formal, fancy, showy. See OSTENTATION, FASHION. *Ant.,* dowdy, informal.

dribble, *v.* slaver, drivel; trickle. See EGRESS, EXCRETION.

drift, *n.* pile, heap, deposit; movement, DEVIATION; TENDENCY, MEANING. See ASSEMBLAGE, MOTION, DIRECTION. —*v.i.* proceed aimlessly; pile up.

drifter, *n.* nomad, hobo (see TRAVEL).

drill, *v.* pierce, bore; train, exercise, practice; quiz. See OPENING, TEACHING, EXERTION, REPETITION.

DRINKING
Swallowing a liquid

Nouns—1, drinking, imbibing, potation, libation; social drinking; bacchanalia; blue law; cocktail party, open *or* cash bar; bring your own bottle *or* booze, BYOB, compotation, keg party; carding; corkage; cask, cellar; distillation; proof.

2, *(substances to drink)* a. drink, beverage, draft, impotation, liquor, nectar, broth, soup; home brew; potion; eye-opener, apéritif, after-dinner drink, digestif, chaser, bracer, refresher, smile, nightcap, one for the road. *Informal,* pick-me-up. b. hard liquor, firewater, alcoholic drink, spirits, the bottle, little brown jug; banger; home brew; brandy, cognac, applejack, Armagnac, hard cider; [bathtub] gin, corn liquor, grain alcohol, grappa, mescal, ouzo, advocaat, rum, slivovitz, tequila, vodka, [corn,

Irish, Scotch, blended, Canadian, bourbon, *or* rye] whiskey. *Informal,* family disturbance, moonshine, hair of the dog [that bit one], hard stuff, demon rum, booze.
Slang, liquid lunch, nooner; hooch, rotgut, alchy, antifreeze, coffin varnish, embalming fluid, juice, goat hair, gunpowder, jungle juice, blue ruin, nose paint, tiger milk,
eyewater, snake medicine, mule, mother's ruin, neck-oil, sauce, white lightning, red-
eye, cactus juice, gauge, panther piss, juniper juice, Mexican milk, leg-opener, stingo,
screech, skag, corpse reviver. **c.** cocktail, mixed drink, nightcap, pick-me-up; alexander, angel's kiss, B&B, banshee, between the sheets, Black *or* White Russian, bloody
Mary, champagne cocktail, cobbler, collins, cooler, daiquiri, fizz, flip, frappé, fuzzy
navel, Gibson, gimlet, gin and tonic, gin fizz, gin rickey, grasshopper, greyhound,
Harvey Wallbanger, highball, Irish coffee, kamikaze, kir, mai tai, Manhattan, Mar-
garita, martini, mimosa, mint julep, Moscow mule, old-fashioned, piña colada, pink
lady, planter's punch, pousse café, prairie oyster, Rob Roy, rusty nail, san garee, san-
gria, screwdriver, shandy, sidecar, Singapore sling, slippery nipple, smash, sour,
spritzer, stinger, stonewall, Tequila sunrise, Tom and Jerry, Tom Collins, white lady,
zombie; grog, [hot] buttered rum, toddy, flip, punch, posset, negus, cup, wassail,
eggnog. *Slang,* electric soup, lunatic soup, giggle water. **d.** liqueur, cordial, bitters,
crème [de cacao, cassis, fraise, framboise, menthe, *etc.*], curaçao, kummel, pastis,
ratafia, sambuca, schnapps, triple sec; Benedictine, Calvados, Cointreau, Drambuie,
Frangelica, Galliano, Grand Marnier, Irish Mist, Kahlúa, Sabra, Tía Maria. **e.** the
grape, [white, red, *or* rosé] wine, malmsey, retsina, champagne; amontillado, blanc
de blanc, blush, rosé, claret, cold duck, dandelion wine, dessert wine, fortified wine,
hard cider, hock, jug wine, port, sack, saké, sherry, sparkling wine, table wine, ver-
mouth; Asti Spumante, Barbera, Bardolino, Barolo, Beaujolais, Bordeaux, Burgundy,
Cabernet Sauvignon, Catawba, Chablis, Chardonnay, Chianti, Cinzano, Côtes du
Rhône, Dom Pérignon, Frascati, Fumé Blanc, Gewürztraminer, Graves, Grenache,
Riesling, Lambrusco, Liebfraumilch, Mâcon, Madeira, Malaga, Margaux, Marsala,
Médoc, Merlot, Moselle, Muscadet, Muscat, Napa Valley, Navarra, Orvieto, Pinot
Blanc *or* Noir, Pouilly-Fuissé *or* -Fumé, St.-Julien, Sauternes, Sonoma, Sylvaner,
Tokay, Valpolicella, Vouvray, Zinfandel. *Informal,* bubbly. *Slang,* sweet lucy, dog
juice, pluck, plug, salbe, schoolboy scotch, mad dog. **f.** beer, ale, bitter, bock [beer],
dark *or* light beer, ice beer, malt liquor, mead, dortmunder, pilsner, porter, pulque,
stout, microbrew[ed beer], draught beer. *Slang,* brew, brewski, piss, sissy beer, suds,
cold pop, road brew, swill, gusto, frosty, goog. **g.** nonalcoholic beverage, virgin
Mary; [mineral, distilled, sparkling, spring, tap *or* Vichy] WATER, mixer, tonic [wa-
ter], soft drink, cola, seltzer, club soda, cream soda, ginger ale, root beer, sarsaparilla;
nectar, [apple, cranberry, orange, tomato, grapefruit, *etc.*] juice, lemonade, limeade;
cider, shrub; coffee, café [au lait, filtre, noir, *or* latte], cappuccino, espresso, caf-
feinated *or* decaffeinated coffee, Sanka, mocha; chocolate, cocoa; [ginseng, Darjeel-
ing, Earl Grey, pekoe, green, herb, *etc.*] tea, tisane; ice cream soda, frappé, milk
shake, syllabub, malt[ed milk], phosphate; kava, kefir, kumiss. *Informal,* decaf.
Slang, java, joe, battery acid. **h.** dram, draft, draught, shooter, double, snort, nip, sip,
sup, gulp, pull, swill; splash, gill, finger, jigger, pony, rock glass, shot glass, snifter,
eighty-six; six-pack; split, fifth, jeroboam, magnum; hogshead, cask, keg. *Informal,*
swig. See MEASUREMENT, RECEPTACLE. **i.** bar rag, cocktail shaker, stirrer, *or* strainer,
corkscrew, crushed ice, ice tongs, soda gun, speed rack, swizzle stick.
3, *(drinking too much)* drunkenness, intoxication; INTEMPERANCE; inebriety, inebria-
tion; ebriety, ebriosity; insobriety; wine bibbing; bacchanals, bacchanalia, libations;
alcoholism, alcohol abuse, dipsomania, oenomania; delirium tremens, DTs, fantods,
jitters; hangover; twelve steps. *Informal,* bust. *Slang,* binge, tear, bat, toot, jag, bender, pink elephants, clanks; the morning after; grog blossom.
4, *(one who drinks too much)* drunkard, drunk; problem drinker, alcoholic, dipsomaniac, inebriate, lush, sot, toper, tippler, bibber, wine bibber, oenophile, wino, guzzler; hard drinker; soaker, sponge, tosspot, pub crawler; thirsty soul, reveler,

carouser, tight skirt; cheap drunk; Bacchanal, Bacchanalian, Bacchante, devotee of Bacchus. *Informal,* boozer, barfly. *Slang,* alchy, groghound, souse, wino, lush, tank, rumhound, dipso, rummy, juicer, glowworm, hooch hound.

5, *(drinking place)* tavern, inn; public house, pub *(both Brit.)*; barroom, taproom, rathskeller, *buvette,* bar [and grill], alehouse, dramshop, saloon, [cocktail] lounge, bottle club, barrelhouse, beer garden *or* hall, honky-tonk, roadhouse, singles bar; bistro, cabaret, café, cantina; publican *(Brit.)*, bartender, barkeep[er], mixologist, beverage host, barback, barmaid *or* -girl, cocktail waitress *or* waiter, steward, bouncer; liquor *or* package store; cash, open *or* no-host bar; round, cocktail hour, happy hour, last call; designated driver. *Informal,* rumshop, watering hole; attitude adjustment hour. *Slang,* gin mill, meat rack, fillmill, happy shop, draft board.

6, brewer, distiller; brewery, microbrewery, distillery, still.

Verbs—**1,** drink, imbibe, quaff, sip, lap; take a drop, tipple, guzzle, squizzle, soak, sot, carouse, tope, swill; take to drink, name one's poison; drink up, drink hard, drink like a fish; drain the cup, take a hair of the dog [that bit one]; wet one's whistle, crack a bottle, pass the bottle; toss off; wash down; barhop; run a tab. *Informal,* booze, swig, prop up the bar, chug-a-lug, knock back. *Slang,* belt the grape, pop some tops, tie one on.

2, be *or* get drunk; fall off the wagon, drink the three outs, bend *or* lift one's elbow; see double. *Slang,* feel no pain; liquor up, lush, get high, hit the bottle *or* the sauce, go on a toot, paint the town red, hang one on, have an edge *or* a load on, have a jag on, crapulate, pass out [cold], honk, get on.

3, make drunk, intoxicate, inebriate, [be]fuddle, besot, go to one's head. *Slang,* plaster, pollute.

Adjectives—**1,** on the rocks, straight up, neat; potable, bibulous.

2, drunk, tipsy, intoxicated, inebrious, inebriate[d], in one's cups, in a state of intoxication, under the table, cut, fresh, merry, elevated, flush[ed], flustered, disguised, top-heavy, overcome, maudlin, crapulous, dead *or* roaring drunk, drunk as a lord, an owl, a top, *etc. Informal,* boozy, mellow, high [as a kite]. *Slang,* off the wagon; faced, [well-] oiled, rat-faced, boiled, soused, shellacked, fried, polluted, tanked, tight, cockeyed, squiffed, stinko, tight, three sheets in *or* to the wind, mellow, out cold, stiff, blotto, feeling no pain, out of it, crispy, wasted, zonked, schnockered, shitfaced, smashed, squiffy, bombed, damaged, ossified, polluted, pixilated, rosy about the gills, spifficated.

3, *(causing drunkenness)* intoxicating, heady.

Phrases—alcohol will preserve anything but a secret; the drunkard's cure is drink again; heaven protects children, sailors, and drunken men.

Quotations—O for a draught of vintage! . . . O for a beaker full of the warm South *(John Keats)*, We drink one another's healths, and spoil our own *(Jerome K. Jerome)*, Candy is dandy but liquor is quicker *(Ogden Nash)*, I have taken more good from alcohol than alcohol has taken from me *(Winston Churchill)*, Better sleep with a sober cannibal than a drunken Christian *(Herman Melville)*, Work is the curse of the drinking classes *(Oscar Wilde)*.

Antonyms, see MODERATION.

---

drip, *v.i.* drop, dribble, trickle; leak, percolate. See WATER.

drip-dry, *adj.* wrinkle-free, no-iron, wash-and-wear, permanent *or* durable press (see CLOTHING).

drive, *v.t.* propel, impel; urge forward, pursue; steer, control; conduct, carry out; ram, hammer, thrust; urge, force, compel, coerce. See COMPULSION, TRAVEL, PROPULSION, ENERGY, HASTE.

drivel, *n.* drool, slaver, slobber; nonsense, babble. —*v.i.* drool, slobber, babble, talk nonsense, dote. See ABSURDITY, LOQUACITY, UNMEANINGNESS, EXCRETION.

driver, *n.* chauffeur, teamster, wagoner, cabman, hack, cabby. See VEHICLE, TRANSPORTATION.

drizzle, *n. & v.* sprinkle, mist, rain, spray. See WATER.

droll, *adj.* comical, amusing. See AMUSEMENT.

drone, *n.* monotone, hum, buzz. See REPETITION.

drool, *v.i.* drivel, slaver. See EXCRETION.

droop, *v.* bend, loll, slouch, sag; sink, languish, decline, waste; wilt. See DEJECTION, DISEASE, WEAKNESS, PENDENCY.

drop, *v.* let fall; give up, abandon; fall, plunge; faint, collapse; cease, terminate, END; drip; dismiss, let go. See DESCENT, RELINQUISHMENT, IMPOTENCE. —*n.* globule, bead; minim; bit, mite; DESCENT. See LITTLENESS, PENDENCY, ROTUNDITY, WATER, WEAKNESS.—**drop in,** [pay a] visit, call on (see SOCIALITY). —**drop out,** withdraw, quit (see RESIGNATION).

dross, *n.* refuse; slag; waste. See USELESSNESS, REMAINDER.

drought, *n.* aridity, DRYNESS, thirst; lack, scarcity. See INSUFFICIENCY. *Ant.,* flood(ing).

drown, *v.* suffocate; submerge, inundate; muffle, overpower, go down for the third time. See WATER, KILLING, SILENCE, DEATH, LOUDNESS, FAILURE.

drowsy, *adj.* sleepy, somnolent; lazy, languid. See WEARINESS.

drudge, *v.i.* toil, slave, grub, plod, hack, grind, plug. See EXERTION.

drug, *n.* medicine, physic, elixir, preparation, prescription, REMEDY; narcotic, dope; white elephant, a drug on the market. —*v.* narcotize, dope; medicate, dose; knock out, put to sleep. See INSENSIBILITY, SUFFICIENCY, DRUGS.

druggist, *n.* apothecary, pharmacist, chemist. See REMEDY.

DRUGS
Medicinal substances

Nouns—**1,** drugs; therapeutic drugs (see REMEDY); drug *or* substance abuse; drug addiction, [chemical] dependency, physical *or* psychological dependence, habit, reverse tolerance; glue sniffing; drug testing; methadone maintenance; drug smuggling. *Informal,* stash. *Slang,* the street; chipping, ice-cream habit, nose habit, jones, tang, monkey on one's back, drugstore johnson; Columbian roulette.

2, a. controlled substance, addictive drug, hard *or* soft drug, body drug, gateway drug; designer drug, recreational drug; cephalotropic drug, psychoactive *or* psychotropic drug; synthetics; stimulant, caffeine, diet pill; [anti]depressant, hallucinogen, psychedelic, tranquilizer, opiate, sedative, ataraxic [drug], aphrodisiac, antispasmodic, atropine, mandrake, nicotine. *Slang,* dope, stuff, junk, bam, chemicals, bang, basketball, biscuit, Nixon, happy dust. **b.** [meth]amphetamine, pep *or* diet pill, desoxyn, Benzedrine, Biphetamine, Dexamyl, Dexedrine, Methedrine. *Slang,* activity booster, bean, benny, blackbird, black beauty, blockbuster, browns, cartwheel, chicken powder, crank, [crystal] meth, football, forward, [purple] heart, dexie, doll, ice, jelly bean, leaper, shards, sparkle, speed, splash. **c.** barbiturate, sleeping pill, amyl nitrate, Amytal, Luminal, Nembutal, Tuinal, Seconal. *Slang,* barbie, blockbuster, downer, fender-bender, geronimo, goofball, gorilla pill, pinks, rainbow, red devil, yellow [jacket]. **d.** cocaine, coca, *Slang,* bernice, big bloke, blow[zeen], bouncing powder, bullet, candy, Cecil, charlie, coke, crack, flake, Gibraltar, girl[friend], gold dust, happy dust, her, hubba, lady snow, nose candy, paradise, perico, Peruvian perfume, pimp, [moon]rock, [lady] snow, toot, white girl *or* lady. **e.** hallucinogenic [drug], psychedelic, utopiate, lysergic acid, LSD, DMT, soma. *Slang,* acid, blotter, blue acid, blue cheer, blue flag, California sunshine, clear light, conductor, contact lens, cube, datura, domes, jet, locoweed, ecstasy, electric Kool-Aid, Lucy in the sky with diamonds, magic mushroom, majoon, orange wedge, Owsley, pearly gate, pink wedge, purple haze, strawberry fields, STP, white lightning, windowpane. **f.** heroin. *Slang,* antifreeze, Aunt Hazel, [black] tar, boy, brown, Chinese white *or* red, chiva, downtown, flea powder, freebase, gow, H, henry, him, horse, hotshot, jolt, junk, Karachi, liquid sky, mortal combat, mud, nag, noise, number eight, peg, poison, pure, scag, smack, snowball, stuff, taste, tecata, red chicken. **g.** marijuana, hashish, bud, hemp, cannabis, indica, sinsimilla, Jamaican ganja, *Slang,* hash, Afgani, African black, airplane, Alice B. Toklas, black gunny, black oil, Columbian gold, dagga, dank, ditch weed, doobie, dopestick, gage, gangster, ganja, grass, griffa, hay, herb, hooch, kif, killer weed, kind green, M, marahoochie, Mary Jane, Maui wowie, jay, joint, juju, killer weed, mezz, michoacán, mota, muggle, number, [hash] oil, owl, Panama red, resin, pinner, pot, rainy day woman, reefer, righteous bush, roach, rope, schwag, shake, shit, sins, smash, smoke, snop, son of one, spliff, stick, tea, Thai stick, the kind, twist, [viper's] weed, yerba; banji, bar, bhang, bomber, boo, bush, Cambodian red. **h.** opium, Demerol, morphine, peace pill. *Slang,* Aunt Emma, black[stuff], Chinese molasses, gow, hop, midnight oil, poppy, sister, unkie, white nurse, toye. **i.** PCP, phencyclidine. *Slang,* angel dust, animal trank, cyclone, crystal [joint], dummy juice, elephant, hog, lovely, love boat, parsley, pig killer, purple rain, rocket fuel, scaffle, soma, supergrass, superweed, water. **j.** peyote, mescal[ine]. *Slang,* beans, big chief, button, cactus, mesc, topi. **k.** sedative, sedative-hypnotic, depressant, codeine, barbital, Quaalude, meperidine, meprobamate, Miltown. *Informal,* downer. *Slang,* Christmas tree, 'lude, quack, soaper. **l.** sodium amytal. *Slang,* blue angel *or* heaven, bluebird. **m.** stimulant, pep pill, ibogaine, MDA, *Informal,* upper. *Slang,* jelly bean. **n.** tranquilizer, Librium, Valium, diazepam, neuroleptic. *Slang,* mother's helper. **o.** *(mixture) Slang,* Thai stick, juice and beans, hot and cold, San Francisco bomb, sheet rock, moon rock, wuwoo, one-on-one, roller coaster, silk and satin, speedball.

3, bag, bindle, brick, cargo, microdot, tab, amp. *Informal,* cap, *Slang,* bale, bird's eye, blank, bundle, can, deck, dime *or* nickel bag, dot, fireplug, K, key, kilo, lid, line, mike, paper, spoon, taste, quill.

4, dose, injection; acid trip, bad trip, panic, jag; [crack, water, *or* marijuana] pipe, narghile, chillum, crutch; dropper, [hypodermic] syringe, outfit, rig, paraphernalia; stash. *Informal,* hypo, needle; scrip. *Slang,* fix; run; toke, toot; wings, tracks; bummer; beaming [up], booting; high, joyride, white light, contact high, buzz, charge, rush, bump, flash; cotton mouth; bong, stem, devil's dick; kit, works, nail, spike, roach clip *or* holder, jefferson airplane.

5, crack house, opium den; balloon *or* bang room. *Slang,* needle park, shooting gallery, copping zone, pot party; tea pad; sleigh ride; kitchen; behind the scales, head shop.

6, withdrawal, detoxification. *Informal,* cold turkey, detox. *Slang,* bogue, belly habit.

7, drug addict, user; trafficker; flower child; guide, conductor. *Slang,* joy-popper, social junker; poison people, acid freak *or* head, A-head, cubehead, dope fiend, dopenik, dopehead, doper, hype, hophead, chip, zombie, globetrotter, viper, explorer's club, freak, junkie, junker, pillhead, poison people, pothead, tea head, shmecker; pusher, source, [dope] peddler, missionary, powder monkey, bagman, bingle, candy man, travel agent, connection, dealer, ice-cream man, hustler, the man, mother; artillery man; chef; take-off artist; croaker; body packer.

Verbs—**1,** take *or* do drugs, chase the dragon (take heroin), cold turkey, have the monkey on one's back; overdose; potentiate; sell *or* deal drugs; buy drugs. *Informal,* hassle. *Slang,* kick the gong around, bang a gong, blow, carry, connect, cook, cap, cop, score, chase the dragon, cut, deal, do dope, drop, fix, flip *or* freak out, freebase, geeze, get high, goof, nod out, hit, hustle, joypop, OD, jazz *or* rock out, pop, channel, mainline, shoot [up], jab, take in the sky, skin-pop, snort, fire a line, tie off, toke, turn on, trip, coast, wig out, blow a stick, gage, *etc.*

2, withdraw. *Slang,* kick the habit.

Adjectives—addicted; high, dusted; carrying, holding. *Informal,* hooked, on the needle, using, wasted, baked, strung out, stoned, on the nod *or* pipe, zoinked, wired, loaded, spaced *or* zoned out, caught in a snowstorm, pinned; sick.

Quotations—Every form of addiction is bad, no matter whether the narcotic be alcohol, morphine or idealism (*Carl Jung*), I'll die young, but it's like kissing God (*Lenny Bruce*), Drugs don't cause today's alarming crime rates, but drug prohibition does (*David Boaz*), Angelheaded hipsters burning for the ancient heavenly connection to the starry dynamo in the machinery of the night (*Allen Ginsberg*), Turn on, tune in and drop out (*Timothy Leary*), Thou hast the keys of Paradise, oh just, subtle, and mighty opium! (*Thomas de Quincy*), A habit is hell for those you love (*Billie Holiday*).

drum, *v.* tap *or* beat time, play the drums. See MUSIC. —*n.* [side, bass *or* snare] drum (see MUSIC).

drunk, *adj.* intoxicated, tipsy. —*n.* drunkard, sot, alcoholic. See DRINKING.

dry, *adj.* arid, thirsty (see DRYNESS); barren, sterile; humorless, grave. See IMPOTENCE, WEARINESS.

DRYNESS
Lack of moisture

Nouns—1, dryness, aridity, aridness; desiccation, dehydration, anhydration, dehumidification; thirst; drainage; curing, mummification, freeze-drying (see PRESERVATION); evaporation.

2, drought; ebb tide, low water.

3, [hair, blow, clothes, *etc.*] drier, dehydrator, dehumidifier, desiccator.

Verbs—dry (up), soak (up), sponge, swab, wipe [dry], towel [off]; evaporate, dehumidify, desiccate; drain, parch, sear, scorch, wither; smoke, dehydrate; air-dry, drip-dry, blow-dry, *etc.*

Adjectives—1, dry, anhydrous, dehydrated, arid; dried, undamped; juiceless, sapless; sere, sear; thirsty, husky; rainless, without rain; sec, brut, fine; dry as a bone, a stick, a mummy, *or* a biscuit, bone-dry, dry-as-dust; waterproof, moisture-proof, watertight; desertlike, unirrigated, waterless, parched.

2, drying, [de]siccative, dehydrating.

Phrases—you never miss the water till the well runs dry.

Quotations—Water, water, every where, nor any drop to drink (*Coleridge*).

Antonyms, see MOISTURE.

---

dual, *adj.* duplex, twofold, double, duplicate, twin, binary. See NUMERATION.

dub, *v.t.* name, call, invest. See NOMENCLATURE.

dubious, *adj.* doubtful, uncertain; questionable, unreliable. See DOUBT. *Ant.,* certain.

duck, *v.* nod, bob; dodge, avoid, elude; dip, immerse, plunge. —*n.* drake. See AVOIDANCE, WATER, BIRDS.

duct, *n.* channel, canal, tube, pipe, flue. See PASSAGE.

ductile, *adj.* tractile, malleable; yielding, pliant; compliant, docile, obedient. See SOFTNESS, OBEDIENCE, ELASTICITY.

dud, *n.* FAILURE; (*pl.*) *informal*, CLOTHING.

due, *adj.* owed, owing, payable, outstanding, unpaid; rightful, proper, fit, appropriate, apropos; lawful, licit. See JUSTICE, RIGHTNESS, EXPEDIENCE, DEBT, DUTY, EFFECT. —*n.* reward, deserts. See COMPENSATION, JUSTICE, ATTRIBUTION.

duel, *n.* single combat, contest, competi-tion, rivalry; affair of honor. See CONTENTION.

duet, *n.* pair, couple, twosome. See NUMERATION.

dues, *n.pl.* assessment, fee; deserts. See PAYMENT, PRICE.

duffer, *n.* peddler; mediocre player, hacker (*inf.*). See SALE, MEDIOCRITY.

dull, *adj.* unsharp, blunt; deadened, numb; stupid; tedious, uninteresting, boring; spiritless, vapid, vacuous; dead, lifeless; sluggish, listless, lethargic; lackluster, dim, cloudy, obscure, stale, jaded. —*v.t.* blunt. See SLOWNESS, BLUNTNESS, DIMNESS, WEARINESS, COLORLESSNESS. *Ant.,* sharp, bright, lively.

duly, *adv.* properly; punctually. See ATTRIBUTION, EARLINESS.

dumbfound, *v.t.* confound, flabbergast, disconcert; astonish. See SURPRISE.

dumbness, *n.* aphonia, muteness, aphony, mutism; deaf-mutism, voicelessness; SILENCE, TACITURNITY, inarticulateness; *informal*, IGNORANCE.

dummy, *n.* [deaf-]mute; puppet, manikin, proxy, agent, stand-in, stooge. See REP-RESENTATION, SUBSTITUTION, SILENCE, IGNORANCE.

dump, *v.* drop, let fall; discharge, unload; abandon, jettison, scrap, junk, discard, ditch (*sl.*); flood the market. See REJEC-TION. —*n.* trash heap, junkpile, midden; STORE, depot, depository; den; *slang,* dive, joint, greasy spoon, flophouse, flea trap. See ABODE, UNCLEAN-NESS.

dumpling, *n.* spaetzle, gnocchi, matzo [balls]. See FOOD.

dumpy, *adj.* stocky, chubby, chunky (see ROTUNDITY).

dun, *v.t.* bill, press for payment. See AC-COUNTING.

dunce, *n.* dullard, moron, fool, dunderhead, simpleton, simple Simon, nitwit; dolt, oaf, clod; bonehead, meathead, boob, dope (*all sl.*). See IGNORANCE, FOLLY. *Ant.,* genius, sage.

dune, *n.* sand hill *or* ridge, mound. See HEIGHT, POWDERINESS.

dung, *n.* excrement, manure, droppings. See EXCRETION.

dungarees, *n.pl.* jeans, overalls, Levi's, chinos. See CLOTHING.

dungeon, *n.* pit, cell; jail, donjon, PRISON; black hole of Calcutta. See DEFENSE, LOWNESS.

dunk, *v.t.* dip (see WATER).

dupe, *n.* gull, victim, cully, cat's-paw; fool; puppet, tool; butt, laughingstock, April fool; sucker, chump (*both inf.*); easy mark, soft touch, pushover, pigeon (*all sl.*). —*v.t.* cheat, defraud, swindle; hoodwink, deceive, delude. See CREDULITY, DECEPTION.

duplicate, *n.* facsimile, duplication, double, reproduction, replica, COPY, reduplication; iteration, REPETITION; renewal; counterpart; gemination, twin. —*adj.* double[d], bifold, biform, bilateral, two-fold, two-sided, duplex; double-faced; twin, ingeminate; second. —*v.* [re]double, reduplicate, geminate, COPY, repeat.

duplicity, *n.* double dealing, two-facedness, treachery, deceitfulness, fraud, guile, hypocrisy. See FALSEHOOD, IM-PROBITY.

DURABILITY
Lastingness

Nouns—1, durability, durableness, lastingness, CONTINUITY, standing; STABILITY, survival, longevity, AGE; distance, protraction, *or* prolongation (of time). See RESISTANCE.

2, (*long period of time*) diuturnity; age, century, eternity, eon, years on end; lifetime; PERPETUITY, PERMANENCE. *Informal,* long haul, blue moon, month of Sundays. *Slang,* dog's *or* coon's age.

Verbs—1, endure, last, stand [up], remain, abide, bear up, hold good, hold on, linger, continue; wear well; tarry, drag on, hold, protract, prolong; tide over; drag, spin, eke, *or* draw out; temporize, gain *or* make time, talk against time; outlast, outlive, survive; land on one's feet, keep body and soul together, keep one's head above water; sit through; last *or* live out, live to fight again; live on borrowed time; take it.

2, perpetuate, immortalize, maintain (see PERPETUITY).

Adjectives—durable, lasting, hardy, heavy-duty; of long duration *or* standing, chronic, long-standing; intransient, intransitive; intransmutable, lifelong, livelong; everlasting, immortal; longeval, long-lived; diuturnal, evergreen, perennial; never-ending, unremitting; perpetual, interminable, eternal; unfailing; lingering, protracted, prolonged, spun-out, long-pending, long-winded; slow.

Adverbs—1, durably, long; for a long time, for an age, for ages, for ever so long, from way back; for many a long day; long ago; all day long, all year round, the live-long day, as the day is long; morning, noon, and night; day in and day out; hour after hour, day after day; for good, permanently.

2, always, ever, evermore, forever, for keeps, for good, till Hell freezes over, till the cows come home; for aye, world without end, perpetually.

Quotations—Endure, and preserve yourselves for better things (*Virgil*), Men must endure their going hence even as their coming hither (*Shakespeare*), His mercy endureth forever (*Bible*).

Antonyms, see TRANSIENTNESS.

---

duration, *n.* term, TIME, period; continuance, persistence. See PERMANENCE.

duress, *n.* coercion; RESTRAINT, imprisonment. See COMPULSION.

during, *prep.* pending, through, in the time of, until. See TIME.

dusk, *n.* twilight, gloaming; semi-darkness, gloom, half-light, shadow; swarthiness. See DIMNESS, DARKNESS.

dust, *n.* powder; earth, soil; dirt, lint, ash, soot, flue. See POWDERINESS, UNCLEANNESS.

DUTY
Requisite service

Nouns—1, duty, moral obligation, accountability, LIABILITY, onus, responsibility; bounden duty; call of duty; allegiance, fealty, tie; engagement, PROMISE; part, function, calling, BUSINESS.

2, *(moral duty)* morality, morals, ethics; Ten Commandments; conscientiousness, conscience, inward monitor, still small voice; sense of duty, VIRTUE; noblesse oblige.

3, *(societal duty)* propriety, fitness, the [proper] thing (see AGREEMENT).

4, *(fulfilling duty)* observance, fulfillment, discharge, acquittal, performance (see COMPLETION).

Verbs—1, be the duty of, be incumbent on, be responsible, behoove, become, befit, beseem; belong to, pertain to; fall to one's lot; devolve on, lie upon, lie on one's head, lie at one's door, rest with, rest on the shoulders of.

2, take upon oneself, PROMISE, be bound to, be sponsor for; incur a responsibility; be *or* stand under obligation; have to answer for, be answerable for, owe it to oneself. *Informal,* pay one's dues.

3, impose a duty, enjoin, require, exact (see COMPULSION); pass the buck, let George do it.

4, enter upon, perform, observe, fulfill, discharge, satisfy, *or* acquit oneself of a duty *or* an obligation; adhere to; act one's part, redeem one's pledge, do justice to, be at one's post; do one's duty; be on good behavior, mind one's Ps and Qs. *Informal,* hold the baby.

Adjectives—1, obligatory, binding, imperative, behooving, incumbent on; obligated, under obligation; obliged, bound, *or* tied by; saddled with; due to, beholden to, bound to, indebted to, duty bound, tied down; compromised; amenable, liable, accountable, responsible, answerable; right, meet, due; moral, ethical, casuistical, conscientious.

2, dutiful, duteous, loyal, diligent, obedient, submissive. See OBEDIENCE.

Adverbs—dutifully, in duty bound, on one's own responsibility, at one's own risk; in the line of duty.

Phrases—the buck stops here; carry the can.

Quotations—Do your duty, and leave the outcome to the gods (*Corneille*), The buck stops here (*Harry S. Truman*), A wife loves out of duty, and duty leads to constraint, and constraint kills desire (*Jean Giraudoux*), I believe that every right implies a responsibility; every opportunity, an obligation; every possession, a duty (*John D. Rockefeller*).

Antonyms, see NEGLECT.

---

dwarf, *n.* midget, pygmy, Lilliputian, runt, shrimp. See LITTLENESS, DEMON. —*v.* stunt; tower over. See SHORTNESS, CONTRACTION, INFERIORITY. *Ant.,* giant.

dwell, *v.i.* live, reside, abide; hang out (*sl.*); *slang,* harp, iterate. See PRESENCE, REPETITION, ABODE, INHABITANT.

dwelling, *n.* See ABODE.

dwindle, *v.i.* diminish, shrink, lessen, run low, waste away. See DECREASE.

dye, *v.t. & n.* COLOR, tint, stain. —dyed in the wool, complete, thoroughgoing (see COMPLETION).

dying, *adj.* moribund, terminal (see DEATH).

dyke, *n., slang,* lesbian, amazon, butch (*inf.*). See FEMALE.

dynamic, *adj.* forceful, vigorous, potent, impelling; propulsive. See POWER, IMPULSE.

dynasty, *n.* lineage, line, succession. See AUTHORITY, POSTERITY.

dysentery, *n.* flux; diarrhea; cramps; the grips, trots, *or* runs (*sl.*). See DISEASE, EXCRETION.

E

each, *adv.* apiece, severally, seriatim, respectively. See SPECIALITY. —*adj.* every. See GENERALITY.

eager, *adj.* desirous, keen, fervent, fervid, hotheaded, earnest, intent; zealous, ardent, agog; avid, anxious, athirst. See ACTIVITY, DESIRE, EXPECTATION, FEELING, HASTE. *Ant.,* indifferent, phlegmatic.

eagle, *n.* bald, sea, *or* golden eagle, erne, ringtail, eaglet, harpy. See ANIMAL.

ear, *n.* head, spike; auricle, concha; handle, knob; heed, observance. See ATTENTION, HEARING.

earful, *n., informal,* harangue, tirade; gossip, tip; a piece of one's mind, bawling out; the lowdown, info (*both sl.*). See NEWS, SPEECH, INFORMATION.

EARLINESS
Occurrence near the beginning of a period of time

Nouns—1, *(early arrival)* earliness, punctuality, promptitude, alacrity, dispatch, expedition, readiness, PREPARATION; HASTE; head start, lead time, advance notice; first to arrive, first on the scene. See UNPREPAREDNESS, BEGINNING, INSTANTANEITY.

2, *(early development)* prematurity, precocity, precipitation, anticipation. See PREDICTION, PRIORITY, OCCASION.

3, *(early hour)* early black, bright, *or* candlelight; early bird. *Informal,* red-eye.

Verbs—1, be early, be beforehand, jump the gun, take time by the forelock, anticipate, forestall; have the start; steal a march upon, get *or* have the jump on, steal one's thunder *or* the spotlight, take the words out of one's mouth; take advantage of; gain time, preempt, bespeak.

2, be up *or* arise before the dawn.

Adjectives—1, *(early in time)* early, timely, punctual, forward; prompt, instant, ready.

2, *(developed early)* premature, precipitate, precocious; prevenient, anticipatory, ahead of time; forward, advanced; imminent.

Adverbs—1, early, soon, anon, betimes, duly, ere *or* before long, punctually, promptly, on time *or* schedule, on the dot, to the minute, in due course *or* season, in [good] time *or* season, in due time, time enough, bright and early.

2, *(before something)* beforehand, prematurely, precipitately, hastily, too soon, before its time; in anticipation; unexpectedly.

3, *(soon)* briefly, shortly, presently, at the first opportunity, by and by, in a while, directly.

Phrases—first come, first served; punctuality is the art of guessing correctly how late the other party is going to be; a stitch in time saves nine; early to bed and early to rise makes a man healthy, wealthy, and wise; strike while the iron is hot; the early bird catches the worm.

Quotations—You come most carefully upon your hour (*Shakespeare*), Lovers ever run before the clock (*Shakespeare*). I was nearly kept waiting (*Louis XIV*), I have noticed that the people who are late are often so much jollier than the people who have to wait for them (*E. V. Lucas*), Punctuality is the virtue of the bored (*Evelyn Waugh*), One who has a reputation for rising early can sleep until noon (*Alphonse Daudet*).

Antonyms, see LATENESS.

---

earmark, *n. & v.t.* See INDICATION.

earn, *v.t.* work for, gain, win; deserve, merit, rate; make a living, be gainfully employed. See ACQUISITION, JUSTICE.

earnest, *adj.* intent, intense, serious, grave, solemn, sober, weighty, purposeful, determined; sincere; IMPORTANT; diligent; eager, impassioned, animated, cordial, zealous, fervent, ardent. See FEELING, IMPORTANCE, RESOLUTION. *Ant.,* careless, frivolous.

earnings, *n.pl.* pay, PAYMENT.

earsplitting, *adj.* See LOUDNESS.

earth, *n.* planet, globe, world; ground, LAND, dirt, soil, mold. See UNIVERSE.

earthbound, *adj.* mundane, temporal. See LIMIT, POSSIBILITY.

earthenware, *n.* crockery, china, pottery, ceramics, stoneware. See MATERIALS.

earthling, *n.* earth-dweller, mortal, terrestrian; flesh and blood. See HUMANITY. *Ant.,* extraterrestrial.

earthly, *adj.* terrestrial; material, worldly, sensual, temporal, mundane, secular; *informal,* possible, conceivable. See IRRELIGION, LAND, POSSIBILITY. *Ant.,* spiritual, celestial.

earthquake, *n.* tremor, seism, quake, shock. See VIOLENCE.

earthshaking, *adj., informal.* See LOUDNESS, IMPORTANCE.

earthwork, *n.* rampart (see DEFENSE).

earthy, *adj.* earthly; popular, vulgar, crude, unrefined; elemental, simple, primitive, down-to-earth; robust, vigorous, Rabelaisian; lewd, racy, bawdy. See SIMPLENESS, IMPURITY, POPULACE. *Ant.,* refined.

ease, *n.* comfort, luxury; rest, repose; CONTENT, enjoyment, complacency; RELIEF; leisure, convenience; FACILITY, readiness, expertness; unconstraint, naturalness. See PLEASURE, ELEGANCE. —*v.* mitigate, lessen, relax; facilitate, smooth, cushion. *Ant.,* discomfort, DIFFICULTY. —**at ease,** relaxed, in repose.

easel, *n.* tripod. See SUPPORT.

eastern, *adj.* east, oriental. See DIRECTION.

easy, *adj.* comfortable, restful, indolent, unconcerned, untroubled; free, unembarrassed, careless, smooth, unconstrained, natural, graceful; effortless (see FACILITY); mild, gentle, indulgent; tractable, compliant; light, unexacting. See ELEGANCE, MODERATION, CONSENT, CONTENT. *Ant.,* difficult, hard, awkward. —**on easy street,** comfortable, well off. See WEALTH.

easygoing, *adj.* happy-go-lucky, cheerful; unconcerned, untroubled, careless; effortless, facile; tractable, compliant. See CONTENT, LENIENCY. *Ant.,* uptight, nervous.

eat, *v.* consume, devour, eat up, feed, fare; erode, corrode, wear, rust. See FOOD, DETERIORATION.

eavesdrop, *v.i.* listen in, spy, snoop, overhear; bug, tap. See HEARING, CURIOSITY.

ebb, *v.i.* recede, fall back, outflow, withdraw; decline; waste, decay. See DECREASE, REGRESSION, WASTE. *Ant.,* flow, INCREASE.

ebullient, *adj.* excited; boiling. See EXCITEMENT, AGITATION.

eccentric, *adj.* elliptic[al], parabolic, hyperbolic; irregular, deviating; peculiar, queer, odd, strange, bizarre, singular; erratic, cranky, abnormal. See IRREGULARITY, FOLLY, INSANITY, UNCONFORMITY, ROTUNDITY. *Ant.,* normal.

ecclesiastical, *adj.* churchly, sacerdotal, priestly, clerical. See CLERGY. *Ant.,* lay.

echelon, *n.* grade, position. See DEGREE, ARRANGEMENT.

echo, *v.* reverberate, resound, reply, ring; repeat, reproduce. See IMITATION, RECOIL, ANSWER, COPY. —*n.* reverberation, REPETITION, response, repercussion.

eclectic, *adj.* selective. See CHOICE, DIFFERENCE.

eclipse, *v.t.* obscure, darken, cloud, hide, conceal; outshine, surpass, overshadow. See DARKNESS, REPUTE, CONCEALMENT.

ecology, *n.* conservation; ecosystem; autecology, *etc.* See ENVIRONMENT.

economics, *n.pl.* See MONEY.

ECONOMY
Avoidance of waste

Nouns—1, economy, thriftiness, frugality, thrift, austerity, care, husbandry, housekeeping, ménage, good housewifery, good management *or* administration, retrenchment, cutback, rollback, belt-tightening; PARSIMONY, cheeseparing, stinginess, scrimping. See ORDER, PRESERVATION, ACCOUNTING, CHEAPNESS.

2, savings, reserves; savings account, Christmas Club; IRA, Roth IRA, Keogh plan; investment account. See CHEAPNESS.

Verbs—economize, save, scrimp; retrench, tighten one's belt; cut corners, skimp, make [both] ends meet, meet one's expenses, pay one's way; husband, save money, lay by *or* away, put by, lay aside, store up; hoard, accumulate, amass, salt away; provide for a rainy day; feather one's nest.

Adjectives—economical, frugal, careful, thrifty, saving, chary, sparing, parsimonious, stingy, scrimping; cost-effective, efficient.

Adverbs—sparingly, frugally, thriftily, economically, carefully, parsimoniously.

Phrases—most people consider thrift a fine virtue in ancestors; a penny saved is a penny earned; thrift is a great revenue.

Quotations—Expenditure rises to meet income (*C. Northcote Parkinson*), Economy is going without something you do want in case you should, some day, want something you probably won't want (*Anthony Hope*), He is almost always a slave who cannot live on little (*Horace*), Nothing hurts worse than the loss of money (*Livy*).

Antonyms, see WASTE.

---

ecosystem, *n.* See ENVIRONMENT.

ecstasy, *n.* rapture, joy, transport, bliss, exaltation; gladness, intoxication, enthusiasm; trance, frenzy, inspiration. See PLEASURE, FEELING, IMAGINATION.

ecumenical, *adj.* See GENERALITY.

eddy, *n.* countercurrent, vortex, whirlpool. See WATER, ROTATION.

EDGE
Extreme border

Nouns—1, edge, verge, brink, brow, brim, curb, margin, LIMIT, boundary, border, skirt, rim, flange, SIDE, mouth, jaws, lip; frame, fringe, flounce, frill, trim[ming], edging, skirting, hem, welt, furbelow, valance, salvage.

2, threshold, entrance, gate[way], coast, bank, shore[line], watershed; quay.

Verbs—edge, verge, border, bound, skirt, rim, fringe; sidle *or* inch along.

Adjectives—border, bordering, rimming, fringing, marginal, skirting; labial, labiated, marginated.

Adverbs—edgewise, edgeways, sidewise, sideways, edge on.

Antonyms, see INTERIOR, MIDDLE.

---

edgy, *adj.* on edge, irritable, nervous. See IRASCIBILITY, EXCITABILITY.

edible, *adj.* palatable. See FOOD.

edict, *n.* decree, bull, law, fiat, proclamation. See COMMAND.

edification, *n.* instruction, enlightenment, education. See TEACHING.

edifice, *n.* BUILDING, structure.

edit, *v.t.* redact, revise, arrange, digest, correct, prepare; select, adapt, compose, compile; issue, publish. See IMPROVEMENT, PUBLICATION.

edition, *n.* redaction; issue, impression, printing. See PUBLICATION.

editorial, *n.* critique, commentary. See JUDGMENT.

editorialize, *v.* expatiate, expound, spout; use the editorial "we." *Slang,* sound off, put in one's two cents. See JUDGMENT, TEACHING.

educate, *v.t.* teach, train, instruct, enlighten, edify, school; develop, cultivate; discipline, form. See TEACHING.

educated, *adj.* lettered, literate. See KNOWLEDGE. *Ant.,* uneducated, ignorant.

educe, *v.t.* draw forth, bring out, develop, elicit; deduce, infer, evoke. See EXTRACTION.

eerie, *adj.* weird, uncanny. See FEAR.

efface, *v.t.* obliterate, erase, expunge, excise, delete, dele, strike, cancel, wipe out, blot. See NULLIFICATION.

EFFECT
Result of a cause

Nouns—1, effect, consequence, result, upshot, issue, outcome, outgowth, denouement; outgrowth, development, aftermath, aftereffect, fallout, butterfly effect, domino effect, ripple effect, trickle-down theory; OCCURRENCE; corollary. *Slang,* payoff. See SEQUENCE.

2, product, output, work, handiwork, performance; creature, creation; offspring, offshoot, spin-off, by-product; fruit, first fruits, crop, harvest; effectiveness.

Verbs—1, effect, CAUSE, create, effectuate, produce, bring about, give rise to.

2, be the effect *or* result of; be due *or* owing to; originate in *or* from; rise, ensue, arise, spring, eventuate, proceed, emanate, come, grow, issue, *or* result from; come out of, follow, come to; cut both *or* two ways, pan out, fare; hinge on.

3, take effect (see OCCURRENCE).

Adjectives—1, owing to, resulting from, due to, attributable to, caused by, dependent upon, derived *or* evolved from; derivative, hereditary.

2, consequent, resultant, contingent, eventual, consequential.

Adverbs—of course, it follows that, so that, in effect, therefore, hence, naturally, consequently, as a consequence, in consequence, in the wake of, through, necessarily, eventually.

Conjunctions—owing to, resulting from, due to; contingent on, following from *or* upon.

Phrases—garbage in, garbage out; great oaks from little acorns grow; what goes up must come down; one [good] thing leads to another.

Quotations—Whatsoever a man soweth, that shall he also reap (*Bible*), Between good sense and good taste there is the same difference as between cause and effect (*Jean de la Bruyère*), The present contains nothing more than the past, and what is found in the effect was already in the cause (*Henri Bergson*), Every positive value has its price in negative terms. . . . The genius of Einstein leads to Hiroshima (*Pablo Picasso*).

Antonyms, see CAUSE.

---

effective, *adj.* efficacious, effectual, productive, adequate, telling, potent, active, operative, dynamic; successful; causative; efficient, capable. See POWER, UTILITY, AGENCY, SUCCESS, VIGOR. *Ant.,* ineffective, useless.

effeminate, *adj.* womanish, unmanly. See WEAKNESS, FEMALE.

effervesce, *v.i.* bubble, hiss, ferment, foam, fizz. See AGITATION.

effete, *adj.* exhausted, spent, depleted; barren, sterile, fruitless; weak, corrupt, decadent. See DETERIORATION, USELESSNESS.

efficient, *n.* effective, effectual, efficacious, operative; skillful, capable, productive, competent; causative. See POWER, SKILL,

AGENCY, CAUSE, UTILITY. *Ant.,* inefficient, ineffectual.

effigy, *n.* dummy, icon, caricature; COPY, counterpart, replica, simulacrum; substitute; Guy Fawkes. See REPRESENTATION.

effort, *n.* EXERTION, endeavor; strain, stress, attempt; achievement; *informal,* push. See ACTION.

effortless, *adj.* easy, facile; natural, simple. See FACILITY.

effrontery, *n.* shamelessness, brazenness, INSOLENCE, audacity.

egg, *n.* egg cell, ovum, embryo; oval. See BEGINNING, REPRODUCTION, ROTUNDITY. —*v.* incite, goad. See CAUSE.

egghead, *n.* intellectual (see INTELLECT).

egg-shaped, *adj.* oviform, oval, ovate, ovoid, elliptical. See ROTUNDITY.

ego, *n.* self, personality, I. See INSUBSTANTIALITY, IDENTITY. **—ego trip,** narcissism, complacency. See IDENTITY.

egoism, *n.* individualism, SELFISHNESS, self-seeking, conceit. See VANITY. *Ant.,* HUMILITY.

egotism, *n.* VANITY, self-exaltation, [self-]conceit. See SELFISHNESS. *Ant.,* HUMILITY.

egregious, *adj.* flagrant, gross. See BADNESS.

EGRESS
Act of going out

Nouns—1, egress, exit, issue, emergence, eruption, emanation, exudation, percolation, weeping, leakage, oozing, dripping; gush, efflux, outpouring, effluence, effusion, drain, drainage, outflow, runoff; discharge (see EXCRETION); export[ation].

2, *(act of leaving)* export, expatriation, emigration, exodus, exile, DEPARTURE.

3, outlet, vent, spout, tab, sluice, floodgate; exit, way out, mouth, pore, OPENING; port, terminus.

4, goer, departer; emigré[e], emigrant, migrant, colonist. *Informal,* refusenik.

Verbs—1, emerge, emanate, issue, pass off; exit, exeunt, depart, ESCAPE; emigrate; export.

2, leak, run out, percolate, exude, strain, drain, ooze, filter, filtrate, dribble, gush, spout, flow, well out, pour, trickle; effuse, debouch, come forth, break *or* burst out, fall out, let out.

Adjectives—emergent, emerging, outgoing, emanative, effluent, eruptive, leaky; migrant.

Adverbs—out, from, away, forth.

Prepositions—out of, from, away from, forth.

Antonyms, see INGRESS.

---

either, *adj.* See CHOICE. *Ant.,* neither.

ejaculate, *v.t.* eject, discharge, spew *or* shoot out; exclaim, blurt out. See PROPULSION, CRY.

EJECTION
Expulsion

Nouns—1, ejection, emission, effusion, rejection, expulsion, eviction, extrusion, discharge, EXCRETION; exfiltration; evacuation, vomiting, regurgitation, eructation. See PROPULSION.

2, deportation, banishment, exile, excommunication, relegation, extradition, dislodgment, DISPLACEMENT; depopulation; dismissal, ouster, firing, layoff, furlough, outplacement, separation; demotion; riddance. *Slang,* the gate, the sack, the ax, the air, the bum's rush, walking papers. See EXCLUSION, RELINQUISHMENT.

3, vomitus; eructation, hiccup. *Slang,* fart, gurk, barking *or* trumpet spider; belch, gas; upchuck, cheese, puke, barf, dry heaves.

4, bouncer, ejector.

Verbs—1, give vent to, let out *or* off, send out, shed, void, eliminate, evacuate, emit, vomit, spew, become ill, be sick; eruct, belch, bring up gas; extrude, effuse, spend; squirt, spurt, spill; throw up *or* heave; spit up. *Informal,* bring up. *Slang,* barf, cack, cascade, upchuck, duke, flash, keck, honk, lose it, toss one's cookies, puke, ralph, retch, york, drive the porcelain bus, dump, deballast, surplus; burp; fart, break wind.

2, eject, reject, expel, discard; exfiltrate; cast out, throw *or* push out, off, away, *or* aside; shovel *or* sweep out; dispose of, get out of one's hair; brush off, cast adrift, turn *or* bundle out; unburden; throw overboard; get rid of, shake off; send packing, turn out, pack off, dismiss, dump; bow out, show the door to; boycott; discharge, cashier, read out of, send flying, kick upstairs; evict, oust, dislodge, relegate, deport, banish, exile, extradite; kick *or* boot out; dehire, deselect, dislocate, select out; excommunicate; run out; clear off *or* out, clean out, make a clean sweep of, purge; displace; give one one's walking papers; smoke out. *Slang,* give the gate, the sack, *or* the bum's rush to, fire, sack, can, give *or* get the air; kiss off, give the pink slip, stuff; show one the door, bounce.

3, be dismissed. *Slang,* get the ax, the sack, the bounce, the gate, *or* the hook.

4, *(remove objects from a carrier)* unpack, unlade, unload, unship.

Adjectives—emitting, emissive, ejective, expulsive, eliminative.

Interjections—begone! get you gone! get away! go away! off with you! go about your business! be off! avaunt! *Slang,* take off! get lost! beat it! scram! drop dead!

Antonyms, see RECEIVING.

---

eke out, *v.t.* manage, just *or* barely make, squeeze out. See DIFFICULTY, PROVISION.

elaborate, *v.* work out, develop, devise, perfect, embellish, refine. See COMPLETION, VARIEGATION. —*adj.* labored, studied, complicated, detailed, painstaking, finished, perfected; intricate, involved. See DISORDER.

elapse, *v.i.* slip away, pass, expire, intervene, glide by. See TIME, COURSE.

ELASTICITY
Great flexibility

Nouns—**1,** elasticity, springiness, spring, resilience, buoyancy, extensibility, ductility, stretch, rebound, adaptability. See VIGOR, EXPANSION.

2, *(elastic material)* rubber, India rubber, caoutchouc, whalebone, elastomer, baleen, gum elastic; rubber ball, rubber *or* elastic band; trampoline, springboard.

3, *(flexible person)* gymnast, contortionist.

Verbs—be elastic, spring back, rebound, stretch, expand; elasticize, vulcanize.

Adjectives—elastic, tensile, springy, resilient, buoyant, extensible, ductile, stretchable, adaptable; rubbery, rubberized.

Antonyms, see INELASTICITY.

---

elate, *v.t.* excite, enliven, exhilarate, exalt, animate, lift up, flush, elevate; please, gratify, gladden, delight. See CHEERFULNESS, EXCITEMENT. *Ant.,* sadden, depress.

elbow, *n.* bend, angle, dogleg. See ANGULARITY, CONVEXITY. —*v.* jab, poke; push, prod, shove; jostle, make one's way through. See IMPULSE.

elder, *adj.* older, earlier, superior, senior; elderly. —*n.* ancestor, senior. See AGE, OLDNESS.

elect, *v.t.* choose, select, decide on, fix upon; call, ordain. See CHOICE.

electric, *adj.* voltaic, magnetic, galvanic; thrilling, exciting, stimulating. See FEELING, POWER.

ELECTRICITY
An entity of nature with positive and negative parts

Nouns—**1,** electricity, electric[al] power; electromagnetism, electromotion; electrical engineering, ELECTRONICS, magnetics; electrolysis.

2, electric current, alternating current, AC, direct current, DC; open *or* closed circuit; electrical circuit *or* field; electric charge, positive *or* negative charge, live circuit; positive *or* negative charge *or* polarity, north *or* south pole, magnetic pole; resistance, reluctance, reactance, impedance, conductance, conduction, capacitance; electromotive force, potential, high *or* low tension; electric POWER, hydroelectric power, nuclear power.

3, *(electric measurements)* amperage, wattage, voltage; amp[ere], watt, angstrom, volt; ohm, mho, coulomb, maxwell, henry, farad, faraday, fresnel, gauss, gilbert, hertz, oersted, tesla, weber; electric meter, voltmeter, ammeter, galvanometer, spectrometer.

4, electric storage, [storage] battery, [dry *or* wet] cell, accumulator; capacitor; atomic, electronic, mercury, nickel-cadmium, solar, voltaic, *or* alkaline battery; alternator, amplifier, armature, attenuator, ballast, bridge, capacitor, circuit breaker, commutator, condenser, conductor, converter, depolarizer, dynamo, electrical cord, extension cord, fuse, generator, ground, insulator, inverter, laser, maser, motor, oscilloscope, patchbay, patchboard, patchcord, phasor, potentiometer, power supply, rectifier, regulator, relay, resistor, resonator, rheostat, rotor, solenoid, switch, transducer, transformer, transmitter.

5, electrician, line[s]man; electrical engineer.

6, power failure, blackout, brownout.

7, power station; nuclear, coal-fired, *or* oil-fired plant, hydroelectric plant; power grid.

Verbs—electrify, charge; shock; generate [electricity]; transform, step up *or* down; plug in; switch on *or* off; short[-circuit].

Adjectives—electric, electrical, photoelectric; hydroelectric; electromotive; solar-powered, battery-powered; [electro]magnetic; charged, live, hot; high- *or* low-tension; positive, negative; diamagnetic, dielectric, electrostatic.

---

electrify, *v.t.* galvanize, magnetize, charge; excite, thrill, stimulate, animate; stun, bewilder, startle. See POWER, ELECTRICITY, WONDER, EXCITEMENT.

electrocute, *v.t.* execute, zap (*sl.*). See KILLING, PUNISHMENT.

electrode, *n.* terminal; anode, cathode; conductor. See POWER.

ELECTRONICS
Science of electrons

Nouns—**1**, electronics, electron physics, electronic engineering, solid-state electronics; musical instrument digital interface, MIDI; electron theory of atoms *or* solids; superconductivity; nuclear *or* particle physics, atomic science, quantum mechanics; atomic energy (see POWER); atomic bomb (see ARMS). See ELECTRICITY.

2, molecule, radical; atom, isobar, isotope; nucleus, nuclear particle, nucleon, proton, neutron, electron; subatomic particle, [up, down, strange, charm, bottom *or* top] quark, baryon, alpha *or* beta particle, flavor, graviton, hadron, hyperon, kaon, lepton, muon, neutrino, photon, positron, tachyon, tardyon, tauon, zino; valence; electron ray *or* beam, cathode *or* anode ray.

3, amplifier, electron *or* vacuum tube, cathode-ray tube, CRT; semiconductor, solid-state device, transistor, thermistor; base, collector, emitter; printed circuit, microcircuit, microchip, integrated circuit, IC, diode; conductance, resistance, impedance; photoelectric cell, photocell, electric eye, photosensitive device; cryotron; electronic circuit, logic gate, flip-flop circuit.

4, a. nuclear fission *or* fusion, fission *or* fusion reaction; atom-smashing *or* -splitting, thermonuclear reaction, chain reaction; cold fusion; bombardment. **b.** nuclear accelerator, linear *or* induction accelerator, betatron, cosmotron, cyclotron, Van de Graaff generator. **c.** nuclear reactor, CANDU reactor, breeder [reactor]; pile, core, rods. **d.** nuclear fuel, fissionable *or* fusionable material.

5, electronic appliance, computer (see COMPUTERS), radio, television (see COMMUNICATION); scanner, [tele]copier, sequencer.

6, electronics engineer; nuclear physicist, atomic scientist.

Verbs—atomize, bombard, cleave, split; *or* smash the atom, fuse.

Adjectives—electronic, anodic, cathodic, solid-state, transistorized, photoelectric; superconductive; atomic, nuclear, subatomic, subnuclear, thermonuclear.

ELEGANCE
Good taste

Nouns—**1**, elegance, refinement, ease, grace, gracefulness, polish, finish, good TASTE, harmonious simplicity, rhythm, harmony, symmetry. See BEAUTY. See AFFECTATION.

2, [good] style, euphony, classicism, purism.

3, purist, classicist, stylist.

Verbs—show elegance *or* refinement; discriminate; round a period.

Adjectives—1, elegant, polished, classic[al], courtly, correct, artistic, chaste, pure, appropriate, refined, graceful, felicitous, in good taste, harmonious; genteel.

2, easy, fluent, flowing, mellifluous, balanced, euphonious; neatly put, well expressed.

Quotations—To achieve harmony in bad taste is the height of elegance (*Jean Genet*), In matters of great importance, style, not sincerity, is the vital thing (*Oscar Wilde*).

Antonyms, see VULGARITY, INELEGANCE.

---

elegy, *n.* dirge, lament, requiem, threnody. See LAMENTATION, POETRY.

element, *n.* component, PART, substance, constituent, ingredient; factor, principle, rudiment, fundamental. See CAUSE, COMPOSITION.

elementary, *adj.* elemental, rudimentary, incipient, primary, fundamental, basic; introductory; simple, uncompounded. See INTRINSIC, SIMPLENESS. *Ant.,* advanced, difficult.

elementary school, primary *or* grade SCHOOL.

elephantine, *adj.* huge, mammoth. See SIZE. *Ant.,* minuscule, tiny.

ELEVATION
Act of raising

Nouns—1, elevation; raising, lifting, erection; upheaval, uplift; exaltation, apotheosis, deification (see DEITY). *Informal,* heave, hike, boost. See ANGULARITY, VERTICAL.

2, (*elevated land*) prominence, eminence; HEIGHT, hill, mount, mountain.

3, (*device for raising*) lever, crank, block and tackle, crane, derrick, forklift, windlass, capstan, winch, crowbar, jimmy, pulley, jack, hoist, dredge, elevator, lift, dumbwaiter, hoist, escalator, moving stairway.

Verbs—elevate, heighten, raise, lift, erect, jack up, set up, stick up, heave, buoy, weigh, pick up; take up, fish up; cast up; dredge (up); uplift; exalt, apotheosize, deify, put on a pedestal; hold up (see SUPPORT). *Informal,* heave, hike, boost.

Adjectives—1, elevated, raised, lifted (up); uplifted; exalted, deified, lofty; on a pedestal; aweigh; erect, VERTICAL.

2, elevating, uplifting; erectile.

3, eminent, prominent.

Quotations—Only passions, great passions, can elevate the soul to great things (*Denis Diderot*).

Antonyms, see DEPRESSION.

---

elevator, *n.* lift; granary, silo. See ELEVATION, STORE.

elf, *n.* sprite, fairy, imp, puck, pixy; gnome, goblin. See MYTHICAL DEITIES, DEMON.

elicit, *v.t.* draw forth, extract, evoke, educe, extort. See EXTRACTION, CAUSE.

elide, *v.t.* omit, suppress. See NEGLECT.

eligible, *adj.* qualified, fitted, suitable, desirable. See EXPEDIENCE. *Ant.,* ineligible, unsuitable.

eliminate, *v.t.* expel, excrete, secrete; remove, get rid of, exclude, set aside, drop, cast out, eradicate; omit, ignore, leave out, NEGLECT, pass over; suppress, extract. See EXTRACTION, EJECTION, EXCLUSION. *Ant.,* add.

elite, *adj.* select, choice, prime. —*n.* [the] elect, choice, cream, flower; chosen people; inner circle, aristocracy, beau *or* haut monde; the four hundred; cream of the crop, crème de la crème. See SUPERIORITY, GOODNESS.

elixir, *n.* potion, essence, quintessence; philosophers' stone. See REMEDY.

elliptical, *adj.* oval, egg-shaped; condensed, cut, lacunal. See ROTUNDITY, SHORTNESS.

elongate, *v.* lengthen, extend, string out. See LENGTH.

elope, *v.t.* run away, decamp, abscond. See MARRIAGE, ESCAPE.

eloquence, *n.* oratory, rhetoric, power; fluency, persuasiveness, volubility. See LOQUACITY, SPEECH. *Ant.,* hesitancy, STAMMERING.

elsewhere, *adv.* somewhere else. See ABSENCE.

elucidate, *v.t.* clarify, illuminate, illustrate; explain, interpret. See INTERPRETATION.

elude, *v.t.* ESCAPE, evade, avoid; dodge, foil, baffle. See AVOIDANCE.

elusive, *adj.* elusory, evasive, slippery, shifty, tricky, baffling; deceptive, illusory, intangible, fugitive. See TRANSIENTNESS, DECEPTION.

emaciated, *adj.* starveling, thin, haggard, wasted, gaunt, drawn, scrawny, skin and bones (*inf.*). See NARROWNESS.

emanate, *v.* effuse, exhale, radiate; flow, proceed, issue, come, spring, arise. See EGRESS, EFFECT, FRAGRANCE.

emancipate, *v.t.* liberate, free, release, deliver, manumit, set free, enfranchise. See LIBERATION. *Ant.*, enslave.

emasculate, *v.t.* unman, castrate, geld, alter, effeminize; devitalize, debilitate; dispirit, demoralize. See WEAKNESS, IMPOTENCE.

embalm, *v.t.* preserve, mummify. See INTERMENT, PRESERVATION.

embankment, *n.* dike, mole, bulwark, bank, wall, levee; barrier, rampart. See DEFENSE, ENCLOSURE.

embargo, *n.* restriction, RESTRAINT, HINDRANCE, PROHIBITION.

embark, *v.t.* ship, board, set sail; sail; begin, engage. See DEPARTURE, UNDERTAKING, BEGINNING. *Ant.*, disembark, complete.

embarrass, *v.t.* discomfort, demoralize, disconcert, discomfit, nonplus, bother, abash, encumber, trouble, hamper, complicate, perplex. See DIFFICULTY, HINDRANCE, DISCONTENT.

embassy, *n.* mission, ministry, legation, consulate. See COMMISSION.

embattled, *adj.* armed, arrayed; fortified. See DEFENSE.

embed, *v.t.* fix, envelop; incorporate. See INCLUSION.

embellish, *v.t.* ORNAMENT; embroider (see EXAGGERATION).

ember, *n.* coal, brand (see FUEL).

embezzle, *v.* steal, misappropriate, misapply, peculate, defalcate. See STEALING.

embitter, *v.t.* sour, envenom, poison, anger, irritate. See RESENTMENT.

emblem, *n.* symbol, token, sign; flag, badge, *etc.* See INDICATION.

embody, *v.t.* incorporate, join, unite, organize, impersonate, personify, incarnate; comprise, contain, include; express. See REPRESENTATION, COMBINATION, SUBSTANCE, WHOLE.

emboss, *v.* knob, stud, engrave, chase. See CONVEXITY, ORNAMENT.

embrace, *v.t.* clasp, clutch, hold, fold, hug; include, comprehend, take in, comprise, involve, embody; encircle, enclose, surround; receive, welcome; take up, adopt, espouse. See CHOICE, INCLUSION, ENVIRONMENT, ENDEARMENT, CIRCUMSCRIPTION.

embroidery, *n.* needlework, crewelwork, gros *or* petit point. See ORNAMENT, EXAGGERATION.

embroil, *v.t.* complicate, throw into DISORDER.

embryo, *n.* fetus, egg, germ, bud; incipience, conception. See BEGINNING.

emcee, *n.* master of ceremonies (see AMUSEMENT).

emend, *v.t.* amend (see IMPROVEMENT).

emerge, *v.i.* issue, appear; arise, come forth. See EGRESS.

emergency, *n.* juncture, crisis; exigency, NECESSITY, pinch, extremity. See CIRCUMSTANCE, DIFFICULTY.

emigrant, *n.* See EGRESS. *Ant.*, immigrant.

emigration, *n.* migration, departure, exodus. See EGRESS. *Ant.*, immigration.

eminence, *n.* height, altitude, ELEVATION; distinction, rank, REPUTE, importance; hill, HEIGHT. See CLERGY.

emissary, *n.* messenger, AGENT.

emit, *v.t.* discharge, emanate, radiate, breathe, exhale, send forth, throw off, issue; deliver, voice, utter. See EJECTION, SPEECH.

emollient, *n.* ointment, balm. See REMEDY, SOFTNESS.

emotion, *n.* FEELING, sentiment, passion, SENSIBILITY, sensation.

empathy, *n.* understanding, comprehension. See PITY, FRIEND.

emperor, *n.* Caesar, kaiser, czar; empress. See AUTHORITY, NOBILITY.

emphasize, *v.t.* accentuate, stress, mark, underline, underscore. See AFFIRMATION, IMPORTANCE.

empire, *n.* realm, domain, imperium; sovereignty, sway. See AUTHORITY, REGION.

empirical, *adj.* experiential, perceptual, practical, firsthand; commonsense, prag-

matic; by trial and error, by feel. See EX-
PERIMENT.

employ, *v.t.* USE, occupy; hire, engage. See
COMPARISON, BUSINESS.

employee, *n.* SERVANT, helper, [hired]
hand; clerk, assistant.

employer, *n.* user, consumer; boss, padrone.
See USE, DIRECTOR.

emporium, *n.* See SALE.

empower, *v.t.* enable, endow, invest; authorize, license, COMMISSION. See PER-
MISSION, POWER.

empress, *n.* czarina, queen, [maha]rani,
begum; consort. See AUTHORITY.

empty, *v.* void, deplete, exhaust, evacuate,
drain, deflate, discharge, unload. See
CONTRACTION, EJECTION. —*adj.* hollow,
vacant, depleted, untenanted, devoid;
hungry; vain, insubstantial, useless, foolish, trivial, unfeeling, fruitless, inane.
See ABSENCE, USELESSNESS, WASTE. *Ant.,*
full, filled.

empyrean, *adj.* heavenly, empyreal, celestial, sublime; fiery. See UNIVERSE.

emulate, *v.t.* rival, vie, compete, strive,
contend. See OPPOSITION, REPUTE, IMI-
TATION.

enable, *v.t.* empower, invest, endow; authorize. See POWER.

enact, *v.t.* decree, make, pass, order, ordain; play, execute, perform, do. See
DRAMA, COMMAND.

enamor, *v.t.* charm, captivate. See LOVE.

encampment, *n.* camp, bivouac (see
ABODE).

enchant, *v.t.* bewitch, conjure; captivate,
please, charm, delight, fascinate. See
PLEASURE, SORCERY.

encipher, *v.t.* encode (see SECRET). *Ant.,*
decipher.

encircle, *v.t.* environ, surround, embrace, encompass, enclose; span, ring, loop, girdle.
See ENVIRONMENT, CIRCUMSCRIPTION.

enclave, *n.* See REGION.

ENCLOSURE
Act of enclosing

Nouns—1, enclosure, containment, CIRCUMSCRIPTION, confinement, imprisonment
(see PRISON); blockade, siege; quarantine.

2, envelope, case, cartridge, RECEPTACLE, wrapper, COVERING, girdle; parenthesis,
bracket, bookend. See REGION.

3, *(enclosed space)* pen, fold; enclave; sheepfold, paddock, pound, coop, sty, pigsty,
stall, kennel, corral, net, kraal, compound; courtyard; patio, yard, *etc.*

4, *(enclosing structure)* wall; hedge, fence, pale, paling, balustrade, rail[ing], dike,
ditch, fosse, moat, levee, embankment; dam. See DEFENSE.

5, *(limiting structure)* barrier, barricade, parapet, rampart, stockade; jail (see
PRISON).

Verbs—enclose, confine, surround, circumscribe, contain, envelop, hedge about *or* in, pen
in, coop up, hem in, impen, impound; fence in, wall in *or* up, close in, dam up, curtain
off, cordon off, quarantine, blockade; confine, imprison; parenthesize, bracket.

Adjectives—enclosed, confined, *etc.*; shut in, walled up; enclosing, parietal, cloistered.

Quotations—Good fences make good neighbors (*Robert Frost*), Something there is that
doesn't love a wall (*Robert Frost*), Stone walls do not a prison make, nor iron bars a
cage (*Richard Lovelace*).

Antonyms, see EXTERIOR, SPACE.

---

encode, *v.t.* encipher (see SECRET).

encompass, *v.t.* surround, encircle; contain. See INCLUSION, ENVIRONMENT.

encounter, *v.t.* meet, come across; engage,
struggle, contend. —*n.* meeting, interview; collision, combat, battle, skirmish,
brush, engagement. See CONTENTION,
IMPULSE, OPPOSITION, OCCURRENCE,
CONTACT.

encourage, *v.t.* animate, strengthen, hearten,

fortify, inspirit, cheer, inspire, reassure,
rally, comfort; abet, embolden, incite,
urge, instigate; help, foster, promote,
advance, advocate. See HOPE, CHEER-
FULNESS, AID. *Ant.,* discourage,
dampen.

encroach, *v.i.* advance, infringe, usurp, invade, trespass, intrude, overstep, violate; make inroads. See ILLEGALITY,
OVERRUNNING.

encumber, *v.t.* burden, hamper, load, clog, oppress; obstruct, hinder, impede, embarrass, retard, check, handicap. See HINDRANCE, DIFFICULTY, DEBT.

encyclopedic, *adj.* extensive, exhaustive, comprehensive. See INCLUSION, COMPLETION, GENERALITY.

END
Terminal point

Nouns—1, end[ing], close, termination, conclusion, wind-up, finis, finish, finale, period, terminus, stopping [point]; halt, cessation, desistance, cloture, abortion, curtailment, stop[page], expiration, halt; end game; bitter end, happy end[ing]. See DISCONTINUANCE, FAILURE.

2, *(end of a line)* extreme, extremity; acme, peak (see HEIGHT); tip, nib, point; tail [end], fag *or* tag end, bitter end; peroration; final *or* last inning, round, *or* lap, *etc.*; homestretch, Z, omega, izzard, zed. *Informal,* shank. See LIMIT.

3, *(end of life)* consummation, COMPLETION, denouement, finish, doomsday, crack of doom, Day of Judgment, final curtain, last stages, last word, expiration, DEATH, end of all things, quietus, finality; the four last things (death, judgment, heaven, and hell); last hurrah. *Slang,* payoff, curtains.

4, *(cause of an ending)* finishing stroke, death blow, knockout, KO, coup de grâce, crowning touch; last straw; straw that breaks the camel's back.

5, *(end destination)* goal, destination, object, purpose (see INTENTION).

Verbs—1, end, close, finish, terminate, conclude, be all over, expire, die (see DEATH); come to a close, run its course, run out, pass away, be through, end up; have done, leave off, go out with a bang, ride off into the sunset. *Informal,* wind up.

2, bring to an end, put an end to, make an end of, lay to rest; determine; complete; stop, turn, *or* cut off; close *or* shut the door, shut up shop, ring down the curtain; abort, call off; call a halt, blow the whistle on, rain out; flag down; stop cold *or* dead, stop in one's tracks, nip in the bud; put out, extinguish. *Slang,* pull a rabbit.

3, cease, halt, arrest, desist, expire, lapse, stop; sign off, log off, hang up; curtail, choke off, cut short (see SHORTNESS); abort, drop. *Slang,* cut out, flame out.

Adjectives—1, ending, final, terminal, definitive, crowning, completing, last [but not least], ultimate, extreme, conclusive, last-ditch.

2, end, at an end, settled, decided, over, played out.

Adverbs—finally, definitely, conclusively; at the last, when the chips are down; in time; once and for all, to the bitter end; all over but the shouting; that is that; in at the kill *or* the death.

Phrases—all good things must come to an end; all's well that ends well; the end crowns the work; the opera isn't over till the fat lady sings; a whistling girl and a crowing hen never came to a good end. *Informal,* the jig *or* game is up.

Quotations—The end is not yet (*Bible*), I am the Alpha and the Omega, the beginning and the end, the first and the last (*Bible*), Better is the end of a thing than the beginning thereof (*Bible*), In my beginning is my end (*T. S. Elliot*), If men could get pregnant, abortion would be a sacrament (*Florynce Kennedy*).

Antonyms, see BEGINNING.

---

endanger, *v.t.* imperil. See DANGER.

ENDEARMENT
Act of endearing

Nouns—1, endearment, caress; fondling, billing and cooing, hand-holding, nuzzling, embrace, kiss, buss, smack, peck, osculation. *Informal,* first base, noogie, French kiss, passion kiss, soul kiss, kissy-face, mouth-to-mouth resuscitation, tongue wrestling. See FLATTERY, FEELING, SEX.

2, courtship, affections, wooing, suit, addresses, advances, liberties; amour, love-making, petting; flirting, flirtation, dalliance, gallantry; coquetry; computer dating, personal ad, personals; wolf whistle. *Informal,* spooning, hanky-panky. *Slang,* come-on, pass, snow job; necking, smooching, queening, rottenlogging. See LOVE.

3, *(symbol of love)* lover's knot, love token, love letter; billet-doux, valentine.

4, affair, liaison, tryst, rendezvous, assignation; blind date, double date; engagement, betrothal, MARRIAGE; honeymoon.

5, suitor, swain, beau, blade, belle; flirt, coquette, femme fatale; philanderer, lover, Don Juan, Casanova, ladies' man; paramour; Mr. Right. *Informal,* loverboy, la-dykiller, smoothie. *Slang,* vamp, gold-digger; wolf, sheik, make-out artist, stud, cock-teaser. See MALE, FEMALE.

6, *(terms of love)* pet name; dear, darling, sweetheart, precious, love, honey, honey-bunch, pet, dollface, *etc. Informal,* sweet talk. *Slang,* sweet nothings.

7, lovers' lane, singles bar. *Slang,* passion pit, meat rack.

Verbs—1, caress, fondle, pet; cosset, coddle, make much of; cherish, foster; hold hands; clasp, hug, cuddle, nuzzle, snuggle, fall all over, enfold, fold in one's arms, nestle; embrace, kiss, buss, smack. *Slang,* sample, pucker up, play tonsil hockey, smash mouth, suck *or* eat face, swap spit, snog, mush, paw.

2, make love, bill and coo, pet; toy, dally, flirt, coquet, philander; court, gallivant, squire, woo, pay addresses; set one's cap for, be sweet on; ogle, cast sheep's eyes on, make eyes at; pop the question. *Informal,* pitch woo, spark, spoon, make time. *Slang,* smooch, neck, make out, play footsie; make a pass at, hit on, make a play for, put the make *or* move on, cop a feel, grease.

3, fall in love with; propose, pop the question; plight one's troth. *Informal,* hit it off. *Slang,* string along.

Adjectives—1, endearing, winsome, lovable, kissable, affectionate, caressing; come-hither.

2, lovesick, lovelorn. *Informal,* spoony.

3, on the make, on the prowl.

Phrases—a courtship is a man's pursuit of a woman until she catches him.

Quotations—Come live with me and be my love (*John Donne*), Shall I compare thee to a summer's day? Thou art more lovely and more temperate (*Shakespeare*), I wasn't kissing her, I was just whispering in her mouth (*Chico Marx*).

Antonyms, see DETRACTION, HATE.

---

endeavor, *v.i.* try, attempt, seek, struggle, strive, essay, labor, aim, offer. —*n.* trial, try, attempt, effort, struggle, EXERTION, offer. See INTENTION, UNDERTAKING.

en déshabillé, *Fr.* in dishabille, in casual dress. See UNPREPAREDNESS.

endless, *adj.* incessant, uninterrupted, unceasing, continuous, perpetual; never-ending, unending, everlasting, continual, undying, eternal; boundless, indefinite, illimitable, unlimited, immeasurable. See CONTINUITY, PERPETUITY, INFINITY.

endmost, *adj.* most remote, furthest. See DISTANCE.

endorse, *v.t.* approve, support, second; recommend; subscribe (to); sign. See APPROBATION.

endow, *v.t.* dower, settle upon, bequeath, bestow, enrich, endue; furnish, invest, clothe. See GIVING.

endowment, *n.* property, fund, foundation; gift, bestowal, dower, dowry; POWER; ability, faculty, aptitude, capacity, talent, bent. See GIVING, SKILL, POSSESSION.

endue, *v.t.* endow, clothe, furnish. See POWER.

endure, *v.* continue, remain, wear, last; abide, bear, suffer, bear up, sustain, undergo; tolerate, put up with, stand, brook, permit. See RESISTANCE, FEEL-ING, DURABILITY, EXISTENCE. *Ant.,* perish, falter.

endways, *adv.* lengthwise, on end (see DIRECTION).

enemy, *n.* foe, opponent (see OPPOSITION). *Ant.,* ally, FRIEND.

ENERGY
Strength in action

Nouns—1, energy, POWER, STRENGTH; VIGOR, vim, punch; intensity, go, dash, drive, high pressure; RESOLUTION; EXERTION, excitation. *Informal,* ginger. *Slang,* pep, moxie, socko, zip, vinegar, juice, flex.

2, *(types of energy)* ACTIVITY; effervescence, fermentation (see AGITATION); radioactivity; actual, potential, atomic, nuclear, wind, alternative, kinetic, electrical, geothermal, solar, *or* dynamic energy, water power; driving force; erg, dyne.

3, *(creator of power)* dynamo, generator; motor, engine; spark plug, battery; FUEL, ELECTRICITY, wind *or* power farm; stimulant.

4, *(energetic person)* life of the party. *Slang,* live wire, human dynamo, go-getter, hustler.

5, *(units of energy)* dyne, erg, joule, calorie, quantum, photon, foot-pound, horsepower.

Verbs—1, energize, galvanize, enliven, stimulate, charge up, intensify. *Slang,* pep up, give a shot in the arm, jazz up, build a fire under.

2, be energetic, have energy. *Slang,* feel one's oats.

Adjectives—energetic, active, intense; keen, vivid, incisive, trenchant, brisk, rousing, electrifying. *Slang,* full of steam, raring to go, full of piss and vinegar, funky, gung ho.

Adverbs—energetically, strongly, with might and main, in earnest. *Informal,* like mad, with hammer and tongs, like gangbusters.

Antonyms, see WEAKNESS.

enervate, *v.t.* weaken, devitalize, unnerve, paralyze, soften, emasculate, unman, debilitate, enfeeble, effeminate. See IMPOTENCE, WEAKNESS. *Ant.,* innervate, invigorate.

en famille, *Fr.* at home; informally. See UNCONFORMITY.

enfant terrible, *Fr.* unruly child, juvenile delinquent. See DISOBEDIENCE.

enfold, *v.t.* envelop, enclose, encompass; embrace. See ENDEARMENT, CIRCUMSCRIPTION.

enforce, *v.t.* compel, force, oblige; urge, lash, goad; strengthen; execute, sanction, put in force. See COMPULSION, CAUSE. *Ant.,* neglect, overlook.

enfranchise, *v.t.* liberate, set free, release; naturalize; empower, license, qualify. See PERMISSION, LIBERATION. *Ant.,* disenfranchise.

engage, *v.t.* bind, obligate, pledge, PROMISE; betroth; hire, enlist, employ, book, retain; reserve, secure; occupy, interest, engross, attract, entangle, involve, interlock; set about, take up; fight, contend. See COMMISSION, UNDERTAKING, ATTENTION, CONTENTION. *Ant.,* disengage, dismiss, discharge.

engagement, *n.* betrothal, obligation, PROMISE, agreement, pledge; appointment, interview; occupation, employment; battle, action, skirmish, brush, encounter. See DUTY, BUSINESS, CONTENTION, SOCIALITY, MARRIAGE.

engender, *v.t.* CAUSE; beget, procreate. See REPRODUCTION.

engine, *n.* motor, machine; device; engine of war. See ARMS, INSTRUMENTALITY, POWER.

engineer, *n.* motorman, hogger (*sl.*); planner, organizer. —*v.t.* plan, direct; contrive, machinate. See VEHICLE, PRODUCTION, PLAN, WIT.

ENGRAVING
Art of making designs by etching

Nouns—1, engraving; line, mezzotint, *or* stipple engraving; drypoint, drawpoint, etching, intaglio, gravure, copperplate, silverpoint; steel *or* wood engraving; xylography, chalcography, glyptography, cerography, lithography, photolithography, glyphography, glyptography, hyalography, pyrography, xylopyrography, zincography; steel engraving; gravure, photogravure, rotogravure; photoengraving, photoetching.

2, *(print from an engraved plate)* proof; [block] print, impression, monotype, plate, etching, aquatint, lithotint, cut, linoleum cut, woodcut, linecut, xylograph; mezzotint, aquatint; restrike, resist. See PRINTING.

3, *(engraving equipment)* graver, brayer, point, scraper, burnisher, burin, etchingpoint, style; plate, stone, woodblock, negative; die, punch, stamp.

Verbs—engrave, grave, enchase, stipple, etch, bute, lithograph.

Adjectives—engraved, sculptured, graven; carved, carven, chiseled; lithographic, xylographic.

---

engross, *v.t.* monopolize, control; absorb; occupy, engage; copy, write, transcribe. See ATTENTION, THOUGHT, WRITING.

engulf, *v.t.* swamp, flood, immerse, engorge, swallow up; encircle, envelop, encompass. See DESTRUCTION, WATER.

enhance, *v.t.* intensify; exaggerate; advance, augment, INCREASE, elevate. See EXAGGERATION, IMPROVEMENT.

enigma, *n.* riddle, mystery, puzzle, conundrum, SECRET. See DIFFICULTY, UNINTELLIGIBILITY.

enjoin, *v.t.* COMMAND, bid, direct, order, instruct, charge; counsel, admonish; prohibit, forbid, restrain; exact, require. See ADVICE, DUTY, PROHIBITION.

enjoy, *v.t.* like, relish, love, gloat over, delight in; experience; hold, possess. See PLEASURE, POSSESSION.

enkindle, *v.t.* inflame. See EXCITEMENT, HEAT, CAUSE.

enlarge, *v.t.* increase, extend, widen, broaden; aggrandize, amplify, magnify, augment, expand, elaborate, expatiate; dilate, distend, swell. See INCREASE, GREATNESS, DIFFUSENESS, BREADTH.

enlighten, *v.t.* brighten, illuminate; educate, civilize, instruct, inform, teach, edify. See LIGHT, TEACHING, INFORMATION. *Ant.,* obfuscate.

enlist, *v.* volunteer, sign up, enroll, recruit, draft, muster, press [into service], impress. See WARFARE, COMPULSION.

enliven, *v.t.* animate, exhilarate, inspirit, quicken, fire, brighten, stimulate, rouse, invigorate; cheer, elate, encourage. See CHEERFULNESS, EXCITEMENT.

en masse, *Fr.* all together; in a group. See ASSEMBLAGE, WHOLE.

enmity, *n.* hostility, unfriendliness, antagonism, OPPOSITION, HATE, ill will; grudge, rancor, anger, spite, animus, animosity, DISLIKE, antipathy; feud, vendetta. *Ant.,* friendship.

ennoble, *v.t.* dignify, exalt, raise, elevate, glorify, uplift. See REPUTE.

ennui, *n.* boredom (see WEARINESS).

enormity, *n.* wickedness, atrociousness; atrocity, outrage; immensity, enormousness, GREATNESS. See GUILT.

enormous, *adj.* monstrous, atrocious, excessive; large, titanic, tremendous, huge, immense, colossal, gigantic, vast, prodigious, stupendous. See SIZE, BADNESS.

enough, *adj.* adequate, sufficient, satisfactory, equal; ample, abundant, plenteous. See SUFFICIENCY. *Ant.,* insufficient.

en passant, *Fr.* in passing; by the way. See OCCASION, TRANSIENTNESS.

enrage, *v.t.* anger, exasperate, provoke, incense, irritate; madden, flame, infuriate. See RESENTMENT.

en rapport, *Fr.* in harmony. See AGREEMENT.

enrapture, *v.t.* transport, enravish, entrance, enchant; please, delight, charm, captivate, bewitch. See PLEASURE.

enrich, *v.t.* endow, aggrandize, make wealthy; embellish, ORNAMENT, adorn, beautify; fertilize; cultivate, develop. See IMPROVEMENT, MONEY. *Ant.,* impoverish.

enroll, *v.* LIST, RECORD, enter, register; enlist, serve.

en route, *adv.* on *or* along the way; in transit, on the road. See TRAVEL.

ensconce, *v.t.* settle; cover, hide. See SECRET.

ensemble, *n.* See WHOLE.

enshrine, *v.t.* consecrate, hallow; cherish; commemorate. See MEMORY, WORSHIP, PIETY.

ensign, *n.* flag; badge, emblem, insignia; standard-bearer. See INDICATION, COMBATANT.

enslave, *v.t.* subjugate, enthrall, suppress, dominate, hold dominion over; oppress, tyrannize; addict. See SUBJECTION, HABIT.

ensnare, *v.t.* [en]trap, catch, net, bag; entangle, ensnarl, entoil (*archaic*); bait, decoy; seduce, entice. See DECEPTION.

ensue, *v.* follow, succeed, supervene, happen, result; pursue, seek after. See EFFECT, SEQUENCE.

ensure, *v.t.* secure, guarantee; protect. See SECURITY, SAFETY, CERTAINTY.

entail, *v.t.* involve, imply, call for, require; CAUSE. See NECESSITY.

entangle, *v.t.* tangle, ravel, mesh, entrap, mat, ensnare, inveigle, twist, snarl; perplex, involve, embroil, embarrass. See DIFFICULTY, DISORDER.

entente, *n.* understanding, entente cordial, accord, AGREEMENT.

enter, *v.* penetrate, pierce; go *or* come in; insert; trespass, invade, board; begin, start, take up; LIST, RECORD, inscribe, enroll, register, file; join. See COMPOSITION, INGRESS, ACCOUNTING.

enterprise, *n.* project, scheme, venture, UNDERTAKING; business; energy; push (*inf.*), go-ahead (*inf.*). See COURAGE.

enterprising, *adj.* energetic, venturesome, adventurous; eager, ambitious, pushing (*inf.*). See COURAGE.

entertain, *v.* receive, welcome; amuse, divert, regale; harbor, shelter, cherish; maintain, keep up; consider, dwell upon, heed. See ATTENTION, THOUGHT, AMUSEMENT.

enthrall, *v.t.* enslave, subjugate; captivate, fascinate, charm. See PLEASURE, SUBJECTION.

enthusiasm, *n.* ecstasy, frenzy, fanaticism; fire, spirit, force; ardor, zeal, fervor, vehemence, eagerness; optimism, assurance. See FEELING, HOPE, EXCITABILITY, VIGOR. *Ant.,* disinterest.

entice, *v.* [al]lure, tempt, attract; induce, coax, cajole, woo; bewitch, enchant, seduce; deceive, hoodwink. See ATTRACTION, PLEASURE. *Ant.,* repel.

entire, *adj.* complete, absolute, unqualified; total, gross, all; WHOLE, intact, undiminished, unimpaired, perfect, unbroken; undivided, unalloyed.

entitle, *v.t.* qualify, fit, capacitate, authorize; name, call, designate, dub, style. See NOMENCLATURE, JUSTICE, PERMISSION.

entity, *n.* thing, being; whole, UNITY; abstraction, EXISTENCE. See SUBSTANCE.

entomb, *v.t.* bury, inter (see INTERMENT).

entourage, *n.* retinue, train. See ASSEMBLAGE, SERVANT.

entr'acte, *n.* interval. See DRAMA.

entrails, *n.* viscera, intestines, bowels; insides, guts. See INTERIOR.

entrance, *n.* entry, INGRESS, entrée, incoming, ingoing; debut, induction; admission, access, admittance, APPROACH; aperture, door, lobby, gate, portal, way, OPENING; BEGINNING, start, commencement, introduction; invasion, penetration. See EDGE. —*v.t.* enrapture, delight; spellbind. See PLEASURE, SORCERY. *Ant.,* exit.

entrap, *v.t.* See ENSNARE.

entreat, *v.t.* REQUEST, beg, crave, pray, beseech, implore, supplicate, plead.

entrench, *v.* establish, dig in, embed; encroach, infringe. See STABILITY, OVERRUNNING.

entre nous, *Fr.* [just] between us. See DISCLOSURE, NEARNESS.

entrepreneur, *n.* producer, angel, impresario; investor. See CHANCE, UNDERTAKING, DRAMA.

entrust, *v.t.* COMMISSION, charge, delegate; confide, trust, consign, commit; charge; show faith *or* reliance in.

entry, *n.* ENTRANCE, memorandum, RECORD, posting, listing; entrant, contestant, contender, competitor. See CONTENTION.

entry-level, *adj.* basic, fundamental; simple. See SIMPLENESS, BEGINNING.

entwine, *v.* twine, interlace, twist, wreathe, weave. See CROSSING.

enumerate, *v.t.* count, tell off, number; name over, mention, recount, rehearse, recapitulate, detail, specify. See NUMERATION.

enunciate, *v.* announce, state, proclaim, declare; pronounce, articulate. See AFFIRMATION, SPEECH.

envelop, *v.t.* cover, wrap, enshroud, enfold, surround, enclose, hide. See CIRCUMSCRIPTION, COVERING.

envelope, *n.* COVERING, wrapper, casing, capsule; film, skin, integument, shell, sheath; receptacle. See ENCLOSURE.

enviable, *adj.* desirable, fortunate. See JEALOUSY.

envious, *adj.* jealous, invidious, covetous. See JEALOUSY.

ENVIRONMENT
Surrounding things or conditions

Nouns—1, environment, encompassment, circumjacence, circumference; atmosphere, ambience, aura, medium, surroundings (see CIRCUMSTANCE); environs, outposts, outskirts, suburbs, purlieus, precincts, neighborhood, vicinity, background, setting, habitat, milieu, stamping ground; ecology, ecosystem, biome. *Informal,* neck of the woods; context. *Slang,* hangout, turf. See NEARNESS, CIRCUMSCRIPTION.

2, environmental science, environmentalism; environmental art, design, *etc.*; bionomics; recycling; ecodefense.

3, environmentalist, ecodefender. *Slang,* eco-freak, posy-sniffer, bunny- *or* tree-hugger; antinuke.

Verbs—environ, lie around *or* about, surround, compass, encompass, enclose, encircle, embrace.

Adjectives—1, circumjacent, circumambient, ambient, surrounding, encompassing, enclosing, suburban, neighboring, vicinal.

2, environmental, ecological, environmentally friendly.

Adverbs—around, about; on every side, on all sides, all around, round about; in the neighborhood *or* vicinity.

Quotations—The supreme reality of our time is . . . the vulnerability of our planet (*J. F. Kennedy*), We have forgotten how to be good guests, how to walk lightly on the earth as its other creatures do (*Stockholm Conference*), Conservation is a state of harmony between men and land (*Aldo Leopold*), We must make our garden grow (*Voltaire*), Pity the Meek, for they shall inherit the earth (*Don Marquis*).

Antonyms, see DISTANCE.

---

envision, *v.t.* visualize, envisage, contemplate, picture. See IMAGINATION.

envoy, *n.* diplomat, AGENT; messenger (see COMMUNICATION); postscript (see ADDITION).

envy, *n.* enviousness, JEALOUSY; covetousness, cupidity, spite; ill will, malice; greenness. —*v.* begrudge; DESIRE, crave, covet, hanker, turn green.

eon, *n.* age, [long] TIME, epoch, dog's *or* coon's age (*inf.*).

ephemeral, *adj.* short-lived, fugitive, transient, transitory, fleeting, evanescent, momentary. See TRANSIENTNESS.

epic, *adj.* heroic, majestic, elevated, noble; Homeric, Virgilian; larger than life, on a grand scale. See GREATNESS. —*n.* saga, edda; epos, tale; rhapsody, eulogy. See POETRY, WRITING.

epicene, *adj.* sexless, bisexual; effeminate. See MALE, FEMALE.

epicure, *n.* epicurean, bon vivant, gourmet. See TASTE, PLEASURE, GLUTTONY.

epidemic, *n.* DISEASE, pestilence, plague, contamination. —*adj.* pestilential, infectious, contagious; raging, rife, pandemic, ubiquitous. See GENERALITY.

epigram, *n.* aphorism, bon mot, saying, MAXIM. See WIT.

epigraph, *n.* inscription, motto. See MAXIM.

epilepsy, *n.* grand *or* petit mal. See DISEASE.

epilogue, *n.* afterword, postscript, postlude; summation; valedictory, last word. See ADDITION, COMPLETION, DRAMA.

epiphany, *n.* APPEARANCE, manifestation; DISCLOSURE. See IMAGINATION.

episode, *n.* digression, excursus; OCCURRENCE, incident, happening, action. See BETWEEN, MUSIC.

epistle, *n.* letter, COMMUNICATION, missive.

epitaph, *n.* inscription, hic jacet, requiescat in pace, RIP. See INTERMENT.

epithet, *n.* byname (see NOMENCLATURE).

epitome, *n.* compendium, abridgment, abstract, synopsis, summary, brief. See SHORTNESS.

epoch, *n.* date; period, era, age. See TIME, CHRONOMETRY.

equable, *adj.* uniform, even, steady; tranquil. See EQUALITY, INEXCITABILITY.

EQUALITY
Identity in magnitude, etc.

Nouns—1, equality, parity, coextension; symmetry, balance, evenness, level, equivalence; balance of power, standoff; equipoise, equilibrium; par, quits; IDENTITY, SIMILARITY; equalization, equation, coordination, adjustment; peer pressure; Equal Rights Amendment, equal opportunity, affirmative action, women's *or* gay liberation. See SYMMETRY, INDIFFERENCE, JUSTICE, COPY.

2, *(equal result)* tie, draw, dead heat, deadlock, standoff, even match, impasse, photo finish; even break, fair shake.

3, match, peer, compeer, equal, mate, fellow, brother, equivalent, parallel, counterpart, colleague; peer group. *Informal,* ditto.

4, tit for tat; a Roland for an Oliver, an eye for an eye.

5, equalizer; equation; equator.

Verbs—1, equal, match, keep pace *or* up with, come up to, be on a level *or* par with, balance, measure up to, be equal to, having nothing on (someone), hold a candle *or* stick to.

2, make equal, equalize, equate, level, balance, trim, adjust, poise, fit, strike a balance, equilibrate, restore equilibrium, readjust; handicap; share and share alike; break even.

Adjectives—1, equal, even, level, coequal, symmetrical, coordinate; on a par with, abreast, coextensive; square, quits, fifty-fifty; up to the mark. *Informal,* even steven, neck-and-neck.

2, equivalent, tantamount; homologous, synonymous, analogous, similar, as broad as it is long, much the same, the same; equalized, drawn, neck-and-neck; half-and-half. *Informal,* quits; fifty-fifty.

Adverbs—equally, both, to the same degree, pari passu; to all intents and purposes, nip and tuck, abreast; on even footing, on equal terms; with the best; up to par, scratch, *or* snuff; all things being equal; from scratch.

Phrases—diamond cuts diamond; the pot calling the kettle black; do as you would be done by; do unto others as you would they should do unto you; all's fair in love and war.

Quotations—A man's a man for a' that (*Robert Burns*), There is no method by which men can be both free and equal (*Walter Bagehot*), All animals are equal, but some animals are more equal than others (*George Orwell*).

Antonyms, see INEQUALITY.

---

equanimity, *n.* evenness, composure, repose, poise; calmness, serenity, tranquility, self-possession, self-control, INEXCITABILITY. *Ant.,* EXCITABILITY.

equator, *n.* great circle, the line. See EQUALITY, DISJUNCTION.

equestrian, *adj.* equine. See ANIMAL. —n. horseman *or* -woman, rider. See TRAVEL.

equilibrium, *n.* balance, equipoise, STABILITY; moderation, neutrality; EQUALITY, parity, symmetry; composure, self-possession, [self-]restraint. See IN-EXCITABILITY. *Ant.,* unbalance, instability.

equip, *v.t.* furnish, outfit, rig [out], provide; accouter, appoint, dress, accommodate, array, attire; arm, gird. See CLOTHING, PREPARATION, PROVISION.

equipage, *n.* carriage; outfit, equipment. See VEHICLE, PROVISION.

equipment, *n.* furnishings, gear, harness, supplies, apparatus, accouterment, appointment, outfit, apparel. See CLOTHING, INSTRUMENTALITY, PROVISION.

equipoise, *n.* equilibrium; counterbalance. See EQUALITY.

equitable, *adj.* fair, just, ethical, honest; unbiased, dispassionate, evenhanded, fair-and-square; deserved, merited, condign, due, on the up-and-up (*inf.*). See JUSTICE. *Ant.*, inequitable, unfair.

equity, *n.* fairness, impartiality; ownership. See JUSTICE, PROPERTY.

equivalent, *adj.* equal, tantamount, synonymous; analogous, correspondent, interchangeable; convertible, reciprocal. —*n.* equal; worth; analogue. See COMPENSATION, SUBSTITUTION, EQUALITY, INTERPRETATION.

equivocation, *n.* equivocalness; quibble, quibbling; evasion, shiftiness; ambiguity, double meaning, double entendre; prevarication, white lie; half-truth, sophistry, casuistry; dodge, subterfuge, smoke screen, red herring. See CONCEALMENT, FALSEHOOD, AVOIDANCE.

era, *n.* See TIME, CHRONOMETRY.

eradicate, *v.t.* abolish; blot out, erase, extirpate, exterminate, weed out, eliminate, uproot. See DESTRUCTION, EXTRACTION.

erase, *v.t.* efface, rub out, expunge, cancel, obliterate, blot out. See NULLIFICATION, DESTRUCTION, EXTRACTION.

erect, *v.t.* raise, exalt; rear; build, construct; establish, set up, institute; create. See ELEVATION, PRODUCTION. —*adj.* upright, straight, VERTICAL, perpendicular; uplifted.

erogenous, *adj.* erotic (see SEX).

erosion, *n.* eating *or* wearing away, disintegration. See DETERIORATION, FRICTION.

erotic, *adj.* sexual, sensual; carnal, lascivious; obscene, pornographic; hot, spicy; sexy, raunchy, X-rated (*all sl.*). See IMPURITY, LOVE, SEX.

erotica, *n.* pornography, blue literature, movie, *etc.* See SEX, IMPURITY.

err, *v.t.* mistake, misjudge; nod, slip, go astray, trip, blunder; sin, transgress; fall, wander, stray. See ERROR, BADNESS, IMPROBITY.

errand, *n.* BUSINESS, COMMISSION, mission, charge, task, message; trip.

errant, *adj.* wandering, roving; deviating. See DEVIATION.

erratic, *adj.* abnormal, eccentric, odd, capricious, queer, peculiar; wandering, off course; uncertain, changeable. See CHANGEABLENESS, IRREGULARITY, DEVIATION. *Ant.*, regular, dependable.

erratum, *n.* misprint, ERROR.

ERROR
Deviation from truth

Nouns—1, error, fallacy; falsity (see FALSEHOOD), untruth; misconception, misapprehension, misunderstanding; inexactness, inaccuracy; anachronism; misconstruction, misinterpretation, miscomputation, MISJUDGMENT, misstatement; aberration. See HETERODOXY, WRONG, NEGLECT, UNSKILLFULNESS.

2, mistake, miss, fault, blunder, misadventure; oversight; misprint, erratum; slip, flaw, trip, stumble; slip of the tongue, lapsus linguae, slip of the pen, lapse; solecism; typographical *or* clerical error; malapropism, blooper, metathesis; bull, break; demerit. *Informal,* boner, howler, typo, booboo. *Slang,* clam, chunk.

3, (*mistaken idea*) delusion, illusion, false impression, self-deception; heresy; hallucination, optical illusion (see DECEPTION).

Verbs—1, be erroneous, mislead, misguide, lead astray, lead into error, beguile, misinform, delude, give a false impression, misstate. *Informal,* not add up, not hold up, not hold water.

2, err, be in error, be mistaken, goof, lapse, slip up; mistake, receive a false impression, be in the wrong, stray, not have a leg to stand on; take for; misapprehend, misconceive, misinterpret, misunderstand, miscalculate, misjudge; be at cross purposes, slip up, slip a cog *or* gear. *Informal,* bark up the wrong tree, back the wrong horse, be all wet, throw the baby out with the bathwater, miss by a mile.

3, make a mistake, blunder, put one's foot in one's mouth; misdo, misapply; trip, stumble, lose oneself, go astray; bungle, botch. *Slang,* fuck up, screw up.

Adjectives—1, erroneous, untrue, fallacious; apocryphal, ungrounded; groundless, unsubstantial; heretical, unsound, illogical; unauthenticated; exploded, refuted.

2, inexact, inaccurate, incorrect, ungrammatical, faulty. *Slang,* off, assbackward. See WRONG.

3, *(misleading)* illusive, illusory, delusive; spurious. See DECEPTION.

4, *(having erroneous ideas)* in error, mistaken, aberrant, wide of the mark, out of line, astray, faulty, at fault, on a false scent, at cross purposes. *Slang,* all wet, off-base.

Adverbs—erroneously, wrongly, by error, by mistake; inaccurately, imprecisely.

Phrases—a miss is as good as a mile; there's many a slip 'twixt cup and lip; to err is human (to forgive divine); you cannot make an omelet without breaking [a few] eggs.

Quotations—Truth lies within a little and certain compass, but error is immense (*Lord Bolingbroke*), The man who makes no mistakes does not usually make anything (*Edward John Phelps*), The report of my death was an exaggeration (*Mark Twain*), The weak have one weapon: the errors of those who think they are strong (*Georges Bidault*).

Antonyms, see TRUTH, GRAMMAR.

---

erudite, *adj.* learned, literate, wise; authoritative. See LEARNING, KNOWLEDGE. *Ant.,* ignorant, unschooled.

eruption, *n.* efflorescence, rash; outbreak, commotion; discharge, expulsion. See DISEASE, EGRESS, VIOLENCE.

escalate, *v.* intensify, worsen (see INCREASE).

escalator, *n.* moving staircase. See ELEVATION.

escapade, *n.* jaunt, adventure, prank; frolic, caper, spree. See AMUSEMENT.

ESCAPE
Get away

Nouns—1, escape, elopement, flight; evasion (see AVOIDANCE); retreat; narrow escape *or* squeak, hairbreadth escape; deliverance, LIBERATION; redeployment; jailbreak, freedom. *Informal,* close call *or* shave. *Slang,* getaway, lam, strategic movement to the rear. See RECESSION, DEPARTURE.

2, *(means of escape)* outlet; puncture, aperture; safety valve, fire escape, ladder, parachute; refuge, sanctuary, asylum; lifeboat, life raft; emergency exit, ejection seat, inflatable slide; escape hatch; escape clause, loophole. See SAFETY, EGRESS.

3, *(one who escapes)* refugee, fugitive, escapee, runaway, runagate, deserter, boat person.

4, *(desire to avoid)* escapism, withdrawal, fantasy, flight. See INSANITY.

Verbs—escape, get off, get well out of, save one's bacon, weather the storm; bolt, elope, abscond, defect; evade (see AVOIDANCE); show *or* take to one's heels, beat a retreat, flee, bail out, make oneself scarce, run away *or* off, [make a] run for it, cut and run, steal away, slip off, take off, vamoose; elude, make off, give one the slip, slip through the fingers, dig [oneself] out; wriggle out of; break out *or* loose, make a getaway; get away with, get off easy; find a loophole; drop, draw, fade, *or* fall back, back out. *Informal,* skip out; get away with murder, get off cheap. *Slang,* skedaddle, skiddoo, scarper, take a powder, fly the coop, take it on the lam, lam out, cheese it, blow ass.

Adjectives—escaping, escaped, fled, free, scot-free, at large, well out of; on the run. *Slang,* on the lam, over the hill.

Quotations—I am escaped with the skin of my teeth (*Bible*), Oh, that I had wings like a dove! for then I would fly away, and be at rest (*Bible*), The best way out is always through (*Robert Frost*).

Antonyms, see RESTRAINT.

---

escarpment, *n.* cliff (see HEIGHT).

eschew, *v.t.* shun, avoid (see AVOIDANCE). *Ant.,* pursue.

escort, *v.t.* accompany, conduct, convoy, guard, walk, attend, usher. —*n.* attendant, companion, conductor, convoy,

bodyguard. See SAFETY, ACCOMPANI-
MENT.

esoteric, *adj.* select, mysterious. See SECRET.

espionage, *n.* intelligence, reconnaissance,
investigation; counterespionage, counterintelligence; cloak-and-dagger *or* undercover work. See INQUIRY.

esplanade, *n.* promenade, boardwalk,
quadrangle, mall. See PASSAGE, HORI-
ZONTAL.

espouse, *v.t.* wed; champion, advocate.
See MARRIAGE, SUPPORT.

esprit de corps, Fr. group spirit; morale.
See COURAGE, CHEERFULNESS.

essay, *n.* composition; attempt, effort. *v.t.*
endeavor, try, attempt. See DISSERTA-
TION, EXPERIMENT.

essence, *n.* being, SUBSTANCE, element, entity, reality, nature, life; extract, distillation; perfume; principle, inwardness;
sense, gist, core, kernel, pith, quintessence, heart, purport. See EXTRACTION,
ODOR, IMPORTANCE, INTRINSIC.

essential, *adj.* substantial, material, constitutional, fundamental, elementary,
absolute; necessary, needful, requisite,
cardinal, indispensable, vital; inherent,
INTRINSIC, basic. See NECESSITY, PART,
IMPORTANCE. *Ant.,* inessential, unimportant.

establish, *v.t.* confirm, fix, settle, secure,
set, stabilize; sustain, install, root, ensconce; appoint, enact, ordain; found,
institute, constitute, create, organize,
build, set up; verify, prove, substantiate; determine, decide. See EVIDENCE,
PRODUCTION, STABILITY, DEMONSTRA-
TION, LOCATION.

estate, *n.* state, status, rank, condition, station, DEGREE; property, fortune, possessions, effects, interest, land, holdings;
ABODE. See POSSESSION, CLASS.

esteem, *n.* RESPECT, regard, favor, admiration, estimation, honor; reverence,
worship. See APPROBATION. *Ant.,* despise.

esthetic, *adj. & n.* See AESTHETIC.

estimable, *adj.* meritorious, worthy. See
APPROBATION.

estimate, *v.t.* consider, gauge, judge; value,
appraise, evaluate, rate, assess, measure; compute, reckon, calculate. —*n.*
JUDGMENT, opinion, appraisal, report,
criticism; calculation.

estrange, *v.t.* alienate, separate, withdraw;
fall out, be unfriendly; disunite, part,
wean; transfer. See DISJUNCTION.

estuary, *n.* arm, inlet, firth, fjord; mouth,
delta. See OPENING.

et cetera, and so on, and so forth. See AD-
DITION, ACCOMPANIMENT.

etch, *v.* engrave, incise, scratch, carve, corrode. See ENGRAVING.

eternal, *adj.* perpetual, endless, everlasting, continual, ceaseless; timeless, infinite, unending; incessant, constant;
immortal, imperishable, deathless. See
DURABILITY, PERMANENCE, PERPETU-
ITY. *Ant.,* ephemeral, temporary.

ethereal, *adj.* airy, delicate, light, tenuous,
fragile, fairy; heavenly, celestial, empyreal. See INSUBSTANTIALITY, HEAVEN.
Ant., earthly, mortal.

ethics, *n.* morals, morality, rules of conduct. See DUTY, VIRTUE.

ethnic, *adj.* native, national, indigenous;
cultural, tribal, racial. See INTRINSIC,
HUMANITY.

etiquette, *n.* manners, decorum, custom,
formality, good form. See FASHION.

Eucharist, *n.* Communion, mass, vi-
aticum, sacrament. See RITE.

eulogize, *v.t.* praise, compliment, celebrate, glorify, laud, panegyrize, extol.
See APPROBATION.

euphoria, *n.* elation, high spirits, PLEA-
SURE, well-being; the pink of condition,
high (*sl.*). See CONTENT.

euthanasia, *n.* mercy killing (see DEATH,
KILLING).

evacuate, *v.t.* empty, clear; eject, expel,
purge; discharge, excrete, defecate,
void, emit; leave, quit, vacate. See DE-
PARTURE, EJECTION, EXCRETION.

evade, *v.t.* avoid, elude; dodge, shun; baffle, foil, parry; ESCAPE, slip away; ignore, violate, NEGLECT; equivocate. See
AVOIDANCE.

evaluate, *v.t.* value, appraise, estimate, assess, PRICE. See MEASUREMENT.

evanesce, *v.i.* disappear, fade away. See
DISAPPEARANCE.

evangelical, *adj.* proselytizing, apostolic,
missionary. See RELIGION, SACRED
WRITINGS.

evaporate, *v.* emanate, pass off, escape;
vaporize, distill; condense, solidify, dehydrate, desiccate; vanish, disappear.

See DRYNESS, INSUBSTANTIALITY, VAPOR, TRANSIENTNESS.

evasion, *n.* elusion, AVOIDANCE, ESCAPE; equivocation; trick, subterfuge. See NONPAYMENT.

even, *adj.* level, equal, smooth, flat, flush, uniform, regular, unvaried, parallel; equable, even-tempered, unruffled, placid; equitable, fair, impartial, just; straightforward, plain, direct; abreast, alongside; true, plumb, straight. See HORIZONTAL, EQUALITY, STRAIGHTNESS, SMOOTHNESS. **—break even,** see EQUALITY. **—get even,** retaliate (see RETALIATION).

even-handed, *adj.* impartial, equitable, fair. See JUSTICE.

evening, *n.* dusk, nightfall, eventide, close of day; gloaming, twilight; sundown, sunset; curfew; eve, even (*poetic*); decline, old age, sunset years. See DIMNESS, TIME, AGE.

event, *n.* OCCASION, OCCURRENCE, happening; affair, episode, incident; gala affair *or* occasion, holiday; experience; circumstance, issue, outcome, result.

eventful, *adj.* bustling; momentous. See OCCURRENCE, IMPORTANCE.

eventual, *adj.* final, ultimate, coming; contingent. See FUTURITY, CHANCE, EFFECT.

ever, *adv.* always, at all times, eternally, perpetually, incessantly, continually, constantly, forever, evermore; once, at any time; in any case, at all. See DURABILITY, PERPETUITY.

everlasting, *adj.* unending, never-ending, without end; ageless, sempiternal; constant, ceaseless, wearisome, perpetual, continual, incessant. See PERPETUITY, DURABILITY.

every, *adj.* each, all; complete, entire. See GENERALITY.

everybody, *n.* everyone, one and all (see WHOLE, GENERALITY). *Ant.,* no one.

everyday, *adj.* habitual, usual, routine, workaday. See HABIT, MEDIOCRITY.

everyone, *n.* everybody, *tout le monde.* See GENERALITY. *Ant.,* no one.

everything, *n.* all, all and sundry, the WHOLE. *Ant.,* nothing.

everywhere, *adv.* wherever; all over, far and wide. See SPACE. *Ant.,* nowhere.

evict, *v.t.* eject, oust, remove, expel, put out, dispossess. See EJECTION.

EVIDENCE
Means of proving

Nouns—1, evidence, facts, premises, data, grounds, DEMONSTRATION, confirmation, corroboration, support, ratification, authentication, acknowledgment, proof; state's, king's, queen's, oral, documentary, hearsay, external, extrinsic, internal, intrinsic, circumstantial, ex parte, presumptive, collateral, *or* constructive evidence; clue; control. See LAWSUIT, TRUTH.

2, testimony, attestation, declaration, deposition, [sworn] statement, AFFIRMATION; examination; exhibit.

3, (*written evidence*) citation, reference, authority, warrant, credential, testimonial; diploma, voucher, affidavit, certificate, INDICATION; RECORD, document; signature, seal, identification. See PROMISE.

4, physical evidence, proof, DEMONSTRATION. *Informal,* smoking gun.

5, witness, indicator, eyewitness, deponent, sponsor, [innocent] bystander, testifier, attestor, onlooker.

Verbs—1, evidence, evince, manifest, display, exhibit, show; betoken, tell of, indicate, denote, imply, argue, bespeak; have *or* carry weight, tell, speak volumes, speak for itself; hold up.

2, rest *or* depend upon; bear witness, give evidence, testify, depose, witness, vouch for; sign, seal, set one's hand and seal, certify, attest, acknowledge. *Informal,* make out.

3, confirm, ratify, corroborate, support, bear out, uphold, warrant, establish, authenticate, prove, cite chapter and verse, substantiate, verify, validate, demonstrate, lend *or* give color to; beg the question. *Informal,* see the color of one's money.

4, *(present evidence)* adduce, attest, cite, quote, refer, bring into court; produce witnesses; collect evidence, examine, make out a case; have *or* get the goods on one.

Adjectives—evidential, documentary; indicative, indicatory, deducible; grounded on, founded on, based on, corroborative, confirmatory; supportive, authentic, conclusive; circumstantial, by inference, according to, a fortiori, prima facie.

Phrases—facts are stubborn things.

Quotations—If it walks like a duck, and quacks like a duck, then it just may be a duck (*Walter Reuther*).

Antonyms, see NEGATION, CONFUTATION.

---

evident, *adj.* apparent, plain, obvious, distinct; broad, unmistakable, palpable, patent, open, manifest, clear; downright, overt, indubitable. See APPEARANCE, CERTAINTY, DEMONSTRATION, VISIBILITY.

EVIL
Immorality

Nouns—1, *(something evil)* evil, ill, harm, hurt; mischief, nuisance; disadvantage, drawback; disaster, casualty, mishap, misfortune, calamity, catastrophe, tragedy, ADVERSITY; abomination, peccancy, atrocity, crime against humanity, bane, curse, scourge, Jonah; evil eye, curse. *Informal,* jinx, [double] whammy. *Slang,* bad news. See IMPROBITY.

2, *(evil quality)* BADNESS, wickedness, sin, vice, iniquity, IMPIETY, immorality, corruption, weakness of the flesh, moral infirmity *or* turpitude, depravity, degeneracy, profligacy. See MALEVOLENCE.

3, *(evil act)* outrage, WRONG, injury, foul play; bad *or* ill turn; disservice, spoliation, grievance, crying evil.

4, den of iniquity, Sodom, Gomorrah; sewer, pit, gutter. *Slang,* the pits. See IMPURITY.

5, see EVILDOER.

Verbs—1, be *or* do evil, sin, harm, hurt, injure, wrong, outrage, dishonor, victimize; stray [from the paths of righteousness], go wrong, err; degenerate, fall [from grace], lapse; relapse.

2, turn to evil, deprave, demoralize, send to the dogs; defile, sully.

Adjectives—1, evil, bad, ill, sinful, peccant, wicked, wrong, vicious, immoral, corrupt, degenerate, depraved, dissolute; unrighteous, unvirtuous; diabolical (see DEMON); fallen, lapsed; callous, hardhearted.

2, harmful, hurtful, noisome, injurious; malevolent; prejudicial, disastrous.

Adverbs—evilly, badly, *etc.*; amiss, wrong, ill, to one's cost.

Phrases—never do evil that good may come of it; two wrongs don't make a right; sufficient unto the day is the evil thereof.

Quotations—Men loved darkness rather than light, because their deeds were evil (*Bible*), The evil that men do lives after them, the good is oft interrèd with their bones (*Shakespeare*), It is necessary only for the good man to do nothing for evil to triumph (*Edmund Burke*), Men alone are quite capable of every wickedness (*Joseph Conrad*), The face of "evil" is always the face of total need (*William S. Burroughs*), Pity the criminal all you like, but don't call evil good (*Fyodor Dostoyevsky*), All human evil comes from this: a man's being unable to sit still in a room (*Pascal*).

Antonyms, see GOODNESS.

EVILDOER
Transgressor

Nouns—1, evildoer; sinner, transgressor, profligate, libertine; oppressor, despot, tyrant (see AUTHORITY); incendiary, anarchist, destroyer, vandal, iconoclast, terrorist; arsonist. *Informal,* bad guy, firebug.

2, a. savage, brute, ruffian, barbarian, caitiff, desperado; godfather, bully, rough, hooligan, hoodlum, gangster, mafioso, good fellow, tough, plug-ugly, hellion, gorilla; fraud, swindler, confidence man, thief (see STEALING); murderer, gunman, killer (see KILLING); villain, miscreant, rascal, knave, cad, scalawag, rogue, badman, scapegrace, rowdy, scamp, apache; pimp, procurer, whoremaster, white slaver; criminal, felon, convict (see PRISON); delinquent, troublemaker; forger; black sheep, blackguard, prodigal son, fallen angel, ne'er-do-well. *Informal,* bad news, perp. *Slang,* hood, mobster; bad actor, cad, cunt, beast, nonce, buck, homeboy, ratfink, scumsucker, shag, skinhead, torpedo. **b.** hag, beldam[e], Jezebel, jade, nag, shrew, fishwife; murderess; ogress, harpy, Fury, maenad; adulteress, paramour, mistress; prostitute, whore (see IMPURITY); dragon, harridan, vixen, virago; witch, siren, Circe, Delilah, Medusa, Gorgon; enchantress, sorceress. *Slang,* megabitch.

3, monster, fiend, DEMON, devil, devil incarnate, fiend in human shape; Frankenstein's monster; cannibal, bloodsucker, vampire, ghoul, vulture, ogre.

4, *(traitor)* culprit, offender, malefactor; recidivist; traitor, betrayer, Judas [Iscariot], Benedict Arnold, Quisling; conspirator, snake in the grass; turncoat, renegade, apostate; informer. *Slang,* rat, squealer, bad *or* rotten egg, bad actor. See IMPROBITY.

Quotations—The soul of a murderer is blind (*Albert Camus*), He that hides a dark soul, and foul thoughts . . . himself is his own dungeon (*John Milton*), All men that are ruined are ruined on the side of their natural propensities (*Edmund Burke*).

        Antonyms, see GOODNESS, BENEVOLENCE.

---

evince, *v.t.* exhibit, display, show, manifest, evidence, demonstrate, disclose, indicate, prove. See DEMONSTRATION.

eviscerate, *v.t.* disembowel. See EXTRACTION, WEAKNESS.

evoke, *v.t.* draw forth, summon, invoke; envision, imagine; suggest, bring to mind; produce, CAUSE. See EXCITEMENT.

evolution, *n.* evolvement, unfolding, growth, expansion, development, elaboration; Darwinism, natural selection; mutation. See CHANGE, IMPROVEMENT.

exacerbate, *v.* aggravate, intensify, worsen; enrage, embitter, irritate, vex. See INCREASE, RESENTMENT.

exact, *v.t.* require, claim, demand; extort, take, wring, wrest, force, impose. See COMMAND, COMPULSION. —*adj.* strict, rigorous; accurate, precise, delicate, nice, fine, correct, literal, verbatim; faithful, lifelike, close; definite, absolute, direct. See RIGHTNESS, SIMILARITY, TRUTH. *Ant.,* approximate.

EXAGGERATION
False magnification

Nouns—**1,** exaggeration, magnification, overstatement, inflation, puffing up, hyperbole, stretch, strain, [high *or* false] coloring, caricature, extravagance. See DISTORTION, FIGURATIVE.

2, Baron Munchausen; fringe, embroidery, traveler's tale, yarn, tall story *or* tale, overestimation; overreaction, tempest in a teapot, much ado about nothing; puffery, BOASTING, rant; travesty, caricature; figure of speech, stretch of the imagination, bananas on bananas; flight of fancy. *Informal,* bloatware, overkill. *Slang,* California *or* Chicago bankroll.

3, exaggerator, puff artist. *Slang,* butter-and-egg man.

Verbs—exaggerate, magnify, pile up, amplify, build up, expand, overestimate, hyperbolize; gild *or* paint the lily; overstate, overdraw, overpraise, overshoot the mark, strain, stretch, strain *or* stretch a point, spin a long yarn, make a mountain out of a molehill; draw the longbow, run riot, glorify, heighten, overcolor, embellish, enhance, embroider, misrepresent, puff, boast, turn geese into swans; bite off more than one can chew. *Informal,* carry on, put on, lay it on [thick *or* with a trowel], make a federal case out of it.

Adjectives—exaggerated, overwrought; bombastic, florid, flowery, magniloquent, high-flown, hyperbolical, fabulous, extravagant, preposterous; egregious, outré; high-flying, tall, steep. *Slang,* maxed out.

Phrases—all mouth and trousers. *Slang,* all piss and wind.

Quotations—The report of my death was an exaggeration (*Mark Twain*), Excess on occasion is exhilarating. It prevents moderation from acquiring the deadening effect of habit (*W. Somerset Maugham*), That was laid on with a trowel (*Shakespeare*), An exaggeration is a truth that has lost its temper (*Kahlil Gibran*).

Antonyms, see TRUTH, MODESTY, DETRACTION.

---

exalt, *v.t.* elevate, raise, lift up, dignify, honor; praise, glorify, magnify, extol, aggrandize, elate, uplift; intensify, heighten. See APPROBATION, REPUTE, INCREASE. *Ant.,* abase.

examination, *n.* test; midterm, final; physical [examination], exam (*inf.*). See INQUIRY.

examine, *v.t.* investigate, inspect, survey, prove, canvass, search; scrutinize, peruse, dissect, scan; test, interrogate, try, question; audit, review. See ATTENTION, INQUIRY, EVIDENCE.

example, *n.* sample, specimen, piece; instance, case, illustration; pattern, type, standard, copy, model, idea; precedent; warning; problem, exercise. See CONFORMITY, IMITATION.

exasperate, *v.t.* anger, enrage, infuriate; irritate, vex, nettle, provoke, roil, peeve, annoy. See RESENTMENT.

ex cathedra, *Lat.* from the seat of AUTHORITY. See CERTAINTY.

excavation, *n.* cavity, hole, pit, mine, shaft, quarry, opening. See CONCAVITY.

exceed, *v.t.* transcend, surpass, excel, outdo, outstrip, beat; overstep, pass, overdo, go beyond. See SUPERIORITY. *Ant.,* fall short of.

exceedingly, *adv., informal,* extremely. See SUPERIORITY.

excel, *v.* exceed, surpass, eclipse, outdo, outstrip. See UNCONFORMITY, VIRTUE, GOODNESS.

except, *prep.* unless, saving, save, but, excepting, barring. See UNCONFORMITY, CIRCUMSTANCE, DEDUCTION.

exception, *n.* EXCLUSION, omission, rejection, reservation, limitation; objection, cavil, complaint; irregularity. See DISAPPROBATION, UNCONFORMITY, DISSENT, EXEMPTION, QUALIFICATION. —**take exception,** object, demur (see DISAPPROBATION).

exceptionable, *adj.* objectionable. See DISAPPROBATION.

exceptional, *adj.* abnormal; unusual, uncommon, extraordinary, rare; special, superior. See UNCONFORMITY, SPECIALITY. *Ant.,* common, ordinary.

excerpt, *n.* extract, quote, citation, selection; sentence, verse, section, passage. See PART.

excess, *n.* immoderation, INTEMPERANCE, dissipation, indulgence; superabundance, superfluity, extravagance, exorbitance; redundance, REMAINDER. See SUFFICIENCY. *Ant.,* moderation.

excessive, *adj.* immoderate, inordinate, extravagant, exorbitant, unreasonable, outrageous; superfluous, extreme. See DEARNESS.

exchange, *n.* reciprocity, substitution; trade, BARTER, commerce; conversion, INTERCHANGE; market. See BUSINESS, TRANSFER.

excise, *n.* tax, duty (see PAYMENT). —*v.t.* delete, expunge (see DEDUCTION).

EXCITABILITY
Capability to be stimulated

Nouns—1, excitability, impetuosity, impatience, intolerance; irritability (see IRASCIBILITY); disquiet[ude], AGITATION, jitters, cold sweat. *Slang,* heebie-jeebies, shakes, shivers, ants in one's pants. See SENSIBILITY, FEELING.

2, (*act of excitement*) VIOLENCE, fierceness, rage, mania, madness (see INSANITY), frenzy, hysterics, fanaticism, mass hysteria. *Slang,* wilding.

3, hothead, madcap; nervous Nellie, nervous wreck, bundle of nerves. *Informal,* Type A. *Slang,* headbanger.

Verbs—1, be excitable *or* impatient, champ at the bit, be in a stew, fidget, toss, jump, twitch, jerk, jitter, have the jitters; choke up.

2, lose one's temper, burst out; fly *or* go off [at a tangent]; explode, flare up, burn; boil [over], foam, fume, seethe, rage, rave, rant, have a fit, run wild, go mad; go into hysterics; run riot, run amuck, go off half-cocked; climb the wall, go off the deep end, go overboard. *Slang,* get one's goat; fly off the handle, flip one's lid, blow one's top *or* one's mind; push the panic button, have kittens, wig out.

Adjectives—1, excitable, seething, hot, boiling, burning; impatient, intolerant; feverish, frenzied, febrile, hysterical, unstrung; highstrung, mettlesome, jumpy, nervous, jittery, edgy, on edge, on pins and needles; skittish; mercurial (see CHANGEABLENESS); impulsive, impetuous, tempestuous, passionate, uncontrolled, ungovernable, irrepressible, madcap. *Informal,* flappable. *Slang,* uptight, goosey, strung out, untied, unglued, unravelled, unstuck, unstrung, unwrapped, all shook up, ape-shit.

2, violent, wild, fierce, fiery, hotheaded, irritable, irascible; demonstrative, boisterous, enthusiastic, impassioned, fanatical, rabid.

Antonyms, see INEXCITABILITY.

EXCITEMENT
State of being excited

Nouns—1, excitement, excitation; stimulation, piquancy, provocation, arousal, incitement; animation, AGITATION, perturbation; intoxication, high pressure; exhilaration, passion, thrill, flame. *Informal,* charge, boot, jolt, charge, kick. *Slang,* high, buzz, rush, jollies. See VIOLENCE.

2, *(excited situation)* fever, commotion, to-do, buzz, dither, fluster, bustle, hurlyburly, hullabaloo, pandemonium, furor[e], upheaval, frenzy, alarums and excursions; rut, orgasm (see SEX). *Informal,* tizzy, lather.

3, EXCITABILITY, turbulence; exuberance, effervescence, ebullition.

Verbs—1, *(excite to action)* excite, move; strike, interest, animate, enliven, inspire, impassion, stir *or* warm the blood; awaken, evoke, provoke; raise, arouse, stir; fire, get going, [en]kindle, set on fire, inflame, fan the flames, heat, warm, foment, raise to fever heat. *Slang,* rev up, jazz up, rattle someone's cage, yank someone around *or* someone's chain.

2, *(make excited)* stimulate, inspirit, stir up, elate, work up, sharpen, spice, whet, incite, give a fillip, put on one's mettle; stir *or* play on the feelings; touch a chord, go to one's heart, touch to the quick; intoxicate, electrify, turn one's head, carry *or* sweep off one's feet, carry away, warm the blood. *Slang,* turn on.

3, be excited, flare up, catch fire; flush, pale, turn color; work oneself up, lose one's grip; seethe, boil, simmer, foam, fume, rage, rave (see EXCITABILITY). *Informal,* race one's motor, blow one's top. *Slang,* flip [out], get off on, cream one's jeans, wig out, go ape, go bananas, freak out.

Adjectives—1, excited; worked, keyed, *or* wrought up, on the qui vive, in a quiver, in a fever, in hysterics; black in the face, overwrought; hit, flushed, feverish; all atwitter; flaming, boiling [over], ebullient, seething, foaming [at the mouth], fuming, raging; wild, frantic, mad, hectic, distracted, beside oneself, out of one's mind *or* wits, ready to burst, stung to the quick. *Informal,* hot and bothered, gung ho, antsy. *Slang,* switched on, ape-shit.

2, exciting, warm, glowing, fervid, swelling, heart-stirring, thrilling; striking; soul-stirring, spine-tingling, agonizing, sensational, hysterical; overpowering, overwhelming, piquant, spicy, heady, provocative, tantalizing. *Informal,* mind-blowing, happening.

Adverbs—excitedly, excitingly, in a dither, all agog; with bated breath.

Quotations—Chaos often breeds life, when order breeds habit (*Henry Adams*), It is not merely cruelty that leads men to love war, it is excitement (*Henry Ward Beecher*).

Antonyms, see INDIFFERENCE, INEXCITABILITY.

exclaim, *v.* cry out, shout, ejaculate, clamor, vociferate; exclaim *or* inveigh against, denounce, condemn. See CRY, SPEECH, DISAPPROBATION.

EXCLUSION
Act of excluding

Nouns—1, exclusion, omission, exception, REJECTION, relegation; preclusion, elimination, DISPLACEMENT; separation, discrimination, exclusiveness, insularity; segregation, apartheid; quarantine, isolation, ostracism; redlining, disinvestment; xenophobia, parochialism; ethnocentrism; PROHIBITION; exile, deportation, banishment, EJECTION; purge. *Informal,* gólden exile.

2, clan, clique (see PARTY); outsider, outcast, untouchable, children of God, persona non grata; foreigner, alien, expatriate; silent treatment, blacklist. *Slang,* shit list.

Verbs—exclude, [de]bar; prohibit, preclude; freeze out, edge out; leave out, rule *or* count out, reject, blackball; lay, put, *or* set aside; relegate, pass over, omit, eliminate, weed out, throw over, throw overboard; strike out; separate, segregate, isolate, insulate, ostracize, weed out; displace; blacklist, redline, disinvest; keep *or* shut out, except; exile, banish, deport, eject. *Informal,* count out, blackball, leave out in the cold, drum out, freeze out. See DEDUCTION.

Adjectives—exclusive, cliquish, clannish; closed; sole, unique; one and only, barring all others; exclusory, exclusive, prohibitive; select, restrictive; excluded, left out, isolated, solitary, banished, inadmissible, unacceptable; segregated, quarantined, isolated, ghettoized; insular, xenophobic, parochial, ethnocentric.

Prepositions—exclusive of, outside of, barring, except; with the exception of; save. *Informal,* outside of.

Quotations—Everywhere I see bliss, from which I alone am irrevocably excluded (*Mary Shelley*).

Antonyms, see INCLUSION.

---

excommunicate, *v.t.* expel, curse, unchurch. See EJECTION.

excoriate, *v.t.* denounce, censure; skin, pare. See CONDEMNATION, DIVESTMENT.

excrement, *n.* See EXCRETION.

excrescence, *n.* outgrowth, protuberance, appendage. See CONVEXITY.

EXCRETION
Act of discharging

Nouns—1, excretion, discharge, elimination, exhalation, exudation, extrusion, ejaculation, effusion, egestion, extravasation, evacuation, dejection, defecation, urination, micturition; secretion, lactation, lacrimation. See EJECTION, SEX, CLEANNESS.

2, *(something excreted)* a. bodily fluid, perspiration, sweat, lather, sweat of one's brow, underarm wetness. b. bowel movement, BM, easement; stool, waste, ejecta, dejecta, excreta, offal, feces, fecal matter, excrement[um], diarrhea, flux, dysentery. *Slang,* trots, runs; shit, turd, caca, poo-poo, crap[ola], clinkers, dingleberry, clart, number two; night soil. c. urine, water, urea. *Slang,* pee-pee, number one, lant. d. pus, suppuration, gleet, ichor. e. hemorrhage, bleeding, flux; nosebleed. f. menstruation, menses, monthlies, period; menstrual flux. *Informal,* the curse. g. *(animal waste)* dung, manure; droppings, pellets, guano; cow-pie, dog-doo. *Slang,* birdshit; buffalo chip, prairie fuel, alley *or* road apple, cow chip, calling card.

3, *(something secreted)* a. mucus, catarrh, phlegm. *Slang,* boogie, bugger, bugaboo, snot, oyster. b. adrenaline, bile, epinephrine, hormone, melatonin, pancreatic juice, sweat. c. vaginal secretion, female spendings. *Slang,* cunt juice. d. saliva, rheum, sputum, spittle, spit, salivation, catarrh. e. semen, sexual discharge. *Slang,* come [off], cum, jism, junk, jizz, wad, joy juice, load, milk, paste, honey, butter, spooge.

4, toilet (see CLEANNESS).

5, gland (see BODY).

Verbs—1, **a.** excrete, eject, discharge, emit; extrude, effuse, extravasate; cast off. **b.** vacuate, void, defecate, have a bowel movement, ease nature *or* oneself. *Informal,* go to the bathroom. *Slang,* shit, poop, dump, crap, take a shit, dump, *or* crap, drop one's load, fill one's pants, clart, cuck, do number two. **c.** urinate, make *or* pass water. *Informal,* relieve oneself, retire, answer nature's call, go to Egypt, powder one's nose, see a man about a dog, wash up, go to the washroom *or* bathroom, make a pit stop, shake the dew off the lily; wet [the bed, *etc.*]. *Slang,* piss, splash, whiz, go pee-pee, take a leak *or* piss, piddle, squirt, take a whiz, tinkle, kill a tree. **d.** perspire, sweat, exude, break out in a sweat *or* a lather. **e.** suppurate, fester, run. **f.** hemorrhage, bleed. **g.** menstruate, have one's period *or* monthlies.

2, secrete, produce; lactate, salivate, dribble, slaver, drool, expectorate, spit, spew; ejaculate, make one's love come down. *Slang,* come, cum, juice, melt, shoot one's wad, cream [one's jeans], get *or* come off, get one's rocks *or* nuts off.

Adjectives—1, excretive, excretory, ejective, eliminative; fecal, urinary; sweaty; suppurative, festering, pussy, purulent; sweaty, clammy, drenched *or* bathed in sweat, sudorific; bloody; menstrual.

2, secretory, lactational, salivary, lachrymal, seminal; glandular, hormonal, endrocine, pancreatic.

Antonyms, see RECEIVING.

---

excruciating, *adj.* torturing, painful, agonizing, racking, acute. See PAIN.

exculpate, *v.t.* exonerate (see VINDICATION). *Ant.,* convict.

excursion, *n.* expedition, trip, sally, tour, outing, journey, jaunt; digression, DEVIATION, TRAVEL.

excuse, *v.t.* pardon, remit, overlook, condone, forgive, extenuate, justify; exonerate, absolve, acquit, exempt, free, apologize. See VINDICATION, EXEMPTION, FORGIVENESS.

execrable, *adj.* abominable, bad, detestable; poor, inferior, wretched. See BADNESS.

execute, *v.t.* perform, do, accomplish, make, administer, enforce, effect; finish, complete, fulfill; kill, put to death, behead, lynch, hang, gas, electrocute; enact; seal, sign. See COMPLETION, PUNISHMENT, ACTION, AGENCY, CONDUCT.

executive, *n.* DIRECTOR, manager, official, administrator, brass (*sl.*).

exemplary, *adj.* commendable; model; typical, illustrative. See APPROBATION, CONFORMITY.

exemplify, *v.t.* typify; illustrate, explain, quote. See CONFORMITY.

exempli gratia, Lat. for example; e.g. See CONFORMITY.

EXEMPTION
Freedom from obligation

Nouns—exemption, FREEDOM, immunity, impunity, privilege, liberty, release, excuse, dispensation, exception, benefit of clergy, executive privilege, absolution, discharge; [bill, act, covenant, *or* deed of] indemnity. See PERMISSION, UNCONFORMITY.

Verbs—exempt, release, discharge, liberate, free, set at liberty; indemnify; let off, pass over, spare, excuse, dispense with, give dispensation; stretch a point.

Adjectives—1, exempt, free, at liberty, scot-free, released, unbound, unencumbered, unaccountable, not answerable, immune, privileged, excusable, off the hook.

2, not having, devoid of, destitute of, without, unpossessed of, unblest with, exempt from, off one's hands; tax-free, untaxed, untaxable, tax-exempt.

Antonyms, see LIABILITY, DUTY.

---

exercise, *n.* drill (see EXERTION); (*pl.*) ceremonies (see RITE). —*v.* perform, USE; train, drill; disturb (see DISCONTENT).

EXERTION
Physical effort
Nouns—1, exertion, ENERGY, effort, strain, tug, pull, stretch, struggle, trouble, pains, endeavor, ACTION; work ethic.

2, *(physical exercises)* **a.** gymnastics, athletics, acrobatics; ariel, backflip, balance beam, dismount, flip, floor exercise, freestyle, handspring, handstand, high bar, horizontal bar, horse, Indian club, iron cross, parallel bars, pommel horse, rings, somersault, springboard, straddle, tilt board, trapeze, tuck, twist, uneven bars, vault, vaulting horse, walkover. **b.** calisthenics, exercise, workout, dancercise; training, sport, play, drill, daily dozen, warm-up, sitting-up exercises, jumping jack, pull- *or* push-up, roadwork, scissors, setting-up exercises.

3, *(physical·labor)* workforce; labor, work, toil, task, travail, manual labor, sweat of one's brow, elbow grease, wear and tear, toil and trouble, yeoman work, uphill work, drudgery, slavery, heavy duty, run for one's money. *Informal,* daylighting.

4, laborer, worker, toiler, drudge, slave; workhorse, packhorse, galley slave, Trojan; carny, roustabout, odd-job man, contingent worker, seasonal employee, migrant worker; exerciser; gymnast; human resources. *Informal,* temp. *Slang,* workaholic, workaphile; obligate runner, redneck.

Verbs—1, exert oneself, put one's back to it, go to *or* take the trouble, set *or* put one's hand to, roll up one's sleeves, strive, strain, pull, tug, ply, struggle, try; lay, fall, *or* turn to; fall over oneself, fall over backward, sink one's teeth into, go out of one's way, go the extra mile, knock oneself out, go for broke. *Informal,* go gangbusters.

2, labor, work, toil, moil, sweat, plug, plod, drudge, slave; buckle down, dig in, bear down, wade into, come to grips; put one's back into, put one's shoulder to the wheel, lay, sail, *or* pitch into; work like a horse; burn the candle at both ends; work one's fingers to the bone, keep one's nose to the grindstone, persevere, take pains, do one's best, bend over backward, strain every nerve, spare no pains, move heaven and earth, burn oneself out, work like a beaver, work one's fingers to the bone; work off; hammer out (see PRODUCTION). *Slang,* sweat blood, go to town, blow one's brains out, break one's neck, burn the midnight oil, bust one's buns.

3, exercise, work out, warm up, train, drill. *Informal,* aerobicize.

Adjectives—laboring; laborious; strained, toilsome, troublesome, wearisome, uphill, Herculean; hardworking, painstaking, strenuous, energetic; workaday.

Adverbs—laboriously, lustily; with might and main, with all one's might, tooth and nail, hammer and tongs, heart and soul; by the sweat of one's brow; energetically. *Informal,* like mad.

Phrases—the laborer is worthy of his hire; if a thing's worth doing, it's worth doing well; many hands make light work; where bees are busy, there is honey; a woman's work is never done; diligence is the mother of good luck; practice makes perfect; Saturday's child works hard for its living.

Quotations—If any would not work, neither should he eat (*Bible*), By working faithfully eight hours a day, you may eventually get to be a boss and work twelve hours a day (*Robert Frost*), I like work: it fascinates me. I can sit and look at it for hours (*Jerome K. Jerome*), Work is the curse of the drinking classes (*Oscar Wilde*), Work is love made visible (*Kahlil Gibran*), Work expands so as to fill the time available for its completion (*C. Northcote Parkinson*), It takes all the running you can do to keep in the same place (*Lewis Carroll*), There are no gains without pains (*Adlai Stevenson*).

Antonyms, see REPOSE.

---

exhale, *v.t.* breathe, expel, emanate, emit, expire, transpire, respire, blow. See EXCRETION, WIND, ODOR. *Ant.,* inhale.

exhaust, *v.t.* drain, empty, let out, deflate; weaken, deplete, overtire, prostrate, fag, fatigue; spend, consume, USE, expend; develop, finish, end. See COMPLETION, WEARINESS.

exhibit, *v.* show, present, display, produce, demonstrate, stage, expose, evince; reveal; flaunt. See EVIDENCE, OSTENTATION.

exhibition, *n.* display, demonstration; parade, spectacle. See DEMONSTRATION, DISCLOSURE.

exhilarate, *v.t.* elate, exalt, inspirit; enliven, animate, cheer, make merry, invigorate, gladden. See CHEERFULNESS.

exhort, *v.* incite, urge, prompt, admonish, egg on (*inf.*). See ADVICE, WARNING, CAUSE.

exhume, *v.t.* dig up, disinter, excavate; discover, locate; call up, recall. See MEMORY, DISCLOSURE, PAST.

exigency, *n.* demand, need, NECESSITY, distress, DIFFICULTY, extremity, urgency, pressure, pinch, crisis, emergency, juncture. See CIRCUMSTANCE.

exiguous, *adj.* meager, scanty, small (see INSUFFICIENCY).

exile, *v.i.* expel, remove, banish, expatriate. See DISPLACEMENT, EJECTION, EXCLUSION, SECLUSION.

EXISTENCE
State of being

Nouns—1, existence, LIFE, being, entity, ens, esse, subsistence, PRESENCE; ontology, existentialism.

2, *(fact of existence)* reality, actuality, authenticity; positiveness, fact, matter of fact, TRUTH; simple, cold, bald, *or* stubborn fact; premise; not a dream, no joke, sober reality, actual existence; historicity. *Informal,* what's what, nitty-gritty, grim reality.

3, details, particulars, data, facts. *Informal,* dope, scoop.

Verbs—exist, be; have being, subsist, live, breathe; stand, obtain, be the case; consist in, lie in, have place, prevail, endure, find oneself; vegetate, come alive *or* to life; come *or* bring into existence (see OCCURRENCE).

Adjectives—1, existing, existent, extant; in existence, current, prevalent.

2, real, actual, positive, absolute, authentic, true; big *or* large as life, big as life and twice as natural; in person, in the flesh; matter-of-fact; substantial, substantive, enduring, well-founded.

Adverbs—actually, really, truly, positively, in fact, in point of fact, for that matter, in reality, indeed, de facto, ipso facto; as far as that goes *or* is concerned.

Quotations—I summed up all systems in a phrase, and all existence in an epigram (*Oscar Wilde*), The cradle rocks above an abyss, and common sense tells us that our existence is but a brief crack of light between two eternities of darkness (*Vladimir Nabokov*), What is hope? nothing but the paint on the face of Existence (*Lord Byron*), Consciousness . . . is the phenomenon whereby the universe's very existence is made known (*Roger Penrose*).

Antonyms, see NONEXISTENCE.

---

exit, *n.* DEPARTURE, withdrawal. See EGRESS.

exodus, *n.* DEPARTURE, flight, migration, EGRESS, issue.

ex officio, Lat. by right of office. See AUTHORITY, LEGALITY.

exonerate, *v.t.* exculpate, free, clear, absolve, acquit. See VINDICATION, ACQUITTAL.

exorbitant, *adj.* excessive, immoderate, inordinate, unreasonable; extravagant,

expensive, dear. See DEARNESS. *Ant.,* modest, reasonable.

exorcise, *v.t.* expel, drive *or* cast out; adjure, conjure. See SORCERY.

exotic, *adj.* foreign, alien; strange, outlandish, outré, bizarre, rare; vivid, colorful, extravagant. See UNCONFORMITY.

expanse, *n.* stretch, spread, reach, extent, BREADTH. See SPACE.

EXPANSION
Act of expanding

Nouns—expansion, INCREASE, enlargement, extension, augmentation, amplification, dilation, aggrandizement, spread, growth, development, turgescence, turgidness, turgidity; obesity, dropsy, tumefaction, tumescence, flare, swell[ing], tumor, tumidity; diastole, distension; puffiness, inflation; overgrowth, hypertrophy; blowup. See ADDITION, ELASTICITY, SPACE.

Verbs—1, expand, widen, enlarge, extend, grow, augment, INCREASE, swell, mushroom, fill out; dilate; deploy; stretch, spread, flare, bell; spring up, bud, burgeon, sprout, put forth, open, burst forth, gain flesh, flesh out *or* up; draw out; outgrow, overrun, be larger than.

2, aggrandize, distend, develop, amplify, blow up, widen, inflate, stuff, pad, cram, exaggerate; fatten.

Adjectives—expanded, larger, swollen, expansive, extensive, widespread, overgrown, exaggerated, bloated, fat, turgid, tumid, hypertrophied, potbellied; obese, puffy, distended, bulbous, full-blown, full-grown, big, developed.

Antonyms, see CONTRACTION.

---

ex parte, *Lat.* from one side only. See MISJUDGMENT, EVIDENCE.

expatiate, *v.i.* enlarge, descant, dilate, expand; rant. See DIFFUSENESS.

expatriate, *n.* exile, displaced person; exurbanite. See DISPLACEMENT, EGRESS.

EXPECTATION
Expectancy

Nouns—1, expectation, expectancy, anticipation, reckoning, calculation, foresight, PREDICTION, imminence, contingency; contemplation, lookout, prospect, outlook, perspective, horizon. See DESTINY, INTUITION, FUTURITY.

2, *(concern about future possibility)* suspense, waiting, anxiety, presentiment; apprehension, pessimism, dread; HOPE, BELIEF, faith. *Slang,* edge city.

Verbs—1, expect, look for, look out for, look forward to; hope for, anticipate, figure *or* plan on, take in stride; have in prospect, keep in view, wait *or* watch for, keep a sharp lookout for, await; bide one's time, hold one's breath, hang on; foresee, prepare for, predict, second-guess, count upon, believe in, take for granted, think likely, bargain for *or* in; push *or* press one's luck.

2, be expected, be in store, be just around the corner.

3, fulfill one's expectations, come as no surprise.

Adjectives—1, expectant, expecting; openmouthed, agape, all agog; ready, curious, eager, anxious, apprehensive, on tenterhooks, on edge.

2, expected, foreseen, in prospect, prospective, in view, impending, imminent. *Informal,* on deck, in the cards.

Adverbs—expectantly, on the watch, with bated breath, with ears pricked up, on edge.

Interjections—no wonder! of course! small wonder!

Phrases—if a man's foresight were as good as his hindsight, we would all get somewhere; it's too late to shut the stable door after the horse has bolted.

Quotations—I am giddy, expectation whirls me round. The imaginary relish is so sweet that it enchants my sense (*Shakespeare*), Expect nothing. Live frugally on surprise (*Alice Walker*), It is folly to expect men to do all that they may reasonably be expected to do (*Richard Whately*).

Antonyms, see DOUBT, UNPREPAREDNESS, SURPRISE, WONDER.

EXPEDIENCE
Desirableness

Nouns—1, expedience, expediency, desirableness, desirability, advisability, eligibility, seemliness, fitness, UTILITY, propriety, opportunism, convenience, timeliness, suitability. See POSSIBILITY.

2, [golden] opportunity, OCCASION, high time; critical *or* crucial moment, zero hour, moment of truth, crunch, pinch; turning point. *Informal*, when push comes to shove, nick of time.

Verbs—1, be expedient, timely, *or* suitable, suit *or* befit the occasion, strike the right note.

2, seize the moment, carpe diem, take the opportunity, commit oneself, take the bull by the horns; capitalize on, make hay while the sun shines, strike while the iron is hot.

Adjectives—expedient, acceptable, convenient, worthwhile, meet, fitting, fit, due, proper, eligible, seemly, becoming, opportune, in season, suitable, timely, well-timed, auspicious, right, seasonable.

Adverbs—expediently, conveniently; in the right place, at the right moment.

Quotations—We do what we must, and call it by the best names (*Emerson*); In every sort of danger, there are various ways of winning through, if one is ready to do and say anything whatever (*Socrates*), Custom adapts itself to expediency (*Tacitus*), You can't learn too soon that the most useful thing about a principle is that it can always be sacrificed to expediency (*W. Somerset Maugham*), No man is justified in doing evil on the grounds of expediency (*Theodore Roosevelt*).

Antonyms, see INEXPEDIENCE.

---

expedite, *v.t.* hasten, dispatch; further, advance. See HASTE, AID. *Ant.*, hinder, delay.

expedition, *n.* HASTE, dispatch, promptness, speed, alacrity; journey, quest, tour, trip, jaunt, excursion; crusade, campaign. See EARLINESS, WARFARE, TRAVEL.

expel, *v.t.* eject, extrude, excrete, discharge, dispel, eliminate; exclude, remove, evict, dislodge, dispossess, oust; excommunicate; banish, exile, deport, expatriate. See EJECTION.

expend, *v.t.* spend, lay out, pay [out], disburse; USE, consume; exhaust; give; WASTE, use up. See PAYMENT.

expendable, *adj.* superfluous, redundant; needless, gratuitous; consumable. See REMAINDER, USELESSNESS.

expenditure, *n.* expense[s], outlay, spending, PAYMENT, cost[s]; disbursement, outgo, overhead; PURCHASE[s]; PRICE. See ACCOUNTING.

expensive, *adj.* costly, dear, high, exorbitant. See DEARNESS. *Ant.*, cheap.

experience, *v.t.* have, know, see, meet, encounter; undergo, suffer, brave, sustain; enjoy, realize, apprehend, understand. See FEELING, KNOWLEDGE, OCCURRENCE.

EXPERIMENT
Trial

Nouns—1, experiment, experimentation, essay, attempt; venture, adventure, speculation; trial, probation, proof (see DEMONSTRATION); [acid *or* litmus] test, check, tryout, assay, ordeal; empiricism, rule of thumb, trial and error; criterion, touchstone, golden rule; biofeedback. *Informal*, go, whack. *Slang*, shot, crack. See INQUIRY.

2, (*experimental action*) feeler, probe; trial balloon, test flight, scout, straw in the wind, speculation, random shot, leap *or* shot in the dark, [first *or* rough] draft; road test; tryout, screen test, audition, dry *or* trial run; road test, test flight; beta test; single *or* double blind; polygraph.

3, laboratory, field station; think tank; proving ground. *Informal*, lab.

4, researcher, tester, experimenter; test driver *or* pilot.

5, laboratory subject, patient; test animal, guinea pig, white rat.

Verbs—1, experiment, essay, try, endeavor, strive, attempt; venture, adventure, speculate, take a chance, tempt fortune, try one's luck *or* hand, have a go at, shoot at, make a go of it, give it a whirl; put on trial, put to the test *or* proof, try *or* check out, crosscheck, shake down, put through one's paces, try on; test, practice upon; try one's strength, test one's wings. *Slang,* milk a duck.

2, grope, feel *or* grope one's way; throw out a feeler, send up a trial balloon, see how the land lies, see how the wind blows, feel the pulse, beat the bushes, try one's fortune; explore, inquire. *Informal,* see how the ball bounces; fiddle, monkey, mess, play, *or* fool around.

Adjectives—experimental, probative, probationary, tentative, empirical, on probation, on trial, on approval.

Adverbs—experimentally, tentatively, on trial, by rule of thumb.

Phrases—if at first you don't succeed, try, try, try again; nothing venture[d], nothing gain[ed]; the proof of the pudding is in the eating.

Quotations—Experience is the name everyone gives to their mistakes (*Oscar Wilde*), Experience keeps a dear school, but fools will learn in no other (*Benjamin Franklin*), Experience gives us the tests first and the lessons later (*Naomi Judd*).

---

expert, *n. & adj.* See SKILL.

expertise, *n.* SKILL, skillfulness, KNOWLEDGE, LEARNING, facility, proficiency, mastery; professionalism, savoir-faire, know-how (*inf.*). See PERFECTION.

expiate, *v.t.* atone for (see ATONEMENT).

expire, *v.* exhale, breathe out, emit; die, perish; END, cease, terminate, stop. See DEATH, WIND.

explain, *v.t.* expound, solve, elucidate, resolve, fathom, account for; demonstrate, construe, interpret, define, describe, develop, detail, criticize, comment. See ANSWER, ATTRIBUTION, INTERPRETATION.

expletive, *n.* oath, IMPRECATION.

explicate, *v.t.* analyze, explain (see INTERPRETATION).

explicit, *adj.* express, written, plain, positive, clear, unambiguous, open, definite; unreserved, outspoken. See INFORMATION, MEANING.

explode, *v.* destroy; burst, detonate, fire, discharge; reject; refute, discredit, expose, disprove. See CONFUTATION, VIOLENCE, EXCITABILITY.

exploit, *v.t.* utilize, profit by, milk, work; abuse, misapply. See USE. —*n.* deed, act, feat, achievement. See COURAGE.

explore, *v.t.* seek, search, fathom, prospect, penetrate, range, examine, investigate, inquire into. See INQUIRY.

explosive, *adj.* See VIOLENCE, DANGER. —*n.* dynamite, TNT, nitroglycerin. See VIOLENCE, ARMS.

exponent, *n.* expounder, representative; backer, defender; power, superscript. See TEACHING, AUXILIARY.

export, *n.* commodity, exportation. See EGRESS, SALE.

expose, *v.t.* disclose, reveal, divulge, unearth, unmask, denude, bare, uncover; exhibit, display; offer, submit; subject to, risk, weather, lay open, endanger, imperil; turn out, cast out, abandon; denounce, brand. See DANGER, DISAPPROBATION, DISCLOSURE, DIVESTMENT, VISIBILITY. *Ant.,* conceal.

exposé, *n.* exposure, unmasking. See DISCLOSURE.

exposition, *n.* explanation, exegesis, elucidation, commentary; show, exhibition, fair; statement, discourse; exposure, abandonment. See DISCLOSURE, INTERPRETATION, REASONING, BUSINESS.

ex post facto, Lat. after the deed [is done], subsequently, retroactively. See LATENESS, PAST.

expostulate, *v.i.* remonstrate, reason; object, protest, rebuke. See ADVICE, DISAPPROBATION, DISSUASION.

expound, *v.t.* state, express, set forth; explain, interpret, elucidate. See TEACHING, SPEECH, INTERPRETATION.

express, *v.t.* squeeze, press out, exude; represent, symbolize, show, reveal, denote, signify, delineate, depict; state, tell, frame, enunciate, expound, couch, utter, voice, communicate, speak; ship. See MEANING, SPEECH, TRANSPORTA-

TION, HASTE, INFORMATION, EXTRACTION. —*adj.* manifest, explicit, precise; special. See SPECIALITY.

expression, *n.* REPRESENTATION, symbolization, INDICATION; statement, utterance, wording, communication; modulation, shading, interpretation; idiom, phrase, term; aspect, look, pose; token; saying. See AFFIRMATION, APPEARANCE, MEANING, SPEECH, NOMENCLATURE.

expressway, *n.* limited access highway, superhighway (see PASSAGE).

expropriate, *v.t.* dispossess (see ACQUISITION).

expulsion, *n.* EJECTION, eviction, ousting, dislodgement, dismissal; banishment, exile, deportation, expatriation, ostracism; EXCRETION, discharge.

expunge, *v.t.* erase; efface. See DEDUCTION, DESTRUCTION.

expurgate, *v.t.* bowdlerize; purge, purify, cleanse; emasculate, castrate. See PURITY.

exquisite, *adj.* accurate, exact, fastidious, appreciative, discriminating; accomplished, perfected; intense, keen, sharp; choice, selected, refined, rare; excellent, delicate, beautiful, matchless, dainty, charming, delightful. See FEELING, SUPERIORITY.

extant, *adj.* surviving, existent. See EXISTENCE. *Ant.,* extinct, lost.

extemporaneous, *adj.* unpremeditated, spontaneous, extempore, improvised, impromptu, offhand, unprepared. See IMPULSE, UNPREPAREDNESS. *Ant.,* planned, rehearsed.

ex tempore, *Lat.* impromptu, offhand. See OCCASION.

extemporize, *v.* improvise, fake (*inf.*), wing it (*inf.*). See UNPREPAREDNESS, INTUITION.

extend, *v.* continue, lengthen, elongate, widen, enlarge, stretch, draw out, prolong, protract, expand, spread, broaden; increase; hold out, proffer, OFFER, impart, bestow. See INCREASE, LENGTH. *Ant.,* shorten.

extension, *n.* widening, enlargement, stretching, EXPANSION, amplification, distension, ADDITION, continuance, continuation, lengthening, protraction, prolongation, protrusion, projection, ramification; comprehension; expanse, sweep, stretch. See INCREASE, SPACE, LENGTH.

extensive, *adj.* broad, comprehensive. See BREADTH, GENERALITY, SPACE. *Ant.,* narrow, limited.

extent, *n.* LIMIT, measure, range; span, longitude, LENGTH, BREADTH; compass, proportions, SIZE.

extenuate, *v.t.* excuse, forgive, pardon, mitigate, palliate; attenuate; diminish, weaken. See VINDICATION, WEAKNESS, DECREASE.

EXTERIOR
Outer surface

Nouns—1, exterior, exteriority, outwardness, externality, extraneousness; superficiality; externalization. See APPEARANCE.

2, *(exterior surface)* outside, face, FRONT, surface, finish, superficies; skin (see COVERING), superstratum, facet, SIDE.

3, outdoors, open air, surroundings.

Verbs—be exterior, be outside; lie around, surround (see CIRCUMSCRIPTION); externalize.

Adjectives—exterior, external, outer, outmost, outside, outermost, outward, outdoor, open-air; round about, outside of, surface, superficial, skin-deep, cosmetic; public; EXTRINSIC.

Adverbs—externally, outwardly, out, without, outward[s]; out-of-doors, in the open air, al fresco.

Antonyms, see INTERIOR.

exterminate, *v.t.* abolish, destroy, annihilate; extirpate, eradicate, root out. See DESTRUCTION.

external, *adj.* EXTERIOR; foreign; perceptible, visible, physical; extraneous, superficial. See VISIBILITY, UNCONFORMITY. *Ant.,* INTERNAL.

extinct, *adj.* extinguished, quenched; exterminated, nonexistent, obsolete; died out, gone. See OLDNESS, PAST, NON-EXISTENCE, DEATH, DESTRUCTION.

extinguish, *v.t.* destroy, annihilate, eradicate, suppress, end; quench, choke, put *or* blow out, douse, snuff; smother, suffocate; quell, subdue. See DARKNESS, DESTRUCTION. *Ant.,* light.

extirpate, *v.t.* uproot, eradicate, destroy (see DESTRUCTION).

extol, *v.t.* praise, applaud, commend, glorify, celebrate, exalt. See APPROBATION. *Ant.,* defame, run down.

extort, *v.t.* elicit, extract, draw, exact; wring, wrench, force; squeeze. See STEALING, COMPULSION, EXTRACTION, THREAT.

extra, *adj.* additional, AUXILIARY, accessory, spare, supplementary, redundant. See ADDITION.

EXTRACTION
Act of removing

Nouns—1, extraction, removal; drawing out, pulling; elimination, extrication, eradication, evulsion; expression, squeezing; extirpation, suction, pumping, aspiration, siphoning, draining, bleeding; excision, cutting out; disinterment, unearthing; extortion, wrenching, exaction.

2, eduction, elicitation, evolution, derivation, bringing forth. See ANCESTRY.

3, *(tool for extracting)* extractor, corkscrew, forceps, pliers, wrench; pump, pulmotor, vacuum cleaner, siphon, aspirator.

4, *(something extracted)* extract, essence, elixir, distillate, decoction, concentrate, juice, *etc.*

Verbs—1, extract; draw, pull, tear, *or* pluck out; wring from, extricate, wrench, extort, exact; root, dig, *or* rout out, weed out; grub up, rake out, uproot, pull up; eviscerate; extirpate, eradicate, eliminate, remove; express, squeeze out; distill; pump, milk, aspirate, siphon, drain, bleed; disinter, unearth, dig up; soak [up]. *Slang,* shake down.

2, educe, elicit, evolve, extract, derive, bring forth *or* out.

Adjectives—extractive; evocative, exacting, extortionate; essential, pure.

Antonyms, see INSERTION.

extracurricular, *adj.* nonscholastic, outside. See SCHOOL.

extradite, *v.t.* deliver, deport, expel; turn *or* hand over. See EJECTION, TRANSFER.

extraneous, *adj.* foreign, alien; ulterior, exterior, external, outlandish; excluded, inadmissible, exceptional. See EXTRINSIC. *Ant.,* INTRINSIC.

extraordinary, *adj.* unusual, singular, uncommon, remarkable, phenomenal, abnormal; eminent, rare, notable. See GREATNESS, UNCONFORMITY, SPECIALITY. *Ant.,* commonplace, ordinary.

extrapolate, *v.t.* surmise, infer, conjecture; estimate. See BELIEF, SUPPOSITION.

extravagant, *adj.* profuse, prodigal, lavish, excessive, extreme; wasteful, profligate, rampant, wild; bombastic, fantastic; high, exorbitant, unreasonable; unreal, flighty, visionary, absurd, fanciful, grotesque. See IMAGINATION, ABSURDITY, DEARNESS, FOLLY, BOASTING, EXAGGERATION, WASTE. *Ant.,* simple, plain.

extravaganza, *n.* spectacle, pageant. See SOCIALITY, DRAMA, IMAGINATION.

extreme, *adj.* remote, utmost, farthest, last, final, ultra, radical, drastic; excessive, inordinate, deep, intense, desperate, outrageous, immoderate, greatest. See END, GREATNESS.

extremist, *n.* radical. See CHANGE.

extremity, *n.* utmost, LIMIT, EDGE, boundary, tip; limb (of the body); destitution, need, distress. See END, POVERTY.

extricate, *v.t.* free, disentangle, loose, liberate, disengage. See LIBERATION, EXTRACTION.

EXTRINSIC
Separate

Nouns—1, extrinsicality, outwardness, extraneousness, foreignness, objectivity. See EXTERIOR, AUXILIARY, CIRCUMSTANCE.

2, (*extrinsic object or action*) accessory, appendage, extra, appurtenance, supplement, adjunct; accident; outreach; contingency, incidental; foreigner, stranger, nondocumented person. *Informal*, foreign devil, face.

Verbs—be extrinsic, lie outside *or* beyond.

Adjectives—1, extrinsical, external, outward, objective, circumstantial, contingent, foreign, impersonal, out-of-body.

2, unessential, nonessential, extraneous, accessory, adventitious, extra, AUXILIARY, incidental, fortuitous, casual.

Antonyms, see INTRINSIC.

---

extroverted, *adj.* outgoing, extrovert (see COMMUNICATION). *Ant.*, introverted.

extrude, *v.* thrust out, expel; protrude, project. See EXPULSION, EJECTION, CONVEXITY.

exuberance, *n.* zest, enthusiasm, VIGOR, ebullience, energy, EXCITEMENT, high spirits, abundance, bounty, effusion. See FEELING, DIFFUSENESS.

exude, *v.* emit, discharge, ooze, leak, trickle, drain. See EGRESS, EXCRETION.

exult, *v.i.* rejoice, vaunt, jubilate, gloat, crow, triumph, glory. See BOASTING, REJOICING.

eye, *v.t.* watch, ogle, stare, view, observe, scrutinize, inspect. See VISION. —*n.* orb, visual organ; optic; eyesight, perception; VISION; opinion, view; hook, loop, OPENING. See CIRCULARITY, BODY.

eyeglasses, *n.pl.* spectacles, glasses (see OPTICAL INSTRUMENTS).

eye-opening, *adj.* enlightening (see DISCLOSURE).

eyesight, *n.* See VISION.

eyesore, *n.* offense, blemish. See UGLINESS.

eyewitness, *n.* bystander, witness. See PRESENCE, EVIDENCE.

F

fable, *n.* parable, allegory, moral tale; apologue; myth, legend, fiction. See DESCRIPTION, FALSEHOOD, FIGURATIVE.

fabled, *adj.* famous, noted; fictional. See REPUTE, FALSEHOOD.

fabric, *n.* cloth, textile, material, tissue; structure, framework. See PRODUCTION, MATERIALS, CROSSING, TEXTURE.

fabricate, *v.t.* build, construct, manufacture; invent, make up, trump up, concoct. See PRODUCTION, IMAGINATION, FALSEHOOD.

fabulous, *adj.* legendary, mythical; incredible, stupendous, prodigious. See DESCRIPTION, EXAGGERATION, DOUBT, NONEXISTENCE.

facade, *n.* FRONT; APPEARANCE, aspect, style; pretense, false front, mask, persona; stimulation, AFFECTATION. See SHALLOWNESS, FALSEHOOD.

face, *n.* facing; countenance, visage, physiognomy, lineaments, features; FRONT, facade, facet, obverse; van, first line; prestige, reputation; effrontery, INSOLENCE; mug, map, puss, phiz (*all sl.*). See APPEARANCE, REPUTE. —*v.* encounter, confront; veneer, plate, sheathe; look out on. See OPPOSITION, COVERING, DIRECTION. —**face down,** abash, stare down, confront. See OPPOSITION. —**face up to,** acknowledge, admit; confront. See DISCLOSURE, OPPOSITION.

face-lift, *n.* renovation (see RESTORATION).

face-off, *n.* confrontation (see OPPOSITION).

facet, *n.* face, surface, plane, bezel, culet; aspect, phase. See EXTERIOR.

facetious, *adj.* whimsical, joking, tongue-in-cheek; ironic[al], sarcastic, satirical, derisive. See WIT, RIDICULE. *Ant.,* serious.

facility, *n.* building, facilities; *informal,* WASHROOM, TOILET. See BUSINESS, PROVISION, UNCLEANNESS, FACILITY.

FACILITY
Ease

Nouns—**1,** facility, ease; easiness; capability, feasibility, practicability; dexterity, SKILL; plain *or* smooth sailing, smooth water, fair wind, clear coast *or* stage; line *or* path of least resistance; full *or* free play (see FREEDOM). See SIMPLENESS.

2, easy task, simple matter, sinecure, child's play. *Informal,* [lead-pipe] cinch, breeze, bed of roses, piece of cake. *Slang,* snap, picnic, duck soup *or* shoot, fun and games; gravy train, no-brainer, pushover, doss, apple pie, easy meat, milk run, skate, sleigh ride.

3, facilitation, expedition, streamlining, easing, smoothing.

4, manageability, submissiveness (see *Adjectives,* 2).

Verbs—**1,** be easy, be feasible; go *or* run smoothly; have full *or* free play (see FREEDOM); work well; flow *or* swim with the stream, drift *or* go with the tide; see one's way; have it easy, have it all one's own way, have the game in one's own hands; walk over the course; win in a walk, win hands down; take in one's stride; make light *or* nothing of; be at home in.

2, (*make easy*) facilitate, smooth, ease, lighten [the labor]; popularize; free, clear; disencumber, disembarrass, disentangle, disengage; disobstruct, unclog, extricate, unravel; leave the matter open; give the reins to; make way for, open the door to; prepare the ground *or* way, smooth *or* clear the ground; leave a loophole; spoon-feed. *Informal,* grease the ways *or* wheels. *Slang,* dumb down.

Adjectives—1, facile, simple, easy, effortless; feasible, practicable; easily managed *or* accomplished, nothing to it, easy as falling off a log, like water off a duck's back, like taking candy from a baby, easy as pie, hands-down; within reach, accessible, easy of access, open to. *Informal,* gut, painless, user-friendly. *Slang,* no sweat.

2, *(easy to manage)* manageable, wieldy, tractable, submissive, yielding, ductile; pliant, soft; glib; unburdened, disburdened, disencumbered, unembarrassed, unloaded, unobstructed, in the clear, untrammeled, unrestrained, free; at ease, dexterous, light; at home, in one's element.

Adverbs—facilely, easily; readily, handily, smoothly, swimmingly, on easy terms, without a hitch; single-handed; without striking a blow.

Phrases—easy come, easy go; easy does it.

Antonyms, see DIFFICULTY.

---

facing, *n.* lining, COVERING. —*adj.* fronting on, OPPOSITE.

facsimile, *n.* duplicate, reproduction, replica. See IDENTITY.

fact, *n.* reality, actuality, CERTAINTY; OCCURRENCE. See EXISTENCE, TRUTH, EVIDENCE. *Ant.,* fiction, FALSEHOOD.

faction, *n.* clique, cabal, splinter party; sect, denomination; DISCORD, dissidence, dissension. See PARTY, HETERODOXY.

factious, *adj.* contentious, dissentious (see DISSENT, CONTENTION). *Ant.,* cooperative.

factor, *n.* component, element, PART, constituent, condition; AGENT.

factory, *n.* manufactory, mill, shop, works, facilities, workshop. See PRODUCTION.

factual, *adj.* real, indisputable, demonstrable. See CERTAINTY, EXISTENCE, TRUTH. *Ant.,* fictitious, unreal.

faculty, *n.* ability, aptitude, POWER, talent, knack; professorate, [teaching] staff. See SKILL, SCHOOL, INTELLECT.

fad, *n.* craze, rage, vogue; fancy, hobby. See CHANGEABLENESS, FASHION.

fade, *v.* pale, dim, bleach, whiten; vanish, disappear; languish, wither, shrivel. See DIMNESS, COLORLESSNESS, NONEXISTENCE, DETERIORATION, DISAPPEARANCE, WEAKNESS, TRANSIENTNESS, OBLIVION.

failing, *n.* fault, frailty, shortcoming; foible. See GUILT, IMPERFECTION.

FAILURE
Nonperformance

Nouns—1, failure, unsuccessfulness, nonsuccess, nonfulfillment; dead failure, abortion, miscarriage, malfunction, outage; bankruptcy (see NONPAYMENT); labor in vain; no go; inefficacy; vain *or* abortive attempt, slip 'twixt cup and lip; no-win situation. See INSUFFICIENCY, NEGLECT.

2, mistake (see ERROR); mess, fiasco, breakdown, collapse, fall, crash, downfall, ruin, perdition, grief; bankruptcy; wild-goose chase; losing game; non pass. *Informal,* has-been. *Slang,* flop, turkey, bomb, washout, glitch, nose dive, tailspin.

3, *(total defeat)* rebuff, defeat, rout, debacle, beating, drubbing; checkmate, stalemate. *Informal,* death knell.

4, *(one who fails)* also-ran, flash in the pan; underdog; house of cards, dud; bankrupt, insolvency, Chapter 11. *Informal,* bust, lemon, loser, dud, schlemiel. *Slang,* flop, goner.

Verbs—1, fail, be unsuccessful, not succeed; labor *or* toil in vain; lose one's labor; bring to naught, make nothing of; roll the stone of Sisyphus; do by halves; lose ground (see REGRESSION); fall short of. *Informal,* peter out, achieve a deficiency. *Slang,* flop, not get to first base, crumb it, go belly-up, stiff.

2, *(fail to accomplish a goal)* miss, miss one's aim, miss the boat *or* bus, miss the mark, miss by a mile, bite off more than one can chew; make a slip, blunder (see ERROR); make a mess of; miscarry, misfire, hang fire, backfire, abort; go up like a rocket and come down like a stick; reckon without one's host, back the wrong horse. *Informal,* blow. *Slang,* bollix up, botch.

3, *(deteriorate)* limp, hobble; fall, lose one's balance; overreach oneself; flounder, falter; stick in the mud, run aground; tilt at windmills; come up against a stone wall; burn one's fingers; break one's back; break down, sink, go under, drown, founder, have the ground cut from under one; get into trouble, get into a mess *or* scrape; come to grief (see ADVERSITY); go to the wall, go under, go to the dogs, go to pot.

4, be defeated, bite the dust, take it on the chin, meet one's Waterloo, have the worst of it, lose the day; come off second best, bring up the rear, lose, lose out; succumb, buckle, drop *or* fall by the wayside; not have a leg to stand on. *Informal,* flunk [out]; have two strikes against one, haul down one's colors. *Slang,* fall down on, lay an egg, fold up, throw in the sponge *or* towel, take a dive, bath, tumble, *or* fall, toss.

5, come to nothing *or* naught, end in smoke; go bankrupt, close its doors, come a cropper, fizzle [out], die *or* wither on the vine; fall through, fall flat; give out, give way, fall down on the job; slip through one's fingers; hang fire; collapse; topple down; go to wrack and ruin; go amiss, go hard with; go wrong, go on a wrong tack, take a wrong turn; sow the wind and reap the whirlwind; jump out of the frying pan into the fire. *Slang,* fold up.

6, cause to fail, fix one's wagon, dash one's hopes, shoot down.

Adjectives—1, failing, unsuccessful; abortive, stillborn; fruitless; bootless; ineffectual, ineffective, inefficacious; inefficient; impotent (see IMPOTENCE); lame, hobbling; insufficient (see INSUFFICIENCY); unavailing, useless (see USELESSNESS).

2, aground, grounded, swamped, stranded, cast away, wrecked, foundered, capsized, shipwrecked; foiled, defeated, vanquished, conquered, struck, borne, *or* broken down; downtrodden, overborne, overwhelmed; all up with; lost, undone, ruined, broken, bankrupt (see DEBT); done up, done for, dead beat, knocked on the head; thrown off one's balance; unhorsed; in a sorry plight; hard hit; left in the lurch; stultified, befooled, hoist by one's own petard; victimized, sacrificed; wide of the mark (see ERROR); thrown away (see WASTE); unattained; uncompleted. *Informal,* whipped, licked, kaput, out of the running. *Slang,* washed out; dished, fucked, in the bag, on the fritz.

Adverbs—unsuccessfully; to little *or* no purpose, in vain, to no avail; about *or* on one's head; about *or* around one's ears.

Phrases—back to the drawing board *or* square one; the bigger they are, the harder they fall; the best laid schemes of mice and men gang aft agley; you cannot make an omelet without breaking eggs. *Slang,* the jig is up.

Quotations—As he rose like a rocket, he fell like the stick (*Thomas Paine*), Half the failures in life arise from pulling in one's horse as he is leaping (*Julius and Augustus Hare*), Down with the defeated! (*Livy*), There is no loneliness greater than the loneliness of failure (*Eric Hoffer*), There is not a fiercer hell than the failure in a great object (*John Keats*), Thou art weighed in the balances, and art found wanting (*Bible*).

Antonyms, see SUCCESS.

---

faint, *v.i.* swoon; lose heart *or* courage; fail, fade, weaken, pass out (*inf.*). —*adj.* pale, indistinct; feeble, weak. See WEAKNESS, COLORLESSNESS, IMPOTENCE, SILENCE, DIMNESS, FAINTNESS.

fainthearted, *adj.* timid, diffident. See COWARDICE. *Ant.,* courageous.

FAINTNESS
Weakness of sound

Nouns—1, faintness, softness, lowness, indistinctness; decrescendo, diminuendo. See SOUND, SILENCE, WEAKNESS.

2, *(faint sound)* murmur, mumble, mutter, whisper, undertone, muffled tone(s); aside, stage whisper; sigh, breath; hum, buzz; rustle, rustling; [pitter-]patter, tap, tinkle, gurgle, burble.

Verbs—whisper, murmur, rustle, mutter, hum, buzz, tap, tinkle; breathe, sigh; rustle, patter, tap, tinkle, gurgle, burble; steal on the ear, speak under one's breath.

Adjectives—faint, soft, low, dim, weak, feeble; indistinct, half-heard; muffled, subdued, bated; piano, pianissimo, decrescendo; distant; whispering, murmuring, *etc.*

Adverbs—faintly, softly, *etc.*; piano, pianissimo; sotto voce, under one's breath, with bated breath, in a whisper, in an undertone; muted, *à la sourdine*; in the distance, out of hearing *or* earshot.

Phrases—speak softly and carry a big stick.

Quotations—A soft answer turneth away wrath (*Bible*), Speak low, if you speak love (*Shakespeare*), Tread softly because you tread on my dreams (*W. B. Yeats*).

Antonyms, see LOUDNESS, SILENCE.

---

fair, *adj.* beautiful, handsome, good-looking, pretty, comely; blond, light; unsullied, unblemished; pleasant, fine; impartial, equitable, unbiased, just; moderate, passable; clear, sunny, cloudless. See BEAUTY, COLORLESSNESS, JUSTICE, PROSPERITY. —*n.* sale, bazaar. See BUSINESS. *Ant.*, unfair, unjust; cloudy, rainy; plain, ugly.

fairly, *adj.* impartially, reasonably; legitimately; tolerably, moderately. See JUSTICE, MODERATION.

fairy, *n.* fay, sprite, pixy, elf, brownie, gnome, leprechaun. See MYTHICAL DEITIES, DEMON.

fairy tale, *n.* fairy story, fable (see IMAGINATION).

fait accompli, *Fr.* fact, done deed (*inf.*). See COMPLETION.

faith, *n.* trust, reliance, confidence, EXPECTATION; BELIEF, creed; loyalty; RELIGION. *Ant.*, DOUBT.

faithful, *adj.* loyal, devoted; conscientious, trustworthy; exact, lifelike. See PROBITY, OBEDIENCE, PIETY. *Ant.*, faithless, unfaithful.

faithless, *adj.* unfaithful, disloyal, untrue, inconstant, treacherous. See IMPROBITY, DOUBT. *Ant.*, faithful.

fake, *n.* counterfeit, imposture, make-believe; impostor. See DECEPTION, FALSEHOOD. —*v.,* *informal,* pretend, feign; imitate; improvise, wing it (*inf.*). See UNPREPAREDNESS, IMITATION. *Ant.*, real, genuine.

fakir, *n.* ascetic, dervish; yogi[n]. See ASCETICISM.

fall, *v.i.* plunge, drop, sink, tumble, topple; perish; be deposed, come to grief; happen, occur, take place; sin, misbehave, lapse. —*n.* slope, declivity; downfall, defeat, comedown; drop, slump; plunge, tumble, header; autumn. See DESCENT, DESTRUCTION, DETERIORATION, OBLIQUITY, BADNESS, FAILURE, DEATH. *Ant.*, rise. —**fall guy,** *slang,* victim, scapegoat, dupe. See DECEPTION, CREDULITY. —**fall off,** DECREASE; separate, withdraw (see SEPARATION).

fallacy, *n.* ERROR, flaw, misconception; false meaning. *Ant.*, TRUTH.

fall back, *n.* retreat; reserve, backup. See ESCAPE, REGRESSION, SUBSTITUTION.

fallible, *adj.* unreliable, untrustworthy. See DOUBT. *Ant.*, infallible.

fallout, *n.* radioactive dust, contamination; aftereffect, EFFECT.

fallow, *adj.* uncultivated, untilled, unsown. See NEGLECT, UNPREPAREDNESS.

FALSEHOOD
Lack of honesty

Nouns—1, falsehood, falseness, dishonesty; falsity, falsification; DECEPTION, untruth; lying, misrepresentation, disinformation, plausible denial; mendacity, perjury, forgery, invention, fabrication; paradox of the liar. *Slang*, cooking.

2, perversion *or* suppression of truth, fiction, romance; perversion, DISTORTION, false coloring; EXAGGERATION, prevarication, equivocation, mystification (see CONCEALMENT); simulation, IMITATION, dissimulation, dissembling; whitewash; sham, make-believe, pretense, pretending, malingering. *Informal*, playacting, bunk. *Slang*, flaking.

3, *(treachery)* lip service; hollowness; duplicity, double-dealing, insincerity, hypocrisy, facade, cant, humbug, sanctimony; pharisaism; Machiavellianism; crocodile tears, mealy-mouthedness, quackery; charlatanism, charlatanry; cajolery, FLATTERY; Judas kiss; perfidy, bad faith, unfairness (see IMPROBITY); misstatement (see ERROR). *Informal*, front. *Slang*, fourflushing.

4, lie, half-truth, white lie, yarn, tall story, fable, fiction, fabrication, pious fraud, song and dance, cock-and-bull story; irony. *Informal*, lollapalooza, whopper, fairy tale, weasel words, hogwash, poppycock. *Slang*, bunk[um], crock [of shit], crap[ola], bullshit.

5, fake, phony, counterfeit, forgery; paste, dummy, shoddy; hoax, fraud; impostor. *Informal*, rip-off, put-on.

6, liar, fibber, fabulist, prevaricator, falsifier, perjurer; charlatan; Ananias, Baron Munchhausen. *Slang*, baby kisser, buller, fourflusher.

7, liars' club. *Slang*, bull session.

Verbs—1, be false, speak falsely, tell a lie, lie, fib, misspeak; lie like a trooper, lie in one's throat, forswear, perjure oneself, bear false witness; belie, falsify, pervert, distort, misquote; put a false construction upon, misinterpret; misinform, mislead; prevaricate, equivocate, quibble; fence, mince the truth, beat about the bush, blow hot and cold, play fast and loose; garble, gloss over, disguise, color, varnish, dress up, embroider; pad the bill; exaggerate. *Slang*, throw the bull; cook.

2, invent, fabricate; trump up, get up; forge, hatch, concoct; romance, imagine (see IMAGINATION); cry "wolf!"; dissemble, dissimulate, palter; feign, assume, put on, pretend, make believe (see AFFECTATION); play false, play a double game; pull out of a hat; act *or* play a part; affect, simulate; palm off, pass off for; counterfeit, sham, make a show of, malinger; cant, fob off, put on, play the hypocrite, sail under false colors, deceive (see DECEPTION); go through the motions. *Informal*, let on, playact, play possum, put on a front. *Slang*, fourflush.

Adjectives—1, false, deceitful, mendacious, untruthful, unveracious, fraudulent, dishonest, make-believe, faithless, truthless, trothless; unfair, uncandid, evasive; uningenuous, disingenuous; hollow, insincere, forsworn; canting; hypocritical, pharisaical, sanctimonious; Machiavellian, two-faced, double-dealing; Janus-faced; smooth-faced, -spoken, *or* -tongued, tongue-in-cheek; mealy-mouthed; less than candid; affected; collusive, collusory, perfidious (see IMPROBITY). *Slang*, full of shit.

2, spurious, deceptive (see DECEPTION); untrue, falsified; ungrounded, unfounded; counterfeit, phony, fake, mock, synthetic; inoperative.

Adverbs—falsely; slyly, crookedly, *etc.*

Phrases—half the truth is often a whole lie; a lie can go around the world and back again while the truth is lacing up its boots; ask no questions and hear no lies.

Quotations—I want that glib and oily art to speak and purpose not (*Shakespeare*), The lie in the soul is a true lie (*Benjamin Jowett*), A little inaccuracy sometimes saves tons of explanation (*Saki*), Without lies humanity would perish of despair and boredom (*Anatole France*), A truth that's told with false intent beats all the lies you can invent (*William Blake*), Since a politician never believes what he says, he is surprised when others believe him (*Charles de Gaulle*), White lies always introduce others of a darker complexion (*William Paley*), O, what a tangled web we weave, when first we practice to deceive! (*Sir Walter Scott*), I detest that man who hides one thing in the depth of his heart and speaks forth another (*Homer*), Only the hypocrite is really rotten to the core (*Hannah Arendt*).

Antonyms, see TRUTH, REASONING.

falter, *v.i.* hesitate, waver, hang back, vacillate; shuffle, stumble, totter; stammer. See DOUBT, SLOWNESS, STAMMERING, FAILURE, HOPELESSNESS.

fame, *n.* REPUTE, renown, prestige, celebrity; honor, distinction, glory, eminence; notoriety. See NEWS.

familiar, *adj.* intimate, close; acquainted, well-versed; common; presumptuous. —*n.* intimate, associate; familiar spirit (see MYTHICAL DEITIES, DEMON). See FRIEND, NEARNESS, SOCIALITY, INSOLENCE. *Ant.*, unfamiliar, reserved, distant.

familiarity, *n.* intimacy, acquaintance, fellowship; KNOWLEDGE; informality, forwardness, impudence. See FRIEND, SOCIALITY, INSOLENCE.

familiarize, *v.t.* acquaint; accustom. See INFORMATION, HABIT.

family, *n.* household; forefathers, children, descendants, lineage, family tree; clan, tribe, kindred; group, association, classification, CLASS. See ANCESTRY.

famine, *n.* starvation; dearth, paucity. See DESIRE, POVERTY, INSUFFICIENCY. *Ant.*, abundance.

famish, *v.* starve, die of hunger, be hungry; pinch, exhaust. See PARSIMONY. *Ant.*, sate.

famous, *adj.* noted, famed, renowned, celebrated, well-known. See REPUTE. *Ant.*, unknown.

fan, *n.* fanner, blower, winnower, flabellum, ventilator; wind; *informal*, devotee, follower, enthusiast, supporter, rooter (*sl.*), addict (*sl.*), groupie (*sl.*). See ACTIVITY. —*v.t.* blow, winnow, cool, refresh, ventilate, stir up; *slang*, strike out (see SPORTS). See AIR, WIND, AGITATION, REFRESHMENT.

fanatic, *n.* zealot, enthusiast, dogmatist. See EXCITABILITY, FEELING, HETERODOXY, INSANITY.

fanciful, *adj.* whimsical, capricious, fantastic, quaint, bizarre; quixotic, imaginary. See UNCONFORMITY, IMAGINATION.

fancy, *n.* IMAGINATION; idea, caprice, whim; preference, DESIRE; reverie, daydream. —*v.t.* imagine; believe, suppose, assume; like, DESIRE, take to. See BELIEF, SUPPOSITION. —*adj.* ornate, showy; superior, extravagant. See ORNAMENT, OSTENTATION. *Ant.*, simple, plain.

fancy-free, *adj.* carefree, unattached. See FREEDOM.

fanfare, *n.* flourish, tantara; CELEBRATION, OSTENTATION.

fang, *n.* tooth, eyetooth, tusk. See SHARPNESS.

fantastic, *adj.* bizarre, grotesque; imaginative, fanciful; extravagant, irrational, absurd. See IMAGINATION, ABSURDITY.

far, *adv.* remotely, distantly, widely, afar. —*adj.* far off, remote, distant. See DISTANCE.

farce, *n.* buffoonery, burlesque, travesty; mockery, fiasco. See WIT, DRAMA.

fare, *v.i.* get on, make out, get along; prosper, thrive; eat, dine, regale oneself. —*n.* passage, carfare, token; luck, outcome; FOOD, diet, table, board, provisions. See TRAVEL, PRICE, EFFECT.

farewell, *interj. & n.* See DEPARTURE.

farfetched, *adj.* forced, strained. See IMPROBABILITY. *Ant.*, believable.

far-flung, *adj.* extensive; dispersed. See DISTANCE.

farm, *n.* ranch, rancho, plantation, farmstead, grange. See ABODE. —*v.* cultivate, till. See AGRICULTURE.

farsighted, *adj.* hypermetropic, eagle-eyed; foresighted, farseeing, longheaded, prudent, provident. See PREDICTION, VISION. *Ant.*, nearsighted, myopic.

fart, *n., vulgar,* flatulence, gas, wind. —*v.i.* break wind. See VAPOR.

farther, *adj.* more distant, further, additional. —*adv.* beyond. See DISTANCE. *Ant.*, nearer.

fascination, *n.* charm, attraction, allurement, captivation; bewilderment; enchantment, spell; obsession. See PLEASURE, WONDER.

fascism, *n.* totalitarianism, authoritarianism; dictatorship; reactionism, nationalism; national socialism, red fascism, falangism, nazism; neofascism. See AUTHORITY.

FASHION
Prevailing mode

Nouns—1, fashion, style, [bon] ton, society; good society, polite society; drawing room, civilized life, civilization; town; haut *or* beau monde, high life, court; world; haute couture, high fashion *or* style; fashionable world; Vanity Fair; show, OSTENTATION.
2, manners, breeding, politeness (see COURTESY); air, demeanor, APPEARANCE; savoir faire; gentlemanliness, gentility, suavity; decorum, propriety, convention, conventionality, punctilio; form, formality; etiquette, social usage, custom, HABIT; mode, vogue, go, rage, furor, fad, craze, chic, TASTE, distinction, wave of the future; dress (see CLOTHING). *Slang,* the last word, le dernier cri, flavor of the month, radical chic.
3, man *or* woman of fashion, man *or* woman of the world; height of fashion; fashion plate; leader of fashion, socialite; arbiter; upper ten thousand, beautiful people (see NOBILITY); elite. *Informal,* upper crust, the four hundred; jet set, smart set, café society. *Slang,* studley, teenybopper.

Verbs—be fashionable, be the rage; follow the fashion, conform to the fashion, get on the bandwagon, go with the stream (see CONFORMITY); keep up appearances, behave oneself (see CONDUCT); set the style *or* fashion; bring into style *or* fashion, come in. *Informal,* be in the swim.

Adjectives—1, fashionable, in fashion, modish, chic, dressy, formal, stylish, smart, chichi, all the rage, sharp [as a tack]; recherché; newfangled, à la mode, comme il faut; presentable; conventional, customary, genteel, continental; well-bred, well-mannered, well-behaved, well-spoken; gentlemanly, ladylike; civil, polite, courteous (see COURTESY); polished, refined, thoroughbred, courtly; distingué; dégagé, suave, jaunty, switched-on; dashing, fast. *Informal,* in, natty, snappy, trendy, gussied up. *Slang,* piss-elegant.
2, out of fashion, démodé (see OLDNESS).

Adverbs—fashionably, stylishly, smartly, nattily, à la mode.

Phrases—fingers were made before forks; better be out of the world than out of the fashion.

Quotations—It is not only fine feathers that make fine birds (*Aesop*), Men should not care too much for good looks; neglect is becoming (*Ovid*), It is only shallow people who do not judge by appearances. The true mystery of the world is the visible, not the invisible (*Oscar Wilde*), In matters of great importance, style, not sincerity, is the vital thing (*Oscar Wilde*), Fashion is something barbarous, for it produces innovation without reason and imitation without benefit (*George Santayana*).

Antonyms, see VULGARITY, UNCONFORMITY.

---

fast, *v.i.* starve, diet, abstain. See ASCETICISM. —*adj.* swift, speedy, fleet, quick, rapid; secure, firm, permanent, steadfast, profound; wild, rakish, dissipated. See VELOCITY, JUNCTION, IMPURITY, TENACITY, FASHION. *Ant.,* gorge [oneself].

fasten, *v.t.* secure, make fast, attach, fix, bind, lock up. See JUNCTION, CLOSURE, RESTRAINT. *Ant.,* unfasten, release.

fastening, *n.* fastener, lock, catch, clasp, latch, hook, CONNECTION; button, zipper, hook [and eye], buckle; nail, tack, staple, screw, bolt, rivet, peg; thread; glue, cement.

fastidious, *adj.* finicky, [over]nice, fussy, crotchety. See TASTE. *Ant.,* gross, tasteless.

fasting, *n.* fast, starvation, hunger, famishment; hunger strike. See ASCETICISM, ATONEMENT.

fat, *adj.* plump, stout, corpulent, obese, portly, chubby; fertile, profitable, fruitful, rich; greasy, unctuous. See SIZE, ROTUNDITY, SMOOTHNESS, PRODUCTION. *Ant.,* thin, emaciated.

fatal, *adj.* deadly, lethal, mortal; fateful, critical. See KILLING, DEATH, IMPORTANCE.

fatalism, *n.* determinism, predestination; submission, apathy, nonresistance; passivity, stoicism. See DESTINY.

fatality, *n.* mortality, deadliness; casualty, accident, DEATH. See ADVERSITY, NECESSITY.

fate, *n.* DESTINY, lot, fortune, doom, predestination, CHANCE. See NECESSITY.

fateful, *adj.* momentous; prophetic; disastrous. See DESTINY, PREDICTION, IMPORTANCE.

father, *n.* sire, forefather; founder, patriarch; priest, pastor; the Father, God. See ANCESTRY, CLERGY, DEITY.

fatherland, *n.* homeland, native country, home. See ABODE.

fathom, *v.t.* measure, take a sounding; plunge, reach the bottom of; investigate, probe, study, delve into. See MEASUREMENT, INQUIRY.

fathomless, *adj.* bottomless, abyssal; cryptic, mystifying, insoluble, puzzling, enigmatic. See DEPTH, UNINTELLIGIBILITY.

fatigue, *v.* weary, tire, exhaust; jade, fag; bore, irk, wear; weaken, debilitate, overstrain, overtax, overwork. —*n.* tiredness, WEARINESS, exhaustion, lassitude, feebleness; exertion, strain; faintness, labor, work, toil, drudgery; ennui, boredom; (*pl.*) work clothes (see CLOTHING). *Ant.,* vigor.

fatten, *v.* feed, flesh out; enrich, INCREASE. See EXPANSION, FOOD, PROSPERITY.

fatuous, *adj.* vain, foolish, inept; inane, silly, dumb (*sl.*), sappy (*sl.*). See FOLLY, ABSURDITY.

faucet, *n.* tap, spigot, cock, spout, valve; spile, bung. See CLOSURE, OPENING.

fault, *n.* failing, shortcoming, peccadillo; flaw, blemish, defect, IMPERFECTION; ERROR, slip, inadvertency; sin, [venial] sin, [minor] vice. See GUILT, FAILURE.

faultfinding, *adj.* captious, carping, caviling, critical, censorious. See DISAPPROBATION.

faultless, *adj.* flawless, perfect, correct, impeccable; irreproachable, *sans peur et sans reproche.* See PERFECTION, INNOCENCE, PURITY. *Ant.,* faulty.

faulty, *adj.* defective; erroneous, wrong. See IMPERFECTION, ERROR. *Ant.,* faultless.

faux pas, *Fr.* a false step; ERROR.

favor, *n.* goodwill, esteem, APPROBATION, approval; partiality, bias, favoritism; patronage, backing; concession, dispensation; kindness, service, good turn; token, badge. See AID, PERMISSION, GIVING, LENIENCY. *Ant.,* disfavor.

favorable, *adj.* auspicious, propitious, advantageous, opportune, commendatory, well-inclined; affirmative. See OCCASION, AID. *Ant.,* unfavorable, disadvantageous.

favorite, *n.* darling, pet; idol, hero, jewel; apple of one's eye; CHOICE, preference; spoiled child *or* darling; teacher's pet, fair- *or* white-haired boy (*all inf.*). —*adj.* dearest; beloved, preferred, CHOICE. See LOVE.

favoritism, *n.* partisanship, partiality; nepotism. See CHOICE.

fawn, *v.i.* cringe, grovel, toady, truckle, cower, ingratiate, curry favor. See SERVILITY, FLATTERY.

fax, *n.* facsimile, telefax (see COMMUNICATION).

fay, *adj.* elfin, impish, pixie, fey; coy, arch; *slang,* effeminate. See MYTHICAL DEITIES, FEMALE.

faze, *v.t.* deter, daunt, ruffle; disconcert, bother, rattle, hold back, interfere with. See HINDRANCE.

FEAR
Anticipation of misfortune

Nouns—1, fear, fearfulness, phobia; timidity, timorousness, diffidence; solicitude, anxiety, worry, CARE, apprehension; apprehensiveness, misgiving, mistrust, DOUBT, suspicion, qualm; hesitation, irresolution; fright, alarm, dread, horror, awe, terror, dismay, consternation, panic, scare, stampede.

2, (*symptoms of fear*) nervousness, restlessness, inquietude, disquietude; flutter, trepidation, fear and trembling, buck fever, jitters, creeps, shivers; goose flesh, bumps, *or* pimples; butterflies [in the stomach]; perturbation, tremor, quivering, shaking, trembling, palpitation, cold sweat; abject fear (see COWARDICE); hangup. *Informal,* funk. *Slang,* heebie-jeebies.

3, *(induced fear)* intimidation, terrorism, reign of terror, THREAT, menace.

4, phobia; acrophobia, agoraphobia, ailurophobia, arachnophobia, claustrophobia, ecophobia, ergophobia, ichthyophobia, pyrophobia, xenophobia, zoophobia, *etc.*; Anglophobia, Francophobia, Germanophobia, *etc.*

5, *(something scary)* bugbear, bugaboo; scarecrow; hobgoblin, DEMON; nightmare, Gorgon, ogre; bête noire.

6, alarmist, fearmonger, scaremonger; terrorist, bomber, arsonist; bogeyman.

Verbs—**1,** fear, stand in awe of, be afraid, have qualms, be apprehensive, distrust, DOUBT; hesitate; funk, cower, crouch; skulk (see COWARDICE); take fright, take alarm, panic, stampede.

2, *(react with fear)* start, wince, flinch, cringe, shy, shrink; fly, flee (see AVOIDANCE); tremble, shake, jump out of one's skin; shiver [in one's boots *or* shoes]; shudder, flutter; tremble like a leaf *or* an aspen leaf, quake, quaver, quail; grow *or* turn pale; blench, stand aghast, throw up one's hands in horror. *Slang,* sweat blood *or* bullets, not be able to say boo to a goose, hit the panic button, shit *or* pee in one's pants.

3, inspire *or* excite fear *or* awe; raise apprehensions; alarm, startle, scare, cry "wolf!", disquiet, dismay; fright[en]; affright, terrify; scare *or* frighten out of one's wits, scare the [living] daylights out of, put the fear of God into; awe, strike terror (into), appall, unman, petrify, horrify; make one's flesh creep, make one's hair stand on end, curl one's hair; make one's blood run cold, turn to ice, *or* freeze, make one's teeth chatter; take away one's breath, make one's heart stand still; make one tremble; haunt; prey *or* weigh on the mind. *Informal,* spook, throw a scare into. *Slang,* scare shitless, scare the shit out of, curl one's hair.

4, *(dissuade with fear)* put in fear, terrorize, intimidate, cow, daunt, take aback, overawe, deter, discourage; browbeat, bully, boss; threaten (see WARNING), menace. *Slang,* bulldoze.

Adjectives—**1,** fearful, fearing, frightened, in fear, in a fright, afraid, scared, timid, timorous, cowardly (see COWARDICE); nervous, diffident, fainthearted, tremulous, shaky, panicky, afraid of one's shadow, mousy, apprehensive, irresolute; restless, fidgety, on pins and needles; having one's heart in one's mouth *or* boots, afraid of one's own shadow; paranoid; careworn, anxious.

2, aghast; alarmed; awestruck, terrified, horrified, horror-, terror-, *or* panic-stricken; frightened *or* scared to death, scared stiff, white as a sheet; pale as death, ashes, *or* a ghost; breathless, in hysterics, paralyzed [with fear]. *Informal,* yellow. *Slang,* chicken, scared shitless.

3, inspiring fear, fearsome, alarming; formidable, redoubtable; forbidding, dreadful, fell; dire, direful; shocking, terrible, terrifying, terrific, spine-chilling, alarmist; tremendous; horrid, horrible, horrific; ghastly; awful, awe-inspiring, eerie.

Adverbs—fearfully, in [mortal] fear, in fear for one's life, for fear, for dear life, with fear and trembling, with the tail between the legs, in a cold sweat.

Phrases—a burnt child dreads the fire; once bitten, twice shy.

Quotations—Present fears are less than horrible imaginings (*Shakespeare*), I will show you fear in a handful of dust (*T. S. Eliot*), The only thing we have to fear is fear itself (*F. D. Roosevelt*), Fear has many eyes and can see things underground (*Cervantes*), If we let things terrify us, life will not be worth living (*Seneca*), Fatigue makes cowards of us all (*George S. Patton*), Always do what you are afraid to do (*Mary Emerson*), Be not afraid of shadows (*Shakespeare*), 'Tis time to fear when tyrants seem to kiss (*Shakespeare*).

Antonyms, see HOPE, COURAGE.

---

fearless, *adj.* courageous, dauntless, daring, valorous, valiant, intrepid, unafraid. See COURAGE. *Ant.,* fearful, afraid.

feasible, *adj.* practicable, possible, workable; suitable. See POSSIBILITY, FACILITY. *Ant.,* impossible, undoable.

feast, *n.* banquet, spread, repast; holiday,

holy day, festival. —*v.* gratify, delight; regale, eat up. See FOOD, RITE, SUFFICIENCY, GLUTTONY, PLEASURE. *Ant.,* famine.

feat, *n.* deed, gest, accomplishment, exploit; stunt. See COURAGE, COMPLETION.

feather, *n.* plume, plumage, down, aigrette, quill; kind, sort, variety. See COVERING, DIFFERENCE, CLASS, ROUGHNESS.

feature, *n.* lineament, aspect; trait, peculiarity, property, characteristic; presentation, film, story. See FORM, INDICATION, IMPORTANCE, FRONT, SPECIALITY, APPEARANCE, PART.

feces, *n.* excrement, defecation, [bowel] movement. See EXCRETION.

fecund, *adj.* fertile, prolific, inventive, creative. See IMAGINATION, PRODUCTION. *Ant.,* barren.

federation, *n.* league, union, [con]federacy, association, alliance. See COOPERATION, PARTY, COMBINATION.

fee, *n.* PAYMENT, pay; COMPENSATION, emolument; assessment, dues, tax; gratuity, tip.

feeble, *adj.* See WEAKNESS. *Ant.,* strong.

feebleminded, *adj.* stupid, weak-minded, unintelligent. See IGNORANCE.

feed, *v.* eat, dine, consume, devour; graze; nourish, nurture, bait; supply, provide, furnish; satisfy, gratify. See FOOD, SUFFICIENCY, FUEL.

feedback, *n.* response, ANSWER.

feel, *v.* TOUCH, TASTE; experience; bear, suffer, endure (see DURABILITY); infer, intuit; explore. —*n.* emotion, FEELING; TOUCH; *informal,* aptitude, understanding. See REASONING, INTELLECT.

feeler, *n.* antenna, tentacle, palp[us], vibrissa, whisker; test, probe, trial balloon. See TOUCH, INQUIRY.

FEELING
Emotional sensation
See also TOUCH, TASTE

Nouns—**1,** feeling, sensation, sentience, emotion, SENSIBILITY, sensitivity; endurance, tolerance, sufferance, experience, response; vibrations; impression, inspiration; warmth, glow, unction, gusto, vehemence; fervor, fervency, fire; heart, breast; heartiness, cordiality; earnestness, eagerness; ardor, élan, zeal, passion, enthusiasm, verve, furor, fanaticism; EXCITEMENT; EXCITABILITY, ecstasy; PLEASURE. *Informal,* vibes. *Slang,* gut reaction.

2, tenderness, affection, fondness, soft place in the heart; sympathy, empathy, concern, caring; PITY, pathos, sympathy, LOVE.

3, *(symptom of emotion)* blush, suffusion, flush; tingling, thrill; turn, shock (see SURPRISE); AGITATION, quiver, throb[bing]; heartstrings, heartthrob; lump in the throat.

4, emotionalism, sensationalism; dramatics, theatrics, histrionics; sob story.

5, bad *or* hard feelings, hostility, animosity (see HATE).

6, sentimentalist. *Informal,* softie.

Verbs—**1,** feel, receive an impression; be impressed with; entertain, harbor, *or* cherish feeling; respond; catch fire, catch infection; enter the spirit of.

2, swell, glow, warm, flush, blush, change color, mantle; turn color, turn pale, turn black in the face; tingle, thrill, heave, pant, throb, palpitate, go pit-a-pat, tremble, quiver, flutter, twitter; wear one's heart on one's sleeve, take to heart; shake, be agitated, be excited, look blue, look black; wince, draw a deep breath. *Informal,* blow off steam. See AGITATION.

3, move, appeal to the emotions, touch the right chord.

Adjectives—**1,** feeling, sentient, sensuous; sensorial, sensory; emotive, emotional; tactile, tactual, tangible, palpable.

2, *(causing sharp emotion)* warm, quick, lively, smart, strong, sharp, acute, cutting, piercing, incisive; keen, exquisite, intense, razor-sharp; trenchant, pungent, racy, piquant, poignant, caustic.

3, *(causing deep emotion)* impressive, deep, profound, indelible; pervading, penetrating, absorbing; deep-felt, heartfelt; swelling, soul-stirring, electric, thrilling, rapturous, ecstatic.

4, *(expressing emotion)* earnest, wistful, eager, breathless; fervent, fervid; gushing, passionate, warmhearted, hearty, cordial, sincere, devout, zealous, enthusiastic, flowing, ardent, burning, consumed with, red-hot, fiery, flaming; seething, boiling; rabid, raving, feverish, delirious, fanatical, hysterical; impetuous, excitable. *Informal,* gung ho.

5, impressed by, moved by, touched, affected, seized by, imbued with; devoured by; wrought up, excited, struck all of a heap; misty- or dewy-eyed; rapt, in a quiver, enraptured.

Adverbs—feelingly, with feeling, heart and soul, with all one's heart, from the bottom of one's heart, at heart, *con amore, con brio,* heartily, devoutly, head over heels.

Quotations—The heart has its reasons which reason knows nothing of (*Pascal*), The desires of the heart are as crooked as corkscrews (*W. H. Auden*), Sentimentality is the emotional promiscuity of those who have no sentiment (*Norman Mailer*), If you want me to weep, you must first feel grief yourself (*Horace*).

Antonyms, see INSENSIBILITY.

---

feign, *v.t.* simulate, pretend, counterfeit, sham. See FALSEHOOD, AFFECTATION.

feint, *n.* diversion, trick; pretense, artifice, evasion; sleight-of-hand, legerdemain; bobbing and weaving; red herring. See CUNNING, DECEPTION.

feisty, *adj.* quarrelsome; frisky. See IRASCIBILITY, ACTIVITY.

felicitate, *v.t.* See CONGRATULATION.

felicitous, *adj.* happy, well-chosen, pertinent, apt, pat, neat. See AGREEMENT, ELEGANCE, SUCCESS. *Ant.,* inapt, unfortunate.

feline, *adj.* catlike, cattish, *etc.;* stealthy, CUNNING; catty. See ANIMAL.

fell, *v.t.* bring, cut, *or* chop down, drop.

See DISJUNCTION. —*adj.* ruthless, terrible. See FEAR. —*n.* pelt, skin (see COVERING).

fellow, *n.* comrade, associate, colleague; compeer, mate, equal; scholar; *informal,* person, man, boy, chap, guy. See HUMANITY, FRIEND, EQUALITY, ACCOMPANIMENT, MALE.

fellowship, *n.* companionship, camaraderie, comradeship; neighborliness, amity; sodality, sorority, fraternity; scholarship, bursary. See SOCIALITY, FRIEND, PARTY, COOPERATION, PAYMENT, ACCOMPANIMENT.

felon, *n.* criminal (see EVILDOER).

felony, *n.* crime (see ILLEGALITY).

FEMALE
The female sex

Nouns—**1,** female, womankind, womanhood, femininity, muliebrity; fair sex, weaker sex; feminist, suffragist (see CHOICE); women's liberation *or* movement, feminism, NOW; mommy track. See HUMANITY, POPULACE.

2, madam, madame, mistress, Mrs., Ms., lady, donna, belle, matron, dowager, goody, gammer; matriarch; crone (see EVILDOER); good woman, goodwife; squaw; wife (see MARRIAGE); matronhood; miss, mademoiselle, bachelorette; spinster; girl, lass (see YOUTH). *Informal,* sweater *or* pinup girl. *Slang,* babe, jane, fox, broiler, baggage, beaver, bitch goddess, cherry, chicken, doll, filly, sweet young thing, forbidden fruit, jail bait, bantam, quail, wench, nooky, pussy, skirt, snatch, [beach] bunny; calico, piece of stuff, frail, dame, skirt, broad, hammer, sister, tamale, tomato, [piece of] ass, poon[tang], bed-bunny, canvasback, bimbo, bimbette, bunny, chippy, cupcake, gash, groupie, band rat *or* moll; [piece of] tail, chassis, sexpot, [easy] lay, easy ride; pink[toes], Miss Ann, Miss Lillian; raven beauty, black velvet, shady lady, café au lait, sapphire, stone fox, brown sugar, brown-skin baby.

3, a. emancipated *or* liberated woman, feminist, new woman, s/he; femme fatale. *Slang,* bra burner. **b.** androgyne. *Slang,* jezebel, virago. **c.** lesbian, female homosexual, sapphist, tribade. *Slang,* bull[-dyke], [diesel *or* granola] dyke, butch, fem[me], gal-boy, fellagirly, lesbo, tootsie, wolf, jasper, velcro, crunchie, lipstick, fairy lady, lesbyterian. **d.** effeminate, pantywaist, weak sister, sissy, old woman, fribble. **e.** prostitute (see IMPURITY); nymphomaniac (see SEX).

4, *(female animal)* hen, bitch, sow, doe, roe, mare, she-goat, nanny-goat, ewe, cow, heifer, filly, jenny, vixen, lioness, tigress.

Verbs—feminize, womanize, emasculate.

Adjectives—1, female, feminine; womanly, ladylike, matronly; womanish, effeminate, unmanly, sissified, old-womanish; maternal; girlish, maidenly. *Slang,* foxy.

2, lesbian, gay, in the life, bi[sexual]. *Slang,* ambidextrous.

Phrases—the hand that rocks the cradle rules the world; a woman's place is in the home; a woman's work is never done; girls will be girls.

Quotations—A woman without a man is like a fish without a bicycle (*Gloria Steinem*), If all men are born free, how is it that all women are born slaves? (*Mary Astell*), I want to be something so much worthier than the doll in the doll's house (*Charles Dickens*), I myself have never been able to find out precisely what feminism is: I only know that people call me a feminist whenever I express sentiments that differ me from a doormat or a prostitute (*Rebecca West*), Woman is the nigger of the world (*Yoko Ono*), Woman was God's second blunder (*Friedrich Nietzsche*), The female of the species is more deadly than the male (*Rudyard Kipling*), A woman is a sometime thing (*Du Bose Heyward/Ira Gershwin*), In my youth there were words you couldn't say in front of a girl; now you can't say "girl" (*Tom Lehrer*), Woman's at best a contradiction still (*Alexander Pope*).

Antonyms, see MALE.

---

feminist, *n.* suffragist, suffragette. See FEMALE.

femme fatale, *Fr.* seductress. See ENDEARMENT, ATTRACTION.

fence, *n.* barrier, barricade, wall, stockade, paling, hedge, railing; *slang,* bagman *or* -woman, receiver [of stolen goods]. —*v.i.* enclose; fight, thrust and parry; parry, evade; *slang,* bootleg, black-market, unload. See DEFENSE, ENCLOSURE, CONTENTION, STEALING, ILLEGALITY.

fend, *v.* defend, protect, take care of; ward, hold, *or* stave off; avert; shift [for oneself], be on one's own. See DEFENSE, REPULSION.

fender, *n.* fire screen; bumper. See HEAT, SAFETY.

feral, *adj.* wild; undomesticated, uncultivated. See VIOLENCE.

ferment, *n.* yeast, leaven; uproar, turmoil, AGITATION, DISORDER. See SOURNESS. —*v.i.* effervesce, work, raise; seethe, arouse.

ferocity, *adj.* fierceness, savagery, brutality, cruelty. See MALEVOLENCE, VIOLENCE.

ferret out, *v.t.* spy, fish, search, *or* hunt out. See INQUIRY.

ferry, *n.* ferryboat, scow, lighter, barge, raft, launch, tender; shuttle, airlift, airdrop. —*v.* convey, transport, shuttle. See TRANSPORTATION.

fertile, *adj.* prolific, productive, fruitful, rich; creative, inventive. See PRODUCTION, IMAGINATION. *Ant.,* infertile, barren.

fertilization, *n.* impregnation, procreation, pollination; enrichment. See PRODUCTION.

fertilizer, *n.* manure, compost, guano. See AGRICULTURE.

fervent, *adj.* fervid, earnest, ardent, eager; vehement, impassioned, intense; hot, glowing. See DESIRE, FEELING, HEAT.

fervor, *n.* intenseness, enthusiasm, ardor, passion, zeal. See ACTIVITY, FEELING, HEAT.

fester, *n.* suppurate, ulcerate, rankle; infect. See DISEASE, DETERIORATION.

festina lente, *Lat.* make haste slowly. See CAUTION.

festive, *adj.* festal, joyful, gladsome (see REJOICING).

festivity, *n.* merrymaking, REJOICING; gaiety, jollity; (*pl.*) festival. See AMUSEMENT, CELEBRATION.

fetal, *adj.* embryonic, larval (see BEGINNING).

fetch, *v.t.* retrieve, bring, carry; heave, deal, yield; sell *or* go for. See TRANSPORTATION, PRICE.

fetid, *adj.* stinking, malodorous, foul, smelly, noisome. See MALODOROUSNESS.

fetish, *n.* charm, amulet, totem, talisman; obsession, mania. See IDOLATRY.

fetter, *v.t.* shackle, manacle, handcuff, [en]chain, put in irons; tie up, tie hand and foot, hobble, hog-tie, strap down; check, restrain. See RESTRAINT.

fetus, *n.* embryo. See BEGINNING.

feud, *n.* CONTENTION, quarrel, strife, conflict; rancor, grudge, rivalry, revenge, vendetta. —*v.i.* quarrel, struggle. See RETALIATION.

feudalism, *n.* vassalage, serfdom. See AUTHORITY, SUBJECTION.

fever, *n.* pyrexia; frenzy, delirium. See DISEASE, AGITATION, HEAT.

feverish, *adj.* febrile, hectic, hot; restless, agitated. See HEAT, EXCITEMENT, EXCITABILITY.

few, *adj.* not many, little; scant[y], meager, scarce, rare; infrequent; several, two or three, hardly any. See RARITY. *Ant.,* many.

fiancé(e), *n.* affianced, betrothed, engaged, *or* pledged [one]; husband- *or* bride-elect, intended (*inf.*). See PROMISE.

fiasco, *n.* FAILURE, miscarriage, slip, misfire; botch, mess. *Ant.,* SUCCESS.

fiat, *n.* decree, COMMAND, edict, mandate; sanction, PERMISSION.

fib, *n.* white lie. See FALSEHOOD. *Ant.,* TRUTH.

fiber, *n.* FILAMENT, thread, strand; shred; TEXTURE, structure.

fickle, *adj.* capricious, unstable, inconstant. See CHANGEABLENESS. *Ant.,* faithful, constant.

fiction, *n.* fabrication, FALSEHOOD; romance, myth, hypothesis. See DESCRIPTION. *Ant.,* fact.

fictitious, *adj.* imaginary, fictional, fictive;

feigned, false. See IMAGINATION, DECEPTION. *Ant.,* factual.

fiddle, *n.* violin (see MUSIC). —*v.i.* trifle. See UNIMPORTANCE.

fidelity, *n.* faithfulness, reliability, loyalty; exactness, accuracy. See TRUTH, PROBITY. *Ant.,* infidelity.

fidget, *v.i.* toss, squirm, twitch, twiddle. See AGITATION, EXCITABILITY.

fidus Achates, *Lat.* faithful Achates; a devoted FRIEND. See PROBITY.

field, *n.* clearing, grassland; expanse, range, plot; playground, links, court, airport, aerodrome, ARENA; scope, sphere, realm; battlefield, WARFARE. See REGION, BUSINESS, AGRICULTURE, SPACE.

fiend, *n.* DEMON, imp; addict, buff, fan, fanatic, enthusiast, nut (*all inf.*). See DESIRE, FEELING, EVILDOER, ACTIVITY. *Ant.,* angel.

fierce, *adj.* ferocious, truculent; tigerish, savage; intense, violent; aggressive, bellicose; vehement. See VIOLENCE, EXCITABILITY. *Ant.,* gentle, mild.

fiery, *adj.* impetuous, passionate, hot-tempered, fervid; irritable; blazing, glowing; inflamed. See HEAT, EXCITEMENT, IRASCIBILITY, EXCITABILITY.

fiesta, *n.* CELEBRATION, holiday, fete, festival.

fight, *n.* battle, affray, brawl, quarrel; contest, struggle; pugnacity. *Slang,* scrap. See CONTENTION, IRASCIBILITY, RESOLUTION.

fighter, *n.* COMBATANT; boxer, prize fighter, pugilist, bruiser, pug (*sl.*).

figment, *n.* invention, fantasy, chimera, pipe dream. See IMAGINATION.

FIGURATIVE
Characterized by symbolism and imagery

Nouns—1, figurativeness, figure of speech, figurative language, device; metaphor, conceit, euphuism; dead metaphor, mixed metaphor; way of speaking, colloquialism, turn of phrase.

2, a. (*simile*) figure, trope; symbolism; analogy; image, imagery. b. (*substitution*) metonymy, metalepsis, enallage, antonomasia, catachresis; synecdoche, euphemism, dysphemism. c. (*roundabout wording*) ambages. d. (*use of opposites*) antiphrasis, antithesis, oxymoron; syllepsis, zeugma, apophasis; irony, sarcasm. e. (*allegory*) type, anagoge, simile, personification, prosopopoeia, allegory, apologue, parable, fable; allusion, meiosis, adumbration. f. (*grammatical separation*) hendiadys. g. (*understatement*) litotes, preterition, paralepsis. h. (*exaggeration*) amplification, emphasis, hyperbole, bombast, exclamation, EXAGGERATION. i. periphrasis, parenthesis, polysyndeton. j. (*form of address*) apostrophe. k. (*omission*) anacoluthon. l. (*change of word order*) inversion, hypallage, hyperbaton, hysteron-proteron, aposiopesis, chiasmus, circumlocution, anastrophe; spoonerism, malapropism. m. *(anticipation)* prolepsis. n. *(repetition)* agnomination, anadiplosis, anaphora, autonomasia, aporia, climax, conversion, ecphonesis, epanaphora, epanodos, epanorthosis, epidiplosis, epiphora, eroteme, gemination, hypozeugma, hypozeuxis, kenning, paradiastole, paregmenon, pleonasm, redundancy, ploce, polyptoton, regression, symploce, repetition.

Verbs—speak figuratively, employ figures of speech, metaphor, *etc.*; verbalize; personify, allegorize, symbolize, adumbrate; apply, allude to.

Adjectives—figurative, metaphorical, flowery, florid, ornate, catachrestic, typical, parabolic, symbolic, allegorical, allusive, anagogical; ironical; colloquial.

Adverbs—figuratively, metaphorically; so to speak, so to say, in a sense, as it were; in a manner of speaking.

Antonyms, see MEANING.

---

figure, *n.* FORM, shape, configuration, outline; body; REPRESENTATION, image, effigy; APPEARANCE; pattern, diagram; figure of speech (see FIGURATIVE); emblem, symbol, NUMBER, digit; figurehead; cast, bust, statue. —*v.* ORNAMENT, decorate; symbolize, represent, signify, delineate, embody; imagine, conceive, picture; draw, outline; compute, calculate, do sums; appear, perform, act; cut a figure, matter, stand out. See IMAGINATION, NUMERATION, ACTION.

figurehead, *n.* prow, rostrum; front man, dummy, puppet. See FRONT, SUBSTITUTION.

figure of speech, *n.* expression, device (see FIGURATIVE).

figurine, *n.* statuette (see SCULPTURE).

FILAMENT
Threadlike fiber

Nouns—1, filament, line; fiber, fibril; funicle, vein, hair, capillament, capillary, cilium, tendril, gossamer; hairline.

2, string, chord, thread, cotton, sewing silk, twine, twist; whipcord, tape, ribbon, strap, strand, cord, rope, lariat, yarn, hemp, oakum, jute.

3, strip, shred, list, band, fillet, ribbon; lath, splinter, shiver, shaving; cable, wire.

4, spinning wheel, [spinning] jenny, mule.

Verbs—roll, spin, shred; braid.

Adjectives—filamentous, filaceous, filar, filiform; fibrous, fibrilous; threadlike, wiry, stringy, ropy; capillary, capilliform; funicular, wire-drawn; anguilliform; flagelliform; hairy, ciliate; gossamer.

---

filch, *v.t.* steal, pilfer (see STEALING).

file, *n.* ARRANGEMENT, classification; LIST, dossier, record, catalog, inventory; folder; row, column; rasp. —*v.t.* classify, arrange, STORE; catalog, record; submit, deliver; rasp. See CONTINUITY, FRICTION.

filial, *adj.* dutiful; sonlike, daughterly. See POSTERITY.

filibuster, *n. & v.i.* See SPEECH.

filigree, *n.* ornamentation, tracery, scrollwork, arabesque. See ORNAMENT.

fill, *v.t.* complete, load, pervade, permeate; plug, cork; occupy, serve well, satisfy; carry out. See LAYER, SUFFICIENCY, PRESENCE, CLOSURE, BUSINESS.

film, *n.* coating, membrane, haze, blur, scum; movie (see DRAMA). See COVERING, NARROWNESS.

filter, *v.* filtrate, strain, sieve; percolate, pass through; purify, refine, leach. See CLEANNESS, EGRESS. —*n.* strainer, sifter, sieve, screen, percolator; cheesecloth; optical *or* audio filter. See OPENING, DISJUNCTION.

filth, *n.* dirt, ordure; obscenity. See UNCLEANNESS, IMPURITY.

fin, *n.* flipper, process, lobe, pinna; propellor, rudder; lug, ear, blade. See NAVIGATION, PART.

finagle, *v.* wangle; maneuver. See CUNNING, DECEPTION.

final, *adj.* last, ultimate; decisive. See END, JUDGMENT.

finale, *n.* ending, conclusion, final curtain. See END.

finance, *v.t.* capitalize, back, fund, subsidize; put up money for; underwrite, guarantee. See DEBT, PAYMENT. —*n.* high finance, banking; budget, purse, treasury. See MONEY, ACCOUNTING, MEANS.

find, *v.t.* discover, detect, espy; get; obtain; learn, ascertain, perceive; provide; decide, declare. See ACQUISITION, DISCLOSURE, JUDGMENT.

fin de siècle, *Fr.* decadent. See DETERIORATION.

finding, *n.* find, discovery, ACQUISITION, windfall; JUDGMENT, verdict. See DISCLOSURE.

fine, *n.* penalty, forfeit, amercement. —*v.t.* amerce, mulct, penalize. See PUNISHMENT. —*adj.* pure, superior, admirable, excellent; small, tiny, slender, flimsy, delicate; worthy, estimable; skilled, accomplished; refined, polished; subtle, nice, keen, sharp; fair, pleasant. See PURITY, BEAUTY, LITTLENESS, NARROWNESS, RARITY.

fine arts, *n.* PAINTING, SCULPTURE, ARCHITECTURE, ENGRAVING, PHOTOGRAPHY.

finery, *n.* frippery, frills, tinsel. See ORNAMENT.

finesse, *n.* craft, CUNNING; SKILL.

finger, *n.* digit; pointer, trigger finger, pinky. See TOUCH. —*v.t.* TOUCH, feel, toy with; *slang,* tell on (see INFORMATION).

finicky, *adj.* finical, fussy; meticulous. See PERFECTION, CARE.

finish, *v.t.* END, terminate, complete, conclude; USE up, polish off. —*n.* COMPLETION, conclusion; poise, polish; surface, patina. See ELEGANCE, EXTERIOR, TEXTURE.

finite, *adj.* limited (see LIMIT).

fink, *n., slang,* [stool]pigeon, rat, informer; strikebreaker, scab. —*v.i.* inform on, squeal, rat; scab. See INFORMATION, IMPROBITY.

fire, *n.* flame, blaze, conflagration, holocaust; enthusiasm, verve. —*v.t.* kindle, ignite; shoot, detonate; inspire, arouse; dismiss, discharge. See HEAT, PROPULSION, EXCITEMENT, FUEL, VIGOR, EJECTION.

firearm, *n.* See ARMS.

firebrand, *n.,* revolutionary, terrorist, hothead (see AGITATION).

firebug, *n., informal,* pyromaniac, incendiary, arsonist. See HEAT, EVILDOER.

fireman, *n.* firefighter; stoker. See INCOMBUSTIBILITY, TRAVEL.

fireplace, *n.* hearth, ingle[nook], chimney. See HEAT.

fireproof, *adj.* See INCOMBUSTIBILITY.

firewood, *n.* faggots, logs, kindling. See FUEL.

fireworks, *n.pl.* pyrotechnics; firecrackers, sparklers, Roman candles, rockets, *etc.* See HEAT.

firm, *adj.* immovable, secure; unalterable, steadfast; solid, hard; steady, vigorous; unalterable, resolute, determined. See STABILITY, PROBITY, DENSITY, RESOLUTION. —*n.* partnership, company, house. See BUSINESS, PARTY.

firmament, *n.* sky, vault of HEAVEN; welkin, empyrean; starry cope. See UNIVERSE.

first, *adj.* earliest, original, prime; leading, chief, fundamental. —*adv.* firstly, originally, at first; before, ahead; sooner, rather. See BEGINNING, PRIORITY, PRECEDENCE.

first-class, first-rate, *adj.* choice, excellent, four-star, top-drawer, A-one, first-water; best, outstanding, palmary; de luxe, swanky, luxurious, ritzy (*sl.*). See SUPERIORITY.

firsthand, *adj.* eyewitness, authentic. See EVIDENCE.

fiscal, *adj.* monetary, financial. See MONEY.

fish, *v.* angle; pull out, dredge; solicit; search. See PURSUIT, DESIRE, FISH, FOOD.

FISH
Aquatic vertebrate animal

Nouns—1, fish, denizen of the deep, Pisces; anadromous, freshwater *or* saltwater fish, tropical fish, game fish; school, shoal; fish hatchery, fishery; fishing (see PURSUIT); panfish (see FOOD).

2, *(parts of a fish)* [dorsal, pectoral, pelvic, ventral, anal, adipose, *or* caudal] fin, spine, nostril, barbel, operculum, keel, tail, gill, gill slit, gill raker, scute, spiracle, priapum, swim bladder, myotome; [placoid, ganoid, ctenoid, *or* cycloid] scale; lateral line, cupula, neuromast, Weberian apparatus, electroreceptor, sucker.

3, *(jawless fishes)* hagfish; [northern, pouched, *or* shorthead] lamprey.

4, *(cartilaginous jawed fishes)* shark; frill, sixgill, cow, bramble, dogfish, rough, saw, horn, bullhead, carpet, blind, zebra, nurse, whale, goblin, crocodile, megamouth, thresher, basking, mackerel, finback, weasel, whaler, requiem, angel, man-eating, *or* hammerhead shark, wobbegong, white-spotted spurdog, sand tiger, mako, tope, catshark, houndshark; ray, platyrhinid, guitarfish; skate, sawfish, electric ray, coffinray, narcinid, narkid, river ray, sting ray, butterfly ray, sixgill ray, eagle ray, cownose ray, shovelnose ray, sharkfin, guitarfish, manta, devil ray; [plownose, shortnose, *or* longnose] chimaera, ratfish, spookfish, elephant fish.

5, *(bony jawed fishes)* a. lungfish, coelacanth, gombessa. b. bichir, reedfish, sturgeon, beluga, paddlefish, gar, bowfin. c. teleost, bonytongue, arapaima, pirarucu, butterflyfish, featherback, mooneye, goldeye, aba, elephantfish; tenpounder, ladyfish, tarpon, bonefish, halosaur, spiny eel; [freshwater, shortfaced, spaghetti, moray, slime, snipe, pike, cutthroat, snake, worm, duckbill, conger, garden, narrowneck, spoonbill, sawtooth, gulper, *or* singlejaw] eel, swallower. d. herring, brisling, sprat, sardine, sardinella, shad, menhaden, mossbunker, pilchard, anchovy, anchoveta, nehu, thryssa. e. milkfish, beaked salmon, shellear, hingemouth; carp, koi, mahseer, rasbora, snow trout, roach, redeye, rudd, bleak, bream, squawfish, bitterling, zebrafish, zebra danio, shiner, goldfish, veiltail, chub, minnow, dace, ide, orfe, tench, loach, sucker; buffalofish, characin, tigerfish, trahira, voladora, pyrrhulina[n], pencil fish, African *or* neon tetra, brycon, piranha, tambaqui, flannelmouth, anastomin, leporinin, headstander, hatchetfish.

6, a. catfish, [velvet, mountain, spinyhead, plated, spinynose, Andes, suckermouth, bullhead, miller's thumb, bagrid, schilbid, torrent, loach, banjo, hillstream, airsac, electric, olyrid, eeltail, upsidedown, thorny, wood, shovelnose, bottlenose, helogene, shark, *or* loweye] catfish, corydora, candirus, madtom, wels, sheatfish, squeaker, longwhisker, carnero. b. [longtail, longsnout, bluntnose, *or* banded] knifefish.

7, pike, muskellunge, muskie, mudminnow, smelt, cap[e]lin, barreleye, spookfish, slickhead, tubeshoulder, salamanderfish, ayu, icefish, noodlefish, galaxiid, peladillo, whitebait, [brook, golden, rainbow, Sunapee, *or* brown] trout, steelhead, [Chinook *or* sockeye] salmon, pike, pickerel, char, whitefish, cisco, grayling.

8, a. lightfish, bristlemouth, hatchetfish, viperfish, dragonfish, snaggletooth, loosejaw; aulopid, bathysaurid, greeneye, harpadontic, Bombay duck, tripod fish. b. lizardfish, pearleye, waryfish, telescopefish, hammerjaw, barracudina, daggertooth, omosudid, lancetfish. c. lanternfish. d. troutperch, cavefish, swampfish, blindfish. e. cod, burbot, mora, melanonid, codlet, codfish, pollock, haddock, hake, rattail, grenadier. f. pearlfish, cuskeel, kingklip, brotula, pearlfish, aphyonid. g. toadfish, midshipman. h. goosefish, monkfish, frogfish, lophichthyid, [humpback, fanfin, needlebeard, wolftrap, hollowchin, *or* double] angler, hand fish, seatoad, gaper, coffinfish, batfish, seadevil, netdevil, dreamer, footballfish, blackdevil.

9, a. clingfish, singleslit. b. annual, profundulid, killifish, mosquitofish, ricefish, medaka, buntingi, Amazon molly, platy[fish], Amistad gambusia, panchax, cuatro ojos, livebearer, guppie, goodeid, pupfish. c. flyingfish, halfbeak, betta, needlefish, saury. d. silverside, topsmelt, jacksmelt, grunion, rainbowfish, blue-eyes. e. opah, velifer, crestfish, inkfish, ribbonfish, oarfish, tube-eye, jellynose fish. **f.** beardfish, squirrelfish, soldier fish, alfoncino, redfish, fangtooth fish, pineapple or pinecone fish, coat-of-mail fish, flashlight or lanterneye fish, roughie, sawbelly, slimehead, spinyfin, fangtooth, pricklefish, bigscale fish, ridgehead, gibberfish, bristlyskin, [orangemouth, redvelvet, or flabby] whalefish, hairyfish, tapetail, mosaicscale fish.

10, a. parazen, dory, orio, tinselfish, boarfish. **b.** sand eel, tubesnout, stickleback; paradox fish; seamoth, trumpetfish, cornetfish, snipefish, shrimpfish, razorfish, pipefish, seahorse. **c.** swampeel, marbled eel. **d.** scorpionfish, rockfish, stonefish, coral croucher, velvetfish, prowfish, pigfish, horsefish, sea robin, gurnard, flathead, sablefish, skilfish, greenling, lingcod, combfish, sculpin, cabezon, ereuniid, oilfish, blob fish, poacher, snailfish, lumpfish, lumpsucker, stonefish, turkeyfish, lionfish.

11, perch, glassfish, snook, barramundi, robalo, gnomefish, discus, wreckfish, cavebass, snook, weakfish, sea trout, squeteague, dottyback, basslet, jawfish, roundhead, bandfish, grunter, banjosid, aholehole, sunfish, tilapia, crappie, darter, bigeye, catalufa, cardinalfish, whiting, tilefish, trevally, bluefish, tailor, moonfish, ponyfish, slipmouth, pomfret, manefish, rover, [red] snapper, fusilier, emperor, tripletail, mojarra, silver biddy, grunt, bonnetmouth, porgy, scup, bream, scavenger, emperor, threadfin, drum[fish], croaker, goatfish, moonfish, fingerfish, sweeper, beachsalmon, archerfish, nurseryfish, galjoenfish, seachub, nibbler, blackfish, tautog, halfmoon, mado, sweep, stripey, spadefish, argusfish, scat, butterflyfish, angelfish, dottyback, hulafish, devilfish, longfin, spiny basslet, alewife, oldwife, armorhead, knifejaw, ragfish, nurseryfish; roosterfish, papagallo, jack, pompano, permit, pilot fish, scad, amberjack, remora, cobia, sergeant fish, dolphin; hawkfish, kelpfish, morwong, trumpeter; mullet; threadfin; ronquil, eelpout, prickleback, wrymouth, gunnel, wolffish, quillfish, prowfish, graveldiver; thornfish, plunderfish, dragonfish, icefish; swallower, sandfish, weeverfish, stargazer, sanddiver, sandburrower, duckbill, sandperch, torrentfish, sandlance; triplefin, blenny; dragonet; rabbitfish, louvar, Moorish idol, surgeonfish, doctorfish, tang; barracuda fish, cutlassfish, mackerel, albacore, tuna, bonito, swordfish, sailfish, marlin, spearfish, billfish, wahoo; medusafish, driftfish, squaretail, butterfish; chameleonfish, leaffish, snakehead, [climbing, kissing, or giant] gourami, pikehead; spiny eel.

12, a. grouper, rock cod, soapfish, podge, cabrilla, kelp bass, butter hamlet, anthias, sea bass. **b.** cichlid, angelfish. **c.** surfperch, damselfish, demoiselle, anemonefish, white ear, garibaldi, clownfish. **d.** wrass, parrotfish, butterfish, rock whiting, rainbow cale, clown coris. **e.** [snake, convict, or mimic] blenny, sand stargazer. **f.** goby, sleeper, gudgeon, mudskipper. **g.** flatfish, flounder, plaice, whiff, halibut, tonguefish, [Dover, lemon, or tongue] sole. **h.** spikefish, triplespine, triggerfish, filefish, leatherjacket, boxfish, cowfish, trunkfish, pursefish, puffer[fish], toado, porcupinefish, ocean sunfish, globefish, balloonfish.

13, *(young fish)* alevin, fry, parr, smolt, grilse, whitebait.

14, *(minute marine animals)* plankton, benthos, nekton, tripton, [bio]seston.

Verbs—spawn; fish, angle (see PURSUIT).

Adjectives—fishy, fishlike, eellike, *etc.*; anguilliform, selachian, *etc.*; piscatory, piscatorial.

Quotations—Who hears the fishes when they cry? It will not be forgotten by some memory that we were contemporaries *(Thoreau)*.

---

fisher, *n.* fisherman *or* -woman, angler, piscator; whaler, clam digger, *etc.* See PURSUIT, FISH.

fishy, *adj.*, *informal*, unlikely, improbable; suspicious. See IMPROBABILITY, DOUBT.

fission, *n.* cleavage, scission, DISJUNCTION; nuclear fission, splitting the atom, atom smashing.

fissure, *n.* cleft, chink, opening, crack, rift, breach. See INTERVAL.

fit, *n.* caprice, whim, fancy, notion; paroxysm, convulsion, seizure, outburst. See

AGITATION. —*v.* equip, furnish, outfit; grace, beautify; accommodate; clothe; suit, meet, conform; adapt. See AGREEMENT, EQUALITY, PREPARATION, CLOTHING. —*adj.* appropriate, suitable, fitting, proper; expedient, advantageous; vigorous, well, sound. See AGREEMENT, HEALTH, VIOLENCE, EXPEDIENCE, DISEASE.

fitful, *adj.* intermittent. See DISCONTINUANCE.

fitting, *adj.* suitable, proper, decorous; expedient. See AGREEMENT, EXPEDIENCE.

fix, *v.t.* stabilize, establish; repair, adjust, mend; settle, decide; place; fasten; prepare; *slang,* bribe; *informal,* spay, castrate. See STABILITY, RESTORATION, JUNCTION, CERTAINTY, LOCATION, DENSITY. —*n., informal,* predicament (see DIFFICULTY).

fixation, *n.* focus, ATTENTION; idée fixe, obsession, compulsion, mania, bee in one's bonnet (*inf.*), hangup (*sl.*). See INSANITY.

fixings, *n.pl.* ingredients (see COMPOSITION).

fixture, *n.* attachment, fitting, appendage. See PERMANENCE.

fizzle, *v.i.* fizz, effervesce, bubble, ferment, foam; sizzle, hiss; *informal,* collapse, disintegrate, fade *or* die out, fail, flop, conk out. See FAILURE, AGITATION.

fjord, *n.* inlet, arm [of the sea]. See WATER.

flabbergast, *v.t.* confound, astonish, SURPRISE.

flabby, *adj.* limp, soft, flaccid; feeble. See SOFTNESS, WEAKNESS.

flaccid, *adj.* flabby, soft. See SOFTNESS.

flag, *n.* banner, pennant, ensign, standard; iris; flagstone. See INDICATION. —*v.i.* droop, pine, languish. See INACTIVITY, DEJECTION, DISEASE.

flagellate, *v.t.* whip, flog (see PUNISHMENT).

flagon, *n.* flask, bottle, carafe, mug. See RECEPTACLE.

flagrant, *adj.* glaring, notorious, outrageous, shocking. See BADNESS.

flagrante delicto, Lat. red-handed. See GUILT, ACTION.

flail, *v.* thrash, flog (see PUNISHMENT).

flair, *n.* judgment, discernment, TASTE; talent, gift, bent, TENDENCY, SKILL; verve, style, bravura, flourish.

flak, *n.* criticism, bad press (see DISAPPROBATION).

flake, *n.* fleck, floccule, scale, chip, shaving; snowflake. See LAYER, COLD.

flaky, *adj.* flocculent, scaly; crumbly; *slang,* eccentric, wacky. See POWDERINESS, LAYER, UNCONFORMITY.

flam, *n.* trick, DECEPTION. —*v.t.* deceive, cheat.

flamboyant, *adj.* extravagant, showy, ostentatious; pompous, strutting, high-flown, grandiloquent, splendiferous (*inf.*). See OSTENTATION.

flame, *n.* blaze, fire; EXCITEMENT, passion, zeal; *slang,* sweetheart. See HEAT, LOVE.

flaming, *adj.* flagrant; fiery; passionate, violent. See HEAT, BADNESS, VIOLENCE.

flange, *n.* rim, collar, EDGE.

flank, *n.* SIDE, wing (of an army). —*v.t.* skirt, circle around.

flap, *n.* tab, fly, lap, tag; FOLD; argument, controversy. See DISCORD, ADDITION. —*v.* swing, sway, flop, beat, wave. See AGITATION.

flare, *v.* blaze [up], burst into flame; shine, glow; spread out, swell, splay. —*n.* torch, flambeau, signal [light]; curvature, swelling; outburst. See LIGHT, EXPANSION.

flash, *v.i.* flare, blaze; burst, streak; gleam, scintillate; retort. See LIGHT.

flashback, *n.* MEMORY, reminiscence; back draft.

flashy, *adj.* gaudy, showy, garish. See ORNAMENT. *Ant.,* plain, dull.

flask, *n.* bottle, vial, flacon, ampoule. See RECEPTACLE.

flat, *adj.* level, smooth, plane; even, flush; positive, exact; dull, stale, insipid; *slang,* penniless. See HORIZONTAL, CERTAINTY, POVERTY, INSIPIDITY. —*n.* plain, shoal; apartment (see ABODE). *Ant.,* curved, uneven.

flatten, *v.* level, smooth [out], grade; raze. See HORIZONTAL, DESTRUCTION.

FLATTERY
Undue adulation

Nouns—1, flattery, adulation, blandishment, cajolery; fawning, wheedling, coquetry, sycophancy, flunkeyism, SERVILITY, toadying, incense, honeyed words, flummery, blarney; lip service, unctuousness. *Informal,* soft soap, sweet talk, stroking. *Slang,* snow job, banana oil, pot-licking, ego massage. See FALSEHOOD.

2, flatterer, adulator; eulogist; toady, flunky, sycophant, courtier; puffer, touter, claquer; parasite, hanger-on (see SERVILITY); coquette. *Slang,* brown-nose[r], ass-kisser, egg-sucker; star-fucker.

Verbs—flatter, adulate, praise to the skies, puff; wheedle, cajole, coax; fawn (upon); blandish, humor, soothe, pet; overpraise, turn one's head; pay court to, court, curry favor with; overestimate, exaggerate (see EXAGGERATION). *Informal,* soft soap, butter up, stroke [one's ego], lick one's boots, lay *or* spread it on thick, pull one's leg, string along. *Slang,* snow, honey up, grease, kiss ass.

Adjectives—flattering, adulatory; mealy- *or* honey-mouthed, honeyed, buttery, fawning, smooth, smooth-tongued; soapy, oily, unctuous, specious, obsequious; fine-spoken, sycophantic, fulsome, courtly.

Adverbs—flatteringly, fulsomely, fawningly, *etc.*

Phrases—flattery, like perfume, should be smelled, not swallowed.

Quotations—I suppose flattery hurts no one, that is, if he doesn't inhale (*Adlai Stevenson*), Imitation is the sincerest form of flattery (*Charles Caleb Colton*), But when I tell him he hates flatterers, he says he does, being then most flattered (*Shakespeare*), Let those flatter who fear: it is not an American art (*Thomas Jefferson*), For flattery is the bellows blows up sin (*Shakespeare*).

Antonyms, see DETRACTION.

---

flatulence, *n.* windiness, belching, eructation, gassiness, gas; conceit, pompousness. See OSTENTATION, VAPOR.

flaunt, *v.* parade, display; brandish. See OSTENTATION.

flavor, *n.* TASTE, seasoning, savor.

flavorless, *adj.* tasteless, flat, insipid. See INSIPIDITY.

flaw, *n.* IMPERFECTION, defect, fault, mar, crack; ERROR, mistake, gust, squall, flurry. See WIND, INTERVAL.

flawless, *adj.* perfect (see PERFECTION).

flay, *v.t.* skin, peel; criticize. See DIVESTMENT, DISAPPROBATION.

fleabag, *n., slang,* flophouse (see ABODE).

flea market, street market, *marché aux puces.* See SALE.

fleck, *n.* speck, speckle, flyspeck, spot. See LITTLENESS.

fledgling, *n.* beginner, novice, tyro (see BEGINNING).

flee, *v.i.* run away, fly, abscond. See AVOIDANCE, ESCAPE.

fleece, *v.t.* swindle, despoil, rob, strip. See STEALING, DECEPTION. —*n.* coat (see COVERING).

fleet, *n.* navy; flotilla, squadron, argosy, armada. See SHIP, COMBATANT, ASSEMBLAGE. —*adj.* swift, speedy, nimble. See VELOCITY.

fleeting, *adj.* transient, transitory (see TRANSIENTNESS).

flesh, *n.* animal tissue, meat, pulp; HUMANITY, materiality, carnality; blood relative. See FOOD, IMPURITY.

fleshly, *adj.* corporeal, bodily; carnal, sensual. See HUMANITY, BODY.

fleshy, *adj.* plump, fat (see ROTUNDITY).

flex, *v.t.* bend, contract (see ELASTICITY).

flexible, *adj.* pliant, limber, lithe, supple; adaptable. See SOFTNESS, ELASTICITY.

flick, *n.* tap; jerk; *slang,* movie. See IMPULSE, TOUCH, MOTION PICTURES.

flicker, *v.i.* waver, flutter, quiver, blink. See IRREGULARITY, LIGHT.

flier, *n.* aviator, aeronaut, airman, astronaut, pilot, co-pilot; leaflet, handbill, circular, birdman (*sl.*), flyboy (*sl.*). See AVIATION, PUBLICATION.

flight, *n.* decampment, hegira, ESCAPE, elopement; course, onrush; covey, flock, shower, volley; wing, squadron. See

AVOIDANCE, MOTION, ASSEMBLAGE, AVIATION, VELOCITY.

flighty, *adj.* light-headed; scatterbrained, capricious, frivolous. See INATTENTION, INSANITY.

flimsy, *adj.* sleazy, gossamer, fragile; tenuous, unsubstantial; feeble, weak. See WEAKNESS.

flinch, *v.i.* wince, shrink, RECOIL. See COWARDICE, FEAR.

fling, *v.t.* throw, cast, hurl, sling. See PROPULSION.

flip, *n. & v.t.* flick, snap; flip-flop. See IMPULSE, CHANGE. —*adj., informal,* pert, flippant. See INSOLENCE.

flippant, *adj.* pert, impertinent; thoughtless, frivolous, flip (*inf.*). See INSOLENCE.

flirt, *n.* coquette, philanderer, vamp (*sl.*). —*v.i.* coquet, philander, dally. See ENDEARMENT. —*v.t.* jerk, fling, throw, toss. See PROPULSION.

flit, *v.i.* fly, dart, take wing. See DEPARTURE, MOTION, TRAVEL, TRANSIENTNESS.

float, *v.* glide, drift, be wafted, hover, soar, be buoyed up. —*n.* ferry, SHIP, raft; launch. See ASCENT.

flock, *n.* drove, herd; covey, flight, bevy; congregation. See MULTITUDE, RELIGION.

flog, *v.t.* thrash (see PUNISHMENT).

flood, *n.* deluge, inundation, torrent, freshet, cloudburst, spate; superabundance. See SUFFICIENCY, WATER, ASSEMBLAGE.

floodgate, *n.* dam, spillway, weir, lock; sluice[-gate], conduit; flume, penstock; control, inhibition. See HINDRANCE, EGRESS.

floor, *n.* flooring, deck, pavement, terrazzo; story, level; rostrum. See COVERING, HORIZONTAL, LAYER.

floozy, *n., slang,* prostitute, tart (see FEMALE, IMPURITY).

flop, *v.i.* fall, drop, thud, plump down; loll, idle; flutter, flap; *slang,* sleep, bed down; *slang,* fail, bust (*inf.*), lay an egg

(*sl.*). See DESCENT, FAILURE, REPOSE. —*n., slang,* FAILURE, bust (*sl.*), turkey (*sl.*).

floppy, *adj.* limp, droopy, baggy. See SOFTNESS.

floral, *adj.* flowery, flowering; horticultural. See VEGETABLE.

florid, *adj.* ruddy, flushed; showy, rococo, flowery. See COLOR, OSTENTATION.

flotilla, *n.* fleet (see NAVIGATION).

flotsam, *n.* wreckage, refuse, odds and ends. See RELINQUISHMENT.

flounce, *v.i.* ruffle, trim; prance, bounce. See EDGE, LEAP.

flounder, *v.i.* wallow, welter, struggle, stagger, fumble, grope. See FAILURE, UNSKILLFULNESS.

flourish, *v.t.* wave, wield, flaunt, brandish. See AGITATION. —*v.i.* grow, prosper, thrive. See PROSPERITY. —*n.* fanfare; ORNAMENT. See MUSIC, OSTENTATION.

flout, *v.* mock, scoff (at). See CONTEMPT, DISRESPECT.

flow, *v.i.* run, glide, trickle, stream, sweep along; circulate; issue. See MOTION, WATER, FLUIDITY.

flower, *n.* bloom, blossom, posy; elite, elect, best, pick; ORNAMENT. See VEGETABLE, GOODNESS.

flowery, *adj.* florid, high-flown, flamboyant; blossomy. See ORNAMENT, OSTENTATION.

flowing, *adj.* running, gliding; fluent, graceful, smooth; loose, billowy. See WATER, ELEGANCE.

flub, *n. & v.* blunder, fumble, goof (*inf.*). See ERROR.

fluctuate, *v.i.* alternate, wave, vacillate, vary, shift. See CHANGEABLENESS, OSCILLATION.

flue, *n.* duct (see PASSAGE, CONDUIT).

fluent, *adj.* flowing, graceful, voluble. See ELEGANCE, LOQUACITY.

fluffy, *adj.* downy, flocculent, cottony. See SOFTNESS.

fluid, *n.* See FLUIDITY. —*adj.* changeable, variable; liquid, flowing. See CHANGEABLENESS, FLUIDITY.

FLUIDITY
Quality of a liquid

Nouns—1, fluidity, liquidity, serosity, liquidness; fluid, liquid, liquor; lymph, juice, sap, serum, plasma, blood, ichor; solubility, solubleness, LIQUEFACTION; fluidics, hydrostatics, hydrodynamics; stream (see WATER). See MOTION, MOISTURE.

2, fluid, liquid, juice, sap, lymph, plasma, blood, ichor; gas, VAPOR; solution, decoction, brew (see DRINKING).

Verbs—be fluid, flow, bleed; liquefy (see LIQUEFACTION).

Adjectives—fluid, liquid, serous, juicy, milky, watery (see WATER); succulent, sappy; affluent, fluent, flowing; liquefied, uncongealed, soluble (see LIQUEFACTION).

Antonyms, see DENSITY.

---

fluke, *n.* stroke of luck, accident; [lucky] break. See CHANCE.

flunk, *v.* fail, flunk out [of]. See FAILURE.

flunky, *n.* lackey; toady. See SERVANT, FLATTERY.

flurry, *n.* squall, gust, scud, blast; hubbub, ferment. See WIND, ACTIVITY. —*v.t.* ruffle, excite, fluster. See AGITATION.

flush, *v.* blush, redden; elate, thrill; rinse; start, rouse. See HORIZONTAL. —*n.* blush, redness, glow, elation, thrill; gush, rush. See HEAT, FEELING, COLOR, CLEANNESS.

fluster, *v.t.* confuse; excite. See EXCITEMENT, INATTENTION.

flute, *n.* groove, FURROW, channel; pipe, piccolo, fife. See MUSIC.

flutter, *v.* flicker, tremble, flap, shake, whip, wave; bustle, fidget, twitter, quiver; agitate, ruffle; hover. See AGITATION, OSCILLATION, FEAR.

flux, *n.* flow, current, course; MOTION, CHANGE, transition; continuum; solvent; EXCRETION.

fly, *v.* soar, wing, aviate; float, wave; speed, bolt, dart; flee, decamp, disperse, scatter. See AVIATION, VELOCITY, ESCAPE.

fly-by-night, *adj.* unreliable, untrusty (see DOUBT).

foam, *n.* froth, suds, lather, spume. —*v.i.* froth, spume. See AGITATION, EXCITABILITY.

focus, *n.* point; focal *or* central point; concentration, CONVERGENCE; center, hub, core, heart, nucleus; sharpness. —*v.* concentrate, converge; centralize, contract; rally, gather, meet. See MIDDLE, VISION.

fodder, *n.* feed, forage (see FOOD).

foe, *n.* enemy, adversary, antagonist, opponent. See OPPOSITION.

fog, *n.* mist, smog, vapor, haze, cloud; uncertainty, OBSCURITY. See CLOUDINESS, MOISTURE.

fogy, *n.* See PERMANENCE.

foible, *n.* whimsy, WEAKNESS.

foil, *v.t.* frustrate, battle, balk, circumvent. See HINDRANCE. —*n.* contrast, setoff; leaf, sheet (of metal); sword, épée. See OPPOSITION, LAYER, ARMS.

foist, *v.t.* palm off (see DECEPTION).

fold, *n.* bend (see FOLD); embrace; pleat; flock, congregation. See RELIGION, ASSEMBLAGE.

FOLD
A bending double

Nouns—fold, plication, crease, double, bend, lapping, plait; wrinkle, corrugation; flap, lapel, turnover, dog-ear; ply (see LAYER); tuck, gather, [accordion] pleat, ruffle, flounce; crow's-feet; paper-folding, origami. See FURROW.

Verbs—fold, double (over), crease, crimp, bend; pucker, knit, corrugate, wrinkle, FURROW; tuck, gather, pleat; double back; turn over, dog-ear; crumple, rumple, crinkle; friz[zle], crisp.

Adjectives—folded, creased, *etc.*; plicate; wrinkled, knitted, puckered; foldable, pliable, flexible.

Antonyms, see SMOOTHNESS, HORIZONTAL.

folder, *n.* booklet; cover, portfolio, loose-leaf [folder]. See WRITING, RECEPTACLE.

foliage, *n.* leafage, verdure. See VEGETABLE.

folk, *n.* people, commonalty, race; kin. See HUMANITY, POPULACE.

folklore, *n.* mythology, legends, old wives' tales. See KNOWLEDGE, MYTHICAL DEITIES.

folksy, *adj.* sociable, friendly; informal, rustic. See SOCIALITY, HUMANITY.

follow, *v.* go *or* come after; succeed; tread on the heels of; come *or* be next; pursue (see PURSUIT); attend, associate with, go with, accompany; adhere to, support; obey, heed; understand; copy, imitate, emulate, practice; ensue, result, be the outcome of. See SEQUENCE, IMITATION, EFFECT, ACCOMPANIMENT, REAR.

follower, *n.* adherent, disciple, cohort. See ACCOMPANIMENT.

following, *n.* followers, adherents; attendance, train, retinue. See ACCOMPANIMENT.

follow-through, *n.* COMPLETION; continuation, follow-up (*inf.*).

FOLLY
Lack of good sense

Nouns—1, folly, silliness, foolishness, inanity, idiocy; frivolity, ineptitude; giddiness; INATTENTION; irrationality, eccentricity (see INSANITY); extravagance, nonsense, ABSURDITY; RASHNESS; stultification, infatuation. *Slang,* meshuggaas; flapdoodle. See SHALLOWNESS.

2, *(foolish person)* fool, dunce, idiot, tomfool, wiseacre, simpleton, imbecile, donkey, ass, [silly] goose, ninny, nincompoop, dolt, numskull, bonehead, boob[y]; trifler, babbler; oaf, lout, loon, ass, dullard, dunderhead, blockhead, loggerhead; half-wit, nitwit, lackwit; harebrain; clod, clodhopper. *Informal,* chump, loony, dingbat, ding-a-ling, chucklehead, fathead, schmuck. *Slang,* jerk, sap, duffer, dumbbell, square, rube, airbrain, airhead, dumbo, muttonhead, clodhead, dimwit, goof, dumb bunny, gonzo, space cadet, schlemazel, donk, flat tire, fruitcake, zip, woodcock, asshole.

3, *(foolish act)* act of folly, indiscretion, blunder; antic (see AMUSEMENT). *Informal,* dumb thing to do.

4, *(people foolish for special reasons)* innocent, milksop, sop (see CREDULITY); dotard, driveler; old fogy, old woman; crone, grandmother; greenhorn, dupe, ignoramus (see IGNORANCE); lubber, bungler, blunderer; madman (see INSANITY); jester (see WIT).

Verbs—1, be a fool, be foolish, fool around, drivel, have rocks in one's head; play the fool, talk nonsense *or* through one's hat, take leave of one's senses, need one's head examined. *Slang,* horse around.

2, make a fool *or* monkey of, stultify, infatuate (see RIDICULE).

Adjectives—1, foolish, silly, senseless, inane, irrational, giddy, fatuous, nonsensical, inept. *Slang,* daft, screwy, goofy, daffy, flaky, out to lunch, dizzy, loony, meshugga, jive-ass.

2, unwise, injudicious, imprudent, unreasonable, without [rhyme or] reason, ridiculous, silly, stupid, asinine, ill-advised, ill-judged, extravagant, idle, useless (see USELESSNESS); inexpedient, frivolous, trivial (see UNIMPORTANCE).

Phrases—ask a silly question and you get a silly answer; a fool and his money are soon parted; fools build houses and wise men live in them; a fool's bolt is soon shot.

Quotations—A knowledgeable fool is a greater fool than an ignorant fool (*Molière*), Fools rush in where angels fear to tread (*Alexander Pope*), A fool sees not the same tree that a wise man sees (*William Blake*), Better a witty fool than a foolish wit (*Shakespeare*), Lord, what fools these mortals be! (*Shakespeare*).

Antonyms, see KNOWLEDGE, REASONING.

---

foment, *v.t.* stir up, incite. See EXCITEMENT.

fond, *adj.* affectionate, tender; foolish, doting. See LOVE.

fondle, *v.t.* pet, caress, cosset, feel up (*sl.*). See ENDEARMENT.

font, *n.* fount[ain], spring, source, basin, baptistery, reservoir; type, case, face. See RECEPTACLE, PRINTING.

FOOD
Nourishment

Nouns—1, food, aliment, nourishment, nutriment; aliment[ation], foodstuffs, sustenance, nurture, subsistence, provender, daily bread, fodder, PROVISION, ration, keep, commons, board; fare, cheer; diet, regimen; bread, staff of life; natural *or* organic food, health food, soul food, Tex-Mex, macrobiotics; additive; comestibles, eatables, victuals, edibles, groceries, convenience food; finger foods; meat, viands; fast food, convenience food; delicacy, dainty; fleshpots; festive board; ambrosia; good cheer; hearty meal; soul food. *Slang,* grub, chow; junk food, eats, vittles, scarf, dog's vomit.

2, cookery, [nouvelle] cuisine, haute cuisine, *cuisine minceur,* cordon bleu, home cooking.

3, meal, repast, feed, spread; mess; dish, plate, course, entrée; pièce de résistance, hors d'oeuvres; REFRESHMENT; refection, collation, picnic, box lunch; feast, banquet, luau (see AMUSEMENT); [continental *or* power] breakfast; *déjeuner,* lunch, luncheon; [high] tea; dinner, supper, snack, dessert; pot luck [supper], wiener roast, barbecue, cookout, fish fry, pot luck; buffet, smorgasbord; table d'hôte; table, cuisine, bill of fare, menu; chow line. *Informal,* brunch; square meal.

4, appetizer, hors d'oeuvres, kickshaw, antipasto, canapé, cold cut, crudités, dim sum, dip, finger food, rollmop, rumaki, spreads, starters, tapas, vorspeise.

5, herb, spice, bouquet garni; allspice, angelica, anise, basil, bay leaf, pepper, capers, caraway seed, cardamom, carob, cayenne, celery seed, chervil, chicory, chili powder, chives, cilantro, cinnamon, cloves, coriander, cubeb, cumin, curry, dill, garlic, fennel, fenugreek, ginger, salt, lemon grass, licorice, mace, marjoram, mint, mustard, nutmeg, oregano, paprika, parsley, poppy seed, rosemary, saffron, sage, sesame seed, sorrel, tarragon, thyme, turmeric, vanilla.

6, a. grain, staff of life, [bleached, enriched, pastry, rice, rye, semolina, unbleached, wheat, *or* white] flour; barley, cornmeal, bran, buckwheat, couscous, farina, grits, hominy, millet, oats, polenta, [basmati, brown, enriched, long-grain, minute, short-grain, wild, *or* white] rice, rye, wheat. b. bread, roll cracker, bagel, baguette, biscuit, muffin, breadstick, brioche, bun, challah, chapati, cornbread, cracknel, croissant, crouton, egg bread, English muffin, goody *or* crackling bread, graham cracker, hardtack, johnny cake, matzo, melba toast, pita, pretzel, pumpernickel, raisin bread, [dinner, Kaiser, *or* sourdough] roll, saltine, sippet, soda biscuit, toast, tortilla, wafer, zwieback; sandwich, dagwood, submarine, hero, hoagy, poorboy, grinder. c. pasta, noodle; bucatini, cannelloni, conchiglie, dumpling, fettuccine, fusilli, gnocchi, knodel, kreplach, lasagne, linguine, lo mein, macaroni, manicotti, mostaccioli, penne, ravioli, rigatoni, rotini, rotelli, spaetzle, spaghetti[ni], tortellini, vermicelli, won ton, ziti.

7, a. meat, red *or* white meat; joint; [pot, rib, pocket, *or* prime rib] roast, [club, Delmonico, flank, New York, porterhouse, rib eye, round, Salisbury, sirloin, skirt, T-bone, *or* tenderloin] steak, chopped beef, beefsteak, sweetbreads, tongue, tournedos, tripe, veal, kabob; spare ribs, beef, brains, brisket, charqui, Châteaubriand, chitterlings, cold cuts, corned beef, filet mignon, flitch, [Danish, baked, *or* processed] ham, hamburger, kidney, lamb, liver, mutton, noisette, pastrami, pork, rack, tripe, chitterlings, bacon; roast, boiled meat, hash, ground beef, chipped beef, jerky; fricandeau, sweetbread; leg of lamb, leg *or* saddle of mutton; chop, cutlet. *Informal,* piano. b. sausage, bratwurst, andouillettes, bangers, bologna, Bratwurst, Braunschweiger, pâté, chorizo, foie gras, forcemeat, frank[furter], galantine, salami, head cheese, hot dog, kielbasa, knockwurst, liverwurst, mortadella, saucisse, scrapple, terrine, weenie, tube steak, zampone. c. FISH, shellfish, seafood; abalone, anchovy, bacalao, calamari, caviar, clam, cod, crawdad, crawfish, crayfish, eel, escargot, finnan haddie, flounder, halibut, kipper, mahimahi, orange roughy, prawn, red snapper, scampi, softshell crab, scrod, surimi, tomalley, turbot; finnan haddie, gravlax, kipper, lox, seviche, sashimi, sushi. *Informal,* deep-sea turkey, two-eyed steak. d. poultry, [stewing, roasting, frying, or broiling] chicken, goose, turkey; game, fowl, capon, duck, grouse, guinea fowl, partridge, pheasant, quail, squab; boar, deer, hare, rabbit, venison; white or dark meat, giblets, sweetbreads, drumstick, thigh, breast; [fried, scrambled, boiled, shirred, or poached] eggs. **e.** fish and chips; stir-fry; headcheese, smegma, jerky, burrito, nacho; hash, stew, ragout, fricassee; chitlins, tripe; surf and turf.

8, [American, blue, cream, cottage, feta, goat, jack, pot, processed, string, cheddar, or Swiss] cheese, Bel Paese, Boursin, Brie, Camembert, Cheshire, colby, Edam, Emmenthaler, fontina, Gorgonzola, Gouda, Gruyère, Havarti, Jarlsberg, Liederkranz, Limburger, Montrachet, mozzarella, Muenster, Neufchâtel, Pont l'Evèque, Port-Salut, provolone, ricotta, Romano, Roquefort, Stilton, Velveeta; clabber, cream, crème fraîche, half-and-half, heavy cream, whipping cream, sour cream; [condensed, dry, evaporated, homogenized, low-fat, nonfat, pasteurized, raw, or skim] milk, buttermilk; butter; yogurt; tofu, bean curd.

9, a. vegetable, legume, artichoke, asparagus, aubergine, [black, butter, fava, garbanzo, green, kidney, lima, mung, navy, pinto, soya, string, wax, or white] bean, lentil, chickpea, bean sprout, beet, onion, bok choy, broccoli, Brussels sprout, cabbage, carrot, cauliflower, celery, chard, chicory, chive, corn, cress, cucumber, eggplant, endive, escarole, finocchio, kale, kohlrabi, leek, [Bibb, Boston, cos, iceberg, or romaine] lettuce, maize, manioc, fungus, [button, chanterelle, morel, oyster, porcini, or shiitake] mushroom, mustard greens, okra, parsnip, [black-eyed, green, snow, or baby] pea, [bell, chile, green, jalapeño, pimiento, red, serrano, wax, or yellow] pepper, potato, pumpkin, radiccio, radish, rhubarb, rutabaga, salsify, scallion, seaweed, shallot, soybean, spinach, [acorn, butternut, summer, winter, or yellow] squash, zucchini, succory, sweet potato, tomato, truffle, turnip, water chestnut, watercress, yam; crudités. *Informal,* veggies. *Slang,* rabbit food. **b.** salad, greens, Caesar salad, salade niçoise, chef's or julienne salad; sauerkraut.

10, a. fruit, [Delicious, golden, Granny Smith, gravenstein, Jonathan, Macintosh, Rome, or winesap] apple, apricot, avocado, banana, berry, blackberry, [black or red] raspberry, blueberry, boysenberry, cranberry, dewberry, elderberry, gooseberry, lingonberry, strawberry, black currant, breadfruit, carambola, cherry, citron, clementine, coconut, crabapple, custard apple, plum, date, fig, [Concord, muscat, or seedless] grape, grapefruit, guava, jujube, kiwi, kumquat, lemon, lime, loquat, mango, [cantaloupe, casaba, honeydew, or winter] melon, watermelon, muskmelon, [mandarin, navel, or Valencia] orange, nectarine, olive, papaya, passion fruit, pawpaw, peach, [Anjou, Bosc, or Bartlett] pear, persimmon, pineapple, plantain, pomegranate, pomelo, prune, quince, raisin, sapodilla, spanspek, tamarillo, tamarind, tangelo, tangerine. **b.** fruit compote or cocktail.

11, nut, seed, acorn, almond, betel nut, black walnut, Brazil nut, butternut, cashew, chestnut, corozo, filbert, hazelnut, hickory, horse chestnut, kola, litchi, macadamia, peanut, pecan, pine nut, pistachio, sesame seed, sunflower seed, walnut.

12, a. dessert, pandowdy, baked Alaska, Bavarian cream, blancmange, cannoli, cassata, charlotte russe, clafoutis, cobbler, compote, coupe, crème brûlée, crème caramel, crêpe suzette, custard, flan, flummery, frappé, frozen custard, fruit cup, gelato, glacé, granita, ice cream, ice, Jell-O, meringue, mousse, parfait, peach Melba, pudding, torte, sherbet, sorbet, soufflé, shortcake, streusel, sundae, syllabub, tiramisu, tortoni, trifle, zabaglione. **b.** cake, angel food cake, cheesecake, chocolate or devil's food cake, cupcake, coffeecake, fruitcake, gâteau, genoise, gingerbread, jelly roll, kuchen, layer cake, marble cake, [buckwheat, griddle, or potato] pancake, blini, blintz, crêpe, flapjack, hotcake, waffle, pound cake, Sacher torte, savarin, stollen, tart, teacake, torte, wedding cake. **c.** pastry, fruit or cream pie; baba au rum, baklava, beignet, cornet, crescent, cruller, crumpet, Danish, doughnut, éclair, feuilletée, frangipane, fritter, madeleine, mille-feuilles, napoleon, pain au chocolat, petit four, phyllo, profiterole, quiche, scone, sopaipilla, strudel, sweet roll, tart, timbale, turnover. **d.** cookie, brownie, fig bar, florentine, fortune cookie, garibaldi, ginger-

snap, lady finger, macaroon, Oreo, panettone, ratafia, shortbread, Toll House, wafer.
e. candy, sweets, bonbon, brittle, butterscotch, candy bar, caramel, confection, cotton candy, fondant, frosting, fudge, halvah, icing, jawbreaker, jellybean, jimmies, sprinkles, jujube, kiss, lemon drop, licorice, lollipop, marchpane, marshmallow, marzipan, nonpareil, nougat, peanut brittle, praline, saltwater taffy, toffee.

13, soup, potage, gruel, porridge, haggis; broth, consommé, purée, avgolemono, broth, bisque, borscht, bouillabaise, bouillon, burgoo, cholent, chowder, cloppino, civet, consommé, cullis, daube, fumet, gazpacho, goulash, gumbo, hasenpfeffer, lobscouse, madrilene, matelote, menudo, minestrone, miso soup, mulligan, mulligatawny, navarin, [Irish or Hungarian] stew, olla podrida, oxtail soup, potage, ragout, ramen, salmi, shark's fin soup, slumgullion, stock, tzimmes, vichyssoise.

14, condiment, anchovy, bitters, aspic, pickle, caper, catsup, chutney, cornichon, gherkin, horseradish, jam, jelly, marmalade, piccalilli, pimiento, relish, salsa, sambal, tahini, wasabi, zest, [balsamic, malt, red wine, rice wine, or white wine] vinegar; dressing, vinaigrette; [barbecue, béarnaise, béchamel, brown, chasseur, chili, cranberry, curry, duck, hollandaise, oyster, pesto, rémoulade, soy, sweet-and-sour, Tabasco, tartar, velouté, white, or Worcestershire] sauce, guacamole, hummus, mayonnaise, satay, tahini.

15, drink (see DRINKING).

16, (act or means of eating) eating, ingestion, mastication, manducation, rumination; GLUTTONY; mouth, jaws, mandible, chops; carousal (see AMUSEMENT); digestion, chyle.

17, food mill or processor, blender, egg beater, grinder; oven (see HEAT); refrigerator (see COLD).

18, a. restaurant, steakhouse, chophouse, chuck wagon, coffee shop, diner, eatery, café, brasserie, trattoria, eating house, roadhouse, drive-in, cafeteria, lunch counter, luncheonette, Automat, canteen; dining room, refectory, mess hall. Informal, greasy spoon, hash house, pit stop. b. blue plate special, early-bird special, plat du jour.

19, a. grocery store, delicatessen, charcuterie. b. kitchen, scullery, galley, cuisine.

20, a. chef, cook, short-order chef or cook; salad chef, pastry chef, etc., confectioner, prep cook, sous-chef. b. headwaiter, host[ess], waitperson, waiter, waitress, waitron, busboy, carhop; sommelier, wine steward, barman, barmaid.

21, eater, brown-bagger; gourmet, gourmand (see GLUTTONY).

22, forage, pasture, pasturage; fodder, feed; wheat, corn, oats, barley, hay, stray, clover, chicken feed; ensilage; pet food, dog or cat food, bird seed.

Verbs—1, eat, feed, fare, devour, swallow, take; gobble, gulp, bolt, snap; fall to; dispatch, partake of, eat up; take, get, wolf, or gulp down; lay or tuck in; lick, pick (at), peck, eat like a bird (see ASCETICISM); gormandize, ingurgitate (see GLUTTONY); bite, champ, munch, crunch, chew, masticate, nibble, gnaw; live, feed, batten, or fatten on, feast upon; browse, graze, crop; regale, carouse; eat heartily, do justice to; banquet; break bread, break one's fast; breakfast, lunch, dine, take tea, sup; eat out; ration (see APPORTIONMENT). Informal, chow down, dig in, put away, inhale, nosh. Slang, pig or pork out, scarf.

2, nourish, nurture; digest; stick to one's ribs.

3, prepare; cook, grill, fry, brown, bake, broil, boil, parboil, toast, roast, charbroil, steam, scald, simmer; warm up, reheat; smoke. Informal, rustle up.

Adjectives—eatable, edible, esculent, comestible, alimentary; cereal; dietetic; fast-food; culinary; nutritive, nutritious; succulent; omnivorous, carnivorous, herbivorous, graminivorous; macrobiotic, organic; kosher.

Adverbs—at table.

Interjections—come and get it!; soup's on!

Phrases—more die of food than of famine; eat to live, not live to eat; the way to a man's heart is through his stomach.

Quotations—I consider supper as a turnpike through which one must pass, in order to get to bed (*Oliver Edwards*), Tell me what you eat and I will tell you what you are (*Anthelme Brillat-Savarin*), We each day dig our graves with our teeth (*Samuel Smiles*), A man hath no better thing under the sun than to eat, and to drink, and to be merry (*Bible*), One cannot think well, love well, sleep well, if one has not dined well (*Virgina Woolf*), Food is our common ground, a universal experience (*James Beard*).

---

fool, *n.* See FOLLY. —*v.* dupe, mislead; idle away; tamper. See DECEPTION, CHANGE, INACTIVITY. —**fool around**, horse *or* monkey around, jerk off (*all sl.*); philander, flirt. See AMUSEMENT, ENDEARMENT, IMPURITY.

foolhardy, *adj.* daring, brash, reckless, venturesome. See RASHNESS.

foolish, *adj.* silly; unwise. See FOLLY, IGNORANCE.

foolproof, *adj.* safe, fail-safe. See STRENGTH.

foot, *n.* base, bottom, footing; hoof, paw; foot soldiers, infantry. —*v.t.* add [up]; *informal*, pay for. See SUPPORT, COMBATANT, PAYMENT.

foothold, *n.* [toe]hold, footing, grip, SUPPORT; BEGINNING, start, access, opportunity, first rung on the ladder.

footing, *n.* foothold; basis, base, foundation, status, rank. See SUPPORT.

footloose, *adj.* free, unattached, at liberty. See FREEDOM.

footman, *n.* lackey (see SERVANT).

footstool, *n.* ottoman, hassock. See SUPPORT.

fop, *n.* dandy, dude, swell, buck, [gay] blade, coxcomb, macaroni, exquisite, Beau Brummel, Dapper Dan, clothes-horse (*sl.*). See AFFECTATION, OSTENTATION.

forage, *n.* fodder, feed, FOOD; pasturage, herbage. —*v.* pasture, graze, feed; hunt, search, beat the bushes; raid, maraud, pillage, plunder, loot, ravage, scrounge around. See STEALING, INQUIRY, PROVISION.

foray, *n. & v.i.* raid, ATTACK; pillage (see STEALING).

forbearance, *n.* [self-]restraint; patience, long-suffering; temperance, clemency, LENIENCY; mercy, pardon. See AVOIDANCE, DISUSE, RESIGNATION.

forbid, *v.t.* prohibit, inhibit, interdict, ban, taboo. See PROHIBITION.

forbidding, *adj.* prohibitive; repellent, fearsome (see FEAR); unpleasant, abhorrent; stern, menacing; unfriendly, distant; disagreeable. See UGLINESS, HINDRANCE, SEVERITY, PROHIBITION.

force, *n.* COMPULSION, coercion; STRENGTH, brawn, POWER, might; MEANING, import, effect; troops, soldiery, army (see COMBATANT). See VIGOR.

forceful, *adj.* powerful; effective, cogent. See STRENGTH, MEANING.

force majeure, Fr. act of God (see CHANCE).

forcible, *adj.* forceful, strong (see STRENGTH).

ford, *n.* wading place; shoal. —*v.* wade, cross. See PASSAGE, SHALLOWNESS.

fore, *adj.* foremost; former, prior, previous. See FRONT.

forebear, *n.* See ANCESTRY.

foreboding, *n.* portent; presentiment, premonition, apprehension. See PREDICTION, WARNING, THREAT.

forecast, *v.t.* predict, divine, prognosticate; foretell, presage, portend. See PREDICTION, PLAN.

foreclose, *v.* dispossess, evict. See EJECTION.

forefathers, *n.pl.* ancestors, forebears, progenitors. See ANCESTRY.

forefront, *n.* vanguard, FRONT.

foregoing, *adj.* preceding, previous, aforesaid. See PRIORITY.

foregone, *adj.* PAST, previous.

foreground, *n.* proscenium, FRONT.

forehead, *n.* brow, sinciput; head, temples. See FRONT.

foreign, *adj.* alien, strange, exotic; extraneous, unrelated. See EXTRINSIC, ABODE.

foreman, forewoman, *n.* supervisor, superintendent, overseer, straw boss (*inf.*). See DIRECTOR.

foremost, *adj.* leading, first, precedent; chief, best, principal. See BEGINNING, PRIORITY, FRONT, SUPERIORITY.

forensic, *adj.* legal, juridical; controversial. See LEGALITY, REASONING.

forerunner, *n.* precursor, predecessor; harbinger; herald, announcer; Elijah, John the Baptist, *etc.*; leader, vanguard, scout, picket. See PRIORITY, PREDICTION.

foresee, *v.t.* anticipate, predict (see PRE-DICTION).

foreshadow, *v.t.* prefigure, foretoken (see PREDICTION).

foresight, *n.* forethought, PREPARATION; foreknowledge, prescience; clairvoyance, prevision. See PREDICTION, CAUTION, EXPECTATION.

forest, *n.* wood[s], tall timber, timberland, woodland; grove, coppice, copse, thicket. See VEGETABLE.

forestall, *v.t.* thwart, prevent. See HINDRANCE, EARLINESS.

forestry, *n.* woodcraft, silviculture; dendrology, forestage; conservation; [re]forestation. See AGRICULTURE.

foretell, *v.t.* presage, portend; forecast, prognosticate, predict. See PREDICTION.

forethought, *n.* prudence, providence; premeditation, anticipation. See PREPARATION, CAUTION.

foretoken, *n.* omen. —*v.t.* foreshadow. See PREDICTION.

forever, *adv.* always, ever, eternally; incessantly, unceasingly. See DURABILITY, PERPETUITY.

forewarn, *v.t.* prepare (see PREPARATION, WARNING).

foreword, *n.* preface, prologue, introduction, avant-propos, preamble; [address] to the reader. See PRECEDENCE.

forfeit, *n.* penalty, fine; deposit. See LOSS, PUNISHMENT.

forge, *v.t.* make, fabricate; invent, counterfeit; hammer. See PRODUCTION, FALSEHOOD, COPY.

forgery, *n.* IMITATION, counterfeit; kited, rubber, bum, *or* phony check (*sl.*). See FALSEHOOD, DECEPTION.

forget, *v.t.* disregard, overlook, dismiss, omit. See NEGLECT, OBLIVION, FORGIVENESS.

forgetful, *adj.* absentminded, amnesiac, oblivious. See OBLIVION.

forgive, *v.t.* pardon (see FORGIVENESS); remit, cancel, nullify (see NULLIFICATION).

FORGIVENESS
Granting of pardon

Nouns—forgiveness, pardon, condonation, grace, remission, absolution, amnesty, oblivion; indulgence; reprieve; excuse, exoneration, exculpation (see ACQUITTAL); conciliation, reconciliation; placability (see PACIFICATION). See OBLIVION.

Verbs—1, forgive, pardon, condone, think no more of, let bygones be bygones, shake hands, forget an injury, forgive and forget, live and let live; excuse, pass over, overlook; wink at (see NEGLECT); bear with; allow for, make allowances for; let one down easily, not be too hard upon, bury the hatchet; write off; let off, remit, absolve, give absolution, reprieve, wipe the slate clean, turn the other cheek; acquit (see ACQUITTAL).

2, beg, ask, *or* implore pardon, excuse oneself; conciliate, propitiate, placate; make one's peace with, make up a quarrel (see PACIFICATION).

Adjectives—forgiving, placable, conciliatory, indulgent; forgiven, pardoned, condoned, *etc.*, unresented, unavenged, unrevenged.

Phrases—to know all is to forgive all; charity covers a multitude of sins.

Quotations—To err is human; to forgive, divine (*Alexander Pope*), I never forgive, but I always forget (*Arthur James Balfour*), Father forgive them; for they know not what they do (*Bible*), It is by forgiving that one is forgiven (*Mother Theresa*).

Antonyms, see RETALIATION.

---

forgo, *v.t.* relinquish, abandon; deny oneself, give up, do without, pass up. See RELINQUISHMENT.

fork, *v.i.* bifurcate, diverge, separate, branch off. See DISJUNCTION, ANGULARITY.

forlorn, *adj.* abandoned, deserted, forsaken; hopeless, wretched, miserable. See RELINQUISHMENT, HOPELESSNESS, DEJECTION.

FORM
External shape

Nouns—1, form, formation, forming, figure, shape; make[up], conformation, configuration; make, frame[work], construction, cut, set, build, trim, cut of one's jib; stamp, type, cast, mold; organization, ARRANGEMENT, disposition, stratification; fashion; contour, outline, silhouette; lines, features, lineaments; skeleton, broad outline; architecture, structure; sculpture. See SYMMETRY, ORDER.

2, feature, lineament, anatomy, profile; turn; phase, aspect, APPEARANCE; posture, attitude, pose.

3, square, rectangle (see ANGULARITY); circle, sphere, cylinder (see CIRCULARITY, ROTUNDITY).

4, *(study of form)* morphology, histology, structural botany; isomorphism.

Verbs—form, shape, figure, fashion, carve, cut, chisel, hew, cast; rough-hew, rough-cast; sketch, silhouette, delineate; block out, hammer out; trim; lick *or* put into shape; model, knead, work up into, set, mold, SCULPTURE; tailor; cast, stamp; build, construct.

Adjectives—formed, formative; plastic, fictile; isomorphous.

Quotations—Form ever follows function (*Louis Sullivan*).

Antonyms, see FORMLESSNESS.

---

formal, *adj.* structural; external, superficial, outward; stylized, conventional, ceremonial, ritual[istic], traditional; solemn, dignified; stuffy, strict, prim; correct, proper. See CONFORMITY, FASHION, AFFECTATION. —*n.* evening dress; black tie, white tie [and tails]. See CLOTHING.

formality, *n.* formalness (see FORMAL); punctilio, convention, etiquette; due course, process, *or* form, red tape; mere formality, lip service. See CONFORMITY, AFFECTATION, FASHION.

formalize, *v.t.* ritualize, standardize, codify. See CONFORMITY, RITE.

format, *n.* form, ARRANGEMENT, PLAN, makeup, layout, design; style.

formation, *n.* shape, ARRANGEMENT, COMPOSITION, fabrication, structure, configuration.

former, *adj.* erstwhile, whilom, sometime, quondam; foregoing, preceding. See PAST, PRIORITY.

formidable, *adj.* appalling, tremendous; arduous, Herculean. See FEAR, DIFFICULTY.

FORMLESSNESS
Lack of shape

Nouns—formlessness, shapelessness, amorphism, informity; deformity, disfigurement, defacement, derangement, mutilation; DISORDER, chaos; DISTORTION.

Verbs—deface, disfigure, deform, mutilate, truncate, misshape; derange, DISORDER, distort.

Adjectives—formless, shapeless, amorphous; unformed, unhewn, uncut, unfashioned, unshapen; rough, rude, rugged, barbarous, chaotic; blank, vague, nebulous, half-baked; misshapen, disordered, distorted.

Quotations—Bah! the thing is not a nose at all, but a bit of primordial chaos clapped on to my face (*H. G. Wells*).

Antonyms, see FORM.

---

formula, *n.* RULE; expression, equation; recipe. See MAXIM.

formulate, *v.t.* frame, devise, concoct, formularize. See METHOD, PLAN.

fornicate, *v.i.* philander, sleep around (*inf.*). See SEX, IMPURITY.

forsake, *v.t.* desert, abandon; renounce, quit, forswear. See RELINQUISHMENT.

forswear, *v.* deny, abjure; commit perjury. See NEGATION, FALSEHOOD.

fort, *n.* fortress, stronghold, fortification. See DEFENSE.

forte, *n.* strong point, specialty (see SPE-CIALITY).

forth, *adv.* forward, onward; out (of), from; away (from). See PROGRESSION.

forthcoming, *adj.* imminent; available. See APPROACH, PREPARATION.

forthright, *adj.* downright, straightfor-ward, frank, candid, outspoken; un-equivocal, explicit, honest, straight from the shoulder (*inf.*). See PROBITY.

forthwith, *adv.* at once, immediately (see INSTANTANEITY).

fortify, *v.t.* strengthen, buttress, barricade; uphold, sustain. See POWER, DEFENSE, STRENGTH.

fortitude, *n.* COURAGE, patience, en-durance. See INEXCITABILITY.

fortress, *n.* fort, citadel. See DEFENSE.

fortuitous, *adj.* casual, CHANCE.

fortunate, *adj.* lucky, blest, to be congrat-ulated; auspicious, propitious, oppor-tune, born under a lucky star *or* with a silver spoon in one's mouth (*inf.*). See PROSPERITY, SUCCESS, OCCASION.

fortune, *n.* fate, lot, DESTINY; CHANCE, luck; wealth, possessions, property; MONEY.

fortune-teller, *n.* clairvoyant, crystal-gazer, astrologer, numerologist, phre-nologist, palmist, palm-reader. See PREDICTION.

forum, *n.* marketplace, agora; court, tri-bunal, COUNCIL; colloquium, sympo-sium, panel, town meeting. See CONVERSATION.

forward, *adj.* FRONT, anterior, foremost; precocious; ready, eager, prompt; enter-prising, aggressive; intrusive, officious; pert, saucy, flip; future, coming. See IN-SOLENCE. —*v.t.* impel, dispatch, deliver, further, advance, encourage. See AID, TRANSPORTATION, PROGRESSION.

fossil, *n.* relic, petrification; fogy. See OLD-NESS, AGE.

foster, *v.t.* nourish, nurture, cherish; en-courage, support. See AID, ENDEAR-MENT.

foul, *adj.* dirty, soiled, disgusting; stormy, unpleasant; obscene, indecent; clogged, choked, entangled; unfair, underhand. See UNCLEANNESS, IMPURITY, IMPRO-BITY. —**fall foul** of, collide; quarrel, conflict [with]. See IMPULSE, DISCORD.

foul-mouthed, *adj.* abusive, blasphemous, profane, ribald. See IMPRECATION.

found, *v.t.* establish, institute, originate; cast. See BEGINNING, FORM.

foundation, *n.* base; basis; endowment; institution. See SUPPORT, PARTY, CAUSE, PREPARATION.

founder, *n.* producer, establisher, origina-tor. See BEGINNING. —*v.i.* sink, be swamped; go lame. See NAVIGATION, FAILURE.

foundling, *n.* waif, orphan, bastard. See YOUTH, RELINQUISHMENT.

foundry, *n.* works, iron- *or* steelworks, smelter; smithy. See PRODUCTION.

fountain, *n.* spring, jet, spray; fount, source. See CAUSE, WATER.

Fourth Estate, *n.* the press, print medium. See PUBLICATION.

fowl, *n.* bird; hen, stewing chicken. See ANIMAL, FOOD.

fox, *n.* reynard, slyboots. See ANIMAL, CUNNING.

foxhole, *n.* pit, trench. See DEFENSE.

foxy, *adj.* clever, sly, CUNNING; attractive, sexy (see BEAUTY).

foyer, *n.* lobby, vestibule, anteroom, entry, entrance hall. See RECEPTACLE, INGRESS.

fracas, *n.* uproar, disturbance. See DISOR-DER, LOUDNESS.

fraction, *n.* PART; half, quarter, eighth, *etc.*; portion, piece, bit; scrap, fragment.

fracture, *n.* break, split, crack, cleft. See DISJUNCTION, BRITTLENESS.

fragile, *adj.* delicate, frail, breakable; tenuous, gossamer. See BRITTLENESS, WEAKNESS.

fragment, *n.* bit, PART, scrap.

fragrance, *n.* perfume, bouquet, ODOR.

frail, *adj.* fragile, brittle, delicate; weak, infirm, weak-willed. See BRITTLENESS, WEAKNESS.

frame, *v.t.* construct, fashion, fabricate; devise, compose, formulate; enclose; *slang,* incriminate, trump up. See PRO-DUCTION, ACCUSATION, PLAN. —*n.* framework, skeleton; EDGE, boundary, confines; temper, state, humor; FORM; shape; plot, conspiracy. See SUPPORT, WILL.

framework, *n.* structure, frame, skeleton, shell; frame of reference. See PRODUC-TION, PLAN.

franchise, *n.* privilege, right, prerogative. See FREEDOM, CHOICE.

frank, *adj.* ingenuous, candid, straightfor-

ward, forthright, sincere, open. See
TRUTH.

frankfurter, *n.* frankfurt, sausage, wiener,
frank (*inf.*), weenie (*sl.*), hot dog, red-
hot. See FOOD.

frantic, *adj.* distraught, frenzied, wild. See
INSANITY, EXCITEMENT.

fraternal, *adj.* brotherly (see FRIEND).

fraternity, *n.* brotherhood, fellowship, secret society, club. See PARTY, SOCIAL-
ITY.

fraternize, *v.i.* associate, band together;
consort *or* mingle with; collaborate. See
SOCIALITY, COMBINATION, IMPROBITY.

fraud, *n.* DECEPTION, swindle; imposture,
artifice; confidence man; impostor,
humbug, bunco (*inf.*). See EVILDOER,
STEALING.

fraught, *adj.* filled with, loaded, laden, beset. See COMPLETION.

fray, *n.* fracas, fight, battle, skirmish;
brawl, melee, free-for-all. See CON-
TENTION. —*v.* ravel, rub, wear. See
FRICTION, DETERIORATION.

frazzle, *v.t.*, *informal*, fray, abrade, wear
out; vex, exasperate, get on one's
nerves. See RESENTMENT, WEARINESS.

freak, *n.* abnormality, fluke, monstrosity;
caprice, sport, whim. See UNCONFOR-
MITY, CHANGEABLENESS. —**freak out,**
slang, lose it, go wild (see EXCITABIL-
ITY).

freckle, *n.* spot, dapple, lentigo (see IM-
PERFECTION).

free, *adj.* at liberty, unrestrained; exempt;
gratuitous, free of charge; lavish, profuse. —*v.t.* unfetter, release; rid [of] (see
EJECTION). See FREEDOM, EXEMPTION,
NONPAYMENT, LIBERALITY.

FREEDOM
Personal liberty

Nouns—**1,** freedom, liberty, independence; self-government *or* -determination; license,
PERMISSION; FACILITY; immunity, EXEMPTION; release, parole, probation, discharge;
civil liberties, civil *or* human rights; free speech, freedom of speech *or* of the press; individualism, self-dependence *or* -reliance, discretion.

2, *(area of free movement)* scope, range, latitude, play; free hand *or* rein; free *or* full
play, full scope; [full] swing, leeway, breathing room *or* space, elbow room, margin,
rope, wide berth; carte blanche, blank check. *Informal*, rope enough to hang oneself.
Slang, room to swing a cat.

3, *(act or means of freeing)* franchise; emancipation (see LIBERATION); enfranchisement; autonomy, self-government, self-determination; liberalism, free trade; nonin-
tervention, noninterference, Monroe Doctrine; Bill of Rights, Magna Carta; glasnost;
women's liberation.

4, *(free person)* free[d]man *or* -woman; burgess, franklin; free agent; individualist;
emancipated woman.

5, *(something unencumbered)* free land, freehold; allodium; mortmain. *Slang*, loose
cannon.

Verbs—**1,** be free, have scope, have the run of, have one's own way, have a will of one's
own, have one's fling; do what one likes, wishes, pleases, *or* chooses, see one's way
clear; go at large, feel at home; fend for oneself; paddle one's own canoe; stand on
one's rights; be one's own man; shift for oneself, stand on one's own [two] feet, hoe
one's own row; take a liberty; make free with, make oneself at home; take leave, take
French leave; go scot-free. *Informal*, please *or* suit oneself. *Slang*, get down, let it all
hang out.

2, set free, liberate, release, let go; parole; permit (see PERMISSION); allow *or* give
scope to, open the door; give [free] rein; give a horse his head; make free of; give the
freedom of; give the franchise, give one carte blanche *or* a blank check; enfranchise;
laissez-faire; live and let live; leave to oneself, leave alone, let alone; deregulate, de-
control; liberalize. *Informal*, give one leeway, give one enough rope, give one the run
of, get off one's case *or* back. *Slang*, butt out, back off.

3, *(remove restraints)* unfetter, untie, loose, unchain, unshackle, unbind; disengage,
disentangle, clear, extricate, unloose. *Slang*, cut one a little slack.

Adjectives—1, free, free as air; independent, at large, loose, scot-free; left alone, left to oneself, on the loose; free and easy; at one's ease; dégagé, quite at home; wanton, rampant, irrepressible, unvanquished; freed, liberated, rid of, hands-off; freeborn; out from under; autonomous, freehold, allodial, on one's own [account *or* hook], under one's own steam; in the clear (see ACQUITTAL).

2, *(free to move)* in full swing, uncaught, unconstrained, unbuttoned, unconfined, unrestrained, unchecked, unprevented, unhindered, unobstructed, unbound, uncontrolled, untrammeled, unsubject, ungoverned, unenslaved, unenthralled, unchained, unshackled, unfettered, unreined, unbridled, uncurbed, unmuzzled; catch as catch can, freewheeling, [footloose and] fancy-free, carefree; out of control; unrestricted, unlimited, unconditional; absolute; discretionary, optional (see CHOICE); exempt; unforced, uncompelled; unbiased, spontaneous. *Slang,* off the hook.

Adverbs—ad libitum, at will, freely, *etc.,* without let or hindrance, no strings attached; on one's own, of one's own free will. *Informal,* all by one's lonesome.

Phrases—live free or die; don't tread on me.

Quotations—Give me your tired, your poor, your huddled masses yearning to breathe free (*Emma Lazarus*), Liberty is, to the lowest rank of every nation, little more than the choice of working or starving (*Samuel Johnson*), Man was born free, and everywhere he is in chains (*Jean-Jacques Rousseau*), Give me liberty, or give me death! (*Patrick Henry*), I am condemned to be free (*Jean-Paul Sartre*), Freedom and slavery are mental states (*Mahatma Gandhi*).

Antonyms, see SUBJECTION, RESTRAINT.

---

free-for-all, *n., informal,* fight, melee, brawl, fracas; knock-down-drag-out [affair]. See CONTENTION.

freelance, *n.* mercenary; freelancer, private contractor, free agent, independent. —*v.i.* be one's own boss, go it alone. See COMBATANT, FREEDOM, EXERTION.

freeloader, *n., slang,* parasite, sponge. See SERVILITY.

freethinker, *n.* skeptic, agnostic, doubter; iconoclast. See IRRELIGION.

freeway, *n.* highway, parkway, boulevard, expressway. See PASSAGE.

freewheeling, *adj., informal,* nonchalant, carefree. See FREEDOM.

freeze, *v.* congeal, turn to ice, make ice; harden; die; immobilize; chill, ice, frost, refrigerate; kill; fix, stabilize. See COLD, DEATH, PERMANENCE. —**freeze out**, exclude (see EXCLUSION).

freight, *n.* cargo, load, shipment; burden. See TRANSPORTATION, GRAVITY.

freighter, *n.* cargo ship, lighter, trader, [tramp] steamer, transport, tanker. See SHIP.

frenetic, *adj.* frantic, frenzied, hectic, distraught, jittery. See EXCITABILITY, VIOLENCE.

frenzy, *n.* fury, AGITATION; EXCITEMENT, enthusiasm; delirium, furor. See VIOLENCE, INSANITY, EXCITABILITY.

FREQUENCY
Repeated occurrence

Nouns—frequency, oftenness; REPETITION, recurrence, persistence; perseverance; prevalence; continuance; OSCILLATION.

Verbs—do frequently; do nothing but, keep on, continue (see CONTINUITY); be frequent, persist; recur; repeat, hammer [away] at (see REPETITION).

Adjectives—frequent, many times, not rare, incessant, continual, constant; everyday, repeated (see REPETITION); habitual (see HABIT).

Adverbs—often, oft, ofttimes, oftentimes, frequently, every time one turns around; repeatedly (see REPETITION); not unfrequently; in rapid succession; many a time, daily, hourly, every day; perpetually, continually, constantly, incessantly, without ceasing, at all times, night and day, day after day; morning, noon and night; ever and anon; most often; commonly, habitually (see HABIT); sometimes, occasionally, between times, at times, [every] now and then, [every] once in a while, [every] now and again, from time to time, often enough, again and again, every so often; more often than not, in general. *Informal,* a lot.

Antonyms, see RARITY.

---

frequent, *adj.* regular (see FREQUENCY). —*v.t.* haunt, hang around *or* out [at] (*inf.*). See HABIT.

fresh, *adj.* novel, recent; new, unfaded, unjaded, unhackneyed, unused; healthy, vigorous; rested, unfatigued; unsalted; cool, refreshing, brisk, keen; inexperienced; *slang,* insolent. See NEWNESS, COLD, HEALTH, REFRESHMENT, INSOLENCE.

freshen, *v.t.* refresh, revive, brace up; renovate, spruce up; ventilate, air out, cool off; deodorize, sweeten. See RESTORATION, CLEANNESS, REFRESHMENT.

freshman, *n.* plebe, underclassman; novice, greenhorn, tenderfoot, frosh (*inf.*). See BEGINNING, SCHOOL.

fret, *v.* agitate, irritate, vex; worry, chafe, rub, fume, complain. See DISCONTENT, PAIN, RESENTMENT, DEJECTION.

fretful, *adj.* restless; peevish, pettish. See AGITATION, DISCONTENT.

friable, *adj.* crumbly (see POWDERINESS).

friar, *n.* monk, brother; fra. See CLERGY.

friction, *n.* rubbing (see FRICTION); conflict, DISCORD.

FRICTION
Rubbing together

Nouns—1, friction, attrition, rubbing; frication, confrication, abrasion; sanding, sandpapering, sandblasting, erosion, limation, rub, scuffing, erasure, grinding, filing, scraping, scouring, chafing, scratching; [therapeutic] massage, rubdown, facial; whirlpool bath, water jet; RESISTANCE. See TRACTION.

2, friction sore, abrasion, scrape, lesion (see PAIN).

3, sandpaper, emery board *or* wheel, grinder, grinding wheel, pumice [stone]; masseur, masseuse.

Verbs—rub, scratch, abrade, file, rasp, scrape, scrabble, grate, scrub, fray, chafe, scuff, graze, curry, buff, scour, polish, rub up; work in; rub down, wear away *or* out; sandpaper, grind (see POWDERINESS); massage, knead.

Adjectives—frictional, abrasive, attritive, erosive; scraping, grinding, *etc.*

Antonyms, see SMOOTHNESS.

FRIEND
Person on intimate terms with another

Nouns—1, friend, acquaintance, neighbor, well-wisher; alter ego; bosom *or* fast friend, gentleman *or* lady friend; partner; fidus Achates; persona grata; associate, compeer, comrade, mate, companion, confrère, colleague, compatriot, compadre, brother, intimate, confidant[e], hail-fellow; countryman. See ACCOMPANIMENT.

2, (*supporter*) patron, Maecenas; tutelary saint, guardian angel, good genius, advocate, partisan, sympathizer; ally; friend-in-need; associate. See BENEVOLENCE.

3, (*informal friend*) best friend, crony, chum, playfellow, playmate; schoolfellow, schoolmate; shopmate, shipmate, messmate, roommate; fellow, boon companion; regular guy *or* fellow. *Informal,* sidekick, homeboy *or* -girl, jasper, cotton-picker, punk. *Slang,* pal, ace, running partner, soul brother *or* sister, asshole buddy, cuz, dude.

4, (*famous friends*) Pylades and Orestes, Castor and Pollux, Nisus and Euryalus, Damon and Pythias, David and Jonathan, Three Musketeers, Achilles and Patroclus.

5, (*quality of being friends*) friendship, friendliness, amity, brotherhood, bonhomie; harmony, concord, peace; cordiality, fraternization; fellowship, familiarity, intimacy, comradeship, common touch. See SOCIALITY, BENEVOLENCE.

Verbs—make friends with, receive with open arms; fraternize (see SOCIALITY), get along with; chase *or* run after; befriend, take up with, warm up to. *Informal,* hit it off, take to, stand in with, go steady. *Slang,* cozy up, shine up to.

Adjectives—friendly, amicable, cordial; hospitable, neighborly, brotherly, sisterly, collegial; hearty, bosom, warmhearted, familiar; on good terms, friends with, in with, on one's good side. *Slang,* tight.

Phrases—a friend in need is a friend indeed; save us from our friends; be kind to your friends: if it weren't for them, you would be a total stranger.

Quotations—We can scarcely hate any one that we know (*William Hazlitt*), One soul inhabiting two bodies (*Aristotle*), Should auld acquaintance be forgot and never brought to mind? (*Robert Burns*), God's apology for relations (*Hugh Kingsmill*), Friends are born, not made (*Henry Adams*), Greater love hath no man than this, that a man lay down his life for his friends (*Bible*), A friend may well be reckoned the masterpiece of nature (*Emerson*), Friendship needs no words—it is solitude delivered from the anguish of loneliness (*Dag Hammarskjöld*), A true friend is the most precious of all possessions and the one we take the least thought about acquiring (*La Rochefoucauld*), Of two close friends, one is always the slave of the other (*Mikhail Lermontov*).

Antonyms, see OPPOSITION.

---

fright, *n.* dread, terror, panic, alarm, consternation. See FEAR.

frightful, *adj.* horrible, shocking; *informal,* unpleasant, disagreeable. See FEAR, UGLINESS.

frigid, *adj.* COLD, icy, freezing; passionless, cold-blooded, formal. See INSENSIBILITY.

frill, *n.* trimming, decoration, ORNAMENT; ruffle, flounce, furbelow; extra, icing [on the cake] (*inf.*). See EDGE.

fringe, *n.* EDGE, border, outskirts; edging; perimeter.

frisk, *v.t.* caper, cavort, frolic; cut up, carry on, horse around (*sl.*); *slang,* search, shakedown, fan. See AMUSEMENT, INQUIRY.

frisky, *adj.* playful, pert, peppy. *Informal,* full of beans. See AMUSEMENT, ACTIVITY.

fritter, *v.t.* squander, WASTE, dissipate. —*n.* battercake (see FOOD).

frivolity, *n.* levity, flightiness, giddiness, FOLLY. See UNIMPORTANCE.

frizzy, *adj.* curly, kinky (see CONVOLUTION).

frock, *n.* gown, dress; smock. See CLOTHING.

frolic, *v.i.* play, gambol, caper, romp, disport. See AMUSEMENT.

from, *prep.* away, out of. See EGRESS.

front, *n.* foreground (see FRONT); figurehead, cover (see SUBSTITUTION). —*v.t.* confront, face (see OPPOSITION). —**front for,** cover (see SUBSTITUTION).

FRONT
Foremost part

Nouns—**1,** front, forefront, fore, forepart; foreground; face, disk, frontage, facade, proscenium, frontispiece; downstage; obverse; BEGINNING. See PRECEDENCE.

2, *(what's in front)* front rank, front lines; flagship; van, vanguard; advanced guard; outpost. See PRIORITY.

3, *(appearance in front)* face, brow, forehead, chin, visage, physiognomy, countenance, features; rostrum; false front; beak; bow, stem, prow, jib, cutting edge; beachhead, bridgehead. *Slang,* dial, map, mug, puss, kisser. See BODY.

Verbs—be *or* stand in front, head [up]; front, face, confront, look in the eye *or* face, defy (see DEFIANCE); bend forward; come to the front *or* the fore.

Adjectives—front, fore, frontal, forward; downstage.

Adverbs—frontward, in front, to the fore; before, in the van, ahead, right ahead; foremost, headmost; in the foreground, in the lee; in one's face, before one's face *or* eyes, dead ahead; face-to-face, vis-à-vis.

Antonyms, see REAR.

---

frontier, *n.* borderland, outskirts; wilderness. See LIMIT, CONTACT.

front-runner, *n.* leader, pacesetter. See PRIORITY.

frost, *n.* rime, hoarfrost, cranreuch; coldness, COLD.

frosting, *n.* icing, decoration (see ORNAMENT, FOOD).

frosty, *adj.* COLD, cool; unfeeling, coldhearted; distant, aloof. See SECLUSION. *Ant.,* warm.

froth, *n.* foam, suds, lather, spume; head, cream, collar; scum; levity, triviality, frivolity. —*v.i.* foam, spume, effervesce, ferment, bubble, fizz. See AGITATION, UNIMPORTANCE.

frown, *v.i.* scowl, lower, glower; look askance. —*n.* scowl. See IRASCIBILITY, DISAPPROBATION, DEJECTION. *Ant.,* smile.

frowsy, *adj.* unkempt, slovenly, frumpy. See UNCLEANNESS, VULGARITY.

frozen, *adj.* glacial, gelid; frostbitten, COLD; motionless, paralyzed, petrified; coldhearted, frigid, insensitive. See INSENSIBILITY. *Ant.,* liquid; thawed, melted.

frugal, *adj.* prudent, saving, provident, thrifty; sparing, stinting. See ECONOMY. *Ant.,* spendthrift.

fruit, *n.* product, yield, harvest; offspring, result, consequence, outgrowth. See PRODUCTION, EFFECT.

fruitful, *adj.* productive, fertile; prolific; profitable. See PRODUCTION, PROSPERITY. *Ant.,* barren, fruitless.

fruition, *n.* realization, attainment. See COMPLETION.

fruitless, *adj.* unavailing, unprofitable, vain; barren. See USELESSNESS.

frump, *n.* dowdy person, slattern. See UNCLEANNESS, VULGARITY.

frustrate, *v.t.* defeat, thwart, circumvent, cross, baffle, nullify. See HINDRANCE, DISAPPOINTMENT.

fry, *v.* sauté, panfry, deep-fry, frizzle, griddle, skillet-cook; *slang,* get the [electric] chair. See HEAT, PUNISHMENT.

fuck, *v.,* *vulgar,* copulate, have sex[ual relations], sleep *or* go to bed with. See SEX. —**fuck up,** *slang,* muddle, screw up, mess up, make a mess of. See ERROR.

fuddy-duddy, *n.* fogy, fussbudget; stuffed shirt. See AGE, AFFECTATION.

fudge, *v.i.* cheat, hedge, welsh; exaggerate. See DECEPTION.

FUEL
Combustible material

Nouns—1, fuel, firing, combustible; inflammable, burnable; ignite; fossil fuel; solar, nuclear, *etc.* ENERGY. See HEAT, POWER.

2, peat, turf; [bituminous, soft, anthracite, hard, buckwheat, grate, lignite, brown, glance, *or* cannel] coal, coal dust, culm, coke, charcoal, briquette; OIL, kerosene, petroleum, [leaded, regular, hi-test, premium, white, *or* unleaded] gasoline, petrol, diesel fuel, jet fuel; [ethyl] alcohol, ethanol, ethyl gasoline; canned heat, paraffin; [natural] gas (see VAPOR); firewood, kindling, fagot, log; cinder, embers; atomic *or* nuclear fuel, plutonium, uranium.

3, (*material for starting a fire*) tinder, punk, amadou, touchwood; [fire]brand, torch; fuse, detonator, cap; spill, wick, [safety *or* friction] match, flint, [cigar, cigarette, *or* butane] lighter; candle.

Verbs—fuel, furnish with fuel; refuel; feed, fire, stoke.

Adjectives—fuel, combustible, inflammable, burnable; fiery; gas-powered, nuclear-powered, *etc.*

Phrases—add fuel to the flames.

Antonyms, see INCOMBUSTIBILITY.

fugitive, *adj.* runaway, fleeing; transient, ephemeral, evanescent, fleeting; transitory. —*n.* runaway, eloper, absconder; refugee, escapee. See AVOIDANCE, ESCAPE, TRANSIENTNESS.

fulfill, *v.t.* satisfy, realize, gratify; execute, discharge; effect, carry out. See COMPLETION.

fulgent, *adj.* shining, resplendent (see LIGHT).

full, *adj.* filled, sated, satiated, glutted, gorged; replete; whole, complete, entire; loose, baggy; sonorous; plump, rounded; brimming. See COMPLETION, SUFFICIENCY. *Ant.*, empty.

full-blooded, *adj.* thoroughbred, pure-bred, whole-blooded; virile. See PURITY, STRENGTH.

full-blown, *adj.* full-fledged, mature; in bloom. See AGE, COMPLETION.

fulminate, *v.* boom, thunder, roar; detonate, explode; rail, berate, excoriate. See VIOLENCE, IMPRECATION, THREAT.

fulsome, *adj.* obnoxious, foul, noisome; unctuous, obsequious, fawning; cloying, excessive; tasteless, offensive. See SERVILITY, VULGARITY.

fumble, *v.* grope, paw; fluff, flub, muff, bungle. See UNSKILLFULNESS, TOUCH.

fume, *v.i.* chafe, fret, rage; smoke, reek. See EXCITABILITY, RESENTMENT, HEAT, DISCONTENT.

fumigate, *v.t.* disinfect (see CLEANNESS).

fun, *n.* sport, diversion, AMUSEMENT. See WIT.

function, *n.* faculty, office, DUTY, role, province; observance. See AGENCY, BUSINESS, RITE. —*v.i.* operate, serve. See ACTION, USE.

functional, *adj.* useful, serviceable. See UTILITY.

functionary, *n.* official, administrator, bureaucrat. See DIRECTOR.

fund, *n.* resources, STORE, cache, reserve, accumulation; slush fund, kitty; (*pl.*) assets, MONEY, capital. —*v.t.* set aside, lay away, STORE; invest in, finance. See MEANS.

fundamental, *adj.* basic, essential, underlying, original, INTRINSIC, rudimentary.

funeral, *n.* obsequies; burial, INTERMENT, entombment.

funereal, *adj.* funebrial, mournful, sad, solemn, somber, lugubrious; black, dark. See DEJECTION, INTERMENT.

funky, *adj.* earthy, bluesy; foul[-smelling], odorous. See SIMPLENESS, MALODOROUSNESS.

funnel, *n.* cone, bottleneck, channel, flue, chimney, shaft. See ROTUNDITY.

funny, *adj.* amusing, droll, comic; absurd, laughable, mirth-provoking, ludicrous; *informal*, strange, odd; (*pl.*) comics. See WIT, ABSURDITY. *Ant.*, unfunny.

fur, *n.* hide, pelt, coat, peltry, skin, pelage; hair, down. See COVERING, ROUGHNESS.

furies, *n.pl.* avengers, Erinyes, Eumenides, Dirae. See DEMON.

furious, *adj.* raging, violent, fierce, storming, turbulent, unrestrained; *informal*, mad, angry. See RESENTMENT, VIOLENCE.

furlough, *n.* leave [of ABSENCE], pass, shore leave, liberty. See PERMISSION.

furnace, *n.* See HEAT.

furnish, *v.t.* equip, outfit; provide, yield, supply. See PREPARATION, PROVISION.

FURNITURE
Movable equipment for office, home, etc.
See also LIGHT, MUSIC.

Nouns—1, furniture, [home] furnishings, household effects, movables.

2, seat, throne, dais; [Adirondack, Bath, Barcelona, barber, basket, butterfly, captain's, fanback, farthingale, folding, lawn, lounge, morris, overstuffed, parlor, porter, rocking, sling, slipper, swivel, wicker, *or* wing] chair, Chippendale, Dante, Savonarola, Carver, *or* scissors chair, cathedra, armchair, easy chair, highchair; divan; bench, banquette, inglenook, form, stool, sofa, chesterfield, davenport, daybed, duchesse, confidente, sedan, lounge, settee, squab, stall; love seat, dos-à-dos, couch, fauteuil, ottoman, settle, bench; saddle; pillion; saddle; pommel.

3, [single, double, twin, queen(-size), *or* king(-size)] bed, waterbed, berth, bunk [bed], charpoy, tester, cot, gurney, hammock, shakedown, cradle, litter, stretcher; bedding, mattress, featherbed, futon, pallet, paillasse, box spring, spring, pillow, bolster; foldaway, folding, *or* rollaway bed, hospital bed, Murphy bed, four-poster, truckle *or* trundle bed, platform bed; chair bed, sofa bed, convertible; crib, cradle, bassinet, car bed; bedstead, canopy, headboard, footboard. *Slang*, rack.

4, table, butterfly table, drum table, capstan table, card *or* folding table, coffee *or* cocktail table, drop-leaf table, extension table, nesting table, pier table, pouch table, teapoy stand, tray table; ambo; bar, counter; basin stand; credence, credenza; end table, night table, nightstand, bed table; worktable, [work]bench, drawing table; billiard *or* pool table; buffet, banquet table, refectory table, dining table, sideboard, dinette, kitchen table; desk, carrel, computer table *or* desk, writing desk, escritoire, kneehole desk, roll-top desk, secretary, tambour; dressing table, vanity, poudreuse; lectern; trolley, TV table, typewriter table.

5, cabinet, armoire, cupboard, press, kitchen cabinet, china cabinet, display case, whatnot, étagère, wardrobe, breakfront, buffet, credenza; Biedermeier cabinet, canterbury, cellarette; bookcase; bureau, chest of drawers, dresser, highboy, tallboy, lowboy, commode, chiffonier, chifforobe, clothes chest; filing cabinet; bin, bunker, caddy, coffer, crate, hamper, basket, trunk, hope chest, hutch, safe, strongbox.

6, footstool, cricket, foldstool, footrest, hassock, tabouret, mora; bar stool, campstool, music stool, piano stool *or* bench; coatrack, hatrack, umbrella stand; tripod; platform, stand, rostrum, dais, podium, pulpit, lectern; music stand; smoking stand.

Verbs—furnish (see PROVISION); decorate.

Adjectives—furnished.

---

furor, *n.* frenzy, commotion, disturbance, EXCITEMENT, hubbub, hullaballoo; craze, mania, fad. See FEELING, DESIRE.

furrier, *n.* fur dealer (see CLOTHING).

FURROW
Trench, wrinkle

Nouns—furrow, groove, rut, scratch, stria, crack, score, incision, slit; chamfer, flute, fluting, dado, rabbet; microgroove; channel, gutter, wheel track, trench, ditch, moat, fosse, trough, kennel; ravine (see INTERVAL); seam, line, corrugation; pleat. See FOLD.

Verbs—furrow, plow, plough; incise, score, cut, seam, channel; engrave (see ENGRAVING), etch, bite in; flute, chamfer; pucker, wrinkle, knit.

Adjectives—furrowed, grooved, *etc.*; ribbed, striated, fluted; corduroy.

Antonyms, see SMOOTHNESS.

---

furry, *adj.* hispid, bushy, shaggy, fuzzy. See ROUGHNESS.

further, *adj.* farther, more, additional. See ADDITION. —*v.t.* AID, advance, promote, expedite.

furthermore, *adv.* moreover, besides, in ADDITION.

furtive, *adj.* stealthy, sly, surreptitious, sneaking, skulking, covert. See CONCEALMENT.

fury, *n.* rage, frenzy; VIOLENCE, turbulence. See INSANITY, DEMON.

fuse, *v.* merge, unite, amalgamate, weld; melt, dissolve. See JUNCTION, COMBINATION, FUEL, UNITY.

fusion, *n.* union, amalgamation, integration, merger. See UNITY, COMBINATION, JUNCTION.

fuss, *n.* ado, bustle, hubbub, confusion, AGITATION; fret, fidget. See ACTIVITY.

fusty, *adj.* musty, stuffy, stale; old-fashioned. See OLDNESS.

futile, *adj.* ineffectual, vain, idle, useless. See USELESSNESS, HOPELESSNESS.

FUTURITY
Time yet to come

Nouns—futurity, [near *or* distant] future, hereafter, time to come; approaching *or* coming years *or* ages; millennium, doomsday, Day of Judgment, crack of doom; remote future; shape of things to come, writing on the wall, straw in the wind; future shock; approach of time, advent, time drawing on, womb of time; DESTINY, POSTERITY, eventuality; prospect (see EXPECTATION); afterworld, next world; foresight; futurism. *Informal,* the sweet by-and-by. See PREDICTION, THREAT, SEQUENCE.

Verbs—approach, await; look forward, anticipate, expect (see EXPECTATION); foresee; come on, draw on; draw near; threaten, impend (see DESTINY).

Adjectives—future, to come, coming, impending (see DESTINY); next, near; near at hand, close at hand; eventual, ulterior, in prospect (see EXPECTATION); futuristic (see NEWNESS).

Adverbs—in [the] future, prospectively, hereafter, tomorrow, the day after tomorrow; in course of time, in process of time, in the fullness of time; eventually, ultimately, sooner or later, in the long run; one of these days; after a while, after a time; from this time, henceforth, thence; thenceforth, whereupon, upon which; soon, on the eve of, on *or* at the point of, on the brink of; about to, close upon, around the corner, in the wind. *Ant.,* see PAST.

Phrases—coming events cast their shadow before; there is no future like the present; tomorrow is another day; tomorrow never comes.

Quotations—I never think of the future. It comes soon enough (*Albert Einstein*), The distinction between past, present, and future is only an illusion, however persistent (*Albert Einstein*), The future ain't what it used to be (*Yogi Berra*), Lord! we know what we are, but know not what we may be (*Shakespeare*), If you want a picture of the future, imagine a boot stamping on a human face—forever (*George Orwell*), Time present and time past are both perhaps present in time future (*T. S. Eliot*), The future is no more uncertain than the present (*Walt Whitman*).

---

fuzz, *n.* down, fluff, fur (see SOFTNESS);
  slang, police, police officer (see SAFETY).

G

gabble, *v.* cackle; chatter, prattle, blab; gibber, gab (*inf.*), chin (*sl.*), jaw (*sl.*). See LOQUACITY.

gad about, *v.* ramble, wander, roam, stray. See DEVIATION, TRAVEL.

gadfly, *n.* stable *or* warble fly; goad, mover. See INSECT, CAUSE.

gadget, *n.* contrivance, device, doohickey; invention, machine; thingamajig, whatchamacallit, contraption, doodad (*all inf.*). See PLAN, INSTRUMENTALITY.

gaff, *n.* spear, hook. See ARMS.

gaffe, *n.* blunder, ERROR.

gag, *v.* muffle, SILENCE; choke, strangle, retch. See EJECTION. —*n., informal,* joke. See WIT.

gaiety, *n.* merriment, frivolity, merrymaking, CHEERFULNESS. *Ant.,* sadness.

gain, *n.* INCREASE, profit; amplification. —*v.i.* benefit; progress; put on weight. —*v.t.* earn; win; reach, attain; persuade. See ACQUISITION. *Ant.,* loss.

gainful, *adj.* profitable, lucrative. See UTILITY.

gainsay, *v.t.* contradict (see NEGATION). *Ant.,* confirm.

gait, *n.* step, pace, stride; trot, gallop, walk, dogtrot; shuffle, saunter. See MOTION, METHOD.

gaiter, *n.* legging, spat[s]. See CLOTHING.

gala, *n.* festival. —*adj.* festive. See CELEBRATION.

galaxy, *n.* ASSEMBLAGE, MULTITUDE; Milky Way.

gale, *n.* WIND, storm, tempest. See REJOICING.

gall, *n.* bitterness, bile, rancor; *slang,* impudence, INSOLENCE. —*v.* irritate, chafe; annoy, exasperate; vex. See PAIN, RESENTMENT.

gallant, *n.* gigolo; squire, cavalier. See ACCOMPANIMENT. —*adj.* chivalrous, polite; brave, courageous; courteous, courtly. See ENDEARMENT. *Ant.,* discourteous.

gallery, *n.* balcony, corridor; veranda, loft; salon. See DRAMA, PAINTING, STORE.

gallivant, *v.i.* roam, wander, gad. See TRAVEL, DEVIATION.

gallop, *n. & v.* run, canter. See TRAVEL.

gallows, *n.* gibbet, scaffold, crosstree, hanging tree, yardarm. See PUNISHMENT.

galore, *adv.* in abundance. See SUFFICIENCY.

galvanize, *v.t.* stimulate, shock; motivate, move [to action]. See CAUSE.

gambit, *n.* attack; stratagem, ruse, artifice, ploy. See CUNNING, GIVING.

gamble, *n.* CHANCE, wager, risk. —*v.* speculate, risk, bet. See GAMBLING.

GAMBLING
Games of chance

Nouns—1, gambling, gaming, risk, betting, dicing, bookmaking, speculation, laying odds; bet, stake, wager, ante, pot, pool, kitty, bank, progressive betting, betting system, spread; jackpot; [even, short, *or* long] odds; house advantage, PC, percentage, vig[orish]; betting system; wheel of fortune, tossup, toss of the dice, Russian roulette, heads or tails, turn of the card[s] *or* wheel; gamble, risk (see CHANCE). *Slang,* flier. 2, casino, gambling *or* gaming house, betting parlor, gambling hall, gaming table[s], roulette wheel, craps table, slot machine, one-armed bandit, *etc.,* pinball machine; shoe, sabot; race track, the turf, the horses, the dogs, parimutuel window[s], racing forms, tout sheets, totalizator, tote board; chip, counter; bucket shop, off-track betting, OTB; wheel of fortune. *Slang,* grind *or* sawdust joint, house, shop, store, trap, creep dive *or* joint.

3, a. game of chance, betting game, crank game. **b.** blackjack, twenty-one, vingt-et-un, first base, card-counting. **c.** [American *or* European] roulette, rouge et noir, canoe, fret, layout; straight-up, column, dozens, split, street, corner, *or* square bet. **d.** craps, dice, crap game, poker dice; win, hardway, pass, don't pass, come *or* don't come bet; boxes, craps, Jonah, fimps, little Phoebe, little Joe, carolina, point, natural, sice, big Joe, cock-eyes, boxcars, snake eyes. *Slang,* Harlem tennis, poor man's roulette. **e.** [draw, stud, closed, *or* open] poker, high- *or* lowball, high-low; bet, raise, call, showdown, openers. **f.** lottery, raffle, drawing, sweepstakes, numbers game, policy; bingo, keno, beano, lotto, big game. **g.** baccarat, chemin-de-fer; [three-card] monte; wheel of fortune; cribbage, bridge, *etc.* (see AMUSEMENT).
4, [degenerate *or* compulsive] gambler, gamester, player, dicer, horseplayer, bettor, crapshooter, pokerface, *etc.*; cheat[er], mark (see DECEPTION); banker, croupier, caller, callman, dealer, ladderman; adventurer, speculator, entrepreneur; bookmaker, tout; kibitzer. *Slang,* bookie, runner, banker, customer's man; vulture capitalist; piket, tinhorn, prof, grind, lowballer, plunger, screamer; sharp[er].
Verbs—gamble, game, speculate; flip a coin, call head or tails, shoot craps, play the ponies, *etc.*; bet, wager, hazard, stake, put up; make a bet, make book, bet on, ante [up]; call, cover, see; check, pass, stand [pat], hit; double down; cheat, use loaded dice *or* marked cards. *Informal,* get a piece of the action, ball the jack, take a flyer, get down. See CHANCE.
Phrases—there are two great pleasures in gambling: winning and losing.
Quotations—Life is a gamble at terrible odds—if it was a bet, you wouldn't take it (*Tom Stoppard*), Gaming corrupts our dispositions and teaches us a habit of hostility against all mankind (*Thomas Jefferson*), [Gambling:] The child of avarice, the brother of iniquity, and the father of mischief (*George Washington*).

---

gambol, *v. & n.* LEAP, cavort, frolic, romp, play. See AMUSEMENT.

game, *n.* AMUSEMENT, diversion, sport, play; contest, match; plan, purpose; prey (see PURSUIT). See CONTENTION, CHANCE, ANIMAL. —*adj., slang,* sporty, gritty, plucky. See COURAGE, RESOLUTION.

gamin, *n.* urchin, street Arab. See YOUTH.

gamut, *n.* scale; scope, extent, compass. See SPACE, MUSIC.

gamy, *adj.* high, rank, rancid; spirited, plucky; racy, off-color. See MALODOROUSNESS, IMPURITY, COURAGE.

gang, *n.* group, band; set, clique; mob, horde. See ASSEMBLAGE, PARTY.

gangling, *adj.* gangly, lanky, gawky, spindly; ungainly, awkward. See NARROWNESS, UNSKILLFULNESS. *Ant.,* stalwart.

gangrenous, *adj.* mortified, necrose. See DISEASE.

gangster, *n.* hoodlum, hooligan, thug, racketeer, tough; syndicate man; mobster, goon, hood (*all sl.*). See EVILDOER.

gap, *n.* INTERVAL, vacancy, break, lacuna, hiatus. See NARROWNESS, DISCONTINUANCE.

gape, *v.* open, spread, yawn; stare, gaze. See OPENING, WONDER.

garage, *n.* carport; service station. See STORE, RESTORATION.

garb, *n.* See CLOTHING.

garbage, *n.* waste, refuse, trash, rubbish, junk, scraps; nonsense. See USELESSNESS, UNMEANINGNESS, UNCLEANNESS, FALSENESS.

garble, *v.* distort, misreport. See FALSENESS, DISTORTION.

garden, *n.* herbary, nursery, pleasance; flower beds. See AGRICULTURE.

garden-variety, *adj.* common, regular, ordinary. See CONFORMITY. *Ant.,* extraordinary.

gargantuan, *adj.* enormous, gigantic. See SIZE. *Ant.,* liliputian.

garish, *adj.* showy, gaudy. See OSTENTATION.

garland, *n.* festoon, wreath, lei. See ORNAMENT, CIRCULARITY.

garment, *n.* CLOTHING, robe, dress, vestment, habiliment.

garner, *v.* harvest, collect, STORE.

garnish, *v.* ORNAMENT, trim, decorate, embellish; season, flavor (see TASTE).

garret, *n.* crawl space, loft, attic. See RECEPTACLE.

garrison, *n.* fort[ress], outpost, stronghold; camp, bivouac; billet, barracks, soldiery. —*v.* occupy, encamp, billet; defend, secure, protect, fortify. See DEFENSE, COMBATANT.

garrulity, *n.* LOQUACITY, wordiness, prolixity, verbosity. *Ant.,* TACITURNITY.

gas, *n.* aeriform *or* elastic fluid; VAPOR, fume, reek; AIR, ether; FUEL, gasoline, petrol; bombast, hot air (*sl.*); gas attack.

gash, *n. & v.* slash, gouge, slit; cut; scratch, score. See DISJUNCTION, INTERVAL.

gasoline, *n.* petrol; leaded *or* no-lead gasoline. See FUEL, OIL.

gasp, *v.* pant, labor, choke; puff; exclaim. See WEARINESS.

gate, *n.* gateway, OPENING, portal; sluice, floodgate; *slang,* admission. See RECEIVING, EJECTION, PASSAGE.

gate-crasher, *n.* intruder, trespasser (see INGRESS, IMPROBITY).

gather, *v.* infer, conclude; congregate, group, amass; collect, harvest, cull, pick, glean; cluster, huddle, herd; pleat; fester, suppurate. See ASSEMBLAGE, SUPPOSITION, ACQUISITION.

gathering, *n.* ASSEMBLAGE, get-together, reception.

gauche, *adj.* awkward, clumsy; uncultured. See UNSKILLFULNESS.

gaudy, *adj.* garish, showy, cheap, blatant, tawdry; gay, bright, flashy. See COLOR, OSTENTATION, VULGARITY. *Ant.,* plain.

gauge, *n.* measure, templet, template; caliber, SIZE. —*v.* measure, estimate, judge, evaluate. See MEASUREMENT, JUDGMENT.

gaunt, *adj.* haggard, bony, lean, emaciated. See NARROWNESS. *Ant.,* plump.

gauze, *n.* net, tulle, malines, scrim, marquisette, gossamer, cheesecloth, bandage. See TRANSPARENCY.

gay, *adj.* lively, vivacious, blithe; homosexual; convivial, festive; bright, colorful. See CHEERFULNESS, COLOR, UNCONFORMITY. *Ant.,* dull; straight.

gaze, *v.* stare, ogle, pore. See VISION.

gazebo, *n.* pavilion, summerhouse. See ABODE.

gazette, *n.* newspaper, tabloid, bulletin. See PUBLICATION.

gear, *n.* CLOTHING, dress; cogwheel; equipment, tools, apparatus; harness, *etc.* See INSTRUMENTALITY, PROVISION.

gelatin, *n.* gel, jelly, aspic, gelée; gluten, pectin, agar-agar. See COHERENCE.

gelid, *adj.* frozen, COLD; icy, frosty, ice-cold. *Ant.,* tepid.

gem, *n.* jewel, stone; prize; work of art. See ORNAMENT, GOODNESS.

gender, *n.* sex; masculine, feminine, neuter. See MALE, FEMALE.

genealogy, *n.* pedigree, descent, ANCESTRY, lineage, stock, POSTERITY.

general, *adj.* universal (see GENERALITY). —*n.* general of the armies, commander in chief. See COMBATANT. *Ant.,* specific.

GENERALITY
Universal reference

Nouns—1, generality, generalization, abstraction, sweeping generalization *or* statement; universality, currency, broadness, collectivity; average; catholicity, catholicism; miscellany, miscellaneousness; prevalence; DISPERSION. *Informal,* dime a dozen.

2, everyone, everybody [and his *or* her brother *or* sister], every last man *or* woman, every man jack, every mother's son, every Tom, Dick, and Harry; all hands, all the world and his wife [*or* brother, *etc.*]; anybody; world community. *Informal,* whole kit and caboodle. *Slang,* the works.

Verbs—be general, prevail, be going about; generalize.

Adjectives—general, generic, collective, current; broad, comprehensive, extensive, sweeping; encyclopedic, widespread, dispersed; universal, catholic, common, all-inclusive, worldwide, global; ecumenical; transcendental; prevalent, prevailing, rife, epidemic, besetting; all over, covered with; every, each and every, every single *or* last, all; unspecified, impersonal; indiscriminate; customary (see HABIT).

Adverbs—generally, in general, generally speaking, on an average; always, for better or worse; for the most part, by and large, on the whole, in the main; in the long run;

whatever, whatsoever; everywhere, wherever; to a man, one and all, all told. *Informal,* across the board.

Phrases—a rising tide lifts all boats; all roads lead to Rome; what everybody says must be true.

Quotations—General notions are generally wrong (*Lady Mary Montagu*).
Antonyms, see SPECIALITY.

---

generate, *v.* make, produce; proliferate, procreate, breed, impregnate; engender. See POWER, PRODUCTION, CAUSE.

generation, *n.* age, descent, lifetime; procreating, breeding, begetting. See PRODUCTION, POSTERITY.

generosity, *n.* BENEVOLENCE, philanthropy, LIBERALITY, munificence, prodigality; altruism, magnanimity. See GIVING, UNSELFISHNESS. *Ant.,* miserliness.

genesis, *n.* creation, origin, formation, BEGINNING, birth. See PRODUCTION.

genetic, *adj.* genic, inherited, hereditary, innate. See PRODUCTION.

genial, *adj.* affable, cordial, jovial, friendly, hearty, pleasant. See CHEERFULNESS. *Ant.,* unfriendly.

genie, *n.* imp, gnome; jinni. See DEMON, MYTHICAL DEITIES.

genitalia, *n.pl.* genitals, sex organs, pudenda, private parts. See BODY.

genius, *n.* spirit, pixy; brilliance, INTELLIGENCE; talent, bent, gift, ability. See SKILL, INTELLECT, MYTHICAL DEITIES.

genocide, *n.* mass murder, decimation, extermination. See KILLING.

genre, *n.* kind, category, species, type, CLASS.

genteel, *adj.* polite, elegant. See COURTESY, ELEGANCE. *Ant.,* crude.

gentile, *adj.* heathen, pagan; Christian; non-Jewish. See HETERODOXY.

gentility, *n.* refinement, ELEGANCE; COURTESY; NOBILITY. See FASHION.

gentle, *adj.* mild, calm; soothing, kindly, tolerant; considerate, courteous, well-bred, high-born; tame, docile. See COURTESY, MODERATION, NOBILITY, DOMESTICATION. *Ant.,* rough, brutal.

gentleman, *n.* aristocrat, cavalier, esquire. See MALE, PROBITY, NOBILITY.

gentleness, *n.* MODERATION, mildness; kindness, amenity, LENIENCY. See COURTESY. *Ant.,* brutality.

gentry, *n.* See NOBILITY.

genuine, *adj.* true, right, real, authentic;

sincere, real, unaffected; honest, valid. See GOODNESS, PURITY, TRUTH. *Ant.,* fake, false.

geometrical, *adj.* geometric, planimetric; patterned, designed, symmetric; formal, stylized. See ORDER, NUMERATION.

geography, *n.* topography, ARRANGEMENT.

geriatric, *adj.* elderly, aged. See OLDNESS. *Ant.,* youthful.

germ, *n.* microorganism; seed, embryo; microbe, bacterium; BEGINNING, rudiment; source, origin, CAUSE. See LITTLENESS.

germane, *adj.* relevant, pertinent, apropos, to the point. See RELATION.

germicide, *n.* germ killer; bactericide, insecticide, antiseptic. See REMEDY.

germinate, *v.* impregnate; sprout, begin. See PRODUCTION.

gesticulate, *v.* gesture, motion, wave, pantomime, mime. See INDICATION.

gesture, *n.* motion, signal, gesticulation. —*v.i.* wave, signal, nod, beckon. See INDICATION.

get, *v.* secure, obtain, procure, acquire; win, earn, attain; understand, comprehend; produce, beget. See ACQUISITION, PRODUCTION, REPRODUCTION.

getaway, *n., slang,* ESCAPE, breakout, flight; head start.

get-together, *n.* social [gathering], meeting. See ASSEMBLAGE.

getup, *n., informal,* rig, outfit, garb; costume. See CLOTHING.

gewgaw, *n.* trinket, knickknack, bauble. See ORNAMENT.

geyser, *n.* hot spring, spout, gusher; Old Faithful. See WATER.

ghastly, *adj.* pale, haggard, deathly, ashen, livid; horrible, terrible, fearsome, hideous. See UGLINESS, COLORLESSNESS, FEAR. *Ant.,* lovely, ruddy.

ghetto, *n.* quarter, slum. See ABODE.

ghost, *n.* apparition, phantom, spirit, shade, specter. See DEMON, INTELLECT.

ghostly, *adj.* ghostlike, spectral, phantasmal. See DEMON.

ghoul, *n.* grave robber, body snatcher; DE-MON, vampire; blackmailer. See EVIL-DOER.

giant, *n.* jumbo, monster, titan, colossus. See SIZE. *Ant.,* midget, dwarf.

gibberish, *n.* jargon, double-talk. See AB-SURDITY, UNMEANINGNESS.

gibe, *n.* sneer, taunt, jeer, RIDICULE. See DISRESPECT.

giddy, *adj.* frivolous, irresponsible; dizzy, flighty, capricious. See INSANITY, FOLLY. *Ant.,* serious, staid.

gift, *n.* present, donation, favor, bounty; contribution, gratuity, tip, largesse; talent, aptitude, ability. See GIVING, POWER, SKILL, LIBERALITY.

gifted, *adj.* talented (see SKILL). *Ant.,* untalented.

gig, *n.* carriage; hairdo; engagement, post. See EXERTION, VEHICLE, BEAUTY.

gigantic, *adj.* titanic, huge, enormous, colossal, immense. See SIZE. *Ant.,* minuscule.

giggle, *v.* chuckle, titter. See REJOICING.

gigolo, *n.* fancy man. See IMPURITY.

gild, *v.t.* aurify (see COVERING).

gimmick, *n.* artifice, trick, angle. See PLAN.

gingerly, *adv.* carefully, prudently, timidly, charily, hesitantly. See CAUTION. *Ant.,* bold, rash.

gird, *v.* bind, strap, secure; encircle, surround; equip, support, fortify. See CIRCUMSCRIPTION, PREPARATION, STRENGTH.

girdle, *n.* band, belt, girth; corset, cummerbund. See CLOTHING, CIRCUMSCRIPTION.

girl, *n.* lass, maid, damsel; SERVANT, clerk. See FEMALE, YOUTH. *Ant.,* boy.

girlfriend, *n.* sweetheart, girl, LOVE, date, steady (*inf.*), flame (*sl.*), moll (*sl.*). *Ant.,* boyfriend.

girth, *n.* outline; circumference, belt, girdle, band. See CIRCUMSCRIPTION.

gist, *n.* MEANING, essence, significance, point. See INTRINSIC.

give, *v.t.* bestow, donate (see GIVING); give up, yield, concede. —*v.i.* give in, give way, surrender, yield. —*n.* ELASTICITY. See RELINQUISHMENT. *Ant.,* take.

give-and-take, *n.* compromise, BARTER; CONVERSATION.

give birth, *v.* bear [a child, young, *etc.*], lie in; whelp, fawn, *etc.* See REPRODUCTION.

give off, *v.t.* exude, emit, produce (see EXCRETION).

giveaway, *n.* disclosure, revelation, dead giveaway; premium, bonus, door prize, handout, come-on, something for nothing; loss leader. See GIVING.

given, *n.* fact, factor, EVIDENCE.

GIVING
Act of bestowing

Nouns—1, giving, bestowal, donation; presentation, presentment; accordance; cession, concession; delivery, giveaway; consignment; dispensation; communication; endowment; investment, investiture; award; almsgiving, charity, LIBERALITY; generosity, philanthropy (see BENEVOLENCE); self-sacrifice, the supreme sacrifice; fund-raising (see REQUEST).

2, (*free gift*) gift, donation, present, cadeau, boon, favor; benefaction, grant; offering, oblation, sacrifice, immolation; gambit; bonus, bonanza.

3, (*money given*) allowance, contribution, subscription, subsidy, tribute; alimony, pension; fee, recompense (see PAYMENT); consideration; bribe, bait; peace offering.

4, (*money given as inheritance*) bequest, legacy, devise, will; dot, appanage; voluntary settlement *or* conveyance, TRANSFER; amortization.

5, (*charity*) alms, charity, largesse, bounty, dole, relief; outdoor relief, home relief; oblation, offertory; honorarium, gratuity, Christmas box, Easter offering, breadline; food stamps; tip, drink money, pourboire, lagniappe, baksheesh, premium. *Slang,* handout.

6, (*one who gives*) giver, grantor; contributor, donor, friend, testator, testatrix; feoffer, settlor; political donor, political action committee, PAC.

7, (*unexpected gift*) godsend, manna, windfall, blessing; pennies from heaven.

Verbs—1, give, donate, bestow, impart, confer, grant, accord, render, award, assign; present, give away, dispense, dispose of, deal, mete, *or* dole out (see APPORTIONMENT); pay *or* squeeze out; come across; make a present, loosen the purse strings, chip in, contribute, subscribe; endow, settle upon, bequeath, will, leave, hand down, devise; hand *or* turn in; deliver, hand, pass, make, *or* turn over; entrust; consign, vest in; concede, cede, yield, part with, spend; pay (see PAYMENT).

2, furnish, supply, make available, help; administer *or* minister to; afford, spare; accommodate *or* favor with; shower down upon, lavish, pour, *or* thrust upon; cross, tickle, *or* grease the palm, bribe; tip; OFFER, sacrifice, immolate. *Informal,* fork over. *Slang,* kick in; cough up.

Adjectives—giving, given; allowed, allowable; donative, concessional; communicable; charitable, eleemosynary; liberal.

Adverbs—ex gratia.

Phrases—a small gift usually gets small thanks; Friday's child is loving and giving; charity begins at home; fear the Greeks bearing gifts; never look a gift horse in the mouth.

Quotations—It is more blessed to give than to receive (*Bible*), God loveth a cheerful giver (*Bible*), Self-sacrifice enables us to sacrifice other people without blushing (*G. B. Shaw*), Don't deprive yourself of the joy of giving (*Michael Greenberg*).

Antonyms, see RECEIVING, ACQUISITION.

---

glacial, *adj.* icy (see COLD). *Ant.,* torrid.

glad, *adj.* happy, content, cheerful, joyful; blithe, beatific; pleased; blissful. See PLEASURE, REJOICING, CHEERFULNESS. *Ant.,* sad.

glade, *n.* clearing, glen, cañada. See MOISTURE.

glamour, *n.* charm, romance, enchantment, allure; sex appeal. See ATTRACTION.

glance, *n.* glimpse, coup d'oeil; ray, beam, look; ricochet, skim, stroke. —*v.i.* peek, glimpse, look; graze, brush, strike; gleam, flash. See VISION, LIGHT.

glandular, *adj.* endocrine, hormonal; adrenal, thryroidal, *etc.* See BODY, EXCRETION.

glare, *n.* scowl, frown, glower; stare. —*v.i.* flare, shine, glitter; blinding light. See LIGHT, VISION.

glaring, *adj.* fierce; bright, dazzling, showy; conspicuous, flagrant, obvious, notorious. See COLOR, VISIBILITY.

glass, *n.* crystal; mirror, lens, slide; beaker, tumbler, goblet, snifter; pane; stained glass, bottle glass, peloton, *etc.*; telescope, spyglass; (*pl.*) spectacles, eyeglasses. See OPTICAL INSTRUMENTS, RECEPTACLE, BRITTLENESS, TRANSPARENCY.

glassy, *adj.* glazed, vitreous, crystalline; mirrory, smooth, polished; clear, bright, transparent; fragile, brittle. See TRANSPARENCY, SMOOTHNESS, BRITTLENESS, UNMEANINGNESS.

glaze, *n.* luster, shine; coating; ice; glass, glassiness. See SMOOTHNESS, COVERING.

gleam, *n.* light, beam, flash, glimmer, ray. —*v.i.* shine, glow, glitter, glimmer. See LIGHT.

glean, *v.* gather [in], harvest; deduce; cull; winnow. See AGRICULTURE, CHOICE, JUDGMENT.

glee, *n.* CHEERFULNESS, delight, joy, merriment, gaiety, mirth. *Ant.,* depression.

glen, *n.* valley, dale. See CONCAVITY.

glib, *adj.* facile, fluent, voluble, insincere. See LOQUACITY, FACILITY, AFFECTATION. *Ant.,* halting, considered.

glide, *v.i.* float, flow, skim; slip, slide, coast; skate, swim, ski. See MOTION, AVIATION.

glimmer, *n.* glance, appearance, view, flash, sight. See VISION. —*v.i.* shine. See LIGHT, DIMNESS.

glimpse, *v. & n.* glance (see VISION).

glint, *n.* luster, brightness, gleam. —*v.i.* flash, gleam, glisten, scintillate. See LIGHT.

glisten, *v.i.* glister, gleam, glint, glitter, coruscate. See LIGHT.

glitch, *n.* malfunction, defect, flaw, snag. See ERROR.

glitter, *v.i. & n.* flash, gleam, twinkle, glisten, glint, sparkle. See LIGHT, OSTENTATION.

glitz, *n., slang,* flash[iness], superficiality. See ORNAMENT, SHALLOWNESS.

gloat, *v.i.* boast, exult, rejoice; stare, gape; revel, glory, delight. See PLEASURE, BOASTING.

glob, *n.* lump, gob, mass (see DENSITY).

global, *adj.* spherical; worldwide. See GENERALITY, ROTUNDITY.

globe, *n.* ball, sphere; earth; orb. See ROTUNDITY.

globule, *n.* glob, drop[let], bead, blob; spherule. See ROTUNDITY.

gloom, *n.* DEJECTION, sadness, dolefulness, melancholy; shadow, shade, dimness, DARKNESS, OBSCURITY; pessimism. *Ant.,* CHEERFULNESS.

gloomy, *adj.* obscure, shadowy; despondent, glum. *Ant.,* bright.

glorify, *v.* exalt, magnify, revere; exaggerate; praise, honor; transform; flatter. See REPUTE, EXAGGERATION, APPROBATION. *Ant.,* denigrate.

glory, *n.* aureole, halo, nimbus; radiance, brilliance; fame, dignity; effulgence; honor, kudos, renown. See BEAUTY, LIGHT, REPUTE.

gloss, *n.* luster, sheen, shine, finish, polish; glaze, veneer; DECEPTION, speciousness. See LIGHT, SMOOTHNESS, SHALLOWNESS.

glossary, *n.* [word]list, lexicon, vocabulary. See LIST.

glove, *n.* mitten, gauntlet. See CLOTHING.

glow, *n.* flush, sheen, LIGHT, radiance, warmth. —*v.* shine, gleam, flush, burn, blaze, flame. See HEAT, FEELING, COLOR, VIGOR.

glower, *n.* scowl, frown, glare. See RESENTMENT.

glowing, *adj.* incandescent; ardent, enthusiastic. See FEELING.

glue, *n.* mucilage, paste, cement, adhesive. —*v.* stick, attach, cement; adhere. See CONNECTION, COHERENCE.

glum, *adj.* morose, sullen, moody, gloomy, low, unhappy. See DEJECTION. *Ant.,* cheerful.

glut, *v.* stuff, cram, choke, pack, jam. —*n.* surplus, surfeit, plethora, saturation, satiety, redundance. See SUFFICIENCY. *Ant.,* dearth.

GLUTTONY
Insatiable appetite

Nouns—1, gluttony, gluttonousness, hunger, hoggishness; greed, greediness; voracity, rapacity, edacity, crapulence; epicurism; good *or* high living; guzzling; good cheer, blow out; feast; gastronomy. See DESIRE, PLEASURE.

2, glutton, epicure, bon vivant, gourmand, gourmandizer, gourmet; apicius, cormorant; gastronome; Vitellius. *Informal,* hog, pig.

Verbs—be gluttonous, gormandize, gorge; overgorge, overeat; engorge, eat one's fill, indulge one's appetite; cram, stuff; bolt, raven, wolf, devour, gobble up; eat out of house and home; have a tapeworm inside, have eyes bigger than one's belly. *Informal,* eat like a horse, make a pig of oneself. *Slang,* blimp out, hoover (up), pit out, scarf up *or* down, throw down. See FOOD.

Adjectives—gluttonous, greedy, hungry, voracious, ravenous, rapacious, edacious, omnivorous, crapulent, swinish, cormorant; gorged, overfed; insatiable.

Phrases—eat to live, not live to eat; you cannot have your cake and eat it [too].

Quotations—Gluttony is an emotional escape, a sign that something is eating us (*Peter De Vries*), More die in the United States of too much food than of too little (*John Kenneth Galbraith*).

Antonyms, see ASCETICISM, MODERATION.

gnarled, *adj.* knotty, burred, cross-grained; misshapen, deformed; rough, wiry, rugged. See DISTORTION, ROUGHNESS.

gnash, *v.t.* grind, champ, crunch, gnaw, bite. See RESENTMENT, LAMENTATION.

gnaw, *v.* chew, masticate, crunch; rankle, irritate, distress. See FOOD, PAIN.

gnome, *n.* dwarf, goblin, elf, kobold, gremlin; aphorism. See DEMON, MYTHICAL DEITIES, MAXIM.

go, *v.i.* go away, leave, depart, withdraw, retire, exit; vanish, disappear, evaporate, evanesce; operate, work, run, function, succeed; proceed, pass; wend, stir;

extend, reach; elapse, pass; wither, fade, die; burst, explode. See DEPARTURE, PASSAGE, DEATH, SUCCESS, MOTION, ENERGY. —**go back on,** *informal,* renege, betray (see NEGATION). —**go over,** *informal,* succeed (see SUCCESS). —**go under,** *informal,* fail (see FAILURE).

goad, *v.* prick, stab, prod, poke, spur; urge, egg [on], incite, impel, drive, needle (*inf.*). See CAUSE.

go-ahead, *n.* approval, green light, PERMISSION.

goal, *n.* object, end, aim; ambition; (*in games:*) finish line, home, cage, goalposts, end zone, basket; field goal, foul. See INTENTION, ARRIVAL.

gob, *n.* lump, dab, dollop (see DENSITY); (*pl.*) piles, lots, heaps, oodles. See MULTITUDE.

gobble, *v.* eat, devour, bolt, wolf, gulp; *slang,* engulf, swallow up, consume, exhaust, take over. See GLUTTONY, FOOD.

go-between, *n.* AGENT, intermediary, broker, middleman, dealer; pander. See BUSINESS.

goblet, *n.* cup, chalice. See RECEPTACLE.

goblin, *n.* gnome, gremlin. See MYTHICAL DEITIES.

goddess, *n.* DEITY, idol, divinity; Olympian. See MYTHICAL DEITIES.

godless, *adj.* unbelieving, faithless; atheistic, agnostic, skeptic[al]; heathen[ish], pagan, infidel; impious, irreligious. See IRRELIGION.

godly, *adj.* divine; pious, reverent, religious, devout. See PIETY. *Ant.,* ungodly.

godsend, *n.* miracle, blessing, manna [from heaven], windfall, boon, [lucky] break. See PROSPERITY.

gofer, *n., slang,* flunky, errand boy *or* girl, underling. See SERVANT.

go-getter, *n., slang,* doer, entrepreneur, drum-beater, hustler, operator; zealot, enthusiast, wheeler-dealer (*sl.*).

goggles, *n.pl.* spectacles, eyeshield (see OPTICAL INSTRUMENTS).

goings-on, *n., informal,* behavior, CONDUCT.

gold, *n.* MONEY, wealth; bullion, aurum; gilding, gilt, goldplate. See COLOR.

goldbrick, *v.t.* shirk, malinger, slack. See AVOIDANCE.

golden, *adj.* gilded, aureate, yellow; gold; precious, priceless; unequaled. See COLOR, DEARNESS.

golden rule, principle, tenet, guideline. See MAXIM.

gold mine, bonanza, [mother] lode; Eldorado. See SUCCESS, MONEY.

gone, *adj.* away, absent (see ABSENCE).

gong, *n.* cymbal, tocsin, tam-tam. See MUSIC.

good, *adj.* worthy; useful, skillful, competent; thorough, complete; valid, genuine; pleasant. See GOODNESS, SKILL, COMPLETION, TRUTH. —*n.* POSSESSION, merchandise. *Ant.,* bad.

good-bye, *n.* DEPARTURE, leavetaking; adieu, aloha, farewell, ciao, *etc. Ant.,* hello, greeting.

good-for-nothing, *n.* knave, rogue, ne'er-do-well, do-nothing; lazybones, loafer, sloth, wastrel, fainéant, bum (*sl.*). See INACTIVITY. —*adj.* no-account, useless, worthless, futile. See USELESSNESS.

good-looking, *adj.* handsome, pretty, comely. See BEAUTY. *Ant.,* homely.

goodly, *adj.* considerable, sizable; excellent, splendid. See SIZE, GOODNESS, BEAUTY.

good-natured, *adj.* easygoing, even-tempered, pleasant, agreeable, amiable, sociable. See CHEERFULNESS, BENEVOLENCE. *Ant.,* ill-natured, disagreeable.

GOODNESS
Quality of being good

Nouns—1, good, goodness; excellence, merit; value, worth, price; welfare, benefit, blessing. See VIRTUE, BENEVOLENCE, PROBITY, UTILITY.

2, (*item of best quality*) masterpiece, chef d'œuvre, prime, flower, cream, pride, elite, pick, classic, flower of the flock, salt of the earth, eighth wonder of the world; prime, heyday, zenith. *Slang,* God's gift to the world. See SUPERIORITY, PERFECTION.

3, (*item of good quality*) gem [of the first water]; bijou, precious stone, jewel, diamond [in the rough], ruby, brilliant, treasure; good thing; rara avis, one in a million. *Slang,* class act, something else, cat's meow *or* pajamas, living end, GQ, good shit.

4, good person, man, *or* woman, model, paragon, prince, angel.

Verbs—1, produce *or* do good, be beneficial, profit (see UTILITY); serve, help, avail, [confer a] benefit; be the making of, do a world of good, make a man *or* woman of; produce a good effect; do a good turn, improve (see IMPROVEMENT).

2, be good, stand the test; pass muster; challenge comparison, vie, emulate, rival.

Adjectives—1, good, beneficial, valuable, of value, excellent, divine, heavenly, goodly; serviceable, useful; advantageous, profitable, edifying, salutary, healthful (see HEALTH); genuine (see TRUTH); moderately good, tolerable (see MEDIOCRITY); elite, prime, tiptop, great, top-drawer, dandy, all wool and a yard wide; up to snuff, par, *or* the mark; above par. *Informal,* grand, topnotch, A-1, dynamite, jim-dandy, out of this world, not half bad. *Slang,* bang-up, swell, bodacious, zanzy, all right, cool, copacetic, bad[ass], hard, hellacious, mad, nasty, out of sight, phat, aces, aggro, bitchin', sweet, awesome, boss, crazy, far out, real gone, george, ginchy, gnarly, jake, keen, knockout, mean, rad[ical], righteous, something else, to die, too much.

2, harmless, unobnoxious, innocuous, innocent, inoffensive.

3, virtuous, moral, creditable, laudable, exemplary (see VIRTUE).

Adverbs—to the good, well and good, for the best, beneficially, in one's favor *or* interest[s], handsome is as handsome does; see no evil, hear no evil, speak no evil. *Slang,* like a mojo.

Quotations—I hope there is a hell for the good somewhere (*Eugene O'Neill*), Good merchandise, even when hidden, soon finds buyers (*Plautus*), Nature made him, and then broke the mould (*Ludovico Ariosto*).

Antonyms, see BADNESS, EVILDOER.

---

goods, *n.pl.* wares, merchandise, stock, effects, commodities; belongings, possessions. See POSSESSION.

goof, *n. & v.* See ERROR, FOLLY.

goof off, *slang,* loaf, loiter, shirk. See INACTIVITY, AVOIDANCE.

gore, *n.* blood (see FLUIDITY).

gorge, *n.* gully, ravine, canyon, pass; feast. See INTERVAL. —*v.* overeat, gormandize, stuff, bolt, gulp. See GLUTTONY.

gorgeous, *adj.* beautiful, superb, magnificent. See BEAUTY. *Ant.,* ugly.

gory, *adj.* bloody; bloodthirsty, sanguinary. See KILLING.

gospel, *n.* good news, glad tidings; dogma, TRUTH. See SACRED WRITINGS, NEWS, RULE.

gossamer, *n.* cobweb; gauze, veil. See TRANSPARENCY.

gossip, *n.* busybody, talebearer, chatterer; reports, rumors. —*v.i.* talk, report, tattle, whisper. See CURIOSITY, INFORMATION, SPEECH, NEWS.

gouge, *v.* scoop, channel, dig, groove, rout out; *informal,* defraud, cheat (see DECEPTION, STEALING). See CONCAVITY, FURROW.

goulash, *n.* stew; jumble, hash. See MIXTURE, FOOD.

gourmet, *n.* epicure, bon vivant; gastronome, gastrophile. See TASTE, GLUTTONY.

govern, *v.* RULE, reign, administrate, preside; hold power, sway, *or* the reins; guide, control; restrain, moderate, temper, curb, bridle, check. See RESTRAINT, AUTHORITY.

governess, *n.* nurse, nanny; preceptress, gouvernante. See TEACHING.

government, *n.* regime, administration; control, rule, regulation; state, economy; kingship, regency, *etc.* See AUTHORITY.

gown, *n.* peignoir, negligee, nightgown; dress, evening gown, robe; vestment, cassock, frock, smock, slip. See CLOTHING.

grab, *v.* take, snatch, seize, capture; clutch; annex. See ACQUISITION.

grab bag, *n.* miscellany, medley, assortment, ASSEMBLAGE.

grace, *n.* delicacy, tact, culture; graciousness, COURTESY; attractiveness, charm; compassion, mercy, clemency; saintliness, PIETY. See PERMISSION, GRATITUDE, FORGIVENESS, ELEGANCE, PITY. —*v.* adorn, honor, decorate; improve. See BEAUTY, TASTE, ORNAMENT, ELEGANCE.

graceful, *adj.* lithesome, lissome, svelte, sylphlike, gainly; easy, fluent; willowy, pleasing, elegant, attractive. See BEAUTY, ELEGANCE. *Ant.,* awkward.

graceless, *adj.* ungracious, tactless; inept, awkward, clumsy, ungainly; inelegant; sinful, corrupt. See UGLINESS, IRRELIGION, IMPENITENCE, INELEGANCE.

gracious, *adj.* gentle, courteous, tactful; kind, thoughtful, benign; affable, obliging; generous; charming, attractive. See BENEVOLENCE, COURTESY. *Ant.,* ungracious.

gradation, *n.* stage, DEGREE.

grade, *n.* level, quality, class; rank, standing; gradation, slope, tilt, slant. See OBLIQUITY, DEGREE.

gradual, *adj.* slow, progressive, moderate, leisurely. See DEGREE, SLOWNESS. *Ant.,* sudden.

graduate, *n.* measure, beaker, grad (*sl.*). See DEGREE. —*v.* measure, classify, grade; calibrate; pass, commence. See ARRANGEMENT, MEASUREMENT, SCHOOL.

graffiti, *n.pl.* See WRITING.

graft, *v.* inoculate, bud, transplant, implant, join, crossbreed. See MIXTURE, INSERTION. —n. corruption, porkbarrel politics. See STEALING, IMPROBITY.

grain, *n.* fruit, cereal, seed, grist, kernel; TEXTURE, temper, TENDENCY; mite, speck, bit (see LITTLENESS).

GRAMMAR
Mode of speaking and writing

Nouns—1, grammar; accidence, syntax, analysis, synopsis, praxis, punctuation, syllabi[fi]cation; agreement. See SPEECH, LANGUAGE, WRITING.

2, a. part of speech; participle; [definite *or* indefinite] article, [abstract, collective, common, compound, count, mass, *or* proper] noun, substantive, [indefinite, relative, possessive, *or* personal] pronoun, [active, passive, strong, weak, transitive, intransitive, linking, reflexive, auxiliary, *or* helping] verb, copula, [positive, comparative, *or* superlative] adjective, adverb, preposition, postposition, interjection, [coordinating] conjunction. b. conjugation, tense: present, historical present, present perfect, past, preterit, future, future perfect, imperfect, perfect, past perfect, pluperfect, progressive, aorist; principal parts, infinitive, past tense, past participle; gerund, [past, perfect, *or* present] participle, modal auxiliary. c. mood, mode: infinitive, indicative, subjunctive, imperative, optative; [middle, active, *or* passive] voice, aspect, inceptive, inchoative. d. [simple, complex, compound-complex, compound, declarative, exclamatory, *or* periodic] sentence, paragraph, [dependent, independent, nonrestrictive, relative restrictive, *or* subordinate] clause, phrase; subject, [direct *or* indirect] object, verb; diagram, parse *or* syntax tree. e. declension, case; ablative, accusative, dative, nominative, locative, vocative, objective; [first, second, *or* third] person; number, singular, plural; gender, masculine, feminine, neuter. f. antecedent, apodosis, apposition, causative, clause, complement, connective, construction, contraction, copula, correlative, [dangling] participle, demonstrative, determiner, dvandva, exophora, expletive, hypotaxis, inflection, intensifier, intensive, interrogative, inversion, marker, particle; prefix, suffix, combining form, element; inflection, inflexion, paradigm, postposition, predicate nominative, prepositional phrase.

3, style; philology, language; phraseology, wording, rhetoric, diction. See SPEECH; WRITING, FIGURATIVE.

4, grammarian, semanticist, linguist. See LANGUAGE.

Verbs—parse, analyze, diagram; punctuate; conjugate, decline, inflect.

Adjectives—grammatical; conditional, copulative, emphatic, epicene, factitive, heteroclite, impersonal, periphrastic, suppletive, volitive; regular, irregular.

Antonyms, see ERROR.

---

grand, *adj.* large, impressive, magnificent, stately, majestic; pretentious, ostentatious; elegant, lofty. See GREATNESS, OSTENTATION, REPUTE.

grandeur, *n.* GREATNESS, magnificence; show, ostentation; splendor, majesty; eminence, stateliness, loftiness. See IMPORTANCE. *Ant.,* smallness.

grandfather, *n.* grandpa, grandsire; gaffer, old man. See ANCESTRY, AGE.

grandiose, *adj.* grand; stately, pompous, bombastic. See BOASTING, OSTENTATION.

grandmother, *n.* granny, grandma, nana, nanny; old woman. See ANCESTRY, AGE.

grand prix, *Fr.,* first prize. See APPROBATION, SUPERIORITY.

grandstand, *n.* bleachers. See VISION. —*v.i.* show off, hot dog (*inf.*). See BOASTING.

grant, *n.* gift, allotment, contribution. —*v.* bestow, give, yield; concede; permit; contribute. See GIVING, PERMISSION, CONSENT, RIGHTNESS, TRANSFER.

granular, *adj.* granulated, grainy, mealy, gritty, sandy. See POWDERINESS.

grapevine, *n., informal,* rumor, rumor mill, pipeline, a little bird. See INFORMATION.

graph, *n.* diagram, chart, plot, PLAN; bar, circle, *etc.* graph.

graphic, *adj.* pictorial, descriptive; vivid, diagrammatic; delineative; picturesque. See REPRESENTATION, DESCRIPTION.

graphic arts, drawing, PAINTING, ENGRAVING, etching, lithography.

grapple, *v.* seize, grasp, clutch, struggle, contend. See OPPOSITION, CONTENTION.

grasp, *v.* hold, clasp, seize; comprehend, understand. See ACQUISITION, INTELLIGENCE, AUTHORITY, RETENTION.

grass, *n.* lawn, greenery, turf, sod, verdure; marijuana. See VEGETABLE, DRUGS.

grassland, *n.* pasture, prairie, meadowland, plain. See LAND.

grassroots, *adj., informal,* people's, of the people, mass. See GENERALITY.

grate, *v.* scrape, grind, rasp, abrade, scratch, rasp. See FRICTION. —*n.* grating (see CROSSING).

grateful, *adj.* appreciative, thankful; welcome, agreeable, refreshing, soothing. See GRATITUDE, PLEASURE. *Ant.,* ungrateful.

gratification, *n.* satisfaction, fulfillment; entertainment, diversion, feast; ease, comfort; indulgence, consummation. See PLEASURE, CONTENT.

grating, *n.* lattice, openwork, grillwork, grid. See CROSSING.

gratis, *adj.* free [of charge], for nothing, complimentary. See NONPAYMENT.

GRATITUDE
Thankfulness

Nouns—gratitude, gratefulness, thankfulness; indebtedness; acknowledgment, recognition, thanksgiving; thanks, praise; paean, Te Deum, WORSHIP, grace; thank-offering; requital.

Verbs—be grateful, thank; give, render, return, offer, *or* tender thanks; acknowledge, requite; thank *or* bless one's [lucky] stars.

Adjectives—grateful, thankful, appreciative, obliged, beholden, indebted to, under obligation.

Interjections—thanks! much obliged! thank you! thank heaven! Heaven be praised! thanks a million! gracias! merci!

Phrases—never look a gift horse in the mouth.

Quotations—A joyful and pleasant thing it is to be thankful (*Bible*), In most of mankind gratitude is merely a secret hope for greater favors (*La Rochefoucauld*), Never in the field of human conflict was so much owed by so many to so few (*Winston Churchill*), A single grateful thought raised to heaven is the most perfect prayer (*Gotthold Ephraim Lessing*).

Antonyms, see INGRATITUDE.

---

gratuitous, *adj.* baseless, uncalled for, unwarranted; free, gratis. See NONPAYMENT, SUPPOSITION.

gratuity, *n.* tip, largesse; present, gift; fee. See LIBERALITY, GIVING, CHEAPNESS.

grave, *n.* sepulcher, tomb, mausoleum; DEATH. See INTERMENT. —*adj.* important, weighty, serious; sedate, dignified; momentous, solemn; dull, somber. See DEJECTION, IMPORTANCE, INEXCITABILITY.

gravel, *n.* stones, pebbles, calculi; rubble, scree; alluvium, detritus, attritus, ballast, shingle, beach. See LAND.

graveyard, *n.* cemetery, burial ground *or* mound. See INTERMENT.

gravity, *n.* weight (see GRAVITY); graveness, IMPORTANCE. *Ant.,* lightness, unimportance.

GRAVITY
Weight

Nouns—1, gravity, gravitation; weight, weighing; heft, heaviness; ponderosity, pressure, burden; ballast, counterpoise; load, lading, freight; lead, millstone. See SIZE, ATTRACTION.

2, (*systems of weight*) avoirdupois, troy, *or* apothecaries' weight; grain, scruple, dram, ounce, pound, load, stone, hundredweight, cental, peck, [short *or* long] ton, carat, pennyweight; gram, picogram, nanogram, microgram, centigram, decigram, dekagram, hectogram, kilogram, quintal, metric ton; assay ton, carat, keel, kip, megaton, troy ounce; arroba, catty, denarius, drachma, kantar, liang, livre, mark, maund, mina, mite, momme, obolus, oka, pound, picul, pocket, pood, rotl, rundlet, ser, shekel, stone, talent, tael, tod, tola, tower pound; tare and tret.

3, *(weighing devices)* balance, scale[s], steelyard, beam, weighbridge, weigh station, spring balance, platform scale.

Verbs—be heavy; gravitate, weigh, press, cumber, load; weigh in at, tip the scales at; weight, weigh down; outweigh, overbalance; gain *or* put on weight.

Adjectives—1, gravitational.

2, weighty, weighted; weighing; heavy, ponderous, ponderable; loaded, sagging; lumpish, lumpy; cumbersome, burdensome; cumbrous, unwieldy, massive, hefty.

Quotations—The fatal law of gravity: when you are down everything falls on you (*Sylvia Warner*), A light wife doth make a heavy husband (*Shakespeare*).

Antonyms, see LEVITY.

---

gravy, *n.* sauce, dressing; *slang,* profit, graft. See FOOD, INCREASE.

gray, *adj.* dun, mousy, slaty, *etc.*; clouded, overcast, drab, dingy, dull, depressing; bleak; aged, old, venerable. See COLOR, CLOUDINESS, DEJECTION, AGE. —gray matter, *informal,* intelligence, brains. See INTELLECT.

graze, *v.* TOUCH, brush; scratch, abrade, rub; pasture, browse, feed, crop. See FOOD, FRICTION.

grease, *n.* OIL, fat; graphite; suet, lard, tallow. —*v.* lubricate; anoint; *slang,* FLATTERY, bribe. See SMOOTHNESS, PAYMENT.

GREATNESS
Magnitude

Nouns—1, greatness, magnitude; dimensions; number; immensity, enormity; might, STRENGTH; intensity, fullness. See SIZE, MULTITUDE, POWER, QUANTITY.

2, eminence, prominence, grandeur, distinction, IMPORTANCE; fame, REPUTE, notability.

Verbs—run high, soar, tower, transcend; rise to a great height; know no bounds; enlarge, INCREASE; expand.

Adjectives—1, great, grand, large, epic, considerable, fair, above par; ample, abundant; full, intense, strong; passing (*archaic*), heavy, plenary, deep, high, *etc.*; signal, at its height, in the zenith; marvelous (see WONDER).

2, goodly, noble, mighty, arch; profound, intense, consummate, utter; extraordinary, remarkable, noteworthy, spanking.

3, vast, immense, enormous, measureless, extreme. *Informal,* whopping, terrific.

Adverbs—greatly, much, in a great measure, to the nth degree, richly, to a large *or* great extent, on a large scale; mightily, powerfully, intensely; remarkably, notably, exceptionally, marvelously. *Informal,* terribly, awfully; no end, plenty, mighty, as you please; by far, far and away, by a long shot.

Quotations—What millions died—that Caesar might be great! (*Thomas Campbell*), A great man is always willing to be little (*Emerson*), A great man is he who does not lose his child's heart (*Mencius*), Be not afraid of greatness: some men are born great, some achieve greatness, and some have greatness thrust upon them (*Shakespeare*).

Antonyms, see LITTLENESS, UNIMPORTANCE.

---

greed, *n.* greediness, DESIRE, cupidity, avidity, avarice. See GLUTTONY, PARSIMONY.

green, *adj.* immature; inexperienced; new, recent; pale, wan. See COLOR, NEWNESS, YOUTH, CREDULITY.

greenery, *n.* vegetation, foliage; greenhouse, nursery. See AGRICULTURE.

greenhorn, *n.* neophyte, beginner; dupe, gull; *slang,* immigrant, newcomer. See BEGINNING, CREDULITY, INGRESS.

greenhouse, *n.* hothouse, solarium, herbarium, conservatory, nursery. See AGRICULTURE.

greet, *v.* address, hail, salute; welcome, receive, entertain, admit. See COURTESY.

gregarious, *adj.* sociable (see SOCIALITY).

gremlin, *n.* goblin, gnome. See MYTHICAL DEITIES, DEMON.

grenade, *n.* bomb, pineapple (*sl.*), egg (*sl.*). See ARMS.

grid, *n.* gridiron, grate, network. See CROSSING.

gridlock, *n.* stoppage, blockage, bottleneck, congestion. See HINDRANCE.

grief, *n.* distress, bereavement, sorrow, dolor; affliction, disaster, trouble, tribulation. See PAIN, DEJECTION, FAILURE. *Ant.*, happiness.

grievance, *n.* complaint, annoyance; injustice, WRONG; tribulation, injury, gripe (*sl.*). See EVIL.

grieve, *v.* distress, PAIN, hurt, sadden, injure; mourn, sorrow, deplore. See LAMENTATION. *Ant.*, rejoice.

grievous, *adj.* intense, sad; severe, flagrant, appalling, atrocious. See PAIN, BADNESS.

grill, *n.* gridiron, CROSSING; bar, tavern. —*v.* broil, roast, toast, sear, panfry, barbecue; question, rake over the coals. See INQUIRY, FOOD, HEAT.

grille, *n.* grating, grid, web, net[work]. See CROSSING.

grim, *adj.* fearful, stern, fierce, forbidding; inflexible; ruthless; grisly, horrible. See RESOLUTION, UGLINESS.

grimace, *n.* face, scowl, leer, expression, moue. See DISTORTION, DEJECTION.

grimy, *adj.* soiled, dirty, foul, filthy. See UNCLEANNESS. *Ant.*, clean.

grin, *n.* smile, smirk. —*v.* bare the teeth; smile; smirk; grin from ear to ear. See REJOICING. *Ant.*, frown.

grind, *v.* pulverize, crush; sharpen, whet, file, polish; masticate, chew, crunch; rasp, grate; oppress, harass. See FRICTION, POWDERINESS.

grip, *n.* handle; handclasp; hold, control; *informal*, suitcase, bag, satchel. —*v.* seize, grasp, clutch, hold. See ACQUISITION, RECEPTACLE, RETENTION.

gripe, *v., informal*, complain, grumble, mutter. See DISCONTENT.

gripping, *adj.* fascinating, engrossing, enthralling. See ATTENTION. *Ant.*, boring.

grisly, *adj.* gruesome, frightful, grim. See UGLINESS.

grit, *n.* sand, roughage, gravel; COURAGE, pluck, stamina, endurance. See RESOLUTION, POWDERINESS.

grizzled, *adj.* grizzly, graying, grayish, white. See COLORLESSNESS.

groan, *n.* LAMENTATION, moan. —*v.i.* grumble, lament, moan.

grocery, *n.* grocery store, green-grocer[y], purveyor's; [super]market; (*pl.*) provisions, victuals, FOOD, supplies. See STORE, PROVISION.

grog, *n.* [hot] buttered rum; hot toddy; potion. See DRINKING.

groggy, *adj.* dizzy, stupefied, sleepy, half-asleep, punchy (*inf.*), out of it (*inf.*). See INATTENTION.

groom, *n.* bridegroom, benedict. See MARRIAGE, SERVANT. —*v.* dress, tend, polish, curry; coach, train. See DOMESTICATION, CLEANNESS.

groove, *n.* HABIT, routine, rut; FURROW; trench, channel, indentation.

groovy, *adj., informal,* wonderful, trendy, hip. See GOODNESS.

grope, *v.i.* feel, essay, fumble; attempt; hunt, search. See FEELING, TOUCH.

gross, *adj.* bulky, large, fat, obese; coarse, crass; brutish, callous, unrefined, insensitive; vulgar, crude, obscene; total, whole; flagrant. See VULGARITY, SIZE, IMPURITY, INELEGANCE.

grotesque, *adj.* strange, unnatural, abnormal; bizarre, fantastic, odd; misshapen, distorted. See UNCONFORMITY, DISTORTION, INELEGANCE, UGLINESS. *Ant.*, common, normal.

grotto, *n.* cave, cavern; bower; crypt, vault; spelunk. See CONCAVITY, RECEPTACLE.

grouchy, *adj., informal,* cross, sharp, sulky, testy, grumpy, gruff, sullen, ill-tempered, sour, out of sorts. See IRASCIBILITY, DISCONTENT. *Ant.*, good-humored.

ground, *n.* earth, terra firma, soil; foundation, basis; CAUSE, reason; viewpoint. See COVERING. —*v.* base, establish; settle, fix; instruct. —*adj.* pulverized, grated; whittled, sharpened, abraded. See LAND, SUPPORT, POWDERINESS, REGION.

groundless, *adj.* unsubstantiated, baseless, unfounded. See INSUBSTANTIALITY.

grounds, *n.pl.* dregs, lees; property, land, estate, yard; motive, reason, CAUSE. See UNCLEANNESS, REMAINDER, EVIDENCE, POSSESSION.

groundwork, *n.* foundation, framework; inception, beginning; basis. See SUPPORT, CAUSE, PREPARATION.

group, *n.* ASSEMBLAGE, company, association; clique, set; collection, cluster, company. —*v.* collect, gather, classify, sort, combine, cluster. See ARRANGEMENT.

groupie, *n., informal,* fan, rooter, demon (see ACTIVITY).

grove, *n.* thicket, coppice, copse. See VEGETABLE.

grovel, *v.* fawn, creep, cringe; wallow, humble (oneself). See SERVILITY, LOWNESS.

grow, *v.* mature, become, develop; increase, extend, expand, enlarge; nurture, raise, cultivate; germinate, breed, sprout; flourish, thrive. See AGRICULTURE, INCREASE, PROSPERITY, CHANGE. —**grow up,** mature, AGE; arise. See BEGINNING.

growl, *v.* mutter, grumble, snarl; complain, howl. See LAMENTATION, THREAT.

growth, *n.* development, evolution, INCREASE; adulthood, maturity; harvest, crop, produce, yield; flora, VEGETABLE; tumor, cancer, node, polyp, mole, tubercule, cyst, excrescence, swelling, protuberance, wen. See DISEASE, CONVEXITY, EXPANSION.

grubby, *adj., informal,* dingy, dirty, shabby, scurvy; ignoble, base, mean. See UNCLEANNESS. *Ant.,* clean.

grudge, *v.* stint, dole; begrudge, withhold. See PARSIMONY, UNWILLINGNESS.

gruel, *n.* porridge, oatmeal, cereal, grout. See FOOD.

grueling, *adj.* arduous, exhausting, strenuous. See EXERTION, SEVERITY. *Ant.,* easy.

gruesome, *adj.* ghastly, fearful, grisly, hideous. See UGLINESS.

gruff, *adj.* bluff, surly, rough, harsh, coarse. See DISCOURTESY.

grumble, *v.* rumble, growl, complain, mutter. See DISCONTENT.

grumpy, *adj.* surly, glum. See IRASCIBILITY.

grungy, *adj.* dirty, grubby, offensive (see UNCLEANNESS).

grunt, *v.* snort, rasp, oink; complain, lament. See LAMENTATION, CRY.

guarantee, *v.* vouch, undertake, warrant; pledge; PROMISE, insure, secure. See SECURITY, CERTAINTY.

guard, *n.* safeguard, shield, baffle; cover, protection; pad, hood; catch; protector, sentinel, watchman, sentry; escort, patrol, convoy; warder, warden; night watchman, keeper, guardian. —*v.t.* protect, defend, shield, watch, patrol. See DEFENSE, SAFETY, COMBATANT.

guardian, *n.* trustee, caretaker, warden. See SAFETY.

guerrilla, *n.* irregular, partisan, rebel; franc-tireur, sniper, terrorist, bush fighter. See WARFARE, COMBATANT.

guess, *n.* surmise, guesswork, SUPPOSITION, assumption, conjecture, theory, guesstimate (*inf.*). —*v.* suppose, divine, predict, surmise, conjecture. See INTUITION.

guest, *n.* visitor, company, caller. See SOCIALITY.

guidance, *n.* direction, management. See TEACHING, ADVICE.

guide, *n.* tracker, leader, instructor, pilot; map, instructions; guidebook, chart, manual; cicerone, dragoman, escort. —*v.* lead, direct, regulate; train. See DIRECTION, INFORMATION, TEACHING, ADVICE, RULE.

guidebook, *n.* guide, manual; Baedeker, Michelin, atlas, vade mecum; gazetteer, directory; instructions, operating manual. See INFORMATION, DIRECTION.

guideline, *n.* principle, ground rule, protocol. See CONFORMITY.

guidepost, *n.* milepost, pointer, blaze. See DIRECTION.

guild, *n.* union, association, club, society. See PARTY.

guile, *n.* DECEPTION, deceitfulness; trickery, CUNNING, craftiness.

guileless, *adj.* artless, innocent, naive, unsuspecting, ingenuous, honest. See INNOCENCE. *Ant.,* worldly-wise.

GUILT
Fact or sense of commission of wrong

Nouns—1, guilt, guiltiness, culpability, chargeability, criminality, IMPROBITY, sinfulness (see BADNESS). See ACCUSATION.

2, *(act of doing wrong)* misconduct, misbehavior, misdoing, malpractice, transgression, dereliction, delinquency; misfeasance, misprision; malefaction, malfeasance.

3, *(wrongful deed)* fault, misdeed, sin, ERROR, lapse, flaw, blot, omission; failing; offense, trespass; misdemeanor, crime, felony; enormity, atrocity, outrage; deadly *or* mortal sin. See ILLEGALITY.

4, *(guilty person)* guilty one (see EVILDOER).

Verbs—be guilty, have on one's head; plead guilty. *Slang,* cop a plea.

Adjectives—guilty, to blame, culpable, sinful, criminal; red-handed, derelict, at fault, censurable, reprehensible, blameworthy, exceptionable (see DISAPPROBATION).

Adverbs—guiltily; in flagrante delicto; in the act.

Phrases—the guilty one always runs.

Quotations—He that first cries out stop thief, is often he that has stolen the treasure (*William Congreve*), Good women always think it is their fault when someone else is being offensive. Bad women never take the blame for anything (*Anita Brookner*), He that is without sin among you, let him first cast a stone at her (*Bible*), The wicked flee when no man pursueth (*Bible*), What hangs people . . . is the unfortunate circumstance of guilt (*R. L. Stevenson*).

Antonyms, see INNOCENCE.

---

guiltless, *adj.* inculpable, innocent, blameless, faultless. See INNOCENCE. *Ant.,* guilty.

guinea pig, subject (see LIABILITY).

guise, *n.* APPEARANCE, aspect, pretense, semblance; costume, mien; cloak, cover. See METHOD.

gulch, *n.* gully, ravine, canyon, arroyo, gorge; riverbed. See INTERVAL.

gulf, *n.* arm (of the sea), bay; chasm, abyss; rift, gap, separation, void, crevasse, pit, deep. See INTERVAL, WATER.

gull, *n.* dupe, pigeon. —*v.t.* cheat, trick. See DECEPTION, CREDULITY.

gullible, *adj.* See CREDULITY.

gully, *n.* arroyo, gulch, trench, ditch, wadi, gorge, ravine. See INTERVAL, CONCAVITY.

gulp, *v.* swallow; choke. See FOOD, CREDULITY, WIND.

gummy, *adj.* sticky, tacky, gluey. See COHERENCE.

gumption, *n., informal,* initiative, self-reliance; common sense. See CUNNING, RESOLUTION.

gun, *n.* firearm (see ARMS).

gunfire, *n.* gunplay, shooting, burst, volley, salvo. See ATTACK.

gung ho, *adj., informal,* enthusiastic (see EXCITEMENT).

gunk, *n.* muck, mire, slime, sludge. See UNCLEANNESS.

gunman, *n., slang,* trigger man, torpedo. See EVILDOER.

gunner, *n.* carabineer, cannoneer, artilleryman; hunter; marksman. See COMBATANT.

gurgle, *v.i.* bubble, babble. See SOUND.

guru, *n.* pundit, mentor; mahatma, yogi, *etc.* See TEACHING.

gush, *v.* pour, flow, jet, spurt; effuse, issue, emit, spout. See EGRESS, WATER.

gushy, *adj., informal,* sentimental, maudlin, mushy. See FEELING. *Ant.,* restrained.

gust, *n.* puff, burst, flurry, blow, breeze, blast. See WIND.

gusto, *n.* PLEASURE, enthusiasm, enjoyment, relish, zest, delight. See FEELING.

gut, *v.* eviscerate, disembowel; burn out, lay waste, demolish. See DESTRUCTION.

guts, *n.pl.* bowels, entrails, innards, viscera; substance, gist, essence; *slang,* determination, endurance, intestinal fortitude, COURAGE. See INTERIOR.

gutsy, *adj., informal,* brave, nervy, plucky (see COURAGE). *Ant.,* cowardly.

gutter, *n.* curb, ditch, spillway, trough. See FURROW.

guttural, *adj.* throaty, rasping, husky, hoarse. See ROUGHNESS.

guy, *n.* shroud, rigging (see SUPPORT); *informal,* chap, fellow (see MALE).

guzzle, *n.* swig (see DRINKING).

gymnasium, *n.* gym, gameroom; ARENA.

gymnastics, *n.pl.* athletics, acrobatics, exercises, calisthenics. See CONTENTION, EXERTION.

gyp, *n.,* *slang,* cheat, swindle. See DECEPTION, STEALING.

gypsy, *n.* nomad, vagrant, idler; flirt, coquette. See TRAVEL.

gyrate, *v.* turn, whirl, twirl, spin, revolve, rotate. See ROTATION.

H

habilitate, *v.t.* clothe, dress; PROVISION. See CLOTHING.

habit, *n.* tendency (see HABIT); costume, uniform (see CLOTHING).

HABIT
Usual mode of action

Nouns—1, habit, habitude, wont, way; prescription, custom, USE, usage; practice; matter of course, prevalence, observance; conventionalism, conventionality; mode, vogue (see FASHION); CONFORMITY; RULE, standing order, precedent, routine, lifestyle; rut, groove, beaten path; banality, familiarity; bad habit, addiction; quirk, trick (see UNCONFORMITY); Procrustean bed; seasoning, hardening, inurement; second nature, acclimatization. *Informal,* same old same old, shtick. See REGULARITY, GENERALITY, FREQUENCY, ORDER, PRECEDENCE.

2, habitué, addict, user, slave (to), frequenter, alcoholic, drunkard (see DRINKING). *Informal,* dope fiend; chocoholic. *Slang,* [hop]head, junkie, freak, mainliner, acidhead. See DRUGS.

Verbs—1, be wont, fall into a custom, conform to (see CONFORMITY); follow the beaten path; get used to, make a practice *or* habit of, get the feel of, take to, get the knack of, learn.

2, be habitual, prevail; come into use, take root; become second nature.

3, habituate, inure, harden, season, caseharden; accustom, familiarize; naturalize, acclimatize; keep one's hand in; train, educate, domesticate; grow on, cling to, adhere to; repeat (see REPETITION); enslave. *Slang,* hook.

Adjectives—1, habitual, customary; accustomed; of everyday occurrence; wonted, usual, general, ordinary, common, frequent, everyday; well-trodden, well-known; familiar, hackneyed, trite, commonplace, conventional, regular, set, stock, established, routine, stereotyped; prevailing, prevalent; current; fashionable (see FASHION); deep-rooted, inveterate, chronic, besetting; ingrained.

2, wont; used to, given to, addicted to, habituated to; in the habit of; seasoned, imbued with; devoted to, wedded to.

Adverbs—habitually; always (see CONFORMITY); as usual, as is one's wont, as a rule, for the most part; all in a day's work; generally, of course, most often, frequently.

Phrases—old habits die hard; you can't teach an old dog new tricks; there is nothing new under the sun; better the devil you know than the devil you don't know.

Quotations—Habit is a great deadener (*Samuel Beckett*), The tradition of all the dead generations weighs like a nightmare on the brain of the living (*Karl Marx*), Custom reconciles us to everything (*Burke*), Familiarity breeds contempt—and children (*Mark Twain*), Customs represent the experiences of mankind (*Henry Ward Beecher*), I don't have any bad habits. They might be bad habits for other people, but they're all right for me (*Eubie Blake*).

Antonyms, see DISUSE, IRREGULARITY.

---

habitat, *n.* habitation; ENVIRONMENT, native heath; quarters. See ABODE.

hack, *v.* chop, hew, slash, cut. —*n.* cough, stutter; hackney, cab. See DISJUNCTION, VEHICLE. —**hack around,** *slang,* loaf, idle; fool around. See INACTIVITY,

AMUSEMENT. —**hack it,** get by, perform, pass muster. See SUCCESS.

hackneyed, *adj.* trite, stale, used, banal, commonplace. See HABIT. *Ant.,* new; profound.

haft, *n.* handle. See SUPPORT.

hag, *n.* harridan, termagant, shrew, witch, crone. See EVILDOER.

haggard, *adj.* drawn, gaunt; cadaverous, skeletal. See UGLINESS, NARROWNESS.

haggle, *v.i.* cavil; bargain, chaffer, dicker. See BARTER.

hail, *n.* greeting, welcome; hailstones. See COLD. —*v.* salute, greet, call, summon; accost, address. See COURTESY, INDICATION.

hair, *n.* mane (see HAIR); FILAMENT; bit, inch (see NARROWNESS, NEARNESS).

HAIR
Body-covering filament

Nouns—1, hair; head of hair, thatch, mop, mane, crop of hair, thatch, shock; gray, silver *or* white hair (see OLDNESS); cowlick, forelock; tresses, locks, ringlet; eyelashes, eyebrows; body hair, underarm hair, chest hair.

2, beard, chin whiskers, facial hair, five o'clock shadow, stubble, three days' growth; down, peach fuzz; full beard, Fu Manchu, imperial beard, dundrearies, Vandyke, Abe Lincoiln, whiskers, sideburns, sidelocks, side whiskers, tuft, burnsides, muttonchops, goatee, stubble; mustache, handlebar mustache, walrus mustache. *Slang,* weepers.

3, wig, wiglet, toupee, peruke, hairpiece, postiche, ramillie, bagwig; fall, switch. *Slang,* rug, lace curtains, artificial turf.

4, **a.** hairstyle, coiffure, hairdo, haircut, permanent wave, set, styling; Afro, artichoke, back combed, bangs, beehive, [coquette *or* windblown] bob, bouffant, [fishtail *or* French] braid, brush cut, bun, butch, buzz cut, chignon, coil, conk, cornrows, crew cut, crimp, curls, DA, dreadlocks, ducktail, feathercut, finger wave, flattop, fluff, French knot *or* twist, fringe, frisette, frizz, fuzz cut, knot, layered cut, lovelock, marcel, mohawk, moptop, natural, pageboy, peyes, pigtail, pixie, pompadour, ponytail, pouf, Prince Valiant, process, psyche knot, queue, quiff, razor cut, roach, shingle, spikes, spit curl, swirl, tail, tonsure, topknot, updo, upsweep, widow's peak. *Informal,* perm. *Slang,* grass, naps, moss, cornrolls, conk, B-52, do, duck's ass, burr cut, fade; jarhead, skinhead. **b.** hair color, coloring; [natural, strawberry, platinum, peroxide *or* bleached] blond[e], brunet[te], tortoiseshell, redhead, towhead; blaze, frosting, streaking, tint.

5, pubic hair. *Slang,* bush, Downshire, fluff, plush, scut.

6, hirsuteness, hairiness, shagginess, furriness, fleeciness, wooliness.

7, *(animals)* fur, pelt, fleece, coat, mane, camel's hair, horsehair; feeler, antenna; plumage, feathers (see BIRD).

8, *(plants)* awn, arista, brush, pile.

9, barber, [hair]stylist, hairdresser, friseur; curler, curling iron, hair dryer, diffuser, hair net, hair spray; hair remover, depilatory.

Verbs—cut, style, perm, coif[fure], wave, wash, pleach, tease, braid, cornrow, comb, brush; tint, tone, color, bleach.

Adjectives—1, hairy, hirsute, shaggy, furry, bushy, tufty, fleecy, woolly; bristly (see ROUGHNESS); crinose, pubescent, ciliate, hispid; clean-cut, close-cropped, ratted, shorn, teased, tousled; bearded, bewhiskered; unshaven, stubbly; goateed; wigged, toupeed. *Slang,* mossy, kinky, nappy.

2, feathery, downy; tufted, pinnate, feathered, plumed, crested.

Quotations—The loose train of thy amber-dropping hair (*John Milton*), Oh they're taking him to prison for the color of his hair (*A. E. Housman*), Never trust a man who combs his hair straight from the left armpit (*Alice Roosevelt Longworth*).

haircut, *n.* barbering, trim, hairdo; crew cut, butch, flattop, fuzz-cut, razor cut. See BEAUTY, HAIR.

hairdo, *n.* coiffure, hairstyle; set, cut, shape; permanent [wave]; bob, pigtail, ponytail, bangs, braids, ringlets; pageboy, chignon, gamin cut, *etc.* See BEAUTY, HAIR.

hairdresser, *n.* coiffeur, coiffeuse, hairstylist; barber, tonsor; wigmaker, *perruquier, perruquière.* See BEAUTY, HAIR.

hairless, *adj.* beardless; bald, bare; clean-shaven, smooth-faced. See DIVESTMENT. *Ant.,* hairy, hirsute.

hairpiece, *n.* toupee, wig (see COVERING).

hair-raising, *adj.* frightening, terrifying. See FEAR.

hair-splitting, *n.* quibbling, nitpicking. See DISSENT.

hairy, *adj.* hirsute; furry; *slang,* dangerous. See ROUGHNESS, DANGER, HAIR. *Ant.,* smooth.

halcyon, *adj.* calm, tranquil, peaceful, quiet, pleasant. See PLEASURE. *Ant.,* stormy.

hale, *adj.* healthy, robust, hearty, vigorous, sound. See HEALTH. —*v.t.* haul, pull. See TRACTION.

half, *n.* hemisphere; bisection; moiety. See NUMERATION. *Ant.,* WHOLE.

half-baked, *adj.* incomplete; immature. See INCOMPLETENESS, EARLINESS.

half-breed, *n.* mestizo, métis[se], mulatto; half-blood, half-caste; mule; hybrid, mongrel. See MIXTURE.

halfhearted, *adj.* indifferent, apathetic, listless, unenthusiastic; insincere; timid. See INDIFFERENCE. *Ant.,* enthusiastic.

half-truth, *n.* white lie, equivocation (see FALSEHOOD).

halfway, *adj.* midway, equidistant, MIDDLE. —*adv.* half, part[ly], BETWEEN, en route; so-so, more or less (*inf.*). See INCOMPLETENESS.

halfway house, *n.* hostel, rehabilitation center, way station. See REMEDY.

half-witted, *adj.* unintelligent, foolish, feeble-minded, moronic; mentally retarded. See IGNORANCE.

hall, *n.* PASSAGE, corridor; auditorium, building; college; dormitory; edifice. See ABODE.

hallelujah! *interj.* praise the Lord! alleluia! hosanna! See RELIGION, REJOICING.

hallmark, *n.* imprint, badge, mark, cachet, stamp; guarantee, authority; characteristic, feature, attribute, trait, SPECIALITY. See INDICATION.

hallow, *v.* bless, sanctify, consecrate, enshrine. See PIETY, CELEBRATION. *Ant.,* desecrate.

hallucination, *n.* phantasm, phantom, mirage; fancy, delusion, chimera, illusion; deception. See ERROR, IMAGINATION.

hallucinogen, *n.* psychedelic [drug], mind-altering drug (see DRUGS).

hallway, *n.* vestibule, lobby, foyer, gallery; PASSAGE, corridor.

halo, *n.* corona, aura, nimbus, glory, aureole. See LIGHT, CIRCULARITY.

halt, *v.* stop, check, arrest, pause, cease. —*n.* stop, interruption, immobility. See END. —*adj., archaic,* crippled, disabled. See IMPOTENCE, DISEASE, STAMMERING. *Ant.,* continue, proceed.

halter, *n.* harness, bridle, tether, hackamore; noose; shoulder strap, waist, brassiere. See CLOTHING, RESTRAINT.

halve, *v.t.* bisect, cleave, cut in two (see DISJUNCTION.

ham, *n., slang,* hambone, ham actor, show-off, grandstand player. —*v., slang,* ham it up, overact, emote, chew the scenery, pull out all the stops. See DRAMA.

hamburger, *n.* chopped *or* ground meat, forcemeat, meatball, meat patty; meat loaf, Salisbury steak, steak tartare; beef *or* cheeseburger. See FOOD.

hamlet, *n.* village, town. See ABODE.

hammer, *v.* strike, beat, drum, pound, ram. —*n.* mallet, gavel, sledge. See IMPULSE, REPETITION, INSTRUMENTALITY.

hamper, *v.* encumber, hinder, impede, trammel, obstruct, fetter, restrict. See HINDRANCE.

hand, *n.* fist, extremity; helper, workman, employee, laborer; handwriting; *informal,* applause, greeting. See WRITING, APPROBATION. —*v.* pass, deliver, convey, give, transmit. See GIVING, SIDE, AGENCY, TOUCH.

handbag, *n.* pocketbook, purse; valise, grip. See RECEPTACLE.

handbill, *n.* notice, announcement, flyer. See PUBLICATION.

handbook, *n.* guide[book], instructions, manual. See INFORMATION, PUBLICATION.

handcuff, *n.* manacle[s], bracelet[s]. —*v.* shackle, fetter. See RESTRAINT.

handful, *n.* fistful, grip; QUANTITY, few, some; *informal,* trouble, problem, nuisance, DIFFICULTY, pain in the neck (*sl.*).

handicap, *v.* penalize, encumber, inconvenience, burden, hamper; disable. See HINDRANCE, EQUALITY, DISTORTION, DISEASE.

handicraft, *n.* craftwork, handiwork; woodcraft, stonecraft, *etc.*; SKILL, workmanship, dexterity, artisanship, artistry, craftsmanship. See BUSINESS.

handily, *adv.* skillfully, neatly, easily, with dispatch. See FACILITY, SKILL. *Ant.,* with DIFFICULTY.

handkerchief, *n.* nose cloth, sudarium; neckerchief; bandanna, foulard; scarf, headcloth, headkerchief. See CLOTHING.

handle, *n.* shaft, hilt, grip, knob; *slang,* name (see NOMENCLATURE). —*v.* manipulate, USE, wield; direct, control, manage; feel, paw, TOUCH; operate, direct, CONDUCT; deal in, trade. See DIRECTION, SALE, CONDUCT.

handler, *n.* trainer, coach; masseur; dealer, jobber, agent. See DOMESTICATION, AGENT.

handmade, *adj.* handcrafted, -wrought, -carved, *etc.*; individualized; crude, makeshift. See PRODUCTION. *Ant.,* machine-made, production line.

hand-me-down, *adj.* secondhand, castoff, discarded. See OLDNESS. *Ant.,* [brand] new.

handout, *n., slang,* alms, offering, charity; handbill. See GIVING, PUBLICATION.

handsome, *adj.* attractive, comely, good-looking, personable; fine; generous, ample; striking. See BEAUTY, LIBERALITY. *Ant.,* ugly.

handwriting, *n.* calligraphy, penmanship. See WRITING.

handy, *adj.* convenient, near, available, ready; adept, dexterous, apt; competent, capable, expert. See SKILL, UTILITY.

handyman, *n.* jack-of-all-trades, odd-job man, factotum, janitor. See SKILL.

hang, *v.* suspend, dangle, sag; attach; depend, be contingent (on); string up, lynch. See PENDENCY, CONNECTION, KILLING, RELATION. —*n., informal,* knack, art, SKILL.

hangar, *n.* shed, housing (see RECEPTACLE).

hanger-on, *n.* dependent, parasite. See SERVILITY, FLATTERY.

hangman, *n.* executioner. See PUNISHMENT.

hangout, *n.* resort, haunt, rendezvous, stamping ground, clubhouse; *slang,* saloon, dive, den. See ABODE.

hangover, *n., informal,* crapulence, nausea, katzenjammer, *gueule de bois;* holdover, atavism, survival, vestige, relic, remnant. See DRINKING, REMAINDER.

hang-up, *n., slang,* thing, obsession, preoccupation; phobia. See FEAR.

hanker, *v.* DESIRE, covet, crave, long for, yearn for.

haphazard, *adj.* CHANCE, casual, aimless, random; hit-or-miss. *Ant.,* planned, orderly.

hapless, *adj.* unlucky, unfortunate. See ADVERSITY.

happen, *v.* befall, eventuate, occur. See CHANCE, OCCURRENCE.

happening, *n.* event, incident, OCCURRENCE.

happy, *adj.* fortunate, lucky; gay, contented, joyous, ecstatic; felicitous, apt; glad. See AGREEMENT, CHEERFULNESS, PLEASURE, OCCASION. *Ant.,* sad.

happy-go-lucky, *adj.* unworried, irresponsible. See INDIFFERENCE.

harangue, *n.* SPEECH; tirade, scolding, diatribe; address, declamation.

harass, *v.* distress, badger, trouble, vex, plague, torment, irritate, needle (*inf.*), heckle, beset; worry, afflict, depress, sadden. See DISCONTENT, MALEVOLENCE.

harbinger, *n.* omen, sign, forerunner, precursor. See PREDICTION.

harbor, *n.* refuge; port, retreat; haven, shelter; mole. —*v.* protect, shield, shelter; cherish, keep. See SAFETY, ARRIVAL.

hard, *adj.* firm, rigid (see HARDNESS); unsympathetic, unloving, unfriendly, callous; strenuous, difficult, puzzling; severe, serious, short, intensive. See INSENSIBILITY. *Ant.,* soft.

hardboiled, *adj., informal,* disillusioned, sophisticated. See SKILL.

hard-core, *adj.* dedicated, faithful; severe, intense. See SENSIBILITY.

harden, *v.* anneal, fire; steel; congeal,

thicken (see HARDNESS); accustom, inure, blunt. See HABIT, INSENSIBILITY.
Ant., soften.

hard feelings, *n.* ill will, bad blood, animosity. See HATE.

hard-hearted, *adj.* cruel, pitiless, ruthless,
merciless, uncompassionate, callous,
unsympathetic, tough, hard as nails
(*inf.*). See INSENSIBILITY. *Ant.,* warm-
or soft-hearted.

hard-line, *adj.* rigid, uncompromising; authoritarian. See OBSTINACY.

hardly, *adv.* scarcely, barely; improbably;
rarely. See RARITY, DIFFICULTY.

HARDNESS
Solidity

Nouns—1, hardness, rigidity, inflexibility, temper, callosity; toughness; petrification,
lapidification, lapidescence; vitrification, ossification; crystallization. See DENSITY,
STRENGTH.

2, (*measurement of hardness*) Mohs' scale: talc, gypsum, calcite, fluorite, apatite,
feldspar, quartz, topaz, sapphire, diamond.

3, horn, callus, flint, marble, rock, crag (see LAND), crystal, granite, adamant, iron,
steel; brick; concrete. *Informal,* Irish confetti. See INORGANIC MATTER.

Verbs—harden, stiffen, petrify, temper, anneal, ossify, vitrify; callous; set, congeal, con-
cretize; bake.

Adjectives—hard, rigid, stubborn, stiff, firm; starch[ed]; stark, unbending, unlimber,
unyielding; inflexible, tense; proof; diamondlike, diamantine, adamant[ine]; concrete, stony, marble, granitic, vitreous; horny, callous[ed], corneous; bony, osseous;
tempered, annealed.

Antonyms, see SOFTNESS, ELASTICITY.

---

hardship, *n.* ADVERSITY, difficulties; calamity, affliction.

hard up, *adj., informal,* poor, needy (see
POVERTY); frustrated; at one's wits' end,
up against it (*sl.*); hungry, sex-starved,
horny (see DESIRE). *Ant.,* well-off.

hardware, *n.* housewares, tools, utensils;
ironmongery, plumbing supplies, *etc.*;
slang, guns, weaponry, ARMS. See IN-
STRUMENTALITY.

hardy, *adj.* sturdy, tough, vigorous; resolute, daring; durable. See COURAGE,
DURABILITY, STRENGTH. *Ant.,* weak.

harebrained, *adj.* giddy, capricious, scatterbrained. See FOLLY, IGNORANCE.

harem, *n.* seraglio; bridal suite, love nest
(*sl.*). See ABODE.

hark, *v.* harken; hear, listen. See HEARING,
ATTENTION. —**hark back,** revert (see
REVERSION).

harlot, *n.* strumpet, cocotte, prostitute;
paramour, courtesan. See IMPURITY.

harm, *n.* DETERIORATION, EVIL, dishonor,
mischief, injury. —*v.* damage, injure;
desecrate, abuse, break. See MALEVO-
LENCE, WRONG.

harmful, *adj.* injurious, hurtful. See DIS-
EASE, BADNESS. *Ant.,* harmless, safe.

harmless, *adj.* innocent, innocuous, inoffensive. See INNOCENCE, SAFETY, GOOD-
NESS.

harmony, *n.* AGREEMENT, concurrence,
concord; accompaniment; ORDER, SYM-
METRY; tunefulness, euphony; congruity; proportion; unison; peace,
amity, friendship. See MUSIC, UNITY,
FRIEND. *Ant.,* DISCORD.

harness, *n.* bridle, traces, hackamore;
gear. —*v.* control, utilize; curb, yoke.
See DOMESTICATION, RESTRAINT, USE.

harp, *n.* lyre, psaltery. See MUSIC. —*v.*
dwell on, repeat, din, iterate, nag,
pester. See REPETITION.

harrowing, *adj.* distressing, wrenching,
tragic, nerve-racking. See PAIN.

harry, *v.* plunder, pillage, ATTACK; distress,
plague, harass, hound. See MALEVO-
LENCE.

harsh, *adj.* acrimonious, ungenial, severe,
rough, ungracious; sharp, sour; discordant, hoarse, grating; brutal, heartless,
cruel; austere, stern; rigorous, hard. See
DISCOURTESY, DISCORD, SEVERITY, IN-
ELEGANCE. *Ant.,* clement, gentle.

harvest, *n.* crop, yield, product, issue, outcome. See EFFECT, STORE, AGRICULTURE.

has-been, *n.* [old] fogy, mossback (see OLDNESS).

hash, *n.* MIXTURE, medley, mix, jumble, mishmash, confusion; botch; rehash; review; *slang,* hashish, marijuana. See FOOD, DRUGS. —*v.t.* mince, chop, dice; botch, bungle; hash over, discuss. See INQUIRY, UNSKILLFULNESS.

hassle, *n., slang,* quarrel, squabble. See DISCORD.

HASTE
Swiftness

Nouns—haste, urgency; dispatch; acceleration, spurt, forced march, rush, dash; VELOCITY; precipitancy, precipitation, precipitousness; impatience, impetuosity; expedition, EARLINESS; hurry, drive, scramble, bustle.

Verbs—1, haste, hasten; make haste, hurry [up], rush, dart, dash, whip on, push on, press; sentry, scuttle along, step lively, dash off, bustle, hustle, barrel, flash, scramble, plunge, bestir oneself (see ACTIVITY); lose no time, make short work of; work against time. *Informal,* make tracks, make good time, step on it. *Slang,* shake a leg, get cracking, make it snappy, hotfoot it, get a move on, get the lead out [of your ass].

2, *(get faster gradually)* speed [up], expedite; precipitate; quicken, accelerate. *Slang,* step on the gas, give 'er the gun, burn rubber; give the bum's rush.

Adjectives—hasty, hurried, cursory, precipitate, headlong, impulsive, impetuous, eager, impatient, hotheaded; pressed for time, hard-pressed, urgent.

Adverbs—hastily, precipitately, helter-skelter, slapdash, full-tilt, headlong, on the run; against time *or* the clock; apace, amain; all at once (see INSTANTANEITY); at short notice, immediately (see EARLINESS); express, posthaste; on the double. *Informal,* in a jiff[y].

Phrases—always in a hurry, always behind; haste is from the Devil; haste makes waste; *festina lente,* hasten slowly.

Quotations—If it were done when 'tis done, then 'twere well it were done quickly (*Shakespeare*), Make haste slowly (*Augustus*), Nothing is more vulgar than haste (*Emerson*), Wisely and slowly; they stumble that run fast (*Shakespeare*).

Antonyms, see SLOWNESS.

hat, *n.* cap, headgear, bonnet; headdress; derby, bowler; turban, cloche. See CLOTHING. —**pass the hat,** solicit donations, take [up] a collection. See REQUEST.

hatch, *v.* invent, contrive, originate; incubate; concoct, devise. See FALSEHOOD, IMAGINATION, PLAN.

hatchet, *n.* ax(e); hatchetman *or* -woman, assassin. See INSTRUMENTALITY, KILLING. —**bury the hatchet,** make peace (see PACIFICATION).

hatchway, *n.* trapdoor (see OPENING).

HATE
Intense dislike

Nouns—1, hate, hatred, abhorrence, loathing; disaffection, disfavor; alienation, estrangement, coolness; enmity, hostility, animosity, RESENTMENT; spite, despite, bad blood; malice (see MALEVOLENCE); implacability (see RETALIATION); repugnance, DISLIKE, odium, unpopularity; detestation, antipathy, revulsion. See FEELING, PREPARATION.

2, *(something hated)* abomination, anathema, aversion, bête noire; enemy (see OPPOSITION).

3, hater; misanthropist, misogynist; racist, bigot, redneck, anti-Semite; xenophobe, homophobe, *etc.*

Verbs—1, hate, detest, despise, abominate, abhor, loathe; shrink from, view with horror, hold in abomination, revolt against, execrate; DISLIKE. *Informal,* have it in for, not be able to stand. *Slang,* hate one's guts.

2, excite *or* provoke hatred, be hateful; repel, envenom, incense, irritate, rile; horrify.

3, be unfriendly, on bad terms, estranged, *etc.*

Adjectives—**1,** *(hating)* averse, set against, hostile; bitter, acrimonious (see DISCOURTESY); implacable, revengeful; on the outs; invidious, spiteful, malicious (see MALEVOLENCE).

2, hated, despised, unloved, unbeloved, unlamented, unmourned, disliked; forsaken, rejected, lovelorn, jilted.

3, *(worthy of being hated)* hateful, obnoxious, abhorrent, despicable, heinous, odious, abominable, repulsive, loathsome, offensive, disgusting, disagreeable; unfriendly.

Phrases—better a dinner of herbs where love is, than a stalled ox where hate is; hatred watches while friendship sleeps.

Quotations—Men love in haste, but they detest at leisure (*Lord Byron*), People must learn to hate (*Nelson Mandela*), I tell you there is such a thing as creative hate (*Willa Cather*), It is human to hate those whom we have injured (*Tacitus*), The price of hating other human beings is loving oneself less (*Eldridge Cleaver*).

Antonyms, see LOVE.

---

haughty, *adj.* overbearing, arrogant, supercilious, proud, lordly, superior. See CONTEMPT, INSOLENCE. *Ant.,* modest, humble.

haul, *v.* drag, pull, draw; transport, deliver; lug; haul up, arraign. See TRANSPORTATION, TRACTION, LAWSUIT.

haunt, *n.* shade, ghost, spirit, spook; resort, rendezvous, retreat, den, hangout (*sl.*). —*v.* frequent, attend; obsess; visit. See FEAR, ABODE.

haute couture, Fr., high FASHION.

haute cuisine, Fr., gourmet cooking, cordon bleu (see FOOD).

haut monde, Fr., upper classes; high society. See FASHION, NOBILITY.

have, *v.* own, hold, retain, possess, keep, maintain. See POSSESSION. —*n., informal,* rich person (see MONEY).

haven, *n.* refuge, sanctuary, asylum, shelter; harbor, port, snuggery; protection. See SAFETY.

have-not, *n., informal,* pauper, poor person (see POVERTY).

havoc, *n.* devastation, DESTRUCTION, wreckage; DISORDER, chaos, confusion; ravagement, vandalism; disaster, catastrophe.

hawk, *n.* falcon, buzzard, kite, harrier, *etc.*; [hard *or* racking] cough; *informal,* hard-liner, warmonger. See WARFARE, DISEASE. —*v.* peddle. See SALE.

hawker, *n.* street salesman, vivandière, street crier (see SALE).

hayseed, *n., informal,* rustic, bumpkin. See POPULACE.

haywire, *adj., slang,* confused, mixed-up, berserk, screwy; out of control, out of commission; balled *or* bollixed up, snafu (*sl.*). See DISORDER, INSANITY.

hazard, *n.* DANGER, CHANCE, risk, peril, gamble; accident, adventure, contingency. —*v.* risk, venture, gamble. See RASHNESS.

haze, *n.* film, opacity, mist, fog; dimness. OBSCURITY. See CLOUDINESS.

head, *n.* pate, poll, noggin (*sl.*), bean (*sl.*); chief, DIRECTOR, manager, leader; title, heading, caption; talent, ability, JUDGMENT; CLASS, category, type, grouping; *slang,* user, addict (see HABIT). See BEGINNING, INTELLECT, HEIGHT. —*v.* lead, direct, precede; guide, rule, control, manage. See DIRECTION, PRIORITY, AUTHORITY.

headache, *n.* migraine, megrim, splitting headache; hangover; problem, burden, difficulty, nuisance, the misery (*inf.*). See PAIN.

headdress, *n.* headgear, millinery; coiffure; plumage, warbonnet. See CLOTHING.

headhunter, *n.* cannibal; recruiter, talent scout. See INQUIRY, PURSUIT.

heading, *n.* title, caption; DIRECTION, course. See NOMENCLATURE.

headland, *n.* promontory, spit, cape, spur. See CONVEXITY, HEIGHT.

headline, *n.* title, banner. —*v.i.* star, feature. See NOMENCLATURE, INDICATION.

headlong, *adj.* hasty, hurried; rash, precipitate; heedless, reckless. See RASHNESS, HASTE.

headmaster, headmistress, *n.* principal. See SCHOOL.

headphone, *n.* headset, receiver, earphone. See HEARING.

headquarters, *n.pl.* main office, base of operations, HQ; government, general staff, chief. See AUTHORITY, ABODE.

headstone, *n.* gravestone; foundation stone, cornerstone; cairn, dolmen, cromlech. See INTERMENT.

headstrong, *adj.* obstinate, willful, stubborn. See OBSTINACY, VIOLENCE.

headway, *n.* PROGRESSION, advance; gain, accomplishment, achievement; clearance. See SPACE.

heady, *adj.* exhilarating, intoxicating. See DRINKING, EXCITEMENT.

heal, *v.* mend, cure; repair, restore; ease. See RESTORATION. *Ant.*, infect.

HEALTH
Physical well-being

Nouns—1, health, healthiness; mental health, SANITY; soundness; vim, vigor, and vitality; STRENGTH, robustness; bloom, prime; *mens sana in corpore sano;* hygeia; clean bill of health; convalescence, recovery, cure (see RESTORATION).

2, *(a condition that promotes health)* salubrity, healthfulness; hygiene, sanitation. See CLEANNESS.

3, health spa *or* club; sanitarium (see REMEDY); health food, organic food, food guide pyramid, low-fat, low-salt, *or* low-cholesterol diet. *Slang,* fat farm, meat rack.

Verbs—1, be healthy; bloom, flourish; look oneself; be in *or* enjoy good health; convalesce, recuperate, recover (see RESTORATION); get better, improve (see IMPROVEMENT); take a new lease on life; cure, restore; exercise. *Informal,* feel like a million [dollars].
2, be salubrious, be healthful, agree with, be good for.

Adjectives—1, healthy, well, sound, hearty, sanguine, hale [and hearty], fresh, green, whole; florid, flush, hardy, staunch, brave, robust, vigorous, toned, trim; unscathed, uninjured, untainted; in shape *or* condition, in the pink [of condition]; sound as a bell, fit [as a fiddle], shipshape; fresh as a daisy *or* a rose, in fine feather *or* fettle, in one's prime; able-bodied, nondisabled. *Informal,* chipper. *Slang,* peppy.
2, healthful, salubrious, salutary, wholesome, prophylactic, benign, bracing, tonic, invigorating; good for; hygienic; innocuous, innocent, harmless, uninjurious, uninfectious, sanitary; lite, low-fat, low-cholesterol, salt-free, meatless, fat-free, sugar-free, *etc.* See GOODNESS.

Phrases—early to bed and early to rise, makes a man healthy, wealthy, and wise; *mens sana in corpore sano,* a sound mind in a sound body.

Quotations—Look to your health (*Izaak Walton*), Health and good estate of body are above all good (*Bible*), The first wealth is health (*Emerson*).

Antonyms, see DISEASE.

---

heap, *n.* pile, load, stack, mound, ASSEMBLAGE; *informal,* great deal, heaps (*inf.*), oodles (*inf.*), piles (*inf.*), scads (*sl.*). See MULTITUDE.

HEARING
Sense of hearing

Nouns—1, hearing, sense of hearing; audition, auscultation; eavesdropping, audibility; acute ear, *etc.*; ear for music; otology, audiology; audiometer; acoustics (see SOUND).
2, ear, auricle, acoustic organ, auditory apparatus, eardrum, tympanum; hearing aid, ear trumpet, speaking trumpet; amplifier, amplification, bone conduction; earphones. *Slang,* cans.
3, hearer, auditor, listener, eavesdropper; audience.
4, hearing, interview, audition, audience; trial (see INQUIRY).

Verbs—1, hear, overhear, take in; eavesdrop, bug; sit in on, audit; hark[en], listen [in], give *or* lend an ear, bend an ear, be all ears, heed, hark, attend, prick up one's ears; turn a deaf ear to. *Slang,* get a load of.

2, become audible, fall upon the ear, listen in, catch *or* reach the ear, be heard; ring, resound. *Informal,* be all ears, drink in.

Adjectives—auditory, aural; auricular; audible, articulate, clear.

Phrases—little pitchers have large *or* big ears; walls have ears.

Antonyms, see DEAFNESS.

---

hearsay, *n.* NEWS, gossip, rumor, talk, report. See INFORMATION. *Ant.,* eyewitness.

hearse, *n.* funeral wagon. See INTERMENT.

heart, *n.* center, substance; kernel, pith, gist, core; breast; spirit, COURAGE; sympathy, affection, understanding; nature, soul. See IMPORTANCE, MIDDLE, FEELING, INTERIOR.

heartache, *n.* sorrow, anguish. See DEJECTION.

heartbroken, *adj.* miserable, wretched, forlorn, disconsolate, anguished. See PAIN, DEJECTION.

heartburn, *n.* cardialgia, pyrosis, PAIN; rue, remorse, RESENTMENT. See JEALOUSY.

hearten, *v.* cheer, encourage, brighten, reassure, comfort, rally. See COURAGE, CHEERFULNESS.

heartfelt, *adj.* sincere, earnest; profound; meaningful, cordial; enthusiastic. See FEELING. *Ant.,* insincere.

hearth, *n.* fireside, fireplace; ingle[nook]; family [circle]. See HEAT, ABODE.

heartless, *adj.* cruel, cold, unfeeling, uncaring, unsympathetic, callous; unkind, inconsiderate, insensitive. See INSENSIBILITY. *Ant.,* kind, warm.

heartrending, *adj.* harrowing; heartbreaking. See DEJECTION.

heartsick, *adj.* unhappy, grieving, forlorn. See DEJECTION.

heartthrob, *n.* sweetheart, honey (see LOVE).

heart-to-heart, *adj.* intimate, confidential, private, off the record, entre nous; frank, candid. See SECRET, PROBITY.

heartwarming, *adj.* encouraging, inspiring, heartening. See HOPE.

hearty, *n.* comrade; sailor, tar. See FRIEND, NAVIGATION. —*adj.* sturdy, robust, strong, well, vigorous, healthy; friendly, cordial; substantial. See FEELING, HEALTH.

heat, *n.* high temperature (see HEAT); passion, rage, vehemence; rut, mating period. See SEX, EXCITEMENT. *Ant.,* COLD.

HEAT
Quality of warmth

Nouns—1, heat, caloric; warmth, ardor, fervor, fervency; incalescence, incandescence; flush, glow; temperature, fever; white heat, blood *or* body heat, fever heat; thermal energy; specific heat; heat of fusion, heat of vaporization; melting point (see LIQUEFACTION).

2, *(cause of fire)* fire, spark, scintillation, flash, combustion, flame, blaze; bonfire, campfire, smudge, forest fire, brand, wildfire, sheet of fire, lambent flame; devouring element; sun; fireworks, pyrotechnics; ashes, cinders.

3, *(hot weather)* torridity, hot weather, [mid]summer, dogdays; heat wave, hot spell, sirocco, simoom; Indian summer; global warming, greenhouse effect.

4, *(study or measurement of heat)* thermology, thermotics, thermodynamics, thermometer, thermostat, calorimeter; thermal unit, British thermal unit, BTU; kelvin, celsius, centigrade, calorie, Fahrenheit; adiabatic process, thermal expansion; first *or* second law of thermodynamics, kinetic theory of heat, law of heat exchange. *Informal,* mercury, glass. See MEASUREMENT.

5, *(heating device)* heating, calefaction, convection; heater, stove, range, cooktop, [convection *or* microwave] oven; [forced] hot air, steam heat, hot water, radiator, register; blast furnace, electric furnace, heat pump, heat exchange[r]; kiln; crematorium; forge, crucible, alembic; Bunsen burner; [acetylene *or* butane] torch, electric welder; crematory, pyre; incinerator; fireplace, hearth, grate, fender, fire screen; brazier, German *or* Holland fireplace *or* stove, Franklin stove; bed warmer, electric blanket, heating pad; chafing dish; heliostat; heat engine; heat sink.

6, see FUEL.

7, hell, blast furnace, hot tub, sauna, steam room. *Slang,* hell-hole.

Verbs—**1,** heat, warm [up], reheat; be hot, glow, flush, sweat, swelter, bask, smoke, reek, stew, simmer, seethe, boil, broil; go up in smoke; smolder; parch, fume, pant; thaw; cook (see FOOD).

2, ignite, set on fire, enkindle; burn, blaze, flame, char, burn to a crisp; cremate. *Slang,* torch.

Adjectives—**1,** hot, warm; mild, genial; tepid, lukewarm, unfrozen; thermal, thermic, calorific; fervent, fervid, feverish; ardent, aglow; red-hot, white-hot, piping-hot; like a furnace *or* oven; hot as fire, like the fires of Hell.

2, sunny, torrid, tropical, estival, canicular; close, sultry, stifling, stuffy, sweltering, suffocating, oppressive; reeking; baking.

3, fiery, incandescent, incalescent; candent, glowing, smoking; on fire; blazing, in flames, alight, afire, ablaze; smoldering, in a glow, feverish, in a sweat; blood-hot, warm as toast; volcanic, plutonic, igneous; isothermal, isothermic.

4, microwavable.

Phrases—cold hands, warm heart.

Quotations—If you can't stand the heat, get out of the kitchen (*Harry S. Truman*), Heat not a furnace for your foe so hot that it do singe yourself (*Shakespeare*).

Antonyms, see COLD.

---

heated, *adj.* feverous, fervent; excited, agitated; passionate, hot; angry. See HEAT, AGITATION, EXCITEMENT, RESENTMENT. *Ant.,* calm, pleasant.

heathen, *n.* pagan, infidel, unbeliever. —*adj.* irreligious, idolatrous, pagan, unconverted; atheistic. See IRRELIGION, IDOLATRY. *Ant.,* believer.

heave, *v.* lift, hoist, raise; throw, pitch, toss; swell, expand; undulate; vomit. See ELEVATION, PROPULSION.

HEAVEN
Abode of the blessed

Nouns—**1,** heaven, above, empyrean; kingdom of heaven *or* God, Abraham's bosom; future state, eternal blessedness, eternity, everlasting bliss, eternal life *or* reward; Paradise, Eden, abode *or* isle of the blessed; celestial bliss, glory; hereafter, afterlife; Golden Age, Utopia, never-never land, millennium, land of Canaan, Land of Beulah, Celestial City, City of God, promised land; Pearly Gates; Land of the Leal; New Jerusalem; Alfardaws, Assama, Garden of Irem; Nirvana; Olympus; Elysium, Elysian fields, garden of the Hesperides, Valhalla, Nirvana, the happy hunting grounds, seventh heaven. *Slang,* kingdom come. See PLEASURE.

2, sky, firmament, welkin, blue empyrean, the ether, heavens. See UNIVERSE.

3, resurrection, translation, apotheosis, ascension, assumption; afterlife, life after death, great beyond, afterworld.

4, See ANGEL, DEITY.

Adjectives—heavenly, celestial, supernal, unearthly, from on high, paradisiac[al]; beatific, elysian, ethereal, Olympian.

Quotations—I will spend my heaven doing good on earth (*St. Teresa*).

Antonyms, see HELL.

---

heavenly, *adj.* celestial (see HEAVEN); blessed, angelic, saintly, holy; *informal,* delectable, delightful, wonderful, marvelous. See GOODNESS. *Ant.,* Satanic.

heavy, *adj.* weighty, heavyset (see GRAVITY); oppressive, tedious, tiresome; dull, gloomy, overcast; strong, pressing, large; somber, dismal, dejected, sad, melancholy; slow, inert, sluggish; grievous, serious. See DEJECTION, IMPORTANCE. *Ant.*, light.

heavy-duty, *adj.* durable, sturdy; tough, rugged. See DURABILITY.

heavy-handed, *adj.* oppressive, tyrannical (see SEVERITY); clumsy, offensive (see UNSKILLFULNESS).

heckle, *v.t.* plague, taunt, harass; challenge, interrupt. See DISCONTENT.

hectic, *adj.* feverish, febrile; excited, agitated, frenetic, wild, turbulent. See EXCITEMENT.

hector, *v.* bully, torment, plague, domineer, bluster. See INSOLENCE, THREAT.

hedge, *n.* shrubbery, hedgerow. See VEGETABLE, ENCLOSURE. —*v.* evade; protect, shelter; hem in, obstruct; temporize. See COMPENSATION.

heed, *n.* ATTENTION, notice, regard, consideration, CARE. —*v.* observe, CARE, notice, attend, regard; consider. See CAUTION. *Ant.*, ignore.

heedful, *adj.* caring, attentive (see CARE).

heedless, *adj.* disregardful, remiss, careless, negligent, thoughtless; unobservant, unnoticing, undiscerning; reckless. See INATTENTION, RASHNESS.

heel, *n.* rear; tilt, cant; *slang,* cad, scoundrel, bounder (*inf.*), rat (*sl.*), louse (*sl.*), SOB (*sl.*). See OBLIQUITY, EVILDOER. —*v.i.* turn around, pivot, swivel. —*v.t.* follow, pursue, go after; *slang,* shadow, tail; supply, furnish, outfit, PROVISION. See PURSUIT, DEVIATION, DISCOURTESY.

hefty, *adj.* weighty; bulky, burly, brawny; beefy, corpulent. See SIZE, GRAVITY.

HEIGHT
Vertical size

Nouns—1, height, altitude, ELEVATION; eminence, pitch; loftiness, tallness, stature, prominence (see CONVEXITY); orogeny, orogenesis, orogenics, orography.

2, *(high place)* mount[ain], cordillera, divide, range, saddle, steptoe, massif, nunatak, alp, palisade, pinnacle, piton, seamount; headland, foreland; promontory, ridge, hogback; dune; vantage ground; down; moor[land]; uplands, highlands; watershed, foothills; heights; knoll, hummock, hill[ock], cuesta, kopje, barrow, mound, knoll, bunker, mole, butte; steeps, bluff, cliff, krantz, crag, crest, tor, pike, esker, escarpment, edge, ledge, brae.

3, *(highest point)* summit, top, vertex, apex, zenith, pinnacle, acme, peak, culmination; meridian; utmost height; capital; crown, point, crest, cap; hilltop, knap, mountain top; housetop, rooftop; head.

4, *(high building or space)* tower, pillar, column, obelisk, monument, steeple, spire, minaret, campanile, turret, dome, cupola, pole, pikestaff, maypole, flagstaff; aerial, mast; topmast, topgallantmast, moonraker; skyscraper, high-rise; ceiling (see COVERING); derrick; attic, garret; balcony. *Slang,* Ethiopian paradise.

5, colossus, giant (see SIZE); mountain climber, mountaineer. *Informal,* beanpole, long drink of water, stringbean.

Verbs—be high, tower, soar, command; hover, cap, culminate; mount, perch, surmount; cover, crown; overtop, top off (see SUPERIORITY); stand on tiptoe; grow, upgrow, rise (see ASCENT); heighten, elevate (see ELEVATION).

Adjectives—high, elevated, eminent, exalted, lofty; tall; gigantic, towering, soaring, elevated, upper; highest, top[most], uppermost; capital, paramount; upland, hilly, mountainous, alpine, aerial; sky-high, tall as a steeple; long-legged *or* -limbed, rangy. *Informal,* high as a kite.

Adverbs—on high, high up, aloft, up, above, aloof, overhead; in the clouds; on tiptoe, on stilts.

Quotations—Happiness makes up in height what it lacks in length (*Robert Frost*).
Antonyms, see LOWNESS.

heinous, *adj.* dreadful, abominable; atrocious, hateful, monstrous. See BADNESS, HATE.

heir, heiress, *n.* legatee, inheritor, beneficiary. See POSSESSION, ACQUISITION.

heirloom, *n.* POSSESSION, keepsake, memento, souvenir.

heist, *n., slang,* burglary (see STEALING).

helicopter, *n.* autogiro, whirlybird. See AVIATION.

HELL
Abode of the damned

Nouns—1, hell, Hades, place of torment; Pandemonium, Tophet; Gehenna, Sheol; hellfire, everlasting fire, fire and brimstone *or* damnation, inferno, perdition; underworld; purgatory, limbo, abyss, void, bottomless pit, infernal, lower, *or* nether regions, netherworld; hell on earth. *Slang,* all-get-out, the other place.

2, Tartarus, Hades, Avernus, Erebus, Styx, Stygian creek, pit of Acheron, Cocytus; infernal regions, inferno, realms of Pluto, Jericho; Amenti, Arallu, Naraka, Nastrond, Nifleheim.

3, Pluto, Rhadamanthus; Charon; Satan (see DEMON).

Adjectives—hellish, infernal, Stygian, Plutonian.

Adverbs—[down] below.

Quotations—Abandon all hope, you who enter! (*Dante*), Hell is other people (*Jean-Paul Sartre*), Hell is oneself (*T. S. Eliot*), The road to Hell is paved with good intentions (*Karl Marx*), Hell, madam, is to love no more (*Georges Bernanos*), Me miserable! which way shall I fly infinite wrath, and infinite despair? Which way I fly is hell; myself am hell (*John Milton*), If there is no Hell, a good many preachers are obtaining money under false pretenses (*Billy Sunday*).

Antonyms, see HEAVEN.

---

hello, *n.* greeting, salutation, welcome; reception. —*interj.* good day! good morning! good afternoon! good evening!; how are you? how do you do? *bonjour! buon giorno! guten Tag!* aloha!; hi! hi there! howdy! how's tricks? ahoy! ciao! (*all inf.*). See COURTESY. *Ant.,* goodbye.

helm, *n.* tiller, wheel; authority, command, scepter. See DIRECTION.

helmet, *n.* headgear, skullcap, casque, headpiece; crest, morion. See CLOTHING, DEFENSE.

help, *n.* SERVANT[s], staff, employees; AID, assistance, succor; relief, REMEDY. —*v.* assist, serve, befriend; relieve, ameliorate, better. See AID, AUXILIARY.

helpful, *adj.* beneficial, contributory, favorable; useful, worthwhile, furthering, improving; serviceable, salutary; remedial. See IMPROVEMENT.

helping, *n.* serving, portion (see APPORTIONMENT).

helpless, *adj.* impotent, powerless; defenseless, vulnerable, resourceless; prostrate, crippled; dependent. See IMPOTENCE. *Ant.,* capable.

helter-skelter, *adj.* confused, disorderly. See DISORDER.

hem, *n.* edging, fringe, frill. See EDGE.

hemorrhage, *v.i.* bleed (see FLUIDITY).

hen, *n.* fowl, chicken, bird, pullet. See ANIMAL.

hence, *adv.* herefrom, away; henceforth, henceforward; so, therefore. See REASONING, DEPARTURE, ATTRIBUTION, EFFECT.

henchman, *n.* hireling, underling; flunky, lackey; tool, puppet; accomplice; stooge, yes-man, ward heeler, errand boy (*all sl.*). See SERVANT, AGENT.

henpecked, *adj.* hag-ridden; browbeaten, nagged, hounded; led by the nose, jumping through hoops. See OBEDIENCE, SUBJECTION.

hep, *adj., slang,* well-informed; hip, in the know, wise (to), up on, cool (*all sl.*). See KNOWLEDGE.

herald, *n.* forerunner, precursor, announcer, messenger, harbinger. —*v.* proclaim, announce, declare; introduce; precede, warn. See PREDICTION, COMMUNICATION, PRECEDENCE.

heraldry, *n.* blazonry, emblazonment. See INDICATION.

herb, *n.* potherb, condiment. See VEGETABLE, REMEDY.

herbicide, *n.* weed killer, defoliant, paraquat, *etc.* See KILLING.

herculean, *adj.* strong; arduous, strenuous. See STRENGTH, DIFFICULTY.

herd, *n.* group, flock, drove; gathering; troop, pack, crowd. See MULTITUDE. —*v.* drive, tend, collect; gather, assemble; corral, group. See ASSEMBLAGE.

herder, *n.* shepherd, shepherdess, cowherd, pasturer, herdboy, cowboy. See DOMESTICATION.

here, *adv.* hereabouts, hither, hitherward. See LOCATION.

hereafter, *adv.* subsequently, henceforth, henceforward, eventually, ultimately. See FUTURITY.

hereditary, *adj.* inheritable, transmissible, heritable, ancestral, patrimonial. See INTRINSIC, POSTERITY, TRANSFER.

heresy, *n.* dissent, HETERODOXY. See DOUBT, ERROR.

heritage, *n.* bequest, inheritance, legacy, hereditament, patrimony. See POSSESSION.

hermaphrodite, *n.* androgyne, epicene; transsexual. See MIXTURE, MALE, FEMALE.

hermetic, *adj.* mystic, magic, alchemic; airtight, vacuum-packed. See CLOSURE.

hermit, *n.* anchorite, recluse, eremite, ascetic, solitary. See ASCETICISM, SECLUSION.

hero, heroine, *n.* victor, defender, champion, redeemer; inspiration, ideal, model, paragon; knight in [shining] armor; main character, protagonist, lead; darling, favorite, idol, big *or* hot shot (*sl.*); submarine [sandwich], hoagie, grinder. See COURAGE, DRAMA, FOOD.

heroic, *adj.* courageous, intrepid, valiant, brave, mighty, fearless, gallant. See COURAGE, BOASTING, UNSELFISHNESS.

heroin, *n.* diamorphine; [big] H, horse, snow, scag (*all sl.*). See DRUGS, HABIT.

hesitate, *v.i.* falter, waiver, shrink, demur; pause. See DOUBT, STAMMERING, UNWILLINGNESS.

HETERODOXY
Departure from orthodoxy

Nouns—1, heterodoxy, syncretism; sectarianism, nonconformity, UNCONFORMITY, secularism, denominationalism, cultism; heresy, schism, ERROR, false doctrine; schismaticism, recusancy; backsliding, apostasy, atheism, IRRELIGION.

2, bigotry (see OBSTINACY); fanaticism, zealotry, iconoclasm; hyperorthodoxy, precisianism, bibliolatry, sabbatarianism, puritanism, IDOLATRY; DISSENT, superstition.

3, (*religious nonconformist*) sectarian, heretic, seceder, separatist, recusant, dissenter, dissident, nonconformist, nonjuror; gentile; zealot, fanatic.

4, sect, denomination, faction, division, schism, organization, group, school, church, following, fellowship, ism, faith.

Verbs—deviate, stray, err, fall into ERROR.

Adjectives—heterodox, sectarian, heretical, denominational, nonconformist, unorthodox, unscriptural, uncanonical, apocryphal; schismatic, recusant, iconoclastic, dissenting, dissident, secular; pantheistic, polytheistic; bigoted, prejudiced, exclusive, narrow, intolerant, fanatical, dogmatical; superstitious, ideological, visionary; idolatrous.

Quotations—Orthodoxy is my doxy; heterodoxy is another man's doxy (*William Warburton*), I am for religion, against religions (*Victor Hugo*), There is only one religion, though there are a hundred versions of it (*G. B. Shaw*), Old religious factions are volcanoes burnt out (*Edmund Burke*), One religion is as true as another (*Robert Burton*).

Antonyms, see RELIGION.

heterogeneous, *adj.* diverse, mixed, conglomerate; unlike, dissimilar. See DIFFERENCE, VARIEGATION.

heterosexual, *adj.* straight (see SEX).

hew, *v.t.* fell; chop, cut, hack; chip. See DISJUNCTION, FORM.

hex, *n.* see SPELL.

heyday, *n.* prime, height, peak, zenith; glory, full bloom, top of one's form; halcyon, golden, *or* palmy days; golden age, YOUTH. See GOODNESS.

hiatus, *n.* INTERVAL, gap, interruption, lacuna, void.

hibernate, *v.i.* winter; become dormant, hole up (*inf.*). See INACTIVITY.

hick, *n.*, *slang*, rustic, rube. See POPULACE.

hidden, *adj.* See CONCEALMENT.

hide, *n.* skin, pelt, coat; leather. See COVERING. —*v.* cover, secrete, cloak, veil; dissemble, falsify; hole up; disguise, camouflage. See CONCEALMENT, SECRET.

hideaway, *n.* hide-out, retreat, hiding [place]. See CONCEALMENT, SECLUSION, ABODE.

hidebound, *adj.* bigoted, prejudiced, narrow; illiberal; unyielding. See NARROWNESS.

hideous, *adj.* frightful, dreadful, horrible, repulsive, unsightly, revolting. See UGLINESS. *Ant.*, beautiful.

hideout, *n.* hiding [place], cover, refuge; safe house. See CONCEALMENT.

hierarchy, *n.* rank, officialdom; order, ranking, succession. See AUTHORITY.

high, *adj.* elevated, lofty, tall; towering, eminent; acute, sharp, shrill; prominent, important, directorial; costly, dear, expensive; overripe, gamy; *informal*, elated; *slang*, drunk. See HEIGHT, DRINKING, DRUGS. *Ant.*, low.

highborn, *adj.* patrician, noble, royal, aristocratic. See NOBILITY.

highbrow, *n.* intellectual, egghead (*sl.*), longhair (*inf.*), brain (*sl.*). —*adj.* intellectual, intelligent, brainy, cultured. See KNOWLEDGE. *Ant.*, lowbrow.

high-class, *adj.* superior, top-quality (see SUPERIORITY). *Ant.*, low-class, plebeian.

high fidelity, *adj.* hi-fi, stereo; quadraphonic. —*n.* home theater. See SOUND. *Ant.*, low fidelity, monophonic.

highest, *adj.* ultimate, supreme (see SUPERIORITY). *Ant.*, lowest.

high-handed, *adj.* arrogant, authoritarian, pushy (*inf.*). See INSOLENCE.

highlight, *n.* centerpiece, main attraction. —*v.t.* spotlight, feature, focus on. See INDICATION, IMPORTANCE.

highly, *adv.* greatly, extremely; generously. See GREATNESS.

high-minded, *adj.* principled, idealistic. See BELIEF.

high-rise, *n.* skyscraper (see BUILDING).

high society, *n.* smart *or* jet set, Four Hundred, *haut monde.* See SOCIALITY.

high-strung, *adj.* taut, tense, edgy, jumpy, temperamental, excitable; volatile. See EXCITABILITY.

high-tech, *adj.* sophisticated, complex (see INTELLECT). *Ant.*, lo-tech.

highway, *n.* road, turnpike, highroad, thoroughfare. See PASSAGE.

highwayman, *n.* thief, robber, footpad, thug, bandit. See STEALING.

hijack, *v.t.*, *slang*, highjack, steal. See STEALING.

hike, *n.* walk, tramp, jaunt, march; *informal*, raise, INCREASE. —*v.* walk, march; hitchhike, thumb a ride; raise, inflate, boost, hitch up, adjust higher. See ELEVATION, TRAVEL.

hilarity, *n.* CHEERFULNESS, mirth, amusement, enjoyment, gaiety, laughter, glee.

hill, *n.* grade, slope; rise, ASCENT; elevation, mound. See HEIGHT, CONVEXITY.

hillbilly, *n.* mountaineer, rustic, bumpkin. See UNSKILLFULNESS, POPULACE.

hilly, *adj.* steep, mountainous. See ASCENT. *Ant.*, flat.

hilt, *n.* handle, heft. See TOUCH. —**to the hilt,** all the way, completely (see COMPLETION).

HINDRANCE
Something that obstructs

Nouns—**1,** hindrance, obstruction, stoppage; interruption, interception, impedition; retardment, retardation; embarrassment, coarctation, stricture, restriction, RESTRAINT, embargo; deterrent, inhibition, PROHIBITION; blockade, CLOSURE; DIFFICULTY. *Informal,* fly in the ointment.

2, (*hindrance through intervention*) interference, interposition (see BETWEEN), obtrusion; disadvantage; discouragement, preventive action, DISSUASION.

3, (*something that hinders movement*) impediment, let, obstacle, obstruction, knot, check, hitch, snag, glitch, contretemps; drawback, objection; stumbling block, blind alley, ill wind; head wind, OPPOSITION; trammel, hobble, tether; counterpoise; bar, stile, turnstile, barrier; barrage; buffer; gate, portcullis; barricade (see DEFENSE);

[brick or stone] wall, breakwater; bulkhead, block, hurdle, buffer, stopper, boom, dam, floodgate, weir; embolism; gridlock, traffic jam. *Informal,* sleeping policeman.

4, *(symbolic hindrance)* encumbrance; clog, drag, stay, stop, detent, catch; preventive, prophylactic; load, burden, onus, handicap, millstone, impedimenta, ball and chain; dead weight; lumber, pack; incubus, old man of the sea; remora; red herring, false trail.

5, *(hindrance to conception)* contraception, birth control, Planned Parenthood; rhythm method, safe period; coitus interruptus; prophylactic [device], sheath, condom, pessary, diaphragm, cervical cap, coil, loop, intrauterine device, IUD, oral contraceptive, contraceptive sponge, [spermicidal] jelly, Norplant, suppository, morning-after pill; douche; [bilateral] tubal ligation, salpingectomy, vasectomy. *Informal,* the pill, elastic [band], specialities. *Slang,* rubber, safe, [eel]skin, propho, Vatican roulette, rubber cookie or ring, safe, catcher's mitt, jimmy [hat], Dutch cap, womb veil, french[ie], French tickler, glove.

6, handicap, disability; deformity, malformation (see DISTORTION); paralysis (see DISEASE).

7, *(hindrance to enjoyment)* damper, wet blanket, hinderer, marplot, killjoy, interloper; opponent (see OPPOSITION). *Informal,* party pooper.

Verbs—**1,** hinder, impede, delay, detain; embarrass, interpose, interfere, meddle; keep, fend, stave, or ward off; obviate; avert, turn aside, draw off, nip in the bud; forestall, retard, slacken, check, let; counteract, countercheck; debar, foreclose, deter, estop, inhibit (see PROHIBITION); shackle, restrain (see RESTRAINT); restrict. *Informal,* drag one's feet. *Slang,* stonewall.

2, obstruct, stop, stay, bar, block [up]; barricade; bar the door, dam up, close (see CLOSURE); put on the brake, put a spoke in the wheel; put a stop to (see END); interrupt, intercept; oppose (see OPPOSITION); fence, hem, or hedge in, cut off; cramp, hamper; clog, [en]cumber; choke; saddle or load with, overload, trammel, tie one's hands; inconvenience, incommode, baffle, faze, discommode. *Slang,* gum up, throw a monkey wrench in the works. *Informal,* cross up.

3, handicap, disable; thwart, foil, frustrate, disconcert, balk, baffle; spoil, mar, clip the wings of, cripple (see DETERIORATION); dishearten, dissuade, deter, discourage; discountenance, throw cold water or a wet blanket on; cut the ground from under one, nip in the bud, take the wind out of one's sails, hang up, undermine; be or stand in the way of; act as a drag, be a millstone around one's neck. *Informal,* cook one's goose, spike one's guns. *Slang,* cramp one's style, louse up.

Adjectives—**1,** hindering, preventive, forbidding, deterrent; obstructive, impeditive, interceptive; in the way of, unfavorable; onerous, burdensome, cumbersome, cumbrous; binding, blocking, obtrusive; in one's hair, inhibitory, preclusive; prophylactic.

2, hindered, waterlogged, heavy-laden; hard-pressed; handicapped, impeded, thwarted, *etc.*; handi-capable.

Antonyms, see AID.

---

hindsight, *n.* retrospect (see MEMORY).

hinge, *n.* joint, pivot, center, axis; crisis. See CAUSE, JUNCTION.

hint, *n.* intimation, suggestion, allusion, reference, implication; tip, trace, reminder, insinuation. —*v.i.* suggest, allude, imply, intimate. See INFORMATION, MEMORY, DISCLOSURE.

hinterland, *n.* country; inland, backwoods, the sticks (*inf.*). See REGION.

hip, *adj., slang,* wise, in, on to; swinging, jazzy; bohemian; cool, gone, beat (all

sl.); with it, making the scene (all sl.). See KNOWLEDGE.

hippie, *n., slang,* hipster, beat[nik], yippie; bohemian, nonconformist; [cool] cat, swinger; hepcat; hip chick (all sl.). See UNCONFORMITY.

hire, *n.* rental, employment; fee, remuneration. —*v.* rent, lease; employ, engage. See COMMISSION, PRICE.

hireling, *n.* mercenary, henchman, minion, SERVANT.

hiss, *n.* sibilation, fizz, sizzle; spit. —*v.*

sibilate, fizz, sizzle; condemn. See DIS-
APPROBATION, DISRESPECT.

history, *n.* RECORD, chronicle, annals, biography; story, narrative, memoirs, autobiography. See DESCRIPTION.

histrionic, *adj.* theatrical; affected, exaggerated, dramatic. See DRAMA, AFFEC-
TATION.

hit, *n., informal,* SUCCESS, smash; favorite; popularity. —*v.* strike, club, batter; touch, contact, reach, find; knock,
smite; *slang,* bump off. See ARRIVAL,
IMPULSE, KILLING.

hitch, *n.* HINDRANCE, knot, obstruction,
obstacle, inconvenience, impediment;
interruption, pause, stop; tug, jerk,
pull; limp, hobble; accident, mischance.
See DIFFICULTY. —*v.* hobble, shuffle,
limp; tie, knot, fasten, yoke; attach. See
JUNCTION.

hitchhike, *v.i., informal,* hitch, thumb [a
ride], bum a ride. See TRAVEL.

hither, *adv.* here, nearer. See DIRECTION.

hit man, *n.* killer, assassin, hatchet man,
trigger (see KILLING).

hit-or-miss, *adj.* haphazard, CHANCE, random, trial-and-error.

hoard, *n.* collection, STORE, reserve, stock,
supply, savings. —*v.* save, preserve, retain, STORE, amass; treasure; hide; accumulate, collect.

hoarse, *adj.* throaty, raucous, husky,
thick, croaking. See ROUGHNESS.

hoary, *adj.* old, aged, venerable, ancient;
frosty, white; gray[ed]. See AGE.

hoax, *n.* DECEPTION, trick; deceit, fraud,
fakery, humbug, canard. —*v.t.* dupe,
deceive, trick, fool, swindle.

hobble, *n.* shackle, bond, binding. —*v.*
limp, stagger; halt, bind, shackle, handicap, limit. See RESTRAINT, SLOWNESS,
FAILURE.

hobby, *n.* avocation, AMUSEMENT, fad,
whim.

hobgoblin, *n.* imp, gremlin; bugaboo,
bugbear. See FEAR, DEMON.

hobnob, *v.i.* consort, associate, socialize,
mix; pal around, chum, hang out with
(*all inf.*). See SOCIALITY.

hobo, *n.* tramp, drifter, vagabond, vagrant; beggar, freight-hopper, rod-rider;
knight of the road, rolling stone;
bum[mer], deadbeat, bo[e], vag (*all sl.*).
See POPULACE, TRAVEL.

hocus-pocus, *n.* magic, sleight-of-hand,
SORCERY; trickery, deceit, DECEPTION.

hock, *v.t., informal,* pawn, pledge (see
BORROWING).

hodgepodge, *n.* MIXTURE, medley, conglomeration; stew, hash, jumble.

hog, *n.* pig, swine, boar, sow; beast; *informal,* glutton (see GLUTTONY). See ANI-
MAL.

hogwash, *n., informal,* trash, nonsense.
See UNMEANINGNESS.

hoist, *n.* elevator, lift, derrick, crane. —*v.t.*
lift, raise, jack, rear. See ELEVATION.

hoity-toity, *adj.* haughty, pretentious. See
AFFECTATION.

hokey, *adj.* phony, mock, sham; ersatz.
See FALSEHOOD.

hold, *n.* grasp, clutch, grip; tenure, POS-
SESSION; control, INFLUENCE, domination; ownership, keeping; anchor, rein.
—*v.* have, occupy, retain, own, possess;
restrain, repress, control, pinion, curb;
check, stop, interrupt, pause; clutch,
grasp, grip, seize; pin, clip, fasten; believe, declare, opine, state, think; insist,
persist; last, endure, continue; cling,
cleave, stick, adhere; keep, defend, protect, guard. See BELIEF, COHERENCE,
DEFENSE, DURABILITY, RESTRAINT, RE-
TENTION, STORE, SUPPORT, COMPOSI-
TION, AUTHORITY.

holding, *n.* property, POSSESSION, tenure;
claim, interest.

holdover, *n.* residue, remnant, REMAINDER.

holdup, *n., informal,* theft, [armed] robbery, stickup, hijack[ing], heist. See
STEALING.

hole, *n.* OPENING, aperture, gap, cavity;
excavation, hollow; slot, puncture; dungeon; cave; space. See CONCAVITY, ABODE,
INTERVAL.

holiday, *n.* vacation, festival, CELEBRA-
TION, recreation. See AMUSEMENT, RE-
POSE.

hollow, *n.* CONCAVITY, depression, dent,
cavity, hole; valley, gully, basin; channel,
groove, furrow. —*adj.* thin, unresonant;
sepulchral, deep, empty, void, unfilled,
vacant; unsound, weak, uncertain, un-
convincing; specious, false, unsubstantiated, inadequate. See ABSENCE.

holocaust, *n.* immolation, burnt offering;
massacre, pogrom. See DESTRUCTION,
KILLING.

holy, *adj.* consecrated, saintly; blessed, sacred, godly. See PIETY, DEITY.

homage, *n.* RESPECT, tribute, honor; deference, allegiance, devotion, veneration; SUBMISSION, reverence. See OBEDIENCE, WORSHIP.

home, *n.* domicile, residence, ABODE, dwelling; shelter, refuge, asylum, sanctuary; habitat, habitation, environment; homeland, native land, fatherland, country, homeland, stateside (*inf.*). See OBEDIENCE.

homecoming, *n.* return, ARRIVAL, journey's end.

homeland, *n.* native land, father- *or* motherland, birthplace. See ABODE.

homeless, *adj.* unhoused; nomadic; outcast, desolate. See DISPLACEMENT.

homely, *adj.* plain; simple, homespun, rustic, unpretentious, down-to-earth. See SIMPLENESS, UGLINESS.

homemaker, *n.* housewife *or* -husband. See DOMESTICATION.

homeowner, *n.* proprietor, householder, cottager. See INHABITANT.

homesick, *adj.* nostalgic, pining [for home], melancholy. See REGRET.

homespun, *adj.* plain, unpretentious, simple. See SIMPLENESS.

homesteader, *n.* squatter, settler, colonist. See INHABITANT.

homicide, *n.* KILLING, murder, manslaughter, assassination.

homogeneity, *n.* uniformity, similarity, likeness. See SIMPLENESS, CONFORMITY, UNITY.

homosexual, *n.* gay; man-woman, woman-man, androgyne, epicene, transvestite, bisexual; lesbian; pervert, deviate; homo, queer, pansy, fairy, fruit, fag[got], swish, queen; lesbo, dyke (*all offensive*). —*adj.* gay, lesbian, homophile, homoerotic. See UNCONFORMITY.

hone, *v.t.* sharpen, whet, grind. See SHARPNESS.

honesty, *n.* candor, frankness; sincerity; trustworthiness, uprightness; truthfulness, veracity, PROBITY.

honk, *v.t.* blare, blat; blow the horn. See LOUDNESS.

honor, *n.* PROBITY, integrity; REPUTE, glory, title, distinction, award; worship, RESPECT, deference. —*v.t.* revere, reward; elevate; recognize; RESPECT; accept (as payable).

honorable, *adj.* estimable, well- *or* highly regarded (see RESPECT).

honorarium, *n.* fee; gratuity, tip; reward. See GIVING, PAYMENT.

honorary, *adj.* nominal, in name only, titular, gratuitous, emeritus. See CHEAPNESS, REPUTE.

hood, *n.* COVERING; cape, cowl, coif; *slang*, hoodlum, gangster. See CLOTHING, EVILDOER. —*v.t.* shield, cover, protect; camouflage; blindfold.

hoodoo, *n.* Jonah, bad luck, jinx; witchcraft, voodoo, obeah; SORCERY.

hoodwink, *v.t.* delude, deceive, fool, hoax; blind. See DECEPTION, BLINDNESS, CONCEALMENT.

hoof, *n.* foot, ungula, dewclaw. See SUPPORT. —*v.* See TRAVEL.

hook, *n.* CURVATURE, crook, bend; gaff. —*v.t.* catch, fasten; curve, bend; link, join. See CONNECTION, PENDENCY.

hookup, *n., informal,* connection, JUNCTION; circuit, rigging; tie-up, union, alliance, merger, cooperation, partnership. See COMMUNICATION.

hooligan, *n., slang,* loafer; thug, strong-arm man, tough, ruffian. See EVILDOER.

hoop, *n.* ring, band. See CIRCULARITY.

hoopla, *n.* EXCITEMENT; ballyhoo, hullabaloo; publicity, fame, celebrity. See PUBLICATION, REPUTE.

hooray, *interj.* See REJOICING.

hop, *n.* LEAP, spring; *informal*, dance. —*v.i.* jump, LEAP, bounce, spring, bound, dance. See AMUSEMENT.

HOPE
Confidence

Nouns—1, hope[s], DESIRE; trust, confidence, optimism, reliance, faith, BELIEF; assurance, secureness, security; reassurance. See SAFETY.

2, (*omen of hope*) good omen *or* auspices, promise; good, fair, *or* bright prospect; clear sky, *la vie en rose*; ray of hope, cheer; silver lining; Pandora's box, balm in Gilead. *Slang*, pie in the sky.

3, *(hope for the future)* assumption, presumption; anticipation, EXPECTATION; hopefulness, buoyancy, optimism, enthusiasm, aspiration.

4, *(false hopes)* castles in the air *or* in Spain, pot of gold at the end of the rainbow; Utopia, millennium, hope of Heaven; daydream, airy hopes, fool's paradise; mirage, chimera. See IMAGINATION.

5, optimist, Pollyanna; aspirant.

Verbs—**1,** hope, trust, confide, rely on, lean upon; pin one's hopes upon (see BELIEF); feel *or* rest assured, feel confident.

2, DESIRE, wish, anticipate; look on the bright side of, see the sunny side, see through rose-colored glasses, make the best of it, hope for the best; put a good face upon; keep one's spirits up; take heart, be of good cheer; flatter oneself.

3, hope against hope, cross one's fingers, clutch *or* grasp at straws, count one's chickens before they are hatched, knock on wood; make a virtue of necessity.

4, give hope, encourage, cheer, [re]assure, buoy up, embolden; be hopeful, see daylight; promise, bid fair, augur well, look up.

Adjectives—**1,** hoping, in hopes, hopeful, confident; secure, certain (see BELIEF); starry-eyed; sanguine, in good heart, buoyed up, buoyant, elated, flushed, exultant, enthusiastic; fearless, undespairing, self-reliant. *Informal,* bullish.

2, within sight of; promising, propitious; of good omen; auspicious, encouraging, cheering, bright, rosy, roseate, rose-colored.

Adverbs—at [the] best, at worst.

Phrases—a drowning man will clutch at a straw; he that lives on hope dances to an ill tune; hope springs eternal; while there's life there's hope; another day, another dollar; every cloud has a silver lining.

Quotations—Hope springs eternal in the human breast (*Alexander Pope*), What is hope? nothing but the paint on the face of Existence (*Lord Byron*), He who has never hoped can never despair (*G. B. Shaw*), Hitch your wagon to a star (*Emerson*), In this best of all possible worlds . . . all is for the best (*Voltaire*), God's in his heaven—all's right with the world! (*Robert Browning*); A woman's hopes are woven of sunbeams; a shadow annihilates them (*George Eliot*), Hope is a waking dream (*Aristotle*), Hope is a good breakfast, but it is a bad supper (*Francis Bacon*), He that lives upon hope will die fasting (*Benjamin Franklin*); Hope: he is a flatterer, a parasite (*Shakespeare*).

Antonyms, see HOPELESSNESS.

HOPELESSNESS
Lack of hope

Nouns—**1,** hopelessness, futility, IMPOSSIBILITY; despair, desperation; despondency, DEJECTION; pessimism, Weltschmerz; hope deferred, dashed hopes; vain expectation, DISAPPOINTMENT. *Slang,* fat chance. See USELESSNESS.

2, forlorn hope, ghost of a chance; bad job; slough of despond, cave of despair, dark night of the soul; catch-22. *Slang,* dead duck.

3, pessimist, Job's comforter; bird of ill omen; cynic, killjoy; legion of the lost ones.

Verbs—lose hope, lose heart, despair, give up *or* over; falter; despond, throw up one's hands, give way. *Informal,* throw in the towel *or* sponge.

Adjectives—**1,** hopeless, desperate, despairing, despondent, in despair, forlorn, inconsolable, dejected, brokenhearted; pessimistic. *Informal,* bearish.

2, out of the question, not to be thought of, futile, impracticable, impossible (see IMPOSSIBILITY); beyond hope, past mending, past recall; at the end of one's rope *or* tether, at one's wits' end; given up, incurable, beyond remedy, irreparable, irremediable; ruined, undone. *Informal,* all up.

Phrases—it's an ill wind that blows nobody any good; a drowning man will clutch at a straw.

Quotations—There is no despair so absolute as that which comes with the first moments of our first great sorrow (*George Eliot*), Human life begins on the far side of despair (*J. P. Sartre*), The optimist proclaims that we live in the best of all possible worlds; the pessimist fears this is true (*James Branch Cabell*), If we see light at the end of the tunnel, it's the light of the oncoming train (*Robert Lowell*), My God, my God, why hast thou forsaken me? (*Bible*)

Antonyms, see HOPE.

---

horde, *n.* mass, group, throng, mob, gang, crowd, pack. See MULTITUDE, ASSEMBLAGE, POPULACE.

horizon, *n.* skyline, sea line, azimuth, edge of the world; limit, circumscription, scope, range, sphere; reach; prospect, outlook. See EXPECTATION, DISTANCE.

HORIZONTAL
Parallel to the earth's surface

Nouns—1, horizontality, horizontalness, flatness; level, plane; stratum (see LAYER); horizon, azimuth; recumbency, lying down, reclination, proneness, supination, prostration; SMOOTHNESS.

2, plane surface, fascia, landscape; floor, platform, [billiard] table; terrace, esplanade, parterre, tableland, plain, plateau, prairie, ledge; plate, platter; tablet, slab; sea level.

Verbs—1, be horizontal, lie, recline, couch; lie down *or* flat; sprawl, loll.

2, lay [down *or* out]; level, flatten, smooth, even, equalize, align; steamroll[er], iron, press; prostrate, knock down, floor, fell, bowl over.

Adjectives—horizontal, level, even, plane, flush; flat [as a pancake *or* flounder], on an even keel; alluvial; calm; smooth as glass; recumbent, lying, prone, supine, couchant, prostrate.

Adverbs—horizontally, on a level, on one's back; on all fours.

Antonyms, see VERTICAL.

---

horn, *n.* antler, cornu, callus, nail; saddle horn, pummel, pommel; blower, tooter, tin horn, ram's horn, shofar, French horn, trumpet, *etc.* (see MUSIC); horn of plenty, cornucopia; powder horn. See HARDNESS, SHARPNESS, RECEPTACLE. —**horn in,** intrude, interrupt. See DISCONTINUANCE.

horny, *adj.* tough, callous[ed], sclerotic; *slang,* oversexed, lecherous, lascivious, hard up (*sl.*). See HARDNESS, DESIRE.

horrendous, *adj.* horrible, frightful. See FEAR.

horrible, *adj.* alarming, dreadful, horrifying, appalling, frightful, horrendous, hideous, abominable, deplorable, revolting, execrable, dire. See FEAR.

horrid, *adj.* horrible, foul, shocking; troublesome, vexatious; nasty, bratty; unpleasant, disagreeable. See UGLINESS, BADNESS. *Ant.,* wonderful.

horrify, *v.t.* appall, shock, awe. See FEAR.

horror, *n.* terror; loathing, disgust, revulsion; detestation, abhorrence; dread, aversion. See HATE, FEAR.

hors de combat, *Fr.,* out of the fight; disabled. See IMPOTENCE, WEARINESS.

hors d'oeuvres, *n.pl.* appetizers, canapés, antipasto, smorgasbord. See FOOD.

horse, *n.* equine; stallion, mare, colt, filly, foal, gelding; steed, mount; trotter, pacer, hackney; nag, hack, pony, charger, courser; dobbin, jennet; cavalry; sawhorse; bronco, mustang, cayuse; Arab. See ANIMAL, TRANSPORTATION, COMBATANT.

horseman, horsewoman, *n.* equestrian, rider; cavalryman, chevalier, jockey. See TRAVEL, COMBATANT.

horseplay, *n.* rowdiness, monkey business. See VULGARITY.

hose, *n.* hosing, tubing; stockings, socks; tights, leotard. See CLOTHING, PASSAGE. —*v.t.* spray, sprinkle, WATER; extinguish, put out. See CLEANNESS.

hospice, *n.* shelter, retreat, rest house. See ABODE, SAFETY.

hospitable, *adj.* neighborly; receptive. See FRIEND, SOCIALITY. *Ant.,* inhospitable, unfriendly.

hospital, *n.* sanitarium, sanatorium; clinic, pesthouse, infirmary. See REMEDY.

hospitality, *n.* SOCIALITY, cordiality, welcome, entertainment. See LIBERALITY.

host, *n.* MULTITUDE, throng, mass, horde, army, legion, array; element; innkeeper, boniface, hostess. See COMBATANT, RITE, SOCIALITY.

hostage, *n.* SECURITY, pledge, guarantee, bond.

hostel, *n.* shelter, lodgings; hotel, hostelry; hospice. See ABODE.

hostile, *adj.* antagonistic, opposed, warlike, unfriendly, belligerent. See OPPOSITION, HATE.

hot, *adj.* heated (see HEAT); peppery, biting. See TASTE, EXCITABILITY, PUNGENCY.

hotbed, *n.* source, CAUSE, generator, inciter; trouble spot, powderkeg.

hot-blooded, *adj.* excitable, impetuous (see EXCITABILITY).

hot dog, *n.* frankfurter, wiener; show-off, grandstander. See FOOD, BOASTING.

hotel, *n.* inn, hostelry. See ABODE.

hotheaded, *adj.* hot, hot-blooded, passionate; quick-tempered, peppery, irascible; willful, headstrong, rash, impetuous. See RASHNESS, IRASCIBILITY, EXCITABILITY.

hothouse, *n.* greenhouse, nursery, conservatory. See AGRICULTURE.

hound, *n.* dog, beagle, basset, bloodhound, dachshund, greyhound, foxhound, *etc.*; *slang*, cur, wretch. See ANIMAL. —*v.t.* plague, worry, pursue, harass, bait, persecute; hunt; drive, incite. See MALEVOLENCE, PURSUIT.

hourly, *adj.* frequent, continual. See FREQUENCY.

house, *n.* ABODE, residence; chamber, legislature; firm, organization, company; family, ANCESTRY, lineage. See BUSINESS. —*v.t.* shelter, protect; cover, contain, harbor. See PARTY, COVERING.

housebreaker, *n.* burgler (see STEALING).

housebroken, *adj.* tamed, domesticated, trained, disciplined. See DOMESTICATION.

household, *n.* establishment; domicile, family. See ABODE.

housekeeping, *n.* housewifery, ménage, ECONOMY.

housewife, *n.* homemaker, lady of the house, hausfrau. See DOMESTICATION.

housing, *n.* shelter, lodging; frame, COVERING. See ABODE, SUPPORT.

hovel, *n.* shanty, hut, cabin, shack, den, shed. See ABODE. *Ant.,* palace, mansion.

hover, *v.i.* fly; poise, hang, linger; waver, vacillate. See DOUBT, NEARNESS.

how, *adv.* whereby, wherewith, why, however. See MEANS, COMPENSATION.

howl, *n.* bellow, shriek, yowl, bay, keen. —*v.i.* wail, complain, ululate, bawl, yowl. See CRY, LAMENTATION, WIND.

hub, *n.* center, midpoint, axis, focus, MIDDLE; nave.

hubbub, *n.* tumult, uproar, racket, disturbance, din. See LOUDNESS.

huckster, *n.* peddler, vendor, hawker. See SALE.

huddle, *v.i.* crowd, group, gather, bunch, collect. See ASSEMBLAGE, CONVERSATION, DISORDER.

hue, *n.* COLOR, tint, shade; tone, complexion, tinge.

huff, *n.* pique, nettle, tiff; offense, umbrage, petulance, tantrum, the sulks. See IRASCIBILITY, RESENTMENT.

hug, *v.* caress, embrace, enfold, clasp; cherish; press, fit. See LOVE, NEARNESS, ENDEARMENT.

huge, *adj.* gargantuan, enormous, gigantic, immense. See SIZE.

hulk, *n.* hull, shell. See COVERING.

hulking, *adj.* bulky, massive, ponderous. See GRAVITY.

hull, *n.* husk, shell, calyx, COVERING. —*v.t.* shuck (see DIVESTMENT).

hullabaloo, *n.* uproar, EXCITEMENT; publicity, ballyhoo, CRY.

hum, *n.* buzz, murmur, drone, bumble. —*v.i.* thrum, drone, buzz, murmur, croon, burr; sing. See REPETITION.

human, *adj.* mortal; earthly; humane, civilized. —*n.* man, woman, child, girl, boy; earthling. See HUMANITY.

humane, *adj.* kind, merciful, tender, sympathetic; civilized. See BENEVOLENCE, PITY.

humanitarian, *n.* altruist, philanthropist, Samaritan, do-gooder. —*adj.* altruistic, generous, benevolent. See BENEVOLENCE.

HUMANITY
The family of man

Nouns—1, humanity, human race, human species, Homo sapiens, naked ape, humankind, ship of fools; mankind, man, womankind; human nature, mortality, flesh [and blood], feet of clay, quintessence of dust; generation; every man jack, every mother's son, lords of creation.

2, *(study of humanity)* anthropology, anthropography, ethnography, ethnology, sociology, praxeology; acculturation; biculturalism, pluralism, nativism.

3, human [being]; person, individual, creature, fellow creature, mensch, gentleperson; mortal; Type A *or* B; somebody, one; [living] soul; earthling; party; MALE, man; FEMALE, woman; Tom, Dick, and Harry; a man and a brother.

4, people; persons, folk, nation; public, society, world, [world] community, global village, general public, nationality, state, realm, commonweal[th], republic, body politic, population, POPULACE; rainbow coalition. See INHABITANT.

5, a. [Negroid, Caucasian, *or* Mongoloid] race; anthropoid, homonid, homonoid, cave man, troglodyte; Cro-Magnon man, Heidelberg man, Java man, Neanderthal man, Peking man, Piltdown man. b. African American, Afro-American, black, Negro, person of color, colored [person *or* folk]. *Slang,* brother, sister; mahogany, brown-skin, lemon, yeller; *(offensive:)* Afro-Saxon, black bean, blackamoor, blackout, blood, blue[skin], boy, buck, chalker, chocolate drop, coon, darky, dewbaby, dinge, dinkebony, Ethiopian, frosty, geechee, jig[aboo], Jim Crow, juba, jungle bunny, kaffir, negative, nigger, oreo, pickaninny, sambo, shade, shadow, shine, skillet, smoke, spade, spook, Uncle Tom, velcro head, zulu. c. Caucasian, white, haole. *Slang,* paleface; *(offensive:)* anglo, blanco, buckra, [Mister] Charlie, cracker, face, frosty, gray boy, gray, hay-eater, hinkty, honky, junk, keltch, Ku Kluxer, lilywhite, long knife, marshmallow, monkey, ofay, paddy, peckerwood, pinkie, red-neck, shitkicker, snake, the man, WASP, white meat, whitey. d. Asian, Oriental. *Slang, offensive,* slant, slope, buddhahead, gink; chink, dink, gook, paddy, riceman; jap, jeep, nip. e. Native American, [American] Indian. *Slang, offensive,* redskin, breed, buck, injun.

Adjectives—human; android, anthropoid; ethnic, racial; mortal, personal, individual; national, civil, communal, public, social; cosmopolitan, universal; ethnocentric.

Phrases—the best of men are but men at best; man is the measure of all things; black is beautiful; one half of the world does not know how the other half lives; *pro bono publico* (for the public good); every Jack has his Jill.

Quotations—The terrorist and the policeman both come from the same basket (*Joseph Conrad*), Man is the measure of all things (*Protagoras*), Nothing is more wonderful than man (*Sophocles*), What a piece of work is a man! (*Shakespeare*), O brave new world that has such people in't (*Shakespeare*), Man is only a reed, the weakest thing in nature; but he is a thinking reed (*Pascal*), The proper study of mankind is man (*Alexander Pope*), Man is the only animal that blushes. Or needs to (*Mark Twain*), Man is a useless passion (*Jean-Paul Sartre*), No man is an Island, entire of itself; every man is a piece of the Continent, a part of the main (*John Donne*), Society is based on the assumption that everyone is alike and no one is alive (*Hugh Kingsmill*), All the world's a stage, and all the men and women merely players (*Shakespeare*).

Antonyms, see ANIMAL.

---

human nature, *n.* human frailty, mortality, HUMANITY.

humble, *adj.* lowly, unassuming, modest (see HUMILITY); poor, obscure, paltry, mean. —*v.t.* abase, shame, humiliate. See MODESTY, OBSCURITY, PIETY.

humbug, *n.* deceiver, imposter, pretender; DECEPTION, hoax, fraud; charlatanry. See FALSEHOOD.

humdrum, *adj.* dull, routine, monotonous, prosaic, tiresome; ordinary, unremarkable. See WEARINESS.

humid, *adj.* moist, damp, wet, dank. See MOISTURE.

humiliate, *v.t.* shame, degrade, debase, demean; humble (see HUMILITY). See DIS-
REPUTE.

HUMILITY
Lack of pride

Nouns—1, humility, humbleness; meekness, lowliness, lowness; [self-]abasement; SUB-
MISSION, resignation; MODESTY, blush, suffusion, confusion.

2, humiliation, degradation, mortification; letdown, comedown, setdown; condescension, affability (see COURTESY). *Slang,* comeuppance. See SERVILITY.

Verbs—1, be humble, deign, vouchsafe, condescend; humble *or* demean oneself, stoop,
submit; yield the palm; lower one's tone, sober down; not have a word to say for oneself; lose face, feel shame, eat dirt, crow, *or* humble pie; blush, redden, change color;
swallow one's pride, hang one's head, come down off one's high horse, look foolish,
feel small. *Informal,* sing small, draw in one's horns.

2, humble, humiliate, abase; let, set, *or* take down; bring to one's knees, cut down to
size, put in one's place, put into the shade (see DISREPUTE); discountenance, stare out
of countenance; confuse, mortify, deflate, disgrace, crush; take down a peg *or* notch.
Slang, high-hat, take *or* knock the piss out of.

Adjectives—1, humble, lowly, meek, as meek as a lamb *or* as Moses; modest, soberminded; unoffended; submissive, servile (see SERVILITY); democratic, affable.

2, humbled, downcast, bowed down, resigned, abashed, ashamed, dashed; out of
countenance; down in the mouth; on one's knees, browbeaten. *Slang,* faced.

Adverbs—humbly, meekly, with one's tail between one's legs, with downcast eyes, on
bended knee; on all fours, cap in hand.

Quotations—Blessed are the meek: for they shall inherit the earth (*Bible*), No one can
make you feel inferior without your consent (*Eleanor Roosevelt*), And whosoever
shall exalt himself shall be abased; and he that shall humble himself shall be exalted
(*Bible*), It is very difficult for the prosperous to be humble (*Jane Austen*), The hum-
blest citizen of all the land, when clad in the armor of a righteous cause, is stronger
than all the hosts of error (*William Jennings Bryan*).

Antonyms, see PRIDE.

---

humor, *n.* disposition, mood, temper;
caprice, drollery, WIT; fun; jest; choler,
melancholy, depression, anger; facetiousness. See FEELING. —*v.t.* indulge,
favor, oblige, gratify. See PERMISSION,
TENDENCY, FLATTERY.

humorist, *n.* comedian (see WIT).

hump, *n.* hunch, lump, bulge, knob, excrescence; humpback; pile, heap; ridge,
hill. See CONVEXITY.

hunch, *n.,* *informal,* intimation, sense,
feeling; inkling, notion, SUPPOSITION,
hint, intuition, guess.

hunchbacked, *adj.* humpbacked, gibbous,
kyphotic. See CURVATURE.

hunger, *n.* DESIRE, craving; famine, hun-
griness, emptiness; appetite, voracity,
greed. —*v.i.* DESIRE, crave, yearn; famish, starve. See GLUTTONY.

hunk, *n.,* *informal,* piece, PART, chunk,
clab, lump, mass, chaw (*inf.*); *slang,*
beefcake (*inf.*). See BEAUTY.

hunt, *n.* chase, drag; PURSUIT, search.
—*v.t.* chase, stalk, follow, trace, pursue,
run, trail, hound. —*v.i.* shoot, poach,
trap, snare, hawk, ferret. See INQUIRY.

hurdle, *n.* DIFFICULTY, HINDRANCE, snag,
impediment; problem, obstacle, challenge.

hurl, *v.t.* throw, project, pitch, toss, fling,
cast, dart. See PROPULSION.

hurrah, *n.* cheer, applause (see APPROBA-
TION).

hurricane, *n.* tempest, cyclone, typhoon,
whirlwind; VIOLENCE, furor. See WIND.

hurry, *v.* press, rush, drive, force; hasten,
speed, accelerate, quicken, facilitate,
scurry. See HASTE, EXPEDITION.

hurt, *n.* damage, PAIN, ache, injury,
wound, bruise, offense; loss, harm; distress, grief. —*v.* ache, PAIN, throb; in-

jure, wound; damage, harm; offend, distress, grieve, bruise. See MALEVOLENCE, DETERIORATION, EVIL.

hurtful, *adj.* injurious, harmful. See BADNESS. *Ant.,* harmless.

hurtle, *v.i.* rush, strike. See IMPULSE.

husband, *n.* mate, spouse; benedict, bridegroom; man. See MARRIAGE. —*v.* economize (see ECONOMY, RETENTION). *Ant.,* wife.

husbandry, *n.* frugality, ECONOMY; farming, AGRICULTURE. See CONDUCT.

hush, *n.* SILENCE, quiet, stillness, calm. —*v.t.* calm, stifle, muffle; soothe, allay, still; hide, suppress. See CONCEALMENT, MODERATION.

husk, *n.* shell, integument, rind, skin. See COVERING.

husky, *adj.* strong, sturdy, powerful, robust, healthy; harsh, throaty, hoarse. See STRENGTH, DRYNESS.

hussy, *n.* wanton, trollop, wench, tramp, slut, baggage. See IMPURITY.

hustle, *v.* jostle, jolt, poke, prod; rush, bustle, hasten; *slang,* push, promote, advertise; *slang,* con, swindle, fleece, deceive, inveigle, lead on, take, sucker, sell a bill of goods; *slang,* solicit, walk the streets. See DECEPTION, HASTE.

hustler, *n., informal,* go-getter, live wire, dynamo; *slang,* gambler, swindler, sharp[er]; *slang,* prostitute. See ACTIVITY, STEALING, IMPURITY.

hut, *n.* shack, shanty, hogan, hovel, shelter, cabin. See ABODE.

hybrid, *n.* MIXTURE, crossbreed, cross, mongrel; mestizo, mulatto, quadroon, octoroon, half-caste, half-breed, Creole. —*adj.* mixed, crossbred; mongrel; half-blooded. See UNCONFORMITY.

hygienic, *adj.* cleanly, sanitary, uncontaminated; wholesome, salutary; clean. See HEALTH, CLEANNESS. *Ant.,* unhygienic, unclean.

hymn, *n.* song of praise *or* devotion; hallelujah, hosanna; canticle, sacred song, spiritual; psalm, paean; psalmody; chant, plainsong; anthem; response; evensong, vespers, matins; noël, nowell, Christmas carol. See RELIGION, MUSIC.

hype, *n.* puff, promotion, plug, blurb. See PUBLICATION.

hyperactive, *adj.* hyper (*inf.*), overactive, frenetic. See AGITATION.

hypnotic, *adj.* mesmeric, fascinating, magnetic; soporific, narcotic, quieting, lethargic; irresistible. See SORCERY.

hypocrisy, *n.* deceit, dissembling, pretense, falsity, insincerity; sanctimony, cant, Phariseeism. See FALSEHOOD, IMPIETY. *Ant.,* honesty, sincerity.

hypodermic, *n.* syringe, needle (see REMEDY).

hypothesis, *n.* condition, SUPPOSITION, theory, postulate, assumption.

hysterical, *adj.* uncontrolled, wild, emotional; convulsive; frenzied, frenetic. See EXCITABILITY.

I

ice, *n.* frost, rime; glacier; sherbet; icicle; *slang,* diamonds. —*v.* freeze, chill. See COLD.

iceberg, *n.* berg, floe, ice pack *or* sheet, glacier. See COLD.

icebox, *n.* refrigerator, Frigidaire. See COLD.

icing, *n.* frosting (see COVERING).

iconoclast, *n.* dissenter, nonconformist, radical (see UNCONFORMITY).

icy, *adj.* frosty, COLD. *Ant.,* steamy, hot.

idea, *n.* THOUGHT, concept, notion; opinion, conceit, BELIEF, impression; principle; invention, imagination.

ideal, *n.* model, paragon; idol, hero; perfect example. —*adj.* visionary; unattainable, Platonic, abstract, Utopian, perfect; impracticable. See IMAGINATION, NONEXISTENCE, PERFECTION.

idealist, *n.* visionary, dreamer; perfectionist, Utopian. See IMAGINATION, PERFECTION.

idée fixe, Fr., fixed idea; obsession. See BELIEF, MISJUDGMENT.

identify, *v.t.* recognize, distinguish, put one's finger on; associate; name. See MEMORY, IDENTITY, NOMENCLATURE.

IDENTITY
Sameness

Nouns—1, identity, identicalness, oneness, sameness; coincidence, coalescence; convertibility; EQUALITY; identification; monotony, synonymity; tautology (see REPETITION); synonym, facsimile (see COPY); alter ego (see SIMILARITY); very *or* actual thing, no other, as much. See UNITY, INTRINSIC.

2, selfness, self, individuality, SPECIALITY; very thing; no other; personality; oneself, I, ego, myself, himself, *etc.*; identity crisis.

Verbs—be identical, coincide, coalesce; treat as *or* render the same *or* identical; diagnose, identify; recognize the identity of.

Adjectives—identical; the same, selfsame, very same, one and the same; coincident, coalescent, coalescing; indistinguishable; one; synonymous, analogous, equivalent (see EQUALITY); much the same, much of a muchness; unaltered; tantamount.

Adverbs—each, apiece, one by one, in detail; identically, to scale.

Phrases—every man is the architect of his own fortune.

Quotations—This above all: to thine own self be true (*Shakespeare*), But I do nothing upon myself, and yet I am mine own executioner (*John Donne*), The men who really believe in themselves are all in lunatic asylums (*G. K. Chesterton*), Rose is a rose is a rose is a rose, is a rose (*Gertrude Stein*), My one regret in life is that I am not someone else (*Woody Allen*), All our knowledge is, ourselves to know (*Alexander Pope*), I do not know myself, and God forbid that I should (*Goethe*), I celebrate myself, and sing myself (*Walt Whitman*).

Antonyms, see DIFFERENCE.

---

ideology, *n.* beliefs, ideas, philosophy. See THOUGHT.

idiocy, *n.* imbecility, vacuity, cretinism, feeblemindedness; foolishness, vapidity, senselessness. See INSANITY, FOLLY. *Ant.,* genius.

idiom, *n.* dialect; language; idiotism, phrase. See SPEECH.

idiomatic, *adj.* colloquial, individual. See LANGUAGE, SPECIALITY.

idiosyncrasy, *n.* peculiarity, mannerism, eccentricity. See SPECIALITY.

idle, *adj.* vain, useless, futile, fruitless, pointless, aimless; out of work, unemployed, inactive, at rest; vacant, empty.

See INACTIVITY, USELESSNESS, UNIMPORTANCE. *Ant.,* active, busy.

IDOLATRY
Worship of idols

Nouns—1, idolatry, idolism; demonism, demonolatry; idol, demon, devil, fire, *or* sun worship; paganism, zoolatry, fetishism; bibliolatry; deification, apotheosis, canonization; hero worship; animism; demon worship, animal worship, *etc.* See HETERODOXY.

2, sacrifice, hecatomb, holocaust; human sacrifice, immolation, infanticide, self-immolation, suttee.

3, idolater, idolatress, idol worshiper, devil worshiper, *etc.*; fetishist, Druid.

4, idol, joss, totem, golden calf, sacred cow, graven image, fetish, avatar, lares et penates, household gods.

Verbs—idolatrize, idolize, WORSHIP (idols, pictures, relics); deify; canonize, make sacrifice.

Adjectives—idolatrous, pagan, heathen; hero-worshiping.

Quotations—The confidence and faith of the heart alone make both God and an idol (*Martin Luther*).

Antonyms, see RELIGION, PIETY.

---

idyllic, *adj.* simple, unspoiled; bucolic, arcadian. See SIMPLENESS.

if, *conj.* supposing, in case that, provided; whether. See SUPPOSITION, QUALIFICATION.

igloo, *n.* ice hut, shelter (see ABODE).

ignis fatuus, Lat., will-o'-the-wisp. See INSUBSTANTIALITY.

ignition, *n.* firing, kindling; combustion. See HEAT.

ignoble, *adj.* vile, base; knavish; detestable, low, common. See VULGARITY, POPULACE, DISREPUTE. *Ant.,* honorable.

ignominious, *adj.* shameful, disgraceful; degrading, humiliating. See DISREPUTE.

ignoramus, *n.* See IGNORANCE.

IGNORANCE
Lack of knowledge

Nouns—1, ignorance, nescience; illiteracy; darkness, blindness; incomprehension, inexperience, simplicity, simpleness, INNOCENCE; stupidity; unawareness. See FOLLY, INSANITY, SHALLOWNESS.

2, *(something not known)* unknown quantity, sealed book, terra incognita, virgin soil, unexplored ground; dark ages. *Slang,* brain fart.

3, *(limited knowledge)* smattering, glimmering; dilettantism, superficiality; bewilderment (see DOUBT); incapacity; blind spot. *Slang,* bozon. See UNSKILLFULNESS.

4, aliterate; idiot savant; innocent, ignoramus, dunce, dolt, know-nothing, dullard, moron; simpleton, oaf, lout, clod, bonehead, blockhead, halfwit, dimwit, idiot; greenhorn, novice (see BEGINNING). *Informal,* dummy. *Slang,* lowbrow, lightfoot, nitwit, dumbbell, dope, stupe, addlebrain, airball, airhead, ass, asshole, birdbrain, bohunk, boob, boor, bumpkin, churl, clyde, conehead, dickhead, dim bulb, ding-a-ling, dingbat, dingdong, dipshit, dipstick, donkey, doorknob, dork, droid, drone, dufus, dumbfuck, dumb bunny, cluck, *or* dora, dweeb, flake, galloot, gimp, gleep, goofball, goofus, grobian, harebrain, klotz, kluck, lamebrain, meatball, meathead, moke, mutant, neanderthal, nincompoop, ninny, palooka, pigmeat, putz, quimp, reject, retard, sausage, shit-for-brains, schlub, shmuck, shnook, simp, turkey, twerp, waldo, yahoo, yinyang, yokel, yo-yo, zero, zib.

Verbs—1, be ignorant, not know, have no idea, conception, *or* notion, not have the remotest idea; not know from Adam; ignore, be blind to; see through a glass darkly; not know what to make of. *Informal,* fly blind. *Slang,* know shit from shinola, know one's ass from a hole in the ground.

2, keep in the dark *or* in ignorance (see CONCEALMENT).

3, act stupid. *Slang,* jeff.

Adjectives—1, ignorant; unknowing, unaware, incognizant, unacquainted; unapprised, unwitting, witless; a stranger to; unconversant; uninformed, uncultivated, unversed, uninstructed, unlettered, none the wiser, uneducated, untaught, uninitiated, untutored, unschooled, preliterate, unguided, unenlightened, crass; behind the times; in the dark, benighted; hoodwinked, misinformed; at sea (see DOUBT). *Informal,* out of it, out of the loop. *Slang,* clueless, airbrained, birdbrained, blockheaded, boneheaded, brain-dead, empty-skulled, harebrained, thick, slow, rooty-poot.

2, shallow, superficial, green, rude, empty, half-learned, illiterate; stupid, half-witted; thick[-headed], as thick as two short planks.

Adverbs—ignorantly, unaware[s], for anything one knows; not that one knows.

Phrases—nothing so bold as a blind mare; a slice off a cut loaf isn't missed; what you don't know can't hurt you.

Quotations—Where ignorance is bliss, 'tis folly to be wise (*Thomas Gray*), Ignorance is not innocence but sin (*Robert Browning*), You know everyone is ignorant, only on different subjects (*Will Rogers*), Against stupidity, the gods themselves struggle in vain (*Friedrich von Schiller*), Lord, what fools these mortals be! (*Shakespeare*), There is no sin except stupidity (*Oscar Wilde*), It is ill-manners to silence a fool, and cruelty to let him go on (*Benjamin Franklin*), There is no darkness but ignorance (*Shakespeare*).

Antonyms, see KNOWLEDGE, INTELLIGENCE.

---

ignore, *v.t.* overlook, pass by, disregard; slight, omit, NEGLECT; snub.

ilk, *n.* kind, family, CLASS.

ill, *adj.* unwell, sick, indisposed; nauseated. See DISEASE. —*adv.* poorly, badly; wrongly, improperly; clumsily. See UNSKILLFULNESS, BADNESS. —*n.* See EVIL.

ill-advised, *adj.* unwise, imprudent. See FOLLY.

ill-bred, *adj.* unmannerly, impolite; boorish, rude, coarse, uncouth; ignoble, base. See DISCOURTESY, POPULACE. *Ant.,* well-behaved.

ILLEGALITY
Lack of legality

Nouns—1, illegality, lawlessness, unlawfulness, unconstitutionality; illegitimacy, bar sinister, bastardy; criminality; outlawry; extralegality; criminology; criminalization. See DISOBEDIENCE, UNCONFORMITY, PROHIBITION, IMPROBITY, WRONG.

2, VIOLENCE, brute force; tyranny, despotism; mob, lynch, martial, *or* drumhead law, law of the streets, kangaroo court; anarchy, nihilism, law unto itself; rebellion, coup d'état, putsch, REVOLUTION.

3, a. offense, crime [of passion, commission, *or* omission], transgression, infringement, infraction, felony, misdemeanor, malfeasance, capital crime, violation, premeditated *or* unpremeditated crime, breach, contravention, delinquency; white- *or* blue-collar crime; crime against humanity; victimless crime; technical violation *or* breach. b. abduction, adultery, assault [and battery], air piracy, skyjacking, arson, assassination, bigamy, blackmail, bootlegging, breaking and entering (see STEALING), bribery, bunko, collusion, fraud, confidence game, conspiracy, contempt of court, counterfeiting, cybercrime, defalcation, embezzlement, defamation, disorderly conduct, extortion, forgery, graft, grand *or* petit larceny, hijacking, homicide (see KILLING), jury tampering, libel, looting, malicious mischief, mayhem, mugging, mutiny, nuisance, numbers racket, obstruction of justice, peculation, perjury, pickpocketing, piracy, poaching, prostitution, racketeering, [statutory, spousal, or date] rape, reckless endangerment, resisting arrest, rumrunning, rustling, safecracking, sedition, shanghaiing, shoplifting, skyjacking, slander, smuggling, sodomy, soliciting, subornation, swindling, terrorism, treason, trespass, usury, vagrancy, vandalism. *Slang,* wilding, Jewish lightning.

4, *(organized crime)* racketeering, confidence *or* bunco game, swindling, *etc.*; underworld. See DECEPTION.

5, *(illegal civil action)* undueness, invalidity, impropriety, absence of right, usurpation, encroachment.

6, criminal, crook, perpetrator, outlaw, lawbreaker, scofflaw (see EVILDOER); illegal immigrant, undocumented person, worker, *etc.*; accessory [before, during, *or* after the fact], accomplice; first offender, hardened *or* career criminal, public enemy; juvenile delinquent, youthful offender; cyberthief; dacoit; mass murderer, serial killer; bastard, natural child. *Slang,* perp, juve.

Verbs—offend against, break, flout, contravene, *or* violate the law; take the law into one's own hands; smuggle, run, poach, encroach, usurp (see STEALING).

Adjectives—illegal, prohibited, unsanctioned, not allowed, verboten, interdit, unlawful, outlaw[ed], illegitimate, illicit, contraband, actionable, criminal, unchartered, unlicensed, unconstitutional; undue, unwarranted, unwarrantable; unauthorized, invalid; crooked, dishonest (see IMPROBITY); informal, unofficial, injudicial, extrajudicial; lawless, arbitrary, licentious; despotic, summary, irresponsible; unanswerable, unaccountable; null and void; bastard, born out of wedlock. *Slang,* hot.

Adverbs—illegally; with a high hand; in violation; outside *or* beyond the law.

Quotations—It's awful hard to get people interested in corruption unless they can get some of it (*Will Rogers*), Crime does not pay—enough (*Clayton Rawson*), All the things I really like to do are either immoral, illegal, or fattening (*Alexander Woollcott*).

Antonyms, see LEGALITY.

---

illegible, *adj.* unreadable, ill-written, scrawled; jumbled, pied. See UNINTELLIGIBILITY. *Ant.,* legible.

illegitimate, *adj.* See ILLEGALITY.

ill-equipped, *adj.* unfit, unsuited; ill-furnished. See UNSKILLFULNESS. *Ant.,* well-suited.

ill-fated, *adj.* ill-starred, doomed; unlucky. See ADVERSITY.

ill-gotten, *adj.* See IMPROBITY.

illicit, *adj.* illegal (see ILLEGALITY); clandestine, SECRET.

illiterate, *adj.* unlettered, unlearned. See IGNORANCE.

ill-mannered, *adj.* ill-bred, rude, coarse, boorish. See DISCOURTESY.

illness, *n.* sickness, DISEASE.

illogical, *adj.* unreasoned, fallacious, specious, implausible, absurd. See ERROR, ABSURDITY.

ill repute, DISREPUTE.

ill treatment, *n.* abuse, cruelty, mistreatment, maltreatment; manhandling; carelessness. See MALEVOLENCE, SEVERITY, WRONG.

illuminate, *v.t.* LIGHT, illumine; clarify, elucidate, explain; decorate, ORNAMENT. See INTERPRETATION, COLOR.

illusion, *n.* delusion, hallucination, VISION, apparition; chimera, mirage, bubble, figment [of the mind *or* IMAGINATION]; dream, fool's paradise; misconception, self-delusion, ERROR; legerdemain. See DECEPTION.

illusory, *adj.* imaginary, fancied, unreal. See DECEPTION.

illustrate, *v.t.* decorate; give as an example, exemplify; explain, clarify. See ORNAMENT, INTERPRETATION, PAINTING, REPRESENTATION.

illustrious, *adj.* renowned, eminent, distinguished, famous, celebrated. See REPUTE.

ill will, *n.* hostility, animosity, hard feelings. See RESENTMENT.

image, *n.* picture, reflection, double, counterpart, likeness; portrait, statue, figure; idea, concept. See SIMILARITY, APPEARANCE, REPRESENTATION, FIGURATIVE.

imagery, *n.* invention, fancy; tropes, metaphors, similes, analogies. See REPRESENTATION, FIGURATIVE.

IMAGINATION
Mental imagery

Nouns—1, imagination, imaginativeness, originality, invention, fancy, creativeness, inspiration; mind's eye; verve, improvisation.

2, *(image of perfection)* ideality, idealism; romanticism, utopianism, castle building; dreaming; reverie, trance, somnambulism. See NONEXISTENCE, INSUBSTANTIALITY.

3, *(types of illusions)* conception, concept, excogitation (see THOUGHT); cloudland, wonderland, dreamland, fairyland; flight of fancy, pipe dream; brainstorm, brainchild; imagery; conceit, figment [of the imagination]; myth, dream, vision, shadow, chimera, gate of horn, ivory gate; phantasm, unreality, illusion, hallucination, mirage, fantasy; whim, whimsy; vagary, rhapsody, romance, extravaganza; bugbear, nightmare; castles in the air *or* Spain; Utopia, Atlantis, Hesperides, Seven Cities of Cibola, Shangri-la, Xanadu, Laputa, Nephelococcygia; New Harmony, Oneida Community, Happy Valley, Agapemone, Arcadia, Avalon, Brook Farm, Cockaigne, El Dorado, Erewhon, [land of] Goshen; fabrication, creation, coinage; fiction, stretch of the imagination (see EXAGGERATION). *Slang,* tripping without luggage. See HEAVEN.

4, imaginer, idealist, romanticist, visionary; romancer, dreamer; enthusiast; rainbow chaser; tilter at windmills.

Verbs—imagine, fancy, conceive, visualize; idealize, realize; drum, make, *or* think up, dream (up), pull out of a hat; daydream; create, originate, cook up, devise, hatch, formulate, invent, coin, fabricate; improvise; set one's wits to work, strain one's imagination; rack, ransack, *or* cudgel one's brains; excogitate, work up, think out; give play to the imagination, indulge in reverie; conjure up a vision; suggest itself (see THOUGHT). *Informal,* see stars, see things.

Adjectives—imagined, made-up, imaginary; starry-eyed; imagining, imaginative; original, inventive, creative, fertile, fecund; fictitious; fabulous, legendary, mythical, mythological; chimerical, visionary; notional; fancy, fanciful, fantastic[al]; whimsical; fairy, fairylike; romantic, high-flown, flighty, extravagant, out of this world, enthusiastic, Utopian, quixotic; ideal, unreal, in the clouds; unsubstantial, out of thin air (see INSUBSTANTIALITY); illusory (see ERROR).

Phrases—dreams go by contraries; dreams retain the infirmities of our character; morning dreams come true.

Quotations—The quick dreams, the passion-wingèd Ministers of thought (*Percy Bysshe Shelley*), The interpretation of dreams is the royal road to a knowledge of the unconscious activities of the mind (*Sigmund Freud*), [Dreams] are the work of poor dramatists (*Max Beerbohm*), Heard melodies are sweet, but those unheard are sweeter (*John Keats*), Where there is no imagination, there is no horror (*A. Conan Doyle*), Vision is the art of seeing things invisible (*Jonathan Swift*), What the imagination seizes as beauty must be truth (*John Keats*), Imagination is more important than knowledge (*Albert Einstein*), I have a dream (*Martin Luther King*).

Antonyms, see TRUTH, WEARINESS.

---

imbalance, *n.* INEQUALITY, asymmetry, instability; difference, disparity.

imbecility, *n.* idiocy. See INSANITY.

imbue, *v.t.* saturate; tinge, COLOR, suffuse; instill, inspire. See TEACHING, MIXTURE.

IMITATION
Following of a model

Nouns—1, imitation; quotation, paraphrase, parody, travesty, burlesque; COPY, forgery (see FALSEHOOD); mockery, mimicry; simulation, pretense, sham, impersonation, imposture; REPRESENTATION; semblance; assimilation. *Informal,* take-off, Simon says, follow the leader.

2, model, prototype, pattern, mock-up; exemplar, paragon, original; type, standard; role model. See CONFORMITY.

3, imitator, mimic, cuckoo, parrot, ape, monkey, mockingbird; counterfeiter, forger. *Informal,* copycat. *Slang,* wannabe.

Verbs—imitate, COPY, catch; match, parallel; mock, take off, mimic, parrot, ape, simulate, [im]personate; act (see DRAMA); represent (see REPRESENTATION); counterfeit, parody, travesty, caricature, burlesque; feign, dissemble (see FALSEHOOD); follow, pattern after; follow suit; take after, model after; emulate, follow in one's footsteps *or* tracks.

Adjectives—imitated, imitating; mock; mimic; modeled after, molded on; quasi, pseudo; paraphrastic; literal; imitative; secondhand; imitable, unoriginal.

Adverbs—imitatively; literally, to the letter, verbatim, literatim; sic; word for word.

Phrases —imitation is the sincerest form of flattery.

Quotations—All art is but imitation of nature (*Seneca*), Life imitates art far more than art imitates life (*Oscar Wilde*), In the matter of slavish imitation, man is the monkey's superior all the time (*Mark Twain*).

Antonyms, see UNCONFORMITY, IDENTITY.

---

immaculate, *adj.* clean, spotless, unsullied; chaste, pure, virgin, untouched. See CLEANNESS, PURITY, INNOCENCE, PERFECTION. *Ant.,* dirty, soiled.

immanent, *adj.* INTRINSIC, innate, inherent; universal (as God).

immaterial, *adj.* unsubstantial, incorporeal, disembodied; impalpable, intangible; irrelevant, impertinent; trivial, unimportant, inconsequential. See INSUBSTANTIALITY, UNIMPORTANCE.

immature, *adj.* half-grown; unripe, green; undeveloped; raw, callow, young, hebetic; unready. See UNPREPAREDNESS, YOUTH, IMPERFECTION, NEWNESS. *Ant.,* mature, adult.

immeasurable, *adj.* limitless (see INFINITY). *Ant.,* finite.

immediate, *adj.* prompt, instant, PRESENT; next, first. See EARLINESS, INSTANTANEITY.

immemorial, *adj.* prehistoric, beyond recollection. See OLDNESS.

immense, *adj.* vast, great, huge, infinite. See SIZE, INFINITY.

immerse, *v.* bathe, dip, baptize, duck, plunge, submerge. See WATER, INSERTION.

immigrant, *n.* newcomer, settler, colonist. See INGRESS. *Ant.,* emigrant, emigré[e].

imminent, *adj.* impending, close at hand, about to occur; near, threatening. See EARLINESS, APPROACH, EXPECTATION, THREAT.

immobile, *adj.* immovable; motionless. See STABILITY, REPOSE.

immoderate, *adj.* intemperate, excessive, extreme, extravagant. See INTEMPERANCE.

immodest, *adj.* forward, bold, vain (see VANITY); suggestive, risqué, revealing, low-cut; unseemly, indecorous, indecent, sexy (*sl.*). See IMPURITY.

immolate, *v.t.* exterminate, sacrifice (see IDOLATRY).

immoral, *adj.* WRONG, EVIL; corrupt, lewd, bawdy; dissolute, licentious, loose, indecent, adulterous. See IMPURITY.

immortal, *adj.* everlasting; divine, godlike; deathless, imperishable. See DURABILITY, PERPETUITY. —*n.* [demi]god, great man. See REPUTE.

immovable, *adj.* fixed, unbudging; firm, steadfast, rocklike; stubborn, obdurate. See STABILITY.

immunity, *n.* EXEMPTION, FREEDOM (from); privilege.

imp, *n.* devil, DEMON; brat, YOUTH.

impact, *n.* brunt, shock, percussion, collision; contact, TOUCH, bump, slam. See IMPULSE.

impair, *v.t.* damage, weaken, wear [out], spoil, mar; vitiate. See DETERIORATION, WEAKNESS.

impale, *v.t.* transfix, pierce. See OPENING.

impart, *v.t.* share, lend; tell, disclose, divulge, reveal, communicate. See GIVING, INFORMATION.

impartial, *adj.* nonpartisan; unprejudiced, unbiased, fair; dispassionate, disinterested. See PROBITY, JUSTICE, LIBERALITY.

impasse, *n.* deadlock; blind alley, stone wall, dead end; standstill. See DIFFICULTY.

impassioned, *adj.* ardent, fervent, heated, passionate, frenzied, excited. See EXCITEMENT.

impassive, *adj.* stolid, phlegmatic, stoical, calm, undemonstrative. See INSENSIBILITY.

impatient, *adj.* eager, hurried, restive, restless; anxious, uneasy, intolerant. See EXCITABILITY, HASTE, DESIRE.

impeach, *v.t.* accuse, charge, indict, arraign; censure, cite, impute; try, court-martial. See ACCUSATION, LAWSUIT.

impeccable, *adj.* faultless, irreproachable (see PERFECTION).

impediment, *n.* HINDRANCE, obstacle.

impel, *v.t.* drive, push, urge; force, constrain; incite, compel, induce. See IMPULSE, MOTION.

impend, *v.i.* threaten, hang over. See APPROACH, THREAT, DESTINY.

impenetrable, *adj.* solid, dense; impermeable, impassable; proof; abstruse, mysterious, esoteric; incomprehensible, unfathomable. See DENSITY, UNINTELLIGIBILITY.

IMPENITENCE
Lack of remorse

Nouns—impenitence, irrepentance, recusance, remorselessness, gracelessness, incorrigibility; hardness of heart, induration, obduracy. See INSOLENCE, DEFIANCE.

Verbs—harden the heart, steel oneself, show no remorse, have no regrets.

Adjectives—impenitent, uncontrite, obdurate; hard[ened]; seared, recusant; unrepentant; relentless, remorseless, graceless, shriftless; lost, incorrigible, irreclaimable; unreclaimed, unreformed; unrepented, unatoned.

Adverbs—impenitently; without regret, remorse, *or* qualms.

Antonyms, see PENITENCE.

imperative, *adj.* peremptory; obligatory, essential, necessary, compulsory; unavoidable. —*n.* command; imperative mood (see GRAMMAR); *informal,* a must. See NECESSITY, DUTY. *Ant.,* unnecessary, avoidable.

imperceptible, *adj.* unnoticeable, indistinguishable; slight, minute, indiscernible. See INVISIBILITY, LITTLENESS.

IMPERFECTION
Lack of perfection

Nouns—1, imperfection, imperfectness, incompleteness, faultiness; deficiency; inadequacy, INSUFFICIENCY, peccancy (see BADNESS); immaturity; MEDIOCRITY, shortcoming, INFERIORITY; UGLINESS. *Slang,* lemon law. See DISORDER.

2, fault, defect, weak point; mar, blemish; flaw, snag, taint, stigma, attainder; bar sinister; WEAKNESS; half-blood; failing, foible, feet of clay; drawback, catch. *Informal,* no great shakes; fly in the ointment. *Slang,* bug, kludge.

3, deformity, disfigurement (see DISTORTION).

Verbs—1, not measure up, not pass muster, fall *or* come short, miss the mark, not come up to par.

2, impair, damage, mar (see DETERIORATION).

Adjectives—1, imperfect, deficient, defective; faulty, unsound, tainted; crude, jerry-built; out of order, out of tune; cracked, leaky; sprung; warped (see DISTORTION); lame, injured (see DETERIORATION); peccant, bad (see BADNESS); frail, weak, infirm; below par. *Informal,* not up to scratch, not much to boast of. *Slang,* on the blink; fouled (up), snafu.

2, blemished, pitted, discolored, impaired, marred, deformed.

Adverbs—imperfectly, almost, to a limited extent, rather (see LITTLENESS); pretty, only; considering, all things considered (see NEARNESS).

Phrases—no rose without a thorn.

Quotations—Thou art weighed in the balance, and art found wanting (*Bible*).

Antonyms, see PERFECTION.

---

imperialism, *n.* colonialism, expansionism; exploitation, "the White man's burden"; communism, capitalism. See AUTHORITY.

imperil, *v.t.* endanger, jeopardize, risk. See DANGER.

imperious, *adj.* lordly; domineering, dictatorial, despotic; imperative, urgent. See AUTHORITY.

imperishable, *adj.* everlasting, indestructible, permanent, undying, immortal. See PERPETUITY.

impermeable, *adj.* impervious, impenetrable. See DEFENSE.

impersonal, *adj.* removed, distant; impartial, fair, businesslike; general, abstract, unemotional. See GENERALITY, INSENSIBILITY, EXTRINSIC, JUSTICE.

impersonate, *v.t.* pose (as), imitate, take off, mimic; personify, play the impostor. See REPRESENTATION, DRAMA, IMITATION.

impertinent, *adj.* insolent, saucy, fresh, cheeky, impudent; irrelevant, inapt, inapposite. See INSOLENCE, DISAGREEMENT.

imperturbable, *adj.* See INEXCITABILITY.

impervious, *adj.* impenetrable, impermeable; safe, proof; invulnerable, immune; oblivious, indifferent, unaware. See DEFENSE, INSENSIBILITY, INDIFFERENCE.

impetuous, *adj.* impulsive, rash, headlong; rushing, unrestrainable. See EXCITABILITY, RASHNESS, VIOLENCE, FEELING, HASTE.

impetus, *n.* IMPULSE, force; stimulus, CAUSE, motive, incentive.

IMPIETY
Lack of piety

Nouns—1, impiety, impiousness; irreverence; profaneness, profanity, profanation; blasphemy, desecration, sacrilege; apostasy, iconoclasm; scoffing; hardening, fall from grace; backsliding, declension, perversion, reprobation, IRRELIGION. See WRONG.

2, [seven deadly] sins: PRIDE, covetousness, lust (see DESIRE), envy (see JEALOUSY), GLUTTONY, anger (see RESENTMENT), sloth (see INACTIVITY); fall from grace, original sin.

3, assumed piety, hypocrisy (see FALSEHOOD); pietism, cant; pious fraud; lip service; misdevotion, formalism; sanctimony, sanctimoniousness; pharisaism; sabbatism, sabbatarianism; sacerdotalism.

4, sinner, EVILDOER; scoffer, blasphemer, profaner, sacrilegist; worldling; backslider, hypocrite, apostate; Pharisee, ranter, fanatic; sons of Belial, children of darkness.

Verbs—profane, desecrate, blaspheme, revile, scoff; swear (see IMPRECATION); commit sacrilege; fall from grace, backslide.

Adjectives—impious; irreligious; desecrating, profane, irreverent, sacrilegious, blasphemous; unhallowed, unsanctified, unregenerate; hardened, perverted, reprobate; hypocritical, canting, sanctimonious, unctuous, pharisaical, overrighteous.

Adverbs—impiously; under the mask, cloak, pretense, form, *or* guise of religion.

Quotations—The sinner is at the heart of Christianity (*Charles Péguy*).

Antonyms, see PIETY.

impinge, *v.i.* encroach, intrude; collide, clash. See ILLEGALITY.

implant, *v.t.* plant, embed, fix, set in; inculcate, instill; graft, engraft. See INSERTION.

implement, *n.* tool, utensil, instrument. — *v.* equip; affect, fulfill; enact, execute. See COMPLETION, INSTRUMENTALITY.

implicate, *v.t.* involve, entangle, embroil; incriminate; connect, associate. See ACCUSATION, INCLUSION, DIFFICULTY.

implication, *n.* involvement, allusion, inference; innuendo, suggestion. See MEANING, ACCUSATION, INFORMATION.

implicit, *adj.* unspoken, tacit, understood, implied, inferred. See MEANING, LATENCY.

implode, *v.* cave in, collapse, puncture. See CONTRACTION.

implore, *v.t.* beg, beseech, entreat, plead. See REQUEST.

imply, *v.t.* hint, suggest, infer, intimate; involve, entail. See EVIDENCE, INFORMATION, LATENCY.

impolite, *adj.* rude, uncivil, ill-mannered. See DISCOURTESY. *Ant.*, polite, courteous.

import, *n.* MEANING, significance, IMPORTANCE; trend, drift, purport; importation, introduction. See INGRESS. —*v.* bring in, introduce; imply, indicate.

IMPORTANCE
Consequence

Nouns—1, importance, import, consequence, moment, prominence, consideration, mark, materialness, primacy; significance, concern; emphasis, interest; distinction, prestige, grandeur, majesty, INFLUENCE, GREATNESS, SUPERIORITY, notability, REPUTE; weight, value, GOODNESS; usefulness (see UTILITY). See MEANING, PRECEDENCE.
2, (*seriousness*) gravity, seriousness, solemnity; no joke, no laughing matter; pressure, urgency, stress; matter of life and death; exigency.
3, (*important events*) memorabilia, notabilia, great doings; red-letter day, milestone, turning point. *Informal*, the big time.
4, (*important items*) essence, substance, gist; main chance, be-all and end-all, cardinal point; buzzword; sum and substance, sine qua non; breath of life; cream, salt, core, kernel, heart, nucleus; key, keynote, keystone, cornerstone; trump [card]; salient points; magnet, hot button, *or* pocketbook issue; essentials, fundamentals. *Informal*, where it's at, name of the game, the long and the short of it. See INTRINSIC.
5, personage, dignitary, figure, prima donna, chief, mogul, magnate, player, somebody. *Informal*, big fish in a small pond. *Slang*, big gun, shot, cheese, wheel, *or* daddy, VIP, bigwig, big enchilada, mugwump.
6, pointer, highlighter.

Verbs—1, import, signify, matter, boot, be somebody, carry weight; cut a figure (see REPUTE); overshadow (see SUPERIORITY); count for something, make history.
2, attach importance to, value, care for; set store by; mark (see INDICATION); underline; put in italics *or* capitals, capitalize, italicize; accentuate, emphasize, feature, point up, stress, lay stress on; get *or* come to the point, get down to brass tacks *or* to cases; make a fuss *or* stir about, make much *or* something of, play up; hit the high spots; hit the bull's-eye.

Adjectives—1, important; of importance, momentous, material, of consequence, consequential, crucial; not to be overlooked, not to be despised, not to be sneezed at; egregious; weighty, influential, big-time; of note (see REPUTE); prominent, salient, signal; memorable, remarkable; worthy of remark *or* notice; never to be forgotten; eventful, significant, telling, trenchant, emphatic, pregnant. *Informal*, earthshaking, bankable.
2, grave, serious, heavy; urgent, pressing, critical, instant, solemn, fateful, fatal. *Informal*, not to be sneezed at.
3, essential, vital, all-absorbing; cardinal, chief, main, prime, primary, principal, capital, foremost, overriding; in the front rank, first-rate; superior (see SUPERIORITY); considerable (see GREATNESS); marked. See PRIORITY.

Adverbs—importantly, materially, in the main, mainly, first and last *or* foremost. *Informal*, joking aside.

Quotations—It has long been an axiom of mine that the little things are infinitely the most important (*Conan Doyle*), The execution of the laws is more important than the making of them (*Thomas Jefferson*), Half of the harm that is done in this world is due to people who want to feel important (*T. S. Eliot*).

Antonyms, see UNIMPORTANCE.

---

importune, *v.* beset, solicit; beg, plead. See REQUEST.

impose, *v.t.* burden (with), inflict; force (upon); levy, tax; delude, take advantage (of), palm off, foist; obtrude. See DECEPTION, COMPULSION.

imposing, *adj.* dignified, awe-inspiring; impressive; grand, stately, commanding. See REPUTE.

imposition, *n.* nuisance, bother, inconvenience, intrusion, infringement, invasion of privacy. See DECEPTION, COMMAND, WRONG.

IMPOSSIBILITY
Lack of possibility

Nouns—1, impossibility, what can never be; HOPELESSNESS; impracticability, infeasibility, insuperability. *Informal*, no go. *Slang*, fat chance, Chinaman's chance, snowball's chance in hell.

2, impossible task, the impossible, what cannot be.

Verbs—have no chance; square the circle, skin a flint, make a silk purse out of a sow's ear, make bricks without straw, build castles in the air; bite off more than one can chew; be in two places at once; ask *or* cry for the moon, promise *or* give the moon. *Slang*, milk a duck.

Adjectives—impossible; absurd, contrary to reason (see ABSURDITY); unreasonable, incredible (see DOUBT); visionary, inconceivable (see IMPROBABILITY); unimaginable, unthinkable, impracticable, impractical, unachievable, unfeasible, unworkable, insuperable, insurmountable; unattainable, unobtainable, out of reach; out of the question; desperate, hopeless; out of print; inaccessible, impassable, impervious, unnavigable, inextricable, ineluctable, *etc. Slang*, in a pig's eye.

Adverbs—impossibly, *etc.*; when hell freezes over, when pigs fly.

Phrases—pigs may fly, but they are very unlikely birds; tell it to the marines.

Quotations—Probable impossibilities are to be preferred to improbable possibilities (*Aristotle*), The difficult we do immediately. The impossible takes a little longer (*U.S. Armed Forces*), Why, sometimes I've believed as many as six impossible things before breakfast (*Lewis Carroll*), If an elderly but distinguished scientist says that something is possible he is almost certainly right, but if he says that it is impossible he is very probably wrong (*Arthur C. Clarke*), To dream the impossible dream, to reach the unreachable star! (*Joe Darion*).

Antonyms, see POSSIBILITY.

---

impostor, *n.* fake[r]; masquerader, pretender, fraud. See DECEPTION.

imposture, *n.* masquerade, pretense; fraud, DECEPTION; impersonation.

IMPOTENCE
Lack of strength

Nouns—1, impotence, inability, disability; disablement, impuissance, incapacity, incapability; inaptness, ineptitude, inefficiency, incompetence; disqualification. See WEAKNESS, UNSKILLFULNESS, INSUFFICIENCY.

2, *(result of impotence)* inefficacy (see USELESSNESS); paralysis; helplessness, prostration, exhaustion, enervation.

3, *(rendering impotent)* emasculation, castration, bilateral orchidectomy.

4, *(impotent person or thing)* eunuch, castrato; cripple; blank cartridge, basket case, flash in the pan, dummy, dud, wimp. *Slang,* cold biscuit, flat tire, iceberg, ice wagon, schmendrick, third sex, abelard, androgyne, capon, gelding, spado, wether.

Verbs—1, collapse, faint, swoon, drop. See DETERIORATION.

2, unman, unnerve, enervate; emasculate, castrate, geld; disable, disarm, incapacitate, disqualify, unfit, invalidate; deaden, cramp, exhaust, weaken, debilitate; demoralize, take the wind out of one's sails; muzzle, cripple, maim, lame, hamstring, hogtie, paralyze, pull *or* draw the teeth of; break the back of; unhinge, unfit. *Slang,* fix, arrange, capsize, change, cut, dehorn, prune, spade, trim, doctor, knacker, mutilate, unsex. See HINDRANCE.

3, be impotent. *Slang,* fire blanks.

Adjectives—1, impotent, powerless, unable, incapable, incompetent; inefficient, ineffective, ineffectual; inept, unfit[ted]; unqualified, disqualified, unendowed; crippled, halt, disabled, paralytic, paralyzed; emasculate[d], sexless, unsexed, fixed; on one's back; done up, dead beat, exhausted, shattered, demoralized; without a leg to stand on, hors de combat, out of commission.

2, harmless, helpless, unarmed; defenseless, unfortified; vincible, pregnable; null and void, nugatory, inoperative, good-for-nothing.

Quotations—It is better to be violent, if there is violence in our hearts, than to put on the cloak of non-violence to cover impotence (*Mahatma Gandhi*), Justice without force is impotent; force without justice is tyranny (*Pascal*), Impotence and sodomy are socially OK, but birth control is flagrantly middle-class (*Evelyn Waugh*).

Antonyms, see POWER.

---

impound, *v.t.* jail, restrain; confine, corral, encage; seize, take, confiscate, expropriate, appropriate. See ENCLOSURE, RESTRAINT, ACQUISITION.

impoverish, *v.t.* pauperize; exhaust, drain; reduce, deplete, rob; weaken. See POVERTY, INSUFFICIENCY, WASTE. *Ant.,* enrich.

impracticable, *adj.* unworkable, inexpedient, not feasible; idealistic, visionary; unrealistic. See DIFFICULTY, IMPOSSIBILITY, INEXPEDIENCE. *Ant.,* practicable, doable.

impractical, *adj.* impracticable; unwise, imprudent, unrealistic; unsound, illogical; harebrained. See IMAGINATION, IMPOSSIBILITY. *Ant.,* practical.

IMPRECATION
Swearing

Nouns—1, imprecation, malediction, malison (*archaic*), curse, denunciation, execration; anathema, ban, fulmination; calumny, calumniation, contumely, invective, diatribe, jeremiad, tirade, vituperation, disparagement, obloquy; abuse, billingsgate, sauce; cursing, profanity, swearing, oath, expletive, barnyard epithet; the finger; THREAT. See DETRACTION, CONDEMNATION, DISAPPROBATION.

2, swearer, curser. *Slang,* garbage mouth, black mouth, foul mouth, potty mouth, latrine lips.

Verbs—imprecate, curse, damn, swear (at); execrate, beshrew, scold; anathematize; vilify, denounce; fulminate, thunder against; threaten; defame. *Slang,* flip *or* throw the bird.

Adjectives—1, imprecatory, denunciatory, abusive, cursing, cursed, accursed.

2, damned, deuced, dratted, all-fired, blamed, blasted, bleeding, bloody, confounded, cotton-picking. *Slang,* frigging.

Interjections—**a.** woe to! woe betide! damn! confound! blast! curse! devil take! hang! out with! a plague *or* pox upon! out upon! **b.** damnation! tarnation! thunderation! by cracky! by jove! dad-blamed! dadburn it! dang! darn! dash! doggone! drat! durn! gol blame! gol darn! what the dickens! what the Sam Hill! *Slang,* dammit! damn! goddamn! damn you! damn your eyes! goddamnit! what the hell! **c.** sheesh! crikey!

criminy! *Slang,* bejesus! good Lord! Christ! Christmas! for Christ's sake! jeez Louise! Jesus [Christ]! Jesus H. Christ! holy jumping mother of Jesus! **d.** shoot! *Slang,* shit! merde! crap[ola]! holy shit! **e.** lawsy! *Slang,* God forbid! good God! **f.** sacre bleu! mon dieu! blimey! hell's bells! holy gosh! mother of God! blow me down! caramba! gadzooks! gee-whittakers! gee-whiz! holy cats! holy moly! I'll be hanged! Jiminy Crickets! Judas Priest! jumping Jehoshaphat! like fun! strike me dead! upon my word! *Slang,* fuckin'-A, sumbitch!, son of a bitch! motherfucker! my ass! fuck you! screw you! penis breath!

Quotations—A plague on both your houses! (*Shakespeare*).

Antonyms, see APPROBATION, WORSHIP.

---

impregnable, *adj.* invincible. See STRENGTH. *Ant.,* pregnable, vulnerable.

impregnate, *v.t.* fertilize, fecundate, pollinate, inseminate, get in trouble (*inf.*), get in a family way (*inf.*), knock up (*sl.*); infuse, soak, permeate, saturate. See REPRODUCTION, INSERTION, MIXTURE.

impresario, *n.* promoter, entrepreneur. See UNDERTAKING, DRAMA.

impress, *v.t.* stamp, mark, print, imprint; dint, dent; inspire, overawe; interest; strike; draft, compel (service), shanghai. See COMPULSION, PRINTING.

impression, *n.* PRINTING, ENGRAVING, mark, stamp; dent; opinion, FEELING; inkling, suspicion. See BELIEF, SENSIBILITY.

impressionable, *adj.* susceptible, suggestible, malleable. See OBEDIENCE.

impressive, *adj.* imposing, awesome, majestic, stately, moving, stirring, weighty, large. See FEELING, OSTENTATION.

imprint, *n.* impress, stamp, impression; cachet, seal, symbol, device; result, effect. —*v.t.* impress, stamp, fix; inscribe, seal; make one's mark on. See INDICATION, PRINTING.

imprison, *v.t.* lock up, confine, detain; hold, jail, incarcerate. See CIRCUMSCRIPTION, RESTRAINT.

IMPROBABILITY
Lack of likelihood

Nouns—improbability, unlikelihood, unlikeliness; small *or* long chance, Chinaman's chance, ghost of a chance; long odds, long shot; incredibility (see DOUBT). See HOPELESSNESS, IMPOSSIBILITY.

Verbs—be improbable *or* unlikely, be a strain on the imagination.

Adjectives—improbable, unlikely, contrary to all reasonable expectation, doubtful, far-fetched; rare, infrequent (see RARITY); unheard-of, implausible, questionable, fishy. *Slang,* in a pig's eye.

Interjections—don't count on it! don't hold your breath! don't bet on it! you should live so long!

Quotations—Faith may be defined briefly as an illogical belief in the occurrence of the improbable (*H. L. Mencken*), When you have eliminated the impossible, whatever remains, *however improbable,* must be the truth (*A. Conan Doyle*), The essence of life is statistical improbability on a colossal scale (*Richard Dawkins*).

Antonyms, see CHANCE, PROBABILITY.

IMPROBITY
Lack of probity

Nouns—**1,** improbity; dishonesty, dishonor; disgrace, DISREPUTE; fraud, DECEPTION; lying, FALSEHOOD; bad faith, infidelity, inconstancy, faithlessness, Judas kiss, betrayal; breach of promise, trust, *or* faith; renegation, renegadism, disloyalty, [high] treason; Watergate; apostasy (see CHANGEABLENESS). *Slang,* Irangate. See GUILT, ILLEGALITY, WRONG.

2, (*dishonest actions*) villainy, baseness, abjection, debasement, [moral] turpitude, laxity; perfidy, perfidiousness, treachery, duplicity, double-dealing; knavery, roguery, rascality, foul play; trickery, venality; collaboration; nepotism, corruption, simony, barratry, graft, jobbery, malfeasance; night of the long knives. *Slang,* dirty pool.

3, vice, depravity, looseness, profligacy. See IMPURITY.

4, knave (see EVILDOER); double-crosser, betrayer, informer; collaborator, Quisling; fair-weather friend. *Informal,* two-timer. *Slang,* rat, [rat]fink. See INFORMATION.

Verbs—**1,** play false; forswear, break one's word, faith, *or* promise, go back on one's word; betray, double-cross, stab in the back, sell out, sell down the river, sell the pass, stab in the back; cuckold, jilt, cheat on, carry on; lie (see FALSEHOOD); live by one's wits; misrepresent; hit below the belt. *Informal,* two-time. *Slang,* rat (on), fink (on), blow the whistle (on), yard (on), chippy (on).

2, sin (see BADNESS).

Adjectives—**1,** dishonest, dishonorable, unscrupulous, fly-by-night; fraudulent (see DECEPTION); knavish, disgraceful, unconscionable; disreputable (see DISREPUTE); wicked, sinful, vicious, criminal.

2, false-hearted, two-faced; crooked, insidious, Machiavellian, dark, slippery; perfidious, treacherous, underhand[ed], perjured; infamous, arrant, foul, base, abject, vile, ignominious, blackguard; corrupt, venal; recreant, inglorious, discreditable, improper; faithless, false, unfaithful, disloyal; treacherous, renegade; untrustworthy, unreliable, undependable, trustless; lost to shame, dead to honor.

Adverbs—dishonestly, like a thief in the night, underhandedly, by fair means or foul, by hook or crook.

Phrases—there is nothing constant but inconstancy; fear the Greeks bearing gifts.

Quotations—Faith unfaithful kept him falsely true (*Lord Tennyson*), We have to distrust each other. It's our only defense against betrayal (*Tennessee Williams*), This was the most unkindest cut of all (*Shakespeare*), Each man kills the thing he loves (*Oscar Wilde*).

Antonyms, see PROBITY.

---

impromptu, *adj.* extemporaneous. See UNPREPAREDNESS. *Ant.,* studied, prepared.

improper, *adj.* indecent, bawdy, lewd, risqué; WRONG, inapt, unsuitable, unfitting, incorrect, out of place, misplaced.

See INEXPEDIENCE, DISAGREEMENT. *Ant.,* proper, appropriate.

impropriety, *n.* misbehavior, VULGARITY, immodesty; bad manners, indecorum; unfitness, unsuitability. See INEXPEDIENCE, DISAGREEMENT, DISCOURTESY.

IMPROVEMENT
Making better

Nouns—**1,** improvement, uplift; melioration, amelioration, betterment, uptick; mend, amendment, emendation; advancement, advance, development, progress, telesis, quantum jump *or* leap, PROGRESSION, ascent; promotion, preferment; elevation, INCREASE; evolution; upward mobility, gentrification, green revolution, urban renewal; cultivation, civilization, culture; crusade, crusading; perestroika.

2, reform, reformation, revision; correction, refinement, enhancement; PERFECTION, purification (see CLEANNESS); repair, RESTORATION; recovery. See RELIEF.

3, reformer, radical, progressive, crusader; new man. *Informal,* do-gooder, new-collar.

Verbs—**1,** improve; better, mend, amend; turn to good account, profit by, reap the benefit of; make good use of, make capital of; make the best of; evolve, develop, advance, ascend, INCREASE; fructify, ripen, mature; come along, gain ground, pick up, come about, rally, take a turn for the better; turn over a new leaf, turn the corner, break new ground; come a long way, recover; gentrify. *Informal,* look up, snap out of it.

2, meliorate, ameliorate; palliate, mitigate; turn the tide; correct, rectify, retrofit; enrich, mellow, fatten; promote, prefer; cultivate, advance, forward, enhance, refine (upon); update; bring forward, bring on; foster (see AID); invigorate, strengthen.

3, touch up, brush up, refurbish, renovate, polish, make the most of, set off to advantage; prune; repair, restore (see RESTORATION); put in order.

4, revise, edit, correct; debug; straighten out; doctor, purify; relieve, refresh, infuse new blood *or* life into; reform, remodel, retrofit, reorganize.

Adjectives—improving, on the mend; improved; progressive; better [off], better for; reformatory, emendatory; reparatory, restorative, remedial; corrigible, improvable.

Adverbs—for the better. *Informal,* over the hump, out of the woods.

Phrases—April showers bring May flowers.

Quotations—Change is certain. Progress is not (*E. H. Carr*), All progress is precarious, and the solution of one problem brings us face-to-face with another problem (*Martin Luther King*), And step by step, since time began, I see the steady gain of man (*J. G. Whittier*), We have made progress in everything, yet nothing has changed (*Derrick Bell*), Is it progress if a cannibal uses knife and fork? (*Stanislaw Lec*).

Antonyms, see DETERIORATION.

---

improvise, *v.* invent, extemporize. See IMAGINATION, UNPREPAREDNESS.

imprudent, *adj.* careless, incautious, rash; unwise, injudicious, ill-advised; foolish. See RASHNESS, FOLLY, UNPREPAREDNESS.

impudence, *n.* INSOLENCE, gall, cheek, effrontery; boldness, DISCOURTESY.

impulse, *n.* thrust, push (see IMPULSE); impromptu, improvisation (see UNPREPAREDNESS).

IMPULSE
Forward thrust

Nouns—**1,** impulse, impulsion, impetus, momentum; push, thrust, shove, jog, nudge, prod, jolt, brunt, throw; explosion (see VIOLENCE); PROPULSION; percussion, concussion, collision, pile-up, clash, encounter, shock, crash, bump; coup; impact; charge, ATTACK; beating, PUNISHMENT.

2, blow, dint, stroke, clap, knock, tap, rap, slap, smack, pat, wallop, dab; fillip; slam, bang; hit, whack, clout, cuff, clip, punch, pasting, bump, thump, pelt, kick; cut, thrust, lunge. *Informal,* bat, swat, lick. *Slang,* sock, the old one-two, knuckle sandwich.

3, hammer, sledgehammer, maul, mallet, flail; ram, battering ram, pile driver, punch, bat; cudgel, weapon; ax.

Verbs—**1,** give impetus; impel, push; start, set going; drive, urge; thrust, prod; elbow, shoulder, jostle, hustle, hurtle, shove, jar, jolt; bump, run, *or* plow into; impinge; flounce. *Slang,* kick-start, jump-start.

2, strike, knock, hit, pelt, jab, clip, lambaste, larrup, wallop, tap, rap, slap, swipe, pat, thump, stub, beat, bang, slam, dash; sock, punch, whack; hit *or* strike hard; batter; pelt, buffet, bruise, belabor, rough up; fetch one a blow, throw a punch; poke at, lunge; kick, butt; make a pass at, take a punch, poke, *or* sock at, strike at, ATTACK; whip (see PUNISHMENT). *Informal,* swat, larrup, beat the [living] daylights out of. *Slang,* knock galley-west, knock off one's block, clobber, ding, hang one on, waste, deck, paste.

3, collide; fall *or* run foul of; throw (see PROPULSION).

Adjectives—impelling, impellent; dynamic, impelled.

Adverbs—impulsively, explosively, *etc.*

Quotations—Distrust all in whom the impulse to punish is powerful (*Friedrich Nietzsche*), A first impulse was never a crime (*Corneille*), May I ask whether these pleasing attentions proceed from the impulse of the moment, or are the result of previous study? (*Jane Austen*).

Antonyms, see THOUGHT, RECOIL.

impulsive, *adj.* impulsive, impromptu, off-hand, natural, unguarded; spontaneous, voluntary. See WILL, UNPREPAREDNESS.

impunity, *n.* EXEMPTION, immunity.

impure, *adj.* obscene, unchaste (see IMPURITY); tainted, unclean, polluted (see UNCLEANNESS).

IMPURITY
Moral uncleanness

Nouns—1, impurity, immodesty, grossness, indelicacy, indecency; pornography, curiosa, obscenity, ribaldry, smut, bawdy, filth, double entendre; coprophilia; pornographic movie, blue film. *Slang,* tits and ass, T&A. See SEX.

2, *(looseness of morals)* laxity, looseness of morals, turpitude, depravity, pollution, profligacy, shame, vice. *Slang,* zipper morals. See BADNESS.

3, *(carnal desire)* concupiscence, lust, carnality, flesh, salacity; pruriency, lechery, lasciviousness, lewdness, lubricity; incontinence, unchastity; debauchery, license, immorality, libertinism, fornication, liaison; wenching, venery, dissipation; incest; perversion; sodomy, pederasty; sadism, masochism; seduction, defloration, defilement, abuse, violation, [acquaintance, date, *etc.*] rape, [criminal] assault; harlotry, whoredom, concubinage, prostitution, fast life, the trade; cuckoldry, adultery, infidelity, conjugal infidelity, criminal conversation; blue *or* dirty movie. *Informal,* extracurricular activities.

4, brothel, bagnio, bawdyhouse, whorehouse, seraglio, house of ill fame, repute, *or* pleasure, disorderly house, bordello, rap club, gentlemen's club; massage parlor; madam, housekeeper, house mother; red-light district, combat zone; escort service. *Slang,* call-house *or* -joint, catflat, cathouse, flesh factory *or* market, heifer barn, ice palace, jag house, kip shop, meat market, monkey-house, parlor house, chicken ranch, band[box], birdcage, cab-joint, doss house, ornery-house; abbess, fleshbroker.

5, **a.** libertine, voluptuary, rake, roué, playboy, debauchee, profligate; gigolo; lecher, satyr; pederast, dirty old man; pimp, pander, Don Juan, Casanova; hustler; male prostitute. *Informal,* rip, masher. *Slang,* cocksman, cockhound, cocksmith, easy lay, easy rider, gay dog, ginch, jazz baby, jinker, piece of snatch *or* trade, sack artist. **b.** courtesan, call girl, doxy, drab, prostitute, working girl, strumpet, harlot, painted lady, bawd, procuress, whore, scarlet woman, wanton, fille de joie, grisette, putain, streetwalker, lady of the evening, daughter of joy, fallen woman, fancy woman, fast woman, concubine, demimondaine, camp follower; tart, forgotten woman, wench, trollop, trull, doxy, bat, beetle, jade, light o' love; nymphomaniac. *Slang,* big twenty, broad-jumper, canvasback, dirty leg, charity dame, moll, *or* girl, chippy, company girl, sporting girl, cracked pitcher, skirt, street sister, zook, blister, bludget, [flat] floozy, hustler, girl at ease, pavement princess, glue neck, jane, quiff, bottom woman, free rise, pro, tenderloin madam, dress for sale, crack, curbstone sailor, nautchbroad, bachelor's wife, pickup, hooker, B-girl, V-girl, barber's chair; dick peddler. **c.** exhibitionist, flasher. *Slang,* dangler, troller. **d.** bastard, baby of love, love child. *Slang,* bell-bastard, incident, left-handed son.

6, adulteration (see DETERIORATION).

Verbs—1, debauch, defile, deflower, rape, ravish, ruin, seduce; prostitute, pander, cater, sell oneself, walk the streets; abuse, violate; adulterate (see DETERIORATION). *Slang,* cop a cherry, dock, crack a pitcher, devirginate, ease.

2, commit adultery, cuckold. *Slang,* bad-time; sleep around, carry on, womanize, chippy around, screw around, turn a trick.

Adjectives—1, impure, immoral, amoral; unclean; immodest, shameless; indecorous, indelicate, indecent, hardcore; loose, coarse, gross, broad, earthy; smutty, foul, ribald, obscene, bawdy, erotic, pornographic, risqué, nasty, rude, filthy, blue, purple; concupiscent, prurient, lustful; lewd, lascivious, lecherous, libidinous, ruttish, salacious; unfaithful, adulterous; incestuous; unchaste, incontinent; light, wanton, licentious, rakish, debauched, dissipated, dissolute, fast; promiscuous, loose, meretricious, of easy virtue, on the streets; differently pleasured; gay. *Informal,* off-color, X-rated. *Slang,* sexy, sultry, raunchy, barnyard.

2, vicious, immoral, dissolute, profligate, sinful, iniquitous.

3, bastard, of unknown birth.

Quotations—Pornography is the attempt to insult sex, to do dirt on it (*D. H. Lawrence*), It is the function of vice to keep virtue within reasonable bounds (*Samuel Butler*), Pleasure's a sin, and sometimes sin's a pleasure (*Lord Byron*), When the passions become masters, they are vices (*Pascal*), It's a bawdy planet (*Shakespeare*), We are punished by our sins, not for them (*Elbert Hubbard*).

Antonyms, see PURITY.

---

impute, *v.t.* ascribe, attribute. See ACCUSATION, ATTRIBUTION, DISREPUTE.

in, *n.* entrée, access. See ENTRANCE. —*adj.* fashionable, in favor; involved. See FASHION, ACCOMPANIMENT. —*adv.* inward(s); accepted, elected. See INGRESS, CHOICE. *Ant.,* out.

inability, *n.* IMPOTENCE, incapacity, powerlessness; UNSKILLFULNESS, incompetence, inefficiency. *Ant.,* ability, knack.

in absentia, *Lat.,* in or during [one's] ABSENCE.

inaccessible, *adj.* unapproachable, incommunicado; sheltered, guarded; restricted, taboo, sacrosanct; aloof, cold, cool, distant, withdrawn. See DISTANCE, PROHIBITION, SECLUSION. *Ant.,* accessible.

inaccurate, *adj.* erroneous, fallacious, incorrect, WRONG; mistaken; inexact, unprecise; misleading. See ERROR. *Ant.,* accurate.

INACTIVITY
Lack of action

Nouns—1, inactivity; inaction; inertness; lull, cessation (see REPOSE); idleness, sloth, laziness, indolence, vegetation; unemployment, dilatoriness, dawdling; malingering; passiveness, passivity, dormancy; stagnation; procrastination; time on one's hands; laissez-faire, noninterference; *dolce far niente,* lotusland. See INSENSIBILITY, INDIFFERENCE, AVOIDANCE.

2, *(slowness of activity)* dullness, languor; sluggishness, SLOWNESS, delay (see LATENESS); torpor, torpidity, torpescence.

3, *(inactive person)* idler, drone, do-little; dummy, silent partner; fifth wheel; lounger, loafer; lubber, slowpoke (see SLOWNESS); opium eater, lotus eater; slug, laggard, sluggard, ne'er-do-well, do-nothing, faineant; clock watcher, good-for-nothing; lumpenproletariat. *Slang,* bum, couch potato, armchair athlete.

4, *(cessation of activity)* halt, pause, standstill, full stop; stalemate, impasse, block, check, checkmate; red light.

Verbs—1, let the grass grow under one's feet; take one's time, dawdle, lag, hang back, slouch, loll, lounge, loaf, laze, loiter, hang around; sleep at one's post or at the switch, flag, languish. *Slang,* hang out.

2, vegetate, lie fallow; waste, consume, kill, or lose time; twiddle one's thumbs; not lift a finger or hand; idle, trifle, fritter, or fool away the time, sit by, sit back, sit on one's hands, not move a muscle, lie down on the job; mark time, piddle, potter, putter, dabble, fiddle-faddle, dally, shilly-shally, dilly-dally; ride at anchor, rest on one's oars, rest on one's laurels; hang fire, postpone. *Informal,* cool one's heels. *Slang,* goof off, dick or fuck around, fart off, frig, lally-gag, pouch out.

Adjectives—1, inactive; motionless, quiescent, stationary; unoccupied, out of circulation, idle, off-duty, at leisure, on the bench, unemployed; indolent, shiftless, lazy, slothful, idle, remiss, slack, torpid, sluggish, languid, supine, heavy, dull, leaden, lumpish; inert, inanimate; listless; dilatory, laggard; lagging, slow; rusty, flagging, lackadaisical, pottering, irresolute; lumpen. *Slang,* outplaced, involuntarily at leisure, between projects.

2, torpid, lethargic, heavy, napping; tranquilizing, soporific, hypnotic; balmy, dreamy; sedative. *Slang,* dopey; out of this world.

Phrases—the devil finds work for idle hands to do; the busiest men have the most leisure.

Quotations—Iron rusts from disuse . . . even so does inaction sap the vigor of the mind (*Leonardo da Vinci*), They also serve who only stand and wait (*Milton*), Idleness is the only refuge of weak minds (*Lord Chesterfield*), It is impossible to enjoy idling thoroughly unless one has plenty of work to do (*Jerome K. Jerome*).

Antonyms, see ACTIVITY, ACTION.

---

inadequate, *adj.* scant, wanting, short, below par; incomplete, partial, deficient, lacking. See INSUFFICIENCY. *Ant.,* adequate.

inadvertent, *adj.* unintentional, adventitious, accidental, CHANCE; heedless, careless, regardless, thoughtless. See INATTENTION.

inadvisable, *adj.* inexpedient, not recommended; impracticable; ill-advised, unwise, imprudent, risky. See INEXPEDIENCE.

inalienable, *adj.* absolute, inviolable, inherent. See INTRINSIC.

inane, *adj.* pointless, senseless, silly; empty, vacuous; idiotic. See UNMEANINGNESS, FOLLY.

inanimate, *adj.* inorganic; lifeless, insentient, unconscious, dead; listless, inactive, inert, supine, dormant, comatose. See DEATH, INACTIVITY.

inappropriate, *adj.* unbecoming, unsuitable, WRONG, improper; inapt, unfitting, inadvisable. See DISAGREEMENT.

inarticulate, *adj.* voiceless, speechless, mute, stammering; unexpressed, unspoken, indistinct; unjointed. See SILENCE, DISJUNCTION, STAMMERING, UNINTELLIGIBILITY.

INATTENTION
Lack of attention

Nouns—1, inattention, inattentiveness; abstraction, absence of mind, preoccupation, distraction; reverie, woolgathering, daydreaming, brown study, detachment; inconsiderateness, oversight; inadvertence, inadvertency; nonobservance, disregard; thoughtlessness, heedlessness (see NEGLECT); insouciance, INDIFFERENCE; RASHNESS. *Slang,* nobody home. See UNPREPAREDNESS, DISRESPECT, CONTEMPT, FOLLY.

2, daydreamer, escapist. *Slang,* space cadet.

Verbs—1, pay no attention, disregard, overlook; pass by, NEGLECT; ignore, think little of, wink at; close *or* shut one's eyes to; disdain, dismiss from one's thoughts *or* mind, reckon without; think no more of; set *or* put aside; turn a deaf ear *or* blind eye to, turn one's back upon, shrug off *or* away, laugh off; set aside; take no notice of, not give one the time of day. *Dialect,* pay no mind. *Slang,* space, zone out, let well [enough] alone.

2, abstract oneself, dream, daydream, woolgather; play possum; moon.

3, escape notice *or* attention; go in one ear and out the other; fall on deaf ears.

4, divert, distract, turn one's head; disconcert, discompose; confuse, perplex, bewilder, fluster, muddle, dazzle; put off. *Informal,* fuddle, rattle, faze. *Slang,* ball up.

Adjectives—1, inattentive; unobservant, unmindful, unheeding, undiscerning; inadvertent, regardless, listless, indifferent; blind, deaf; cursory; inconsiderate, offhand, thoughtless; heedless, careless, insensate.

2, absent[minded], abstracted, flighty, detached, distraught, distrait; lost in thought; rapt, in the clouds, in a fog; bemused, punch-drunk, slap-happy; preoccupied; engrossed; off [one's] guard; napping, dreamy, woolgathering, sleeping, asleep, groggy, dead to the world. *Informal,* asleep at the switch, out to lunch. *Slang,* spacey.

Antonyms, see ATTENTION, THOUGHT.

inaudible, *adj.* unhearable; faint, muffled. See SILENCE. *Ant.,* audible, loud.

inaugurate, *v.t.* install, induct, invest; start, launch, initiate, institute, open. See BEGINNING.

inauspicious, *adj.* unpropitious, ill-omened, unfavorable, unlucky. See BADNESS. *Ant.,* auspicious, promising.

inborn, *adj.* native, innate, inbred, inherent. See INTRINSIC. *Ant.,* learned.

incalculable, *adj.* inestimable, immeasurable; vast. See INFINITY.

in camera, *Lat.,* privately. See CONCEALMENT.

incandescent, *adj.* glowing, brilliant; white-hot. See LIGHT.

incantation, *n.* magic words, mumbo jumbo, conjuration. See SORCERY.

incapable, *adj.* powerless, unable, incompetent; unqualified, unfitted, untrained. See IMPOTENCE.

incapacity, *n.* disability, IMPOTENCE, incompetence; inability, lack, deficiency. See IGNORANCE.

incarcerate, *v.t.* imprison (see RESTRAINT).

incarnate, *v.t.* shape, form, embody; animate, quicken. See SUBSTANCE.

incendiary, *n.* pyromaniac, firebug; arsonist. See DESTRUCTION.

incense, *v.t.* inflame, heat; infuriate, anger, ire; perfume, scent, thurify. See RESENTMENT. —*n.* perfume, fragrance, scent, ODOR, bouquet; frankincense, musk, myrrh, sandalwood. See FLATTERY, RITE.

incentive, *n.* stimulus, goad, spur; motive, CAUSE; provocation.

inception, *n.* start, BEGINNING.

incessant, *adj.* endless, continual, unceasing; uninterrupted. See FREQUENCY, CONTINUITY, REPETITION. *Ant.,* intermittent.

incest, *n.* sexual abuse, molestation. See IMPURITY.

inch, *v.* creep, crawl; EDGE, worm. See SLOWNESS.

incident, *n.* occasion; event, episode, happening. See OCCURRENCE. —*adj.* dependent, pertaining; likely. See QUALIFICATION.

incidental, *adj.* secondary, minor, subordinate; casual, CHANCE; current. See CIRCUMSTANCE.

incinerate, *v.t.* burn, cremate. See HEAT, INTERMENT.

incipient, *adj.* See BEGINNING.

incision, *n.* cut, gash, notch. See FURROW, INTERVAL.

incisive, *adj.* trenchant, penetrating; perceptive, discerning. See SHARPNESS, FEELING, INTELLECT.

incite, *v.t.* stir, urge, impel; actuate, provoke, instigate; encourage, stimulate; spur, goad, fan the flames (*inf.*). See CAUSE, EXCITEMENT.

inclement, *adj.* harsh, tempestuous, raw. See SEVERITY, ADVERSITY. *Ant.,* pleasant.

inclination, *n.* propensity, leaning, bent, predisposition; fondness, liking; predilection; slope, slant, ramp. See TENDENCY, WILL, OBLIQUITY.

incline, *v.* slant, slope, tilt; pitch, lurch; tend, influence, bias. See TENDENCY. —*n.* OBLIQUITY, grade; gradient, slant, bias, slope (see *v.*); ramp, ASCENT, upgrade; downgrade, DESCENT.

INCLUSION
Fact of being contained

Nouns—inclusion, admission, acceptance; comprehension, incorporation, subsumption; COMPOSITION, contents. See PART, GENERALITY.

Verbs—include, comprise, comprehend, embody, contain, admit, embrace, take in, receive, take up, subsume; inclose, circumscribe (see CIRCUMSCRIPTION); compose, incorporate, encompass; reckon *or* number among; cut *or* count in, implicate; refer to, place under, take into account *or* consideration; pertain *or* relate to.

Adjectives—included, including, inclusive; subsumptive; compendious, comprehensive, encyclopedic, omnibus; of the same class.

Adverbs—inclusively, comprehensively, *etc.*

Quotations—Life being all inclusion and confusion, and art being all discrimination and selection (*Henry James*).

Antonyms, see EXCLUSION.

incognito, *adj.* See CONCEALMENT.

incognizant, *adj.* unaware (of). See IGNO-RANCE.

incoherence, *n.* UNINTELLIGIBILITY, irra-tionality, inconsistency; incongruity; maundering, raving; immiscibility; loose-ness, FREEDOM. See DISJUNCTION.

INCOMBUSTIBILITY
Resistance to fire

Nouns—1, incombustibility, uninflammability, nonflammability; fireproofing, fire re-sistance.

2, [fire] extinguisher; fire engine, hook and ladder [truck]; [automatic] sprinkler, [fire] hydrant, fireplug, fire hose; carbon tetrachloride, foam, [wet] blanket; fireproofing, asbestos; fire wall *or* curtain.

3, firefighter, fireman; fire warden; volunteer fireman; fire *or* bucket brigade, fire de-partment.

Verbs—fireproof, flameproof; extinguish, snuff, put *or* stamp out, quench, douse, smother, damp; burn *or* go out, die.

Adjectives—incombustible, non[in]flammable, flameproof, fireproof, unburnable; fire-resistant; quenched, [snuffed] out.

Antonyms, see FUEL.

---

income, *n.* revenue; dividends; interest; re-ceipt[s], emoluments, fees, earnings; profit. See RECEIVING.

incomparable, *adj.* peerless, matchless, nonpareil, inimitable. See SUPERIORITY.

incompatible, *adj.* inharmonious, incon-sistent, antipathetic, incongruous, un-congenial; clashing, discordant, disagree-ing. See DISAGREEMENT.

incompetence, *n.* inability, inefficiency; IMPOTENCE; unfitness, incapability, in-capacity, UNSKILLFULNESS. *Ant.,* com-petent, capable.

INCOMPLETENESS
Lack of something

Nouns—1, incompleteness, short measure, half measures, INSUFFICIENCY, deficiency, IMPERFECTION, inadequacy, DISCONTINUANCE; immaturity (see UNPREPAREDNESS). See PART.

2, noncompletion, nonfulfillment, nonperformance, nonexecution.

3, deficit, want, lack, defalcation, omission, caret; INTERVAL, break, gap, missing link; loose end.

Verbs—1, be incomplete; fall short, lack, want; need (see INSUFFICIENCY).

2, leave unfinished, leave undone, let alone, let slide, let slip; lose sight of, hang fire, do things by halves, lie down on the job.

Adjectives—1, incomplete, uncompleted, unfinished, left undone, half-baked; imper-fect, defective, deficient, partial, wanting, failing; in default, in arrears, short (of); hollow, meager, skimpy, poor, lame, half-and-half, perfunctory, sketchy, crude; muti-lated, garbled, mangled, docked, lopped, truncated, catalectic. *Slang,* half-assed.

2, unaccomplished, unperformed, unexecuted; in progress, going on, in hand, pro-ceeding, under way, under construction.

Adverbs—incompletely; by halves, partly, partially; on paper, on the drawing board, in the blueprint *or* planning stage.

Quotations—A single man . . . is an incomplete animal. He resembles the odd half of a pair of scissors (*Benjamin Franklin*), A man in love is incomplete until he has mar-ried. Then he's finished (*Zsa Zsa Gabor*).

Antonyms, see COMPLETION.

incomprehensible, *adj.* unintelligible; unfathomable, abstruse, inscrutable. See UNINTELLIGIBILITY. *Ant.,* understandable, clear.

inconceivable, *adj.* unimaginable, unthinkable, incredible. See IMPOSSIBILITY, UNINTELLIGIBILITY.

incongruity, *n.* disharmony; inconsistency, incompatibility, absurdity. See DIFFERENCE, DISAGREEMENT.

inconsequential, *adj.* inconsequent, irrelevant; trivial. See UNIMPORTANCE, DISAGREEMENT. *Ant.,* important.

inconsiderate, *adj.* careless, heedless, thoughtless; tactless, neglectful. See NEGLECT. *Ant.,* considerate, kind.

inconsistency, *n.* CHANGEABLENESS, fickleness; incompatibility; contrariness, contradiction.

inconspicuous, *adj.* unnoticeable, unobtrusive. See INVISIBILITY.

inconstant, *adj.* unstable, irregular; fickle, changeable, faithless. See CHANGEABLENESS. *Ant.,* constant, unchanging.

incontrovertible, *adj.* irrefutable, incontestable, conclusive. See EVIDENCE.

inconvenient, *adj.* awkward, embarrassing, troublesome; inopportune, untimely. See INEXPEDIENCE, DIFFICULTY.

incorporate, *v.* embody; federate, merge, consolidate; unite, blend, join. See JUNCTION, INCLUSION, COMBINATION, SUBSTANCE.

incorrect, *adj.* WRONG, erroneous, fallacious; mistaken, false, untrue, inaccurate. See ERROR. *Ant.,* correct, precise.

incorrigible, *adj.* irreclaimable, beyond redemption; intractable, hopelessly delinquent. See OBSTINACY, HOPELESSNESS.

incorruptible, *adj.* trustworthy, reliable, inviolable. See CERTAINTY.

INCREASE
Act of making larger

Nouns—1, increase, augmentation, enlargement, extension; dilation, EXPANSION; advance, appreciation; gain, profit, increment, accretion; accession, ADDITION; development, growth; aggrandizement, aggravation; intensification, magnification, multiplication; rise, ascent; exacerbation; spread, DISPERSION; flood tide; population explosion. Butterfly effect. *Slang,* gravy. See IMPROVEMENT.

2, booster; [capital] gains, profits; cash cow.

Verbs—1, increase, augment, add to, enlarge, extend; supplement, eke out; dilate, sprout, expand, swell, burgeon, bud, puff up; grow, wax, get ahead, gain strength; fatten; advance, escalate; develop, grow, run up, shoot up; rise, ascend; amplify, build up, raise, step *or* jack up, punch up, hike. *Informal,* soup up.

2, aggrandize, exalt; deepen, heighten, strengthen, intensify, enhance, magnify, redouble; parlay; let out; accrue; aggravate, exasperate, exacerbate; add fuel to the fire *or* flames, spread, disperse; appreciate, inflate, mushroom, escalate, go up. *Informal,* snowball.

Adjectives—increased, increasing, multiplying, enlarged, on the increase, undiminished; additional, extra, added (see ADDITION); swollen, turgid, tumid, bloated, distended; larger, bigger.

Adverbs—increasingly, *etc.*; even, all the; crescendo.

Quotations—Population, when unchecked, increases in a geometric ratio. Subsistence increases only in an arithmetical ratio (*Thomas Malthus*), In much wisdom is much grief: and he that increaseth knowledge increaseth sorrow (*Bible*), When everything else physical and mental seems to diminish, the appreciation of beauty is on the increase (*Bernard Berenson*), Every increased possession loads us with a new weariness (*John Ruskin*).

Antonyms, see DECREASE.

---

incredible, *n.* unbelievable, inconceivable; absurd, preposterous. See DOUBT, WONDER.

INCREDULITY
Lack of belief

Nouns—1, incredulity, incredulousness, skepticism; want of faith (see IRRELIGION); DOUBT, distrust, suspicion, suspiciousness, scrupulosity, unbelief, disbelief; sophistication, ungullibility. See SURPRISE.

2, unbeliever, disbeliever, skeptic; infidel, heretic.

Verbs—distrust, DOUBT, disbelieve, refuse to believe, reject (see REJECTION); ignore, dispute, question. *Informal,* not swallow.

Adjectives—incredulous, skeptical; sophisticated, ungullible; unbelieving, unconvinced; doubtful, dubious, distrustful, questioning, quizzical, disputing; hesitant, uncertain, suspicious, scrupulous, apprehensive, wary, chary, qualmish; faithless, heretical. *Slang,* leery, not born yesterday.

Quotations—It was the epoch of incredulity (*Charles Dickens*).

Antonyms, see CREDULITY.

---

increment, *n.* growth, INCREASE.

incriminate, *v.t.* blame, indict, inculpate; impeach, put under suspicion; implicate, entangle; put the finger on, frame, pin the rap on (*all sl.*). See ACCUSATION.

incubate, *v.* hatch, brood, sit, gestate. See REPRODUCTION.

inculcate, *v.t.* ingrain, instill, implant. See TEACHING.

inculpate, *v.t.* accuse, incriminate. See ACCUSATION.

incumbent, *n.* in, officeholder, public servant. See AUTHORITY.

incur, *v.t.* acquire, bring about. See LIABILITY.

incurable, *adj.* hopeless, doomed; irremediable; unhealable. See DISEASE, HOPELESSNESS. *Ant.,* curable.

incursion, *n.* encroachment, inroad, invasion; ATTACK, foray, raid. See INGRESS.

indebted, *adj.* obligated, beholden. See DEBT, GRATITUDE.

indecent, *adj.* immoral, obscene, improper; salacious, lewd, lascivious, bawdy; immodest. See IMPURITY.

indecision, *n.* irresolution, hesitation, uncertainty, vacillation, shilly-shally. See DOUBT.

indecorous, *adj.* unseemly. See DISCOURTESY.

indeed, *adv.* in fact, truly. See EXISTENCE.

indefatigable, *adj.* tireless, untiring, relentless, patient. See ENERGY.

indefinite, *adj.* unclear, undefined, blurred; vague, uncertain, unspecified; indeterminate; equivocal. See OBSCURITY, DOUBT. *Ant.,* definite, precise.

indelible, *adj.* unforgettable (see MEMORY).

indelicate, *adj.* immodest; gross, unrefined, coarse. See VULGARITY.

indemnity, *n.* protection, SECURITY; COMPENSATION, EXEMPTION.

indent, *v.t.* impress, hollow, dent, dint, notch; knock in, set in, incise, cut; pit, dimple. See CONCAVITY.

independence, *n.* FREEDOM, liberty; self-reliance; self-government, autonomy; self-sufficiency. *Ant.,* slavery.

independent, *adj.* absolute, free, self-governing, self-reliant; unconnected, separate (from), exclusive (of); well-off, comfortable, well-to-do. —*n.* nonpartisan; freelance, lone wolf. See FREEDOM.

indescribable, *adj.* inexpressible, ineffable (see UNMEANINGNESS).

indestructible, *adj.* unbreakable, invulnerable. See PERMANENCE.

index, *n.* measure, scale, table, LIST; pointer, INDICATION. —*v.t.* tabulate, categorize, post; catalog, register, order; point out. See ARRANGEMENT.

INDICATION

Directing attention to; implication

Nouns—1, indication; symbolism, symbolization; denotation, connotation, signification; specification, designation; sign, symbol; index, indicator; dial; point[er], marker; exponent, note, token, symptom; manifestation, expression; type, figure, emblem, cipher, device; trademark; REPRESENTATION; epigraph, motto; lineament, feature, trait, characteristic, syndrome, earmark, peculiarity, property (see SPECIALITY); footprint, fingerprint; diagnosis (see IDENTITY). See EVIDENCE, RECORD.

2, *(physical indication)* gesture, gesticulation; pantomime; wink, glance, leer; nod, shrug, beck, touch, nudge; dactylology, sign language; cue, implication, suggestion, hint (see INFORMATION), clue, key; scent, track, spoor, hide or hair.

3, signal, rocket, blue light, watchfire, watchtower; telegraph, semaphore, flagstaff; cresset, fiery cross; calumet, white flag.

4, *(written indication)* mark, line, stroke, dash, score, stripe, scratch, tick, backslash, dot, point, notch, nick, crosshair; universal product code, UPC, bar code; asterisk, star, dingbat, dagger, obelisk, bullet, punctuation; period, comma, colon, semicolon, interrogation point, question mark, exclamation point, quotation marks, dash; parentheses, braces, [square] brackets; red letter, italics, sublineation, underlining, underscoring, redlining; accent, diacritical mark, acute, grave, circumflex, macron, dieresis, tilde, cedilla; degree.

5, identification, badge, caste mark; criterion; countercheck, countermark, countersign, counterfoil; tab, tally, label, ticket, coupon, billet, letter, counter, card, bill; button; stamp; imprint, avatar, colophon; trademark, service mark, brand, hallmark; signature, autograph; credentials; attestation; cipher; seal, signet; superscription, endorsement; marginalia; title, heading, docket, caption; shibboleth, watchword, catchword, catchphrase, byword, password, personal identification number, PIN; license plate, vanity plate; prompt; open sesame; cachet; insignia, ensign; regalia; banner, flag, colors, streamer, standard, eagle, oriflamme, tricolor, Stars and Stripes; pennon, pennant, jack, ancient *(obsolete)*, gonfalon, union jack; bunting; heraldry; crest; [coat of] arms, armorial bearings, hatchment, scutcheon, escutcheon; shield, supporters. *Slang*, high sign.

6, beacon, cairn, road sign, post, staff, flagstaff, hand, pointer, vane, cock, weathervane, guidepost, signpost; landmark, lighthouse; polestar, lodestar; blaze; address, direction, name; plaque, sign[board], milestone; traffic signal *or* light, stoplight; joy stick, light pen.

7, *(aural indication)* call, bugle, trumpet, bell, siren, alarum, cry; curfew.

Verbs—1, indicate, denote, betoken, imply, argue, testify (see EVIDENCE); connote, designate, specify, point out, manifest, reveal, disclose, exhibit; represent, stand for; typify, symbolize.

2, signal; warn, wigwag, semaphore, flag; beck[on], hail; nod; wink, glance, leer, nudge, shrug, gesticulate, gesture.

3, wave; unfurl, hoist *or* hang out a banner; wave the hand; give a cue, show one's colors; give *or* sound an alarm; sound the tocsin, beat the drum; raise a [hue and] cry.

4, note, mark, stamp, earmark; tab, label, ticket, docket; dot, spot, score, dash, trace, chalk; print.

Adjectives—indicating, indicative, indicatory; denotative; connotative; diacritical, representative, representational, significant, suggestive; typical, symbolic, symptomatic, characteristic, demonstrative, diagnostic, exponential, emblematic.

Adverbs—indicatively; in token of; symbolically.

Antonyms, see CONCEALMENT.

---

indict, *v.i.* accuse, charge, bring accusation against, bring *or* proffer charges; impeach, arraign. See ACCUSATION, LAWSUIT.

INDIFFERENCE
Lack of interest

Nouns—1, indifference, neutrality; coldness, frigidity (see INSENSIBILITY); unconcern, insouciance, nonchalance; INATTENTION, lack of interest, anorexia, apathy; supineness; disdain (see CONTEMPT); carelessness, NEGLECT. *Informal,* no skin off one's nose.

2, sameness, equivalence, EQUALITY; MEDIOCRITY.

Verbs—be indifferent *or* neutral, be all the same *or* all one; take no interest in, have no desire, taste, *or* relish for, not care for, care nothing for *or* about, not give *or* care a hang, a rap, two straws, *or* a damn, not care a tinker's damn; not bat an eye[lash], not care a straw (see UNIMPORTANCE); not mind; set at naught, make light of; spurn, disdain (see CONTEMPT). *Slang,* not give a [flying] fuck *or* a shit.

Adjectives—1, indifferent, neutral, cold, frigid, lukewarm; impervious; cool [as a cucumber]; on the fence, neither fish nor fowl, middle-of-the-road; unambitious, complacent; unconcerned, insouciant, dispassionate, easygoing, devil-may-care, happy-go-lucky, careless, listless, lackadaisical; halfhearted; unambitious, unaspiring, undesirous, unsolicitous, unattracted; all one (to). *Slang,* insensate.

2, unattractive, unalluring, undesired, undesirable, uncared for, unwished, unvalued; insipid; vain.

Adverbs—indifferently, like water off a duck's back; for the devil of it, for aught one cares.

Interjections — never mind! who cares! what's the difference!

Quotations—Science may have found a cure for most evils; but it has found no remedy for the worst of them all—the apathy of human beings (*Helen Keller*), Take sides. Neutrality helps the oppressor, never the victim. Silence encourages the tormentor, never the tormented (*Elie Wiesel*), Our sympathy is cold to the relation of distant misery (*Edward Gibbon*), All politics are based on the indifference of the majority (*James Reston*).

Antonyms, see DESIRE, CURIOSITY, TASTE.

---

indigenous, *adj.* native; innate, inborn; inherent, natural (to). See INTRINSIC, INHABITANT. *Ant.,* alien, foreign.

indigent, *adj.* poor, poverty-stricken (see POVERTY). *Ant.,* wealthy.

indigestion, *n.* dyspepsia, gastritis, heartburn, stomachache, sour stomach, acidosis, flatulence, colic. See DISEASE.

indignation, *n.* RESENTMENT, ire, wrath; displeasure, vexation.

indignity, *n.* slight, humiliation. See DISRESPECT.

indirect, *adj.* oblique; roundabout, circuitous; underhand, crooked, furtive; hinted, implied, inferential. See CIRCUITY, DEVIATION, OBLIQUITY. *Ant.,* direct, straight.

indiscretion, *n.* carelessness, recklessness; blunder, faux pas, lapse, slip. See RASHNESS, WRONG.

indiscriminate, *adj.* random, heterogeneous, CHANCE; uncritical, injudicious (see INDISCRIMINATION). See MIXTURE, DISORDER, GENERALITY.

INDISCRIMINATION
Lack of discrimination

Nouns—1, indiscrimination, lack of taste *or* discrimination; casualness, indiscretion, imprudence; tactlessness, insensitivity, INSENSIBILITY; GENERALITY; promiscuity.

2, lack of distinction, indistinction, vagueness; UNIFORMITY; impersonality.

Verbs—be indiscriminate, mix up, blur *or* overlook distinctions.

Adjectives—indiscriminate, uncritical, injudicious; wholesale; undemanding, unparticular; casual, indiscreet, imprudent; untactful, tactless, insensitive.

Adverbs—indiscriminately.

indispensable, *adj.* vital, needful, necessary; essential, required. See NECESSITY. *Ant.,* disposable.

indisposed, *adj.* ill; unwilling. See DISEASE, DISSUASION. *Ant.,* well, healthy.

indistinct, *adj.* inaudible; imperceptible, unclear, foggy, blurry, shadowy; vague, obscure, dim; faint. See DIMNESS, INVISIBILITY. *Ant.,* distinct, clear.

individual, *adj.* particular, single, peculiar, special; specific; personal, proper. —*n.* person; personality, entity; somebody, anybody. See SPECIALITY. *Ant.,* group.

individuality, *n.* UNCONFORMITY, uniqueness; personality; peculiarity, originality; character. See SPECIALITY, IDENTITY, UNITY.

indivisible, *adj.* one; inseparable, indissoluble. See UNITY, WHOLE.

indoctrinate, *v.t.* inculcate; brainwash. See TEACHING, BELIEF.

indolence, *n.* sloth, idleness, laziness, sluggishness; INACTIVITY.

indomitable, *adj.* invincible, unconquerable. See STRENGTH.

indorse, *v.t.* See ENDORSE.

indubitable, *adj.* sure, irrefutable, incontrovertible. See CERTAINTY.

induce, *v.t.* CAUSE, bring about, incite; infer; urge, persuade, impel, influence; effect.

induction, *n.* inauguration, installation; inference, REASONING, conclusion; generalization. See COMMISSION.

indulge, *v.t.* pamper, spoil, favor, humor; gratify; take PLEASURE (in); revel. See INTEMPERANCE, PERMISSION, LENIENCY.

industrious, *adj.* active, busy, hardworking; diligent, assiduous, sedulous. See ACTIVITY. *Ant.,* lazy, indolent.

industry, *n.* labor, work; occupation, trade, BUSINESS, ACTIVITY; diligence.

inebriate, *v.t.* intoxicate (see DRINKING).

ineffective, *adj.* useless, vain, unavailing; impotent, worthless; weak, inefficient. See USELESSNESS, FAILURE, IMPOTENCE.

ineffectual, *adj.* futile, unproductive, barren, ineffective. See USELESSNESS, FAILURE.

inefficient, *adj.* ineffective, incompetent. See USELESSNESS, IMPOTENCE.

INELASTICITY
Lack of flexibility

Nouns—inelasticity; flabbiness, limpness, flaccidity, laxity, SOFTNESS; inductibility, inflexibility, stiffness, HARDNESS; inextensibility.

Verbs—stiffen, rigidify, tense.

Adjectives—inelastic, unstretchable, inextensible; flabby, flaccid, limp, lax, soft; inductile, inflexible, irresilient, rigid, unyielding, unpliant.

Antonyms, see ELASTICITY.

INELEGANCE
Lack of elegance

Nouns—inelegance, gracelessness, leadenness, harshness, tastelessness, VULGARITY; stiffness; barbarism; solecism, cacology, circumlocution; mannerism, artificiality (see AFFECTATION); lack of polish, class, *or* finish. See UNSKILLFULNESS.

Adjectives—inelegant, graceless, ungraceful, clumsy; dowdy; harsh, abrupt; dry, stiff, cramped, formal, forced, labored, leaden; artificial, mannered, ponderous, pompous; turgid, affected, euphuistic; awkward, inept, clumsy (see UNSKILLFULNESS); slouching, ungainly, gawky, lumpish, lumbering, hulking, unwieldy; barbarous, barbaric, uncouth, vulgar, gross; grotesque, ludicrous; rugged, rough, gross, rude, crude, halting. *Slang,* klutzy, clunky.

Antonyms, see ELEGANCE.

---

ineligible, *adj.* unqualified, disqualified, inadmissible; unfit, WRONG. See INEXPEDIENCE. *Ant.,* eligible, apt.

inept, *adj.* incompetent, unskilled, clumsy, all thumbs. See UNSKILLFULNESS, FOLLY, INELEGANCE. *Ant.,* skillful.

INEQUALITY
Lack of equality

Nouns—inequality, disparity, imparity, odds, DIFFERENCE; unevenness; imbalance, partiality, double standard; shortcoming; makeweight; SUPERIORITY; INFERIORITY. See INJUSTICE.

Verbs—be unequal, countervail; tip the scale; kick the beam; topple (over); overmatch; not come up to; trim, trim ship.

Adjectives—unequal, uneven, disparate, partial; off balance, unbalanced, overbalanced; top-heavy, lopsided; unequaled, matchless, peerless, unique, inimitable.

Quotations—All is uneven, and everything is left at six and seven (*Shakespeare*), What is a communist? One who hath yearnings for equal division of unequal earnings (*Ebenezer Elliott*), Make all men equal today, and God has so created them that they shall all be unequal tomorrow (*Anthony Trollope*), His lordship may compel us to be equal upstairs, but there will never be equality in the servants' hall (*J. M. Barrie*).

Antonyms, see EQUALITY.

---

inequitable, *adj.* unfair, unjust (see INJUSTICE).

inert, *adj.* static, dormant; stagnant, dead. See INACTIVITY.

inertia, *n.* stillness; laziness, lethargy; passivity. See INACTIVITY, REPOSE.

in esse, Lat., in EXISTENCE.

inestimable, *adj.* priceless, invaluable, beyond price *or* value, too precious for words. See DEARNESS, USE.

inevitable, *adj.* inescapable, unavoidable. See CERTAINTY, DESTINY.

inexact, *adj.* unprecise, incorrect, wrong, erroneous; vague, loose, undefined, indefinite, unspecified. See ERROR, OBSCURITY.

INEXCITABILITY
Patience

Nouns—1, inexcitability, imperturbability; even temper, equanimity, equilibrium, tranquillity, dispassion; tolerance, patience; hebetude, hebetation; INSENSIBILITY. See SUBMISSION, MODERATION, RESTRAINT.

2, coolness, calmness, composure, placidity, indisturbance, imperturbation, aplomb, sangfroid, serenity; quiet, quietude; peace of mind.

3, staidness, gravity, sobriety, Quakerism; fortitude, stoicism; self-possession, self-control, self-command, self-restraint; presence of mind, patience of Job.

Verbs—1, not get excited, be composed, laissez-faire, take things as they come; take it easy, live and let live; take in good part.

2, acquiesce, submit, yield (see SUBMISSION); resign *or* reconcile oneself to; brook, swallow, pocket, stomach; make light of, make the best of, make a virtue of necessity; put a good face on, keep one's countenance. *Slang,* keep one's cool.

3, compose, appease, moderate; repress, restrain; master one's feelings, keep one's head, keep one's wits about one; bite one's lips *or* tongue, count to ten; get it all together, calm *or* cool down. *Informal,* simmer down. *Slang,* hold one's horses, keep one's shirt on, keep one's cool.

Adjectives—1, inexcitable, unexcitable; imperturbable; unsusceptible, insensible; dispassionate, cold-blooded, enduring, stoical, Platonic, philosophical, staid, soberminded; nonchalant, coolheaded, demure, sedate.

2, easygoing, peaceful, placid, calm; quiet, tranquil, serene; cool [as a cucumber], undemonstrative, temperate; composed, collected. *Slang,* laid-back.

3, patient [as Job]; submissive; tame; content, resigned, chastened, subdued, lamblike; gentle [as a lamb]; mild [as milk]; armed with patience, long-suffering.

Adverbs—inexcitably, *etc.*; in cold blood.

Phrases—all commend patience, but none can endure to suffer; all things come to those who wait; patience is a virtue.

Quotations—Beware the fury of a patient man (*John Dryden*), Patience, that blending of moral courage with physical timidity (*Thomas Hardy*), A calm despair, without angry convulsion or reproaches directed to heaven, is the essence of wisdom (*Alfred de Vigny*).

Antonyms, see EXCITABILITY, EXCITEMENT.

---

inexcusable, *adj.* unpardonable, unforgivable, unjustifiable. See INJUSTICE.

inexhaustible, *adj.* limitless, endless, unfailing. See SUFFICIENCY, INFINITY.

inexorable, *adj.* unrelenting, unyielding, inflexible, firm. See SEVERITY.

<h2 style="text-align:center">INEXPEDIENCE</h2>
Inconvenience

Nouns—inexpedience, inexpediency; undesirableness, undesirability; discommodity, impropriety, ineligibility, inaptitude; unfitness (see DISAGREEMENT); inconvenience; disadvantage, untimeliness.

Verbs—come amiss; embarrass, hinder (see HINDRANCE); inconvenience, put upon *or* out.

Adjectives—inexpedient, undesirable; inadvisable, inappropriate; improper, objectionable; deleterious; unapt, inconvenient, embarrassing, disadvantageous, unfit, ineligible; incommodious, discommodious, ill-contrived *or* -occasioned, inopportune, untimely, unseasonable; out of place, unseemly; ill-advised, injudicious; clumsy, awkward.

Antonyms, see EXPEDIENCE.

---

inexpensive, *adj.* See CHEAPNESS. *Ant.,* expensive, pricey.

inexperienced, *adj.* green, raw, untrained, fresh; naive. See UNSKILLFULNESS, YOUTH. *Ant.,* experienced, sophisticated.

inexpressible, *adj.* unutterable, ineffable, beyond words, indescribably. See UNMEANINGNESS, WONDER, PIETY.

in extremis, Lat., at the very end; near DEATH.

infallible, *adj.* reliable, dependable, trustworthy, right; unfailing, unerring, unerrable, certain. See CERTAINTY. *Ant.,* fallible, human.

infamous, *adj.* shameful, abominable, disgraceful, unspeakable, contemptible; heinous, atrocious, base, discreditable. See IMPROBITY, DISREPUTE.

infancy, *n.* babyhood, childhood; BEGIN-NING, cradle, genesis. See YOUTH, IGNORANCE.

infant, *n.* baby (see YOUTH). —*adj.* incipent (see BEGINNING).

infantile, *adj.* childish, puerile, immature. See YOUTH. *Ant.,* mature, adult.

infantry, *n.* soldiery, troops, foot soldiers. See COMBATANT.

infatuation, *n.* enamorment, fascination (by); passion, folly, gullibility, dotingness. See LOVE.

infection, *n.* epidemic, contagion, plague, contamination; illness; taint, toxicity, gangrene, poisoning. See DISEASE, TRANSFER.

infectious, *adj.* contagious (see TRANSFER).

infer, *v.t.* gather, reason, deduce, conclude, opine; presume; construe. See REASONING.

<h2 style="text-align:center">INFERIORITY</h2>
Quality of being lesser

Nouns—1, inferiority, minority, subordinacy; inadequacy, deficiency (see INSUFFICIENCY); minimum; smallness; IMPERFECTION; poorness, meanness; subservience. See INEQUALITY, MEDIOCRITY, LITTLENESS.

2, inferior, subordinate, junior, underling; second best, runner-up, also-ran; second fiddle. *Slang,* second-stringer, long shot, munchkin.

Verbs—not pass [muster], not measure up to; play second fiddle; scrape the bottom of the barrel. *Informal*, take a backseat, get the short end of the stick. *Slang*, suck.

Adjectives—inferior, smaller; minor, junior, less[er], deficient, minus, lower, subordinate, secondary; second-rate, second-class, imperfect; short, inadequate, out of depth; subaltern; abysmal; weighed in the balance and found wanting, below par; not fit to hold a candle to. *Slang*, lame-ass, nowhere, ticky-tacky, rooty-poot.

Adverbs—below; behind, beneath; below par; short of, in the hole; at the bottom of the scale; at a low ebb. *Informal*, not up to snuff.

Phrases—always a bridesmaid, never a bride; you can't make a silk purse out of a sow's ear.

Quotations—A man who has not been in Italy is always conscious of an inferiority (*Samuel Johnson*), No one can make you feel inferior without your consent (*Eleanor Roosevelt*).

Antonyms, see SUPERIORITY.

---

infernal, *adj.* hellish, Plutonian, Stygian; fiendish, diabolical, demoniac[al]; *informal*, annoying, troublesome. See DEMON, HELL.

inferno, *n.* HELL; conflagration, HEAT.

infest, *v.t.* overrun, invade, pervade; molest, torment. See PRESENCE, DISEASE.

infidelity, *n.* betrayal, treachery; faithlessness, fickleness; adultery; skepticism, unbelief. See PROBITY, IRRELIGION. *Ant.,* faithful, true.

infighting, *n.* dissension, factiousness, bickering, DISSENT.

infiltrate, *v.* penetrate, pervade, permeate; enter, worm in, mix with, assimilate into. See INGRESS, MIXTURE, PASSAGE.

infinitesimal, *adj.* tiny, minute (see LITTLENESS). *Ant.,* momumental.

INFINITY
Limitless number

Nouns—infinity, infinitude, infiniteness; immensity, limitlessness, inexhaustibility, immeasurability, incalculability, illimitability, interminability; eternity, PERPETUITY; endlessness. See SPACE, UNIVERSE.

Verbs—be infinite, boundless, *etc.*; go on *or* endure forever; immortalize; have no bounds, limit, *or* end.

Adjectives—infinite, immense; numberless, countless, sumless, measureless; innumerable, immeasurable, incalculable, illimitable, interminable, endless, unfathomable, bottomless, inexhaustible; indefinite; without number, limit, end, *or* measure, beyond measure; incomprehensible; limitless, boundless; untold, unnumbered, unmeasured, unbounded; perpetual, eternal.

Adverbs—infinitely, *etc.*; ad infinitum; perpetually.

Phrases—their name is legion.

Quotations—To see a world in a grain of sand and a heaven in a wild flower, hold infinity in the palm of your hand and eternity in an hour (*William Blake*), Suffering is permanent, obscure, and dark, and shares the nature of infinity (*William Wordsworth*), I can't help it, the idea of the infinite torments me (*Alfred de Musset*), The eternal silence of these infinite spaces terrifies me (*Blaise Pascal*).

Antonyms, see LIMIT.

---

infirmary, *n.* clinic (see REMEDY).

infirmity, *n.* fault; feebleness, WEAKNESS; illness, DISEASE.

inflame, *v.* anger, excite, arouse; incite, animate, kindle; heat, blaze up; aggravate, provoke, irritate; redden, flush. See VIOLENCE, EXCITEMENT.

inflammable, *adj.* burnable, combustible. See FUEL.

inflammation, *n.* ache, soreness, tenderness (see PAIN).

inflammatory, *adj.* incendiary, instigative (see CAUSE).

inflate, *v.* puff *or* blow up, aerate; expand,

dilate, swell, distend; exaggerate. See WIND, INCREASE, EXPANSION, EXAGGERATION.

inflect, v. bend, turn, curve; modulate, vary; conjugate, decline. See CURVATURE, CHANGE, GRAMMAR.

inflexible, adj. unbending, rigid, unyielding; firm, steadfast, stubborn; grim, stern. See HARDNESS, RESOLUTION, INELASTICITY. Ant., flexible, pliant.

inflict, v.t. burden or trouble with; impose, put upon; do (to); give. See PUNISHMENT, COMPULSION.

infliction, n. scourge, affliction; ADVERSITY; curse, disgrace; imposition; administering (to). See COMPULSION.

INFLUENCE
Power to effect decision

Nouns—1, influence, IMPORTANCE, weight, pressure, preponderance; predominance, predominancy (see SUPERIORITY); POWER, sway; ascendancy; hegemony, reign, control, AUTHORITY; bias, protection, patronage, auspices (see AID); purchase, support; play, leverage, impact, spin; cocktail diplomacy. Informal, clout. Slang, pull, drag, juice; casting couch. See CAUSE.

2, patron, friend at court, power behind the throne, woman behind the man, old boy network, peer pressure, power broker, spin doctor. Slang, rainmaker.

Verbs—1, have influence, be influential; carry weight, weigh, tell; have a hold upon, sway, bias, pull the strings, militate; bear or work upon; swing one's weight; gain headway, have, get, or gain the upper hand. Informal, have the inside track, have it all over. Slang, have an in.

2, affect, impact or play on, make an impression on; prejudice; bribe (see PAYMENT); bring into line, lead by the nose, have a way with; move, budge, prompt, persuade, motivate, lean on; prevail upon, outweigh, overweigh; override, overbear. Slang, have in one's pocket; cut ice.

Adjectives—influential, important (see IMPORTANCE); weighty; prevailing upon, proactive.

Adverbs—influentially, with telling effect.

Phrases—money talks.

Quotations—Life is a search after power (Emerson), All power, of whatever sort, is of itself desirable (Samuel Johnson), How to win friends and influence people (Dale Carnegie), A teacher affects eternity; he can never tell where his influence stops (Henry Adams).

Antonyms, see UNIMPORTANCE.

---

influx, n. inflow, INGRESS, infiltration; inroad, invasion, ARRIVAL; immigration.

inform, v. communicate, make known, tell; instruct. See INFORMATION, COMMUNICATION, TEACHING.

informal, adj. casual, free, easy, unofficial; unconventional, unceremonious. See UNCONFORMITY, ILLEGALITY.

INFORMATION
What one is told

Nouns—1, information, enlightenment, acquaintance, KNOWLEDGE; data; publicity (see PUBLICATION); COMMUNICATION, intimation; notice, notification; word, ADVICE, annunciation; announcement; representation, presentment, infographics, infomercial; case, estimate, specification, report, monition; release, communiqué, dispatch, press kit; tidings, bulletin, NEWS, intelligence, dope; returns, RECORD; account, DESCRIPTION; statement, AFFIRMATION; information literacy; information explosion, information highway. Informal, inside story, promo, a thing or two, two cents; info[r]mercial. Slang, info, lowdown, scuttlebutt, spin, cold-lamping.

2, mention, acquainting; instruction, TEACHING; outpouring; intercommunication, communicativeness; hint, suggestion, innuendo, implication, allusion, inkling, whisper, passing word; word, bug, *or* flea in the ear; subaudition, cue, byplay; gesture (see INDICATION); gentle *or* broad hint; whisper campaign; word to the wise; insinuation; subliminal suggestion. *Slang,* hot tip.

3, informer, informant, authority, teller, spokesperson, intelligencer, publisher, broadcaster, newscaster, commentator, reporter, mouthpiece; informer, talebearer, scandalmonger, tattletale, tout, eavesdropper; detective, spy (see INQUIRY); crier, herald; newsmonger; messenger (see AGENT); amicus curiae; pilot, guide. *Informal,* squealer, tipster. *Slang,* snitcher, [stool] pigeon, nark, rat, fink, cheese-eater, pig brother.

4, guidebook, handbook; manual; map, PLAN, chart, gazetteer; itinerary (see TRAVEL). See DIRECTION.

5, rumor, gossip, hearsay; scandal, tidbit, canard; item, topic, talk of the town, common currency, byword, household word. *Informal,* earful, [prittle-]prattle; sack mouth. *Slang,* juice, skinny, pop junk.

Verbs—**1,** inform, tell, acquaint, impart, convey, make acquainted with, apprise, advise, enlighten, awaken; give a piece of one's mind, tell one plainly, speak volumes, open up; let fall, mention, express, intimate, represent, communicate, make known; publish (see PUBLICATION); notify, signify, specify, disclose (see DISCLOSURE); undeceive, correct, disabuse, open the eyes of; let one know; give one to understand; give notice; point out; instruct, teach; direct the ATTENTION to. *Informal,* fill one in on, put wise, cue *or* clue in.

2, announce, annunciate, report; bring, send, leave, *or* give word; retail, render, *or* give an account (see DESCRIPTION); state, affirm (see AFFIRMATION).

3, hint, give an inkling of, imply, insinuate, intimate, get *or* drive at; allude to, suggest, prompt, give the cue, breathe; get to; tattle, spill, whisper; have something on, get the goods on; inform on, betray, turn state's evidence. *Informal,* tip off; put a flea *or* bug in one's ear; tell on, let in on, spill the beans, let the cat out of the bag. *Slang,* rat, blab, [drop a] dime, flip, finger, snitch, double-cross, squeal, fink, riff; sell down the river, turn in, finger.

4, be informed, know (see KNOWLEDGE); learn, receive news, get wind *or* scent of; gather (from); awaken to, open one's eyes to; become alive *or* awake to; hear, overhear, find out, understand; come to one's ears, come to one's knowledge, reach one's ears. *Informal,* catch on. *Slang,* get wise to, wise up.

5, gossip. *Slang,* bad-mouth.

Adjectives—informative, informational, reported, published; expressive, explicit, open, clear, plainspoken; declaratory, expository; communicative, communicatory; informed, knowledgeable.

Phrases—gossip is the lifeblood of society; gossip is vice enjoyed vicariously; those who live in glass houses shouldn't throw stones; dead men tell no tales; never tell tales out of school; information is power.

Quotations—Enter Rumor, painted full of tongues (*Shakespeare*), Be thou as chaste as ice, as pure as snow, thou shalt not escape calumny (*Shakespeare*), Love and scandal are the best sweeteners of tea (*Henry Fielding*), Every man is surrounded by a neighborhood of voluntary spies (*Jane Austen*), The smallest fact is a window through which the infinite may be seen (*Aldous Huxley*), Get your facts first, and then you can distort them as much as you please (*Mark Twain*), Everybody gets so much information all day long that they lose their common sense (*Gertrude Stein*).

Antonyms, see CONCEALMENT.

---

infraction, *n.* breach, violation; infringement, transgression. See ILLEGALITY, DISOBEDIENCE.

infra dignitatem, Lat., beneath one's dignity. See DISREPUTE.

infrequent, *adj.* rare, few; uncommon, unusual; scarce, odd. See RARITY. *Ant.,* frequent.

infringement, *n.* trespass, encroachment; infraction, breach; plagiarism, violation. See ILLEGALITY, DISOBEDIENCE.

infuriate, *v.t.* enrage, anger, madden, incense; incite, provoke, nettle, peeve, rankle, rile, make one's blood boil. See RESENTMENT. *Ant.,* calm, pacify.

infuse, *v.t.* steep, soak; introduce, implant, instill; tinge, imbue; pour into, mix in. See MIXTURE, INSERTION.

ingenious, *adj.* clever, inventive. See IMAGINATION, SKILL.

ingenuity, *n.* SKILL; cleverness; inventiveness; originality.

ingenuous, *adj.* artless, naive, simple; candid, frank, open; trusting, unsuspecting. See SIMPLENESS.

ingest, *v.t.* eat, drink, *etc.*; absorb, assimilate. See FOOD, RECEIVING.

ingrained, *adj.* fixed, implanted; inveterate, chronic, established. See HABIT.

ingratiating, *adj.* charming, winsome, winning, captivating; attractive, pleasing. See COURTESY.

INGRATITUDE
Lack of appreciation

Nouns—1, ingratitude, ungratefulness, unthankfulness.

2, ingrate, wretch, a serpent in one's bosom.

Verbs—be ungrateful, lack appreciation, look a gift horse in the mouth; bite the hand that feeds one, kick down the ladder.

Adjectives—ungrateful, unappreciative, unmindful, unthankful; thankless, ingrate; forgotten, unacknowledged, unthanked, unrequited, unrewarded; ill-requited.

Quotations—Blow, blow, thou winter wind, thou are not so unkind as man's ingratitude (*Shakespeare*), How sharper than a serpent's tooth it is to have a thankless child (*Shakespeare*), Power takes as ingratitude the writhing of its victims (*Rabindranath Tagore*), My first qualification for this great office is my monumental personal ingratitude (*Fiorello La Guardia*).

Antonyms, see GRATITUDE.

---

ingredient, *n.* component, PART, element, constituent. See COMPOSITION.

INGRESS
Act of entering

Nouns—1, ingress; entrance, entry, entrée, introgression; influx; intrusion, inroad, incursion, invasion, irruption; penetration, interpenetration; import, infiltration; access, admission, admittance, reception; insinuation (see BETWEEN); INSERTION. See APPROACH.

2, port of entry; antechamber (see RECEPTACLE); inlet; way in; mouth, door, OPENING, path, way; conduit, channel, PASSAGE; immigration.

3, incomer, immigrant, colonist, alien; entrant; newcomer; fifth column; illegal alien (see ILLEGALITY).

Verbs—enter, step in[side]; go, come, pour, flow, creep, slip, pop, break, *or* burst in; gain entrée; set foot on; burst *or* break in upon; invade, intrude; insinuate itself *or* oneself; penetrate, interpenetrate; infiltrate; find one's way into, wriggle into, worm oneself into; trespass; give entrance to, receive, insert; bore from within. *Informal,* breeze in. *Slang,* crash [the gate].

Adjectives—ingressive; incoming, ingoing, inward; entrant.

Phrases—a door must be either shut or open; when one door shuts another opens.

Quotations—Not many sounds in life . . . exceed in interest a knock at the door (*Charles Lamb*).

Antonyms, see EGRESS.

ingrown, *adj.* embedded; entrenched, inveterate. See HABIT, INTRINSIC.

INHABITANT
One who inhabits

Nouns—1, inhabitant, habitant; resident, [in]dweller, roomer, occupier, occupant; householder, boarder, renter, lodger, tenant; inmate; incumbent, sojourner, locum tenens, settler, colonist, squatter, nester; backwoodsman, islander; mountaineer; flatlander; denizen, citizen, burgher, burgess, townsman; villager, cottager; compatriot, fellow citizen. *Informal,* city slicker; sooner; hayseed. *Slang,* hick, rube. See LOCATION, ABODE.

2, native, indigene, aborigine; newcomer.

3, population, POPULACE, public, people (see HUMANITY); colony, settlement; household; garrison, crew.

Verbs—inhabit, be present (see PRESENCE); dwell, reside, sojourn, occupy, lodge; be *or* hail from; settle (see ABODE); squat; colonize, billet.

Adjectives—indigenous; native, natal; aboriginal, primitive; domestic, domiciled, naturalized, vernacular, domesticated; domiciliary.

---

inhale, *v.* breathe (in). See WIND. *Ant.,* exhale.

inherent, *adj.* native, innate; INTRINSIC, essential.

inherit, *v.t.* succeed (to); get, acquire, receive; possess. See ACQUISITION.

inhibit, *v.* circumscribe, restrain; hamper, check, cramp; repress, suppress; forbid, prohibit. See RESTRAINT, PROHIBITION.

inhospitable, *adj.* unfriendly, unwelcoming. See MALEVOLENCE.

inhuman, *adj.* cruel, barbarous, bestial, brutal, savage; supernatural. See MALEVOLENCE.

inimitable, *adj.* incomparable, matchless (see PERFECTION).

iniquity, *n.* vice, immorality; sin, wickedness, transgression, crime, wrongdoing; injustice. See EVIL, WRONG, IMPROBITY, ILLEGALITY.

initial, *adj.* first, BEGINNING, introductory, primary. —*n.* letter, monogram.

initiate, *v.t.* admit, introduce, take in; start, commence, inaugurate, institute. See BEGINNING.

inject, *v.t.* insert, introduce; wedge *or* force in; inoculate; intersperse, interject. See INSERTION.

injudicious, *adj.* unwise, imprudent. See FOLLY.

injunction, *n.* COMMAND, order, admonition, direction; requirement; PROHIBITION.

injure, *v.t.* wound, hurt; damage, abuse, deface, mar, impair; WRONG, disgrace, dishonor, insult, mistreat, maltreat. See DETERIORATION, EVIL, MALEVOLENCE.

INJUSTICE
Lack of justice

Nouns—1, injustice, unjustness, unfairness; bias, warp, twist, partiality, prejudice, inequity, inequitableness; bigotry, black justice; pedantry; unsportsmanlike conduct; favoritism, nepotism, partisanship; sexism, machismo; ageism, racism, lookism; unjustifiability, *etc.* See IMPROBITY, ILLEGALITY, MISJUDGMENT, INEQUALITY.

2, disservice, injury, WRONG.

Verbs—be unjust, unfair, *or* inequitable, do injustice to, favor, play favorites, show partiality, bias, warp, twist, prejudice; hit below the belt. *Slang,* give a raw deal.

Adjectives—unjust, unfair, unsporting, partial, prejudiced, jaundiced, shortsighted, bigoted, inequitable, partisan, nepotistic, biased, onesided; undue, unjustifiable, inexcusable, unpardonable, unforgivable, indefensible.

Adverbs—unjustly, unfairly, inequitably, *etc.*

Phrases—no tree takes so deep a root as a prejudice; there's none so blind as those who will not see.

Quotations—Bigotry may be roughly defined as the anger of men who have no opinions (*G. K. Chesterton*), Bigotry tries to keep truth safe in its hand with a grip that kills it (*Rabindranath Tagore*), The so-called white races are really pinko-grey (*E. M. Forster*), I, too, sing America. I am the darker brother. They send me to eat in the kitchen when company comes (*Langston Hughes*), I want to be the white man's brother, not his brother-in-law (*M. L. King*), It comes as a great shock to see Gary Cooper killing off the Indians, and, although you are rooting for Gary Cooper, that the Indians are you (*James Baldwin*), We are all precious in God's sight—the real rainbow coalition (*Jesse Jackson*).

Antonyms, see JUSTICE.

---

ink, *n.* See WRITING.

inkling, *n.* clue, suggestion, hint, whisper; surmise. See INFORMATION, SUPPOSITION.

inky, *adj.* black, stained. See COLOR.

inlay, *v.t.* inset, insert (see INSERTION).

inlet, *n.* creek, cove; entrance, INGRESS; channel. See OPENING.

in loco parentis, *Lat.,* in the place of a parent. See SUBSTITUTION.

inmate, *n.* prisoner, *détenu;* tenant, occupant. See INHABITANT, PRISON.

in medias res, *Lat.,* in the MIDDLE of things.

in memoriam, *Lat.,* in MEMORY (of).

inmost, *adj.* innermost, deepest, most private. See INTERIOR.

inn, *n.* hotel, hostelry; tavern, bar and grill. See ABODE, DRINKING.

innards, *n.pl.* entrails, vitals, viscera; mechanism, works. See BODY, INTERIOR.

innate, *adj.* natural, inborn; inherent; congenital. See INTRINSIC, INTUITION. *Ant.,* learned.

inner, *adj.* inward, internal, INTERIOR, inside; private, concealed. —**inner circle,** coterie, clique, set (see PARTY).

innermost, *adj.* inmost, most private *or* personal. See INTERIOR.

innkeeper, *n.* host, hostess; taverner, tavernkeeper; landlord; hotelier, boniface. See PROVISION.

INNOCENCE
Lack of guilt

Nouns—1, innocence, guiltlessness, blamelessness, incorruption, impeccability, clean bill of health, clean hands, clean slate; benefit of the doubt; PURITY, VIRTUE, virginity, chastity; artlessness, naiveté, candor, SIMPLENESS; immaculacy, CLEANNESS. See PROBITY.

2, *(innocent person)* innocent, child, lamb, dove, saint, newborn babe, naïf; virgin, maid; babe in the woods. *Slang,* canned goods, salt-water Negro, choirboy.

Verbs—be innocent, have a clear conscience; exonerate, acquit (see ACQUITTAL); exculpate (see VINDICATION); whitewash; keep one's nose clean; give the benefit of the doubt.

Adjectives—innocent, not guilty, unguilty, guiltless, faultless, sinless, stainless, bloodless, spotless, *sans peur et sans reproche,* clean, immaculate, unspotted, unblemished, unerring; unsullied, undefiled (see PROBITY); unravished, virginal, pure, white as snow, virtuous; Arcadian, artless, guileless, naive, simple, unsophisticated; inculpable, unculpable, unblamed, unblamable, blameless, above suspicion; irreproachable, irreprovable, irreprehensible; unexceptionable, unobjectionable, unimpeachable; harmless, inoffensive, innocuous; dovelike, lamblike; innocent as a lamb, saint, child, babe unborn, *etc.*; more sinned against than sinning, unreproved, unimpeached. *Informal,* in the clear.

Adverbs—innocently, *etc.*; with clean hands; with a clear conscience.

Quotations—It is better that ten guilty persons escape than one innocent suffer (*William Blackstone*), Innocence is like a dumb leper who has lost his bell, wandering the world meaning no harm (*Graham Greene*), In maiden meditation, fancy-free (*Shakespeare*), God will not cast away an innocent man (*Bible*), The innocent are God's elect (*St. Clement*).

Antonyms, see GUILT.

---

innocuous, *adj.* harmless, mild, inoffensive. See HEALTH, INNOCENCE, GOOD. *Ant.,* harmful, dangerous.

innovation, *n.* CHANGE, NEWNESS, novelty; variation; departure.

innuendo, *n.* implication, intimation, allusion. See INFORMATION.

innumerable, *adj.* countless, uncountable; numberless. See INFINITY. *Ant.,* countable, finite.

inoculate, *v.t.* vaccinate, variolate, immunize, infect. See INSERTION, REMEDY.

inoffensive, *adj.* innocuous, harmless; unaggressive; blameless. See INNOCENCE. *Ant.,* offensive, harmful.

inoperative, *adj.* ineffective, not working, malfunctioning, on the fritz (*inf.*). USELESSNESS.

inopportune, *adj.* unseasonable, untimely, ill-timed; inconvenient, awkward. See INEXPEDIENCE. *Ant.,* convenient, proper.

inordinate, *adj.* excessive, disproportionate, unreasonable. See EXAGGERATION.

INORGANIC MATTER
The inanimate world

Nouns—1, inorganic matter, mineral, mineral world *or* kingdom, unorganized, inanimate, *or* lifeless matter, inorganization; lithification, petrification; petrifaction; brute matter; stone, metal, chemicals. See MATERIALS.

2, a. mineral, noble mineral; acanthite, actinolite, adamite, alabaster, amphibole, anhydrite, apatite, aragonite, argentite, asbestos, aventurine, azurite, babingtonite, barite, bauxite, beryl, bismuth, borax, brookite, calcite, carnalite, carnotite, celestite, chalcedony, chlorite, chromite, cinnabar, columbite, copalite, corundum, cryolite, cuprite, dendrite, diaspore, dolomite, emery, epsomite, feldspar, fluorite, gadolinite, galena, garnet, graphite, gypsum, halite, hematite, jamesonite, kaolinite, kernite, kyanite, lazurite, leucite, limonite, magnesite, malachite, manganite, marcasite, mesolite, mica, orpiment, pargasite, pyrite, pyroxene, quartz, realgar, rhodonite, serpentine, siderite, smaltite, sodalite, stannite, sulfur, talc, tourmaline, trona, ulexite, uraninite, wolframite, zincite. b. gem[stone]; agate, alexandrite, almandine, amber, amethyst, aquamarine, beryl, bloodstone, carbuncle, carnelian, cat's eye, chalcedony, chrysoberyl, chrysolite, citrine, diamond, emerald, ·garnet, heliotrope, hyacinth, jacinth, jade, jasper, jet, lapis lazuli, malachite, melanite, moonstone, morganite, nephrite, onyx, opal, peridot, quartz, ruby, sapphire, sard[onyx], spinel, sunstone, tiger's-eye, topaz, tourmaline, turquoise, zircon.

3, metal (see 5,); alloy; alnico, amalgam, babbitt [metal], brass, bronze, carboloy, [carbon, Damascus, graphite, *or* stainless] steel, cast iron, chrome, coin nickel, constantan, damask, electrum, elinvar, invar, permalloy, perminvar, pewter, pinchbeck, solder, spiegeleisen, sterling silver, tombac, white gold, wrought iron.

4, [igneous, extrusive, intrusive, mantle, metamorphic, plutonic, stratified, volcanic, *or* sedimentary] rock, aggregate, batholith, bedrock, boulder, composite, evaporite, laccolith, mélange, moraine, scree, talus; andesite, anorthosite, aplite, basalt, breccia, brownstone, buhr[stone], calc-silicate, chalk, chert, clinkstone, coal, conglomerate, dacite, diabase, diorite, dolerite, dolomite, dripstone, dunite, felsite, flint, gabbro, gneiss, granite, greenstone, grit, gypsum, halite, hematite, hornblende, hornfels, ironstone, lava, limestone, marble, marl, mudstone, obsidian, oolite, pitchstone, porphyry, pumice, quartzite, rock salt, rottenstone, sandstone, schist, scoria, serpentine, shale, skarn, slage, soapstone, stalactite, stalagmite, stinkstone, touchstone, trachyte, trap, traprock, travertine, tufa, tuff, volcanic ash.

5, chemical, organic compound; [chemical] element, actinium, aluminum, americium, antimony, argon, arsenic, astatine, barium, berkelium, beryllium, bismuth, boron, bromine, cadmium, calcium, californium, carbon, cerium, cesium, chlorine, chromium, cobalt, columbium, copper, curium, dysprosium, einsteinium, erbium, europium, fermium, fluorine, francium, gadolinium, gallium, germanium, gold, hafnium, hahnium, helium, holmium, hydrogen, indium, iodine, iridium, iron, krypton, lanthanum, lawrencium, lead, lithium, lutetium, magnesium, manganese, mendelevium, mercury, molybdenum, neodymium, neon, neptunium, nickel, niobium, nitrogen, nobelium, osmium, oxygen, palladium, phosphorus, platinum, plutonium, polonium, potassium, praseodymium, prometium, protactinium, radium, radon, rhenium, rhodium, rubidium, ruthenium, rutherfordium, samarium, scandium, selenium, silicon, silver, sodium, strontium, sulfur, tantalum, technetium, tellurium, terbium, thallium, thorium, thulium, tin, titanium, tungsten, uranium, vanadiu, wolfram, xenon, ytterbium, yttrium, zinc, zirconium.

6, earth sciences; mineralogy, [physical *or* structural] geology, geomorphology, geophysics, lithology, orography, petrology, geognosy, geoscopy, metallurgy, lithology, petrology; inorganic chemistry, geochemistry. See ORGANIC MATTER.

Verbs—mineralize, petrify, lithify; turn to dust.

Adjectives—inorganic, mineral, unorganized, inanimate, lifeless, azoic, inert, insentient, insensible, insensate, unfeeling.

Antonyms, see ORGANIC MATTER.

---

in ovo, Lat., in the egg. See UNPREPAREDNESS.

in posse, Lat., possible, in [the realm of] POSSIBILITY.

input, *n.* INFORMATION, knowledge; contribution, two cents (*inf.*). Ant., output.

—*v.t.* enter, type *or* feed in. See COMPUTERS.

inquest, *n.* INQUIRY, hearing.

inquietude, *n.* uneasiness, FEAR; restlessness, AGITATION.

INQUIRY
Search for information

Nouns—**1,** inquiry, enquiry; question, REQUEST; search, research, quest, PURSUIT; examination, test, intelligence test; review, scrutiny, investigation, inspection, probe; trial, hearing; inquest, inquisition; exploration, ventilation; sifting, calculation, analysis, dissection, reverse engineering; audit; resolution; induction; Baconian method; autopsy, post mortem; strict, close, searching, *or* exhaustive inquiry; narrow *or* strict search; study, consideration. *Informal,* exam. See CURIOSITY, THOUGHT, LEARNING.

2, *(act of inquiring)* questioning, interrogation, grilling, third degree, interrogatory; interpellation; challenge, examination, cross-examination, catechism; questionnaire; feeler, Socratic method, leading question; koan; discussion (see REASONING); reconnoitering, reconnaissance; prying, espionage, spying, intelligence, counterintelligence; [aptitude, achievement, intelligence, IQ, *or* placement] test, Scholastic Aptitude Test, [P]SAT, Graduate Record Examination, GRE, true-false *or* multiple-choice test, makeup test, quiz, oral *or* written exam[ination], standardized test; oral, rectal, *etc.* examination (see REMEDY). *Slang,* fishing expedition.

3, *(subject of inquiry)* question, query, problem, topic, talking point, proposition, desideratum, point to be solved, subject *or* field of inquiry, subject of controversy; point *or* matter in dispute; moot point; [question at] issue; bone of contention (see DISCORD); fair *or* open question; frequently asked question, FAQ; enigma (see SECRET); knotty point (see DIFFICULTY); sixty-four-thousand-dollar question.

4, *(one who inquires)* inquirer, investigator, inquisitor, inspector, querist, examiner, prober, cross-examiner, watchdog committee; spy, secret *or* intelligence agent, operative, undercover agent, counterspy, double agent; detective, operative, private eye *or* detective, plainclothesman, house detective; federal, government, *or* treasury agent; catechist; analyst; busybody (see CURIOSITY); secret service, intelligence community, military, naval, *etc.* intelligence, FBI, CIA. *Informal,* op. *Slang,* shamus, gumshoe; mole; [private *or* house] dick, G-man, T-man, the Company, cousins.

Verbs—1, inquire, seek, search; look for, look about for, look out for; scan, reconnoiter, explore, sound, rummage, ransack, pry, peer, look round; cast about *or* around, scrounge around; scavenge; look *or* go through *or* over; spy; peer *or* pry into every hole and corner; trace; ferret out, unearth, leave no stone unturned; smell, sniff, feel, sound, seek, *or* search out, run down, hunt up, nose *or* poke about *or* around, seek a clue, hunt, track, trail, hound; follow the trail *or* scent, dowse; pick one's way; pursue (see PURSUIT); thresh *or* smoke out; fish, feel, *or* grope for. *Slang,* shake down.

2, *(make inquiries)* investigate, check [up] on; follow up; look up, look at *or* into; preexamine; discuss, comb, canvass, agitate; browse; examine, study, consider, calculate, monitor; delve into, prove, sound, fathom; scrutinize, analyze, anatomize, dissect, sift, winnow; audit, review, take stock of; take into consideration (see THOUGHT); take counsel (see ADVICE). *Informal,* kick around, hash over. *Slang,* clock, make, moose around.

3, *(ask a question)* ask, question, demand; ventilate; grapple with *or* go into a question; interrogate, catechize, quiz, grill, pump, cross-question, cross-examine, give the third degree; pick the brains of; frisk; feel out.

Adjectives—inquiring, inquisitive, curious; catechetical, inquisitorial, analytic; in search *or* quest of; on the lookout for, interrogative; in question *or* dispute, in issue, under discussion, investigation, *or* consideration; subjudice, moot, proposed; doubtful (see DOUBT).

Adverbs—what? why? wherefore? whence? whither? where? how goes it? how is it? what is the reason? what's the matter? what's in the wind? what on earth? when? who? how come? what's up? what's new?

Phrases—ask a silly question and you get a silly answer; ask no questions and hear no lies; seek and ye shall find.

Quotations—In examinations, those who do not wish to know ask questions of those who cannot tell (*Sir Walter Raleigh*), One hears only those questions for which one is able to find answers (*Friedrich Nietzsche*), Try to love the questions themselves (*Rainer Maria Rilke*), It is better to ask some of the questions than to know all of the answers (*James Thurber*), Some questions don't have answers, which is a terribly difficult lesson to learn (*Katharine Graham*).

Antonyms, see ANSWER.

---

inquisition, *n.* examination, questioning; tribunal; cross-examination; probe, investigation, INQUIRY. See SEVERITY.

inquisitive, *adj.* questioning; curious, prying, meddlesome, busybodyish. See CURIOSITY.

in re, *Lat.,* in the matter of; concerning. See RELATION.

inroad, *n.* raid, encroachment. See ATTACK.

INSANITY
Lack of mental soundness

Nouns—1, insanity, lunacy, derangement, craziness, feeblemindedness; abnormal behavior, pathology; affective disorder; nervous breakdown; antisocial, compulsive, cyclothymic, passive-aggressive, *or* psycopathic personality, character disorder; manic depression, bipolar disorder; neurosis, anxiety; hypochondria, psychosis, psychopathy, schizophrenia, hebephrenia, split *or* multiple personality, paranoia, dementia praecox, psychosexual disorder; autism; madness, mental illness, abnormality, aberration; posttraumatic stress disorder, battle *or* combat fatigue; seasonal affective disorder, SAD; dementia, frenzy, raving, delirium, hallucination; mass hysteria; lycanthropy; rabies, hydrophobia; Oedipus *or* Electra complex; disordered reason *or* intellect; diseased, unsound, *or* abnormal mind; idiocy, imbecility; anility, senility, dotage (see AGE). *Slang,* blue devils. See UNCONFORMITY, FOLLY.

2, *(symptoms)* vertigo, dizziness, swimming, disorientation; sunstroke, moon-madness; [nervous] breakdown, collapse; euphoria, mania, hysteria; paranoia, fixation; amnesia, fugue; delusion, hallucination; infantilism; insomnia; melancholia; koro; malaise; persecution complex; defense mechanism, denial, displacement, negation, procrastination, projection, rationalization, reaction formation, regression, repression, substitution.

3, *(obsession)* mania; monomania, megalomania, nymphomania, satyriasis, bibliomania, pyromania, logomania, theomania, kleptomania, dipsomania, Anglomania; delirium tremens; hypochondriasis, melancholia, hysteria (see DEJECTION); obsession, fixation; shell shock; phobia (see FEAR). *Slang,* hangup.

4, *(insane person)* madman, madwoman, maniac, bedlamite, lunatic; demoniac, dipsomaniac, megalomaniac; neurotic, psychotic, psychopath, schizophrenic, catatonic, paranoiac; idiot, imbecile, cretin, moron, lunatic; Jekyll and Hyde. *Informal,* couch case, lunatic fringe. *Slang,* nut, crank, loon[y], bat, bug, screwball, oddball, case, crackpot, fruitcake, mental, space cadet, wacko, loony tune.

5, *(hospital for the insane)* [insane *or* lunatic] asylum, sanitarium, sanatorium, mental hospital *or* institution, [mental] home, bedlam (*archaic*), madhouse; psychiatric ward; halfway house; straitjacket, padded cell. *Slang,* nuthouse, nut factory, nuthatch, bughouse, loony bin, booby hatch, funny farm, psycho ward, snake pit, nuttery.

6, *(doctor who treats insanity)* psychiatrist, alienist (see INTELLECT).

7, psychology, psychotherapy, psychoanalysis, bioenergetics, metapsychology, parapsychology, psychobiology, psychopathology, psychophysics, psychophysiology, somatopsychology; associationism, behaviorism, cultural relativism, functionalism, gestalt, nativism, personality theory, transactional analysis, structuralism.

Verbs—**1,** be insane, be out of one's mind; lose one's senses *or* reason; lose one's faculties *or* wits; go mad, run mad *or* amuck, rave, rant, dote, ramble, wander; drivel; take leave of one's senses, go into a tailspin *or* nosedive, break *or* crack up, go to pieces; lose one's head. *Informal,* come apart at the seams. *Slang,* have a screw loose, have bats in the belfry, not have all one's marbles *or* buttons; go off one's nut *or* rocker, go postal, see things, flip [one's lid], flip *or* freak out, wig out.

2, drive mad *or* crazy, craze, distract, shatter, unhinge, madden, dement, addle the wits of, derange; infatuate, obsess, turn the brain, turn one's head, go to one's head.

3, commit, put away, institutionalize, lock up (see RESTRAINT); certify.

Adjectives—**1,** insane, mad, lunatic; crazy, crazed, non compos mentis, unhinged, unbalanced, disturbed; paranoid, manic; criminally insane, psychopathic, psychotic, psychoneurotic, manic-depressive; not right, touched; bereft of reason; unhinged, unsettled in one's mind; insensate, reasonless, beside oneself, demented, daft; frenzied, frenetic; possessed [of a devil]; far gone, maddened, moonstruck; scatterbrained, crackbrained, off one's head; maniacal; delirious, irrational, light-headed, incoherent, rambling, doting, wandering; amuck, frantic, raving, stark mad, staring mad. *Slang,* overdrawn, crazy as a bedbug *or* a loon, loco, psycho, nutty [as a fruitcake], screwy, gonzo, meshugga, out to lunch, kooky, wacky, wacko, whacked out, dementoid, gomer, loony tunes, bananas, off the wall, ape[shit], around the bend, off one's trolley *or* rocker, freaky, bonkers; tetched, pixilated, bughouse; mental (*Brit.*).

2, *(acting as if insane)* rabid, giddy, dizzy, cuckoo, daft, vertiginous, wild, slap-happy; mazed, flighty; distracted, distraught; mad as a hatter *or* March hare; of unsound mind; touched [in one's head], not in one's right mind; in a fog *or* haze; out of one's mind, head, senses, *or* wits; on the ragged edge. *Informal,* daffy. *Slang,* off one's nut, haywire, barmy, balmy, zoned.

3, *(obsessive)* fanatical, obsessed, infatuated; odd, eccentric (see UNCONFORMITY); hipped; hypochondriac; idiot, imbecile, silly.

4, monomaniacal, kleptomaniacal, *etc.* (see *Nouns,* 3).

Adverbs—insanely; like one possessed; maniacally, *etc.*

Phrases—whom the gods would destroy, they first make mad.

Quotations—There is a pleasure sure, in being mad, which none but madmen know! (*John Dryden*), Is there no way out of the mind? (*Sylvia Plath*), Even paranoics have enemies (*Delmore Schwartz*), When we remember that we are all mad, the mysteries disappear and life stands explained (*Mark Twain*), We are all born mad. Some remain so (*Samuel Beckett*), There is no great genius without some touch of madness (*Seneca*), Sanity is very rare (*Emerson*), Sanity is madness put to good uses (*George Santayana*), If you talk to God, you are praying. If God talks to you, you have schizophrenia (*Thomas Szasz*).

Antonyms, see SANITY.

---

insatiable, *adj.* greedy, voracious; insatiate, unappeasable, quenchless, unquenchable. See DESIRE, GLUTTONY. *Ant.,* full, sated.

inscribe, *v.t.* write; mark, engrave; enter, enroll, LIST. See WRITING, ENGRAVING.

inscrutable, *adj.* unfathomable (see UNINTELLIGIBILITY). *Ant.,* an open book.

insect, *n.* bug; fly, moth, beetle, ant, *etc.* See ANIMAL.

insecticide, *n.* pesticide (see KILLING).

insecurity, *n.* DANGER, uncertainty, risk, hazard, jeopardy.

insensate, *adj.* inanimate; unfeeling, cold. See INSENSIBILITY.

INSENSIBILITY
Lack of physical or emotional feeling

Nouns—1, *(physical numbness)* insensibility, insensibleness; impassibility, impassibleness, impassivity; inappetency, apathy, phlegm, dullness, hebetude, supineness, lukewarmness. See OBLIVION.

2, *(emotional numbness)* coldness, cold fit, cold blood, cold heart; frigidity, sangfroid; stoicism; imperturbability, INEXCITABILITY; nonchalance, unconcern, dry eyes; insouciance, INDIFFERENCE; RASHNESS, callousness; heart of stone, marble, deadness; thickness of skin. See INACTIVITY.

3, *(state of insensibility)* coma, trance, sleep, suspended animation; numbness, unfeeling; stupor, stupefaction, paralysis, palsy. *Slang,* la-la-land. See REPOSE.

4, *(cause of insensibility)* anesthesia, anesthetic, analgesia, narcosis; ether, chloroform, nitrous oxide, opium; saddle-block *or* spinal [anesthesia]; refrigeration, cryotherapy; acupuncture, acupressure; painkiller, novocaine, xylocaine, *etc.*; stun gun.

5, insensate. *Slang,* gork.

Verbs—1, *(become insensitive)* black *or* pass out, faint, draw a blank; have a rhinocerous hide. *Slang,* nod out, snow out, zone out, flake out.

2, *(make insensitive)* desensitize, blunt, obtund, [be]numb, paralyze, drug, chloroform, deaden, hebetate, stun, stupefy, daze, knock out. *Slang,* zap.

3, show insensibility, not mind *or* care, not be affected by; have no desire for, not care a straw (see INDIFFERENCE); disregard (see NEGLECT); set at naught; turn a deaf ear to.

4, inure, harden [the heart]; steel, caseharden, sear.

Adjectives—1, *(physically insensitive)* insensible, senseless, unconscious, insensate; numb[ed]; comatose; anesthetic, stupefied, chloroformed; dead to the world, dead[ened]; narcotic. *Informal,* out like a light, out cold, under.

2, *(emotionally insensitive)* insensitive, insensate; impassive, impassible; dispassionate; blind, deaf, *or* dead to; unsusceptible, insusceptible; unimpressionable, passionless, spiritless, heartless, soulless, hardhearted; unfeeling, indifferent, lukewarm, careless, regardless; inattentive, neglectful; callous, thick-skinned, pachydermatous, impervious; hard, hardened, inured, casehardened; steeled against; proof against; imperturbable, inexcitable, unfelt; unconcerned, nonchalant, insouciant, sans souci.

3, *(lacking certain types of emotional feeling)* unambitious; unaffected, unruffled, unimpressed, uninspired, unexcited, unmoved, unstirred, untouched, unshocked, unstruck; unblushing, shameless; unanimated, vegetative; apathetic, phlegmatic; dull, frigid; cold, cold-blooded, coldhearted; cold as marble *or* charity; flat, obtuse, inert, supine, languid, halfhearted.

Adverbs—insensibly, *etc.*; in cold blood; with dry eyes.

Quotations—Cast a cold eye on life, on death. Horseman, pass by! (*William Butler Yeats*), A man who so much resembled a baked Alaska—sweet, warm and gungy on the outside, hard and cold within (*Francis King*).

Antonyms, see SENSIBILITY, FEELING.

---

inseparable, *adj.* close, indivisible, thick as thieves (*inf.*). See FRIEND.

INSERTION
Act of putting in

Nouns—**1,** insertion, introduction, interpolation; injection, inoculation; implantation; ADDITION; INTERMENT; penetration. See BETWEEN.

2, insert, inset, inlay; entering wedge (see INGRESS); adjunct; parenthesis.

Verbs—insert, interpolate, inset, inlay; put, press, pack, *or* stuff in; inject, inoculate; introduce, insinuate, impregnate, implant, graft, bud; intervene (see BETWEEN); infuse, instill; add; bury, inter; immerse, submerge; pierce (see OPENING).

Adjectives—interpolative, parenthetical, *etc.*

Antonyms, see EXTRACTION.

---

inside, *adj.* internal, INTERIOR; indoor; privileged, specialized. —*adv.* within; indoors, out of the cold. —*n.* INTERIOR; private, personal. See SPECIALITY. *Ant.*, outside, out of doors.

insider, *n.* initiate, member [of the inner sanctum]. See SPECIALITY.

insidious, *adj.* deceitful; treacherous. See DECEPTION, IMPROBITY.

insight, *n.* discernment, perceptiveness, perception; INTUITION; penetration, understanding. See KNOWLEDGE.

insignia, *n.pl.* badges [of office], emblems. See INDICATION.

insignificant, *adj.* meaningless; unimportant, inconsequential, trivial, small, worthless. See CHEAPNESS, UNIMPORTANCE. *Ant.*, significant, important.

insincere, *adj.* false, deceptive; hypocritical, two-faced; halfhearted, untrue, affected. See AFFECTATION, FALSEHOOD. *Ant.*, honest, sincere.

insinuate, *v.t.* hint, suggest, intimate; ingratiate (oneself), curry favor; insert, instill. See INFORMATION, INSERTION, BETWEEN.

INSIPIDITY
Lack of taste or interest

Nouns—insipidity, vapidity; tastelessness, weakness; dullness, MEDIOCRITY, INDIFFERENCE.

Adjectives—**1,** *(lacking taste)* insipid, tasteless, flavorless, savorless, unseasoned, zestless; weak, stale, flat, mild, bland; milk-and-water, watery.

2, *(lacking interest)* uninteresting, unentertaining, prosaic, prosy, jejune, tame, dull, dry; vapid, flat, banal; mawkish, wishy-washy; spiritless, lacklustrous, pointless, lifeless, amort, dead.

Quotations—There is nothing upon the face of the earth so insipid as a medium. Give me love or hate! (*Fanny Burney*).

Antonyms, see TASTE, PUNGENCY.

---

insist, *v.i.* state, maintain, hold to; persist, urge, press; demand. See AFFIRMATION, COMPULSION, OBSTINACY.

insnare, *v.t.* See ENSNARE.

INSOLENCE
Rudeness

Nouns—**1,** *(overbearing behavior)* insolence, arrogance; hauteur, haughtiness, airs; overbearance; presumption, assertiveness, bravado, pomposity, snobbery; DEFIANCE.

2, *(impertinent behavior)* impertinence; sauciness, flippancy, petulance, bluster; familiarity; cheek, swagger[ing], bounce; impudence, assurance, audacity; hardihood, front, face, shamelessness, effrontery, PRIDE, VANITY. *Informal,* brass, sauce. *Slang,* gall, nerve, sass, crust, lip. See DISCOURTESY.

3, smart aleck. *Informal,* smart or wise guy. *Slang,* smarty pants, weisenheimer, minx, cool hand, smart-mouth, wiseass, wiseacre.

Verbs—**1,** bluster, vapor, swagger, swell, give oneself airs, snap one's fingers; swear (see AFFIRMATION); roister; arrogate; assume, presume; make bold, make free; take a liberty, patronize. *Slang,* have a nerve, stiff.

2, outface, outlook, outstare, outbrazen, outbrave; stare out of countenance; brazen out; lay down the law; talk or act big; talk back, get on a high horse; toss the head, carry with a high hand; overreach. See THREAT.

Adjectives—**1,** insolent, haughty, arrogant, imperious, high-handed, high and mighty, stuck-up, cocky, uppity; contumelious, supercilious, snobbish, overbearing, overweening, lordly, assertive, bold, high-flown; nervy. *Slang,* high-hat, fresh, bodacious.

2, flippant, pert, cavalier, saucy, sassy, forward, impertinent, malapert; precocious, assuming, would-be, bumptious; bluff; brazen, shameless, aweless, unblushing, unabashed; boldfaced, barefaced, brazen-faced; familiar, impudent, audacious, presumptuous, free and easy; roistering, blustering, hectoring, swaggering, vaporing. *Informal,* flip.

Adverbs—insolently, *etc.*; with a high hand; where angels fear to tread.

Quotations—Victory is by nature insolent and haughty (*Cicero*), Rudeness is better than any argument; it totally eclipses intellect (*Arthur Schopenhauer*), Good breeding consists in concealing how much we think of ourselves and how little we think of the other person (*Mark Twain*), He has to learn that petulance is not sarcasm, and that insolence is not invective (*Benjamin Disraeli*).

Antonyms, see SERVILITY.

---

insolvency, *n.* FAILURE, bankruptcy; lack of funds. See DEBT.

insomnia, *n.* sleeplessness; wakefulness. See ACTIVITY.

inspect, *v.t.* examine, scrutinize; check (up); oversee; investigate, look into. See ATTENTION, VISION.

inspiration, *n.* breathing, inhalation; happy thought, brainstorm, brainwave. See CAUSE, FEELING, PIETY, IMAGINATION.

inspire, *v.* breathe (in); stimulate, animate, [en]liven; spur, give an incentive. See CAUSE, WIND.

instability, *n.* CHANGEABLENESS, unsteadiness, inconstancy.

install, *v.t.* put in, set up; induct, seat, inaugurate, invest. See LOCATION, CELEBRATION, BEGINNING.

installment, *n.* down payment, time payment, layaway plan; episode, PART; installation, setting up, putting in. See COMMISSION.

instance, *n.* case, example, illustration, demonstration. See CONFORMITY.

instant, *adj.* sudden, immediate, direct, instantaneous. See INSTANTANEITY. —*n.* second, moment; minute; twinkling, jiffy. See NECESSITY, PRESENT.

INSTANTANEITY
Immediate occurrence

Nouns—1, instantaneity, instantaneousness, immediacy, precipitancy (see RASHNESS); suddenness, abruptness; moment, minute, second, instant, split second, nanosecond; twinkling, trice, flash, breath, crack, burst, flash of lightning, less than no time; jackrabbit start. See TIME, EARLINESS, TRANSIENTNESS.

2, very minute, very time, very hour; PRESENT time, right, true, exact, *or* correct time. *Informal,* jiffy. *Slang,* half a shake, sec. See CHRONOMETRY.

Verbs—think on one's feet; stop in one's tracks, stop on a dime.

Adjectives—instantaneous, momentary, sudden, instant, abrupt; extemporaneous; precipitate, immediate, hasty (see HASTE); quick as thought *or* lightning.

Adverbs—instantaneously, instantly, immediately, [right] now, right off, right away, then and there, here and now; in less than no time; presto, subito, instanter, suddenly, at a stroke, word, *or* blow, at the drop of a hat; in a moment, in the twinkling of an eye, in a flash, at one jump, in the same breath, [all] at once; plump, slap; at one fell swoop; at the same instant; straight off, directly, immediately, cold turkey, ex tempore, on the spot, on the spur of the moment; just then; slapdash. *Informal,* in a jiffy, like a shot, yesterday, in nothing flat, in two shakes, before one can say Jack Robinson. *Slang,* like a bat out of hell.

Antonyms, see LATENESS, PERPETUITY.

in statu quo, Lat., in the same condition, unchanged. See STABILITY, PERMANENCE.

instead, *adv.* in place *or* lieu (of). See SUBSTITUTION.

instigate, *v.t.* incite, provoke; initiate, stimulate, urge, promote. See CAUSE.

instill, *v.t.* inculcate, implant, impart; pour in, mix in, infuse. See MIXTURE, TEACHING, INSERTION.

instinct, *n.* knack, aptitude; impulse, prompting, discernment; INTUITION. See INTRINSIC. *Ant.,* LEARNING, KNOWLEDGE.

institute, *v.t.* found, inaugurate; organize, start, begin, commence; originate, or-ganize. See BEGINNING. —*n.* institution; SCHOOL, college; foundation; society; museum; hospital, *etc.* See PARTY.

institutionalize, *v.t.* commit [to an institution], incarcerate; establish. See COMMISSION, CONFORMITY.

instruction, *n.* TEACHING, tutelage, education; training, coaching; COMMAND, order, direction, directive; ADVICE. See INFORMATION.

instructive, *adj.* informative, educational, enlightening. See LEARNING, TEACHING.

instrument, *n.* implement (see INSTRUMENTALITY); flute, oboe, *etc.* (see MUSIC); document, deed, paper, RECORD, charter; MEANS, AGENCY.

INSTRUMENTALITY
Means to an end

Nouns—1, instrumentality; instrument, AID; subservience, subserviency; vehicle, hand, expedient (see PLAN); MEANS, AGENCY.

2, *(means)* stepping-stone; [master *or* skeleton] key, latchkey, passkey; open sesame; passport, passe-partout, safeconduct, pass, *etc.*

3, *(tools)* a. hardware, equipment; gadget, contraption; automaton, robot, nanobot, foglet; instrument, tool, device, implement, appliance, apparatus, contrivance, machine. b. [ball-peen *or* claw] hammer, beetle, club, fuller, hatcher, mallet, maul, pestle, ram, scutch, sledge[hammer], tamp, triphammer. c. adz, alpenstock, awl, barb, bill, bodkin, burin, chisel, cleaver, clipper, colter, crampon, crochet, dibble, draw-shave, edger, frow, gouge, grapnel, graver, hardy, hatchet, hook, inshave, nibbler, nippers, peavey, pick, pike, punch[eon], scissors, scraper, scythe, shears, sickle, snips, spur, stylus, tang, trier, wedge. See SHARPNESS. **d.** buffer, file, darby, die, flatiron, flatter, float, grindstone, hone, jointer, lathe, oilstone, plane, putty knife, rasp, router, sander, sandpaper, scraper, shaper, shavehook, slipstone, spokeshave, steel wool, strop, swage, tamper, trowel, waterstone, whetstone. See SMOOTHNESS. **e.** azibiki, backsaw, bayonet, bucksaw, chain saw, circular saw, coping saw, crosscut saw, dozuki, hacksaw, handsaw, jigsaw, keyhole saw, compass saw, ripsaw, ryoba, saw, whipsaw. **f.** bail, bar, crowbar, cultivator, entrenching tool, fork, hoe, lever, loy, mattock, pitchfork, plow, pry, prize, jimmy, rake, scoop, shovel, spade, spatula, sput, trowel. *Informal,* Army banjo. See CONCAVITY. **g.** auger, drill, bit, bore, brace, chaser, chuck, corkscrew, gimlet, jackhammer, mandrel, reamer, snake, tap, wimble, broach, burr. **h.** wrench, spanner. **i.** anchor, brace, chuck, clamp, claw, clip, forceps, grip, impact driver, pincers, pinchcock, pliers, stapler, nailer, puller, riveter, [Phillips, flathead, offset, *or* Allen] screwdriver, screw gun, tongs, tweezers, vise. **j.** alligator clip, arbor, bearing, bibcock, bolt, brace, brad, buckle, bushing, cable, caster, chain, chevron, clevis, collar, cotter, elbow, eye[bolt], flange, gasket, gooseneck, grommet, hasp, hinge, knob, knuckle, latch, nail, nipple, nut, pin, pipe, plug, rivet, screw, setscrew, shackle, spring, staple, stirrup, stud, switch, tack, thumbscrew, thumbtack, valve, washer, wye. See CONNECTION. **k.** jack; motor, engine, treadle, pedal; gear, paraphernalia, machinery; pulley, block and tackle, crane, derrick; belt, conveyor belt; wheels, gears, cam, clockwork, cog, flywheel; can opener, scissors, shears, lawnmower, *etc. Slang,* droid, Jaws of Life, church key. **l.** gadget. *Informal,* watchamacallit, thingamy. *Slang,* dofunny, dojigger, gewgaw, hicky, wing-ding, dufus, dingbat, doodad, fandangle, gilhooley, gimcrack, gizmo, knack, majig, whazzit, widget.

Verbs—be instrumental, subserve.

Adjectives—instrumental; useful (see UTILITY); ministerial, subservient.

Adverbs—instrumentally; through, by, per; whereby, thereby, hereby; by the agency of.

Quotations—Man is a tool-using animal . . . Without tools he is nothing, with tools he is all (*Thomas Carlyle*), One machine can do the work of fifty ordinary men. No machine can do the work of one extraordinary man (*Elbert Hubbard*), One servant is worth a thousand gadgets (*Joseph Schumpeter*).

Antonyms, see USELESSNESS.

---

insubordinate, *adj.* disobedient, intractable; mutinous, insurgent; stubborn, obsti-nate, too big for one's britches (*inf.*). See DISOBEDIENCE, DEFIANCE.

INSUBSTANTIALITY
Lack of substance

Nouns—**1,** *(lacking substance)* insubstantiality; nothingness, nihility; nothing, naught, nil, nullity, zero, cipher, no one, nobody; never a one; no such thing, none in the world; nothing whatever, nothing at all, nothing on earth; not a particle (see LITTLENESS); all talk, moonshine, stuff and nonsense; shadow; phantom; dream (see IMAGINATION); ignis fatuus; [thin] air; bubble; mockery; hollowness, blank, void (see ABSENCE); inanity, fool's paradise. *Slang,* goose egg. See NONEXISTENCE, UNIMPORTANCE.

2, *(lack of material being)* immateriality, immaterialness, intangibility; incorporeality, disembodiment; spirit, soul, ego; spiritualism, spirituality.

Verbs—immaterialize, dematerialize; disembody, spiritualize (see DISAPPEARANCE).

Adjectives—insubstantial, unsubstantial; bodiless, incorporeal, spiritual, immaterial, intangible, unearthly; psychical, supernatural; visionary, imaginary (see IMAGINA-

TION); dreamy; shadowy, ethereal, aerial, airy, spectral; weightless; vacant, vacuous, empty (see ABSENCE), blank, hollow; nominal, null; inane.

Quotations—All that we see or seem is but a dream within a dream (*Edgar Allan Poe*), We are such stuff as dreams are made on, and our little life is rounded with a sleep (*Shakespeare*), Nothingness haunts being (*J. P. Sartre*).

Antonyms, see SUBSTANCE.

---

insufferable, *adj.* unendurable, unbearable, insupportable, intolerable, past bearing *or* enduring, more than flesh and blood can bear; agonizing, excruciating. See PAIN.

INSUFFICIENCY
Lack of necessary amount

Nouns—1, insufficiency; inadequacy, inadequateness; incompetence, IMPOTENCE; deficiency, INCOMPLETENESS, IMPERFECTION, shortcoming, emptiness, poorness, depletion, vacancy, flaccidity; ebb tide; low water; bankruptcy, insolvency (see DEBT, NONPAYMENT).

2, paucity; stint; scantiness, smallness, none to spare; bare necessities, scarcity, dearth; want, need, deprivation, lack, POVERTY; inanition, starvation, famine, drought; dole, pittance; short allowance *or* rations, half-rations.

Verbs—1, not suffice, fall short of (see FAILURE); run dry, run *or* give out, run short; want, lack, need, require; be caught short, be in want, live from hand to mouth; miss by a mile.

2, exhaust, deplete, drain of resources; impoverish (see WASTE); stint, begrudge (see PARSIMONY); cut back, retrench; bleed white.

Adjectives—1, insufficient, inadequate; too little, not enough; unequal to; incompetent, impotent; weighed in the balance and found wanting; perfunctory (see NEGLECT); deficient, wanting, lacking, imperfect, marginal; ill-furnished, -provided, *or* -stored; badly off.

2, slack, at a low ebb; empty, vacant, bare; out of stock; short (of), out of, destitute (of), devoid (of), denuded (of); dry, drained; in short supply, not to be had for love *or* money, not to be had at any price; empty-handed; short-handed. *Slang,* strapped.

3, meager, poor, thin, sparing, spare, skimpy, stinted; starved, half-starved, famine-stricken, famished; jejune; scant, small, scarce; scurvy, stingy; at the end of one's tether; without resources (see MEANS); in want, poor (see POVERTY); in DEBT. *Slang,* shy of, fresh out of.

Adverbs—insufficiently, *etc.*; in default, for want of; failing.

Phrases—man cannot live by bread alone.

Quotations—Men can starve from a lack of self-realization as much as they can from a lack of bread (*Richard Wright*), As a human being, one has been endowed with just enough intelligence to be able to see clearly how utterly inadequate that intelligence is when confronted with what exists (*Albert Einstein*).

Antonyms, see SUFFICIENCY.

---

insular, *adj.* isolated; islanded, insulated; aloof; narrow[-minded], limited, illiberal; isolationist. See NARROWNESS.

insulate, *v.t.* cover, protect, shield; set apart, isolate, detach. See EXCLUSION, COVERING.

insult, *v.t.* slap, abuse, affront, offend. See DISCOURTESY. —*n.* outrage; slap, affront. See DISRESPECT.

insuperable, *adj.* insurmountable. See IMPOSSIBILITY.

insurance, *n.* guarantee, warranty, coverage, protection; insurance policy; assurance, SECURITY.

insurgent, *adj.* rebellious, insubordinate, mutinous, in revolt, uprising. —*n.* rebel, insubordinate, mutineer, revolu-

tionary, insurrectionist. See REVOLU-
TION, DISOBEDIENCE.

insurmountable, *adj.* insuperable. See IM-
POSSIBILITY.

insurrection, *n.* uprising, riot, eruption;
mutiny, REVOLUTION, insurgence. See
OPPOSITION, DISOBEDIENCE.

intact, *adj.* whole, unimpaired, uninjured;
untouched. See PERFECTION, PRESERVA-
TION.

intake, *n.* consumption, ingestion, assimilation; receipts. See RECEIVING.

intangible, *adj.* immaterial, vague, impalpable; unspecific; abstract. See INSUB-
STANTIALITY. *Ant.,* tangible, concrete.

integral, *adj.* INTRINSIC, component; entire, combined, unified. See COMPLE-
TION.

integrate, *v.t.* unite, fuse; synthesize,
blend; complete. See UNITY.

integrity, *n.* honor, honesty, PROBITY, uprightness; wholeness, completeness,
oneness. See WHOLE. *Ant.,* dishonesty,
immorality.

INTELLECT
Mental capacity

Nouns—1, intellect, intellectuality, mentality, brain[s], mind, understanding, reason
(see REASONING), rationality; faculties, senses, consciousness, observation (see AT-
TENTION); perception, apperception, INTELLIGENCE; INTUITION, association of ideas;
conception, JUDGMENT, wits, mental capacity, genius; logic, THOUGHT, meditation;
the five wits, the ghost in the machine. *Slang,* marbles, smarts.

2, *(location of intellect)* soul, spirit, psyche, ghost, inner man, heart, breast, bosom;
seat of thought, brain; subconscious, id; head, cerebrum, cranium; gray matter.
Slang, upper story, noodle.

3, *(study of intellect)* psychology, psychopathology, psychotherapy, psychiatry, psychoanalysis, psychometry; ideology; philosophy; phrenology, craniology, cran-
ioscopy; ideality, idealism; transcendentalism, spiritualism, immateriality.

4, psychologist, psychopathologist, alienist, psychiatrist, psychometrist, psychotherapist, psychoanalyst, hypnotherapist, analyst, counselor, therapist. *Slang,* head
shrinker, shrink, head doctor, squirrel.

5, intellectual (see INTELLIGENCE).

Verbs—intellectualize (see THOUGHT); note, notice, mark; take notice, take cognizance;
be aware *or* conscious; realize; appreciate; ruminate; fancy, imagine (see IMAGINA-
TION).

Adjectives—intellectual, mental, rational, subjective, metaphysical, spiritual, ghostly;
psychical, psychological; cerebral; percipient, aware, conscious; subconscious; immaterial; logical, reasoning, reasonable; thoughtful, thinking, meditative, contemplative.

Quotations—Minds are like parachutes. They only function when they are open (*James
Dewar*), 'Tis the mind that makes the body rich (*Shakespeare*), A good mind is a lord
of a kingdom (*Seneca*), Intellectual passion drives out sensuality (*Leonardo da Vinci*).
Antonyms, see INSANITY.

intellectual, *n.* pundit, brain (see KNOWL-
EDGE). —*adj.* mental (see INTELLECT).

INTELLIGENCE
Capacity to learn

Nouns—1, intelligence, capacity, comprehension, apprehension, understanding; parts,
sagacity, [mother] wit, esprit; intelligence quotient, IQ, acuteness, shrewdness, CUN-
NING; acumen, subtlety, penetration; perspicuity, perspicacity, percipience; discernment, good JUDGMENT; levelheadedness, common sense, discrimination; refinement
(see TASTE); KNOWLEDGE; head, brains, mind, INTELLECT; eagle eye; genius; inspiration, soul; talent, aptitude (see SKILL). *Informal,* horse *or* cat sense, little gray cells.

2, genius, intellectual, intellect, pundit; scholar (see LEARNING); idiot savant; intelligentsia, literati. *Slang,* pointy-head, egghead, beard, highbrow.

Verbs—**1,** be intelligent, have all one's wits about one; understand, grasp, comprehend, figure *or* make out; come to terms *or* grips with; take a hint; see through, take in, see at a glance, see with half an eye; dawn on one; penetrate; discern (see VISION). *Informal,* sink *or* soak in; catch *or* latch on (to).

2, be levelheaded, have one's feet on the ground, have one's head screwed on the right way, have a good head on one's shoulders.

3, understand, fathom, grasp, comprehend. *Slang,* colly. See MEANING.

Adjectives—intelligent, quick, keen, brainy, acute, alive, awake, bright, brilliant, sagacious, sharp; nimble- *or* quick-witted; wide awake; CUNNING, canny, arch, shrewd, astute; clearheaded *or* -eyed; farsighted; discerning, perspicacious, penetrating, subtle, perceptive, piercing, sharp [as a tack *or* needle]; alive to, aware of (see KNOWLEDGE); clever (see SKILL). *Informal,* not so dumb, no flies on, not just a pretty face. *Slang,* not born yesterday, laser-eyed.

Phrases—genius is an infinite capacity for taking pains; genius without education is like silver in the mine; skill without genius is not much, but genius without skill is nothing.

Quotations—The true genius is a mind of large general powers, accidentally determined to some particular direction (*Samuel Johnson*), Genius is one percent inspiration, ninety-nine percent perspiration (*Thomas Edison*), A man of genius makes no mistakes (*James Joyce*), The height of cleverness is to be able to conceal it (*La Rochefoucauld*), Common sense is nothing more than a deposit of prejudices laid down in the mind before you reach eighteen (*Albert Einstein*), Genius is an African who dreams up snow (*Vladimir Nabokov*), Everybody is born with genius, but most people only keep it a few minutes (*Edgard Varèse*), Towering genius disdains a beaten path (*Abraham Lincoln*).

Antonyms, see IGNORANCE.

---

intelligentsia, *n.pl.* intellectuals, literati, illuminati, clerisy. See KNOWLEDGE. *Ant.,* hoi polloi, unlettered.

intelligible, *adj.* clear, explicit; articulate, comprehensible; lucid, perspicuous; legible, precise; obvious. See MEANING. *Ant.,* unintelligible.

INTEMPERANCE
Lack of moderation

Nouns—**1,** intemperance, indulgence, overindulgence, high living, self-indulgence; voluptuousness; epicurism, epicureanism, sybaritism (see GLUTTONY); drunkenness, DRINKING; prodigality (see WASTE); dissipation, licentiousness, debauchery; crapulence, incontinence; excess, too much; sensuality, animalism, carnality; PLEASURE, luxury, luxuriousness; lap of pleasure *or* luxury. See DRUGS.

2, revel[s], revelry; debauch, carousal, jollification, drinking bout, wassail, saturnalia, orgy.

3, drunkard, addict, voluptuary, sybarite, glutton, rake, roué, gourmand, sensualist, etc.

Verbs—indulge, overindulge, exceed; live well *or* high, live on the fat of the land; wallow, plunge into dissipation; revel, rake, live hard, cut loose, run riot, sow one's wild oats; slake one's appetite *or* thirst; swill; pamper; burn the candle at both ends.

Adjectives—intemperate, inabstinent; sensual, self-indulgent; voluptuous, luxurious, licentious, wild, dissolute, dissipated, rakish, fast, debauched; brutish; crapulous, crapulent, swinish, piggish; epicurean, sybaritical; bred in the lap of luxury; indulged, pampered, full-fed, prodigal. *Slang,* off the wagon.

Adverbs—intemperately, immoderately, to excess, excessively, without restraint. *Slang*, up the butt *or* ying-yang.

Quotations—The road of excess leads to the palace of wisdom (*William Blake*), Nothing succeeds like excess (*Oscar Wilde*), Can one desire too much of a good thing? (*Shakespeare*), Too much of a good thing can be wonderful (*Mae West*), Never . . . murder a man who is committing suicide (*Woodrow Wilson*), Let us eat and drink; for tomorrow we shall die (*Bible*).

Antonyms, see MODERATION.

---

intend, *v.* See INTENTION.

intended, *n.* fiancé[e], betrothed, future. See MARRIAGE. —*adj.* intentional (see INTENTION.)

intense, *adj.* violent, sharp, strong; passionate, ardent, vivid; deep, dark; poignant, keen, acute; extreme. See FEELING.

intensify, *v.* deepen, strengthen, heighten, sharpen; concentrate; aggravate (see INCREASE). See STRENGTH.

intensity, *n.* depth; feeling; power, force, strength, VIGOR; darkness, brilliance; extremity. See DEGREE, ENERGY, VIOLENCE.

intensive, *adj.* extreme, acute, thorough. See COMPLETION.

intent, *n.* See INTENTION. —*adj.* earnest, sincere; absorbed, engrossed; bent (on). See ATTENTION, RESOLUTION.

INTENTION
Purpose

Nouns—1, intention, intent, intentionality; purpose; project, PLAN, UNDERTAKING; predetermination; design, ambition; contemplation, mind, animus, view, purview, proposal; lookout; decision, determination, resolve, RESOLUTION; set *or* settled purpose, wish, DESIRE, motive. See WILL, MEANING.

2, final cause, raison d'être, end in itself; object, aim, end; drift, tenor, TENDENCY; goal, target, prey, quarry, game; destination, mark. See PURSUIT.

Verbs—intend, purpose, design, mean; have to; propose to oneself, harbor a design; have in view *or* mind; have an eye to; labor for; be after, aspire after, endeavor; aim *or* drive at; take aim, set before oneself; study to; hitch one's wagon to a star; take upon oneself, undertake, take into one's head; meditate, contemplate; think, dream, *or* talk of; premeditate; compass, calculate; plan *or* figure on, destine, propose, predetermine; project, PLAN, have a mind to (see WILLINGNESS); DESIRE, pursue.

Adjectives—intended, intentional, advised, studied, express, determinate, prepense, bound for; intending, minded; bent upon, earnest, resolute; at stake; on the fire, in view, in prospect.

Adverbs—intentionally, *etc.*; advisedly, wittingly, knowingly, designedly, purposely, on purpose, by design, studiously, pointedly; with intent; deliberately, with premeditation; with one's eyes open, in cold blood; to all intents and purposes; with a view *or* eye to; by way of, so as to, in order to *or* that, to the end that, with the intent that; for the purpose of, with the view of, in contemplation of, on account of; in pursuance of, pursuant to.

Quotations—The will to do, the soul to dare (*Sir Walter Scott*), The road to Hell is paved with good intentions (*Karl Marx*), The evil that is in the world almost always comes of ignorance, and good intentions may do as much harm as malevolence if they lack understanding (*Albert Camus*).

Antonyms, see CHANCE.

---

inter, *v.t.* bury, entomb, inearth. See INTERMENT.

interact, *v.i.* cooperate; interplay, mesh. See COOPERATION.

intercede, *v.i.* mediate, arbitrate; intervene, interpose. See COMPROMISE.

intercept, *v.t.* stop, interrupt, check, hinder; catch, nab, seize; cut off. See HINDRANCE.

INTERCHANGE
Exchange of something for its equal

Nouns—interchange, exchange, interchangeableness, interchangeability; permutation, intermutation; reciprocation, reciprocity, transportation, shuffling, give-and-take; alternation; hocus-pocus; BARTER; a Roland for an Oliver, tit for tat, an eye for an eye, RETALIATION; crossfire, battledore and shuttlecock; quid pro quo, musical chairs; fungible. See TRANSFER, SUBSTITUTION.

Verbs—interchange, exchange, counterchange, transpose, bandy, shuffle, change hands, change partners, take turns, switch, swap, permute, reciprocate, commute; cash in; give *or* put and take, pay back, requite, return the compliment, put the shoe on the other foot, give a dose *or* taste of one's own medicine; retaliate (see RETALIATION). *Informal*, flip-flop.

Adjectives—interchanged, interchanging, interchangeable, fungible, reciprocal, mutual, communicative, intercurrent.

Adverbs—in exchange, vice versa, backward[s] and forward[s], by turns, turn and turn about; in exchange for, against, in consideration of; from hand to hand; in kind, in turn; each other, one another.

Phrases—one good turn deserves another.

Antonyms, see IDENTITY.

---

intercourse, *n.* COMMUNICATION, CONVERSATION, converse, communion; coitus, [sexual] congress, SEX; SOCIALITY; fellowship, association; commerce, dealings, trade, BUSINESS.

interdict, *v.t.* forbid, [de]bar, proscribe, prohibit. See PROHIBITION.

interest, *v.* concern; touch, affect; fascinate, engross, intrigue; hold [the attention], engage, absorb. See EXCITEMENT.
—*n.* concern; welfare, benefit; payment, sum, advantage, profit; PART, share, holding; claim, title. See DEBT, IMPORTANCE, POSSESSION.

interface, *n.* link, CONNECTION; user interface, GUI. See COMPUTERS.

interfere, *v.i.* butt in, meddle, interpose; hinder, hamper; clash, obstruct, collide, oppose. See HINDRANCE, BETWEEN.

interference, *n.* HINDRANCE; opposition, conflict; static, noise, jamming.

interim, *n.* meantime (see BETWEEN).

INTERIOR
Inside of something

Nouns—interior, interiority; intrinsicality (see INTRINSIC); inside[s], subsoil, substratum; contents (see COMPOSITION), substance, bowels, belly, intestines, guts, chitterlings (see BODY); womb; lap; [innermost] recesses; cave (see CONCAVITY).

Verbs—be inside *or* within; place *or* keep within; enclose, circumscribe (see CIRCUMSCRIPTION); intern; imbed, insert (see INSERTION); imprison (see RESTRAINT).

Adjectives—interior, internal; inner, inside, inward, inmost, innermost; deep-seated; intestinal; inland; subcutaneous; interstitial (see BETWEEN); inwrought; enclosed; intramural; domestic, indoor, vernacular; endemic.

Adverbs—internally, inwardly, inward[s], inly; herein, therein, wherein; indoors, within doors; at home, in the bosom of one's family.

Prepositions—in, inside, within.

Antonyms, see EXTERIOR.

interject, *v.t.* insert, interpolate (see INSERTION).

interlock, *v.* interlink, interconnect (see CONNECTION).

interloper, *n.* intruder, trespasser; meddler, interferer, intermeddler. See BETWEEN.

interlude, *n.* intermission, intermezzo, entr'acte; pause, interval, episode, gap, space. See TIME, DRAMA.

intermediary, *n.* go-between, mediator; arbiter, arbitrator, umpire, referee; middleman. See BETWEEN.

intermediate, *adj.* BETWEEN; MIDDLE, intervening; halfway. See MEAN.

INTERMENT
Burial

Nouns—1, interment, burial, sepulture, inhumation, inurnment; cryonics (see COLD). 2, *(burial rites)* obsequies, exequies, funeral [rites], last rites, extreme unction; embalming; wake; pyre, funeral pile, cremation, immolation; perpetual care; [death] knell, passing bell, tolling; dirge (see LAMENTATION); death watch, vigil; deep six; dead *or* death march, taps, threnody, funeral procession, exequy, muffled drum; elegy, eulogy, panegyric, funeral oration; epitaph; obituary, death notice; autopsy, necropsy, postmortem. *Informal,* obit. See DEATH.

3, *(burial equipment)* grave clothes, shroud, winding sheet, cerement; coffin, casket, burial case, shell, sarcophagus, urn, pall, bier, hearse, catafalque, cinerary urn; crematory, crematorium; human remains pouch, body bag. *Slang,* dead *or* meat wagon, bonebox, Chicago *or* pine overcoat, eternity-box, six-foot bungalow, tree suit, pine drape; glad bag, mummy sack.

4, *(burial location)* grave, pit, sepulcher, tomb, vault, crypt, catacomb, mausoleum, golgotha, house of death, narrow house; cemetery, necropolis, ossuary; burial place *or* ground; graveyard, churchyard; lych gate; God's acre, memorial park; tumulus, cromlech, dolmen, kurgan, barrow, cairn; bonehouse, charnel house, morgue, mortuary, cist, columbarium; cinerarium, monument, marker, cenotaph, shrine; canopic jar; stele, gravestone, headstone, slab, tombstone; memorial, pyramid. *Slang,* boneyard, Boot Hill, marble orchard, cold storage, deep six, city of the dead, potter's field.

5, undertaker, embalmer, mortician, undertaker, funeral director; funeral home; pallbearer, mourner; sexton; gravedigger; coroner; body snatcher, graverobber. *Slang,* black coat, cold cook, planter.

Verbs—inter, bury; lay in the grave, consign to the grave *or* tomb, lay to rest; entomb, inhume, inurn; lay out; lie in state; perform a funeral; cremate, immolate; embalm, mummify. *Slang,* push up daisies.

Adjectives—funereal, funebrial, funerary; mortuary, sepulchral, cinerary; elegiac; necroscopic.

Adverbs—in memoriam; post-obit, postmortem; beneath the sod.

Interjections—rest in peace, requiescat in pace, R.I.P.

Quotations—Bury my heart at Wounded Knee (*Stephen Vincent Benét*), Friends, Romans, countrymen, lend me your ears; I come to bury Caesar, not to praise him (*Shakespeare*), One of the crying needs of the time is for a suitable burial service for the admittedly damned (*H. L. Mencken*).

Antonyms, see DISCLOSURE.

intermezzo, *n.* interlude, entr'acte (see MUSIC, BETWEEN).

interminable, *adj.* endless (see CONTINUITY).

intermission, *n.* pause, interval, break; entr'acte. See DRAMA, DISCONTINUANCE.

intermittent, *adj.* fitful, off-and-on, recurrent; periodic, discontinuous, interrupted, broken; flickering. See IRREGULARITY, DISCONTINUANCE.

intern, *v.t.* detain, hold; shut up *or* in, confine. —*n.* interne, internee; prisoner; student *or* resident doctor. See RESTRAINT, REMEDY.

internal, *adj.* inner, enclosed, inside, INTERIOR; innate, inherent; domestic, inland. See INTRINSIC.

internalize, *v.t.* subjectivize, assimilate. See INTERIOR, SECRET.

international, *adj.* worldwide, global, universal. See HUMANITY.

Internet, *n.* information highway, World Wide Web, net. See COMMUNICATION.

interpose, *v.* step in *or* BETWEEN; interfere, meddle; mediate, arbitrate; intervene, interrupt. See HINDRANCE, DISCONTINUANCE.

INTERPRETATION
Meaning

Nouns—1, interpretation, definition; explanation, explication; solution, ANSWER; rationale, concept; strict interpretation; DEMONSTRATION; MEANING; acception, acceptation, acceptance; light, reading, lection, construction, version; subtext; semantics. *Informal,* spin, take. See TEACHING.

2, translation, rendering, rendition, paraphrase, construct; literal *or* free translation; secret, clue; dissertation; ATTRIBUTION. *Informal,* trot, bicycle. *Slang,* pony.

3, *(analysis)* exegesis; expounding, exposition, megillah; comment, commentary; inference, deduction (see REASONING); illustration, exemplification; glossary, annotation, scholium, note, elucidation; symptomatology; reading of signs, semeiology; diagnosis, prognosis; metoposcopy; paleography, philology; equivalent, synonym; polyglot.

4, *(code interpretation)* decipherment, decodement; cryptography, cryptanalysis; key, solution, ANSWER, light.

5, lecture, sermon, tract; discussion, disquisition; treatise, discourse, exposition, study; critique, criticism; essay, theme, thesis.

6, interpreter, explainer, translator; expositor, exponent, expounder; demonstrator, definer, simplifier, popularizer; oracle, teacher; commentator, annotator, scholiast; constructionist; diagnostician; decoder, cryptographer, cryptanalyst. *Informal,* spin meister *or* doctor.

Verbs—interpret, explain, define, construe, translate, render; do into, turn into; paraphrase, restate; read; spell *or* make out; decipher, unravel, disentangle; illuminate, clarify, find the key of, make sense of, make heads or tails of, enucleate, resolve, solve, get at, clear up, get to the bottom of; read between the lines; account for; find *or* tell the cause of; throw *or* shed light on; clear up, elucidate; illustrate, exemplify; unfold, expound, comment upon, annotate, gloss; key; popularize; understand by, put a construction on, be given to understand; put *or* get across, get over, get through to. *Informal,* psych out.

Adjectives—interpretive, interpretative; definitive; inferential, deductive, explanatory, expository; explicative, explicatory, exegetical, illustrative; polyglot; literal; paraphrastic, metaphrastic; cosignificative, synonymous, equivalent.

Adverbs—interpretively, interpretatively, in explanation; that is to say, id est, videlicet, to wit, namely, in short, in other words; literally, strictly speaking, in plain words *or* English; more simply.

Quotations—A translation is no translation unless it will give you the music of a poem along with the words of it (*John Synge*), Translations (like wives) are seldom strictly faithful if they are in the least attractive (*Roy Campbell*), Interpretation is the revenge of the intellect upon art (*Susan Sontag*).

Antonyms, see UNMEANINGNESS, DISTORTION.

interrogation, *n.* INQUIRY, inquisition, questioning; probe, investigation, [cross-] examination.

interrupt, *v.* stop, check; suspend, cut short, hinder, obstruct; butt in, interpose, break in. See HINDRANCE, DISCONTINUANCE.

intersect, *v.i.* cut, bisect; interrupt; meet, cross. See CROSSING.

intersperse, *v.* scatter (see BETWEEN, DISPERSION).

intertwine, *v.t.* [inter]mingle, interlace, interweave. See MIXTURE, CROSSING.

INTERVAL
Distance between

Nouns—interval, interspace; separation, DISJUNCTION; break, fracture, gap; hole, OPENING; chasm, hiatus, caesura; interruption, interregnum; interstice, lacuna, cleft, mesh, crevice, chink, cranny, crack, chap, slit, fissure, scissure, rift, flaw, breach, rent, gash, cut, incision, leak; haha, gorge, defile, ravine, coulee, canyon, crevasse, abyss, abysm; gulf; inlet, firth, frith, strait, gulch, gully; pass, FURROW; parenthesis (see BE-TWEEN); void (see ABSENCE). See DEPTH, INCOMPLETENESS, DISCONTINUANCE.

Verbs—set at intervals, separate, space, gape, open.

Adjectives—with an interval, far between; spaced.

Adverbs—at intervals, discontinuously.

Antonyms, see CONTACT, COMPLETION, CONTINUITY.

---

intervene, *v.i.* interfere, interrupt, interpose; come between; mediate, arbitrate; intercede; occur, happen, take place. See BETWEEN, DISCONTINUANCE.

interview, *v.t.* converse with, question. — *n.* questioning, CONVERSATION, consultation, meeting. See INQUIRY.

intestine, *n.* bowel, alimentary canal, guts *(inf.)*. See BODY.

intimate, *adj.* close, friendly, familiar; private, personal. See NEARNESS. —*v.t.* hint, suggest, imply; announce, impart. See INFORMATION, DISCLOSURE. —*n.* FRIEND, crony, boon *or* bosom companion. *Ant.*, public, impersonal.

intimidate, *v.t.* subdue, cow, bully, scare, frighten, overawe. See FEAR, THREAT.

intolerable, *adj.* beyond endurance, unbearable, insupportable, insufferable. See PAIN.

intolerance, *n.* bigotry, bias, prejudice; dogmatism, narrowness. See JEALOUSY, EXCITABILITY.

intonation, *n.* inflection *or* modulation [of voice]; tuning. See SOUND, MUSIC.

in toto, *Lat.*, in full; wholly. See COMPLETION.

intoxicate, *v.* inebriate, [be]fuddle; exalt, elate, overjoy; poison. See DRINKING, EXCITEMENT.

intractable, *adj.* unmanageable, ungovernable; obstinate, perverse; refractory, rebellious. See OBSTINACY. *Ant.*, obedient.

intransigent, *adj.* uncompromising, unrelenting, inflexible. See RESOLUTION.

intrepid, *adj.* fearless, undaunted (see COURAGE).

intricate, *adj.* complicated, complex; involved, devious, cunning. See DISORDER, CONVOLUTION. *Ant.*, simple.

intrigue, *n.* plot, conspiracy, skullduggery; spying, espionage, scheming; love affair, amour. See LOVE. —*v.* fascinate, interest; plot, PLAN, scheme; spy. See ATTENTION.

INTRINSIC
Innate quality

Nouns—1, intrinsicality, inbeing, inherence, inhesion; subjectiveness; ego; essence, essentialness, essentiality, essential part, quintessence, incarnation; quiddity, gist, pith, core; marrow, sap, lifeblood, backbone, heart, soul; important part (see IMPORTANCE); principle. See PART.

2, nature, constitution, character, quality, property, crasis, diathesis, the nature of the beast; ring [of truth, *etc.*]. See IDENTITY.

3, HABIT, temper, temperament; spirit, humor, grain; moods, features, aspects; peculiarities (see SPECIALITY); idiosyncrasy; idiocrasy (see TENDENCY); diagnostics; endowment, capacity, capability (see POWER).

Verbs—inhere, be *or* run in the blood, be born to.

Adjectives—intrinsic[al]; subjective; fundamental, normal; implanted, inherent, essential, elementary, basic, natural; innate, inborn, inbred, ingrained, inwrought; radical; incarnate; thoroughbred, hereditary, inherited, immanent; congenital, connate, running in the blood; ingenerate, indigenous; in the grain, bred in the bone, instinctive;

inward, internal, INTERIOR; to the manner born; virtual; characteristic; invariable, incurable, ineradicable, fixed, *etc.*

Adverbs—intrinsically, at bottom, in the main, in effect, practically, virtually, substantially, fairly. *Slang,* like stink on shit.

Quotations—All progress is based upon a universal innate desire of every organism to live beyond its means (*Samuel Butler*).

Antonyms, see EXTRINSIC.

---

introduce, *v.t.* usher, bring in; present, acquaint (with); insert, interpolate; initiate, institute. See BEGINNING, PRECEDENCE, BETWEEN, INSERTION.

introduction, *n.* preface, forward, prelude; presentation, [new] acquaintanceship; INSERTION. See COURTESY, PRECEDENCE, DRAMA.

introspective, *adj.* introverted; preoccupied, self-absorbed. See ATTENTION. *Ant.,* extroverted.

intrude, *v.i.* interlope, intervene, interfere; butt in, trespass, encroach; overstep, obtrude. See BETWEEN, INGRESS.

intrusive, *adj.* intruding, interfering (see BETWEEN).

intrust, *v.t.* See ENTRUST.

INTUITION
Innate knowledge

Nouns—intuition, intuitiveness, insight, perceptivity, instinct; apprehension, presentiment (see EXPECTATION); rule of thumb; clairvoyance, sixth sense, extrasensory perception, ESP, second sight. See INTELLECT, KNOWLEDGE, PREDICTION.

Verbs—sense, feel; guess, hazard a guess, talk at random, play [it] by ear; intuit. *Informal,* not have a leg to stand on; feel it in one's bones. *Slang,* fly by the seat of one's pants.

Adjectives—intuitive, instinctive, impulsive, automatic; perceptive; independent of reason, natural, innate, gratuitous, hazarded; unconnected. *Informal,* gut.

Adverbs—intuitively, instinctively, by intuition; illogically; without rhyme or reason.

Quotations—It is only with the heart that one can see rightly; what is essential is invisible to the eye (*Antoine de Saint-Exupéry*), A moment's insight is sometimes worth a life's experience (*Oliver Wendell Holmes*).

Antonyms, see REASONING.

---

inundate, *v.t.* flood, deluge. See WATER, SUFFICIENCY.

inure, *v.t.* toughen, accustom, familiarize, harden, habituate. See HABIT, STRENGTHEN.

invade, *v.t.* enter, encroach, violate, penetrate, trespass; ATTACK, assail, harry. See INGRESS.

invalid, *adj.* void, null, worthless, useless, valueless, unusable. See NULLIFICATION.

invalid, *n.* sufferer, patient, case, shut-in; cripple. —*adj.* sickly, ill, unhealthy, unwell, weak. See DISEASE.

invalidate, *v.t.* nullify, cancel, annul, void. See NULLIFICATION.

invaluable, *adj.* inestimable, priceless. See DEARNESS, UTILITY.

invariable, *adj.* unvarying, constant, steady; fixed, uniform; monotonous; permanent. See PERMANENCE, STABILITY, REGULARITY.

invasion, *n.* encroachment, infringement, violation; invasion of privacy; ATTACK. See WARFARE, INGRESS, BETWEEN.

invective, *n.* denunciation, vituperation, vilification. See IMPRECATION.

inveigle, *v.i.* lure, attract, ensnare, cajole, persuade, allure, entice. See DECEPTION.

invent, *v.t.* devise, conceive, contrive, originate; imagine, fabricate, improvise; create, spin, forge, design; feign. See IMAGINATION, FALSEHOOD.

inventory, *n.* tally, count; accounting, LIST; stock, goods, merchandise. See STORE.

INVERSION
Reversal

Nouns—1, inversion, eversion, retroversion, introversion; contrariety, contrariness (see OPPOSITION); reversal; turn of the tide; overturn; somersault, somerset; revulsion; turnabout, about-face, volte-face. *Informal,* spill. See CHANGE, INTERCHANGE.

2, inverse, reverse, flip of the coin.

3, transposition, metastasis, anastrophe; tmesis, parenthesis; metathesis; palindrome; pronation and supination. See GRAMMAR.

Verbs—turn, go, *or* wheel around *or* about, cut *or* double back; backfire; turn *or* topple over; capsize; invert, retrovert, introvert, reverse, evert; overturn, upset, turn topsy-turvy; transpose, put the cart before the horse; turn the tables, turn turtle, keel over.

Adjectives—inverted, wrong side out; inside out, upside down; bottom upward, bottoms up; on one's head, topsy-turvy; inverse; reverse, opposite; in reverse; top-heavy.

Adverbs—inversely, counter, heels over head, head over heels, end for end, vice versa.

Antonyms, see DIRECTION.

---

invest, *v.* endue, endow, clothe, array; surround, hem in, besiege, beleaguer; install, induct; dress, adorn; confer; spend. See CLOTHING, POWER, COMMISSION, ATTACK, PURCHASE.

investigate, *v.t.* inquire, examine, question; search, probe. See INQUIRY.

investor, *n.* [finance, venture, *etc.*] capitalist, financier. See MONEY.

inveterate, *adj.* habitual, hardened; fixed, set. See HABIT, RESOLUTION.

invidious, *adj.* hateful, offensive; unfair, injurious; mean[-spirited]. See HATE, INJUSTICE, MALEVOLENCE.

invigorate, *v.t.* strengthen, liven, refresh, enliven, restore, energize, animate. See POWER, STRENGTH, REFRESHMENT. *Ant.,* weaken.

invincible, *adj.* unconquerable, indefatigable, unyielding, indomitable. See STRENGTH, POWER. *Ant.,* vulnerable.

inviolable, *adj.* invulnerable, unassailable. See SAFETY, PURITY.

INVISIBILITY
Lack of visibility

Nouns—invisibility; nonappearance, imperceptibility, indistinctness; mystery, delitescence (see CONCEALMENT). See LATENCY, TRANSPARENCY.

Verbs—lurk, escape notice, blush unseen; conceal, veil, put out of sight; not see, lose sight of; dematerialize.

Adjectives—invisible, imperceptible, indiscernible, unapparent, nonapparent; out of sight, not in sight; behind the scenes *or* curtain; inconspicuous; unseen, covert, latent; eclipsed, under an eclipse; dim, faint (see DIMNESS); indistinct, indistinguishable; shadowy, indefinite, unseen; ill-defined *or* -marked; blurred, out of focus, misty (see OBSCURITY); clouded (see CLOUDINESS), veiled.

Quotations—I am invisible . . . simply because people refuse to see me (*Ralph Ellison*), The poet ranks far below the painter in the representation of visible things, and far below the musician in that of invisible things (*Leonardo da Vinci*), The artist must be in his work as God is in creation, invisible and all-powerful; one must sense him everywhere but never see him (*Gustave Flaubert*), What is essential is invisible to the eye (*Antoine de Saint-Exupéry*).

Antonyms, see VISIBILITY.

---

invite, *v.t.* summon, ask; tempt, attract, lure; solicit; bid; challenge; court. See REQUEST, OFFER.

invoice, *n.* LIST, bill, summation. See ACCOUNTING.

invoke, *v.t.* beseech, plead, beg; call, summon; utilize; wish, conjure; attest. See REQUEST, USE.

involuntary, *adj.* spontaneous, instinctive, automatic, reflex. See NECESSITY, UNWILLINGNESS. *Ant.,* voluntary, intentional.

involve, *v.t.* imply, entail, include; complicate, entangle, inculpate, implicate, incriminate, commit; mean.. See COMPOSITION, DIFFICULTY, RELATION, DISORDER, ATTENTION, MEANING, ACCUSATION.

invulnerable, *adj.* impregnable, invincible; unassailable, impenetrable; immune, proof; perfect, flawless, unimpeachable. See DEFENSE, SAFETY, STRENGTH. *Ant.,* vulnerable, assailable.

inward, *adj.* inside, private; in, interior, incoming; mental, spiritual, hidden. See INTERIOR. *Ant.,* outward.

iota, *n.* bit, jot, particle, tittle, mite. See LITTLENESS.

ipse dixit, *Lat.,* out of the horse's mouth; assertion. See AUTHORITY, CERTAINTY.

ipso facto, *Lat.* by its nature. See EXISTENCE.

IRASCIBILITY
Tendency to become angry

Nouns—1, irascibility, temper; crossness; petulance, irritability, pugnacity, contentiousness, EXCITABILITY; bad, hot, fiery, *or* quick temper, hot blood; ill humor, surliness, sullenness, churlishness, DISCOURTESY. *Informal,* crankiness; boiling point. See MALEVOLENCE, SENSIBILITY, DEJECTION.

2, *(outburst of anger)* fury, huff, miff, anger, RESENTMENT.

3, hothead, blusterer; shrew, vixen, virago, termagant, scold, Xanthippe; spitfire. *Informal,* fire-eater, crank, grouch, crosspatch. *Slang,* ugly customer, sourpuss, sorehead.

Verbs—have a temper, have a devil in one; flare *or* fire up, be angry (see RESENTMENT); sulk, mope, fret, frown, glower; get up on the wrong side of the bed. *Informal,* be *or* get sore.

Adjectives—irascible, bad-, quick-, *or* ill-tempered, hotheaded, irritable, crabbed; excitable; thin-skinned, edgy, sensitive, Type A; hasty, overhasty, quick, warm, hot, testy, touchy, huffy; pettish, petulant; waspish, snappish, cranky, disgruntled, out of sorts, cross [as a bear], grumpy, peppery, fiery, passionate, choleric, shrewish; querulous, captious, moody, moodish; quarrelsome, contentious, disputatious; pugnacious, feisty, bellicose; cantankerous, churlish, discourteous (see DISCOURTESY); fractious, peevish; in a bad temper; angry (see RESENTMENT). *Informal,* grouchy, ugly, sore, cross as two sticks, cross as a bear.

Adverbs—irascibly, irritably, *etc.*; against the grain.

Phrases—don't get mad, get even.

Quotations—Envy and wrath shorten the life (*Bible*), Let not the sun go down on your wrath (*Bible*), Anger is a brief madness (*Horace*), Speak when you are angry and you will make the best speech you will ever regret (*Ambrose Bierce*), Anger makes dull men witty, but it keeps them poor (*Elizabeth I*), Anger is never without a reason, but seldom with a good one (*Benjamin Franklin*).

Antonyms, see COURTESY, CHEERFULNESS.

irate, *adj.* See RESENTMENT.

iridescent, *adj.* opalescent, prismatic; colorful, glowing. See COLOR, VARIEGATION.

irk, *v.t.* annoy (see DISCONTENT).

irksome, *adj.* troublesome, irritating, tiresome, tedious, wearisome. See DIFFICULTY, DISCONTENT.

iron, *n.* flatiron, mangle. —*v.t.* press, mangle. See SMOOTHNESS.

ironclad, *adj.* armored; unassailable, unbreakable, inflexible. See SAFETY, INFLEXIBILITY.

irony, *n.* RIDICULE, satire, sarcasm. See FIGURATIVE.

irrational, *adj.* unreasonable, insensible; brainless, brutish, reasonless, absurd. See FOLLY. *Ant.,* rational, reasonable.

irrefutable, *adj.* unimpeachable, reliable; conclusive. See CERTAINTY.

IRREGULARITY

Nouns—irregularity, variability, DEVIATION, caprice, uncertainty; tardiness, unpunctuality (see LATENESS); intermittence, fitfulness, inconstancy. See CHANGEABLENESS, UN-CONFORMITY, DISCONTINUANCE, ROUGHNESS, DISORDER.

Verbs—fluctuate, intermit, come and go; flare up.

Adjectives—irregular, uncertain, unpunctual, capricious, inconstant, desultory, fitful, intermittent, flickering; sporadic, erratic, eccentric, spasmodic, checkered, variable, unstable, changeable, unpredictable, undependable.

Adverbs—irregularly, by fits and starts, off and on, out of turn, from time to time.

Antonyms, see REGULARITY.

---

irrelevant, *adj.* inappropriate, unfitting, unrelated, inconsistent, inapplicable. See DISAGREEMENT.

IRRELIGION
Lack of religious belief

Nouns—1, irreligion, irreligiousness, ungodliness, godlessness, IMPIETY; IDOLATRY; HETERODOXY.

2, *(questioning philosophies)* skepticism (see DOUBT); unbelief, disbelief; lack *or* want of faith; agnosticism, atheism; materialism, positivism; nihilism, infidelity, freethinking, rationalism, heathenism, paganism; anti-Christianity.

3, atheist, skeptic, doubting Thomas; apostate, renegade; unbeliever, infidel; heathen, pagan, alien, gentile; freethinker, rationalist, materialist, positivist; nihilist; agnostic; heretic.

Verbs—disbelieve, lack faith; DOUBT, question; scoff; curse God [and die].

Adjectives—irreligious, undevout; godless, godforsaken, graceless, ungodly, unholy, unsanctified, unrighteous, unhallowed; atheistic, agnostic; skeptical, freethinking; unbelieving, unconverted; doubting, faithless; unchristian, non-Christian, anti-Christian; gentile; heathen, pagan; materialistic, worldly, mundane, earthly, earthbound, carnal; secular.

Quotations—There are no atheists in the foxholes (*William Cummings*), An atheist is a man who has no invisible means of support (*Fulton Sheen*).

Antonyms, see RELIGION, PIETY.

---

irreparable, *adj.* irremediable, hopeless. See HOPELESSNESS.

irreplaceable, *adj.* essential, indispensable (see NECESSITY).

irreproachable, *adj.* faultless, above suspicion, unimpeachable. See INNOCENCE.

irresistible, *adj.* overpowering, overwhelming, stunning, puissant. See POWER, NECESSITY.

irresolute, *adj.* infirm of purpose, of two minds, halfhearted; dubious, undecided, unresolved, undetermined; hesitating, on the fence; at a loss; vacillating, unsteady, changeable, fickle, capricious, volatile; weak, timid, cowardly. See DOUBT, FEAR, CHANGEABLENESS.

irrespective, *adj.* regardless, independent (of), despite. See QUALIFICATION.

irresponsible, *adj.* negligent, remiss; reckless, unburdened. See CHANGEABLENESS, IMPROBITY, NEGLECT.

irreverent, *adj.* See DISRESPECT.

irrevocable, *adj.* irreversible, past recall, done, absolute. See NECESSITY.

irrigate, *v.t.* WATER, moisten, flood, flush. See CLEANNESS.

irritable, *adj.* fretful, petulant, peevish, touchy, sensitive. See IRASCIBILITY.

irritate, *v.t.* annoy, provoke, vex, bother, trouble; irk, exasperate, chafe, nettle, ruffle. See EXCITEMENT, VIOLENCE, RESENTMENT.

Islamic, *adj.* Muhammedan, Muslim; Shiite, Sunni. See RELIGION.

island, *n.* isle, ait; cay, key; atoll, [coral] reef, ledge. See LAND.

isolate, *v.t.* segregate; insulate, separate, quarantine. See DISJUNCTION, EXCLUSION.

issue, *n.* product, offspring, progeny (see POSTERITY); discharge; outcome, result; question, dispute (see INQUIRY). —*v.* leave, depart, debouch, emerge; circulate, dispatch, send, publish; emit, discharge, exude, eliminate; spout, spurt; flow, spring. See DEPARTURE, EFFECT, EGRESS, MONEY, PUBLICATION.

itch, *n.* itching, tickling, prickly sensation; mange, manginess; *cacoëthes, cacoëthes scribendi* (writer's itch); the itch, scabies, psora; itchiness; burning, tingling; DE-SIRE, craving, hankering. —*v.i.* tingle, prickle, burn; crave, long for, yearn, hanker. See SENSIBILITY.

item, *n.* piece, detail, particular; entry, article; term, paragraph, PART. See INFORMATION, UNITY.

itemize, *v.* detail, particularize, spell out, lay it on the line (*inf.*). See SPECIALITY.

itinerant, *adj.* wandering, nomadic, wayfaring, peripatetic, traveling. See TRAVEL.

itinerary, *n.* journey, route, circuit, course; guidebook. See TRAVEL, DIRECTION.

ivories, *n.pl.* [piano] keys; dice, bones, cubes. See MUSIC, AMUSEMENT.

J

jab, *n. & v.* punch, blow; prod, poke. See IMPULSE.

jabber, *n.* gibberish, babble, blather, nonsense, jabberwocky; prattle, talk, gossip, chatter. —*v.i.* talk, rattle on, prattle, chatter, gibber, gabble. See UNMEANINGNESS.

jack, *n.* man, fellow; knave, bower; lever; sailor, hand; jack-of-all-trades; ass, mule, donkey, rabbit; *slang,* money; applejack. See ANIMAL, ELEVATION, MALE.

jackal, *n.* wild dog, henchman, hireling, dog robber (*sl.*). See ANIMAL, SERVANT.

jackass, *n.* donkey; blockhead, dolt, jerk. See ANIMAL, IGNORANCE.

jacket, *n.* coat, sack *or* suit coat, dinner *or* smoking jacket, tuxedo, sport coat; jerkin; windbreaker, pea jacket *or* coat; peel, rind, skin. See CLOTHING, COVERING.

jackknife, *n.* pocketknife, penknife, switchblade, shiv (*sl.*). See SHARPNESS.

jackpot, *n.* [grand] prize, bonanza. See APPROBATION.

jaded, *adj.* weary, surfeited, blasé, dulled. See WEARINESS.

jag, *n.* bender, binge, toot. See DRINKING.

jagged, *adj.* sharp, rough, snaggy, notched, pointed, zigzag. See ROUGHNESS.

jail, *n.* See PRISON.

jalopy, *n., informal,* crate, bus, clunker, junker. See VEHICLE.

jam, *n.* crowd, press, crush; blockage, impasse; jelly, preserve; *slang,* predicament. See FOOD, DIFFICULTY. —*v.* crowd, press, crush; wedge, shove, push, cram; block. See HINDRANCE, IMPULSE.

jamboree, *n.* carousal, celebration. See AMUSEMENT.

jangle, *n.* DISCORD, clangor; ringing, jingle; bickering, dispute. —*v.* clash, clang, rattle, ring, jingle; upset. See DISCONTENT.

janitor, *n.* caretaker, superintendent, custodian; concierge. See CLEANNESS, SAFETY.

jar, *n.* clash, conflict, DISCORD; vessel, Mason jar, jug, cruse. —*v.* shock, jolt; jounce, shake, rattle; clash. See DISAGREEMENT, IMPULSE, RECEPTACLE.

jargon, *n.* lingo, shoptalk, patois, cant, argot, jive (*sl.*); double-talk; gibberish. See CONCEALMENT, UNMEANINGNESS.

jaundice, *n.* jaundiced eye, JEALOUSY; bitterness, rancor, hate; prejudice, bias, bigotry, narrowness. —*v.t.* predispose, prejudice, bias, color, distort. See RESENTMENT.

jaunt, *n.* excursion, ride, escapade, lark, stroll. See TRAVEL.

jaunty, *adj.* stylish, sprightly, smart, dapper, sporty (*inf.*); gay, breezy, brisk, debonair; jolly, ebullient, vivacious, cavalier, cocky (*inf.*) See FASHION, CHEERFULNESS, OSTENTATION.

jaw, *n.* mandible, jawbone. —*v.i.* chatter, talk, jabber. See LOQUACITY.

jazz, *n.* ragtime, blues, hot jazz, le jazz hot, Dixieland, swing, bop, bebop; cool, progressive, West Coast, *or* modern jazz; *slang,* nonsense, foolishness. See MUSIC, UNMEANINGNESS.

jazzy, *adj.* flashy, showy; syncopated. See OSTENTATION, MUSIC.

JEALOUSY
Feeling of envy

Nouns—jealousy, envy, covetousness, cupidity, DESIRE, heartburn, jaundice, jaundiced eye; green- *or* yellow-eyed monster; distrust, mistrust, umbrage, spite, RESENTMENT; suspicion, DOUBT; anxiety (see CARE).

Verbs—1, envy, turn green, covet; distrust, resent; suspect, DOUBT.

2, fill with envy, put one's nose out of joint, make one's mouth water.

Adjectives—jealous, jaundiced, green [with envy], covetous, envious; distrustful, resentful; doubtful, suspicious; anxious, concerned; apprehensive, watchful; intolerant, zealous, umbrageous.

Phrases—envy feeds on the living—it ceases when they are dead; the grass is always greener on the other side of the fence; nice work if you can get it.

Quotations—Love is strong as death; jealousy is cruel as the grave (*Bible*), Oh! how bitter a thing it is to look into happiness through another man's eyes (*Shakespeare*), The green-eyed monster which doth mock the meat it feeds on (*Shakespeare*), To jealousy, nothing is more frightful than laughter (*Françoise Sagan*), Jealousy is always born with love, but does not always die with it (*La Rochefoucauld*).

Antonyms, see BELIEF.

---

jeer, *v.* sneer, scoff, taunt, gibe, mock; RIDICULE, make fun of, belittle. —*n.* taunt, gibe, mockery; hoot, catcall, hissing. See CONTEMPT, DISRESPECT.

jejune, *adj.* insipid, dull; childish, immature; ignorant, uninformed. See WEARINESS, YOUTH, IGNORANCE.

jelly, *n.* gelatin, aspic; jam, preserve; mush. See FOOD.

je ne sais quoi, *Fr.,* I don't know what; an indefinable something. See SPECIALITY, INTRINSIC.

jeopardy, *n.* DANGER, risk, peril, hazard, THREAT.

jerk, *v.* twist, tweak, pull, snap; start, twitch, jitter, jump. —*n.* start, jump, twitch; spasm; pull, snap; *slang,* nitwit, fool, nobody. See EXCITABILITY, TRACTION, FOLLY.

jerky, *adj.* spasmodic, twitching, spastic. See AGITATION. *Ant.,* smooth.

jerry-built, *adj.* flimsy, gimcrack, tacky. See BADNESS, BUILDING.

jest, *n.* joke, jape; WIT, humor, clowning; practical joke; jocularity, pun, gag, wisecrack, witticism, bon mot; sport, fun; make-believe, fooling. —*v.i.* fool, joke; crack wise, gag; play the fool.

jester, *n.* WIT, joker, gagman, comedian; fool, clown, buffoon.

jet, *v.* stream, spurt, gush, shoot, spout, pour, rush, squirt. —*n.* stream, fountain; outgush, spurt; jet plane (see AVIATION). See WATER. —*adj.* black, pitch[y]; ebon[y]. See COLOR.

jetsam, *n.* castoff, castaway, lagan. See RELINQUISHMENT.

jet set, *informal,* smart set, beautiful people. See SUPERIORITY.

jetty, *n.* pier, wharf, breakwater, seawall. See SUPPORT.

jeunesse dorée, *Fr.,* gilded youth. See WASTE, YOUTH.

jewel, *n.* stone, gem; diamond, ruby, sapphire, *etc.* See ORNAMENT, GOOD.

jewelry, *n.* gems, beads, trinkets, stones; bracelets, bangles, necklaces, *etc.* See ORNAMENT.

jezebel, *n.* trollop, strumpet, hussy. See FEMALE, BADNESS.

jibe, *v.i.* agree, be in harmony, be consistent. See AGREEMENT.

jiffy, *n., informal,* moment, instant, flash. See INSTANTANEITY.

jiggle, *v.* fidget, twitch. See AGITATION.

jilt, *v.t.* reject *or* cast off (a lover); leave in the lurch. See DISAPPOINTMENT.

jimmy, *n.* pry, lever, crowbar. —*v.t.* pry open. See OPENING.

jingle, *n.* clink, tinkle, ring; jangle. See SOUND, POETRY.

jingo, *n.* See CHAUVINIST.

jinx, *n., informal,* curse, evil eye, bad luck, plague, [double] whammy (*sl.*). —*v.* curse, hex, bewitch, bedevil. See SORCERY.

jitter, *v.i.* twitch, fidget, jerk, jump, vibrate. —*n.* vibration; (*pl.*) heebie-jeebies, shakes, nervousness. See EXCITABILITY.

job, *n.* work, occupation, calling; piece of work, stint; position, situation, duty. See BUSINESS, ACTION.

jock, *n., slang,* athlete; he-man; jockstrap. See SPORTS, CLOTHING.

jockey, *v.* maneuver; cheat, trick. See CUNNING, DECEPTION. —*n.* rider, racer (see VELOCITY).

jocularity, *n.* humor; mirth, laughter; jesting, joshing, kidding; WIT.

jog, *v.* jiggle, push, shake, jostle; trot, amble. See IMPULSE, TRAVEL.

john, *n., slang,* toilet, latrine; client, customer. See CLEANNESS, SALE.

joie de vivre, *Fr.,* joy of life; enthusiasm. See CHEERFULNESS.

join, *v.* unite (see JUNCTION); federate, associate, affiliate; become a member; marry. See CONTACT, UNITY. *Ant.,* separate.

joint, *n.* connection, link, juncture; articulation; *slang,* dive, den, haunt, hangout. See JUNCTION, ABODE. —*adj.* combined, shared, common [to both parties]. See PARTY.

joke, *n.* jest, gag, wisecrack, witticism, bon mot; fooling, kidding, joshing. —*v.i.* josh, jest, gag. See WIT.

joker, *n.* kidder, practical joker, cutup; rogue, rascal, scamp. See WIT, EVILDOER.

jolly, *adj.* joyous, frolicsome, mirthful; buoyant, elated. See CHEERFULNESS. *Ant.,* morose.

jolt, *v.* shake [up], shock, stun, give a kick in the pants (*sl.*); lurch, pitch; bump, collide, crash. See IMPULSE, SURPRISE.

jostle, *v.t.* push, bump; elbow, shoulder; collide with. See IMPULSE.

jot, *n.* trace, iota, speck. See LITTLENESS. —jot down, note, make a note of. See WRITING.

jounce, *v.* shake, shock, bump. See AGITATION.

journal, *n.* diary, daybook, RECORD, log; newspaper, magazine, periodical. See PUBLICATION, CHRONOMETRY, ACCOUNTING, DESCRIPTION.

journalist, *n.* newsman, newspaperman, reporter; writer, editor, copyreader. See RECORD, NEWS.

journey, *n.* trip, tour; voyage, cruise, crossing; expedition; tramp, hike; pilgrimage, hadj; caravan; trek. —*v.* TRAVEL; voyage, sail, cross; tour, roam, range, venture, explore; ride, drive, motor. See MOTION.

journeyman, *n.* craftsman *or* -woman, artisan, skilled worker. See EXERTION, SKILL.

jovial, *adj.* genial, cordial; gay, merry; jolly, convivial. See CHEERFULNESS. *Ant.,* morose.

joy, *n.* REJOICING; PLEASURE, happiness, delight, mirth, gaiety, fun (*inf.*); joie de vivre.

joyless, *adj.* cheerless, sad (see DEPRESSION). *Ant.,* joyful.

jubilant, *adj.* joyful; triumphant, exultant; elated, REJOICING, in high spirits. See CHEERFULNESS. *Ant.,* sad, morose.

jubilee, *n.* CELEBRATION; anniversary; REJOICING.

judge, *n. & v.* See LAWSUIT, JUDGMENT.

JUDGMENT
Act of evaluating

Nouns—1, judgment, adjudication, arbitration; result, conclusion, upshot; deduction, inference, corollary (see REASONING); decision, determination, finding, opinion, ruling, verdict, settlement, award, decree, sentence; CONDEMNATION, doom, day of judgment, Judgment Day; res judicata; op ed.

2, *(legal judge)* judge, mullah; jurist, tribunal, court, *etc.* (see LAWSUIT); judgment seat.

3, estimation, valuation, assessment, appraisal, appreciation, consideration, judication; opinion, notion, THOUGHT, viewpoint, BELIEF; estimate, commentary, critique; diagnosis (see IDENTITY); CHOICE, vote; discernment, discretion, TASTE; INTELLIGENCE, INTELLECT, reason, sagacity; sense.

4, *(one who evaluates)* arbiter, umpire, referee; judicator; master, moderator, mediator, conciliator; censor, critic, commentator, connoisseur, authority, expert.

Verbs—1, judge, conclude; come to, arrive at, *or* draw a conclusion, find; make up one's mind, cross the Rubicon; ascertain, determine, deduce; settle, give an opinion; decide, try, *or* hear a case *or* cause; pronounce, rule, pass judgment, sentence, condemn, doom (see CONDEMNATION); adjudge, adjudicate, arbitrate, sit in judgment; bring in a verdict; confirm, decree, award; pass under review; editorialize.

2, estimate, appraise, value, assess; deem, gauge; review, consider, believe; form an opinion about, take the measure of, jump to a conclusion, put two and two together; comment, criticize, examine, inquire. *Informal,* size up.

Adjectives—1, judicial, judiciary, judicatory, forensic, legal; determinate, conclusive; censorious, condemnatory; tribunal.

2, discerning, discriminating, sensible, astute, judicious, circumspect; intelligent, rational, reasonable, sagacious, wise.

Adverbs—therefore, wherefore, this being so *or* the case; all things considered, in light *or* view of, all things being equal, on the whole; in one's opinion.

Phrases—every man to his taste; one man's meat is another man's poison; there is no accounting for tastes; it's difference of opinion that makes the horse race; all cats are gray in the dark; beauty is in the eye of the beholder; discretion is the better part of valor; judge not, that ye be not judged.

Quotations—Taste is the feminine of genius (*Edward Fitzgerald*), Could we teach taste or genius by rules, they would be no longer taste and genius (*Joshua Reynolds*), A man is a critic when he cannot be an artist, in the same way that a man becomes an informer when he cannot be a soldier (*Gustave Flaubert*).

Antonyms, see ERROR, MISJUDGMENT.

Judgment Day, doomsday, day of reckoning, atonement, *or* judgment; last trumpet. See DESTINY.

judicious, *adj.* prudent, sound. See JUDGMENT. *Ant.,* injudicious.

jug, *n.* bottle, urn, pitcher, flagon, tankard. See RECEPTACLE.

juggle, *v.* manipulate; conjure; trick, cheat. See DECEPTION.

juice, *n.* fruit drink, beverage; fluid, liquid; *slang,* [electric] current. See DRINKING, FLUIDITY, POWER.

juicy, *adj.* moist, sappy, succulent; rich, tasty, tempting. See FLUIDITY. *Ant.,* dry, desiccated.

jumble, *n.* mixup, confusion, DISORDER; pi. —*v.* mix up, disarrange, muddle, mess.

jumbo, *adj.* huge (see SIZE).

jump, *n. & v.* hop, LEAP, bound, spring, vault; start, twitch, jerk. See EXCITABILITY.

jumpy, *adj.* nervous, jittery. See EXCITABILITY. *Ant.,* calm.

JUNCTION
Act or point of meeting

Nouns—1, junction, CONNECTION, conjunction, COHERENCE; joining, joinder, union, annex, annexation, attachment; ligation, accouplement, inosculation, anastomosis; MARRIAGE, knot, wedlock; hookup, network, communication, concatenation; fusion, blend, merger. See CROSSING, UNITY.

2, joint, joining, juncture, pivot, hinge, articulation, seam, suture, stitch; coupler, coupling; chain, link; miter, mortise, tenon, dovetail; interface, jumper; strong force.

Verbs—join, unite, knot, knit, conjoin, connect, hitch, affiliate, associate, couple; put, piece, *or* hold together; roll into one, combine, compound, incorporate; skewer; inosculate, anastomose; copulate. See CONNECTION.

Adjectives—1, joined, joint; conjoint, conjunct, conjunctive, corporate, compact, hand in hand; close-knit, conjugate.

2, segmented, jointed, articulate.

3, blent, blended, wedded, married, merged, fused. See MIXTURE.

Adverbs—jointly, in conjunction with, fast, firmly, intimately.

Antonyms, see DISJUNCTION.

---

juncture, *n.* joint, point, connection; contingency, emergency. See JUNCTION, CIRCUMSTANCE, OCCASION.

jungle, *n.* wilderness, bush. See VEGETABLE, DIFFICULTY, ABODE.

junior, *n. & adj.* younger, lesser, subordinate. See INFERIORITY.

junk, *n.* rubbish, waste, refuse, trash, dis-

card, castoffs; scrap, salvage, wreck, wreckage; stuff, miscellany, claptrap. See SHIP, USELESSNESS. —*v.t.* scrap, wreck, tear down, dismember; salvage; discard, cast off, jettison. See DISUSE.

junket, *n.* picnic, excursion. See FOOD, TRAVEL.

junkie, *n., slang,* addict, user, abuser; devotee. See DRUGS, HABIT.

junkyard, *n.* dump[site], landfill, scrapyard. See REJECTION.

junta, *n.* meeting, COUNCIL.

junto, *n.* cabal (see PARTY).

jurisdiction, *n.* judicature; administration; province, dominion, control; magistracy, AUTHORITY; municipality, corporation, bailiwick. See LEGALITY.

jurist, *n.* judge; legal expert. See LAWSUIT, LEGALITY.

jury, *n.* trial, grand, *or* petit jury; panel; board of judges. See LAWSUIT.

jury-rigged, *adj.* ad hoc, makeshift, stopgap. See INSTANTANEITY.

just, *adj.* fair, RIGHT; impartial, nonpartisan; lawful, legal, legitimate; exact, accurate, precise. See PROBITY. *—adv.* precisely, exactly; almost, nearly, within an ace of. See JUSTICE. *Ant.,* unjust, unfair.

JUSTICE
Conformity to moral principles

Nouns—1, justice, justness, fairness, fair treatment, impartiality, equity, equitableness; poetic justice, rough justice, deserts; nemesis (see PUNISHMENT); scales of justice; fair play, fair trial, trial by jury; affirmative action. *Informal,* square deal, straight shooting, fair *or* square shake. See LAWSUIT, LEGALITY, PROBITY.

2, *(fairness)* due, dueness, rightfulness, RIGHTNESS, VINDICATION.

Verbs—1, do justice to, be fair, treat fairly, deal fairly with, be impartial, see justice done, play fair, give the devil his due. *Informal,* give a square deal, play the game, give a sporting chance.

2, be just, right, *or* due; have right, title, *or* claim to; be entitled to; have a claim upon, belong to, deserve, earn, merit, be worthy of. *Informal,* rate, have it coming.

3, *(ask for justice)* demand, claim, call upon for, reclaim, exact, insist on, take one's stand, make a point of, require, lay claim to.

Adjectives—1, just, fair, impartial, equal, fair and square, dispassionate, disinterested, unbiased, even-handed.

2, having a right to, entitled to, deserving, meriting, worthy of; deserved, merited.

Adverbs—justly, rightfully, duly, by right, by divine right, fairly, in justice, as is just *or* fitting. *Informal,* on the level, aboveboard, on the square.

Phrases—all's fair in love and war; give and take is fair play; there are two sides to every question; we all love justice—at our neighbor's expense; what goes around comes around; what's sauce for the goose is sauce for the gander; turnabout is fair play.

Quotations—Life for life, eye for eye, tooth for tooth (*Bible*), Judge not, that ye be not judged (*Bible*), Justice is truth in action (*Benjamin Disraeli*), In England, justice is open to all—like the Ritz Hotel (*James Mathew*), There is no such thing as justice—in or out of court (*Clarence Darrow*), I shall temper . . . justice with mercy (*John Milton*), Everywhere there is one principle of justice, which is the interest of the stronger (*Plato*).

Antonyms, see INJUSTICE.

---

justify, *v.* exonerate, excuse, warrant, vindicate, acquit, absolve; prove right, free from blame. See VINDICATION.

jut, *v.i.* protrude, project, beetle, stand out, overhang. See CONVEXITY.

juvenile, *n.* youngster, minor, adolescent. *—adj.* puerile, young, undeveloped, immature; childish. See YOUTH. *Ant.,* mature.

juxtapose, *n.* See NEARNESS.

K

kaleidoscopic, *adj.* variegated, varying; colorful. See COLOR, CHANGEABLENESS.

kaput, *adj., informal,* ruined, done for, destroyed. See FAILURE, DESTRUCTION.

karma, *n.* fate, DESTINY.

keel, *v.* turn (over), keel over, fall down, drop like a log. See OBLIQUITY, INVERSION. —*n.* bar *or* false keel; centerboard. See SHIP.

keen, *adj.* piercing, stinging, nippy; sharp, edged, cutting, razorlike; eager, enthusiastic, ardent; acute, clever, shrewd, quick. See DESIRE, SHARPNESS, FEELING, INTELLIGENCE, COLD. —keen on, eager to, enthusiastic about. See DESIRE.

keep, *v.* retain, hold, have, possess; receive, preserve; celebrate (holidays), maintain; sustain, continue; hold back, save, cling to, detain. See POSSESSION, PRESERVATION. —*n.* subsistence, maintenance; donjon, dungeon; PRISON, prison tower, cell, jail. See DEFENSE, FOOD. —for keeps, *informal,* permanently. See PERMANENCE.

keeper, *n.* custodian; jailer, warden, watchman, watchdog; gamekeeper, ranger; doorman, tiler; curator; protector, guardian; observer (of rites), celebrator, preserver; supporter, maintainer. See SAFETY, PRISON, DEFENSE.

keep out, *v.t.* shut out, exclude, bar. See EXCLUSION.

keepsake, *n.* memento, souvenir, reminder, token. See MEMORY.

keg, *n.* barrel, cask. See RECEPTACLE.

kelp, *n.* seaweed, [sea] wrack. See VEGETABLE.

ken, *n.* KNOWLEDGE, scope.

kennel, *n.* doghouse, stall; hovel, hut, hutch. See ABODE.

kernel, *n.* nub, gist, core, pitch, point, center, essence; grain, nut, seed, nucleus. See MEANING, IMPORTANCE, MIDDLE.

kettle, *n.* pot, caldron, boiler; teakettle. See RECEPTACLE.

key, *n.* answer, solution, codebook, decipherment; pitch, tonality, register; cay. See SOUND, OPENING, INTERPRETATION, MUSIC, CAUSE, COLOR, INSTRUMENTALITY. —keyed up, tense; excited, worked up. See EXCITEMENT.

keynote, *n.* characteristic, key principle. See IMPORTANCE.

keystone, *n.* cornerstone, quoin; essence, high point. See IMPORTANCE.

kibbutz, *n.* commune, collective farm, community. See ASSEMBLAGE.

kibitz, *v.i.* advise, comment; butt in, interfere, meddle. See ADVICE, BETWEEN.

kick, *v.* punt; spurn; stamp; *slang,* complain, gripe, bellyache, grumble. —*n.* RECOIL; thrill, excitement, fun; *slang,* complaint, grievance, gripe. See IMPULSE, OPPOSITION.

kickback, *n., informal,* backfire; refund, discount, rebate; rakeoff; cut, commission; bribe, payoff, payola. See PAYMENT.

kickoff, *n.* BEGINNING, start, onset, launch.

kid, *n.* kidling; kidskin; *informal,* child, YOUTH. —*v., slang,* tease, make fun of; deceive, fool. See DECEPTION.

kidnap, *v.* carry off, abduct. See STEALING.

kill, *v.t.* slay (see KILLING); destroy, extinguish, nullify, cancel, veto. See NULLIFICATION. —*n.* creek, river; prey, quarry. See WATER, KILLING.

KILLING
Act of one that kills

Nouns—1, killing, homicide, manslaughter, murder, assassination, murder most foul; bloodshed, bloodletting, slaughter, carnage, butchery, extermination, decimation, annihilation, genocide, final solution, ethnic cleansing, depopulation, pogrom, massacre, war, WARFARE; biocide, holocaust, pogrom, purge, hecatomb, parricide, fratricide, patricide, matricide, infanticide, regicide; ritual murder *or* suicide; serial killing; mercy killing, euthanasia; mark of Cain. *Slang,* hit; snuff film. See DEATH.

2, *(method of killing)* death blow, finishing stroke, coup de grâce, quietus; execution, capital PUNISHMENT, firing squad, gassing, electrocution, evisceration, disembowelment, defenestration; execution; martyrdom; poisoning, injection; suffocation, smothering, strangulation, choking, garrote, gallows, hanging, beheading, [burning at the] stake, stoning, lapidation, decapitation, crucifixion, guillotine, immolation, vaporization, violent death, burial alive; [assisted] suicide, self-destruction, suttee, seppuku, hara-kiri, felo-de-se, wrist slitting, immolation; drive-by shooting; final solution; traffic death, fatal accident, casualty, fatality. *Slang,* Dutch act *or* cure, electric cure, joy ride, air dance, necktie party *or* sociable; bough, chates, forks, furca, leafless tree, stalk, swing. See PUNISHMENT.

3, butcher, slayer, murderer, Cain, assassin, cutthroat, garrotter, bravo, thug; executioner, hangman, headsman, firing squad, sniper; regicide, matricide, parricide, fratricide, infanticide; suicide, solitaire; serial killer; poison, germicide, insecticide, Agent Orange; gun, rifle (see ARMS). *Slang,* hatchet *or* finger man, hit man, necktie party, ice man, rat boy.

4, *(killing of animals)* hunting, coursing, shooting; sportsman, huntsman (see PURSUIT); slaughterhouse, shambles, abattoir, packing house; charnel house.

Verbs—1, kill, put to death, slay, dispatch, shed blood; murder, assassinate, butcher, slaughter, immolate, massacre, annihilate; do away with, put an end to, put away, put to sleep; carry off, lay low; run over; pick off; do for, put out of the way, sluice; sign one's death warrant; disappear. *Slang,* liquidate, bump off, brain, take for a ride, knock off, wipe out, zap, do in, rub out, blow away, grease, snuff out, zap, cack, deep six, dust, drill, frag, hose, off, waste, burke, cap, chill, nuke, take out *or* down, grease, smoke, stiff, whack, cream, hush, jugulate.

2, execute; strangle, garrote, hang, lynch, throttle, choke, stifle, poison, gas, electrocute, suffocate, disembowel, bury alive, draw and quarter, stone, smother, asphyxiate, drown, behead; put to the sword, stone, deal a death blow, wade knee-deep in blood. *Slang,* cook, dance, nub, scrag, sizzle, fry, burn, ding, hose down, smoke, string up.

3, kill oneself, blow out one's brains, commit suicide, take one's own life. *Slang,* pull the plug, see oneself off, eat one's gun.

Adjectives—1, killing, murderous, sanguinary, bloodstained, bloodthirsty, homicidal, red-handed; bloody, ensanguined, gory.

2, mortal, fatal, lethal, deadly, internecine, suicidal, biocidal.

Phrases—murder will out.

Quotations—Assassination has never changed the history of the world (*Benjamin Disraeli*), Television has brought back murder into the home—where it belongs (*Alfred Hitchcock*), Kill a man, and you are an assassin. Kill millions of men, and you are a conqueror. Kill everyone, and you are a god (*Jean Rostand*), For who would bear the whips and scorns of time . . . when he himself might his quietus make with a bare bodkin? (*Shakespeare*), Guns aren't lawful; nooses give; gas smells awful; you might as well live (*Dorothy Parker*), Assassination is the extreme form of censorship (*G. B. Shaw*), Murder most foul, as in the best it is, but this most foul, strange, and unnatural (*Shakespeare*).

Antonyms, see LIFE, REPRODUCTION.

killjoy, *n.* spoilsport, wet blanket, party pooper, grinch; Cassandra, prophet[ess] of doom. See DEJECTION, DESTINY.

kin, *n.* kin[s]folk, kinsman, kinswoman; blood relative *or* relation, family, clan; siblings, cousins, folks (*inf.*). See ANCESTRY, POSTERITY.

kind, *n.* sort, species, CLASS, type, ilk, breed, character, nature. —*adj.* kindly, kindhearted; gentle, tender, sympathetic, mild, friendly, obliging, benign, solicitous, lenient; helpful. See BENEVOLENCE, LENIENCY.

kindergarten, *n.* nursery school, playschool. See SCHOOL.

kindle, *v.* ignite, start, fire, set ablaze; stir, excite, rouse, provoke. See EXCITEMENT, CAUSE.

kindling, *n.* tinder, FUEL, firewood, combustibles.

kindred, *n.* consanguinity; relatives, kinfolk[s], kinsmen; clan, tribe; brothers, sisters, cousins, parents, *etc.*; kindred spirits, congenial people. —*adj.* related, akin, allied; congenial. See RELATION, BENEVOLENCE.

king, *n.* ruler, monarch, emperor, sovereign; royalty. See AUTHORITY.

kingdom, *n.* domain, empire, realm. See REGION, AUTHORITY.

kingly, *adj.* royal, majestic, regal, imperial; noble, magnificent. See AUTHORITY.

kingpin, *n., slang,* boss, chief, top dog. See DIRECTOR.

kink, *n.* curl, twist; cramp, crick; quirk, crotchet, notion. See CONTRACTION, CONVOLUTION, UNCONFORMITY.

kinky, *adj.* twisted; quirky, eccentric. See UNCONFORMITY, CONVOLUTION.

kinsman, *n.* relative, blood relation; clansman. See ANCESTRY.

kiosk, *n.* newstand, bandstand, *etc.*; pavilion. See BUILDING, RECEPTACLE.

kismet, *n.* fate, DESTINY.

kiss, *n.* smack, osculation, caress, merest TOUCH. See ENDEARMENT. —*v.* caress, osculate; brush [lightly], TOUCH, graze.

kit, *n.* pack, sack, bag, knapsack; Dop kit; collection, gear, outfit, supplies; do-it-yourself kit. See RECEPTACLE.

kitchen, *n.* scullery, galley, cookhouse, kitchenette. See RECEPTACLE.

kite, *n.* See AVIATION.

kitsch, *n.* camp, VULGARITY.

kittenish, *adj.* playful, frisky (see AMUSEMENT).

kitty, *n.* fund, collection, pool. See STORE, MONEY.

klutz, *n., slang,* oaf, blockhead, dolt. See UNSKILLFULNESS, IGNORANCE.

knack, *n.* adeptness, ability, aptitude, talent; dexterity, handiness, trick, SKILL.

knapsack, *n.* haversack, pack; mochila, rucksack, kit [bag], bag, case; poke, turkey, bindle (*all sl.*). See RECEPTACLE.

knave, *n.* rogue, rascal, villain, scamp, scapegrace, blackguard, reprobate, miscreant; jack, bower; churl, menial, servant. See EVILDOER, CUNNING.

knead, *v.t.* press, squeeze, massage, manipulate, work. See MIXTURE, FORM, FRICTION.

kneel, *v.i.* bend (to pray), genuflect. See DEPRESSION.

knell, *n.* funeral *or* death bell. See DEATH.

knickknack, *n.* bric-a-brac, trifle, trinket, gewgaw. See ORNAMENT, UNIMPORTANCE.

knife, *n.* blade, edge, point, steel, shiv (*sl.*), toothpick (*sl.*); carving knife; snickersnee, dagger, poniard, dirk, bodkin, stiletto; scalpel, lancet. See ARMS, SHARPNESS. —*v.t.* stab, cut, slice, slash; wound; *informal,* knife in the back, betray. See IMPROBITY.

knight, *n.* knight-errant; cavalier, chevalier; paladin, champion, Galahad; Templar; noble. See DEFENSE, NOBILITY.

knit, *v.* weave, interlace; draw together, contract, FURROW, wrinkle. See JUNCTION.

knob, *n.* knot, lump, node, protuberance, boss; handle; hill. See CONVEXITY.

knock, *v.* pound, strike, hit, rap, tap; tamp; bump, collide; *informal,* belittle, depreciate. —*n.* stroke, bump; rap[ping]; *informal,* slur, aspersion. See IMPULSE, DISAPPROBATION.

knoll, *n.* hill, hillock, rise, mound, hummock. See HEIGHT.

knot, *n.* snarl, tangle; puzzle, problem; cluster, group; lump, node. —*v.* tangle, snarl; tie, bind, fasten. See DIFFICULTY, CROSSING, DENSITY, CONNECTION, ASSEMBLAGE.

knotty, *adj.* difficult, intricate, complex. See DIFFICULTY.

know-how, *n., informal,* expertise, SKILL, savvy (*sl.*).

KNOWLEDGE
Cognizance

Nouns—1, knowledge, cognizance, cognition, acquaintance, ken, privity, familiarity, comprehension, apprehension, recognition, appreciation; INTUITION, conscience, consciousness, awareness, perception, precognition; light, enlightenment; facts of life; experience, the university of life, tree of life; glimpse, insight, inkling, glimmer, suspicion, impression.

2, science, philosophy, theory, doctrine, epistemology; encyclopedia; erudition, LEARNING, lore, scholarship, reading, letters, literature, book learning, INFORMATION, store of knowledge, education, culture; attainments, accomplishments, proficiency, SKILL, wisdom, omniscience. *Informal,* know-how.

3, sage, wise man, luminary, magus, savant, philosopher, Nestor, Solon, pundit; highbrow; graduate, academician, academist; master, doctor; fellow, don; mathematician, scientist, littérateur, intellectual, intelligentsia; learned *or* literary man; man of learning, letters, *or* education; bookworm, scholar (see LEARNING); literati, cognoscenti. *Informal,* wise guy, weisenheimer.

Verbs—1, know, ken, wot (*archaic*), be aware of; ween, trow; possess; apprehend, conceive, comprehend, realize, understand, appreciate, fathom, make out; recognize, discern, perceive, see, experience; feel *or* know in one's bones. See INTELLIGENCE.

2, know full well, know like the back of one's hand; have in one's head, have at one's fingertips, know by heart, be master of, know what's what, know one's way around, have been around, have one's eyes open. *Slang,* know the score, know one's stuff, know shit from shinola, know one's ass from a hole in the ground.

3, see one's way, discover, learn, study, ascertain, see the elephant.

Adjectives—1, knowing, cognitive, conscious, cognizant, aware, perceptive.

2, aware of, cognizant of, conscious of, apprised of, told, acquainted with, privy to, no stranger to, up to, alive to; proficient in, versed in, at home with; conversant *or* familiar with; not born yesterday, nobody's fool; sophisticated, cosmopolitan. *Slang,* hip, hep, wise, wised up, with it, in the know, fly.

3, knowledgeable, erudite, scholarly, instructed, learned, lettered, literary, educated, well-informed, well-read, well-grounded, well-educated, enlightened, shrewd; bookish, scholastic, solid, profound, accomplished, omniscient; sage, wise, intellectual; emeritus. *Slang,* bright collar.

4, known, ascertained, well-known, recognized, proverbial, familiar, hackneyed, trite, commonplace.

5, knowable, cognizable, ascertainable, perceptible, discernible, comprehensible.

Phrases—experience is the best teacher; live and learn; once bitten, twice shy; a little knowledge is a dangerous thing; know thyself.

Quotations—The years teach much which the days never know (*Emerson*), All experience is an arch to build upon (*Henry Adams*), I've looked at life from both sides now . . . I really don't know life at all (*Joni Mitchell*), An intellectual is someone whose mind watches itself (*Albert Camus*), I know nothing except the fact of my ignorance (*Socrates*), Knowledge itself is power (*Francis Bacon*), There is nothing so absurd but some philosopher has said it (*Cicero*), There are no such things as applied sciences, only applications of science (*Louis Pasteur*), It is much easier to make measurements than to know exactly what you are measuring (*J. W. N. Sullivan*), All science is either physics or stamp collecting (*Ernest Rutherford*), The aim of science is not to open the door to infinite wisdom, but to set a limit to infinite error (*Bertolt Brecht*), Modern science was largely conceived as an answer to the servant problem (*Fran Lebowitz*).

Antonyms, see IGNORANCE, FOLLY.

know-nothing, *n.* illiterate, ignoramus. See IGNORANCE.

knuckle down, apply oneself (see RESOLUTION).

knuckle under, submit, yield (see SUBMISSION).

kooky, *n., slang,* eccentric, odd[ball], strange. See UNCONFORMITY.

kosher, *adj., informal,* proper, legitimate, conventional; genuine, approved. See RIGHTNESS, TRUTH.

kowtow, *v.i.* salaam, bow down, genuflect; fawn, cringe. See OBEDIENCE, RESPECT, SERVILITY.

kudos, *n.* glory, praise, tribute. See APPROBATION.

kvetch, *v.i., slang,* gripe, complain, beef. See DISCONTENT.

L

label, *n.* tag, tab, mark, sticker; slip, ticket; price tag; epithet, title; record, INDICATION, handle (*inf.*). —*v.t.* identify, tag, name; distinguish, describe. See NOMENCLATURE.

labor, *n.* work, toil, effort; travail, task; proletariat. See EXERTION, POPULACE.

laboratory, *n.* workplace; research center, lab. See BUSINESS.

labored, *adj.* heavy, difficult; stiff, formal, unnatural. See DIFFICULTY, INELEGANCE. *Ant.,* easy.

laborer, *n.* worker, work[ing]man *or* -woman, wage earner. See EXERTION.

laborious, *adj.* hard, arduous, tiresome, irksome; diligent, assiduous. See EXERTION. *Ant.,* effortless.

labyrinth, *n.* maze, tangle, meander; complexity, intricacy. See DISORDER, CONVOLUTION, SECRET.

lace, *n.* cord, lacing; braid; openwork, network. See ORNAMENT. —*v.t.* weave, twine; interlace; bind, tie; flavor, mix, spike; *informal,* whip, lash. See MIXTURE, CROSSING, PUNISHMENT.

lacerate, *v.t.* tear, mangle; harrow, distress. See PAIN.

lack, *n.* want, deficiency, shortage, need. —*v.t.* need, require. See INSUFFICIENCY, POVERTY. *Ant.,* SUFFICIENCY.

lackadaisical, *adj.* languid, listless, casual. See NEGLECT. *Ant.,* careful, intense.

lackey, *n.* footman, SERVANT.

lackluster, *adj.* dull. See DIMNESS. *Ant.,* brilliant.

laconic, *adj.* concise, pithy. See SHORTNESS, DIFFUSENESS. *Ant.,* wordy.

lacquer, *n.* varnish, shellac. See SMOOTHNESS, COVERING.

lacuna, *n.* gap, interruption, break. See DISCONTINUANCE.

lad, *n.* boy, YOUTH, stripling.

laden, *adj.* loaded, burdened, encumbered. See HINDRANCE.

ladle, *n.* spoon, dipper; metal pot. See RECEPTACLE.

lady, *n.* gentlewoman, madam, dowager; noblewoman. See NOBILITY, FEMALE.

ladylike, *adj.* womanly, feminine; genteel, well-bred. See FEMALE. *Ant.,* unladylike.

lag, *v.i.* linger, drag, fall behind, hang back. See SLOWNESS.

laggard, *n.* lingerer, loiterer (see SLOWNESS).

lagoon, *n.* laguna; pool, pond, cove; estuary, sound. See WATER.

laid-back, *adj.* relaxed, calm, casual, easygoing. See INDIFFERENCE, NEGLECT. *Ant.,* tense, serious.

laid up, *adj.* bedridden, sick in bed, confined; amassed, stockpiled. See REMEDY, STORE.

lair, *n.* den, covert, burrow, cave. See ABODE.

laissez-faire, Fr., noninterference. See PERMISSION, FREEDOM, INACTIVITY, NEGLECT.

LAITY
Outside the clergy

Nouns—1, laity, laic; flock, fold, congregation; assembly; churchgoers; parishioners; parish, brethren, people. See RELIGION.

2, lay person, layman, laywoman, lay brother *or* sister, catechumen.

Verbs—laicize, secularize, democratize, popularize.

Adjectives—lay, laic[al], nonclerical, nonreligious; secular, civil, temporal, profane, congregational, popular; nonprofessional, nonexpert, unprofessional.

Antonyms, see CLERGY.

---

lake, *n.* loch, lough; pond, pool, tarn, lakelet, mere. See WATER.

lame, *adj.* crippled, halt; weak, ineffectual. See DISEASE, FAILURE, WEAKNESS.

LAMENTATION
Act of mourning

Nouns—1, lamentation, lament, wail, complaint, plaint, murmur, mutter, grumble, groan, growl, moan, whine, whimper, sob, sigh, cry, outcry, scream, howl. *Slang,* gripe, beef, bellyaching. See DEJECTION.

2, *(signs of mourning)* tears, weeping, lachrymation, languishment; condolence (see PITY).

3, *(mourning clothing)* mourning weeds, crepe, sackcloth and ashes; knell, dirge, coronach, keen, requiem, elegy, monody, threnody, jeremiad.

4, lamenter, mourner; grumbler; Niobe, Jeremiah, Rachel.

Verbs—1, lament, mourn, deplore, grieve, weep over, bewail; regret (see PENITENCE); condole with, commiserate; fret, wear mourning, wear sackcloth and ashes.

2, sigh, heave a sigh; wail, bawl, cry, weep, sob, greet (archaic), blubber, snivel, whimper, pule, shed tears; burst into tears, cry one's eyes out; scream, mew, growl, groan, grunt, moan, roar, bellow; frown, scowl, make a wry face, gnash one's teeth, wring one's hands, tear one's hair, beat one's breast.

3, complain, murmur, mutter, whine, grumble, clamor, make a fuss about. *Slang,* gripe, bellyache, kvetch, pitch a bitch. See DISCONTENT.

Adjectives—lamenting, in mourning, in sackcloth and ashes, sorrowful, sorrowing, unhappy, mournful, tearful, lachrymose, plaintive, querulous, in tears, with tears in one's eyes; elegiac[al].

Interjections—alas! alack! O dear! too bad! sorry! woe is me! alas the day! alackaday! waly waly! what a pity! O tempora, O mores!

Quotations—Blessed are they that mourn, for they shall be comforted (*Bible*), One woe doth tread upon another's heel, so fast they follow (*Shakespeare*).

Antonyms, see CELEBRATION, REJOICING.

---

lamina, *n.* LAYER, stratum, sheet, plate, scale.

laminate, *v.t.* stratify, plate, veneer, overlay. See LAYER.

lamp, *n.* LIGHT, lantern, floor *or* table lamp; [light] bulb; headlamp.

lampoon, *n.* satire, spoof (see DETRACTION).

lance, *n.* dart, spear, pike, javelin, shaft. See ARMS. —*v.* spear; pierce, prick, puncture; hurl, throw, fling, propel, send flying. See OPENING, PROPULSION.

LAND
Surface of the earth

Nouns—1, land, earth, ground, dry land, terra firma, terra incognita. See INORGANIC MATTER, CONCAVITY, HEIGHT, DEPTH.

2, *(inland area)* continent, Europe, Asia, Eurasia, North *or* South America, Australia, Africa, Antarctica; Gondwana[land], Laurasia, Pangaea, supercontinent; mainland, peninsula, delta; neck of land, isthmus, island; oasis, desert; lowland, highland; promontory; pasture, grassland; glacier, iceberg (see COLD); volcano; real estate, property, acres.

3, *(coastal area)* coast, shore, seashore, lakeshore, strand, beach, bank, lea, seaside, seacoast, rock-bound coast, alluvium; barrier beach. See EDGE.

4, *(composition of land)* soil, glebe, clay, loam, marl, mold, topsoil, sod, subsoil, clod; rock, crag, boulder, stone, shale, chalk, gravel, rubble, dust, sand, sediment, sludge, detritus, placer, eluvium, lava, loess, marl.

5, *(study of land)* geography, geology, geophysics, geochemistry, geobotany, geodynamics, geognosy, geomorphology, mineralogy, lithology; hydrology (see WATER); geographer, geologist, *etc.*

6, landlubber, landsman.

Verbs—land, light, alight, ground; disembark, come *or* go ashore. See ARRIVAL.

Adjectives—earthly, terrestrial; continental, midland, littoral, riparian, alluvial, landed, territorial; earthy.

Adverbs—ashore, on shore, land, *etc.*; aground, on solid ground.

Interjections—land ahoy!

Quotations—Conservation is a state of harmony between men and land (*Aldo Leopold*).

Antonyms, see WATER, AIR.

landing, *n.* docking, alighting, landfall, disembarkation; wharf, dock, levee, pier; runway, airstrip; three-point landing. See ARRIVAL, SUPPORT.

landlady, landlord, *n.* proprietor, owner; host, innkeeper, boniface; landholder, landowner. See POSSESSION.

landlubber, *n.* landsman; raw seaman. See LAND, NAVIGATION.

landmark, *n.* milestone, marker, INDICA-TION; cairn, menhir, monolith; turning point, highlight.

landscape, *n.* countryside; vista, view; landscaping, park; cityscape. See APPEARANCE.

landslide, *n.* avalanche, landslip; sweep, runaway, no contest, walkover (*inf.*), shoo-in (*inf.*). See DESCENT, SUCCESS.

lane, *n.* path, byway, passageway; corridor, track. See PASSAGE.

LANGUAGE
System of communication

Nouns — 1, language, tongue, lingo, vernacular, mother tongue, protolanguage; living *or* dead language; idiom, parlance, phraseology; wording; dialect, patois, cant, jargon, lingo, jive, flash, slang, argot; Black Talk, African American English, ebonics, geechee; regionalism, provincialism; archaism; buzzword, commercialese; coinage, neologism, nonce word, derivation, portmanteau word, etymon, ghost word, loan translation, loanword; cognate, paronym, combining form; artificial language, programming *or* computer language (see COMPUTERS); pig *or* dog Latin, pidgin English, bêche-de-mer, creole, acrolect, basilect; Esperanto, Ito, Basic English, lingua franca; thieves' Latin; academese, journalese; double Dutch (see UNMEANINGNESS); sign language, finger spelling, manual alphabet; language pollution, language police. *Slang*, jive, gobbledygook. See MEANING, COMMUNICATION.

2, a. Indo-European; Indo-Iranian, Indic, Indo-Aryan, Sanskrit, Prakrit, Pali, Assamese, Bengali, Oriya, Punjabi, Sindhi, Pahari, Kashmiri, Dard, Gujarati, Marathi, Sinhalese, Hindi, Urdu, Bihari, Rajasthani, Romany; Iranian, Avestan, Persian, Pahlavi, Sogdian, Scythian, Tajik, Kurdish, Baluchi, Pashto, Ossetic; Anatolian, Hittite, Luwian, Lycian, Lydian; Armenian; Hellenic, Greek; Tocharian; Italic, Latin, Romance language, Spanish, Ladino, Portuguese, Catalan, French, Cajun, Quebecois, Provençal, Italian, Sardinian, Rhaeto-Romanic, Rumanian, Faliscan, Umbrian, Oscan; Celtic, Goidelic, Irish, Manx, Scots Gaelic, Brythonic, Welsh, Cornish, Breton, Gaulish; Germanic, [Old, Middle, *or* Modern] English, Frisian, Dutch, Afrikaans, Anglo-Saxon, German, Yiddish, Norse, Icelandic, Faeroese, Norwegian, Swedish, Danish, Gothic; Albanian; Baltic, Prussian, Latvian, Lithuanian; Slavic, Polish, Czech, Sorbian, Slovak, Ukrainian, Byelorussian, Russian, Slavonic, Bulgarian, Macedonian, Serbo-Croatian, Slovene. b. Sino-Tibetan, Tibeto-Burman, Karen, Burmese, Tibetan, Chinese, Mandarin; Tai, Thai, Lao, Shan. c. Austronesian, Malayo-Polynesian. d. Uralic; Finnic, Finnish, Estonian; Ugric, Hungarian. e. Afro-Asiatic, Hamito-Semitic; Semitic, Akkadian, Arabic, Aramaic, Ethiopic, Hebrew, Phoenician; Egyptian; Berber, Tuareg, Kabyle; Cushitic, Somali, Oromo; Chadic. Hausa. f. Niger-Kordofanian, Niger-Congo, Kordofanian; Kwa, Ewe, Ibo, Yoruba, Bantu, Kikuyu, Swahili, Tswana, Zulu; Mande, Mende, Malinke, Bambara, Kpelle; Gur, Mossi. g. Ainu. h. Munda. i. Dravidian; Tamil, Telugu, Kannada, Malayalam, Brahui. j. Altaic;

Turkic, Turkish, Azerbaijani, Turkmen, Uzbek, Kirghiuz, Yakut; Mongolian, Mongolic, Buriat, Khalkha; Tungusic, Manchu, Evenki, Even, Nanay. **k.** Basque.

3, *(study of language)* [applied, comparative, computational, descriptive, structural, *or* anthropological] linguistics, metalinguistics, GRAMMAR, lexicography, lexicology, etymology, morphology, dialectology, pragmatics; semantics, general semantics, semiotics, MEANING, denotation, connotation; WRITING, literature, philology, classics, letters, belles lettres, humanities, Muses; gift of tongues; dictionary, thesaurus, word treasury, glossary, lexicon, vocabulary.

4, word, phone, phoneme, morpheme, lexeme, syllable, stem, root; phrase, sentence; homograph, homonym, homophone, synonym; syntax, idiom; utterance, remark, statement, pronouncement, observation, comment, obiter dictum; question, INQUIRY; ANSWER, reply; aside, apostrophe, rhetorical question.

5, linguist, philologist, grammarian; semanticist, etymologist, lexicographer.

Adjectives—lingual, linguistic, lexical; verbal, idiomatic, colloquial, dialectic, vernacular, provincial; polyglot; polysynthetic; literary; demotic.

Quotations—Language is fossil poetry (*Emerson*), Language is the dress of thought (*Samuel Johnson*), A definition is the enclosing a wilderness of idea within a wall of words (*Samuel Butler*), Slang is a language that rolls up its sleeves, spits on its hands and goes to work (*Carl Sandburg*).

Related categories, GRAMMAR, WORD, WRITING.

---

languid, *adj.* weak, feeble, weary; listless, spiritless, apathetic. See INSENSIBILITY, WEARINESS. *Ant.,* energetic.

languish, *v.i.* weaken, fail, fade, decline; pine, droop. See DISEASE, DEJECTION, WEAKNESS.

languor, *n.* WEARINESS, lassitude, listlessness; indolence, inertia. See INACTIVITY, SLOWNESS. *Ant.,* energy, vitality.

lank, *adj.* lanky; lean, spare, gaunt, bony. See NARROWNESS. *Ant.,* stout, fleshy.

lantern, *n.* lamp, searchlight, torch, LIGHT; jack-o'-lantern.

lap, *v.* FOLD, wrap; lick; overlap; ripple. See SUPERIORITY, COVERING, DRINKING, TOUCH.

lapse, *n.* passage, interval; oversight, peccadillo, ERROR. —*v.i.* pass, glide away; deteriorate; err. See TIME, BADNESS, REVERSION, DESCENT, PAST.

lapsus linguae, *Lat.,* slip of the tongue. See ERROR.

larceny, *n.* theft, STEALING.

larder, *n.* pantry, commissary; provisions, stores. See STORE.

large, *adj.* big, huge, colossal, enormous, immense; large-scale. See SIZE. *Ant.,* small.

largess, *n.* LIBERALITY, generosity, BENEVOLENCE; gratuity, perquisite. *Ant.,* miserliness.

lariat, *n.* rope, lasso, line, riata, rawhide, cable, catgut. See FILAMENT.

lark, *n.* frolic, romp, gambol, caper, spree; prank, joke; caprice, whim, fancy, adventure, jaunt. See AMUSEMENT.

larva, *n.* cocoon, pupa, chrysalis; maggot. See ANIMAL.

lascivious, *adj.* lustful, lewd, salacious, unchaste, wanton. See IMPURITY.

lash, *v.t.* beat, whip, flog, scourge; berate, rebuke, satirize. See PUNISHMENT, DISAPPROBATION.

lass, *n.* lassie; colleen, miss, maid, maiden. See FEMALE.

lasso, *n.* lariat, noose. —*v.t.* catch, rope. See HINDRANCE.

last, *v.i.* endure, persist, continue, abide. See TIME, DURABILITY. —*adj.* final, ultimate; latest. See END, NEWNESS, PAST. *Ant.,* first.

latch, *n.* catch, latchet, hasp, clasp, lock; bolt, bar; coupling. See CLOSURE, CONNECTION.

late, *adj.* tardy (see LATENESS); new, recent; former, sometime; deceased. See NEWNESS, PAST, DEATH. *Ant.,* early.

latecomer, *n.* recent arrival, Johnny-come-lately. See LATENESS. *Ant.,* early arrival, early bird.

lately, *adv.* recently, of late. See LATENESS.

LATENCY
Quality of being hidden

Nouns—latency, passivity, inertia, dormancy, abeyance; ambiguity, mystery, SECRET; INVISIBILITY, imperceptibility; CONCEALMENT; more than meets the eye *or* ear; POSSIBILITY.

Verbs—lurk, smolder, underlie; lie hidden; keep back, conceal, veil, hide; laugh up one's sleeve; still waters run deep.

Adjectives—latent, lurking, smoldering, delitescent; hidden, concealed; implied, unapparent, in the background, invisible, unseen; dark, unknown, unsuspected, undiscovered; unsaid, untold, unspoken, unsung, unwritten, unpublished, unexposed, undisclosed; undeveloped, potential; dormant, quiescent; suspended, in abeyance, inactive, inert; veiled, covert, obscure.

Adverbs—in secret, under cover, in the background, behind the scenes, behind one's back, between the lines, on the tip of one's tongue; in suspense.

Antonyms, see APPEARANCE, DISCLOSURE.

LATENESS
Coming after the expected time

Nouns—1, lateness, tardiness, SLOWNESS, unpunctuality; delay, procrastination, deferring, deferment, postponement, adjournment, prorogation, retardation, respite; protraction, prolongation.

2, stop, stay, continuation, reprieve, moratorium; waiting list, rain check; afterthought; hang-up; lag (see SEQUENCE).

3, Johnny-come-lately, Monday-morning quarterback.

Verbs—1, be late, tarry, wait, stay, bide, take time; dawdle, [dilly-]dally, linger, loiter, stick around, take one's time, drag one's feet *or* heels, gain time, bide one's time; hang fire, stand over, lie over; fall *or* get behind.

2, put off, defer, delay, lay over *or* aside, shelve, suspend, stave off, waive, retard, remand, postpone, put over, put on ice, adjourn, procrastinate, spin *or* draw out, prorogue, hold *or* keep back, tide over, temporize, play for time, get in under the wire, sleep on it; stand up, keep waiting, hold up.

3, lose an opportunity, be kept waiting, dance attendance; cool one's heels, [a]wait; miss *or* lose out, miss the boat *or* bus. *Slang,* sweat it out.

Adjectives—late, tardy, slow, behindhand, belated, backward, unpunctual, dilatory, delayed, delaying, procrastinating, in abeyance, on the shelf; on hold; untimely; eleventh-hour.

Adverbs—late, backward; late in the day, at the eleventh hour, at length, ultimately, finally, behind time, too late, after hours, ex post facto; in arrears (see DEBT); later on; slowly, leisurely, deliberately, at one's leisure; in the nick of time, about time; down to the wire; better late than never; on the back burner.

Interjections—too late! now or never!

Phrases—delays are dangerous; never put off till tomorrow what you can do today; procrastination is the thief of time; he who hesitates is lost; it is no use crying over spilt milk; it is too late to shut the stable door after the horse has bolted; better late than never.

Quotations—Never do today what you can do as well tomorrow (*Aaron Burr*), Delay is preferable to error (*Thomas Jefferson*), He who hesitates is sometimes saved (*James Thurber*).

Antonyms, see EARLINESS.

---

latent, *adj.* See LATENCY.

lateral, *adj.* sidelong. See SIDE.

latest, *adj.* last, freshest, newest; in fash-

ion, le dernier cri, hot off the press (*inf.*), in (*inf.*). See NEWNESS.

lather, *n.* foam, froth, suds, spume, bubbles; head; shaving cream; EXCITEMENT, AGITATION, frenzy, stew, tizzy (*sl.*).

latitude, *n.* range, extent, scope, FREEDOM, BREADTH, SPACE.

latter, *adj.* later, last mentioned. See PAST.

lattice, *n.* network (see CROSSING).

laud, *v.t.* praise, extol, eulogize. See APPROBATION. *Ant.*, criticize.

laugh, *v.i.* guffaw, snicker, giggle, titter, chuckle. See REJOICING. **—laugh at,** RIDICULE.

laughable, *adj.* ludicrous, amusing, comic, absurd; facetious, humorous. See ABSURDITY.

laughingstock, *n.* fool, target, butt, game, fair game, April fool; mockery, monkey, buffoon, fall guy (*sl.*). See RIDICULE.

laughter, *n.* laughing, guffaw, snicker, giggle, titter, chuckle. See REJOICING. *Ant.*, tears, crying.

launch, *v.t.* float, start, get going; throw, cast, hurl. See BEGINNING, PROPULSION, ASTRONAUTICS.

launder, *v.t.* wash (see CLEANNESS).

laurels, *n.pl.* honor, glory, fame (see REPUTE).

lavatory, *n.* washroom; basin. See CLEANNESS.

lavish, *adj.* prodigal, profuse, bountiful, liberal. **—v.t.** give liberally; squander. See LIBERALITY. *Ant.*, stingy, ungenerous.

law, *n.* statute, ordinance, regulation, mandate; RULE, MAXIM; precept, axiom, jurisprudence. See LEGALITY, PERMISSION.

law-abiding, *adj.* obedient, upright. See PROBITY.

lawbreaker, *n.* felon, miscreant, criminal, wrongdoer. See ILLEGALITY, EVILDOER.

lawful, *adj.* legal, legitimate; permissible; valid. See LEGALITY. *Ant.*, illegal.

lawless, *adj.* disorderly, unruly, insubordinate, mutinous. See ILLEGALITY, DISOBEDIENCE. *Ant.*, lawful, law-abiding.

lawmaker, *n.* legislator, representative, lawgiver. See AUTHORITY.

lawn, *n.* green, greenyard, greensward. See AGRICULTURE.

LAWSUIT
Legal action

Nouns—1, lawsuit, suit, action, cause, litigation, proceedings, dispute; hearing, trial; verdict, JUDGMENT, award; recovery, damages. See LEGALITY.

2, *(legal actions)* citation, arraignment, prosecution, impeachment; ACCUSATION, true bill, indictment; apprehension, arrest; commitment, committal; imprisonment; brief; writ, summons, subpoena, habeas corpus, pleadings, declaration, bill, claim, bill of right, affidavit, answer, replication, plea, demurrer, rejoinder, rebuttal, summation; appeal, motion, writ of error, case, decision, precedent, reports; plea bargaining. See RESTRAINT.

3, a. judge, justice, magistrate, surrogate, referee, chancellor; jurist, justice, [the] court; chancellor; judge of assize, recorder, justice of the peace, JP, magistrate; his worship, his honor, his Lordship, Lord Chancellor, Chief Justice; archon, tribune, praetor; mufti, cadi, mullah; judge advocate. *Slang,* beak. **b.** coroner, sheriff, constable, bailiff, officer, policeman, gendarme, myrmidon of the law. **c.** suitor, litigant, plaintiff, accused, alleged, defendant, appellant, claimant; adversary; agent. **d.** lawyer, legal adviser; district *or* prosecuting attorney, attorney general, prosecutor; advocate, barrister, solicitor, counsel, counselor[-at-law], family *or* matrimonial lawyer; King's *or* Queen's counsel; attorney[-at-law *or* -in-fact]; bencher; bar; pleader; Portia; a Daniel come to judgment. *Informal,* DA; sea lawyer. *Slang,* [mouth]piece, lip, snollygoster, ambulance-chaser, Philadelphia lawyer, shark, shyster. **e.** jury, grand *or* petty jury; tribunal, court, forum, bench; circuit, juror, juryman, jury foreman; twelve good men and true. **f.** court, tribunal, judicatory; court of law, equity, chancery, *or* appeals, appellate court, Supreme Court; woolsack, drumhead; court-martial. *Slang,* kangaroo court. **g.** courtroom, chambers, dock jury-box, witness-box *or* -stand.

4, action, case, proceeding, prosecution, litigation, civil *or* criminal action *or* case, class action, assumpsit, inquest; arrest, arraignment, bench warrant, subpoena, citation; search warrant; true bill, indictment, presentment, information, allegation, accusation, counterclaim, counterplea, cross-claim *or* -complaint; preliminary *or* pretrial hearing, voir dire; admission, confession; affidavit, appeal, certiorari; fact-finding, discovery, interrogatories; testimony, EVIDENCE, direct *or* indirect examination, rebuttal, objection, protest; plea bargaining; instructions; transcript; adjournment, cessation, continuance; gag rule; [binding *or* nonbinding] arbitration; assignment, assize, bail, challenge, charge.

Verbs—sue, litigate; bring *or* go to trial, put on trial, accuse, hale to court; prefer a claim, file; serve, cite, apprehend, arraign, prosecute, bring an action against, indict; impeach, commit, arrest (see RESTRAINT), summon[s], call up, swear out a warrant, give in charge; empanel a jury, implead, join issue, try; set in judgment, plea-bargain; judge, adjudicate; rule, award, affirm, deny. *Slang,* cop a plea.

Adjectives—litigious, litigant, contentious; judicial, legal, appellate.

Adverbs—on trial, on the bench.

Phrases—hard cases make bad laws; ignorance of the law is no excuse for breaking it; a man who is his own lawyer has a fool for a client; the long arm of the law; nolle prosequi; nolo contendere; tell God the truth but give the judge money.

Quotations—The rusty curb of old father antick, the law (*Shakespeare*), Laws, like houses, lean on one another (*Edmund Burke*), Laws were made to be broken (*Oliver North*), A lawyer with his briefcase can steal more than a hundred men with guns (*Mario Puzo*), The first thing we do, let's kill all the lawyers (*Shakespeare*), When a judge sits in judgment over a fellow man, he should feel as if a sword is pointed at his own heart (*Talmud*).

---

lawyer, *n.* See LAWSUIT.

lax, *adj.* loose, flaccid, limp, slack; remiss, careless, weak; relaxed, lawless, chaotic, disorderly; unbridled; anarchical, unauthorized. See LATENESS, SOFTNESS, NEGLECT, IMPURITY. *Ant.,* strict, tense.

laxative, *n.* physic, cathartic, purgative, eliminant; enema, irrigation, cleansing. See REMEDY.

laxity, *n.* laxness, looseness, slackness, flaccidity, limpness; toleration, lenity, freedom, relaxation, remission, loosening, DISORDER, disorganization, chaos. See NEGLECT. *Ant.,* severity, strictness.

lay, *adj.* secular, noncleric, nonprofessional. —*v.t.* put, place, deposit; allay, suppress; wager, bet; impose; impute, ascribe; present. —*n.* ballad, song (see MUSIC). See LOCATION, RELIEF, ATTRIBUTION, HORIZONTAL.

LAYER
Thickness set upon another

Nouns—1, layer, stratum, couch, bed, zone, substratum, floor, stage, story, tier, slab, FOLD, flap, ply, veneer, lap, table, tablet, board, plank, platter, course. See HORIZONTAL.

2, plate, lamina, sheet, flake, foil, wafer, scale, coat, peel, membrane, film, leaf, slice, rasher, shaving, integument, seam, pane. See COVERING, PART.

3, stratification, shale, scaliness, squamosity, lamination.

Verbs—slice, shave, pare, peel; plate, coat, veneer, cover, laminate, stratify.

Adjectives—lamellar, lamellate, laminated, micaceous; schistose, scaly, squamous, filmy, membranous, flaky, scurfy, foliated, foliaceous, stratified, stratiform, tabular, discoid.

---

layman, laywoman, *n.* See LAITY.

layoff, *n.* temporary dismissal, furloughing, suspension. See EJECTION.

layout, *n.* design, ARRANGEMENT, makeup.

lazy, *adj.* indolent, slothful; slow, sluggish. See INACTIVITY. *Ant.,* industrious, quick.

leach, *v.* percolate, filter, lixiviate. See CLEANNESS.

lead, *v.t.* conduct, direct; precede; open, start; bring; spend, pass. See AUTHORITY, DIRECTION, BEGINNING, PRECEDENCE.

leaden, *adj.* gray, somber; slow, heavy,

gloomy, cheerless. See DIMNESS, INAC-
TIVITY.

leader, *n.* guide, bellwether; DIRECTOR,
conductor; head, commander, chief. See
AUTHORITY, MUSIC, PRECEDENCE.

leadership, *n.* superintendence, chieftain-
ship, stewardship, guidance. See AU-
THORITY.

leaf, *n.* frond, blade; lamina, sheet, flake;
sheet, page. See VEGETABLE, LAYER.

leafage, *n.* foliage, leaves, verdure. See
VEGETABLE.

leaflet, *n.* pamphlet, circular, handbill,
handout. See PUBLICATION.

league, *n.* band, coalition, covenant, [con-]
federation, confederacy, junta, cabal.
—*v.i.* confederate, unite, join. See
PARTY.

leak, *v.i.* seep, OOZE, escape. See EGRESS,
DISCLOSURE, WASTE.

lean, *v.i.* slant, incline; depend, rely; tend.
See SUPPORT, TENDENCY. —*adj.* spare,
meager; lank, gaunt. See NARROWNESS.

lean-to, *n.* shelter, hut, shack. See ABODE.

LEAP
Spring through the air

Nouns—1, leap, jump, hop, spring, bound, vault; bounce (see RECOIL).

2, dance, caper; curvet, prance, skip, gambol, frolic, romp, buck.

3, leaper, jumper, kangaroo, jerboa, chamois, goat, frog, grasshopper, flea, hoptoad;
jumping bean, jumping jack, pogo stick; spring.

4, high jump, broad *or* long jump, pole vault; lover's leap; springboard; leap frog,
hopscotch; hop, skip, and jump.

Verbs—leap, jump, hop, spring, bound, pounce, vault, cut capers, trip, skip, dance,
prance, gambol, frolic, romp, cavort, caper, curvet, foot it, bob, bounce, flounce,
frisk, start [up].

Adjectives—leaping, bounding, springy, saltatory, frisky, lively, bouncy, frolicsome,
skittish.

Antonyms, see DESCENT.

LEARNING
Acquisition of knowledge

Nouns—1, learning, assimilation, absorption; erudition, KNOWLEDGE; humanity, wisdom, breeding; study, education, schooling; reading, INQUIRY, contemplation; apprenticeship, pupilage, tutelage, novitiate, matriculation. *Informal,* school of hard
knocks. See SCHOOL.

2, learner, beginner, novice, neophyte, adherent; student, scholar, pupil, schoolboy *or*
-girl; robin, bluebird, cardinal; apprentice, plebe, abecedarian; disciple, follower,
apostle; self-taught man *or* woman. *Slang,* cereb, swot, gomer, geek.

3, class, master class, learning curve, open classroom; tracking.

4, scientist, savant, scholar, pedant, pedagogue; man of learning (see KNOWLEDGE);
intelligentsia, literati, clerisy; bookworm, egghead. *Informal,* longhair.

Verbs—1, learn, acquire knowledge, pick up, ascertain, hear (of), discover; come to
one's knowledge; master; learn by rote *or* heart, commit to MEMORY, memorize, absorb, assimilate, digest, fix in one's mind; acquaint oneself; sit at the feet of; learn by
experience, learn the hard way (see DIFFICULTY); remember, bear in mind, bethink
oneself; glean; learn a lesson, run through; serve one's apprenticeship. *Informal,* learn
the ropes; get the hang *or* knack of, catch on. *Slang,* get wise.

2, study, lucubrate, burn the midnight oil, keep one's nose in a book, cram. *Informal,*
hit the books, crack a book, bone up. *Slang,* grind.

Adjectives—learned, cultured, knowledgeable, erudite, literate; schooled, well-read,
well-informed, wise; bookish; studious, scholastic, scholarly, academic, industrious;
teachable, malleable.

Phrases—never too old to learn; there is no royal road to learning; a burnt child dreads
the fire; experience is the best teacher.

Quotations—Better build schoolrooms for "the boy" than cells and gibbets for "the man" (*Eliza Cook*), Studies serve for delight, for ornament, and for ability (*Sir Francis Bacon*), If I have seen further it is by standing on the shoulders of giants (*Isaac Newton*), If you think education is expensive, try ignorance (*Derek Bok*), A little learning is a dangerous thing (*Alexander Pope*), They know enough who know how to learn (*Henry Adams*), I find no other pleasure than learning (*Inigo Jones*).

Antonyms, see TEACHING.

---

lease, *n.* leasehold; contract. —*v.t.* rent, let, demise; hire. See COMMISSION.

leash, *n.* leader, thong; trio. See RESTRAINT, NUMERATION.

least, *adj.* smallest, minimum. See INFERIORITY, LITTLENESS.

leather, *n.* skin, hide; cowhide, calfskin, etc. See COVERING, MATERIALS.

leathery, *adj.* tough, tanned, coriaceous. See HARDNESS. *Ant.*, supple.

leave, *v.t.* abandon, surrender; quit, forsake; deliver; cease, desist, forgo; bequeath; relinquish. See RELINQUISHMENT, GIVING. —*v.i.* go away, depart; omit, postpone. See DEPARTURE, NEGLECT. —*n.* PERMISSION; weekend, *etc.* pass.

leaven, *n.* yeast, ferment; CAUSE, generator. See LEVITY.

leavetaking, *n.* farewell, withdrawal, valediction; adieu, Godspeed. See DEPARTURE.

leavings, *n.pl.* residue, leftovers, refuse, rubbish; REMAINDER.

lecher, *n.* roué, rake, profligate, satyr, le[t]ch (*sl.*). See IMPURITY.

lecture, *v.t.* address, discourse, expound; reprove, rebuke, scold. See TEACHING, DISAPPROBATION, SPEECH.

ledge, *n.* shelf, rim, bench; berm, reef. See HEIGHT, HORIZONTAL.

ledger, *n.* journal, register; books. See ACCOUNTING.

leech, *n.* bloodsucker, parasite, bleeder; toady. See SERVILITY.

leer, *n.* smirk, wink, oblique look. —*v.* ogle, make eyes, grimace, look *or* eye askance. See VISION.

leery, *adj., informal,* wary, distrustful, suspicious. See CAUTION.

leeway, *n.* room, latitude, margin, elbow room. See SPACE.

LEFT
To the left side

Nouns—1, left, sinistrality, sinistration; left hand, left side, near side; port[side], larboard; verso. *Informal,* wrong side.

2, left wing, radical (see CHANGE); liberal, progressive.

3, lefthander. *Slang,* lefty, southpaw, portsider.

Verbs—be left-handed; turn left; have two left feet. *Slang,* hang a louie, louis, *or* ralph.

Adjectives—1, left, sinister, sinistrous, left-hand[ed], awkward, near, port[side], larboard[ed]; counterclockwise.

2, left wing, radical, liberal, progressive.

3, left-handed. *Slang,* southpaw.

Adverbs—port, larboard; left-handedly, leftward[s]. *Informal,* from left field (*unexpectedly or unfairly*).

Quotations—Let not thy left hand know what thy right hand doeth (*Bible*).

Antonyms, see RIGHT.

---

leftover, *adj.* remaining, spare, surplus, extra, superfluous. —*n.pl.* REMAINDER, remains, leavings, scraps, odds and ends.

left-wing, *adj.* leftist, progressive, liberal. See LEFT.

leg, *n.* limb, SUPPORT; course, tack, lap; side. —**shake a leg**, *slang,* hurry, hasten (see HASTE).

legacy, *n.* bequest (see GIVING).

LEGALITY
Lawfulness

Nouns—1, legality, legitimacy, legitimateness, legalization, constitutionalism, constitutionality, lawfulness, legal process, due process of law, Miranda rights.

2, legislation, legislature, law, code, codex, constitution, charter, enactment, statute, bill, canon, precept, ordinance, regulation; bylaw; decree, order; sanction, AUTHORITY.

3, jurisprudence, codification, equity; common, civil, statute, *or* constitutional law; ecclesiastical *or* divine law, law of Moses, unwritten law; family law; military *or* maritime law; Uniform Code of Military Justice.

4, jurisdiction, administration, province, dominion, domain, bailiwick, magistracy, AUTHORITY, police power, eminent domain. See PERMISSION.

Verbs—1, legalize, legitim[at]ize, validate, authorize, sanction; enact, ordain, decree, order, pass a law, legislate; codify, formulate, regulate.

2, administer, govern, rule; preside, judge, arbitrate.

Adjectives—1, legal, legitimate, according to law, vested, constitutional, chartered, legalized, lawful, valid, permitted, statutory; official, ex officio; legislative. *Slang,* legit; kosher.

2, jurisdictional, judicatory, judiciary, judicial, juridical; judging, judicious; forensic.

Adverbs—legally, legitimately, by law, in the eye of the law. *Slang,* on the square, on the up and up, on the level.

Quotations—Useless laws weaken the necessary laws (*Montesquieu*), Laws too gentle are seldom obeyed; too severe, seldom executed (*Benjamin Franklin*).

Antonyms, see ILLEGALITY.

---

legate, *n.* AGENT. See COMMISSION.

legation, *n.* mission, embassy, consulate. See AGENCY.

legend, *n.* tradition, tale, saga; myth, edda; inscription, motto. See DESCRIPTION.

legendary, *adj.* fabled, storied; mythological, traditional, historical; unreal, illusory; famous, celebrated, of REPUTE. See IMAGINATION, DESCRIPTION.

leggings, *n.pl.* gaiters, spats, puttees, chaps. See CLOTHING.

legible, *adj.* readable, decipherable, clear, plain. See WRITING.

legion, *n.* horde, MULTITUDE; army, corps. See COMBATANT.

legislator, *n.* lawmaker, congressman, senator, parliamentarian. See COUNCIL.

legislature, *n.* congress, parliament. See COUNCIL.

legitimate, *adj.* lawful, legal; proper, valid; genuine, logical, justifiable. See LEGALITY, TRUTH. *Ant.,* illegitimate, invalid.

leisure, *n.* spare time, idle hours, time on one's hands; holiday, vacation; SLOWNESS, deliberation; rest, ease, idleness, REPOSE. See TIME, OCCASION.

lemon, *n.* citron; *informal,* dud, FAILURE, bomb. See VEGETABLE.

lend, *v.* advance, accommodate with, finance; loan; entrust; pawn; lend-lease; let, demise, lease, sublet. See DEBT, COMMISSION. *Ant.,* borrow.

LENGTH
Linear measure

Nouns—1, length, lengthiness, longitude, span, extent, stretch, DISTANCE, dimension, footage, yardage, mileage. See MEASUREMENT, SPACE.

2, *(line measure)* line, bar, stripe, string, row, streak; spoke, radius, diameter.

3, *(making longer)* lengthening, prolongation, production, protraction, tension, extension, elongation.

4, *(linear measurement)* line, nail, inch, hand, palm, foot, cubit, yard, ell, fathom, pole, rod, furlong, mile, league, chain; meter; centimeter, *etc.*; kilometer; land measure, surveyors' measure.

Verbs—1, stretch out, extend, sprawl, reach to, stretch to.

2, lengthen, extend, elongate, stretch, prolong, string out, produce, protract, let out, draw out, spin out.

3, enfilade, rake; look along; view in perspective.

Adjectives—1, long, lengthy, outstretched, lengthened, elongated, protracted, interminable, no end of, unshortened, over all.

2, linear, longitudinal, oblong, lineal.

Adverbs—lengthwise, at length, longitudinally, endwise, along, tandem, in a line, in perspective; from end to end, from stem to stern, from head to foot, from top to bottom, from head to toe; cap-a-pie; from dawn to dusk; fore and aft.

Antonyms, see SHORTNESS.

LENIENCY
Mercifulness

Nouns—leniency, lenience, lenity, MODERATION, tolerance, toleration, mildness, gentleness, favor; indulgence, clemency, mercy, forbearance, quarter, patience; compassion, ruth, PITY. See LIBERALITY, RELIEF.

Verbs—tolerate, bear with, give quarter; spare, spare the rod [and spoil the child], PITY; indulge, put up with, bear with, baby, pamper, coddle, spoil. *Slang,* pull one's punches; let one down easy.

Adjectives—lenient, mild, gentle, soft, tolerant, indulgent; moderate, easygoing; clement, compassionate, forbearing, merciful.

Phrases—live and let live.

Quotations—Patience and delay achieve more than force and rage (*La Fontaine*), Sorrow and silence are strong, and patient endurance is godlike (*Longfellow*).

Antonyms, see SEVERITY.

---

lens, *n.* refractor, eyeglass, magnifying glass, reading glass. See OPTICAL INSTRUMENTS.

leper, *n.* pariah, untouchable, outcast. See EXCLUSION.

leprechaun, *n.* sprite, puca, pixie. See MYTHICAL DEITIES.

lesbian, *n.* homosexual, tribade, sapphist. See FEMALE.

lesion, *n.* injury, wound, trauma, sore. See DISEASE.

less, *adj.* inferior, not so much, minor. —*adv.* under, short of. See INFERIORITY, DEDUCTION, ABSENCE. *Ant.,* more, superior.

lessen, *v.t.* reduce, diminish, mitigate, abate, shorten. See DECREASE, MODERATION. *Ant.,* INCREASE, worsen.

lesson, *n.* instruction, task, exercise, example; admonition, reprimand. See TEACHING, WARNING.

lest, *conj.* for fear that. See LIABILITY.

let, *v.t.* allow, permit; propose, CAUSE; assign; lease, rent. See PERMISSION.

letdown, *n.* letup, abatement, fall; comedown, setback, drawback; DISAPPOINTMENT, disillusion; blow, anticlimax.

let go, NEGLECT, ignore; exempt, excuse; fire, dismiss, lay off. See EXCLUSION, PERMISSION.

lethal, *adj.* deadly, fatal, mortal, KILLING, toxic, poisonous; virulent, pernicious, noxious, hurtful, malignant, injurious.

lethargy, *n.* lassitude, sluggishness, indifference, apathy, stupor. See INACTIVITY, INSENSIBILITY, WEARINESS. *Ant.,* energy, vitality.

letter, *n.* character, symbol; cuneiform, hieroglyphic; capital, majuscule; small letter, minuscule; consonant, vowel, digraph, diphthong; missive, note. See WRITING, COMMUNICATION.

lettered, *adj.* learned, educated, literate. See LEARNING. *Ant.,* unlettered, uneducated, illiterate.

letup, *n.* lessening, slowup, slowdown, abatement, mitigation, alleviation; pause, lull, truce, cease-fire; interim, interlude, respite, relief; slack season, breathing spell. See MODERATION, REPOSE, DISCONTINUANCE, DECREASE.

levee, *n.* embankment, dike. See DEFENSE.

level, *adj.* HORIZONTAL; flat; even; aligned;

cool, well-balanced. —*v.t.* raze; flatten;
equalize. See DESTRUCTION, SMOOTH-
NESS, EQUALITY.

levelheaded, *adj.* sane, sensible, practical.
See SANITY. *Ant.,* irrational.

lever, *n.* crowbar, pry, prize, jimmy; tool.
See ELEVATION, INSTRUMENTALITY, IN-
FLUENCE.

leverage, *n.* advantage; purchase, hold.
See INFLUENCE.

leviathan, *n.* monster, behemoth. See SIZE.

levity, *n.* frivolity (see FOLLY); lightness
(see LEVITY).

LEVITY
Lightness in weight

Nouns—1, levity, lightness, buoyancy, imponderability, weightlessness, volatility, airi-
ness, levitation; fermentation, effervescence, ebullience.

2, *(light object)* feather, fluff, down, thistledown, cobweb, gossamer, straw, cork,
bubble, mote, dust, air, ether; lightweight, featherweight.

3, *(substance causing lightness)* leaven, ferment, yeast, barm, baking soda *or* powder;
zyme, enzyme, diastase, pepsin.

Verbs—1, lighten, levitate, float, swim, rise, soar, hang, waft; uplift, upraise, buoy up,
unburden.

2, leaven, raise, work, ferment; effervesce.

Adjectives—1, light, airy, feathery, fluffy, puffy, vapory, zephyry; subtle; weightless,
ethereal, sublimated, volatile; buoyant, floating; portable; imponderable, imponder-
ous.

2, foamy, yeasty, barmy, frothy; effervescent; fermentative, fermenting; zymotic,
zymic, enzymic, diastatic, peptic.

Quotations—He who would travel happily must travel light (*Antoine de Saint-Exupéry*).

Antonyms, see GRAVITY.

---

levy, *n.* assessment; tax; draft, conscription. See ASSEMBLAGE, PRICE.

lewd, *adj.* lascivious, obscene, salacious,
indecent, unchaste. See IMPURITY.

lexicon, *n.* dictionary, vocabulary, wordbook. See PUBLICATION, LANGUAGE.

LIABILITY
Responsibility

Nouns—1, liability, liableness, responsibility, POSSIBILITY, probability, contingency, susceptibility; DUTY; liabilities, debts (see DEBT); drawback (see HINDRANCE). See TENDENCY.

2, person responsible, responsible person.

Verbs—be liable, incur, lay oneself open to, risk, run the risk, stand a chance, lie under,
expose oneself to, open a door to; be responsible for, answer for.

Adjectives—liable, subject, in danger, open to, exposed to, apt to, dependent on, responsible, answerable, accountable, incurring; contingent, incidental, possible, on *or*
in the cards, at the mercy of.

Adverbs—responsibly, *etc.*; at the risk of. *Informal,* likely.

Conjunctions—lest, for fear that.

Quotations—I believe that every right implies a responsibility; every opportunity, an
obligation; every possession, a duty (*John D. Rockefeller*), To be a man is, precisely,
to be responsible (*Antoine de Saint-Exupéry*), Only aim to do your duty, and mankind
will give you credit where you fail (*Thomas Jefferson*).

Antonyms, see EXEMPTION.

---

liaison, *n.* affair; CONNECTION. See LOVE.

liar, *n.* prevaricator, equivocator, falsifier,

fibber, deceiver. See DECEPTION, FALSE-
HOOD. *Ant.,* honest person.

libel, *n.* defamation, calumniation, aspersion. See DETRACTION.

liberal, *adj.* progressive, leftist; tolerant, permissive; bountiful, generous. See LEFT, LENIENCY, LIBERALITY. *Ant.,* conservative.

LIBERALITY
Generosity

Nouns—1, liberality, generosity, UNSELFISHNESS, munificence, largesse, bounty; charity, hospitality, beneficence, philanthropy; prodigality; fullness, broadness, BREADTH.

2, tolerance, catholicity, bigness, broad-mindedness, impartiality, lack of *or* freedom from bigotry, magnanimity. See JUSTICE.

3, gift, donation, present, gratuity, benefaction; giver, benefactor, philanthropist. *Informal,* big tipper. See GIVING, BENEVOLENCE.

Verbs—spend freely, shower down upon, open one's purse strings, spare no expense, give carte blanche, lavish; liberalize, broaden.

Adjectives—1, liberal, free, generous, handsome, charitable, beneficent, philanthropic; bounteous, bountiful, unsparing, ungrudging, unstinting, lavish, profuse; open- *or* freehanded, open- *or* largehearted; hospitable, unselfish, princely, prodigal, munificent.

2, tolerant, catholic, progressive, broad- *or* large-minded, magnanimous, impartial, unbigoted, open-minded, receptive.

Adverbs—liberally, generously, *etc.*; with both hands.

Interjection—keep the change!

Quotations—God loveth a cheerful giver (*Bible*), Defer not charities till death (*Francis Bacon*).

> *Antonyms,* see ECONOMY, PARSIMONY, SELFISHNESS.

LIBERATION
Setting free

Nouns—1, liberation, emancipation, enfranchisement, manumission, freeing; Emancipation Proclamation; ESCAPE, FREEDOM, liberty; deliverance, extrication, release, riddance; rescue, ransom; redemption, salvation, saving, absolution (see ACQUITTAL); discharge, dismissal, demobilization. *Informal,* bail-out. *Slang,* kiss-off.

2, liberator, emancipator, freer, deliverer, rescuer; redeemer, savior.

Verbs—1, liberate, free [from bondage], set free, set at liberty, give one's freedom; disenthrall; emancipate, enfranchise, manumit; deliver, extricate, release, ransom, reclaim; snatch from the jaws of death; redeem, absolve, save; acquit. *Slang,* spring.

2, discharge, dismiss, disband, demobilize; parole; let go, turn, set, cut, *or* let loose, let out, let slip; turn *or* cast adrift; rid, shake off, be *or* get rid of; unfetter, untie, unleash, unloose[n], unlock, unbolt, unbar, uncork, unbind, unhand, unchain, unshackle; disengage, disentangle, disencumber; clear. *Slang,* sack.

3, gain one's liberty, go [scot-]free, get off *or* out, get clear *or* free of (see ESCAPE).

Adjectives—liberated, freed, saved, *etc.*; free, out of harness, unfettered, at liberty, off the hook, at large; out of bondage, on parole, free as a bird; liberative, liberatory. *Slang,* saved by the bell.

Quotations—In giving freedom to the slave, we assure freedom to the free (*Abraham Lincoln*), The moment the slave resolves that he will no longer be a slave, his fetters fall. He frees himself and shows the way to others. Freedom and slavery are mental states (*Mahatma Gandhi*), The God who gave us life, gave us liberty at the same time (*Thomas Jefferson*).

> *Antonyms,* see RESTRAINT.

libertarian, *n.* individualist, free will advocate. See SPECIALITY.

libertine, *n.* See IMPURITY.

liberty, *n.* FREEDOM, independence, emancipation; right, license, privilege. See PERMISSION, EXEMPTION. *Ant.*, slavery. servitude.

libido, *n.* sex drive (see DESIRE).

library, *n.* athenaeum, bookroom. See STORE.

libretto, *n.* script; scenario, book, dialogue, text, words; plot, story, synopsis, promptbook. See DRAMA, WRITING.

license, *n.* PERMISSION, authority; FREEDOM, licentiousness. See IMPURITY.

lick, *v.* lap (up), tongue; dart across (see TOUCH); *informal,* beat, thrash, flog; *informal,* overcome, defeat, rout. See IMPULSE, PUNISHMENT, SUCCESS. —*n.* lap, licking, sip, taste, sup; bit, jot, modicum; *slang,* try, essay, chance; *slang,* hot lick, blue note, vamp, improvisation, riff. See FOOD, TOUCH, MUSIC.

lid, *n.* top, cover, cap, crown, CLOSURE; censorship.

lie, *v.i.* prevaricate, falsify, deceive; recline, rest, be situated; extend. See FALSEHOOD, DECEPTION, LOCATION, HORIZONTAL. *Ant.*, fact, TRUTH. —lie detector, polygraph (see INQUIRY).

lieutenant, *n.* deputy, assistant. See AGENT.

LIFE
Fact of existence

Nouns—1, life, vitality, EXISTENCE, being, living, animation, this mortal coil; vital force, flame, *or* spark, biorhythm; respiration, breath [of life], lifeblood, life force, vivification, revivification, resurgence. See REPRODUCTION, ORGANIC MATTER.

2, life sciences; physiology, zoology, botany, biology, embryology, biochemistry, biophysics, anatomy, bacteriology, biometry, bionics, biotechnology, bryology, cell biology *or* physiology, cytology, dendrology, embryology, endocrinology, entomology, enzymology, epidemiology, ethology, evolution, exobiology, genetics, hematology, herpetology, immunology, mammalogy, microbiology, molecular biology, mycology, neurobiology, ornithology, paleontology, parasitology, phycology, physiology, phytology; behaviorism, ecology.

3, *(life functions)* anabolism, catabolism, chemosynthesis, cytokinesis, exocytosis, glycolysis, mitosis, osmosis, photosynthesis, respiration, breathing, atrophy, autoregulation, biosynthesis, catabolism, defecation, digestion, excretion, expiration, extension, feedback, fermentation, inspiration, metabolism, micturition, respiration, secretion, ventilation. See REPRODUCTION.

4, the living, the quick (see HUMANITY).

Verbs—1, live, be alive, be, breathe, respire, subsist, exist, walk the earth.

2, see the light, be born, come into the world, draw breath, quicken, come to [life]. See RESTORATION.

3, give birth to, bring to life, put life into, [re]vitalize, revive, vivify, [re]animate, keep alive, keep body and soul together, keep the wolf from the door, support life.

Adjectives—1, living, alive, vital, existing, extant, in the flesh, in the land of the living, breathing, quick, animated, lively, alive and kicking.

2, life-giving, generative, fecund, seminal, germinal; vivifying, animative, invigorating, exhilarating.

3, pro-life, right-to-life.

Phrases—life's a bitch, and then you die.

Quotations—Life is as tedious as a twice-told tale, vexing the dull ear of a drowsy man (*Shakespeare*), Life is an incurable disease (*Abraham Cowley*), Life, like a dome of many-colored glass, stains the white radiance of Eternity until Death tramples it to fragments (*Percy Bysshe Shelley*), The mass of men lead lives of quiet desperation (*Henry Thoreau*), Life would be tolerable but for its amusements (*Sinclair Lewis*), Life is just one damned thing after another (*Elbert Hubbard*), Life is just a bowl of cherries (*Lew Brown*), Life is first boredom, then fear (*Philip Larkin*), A living dog is better than a dead lion (*Bible*).

Antonyms, see DEATH.

life-giving, *adj*. See LIFE.

lifeless, *adj*. inanimate, inert, sluggish, spiritless. See DEATH. *Ant.*, lively, full of life.

lifelike, *adj*. realistic, natural, accurate. See SIMILARITY.

life preserver, lifesaver, life belt *or* jacket, Mae West, water wings, flotation device. See SAFETY.

lifestyle, *n*. conduct, behavior, modus vivendi. See HABIT.

lifetime, *n*. lifespan, life expectancy. See DURABILITY.

lift, *v.t*. raise, elevate, exalt; uplift; *informal*, steal. See ELEVATION, STEALING.

liftoff, *n*. launch, blastoff. See BEGINNING. *Ant.*, landing, touchdown.

ligature, *n*. bond, tie, slur, surgical thread. See CONNECTION.

light, *adj*. airy (see LEVITY); frivolous, jesting, jocular, lightsome; giddy, dizzy, flighty; wanton; nimble, agile; flippant, pert, insouciant; humorous; trivial. See CHEERFULNESS, UNIMPORTANCE, IMPURITY, CHANGEABLENESS. *Ant.*, heavy; dark.

LIGHT
Illumination

Nouns—1, light, ray, beam, stream, gleam, streak, pencil; sunbeam, moonbeam, aurora, day, sunshine, light of day, sun, daylight, daybreak, noonday, sunlight; moonlight, starlight. *Informal*, lite.

2, *(intermittent light)* glow, glimmer[ing]; glitter, shimmer, flicker, glint; spark, scintilla, sparkle, scintillation, flash, blaze, coruscation, flame, fire, lightning bolt.

3, *(radiant light)* luster, sheen, gloss; tinsel, spangle; brightness, brilliancy, splendor, effulgence, dazzle, glare, resplendence, dazzlement, phosphorescence, incandescence, fluorescence, luminousness, luminosity, lucidity, radiation, irradiation, radiance, illumination, reflection, refraction; diffraction, dispersion.

4, *(science of light)* photology, photometry, photics, optics, catoptrics, photography, heliography, radioscopy, holography, optronics; quantum theory of light; spectrum, ultraviolet. *or* infrared light, black *or* white light, coherent light, incident light, polarized light, monochromatic *or* polychromatic light; lumen, candela, candle[power].

5, *(source of light)* luminary, illuminant; electric, fluorescent, arc, neon, gas, halogen, *etc.* light, Tensor light, track lighting; candlelight, lamplight, firelight; laser; candle, taper, [arm, desk, floor, gooseneck, phoebe, table, Tiffany, *or* Venetian] lamp, torch, torchiere, brand, flambeau, [Chinese] lantern, searchlight, flashlight, nightlight; bulb, globe, mantle, jet; chandelier, candelabrum, sconce, candlestick; limelight, footlights, spotlight; rocket, flare, beacon, flasher; fireworks, pyrotechnics; halo, aureole, nimbus, gloriole, aura, glory. *Slang*, glim.

Verbs—1, shine, glow, glitter, spangle, glister, glisten, flicker, twinkle, gleam, flare, glare, beam, shimmer, glimmer, sparkle, scintillate, coruscate, flash, glint, blaze, be bright, reflect light, dazzle, radiate, shoot out beams; beat down.

2, lighten, enlighten; light [up], clear up, brighten, irradiate, shine, give *or* shed light, throw light upon, illume, illumine, illuminate; strike a light, kindle.

Adjectives—1, shining, alight, luminous, luminescent, lucid, lucent, luciferous, light, lightsome, bright, vivid, resplendent, lustrous, shiny, beamy, scintillant, radiant, lambent; glossy, sunny, cloudless, clear, unclouded; glinting, gleaming, beaming, effulgent, splendid, resplendent, glorious, blazing, brilliant, ablaze, meteoric, phosphorescent, glowing; lighted, lit, ablaze, on.

2, actinic, photographic, heliographic, optic, optical, holographic.

Quotations—She [Eleanor Roosevelt] would rather light candles than curse the darkness, and her glow has warmed the world (*Adlai Stevenson*), And God said, Let there be light: and there was light (*Bible*), It is better to light one candle than to curse the darkness (*Christopher Society*), Thy word is a lamp unto my feet, and a light unto my path (*Bible*), We are a nation of communities . . . a brilliant diversity spread like stars, like a thousand points of light in a broad and peaceful sky (*George H. W. Bush*).

Antonyms, see DARKNESS.

light-headed, *adj.* giddy, dizzy; frivolous; drunk. See FOLLY, DRINKING.

lightness, *n.* LEVITY; gaiety, volatility; nimbleness, grace; paleness. See ACTIVITY, COLORLESSNESS. *Ant.,* heaviness, seriousness.

lightning, *n.* thunderbolt, levin, firebolt, fulmination. See VELOCITY, LIGHT.

lightweight, *adj.* weak, powerless, impotent. See WEAKNESS, UNIMPORTANCE.

likable, *adj.* lovable, adorable, charming. See LOVE. *Ant.,* unlikable.

like, *adj.* similar, resembling, characteristic. See SIMILARITY. —*v.t.* enjoy, desire, fancy. See PLEASURE, LOVE, APPROBATION. *Ant.,* different, dissimilar; DISLIKE.

likely, *adj.* credible; suitable; promising. See LIABILITY, AGREEMENT, CHANCE, POSSIBILITY. *Ant.,* unlikely.

liken, *v.t.* compare. See RELATION.

likeness, *n.* portrait, effigy, counterpart; SIMILARITY; resemblance. See REPRESENTATION.

likewise, *adv.* moreover, also; similarly, in like manner. See SIMILARITY, ADDITION.

liking, *n.* fondness, inclination, preference. See DESIRE, LOVE. *Ant.,* DISLIKE.

lilt, *n.* swing, cadence (see OSCILLATION).

limb, *n.* branch; arm, leg, member. See PART, INELASTICITY.

limber, *adj.* flexible, supple, pliable; lithe. See SOFTNESS. *Ant.,* stiff, inflexible.

limbo, *n.* land of the lost, no-man's-land, neither here nor there, nowhere, borderland, OBLIVION. See HELL.

limelight, *n.* spotlight, footlights; publicity, notoriety, fame. See PUBLICATION.

LIMIT
Boundary

Nouns—limit, boundary, bounds, confines; curbstone, term, EDGE; compass; bourne, verge, pale; termination, terminus, END, terminal, extremity; stint; frontier, precinct, border, marches, boundary line, landmark, line of demarcation, point of no return, Rubicon, turning point; ceiling; deadline; Berlin wall, Iron *or* Bamboo Curtain. See RESTRAINT, CIRCUMSCRIPTION, QUALIFICATION.

Verbs—limit, restrict, bound, confine, define, circumscribe, restrain, qualify, draw the line.

Adjectives—definite, finite, determinate, terminal, frontier, limited, circumscribed, restricted, confined, earthbound.

Adverbs—thus far, so far and no farther, just so far; to death; within bounds.

Quotations—No natural boundary seems to be set to the efforts of man; and in his eyes, what is not yet done is only what he has not yet attempted to do (*Alexis de Tocqueville*).

Antonyms, see FREEDOM, INFINITY.

limitless, *adj.* endless, inexhaustible, unbounded. See SUFFICIENCY, INFINITY.

limp, *adj.* limber, flaccid, flabby, soft. See SOFTNESS. —*v.t.* hobble, hitch; drag. See FAILURE.

limpid, *adj.* transparent, clear, lucid. See TRANSPARENCY.

line, *v.t.* interline, face; delineate. —*n.* mark; cord, string; crease, wrinkle; verse, note; route, system; vocation, calling; lin-

eage; row, file. See INDICATION, FILAMENT, POETRY, BUSINESS, ANCESTRY, CONTINUITY, FURROW, LENGTH, NARROWNESS, STRAIGHTNESS.

lineage, *n.* ANCESTRY, family, pedigree, POSTERITY.

lineament, *n.* feature, characteristic, singularity. See APPEARANCE, FORM.

linear, *adj.* aligned, straight; lineal. See CONTINUITY.

lineup, *n.* program, calendar; batting order. See LIST, ARRANGEMENT.

linger, *v.i.* delay, dally, loiter, dawdle, poke; remain, persist. See LATENESS, DURABILITY, SLOWNESS.

lingerie, *n.* underthings, underwear, undies (*inf.*), unmentionables (*inf.*). See CLOTHING.

lingo, *n.* language, SPEECH, tongue; argot, cant, jive (*sl.*), *etc.*; shop talk.

lingua franca, *n.* dialect, pidgin, creole. See LANGUAGE.

linguist, *n.* polyglot, philologist, etymologist. See SPEECH.

liniment, *n.* lotion, salve, ointment, embrocation. See REMEDY.

lining, *n.* inner coating *or* COVERING, interlining; filling, stuffing; wainscot[ing]; gasket, washer; facing, sheathing, bushing; ceiling.

link, *n.* tie, bond; component, liaison. — *v.t.* join, unite, couple. See JUNCTION, RELATION, CONNECTION, PART.

lint, *n.* fluff, fuzz, threads; gauze, dressing. See COVERING, REMEDY.

lion, *n.* lioness, cat; hero, celebrity. See ANIMAL, REPUTE.

lionize, *v.t.* adulate, idolize (see REPUTE).

lip, *n.* EDGE, verge; labium, flange; *slang*, impertinence. See CONVEXITY, INSOLENCE. —**lip service,** false homage, mouthing (see FALSEHOOD).

LIQUEFACTION
Making liquid

Nouns—liquefaction, liquescence, liquidization, fluidization; melting, thaw; condensation, colliquation, dissolution, fusion; solution, infusion, lixivium, flux, decoction; solvent, menstruum, dissolvent, resolvent; liquefacient; liquefier. See FLUIDITY.

Verbs—liquefy, liquesce; run, melt, thaw, dissolve, resolve; deliquesce; liquidize, liquate, fluidize, condense; hold in solution, fuse, percolate, milk.

Adjectives—liquefied, fusil, condensed; melted, molten, thawed, *etc.*; in solution *or* suspension; liquefactive, liquescent, colliquative; liquifiable, soluble, dissoluble, dissolvable; solvent, melting.

Antonyms, see DENSITY, VAPOR.

---

liqueur, *n.* cordial, digestif, pousse-café. See FOOD, DRINKING.

liquid, *adj.* fluid, smooth, flowing. See FLUIDITY.

liquidate, *v.t.* pay, settle, wind up; *slang*, kill. See PAYMENT, KILLING.

liquor, *n.* liquid, fluid, broth, stock, juice, essence; spirits, *etc.* (see DRINKING). See FLUIDITY, FOOD.

lissome, *adj.* limber, lithe, agile. See SOFTNESS, ELASTICITY. *Ant.,* stiff, inflexible.

LIST
Enumeration

Nouns—1, list, catalog, beadroll, RECORD, register, cadastre, registry, directory; tabulation, tally [sheet], file; tariff, schedule; menu; docket, calendar; waiting list, honor roll, hit parade; lineup, roll, muster [roll]; enrollment, roster, slate, checklist; census, statistics, poll, ballot; bill [of lading], invoice, ledger, inventory; table, index; catalogue raisonné; glossary, vocabulary; wordbook, lexicon, dictionary, thesaurus; syllabus; portfolio, prospectus, canon, synopsis; Domesday Book, Blue Book, Social Register, Who's Who; Yellow, Blue, *or* White Pages; active, black, retired, sick, *etc.* list; registration, registry; matriculation; job bank; leaderboard. *Informal,* laundry list. See CLASS.

2, registrar, cataloger, indexer, tabulator; actuary, statistician; computer.

Verbs—1, list, catalog, RECORD, register, inventory; tally, file, tabulate; index, post, enter, set *or* jot down, inscribe; enroll, matriculate; itemize, schedule, chronicle; enumerate, rattle *or* reel off; blacklist.

2, list, incline, careen (see OBLIQUITY).

Adjectives—fair-trade, fixed, retail; inventorial.

Quotations—I've got a little list (*W. S. Gilbert*), History . . . is little more than the register of the crimes, follies, and misfortunes of mankind (*Edward Gibbon*).

---

listen, *v.i.* harken, attend; hear; grant; heed. See HEARING, ATTENTION.

listless, *adj.* indifferent, languid, spiritless, apathetic, lethargic. See INACTIVITY. *Ant.,* energetic, lively.

litany, *n.* prayer, invocation, devotions. See RITE.

literacy, *n.* reading, letters, scholarship. See LEARNING.

literal, *adj.* verbatim, word-for-word, exact, prosaic. See MEANING.

literary, *adj.* bookish, scholarly, long-haired (*sl.*). See KNOWLEDGE, WRITING.

literate, *adj.* lettered, educated. See LEARNING. *Ant.,* illiterate.

literature, *n.* books, belles-lettres, letters. See WRITING.

lithe, *adj.* lissome, supple, limber, flexible; spry, slender, willowy, sylphic, svelte. See SOFTNESS, ELASTICITY. *Ant.,* stiff.

litigate, *v.* contest, dispute, sue, prosecute. See LAWSUIT.

litigious, *adj.* actionable; contentious, disputatious. See LAWSUIT.

litter, *n.* DISORDER, scraps; bedding; stretcher, palanquin; offspring, birth. See VEHICLE, USELESSNESS, POSTERITY.

LITTLENESS
Small size

Nouns—**1,** littleness, smallness, minuteness, diminutiveness; thinness, NARROWNESS; epitome, abstract, brief (see SHORTNESS); microcosm; rudiment, miniature; vanishing point. See INSUBSTANTIALITY, POWDERINESS, PART, INVISIBILITY.

2, *(small animal)* animalcule, monad, mite, insect, fly, midge, gnat, shrimp, peewee, minnow, worm, maggot, entozoïn, ameba, microbe, germ, bacterium, grub, tomtit, runt, mouse, small fry, mustard seed, peppercorn, pebble, grain of sand, molehill.

3, *(small object)* point; atom, molecule, ion, electron, neutron, hadron; fragment, particle, crumb, powder; pinpoint, [micro]dot, speck, mote, jot, iota; decimal, fraction; modicum, minimum; minutiae; trifle; soupçon, suspicion, shade, scintilla, smidgeon; grain, bit, fleck, scruple, granule, minim; sip, dab, drop[let], dash, driblet, sprinkling, tinge; bloom; scrap, tag, splinter, chip, sliver, morsel, crumb; bite, snick, snack; thimbleful; nutshell; notebook computer; fine print.

4, *(small person)* dwarf, midget, pygmy; shrimp, peanut, pipsqueak, runt, peewee, bantam; Tom Thumb, Lilliputian, Alberich. *Slang,* half-pint, short stuff.

5, *(study of small things)* micrography, microscopy, micrology, microphotography; microscope, electron microscope, micrometer, vernier.

Verbs—belittle; dice; tweak; decrease, diminish, contract (see CONTRACTION).

Adjectives—**1,** little, small, minute, diminutive, micro[scopic], inconsiderable, exiguous, puny, wee, tiny; petty (see UNIMPORTANCE); petite, peewee, teeny[-weeny], midget, runty, stubby, bantam, elfin, dainty, dinky, minikin, knee-high, miniature, pygmy, nanoid, undersized, dapper, dwarf[ed], dwarfish, compact, stunted, limited, cramped, Lilliputian; pocket[-size], portable, short; thin, weazened, scant, scrubby; granular, powdery, shrunken. *Informal,* pint-size, itsy-bitsy, itty-bitty, runty, sawed-off, shrimpy.

2, impalpable, imperceptible, invisible, infinitesimal, atomic, molecular.

Adverbs—little, slightly, in a small compass, on a shoestring, in a nutshell, on a small scale; partly, partially; some, rather, somewhat; scarcely, hardly, barely, less than; merely; at [the] least.

Phrases—the best things come in small packages; the devil is in the details.

Quotations—Little things affect little minds (*Benjamin Disraeli*), I neglect God and his Angels for the noise of a fly, for the rattling of a coach, for the whining of a door (*John Donne*), It has long been an axiom of mine that the little things are infinitely the most important (A. *Conan Doyle*), Our life is frittered away by detail (*Henry Thoreau*).

Antonyms, see SIZE, GREATNESS.

---

liturgy, *n.* ritual, RITE, ceremony, service, worship; prayer book.

live, *v.i.* exist, be alive; abide; subsist, survive. See LIFE, ABODE.

livelihood, *n.* living, living wage; MEANS, wherewithal, resources, support, [up] keep, subsistence, sustenance, daily bread, job. See BUSINESS.

liveliness, *n.* animation, vivacity, sprightliness, pep (*sl.*). See ACTIVITY, CHEERFULNESS, FEELING, VIGOR.

live wire, hustler, dynamo, doer. See ACTIVITY.

livid, *adj.* pallid, ashen. See COLORLESSNESS.

living, *adj.* [a]live, quick, existing. See LIFE. —*n.* See LIVELIHOOD.

lizard, *n.* lacerta, saurian; gecko, chameleon. See ANIMAL.

load, *n.* burden; cargo, lading, shipment; charge. See GRAVITY, TRANSPORTATION.

loaded, *adj., slang,* drunk; rich, rolling in money. See DRINKING, PROSPERITY.

loafer, *n.* idler, lounger, vagrant, bum (*sl.*). See INACTIVITY.

loan, *n.* lending, borrowing; advance, credit, touch (*sl.*); sinking fund; mortgage. —*v., informal,* give or extend credit; underwrite, finance. See DEBT, MEANS. —**loan shark,** usurer, moneylender, shylock (*inf.*). See BORROWING.

loathe, *v.t.* detest, abhor, abominate. See HATE. *Ant.,* LOVE.

lob, *v.* toss, pitch (see IMPULSE).

lobby, *n.* foyer, hall, vestibule; lobbyism; pressure group, bloc, party, lobbyists, advocates. See RECEPTACLE, INFLUENCE. —*v.* solicit, ask favors; promote, bring pressure [to bear]; plump for, root for, pull strings.

lobbyist, *n.* powerbroker, influence peddler. See INFLUENCE.

local, *adj.* restricted, narrow, provincial; native, endemic. See REGION. *Ant.,* national, international.

locale, *n.* See LOCATION.

LOCATION
Place where something is

Nouns—1, location, localization, lodgment, stowage, collocation, packing, establishment, settlement, installation, fixation; placement, setting, insertion; ground zero. See REGION.

2, place, situation, locality, locale, site, depot, position, post, stand, neighborhood, ENVIRONMENT, whereabouts, bearings, orientation; attitude, aspect, viewpoint, standpoint, spot; colony. See ABODE

3, colonization, domestication, habitation, naturalization.

Verbs—1, place, situate, locate, localize, make a place for, put, lay, set [down], posit, plunk down, slap down, seat, station, lodge, quarter, post, park, double-park, install, house, stow, establish, set up; fix, pin, root, graft, plant, lay down, deposit; cradle; moor, anchor, tether, picket; pack, tuck in; vest, replace, put back; billet on, quarter upon, saddle with, load, freight, put up.

2, inhabit, domesticate (see ABODE).

Adjectives—located, placed, situate[d], ensconced, embedded, rooted, domesticated, vested in.

Adverbs—here, there, here and there; hereabout[s], thereabout[s], whereabout[s]; in place.

Phrases—a place for everything and everything in its place.

Quotations—Home is the place where, when you have to go there, they have to take you in (*Robert Frost*), All places are distant from heaven alike (*Robert Burton*).

Antonyms, see DISPLACEMENT.

lock, *v.t.* fasten, secure, make fast. See CLOSURE, JUNCTION.

locker, *n.* chest, cabinet, safe; lockbox, foot locker. See RECEPTACLE.

locket, *n.* pendant, charm. See ORNAMENT.

lockup, *n., informal,* jail, PRISON.

loco, *adj., slang,* crazy (see INSANITY).

loco citato, Lat., in the place cited; *loc cit.* See LOCATION.

locum tenens, Lat., substitute. See SUBSTITUTION, INHABITANT.

lode, *n.* deposit, vein, seam. See INORGANIC MATTER.

lodestone, *n.* loadstone; magnet, allurement. See ATTRACTION.

lodge, *v.i.* dwell, sojourn; settle; file. —*v.t.* shelter, harbor; deposit; file. —*n.* den; chapter, post. See ABODE, PARTY, LOCATION, STABILITY.

lodger, *n.* guest, roomer, boarder, transient; lessee, tenant. See INHABITANT.

lodging, *n.* accommodation. See ABODE.

loft, *n.* attic, garret; hayloft; studio. See ABODE, STORE.

lofty, *adj.* towering, high; haughty, patronizing; distinguished, noble; sublime; elevated; exalted. See HEIGHT, REPUTE. *Ant.,* pedestrian, deep.

log, *n.* timber, firewood; logbook, RECORD, diary, journal. See FUEL.

loggerhead, *n.* —**at loggerheads,** in dispute, arguing. See DISCORD.

logical, *adj.* rational, reasonable, sane. See REASONING. *Ant.,* illogical.

logo, *n.* logotype, [registered] trademark. See BUSINESS, INDICATION.

logy, *adj.* sluggish, dull, torpid. See WEARINESS.

loincloth, *n.* breechclout, breechcloth. See CLOTHING.

loiter, *v.i.* linger, poke, dawdle, lag. See SLOWNESS.

loll, *v.i.* lounge, lie down, sprawl; idle. See INACTIVITY, HORIZONTAL.

lone, *adj.* solitary, lonely; single, unmarried. See SECLUSION, CELIBACY.

lonely, *adj.* lonesome, solitary, lone, desolate, alone. See SECLUSION.

loner, *n., informal,* individualist, solitaire; hermit. See SECLUSION, ASCETICISM.

long, *adj.* lengthy, elongated; tedious; extended, protracted. See LENGTH. —*adv.* in great degree, for a time. See DURABILITY.

longevity, *n.* See AGE, DURABILITY.

longing, *n.* yearning, craving, hankering, hunger. See DESIRE.

long-lived, *adj.* persistent, hardy, durable. See DURABILITY. *Ant.,* short-lived.

longshoreman, *n.* See STEVEDORE.

long shot, *n.* long odds, outside CHANCE, gamble. See IMPROBABILITY. *Ant.,* sure thing.

long-suffering, *adj.* forbearing, stoic, submissive, patient. See LIBERALITY, FORGIVENESS.

long-winded, *adj.* tedious. See DIFFUSENESS, WEARINESS.

look, *v.i.* behold; perceive, discern; inspect; scan; stare; seem, appear. —*n.* glance, view; APPEARANCE, aspect. See VISION, ATTENTION.

lookout, *n.* vigilance, concern (*inf.*); observatory; watch, sentinel; prospect, vista. See VISION, WARNING, BUSINESS, CARE, EXPECTATION, DEFENSE.

loom, *v.t.* appear, come into sight; be imminent, forebode. See ARRIVAL, PREDICTION.

loony, *adj., informal,* crazy, wacky (see INSANITY). —**loony bin,** *informal,* insane asylum, booby hatch. See INSANITY.

loop, *n.* ring, circle, noose, eyelet, ambit. See CIRCULARITY.

loophole, *n.* peephole, OPENING; alternative, way out, escape hatch. See ESCAPE.

loose, *adj.* free, detached; flowing, unbound; vague, incoherent, diffuse; unrestrained, slack; dissipated, wanton, dissolute. See DISJUNCTION, IMPURITY. —*v.t.* free; loosen, unbind, undo; relax. See FREEDOM. *Ant.,* restrained, tethered, bound; tighten.

loot, *n.* booty, spoil, plunder. See ACQUISITION.

lop, *v.* chop, snip, clip, dock, nip, cut off. See SHORTNESS.

lopsided, *adj.* asymmetrical, askew, aslant; unbalanced, unequal; one-sided, off-center, cockeyed, gimpy (*sl.*). See INEQUALITY.

LOQUACITY
Talkativeness

Nouns—1, loquacity, loquaciousness, talkativeness, volubility, garrulity, multiloquence, flow of words, gift of gab, eloquence, fluency. *Slang,* flannel mouth. See SPEECH.

2, DIFFUSENESS, expatiation, dilation; REPETITION, prolixity. *Slang,* diarrhea of the mouth, motormouth.

3, jaw, gab[ble], jabber, chatter, prattle, patter, gossip, cackle, twaddle, blabber, blather, blarney, small talk. *Slang,* gas, hot air, yak[ety]-yak, skinny.

4, talker, chatterer, chatterbox, babbler, ranter, driveler, gossip, magpie, jay, parrot. *Slang,* windbag.

Verbs—run *or* go on, descant; protract, spin out, dwell on, harp on; talk glibly, patter, prate, palaver, chatter, prattle, blabber, drivel, jabber, jaw, babble, gabble, talk oneself hoarse; digress, perorate, maunder, ramble; gossip. *Slang,* shoot the breeze, shoot off one's mouth, run off at the mouth, gas.

Adjectives—loquacious, talkative, garrulous, voluble, fluent, gossipy; rambling; glib, effusive, gushy, eloquent, chattering, chatty, openmouthed; long-winded, long-drawn-out, discursive; loudmouthed.

Adverbs—at length; in extenso; ad nauseam.

Quotations—Continual eloquence is tedius (*Pascal*), Talkativeness is one thing, speaking well another (*Sophocles*), Talkers are no good doers (*Shakespeare*), Here comes the orator! with his flood of words, and his drop of reason (*Benjamin Franklin*), I have heard talk and talk, but nothing is done. Good words do not last long unless they amount to something (*Chief Joseph the Younger*).

Antonyms, see TACITURNITY.

---

lord, *n.* DIRECTOR; nobleman, aristocrat; God. See NOBILITY, DEITY. *Ant.,* serf, peasant.

lordly, *adj.* noble, imposing; imperious, arrogant, insolent, dictatorial. See REPUTE, INSOLENCE, NOBILITY. *Ant.,* lowly.

lore, *n.* erudition, scholarship, learning. See KNOWLEDGE.

LOSS
Failure to keep

Nouns—loss; perdition; forfeiture, forfeit, lapse, detriment, privation, bereavement, deprivation, dispossession, riddance, WASTE, dissipation, expenditure, leakage; brain drain; DESTRUCTION. See NONEXISTENCE, DEJECTION.

Verbs—lose; incur *or* meet with a loss; miss, mislay, let slip, allow to slip through the fingers; forfeit, get rid of, WASTE, dissipate, squander; write *or* charge off. *Slang,* lose one's shirt, drop a bundle, take a bath.

Adjectives—1, losing, not having; shorn, deprived, rid *or* quit of, denuded, bereaved, bereft, minus, cut off, dispossessed, out of pocket.

2, lost, long-lost; dissipated, wasted, forfeited, missing, gone, irretrievable, destroyed, off one's hands.

Phrases—a fool and his money are soon parted; finders keepers [losers weepers]; one man's loss is another man's gain; you cannot lose what you have never had.

Quotations—In every friend we lose a part of ourselves, and the best part (*Alexander Pope*), All, all are gone, the old familiar faces (*Charles Lamb*), Where have all the flowers gone? (*Pete Seeger*), Nothing hurts worse than the loss of money (*Livy*).

Antonyms, see ACQUISITION.

lot, *n.* fate, DESTINY, fortune; batch, sum; parcel. See ASSEMBLAGE, CHANCE, QUANTITY.

lotion, *n.* wash, liniment; tonic, skin bracer. See REMEDY, OIL.

lots, *n.pl.* a great deal, many, oodles. See MULTITUDE.

lottery, *n.* raffle, draw, lotto; allotment; fortune, CHANCE.

loud, *adj.* flashy (see OSTENTATION, VULGARITY); sonorous (see LOUDNESS). *Ant.,* soft; restrained.

loudmouthed, *adj.* See LOUDNESS.

LOUDNESS
High audibility

Nouns—1, loudness, noisiness, vociference, sonorousness, vehemency, intensity, power; stridency, raucousness, cacophony; decibel, bel. See ROTUNDITY.

2, *(loud echo)* resonance, reverberation, echo, ringing, tintinnabulation; roll, rumble, drumming, tattoo, rat-a-tat, rub-a-dub.

3, *(loud noise)* din, clamor, clang, clangor, fracas, bluster, rattle, clatter, noise, roar, uproar, racket, pandemonium, hubbub, shrillness, hullaballoo; charivari; trumpet blast, fanfare, ring, peal, toll, alarum, blast, boom, thunder, thunderclap; white noise; boiler factory; big mouth, loudmouth. *Slang,* barking *or* trumpet spider.

4, *(producer of loud sounds)* amplifier; [loud]speaker, bullhorn, megaphone. *Slang,* amp, boom box, boom car, bitch box.

Verbs—peal, ring, swell, clang, boom, thunder, fulminate, roar, resound, pop, reverberate; shout, scream, CRY, vociferate, bellow, crack, crash, bang, blare, rend the air, detonate, fill the air, ring in the ear, pierce the ears, deafen, stun, make the rafters ring; drown out. *Informal,* raise the roof. *Slang,* belt out, bump.

Adjectives—loud; sonorous, rotund; high-sounding, big-sounding, deep, full, powerful, noisy, clangorous, thunderous, thundering, dinning, deafening, earsplitting, obstreperous, blatant, rackety, uproarious, boisterous, earthshaking, shrill, clamorous, vociferous, stentorian, enough to wake the dead; loudmouthed, bigmouthed.

Adverbs—loudly, noisily, aloud, at the top of one's voice *or* lungs, lustily, to beat the band; in full cry.

Antonyms, see SOFTNESS.

---

loudspeaker, *n.* cone or electrodynamic speaker, tweeter, [sub]woofer. See LOUDNESS, SOUND.

lounge, *n.* sofa, settee, chaise longue, davenport, divan, daybed; lobby, bar. See SUPPORT, RECEPTACLE. —*v.* relax, REPOSE, loll, slouch, sprawl, make oneself comfortable. See INACTIVITY.

louse, *n.* vermin, bug, parasite; *Slang,* lout, cad, rascal, bounder, dog, stinker, SOB, rat. See ANIMAL, EVILDOER.

lousy, *adj., slang,* see BADNESS.

lout, *n.* bumpkin, clod, oaf, boor, hick, rube (*sl.*). See POPULACE.

louver, *n.* turret, dome, cupola; air vent; shutter, blind, jalousie. See OPENING.

LOVE
Strong affection

Nouns—1, love, fondness, liking; inclination, DESIRE; regard, admiration, affection, tenderness, heart, attachment, yearning; gallantry; passion, flame, devotion, infatuation, adoration; spark, ardor, tender passion; idolatry. See ENDEARMENT, FEELING, PLEASURE, MARRIAGE.

2, *(caring love)* BENEVOLENCE, brotherly *or* sisterly love, mother *or* maternal love, father *or* paternal love, parental affection.

3, *(symbol of love)* Cupid, Venus, Eros; true lover's knot, engagement ring, love token.

4, love affair, amour, liaison, intrigue, entanglement, fling, romance, *affaire d'amour or de cœur,* amourette, love story, plighted troth, courtship. *Informal,* calf *or* puppy love.

5, a. lover, suitor, follower, admirer, adorer, wooer, beau, honey, sweetheart, inamorato, swain, young man, boy friend, flame, love, true love, fair-haired boy; Lothario, Romeo, Casanova, Don Juan, gallant, paramour, amoroso; fiancé. *Slang,* wolf, lover boy, main man, main squeeze, ponce, make-out artist, stud, stage-door Johnny, ace, daddy, fancy man. **b.** inamorata, ladylove; idol, darling, duck, angel, goddess, true love, girl, sweetheart, beloved, girl *or* lady friend; betrothed, affianced, fiancée. *Informal,* steady, honeybunch, date, sweetie, jo. *Slang,* fancy woman. **c.** favorite, apple of one's eye, light of one's life. **d.** lovers, lovebirds. **e.** lovers' lane, lover's leap.

Verbs—**1,** love, like, fancy, care for, favor, become enamored, fall *or* be in love with; go with, go together, keep company; revere, take to, make much of, hold dear, prize, hug, cling to, cherish, pet; adore, idolize, love to distraction, dote on, desire; throw oneself at, lose *or* give one's heart. *Informal,* go steady, pin. *Slang,* go for, fall for, take a shine to, shine up to, be sweet on, be nuts about, carry a torch for.

2, win, gain, *or* engage the love, affections, *or* heart, disarm; sweep off one's feet; keep company; take the fancy of; attract, endear, charm, fascinate, captivate, bewitch, seduce, enamor, enrapture, turn the head. *Informal,* throw oneself at the head of. See ATTRACTION.

3, have an affair; go steady. *Slang,* carry on, fool around.

Adjectives—**1,** loving, fond of; taken with, smitten, attached to, enamored, charmed, in love, lovesick, lovelorn; affectionate, tender, sweet on, amorous, amatory, amative, erotic, uxorious, ardent, passionate, romantic, rapturous, devoted. *Slang,* going steady, pinned; stuck on.

2, loved, beloved, well beloved, dearly beloved. See ENDEARMENT.

3, lovable, adorable, winsome. See BEAUTY, ATTRACTION.

Phrases—love is blind; love makes the world go round; cold hands, warm heart; every Jack has his Jill; Friday's child is loving and giving; love me, love my dog; make love, not war.

Quotations—The course of true love never did run smooth (*Shakespeare*), Then must you speak of one who loved not wisely but too well (*Shakespeare*), The magic of first love is our ignorance that it can ever end (*Benjamin Disraeli*), In the spring a young man's fancy lightly turns to thoughts of love (*Lord Tennyson*), How do I love thee? Let me count the ways (*Elizabeth Barrett Browning*), 'Tis better to have loved and lost than never to have loved at all (*Lord Tennyson*), All you need is love (*Lennon/McCartney*), Love means not ever having to say you're sorry (*Erich Segal*), We are easily duped by those we love (*Molière*).

Antonyms, see HATE, DISLIKE.

---

loveless, *adj.* unloved, lovelorn, rejected. See HATE. *Ant.,* beloved.

lovelorn, *adj.* lovesick; jilted. See LOVE, HATE.

lovely, *adj.* beautiful, delightful, comely, exquisite, captivating. See BEAUTY.

lovemaking, *n.* sexual intercourse, dalliance; petting, fondling, kissing, making out (*inf.*). See ENDEARMENT.

lover, *n.* suitor, wooer, sweetheart, beau, boy- *or* girlfriend. See LOVE.

lovesick, *adj.* languishing, lovelorn. See LOVE.

low, *adj.* deep (see LOWNESS, DEPTH); moderate, simple; inferior, lowdown, base, mean, coarse; soft, feeble; dejected, depressed. See MODERATION, INFERIORITY, SOFTNESS, DEPRESSION. *Ant.,* high, superior.

lowborn, *adj.* humble, plebeian, common. —*n., slang,* vulgarian, illiterate, idiot. See POPULACE. *Ant.,* highborn, noble.

lowbrow, *adj.* unintellectual, uneducated. See IGNORANCE. *Ant.,* highbrow, intellectual.

low-class, *adj.* base, common, coarse. See INFERIORITY. *Ant.,* classy, well-born.

low-cut, *adj.* décolleté (see DIVESTMENT).

lower, *v.i.* lour, glower, scowl; be imminent, impend, APPROACH. —*adj. & v.* See LOWNESS, DEJECTION.

lowland, *n.* bottom[land], marshland, downs; dale, dell. See LAND, LOWNESS.

lowlife, *n.* bum, good-for-nothing, wastrel. See BADNESS.

lowly, *adj.* humble, meek. See HUMILITY, LOWNESS.

LOWNESS
Lack of height

Nouns—1, lowness, shortness, flatness, deepness, DEPTH; debasement, DEPRESSION, prostration. See INFERIORITY.

2, *(low location)* lowlands; basement, cellar, dungeon, ground floor, hold; low water; low tide, ebb tide, neap tide, bottom floor, bedrock; rock bottom.

3, *(low voice)* [contr]alto, baritone, bass-baritone, bass, basso buffo; contrabass, tuba, contrabassoon, bass clarinet, *etc.* See SOUND, MUSIC.

Verbs—1, lie low, lie flat, underlie; crouch, slouch (see DEPRESSION); flatten, wallow, grovel, crawl. *Informal,* touch *or* hit bottom. *Slang,* zero out.

2, lower, depress, let *or* take down, debase, reduce, drop, sink; humble, humiliate. See HUMILITY, CONCAVITY.

Adjectives—low, neap, debased, nether, nethermost, sunken, fallen, flat, level with the ground, lying low, crouched, squat, prostrate, depressed, deep; bass, deep[-toned].

Adverbs—under, beneath, underneath, below, down, downward[s], at the foot of, underfoot, underground, downstairs, belowstairs, at a low ebb, lowly. See INFERIORITY.

Antonyms, see HEIGHT, ELEVATION.

---

low-priced, *adj.* See CHEAPNESS. *Ant.,* high-priced, expensive.

loyal, *adj.* faithful, true, devoted. See PROBITY, OBEDIENCE. *Ant.,* disloyal, unfaithful.

lozenge, *n.* pill, troche, tablet; diamond. See REMEDY, FORM.

LSD, *n.* acid (see DRUGS).

lubrication, *n.* greasing, oiling; oiliness; anointing, anointment, unction, unctuousness. See SMOOTHNESS, OIL.

lucid, *adj.* clear, limpid, transparent, understandable; sane, rational; shining. See TRANSPARENCY, SANITY. *Ant.,* obscure, irrational.

luck, *n.* CHANCE, [good] fortune. See PROSPERITY, DESTINY.

lucky, *adj.* fortunate, opportune, auspicious; CHANCE, fortuitous. See OCCASION. *Ant.,* unlucky.

lucrative, *adj.* profitable, well-paying, gainful, moneymaking, productive. See ACQUISITION. *Ant.,* unprofitable.

lucre, *n.* MONEY, wealth, riches. See PROSPERITY.

ludicrous, *adj.* ridiculous, absurd (see ABSURDITY).

lug, *v.* tote, transport, convey, carry; draw, drag. See TRACTION, TRANSPORTATION.

luggage, *n.* baggage, impedimenta, bag and baggage. See POSSESSION, TRANSPORTATION.

lugubrious, *adj.* mournful, doleful, dejected. See DEJECTION. *Ant.,* cheerful.

lukewarm, *adj.* tepid; moderate, temperate, insipid, so-so, neither here nor there, indifferent (see INDIFFERENCE). See HEAT.

lull, *n.* calm, intermission. See REPOSE.

lullaby, *n.* sleep song (see MUSIC, REPOSE).

lumber, *n.* wood, logs, timber; planks, boards, paneling, *etc.* See MATERIALS. —*v.* trudge, plod, hobble, bumble. See SLOWNESS.

luminary, *n.* heavenly body, sun, star, *etc.*; wise man, shining light; celebrity, notable. See UNIVERSE, KNOWLEDGE, REPUTE.

luminous, *adj.* luminary, lighted, glowing; incandescent, radiant, lit, alight, self-luminous; phosphorescent, luminescent; bright, resplendent; clear, lucid. See LIGHT, MEANING.

lump, *n.* protuberance, swelling, chunk, mass; consolidation, aggregation. See CONVEXITY, ASSEMBLAGE, DENSITY.

lunatic, *n.* madman, bedlamite, maniac, psychopath. See INSANITY.

lunch, *n.* luncheon, snack, collation, midday meal, spread, bite (*inf.*). See FOOD.

luncheonette, *n.* lunchroom, cafeteria, eatery, coffee shop. See FOOD.

lung, *n.* lights, bellows. See WIND.

lunge, *v.i.* surge, thrust, jab; lurch, LEAP, plunge. —*n.* thrust, surge. See IMPULSE, ATTACK.

lurch, *v.i.* sway, pitch, stagger, stumble. See DESCENT.

lure, *v.t.* entice, decoy, tempt, coax. See ATTRACTION.

lurid, *adj.* pallid, ghastly; glaring, eerie; sinister, sensational. See DARKNESS, COLORLESSNESS.

lurk, *v.i.* skulk, slink, sneak, prowl. See CONCEALMENT, LATENCY.

luscious, *adj.* sweet, delicious, ambrosial. See SWEETNESS.

lush, *adj.* luscious, juicy, succulent; tender, ripe; luxurious. See SWEETNESS. —*n.,* *slang,* drunkard, sot, barfly. See DRINKING.

lust, *n.* DESIRE, carnality, sex, sensuality, lasciviousness; satyriasis, nymphomania; voracity, avarice, greed, drive, itch, the hots (*sl.*), yen (*sl.*). —*v.i.* covet, crave, hunger, DESIRE, yearn, *etc.* See IMPURITY.

luster, *n.* gloss, sheen, brightness, splendor; radiance, brilliance, fame. See REPUTE, LIGHT.

lusty, *adj.* robust, vigorous, hearty, sturdy. See SIZE.

luxuriant, *adj.* lush, abundant, profuse; florid, fertile, rich. See SUFFICIENCY.

luxurious, *adj.* sumptuous, elegant; voluptuous, self-indulgent. See PLEASURE.

luxury, *n.* self-indulgence, prodigality; dainty; elegance, sumptuousness, extravagance. See PLEASURE, INTEMPERANCE.

lynching, *n.* hanging, murder, necktie party (*sl.*); tar and feathering; mob rule, kangaroo court. See PUNISHMENT, KILLING.

lyric, *n.* poem, song. See POETRY. —*adj.* melodic. See MUSIC.

M

macabre, *adj.* ghastly, grisly; eerie, weird; morbid, hideous, grotesque, gruesome. See DEATH.

Machiavellian, *adj.* ruthless, scheming, manipulative; opportunistic. See CUNNING, DECEPTION, PLAN.

machinate, *v.i.* plot, PLAN. See CUNNING.

machine, *n.* apparatus, contrivance, mechanism, device; motor, engine; airplane, car, bicycle, robot; organization, cabal; machinery. See VEHICLE, INSTRUMENTALITY, PARTY.

machismo, *n.* virility (see MALE).

macrocosm, *n.* UNIVERSE; totality, COMPLETION.

mad, *adj.* crazy, insane; rabid; frantic, foolish, turbulent; *informal,* angry. See INSANITY, RESENTMENT. *Ant.,* sane.

madam, *n.* procuress, bawd (see IMPURITY).

madcap, *adj.* wild, flighty. See EXCITABILITY.

madden, *v.t.* infuriate, enrage, incense, craze; drive mad, derange; make one's blood boil. See RESENTMENT.

made-up, *adj.* fabricated, imagined, fanciful, make-believe, fictitious, made of whole cloth. See IMAGINATION, FALSEHOOD. *Ant.,* real, true, factual.

madhouse, *n.* asylum. See INSANITY.

madman, madwoman, *n.* See INSANITY.

maelstrom, *n.* whirlpool, vortex, eddy. See ROTATION.

maestro, *n.* conductor; mentor, DIRECTOR. See MUSIC, TEACHING.

magazine, *n.* storehouse, arsenal, reservoir; periodical, weekly, glossy. See STORE, PUBLICATION.

magic, *n.* SORCERY; witchery, glamour, spell; legerdemain. —*adj.* magic[al], mystic[al], occult; enchanting. See DECEPTION.

magician, *n.* witch, wizard, sorcerer; prestidigitator, conjurer. See SORCERY.

magisterial, *adj.* arbitrary, dictatorial; arrogant, pompous; authoritarian, imperious. See PRIDE, CERTAINTY.

magistrate, *n.* judge (see LAWSUIT).

magnanimous, *adj.* generous, high-minded, great-souled. See LIBERALITY, BENEVOLENCE. *Ant.,* ungenerous, small-minded.

magnate, *n.* mogul (see IMPORTANCE).

magnet, *n.* lodestone. See ATTRACTION, POWER.

magnetism, *n.* ATTRACTION, magnetic force; charm, animal magnetism. See POWER.

magnificent, *adj.* grand, splendid; awe-inspiring; noble, superb. See BEAUTY, OSTENTATION. *Ant.,* insignificant, paltry.

magnify, *v.t.* enlarge, augment; laud, glorify. See INCREASE, APPROBATION, EXAGGERATION.

magniloquent, *adj.* pompous, boastful, bombastic. See BOASTING.

magnitude, *n.* SIZE, bulk; extent; immensity. See GREATNESS.

***magnum opus,* Lat.,** masterpiece. See SKILL.

maid, *n.* girl, lass, maiden, miss; virgin, spinster; SERVANT, domestic. See YOUTH, CELIBACY.

maidenhead, *n.* virginity (see PURITY).

maidenly, *adj.* modest; gentle; girlish. See YOUTH, VIRTUE.

mail, *n.* post, letters, correspondence. —*v.t.* post, send, forward. See COMMUNICATION.

maim, *v.t.* cripple, disfigure, mutilate, lame, impair. See DETERIORATION.

main, *n.* conduit, pipe; strength, POWER; sea, ocean. —*adj.* chief, principal; sheer. See IMPORTANCE.

mainland, *n.* continent, landmass. See LAND.

mainline, *v.i., slang,* inject, shoot up. See DRUGS.

mainly, *adv.* principally, primarily; mostly, largely, on the whole; above all, more than anything. See IMPORTANCE.

mainstay, *n.* SUPPORT, supporter.

mainstream, *n.* main current (see IMPORTANCE).

maintain, *v.t.* SUPPORT, carry; preserve, keep; possess, have; uphold, allege, affirm. See PRESERVATION, AGENCY, RETENTION, AFFIRMATION.

maître d'hôtel, *Fr.* butler, headwaiter, majordomo, maître d'. See SERVANT.

majestic, *adj.* noble, august, stately, imposing, grand. See OSTENTATION, PRIDE.

majesty, *n.* stateliness, grandeur; sovereignty. See GREATNESS, AUTHORITY, OSTENTATION.

major, *adj.* principal, chief; greater, senior. See SUPERIORITY. *Ant.,* minor.

majority, *n.* adulthood; preponderance, excess, SUPERIORITY. *Ant.,* minority.

make, *v.t.* create, produce; prepare; obtain, cause, compel; amount to. See PRODUCTION, COMPULSION, FORM.

make-believe, *n.* fantasy, unreality, fiction, imagination; pretense, feigning, imitation, fakery, DECEPTION. —*adj.* made-up; feigned, sham, whimsical, imitation, fake, phony. See FALSEHOOD. *Ant.,* true, factual.

make do, get by, manage, make shift. See SUFFICIENCY.

makeshift, *n.* expedient, substitute, stopgap. See SUBSTITUTION.

makeup, *n.* COMPOSITION; personality; placement; cosmetics, beautification. See BEAUTY.

makings, *n.pl.* ingredients, components (see COMPOSITION).

maladjusted, *adj.* unfit, ineffectual. See UNSKILLFULNESS.

maladroit, *adj.* clumsy, inexpert, awkward, inept. See UNSKILLFULNESS. *Ant.,* skillful, expert.

malady, *n.* DISEASE, sickness, illness, infirmity.

malaise, *n.* uneasiness, anxiety, disquiet. See AGITATION, CARE.

malcontent, *n.* grumbler, faultfinder, griper (*inf.*); insurgent, rebel. See DISCONTENT. *Ant.,* satisfied person.

mal de mer, Fr., seasickness. See DISEASE.

mal de siècle, Fr., world-weariness. See DEJECTION.

MALE
Masculine

Nouns—1, male, man, he, homo, gentleman, sir, master, yeoman, wight, swain, blade, chap, gaffer, husband, bachelor, Mr., mister; boy, stripling, YOUTH, lad; homme; hombre; macho; lady's man, lady-killer; male bonding; male chauvinist pig. *Informal,* fellow. *Slang,* hetero, one-way street; guy, bloke (*Brit.*), bimbo, bozo, buck, colt, hardleg, hunk, hardbody, pair of pants, buffalo, cave man, joe, cunt; blood, clink, brown sugar; geezer. See POPULACE, HUMANITY, MARRIAGE.

2, (*male animal*) cock, drake, gander, dog, boar, stag, hart, buck, horse, stallion, tomcat, ram, billygoat, bull, rooster, cob, capon, ox, gelding, steer.

3, (*male quality*) manhood, manliness, maleness, masculinity, virility, machismo.

4, homosexual, gay, epicene. *Slang,* third sex, closet queen, drag queen, angel, aspro, buttercup, capon, chicken, [midnight] cowboy, daisy, dandy, fag, faggot, fairy, femme, fruit[cake], homo, nancy, pansy, pervert, pixy, queer, sissy, sister, swish, angel[ina], chickenhawk, cookie-pusher, farl[e]y, flamer, kiki, lavender, mary ann, rough trade, flip, half a man, Miss Thing, mother, cake eater, capon, cupcake, daughter, invert.

Verbs—masculinize; act male. *Slang,* foop.

Adjectives—1, male, masculine, manly, boyish, manlike, mannish; macho.

2, homosexual, gay, bi[sexual]. *Slang,* ambidextrous, in the life.

Phrases—boys will be boys; the way to a man's heart is through his stomach.

Quotations—Man is nature's sole mistake! (*W. S. Gilbert*), All men are rapists, and that's all that they are. They rape us with their eyes, their laws, and their codes (*Marilyn French*), Somehow a bachelor never gets over the idea that he is a thing of beauty and a boy forever (*Helen Rowland*), A man is a god in ruins (*Emerson*).

Antonyms, see FEMALE.

malediction, *n.* IMPRECATION, curse, anathema, execration.

malefactor, *n.* EVILDOER, wrongdoer, criminal, felon.

MALEVOLENCE
Ill will

Nouns—1, malevolence; evil *or* bad intent; misanthropy, ill nature, cynicism; enmity, HATE; malignity, malice, malice aforethought, maliciousness, spite, RESENTMENT, venom, rancor, bitterness; virulence, spleen, mordacity, acerbity, churlishness, hardness of heart, obduracy; ill treatment; cruelty, cruelness, brutality, savagery, ferocity, barbarity, barbarism, inhumanity, man's inhumanity to man; sadism, torture; Schadenfreude; truculence, ruffianism; heart of stone, evil eye, cloven foot *or* hoof, poison pen; sexual harassment. See EVIL.

2, ill *or* bad turn; affront (see DISRESPECT).

3, misanthrope, misanthropist, man-hater, misogynist, woman-hater, gaybasher, cynic; sadist. *Slang,* skunk, sky, bad actor, saw.

Verbs—1, bear *or* harbor a grudge, bear malice.

2, hurt, injure, harm, WRONG, do harm; malign, molest (see DISCONTENT); wreak havoc, do mischief, hunt down, hound, persecute, oppress, grind, maltreat, mistreat, bedevil, ill-treat, abuse, misuse, ill-use, do one's worst, show *or* have no mercy; dehumanize. *Informal,* have it in for. *Slang,* do one dirt, rub it in, do a number on, dump on, fuck around with, cheese off, mess with, get on one's case.

Adjectives—1, malevolent, ill-disposed, ill-intentioned, evil-minded, misanthropic, malicious, malign, malignant, rancorous, spiteful, caustic, bitter, mordant, acrimonious, virulent, malefic, maleficent, venomous, invidious. *Slang,* jive-ass, on the rag.

2, unkind, unfriendly, antisocial; cold-blooded, coldhearted, hardhearted, stonyhearted, selfish, unnatural, ruthless, relentless. See DISCOURTESY, SELFISHNESS.

3, cruel, brutal, savage, ferocious, inhuman, sadistic, barbarous, fell, truculent, bloodthirsty, murderous, atrocious, fiendish, heinous, unrelenting, demoniacal, diabolic[al], devilish, infernal, hellish, Satanic.

Quotations—He has enough of misanthropy to be a philanthropist (*Walter Bagehot*), Man's inhumanity to man makes countless thousands mourn! (*Robert Burns*), Cruelty, like every other vice, requires no motive outside itself (*George Eliot*), Cynicism is intellectual dandyism without the coxcomb's feathers (*George Meredith*), [A cynic is] a man who knows the price of everything and the value of nothing (*Oscar Wilde*), Cynicism is an unpleasant way of saying the truth (*Lillian Hellman*), Man delights not me; no, nor woman either (*Shakespeare*), If you pick up a starving dog and make him prosperous, he will not bite you. This is the principal difference between a dog and a man (*Mark Twain*).

Antonyms, see BENEVOLENCE.

---

malformation, *n.* DISTORTION, deformity.

malfunction, *v.i.* go amiss *or* wrong, fail, go haywire. —*n.* FAILURE, defect, misfire, miscarriage.

malice, *n.* MALEVOLENCE, spite, ill will, animosity. *Ant.,* goodwill.

malign, *v.t.* libel, slander, defame; calumniate, asperse, traduce, besmirch; backbite. See DETRACTION, MALEVOLENCE. *Ant.,* praise.

malignant, *adj.* malign, vicious, criminal; harmful, virulent, pernicious; fatal, incurable. See BADNESS. *Ant.,* benign.

malinger, *v.i.* feign, shirk, slack, gold-brick, soldier (*inf.*). See AVOIDANCE, DISEASE, FALSEHOOD.

mall, *n.* promenade, allée, avenue, parkway; shopping center. See PASSAGE, SALE.

malleable, *adj.* adaptable; tractable. See SOFTNESS, LEARNING. *Ant.,* obstinate, obdurate.

mallet, *n.* hammer, club, maul. See SCULPTURE, INSTRUMENTALITY.

malnutrition, *n.* deficiency; emaciation, anemia, marasmus; cachexia, gout, scurvy, pellagra, hookworm; obesity. See DISEASE.

MALODOROUSNESS
Bad smell

Nouns—1, malodorousness, malodor, fetor, fetidness, bad smell, funk, fust, smelliness, bad ODOR, stench, stink, foul odor, effluvium, rankness, goatishness, goatiness, mephitis, miasma, mustiness, rancidness, rancidity, foulness; opprobrium (see DISREPUTE). See UNCLEANNESS.

2, *(something that smells bad)* polecat, skunk, stoat, rotten egg, asafoetida, skunk cabbage, stinkpot, stinker, stink bomb; stinkweed; bad breath, halitosis, body odor, BO; medlar. *Slang,* fart, burnt cheese.

Verbs—smell bad, reek, stink [in the nostrils], stink like a polecat, smell offensively; putrefy. *Informal,* smell to high heaven, smell up. *Slang,* fart, cut one, drop a rose.

Adjectives—malodorous, fetid, olid, smelling, stinking, stinky, smelly, high, bad, foul, strong, offensive, fulsome, noisome, gassy, rank, rancid, graveolent, gamy, corky, tainted, fusty, musty, moldy, stuffy, putrid, suffocating, mephitic, nidorous, putrescent, goaty, goatish. *Slang,* stanky.

Antonyms, see ODOR.

---

malpractice, *n.* wrongdoing, misdemeanor, malfeasance, misconduct. See GUILT, ILLEGALITY.

maltreat, *v.t.* abuse, ill-treat, misuse. See MALEVOLENCE, WRONG.

mammoth, *adj.* huge, giant, gigantic, tremendous, prodigious, colossal, enormous. —*n.* elephant, behemoth. See SIZE.

man, *n.* See MALE, HUMANITY. —*v.* run, operate; staff. See DEFENSE. —**man about town,** sophisticate, man of the world, cosmopolitan, playboy. See MALE, KNOWLEDGE.

manacle, *n.* shackle, handcuff. See RESTRAINT.

manage, *v.t.* administer, conduct; control; afford; contrive, bring about, manipulate. See AUTHORITY, SUFFICIENCY. —*v.i.* See PROVISION.

manageable, *adj.* tractable, docile, obedient; wieldy, governable. See FACILITY. *Ant.,* obdurate, intractable.

management, *n.* DIRECTION, control, administration; directorate, administrative body. See ORDER.

manager, *n.* See DIRECTOR.

mañana, *Span.,* tomorrow. See LATENESS.

mandate, *n.* COMMAND, edict, statute, ordinance; COMMISSION.

mandatory, *adj.* required, compulsory, binding, obligatory. See COMPULSION, NECESSITY.

maneuver, *n.* artifice, stratagem, tactic. See CUNNING, PLAN.

manful, *adj.* brave, resolute. See BRAVERY.

manger, *n.* trough, bin, crib, feed box. See RECEPTACLE.

mangle, *v.t.* break, crush, mutilate; disfigure, mar; press, iron. See DETERIORATION. —*n.* iron, press. See SMOOTHNESS.

mangy, *adj.* itchy, scurvy, scaly, scrofulous; shabby, seedy, shoddy, ragged; sordid, squalid, wretched. See DISREPUTE, TOUCH.

manhandle, *v.t.* maul, batter, paw, maltreat, push around. See MALEVOLENCE, WRONG.

manhood, *n.* adulthood, maturity; virility, manliness. See AGE, MALE.

manhunt, *n.* See PURSUIT.

mania, *n.* madness, frenzy, lunacy; INSANITY; obsession, craze. See DESIRE, EXCITABILITY.

maniac, *n.* madman (see INSANITY).

manic, *adj.* maniacal, insane, frenzied. See INSANITY.

manicure, *v.t.* trim, clip, cut, pare, file; polish, buff, lacquer. See BEAUTY.

manifest, *v.t.* bring forward, show, display, evidence, trot out, bring to light; demonstrate; proclaim, publish, disclose. —*adj.* apparent, obvious, evident; salient, striking, prominent; flagrant; pronounced; definite, distinct; conspicuous, unmistakable, plain, clear; open, overt; patent. See INDICATION, APPEARANCE.

manifestation, *n.* plainness, VISIBILITY; demonstration; exhibition; display, show[ing], showing off; indication, publicity, DISCLOSURE, revelation, openness, prominence, conspicuousness. See INDICATION.

manifesto, *n.* proclamation, statement, pronouncement; credo, theory, BELIEF.

manifold, *adj.* multiple, diverse, multiform; copied, repeated. See MULTITUDE.

manipulate, *v.t.* operate, control, manage; influence; juggle, falsify. See USE, CONDUCT, TOUCH.

mankind, *n.* HUMANITY.

manly, *adj.* masculine (see MALE). *Ant.*, feminine.

man-made, *adj.* manufactured, created, fabricated. See PRODUCTION.

mannequin, *n.* dummy, doll; [fashion] model, cover girl. See BEAUTY.

manner, *n.* kind, sort; habit; CLASS; style, mode; CONDUCT, behavior; way. METHOD.

mannered, *adj.* affected, artificial, theatrical. See AFFECTATION.

mannerism, *n.* eccentricity, peculiarity, idiosyncrasy; AFFECTATION.

manners, *n.pl.* conduct, behavior, deportment; COURTESY, politeness. See FASHION.

mannish, *adj.* unwomanly, unfeminine; mannified. See FEMALE.

manor, *n.* mansion, hall, hacienda; estate, territory, demesne. See ABODE.

manpower, *n.* working force, staff; strength, capacity, potential; warpower, army, fighting force; womanpower. See SERVANT, COMBATANT.

mansion, *n.* house, manor, hall, villa. See ABODE.

manslaughter, *n.* homicide, murder. See KILLING.

mantle, *n.* COVERING; cloak, cape, robe. See CLOTHING.

manual, *adj.* nonautomatic, hand. —*n.* guide, handbook, text[book]; keyboard, control, dial; system, exercise, regimen. See INFORMATION, DIRECTION. —**manual labor**, drudgery, sweat of one's brow, toil. See EXERTION.

manufacture, *v.t.* make, produce, fabricate, invent. See PRODUCTION.

manure, *n.* fertilizer, compost, dung. See UNCLEANNESS.

manuscript, *n.* script, handwriting, [author's] original. See WRITING.

many, *adj.* numerous, multitudinous, manifold. See MULTITUDE.

many-sided, *adj.* versatile; multilateral, polyhedral. See SIDE.

map, *n.* PLAN, chart, projection; diagram; *slang*, FACE.

mapmaker, *n.* cartographer, surveyor. See PLAN.

mar, *v.t.* disfigure, deface, blemish, scratch, impair. See DETERIORATION, IMPERFECTION.

marathon, *adj.* nonstop, continuous, arduous; long, endless. See VELOCITY, CONTENTION, DURABILITY.

maraud, *v.* raid, plunder, freeboot, pillage. See STEALING.

marble, *adj.* hard, vitreous, unyielding; lifeless, insensible, cold; white, pale, colorless; variegated, particolored, pied, striated, mottled. See COLOR, HARDNESS, INSENSIBILITY.

march, *v.i.* tramp, pace, parade, file, advance. See TRAVEL.

mare nostrum, *Lat.*, our sea, ocean. See WATER.

margin, *n.* EDGE, border, rim, brink, verge, limit; leeway. See SPACE, FREEDOM.

marijuana, *n.* marihuana; hemp, cannabis, hashish, bhang, ganja[h]; tea, pot, hay, grass, smoke, reefer, Mary Jane, Acapulco gold (*all sl.*). See HABIT.

marina, *n.* boat basin, dock[age]. See SAFETY, NAVIGATION.

marinate, *v.t.* preserve, cure, pickle. See PRESERVATION.

marine, *adj.* nautical, naval; pelagic, maritime. See NAVIGATION.

mariner, *n.* sailor, seaman, tar (*inf.*), salt (*inf.*). See NAVIGATION.

marionette, *n.* puppet; manikin. See REPRESENTATION.

marital, *adj.* hymeneal, spousal. See MARRIAGE.

maritime, *adj.* pelagic, oceanic; coastal, littoral, seaside; seafaring, nautical. See WATER, NAVIGATION.

mark, *n.* goal; imprint, stain; label, badge; token, symptom; symbol; standard, demarcation. See INDICATION. —*v.t.* inscribe, stain; note; check, indicate; delimit. See ATTENTION, SPECIALITY. —**mark down**, reduce [in price], cheapen. See REDUCTION.

marked, *adj.* noticeable, conspicuous; watched, followed. See SPECIALITY, INDICATION, VISIBILITY.

marker, *n.* indicator, INDICATION, sign; counter, chip; *slang,* IOU, chit.

market, *n.* marketplace, mart (see BUSINESS); demand. See SALE.

marketable, *adj.* salable, commercial. See SALE.

marksman, *n.* sharpshooter, dead shot, crackshot. See PROPULSION.

maroon, *v.t.* abandon, isolate. See RELINQUISHMENT.

marquee, *n.* sign[board], billboard. See PUBLICATION.

MARRIAGE
Legal union

Nouns—1, marriage, matrimony, wedlock, union; intermarriage, nuptial tie, married state, bed and board, cohabitation, POSSLQ (person of the opposite sex sharing living quarters), wedded bliss; mixed marriage; open marriage, endogamy, exogamy; engagement; criminal conversation *or* correspondence. *Slang,* ball and chain, love in a cottage, light housekeeping. See JUNCTION, UNITY, COMBINATION.

2, *(marriage proceedings)* engagement, betrothal, understanding, proposal; wedding, nuptials, Hymen, espousal; leading to the altar; epithalamium; temple of Hymen; honeymoon; sea of matrimony.

3, *(people)* **a.** fiancé[e], betrothed; bride, [bride]groom; bridesmaid, maid *or* matron of honor, best man, usher; spouse, mate, partner, significant other, live-in lover, housemate, helpmate, helpmeet. *Slang,* man-eater, mantrap, pillow-mate. **b.** married man, Benedict, husband, man, good provider, consort, squaw-man, domestic partner. *Slang,* main on the hitch. **c.** married woman, bride, wife, concubine, frau, goodwife, rib, better half, squaw, lady, matron, domestic partner. *Slang,* bachelor's wife, mouse, old saw, warden, ball and chain; bitch's bind, fishwife. **d.** [married] couple, pair, husband and wife, bride and groom, newlyweds; Darby and Joan, Mr. and Mrs., lovebirds, loving couple; May and January; dual *or* double income no children, DINK. *Slang,* salt-and-pepper. **e.** matchmaker, marriage broker. *Informal,* old man *or* woman, little woman. **f.** cradle snatcher.

4, *(marriage law)* monogamy, bigamy, polygamy, polygyny, polyandry, Mormonism; morganatic marriage, common-law marriage, concubinage. *Informal,* light housekeeping.

Verbs—1, marry, wive, take a wife; be married, be spliced; wed, espouse; rob the cradle; give away, give in marriage. *Slang,* get hitched, walk down the aisle, tie the knot.

2, marry, join, couple, unite, make one, tie the nuptial knot; join *or* unite in marriage; elope; live together, cohabit; bundle. *Slang,* shack up with, play house.

3, propose; betroth, affiance, plight troth; bespeak; pin; match; publish banns.

Adjectives—1, matrimonial, marital, conjugal, connubial; wedded, nuptial, hymeneal, spousal, bridal; engaged, betrothed, affianced; marriageable, nubile, available, eligible. *Slang,* spliced. See AGE.

2, living together. *Slang,* shacked up.

Phrases—marry in haste, repent at leasure; marriages are made in heaven; always a bridesmaid, never a bride; a deaf husband and a blind wife are always a happy couple; to marry is to learn to be alone; marriage is a lottery.

Quotations —A man in love is incomplete until he has married. Then he's finished (*Zsa Zsa Gabor*), I married beneath me, all women do (*Nancy Astor*), A husband is what is left of a lover after the nerve has been extracted (*Helen Rowland*), I have always thought that every woman should marry, and no man (*Benjamin Disraeli*), It is better to marry than to burn (*Bible*), In married life, three is company and two is none (*Oscar Wilde*), Two can live cheaper than one (*Ring Lardner*), The heart of marriage is memories (*Bill Cosby*), When a marriage has equal partners, then I fear not (*Aeschylus*), Marriage is a desperate thing (*John Selden*), Keep your eyes wide open before marriage, half shut afterwards (*Benjamin Franklin*), Many a good hanging prevents a bad marriage (*Shakespeare*).

Antonyms, see CELIBACY, DIVORCE.

---

marrow, *n.* essence, core, pith; vitality. See IMPORTANCE, ENERGY.

marry, *v.t.* See MARRIAGE.

marsh, *n.* swamp (see WATER).

marshal, *v.t.* array, dispose, order, arrange; mobilize, activate, assemble, collect, utilize. See ARRANGEMENT. —*n.* officer, AUTHORITY, sheriff.

mart, *n.* See BUSINESS.

martial, *adj.* military, warlike, soldierly. See WARFARE. —**martial arts,** self-defense; judo, karate, aikido, kung fu, *etc.* See SPORTS.

martyr, *n.* victim, sacrifice, scapegoat; symbol, example; sufferer; saint. See PUNISHMENT.

martyrdom, *n.* martyrship; sacrifice, suffering, PAIN, torture, agony; heroism, asceticism; saintliness, long-suffering. See KILLING, PUNISHMENT.

marvel, *n.* See WONDER.

marvelous, *adj.* wonderful, prodigious, surprising, extraordinary. See WONDER. *Ant.,* commonplace.

mascot, *n.* pet, talisman. See SORCERY.

masculine, *adj.* manly, virile. See MALE. *Ant.,* feminine.

mash, *v.t.* crush, smash, squeeze, compress, bruise, batter. See POWDERINESS, SOFTNESS.

mask, *n.* false face, disguise, CONCEALMENT; effigy; shield; masquerade, pretense. —*v.t.* screen, conceal, hide. See DECEPTION.

masochism, *n.* algolagnia, sadism. See PLEASURE, PAIN.

masquerader, *n.* masker, domino, mummer; impostor. See DECEPTION, AMUSEMENT.

Mass, *n.* Divine Service, Eucharist, Communion. See RITE.

mass, *n.* bulk, SIZE; lump, wad, accumulation. See DENSITY, POPULACE.

massacre, *n.* KILLING, slaughter, butchery, carnage.

massage, *v.t.* rub [down]; knead, stroke; manipulate. See FRICTION, TOUCH.

massive, *adj.* bulky, ponderous, solid, imposing. See SIZE.

mast, *n.* pole, timber, upright, column, spar. See SHIP.

master, *n.* superior, DIRECTOR; crowned head, emperor (see AUTHORITY); expert, ARTIST, adept. See RULE, SKILL, MALE, POSSESSION.

masterful, *adj.* masterly, skillful; authoritative. See SKILL, AUTHORITY.

mastermind, *v.t.* PLAN, devise.

master of ceremonies, *n.* emcee, MC, host, toastmaster. See DIRECTOR.

masterpiece, *n.* masterwork, chef d'œuvre. See SKILL, GOOD, PERFECTION.

mastery, *n.* rule, victory; ascendency, supremacy; SKILL. See AUTHORITY.

masturbation, *n.* onanism, self-abuse, autoeroticism, self-pleasuring. See SEX.

mat, *n.* pad, rug, runner, doormat, doily. —*v.* tangle, snarl; plait, braid, weave, entwine. See CROSSING, TEXTURE.

match, *n.* lucifer, vesta; linstock; fuse; complement, equal, peer; contest, bout; union, matrimony. See EQUALITY, CONTENTION, MARRIAGE, SYNCHRONISM, IMITATION.

matchless, *adj.* unequaled, peerless, unrivaled. See SUPERIORITY, INEQUALITY.

matchmaker, *n.* marriage broker, go-between. See MARRIAGE.

mate, *n.* companion, chum, comrade; counterpart; consort, spouse; husband, wife. See FRIEND, MARRIAGE, AUXILIARY.

material, *adj.* bodily, corporeal (see SUBSTANCE). —*n.* cloth, fabric; matter, SUBSTANCE; written matter. See MATERIALS.

materialistic, *adj.* material, worldly; pleasure-seeking, hedonistic, sybaritic, epicurean; greedy, avaricious, mercenary. See IRRELIGION, PLEASURE, GLUTTONY.

materialize, *v.t.* produce, create, realize, give SUBSTANCE; conjure, call, *or* whip up, summon, produce [out of thin air]. —*v.i.* appear, enter, show. See APPEARANCE.

MATERIALS
Substances used to produce goods

Nouns—1, materials, raw materials, substances, stuff; stock, staples; FUEL; grist; stores, goods, provisions (see STORE); MEANS; baggage, personal property.

2, a. wood, lumber, timber, clapboard, decking, excelsior, fencing, flooring, green lumber, hardwood, heartwood, paneling, parquet, plywood, rattan, sapwood, thatch, veneer, weatherboard, wicker; pine, fir, cedar, cypress, spruce, hemlock, juniper, larch, yew; alder, ash, beech, elm, apple, balsa, bamboo, banyan, basswood, birch, cherry, walnut, calamander, cherry, chestnut, dogwood, ebony, elm, eucalyptus, hum, hazel, hickory, ironwood, linden, magnolia, mahogany, maple, oak, pecan, plane, poplar, rosewood, sandalwood, sen, sumac, sycamore, teak, willow, zebrawood. b. clay, brick, bricks and mortar, plaster, tile, adobe, aggregate, asphalt, bitumen, blacktop, brickface, brownstone, capstone, cinderblock, cobblestone, copestone, cork tile, ferroconcrete, firebrick, flag[stone], freestone, shingle, siding, crockery, ceramics, composition; putty; concrete, cement (see COHERENCE). c. paper, pasteboard, cardboard, crepe paper, grass paper, kraft paper, millboard, paperboard, papier-mâché, rice paper, strawboard, tagboard, tarpaper, wallpaper. d. artificial turf. e. metal, stone, ore, iron, copper, *etc.* (see INORGANIC MATTER).

3, plastic[s]; synthetic resin; celluloid, cellophane, vinyl, Vinylite, [poly]styrene, Bakelite; hard rubber, Neolite; synthetic rubber, butyl, butadiene; synthetic fiber, acetate, Acrilan, Banlon, Dacron, Fortrel, Gore-Tex, Lastex, Orlon, Sarelon, Thinsulate, Teflon; acrylic, polyester, nylon, rayon, mousseline, spandex; fiber, viscose, Celanese; leatherette; durable *or* permanent press, wash-and-wear; fiberfill.

4, a. goods, fabric, cloth, material, knit, plush, textiles. b. wool, alpaca, Angora, astrakhan, baize, combing wool, drugget, cashmere, worsted, loden, saxony, mackinaw, cassimere, stuff, frieze, paisley, serge, shahtoosh, stammel, shalloon, melton, merino, petersham, vicuna, vigogne, prunella, qiviut, rag, cheviot, gabardine, castor swansdown, tartan, Shetland wool, Donegal *or* Harris tweed, Kendal green, kersey, wadmal, duffel, beaver. c. cotton, chino, chintz, balbriggan, poplin, sateen, lisle, galatea, jaconet, motley, terry, lawn, duck, tarlatan, cheesecloth, monk's cloth, oxford, stockinette, gingham, percale, Pima, nainsook, nankeen, organdy, calico, denim, jean, dungaree, jersey, drill[ing], dimity, khaddar, khaki, marseilles, candlewick, mackintosh. d. silk, brocade, messaline, samite, sarcenet, pongee, taffeta, tabby, organzine, shantung, barathea, barege, tussah, charmeuse; satin, duchesse. e. linen, byssus, cambric, muslin, mull, batiste; crepe, Canton crepe, crepe de Chine, crepon. f. burlap, hessian, gunny, pedaline, canvas, sailcloth; haircloth; mohair, horsehair, camel's hair, sackcloth. g. batik, broadcloth, challis, cloque, chambray, cretonne, crinoline, moquette, scrim, seersucker, ratine, ratteen, shirting, tattersall, shoddy, sicilienne, rep, russet, moreen, zibeline, surah, satin, mousseline de laine *or* soie, damask, tapa, bengaline, chenille, mat, panne, paramatta, poult-de-soie, ticking, velour, velvet[een], Venetian cloth, duvetyn, ecru, madras, moiré, watered fabric, whipcord, malines, marocain, pique, plaid, pointelle, organza, marquisette, etamine, luster, lamé, voile, gauze, tiffany, veiling, tissue, tulle, toile, toweling, tricot, leno, Georgette, faconne, linsey-woolsey, gossamer, harrateen, jacquard, jardiniere, grenadine, grogram, homespun, hopsack, huck[aback], ikat, grosgrain, faille, ninon, felt, flannel, flannelette, fleece, foulard, brocatelle, fustian, chiffon, chiné, cavalry twill, tricotine, corduroy, cord, covert, crash, buckram, bunting, bombazine, bouclé, brilliantine, bayadere. h. lace, tatting, bobbin *or* pillow lace, torchon, bobbinet, duchesse, gros point, guipure, illusion, mignonette, [needle]point [lace], raised point, reticella, rose point, tambour; Alençon, Breton, Brussels lace, Carrickmacross, Dieppe lace, Mechlin, Milan point, Tenerife, Valenciennes, Venetian point. i. cerecloth, oilcloth; camlet.

5, leather, skin, fur, pelt; alligator, badger, bearskin, beaver, black marten, karakul lamb, broadtail, lambskin, sheepskin, shearling, nappa, mocha, krimmer, buckskin, deerskin, buff, cowhide, cabretta, calfskin, capeskin, chamois, chevrette, chinchilla, rabbit, cony, raccoon, cookskin, doeskin, ermine, [silver, red, or white] fox, [wild, frosted, or ranch] mink, sable, horsehide, kid[skin], leopard, maribou, marmot, marten, miniver, moleskin, morocco, muskrat, coypu, nutria, otter, pigskin, pig suede, puma, cougar, rawhide, sealskin, horsehide, sharkskin, shagreen, skunk, suede, swakara, squirrel, vair; patent leather; Cordovan, Levant.

6, urea, casein, lignite, lignin, wood flour; resin, rosin, gum, lac; bitumen, pitch, tar, asphalt, gilsonite.

Adjectives—plastic, synthetic; cloth, textile, wooden, woody, paper[y]; steel, *etc.*

---

matériel, *n.* equipment, supplies. See PRO-VISION.

maternal, *adj.* motherly, motherlike. See ANCESTRY, FEMALE.

mathematics, *n.* computation, calculation, reckoning, arithmetic. See NUMERA-TION.

matriarch, *n.* materfamilias, matron, dowager, queen bee (*inf.*). See FEMALE, AUTHORITY.

matriculate, *v.* enroll, register. See RECORD.

matrimony, *n.* MARRIAGE, espousal; nuptials. See RITE, MIXTURE.

matrix, *n.* array; mold, FORM. See NUMER-ATION.

matron, *n.* married woman, wife; widow. See FEMALE, MARRIAGE.

matter, *n.* SUBSTANCE, material; subject, topic, BUSINESS; affair; cause, ground; predicament, difficulty. —*v.i.* signify, import; count. See IMPORTANCE, THOUGHT.

matter-of-fact, *adj.* prosaic, unimagina-tive, formal. See SIMPLENESS, WEARI-NESS.

mattress, *n.* bedding; tick, bolster, pallet; futon; featherbed. See SUPPORT.

mature, *adj.* ripe, developed, full-grown, adult. —*v.i.* ripen, develop, grow up. See AGE, COMPLETION, CHANGE, PREP-ARATION, OLDNESS.

maudlin, *adj.* weepy, teary, sobby; senti-mental; drunk. See FEELING.

maul, *v.t.* manhandle, pummel, batter, beat up. See PUNISHMENT.

maunder, *v.i.* digress, wander. See DIF-FUSENESS.

mausoleum, *n.* vault, sepulcher; pyramid, mastaba. See INTERMENT, FEELING.

maven, *n.* expert, authority, specialist. See SKILL.

maverick, *n.* loner, lone wolf, noncon-formist, dissenter. See UNCONFORMITY. *Ant.,* conformer.

mawkish, *adj.* nauseous, offensive; effu-sive, maudlin. See REPULSION, FEELING.

MAXIM
Saying

Nouns—1, maxim, aphorism, gnome, apothegm, dictum, saying, adage, saw, proverb; sentence, mot, motto, catchphrase, word, moral, byword, household word; axiom, theorum, scholium, truism, TRUTH, formula, principle, law, conclusion, reflection, proposition, protasis; precept, RULE, golden rule; well-turned phrase; epigram, slo-gan, device; epitaph; buzzword. See WIT.

2, (*trite saying*) commonplace, bromide, cliché; platitude, twice-told tale, text; wise, trite, or hackneyed saying. *Informal,* old song or story. *Slang,* chestnut.

Verbs—aphorize, epigrammatize.

Adjectives—aphoristic, proverbial, axiomatic, epigrammatic; sententious, bromidic, platitudinous, commonplace; terse, succinct.

Adverbs—aphoristically, proverbially, as the saying goes, as they say, to coin a phrase.

Phrases—a proverb is the child of experience; the maxims of men disclose their hearts.

Quotations—I hate quotation. Tell me what you know (*Emerson*), A proverb is one man's wit and all men's wisdom (*Lord John Russell*), It is a good thing for an uned-ucated man to read books of quotations (*Winston Churchill*), Proverbs are the sanctuary of the intuitions (*Emerson*), Famous remarks are very seldom quoted correctly (*Simeon Strunsky*).

Antonyms, see ABSURDITY.

---

maximize, *v.t.* INCREASE, expand. *Ant.,* minimize.

maximum, *adj.* supreme, utmost; greatest, highest. —*n.* most, utmost. See SUPERIORITY. *Ant.,* minimum.

may, *v.* can; might; be allowed, permitted, *etc.* See PERMISSION.

maybe, *adv.* perhaps, mayhap, perchance; possibly, conceivably, feasibly. See DOUBT, POSSIBILITY.

mayhem, *n.* injury, mutilation, damage, harm, DESTRUCTION, violence.

mayor, *n.* administrator, president; burgomaster, magistrate, major domo; city manager. See AUTHORITY.

maze, *n.* labyrinth, network; bewilderment, perplexity. See DISORDER, CONVOLUTION, DIFFICULTY.

mazel tov, *Yiddish,* good luck, congratulations. See CONGRATULATION.

mea culpa, *Lat.,* I am to blame. See GUILT.

meadow, *n.* mead, lea, pasture, mowing. See LAND.

meager, *adj.* spare, scanty, sparse, poor; lean, gaunt. See INSUFFICIENCY, NARROWNESS.

meal, *n.* repast, refection; breakfast, dinner, lunch, *etc.*; powder, grits. *Slang,* feed, eats. See FOOD, POWDERINESS.

mealy, *adj.* powdery (see POWDERINESS).

mealymouthed, *adj.* evasive, insincere. See FALSEHOOD, COURTESY.

mean, *adj.* humble; ignoble; insignificant; stingy, miserly; sordid, niggardly. See PARSIMONY, SERVILITY, BADNESS.

MEAN
Midway

Nouns—mean, medium; average, normal, RULE, balance; MEDIOCRITY, generality; golden mean, middle course, middle compromise, neutrality, MODERATION, middle of the road. *Informal,* fence-sitting. See MIDDLE.

Verbs—split the difference, reduce to a mean, strike a balance, pair off; average, divide; take a middle course.

Adjectives—mean, intermediate, MIDDLE, medial, medium, average, mediocre, middle-class, commonplace, normal; median.

Adverbs—on the average, in the long run, taking all things together, in round numbers.

Quotations—We know what happens to people who stay in the middle of the road. They get run over (*Aneurin Bevan*), You will go most safely in the middle (*Ovid*).

Antonyms, see INFERIORITY, SUPERIORITY, BEGINNING, END.

---

meander, *v.i.* wind, drift, twist, turn; go with the wind, the tide, *or* the current; float *or* move aimlessly; wander, roam, ramble. See DEVIATION, CONVOLUTION.

MEANING
Significance

Nouns—1, meaning, significance, signification, force; sense, expression; import, purport, implication, drift, tenor, spirit, bearing; scope, purpose, aim, intent, INTENTION, object, thrust; allusion, suggestion, synonym; INTERPRETATION, connotation, subtext, spin; supertitle. *Informal,* take. See IMPORTANCE.

2, matter, subject [matter], argument, text, sum and substance, gist, pith, kernel, meat.

Verbs—1, mean, signify, stand for, denote, express, import, purpose, convey, imply, connote, infer, indicate, tell *or* speak of; touch on; point *or* allude to, drive at, have in mind, put across, intend, aim at, declare; understand by, interpret (see INTERPRETATION).

2, have meaning, make sense, hang together. *Informal,* add up.

Adjectives—meaning, meaningful, expressive, suggestive, articulate, allusive, signifi-cant, eloquent, pithy, full of or pregnant with meaning; declaratory, intelligible, lit-eral; synonymous, tantamount, equivalent; explicit, express, implied, implicit.

Adverbs—meaningly, significantly, *etc.*; to that effect, that is to say, to all intents and purposes; word for word.

Quotations—The meaning doesn't matter if it's only idle chatter of a transcendental kind (*W. S. Gilbert*), No one means all he says, and yet very few say all they mean, for words are slippery and thought is viscous (*Henry Adams*), Everything has its hid-den meaning which we must know (*Maxim Gorky*).

Antonyms, see UNMEANINGNESS.

---

meaningless, *adj.* insignificant, without rhyme or reason; senseless, aimless; nonsensical. See UNMEANINGNESS, AB-SURDITY. *Ant.,* meaningful.

MEANS
Resources

Nouns—means, resources, wherewithal, MONEY, wealth, capital, backing; MATERIALS, ways and means, stock in trade, PROVISION, STORE, appliances, conveniences; expe-dients, measures, two strings to one's bow, bag of tricks, cards to play; aid, medium, instrument, INSTRUMENTALITY. *Informal,* ace in the hole; enough rope.

Verbs—have means, have the power; enable, empower; back, finance, underwrite, cap-italize, fund.

Adverbs—by dint or means of, by virtue of, through the medium of, with, per, by all means; wherewith, herewith, therewith, wherewithal, how, in what manner, through, by the instrumentality of, with the aid of, by the agency of, with the help of; by fair means or foul; somehow or other, anyhow, somehow; by hook or [by] crook. *Infor-mal,* by the seat of one's pants.

Phrases—fight fire with fire; the end justifies the means; give a man enough rope and he will hang himself; if you can't beat 'em, join 'em; the pen is mightier than the sword; set a thief to catch a thief; all roads lead to Rome.

Quotations—The color of the cat doesn't matter as long as it catches the mice (*Deng Xiaoping*), A little harm done to a great good end (*Shakespeare*), Whoever wills the end, wills also . . . the means (*Immanuel Kant*), If there are obstacles, the shortest line between two points may be the crooked line (*Bertolt Brecht*), No man is justified in doing evil on the grounds of expediency (*Theodore Roosevelt*).

Antonyms, see IMPOTENCE, POVERTY.

---

mean-spirited, *adj.* abject, groveling; con-temptible, petty. See NARROWNESS. *Ant.,* generous.

meantime, *n.* meanwhile, interim. See BE-TWEEN.

measure, *n.* QUANTITY, extent; gauge; standard; amount, allotment; [legisla-tive] bill; step, course. See MEASURE-MENT, APPORTIONMENT, DEGREE, RULE.

measureless, *adj.* without measure, im-measurable, immensurable; infinite, endless, fathomless; vast, astronomical. See GREATNESS, INFINITY.

MEASUREMENT
Determination of size

Nouns—1, measurement, measure, admeasurement, mensuration, survey, valuation, appraisement, appraisal, metage, assessment, determination, assize, estimate, estima-tion; dead reckoning, reckoning, gauging.

2, *(unit of measure)* ampere, joule, meter, gram, *etc.* See SIZE, LENGTH, DISTANCE, QUANTITY, BREADTH, NUMERATION, GRAVITY.

3, *(measuring devices)* criterion, standard, benchmark; measure, standard, rule[r], foot-rule, yardstick, balance, sextant, quadrant, compass, calipers, gauge, meter, line, rod, check; level, plumb line, lead, log, tape, [T] square, index, scale; Beaufort scale (see WIND); biofeedback; black box; breathalyzer; engineer's, Gunter's, *or* surveyor's chain; graduated scale, vernier, anemometer, dynamometer, thermometer, barometer, bathometer, galvanometer, goniometer, speedometer, micrometer, hydrometer, tachometer, altimeter, hygrometer, ammeter, voltameter, voltmeter; pedometer; radiometer, potentiometer, sphygmomanometer, *etc.*

4, *(indicators of location)* coordinates, ordinate and abscissa, polar coordinates, latitude and longitude, declination and right ascension, altitude and azimuth.

5, *(study of measurements)* geometry, stereometry, chronometry, barometry, thermometry, hypometry; surveying, geodesy, geodetics, orthometry, topography, micrometry, altimetry, anthropometry, electrometry, craniometry.

6, measurer, surveyor, geometer, geodetist, topographer.

Verbs—measure, meter, value, assess, evaluate, rate, appraise, estimate, set a value on, appreciate, size up, span, pace, step; gauge, plumb, weigh, probe, sound, fathom, quantize; heave the lead; survey, graduate, calibrate.

Adjectives—measuring, metric[al], measurable; geodetic[al]; barometric[al]; latitudinal, longitudinal, *etc.*

---

meat, *n.* pith, essence, SUBSTANCE, core. See FOOD, MEANING.

mechanic, *n.* mechanician, repairman, serviceman. See AGENCY.

mechanical, *adj.* machinelike, automatic, power-driven, powered; involuntary, unreasoning. See POWER, NECESSITY.

mechanism, *n.* apparatus, contraption (see INSTRUMENTALITY).

medal, *n.* medallion, medalet; badge, decoration, order, prize, award, ribbon. See APPROBATION.

medallion, *n.* medal, plaque, relief, coin. See SCULPTURE, REPUTE.

meddle, *v.i.* tamper; interfere, intrude. See BETWEEN.

meddlesome, *adj.* officious, obtrusive, interfering. See BETWEEN, CURIOSITY.

media, *n.pl.* mediums; magazines, newspapers, journals, house organs; radio, television; billboards, posters, *etc.* See COMMUNICATION.

mediation, *n.* intermediation, intercession, intervention; interference; parley, negotiation, arbitration; COMPROMISE. See PACIFICATION, AGENCY.

medic, *n.* doctor, paramedic, medico (*inf.*). See REMEDY.

medicine, *n.* medicament, medication, REMEDY; therapy, physic; medical profession.

medieval, *adj.* feudal, knightly, courtly; antiquated, old-fashioned, outdated, quaint. See OLDNESS.

MEDIOCRITY
Average capacity or worth

Nouns—**1,** mediocrity, middle course, moderate degree, medial standard, moderate *or* average circumstances; normality, average, golden MEAN; MODERATION, temperance, respectability; middle classes, bourgeoisie. See INFERIORITY, INSIPIDITY.

2, mediocrity, nobody, nothing special; silent majority. *Informal,* small potatoes, no great shakes. *Slang,* ham fat. See UNIMPORTANCE.

Verbs—jog on, go *or* get on tolerably, fairly, *or* quietly; get along, get by, pass [in the dark], muddle through. *Slang,* underwhelm.

Adjectives—mediocre, ordinary, commonplace, everyday; moderate, middling, normal, average, MEAN, medium, medial; indifferent, passable, tolerable, *comme ci comme ça,* presentable, bearable, better than nothing; second- *or* third-class; respectable, not bad, fair, so-so, second-rate, run of the mill *or* mine, of poor quality; pretty well *or* good; good *or* well enough; middle-class, bourgeois. *Informal,* no great shakes, fair to middling, nothing to write home about, namby-pamby, of sorts. *Slang,* no ball of fire.

Quotations—The world is a republic of mediocrities, and always was (*Thomas Carlyle*), The only sin is mediocrity (*Martha Graham*), Some men are born mediocre, some men achieve mediocrity, and some men have mediocrity thrust upon them (*Joseph Heller*), Blessed are those who have no talent! (*Emerson*), Women want mediocre men, and men are working hard to be as mediocre as possible (*Margaret Mead*).

Antonyms, see PERFECTION, SUPERIORITY.

---

meditate, *v.* muse, ponder, cogitate; PLAN, intend, contemplate, purpose. See THOUGHT.

medium, *n.* MEAN; surrounding; go-between, agent; agency, instrumentality, MEANS; spiritualist, clairvoyant. See BETWEEN, ENVIRONMENT, MEDIOCRITY.

medley, *n.* jumble, miscellany, variety, MIXTURE. See DISORDER.

meek, *adj.* subdued, humble, patient, submissive. See HUMILITY. *Ant.,* bold.

meet, *v.* encounter, intersect; oppose; greet, welcome; satisfy; refute; assemble, gather; contend. See AGREEMENT, ASSEMBLAGE, CONTACT. —*adj.* fitting. See EXPEDIENCE.

meeting, *n.* encounter, assembly, JUNCTION; duel; tangency. See CONTACT, CONVERGENCE.

melancholy, *adj.* dejected, dispirited, sad, depressed, blue (*inf.*). See DEJECTION. *Ant.,* happy.

mélange, *n.* medley, MIXTURE.

melee, *n.* CONTENTION, combat, brawl, ruckus; DISORDER, turmoil.

mellow, *adj.* soft, rich, ripe; mellifluous; subdued, delicate. See SOFTNESS, AGE, DRINKING. —*v.* ripen, soften. See CHANGE.

melodious, *adj.* melodic, melic, melopoeic; tuneful, lilting, lyric[al], singable, cantabile; bel canto. See MUSIC.

melodrama, *n.* tragicomedy, seriocomedy;

penny-dreadful, thriller, shocker; sentimentality, bathos; bravado, derring-do; *slang,* tearjerker. See DRAMA, SENSIBILITY.

melody, *n.* tune, theme, song, aria, air. See MUSIC.

melon, *n.* fruit, cantaloupe, honeydew, casaba, Persian melon, watermelon, *etc.*; *slang,* graft. See MONEY, FOOD.

melt, *v.* disappear, vanish; fuse, thaw, dissolve, soften; dwindle; blend. See PITY, DISAPPEARANCE, LIQUEFACTION. *Ant.,* freeze, solidify.

member, *n.* unit, constituent, element, PART; fellow, adherent, partner, *etc.*

membership, *n.* members, body, whole, entirety; affiliation, participation, inclusion, admission. See PARTY.

membrane, *n.* film, lamina, sheet, sheath, LAYER.

memento, *n.* keepsake, souvenir, reminder, relic, token, memorial. See RECORD, MEMORY.

memoir, *n.* RECORD; reminiscence, autobiography. See DESCRIPTION, MEMORY.

memorable, *adj.* noteworthy, signal, outstanding; unforgettable. See IMPORTANCE, MEMORY. *Ant.,* forgettable.

memorandum, *n.* RECORD, note, reminder, memo.

memorial, *adj.* commemorative. —*n.* monument, shrine, tablet; anniversary; petition. See MEMORY, RECORD.

MEMORY
Retention of thought

Nouns—**1**, memory, remembrance, RETENTION, retentiveness, reminiscence, recognition, recurrence, recollection, retrospect, retrospection, afterthought; computer memory (see COMPUTERS). See THOUGHT, PAST.

2, reminder, suggestion, prompting, hint, cue; token, memento, souvenir, keepsake, relic, memorandum, memo, memoir; memorial, commemoration, anniversary, Memorial Day, Veterans' Day, Decoration Day, *etc.*; monument; memorabilia; flashback. See RECORD, CELEBRATION.

3, art of memory; artificial memory, mnemonics, mnemotechnics; Mnemosyne; retentive *or* photographic memory, total recall; déjà vu; rote, repetition; flash *or* cue card, nudge; prompter. *Informal,* a string around a finger.

Verbs—**1**, remember, retain the memory of; keep in view, bear in mind, hold in memory, remain in one's memory, mind, *or* head; recur to the mind, flash across the memory; haunt, run in the head; take a walk down memory lane.

2, *(be reminded of)* recognize, recollect, bethink oneself, recall, call up, identify, retrace, look *or* hark back, think back upon, review, call to mind, ring a bell, carry one's thoughts back, reminisce; rack one's brain.

3, *(remind)* suggest, prompt, put *or* keep in mind, remind, call *or* summon up; renew; tax, jog, refresh, *or* awaken the memory, ring a bell; dig up, exhume. *Slang,* rub it in (see REPETITION).

4, memorize; have, learn, know, *or* say by heart *or* rote; repeat, have at *or* on the tip of one's tongue; commit to memory; con, fix, make a note of. *Informal,* busk. See LEARNING.

5, keep the memory alive, keep in memory, commemorate, memorialize, honor the memory of, enshrine.

Adjectives—remembering, remembered, mindful, reminiscent, retentive, retained in the memory, fresh, alive, green, unforgotten, within one's memory, indelible; uppermost in one's thoughts; memorable, memorial, commemorative.

Adverbs—by heart *or* rote, without prompting, word for word; in memory of, in memoriam, for old times' sake.

Phrases—our memory is always at fault, never our judgment; nostalgia ain't what it used to be.

Quotations—Memories are quenting horns whose sound dies on the wind (*Guillaume Apollinaire*), Midnight shakes the memory as a madman shakes a dead geranium (*T. S. Eliot*), In plucking the fruit of memory one runs the risk of spoiling its bloom (*Joseph Conrad*), Memory is the mother of all wisdom (*Aeschylus*), Some memories are realities, and are better than anything that can ever happen to one again (*Willa Cather*), Good memories are lost jewels (*Paul Valéry*), In memory everything seems to happen to music (*Tennessee Williams*), Americans are impatient with memory (*Jamaica Kincaid*), I summon up remembrance of things past (*Shakespeare*).

Antonyms, see OBLIVION.

---

menace, *n.* THREAT, danger, hazard, peril. —*v.t.* threaten, intimidate, bully; impend, loom. See WARNING.

ménage, *n.* household; housekeeping, husbandry. See ABODE, ECONOMY.

menagerie, *n. Tiergarten,* zoo. See ANIMAL, DOMESTICATION.

mend, *v.* repair, restore, correct, improve. See IMPROVEMENT, RESTORATION.

mendacity, *n.* untruthfulness, untruth, FALSEHOOD, duplicity.

mendicant, *n.* beggar, pauper. See POVERTY.

menial, *n.* SERVANT, slave, flunky. —*adj.* humble, servile; degrading, mean. See SERVILITY.

menopause, *n.* change of life, climacteric; middle age. See CHANGE, AGE.

mens sana in corpore sano, *Lat.,* a healthy mind in a healthy body. See HEALTH, SANITY.

mental, *adj.* intellectual, cognitive, rational, psychological. See INTELLECT.

—mental hospital, asylum, madhouse (see INSANITY). —mental illness, INSANITY.

mentality, *n.* INTELLECT, intelligence, mind, understanding.

mention, *v.t.* communicate, designate, let fall; cite, speak of. See INFORMATION, SPEECH.

mentor, *n.* teacher (see TEACHING).

menu, *n.* bill of fare, fare, diet, list, carte. See FOOD.

mercantile, *adj.* commercial (see BARTER).

mercenary, *adj.* calculating, selfish, sordid, venal, grasping, avaricious. See PARSIMONY. *Ant.,* altruistic, unselfish.

merchandise, *n.* wares, commodities. —*v.t.* buy, sell. See SALE.

merchant, *n.* trader, dealer. See SALE, PROVISION.

merciful, *adj.* compassionate; lenient. See LENIENCY, PITY. *Ant.,* merciless.

merciless, *adj.* cruel, pitiless, relentless. See SEVERITY. *Ant.,* merciful.

mercy, *n.* PITY, LENIENCY, forbearance, compassion. —**mercy killing,** euthanasia (see KILLING).

mere, *adj.* nothing but, plain, bare, simple. See SIMPLENESS.

merely, *adv.* barely, simply, only, purely. See LITTLENESS.

merge, *v.* unite, blend, coalesce, absorb. See MIXTURE, JUNCTION, COMBINATION.

merger, *n.* alliance, association, COMBINATION.

meridian, *n.* longitude; height, culmination, zenith, apex, apogee, summit; midday. See CIRCULARITY, CHRONOMETRY.

merit, *n.* desert[s], reward, due; worth, excellence; VIRTUE. See GOODNESS.

mermaid, *n.* naiad, nymph, siren, silkie. See MYTHICAL DEITIES.

merry, *adj.* jovial, mirthful, gay, vivacious. See CHEERFULNESS.

merry-go-round, *n.* carousel, whirligig. See AMUSEMENT, ROTATION.

merrymaking, *n.* revelry, partying, conviviality. See REJOICING.

mesh, *n.* meshwork; network, web, net; lacework; tangle, snarl; lattice, trellis, grille, grate, gridiron, sieve. See CROSSING, INTERVAL.

mesmerize, *v.t.* hypnotize; fascinate, captivate. See SORCERY.

mess, *n.* DIFFICULTY, predicament; DISORDER, litter, jumble; botch. See FAILURE, FOOD. —*v.* dishevel, mess up; litter, clutter; disarrange, DISORDER. *Ant.,* ORDER.

message, *n.* COMMUNICATION, dispatch, note. See NEWS.

messenger, *n.* emissary, envoy, apostle, missionary; courier, carrier, bearer, errand boy, runner, gofer (*sl.*). See AGENT, COMMISSION.

mess hall, *n.* dining room *or* hall, refectory, cafeteria. See FOOD.

messy, *adj.* untidy, sloppy. See DISORDER, UNCLEANNESS. *Ant.,* neat.

metal, *n.* mineral, element, alloy, ore. See INORGANIC MATTER.

metamorphosis, *n.* transformation, transubstantiation. See CHANGE.

metaphorical, *adj.* allegorical, FIGURATIVE.

metaphysical, *adj.* abstruse, speculative, esoteric, transcendental. See THOUGHT.

mete, *v.t.* apportion, administer, apply (see APPORTIONMENT).

meteor, *n.* meteoroid, meteorite, shooting star. See UNIVERSE.

meteoric, *adj.* sudden, rapid, fast, shooting. See LIGHT, VELOCITY.

meteorology, *n.* weather science *or* forecasting; climatology, barometry, *etc.* See WIND.

meter, *n.* rhythm, cadence, lilt; gauge. See POETRY, MEASUREMENT.

METHOD
Systematic procedure

Nouns—method, way, manner, wise; gait, form, mode, MEANS, style, FASHION, design, tone, behavior, guise; *modus operandi, modus vivendi,* procedure, process, practice, regimen, system, technique, methodology, strategy, tactics, routine, line of CONDUCT, lifestyle; system, PLAN, scheme, formula, RULE. See AGENCY, ORDER, USE.

Verbs—methodize, systematize, arrange, regularize, organize, formulate.

Adjectives—methodical, systematic, schematic, stylistic, modal, procedural, planned, arranged, orderly, routine.

Adverbs—how; in what way, manner, *or* mode; so, thus, in this way, after this fashion; one way or another, anyhow, by any means, somehow or other, however; by way of, via, on the high road to.

Phrases—where there's a will there's a way.

Quotations—Though this be madness, yet there is method in it (*Shakespeare*), There are some enterprises in which a careful disorderliness is the true method (*Herman Melville*), Method goes far to prevent trouble in business (*William Penn*), There's a way to do it better—find it (*Thomas Edison*).

Antonyms, see DISORDER.

meticulous, *adj.* fastidious, exacting, scrupulous. See TASTE, TRUTH. *Ant.,* sloppy, careless.

métier, *n.* profession, vocation; SPECIALITY. See BUSINESS.

metropolitan, *adj.* civil, urban, oppidan, citywide, cosmopolitan, urbane, sophisticated, worldly. See ABODE.

mettle, *n.* spirit, temperament, COURAGE, disposition, VIGOR.

mettlesome, *adj.* high-strung, courageous, plucky. See COURAGE, EXCITABILITY.

microbe, *n.* bacterium, germ. See LITTLENESS.

microcosm, *n.* world in miniature. See LITTLENESS.

microorganism, *n.* microbe, germ, bacterium. See DISEASE.

microphone, *n.* pickup, lavaliere, mike, mic (*inf.*). See COMMUNICATION.

microprocessor, *n.* integrated circuit, chip. See COMPUTERS.

microscopic, *adj.* minute, tiny, infinitesimal. See LITTLENESS.

microwave, *v.* [micro-]cook, nuke (*inf.*). See FOOD.

midday, *n.* noon (see CHRONOMETRY).

MIDDLE
Central location

Nouns—1, middle, midst, MEAN, medium, middle term, midpoint; center, core, hub, kernel; umbilicus; halfway house; nave, navel, nucleus; heart, axis, bull's-eye; marrow, pith; equidistance, bisection, half distance, equator, dead center; center, inner, *or* core city; midriff; interjacence (see BETWEEN).

2, centrality, centralness, focalization; concentration, focus (see CONVERGENCE); cynosure; magnetism; center of attraction; COMBINATION, merging.

Verbs—center (on), focus, concentrate; meet, unite, converge.

Adjectives—middle, medial, median, mean, mid; midmost, intermediate, equidistant, central, focal, axial, equatorial, concentric, convergent.

Adverbs—in the middle, midway, halfway, midships; in medias res, in the thick of it, smack dab in the middle.

Antonyms, see EXTERIOR, END.

middle-aged, *adj.* mature, in [one's] prime, *d'un certain âge*. See AGE.

middle-class, *adj.* common, ordinary; bourgeois, conservative, conventional. See MEDIOCRITY, PERMANENCE.

middleman, *n.* go-between, intermediary, AGENT. See COMPROMISE.

middling, *adj.* medium (see MEDIOCRITY).

midget, *n.* dwarf, pygmy, homunculus, shrimp (*sl.*). See LITTLENESS, SHORTNESS. *Ant.,* giant.

midmost, *adj.* central, MIDDLE, mean.

midnight, *n.* witching hour. See CHRONOMETRY, DARKNESS.

midst, *n.* center, MIDDLE.

midtown, *n.* city *or* urban center, city core. See REGION.

midway, *adj.* halfway, MIDDLE. —*n.* carnival, sideshow. See AMUSEMENT.

mien, *n.* APPEARANCE, air, demeanor, bearing. See CONDUCT.

miff, *v.t.,* *informal,* offend, provoke, iritate. See IRASCIBILITY.

might, *n.* POWER, force, STRENGTH, VIGOR.

mighty, *adj.* powerful, momentous, forceful. See POWER. *Ant.,* weak, powerless.

migrate, *v.i.* journey, TRAVEL; emigrate, immigrate.

mild, *adj.* gentle, easy, bland, soft, harmless; lenient, tolerant, merciful, humane, generous, forbearing; weak, neutral; placid, tranquil, temperate, moderate; comfortable, clement; meek, submissive, conciliatory. See MODERATION, INSIPIDITY, LENIENCY. *Ant.,* harsh, forceful, severe.

mildew, *n.* mold, decay, rot, must. See DETERIORATION.

milestone, *n.* landmark, milepost; giant step, progress, advance. See OCCURRENCE, INDICATION, IMPORTANCE.

milieu, *n.* ENVIRONMENT.

militant, *adj.* aggressive, warlike, pugnacious, bellicose. See WARFARE. *Ant.,* peaceful.

military, *adj.* martial, soldierly. See WAR-
FARE.

militate, *v.i.* operate (for *or* against). See
ACTION, INFLUENCE.

militia, *n.* standing army, reserves, min-
utemen, soldiery, National Guard. See
COMBATANT.

milk, *v.* extract; extort, bleed; get the most
out of, exploit; interrogate, question,
play for all it's worth (*inf.*). See EX-
TRACTION, STEALING, LIQUEFACTION.

milky, *n.* lacteal; white, pale, chalky; spiritless, timorous. See COLOR, FEAR.

mill, *n.* grinder, millstone, millrace; factory, plant, works, shop; (*pl.*) industry.
See BUSINESS, CONTENTION. —*v.i.* stir,
wander. See CIRCULARITY. —*v.t.* grind,
pulverize. See POWDERINESS.

millennium, *n.* chiliad; heaven on earth,
PROSPERITY.

millstone, *n.* burden, deadweight; handicap. See HINDRANCE.

mimic, *v.t.* mime, imitate, impersonate;
ape, COPY; mock. See IMITATION, DRAMA.

mince, *v.t.* chop, dice; moderate. See DIS-
JUNCTION, MODERATION. —*v.i.* flounce,
sashay (*inf.*). See AFFECTATION.

mind, *n.* consciousness, understanding;
INTELLECT; purpose, intention, opinion. See WILL, DESIRE. —*v.t.* heed,
obey; notice, tend; object to. See ATTEN-
TION, CARE, BELIEF, DISLIKE.

mind-boggling, *adj.* astounding, amazing
(see WONDER).

mindful, *adj.* aware, heedful, cautious;
careful; watchful, alert. See CAUTION,
MEMORY, ATTENTION.

mindless, *adj.* thoughtless, heedless, careless, negligent, absent[minded]; senseless, insane; blind, deaf, dumb. See
INATTENTION.

mind reader, *n.* telepathist, thought reader.
See PREDICTION.

mine, *n.* lode, vein, deposit; open pit, burrow, excavation; explosive, bomb;
source, treasure trove. See CONCAVITY,
STORE.

mineral, *n.* inorganic substance, ore (see
INORGANIC MATTER).

mingle, *v.* blend, mix, merge, intermingle,
conjoin; associate. See MIXTURE, SO-
CIALITY.

miniature, *adj.* diminutive, minuscule,
minute, petite, minikin; dwarf, pygmy,

Lilliputian. —*n.* scale model, reduction.
See LITTLENESS.

minimal, *adj.* least, smallest, minimum.
See LITTLENESS. *Ant.,* maximum.

minimize, *v.* reduce, lessen; belittle, gloss
over, run down, deprecate, detract
from. See DETRACTION, UNIMPOR-
TANCE. *Ant.,* maximize.

minimum, *n.* modicum; least amount *or*
quantity. See LITTLENESS. *Ant.,* maximum.

minion, *n.* subordinate; henchman. See
SERVANT, SERVILITY, AGENT.

minister, *n.* legate, envoy, ambassador;
cabinet officer, clergyman, pastor, *etc.*
See CLERGY, AGENT. —*v.* attend, CARE
for.

ministry, *n.* state officers; diplomatic service; priesthood, CLERGY.

minor, *adj.* lesser, inferior, secondary. See
INFERIORITY, YOUTH.

minority, *n.* few, handful; smaller group;
nonage, childhood. See YOUTH, INFERI-
ORITY, RARITY. *Ant.,* majority; maturity, adulthood.

minstrel, *n.* poet, troubadour, jongleur,
bard. See POETRY, MUSIC.

mint, *v.t.* coin (see MONEY).

minus, *adj.* less, lacking; negative. See
LOSS, ABSENCE, DEDUCTION. *Ant.,* plus.

minuscule, *adj.* small, miniature; lowercase. See LITTLENESS, WRITING. *Ant.,*
full-size; capital.

minute, *adj.* minuscule, tiny; meticulous,
precise, exact. See LITTLENESS, CARE. —*n.*
moment; summary, draft; (*pl.*) RECORD,
log. See TIME.

minutiae, *n.pl.* details, trivia. See UNIM-
PORTANCE.

miracle, *n.* WONDER, marvel, prodigy; impossibility, fluke, phenomenon; divine
intervention, deus ex machina. See
IMAGINATION.

miraculous, *adj.* preternatural, supernatural, prodigious, wondrous. See WON-
DER.

mirage, *n.* optical illusion, fata morgana.
See DECEPTION, DISAPPOINTMENT, IMAG-
INATION.

mire, *n.* mud, muck, dirt; quagmire,
marsh. See UNCLEANNESS, COHERENCE.

mirror, *n.* looking glass, glass, reflector;
cheval *or* pier glass, *etc.* See OPTICAL
INSTRUMENTS.

mirth, *n.* hilarity, jollity, merriment, glee. See CHEERFULNESS. *Ant.*, gloom.

misanthrope, *n.* misanthropist, man-hater, cynic, egotist; woman-hater, misogynist. See MALEVOLENCE.

misapprehend, *v.t.* misunderstand, mistake, misinterpret. See ERROR.

misbegotten, *adj.* illegitimate, bastard; illicit, illegal. See DISCOURTESY, GUILT.

misbehavior, *n.* misconduct, mischief, disobedience, BADNESS, WRONG.

miscalculate, *v.t.* misjudge, err, misreckon. See MISJUDGMENT, DISAPPOINTMENT, SURPRISE.

miscarry, *v.i.* fail, go wrong, fall through; abort. See FAILURE.

miscellaneous, *adj.* heterogeneous, indiscriminate, mixed, many-sided; diversified, varied. See MIXTURE, GENERALITY.

miscellany, *n.* anthology, analecta; medley, MIXTURE.

mischief, *n.* harm, injury; trouble; prank. See EVIL.

misconception, *n.* delusion, mistake, misunderstanding. See ERROR, MISJUDGMENT.

misconduct, *n.* impropriety, misdemeanor, misbehavior, mismanagement, monkey business (*inf.*). See GUILT, WRONG.

misconstrue, *v.t.* misunderstand, misrepresent, get *or* take wrong, take amiss. See MISJUDGMENT.

miscreant, *n.* See EVILDOER.

misdeed, *n.* offense, WRONG, malefaction. See GUILT.

misdemeanor, *n.* crime, infraction, malfeasance. See ILLEGALITY.

misdirect, *v.t.* misguide, mislead, throw off the track; mismanage. See ERROR, DECEPTION.

mise en scène, *Fr.*, stage setting. See DRAMA, APPEARANCE.

miser, *n.* hoarder, niggard, moneygrubber, skinflint, penny pincher (*sl.*), tightwad (*sl.*). See PARSIMONY. *Ant.*, altruist, benefactor.

miserable, *adj.* wretched, forlorn, doleful; mean, contemptible, paltry. See UNIMPORTANCE. *Ant.*, happy, wealthy.

misery, *n.* wretchedness, POVERTY; distress, anguish. See PAIN.

misfire, *v.* fail, abort; fizzle, sputter; backfire. See FAILURE.

misfit, *n.* mismatch, poor fit; neurotic; rejectee, odd man [out]; schlemiel, oddball, schnook, jerk, queer (*all sl.*). See UNCONFORMITY.

misfortune, *n.* mishap, disaster, calamity, catastrophe; bad luck; ADVERSITY. See EVIL. *Ant.*, good fortune.

misgiving, *n.* DOUBT, apprehension, premonition; qualm. See FEAR.

misguide, *v.t.* mislead, lead astray. See ERROR.

mishandle, *v.t.* maltreat; mismanage, misguide. See ERROR, WRONG.

mishap, *n.* accident, mischance, misfortune. See ADVERSITY, EVIL.

mishmash, *n.* jumble, mess, farrago. See DISORDER.

misinformation, *n.* misintelligence; misteaching, misguidance, misdirection; misinstruction, misleading, perversion; sophistry. See DECEPTION.

misinterpretation, *n.* misunderstanding (see MISJUDGMENT); misrepresentation, perversion, exaggeration, false construction, falsification. See DISTORTION, ERROR.

MISJUDGMENT
Incorrect reasoning

Nouns—1, misjudgment, miscalculation, misconception, miscomputation, ERROR, hasty *or* snap conclusion, misinterpretation, misapprehension, misunderstanding, misconstruction, misapplication, mistake; overestimation, underestimation. See DISAPPOINTMENT, EXAGGERATION, INJUSTICE.

2, (*advance misconception*) prejudgment, prejudication, foregone conclusion, preconception, predilection, presumption, presentiment, preconceived idea, idée fixe.

3, partisanship, clannishness, provincialism; hobby, fad, quirk, crotchet; partiality, infatuation, blind side *or* spot, mote in the eye.

Verbs—1, misjudge, misestimate, misconceive, misreckon, miscompute, miscalculate, jump *or* rush to conclusions; overestimate, underestimate. *Informal,* bet on the wrong horse, lowball.

2, forejudge, prejudge, presuppose, prejudicate, dogmatize.

Adjectives—misjudging, wrongheaded, besotted, infatuated, fanatical, dogmatic, [self-] opinionated, crotchety, impractical, unreasoning.

Quotations—No one in this world, so far as I know . . . has ever lost money by underestimating the intelligence of the great masses of the plain people (*H. L. Mencken*), Truth lies within a little and certain compass, but error is immense (*Lord Bolingbroke*), If all else fails, immortality can always be assured by a spectacular error (*J. K. Galbraith*), Mistakes live in the neighborhood of truth and therefore delude us (*Rabindranath Tagore*).

Antonyms, see JUDGMENT.

---

mislay, *v.t.* misplace, lose. See LOSS.

mislead, *v.t.* deceive, delude, lead astray. See ERROR, DECEPTION.

mismanage, *v.t.* botch, mishandle; misconduct, maladminister. See UNSKILLFULNESS.

misnomer, *n.* misnaming (see NOMENCLATURE).

misogyny, *n.* sexism, sex discrimination, misanthropy. See MALEVOLENCE.

misplace, *v.t.* derange; mislocate, displace, mislay. See LOSS, DISPLACEMENT.

misprint, *n.* typographical ERROR, typo (*inf.*).

mispronounce, *v.t.* misspeak, missay; garble. See STAMMERING.

misquote, *v.t.* miscite, misrepresent; twist, garble, distort. See DISTORTION, FALSEHOOD.

misrepresentation, *n.* misstatement, DISTORTION, exaggeration, perversion, falsification; caricature, burlesque, travesty; mimicry, mockery, parody, takeoff, imitation. See FALSEHOOD.

misrule, *n.* mismanagement, misgovernment; confusion, tumult, DISORDER. See UNSKILLFULNESS.

miss, *v.* fail; omit, skip, overlook; avoid; escape; lose. See FAILURE, NEGLECT, DESIRE, LOSS.

misshapen, *adj.* deformed, malformed, distorted, grotesque. See DISTORTION, FORMLESSNESS, UGLINESS.

missile, *n.* projectile, trajectile; guided missile. See ARMS.

missing, *adj.* omitted; gone, absent; lacking. See ABSENCE, LOSS. *Ant.,* present.

mission, *n.* errand, task, assignment; calling; deputation. See BUSINESS, COMMISSION.

missionary, *n.* evangelist, proselytizer, emissary. See CLERGY, COMMISSION.

misspeak, *v.i.* make a blunder, trip over one's tongue, put one's foot in one's mouth (*inf.*). See SPEECH, ERROR.

misspent, *adj.* squandered, wasted. See WASTE.

misstatement, *n.* ERROR, mistake; misrepresentation, perversion, FALSEHOOD.

misstep, *n.* stumble, false step; impropriety, lapse, slip; sin. See ERROR.

mist, *n.* fog, haze, vapor, drizzle. See CLOUDINESS, MOISTURE.

mistake, *v.t.* misunderstand, err, misidentify. —*n.* ERROR, blunder, misunderstanding, slip.

mistreat, *v.t.* maltreat; mishandle, abuse, neglect; treat shabbily, oppress, victimize, overburden. See SEVERITY, MALEVOLENCE, WRONG.

mistress, *n.* possessor, employer; matron, head, teacher; paramour, sweetheart. See TEACHING, EVILDOER, FEMALE.

mistrust, *n. & v.* See DISTRUST.

misty, *adj.* indistinct, obscure, blurry; *informal,* tearful, weepy. See OBSCURITY, DEJECTION.

misunderstanding, *n.* misapprehension; quarrel, disagreement, falling-out. See CONTENTION, ERROR, DISCORD, MISJUDGMENT.

misuse, *n.* misusage, misemployment, misapplication, misappropriation; abuse, profanation, perversion, prostitution, ill use, ill-usage; desecration; WASTE. —*v.t.* misemploy, misapply, misappropriate; ill-use.

mite, *n.* louse, insect, chigoe, chigger, *etc.*; coin, penny, sou. See LITTLENESS.

mitigate, *v.t.* lessen, moderate, ameliorate,

palliate, allay, relieve. See RELIEF, MOD-
ERATION, VINDICATION.

mixed bag, potpourri, medley, assortment, hodgepodge. See MIXTURE.

MIXTURE
Combination of two or more things

Nouns—1, mixture, admixture, commixture, intermixture, alloyage; matrimony, JUNC-
TION, COMBINATION, union, amalgamation; permeation, imbuement, impregnation,
infusion, suffusion, transfusion, infiltration; seasoning, sprinkling; adulteration; assortment, variety; miscegenation, interbreeding, intermarriage, mixed marriage; hy-
bridization, crossing, crossbreeding; multiculturism, pluralism, biculturalism. *Slang,*
gender-bender. See BETWEEN, INSERTION.

2, *(slight addition)* tinge, tincture, sprinkling, spice, seasoning, infusion, soupçon. See
LITTLENESS.

3, *(mixture of elements)* alloy, amalgam, compound, blend, mélange, miscellany,
melting pot, medley, olio, mess, hodgepodge, brew, patchwork, odds and ends, jumble; salad, sauce; hash, mash; gallimaufry, salmagundy, potpourri, goulash, mosaic;
crazy quilt, mishmash; pi; mixed blessing. *Slang,* dog's breakfast

4, *(mixed races or sexes)* half-breed, half-caste, half-blood, mulatto; quadroon, octoroon; cross, hybrid, mongrel; ladino, mestizo; Eurasian; mustee, métis, métisse; bisexual; hermaphrodite, androgyne, epicene. *Slang,* high yellow, keltch, lemon,
mahogany, sepia[n], cascos, free issue, griffe, marabou, black and tan, brown, café au
lait, caste, grifane, pinky, mango, mameluco, mustalfino, pepper and salt, quarteron,
sang-mêlé, white Negro, yola; half and half, kiki, switch-hitter, moff, panatrope,
scrat, will-jill.

5, *(device or event)* mixer, blender, food processor, eggbeater; social, John Paul Jones,
tea dance.

Verbs—mix, join, combine, commix, intermix, merge, mix up with, mingle, commingle,
intermingle, stir up, knead, brew, impregnate with, intertwine, graft, interweave, associate with; instill, imbue, transfuse, infuse, suffuse, infiltrate, tinge, lace, tincture,
season, sprinkle, blend, cross, allow, amalgamate, throw together with, compound,
adulterate, contaminate, infect; run into. *Slang,* swing both ways.

Adjectives—mixed, composite, half-and-half; hybrid, mongrel; combined, united;
amalgamated, alloyed; multicultural; impregnated (with), ingrained; heterogeneous,
motley, variegated, miscellaneous, promiscuous, indiscriminate, miscible.

Prepositions—among[st], amid[st], with, in the midst of.

Antonyms, see DISJUNCTION.

---

mixup, *n.* confusion, imbroglio, muddle,
contretemps; mixture, hodgepodge;
disagreement, CONTENTION, quarrel,
brawl, hassle (*sl.*), rhubarb (*sl.*).

moan, *v.* wail, sigh, groan, bewail, lament.
See LAMENTATION.

moat, *n.* trench. See FURROW, DEFENSE.

mob, *n.* rabble, riffraff; hoi polloi; common herd, canaille; crowd, POPULACE.
See ASSEMBLAGE.

mobile, *adj.* movable, loose, free, animate.
See MOTION.

mobilize, *v.* motorize, activate, set in action; summon, muster, rally; arm,
equip. See MOTION, WARFARE.

mobster, *n., slang,* gangster, racketeer. See
EVILDOER.

mock, *v.t.* RIDICULE, mimic, tantalize, jeer
at; disappoint. See DISRESPECT. —*adj.*
false, IMITATION, sham, pseudo. See
DECEPTION, SIMILARITY.

mock-up, *n.* layout, dummy, model; reproduction, COPY. See PLAN.

mod, *adj., informal,* modern, up-to-date.
See NEWNESS.

mode, *n.* state, manner, METHOD, custom;
FASHION, style.

model, *n.* prototype, pattern, mock-up;
COPY, miniature, replica; style, type;
mannequin, lay figure; exemplar,
paragon. See REPRESENTATION, GOOD-
NESS, FORM, PERFECTION, IMITATION,
SCULPTURE.

MODERATION
Keeping within limits

Nouns—1, moderation, moderateness, temperance, continence, temperateness, gentleness; self-restraint, self-control, ASCETICISM, abstinence; teetotalism, soberness, sobriety; quiet, tranquillity, INEXCITABILITY; relaxation, abatement, remission, mitigation, tranquilization, assuagement, PACIFICATION; letup, alleviation; juste milieu, golden MEAN. See RELIEF, DECREASE.

2, *(that which moderates)* sedative, palliative, lenitive, balm, opiate, anodyne; lullaby; moderator, temperer.

3, *(moderate action)* LENIENCY, lenity, tolerance, toleration, clemency, PITY; sweetness and light.

4, *(nondrinker)* abstainer, nondrinker, teetotaler, dry, Prohibitionist; designated driver; WCTU (Women's Christian Temperance Union), Anti-Saloon League, Alcoholics Anonymous.

Verbs—1, keep within bounds, sober up, settle down, keep the peace, relent; abstain, be temperate, take the pledge, swear off; hold one's temper, take it easy, go easy; pull in one's horns; detoxify. *Informal,* count to ten. *Slang,* hang loose, keep cool, chill [out]; detox.

2, moderate, soften, mitigate, temper, mollify, dull, blunt, subdue, chasten, tone down, lessen, check, palliate; tranquilize, assuage, appease, lull, soothe, still, calm, cool, quiet, hush, quell, sober, pacify, tame, allay, slacken, smooth, alleviate, deaden, smother; pour oil on troubled waters; cool off, tone down, taper off, ease off *or* up, let up.

3, tolerate, bear with; indulge, spare the rod; spare; give quarter; PITY. *Slang,* pull one's punches; let one down easy.

Adjectives—moderate, lenient, gentle, easy, mild, soft, tolerant, easygoing, forbearing; sober, temperate, dry; tranquil, reasonable, tempered; tame, lulling, hypnotic, sedative, palliative. *Informal,* on the [water] wagon; laid back.

Adverbs—moderately, gingerly, within bounds *or* reason.

Phrases—less is more; moderation in all things; keep no more cats than will catch mice; enough is as good as a feast.

Quotations—We know what happens to people who stay in the middle of the road. They get run down (*Aneurin Bevan*), Moderation in all things (*Terence*), To many, total abstinence is easier than perfect moderation (*St. Augustine*), Pure reason avoids extremes, and requires one to be wise in moderation (*Molière*), And let me remind you also that moderation in the pursuit of justice is no virtue! (*Barry Goldwater*), I see no objection to stoutness, in moderation (*W. S. Gilbert*), Excess on occasion is exhilarating. It prevents moderation from acquiring the deadening effect of habit (*W. Somerset Maugham*).

Antonyms, see VIOLENCE, INTEMPERANCE, DRINKING.

---

modern, *adj.* contemporary; late, recent; up-to-date. See NEWNESS, PRESENT. *Ant.,* old-fashioned.

modernism, *n.* modernity, height of fashion; surrealism, dada, *etc.*; liberalism. See NEWNESS, PAINTING.

modernize, *v.* renovate, update. See RESTORATION.

MODESTY
Timidity

Nouns—modesty; HUMILITY; diffidence, timidity, bashfulness; shyness, unobtrusiveness; shame; reserve, constraint; demureness.

Verbs—1, be modest, retire, give way to, retire into one's shell, keep in the background, keep one's distance, hide one's light under a bushel; not dare to show one's face.

2, hide one's face, hang one's head, eat humble pie; blush, redden, change color; feel small. *Informal,* eat crow, draw in one's horns.

Adjectives—modest, diffident, humble, timid, timorous, bashful, shy, nervous; coy; sheepish, shamefaced, blushing; overmodest, unpretentious, unobtrusive, unassuming, unaspiring, reserved, demure, self-effacing, decent; common as an old shoe.

Adverbs—modestly, humbly, meekly; quietly, privately; without ceremony; with downcast eyes, on bended knee.

Quotations—Modest doubt is called the beacon of the wise (*Shakespeare*), It is difficult for a rich person to be modest, or a modest person rich (*Epictetus*), [Of Clement Attlee:] A modest man who has a good deal to be modest about (*Winston Churchill*), I have often wished I had time to cultivate modesty . . . But I am too busy thinking about myself (*Edith Sitwell*).

Antonyms, see VANITY.

---

modicum, *n.* little, pittance, bit. See LITTLENESS, APPORTIONMENT.

modification, *n.* CHANGE, alteration, mutation; limitation, QUALIFICATION, modulation.

modify, *v.t.* CHANGE, vary, alter; limit, reduce; temper, soften.

modish, *adj.* chic, stylish, fashionable, à la mode, smart. See FASHION.

modulation, *n.* regulation, abatement, inflection, modification. See CHANGE, SOUND.

module, *n.* unit, component, PART.

modus operandi, *Lat.,* METHOD of working. See PLAN.

modus vivendi, *Lat.,* lifestyle, way of life. See METHOD.

mogul, *n.* autocrat, ruler; capitalist, entrepreneur, financier, tycoon, bigwig (*inf.*), bigshot (*inf.*). See IMPORTANCE.

Mohammedan, *n.* Mussulman, Moslem, Islamite. —*adj.* Moslem, Islamic. See RELIGION.

MOISTURE
Dampness

Nouns—1, moisture, moistness, humidity, dampness, wet[ness], dankness, clamminess; hygrometry. See WATER.

2, dew, fog, mist. See CLOUDINESS, VAPOR.

3, wetlands, marsh[land], swamp[land], everglade, chott, pocosin, glade, salina, salt marsh, alluvial *or* coastal plain, delta; morass, moss, fen, [peat] bog; mire, quag[mire], quicksand; slough; sump, swale; wallow, wash, bottoms, mud, slush.

Verbs—moisten, wet, sponge, sprinkle, damp[en], bedew, saturate, soak, drench, water; soak [up].

Adjectives—moist, damp, watery, humid, wet, dank, clammy, muggy, dewy, juicy, wringing wet, wet through, wet to the skin, saturated; soggy, reeking, dripping, soaking, soft, sodden, sloppy, muddy, swampy, marshy, paludal.

Quotations—Let's get out of these wet clothes and into a dry martini (*Robert Benchley*), What would the world be once bereft of wet and wildness? (*Gerard Manley Hopkins*).

Antonyms, see DRYNESS.

---

mold, *n.* matrix, die; FORM, shape, figure; stamp, cast; fungus, growth. —*v.t.* frame, shape, model, cast; knead, work. See SCULPTURE.

molding, *n.* necking, surbase, baseboard, platband; cornice, fillet, tringle, chaplet, *etc.*; edging, border, ornamentation. See ORNAMENT.

moldy, *adj.* musty, mildewed, fusty; stale, antiquated. See UNCLEANNESS, DETERIORATION, OLDNESS.

molecule, *n.* particle, atom, mite, micron. See LITTLENESS.

molehill, *n.* trifle, feather (see UNIMPORTANCE).

molest, *v.t.* disturb, annoy, vex, pester, harass. See PAIN, MALEVOLENCE.

mollify, *v.t.* placate, pacify, soothe, appease, calm; soften. See RELIEF, SOFTNESS. *Ant.,* antagonize.

mollycoddle, *n.* milksop, sissy, pantywaist (*sl.*). See COWARDICE. —*v.t.* pamper, coddle, spoil. See LENIENCY.

molt, *v.t.* shed; cast *or* slough off. See DIVESTMENT.

molten, *adj.* melted, fused, liquefied. See LIQUEFACTION, HEAT.

moment, *n.* IMPORTANCE, consequence, significance; instant, trice, flash; the PRESENT. See INSTANTANEITY.

momentary, *adj.* simultaneous, immediate (see INSTANTANEITY).

momentous, *adj.* important, consequential, great, notable, signal; serious, solemn, memorable; influential. See IMPORTANCE. *Ant.,* unimportant, trivial.

momentum, *n.* impetus, moment. See IMPULSE.

monarch, *n.* sovereign, ruler, potentate, king. See AUTHORITY.

monastery, *n.* cloister, lamasery, abbey, convent, priory. See TEMPLE.

monasticism, *n.* monkhood, monachism, friarhood. See CLERGY.

MONEY
Medium of exchange

Nouns—**1,** money, finance, funds, treasure, capital, assets; ways and means, wherewithal; money matters, economics, the dismal science; resources, backing (see MEANS); purse strings. *Informal,* mad money. *Slang,* green power, fast *or* quick buck, scratch, almighty dollar, dash, jack, grease, mazooma, spondulix, tinkle, bread, dust, dough, dinero, gelt, do-re-mi, tusheroon, wine, the needful; megabucks; voodoo economics.

2, *(accounting)* sum, amount; balance, balance sheet; proceeds, accounts, lump sum, round sum; principal, interest. See ACCOUNTING.

3, *(metal money)* gold, silver, copper, nickel; bullion, ingot, nugget, gold brick; currency, circulating medium; coinage, specie, coin, cash, cold *or* hard cash; [legal] tender, money in hand, ready money; petty cash; pocket, spending, mad, *or* pin money; change, small coin, stiver, mite; plastic money. *Informal,* boodle, [filthy] lucre, easy money, pelf, mad money, wad, wampum, megabucks, bundle. *Slang* brass, gelt, mazuma, filthy lucre, moolah, mopus, shekels, simoleons, beans, chips, berries.

4, wampum; paper money, money order, note, bank note, promissory note, IOU, bond, bill [of exchange]; food stamp; silver certificate; draft, check, cheque, traveler's check; debit *or* credit card; scrip; order, warrant, coupon, debenture, assignat, greenback; plastic money, debit *or* credit card. *Slang,* paper, blue chips, cabbage, kale, long green, alfalfa, green stuff, lettuce, [long] green, folding money; glory roll.

5, *(currency)* **a.** *(United States)* dollar, cent, [golden] eagle. *Slang,* buck, Jewish flag, lettuce, coconut, simoleon, smacker, scoot, clam, cholly, bean, year, ace, two-spot, fin, fiver, five-spot, nickel note, sawbuck, ten-spot, grand, century, bone, honeybee, dime, sawbuck, simoleon, meter, thin one, two bits, four bits; bill, yard, G note, C note; red cent, dead presidents. **b.** *(Europe)* [pound] sterling, crown, farthing, penny, shilling, groat, sovereign, guinea, pence, pony, quid, tenner, sixpence, ha'penny, noble; centavo, centimo, peseta, doubloon, piaster, real; escudo, forint, guilder, tenge, tolar, koruna, kuna, krona, som, kone, zloty, schilling, lat, lek, leu, lev, lit, markka; Mark, pfennig; franc, sou, centime, napoleon; florin; lira, ducat; drachma, obol, denar; Eurodollar, Euro, Emu. *Informal,* quid, tuppence, tenner. *Slang,* bob, tanner.

c. *(Asia)* afgani, baht, won, yuan, yen, dong, taka, dram, rupee, riel, ruble, korbovanets, kyat, tugrik, kip, manat, pataca; shekel. d. *(Africa)* birr, rial, riyal, cedi, dalasi, dinar, zaire, dirham, kwacha, kwanza, metical, shilling, naira, rand, ngultrum, ouguiya, pa'anga, leone, lilangeni, loti, pula. e. *(South America)* austral, balboa, bolivar, colon, cordoba, sucre, cruzeiro real, gourde, quetzal, guarani, inti, lempira, peso, f. *(Other)* dobra, kina, ringgit, rufiyaa, rupiah, tala, vatu; petrodollar, xenocurrency.

6, wealth, opulence, affluence, riches, fortune, king's ransom; competence, solvency; PROSPERITY; worth, substance; property; bonanza, mint, gold mine, Golconda, El Dorado, purse of Fortunatus. See POSSESSION. *Slang,* arm and a leg, bale of hay.

7, *(false money)* counterfeit, false, *or* bad money, stage money; base coin, flash note. *Informal,* funny money, slug. See DECEPTION.

8, DEARNESS, costliness.

9, rich man, capitalist, financier, millionaire, multimillionaire, billionaire; nabob, Croesus, Dives, Maecenas, Midas, Barmecide; plutocrat, tycoon, baron; carriage trade; heir[ess]. *Slang,* moneybags, zillionaire.

10, numismatics, science of coins, coin collecting.

Verbs—1, monetize, issue, circulate; coin, mint; counterfeit, forge; amount to, come to, total.

2, have *or* roll in money, wallow in wealth, have a bundle, make a fortune, feather one's nest, strike it rich, burn a hole in one's pocket. *Informal,* have money to burn, hit the jackpot, make a killing. *Slang,* stink of money.

3, enrich, make rich, line one's pockets; cash a check. *Slang,* clock a grip.

Adjectives—1, monetary, pecuniary, fiscal, financial, numismatical, bankable, disposable.

2, wealthy, rich, affluent, opulent, well-to-do, well off, made of money, born with a silver spoon in one's mouth. *Informal,* flush. *Slang,* well-heeled, in the chips; filthy rich; loaded.

3, dear, expensive, costly; precious, extravagant, at a premium.

Phrases—money is power; money makes money; money talks; time is money; you cannot serve God and Mammon; bad money drives out good; money isn't everything; the almighty dollar is the only object of worship.

Quotations—If possible honestly, if not, somehow, make money *(Horace)*, The love of money is the root of all evil *(Bible)*, Money speaks sense in a language all nations understand *(Aphra Behn)*, Money is coined liberty *(Dostoevsky)*, I don't care too much for money, for money can't buy me love *(Lennon/McCartney)*, Those who have some means think that the most important thing in the world is love. The poor know that it is money *(Gerald Brenan)*, The trouble with the profit system has always been that it was highly unprofitable to most people *(E. B. White)*, Every man thinks God is on his side. The rich and powerful know he is *(Jean Anouilh)*, Money, it turned out, was exactly like sex. You thought of nothing else if you didn't have it and thought of other things if you did *(James Baldwin)*, If you want to know what the Lord God thinks of money, you have only to look at those to whom he gives it *(Maurice Baring)*, To be clever enough to get all the money, one must be stupid enough to want it *(G. K. Chesterton)*, Honesty is incompatible with amassing a large fortune *(Mohandas Gandhi)*, For money you would sell your soul *(Sophocles)*, Let me tell you about the very rich. They are different from you and me *(F. Scott Fitzgerald)*.

Antonyms, see POVERTY.

---

moneylender, *n.* usurer, Shylock. See BORROWING.

mongrel, *n.* crossbreed, hybrid, half-caste; cur, mutt, stray. —*adj.* crossed, mixed, hybrid; impure. See MIXTURE.

moniker, *n., slang,* name, nickname, handle *(inf.)* (see NOMENCLATURE).

monitor, *n.* monitress; overseer, disciplinarian, censor; master, controller; watchdog, troubleshooter. —*v.* keep order, watch, oversee, supervise; check, regulate, sample; listen in (on). See CARE, COMMUNICATION, AUTHORITY, DIRECTOR.

monitory, *adj.* cautionary, WARNING.

monk, *n.* friar, brother, cleric; pilgrim, palmer, mendicant; ascetic, hermit, anchorite, cenobite, eremite, recluse, solitary; abbot, prior, father, abbé. See CLERGY, CELIBACY, ASCETICISM.

monkey, *n.* simian, primate, ape; imitator, mimic. See ANIMAL, IMITATION.

monocle, *n.* eyeglass, eyepiece, lens, lorgnon. See OPTICAL INSTRUMENTS.

monolith, *n.* obelisk, monument, pillar; cromlech, dolmen, *etc.* See RECORD.

monologue, *n.* recitation, monodrama; soliloquy, apostrophe; SPEECH; reverie, stream of consciousness. See DRAMA.

monopolize, *v.t.* engross, absorb, appropriate, corner. See ATTENTION.

monopoly, *n.* trust, cartel, syndicate, pool; corner. See RESTRAINT, POSSESSION.

monotonous, *adj.* wearisome, humdrum, tedious; unvaried, repetitious. REPETITION, WEARINESS.

monsoon, *n.* trade WIND; rainy season, rains. See WATER.

monster, *n.* monstrosity, freak; prodigy; giant; DEMON, brute. See UNCONFORMITY, SIZE, UGLINESS, EVILDOER. *Ant.,* midget.

monstrous, *adj.* huge, enormous; hideous, terrifying, revolting; fiendish, heinous; abnormal, freakish. See SIZE, UGLINESS, UNCONFORMITY, DISTORTION.

monument, *n.* memorial, cenotaph, tombstone. See INTERMENT, RECORD.

mooch, *v., slang,* cadge, borrow, sponge (*inf.*), bum (*inf.*); lift (*inf.*), snitch (*sl.*). See REQUEST.

mood, *n.* temper, humor, disposition, inclination. See TENDENCY, FEELING.

moody, *adj.* capricious, variable; gloomy, pensive, sad; peevish, testy; sullen, glum. See DEJECTION, IRASCIBILITY.

moon, *n.* satellite; month; lunation. See UNIVERSE.

moonshine, *n.* nonsense, idle talk; *informal,* home brew, bootleg; booze, hooch, white lightning, mountain dew (*all sl.*). See DRINKING, DIMNESS.

moor, *n.* heath, moorland, down, brae. See HORIZONTAL, MOISTURE.

moot, *adj.* mooted, debatable, suspect. See DOUBT.

mop, *n.* floor mop, dry mop; brush, broom; tuft. —*v.t.* swab, wipe. See CLEANNESS.

mope, *v.i.* brood, fret, sulk, pout. See DEJECTION, IRASCIBILITY.

moral, *adj.* ethical; righteous, just, virtuous; logical, probable. See VIRTUE, DUTY. *Ant.,* immoral.

morale, *n.* spirit, cheer, nerve, COURAGE, faith, hope; esprit de corps; gumption, RESOLUTION, determination.

morality, *n.* VIRTUE, righteousness, uprightness, rectitude, ethics, morals. See DUTY. *Ant.,* immorality.

morals, *n.pl.* principles, ethics, norms; value system. See VIRTUE, DUTY.

morass, *n.* marsh, bog. See MOISTURE.

moratorium, *n.* delay. See LATENESS.

morbid, *adj.* unhealthy, diseased; gloomy, unwholesome. See DISEASE.

mordant, *adj.* mordacious, biting, sarcastic. See PUNGENCY, MALEVOLENCE.

more, *adj. & adv.* additional, in ADDITION, added, beside[s], to boot, over and above, further.

morgue, *n.* mortuary, death *or* charnel house, deadhouse; files, records, dead records file. See DEATH, RECORD.

moribund, *adj.* dying (see DEATH).

morning, *n.* morn, morningtide, forenoon, ante meridian, A.M., [crack of] dawn, daybreak, break of day; aurora; sunrise, sunup, cockcrow. See TIME, BEGINNING.

moron, *n.* simpleton, half-wit, imbecile. See IGNORANCE.

morose, *adj.* sulky, sullen, gloomy, crabbed, glum, dour. See DEJECTION, IRASCIBILITY.

morsel, *n.* mouthful, bite, crumb, scrap, bit. See LITTLENESS.

mortal, *adj.* human, ephemeral; fatal, deadly; dire; implacable. See HUMANITY, TRANSIENTNESS, KILLING.

mortar, *n.* cannon, howitzer; cement, bond; vessel, cup; grinder, crucible. See ARMS, CONNECTION.

mortgage, *n.* pledge, SECURITY, encumbrance, loan, bond, debenture; PROM-

ISE. —*v.* borrow, pledge, hypothecate. See DEBT.

mortification, *n.* humiliation, vexation, embarrassment, chagrin. See ASCETICISM, HUMILITY.

mortify, *v.t.* humiliate, embarrass, chagrin; decay. See HUMILITY, DETERIORATION, ASCETICISM.

mortuary, *n.* MORGUE, funeral home. —*adj.* funerary, funereal. See INTERMENT.

mosaic, *n.* tilework, inlay, [in]tarsia; jigsaw puzzle; tesserae, tessellation; MIXTURE, montage, kaleidoscope. —*adj.* mosaical, motley; tessellated; pieced, joined. See ORNAMENT, VARIEGATION.

mosque, *n.* See TEMPLE.

moss, *n.* liverwort; club, peat, *etc.* moss. See VEGETABLE.

most, *adj.* greatest, most numerous; the majority of, nearly *or* almost all. See SUPERIORITY, MULTITUDE. *Ant.,* least.

mot, *n.* witticism, quip, epigram. See MAXIM.

mote, *n.* speck [of dust], iota, trace, particle. See LITTLENESS.

motel, *n.* motor court *or* hotel; stopover, inn; cabins. See ABODE.

moth-eaten, *adj.* worn, shabby, tattered, ragged. See DETERIORATION.

mother, *n.* parent, mama; abbess, prioress; matron, matriarch. See ANCESTRY, CLERGY, FEMALE.

motherhood, *n.* maternity (see FEMALE).

motif, *n.* [musical] theme; subject, topic, concept. See MUSIC, THOUGHT.

MOTION
Movement

Nouns—1, motion, movement, move, mobility, movableness; APPROACH; mobilization; restlessness, unrest; kinematics, kinetics; sprite.

2, *(motion forward)* progress, locomotion; journey, voyage, transit, TRAVEL; speed, VELOCITY, rate, clip. See PROGRESSION.

3, *(fluid motion)* stream, flow, flux, run, course, flight, drift, DIRECTION. See FLUIDITY.

4, *(motion on foot)* step, pace, tread, stride, gait, footfall, carriage.

Verbs—1, be in motion, move, go; hie; budge, stir; pass, flit, hover round; shift, slide, glide; roll on, flow, stream, run, drift, sweep along; wander, walk, get around; dodge; keep moving, pull up stakes. *Slang,* doss, haul ass, tool along, truck.

2, put *or* set in motion, move, impel, propel, mobilize, motivate.

3, motion, signal, gesture, direct, guide (see INDICATION).

4, walk, step, pace, tread, stride. *Slang,* galumph.

Adjectives—moving, in motion, astir, transitional, motory, motive, shifting, movable, mobile; mercurial, restless, changeable, nomadic, erratic; kinetic. *Slang,* cooking [with gas].

Adverbs—under way, on the move, on the wing, on the march.

Quotations—Between the idea and the reality, between the motion and the act, falls the Shadow (*T. S. Eliot*), To every action there is always opposed an equal reaction (*Isaac Newton*), America is a land of wonders, in which everything is in constant motion (*Alexis de Tocqueville*).

Antonyms, see INACTIVITY, STABILITY.

---

motionless, *adj.* still, immobile, stationary, inert, fixed. See INACTIVITY.

MOTION PICTURES

Nouns—1, motion *or* moving pictures, cinema, the silver screen; silent film, talking picture, picture show; rating, Motion Picture Rating Association, G, PG, PG-13, R, NC-17, X; production company, majors, motion picture studio, independent producer; coproduction, distribution, release; double bill, double feature, [sneak] preview, trailer. *Informal,* movies, talkie. *Slang,* flick, indie. See PHOTOGRAPHY, DRAMA.

2, A, B, *or* C picture, genre film, star vehicle; feature film, melodrama, romantic, slapstick, *or* screwball comedy; musical, newsreel, documentary, short subject, travelogue, coming attractions; cartoon, [computer-]animated film; action adventure, cinema verité, film noir; detective *or* gangster film, law-and-order film, thriller, shocker, slasher film; disaster film; science fiction, space opera; avant-garde *or* experimental film, art film, new wave, *nouvelle vague*; exploitation film; horror film; costume film, period piece; western, cowboy film, horse opera; blue, pornographic, *or* X-rated film; promotional *or* industrial film; remake, sequel, prequel. *Informal,* chiller, sci-fi, tearjerker. *Slang,* whodunit, sexploitation, blaxploitation, oater, spaghetti western, shoot-'em-up, crash-and-burn film, skin flick, splatter movie, porn, stag movie, snuff film.

3, cinematography; academy leader; acetate base; frame, footage; Cinerama, Cinemascope, Todd-AO Technicolor, wide-screen *or* rear[-screen] projection, stereoscope, Foley, rotoscope; camera, camera track, anamorphic lens, parallax, dolly, crane; kinetoscope, Movieola; film, celluloid, safety film; back projection; optical effect, close up, wipe, blackout, dissolve, iris-in *or* -out, fade-in *or* -out; bridging shot, long shot, insert, pan, moving shot, tracking *or* dolly shot, montage, cut-in, pixilation, jump cut, smash cut, establishing *or* master shot, glass shot, head shot, process shot, split screen, squeezed print, hold, exterior *or* interior shot, library *or* stock shot, stop-action photography, favoring shot, freeze frame, stop motion, time-lapse photography; [film] clip, dailies, rushes, composite *or* married print, workprint, rough cut, final cut, locked cut, looping, continuity, crosscutting, cross-fade, flashback, flash forward, cut[away]; animation, cel; retake, reshoot; location, backlot, set, sound stage, scenery, backdrop, background, cyclorama, gobo, ground, key light, klieg light, skypan; special effects, over- *or* undercranking, slow motion; clap[per]board; edit, splice; dubbing, voice-over; pre- *or* postproduction; background music, film score. *Slang,* FX, inki dink, slo-mo, sticks.

4, screenplay, [shooting] script; storyboard, treatment; adaptation, rewrite; property; back- *or* front-end deal, development, option; pitch meeting; colorization.

5, a. filmmaker, head of production, line producer; cineaste, [assistant] director, auteur, [executive *or* associate] producer; screenwriter, script doctor, script girl, script reader, script supervisor; casting director, lighting director, editor, sound editor; crew, first, second, *etc.* unit, cinematographer, cameraman, flying rig, focus puller, gaffer, greensman, grip, wrangler; animator, in-between; dresser. *Slang,* best boy, gaffer's assistant, hammer. **b.** cast; actor, actress, extra, method actor; [male *or* female] lead, principal, leading lady *or* man, stand-in, body double, stunt man *or* woman; [silent] bit, cameo, heavy, ingénue, love interest; screen test, typecasting; agent, talent scout; breakdowns; billing, credits; call. *Informal,* talent. *Slang,* buzz, heat.

6, movie house *or* theater, picture palace, Cineplex, multiplex, nickelodeon; cinematheque, revival house; projection booth; drive-in [theater].

7, Academy Awards, Oscars, Golden Globes.

Verbs—intercut, synchronize, cheat [to camera], score, screen.

Adjectives—cinematic; in production, in the can; offscreen, rolling, wide-screen, featured.

Adverbs—on location.

Quotations—A trip through a sewer in a glass-bottomed boat (*Wilson Mizner*), Pictures are for entertainment, messages should be delivered by Western Union (*Samuel Goldwyn*), The words "Kiss Kiss Bang Bang" . . . are perhaps the briefest statement imaginable of the basic appeal of movies (*Pauline Kael*).

---

motivate, *v.* induce, move; draw on, give an impulse to, inspire, prompt, stimulate, inspirit, [a]rouse, animate, incite, provoke, instigate, INFLUENCE, bias, sway; tempt, seduce; bribe, suborn; enforce, impel, propel, whip, lash, goad. See CAUSE.

motive, *n.* motivation, reason, ground, CAUSE; purpose, design; occasion; principle, mainspring, keystone; INTENTION, inducement, consideration, attraction; temptation, enticement; bewitchment, spell, fascination; influence, impulse, incitement, instigation; inspiration, encouragement; incentive, stimulus, spur, goad, bribe, bait; sop.

motley, *adj.* colorful, many-colored, variegated; assorted, jumbled, heterogeneous, diverse, kaleidoscopic, crazy-quilt, incongruous. See MIXTURE.

motor, *n.* engine (see POWER, INSTRUMENTALITY).

motorboat, *n.* speedboat, launch, cruiser; runabout, hydroplane. See SHIP.

motorcade, *n.* caravan, parade, procession. See SEQUENCE.

motorcycle, *n.* motocycle, [motor]scooter, motorbike, putt-putt (*inf.*). See VEHICLE.

motorist, *n.* automobilist, Sunday driver (*inf.*), road hog (*inf.*); driver, chauffeur; speeder. See TRAVEL.

mottled, *adj.* spotted, blotched, dappled; motley. See COLOR.

motto, *n.* MAXIM, adage, precept, device.

mould, *n. & v.* See MOLD.

mound, *n.* heap, hillock, knoll, hill, tumulus. See HEIGHT.

mount, *v.t.* ascend, rise, soar, go up, climb; set, place. See ASCENT, HEIGHT.

mountain, *n.* hill, peak, elevation, alp, mount. See HEIGHT.

mountaineer, *n.* highlander, mountain climber, hillbilly (*sl.*). See ASCENT.

mountainous, *adj.* hilly, craggy, peaked; towering, sheer, lofty, precipitous; rugged, massive; Alpine, cordilleran. See HEIGHT.

mountebank, *n.* charlatan, quack. See DECEPTION.

mourn, *v.* lament, sorrow, grieve; bewail, bemoan, deplore. See LAMENTATION.

mourner, *n.* lamenter; mute, pallbearer. See INTERMENT, LAMENTATION.

mournful, *adj.* sorrowful; gloomy, dreary. See DEJECTION, LAMENTATION. *Ant.,* cheerful.

mousy, *adj.* drab, colorless; quiet. See COLOR, TACITURNITY.

mouth, *n.* oral cavity, lips, kisser (*sl.*), trap (*sl.*); muzzle; entrance, exit, inlet, outlet. See OPENING, EDGE, EGRESS, INGRESS.

mouthpiece, *n.* reed, embouchure, lip, bit, pipe stem, *etc.*; *slang,* spokesman, parrot, speaker, lawyer. See MUSIC, SPEECH, LAWSUIT.

movable, *adj.* portable, mobile; changeable. See CHANGEABLENESS, MOTION.

move, *v.* transport, impel, actuate, incite, arouse, INFLUENCE, propose; stir, act; remove. See CAUSE, EXCITEMENT, OFFER.

movement, *n.* MOTION, gesture; maneuver; progress; crusade, drive; works, workings. See ACTIVITY.

movie, *n.* MOTION PICTURES. See DRAMA.

moving, *adj.* motile; stirring; touching, affecting; impressive, exciting. See MOTION, FEELING.

mow, *v.t.* cut, clip, reap, scythe. See AGRICULTURE, SHORTNESS.

moxie, *n., slang,* COURAGE, pluck, spunk.

much, *n.* abundance, ample, plenty, a lot, a great deal, a volume; wealth, sufficiency. —*adj.* many; abundant, ample, copious, plentiful, profuse. See GREATNESS. *Ant.,* little.

muck, *n.* dirt, foulness, filth, slime, mud; pornography, smut, obscenity. See UNCLEANNESS.

muckraker, *n.* reformer, scandal- *or* gossipmonger. See DETRACTION.

mud, *n.* mire, muck, ooze, gumbo. See UNCLEANNESS, COHERENCE.

muddle, *n.* confusion, mess, DISORDER, befuddlement. See ABSURDITY. —**muddle through,** manage, scrape along. See SUFFICIENCY.

mudslinger, *n.* slanderer, muckraker; character assassin. See DETRACTION.

muffin, *n.* bun, roll. See FOOD.

muffle, *v.t.* deaden, stifle, mute, dampen; wrap up, swathe, envelop. See SILENCE, CONCEALMENT.

muffler, *n.* scarf, comforter; silencer, deadener. See CLOTHING, SILENCE.

mug, *n.* cup, stein, tankard; *slang,* face, puss, kisser; *slang,* fool, dolt, clod; *slang,* gangster, mobster, thug. See RECEPTACLE, FRONT. —*v., slang,* pose, posture, make faces, ham [it up] (*sl.*); assault, assail, attack, stick up, hold up. See DRAMA, FEELING, STEALING.

muggy, *adj.* dank, oppressive, sultry, sticky. See MOISTURE.

mule, *n.* hinny, crossbreed; intransigent, pighead. See ANIMAL, OBSTINACY.

mulish, *adj.* obstinate, stubborn, headstrong. See OBSTINACY.

mull, *v.* think, reflect, consider, ruminate, ponder. See THOUGHT.

multilateral, *adj.* many-sided, multifaceted. See SIDE.

multiformity, *n.* variety, diversity; multifariousness, diversification. See DIFFERENCE.

multiple, *adj.* manifold, numerous. See MULTITUDE.

multiplication, *n.* procreation, REPRODUCTION; INCREASE, productiveness. See NUMERATION, MULTITUDE.

multiply, *v.* INCREASE, accrue; propagate proliferate; spread. See NUMERATION, REPRODUCTION. *Ant.*, divide.

MULTITUDE
Large number

Nouns—1, multitude, numerousness, multiplicity, profusion, plurality. See QUANTITY.

2, legion, host, horde, crowd, [great] numbers, quite a few, quite a number, good *or* great many, array, army, sea, galaxy, scores, peck, bushel, swarm, bevy, cloud, flock, herd, drove, flight, covey, hive, brood, litter, farrow. *Informal,* lots, gobs, stacks, heaps, scads, oodles, barrels, rafts, piles, millions, passel, any number. See POPULACE.

3, greater number, majority; INFINITY; multiplication. See INCREASE.

Verbs—1, be numerous, swarm, teem, crowd; outnumber, multiply, proliferate, swarm like locusts.

2, produce in multitudes, churn out.

Adjectives—many, several, sundry, divers, various, not a few, many a; plural; ever so many, numerous, endless, countless, numberless, myriad, legion, profuse, manifold, multiplied, multitudinous, multiple, teeming, swarming, pullulating, populous, crowded, thick, studded; a world of, no end of, thick as fleas, infinite, untold. *Slang,* lousy with, alive with.

Adverbs—galore; in force, en masse; by the dozen, hundreds, *or* thousands; countlessly, numberlessly, infinitely, *etc. Informal,* hand over foot.

Phrases—the more the merrier; there is safety in numbers; too many cooks spoil the broth; two is company, but three is none *or* a crowd.

Quotations—I am large, I contain multitudes (*Walt Whitman*), There is but little virtue in the action of masses of men (*Henry Thoreau*), The people are a many-headed beast (*Horace*).

Antonyms, see RARITY, UNITY.

---

mum, *adj.* mute, dumb, speechless, inarticulate; tight-lipped. See SILENCE. *Ant.*, talkative.

mumble, *v.t.* mutter, murmur, mouth. See STAMMERING.

mumbo-jumbo, *n.* fetish; incantation, hocus-pocus; gibberish, jargon, nonsense. See SORCERY.

mummy, *n.* corpse, cadaver. See DEATH.

munch, *v.* chew, masticate, crunch, nibble, eat. See FOOD.

mundane, *adj.* worldly, earthly; temporal, carnal. See IRRELIGION.

municipal, *adj.* civic, civil, city; local; governmental. See ABODE, AUTHORITY.

munificent, *adj.* generous, liberal, lavish, bounteous, bountiful, freehanded, openhanded; benevolent, philanthropic, charitable, altruistic; unsparing, princely, profuse. See LIBERALITY. *Ant.*, ungenerous, stingy.

munitions, *n.pl.* See ARMS.

mural, *n.* wall painting, fresco; mosaic; shoji. See PAINTING.

murder, *n.* homicide, manslaughter. See KILLING.

murderer, *n.* assassin, manslayer, cutthroat; killer, butcher. See KILLING.

murderous, *adj.* bloodthirsty, sanguinary, deadly, brutal. See KILLING.

murk, *n.* gloom, haze, dusk, dark, blackness, obscurity. See CLOUDINESS, DARKNESS.

murky, *adj.* dark, gloomy; obscure, hazy. See OBSCURITY, DARKNESS.

murmur, *v.i.* mumble, mutter, grumble;

rustle, purl, ripple; whisper, breathe. See LAMENTATION.

muscle, *n.* thew, tendon, sinew; musculature, build, physique, huskiness, beef, weight, burliness; STRENGTH, brawn, power; armed might, arms, firepower.

muscular, *adj.* strong, brawny, sinewy, vigorous. See STRENGTH.

muse, *v.i.* ponder, meditate, dream, ruminate. See THOUGHT.

musette, *n.* bagpipe, chanter. See MUSIC.

museum, *n.* gallery, repository, archives. See STORE.

mush, *n.* porridge, pottage, oatmeal, cereal; pap, sop, corn (*sl.*); *informal,* sentimentality, emotionalism, romance. See FEELING, SOFTNESS, FOOD.

mushroom, *v.i.* boom, INCREASE, expand, swell, puff up, snowball (*inf.*). See EXPANSION.

mushy, *adj.* pulpy; sentimental, mawkish, maudlin. See SENSIBILITY.

MUSIC
Organized sound

*Nouns—*1, music; classical, semiclassical, *or* popular music, rock [& roll] music, country [and western] music, world music; acid, punk, hard metal, hard, *or* soft rock; soul [music], blues; swing, jive, boogie-woogie, progressive jazz, bop, bebop, third stream, stomp; hillbilly *or* country music, rockabilly; western music; concert, light, *or* dinner music, Tafelmusik, Muzak, Hausmusik; electronic music, musique concrète; serial music, minimalism. *Informal,* longhair *or* pop music, pops, canned music.

2, composition, opus, arrangement, movement; full score, [musical] score, [piano] vocal score, miniature score, piano-conductor score; book, fake book. *Slang,* maps.

3, instrumental music; chamber music, incidental music, suite; solo, duo, duet, trio [sonata], quartet, quintet, sextet, septet, octet, nonet, dectet; prelude, sonata, rondo, rondeau, pastorale, concerto, concertino, concerto grosso, concert, musicale, overture, symphony, divertissement, fantasy, fantasia, partita; cadenza, cadence; fugue, toccata, round, canon; serenade, nocturne, prelude, adagio, minuet; lullaby; dirge, pibroch; march.

4, vocal music; [Gregorian *or* Anglican] chant, psalm, psalmody, plainsong, response, evensong; hymn, anthem; melody, strain, tune, air; song, canticle, lay, ballad, ditty, carol, pastoral, recitative, aria; sea chantey, work song, folk song, popular song, ballad, jingle; yodeling, crooning; part song, descant, glee, madrigal, catch, round, canon, chorus, antiphony; cantata, oratorio; [light *or* comic] opera, operetta, music[al] theater, musical comedy.

5, dance music, syncopation, ragtime, jazz; bolero, fandango, tango, mazurka, gavotte, minuet, polka, waltz, two-step, fox trot, reel, jig, hornpipe, conga, rumba, samba, cha-cha; rock [& roll]. See DANCE.

6, *(popular music)* **a.** rock, [deep *or* acid] house, acid rock, acoustic rock, techno, jungle, trip-hop, electronica, alternative rock, disco, doo-wop, folk rock, funk, groove, fusion, gangsta rap, glitter rock, hard rock, heavy metal, hip-hop, jungle, Motown, new wave, bluebeat, power pop, psychedelic music, punk rock, rhythm and blues, rap, rave, reggae, rock & roll, scratch, shockabilly, grunge, homocore, ska, soft rock, soul, stadium rock, surf music, thrash, zydeco. *Slang,* cock rock. **b.** jazz, groove, hambone, barrelhouse, [be]bop, big band, blues, boogie-woogie, fusion, high life, naked *or* gutbucket jazz, honky-tonk, cool jazz, Dixieland, hot jazz, swing, ragtime, progressive jazz, New Orleans *or* Kansas City jazz, ragtime. **c.** country [and western] music, rockabilly, western rock, downhome, bluegrass, folk music, gospel, jug band, protest music, skiffle. **d.** popular music, easy listening. *Slang,* ear candy, elevator music.

7, world music, raga, klezmer, Cajun, Goa, gagaku, mbaqanga, salsa, soca, zouk, lambada, zydeco.

8, *(musical instruments)* **a.** musical instrument; orchestra, [marching] band, chamber orchestra, palm court orchestra, combo, dance band; jug band, jazz band; mariachi, gagaku orchestra, gamelan. *Slang,* ax. **b.** strings, winds, drums, percussion, woodwinds, reeds, brass, horns. **c.** harp, lyre, lute, dulcimer, mandolin, guitar, gittern, cithern, cither, zither, theorbo, psaltery, ukulele, banjo, koto, sitar; violin, fiddle, Cremona, Stradivarius, Amati, Guarnerius; [violon]cello, viol, viola, viola da braccio *or* da gamba, bass viol. *Slang,* air guitar. **d.** piano[forte], grand, baby grand, spinet, upright [piano]; harpsichord, clavichord, virginal; fortepiano; celeste, keyboard glockenspiel. *Slang,* eighty-eights. **e.** [pipe *or* electronic] organ, harmonium, barrel organ; hurdy-gurdy, Aeolian harp, calliope; siren; pipe, pitchpipe, flute, fife, piccolo, flageolet, clarinet; oboe, hautboy, shawm, bassoon, bombarde; cornet, bugle, trumpet, [French] horn, serpent, saxhorn, trombone, sackbut, saxophone; accordion, concertina; bagpipes, whistle, ocarina; althorn, tuba; harmonica, Melodica; mouth organ, kazoo; jew's harp, gewgaw. *Slang,* squawk box; squeeze box; sax[e]; harp[oon]; licorice stick. **f.** cymbal, bell, gong, tambour, tambourine, snare *or* trap drum, bass drum, bongo, tomtom; kettledrum, tympanum; timbal, timbrel; steel drums; castanets; musical glasses, sounding board, rattle, bones; triangle; Jew's harp; xylophone, marimba, vibraphone *or* -harp; glockenspiel. *Slang,* skins, woodpile. **g.** baton, wand, stick; drumsticks; music stand, podium; metronome; tuning bar, box, fork, *or* hammer.

9, *(musical terms)* staff, key, bar, space, [C, G, F, treble, soprano, mezzo-soprano, alto, tenor, baritone, violin, *or* bass] clef, [key *or* time] signature, note, grace note, tone, rest; tie, slur; pitch; accent, accidental; barline; [pentatonic, whole tone, minor, *or* major] scale, mode, gamut, degree; [double] flat *or* sharp; microtone, quartertone, interval, unison, second, semitone, whole tone, third, fourth, fifth, sixth, seventh, octave, diabolus in musica; supertonic, mediant, subdominant, dominant, superdominant, submediant, subtonic, leading tone; beat, downbeat, upbeat, tempo, rhythm, polyrhythm, rubato, syncopation; harmony, changes, counterpoint, homophony, dissonance, consonance; ornament, embellishment, mordent, trill, turn, roulade, coloratura, tremolo; touch, expression, solmization, fingering; [basso] continuo; theme, melody, tune, tone row; chord, triad, tone cluster, voicing; triplet, quintuplet, duplet; glissando, portamento; solo, duet, duo, trio, quartet, quintet; accompaniment, second. *Slang,* lick.

10, *(the music business)* performance, execution, set, set list; tour, roadie; jam session, hootenanny; eisteddfod, concert *or* recital hall; opera house; rock concert, mosh pit, crowd surging, head walking; airplay, playlist, disc jockey, deejay, DJ, video jockey, VJ, American Bandstand; recording, session, A- *or* B-side, cut, single, album, cassingle, LP, 45, long *or* extended play, compact disc, CD, cassette, DAT, eight-track tape, jukebox, karaoke, music video; cover, soundalike, original, standard, oldie, crossover hit, race record; *Billboard, Downbeat,* fanzine; MTV, Much Music, Tin Pan Alley; Grammy, hit parade, charts. *Informal,* payola; groupie, headbanger, metalhead, deadhead. *Slang,* def jam, gig, platter, beat box, ghetto blaster, rasta box.

11, *(musicians)* **a.** musician, artist[e], performer, sideman, player; band, ensemble; [pickup *or* studio] band, garage band; pop group, rock band; talent. *Slang,* muso, solid sender, longhairs. **b.** instrumentalist; organist, pianist; flutist, flautist, fifer, oboist, clarinetist, bassoonist, saxophonist; violinist, fiddler, violist, cellist, bassist; harper, harpist; bugler, trumpeter, horn player, trombonist; percussionist, tympanist, drummer; accordionist. *Slang,* hide-beater, mice. **c.** vocalist, melodist, singer, warbler, backup singer, minnesinger, troubadour, minstrel, bard, chanter, cantor, chantress, songstress, caroler, chorister; crooner, blues singer, folk singer, yodeler, calypso singer, scat singer, patter singer; soprano, mezzo[-soprano], [contr]alto, countertenor, tenor, baritone, bass-baritone, bass, buffo, falsettist, castrato; songbird, nightingale, philomel, thrush, mockingbird; Orpheus, Apollo, the Muses, Euterpe, Terpsichore; siren, Lorelei. *Slang,* bird, canary, chorine. **d.** dancer, coryphée, ballet dancer, ballerina. See AMUSEMENT. **e.** conductor, bandmaster, choirmaster; leader, concertmaster, first violin; composer, arranger, orchestra, scorer.

12, *(study of music)* musicology, ethno[musicology], world music, eurythmics, orchestration, instrumentation, music theory.

Verbs—compose, arrange, adapt, set to music, transpose, melodize, harmonize, orchestrate, score; accompany; execute, perform, play, sing, pipe, fiddle, beat the drum, blow *or* sound the horn, twang, plunk, pluck, pick, thrum, strum; strike up, tune up; keep time; sing, chant, hum, warble, carol, chirp, chirrup, trill, twitter, whistle, intone, lilt. *Informal,* belt. *Slang,* scratch, kick, rap, break, bust out, chat, cut, drop, freak, jam, throw out, bear down, blow down, count it off, busk.

Adjectives—1, musical, instrumental, vocal, choral, singing, lyric, operatic; harmonious, melodious, tuneful, melodic, symphonic, orchestral; classical, popular. *Informal,* longhair, pop.

2, in tune, on pitch; chromatic, atonal, diatonic, enharmonic, pentatonic; parlando; pianissimo, piano, mezzo-piano *or* -forte, forte, fortissimo; major, minor, augmented diminished, perfect.

Adverbs—adagio, lento, andante, andantino, allegretto, allegro, vivace, presto, vivo; rallentando, ritardando, ritenuto, stringendo; diminuendo, crescendo; legato, sostenuto, marcato, staccato.

Quotations—If music be the food of love, play on (*Shakespeare*), Music has charms to soothe a savage breast (*William Congreve*), Jazz music is to be played sweet, soft, plenty rhythm (*Jelly Roll Morton*), The hills are alive with the sound of music (*Oscar Hammerstein II*), Playing "bop" is like Scrabble with all the vowels missing (*Duke Ellington*), A musician, if he's a messenger, is like a child who hasn't been handled too many times by man, hasn't had too many fingerprints across his brain (*Jimi Hendrix*), Today if something is not worth saying, people sing it (*Pierre-Augustin Caron de Beaumarchais*), [Of Negro spirituals:] Every tone was a testimony against slavery, and a prayer to God for deliverance from chains (*Frederick Douglass*), The heart of the melody can never be put down on paper (*Pablo Casals*), Opera . . . could not have been foreseen by any logical process (*Sir Kenneth Clark*), Opera's no business, it's a disease (*Oscar Hammerstein I*).

---

musket, *n.* firearm; flintlock, blunderbuss; brown Bess. See ARMS.

musketeer, *n.* rifleman, soldier. See COMBATANT.

muss, *n.* DISORDER, tangle, confusion, mix-up, mess, muddle.

must, *v.* ought, should, had better, have [got] to, need, needs must, have no choice [but to]; be required, obliged, bound, compelled, doomed, destined, *etc.* See NECESSITY.

mustache, *n.* hairline, toothbrush, Charlie Chaplin, Hitler, Kaiser Wilhelm, waxed, handlebar, *or* walrus mustache; soup strainer, tickler, cookie duster (*all sl.*). See ROUGHNESS.

muster, *v.t.* assemble, collect, gather, mobilize; poll. See ASSEMBLAGE.

musty, *adj.* stale, fusty, moldy. See DETERIORATION.

mutation, *n.* CHANGE, variation, deviation; mutant, freak, aberrancy, monster.

mute, *v.* See SILENCE.

mutilate, *v.t.* maim, destroy, cripple; disfigure, deface, mar. See DISTORTION, DETERIORATION, FORMLESSNESS.

mutiny, *n.* rebellion, revolt, uprising, insurrection, insurgence. See DISOBEDIENCE.

mutter, *v.* murmur, grumble, mumble, growl. See LAMENTATION, STAMMERING.

mutual, *adj.* reciprocal, common, joint, correlative. See INTERCHANGE, PARTY.

muzzle, *v.i.* restrain, bridle, gag, SILENCE, throttle.

myriad, *adj.* innumerable, multitudinous, teeming. See MULTITUDE.

mystery, *n.* SECRET, enigma, puzzle, cabala; rite, sacrament. See CONCEALMENT, LATENCY, OBSCURITY, UNINTELLIGIBILITY.

mystic, *adj.* hidden, SECRET; mysterious; esoteric, occult. See CONCEALMENT.

mystify, *v.t.* puzzle, perplex, bewilder, obscure, confound, baffle. See CONCEALMENT, DECEPTION.

mystique, *n.* aura, mystery, charisma. See SPECIALITY.

myth, *n.* legend, tradition; phantasy, fiction. See IMAGINATION.

mythical, *adj.* unreal; fabulous, fictitious, mythological. See IMAGINATION, MYTHICAL DEITIES.

MYTHICAL DEITIES

Nouns—1, mythical deities, heathen gods and goddesses; god[dess], DEITY, divinity, demigod; pantheon, mythology, folklore.

2, *(Greece)* Zeus, [Phoebus] Apollo[n], Ares, Hephaestus, Hermes, Poseidon, Hades, Eros, Helios, Dionysus, Aeolus, Comus, Hymen, Hypnus, Morpheus, Plutus, Priapus, Thanatos, Zephyrus; Hera, [Pallas] Athena, Artemis, Aphrodite, Amphitrite, Chloris, Demeter, Eos, Eris, Hebe, Hecate, Hestia, Hygeia, Nemesis, Nike, Nyxe, Selene, Tyche; *(Titans)* Uranus, Gaea, Cronos, Oceanus, Coeus, Crius, Hyperion, Rhea, Mnemosyne, Themis, Phoebe, Dione, Cyclops, Helios.

3, *(Rome)* Jupiter, Jove, Apollo, Mars, Vulcan, Mercury, Neptune, Pluto, Orcus, Dis, Mors, Saturn, Cupid, Bacchus, Liber, Comus, Faunus, Janus, Pan, Picus, Sol, Somnus; Juno, Minerva, Diana, Venus, Aurora, Ceres, Flora, Juventas, Kore, Persephone, Luna, Nox, Pomona, Proserpina, Psyche, Salacia, Vesta, Victoria.

4, *(Scandinavia)* Woden, Odin, Thor, Balder, Loki, Bragi, Njord; Freya, Frigg, Sigurd, Brynhild, Gudrun, Fafnir, the Valkyries.

5, *(India)* Janaki, Sita, Ravana, Kama, Hanuman, Kubera, Mahakala, Surya.

6, *(Egypt)* Ra, Ptah, Osiris, Horus, Set[h], Anubis, Thoth, Amun-Ra, Geb; Isis, Hathor, Nut.

7, *(Middle East)* Baal, Bel, Astarte, Ashtoreth, Ishtar, Ashur, Anshar, Anu, Ea, Enlil, Marduk, Mot, Sin, Tammuz; Cybele, Gula.

8, *(Far East)* Benten, Daikoku, Emma-O, Fu-hsing; Kuan-Yin.

9, *(Americas)* Huitzilopochtli, Inti, Tialoc, Xipe, Xochipilli; Pauguk, Thunderbird.

10, *(Celtic)* Lug, Rhiannon, Tuatha Dé Danann.

11, *(Oceania)* Maui.

12, *(mythical water creature)* nymph, dryad, hamadryad, naiad, nereid, oread; sylph; salamander, undine; Pan, faun, satyr; mermaid, merman.

13, *(mythical land creature)* fairy, fay, sprite, elf, brownie, pixie, pixy, Puck, Robin Goodfellow, dwarf, gnome, troll, kobold, peri, hobgoblin, leprechaun; wee folk, little *or* good people, good neighbors; manitou; fairy godmother *or* -father.

14, *(evil spirit)* familiar spirit, familiar, genius, genie, jinni; chimera; DEMON, incubus, succubus, vampire, harpy, werewolf; ogre, ogress.

Adjectives—mythical, mythological, legendary; fairylike, nymphlike, elfin, fey.

Quotations—Science must begin with myths, and with the criticism of myths (*Karl Popper*), It is convenient that there be gods, and, as it is convenient, let us believe that there are (*Ovid*).

N

nab, *v.t., informal,* grab, catch, seize; latch on to; corner, tree, ensnare; take prisoner, collar (*sl.*), pinch (*sl.*). See RESTRAINT.

nadir, *n.* low point, bottom, the pits (*sl.*). See DEPTH, LOWNESS. *Ant.,* zenith.

nag, *n., informal,* pony; jade, hack, plug (*sl.*). See ANIMAL. —*v.* pester, badger, scold; fret, complain; irritate, annoy, plague. See DISCONTENT, EVILDOER.

nail, *n.* fingernail, toenail, ungula; talon, claw; tack, brad, spoke; hobnail, clout; pin, peg. —*v.t.* pin, fix; *informal,* capture, catch. See JUNCTION, RESTRAINT.

naive, *adj.* ingenuous, unsophisticated, unworldly, artless. See SIMPLENESS, CREDULITY. *Ant.,* knowing, sophisticated.

naked, *adj.* uncovered, stripped, bare; nude, unclothed, unclad, unappareled; plain, undisguised. See DIVESTMENT, SIMPLENESS. *Ant.,* clothed, covered.

namby-pamby, *adj.* insipid, mediocre; sentimental, maudlin; weak, pansyish, effeminate. See INSIPIDITY, SENSIBILITY, WEAKNESS. *Ant.,* strong.

name, *n.* nomen (see NOMENCLATURE); reputation, fame, REPUTE. —*v.t.* [en]title, call, designate, christen; appoint, nominate; style; mention, specify. See COMMISSION.

nameless, *adj.* anonymous, unnamed; obscure, unknown, unchristened, illegitimate; untitled, inglorious, unnamable, abominable, indescribable. See NOMENCLATURE, DISREPUTE.

namely, *conj. & adv.* to wit, as follows, specifically, viz., videlicet, that is [to say], i.e. See SPECIALITY, INTERPRETATION.

nanny, *n.* nurse[maid], amah, ayah, baby-sitter. See SAFETY.

nap, *n.* doze, sleep; pile, surface, TEXTURE. See REPOSE.

nape, *n.* scruff, scuff, nuque, scrag. See CONNECTION.

napkin, *n.* linen, serviette, wipe (*sl.*); towel, diaper, handkerchief; sanitary napkin, maxi- *or* minipad, tampon. See CLEANNESS.

narcissism, *n.* self-love, VANITY. *Ant.,* selfless.

narcotic, *n.* soporific, anesthetic; opiate, anodyne; dope, drug; sedative, tranquilizer. —*adj.* stupefying, narcotizing, tranquilizing. See INSENSIBILITY, REMEDY, HABIT, DRUGS.

narrate, *v.* describe, tell, relate; recount, recite; inform, rehearse; record, state, report, retail. See DESCRIPTION.

narrative, *n.* story, tale, anecdote, DESCRIPTION.

narrow, *adj.* limited, restricted (see NARROWNESS).

narrow-minded, *adj.* bigoted; small, mean, intolerant. See NARROWNESS, MISJUDGMENT. *Ant.,* broad-minded.

NARROWNESS
Restricted width

Nouns—1, narrowness, closeness, exiguity, LITTLENESS; thinness, tenuity, emaciation; narrowing; tapering, CONTRACTION; finger's- *or* hair's-breadth, line; strip, streak, vein.

2, shaving, chip; FILAMENT, thread, hair; sylph; neck, waist, isthmus, hourglass; pass; ravine, narrows, strait, gap; film, membrane (see LAYER).

3, skeleton, shadow, spindleshanks, lantern jaws, skin and bone[s]. *Slang,* rattlebones, long drink of water, stringbean.

Verbs—narrow, taper [off]; slice, shave, pare, trim, thin [down *or* out], slim, reduce, attenuate; waste away.

Adjectives—1, narrow, close; slender, thin, fine, gracile; threadlike, finespun, slim; wasp-waisted; scant[y]; tenuous, spare, delicate; contracted.

2, emaciated, lean, meager, gaunt, sinewy, rawboned, lank[y], gangling, gawky, scraggy, gangly, bony, reedy, skinny, thin as a rail, wasp-waisted, bareboned, flat-chested; svelte; starved, attenuated, shriveled, worn to a shadow; slender-waisted, waspish.

3, confined, limited; cramped, pinched, close, tight, constricted.

Adverbs—barely, only, just.

Quotations—Strait is the gate, and narrow is the way, which leadeth unto life, and few there be that find it (*Bible*), I'm fat, but I'm thin inside. Has it ever struck you that there's a thin man inside every fat man? (*George Orwell*), We hope that the world will not narrow into a neighborhood before it has broadened into a brotherhood (*L. B. Johnson*).

Antonyms, see BREADTH, LIBERALITY.

---

narrows, *n.pl.* strait, channel (see NARROWNESS, NAVIGATION).

nasal, *adj.* rhinal, adenoidal; twangy. See BODY, SPEECH.

nascent, *adj.* rudimentary, embryonic (see BEGINNING).

nasty, *adj.* foul, filthy; distasteful, disgusting, horrid; dirty; nauseating, loathsome; indecent, obscene; ill-tempered, disagreeable, dangerous. See UNCLEANNESS, IMPURITY, DISCOURTESY.

nation, *n.* country, state, realm; republic, kingdom, empire; sovereignty, AUTHORITY, polity, body politic; commonwealth, community; tribe, people. See HUMANITY.

national, *adj.* federal, countrywide, nationwide; governmental, public; nationalistic, patriotic. See AUTHORITY. —*n.* citizen, subject. See INHABITANT, SUBJECTION.

nationalism, *n.* patriotism, civism, paternalism; chauvinism, spread-eagleism (*inf.*); socialism, totalitarianism. See PRIDE, AUTHORITY.

nationality, *n.* citizenship; nation. See HUMANITY, REGION.

native, *n.* INHABITANT, aborigine, countryman. —*adj.* indigenous; innate, inherent; aboriginal; endemic, natal, natural. See INTRINSIC.

Native American, *n.* [American] Indian (see HUMANITY).

nativity, *n.* birth. See REPRODUCTION, BEGINNING.

natty, *adj., informal,* smart, chic, stylish, modish, dapper, snappy (*inf*). See FASHION. *Ant.,* dowdy, square.

natural, *adj.* unaffected, spontaneous, artless, unstudied; unsophisticated, naive, ingenuous; normal, ordinary, regular; unadorned, unadulterated; inherent, innate, inborn. See SIMPLENESS, INTRINSIC, CONFORMITY, INTUITION, UNPREPAREDNESS. *Ant.,* unnatural, affected.

naturalist, *n.* zoologist, herpetologist, botanist, horticulturalist, ichthyologist, geologist, arborist, arboriculturist, *etc.* See ANIMAL, VEGETABLE.

naturalize, *v.t.* confer citizenship on, admit (see REGION).

nature, *n.* character, type, sort, kind; essence, basis, essential; constitution, quality; disposition, structure; temperament, bent, CLASS, form; heart; creation, universe. See FEELING, INTRINSIC, TENDENCY.

naturist, *n.* nudist (see DIVESTMENT).

naughty, *adj.* disobedient, wayward, mischievous, troublesome, perverse; improper. See DISOBEDIENCE, IMPURITY. *Ant.,* obedient, nice.

nausea, *n.* qualm, seasickness, queasiness; disgust, aversion, loathing. See DISEASE, DISLIKE.

nauseate, *v.t.* sicken, disgust, revolt. See PAIN, DISEASE.

nautical, *adj.* marine, maritime; ocean-going. See NAVIGATION.

naval, *adj.* nautical, maritime. See NAVIGATION, COMBATANT, WARFARE.

navel, *n.* belly button. See BODY.

NAVIGATION
Travel on water

Nouns—1, navigation; celestial navigation, dead reckoning; circumnavigation; pilotage, steerage; seamanship; navigability.

2, *(active boating)* boating, yachting, yacht racing, sailing, cruising, voyaging, seafaring; oarsmanship, rowing, sculling, crew, canoeing, paddling, kayaking; boardsailing, sailboarding. See SHIP, TRAVEL.

3, *(travel in a boat)* voyage, sail, cruise; leg; crossing; boat *or* yacht race, regatta (see CONTENTION); maneuvers.

4, *(navigational terms)* progress, way; headway, sternway, leeway; sideslip; seaway, [inland *or* coastal] waterway, sea lane (see PASSAGE); buoy (see INDICATION); preacher, deadhead.

5, *(one who works on a boat)* navigator, sailor, mariner, seaman, seafarer, tar, jack, old salt, able seaman, AB; bluejacket, marine, naval cadet, midshipman, middy; captain, skipper, mate; ferryman, bargeman, bargee; longshoreman, stevedore; gondolier, rower, sculler, canoeist, paddler, oarsman; boatswain, coxswain, bosun, steersman, leadsman, helmsman, pilot (see DIRECTION); crew, watch, all hands; shellback. *Slang,* sea dog, barnacle.

6, *(boat storage)* anchorage, dock[age], [boat] basin, wharf, quay, port, harbor; marina.

Verbs—1, navigate, sail, steam, cruise; take bearings, pilot, steer, helm (see DIRECTION); cast off, set sail, put to sea, take ship, weigh anchor, get under way, spread sail, have sail (see DEPARTURE); make [head]way, plow the deep, buffet the waves, ride the storm, hug the shore; sail against *or* into the wind, warp, luff, scud, float, coast; hold a course; drift, yaw; careen, list (see OBLIQUITY); tack, jibe, come about; back water; heave into sight, heave to; nose in, bring to; lie *or* lay to; circumnavigate; put in, cast anchor, moor, dock (see ARRIVAL); shipwreck, beach, go aground; scuttle; capsize, founder, sink.

2, row, oar, paddle, feather, pull, scull, punt, raft, float.

Adjectives—sailing, seafaring, nautical, maritime, marine, naval, afloat; seagoing, oceangoing; adrift, afloat, aweigh; navigable.

Adverbs—under way, sail, canvas, *or* steam; before *or* against the wind; at anchor; aft, abaft, astern; aground; overboard; on board [ship], on deck, topside; aloft.

Interjections—ahoy! ship ahoy! avast! belay! steady as you go!

Phrases—the good seaman is known in bad weather; heaven protects children, sailors, and drunken men.

Quotations—There is nothing more enticing, disenchanting, and enslaving than the life at sea (*Joseph Conrad*), There is *nothing*—absolutely nothing—half so much worth doing as simply messing about in boats (*Kenneth Grahame*), He that will learn to pray, let him go to sea (*George Herbert*), His heart was mailed with oak and triple brass who first committed a frail ship to the wild seas (*Horace*), Being in a ship is being in jail, with the chance of being drowned (*Samuel Johnson*).

---

navy, *n.* fleet; ships, warships. See COMBATANT, WARFARE.

Nazi, *n.* & *adj.* fascist, Hitlerite, racist; National Socialist, NSDAP; reactionary, economic royalist; brownshirt, black-

shirt; authoritarian, totalitarian. See AUTHORITY.

Neanderthal, *adj.* savage, barbarous; uncivilized, unrefined. See VIOLENCE. *Ant.,* refined, cultured.

NEARNESS
Proximity without touching

Nouns—1, nearness, closeness, proximity, propinquity, apposition, approximation, vicinity, neighborhood, adjacency; APPROACH, CONVERGENCE; likeness, SIMILARITY. See FUTURITY.

2, short distance, step, *or* way; shortcut; earshot; close-up, close quarters, close range, stone's throw, hair's-breadth; span.

3, purlieus, neighborhood, vicinage, environs, suburbs, outskirts, confines, borderland. See ENVIRONMENT.

4, bystander, neighbor; abutter, tangent (see CONTACT). *Informal*, tailgater.

Verbs—1, adjoin, hang about, touch *or* border on, verge upon; stand by, approximate, tread on the heels of, cling to, clasp, hug; hover over.

2, near, draw *or* come near, APPROACH; converge, crowd, press. *Informal*, tailgate.

Adjectives—near, nigh, close *or* near at hand; close, neighboring; adjacent, adjoining, proximate; impending, imminent, oncoming, at [close] hand, handy; near the mark; intimate, close to home.

Adverbs—1, near, nigh; hard, close, *or* fast by; close to, at the point of; within reach, call, *or* earshot, next door to, within an ace *or* inch of, on hand, at one's door[step], at one's elbow, but a step, not far from, at no great distance; on the verge *or* brink of; on the outskirts, in the neighborhood of, in the offing, around the corner, at one's fingertips, on the tip of one's tongue, under one's nose, on one's heels, in one's pocket; within a stone's throw, in sight of, at close quarters; cheek by jowl; beside, alongside, side by side, tête-à-tête; in juxtaposition, at the threshold, bordering upon, in the way.

2, nearly, almost, about, thereabouts, circa, *or* so; roughly, in round numbers; approximately, more *or* less, as good as, well nigh; all but.

Quotations—Stand by thyself, come not near me: for I am holier than thou (*Bible*).

Antonyms, see DISTANCE.

---

nearsighted, *adj.* shortsighted, myopic. See VISION. *Ant.,* farsighted.

neat, *adj.* tidy, orderly; compact, trim, shapely; pure, unmixed; deft, skillful, adroit; pat, felicitous. See CLEANNESS, SIMPLENESS, ORDER. *Ant.,* messy, disorderly.

nebulous, *adj.* nebular; cloudy, hazy; amorphous, indistinct, unclear, confused, vague, turbid. See DIMNESS, FORMLESSNESS.

necessity, *n.* need (see NECESSITY); COMPULSION; POVERTY.

NECESSITY
What must happen

Nouns—1, necessity, necessitation, obligation, COMPULSION, subjection; needfulness, essentiality, indispensability; dire *or* cruel necessity, inexorable fate; what must be; force majeure.

2, requirement, need, want, requisite, demand; urgency, exigency; bread and butter, breath of life; sine qua non, matter of life and death; stress, pinch. See CERTAINTY, POVERTY, DESIRE.

3, DESTINY, fatality, foredoom, foreordination.

4, reflex, reaction, automatic response; RECOIL.

5, Fates, Parcae, three Sisters, book of fate; God's will, will of heaven, will of Allah; wheel of fortune; Hobson's choice; last shift *or* resort.

Verbs—1, lie under a necessity; be doomed *or* destined, be in for, be under the necessity of, have no choice *or* alternative, cannot [help] but, have one's back to the wall, be driven into a corner; burn one's bridges *or* boats. *Informal*, take it or leave it.

2, necessitate, demand, require, call for, entail; must; destine, doom, foredoom, predestine, preordain; compel, force, oblige, constrain.

Adjectives—1, necessary, needful, required, requisite, essential, imperative, indispensable, in demand; compulsory, obligatory, uncontrollable, inevitable, unavoidable, irresistible, irrevocable, inexorable, ineluctable; urgent, exigent, pressing, crying; instant.

2, fated, destined, preordained, fateful, doomed; hooked (see HABIT).

3, involuntary, instinctive, automatic, blind, mechanical, unconscious, unwitting, unthinking, impulsive. *Informal,* knee-jerk.

Adverbs—necessarily, of necessity, of course, needs must, perforce, willing or unwilling, willy-nilly, compulsorily; like it or not.

Phrases—any port in a storm; beggars can't be choosers; necessity is the mother of invention; sink or swim.

Quotations—Necessity never made a good bargain (*Benjamin Franklin*), The superfluous, a very necessary thing (*Voltaire*), Necessity knows no law (*Publilius Syrus*), The true creator is necessity, which is the mother of our invention (*Plato*), I know this—a man got to do what he got to do (*John Steinbeck*), Great necessities call out great virtues (*Abigail Adams*).

Antonyms, see WILL, CHOICE.

---

neck, *n.* channel, isthmus, strait, pass; cervix; constriction, narrowing; scruff, nape. See NARROWNESS, CONVEXITY, CONNECTION. —*v.i., slang,* make love, pet, make out (*inf.*), smooch (*inf.*). See ENDEARMENT.

necklace, *n.* beads, chain, string, pearls; pendant, lavaliere; collar, choker. See PENDENCY, ORNAMENT, CIRCULARITY.

necktie, *n.* tie, cravat, scarf; string, bow, four-in-hand, Ascot, Windsor, half-Windsor, black, white, *etc.* tie; neckwear. See CLOTHING.

necrology, *n.* obituary. See DEATH.

necromancy, *n.* SORCERY, enchantment, magic.

nectar, *n.* honey[dew]. See SWEETNESS.

need, *n.* NECESSITY, requirement; DESIRE, want, privation, lack, POVERTY; USE. —*v.t.* require, crave, claim, demand, yearn; lack, want.

needful, *adj.* necessary, requisite (see NECESSARY). *Ant.,* needless.

needle, *n.* obelisk, Cleopatra's needle; thorn, prickle; stylus; syringe. See SHARPNESS. —*v.t., informal,* rib, josh, tease, RIDICULE, heckle, prick, goad; harass, torment, ride. See DISCONTENT.

needless, *adj.* unnecessary, pointless, purposeless, superfluous. See USELESSNESS. *Ant.,* needful.

needlework, *n.* darning, stitching, sewing, embroidery, lace[work], needlepoint, tatting, appliqué; sampler, brocade. See ORNAMENT.

needy, *adj.* in want, destitute, indigent, moneyless, impecunious, penniless, poverty-stricken; poor as a churchmouse. See POVERTY. *Ant.,* satisfied, well-off.

ne'er-do-well, *n.* wastrel, loafer, idler, do-nothing, fainéant, good-for-nothing, bum (*sl.*), deadbeat, no-good. See INACTIVITY.

nefarious, *adj.* evil, detestable, base, wicked. See BADNESS.

NEGATION
Denial of truth

Nouns—negation, negativeness, abnegation, denial, deniability, disavowal, disclaimer, abjuration, contradiction, contravention, repudiation, retraction, refutation, rebuttal, disproof, CONFUTATION, REFUSAL, PROHIBITION. See NULLIFICATION, UNWILLINGNESS.

Verbs—negate, deny, contradict, contravene, controvert, gainsay, forswear, disown, disaffirm, disclaim, disavow, recant, revoke, abrogate, veto; dispute, impugn, traverse, call in question, doubt, give the lie to, disprove, explode, belie; repudiate, set aside, ignore, confute, rebut, refute, qualify, refuse.

Adjectives—negative, negatory, denying, denied, contradictory, contrary, recusant, dissenting.

Adverbs—no, nay, not, nowise, not a bit, not at all, not in the least, no such thing, nothing of the kind, quite the contrary, far from it, on no consideration, on no account, in no respect, by no means, for the life of me; let alone, less than; negatively, never, not ever; perish the thought, not for the world, anything but. *Dialect,* nohow. *Informal,* not on your life; nary a. *Slang,* like fun, fat chance, not by a long shot, nothing doing; in a pig's eye *or* ass, in your eye.

Quotations—This night, before the cock crow, thou shalt deny me thrice (*Bible*).

Antonyms, see AFFIRMATION.

---

negative, *adj.* denying (see NEGATION); minus (see DEDUCTION). —*n.* NEGATION. See PHOTOGRAPHY. *Ant.,* positive; plus.

negativism, *n.* skepticism, pessimism. See HOPELESSNESS. *Ant.,* positivism, optimism.

NEGLECT
Disregard

Nouns—1, neglect, negligence, carelessness, heedlessness, thoughtlessness, dereliction, delinquency; omission, oversight, laches, default; benign neglect; RASHNESS; procrastination. See INDIFFERENCE, INSUFFICIENCY.

2, *(neglect of preparation)* laxity, laxness, slackness, looseness, slovenliness; UNPREPAREDNESS, improvidence, unreadiness; disregard, nonobservance, evasion (see AVOIDANCE); nonperformance, FAILURE. *Informal,* a lick and a promise. See RELINQUISHMENT.

3, *(lack of attention)* INATTENTION, absence of mind, preoccupation, woolgathering.

4, neglecter, trifler, procrastinator, waster, wastrel, drifter, slacker; Micawber.

Verbs—1, neglect, let slip, let go, lay aside, lose sight of, overlook, disregard, ignore, leave out of account; pass over, up, *or* by, elide; sit out; let pass, wink at, connive at, gloss over, blink at, eliminate, leave out in the cold; leave in the lurch.

2, be lax, loose, remiss, slack, *etc.*; relax; let be, ignore, laissez-faire; hold a loose rein, give enough *or* too much rope.

3, scamp, do by halves, cut, slight, skimp, trifle with, slur, slur *or* skip over, skim the surface; miss, skip, omit; postpone, procrastinate (see LATENESS); close *or* shut one's eyes to, turn a deaf ear to, forget, be caught napping, let the grass grow under one's feet.

Adjectives—1, neglectful, negligent, lax, slack, heedless, half-baked, careless, forgetful, perfunctory, remiss, inconsiderate; unprepared, unready, off one's guard, unwary, unguarded, unwatchful, delinquent; casual, offhand, cursory; supine, asleep, indolent, inattentive, unobservant, unmindful, unheeding, thoughtless, inadvertent; indifferent, imprudent, slovenly, inexact, inaccurate, improvident, asleep at the switch. *Informal,* out to lunch.

2, neglected, unheeded, uncared for, unnoticed, unattended to, unmissed, shunted, shelved, unused, abandoned, unweighed, unexplored, hid under a bushel, unsung, out in the cold; fallow, untilled, uncultivated.

Adverbs—neglectfully, negligently, anyhow, in an unguarded moment.

Interjections—never mind! let it be!

Quotations—Full many a flower is born to blush unseen and waste its sweetness on the desert air (*Thomas Gray*), Men should not care too much for good looks; neglect is becoming (*Ovid*), A little neglect may breed great mischief . . . for the want of a nail the shoe was lost; for the want of a shoe the horse was lost; and for the want of a horse the rider was lost (*Benjamin Franklin*).

Antonyms, see CARE, DUTY, SEVERITY.

negligee, *n.* deshabille, morning dress, peignoir, kimono, robe de chambre, nightgown. See CLOTHING.

negligent, *adj.* See NEGLECT.

negligible, *adj.* slight, insignificant. See LITTLENESS, UNIMPORTANCE.

negotiable, *adj.* conveyable, assignable, transferable; spendable. See TRANSFER, POSSIBILITY. *Ant.*, non-negotiable.

negotiate, *v.* accomplish, arrange; bargain, dicker, contract, overcome, achieve, effect; *informal,* handle. See BARTER, COMPROMISE.

Negro, *n.* African, Ethiopian, Sudanese, *etc.*; black, African *or* Afro-American. See HUMANITY.

neighbor, *n.* See FRIEND.

neighborhood, *n.* community, vicinity, district, REGION, environs, presence, venue. See NEARNESS, ENVIRONMENT, LOCATION.

neighborly, *adj.* hospitable; friendly. See FRIEND, SOCIALITY. *Ant.*, unneighborly, unfriendly.

neither, *adj.* See NEGATION. *Ant.*, both.

nemesis, *n.* bane, bugbear (see OPPOSITION).

neology, *n.* neologism. See SPEECH.

neophyte, *n.* beginner, tyro, novice; initiate, debutant, greenhorn (*inf.*), greeny (*inf.*), rookie (*sl.*). See LEARNING, BEGINNING.

ne plus ultra, Lat., that which is peerless; the ultimate. See PERFECTION, DISTANCE.

nepotism, *n.* favoritism, patronage; partiality, favor. See INJUSTICE.

nerd, *n., slang,* bookworm, grind (*inf.*); expert, technie (*inf.*). See LEARNING, SKILL.

nerve, *n.* COURAGE, STRENGTH, vigor, vitality; grit, determination, resolution. —*v.t.* embolden, steel, strengthen, invigorate.

nerveless, *adj.* listless; cowardly. See COWARDICE, WEAKNESS. *Ant.*, nervy, bold.

nervous, *adj.* jumpy, jittery, fidgety, uneasy; tense, fearful; sensitive, neurotic; high-strung; timid. See EXCITEMENT, AGITATION, FEAR. *Ant.*, relaxed. —**nervous breakdown,** collapse, neurasthenia, crackup (*inf.*). See INSANITY.

nervy, *adj.* bold, brash. See COURAGE, INSOLENCE. *Ant.*, nerveless, timid.

nest, *n.* aerie, hammock, lair, den; hotbed, coterie; nursery, cradle; resort, haunt, retreat. See CAUSE, ABODE.

n'est-ce pas?, Fr., isn't it [true]? See INQUIRY.

nest egg, *n.* reserve [fund], savings; rainy-day fund, hope chest. See STORE, MONEY.

nestle, *v.i.* lodge, snuggle, lie, cuddle. See ENDEARMENT, ABODE.

net, *n.* netting; seine, web, snare, mesh; trap, catch; REMAINDER. See DECEPTION, CROSSING.

nether, *adj.* under, lower (see LOWNESS).

nettle, *v.* trouble, irritate; prickle; ruffle, annoy, provoke; vex, offend. See DISCONTENT.

network, *n.* reticulation; net[ting], mesh, interlacing, openwork; hookup, web, interconnection. See CROSSING.

neurosis, *n.* nervous *or* mental disorder, illness, sickness, *or* disease; psychoneurosis, melancholia, nervous breakdown; phobia, mania, obsession, compulsion, hypochondria; psychosis, INSANITY. See FEAR.

neuter, *adj.* sexless, unsexual; emasculated, castrated, gelded. —*v.t.* emasculate, castrate, geld; spay, fix. See IMPOTENCE. *Ant.*, MALE, FEMALE.

neutral, *adj.* nonpartisan; indifferent, disinterested, unconcerned; undecided, irresolute, indeterminate; inert, inactive; impartial; neuter, asexual, sexless; barren, unfruitful, sterile. See INDIFFERENCE, LIBERALITY, MEDIOCRITY.

neutralize, *v.t.* nullify, cancel; offset, negate, counterbalance; destroy, defeat, overpower. See COMPENSATION, NULLIFICATION.

never, *adv.* ne'er, nevermore, not ever, at no time. See NEGATION, REFUSAL.

nevertheless, *adv.* nonetheless, anyway, still, yet, just the same, for all that, notwithstanding; in any event, however that may be, regardless. See COMPENSATION.

new, *adj.* fresh, unused; unfamiliar, different; unaccustomed. See NEWNESS, DIFFERENCE. *Ant.*, old, familiar.

newborn, *adj.* recent; hatched, neonatal, new-fledged. See NEWNESS.

newcomer, *n.* immigrant, alien, foreigner, Johnny-come-lately (*inf.*); initiate. See ARRIVAL.

newfangled, *adj.* novel. See NEWNESS, FASHION.

newlywed, *n.* bride, blushing bride, [bride]groom. See MARRIAGE.

NEWNESS
Recent occurrence

Nouns—1, newness, recentness, currency, freshness, greenness, novelty, immaturity, YOUTH; innovation, renovation; neoism, neologism, language pollution; update; new blood; invention. See PRESENT, RESTORATION.

2, modernism, modernity; latest fashion, latest thing, last word, cutting *or* leading edge, new wave, radical chic; mushroom, nouveau riche, upstart, parvenu. *Slang*, salt-water Negro.

Verbs—renew, restore, modernize, renovate, remodel, reinvent the wheel, retrofit.

Adjectives—1, new, novel, recent, fresh, green, young, evergreen, raw, crisp, immature, virgin, untried, not dry behind the ears; untrodden, unbeaten.

2, late, modern, current, neoteric, new-fashioned, newfangled, just out, up to the minute, cutting *or* leading edge, technotronic, brand-new, vernal, renovated, fresh as a daisy, up-to-date, state-of-the-art, abreast of the times; jet *or* space age; hot off the press, first run, new off the irons; a-go-go.

Adverbs—newly, freshly, afresh, anew, lately, just now, only yesterday, latterly, of late, not long ago, a short time ago.

Phrases—the best thing since sliced bread; a new broom sweeps clean; there is nothing new under the sun; you can't put new wine in old bottles.

Quotations—Discovery consists of seeing what everybody has seen and thinking what nobody has thought (*Albert von Szent-Györgyi*), Nothing has yet been said that's not been said before (*Terence*), What a good thing Adam had. When he said a good thing he knew nobody had said it before (*Mark Twain*), We stand today at the edge of a new frontier (*J. F. Kennedy*).

Antonyms, *see* OLDNESS.

NEWS
Information of public events

Nouns—1, news, INFORMATION, intelligence, journalism; tidings, word, ADVICE; KNOWLEDGE, revelation; message, COMMUNICATION, account, dispatch, bulletin, communiqué; hard *or* soft news. See PUBLICATION.

2, newspaper, newsweekly, newsmagazine, newsletter, calendar, scandal sheet, tabloid; bulldog *or* early edition; newscast, newshour; article, column, feature, editorial, op-ed column, feuilleton; news flash, exposé; news channel; report, rumor, hearsay, buzz, bruit, fame, talk, gossip, table talk, town talk, scandal, tittle-tattle, canard, whisper; good news, glad tidings, gospel, evangel; story, copy, spot, piece, squib, press release; pipeline, earful, hot line; obituary; news bureau, newsroom, city room *or* desk, copy desk; assignment, beat; dispatch, byline; [news] blackout. *Informal*, grapevine, scoop, obit. *Slang*, beat. See PUBLICATION, WRITING, RECORD.

3, journalism, broadcast *or* print journalism, photojournalism, pictorial journalism, reportage, yellow journalism; mass media, the press, press corps, fourth estate; news agency, wire service, United Press International, UPI, Associated Press, AP, Reuters; press association; press box, press card.

4, journalist, newsman, correspondent, narrator, announcer, [cub] reporter, staffer, stringer, [gossip, fashion, *etc.*] columnist, graveyard *or* lobster shift; [managing *or* senior] editor, bureau chief, city editor; broadcaster, newscaster, anchor, commentator, talking head, news analyst; press agent, publicist, press secretary; newsmonger, scandalmonger, informer, talebearer, telltale, tattletale; gossip, tattler, blabber, chatterer. *Slang*, reptile.

Verbs—report, disseminate, publish, notify, broadcast, televise; rumor, gossip, chatter, tattle, prate; make news, make the headlines, sensationalize. *Informal*, scoop.

Adjectives—reported, rumored, circulated, in circulation; rife, current, floating, going around, all over [the] town, the talk of the town, in every mouth, at second hand; newsworthy, fit to print; newsy.

Adverbs—as the story goes *or* runs, as they say, it is said.

Phrases—no news is good news.

Quotations—The nature of bad news infects the teller (*Shakespeare*), There are laws to protect the freedom of the press's speech, but none that are worth anything to protect the people from the press (*Mark Twain*), When a dog bites a man, that is not news, because it happens so often. But if a man bites a dog, that is news (*John B. Bogart*), I read the newspapers avidly. It is my one form of continuous fiction (*Bevan*), Rock journalism is people who can't write interviewing people who can't talk for people who can't read (*Frank Zappa*), All the news that's fit to print (*Adolph Simon Ochs*).

---

newsletter, *n.* calendar, journal (see PUBLICATION, NEWS).

newspaper, *n.* paper; daily, journal, weekly, gazette, sheet, tabloid. See PUBLICATION, RECORD, COMMUNICATION, NEWS.

New Testament, *n.* See SACRED WRITINGS.

next, *adv.* beside, nearest; after, later. —*adj.* adjacent, adjoining, bordering, contiguous; following, ensuing, succeeding, successive. See SEQUENCE, FUTURITY. *Ant.,* preceding.

nib, *n.* point, END; beak, bill.

nibble, *v.* browse, gnaw, graze; nip, peck, pick at; snack, nosh. —*n.* nip, chew, bite, morsel, bit, snack. See FOOD.

nice, *adj.* pleasing, agreeable, attractive, enjoyable; tasteful, proper, genteel; precise, accurate, exact, meticulous; delicate, fine, sensitive, appealing; overrefined, critical, squeamish. See PLEASURE, TASTE. *Ant.,* awful.

nicety, *n.* precision, accuracy; distinction, detail, subtlety. See RIGHTNESS.

niche, *n.* hollow, recess; corner, nook. See ANGULARITY.

nicht wahr?, *Ger.,* [is it] not true? See INQUIRY.

nick, *n.* notch, chip, gouge, jag, indentation. —*v.t.* cut, chip, dent, jag, gouge. See FURROW.

nickelodeon, *n.* theater, movie house; jukebox. See SOUND, MUSIC, PHOTOGRAPHY.

nickname, *n.* pet name, diminutive, sobriquet; appellation. See NOMENCLATURE.

nifty, *adj.,* *slang,* smart, stylish. See FASHION, GOODNESS.

niggardly, *adj.* cheap, stingy, miserly, close, parsimonious, ungenerous; grudging; tight; mean. See PARSIMONY, UNIMPORTANCE. *Ant.,* generous.

niggle, *v.* trifle (with), dally, nickle-and-dime (*inf.*); cheat. See CHEAPNESS, DECEPTION, UNIMPORTANCE.

night, *n.* DARKNESS, evening, nightfall, midnight, nighttime, eventide. *Ant.,* day[time].

nightclothes, *n. pl.* nightgown *or* -shirt, pajamas, robe de nuit, nightie (*inf.*), PJ's (*inf.*). See CLOTHING.

nightclub, *n.* cabaret, café, supper club; discotheque, nightspot, speakeasy, joint (*inf.*), nightery (*inf.*). See ABODE, DRINKING, AMUSEMENT.

nightgown, *n.* nightdress, nightie (*inf.*). See CLOTHING.

nightmare, *n.* bad dream, hallucination; cauchemar; incubus, succubus, demon, night hag; terror, fright, daymare. See FEAR, IMAGINATION.

nihilism, *n.* lawlessness, anarchy. See ILLEGALITY, NULLIFICATION.

nil desperandum, *Lat.,* despairing of nothing. See COURAGE.

nimble, *adj.* spry, active, sprightly, supple, agile, lively, brisk, alert, acute, quick. See VELOCITY, SKILL, CUNNING. *Ant.,* awkward, slow.

nincompoop, *n.* simpleton, chump (see IGNORANCE, CREDULITY).

nip, *v.t.* nibble, bite; cut, snip, pinch, chip, shorten; sip. —*n.* pinch, bite; sip; chill. See DEDUCTION, DISJUNCTION, CONTRACTION, COLD, STEALING.

nipple, *n.* dug, mammilla, pap[illa], teat; tit. See CONVEXITY, BODY.

nippy, *adj*. sharp, biting, COLD; tangy, spicy, peppery. See FOOD.

nirvana, *n*. bliss, ecstasy, HEAVEN, paradise; nibbana.

nitpick, *v.i*. find fault, carp, quibble, catch at straws, split hairs. See FALSEHOOD.

nitty-gritty, *n., slang*, essentials, facts (see IMPORTANCE).

nitwit, *n., slang*, bonehead, jughead, fool, dimwit (*sl.*). See FOLLY.

nix, *v.t., slang*, veto, naysay (see NEGATION).

nixie, *n*. water sprite *or* nymph, undine. See MYTHICAL DEITIES.

no, *adv*. none, not. See NEGATION.

NOBILITY
High rank

Nouns—**1**, nobility, aristocracy, quality, gentility, rank, condition, title, distinction, [blue] blood, [high] birth, high degree; pedigree, lineage. See POSTERITY, ANCESTRY, SUPERIORITY, PRIDE, FASHION.

2, the nobility, aristocracy, peerage, upper classes, haut monde, elite, noblesse, gentry, fashionable world, beau monde, high society, crème de la crème, the upper ten thousand.

3, noble[man], lord, peer, grandee, magnifico, hidalgo, don, aristocrat, gentleman, patrician. *Slang*, swell, nob, toff (*Brit.*).

4, king, emperor, prince, crown prince, duke, marquis, marquess, earl, viscount, baron[et], knight, chevalier, squire, count, laird, thane, seignior, esquire, kaiser, czar, margrave; emir, sheik, rajah, maharajah, sultan. See AUTHORITY.

5, queen, empress, princess, begum, rani, ranee, maharani, sultana, czarina; duchess, marchioness, countess; lady, dame.

6, personage, crème de la crème, notable, celebrity, socialite; First Families. *Slang*, upper crust, Four Hundred. See IMPORTANCE, REPUTE.

Verbs—ennable, confer a title (on), knight, dub, esquire; wear the purple.

Adjectives—noble, exalted, princely, royal, lordly, titled, patrician, aristocratic, wellborn, highborn, of gentle blood, of family, genteel, blue-blooded.

Quotations—Nobility is a graceful ornament to the civil order (*Edmund Burke*), Titles distinguish the mediocre, embarrass the superior, and are disgraced by the inferior (*G. B. Shaw*), When I want a peerage, I shall buy it like an honest man (*Lord Northcliffe*), An aristocracy in a republic is like a chicken whose head has been cut off (*Nancy Mitford*), I think the king is but a man, as I am: the violet smells to him as it doth to me (*Shakespeare*), Royalty is the gold filling in a mouthful of decay (*John Osborne*), Uneasy lies the head that wears a crown (*Shakespeare*), What is aristocracy? A corporation of the best, of the bravest (*Thomas Carlyle*).

Antonyms, see POPULACE.

---

nobody, *n*. nonentity, cipher, upstart, jackanapes, jerk (*sl.*), twirp (*sl.*). See UNIMPORTANCE. *Ant.,* somebody.

nocturnal, *adj*. nightlike, nightly; nighttime; noctivagant, noctambulant; dark, black as night. See DARKNESS. *Ant.,* diurnal, daytime.

nocturne, *n*. night piece *or* music, evensong, Nachtmusik; serenade. See MUSIC.

nod, *n*. salute, greeting, recognition; sign, signal; permission, agreement. —*v.t*. dip, incline, bob. —*v.i*. greet, signal, sign; sleep, nap, doze, drowse. See COMMAND, INACTIVITY, INDICATION, ASSENT.

node, *n*. DIFFICULTY, nodus, Gordian knot; protuberance, CONVEXITY, lump, bump, knurl, gnarl; nodosity, nodule, tumescence. See DISEASE.

no-good, *adj*. worthless, good-for-nothing. See USELESSNESS.

noise, *n*. uproar, hubbub, din, racket, clamor, pandemonium; crash, rattle, clatter. See LOUDNESS, SOUND. *Ant.,* SILENCE, quiet.

noiseless, *adj*. soundless, quiet, silent, hushed. See SILENCE. *Ant.,* noisy.

noisome, *adj*. destructive, harmful, baneful, EVIL; fetid, malodorous, rank, foul[-smelling]; disgusting, loathsome. See BADNESS, MALODOROUSNESS.

nolens volens, Lat., willy-nilly. See NECES-
SITY, UNWILLINGNESS.

nomad, *n.* wanderer, gypsy, rover. See
TRAVEL.

no-man's-land, wasteland; battlefield, field
of battle. See CONTENTION.

nom de guerre, Fr., pseudonym. See
NOMENCLATURE.

nom de plume, Fr., pen name. See NOMEN-
CLATURE.

NOMENCLATURE
Naming

Nouns—1, nomenclature; naming, nomination, terminology, glossology, baptism,
christening; nomenclator. See INDICATION.

2, name, appellation, appellative, designation, title, head[ing], denomination, byname, epithet; label; proper *or* Christian name, first name, cognomen, patronymic,
nomen, praenomen, surname, nickname, maiden *or* birth name; synonym, antonym;
honorific, title; signature; anonymity; eponym; alias, pseudonym, incognito, pen
name, *nom de guerre, nom de plume;* misnomer, misnaming, malapropism. *Informal,*
such-and-such, so-and-so. *Slang,* moniker, handle, tag.

3, term, expression, noun, word, byword, technical term, cant.

Verbs—1, name, call, term, denominate, designate, identify, style, entitle, label, dub,
christen, baptize, characterize, specify, label; misname, nickname. *Informal,* make.

2, be called, go by, answer to the name of.

Adjectives—named, [so-]called, hight, yclept; known as, alias, AKA, cognominal, titular, nominal; pseudonymous, soi-disant, self-styled; nameless, anonymous; né[e].

Prepositions—cum.

Quotations—What's in a name? that which we call a rose by any other name would
smell as sweet (*Shakespeare*), The naming of a man is a numbing blow from which
he never recovers (*Marshall McLuhan*).

---

nominal, *adj.* titular, [so-]called, known as;
in name only, token; slight, little; moderate, reasonable. See NOMENCLATURE.

nominate, *v.t.* propose, name; suggest; appoint. See COMMISSION.

nominee, *n.* appointee, designee, candidate, aspirant; grantee. See COMMIS-
SION.

nonalcoholic, *adj.* abstemious, teetotal;
nonintoxicating; unfermented. See MOD-
ERATION. *Ant.,* alcoholic.

nonaligned, *adj.* neutral, independent. See
FREEDOM. *Ant.,* partisan.

nonbeliever, *n.* See UNBELIEVER.

nonchalance, *n.* INDIFFERENCE, insouciance, unconcern; casualness, carelessness. See INATTENTION.

non-Christian, *adj.* pagan, heretic, heathen, infidel; Antichrist. See IRRELIGION.

noncombatant, *n.* nonbelligerent; civilian.
See PACIFICATION. *Ant.,* COMBATANT,
hawk.

noncommittal, *adj.* neutral, nonpartisan;
ambiguous, vague; careful, cautious,
circumspect, closemouthed, politic. See
CAUTION. *Ant.,* committed, partisan.

non compos mentis, Lat., not of sound
mind. See INSANITY.

nonconformity, *n.* See UNCONFORMITY.
Ant., CONFORMITY.

nondenominational, *adj.* ecumenical, in-
terdenominational, nonsectarian. See
GENERALITY.

nondescript, *adj.* indefinable, unclassifiable,
indescribable, random; odd; casual,
undistinguished. See UNCONFORMITY.

none, *pron.* no one, nothing. See NEGA-
TION, NONEXISTENCE.

nonentity, *n.* nothing, negation; nobody;
nullity. See NONEXISTENCE, UNIMPOR-
TANCE. *Ant.,* entity, player (*inf.*).

nonessential, *adj.* unimportant, irrelevant,
unnecessary, incidental. See UNIMPOR-
TANCE. *Ant.,* essential, necessary.

nonesuch, *n.* rarity, unicum, paragon, exemplar; nonpareil, one in a thousand *or*
million. See PERFECTION, UNCONFOR-
MITY.

nonetheless, *adv.* however, nevertheless.
See QUALIFICATION.

NONEXISTENCE
Lack of being

Nouns—1, nonexistence, inexistence, nonentity, nonsubsistence, negativeness, nullity, nihility, blank, nothingness, ABSENCE, no such thing, void, vacuum, OBLIVION. *Slang,* diddly[squat], dick, jack [shit]. See DISAPPEARANCE, INSUBSTANTIALITY.

2, annihilation, extinction, obliteration, NULLIFICATION, DESTRUCTION.

3, nonperson, unperson; vaporware.

Verbs—1, not exist, be null and void, cease to exist, pass away, perish, become extinct, die out; disappear, fade (see DISAPPEARANCE); go, be no more, die (see DEATH).

2, annihilate, render null [and void], nullify, abrogate, destroy, obliterate, extinguish, remove. See DESTRUCTION, KILLING.

Adjectives—1, nonexistent, inexistent, null [and void], negative, blank, missing, omitted, absent.

2, unreal, baseless, unsubstantial, imaginary, visionary, ideal, fabulous, legendary, chimerical, supposititious, vain. See IMAGINATION.

3, unborn, uncreated, unbegotten, unconceived, unproduced, unmade.

4, annihilated, extinct, exhausted, perished, gone, lost, departed, defunct.

Quotations—A thing of beauty is a joy forever, its loveliness increases; it will never pass into nothingness (*John Keats*), Nothing can be created out of nothing (*Lucretius*), Nothing exists except atoms and empty space; everything else is opinion (*Democritus*).

Antonyms, see EXISTENCE.

---

nonfiction, *n.* reality; history, [auto]biography, article, DISSERTATION; journalism, exposé. See WRITING, PUBLICATION. *Ant.,* fiction.

nonpareil, *adj.* unequaled, matchless, incomparable, in a class by itself. See PERFECTION, SUPERIORITY. —*n.* See NONESUCH.

nonpartisan, *adj.* neutral, uncommitted, disinterested; impartial, unbiased, broad-minded. —*n.* independent, neutral, freethinker, sideliner; judge, arbiter, umpire. See INDIFFERENCE.

NONPAYMENT
Lack of payment

Nouns—1, nonpayment, default, delinquency; protest, repudiation, evasion, reneging, kiting; unprofitableness; bad debt; cancellation, write-off, moratorium, rent strike; insolvency, bankruptcy, insufficient funds, return item, stop payment, INSUFFICIENCY, a run on the bank. See DEBT, POVERTY, ECONOMY.

2, free admission, free *or* complimentary seats, [free] pass, Annie Oakley; labor of love. *Slang,* comp, freebie. See CHEAPNESS.

3, bankrupt, insolvent, debtor; absconder, welsher, defaulter, lame duck, *etc.;* tax dodger. *Informal,* deadhead. *Slang,* deadbeat.

Verbs—1, not pay, stop payment; run up bills, go into debt *or* the red; go bankrupt, fail, crash, go under, fold [up]; protest, dishonor, repudiate, nullify; default; write off, wipe the slate clear, declare a moratorium, cancel. *Informal,* welsh. *Slang,* go broke, skip out, shoot the moon, fly kites.

2, give way, pass out [tickets, *etc.*]. *Informal,* paper the house.

Adjectives—1, defaulting, in default; insolvent, bankrupt; in DEBT, in arrears; unpaid, unrequited, unrewarded.

2, gratuitous, gratis, free, for nothing, pro bono; without charge, untaxed; scot-free; free of cost, complimentary; honorary. *Informal,* on the house, dime a dozen; five-and-ten.

Antonyms, see PAYMENT, PRICE.

nonplus, *v.t.* perplex, confound, baffle; bring up short *or* to a standstill, stop dead [in one's tracks], squelch, throw [for a loop]. See HINDRANCE, OBSCURITY, DIFFICULTY.

nonsense, *n.* ABSURDITY, senselessness, silliness, trash, foolishness. See UNMEANINGNESS.

non sequitur, *Lat.,* sophism, illogicality. See UNMEANINGNESS.

nonstop, *adj.* ceaseless, incessant, round-the-clock. See CONTINUITY.

nonviolence, *n.* MODERATION, pacifism.

nook, *n.* retreat, corner, cover, niche, recess. See ANGULARITY.

noon, *n.* noontime, midday, noonday, lunchtime. See CHRONOMETRY.

noose, *n.* hitch, catch; loop, halter, ring, lariat, lasso. See CIRCULARITY.

norm, *n.* normalcy; norma, model, standard, par, criterion, yardstick, rule of thumb; precept, canon, fashion. See CONFORMITY, MEASUREMENT.

normal, *adj.* ordinary, regular, average, usual, typical. See CONFORMITY, SANITY, INTRINSIC, MEAN, REGULARITY. *Ant.,* abnormal, atypical.

north, *adj.* northerly, northern, northward; arctic, polar. See DIRECTION. *Ant.,* south. —**North Star,** Polaris, polar star, lodestar. See UNIVERSE.

nose, *n.* proboscis, snout, muzzle, beak, schnozzle (*sl.*); nasal *or* olfactory organ; nostrils. See CONVEXITY.

nosedive, *n.* plunge, DESCENT, fall; crash. See AVIATION.

nosegay, *n.* posy, bouquet, corsage. See ODOR.

nosh, *n., slang,* snack, lunch, bite (*inf.*). See FOOD.

nostalgia, *n.* homesickness; pathos, REGRET, wistfulness; nostomania.

nosy, *adj.* inquisitive, meddlesome, prying, snoopy. See CURIOSITY.

nota bene, *Lat.,* note well. See INDICATION.

notable, *adj.* celebrated, noted, noteworthy, distinguished, renowned, famous, remarkable. See REPUTE, NOBILITY. *Ant.,* unknown, unimportant.

notarize, *v.t.* certify, attest, witness, stamp, validate. See RECORD.

notation, *n.* note; comment, annotation; entry. See WRITING, INDICATION, INTERPRETATION.

notch, *n.* nick, gut, gash, score; groove, rut, pit, pock; cleft, dent, dint, indentation; dimple; defile, pass, gap, opening, hole; serrature, tooth; crenel, scallop; embrasure, battlement, machicolation, castellation; tally, mark, DEGREE, calibration, step, peg. —*v.t.* nick, cut, gash, score, dent, indent, jag; scarify; crimp, scallop; crenulate; tally, calibrate, mark (in degrees), peg. See ANGULARITY, INDICATION, INTERVAL, FURROW.

note, *n.* letter, missive; acknowledgment, comment, reminder; observation, memo[randum], notation; explanation, remark, annotation; distinction, fame; tone, sound, pitch. See COMMUNICATION, ATTENTION, INDICATION, RECORD, REPUTE, MUSIC. —*v.t.* observe, notice, remark, attend, need, jot. See INTELLECT, MEMORY.

notebook, *n.* notepad, memo pad *or* book, steno[grapher's] pad; portable *or* laptop [computer]. See WRITING, COMPUTERS.

noted, *adj.* See NOTABLE.

noteworthy, *adj.* extraordinary, notable, remarkable, considerable, exceptional. See UNCONFORMITY, IMPORTANCE. *Ant.,* insignificant, unimportant.

nothing, *n.* zero, cipher, nought, blank; nothingness; nonentity, bagatelle, trifle, zilch (*sl.*). See UNIMPORTANCE, INSUBSTANTIALITY, NONEXISTENCE. *Ant.,* something.

notice, *n.* ATTENTION, observation, recognition, perception; circular, poster, bulletin; placard, announcement; WARNING, sign; consideration; review. See PUBLICATION, INFORMATION. —*v.t.* see, observe, perceive, regard, heed, detect, recognize, note. See VISION.

noticeable, *adj.* striking, conspicuous, perceptible, prominent, observable. See VISIBILITY. *Ant.,* unnoticeable, imperceptible.

notify, *v.* inform, warn, apprise, advise, tell, acquaint. See INFORMATION, PUBLICATION.

notion, *n.* idea, THOUGHT, opinion; fancy, caprice, inclination; BELIEF, conception. See SUPPOSITION, CHANGEABLENESS.

notoriety, *n.* flagrancy, blatancy, notoriousness, DISREPUTE. See PUBLICATION. *Ant.,* anonymity.

notwithstanding, *adv.* nevertheless, although, however, yet. —*prep.* despite, even. See COMPENSATION.

nourish, *v.t.* nurture, sustain, feed, foster, support, maintain. See AID, FOOD, PROVISION.

nouveau riche, Fr., parvenu; social climber, snob. See VULGARITY, MONEY.

novel, *n.* story, book, romance, epic; novella. See DESCRIPTION, WRITING. —*adj.* new, unusual, different, remarkable, unique. See NEWNESS.

novelist, *n.* romancer, fictionist. See WRITING.

novelty, *n.* NEWNESS, originality, singularity, innovation, new departure, change, revolution; fad, fashion, le dernier cri, craze; marvel, freak, curiosity, neology, neoterism. *Ant.,* OLDNESS.

novice, *n.* beginner, student, amateur, probationer, neophyte, apprentice; tyro, greenhorn. See BEGINNING, LEARNING, PREPARATION.

now, *adv.* immediately, here, presently, today, yet. See PRESENT.

noway, *adv.* nowise, by no means, in no case, not on one's life (*inf.*). See NEGATION.

nowhere, *adv.* [in] no place, neither here nor there, absent. See ABSENCE.

noxious, *adj.* noisome, harmful, poisonous, injurious, deleterious, pernicious. See BADNESS.

nozzle, *n.* spout, outlet, vent, valve, faucet, nose, OPENING.

nth degree, utmost, highest degree, maximum. See SUPERIORITY.

nuance, *n.* variation, modulation, shade, subtlety, nicety, fine point, distinction; suggestion, innuendo, hint. See DIFFERENCE.

nub, *n.* knob, stud; *informal,* gist, essence. See CONVEXITY, IMPORTANCE.

nubile, *adj.* marriageable; pubescent, ripe, developed. See MARRIAGE.

nuclear, *adj.* atomic, thermonuclear; core, central. See POWER, MIDDLE. —**nuclear power,** atomic *or* [thermo]nuclear energy. See POWER.

nucleus, *n.* center, heart, core, kernel; basis, foundation. See MIDDLE, IMPORTANCE.

nude, *adj.* naked, stripped, bare, unclad, unclothed, exposed, [in the] raw (*inf.*). See DIVESTMENT. *Ant.,* clothed.

nudge, *n.* push, poke, prod. —*v.t.* poke, prod, push, jog. See INDICATION, IMPULSE, MEMORY.

nudism, *n.* naturism, gymnosophy. See DIVESTMENT.

nugatory, *adj.* useless, ineffectual, worthless, futile; helpless. See USELESSNESS, IMPOTENCE.

nugget, *n.* lump, hunk; slug. See SIZE, MONEY.

nuisance, *n.* pest, annoyance, irritation, bore, bother. See EVIL.

nuke, *v.t., slang,* destroy, wipe out, vaporize; microwave. See DESTRUCTION, HEAT.

null, *adj.* invalid; nonexistent. See NULLIFICATION, NONEXISTENCE.

NULLIFICATION
Invalidation

Nouns—nullification, abrogation, annulment, cancellation, revocation, repeal, rescission, defeasance, renege; dismissal, deposal, deposition, dethronement, disestablishment, disendowment, deconsecration; abolition, abolishment, dissolution; destruction; counterorder, countermand; nolle prosequi; thumbs down, veto. See NEGATION.

Verbs—1, nullify, abrogate, abjure, annul, cancel, destroy, abolish, revoke, repeal, reverse, retract, rescind, recall, overrule, override, set aside, dissolve, quash, invalidate, nol-pros, void, declare null and void, veto, disestablish, disendow, deconsecrate; delete, erase, cross [out], bleep *or* blip out; swallow *or* eat one's words, take back. *Informal,* scrub.

2, countermand, counterorder, set aside, do away with, throw overboard, throw to the dogs, scatter to the winds.

3, cast off, out, aside, away, *or* adrift, dismiss, discharge, discard; get rid of. *Informal,* fire. *Slang,* sack, bounce; send packing; give the gate *or* the boot *or* one's walking papers; give the pink slip.

4, depose, divest of office, throw down; cashier, displace, break, oust, unseat, unsaddle, dethrone, unfrock, ungown, disbar, disbench; disinherit, disown, cut off.

Adjectives—null, [null and] void, invalid.

Quotations—Pray, v. To ask that the rules of the universe be annulled in behalf of a single petitioner, confessedly unworthy (*Ambrose Bierce*), The moving finger writes; and, having writ, moves on: nor all thy piety nor wit shall lure it back to cancel half a line, nor all thy tears wash out a word of it (*Edward Fitzgerald*).

Antonyms, see AFFIRMATION, CELEBRATION.

---

nullity, *n.* nothingness, NONEXISTENCE.

numb, *adj.* unfeeling, deadened, frozen, benumbed; dazed, shocked; anesthetized; narcotized, drugged, paralyzed; dull, torpid, insensitive; desensitized; lifeless. —*v.t.* deaden, benumb, freeze; narcotize, drug, desensitize; stupefy, paralyze. See INSENSIBILITY, COLD.

NUMERATION
Counting

Nouns—**1,** numeration, numbering, counting, tally, enumeration, pagination, summation, reckoning, computation, calculation, cybernetics, MEASUREMENT; statistics, poll, census, roll call, recapitulation; recount; batting average, grade-point average; magic square.

2, *(study of numbers)* arithmetic, [simple, elementary, higher, *or* applied] mathematics, [propositional, differential, *or* integral] calculus, [Boolean, Euclidean, non-Euclidean, linear, matrix, *or* analytic] algebra, quadratics, [Cartesian, plane, solid, *or* descriptive] geometry, trigonometry, fractals, vector analysis; number, set, game *or* group theory; mathematical biology, physics, *etc.*; addition, subtraction, multiplication, division; [linear, cubic, quadratic, differential, *or* simultaneous] equation; even *or* odd number, mixed number; [square, cube, *etc.*] root, power; exponent, index, prime, factorial; reduction, approximation, differentiation, integration; formula, function, [arithmetic, geometric, algebraic, *or* Fibonacci] series.

3, *(calculating device)* abacus, logometer, slide rule, table, Napier's rods, logarithm, log, antilogarithm; calculator, calculating machine, adder, adding machine, cash register; protractor, trammel; computer, electronic computer *or* brain, mainframe [computer], mini-, micro-, *or* personal computer, [micro]processor, punch-card *or* -tape reader. *Slang,* magic brain, number cruncher. See COMPUTERS.

4, *(mathematical terms)* total, amount, QUANTITY; sum, difference, product, multiplier, multiplicand, addend, aggregate, coefficient, dividend, divisor, factor, quotient, subtrahend, minuend, fraction, mixed number, numerator, denominator, decimal, reciprocal; Arabic *or* Roman numbers *or* numerals; [trigonometric, circular, algebraic, composite, periodic, polynomial, transcendental, *or* continuous] function; mean, average (see MIDDLE); constant, variable, unknown, derivative, differential; equation; set, domain; surd, imaginary number, irrational number; four-color problem, golden section *or* mean, pons asinorum; binomial; matrix, set, vector, universe; abscissa, asymptote, axis, coordinates; sine, cosine, tangent, cotangent.

5, ratio, proportion, progression; arithmetic[al] *or* geometric[al] progression; percentage. See DEGREE.

6, a. UNITY; duality, dualism, biformity; triality, trinity; quaternity. **b.** duplication, duplicate; triplication, triplicate; trebleness, trine; quadruplication, quadruplicate, *etc.* **c.** bisection, bipartition, halving; trisection, tripartition; quadrisection, quadripartition, quartering, quarter; quinquesection; decimation.

7, a. [prime, cardinal, *or* ordinal] number, symbol, numeral, figure, cipher, digit, [pos-

itive *or* negative] integer, natural number, counter, round number; folio. **b.** one, single, unity, ace; two, deuce, couple, brace, pair, binomial, square; three, trey, triad, triplet, trio, leash, trinomial, third power, cube; four, tetrad, quartet, quaternion; five, quintet; six, sextet, half a dozen; seven, septet; eight, octet; nine, ennead; ten, decad[e], tithe; twelve, dozen; thirteen, baker's *or* devil's dozen; twenty, score; hundred, century, centenary; number of the beast; thousand, million, billion, trillion, googol, googolplex; zero (see INSUBSTANTIALITY). *Informal,* jillion. *Slang,* goose egg.
c. cardinal *or* ordinal number.

8, mathematician, arithmetician, calculator, abacist, algebraist, statistician, enumerator, counter. *Slang,* bean counter.

Verbs—**1,** number, count [off], tell [off], tally, enumerate, poll, count heads *or* noses, recapitulate; paginate, foliate; score, cipher, compute, calculate, figure, sum up, ring up, cast up, total, add, subtract, multiply, divide; round off.

2, check, prove, demonstrate, balance, audit, take stock (see ACCOUNTING); recount.
3, *(increase numerically)* double, couple, pair [off *or* up], yoke, square; triple, treble, triplicate, cube; quadruplicate, *etc.*
4, *(divide)* bisect, halve, trisect, quarter, decimate.

Adjectives—**1,** numeral, numerical, arithmetic[al], geometric[al], analytic, algebraic, statistical, numerable, computable, divisible, reciprocal, whole, prime, fractional, decimal, proportional; Arabic, Roman, binary, octal; exponential, logarithmic, differential, integral, positive, negative; rational, irrational; radical, real, imaginary, impossible; approximate, round; exact; perfect.

2, one, first, annual, single, unique; two, second, double, duplicate, twain, dual, biannual, biennial, binary, binomial, twin, duplex; three, third, triple, treble, triform, trinary, trinal, trinomial, tertiary, trine, triplicate, threefold; four, fourth, quadruple, quadruplicate, quarter, quaternary, quaternal, quadratic; five, fifth, quintuple, quinary; sixth, sextuple; seventh, septuple; eight, octuple; tenth, decimal, tenfold; twelfth, dozenth, duodenary; hundredth, centennial, centenary, centuplicate; thousandth, millennial.

3, bisected, bipartite, bifid; trisected, tripartite, trifid; quartered, quadripartite; quinquepartite, quinquefid; octifid; tenth, decimal; twelfth, duodecimal; sixtieth, sexagesimal, sexagenary; hundredth, centesimal; thousandth, millesimal.

Adverbs—twice, double; thrice, trebly, triply, thirdly; fourthly; for one thing.

Prepositions—plus, minus, times.

Phrases—there is safety in numbers; third time lucky.

Quotations—Mathematics are a species of Frenchman; if you say something to them, they translate it into their own language and presto! it is something entirely different (*Goethe*), There are three kinds of lies: lies, damned lies and statistics (*Benjamin Disraeli*), Numbers are intellectual witnesses that belong only to mankind (*Honoré de Balzac*), There is divinity in odd numbers (*Shakespeare*).

Antonyms, see UNITY.

---

numerous, *adj.* many, myriad, multitudinous, plentiful, numberless, various, thick. See MULTITUDE. *Ant.,* few.

numskull, *n.* numbskull, dolt, Dummkopf, meathead (*sl.*), bonehead (*sl.*). See IGNORANCE.

nun, *n.* sister, ecclesiastic, religieuse. See CLERGY.

nunnery, *n.* convent, cloister, cenacle, sisterhood, order. See TEMPLE.

nuptial, *adj.* connubial, bridal. —*n.* MARRIAGE, wedding.

nurse, *n.* attendant, nursemaid, nanny (*inf.*). See SAFETY. —*v.i.* foster, tend, serve, cherish; suckle, give suck; entertain, manage. See REMEDY.

nursery, *n.* nursery school, crèche (see SCHOOL); the cradle, infancy, babyhood; conservatory, green- *or* hothouse; hatchery, incubator; spawning ground. See AGRICULTURE.

nurture, *v.t.* sustain, support, feed, nourish; foster, cherish; educate, train, rear. See AID, PREPARATION, FOOD.

nut, *n.* kernel, stone, nutmeat; seed, core; *slang,* eccentric, crank, crackpot (*sl.*), kook (*sl.*). See FOOD, INSANITY.

nutrient, *n.* FOOD, nutriment, health food.

nutritious, *adj.* nutritive, wholesome, digestible, nourishing. See FOOD, HEALTH.

nutshell, *n.* husk, hull, COVERING; synopsis, digest, minimum. See SHORTNESS.

nutty, *adj.* nutlike, meaty, rich, tasty; *slang,* crazy, insane, cracked (*inf.*), kooky (*sl.*), off one's nut (*sl.*), nuts (*sl.*). See INSANITY. *Ant.,* sane.

nuzzle, *v.* nose, muzzle; burrow, snuff, root, pry; suckle; cuddle, nestle, press, snuggle. See ENDEARMENT.

nymph, *n.* dryad, naiad, houri, undine; larva. See MYTHICAL DEITIES, ANIMAL.

O

oaf, *n.* lout, simpleton, dullard, dunce, blockhead, idiot, dope (*sl.*), jerk (*sl.*). See IGNORANCE.

oar, *n.* paddle, blade, sweep, scull, pole. See SHIP. —*v.* row, paddle, propel, stroke; scull. See NAVIGATION.

oarsman, *n.* rower, paddler, *etc.;* crewman, bowman, helmsman; gondolier; thalamite, zygite, thranite. See NAVIGATION.

oasis, *n.* waterhole, wallow; refuge, shelter. See SAFETY, RELIEF.

oath, *n.* curse, epithet, expletive, IMPRECATION, profanity; pledge, bond. See AFFIRMATION.

obdurate, *adj.* flinty, adamant, unyielding, inflexible; stubborn, adamantine, hardened, unshakable, unfeeling, hardhearted; firm. See IMPENITENCE, OBSTINACY. *Ant.,* obedient, bending.

OBEDIENCE
Submission to authority

Nouns—1, obedience, compliance; SUBMISSION, nonresistance; malleability, tractability, ductility; acquiescence, observance; obsequiousness, SERVILITY. See SUBJECTION. 2, allegiance, loyalty, fealty, homage, deference, obeisance, devotion. See RESPECT.

Verbs—obey, comply, submit; observe, respect, abide by, meet, fulfill, carry out, make good; perform, satisfy, discharge (see COMPLETION); kneel *or* bow to, kowtow, salaam, make an obeisance; be at the beck and call of, do one's bidding, do what one is told, heel, walk the chalk [line], toe the line *or* mark; jump through a hoop; serve (see SERVANT).

Adjectives—obedient, observant, acquiescent, dutiful, complying, compliant, loyal, faithful, devoted; at one's command, at one's orders, at one's [beck and] call; tame[d], under control, in line; restrainable; resigned, passive; tractable, docile, submissive; henpecked; pliable, pliant, unresisting, ductile. *Slang*, pussy-whipped.

Adverbs—obediently, *etc.;* in compliance with, in obedience to; as you please, if you please; to heel.

Quotations—Obedience is the mother of success, and the wife of security (*Aeschylus*), It is much safer to obey than to rule (*Thomas à Kempis*), Learn to obey before you command (*Solon*), Rebellion to tyrants is obedience to God (*John Bradshaw*).

Antonyms, see DISOBEDIENCE.

---

obeisance, *n.* homage, deference, OBEDIENCE; bow, salaam, kowtow, curtsy, genuflection; prostration. See COURTESY, SUBMISSION.

obelisk, *n.* monolith, needle, shaft; dagger, obelus. See HEIGHT, RECORD, INDICATION.

obese, *n.* fat, overweight, stout, plump, fleshy, bulky; corpulent, ponderous; adipose. See EXPANSION, ROTUNDITY. *Ant.,* thin, lanky, underweight.

obey, *v.* See OBEDIENCE. *Ant.,* disobey.

obfuscate, *v.t.* darken, obscure; bewilder. See DARKNESS, UNINTELLIGIBILITY. *Ant.,* clarify, enlighten.

obiter dictum, Lat., passing remark; comment. See SPEECH.

obituary, *n.* obit (*inf.*), necrology; obsequies, exequy; eulogy. See DEATH.

object, *n.* thing, item; goal, aim, purpose, objective. See SUBSTANCE, INTENTION. —*v.i.* disapprove, demur, challenge, protest, resist, kick. See DISAPPROBATION, DISSENT, UNITY.

objection, *n.* remonstrance, protest; drawback, criticism; barrier, obstacle; exception, protestation. See DISAPPROBATION, HINDRANCE, DISSENT. *Ant.,* acceptance, AGREEMENT.

objectionable, *adj.* censurable, culpable; unpleasant, undesirable, obnoxious, offensive, harmful. See DISAPPROBATION. *Ant.,* acceptable, OK.

objective, *adj.* unemotional, unprejudiced, unbiased, impersonal. See EXTRINSIC. —*n.* object, goal, aim, ambition. See INTENTION.

oblation, *n.* offering, sacrifice, corban; WORSHIP; expiation.

obligation, *n.* DUTY, PROMISE; DEBT; agreement, bond, incumbency, responsibility, liability, indebtedness; contract, mortgage. See COMPULSION; NECESSITY.

oblige, *v.* compel, force, constrain, bind, impel; accommodate, favor, assist, gratify, please. See AID, COMPULSION.

obliging, *adj.* accommodating, helpful, considerate. See COURTESY. *Ant.,* unhelpful.

OBLIQUITY
Slanting position

Nouns—1, obliquity, obliqueness, DEVIATION, divergence; inclination, slope, slant; crookedness; leaning; bevel, tilt; bias, list, swag, cant, twist, DISTORTION; bend (see CURVATURE); ANGULARITY; tower of Pisa; indirectness (see CIRCUITY).

2, *(amount of obliquity)* acclivity, rise, ASCENT, gradient, upgrade, rising ground, hill, bank; ramp, incline, grade; steepness, diagonality; cliff, precipice (see VERTICAL); escarpment, scarp; declivity, downgrade, downhill, dip, fall, DESCENT.

3, *(measurement of angle)* clinometer; [co]sine, [co]tangent; angle, hypotenuse; diagonal; zigzag; talus.

Verbs—diverge, deviate; slope, slant, lean, incline, shelve, stoop; rise, ascend; decline, descend; bend, heel, careen, sag, cant, sidle; sway, bias; crook; tilt; distort.

Adjectives—1, oblique, inclined; sloping, tilted, recumbent, clinal, askew, aslant, indirect, wry, awry, crooked; knock-kneed, distorted (see DISTORTION); beveled, out of the perpendicular; diagonal; transverse, CROSSING; curved (see CURVATURE).

2, uphill, rising, ascending, acclivitous; downhill, falling, descending; declining, anticlinal; steep, sheer, abrupt, precipitous, breakneck; not straight, not true.

Adverbs—obliquely, diagonally; on one side; askew, askant, askance, edgewise; out of plumb; at an angle; sidelong, sideways; slopewise, slantwise; by a side wind; out of kilter.

Antonyms, see DIRECTION, STRAIGHTNESS.

---

obliterate, *v.t.* efface, erase, expunge, cancel; rub, sponge, *or* scratch out, blot out, take out; dele, delete, strike out, wipe out, wash out; wipe away; deface, leave no trace. See DESTRUCTION, OBLIVION, NONEXISTENCE.

OBLIVION
Forgetfulness

Nouns—oblivion, obliviousness, forgetfulness, obliteration (of the past); INSENSIBILITY; failure, loss, *or* lapse of memory, amnesia, memory hole; waters of Lethe *or* oblivion, nepenthe; limbo. *Slang,* brain fart, senior moment. See INATTENTION, NONEXISTENCE.

Verbs—1, forget, be forgetful, have on the tip of one's tongue; come in one ear and go out the other; misremember; forget oneself; unlearn, efface, obliterate; think no more of; drown one's sorrows *or* troubles; get over, put behind one. *Informal,* file and forget, kiss *or* laugh off; draw a blank; blow *or* fluff one's lines.

2, fall, sink, *or* fade into oblivion; let the dead bury the dead; let bygones be bygones (see FORGIVENESS); slip *or* escape the memory; fade; lose, lose sight of.

Adjectives—oblivious, forgetful, mindless, nepenthean, Lethean; forgotten, unremembered, past recollection, bygone, buried *or* sunk in oblivion; clean forgotten; gone out of one's head. *Informal,* out to lunch.

Adverbs—in limbo; out of sight, out of mind.

Phrases—out of sight, out of mind.

Quotations—In violence, we forget who we are (*Mary McCarthy*), One keeps on forgetting old age up to the very brink of the grave (*Colette*), Forgive but never forget (*J. F. Kennedy*), A good memory is often a great help; but knowing just when to forget things sometimes counts for more (*Philander C. Johnson*).

Antonyms, see MEMORY.

---

oblong, *adj.* elongate, rectangular; elliptical, oval. See LENGTH.

obloquy, *n.* traduction, slander, calumny, denunciation, DETRACTION; odium, shame, disgrace, opprobrium, humiliation, DISREPUTE, ignominy.

obnoxious, *adj.* repulsive, loathsome, hateful, offensive, odious. See HATE, BADNESS, VULGARITY.

oboe, *n.* hautboy; English horn, shawm, schalmei, musette, oboe d'amore, bass *or* baritone oboe, heckelphone. See MUSIC.

obscene, *adj.* foul, lewd, dirty, indecent, coarse, smutty. See IMPURITY, UNCLEANNESS, VULGARITY.

OBSCURITY
Shade

Nouns—1, obscurity, DIMNESS, DARKNESS, obscuration, obfuscation, opacity; whiteout; shade, cloud, gloom, duskiness, *etc.* See CONCEALMENT, INVISIBILITY, CLOUDINESS.

2, unclearness, indefiniteness, vagueness; UNTELLIGIBILITY; ambiguity; intricacy, involution, CONVOLUTION; abstruseness, mystery; terra incognita. *Informal,* twilight zone, zoo event.

3, lowliness, inconspicuousness; SECLUSION, privacy.

Verbs—obscure, shade, cloud, darken, conceal, hide; dim, bedim, becloud, befog, confuse, bewilder, baffle, befuddle, fluster, mystify, perplex, obfuscate. *Slang,* befuzz.

Adjectives—1, obscure, dim, unlighted, unilluminated, rayless, dusky, dark, darksome, muddy, muzzy; shadowy, murky, hazy, misty, seen through a mist, foggy, smoky, shaded, clouded, nebulous; gloomy, somber, opaque, indistinct, undiscernible, bleary; invisible.

2, unclear, indefinite, vague, undecided; unintelligible, ambiguous, enigmatical, equivocal, indefinable, doubtful, difficult; involved, confused, complex, intricate, abstruse, transcendental, indeterminate, inexact, inaccurate; mystic[al], mysterious, cabalistic, cryptic, recondite, hidden, concealed, blind.

3, nameless, unknown, unnoticed, unnoted, inconspicuous; undistinguished, uncelebrated, unhonored, renownless, inglorious; secluded, retired, remote, private.

Phrases—neither fish, nor flesh, nor good red herring.

Quotations—Human life is but a series of footnotes to a vast obscure unfinished masterpiece (*Vladimir Nabokov*), Suffering is permanent, obscure, and dark, and shares the nature of infinity (*William Wordsworth*), I strive to be brief, and I become obscure (*Horace*).

Antonyms, see LIGHT, CERTAINTY, TRANSPARENCY.

---

obsequies, *n.pl.* funeral *or* burial service. See INTERMENT.

obsequious, *adj.* abject, fawning, sycophantic, cringing, servile, truckling, compliant. See SERVILITY, RESPECT. *Ant.,* dominant.

observance, *n.* performance, compliance, adhesion, OBEDIENCE; fulfillment, satisfaction, discharge; acquittance, acquittal; acknowledgment; fidelity, orthodoxy, ceremony, RITE, punctilio, protocol. See ATTENTION, VISION, HABIT.

observant, *adj.* attentive, mindful; vigilant. See ATTENTION, CARE. *Ant.,* unobservant, inattentive.

observation, *n.* notice, perception, regard;

comment, consideration, remark. See AFFIRMATION, ATTENTION, VISION.

observe, *v.* see (see VISION); comply with, respect, acknowledge, abide by; obey, cling to, adhere to, be faithful to, meet, fulfill; carry out, carry into execution, execute, perform, keep, satisfy, discharge, do one's duty; perform, fulfill, *or* discharge an obligation; acquit oneself; perform an office; keep one's word *or* promise; keep faith with; officiate. See CARE, ATTENTION.

obsess, *v.t.* haunt, beset, besiege. See INSANITY, SORCERY.

obsession, *n.* preoccupation, fixation, mania, phobia, compulsion, *idée fixe,* bee in one's bonnet (*inf.*), hang up (*sl.*). See INSANITY, SORCERY.

obsolescence, *n.* DISUSE, disappearance; antiquity. See OLDNESS.

obsolete, *adj.* past, extinct, outworn, disused, discarded, antiquated, dead, out-of-date. See OLDNESS, DISUSE. *Ant.,* new, state-of-the-art.

obstacle, *n.* HINDRANCE, difficulty, barrier, obstruction, snag, impediment, barrage, baffle.

OBSTINACY
Refusal to comply

Nouns—1, obstinacy, stubbornness, TENACITY, doggedness; obduracy, obduration, inssitence, RESOLUTION; intransigency, immovability, inflexibility, hardness, willpower; self-will, will of iron, will *or* mind of one's own; contumacy, pigheadedness, perversity, contrariness, recalcitrance, indocility. *Informal,* cussedness, hard head and a soft behind. See CERTAINTY, UNWILLINGNESS, RESISTANCE, DISOBEDIENCE, HETERODOXY.
2, pighead, stickler, mule, diehard, intransigent, holdout. *Informal,* bitter-ender, stand-patter, hard nut to crack, tough customer, young Turk.

Verbs—be obstinate, stickle, insist, persist, persevere; fly in the face of facts, be wedded to an opinion, hug a belief; have one's own way *or* will; have the last word, die hard, fight to the last ditch, not yield an inch, stand firm. *Informal,* stand pat, fight city hall.

Adjectives—1, obstinate, stubborn, tenacious, persevering, pertinacious, persistent, dogged; obdurate, indurate, insistent, resolute, firm, sturdy, immovable, inflexible, unmoving, unyielding, unbending, not to be moved; rigid, set, settled, fixed, hard; unchangeable, intransigent, inexorable, determined; bullheaded, pigheaded, headstrong, *entêté,* mulish, stubborn as a mule, tough. *Informal,* bitter-end, diehard, hardline, hardcore.
2, self-willed, willful, perverse, heady, headstrong, refractory, unruly, intractable, incorrigible, contumacious, difficult, balky, contrary, froward, cantankerous, recalcitrant; stiff-necked *or* -backed, hidebound; deaf to advice, impervious to reason; out of hand. *Informal,* cussed.

Phrases— a determined fellow can do more with a rusty monkey wrench than a lot of people can with a machine shop; if at first you don't succeed, try, try again; slow and steady wins the race; we shall overcome; quitters never win, winners never quit.

Quotations—I prefer an accommodating vice to an obstinate virtue (*Molière*), Perseverance, dear my lord, keeps honor bright (*Shakespeare*), Obstinacy in a bad cause, is but constancy in a good (*Thomas Browne*), She's as headstrong as an allegory on the banks of the Nile (*Richard Sheridan*), Pick yourself up, dust yourself off, start all over again (*Dorothy Fields*), If at first you don't succeed, try, try again. Then quit. No use being a damn fool about it (*W. C. Fields*).

Antonyms, see UNCERTAINTY, CHANGEABLENESS.

obstreperous, *adj.* noisy, clamorous, vociferous; recalcitrant, unruly, riotous. See VIOLENCE, DISOBEDIENCE.

obstruct, *v.t.* block, stop, impede, choke, retard, clog; occlude, shut; dam, foul; barricade, blockade; delay; check, hedge, overgrow; encumber. See HINDRANCE, CLOSURE.

obtain, *v.t.* acquire, set; prevail. See EXISTENCE, ACQUISITION.

obtrude, *v.* intrude, thrust, interfere. See BETWEEN.

obtuse, *adj.* stupid, dull; blunt. See IGNORANCE, INSENSIBILITY, BLUNTNESS. *Ant.,* sharp.

obverse, *n.* face, FRONT, counterpart. See SIDE.

obviate, *v.t.* preclude, debar. See HINDRANCE.

obvious, *adj.* manifest, patent, clear, evident, plain; undisguised, unconcealed. See VISIBILITY, SHALLOWNESS. *Ant.,* obscure, hidden.

OCCASION
Opportunity

Nouns—occasion, opportunity, opening, room; CIRCUMSTANCE, event, opportuneness; crisis, turn, juncture, psychological moment, conjuncture; turning point; given time; nick of time; chance of a lifetime, golden opportunity, window of opportunity; clear field; spare time, leisure. *Informal,* new deal. See CAUSE.

Verbs—1, seize *or* take advantage of an opportunity; suit the occasion; strike while the iron is hot, make hay while the sun shines, take time by the forelock; take the bull by the horns. *Informal,* cash in on. *Slang,* get the jump on, jump the gun (see EARLINESS).

2, miss one's opportunity *or* chance, let slip through one's fingers, have shot one's bolt.

Adjectives—opportune, seasonable; providential, lucky, fortunate, happy, favorable, propitious, auspicious, critical; timely, well-timed; apropos, suitable (see AGREEMENT).

Adverbs—opportunely, *etc.;* in due time, course, *or* season, in proper time; for the nonce; in the nick of time, in the fullness of time; just in time, at the eleventh hour; now or never; by the way, by the by; en passant, à propos; parenthetically, while on the subject; ex tempore; on the spur of the moment; on the spot (see EARLINESS); when the coast is clear.

Phrases—all is fish that comes to the net; every dog has his day; no time like the present; opportunity never knocks twice at any man's door; when the cat's away, the mice will play.

Quotations—How oft the sight of means to do ill deeds makes ill deeds done! (*Shakespeare*).

Antonyms, see INEXPEDIENCE.

---

occasional, *adj.* incidental, irregular, casual. See RARITY, EXPEDIENCE, CIRCUMSTANCE. *Ant.,* frequent.

occult, *adj.* mystic, mysterious, supernatural, SECRET, hidden. See SORCERY.

occupant, *n.* tenant, lodger, transient, occupier, INHABITANT, roomer. See POSSESSION.

occupation, *n.* tenure, occupancy, holding, tenancy, POSSESSION, habitation; work, trade, BUSINESS, employment, calling, profession, pursuit.

occupy, *v.t.* hold, inhabit, keep, fill, tenant, have; take, beset, garrison; interest, engage, engross, busy, employ. See ABODE, ATTENTION, BUSINESS, PRESENCE.

OCCURRENCE
Happening

Nouns—1, occurrence, eventuality, event, incident, affair, episode, milestone, transaction, proceeding, business, concern, CIRCUMSTANCE, particular; fact, matter of fact, phenomenon; happenstance, goings-on; adventure, happening; accident (see CHANCE), casualty.

2, the world, life, things, doings, affairs; things in general, affairs in general, the times, state of affairs, order of the day; course, tide, stream, current, run *or* march of events; ups and downs of life.

Verbs—1, occur, happen, take place, be; concur, accompany, coincide (see SYNCHRO-NISM); come, become of, come off, come true, come about, come into EXISTENCE, come into view, come to mind, come forth, come to pass, come on, pass; appear (see APPEARANCE), offer *or* present itself, be met with, be found, come one's way, meet the eye; fall, fall *or* turn out; run, be afoot; fall in, befall, betide, bechance; prove, super-vene, eventuate, transpire, hap; draw on, turn up, crop up, spring up; issue, ensue, re-sult (see EFFECT); arrive, arise, rise, start, hold, take its course. *Informal,* come off, go [off], go down.

2, meet with, experience; fall to the lot of; be one's chance, fortune, *or* lot; find, en-counter, undergo; pass *or* go through.

Adjectives—occurring, happening, going on, under way, current, prevailing; in the wind, afloat, on foot, at issue, in question; incidental, eventful, episodic, stirring, bustling, full of incident.

Adverbs—eventually, in the event of, in case; in the [natural] course of things; as things go, as times go, as the world goes, as the tail wags, as the tree falls, as the cat jumps; as it may turn out, as it may happen.

Quotations—I claim not to have controlled events, but confess plainly that events have controlled me (*Abraham Lincoln*), History, n.: an account mostly false, of events mostly unimportant, which are brought about by rulers, mostly knaves, and soldiers, mostly fools (*Ambrose Bierce*).

Antonyms, see INACTIVITY.

---

ocean, *n.* sea (see WATER).

ocular, *adj.* optic, visual; retinal, conjunctival; perceptible, visible. See VISION.

oculist, *n.* ophthalmologist, eye doctor. See VISION.

odd, *adj.* strange, unusual, unnatural; curious, quaint, queer, bizarre, droll; singular, single; casual, occasional; un-matched, unpaired, lone; extra, left. See REMAINDER, UNCONFORMITY. *Ant.,* normal, usual.

oddball, *n.* eccentric, nonconformist (see UNCONFORMITY).

oddity, *n.* curiosity, freak; singularity, strangeness, peculiarity; quaintness, ec-centricity, oddness; crank, eccentric. See INSANITY, UNCONFORMITY.

odds, *n.* DIFFERENCE, probability, advan-tage; disparity. See CHANCE, INEQUALITY. —**odds and ends,** miscellany, bric-à-brac, sundries. See ASSEMBLAGE.

ode, *n.* poem, lyric; psalm, canticle, hymn; monody. See POETRY.

odious, *adj.* disgusting, repugnant, de-testable, offensive, loathsome, hateful. See HATE. *Ant.,* lovable.

ODOR
Pleasant smell

Nouns—1, odor, odorousness, smell, scent, effluvium; emanation, exhalation; fume, essence, trail, redolence; PUNGENCY; fragrance, aroma, perfume, bouquet, ambrosia, ester; sense of smell, olfaction. See MALODOROUSNESS.

2, incense; frankincense, myrrh; pastille; perfumes of Arabia; attar; balsam; berg-amot, balm, civet, musk, potpourri; cachou; pomander, potpourri; nosegay; scent, scentbag; sachet, smelling salts, vinaigrette; [eau de] cologne, toilet water. *Slang,* rape fluid.

Verbs—1, be fragrant, have an odor *or* perfume, smell sweet; smell of, exhale; give out a smell; scent, perfume, embalm.

2, smell, scent; snuff [up]; sniff; nose, inhale; get wind of. *Slang,* schmeck.

Adjectives—odorous, odoriferous; [strong-]smelling; strong-scented; redolent, aro-matic, savory, sweet, fragrant, pungent, spicy, balmy, sweet-smelling *or* -scented, per-fumed, fragrant as a rose; muscadine, ambrosial; reeking (see MALODOROUSNESS); olfactory. *Slang,* funky.

Antonyms, see ODORLESSNESS, MALODOROUSNESS.

ODORLESSNESS
Lack of smell

Nouns—1, odorlessness, inodorousness, scentlessness; deodorization, disinfection, purification, fumigation.

2, deodorizer, [stick, roll-on, *or* spray] deodorant, disinfectant; antiperspirant; fumigant; chlorophyll; mouth freshener, mouthwash.

Verbs—deodorize, fumigate, air, ventilate.

Adjectives—odorless, inodorous, scentless, unscented; deodorized.

Quotations—Of nothing—in the U.S.—are you allowed to get the real odor or savor. Everything is sterilized and wrapped in cellophane (*Henry Miller*).

Antonyms, see ODOR, MALODOROUSNESS.

---

odyssey, *n.* wandering, TRAVEL, journey; quest, pilgrimage.

off, *adv.* away, at a DISTANCE. —*adj.* disconnected, discontinued; in error, mistaken; tainted, rank, stale, high; substandard, below par, not up to scratch. See DISTANCE, SEPARATION, DETERIORATION, INFERIORITY.

offal, *n.* garbage, rubbish, refuse, waste; ordure, filth, excrement. See EXCRETION, UNCLEANNESS.

offbeat, *adj.* unfamiliar, unconventional, unorthodox, weird, queer, wacky (*sl.*), kooky (*sl.*). See UNCONFORMITY.

off-chance, *n.* IMPROBABILITY, unlikelihood.

off-color, *adj., informal,* improper, indelicate; risqué, racy, dirty. See IMPURITY.

offend, *v.* break the law, err, WRONG, sin, trespass; give offense, displease, upset, vex, provoke, hurt, aggravate, rub the wrong way; disgust; affront, spite, insult, hurt one's feelings. See ILLEGALITY, PAIN, RESENTMENT, IMPROBITY.

offender, *n.* lawbreaker, culprit. See GUILT, ILLEGALITY.

offense, *n.* insult, affront, DISCOURTESY; aggression, ATTACK; transgression, fault, crime, sin, WRONG. See GUILT, ILLEGALITY.

OFFER
Present for acceptance

Nouns—1, offer, proffer, presentation, tender, bid, overture, advance; ultimatum, last word, final offer; proposal, proposition, motion, invitation; asking price; candidature, candidacy; offering (see GIVING). *Slang,* come-on. See WILL, PURCHASE, REQUEST.

2, bidder; by-bidder, Peter Funk. *Slang,* come-on man, capper.

Verbs—1, offer, proffer, present, tender, extend, hold forth, bid, make an offer; suggest, propose, prefer, move, make a motion; advance, make advances; serve up; invite, hold out, submit, exhibit, put forward, put up; place in one's way *or* at one's disposal, lay at one's feet; offer for SALE, hawk about; press, urge upon; furnish, propound, show, give.

2, offer *or* present oneself, volunteer, come forward, be a candidate, throw one's hat in the ring; stand for, seek; be at one's service; bribe (see PAYMENT).

Adjectives—offering, offered; on the market, for sale, to let, for hire.

Quotations—I have nothing to offer but blood, toil, tears, and sweat (*Winston Churchill*), I'll make him an offer he can't refuse (*Mario Puzo*).

Antonyms, see REQUEST.

---

offering, *n.* offertory; oblation, contribution, donation, charity. See GIVING.

offhand, *adv.* casually, impromptu, extemporaneously; abruptly, carelessly.

—*adj.* casual, abrupt, extemporaneous, careless; unpremeditated, unplanned, impromptu. See UNPREPAREDNESS. *Ant.*, thought out, considered.

office, *n.* headquarters, department, bureau, room, branch; position, status, rank, function; post, job, duty, service. See AGENCY, BUSINESS, RITE.

officer, *n.* policeman; functionary, official, bureaucrat; president, vice president, secretary, treasurer; registrar; mayor, governor. See DIRECTOR, AUTHORITY.

official, *n.* officer, functionary, dignitary. —*adj.* authoritative, functional, authentic, authorized; formal. See LEGALITY, AUTHORITY. *Ant.,* unofficial.

officiate, *v.* preside, serve, supervise, direct, function. See BUSINESS, RITE.

officious, *adj.* interfering, meddlesome, obtrusive, pushy, presumptuous; bossy. See BETWEEN, AUTHORITY, SEVERITY.

off-limits, *adj.* forbidden, prohibited, taboo. See PROHIBITION.

offset, *v.t.* neutralize, balance, counteract, cancel [out], counterbalance, counterpoise. See COMPENSATION.

offshoot, *n.* ramification, incidental, result; branch, shoot, sprout; scion. See EFFECT.

offspring, *n.* children (see POSTERITY); EFFECT.

off-the-record, *adj.* unofficial, informal. See UNCONFORMITY.

often, *adv.* ofttime[s], oftentime[s], frequently, repeatedly, recurrently, oft. See FREQUENCY. *Ant.,* seldom.

ogle, *v.t.* leer at, stare at, make eyes at. See ATTENTION.

ogre, *n.* giant[ess], man-eater, cannibal; monster, beast, DEMON, fiend; cyclops, ogress, orgillon; bogy, bugbear, golliwog. See EVILDOER, FEAR.

oil, *n.* grease (see OIL); oil paint (see PAINTING). —*v.* lubricate, grease (see OIL); placate, flatter. See FLATTERY, SMOOTHNESS, SERVILITY.

OIL
Friction-reducing fluid

Nouns—1, oil, fat, lipid, grease, wax; mineral, animal, *or* vegetable oil, ethereal, volatile, *or* essential oil; lubricant, lubricator; ointment, demulcent, liniment, lotion, embrocation, Vaseline, glycerine, pomade, brilliantine, unguent, emollient; suntan *or* tanning lotion *or* oil, face *or* cold cream, *etc.*; lard, tallow, beeswax, lanolin, spermaceti, paraffin; canola, rapeseed; black gold, petroleum, gasoline, gas oil, diesel oil, naphtha, benzine, kerosene (see FUEL); benzene, toluene. *Informal,* gas.

2, lubrication, oiling, oiliness; unction, unctuosity, lubricity; lubritorium, grease rack *or* pit. *Slang,* grease *or* lube job.

Verbs—oil, lubricant, grease; anoint; lather, soap, wax, slick [up], smear, smooth, butter, lard, make slippery.

Adjectives—oily, greasy, slippery, lubricous, slick, smooth, lubricant, emollient; fat[ty], adipose, gummy, mucous, slimy, soapy, oleose, sebaceous, oleaginous.

Antonyms, see DRYNESS.

---

ointment, *n.* unguent, balm, pomade, salve, cream. See REMEDY, OIL.

OK, *adj., informal,* okay, approve, endorse. See AGREEMENT, PERMISSION. *Ant.,* objectionable.

old, *adj.* aged, old-age, elderly; experi-enced; antique, antiquated, olden. See OLDNESS, AGE. *Ant.,* young; new.

old-fashioned, *adj.* out-of-date, dated, out of style, old hat. See OLDNESS. *Ant.,* modern, up-to-date.

OLDNESS
Relating to time past

Nouns—1, oldness, AGE, antiquity; maturity; decline, decay.

2, archaism, obsolescence; relic [of the past], missing link; antiquities, fossils; antiquarianism; antiquary (see PAST). *Informal,* back-number, has-been. *Slang,* dusty line.

3, tradition, prescription, custom, neoism, immemorial usage, common law (see HABIT, RULE).

Verbs—be old, have had *or* seen its day, have seen better days; become old, AGE, fade, obsolesce, whiten, turn gray *or* white; date.

Adjectives—1, old, older, oldest, eldest, ancient, antique; of long standing, time-honored, venerable.

2, prime; primitive, primeval, primordial, primordinate; medieval, olden, of old; aboriginal (see BEGINNING); diluvian, antediluvian; prehistoric, patriarchal, preadamite; fossil, paleozoic, preglacial, antemundane.

3, archaic, classic, medieval, pre-Raphaelite; immemorial, traditional, prescriptive, customary; inveterate, rooted; antiquated, obsolete, of other times, of the old school, out-of-date, out of fashion *or* style; stale, outmoded, old-fashioned, old-style, dated, superannuated, behind the times; exploded; gone out *or* by; passé, run out; timeworn; crumbling (see DETERIORATION); extinct; hand-me-down, secondhand, discarded, castoff; old as the hills, Methuselah, *or* history. *Informal,* old-fangled, rinky-dink, old hat. *Slang,* joany.

Phrases—history repeats itself.

Antonyms, see NEWNESS.

Old Testament, *n.* See SACRED WRITINGS.

old-timer, *n., informal,* veteran, old hand *or* soldier, warhorse, oldster. See AGE. *Ant.,* youth, newcomer.

oligarchy, *n.* clique, junta; aristocracy, autocracy. See AUTHORITY.

omen, *n.* WARNING, foreboding; portent, PREDICTION; presage, THREAT.

ominous, *adj.* inauspicious, bodeful, fateful. See WARNING, PREDICTION, THREAT. *Ant.,* unthreatening.

omission, *n.* EXCLUSION, exception, elimination, cut; failure, NEGLECT, dereliction; apostrophe, ellipsis; deficit, shortage; evasion. See GUILT. *Ant.,* inclusion.

omit, *v.t.* NEGLECT, skip, spare, overlook; delete, remove, reject; evade, except, exclude, miss, drop; pass, forget. *Ant.,* add, include.

omnibus, *n.* bus; collection, compilation; reader, portable. See VEHICLE, PUBLICATION. —*adj.* inclusive, catchall, comprehensive, all-embracing, extensive. See INCLUSION.

omnipotent, *adj.* all-powerful, almighty. See DEITY, POWER.

omnipresent, *adj.* ubiquitous, pervasive. See GENERALITY.

omniscient, *adj.* all-seeing, all-knowing. See DEITY, KNOWLEDGE.

omnivorous, *adj.* devouring, all-consuming, gluttonous. See FOOD, GLUTTONY, DESIRE.

on, *adv.* forward, onward, ahead. See PROGRESSION. —*prep.* upon, at; near; *informal,* at one's expense. See RELATION, LOCATION, CONTACT, HEIGHT, COVERING.

once, *adv.* formerly, previously, latterly. See TIME, PAST. —*conj.* as soon as, whenever. See TIME.

once-over, *n., slang,* glance, look, scrutiny, survey; run-through; the eye, sizing-up, double-O (*sl.*). See VISION, INQUIRY.

oncoming, *adj.* impending, menacing. See APPROACH, NEARNESS.

one, *adj.* individual, sole, only, solitary, single. See NUMERATION.

onerous, *adj.* difficult, troublesome, burdensome, wearing, oppressive. See DIFFICULTY. *Ant.,* light, easy.

one-sided, *adj.* unfair, biased, partial; prejudiced; unbalanced, lopsided, asymmetric, awry; unilateral. See DISTORTION, MISJUDGMENT, SIDE.

ongoing, *adj.* continuing, actual, prevalent. See PRESENT.

onlooker, *n.* spectator, observer, watcher, viewer, witness, bystander; nonparticipant. See PRESENCE, VISION.

only, *adv.* solely, singly, exclusively, merely, but. —*adj.* sole, solitary, apart, alone, unique. See UNITY, SIMPLENESS, LITTLENESS.

onset, *n.* ATTACK, onslaught; opening, BEGINNING, outbreak.

onslaught, *n.* onset, ATTACK, charge, assault, offensive, thrust, drive; blame, censure, accusation, DETRACTION.

onus, *n.* burden, charge. See DUTY, COMPULSION, HINDRANCE.

onward, *adv.* forward, ahead. See PRO-
GRESSION.

ooze, *v.* seep, leak, filter; drip, percolate.
See EGRESS.

OPACITY
Nontransparency

Nouns—opaqueness, nontransparency, DIMNESS, filminess, CLOUDINESS, murk[iness], muddiness, OBSCURITY.

Verbs—opaque, obscure, darken; [be]cloud, muddy [up].

Adjectives—opaque, nontransparent, dark, obscure, murky, cloudy, muddy.

---

opaque, *adj.* obscure, nontransparent (see OPACITY); stupid, unintelligent; unintelligible, obtuse; dark, dull. See UNINTELLIGIBILITY, IGNORANCE, DARKNESS, OBSCURITY.

open, *adj.* unclosed (see OPENING); un-filled, unengaged; free, public; unrestrained, unrestricted; frank, overt; spread out, unfolded, revealed. —*v.* unfasten; unfold, spread out; reveal, disclose; start, initiate, commence. See TRUTH, DISCLOSURE. *Ant.,* close(d).

OPENING
Open space

Nouns—1, opening, hole, foramen; aperture, yawning, oscitancy, dehiscence; chasm (see INTERVAL); breach.

2, *(small opening)* puncture, perforation, scuttle; pinhole, keyhole, loophole, porthole, peephole, pigeonhole; eye, eyelet, slot, oriel; porousness, porosity. *Slang,* glory hole.

3, *(passageway)* outlet, EGRESS; inlet, INGRESS; port; vent, vomitory; embouchure; crater, orifice, mouth, sucker, muzzle, throat, gullet; estuary; pore; nozzle, tap, spigot; bore, caliber.

4, *(opening in a building)* door, doorway, entrance, entry, portal, porch, gate, astiary, postern, wicket, trapdoor, hatch; arcade; gateway, hatchway, gangway; embrasure, window, casement, light; dormer; lantern; skylight, fanlight; lattice, louver. *Slang,* gazer. See BUILDING.

5, sieve, screen, filter, colander; honeycomb; notch, cleft, embrasure.

6, *(device for opening)* opener, key, skeleton key, passkey, master key; passe-partout; latch; passport, password, pass (see INDICATION); can opener, church key; punch, gouge; piercer, borer, augur, gimlet, stylet, drill, awl, bradawl; corkscrew; dibble; trocar, trepan, probe; bodkin, needle, stiletto; reamer; warder; lancet; spear.

Verbs—1, open, gape, gap, yawn, bilge; fly *or* hang open; ope (*poet.*); unfurl, unroll; dehisce.

2, perforate, pierce, run through, tap, bore, drill; mine; tunnel; transfix; enfilade, impale, spike, spear, gore, spit, stab, pink, puncture, lance, stick, prick, riddle, punch; stave in; cut a passage through, make way *or* room for, open up *or* out; cut, expose, lay *or* break open, breach, broach. *Slang,* loid.

Adjectives—open, perforate[d], wide open, ajar, agape; unclosed, unstopped; ope (*poet.*), oscitant, gaping, yawning, cavernous; patent; tubular, cannular, fistulous; pervious, permeable; foraminous; vesicular, vascular, porous, follicular, honeycombed; notched, nicked, crenate; infundibular, riddled; tubulous, tubulated; opening; aperient.

Quotations—Each flower is a soul opening out to nature (*Gérard de Nerval*).

Antonyms, see CLOSURE.

---

open-minded, *adj.* broad-minded, impartial, unbiased; candid, receptive, tolerant, understanding, worldly. See LIBERALITY. *Ant.,* closed-minded, biased.

opera, *n.* grand opera (see MUSIC); libretto. See DRAMA.

operate, *v.* conduct, manage, direct, go, run, work, function, act. See ACTION, AGENCY.

operative, *adj.* effective, operating, acting, working, functioning, effectual. See AGENCY. —*n.* workman; detective, spy. See INQUIRY, CONCEALMENT.

operator, *n.* worker, handler; speculator. See COMMUNICATION, AGENCY, EXERTION.

operetta, *n.* musical comedy, comic opera (see MUSIC).

opiate, *n.* narcotic, palliative, drug, sedative, tranquilizer, analgesic. See INSENSIBILITY, REMEDY, HABIT.

opinion, *n.* idea, thought, BELIEF, conviction; theory, view, JUDGMENT; notion, mind, tenet, dogma; verdict; speculation; public opinion, poll, survey.

opinionated, *adj.* convinced; unconvincible, bigoted, dogmatic, prejudiced, hidebound, positive. See MISJUDGMENT. *Ant.,* open[-minded].

opium, *n.* papavarine; poppy, hops, mud, the pipe (*all inf.*). See REMEDY, HABIT.

opponent, *n.* See OPPOSITION.

opportune, *adj.* fortuitous, timely, seasonable, felicitous, suitable, apt, apropos. See OCCASION, EXPEDIENCE. *Ant.,* inopportune, inappropriate.

opportunism, *n.* See EXPEDIENCE.

opportunity, *n.* opening; chance, OCCASION; space, scope, place; leisure. See EXPEDIENCE.

oppose, *v.t.* contrast, confront; combat, counter, resist, hinder; contradict, refute, cross; repel, withstand; obstruct; contravene. See OPPOSITION, CONFUTATION, NEGATION, RESISTANCE. *Ant.,* support.

OPPOSITION
Act of opposing

*Nouns—*1, *(antagonism)* opposition, antagonism, antipathy; enmity, HATE; repugnance, oppugnancy, oppugnation, impugnation; contravention, contradiction; counteraction; counterplot; titanism; confrontation, showdown, face-off; crossfire, undercurrent, riptide, undertow, headwind; race; RESISTANCE; HINDRANCE; contrariness, DEFIANCE. See DISSENT.

2, *(position opposite)* opposition, contraposition, polarity; INVERSION; opposite side, reverse, inverse, converse; counterpart; antipodes, opposite poles, north and south, east and west, heads or tails, anode and cathode, feast or famine.

3, *(result of opposition)* insurrection, rebellion, riot, REVOLUTION; strike, lockout, walkout; boycott.

4, *(one who opposes)* enemy, foe, rival, opponent, adversary, antagonist, foeman; assailant; archenemy, nemesis; foil; disputant, competitor. See CONTENTION.

*Verbs—*1, oppose, counteract, run counter to, withstand, resist, counter, restrain, hinder (see HINDRANCE); antagonize, oppugn, fly in the face *or* teeth of, kick against, fall foul of; set *or* pit against; defy, face, confront, cope with; make a stand [against]; protest against, vote against, raise one's voice against; disfavor, turn one's back upon; set at naught, slap in the face, slam the door in one's face; freeze out; be *or* play at cross purposes; thwart, foil; play off.

2, stem, breast, encounter; stem *or* breast the tide, current, *or* flood, swim against the current *or* stream, go against the grain; beat up against; grapple with, contend (see CONTENTION); do battle (see WARFARE); contradict, contravene; belie; run *or* beat against; militate against; come in conflict with; emulate, compete, rival, vie with; side against.

3, be opposite, oppose, juxtapose, contrapose; subtend.

*Adjectives—*1, opposing, opposed; adverse, antagonistic; contrary; at variance (see DISAGREEMENT); at issue, at war with; unfavorable, unfriendly; hostile, averse, inimical, cross, unpropitious; up in arms; resistant; competitive, emulous.

2, opposite, reverse, inverse; head-on; antipodal; fronting, facing, diametrically opposite.

Adverbs—contrarily, conversely; to *or* on the contrary, then again; vice versa; at cross purposes; against the grain, stream, wind, tide, *or* current; with a head wind, in spite of, in despite of, in defiance of; in the way, teeth, *or* face of; across; athwart. *Slang*, in your face, NIMBY, not in my backyard.

Prepositions—over, against; over *or* up against; face to face, vis-à-vis; counter to, in conflict with; versus, contra.

Phrases—the enemies of my enemies are my friends; fight fire with fire.

Quotations—He that is not with me is against me (*Bible*), Love your enemies, do good to them that hate you (*Bible*), A man cannot be too careful in the choice of his enemies (*Oscar Wilde*), You shall judge of a man by his foes as well as by his friends (*Joseph Conrad*), Your friends sometimes go to sleep; your enemies never do (*Thomas Reed*).

Antonyms, see COOPERATION, SIDE, FRIEND.

---

oppress, *v.t.* persecute, burden, crush, afflict, grieve, load, depress; overbear, compress, overtax, overburden; tyrannize. See MALEVOLENCE, BADNESS, SEVERITY, SUBJECTION, WRONG.

oppressive, *adj.* tyrannical, cruel, burdensome, onerous, grievous. See SEVERITY, BADNESS.

oppressor, *n.* persecutor, bully, boss, slave driver, Simon Legree, master; tyrant, martinet, dictator. See SEVERITY.

opprobrious, *adj.* abusive, insulting, offensive, slanderous, derogatory, contemptuous, malicious. See DISREPUTE, DETRACTION.

opt, *v.i.* decide; approve (of), vote for, elect, choose, select, pick, favor. See CHOICE.

OPTICAL INSTRUMENTS
Devices for modifying vision

Nouns—1, optical instruments, [plano-convex *or* -concave, biconvex, converging *or* diverging miniscus, *or* biconcave] lens, achromatic lens; spectacles, glasses, bifocals, pince-nez, eyeglass, reading glasses, monocle, lorgnon, lorgnette, quizzing glass, goggles; aviator glasses, granny glasses, horn rims; Polaroid lenses, [hard *or* soft] contact lenses; sunglasses, dark glasses; spyglass, magnifying glass; opera glass[es], fieldglass, binoculars; glass eye; telescope, periscope, spectroscope, microscope; optics, optometry. *Slang*, specs, cheaters, peepers, shades.

2, *(reflecting device)* mirror, glass, looking glass, pier glass, cheval glass, shaving mirror, girandole mirror, trumeau; reflection; optical fiber.

3, *(recording or projecting device)* camera, camera lucida, camera obscura; motion-picture camera; kinescope, television camera; stereoscope, stereopticon, viewer, magic lantern, kaleidoscope; projector.

4, optometrist; lens grinder; oculist, optician; microscopist, spectroscopist.

5, *(light sensitive device)* electric eye, photoelectric *or* photovoltaic cell.

Adjectives—optic[al], optometrical; microscopic, telescopic, stereoscopic, three-dimensional, 3-D; [be]spectacled, monocled.

Quotations—Men seldom make passes at girls who wear glasses (*Dorothy Parker*), Women have served all these centuries as looking-glasses possessing the magic and delicious power of reflecting the figure of man at twice its natural size (*Virginia Woolf*).

---

optimal, *adj.* optimum, prime, best. See GOODNESS. *Ant.*, minimal, worst.

optimism, *n.* hopefulness, HOPE, cheerfulness, enthusiasm; confidence, assurance. *Ant.*, pessimism, skepticism, cynicism.

option, *n.* CHOICE, preference, discretion, alternative; privilege; right; first call, choice, *or* say; put, call. See RIGHTNESS.

optional, *adj.* discretionary, voluntary, elective, nonobligatory. See CHOICE. *Ant.*, obligatory, required.

opulent, *adj.* wealthy; abundant. See MONEY, SUFFICIENCY.

opus, *n.* work, publication, composition, work of art, *etc.* See EXERTION.

oracle, *n.* prophet, seer (see PREDICTION).

oral, *adj.* verbal, vocal, spoken, unwritten. See SPEECH. *Ant.,* verbal.

orange, *n.* tangerine, tangelo; sweet, blood, mandarin, navel, *etc.* orange. See VEGETABLE, COLOR.

oration, *n.* SPEECH, declamation, discourse, address.

oratory, *n.* SPEECH, elocution, declamation, eloquence, expression.

orb, *n.* sphere, globe; orbit, circuit. See ROTUNDITY, CIRCULARITY.

orbit, *n.* path, track, CIRCUIT, revolution, course; region, range, sphere, realm, scope; province, sphere of INFLUENCE. See ASTRONAUTICS, BUSINESS.

orchard, *n.* fruit garden, grove, vineyard, plantation. See AGRICULTURE.

orchestra, *n.* symphony, sinfonia; band; parterre, ground floor. See MUSIC, DRAMA, ARENA.

ordain, *v.* install, appoint, invest, frock; decree, [pre]destine. See CLERGY, COMMISSION.

ordeal, *n.* trial, strain, cross, tribulation, test. See ADVERSITY, EXPERIMENT.

order, *n.* orderliness (see ORDER); COMMAND; class, kind, rank; society, fellowship, guild (see PARTY); succession, SEQUENCE.

ORDER
Prescribed mode of procedure

Nouns—1, order, orderliness, REGULARITY, uniformity, SYMMETRY, harmony, precision; METHOD, system, disposition, ARRANGEMENT; pecking order; composition; coordination, subordination; infrastructure; management, regimentation, discipline, ECONOMY; PLAN, FORM, array; course, routine, even tenor, HABIT. See CONFORMITY.

2, gradation, graduation, progression, series, sequence, classification, ordering; rank, place, step, DEGREE; CLASS, kind, sort, set; category, division. See CONTINUITY.

Verbs—1, be in order; form, fall in, draw up; arrange, range, *or* place itself; fall into place *or* rank, take one's place, rally round.

2, [put in] order, make *or* restore order; organize, regulate, regularize; classify, alphabetize; arrange, range, array, align, trim, dispose, place; LIST, file [away], put away; regroup. *Slang,* get one's act, head, *or* shit together, get one's ass in gear.

Adjectives—orderly, regular; in order, in good form, in trim, in place, in its proper place, fixed; neat, tidy, trim, spruce; methodical, classified, symmetrical, shipshape; cosmic; uniform, geometric[al]; businesslike, systematic, schematic. *Informal,* in apple-pie order, together.

Adverbs—orderly, in order; methodically, in [its] turn, step by step, by regular steps, stages, intervals, *or* gradations; seriatim, systematically, by *or* like clockwork.

Quotations—A place for everything and everything in its place (*Mrs. Beeton*), good order is the foundation of all good things (*Edmund Burke*), Chaos often breeds life, when order breeds habit (*Henry Adams*).

Antonyms, see DISORDER.

---

ordinance, *n.* law, regulation, order, decree; appointment, destiny; RULE, enactment. See COMMAND.

ordinary, *adj.* usual, medium, average, unremarkable, commonplace, regular, common; inferior, low; middling, second-rate; mediocre, undistinguished. See CONFORMITY, HABIT, SIMPLENESS, MEDIOCRITY. *Ant.,* unusual, special.

ordnance, *n.* guns, cannon, artillery. See ARMS.

organ, *n.* hand organ, hurdygurdy, barrel organ, organette, regal, organophone, harmonium, calliope; pipe *or* electronic organ; melodeon; PUBLICATION, journal; component, PART, member; gland, heart, *etc.* See MUSIC.

organic, *adj.* bodily (see BODY); animate, biological (see ORGANIC MATTER); systematized, structural. See ORDER, FORM.

ORGANIC MATTER
The animate world

Nouns—1, organic matter, organization, organized nature *or* world, animated *or* living nature, living beings; biogenesis, evolution, microevolution, natural selection; genetic engineering, biotechnology, genetic code, genetic engineering *or* isolation, gene counseling, gene pool, gene therapy *or* splicing, crossbreeding, backcrossing; human genome.

2, five kingdoms, Animalia, Plantae, Fungi, Protista, Monera; agnatha, amphibia, annelida, anthophyta, arachnida, arthropoda, aves, bryophyta, chondrichthyes, chordata, coniferophyta, crustacea, echinodermata, eumetazoa, eutheria, insecta, invertebrata, mammalia, mesozoa, metatheria, metazoa, mollusca, nematoda, osteichthyes, parazoa, prototheria, protozoa, pterophyta, reptilia, sarcodina, vertebrata; flora, fauna, biota; organic remains, fossils, petrified organisms. See ANIMAL, HUMANITY, VEGETABLE, LIFE.

3, organism, plankton; cell, plasma, protoplasm, cytoplasm, ectoplasm, *etc;* [recombinant *or* junk] DNA, RNA, *etc.,* adenosine, thymine, cytosine, guanine, adenine, purine, pyrmidine, transposon, cosmid, double helix, exon, nucleic acid, plasmid; ovum, egg *or* sperm cell, spermatozoon, gamete, semen, seed; spore; nucleus; genome, karyotype, [X, Y, *or* Z] chromosome, autosome, prophase, chromatid, homolog; cell division, mitosis; gene, nucleotide, allele, genome, plasmid, adenovirus, operon, codon, liposome, oncogene, retrovirus, exon, intron, heterozygote, homozygote, imprinted gene, minos, pseudogene, damper gene, obesity gene, retrotransposon, stuttering gene, suicide gene, gay gene. See REPRODUCTION.

4, [alpha *or* beta] cell, adipocyte, basophil, calmodulin, centriole, chloroplast, cytochrome, cytokinesis, cytoplasm, cytoskeleton, desmosome, endocytosis, erythrocyte, eukaryote, exocytosis, glial cell, clycolysis, granulocyte, leukocyte, lymphocyte, lysosome, megakaryocyte, memory cell, microphage, mitochondria, monocyte, neutrophil, nucleolus, organelle, osteoplast, oxyntic cell, parietal cell, peroxisome, phagocytosis, plasma cell, platelet, prokaryote, ribosome.

5, biology, natural history; organic chemistry, anatomy, zoology, botany, bacteriology, biochemistry, bionics, proteomics, genomics, biophysics, embryology, microbiology, molecular biology, biotechnology, cytology, chromosomology, genetics; biologist, zoologist, *etc.*

Adjectives—organic, vital, biotic, biological; protoplasmic, plasmic, plasmatic, cellular, nuclear; chromosomal, haploid, diploid; embryonic, germinal; structural, anatomic[al].

Quotations—The biologist passes, the frog remains (*Edmond Rostand*), The essence of life is statistical improbability on a colossal scale (*Richard Dawkins*), All things are artificial, for nature is the art of God (*Thomas Browne*), Nature is not a temple, but a workshop, and man's the workman in it (*Ivan Turgenev*), Everything from an egg (*William Harvey*).

Antonyms, see INORGANIC MATTER.

---

organization, *n.* ARRANGEMENT, classification, CLASS; association, society, club, establishment, enterprise; organism. See PARTY, ORGANIC MATTER, FORM.

orgasm, *n.* paroxysm, spasm; climax. See VIOLENCE, SEX.

orgy, *n.* debauch, carouse, dissipation; rite; revelry, carousal. See INTEMPERANCE.

orient, *v.t.* orientate; find one's bearings,

locate; acquaint, familiarize, adapt, adjust; indoctrinate, educate, train. See DIRECTION.

orifice, *n.* See OPENING.

origin, *n.* BEGINNING, CAUSE, commencement; descent, source, fountainhead, derivation, rise, ANCESTRY.

original, *adj.* novel, unique; primary, initial; earliest, primal, aboriginal; creative, inventive. See BEGINNING, IMAGINATION, UNCONFORMITY, SPECIALITY. *Ant.*, secondhand, plagiarized, later.

originate, *v.* start, invent, begin, inaugurate, initiate, CAUSE; proceed, spring. See BEGINNING, IMAGINATION.

ORNAMENT
Anything that beautifies

Nouns—1, ornament, ornamentation, ornateness; adornment, decoration, embellishment, dressing, décor.

2, garnish, polish, varnish, gilding, lacquer, enamel; cosmetics (see BEAUTY); ormolu.

3, *(design)* pattern, diaper, powdering, paneling, lining, graining; detail, TEXTURE, richness; mosaic; tracery, filigree, molding, filet, flourish, fleur-de-lis, arabesque, fret, astragal, zigzag, acanthus, pilaster.

4, *(trimming)* pargeting, embroidery, needlework; brocade, brocatel, lace, fringe, trapping, border, guilloche, edging, trimming, frill; hanging, tapestry, arras.

5, *(ornamental attachment)* wreath, festoon, garland, chaplet, flower, nosegay, corsage, bouquet, posy, lei; crepe paper; tassel, shoulder knot, epaulet, braid, aiguillette, frog; star, rosette, bow; feather, plume, plumage, panache, aigrette, fine feathers; agrafe, bodkin, boutonniere, netsuke; band, armlet; bow, cordon.

6, jewelry, parure, bijoutry; bijou, trinket, bauble, bibelot, gewgaw, knickknack, gimcrack, locket, diadem, coronet, aigrette, necklace, rivière, bracelet, anklet, earring, carcanet, chain, fob, chatelaine, brooch, girandole, pin, cameo, scrimshaw, torque, intaglio, labret, nose ring; slave bracelet, costume jewelry; jewel, gem, precious stone; diamond, brilliant, beryl, emerald, chalcedony, agate, heliotrope; girasol; onyx, sardonyx; garnet, lapis lazuli, opal, peridot, chrysolite, sapphire, ruby; spinel, topaz; turquoise; zircon, jacinth, hyacinth, carbuncle, rhinestone, amethyst; pearl, coral; sequin. *Informal*, glass.

7, *(ornament in bad taste)* finery, frippery, gewgaw, gimcrack, tinsel, spangle, clinquant, brummagem, pinchbeck, paste, glass; knickknack, bric-a-brac, curio; gaudiness (see VULGARITY).

8, *(ornamental drawing)* illustration, illumination, vignette; headpiece, tailpiece, scroll, flowers, rhetoric, work of art.

Verbs—1, ornament, embellish, decorate, adorn, grace, beautify, smarten; furbish, polish; blazon, beset; gild, varnish, whitewash, enamel, japan, lacquer, paint, grain, enrich, silver, chrome.

2, garnish, trim, [be]dizen, prink, primp, prank; trip out; [be]deck, [be]dight, array; dress up, [be]spangle, powder, embroider, work; chase, emboss, fret; stud; make up; emblazon, illuminate; illustrate. *Informal*, spruce up. *Slang*, doll up, jazz up.

Adjectives—1, ornamented, beautified; ornate, rich, gilt, gilded; tasselated, festooned, ornamental, decorative, becoming, smart, gay, flowery, glittering; spangled. See BEAUTY.

2, pranked out, bedight, well-groomed, fresh as a daisy; in full dress *or* fashion, *en grande toilette*; in best bib and tucker, in Sunday best, showy, flashy, sporty, fancy; gaudy, garish (see OSTENTATION); gorgeous. *Slang*, sharp, snazzy, Sunday-go-to-meeting; in glad rags; dressed to kill, all dressed up like a Christmas tree, ragged out *or* up.

Quotations—There is material enough in a single flower for the ornament of a score of cathedrals (*John Ruskin*), Respecting all ornament . . . Was it done with enjoyment—was the carver happy while he was about it? (*John Ruskin*), Nobility is a graceful ornament to the civil order. It is the Corinthian capital of polished society (*Edmund Burke*).

Antonyms, see SIMPLENESS.

ornate, *adj.* See ORNAMENT. *Ant.*, simple, plain.

ornery, *adj.* contrary, difficult, cantankerous; irascible. See DISOBEDIENCE, IRASCIBILITY.

orphan, *n.* waif, stray, gamin[e], urchin; foundling. See RELINQUISHMENT.

orphanage, *n.* home, foundlings' home, shelter, refuge. See ABODE.

orthodox, *adj.* approved, conventional; sound, strict, faithful; Christian; evangelical, scriptural, textual, literal, canonical. See RELIGION, BELIEF, CONFORMITY. *Ant.*, unorthodox.

oscillate, *v.i.* vibrate (see OSCILLATION); hesitate, shilly-shally, hem and haw, blow hot and cold. See DOUBT, CHANGEABLENESS

OSCILLATION
Fluctuation

Nouns—oscillation; vibration, libration, nutation, undulation; pulsation, pulse; fluctuation, vacillation, wavering; wave, swing, beat, shake, wag, seesaw, dance; alternation, reciprocation; coming and going; ebb and flow, flux and reflux, ups and downs; trill, tremolo. See REGULARITY, CHANGEABLENESS.

Verbs—oscillate; vibrate, librate, reciprocate, alternate, undulate, wave; rock, swing; flutter, pulsate, beat; wag; tick; play; fluctuate, dance, curvet, reel [to and fro], quake; quiver, quaver; shake, flicker; wriggle; roll, toss, pitch; flounder, stagger, totter; move or bob up and down; pass and repass, ebb and flow, come and go; waver, teeter, seesaw, vacillate; take turns, change off.

Adjectives—oscillating, oscillatory, undulatory, pulsatory, libratory; vibratory, pendulous; wavering, fluctuating; every other; irresolute.

Adverbs—to and fro, up and down, back and forth, backward and forward, seesaw, zigzag, in and out, from side to side, from pillar to post.

Quotations—Is it a fact, or have I dreamt it—that, by means of electricity, the world of matter has become a great nerve, vibrating thousands of miles in a breathless point of time? (*Nathaniel Hawthorne*).

Antonyms, see STABILITY.

---

ossify, *v.* harden, callous, horrify. See HARDNESS.

ostensible, *adj.* apparent, outward; professed, pretended. See APPEARANCE.

OSTENTATION
Pretentious display

Nouns—1, ostentation, ostentatiousness, display, show, flourish, parade; pomp, array, state, solemnity; dash, splash, glitter, strut; bombast, pomposity (see BOASTING); tinsel, tawdriness; pretense, pretension, pretentiousness, flatulence; airs, showing off; showmanship; veneer, AFFECTATION; magnificence, splendor. *Informal,* front, dog. *Slang,* swank, side, ritz[iness], razzle-dazzle, glitz. See VANITY, PRIDE, ORNAMENT, VULGARITY.

2, (*elaborate event*) pageant[ry], demonstration, panoply, exhibition, flying colors, tomfoolery; flourish *or* fanfare [of trumpets]; color guard; spectacle, procession; fete (see CELEBRATION). *Slang,* grandstand play.

3, (*elaborate clothing*) dress; court dress, full dress, black tie, white tie [and tails], evening dress *or* gown, ball dress, fancy dress; full regalia, tailoring; millinery, frippery; foppery, equipage. *Slang,* glad rags, Sunday best. See CLOTHING, FASHION.

4, (*elaborate ceremony*) ceremony, ceremonial; ritual; form, formality; etiquette; punctilio, punctiliousness; stateliness, RITE; protocol.

5, exhibitionist, show-off; showman. *Slang,* grandstander. See AFFECTATION.

Verbs—put oneself forward, court attention, splurge; star, figure; make a show *or* display; glitter; show off, parade; display, exhibit, put forward; sport, brandish, blazon forth; dangle, flaunt, emblazon, prink, primp; set off, mount, have framed; put a good face upon. *Informal,* cut a figure, cut a dash, cut a wide swath, make a splash, play to the gallery, trot out, put on the dog, show off; wear one's heart on one's sleeve. *Slang,* grandstand, put on a front, strut one's stuff, doll up, wank.

Adjectives—ostentatious, showy, dashing, pretentious, impressive; jaunty; grand, pompous, palatial; high-sounding, turgid, garish, gaudy [as a peacock]; conspicuous, flaunting, flashing, flamboyant, flaming, glittering, florid, flowery; gay, splendid, magnificent, sumptuous, grandiose, de luxe; theatrical, dramatic, spectacular; ceremonial, ritual; dressy, fancy; solemn, stately, majestic, formal, stiff, ceremonious, punctilious, starched; in best bib and tucker, in Sunday best, on parade; blatant. *Slang,* ritzy, artsy, Day-Glo.

Adverbs—ostentatiously, pompously, *etc.;* with a flourish of trumpets, with flying colors; in a big way.

Antonyms, see SIMPLENESS, MODESTY.

---

ostracize, *v.t.* exclude, banish, bar, blackball; outcast. See EXCLUSION.

other, *adj.* different, separate, distinct; former; another, additional. See DIFFERENCE.

otherwise, *adv.* else, if not, besides; contrarily, contrariwise; conversely, vice versa; quite the contrary; alias. See DIFFERENCE.

otherworldly, *adj.* unworldly, religious, spiritual, supernatural, extramundane, unearthly, out of this world; idealistic, unreal. See UNCONFORMITY, UNIVERSE, HEAVEN.

oust, *v.t.* depose, evict, remove, dismiss, dislodge. See EJECTION.

out, *adv.* without, outside; outdoors; démodé. See EXTERIOR, DISUSE.

out-and-out, *adj.* absolute, complete (see COMPLETION).

outbreak, *n.* outburst, eruption; rebellion, uprising, revolt, insurrection; disturbance. See DISOBEDIENCE, VIOLENCE, BEGINNING, ATTACK.

outburst, *n.* eruption, explosion, blowup; outpouring, flood, breakthrough; paroxysm, spasm, upheaval; uproar. See VIOLENCE.

outcast, *n.* pariah, derelict, exile; castaway, outsider, outlaw; leper. See UNCONFORMITY, DISPLACEMENT.

outclass, *v.t.* outdo, outrival. See SUPERIORITY.

outcome, *n.* issue, termination, end, result, consequence, outgrowth, upshot. See EFFECT.

outcry, *n.* clamor, tumult, exclamation, shout, uproar. See CRY, DISAPPROBATION.

outdated, *adj.* obsolete, out-of-date, antiquated. See OLDNESS. *Ant.,* up-to-date.

outdistance, *v.t.* See OVERRUNNING.

outdo, *v.t.* excel, exceed, surpass, outstrip, beat. See SUPERIORITY.

outdoor, *adj.* open-air, out-of-door[s], alfresco; drive-in. See EXTERIOR.

outer, *adj.* outside, outward, external, EXTERIOR.

outfit, *n.* ensemble, garments, suit; group, unit; equipment, gear. See CLOTHING, PROVISION.

outflow, *n.* effluence, efflux, outpouring, issue, effusion, escape. See EGRESS, PAYMENT.

outgoing, *adj.* extrovert; retiring. See COMMUNICATION, DEPARTURE.

outgrowth, *n.* development, result, outcome, offshoot; excrescence. See EFFECT, CONVEXITY.

outhouse, *n.* outbuilding; privy. See ABODE, UNCLEANNESS.

outing, *n.* excursion, junket, field day, picnic. See TRAVEL.

outlandish, *adj.* bizarre, outré, eccentric, foreign, grotesque, queer. See UNCONFORMITY.

outlast, *v.* outlive, survive, outwear. See DURABILITY.

outlaw, *n.* criminal, bandit, fugitive, outcast; desperado. See EVILDOER, ILLEGALITY.

outlay, *n.* expenditure, disbursements, outgo. See PAYMENT.

outlet, *n.* loophole, port; sluice, floodgate; faucet, tap, spout, conduit; exit, vent, OPENING. See EGRESS, ESCAPE.

outline, *n.* profile, tracing, tracery; bounds, boundary; EDGE, circumference, perimeter; [rough] sketch, PLAN, blueprint, schematic, scheme, drawing, draft; synopsis, summary, résumé; diagram, chart, map. —*v.t.* sketch; diagram; model, block in, PLAN; boil down, summarize, trace, draw, depict, delimit, design, picture, demonstrate. See APPEARANCE, DESCRIPTION, SHORTNESS, FORM.

outlive, *v.t.* survive, outlast. See DURABILITY.

outlook, *n.* APPEARANCE, prospect, probabilities, forecast; scene, view, vista. See EXPECTATION.

outlying, *adj.* distant, suburban, remote; frontier. See DISTANCE.

outmoded, *adj.* outdated, out-of-date; timeworn, stale; superseded, square (*sl.*). See OLDNESS, DISUSE. *Ant.,* modern, up-to-date.

out-of-date, *adj.* See OLDNESS.

out-of-the-way, *adj.* off the beaten track, secluded, isolated; bizarre, out of the ordinary, outlandish. See DISTANCE, UNCONFORMITY.

outpost, *n.* sentry, scout, picket, vanguard; border, march, frontier; outstation, fort. See DISTANCE, ENVIRONMENT, DEFENSE.

outpouring, *n.* effusion, spate, flood. See SUFFICIENCY, SENSIBILITY, WATER.

output, *n.* produce, yield, harvest, product. See PRODUCTION, EFFECT.

outrage, *n.* VIOLENCE, WRONG, affront, harm, damage, injury, abuse; transgression, infraction, violation. See EVIL, BADNESS, DISRESPECT.

outrageous, *adj.* offensive, shocking. See DISREPUTE.

outreach, *n.* extent, INFLUENCE; community service (see BENEVOLENCE).

outright, *adj.* complete, unqualified, unmitigated, consummate, out-and-out. See COMPLETION.

outrun, *v.t.* overtake, outdistance, outstrip. See SUPERIORITY.

outset, *n.* BEGINNING, start, commencement; DEPARTURE.

outshine, *v.t.* outdo, eclipse, excel, overshadow. See REPUTE.

outside, *adj.* EXTERIOR, outer, external, outward. *Ant.,* inside.

outsider, *n.* alien, stranger, foreigner; layman; onlooker, passerby, intruder, pariah, rebel, *etc.* See EXTRINSIC, LAITY. *Ant.,* insider.

outskirts, *n.pl.* suburbs, environs, surroundings; border, edge; purlieus. See NEARNESS, DISTANCE, ENVIRONMENT.

outsmart, *v.t.* See CUNNING.

outspoken, *adj.* frank, bluff, unreserved, blunt, loud, plainspoken. See SIMPLENESS, SPEECH. *Ant.,* reticent, taciturn.

outstanding, *adj.* prominent, exceptional, conspicuous, remarkable, noticeable, eminent; unpaid, uncollected, owing, due, unsettled. See DEBT, REMAINDER, CONVEXITY, IMPORTANCE, SUPERIORITY. *Ant.,* conventional, common, unexceptional.

outstretched, *adj.* extended, proffered, offered; expanded, outspread. See BREADTH, OFFER.

outstrip, *v.t.* outspace, outrun, excel, exceed, outdo, outdistance; eclipse, surpass. See SUPERIORITY, OVERRUNNING.

outward, *adj.* EXTERIOR, outer, outside, out; visible (see VISIBILITY). *Ant.,* inward.

outweigh, *v.t.* overweigh, outbalance, overbalance, exceed. See SUPERIORITY.

outwit, *v.t.* frustrate, circumvent, outsmart. See DECEPTION.

oval, *adj.* elliptical, ovoid, ovate. See CIRCULARITY.

ovation, *n.* applause, kudos, tribute; acclamation, cheers, APPROBATION.

oven, *n.* stove, range, roaster, broiler; hearth; furnace, kiln; rotisserie, rotary oven, Dutch oven, hibachi; convection *or* microwave oven. See HEAT.

over, *adv.* past, across, by; again; beyond; extra, above, more, remaining, left. — *prep.* on, above. See END, OPPOSITION, REPETITION, SUPERIORITY. *Ant.,* under.

overact, *v.i.* overplay, ham [it up] (*inf.*), chew the scenery (*inf.*). See EXAGGERATION.

overactive, *adj.* hyperactive, frenetic. See AGITATION.

overall, *adj.* blanket, all-inclusive. See INCLUSION.

overawe, *v.t.* intimidate, daunt, abash, cow; impress. See FEAR.

overbalance, *v.t.* surpass, unbalance, overweigh. See SUPERIORITY.

overbearing, *adj.* domineering, bullying, lordly, arrogant, dictatorial; overwhelming. See INSOLENCE.

overcast, *adj.* cloudy, murky, shadowy, gloomy, dark, leaden. See CLOUDINESS.

overcautious, *adj.* overcareful, timorous, fearful, unenterprising. See CAUTION.

overcharge, *v.* rook, fleece, cheat, extort;

scalp, gyp, do (*all inf.*). See DEARNESS. *Ant.*, undercharge.

overcoat, *n.* greatcoat, duster, topcoat, ulster, raglan, petersham. See CLOTHING.

overcome, *v.* conquer, subdue, defeat, overthrow, surmount. See SUCCESS. — *adj.* subdued, conquered, defeated, broken, crushed, downcast. See FAILURE.

overconfident, *adj.* reckless, cocksure, cocky, complacent, brash, incautious, cheeky (*inf.*), nervy. See RASHNESS. *Ant.*, insecure.

overcrowded, *adj.* populous, jam-packed, teeming. See MULTITUDE.

overdo, *v.* overtask, overstrain, *etc.;* go to far, carry to extremes. See EXAGGERATION.

overdue, *adj.* past due, late, delayed. See LATENESS.

overeat, *v.i.* stuff oneself, overindulge. See GLUTTONY.

overestimation, *n.* See EXAGGERATION.

overflow, *v.* inundate; flood; brim *or* well over, boil over, run over. —*n.* inundation, flooding, deluge, alluvion; spate, profusion, excess. See SUFFICIENCY, WATER, OVERRUNNING.

overgrown, *adj.* overrun, weedy; swollen, bloated, oversize, outsize. See SIZE, EXPANSION, OVERRUNNING.

overhang, *v.t.* project over, jut; impend, threaten. See CONVEXITY, PREDICTION.

overhaul, *v.t.* examine, check, inspect; repair, renovate. See RESTORATION.

overhead, *n.* costs, expenditure, outlay, capital, investment. See PRICE. —*adv.* above (see HEIGHT).

overhear, *v.t.* catch; eavesdrop. See HEARING, CURIOSITY.

overjoyed, *adj.* delighted, enraptured. See PLEASURE.

overkill, *n.* overdoing, overemphasis (see EXAGGERATION).

overlap, *v.* imbricate, shingle; overhang, overlie; superimpose. See COVERING.

overlay, *v.t.* superimpose, cover. See COVERING, LAYER.

overlook, *v.t.* look out on, command [a view of]; oversee, manage, direct, supervise; pass over *or* by, ignore, omit, disregard, skip; forgive, indulge, excuse, condone, wink at. See DIRECTION, NEGLECT, FORGIVENESS.

overlord, *n.* master, liege [lord] (see AUTHORITY).

overpass, *n.* bridge, walkway. See PASSAGE.

overpower, *v.t.* overwhelm, subdue. See SUCCESS.

overrated, *adj.* overestimated, exaggerated, pumped up. See EXAGGERATION. *Ant.*, underrated.

override, *v.t.* annul (see OVERRULE); prevail. See SUPERIORITY.

overrule, *v.t.* override, reverse, set aside, contravene, rescind, veto, cancel, countermand. See NULLIFICATION, REJECTION.

OVERRUNNING
Exceeding

Nouns—overrunning, overflowing, overspreading; overstepping, transgression, encroachment, incursion, intrusion, infringement, extravagation, transcendence; infestation; invasion. See EXAGGERATION.

Verbs—1, overrun, run *or* spread over, overspread, overgrow, infest, grow over, run riot; run down, run [roughshod] over, trample on; overswarm, overflow, overwhelm, deluge, inundate.

2, outrun, outstrip, outpace, outstride, outdistance, outrace, pass, go beyond, go by, shoot ahead of, override, outride; outrival, outdo, beat (see SUPERIORITY); overshoot [the mark].

3, overstep, transgress, trespass, encroach, infringe, intrude, invade.

Adjectives—overrun, infested, plagued; overspread, overgrown.

Adverbs—ahead, in advance, beyond the mark, beyond the pale.

Antonyms, see INSUFFICIENCY, FAILURE.

overseas, *adj.* transoceanic, ultramarine, foreign, colonial. —*adv.* beyond the sea, abroad, away, over there (*inf.*). See DISTANCE.

oversee, *v.t.* manage, superintend, direct, supervise, command; overlook. See AUTHORITY.

overshadow, *v.t.* eclipse, show up (*inf.*). See SUPERIORITY.

overshoe, *n.* boot, arctic, galosh, rubber. See CLOTHING.

oversight, *n.* omission, ERROR, blunder, slip; management, directorship, supervision. See AUTHORITY, NEGLECT.

overstate, *v.t.* exaggerate, overclaim, overdo, overdraw, overembellish. See EXAGGERATION. *Ant.,* understate, minimize.

overstep, *v.i.* transgress, trespass, cross, encroach, exceed; intrude, infringe. See OVERRUNNING.

overt, *adj.* open, exposed, plain to see. See DISCLOSURE, OPENING. *Ant.,* concealed, secret.

overtake, *v.t.* catch [up with], pass, reach, overhaul. See ARRIVAL.

overthrow, *v.t.* overcome, defeat, upset, abolish, confute; overturn, demolish, ruin. See DEPRESSION, SUCCESS, CONFUTATION, REVOLUTION.

overtone, *n.* suggestion, connotation, hint, implication, intimation, innuendo, insinuation, inference, undertone. See INFORMATION. *Ant.,* undertone.

overture, *n.* advance, approach, proposal, bid; prelude, preliminary, introduction. See OFFER, PRECEDENCE.

overturn, *v.t.* invert, upset, reverse; overthrow, destroy. See CHANGE, CONFUTATION, DESTRUCTION, INVERSION.

overview, *n.* survey, review, synopsis. See SHORTNESS.

overweight, *adj.* obese, fat, adipose, chubby, chunky. See ROTUNDITY.

overwhelm, *v.t.* overpower, crush, submerge, overcome. See DESTRUCTION, CONFUTATION, WATER. *Ant.,* underwhelm (*inf.*).

overwork, *v.* overdo, tire, weary, exhaust, overtax, overburden, overtask. See EXERTION.

overwrought, *adj.* elaborate, pretentious, ornate; overworked, tired; distraught, hysterical, nervous, frenetic, highstrung. See ORNAMENT, EXCITEMENT.

ovum, *n.* cell, egg, seed. See ORGANIC MATTER, REPRODUCTION.

owe, *v.i.* be indebted, be in DEBT. See ATTRIBUTION.

own, *v.* admit, confess, concede, acknowledge; possess, have, hold. See DISCLOSURE, POSSESSION, SPECIALITY.

ownership, *n.* POSSESSION, proprietorship, title.

oxymoron, *n.* self-contradiction, paradox, ABSURDITY.

P

pace, *n.* rate, speed, VELOCITY; step, measuring step; stride; gait, amble, rack, single-foot. —*v.* walk, step, stride; walk to and fro; measure; lead, set the pace. See MOTION, PRECEDENCE, TRAVEL.

pachyderm, *n.* elephant, rhinoceros, hippopotamus. See ANIMAL.

pacific, *adj.* peaceable, conciliatory; calm. See PACIFICATION, CONTENT. *Ant.,* warlike, contentious.

pacifier, *n.* soother, teether, teething ring; conciliator, alleviator, mediator. See PACIFICATION, MODERATION.

PACIFICATION
Making peace

Nouns—**1,** pacification, conciliation; reconciliation, reconcilement; propitiation, appeasement, mollification, mediation; shaking of hands, accommodation, arrangement, adjustment, COMPROMISE; shuttle diplomacy; deed of release; pacifism; glasnost; peaceful coexistence; nonviolence, satyagraha; peace dividend.

2, peace offering; peace treaty, Carthaginian peace; peace, truce, armistice, cease-fire; suspension of hostilities; breathing spell, détente; flag of truce, white flag, olive branch; peace pipe, calumet. *Slang,* flower power.

3, pacifier, peacemaker, conciliator, Type B; pacifist, antiwar activist. *Slang,* flower child; peacenik, jodie, conshie.

Verbs—**1,** pacify, tranquilize, compose; allay (see MODERATION); reconcile, [re]unite, propitiate, placate, conciliate, meet halfway, hold out the olive branch, accommodate, heal the breach, make peace, restore harmony, bring to terms, pour oil on troubled waters, handle with kid gloves.

2, settle differences, arrange matters; set straight; make up (a quarrel), come to an understanding, come to terms; bridge over, hush up; make it up, make matters up; mend one's fences; patch up; shake hands. *Informal,* bury the hatchet *or* the tomahawk, smoke the peace pipe.

3, disarm, demilitarize, sheathe the sword, denuclearize; raise a siege; lay down one's arms, beat swords into plowshares; come around.

Adjectives—pacific, peaceful, calm; peaceable, unwarlike, peace-loving, peace-making; pacifying, soothing, mollifying; appeasing; pacificatory, propitiatory, conciliatory; pacified, CONTENT; pacifist, antiwar.

Phrases—after a storm comes a calm.

Quotations—The peace of God, which passeth all understanding (*Bible*), Peace hath her victories no less renowned than war (*John Milton*), In the arts of peace Man is a bungler (*G. B. Shaw*), It is easier to make war than to make peace (*Georges Clemenceau*), Nothing will end war unless the people themselves refuse to go to war (*Albert Einstein*), Peace is nothing but slovenliness, only war creates order (*Bertolt Brecht*), The work, my friend, is peace. More than an end of this war—an end to the beginning of all wars (*F. D. Roosevelt*), Pacifism is simply undisguised cowardice (*Adolf Hitler*), Nonviolence is a powerful and just weapon . . . It is a sword that heals (*Martin Luther King*).

Antonyms, see CONTENTION, WARFARE, RESENTMENT.

pack, *n.* stow, bale, package, packet; load, burden, bundle; knapsack; crowd, mob, multitude; herd, flock, bevy, covey. See ASSEMBLAGE. —*v.* stow, bale, package; cram, tamp; cake, solidify; add to; stuff; load, burden. See ARRANGEMENT.

package, *n.* parcel, pack[et], carton. See ASSEMBLAGE, ENCLOSURE. —**package store,** liquor store (see DRINKING).

pack animal, *n.* beast of burden; horse, donkey, *etc.* See TRANSPORTATION, ANIMAL.

packet, *n.* package; packet boat, paquebot; mail boat, steamer, coaster. See SHIP.

packing, *n.* contents, filler, stuffing, wadding; closure, stopper, bung, plug; pad, cushioning, buffer; lute, seal, gasket. See ENCLOSURE, COMPOSITION.

pact, *n.* compact, covenant, treaty; bargain, AGREEMENT.

pad, *n.* cushion, mat, buffer; [writing] tablet; *slang,* flat, room[s] (see ABODE). —*v.* cushion, stuff, wad; enlarge, overstate, inflate. See SOFTNESS, SUPPORT, WRITING.

padding, *n.* pads, cushion, wadding; fill-ins, additions; excess, extras, surplus; REPETITION, tautology; featherbedding. See COMPOSITION, COVERING.

paddle, *n.* oar, scull, sweep, flipper, pole. —*v.* canoe, row, ply the oar; backwater, feather, steer; beat, thrash, spank, drub; toddle, pad, waddle. See NAVIGATION, PUNISHMENT, TRAVEL.

padlock, *n.* See CLOSURE.

paean, *n.* song *or* hymn of joy *or* praise, hosanna, hallelujah. See REJOICING, MUSIC.

pagan, *adj.* heathen, ungodly; idolatrous. —*n.* heathen, idolater. See IRRELIGION, IDOLATRY. *Ant.,* godly, religious.

page, *n.* SERVANT, attendant, call boy, page boy, bellboy; folio, leaf. —*v.* summon, call; number pages, foliate, paginate. See NUMERATION, COMMAND.

pageant, *n.* exhibition, show, parade, display, spectacle. See OSTENTATION, CELEBRATION.

pail, *n.* bucket, can, canister, pot, pan, kettle. See RECEPTACLE.

PAIN
Suffering

Noun—1, pain, suffering, sufferance; hurt, cut; discomfort, painfulness; discomfort, malaise; nightmare; anguish, agony, misery, excruciation, torment, torture, rack; Weltschmerz; distress, affliction (see ADVERSITY). See DEJECTION, HELL, DISEASE, LAMENTATION, PUNISHMENT.

2, *(symptoms)* aches and pains; ache, aching, sore[ness]; smart, sting, burn[ing], tingle; acute, sharp, piercing, throbbing, shooting, gnawing, *or* burning pain; twinge, pang, stab, pinch; cramp, paroxysm, spasm (see AGITATION, VIOLENCE); gripe, stomachache, heartburn, colic; headache, migraine; backache, earache, toothache, *etc. Informal,* tummy-ache, collywobbles, gripes, mulligrubs.

3, *(causes)* shock, blow; distress, affliction, woe, bitterness; lovesickness; heartache; misery, tribulation, wretchedness, desolation; despair; extremity, prostration, depth of misery; hell on earth. See ADVERSITY.

4, instrument of torture (see PUNISHMENT).

Verb—1, feel, experience, suffer, endure, *or* undergo pain; suffer, ache, smart; sting, tingle, shoot; twinge, twitch, writhe, wince; make a wry face, cry out; go through the mill, have one's cross to bear.

2, *(cause physical pain)* give, cause, *or* inflict pain; pain, hurt, wound, chafe, sting, bite, gnaw, gripe; pinch, tweak, grate, gall, fret, prick, pierce, wring, convulse; harrow, torment, torture, rack, agonize, crucify, excruciate; break on the wheel, put on the rack; spank, beat, thrash, flog (see PUNISHMENT).

3, *(cause moral pain)* sicken, disgust, revolt, nauseate, disenchant; repel, offend, shock, stink in the nostrils; turn the stomach; make one sick, set the teeth on edge; rankle, gnaw, corrode. See DISCONTENT.

Adjectives—1, in pain, suffering, pained, harrowed, afflicted, aching, griped, sore, raw; on the rack; agonized, tortured, crucified, racked, broken on the wheel.

2, painful, hurting, hurtful; dolorous; cutting, consuming, racking, excruciating, searching, grinding, grating, agonizing.

3, intolerable, insufferable, insupportable, unbearable, unendurable; more than flesh and blood can bear; enough to drive one mad.

4, distressing, afflicting, afflictive; grievous; woeful, rueful, mournful, deplorable, lamentable; affecting, touching. See ADVERSITY.

Phrases—crosses are ladders that lead to heaven; no pain no gain.

Quotations—If you bear the cross gladly, it will bear you (*Thomas à Kempis*), He jests at scars, that never felt a wound (*Shakespeare*), Suffering is permanent, obscure and dark, and shares the nature of infinity (*Wordsworth*), What does not kill me makes me stronger (*Friedrich Nietzsche*).

Antonyms, see PLEASURE.

---

painkiller, *n.* alleviative, lenitive, anodyne, paregoric, analgesic, [local *or* general] anesthetic, narcotic, morphine, codeine, sleeping pills; Novocaine, Xylocaine, *etc.* See RELIEF, INSENSIBILITY.

painless, *adj.* causing no pain; easy [to take]. See INSENSIBILITY, FACILITY. *Ant.*, painful.

pains, *n.pl.* EXERTION, labor, effort; attention, seriousness.

painstaking, *adj.* careful, particular, meticulous, scrupulous; diligent. See EXERTION, CARE. *Ant.*, careless, sloppy.

PAINTING
Drawing with paint

Nouns—**1**, painting, depicting; drawing; drafting; design; chiaroscuro; chih-hua, chinoiserie; cerography; composition, treatment, perspective, balance, technique; coloration; impasto; REPRESENTATION; house painting. See SCULPTURE, ENGRAVING.

2, a. school, style; aestheticism, antiart, archaism, primitivism; the grand style, fine *or* high art, commercial art, academic art, grand manner, folk art, genre, portraiture. **b.** cave art; Byzantine, Gothic, Hellenic; Mannerism, classicism, baroque, rococo, tenebrism; romanticism, impressionism, Fontainebleau School, plein air, divisionism, postimpressionism, realism; Barbizon school, cloissonism, decadent art, neo-impressionism, neoclassicism, divisionism, intisme, pre-Raphaelite. **c.** abstract expressionism, abstract *or* concrete art, art brut, deco, *or* nouveau, Hudson River School, Bauhaus, conceptual art, constructivism, cubism, Dada[ism], de Stijl, expressionism, Fauvism, funk, futurism, hyperrealism, Jugendstil, kinetic art, lyrical abstraction, merz, minimal art, minimalism, modernism, neoplasticism, new objectivity, new secession, new wave, Orphism, photorealism, pointillism, pop *or* op art, Postimpressionism, postmodernism, postmodernism, proletarian art, social realism, suprematism, surrealism, synchronism, tachism, verism, vorticism. **d.** hard-edge, action paintism, video art, ashcan school, antiart, colorfield, distressed art, fantastic realism, Blaue Reiter, Brucke, New York School; Kamakura, Ming, T'Ang, Mogul School, Tantra art, Yamato-e.

3, *(types of paintings)* painting, picture, piece, tableau, canvas; oil painting; fresco, cartoon; [pencil *or* watercolor] drawing; sketch, outline; study, scene, view; illustration; altarpiece, anastasis, batik, cabinet picture, calathus, capriccio, cherub, cityscape, contrapposto, deieisis, diablerie, diorama, diptych, dreamscape, easel painting, ecce homo, ex-voto, figure, finger painting, fusuma, genre, grotesque, history painting, icon, kakemono, kalathos, kwacho, landscape, life drawing, maesta, makemono, mandala, memento mori, miniature, mosaic, mural, namban, nature morte, nocturne, nude, panel painting, panorama, pantocrator, pastoral, pictograph, Pietà, polyptych, portrait, prospect, psalter, putto, rotulus, scene, seascape, self-portrait, silhouette, stick figure, still life, study, tanka, tondo, triptych, triskelion, trompe l'œil, uchiwa-ye, ukiyo-e, vanitas, vignette, wall painting, wen-jen-hua.

4, picture, cooperative, *or* art gallery, museum; studio, atelier; exhibition, vernissage, show[ing], retrospective, group show, juried show, private collection; auction; artist's rep[resentative], collector, curator, docent, patron.

5, *(painting methods)* palette, pallet, pallet cup, palette knife, mahlstick; easel; frame, stretcher; [paint]brush, air brush, spray gun; palette knife, spatula; pencil, charcoal, crayons, chalk, pastel; brush stroke, scumbling; [short *or* thick] paint, water color, oils, oil paint; primer, gesso, underpainting, imprimatura, sizing; oxgall; aquarelle, [transparent *or* opaque] watercolor, gouache, designer's colors, aquatint; varnish, tempera, distemper, [true *or* dry] fresco, enamel, encaustic painting, acetate color; aniline dye, impasto, lake, liver; finger paint, sgraffito; poster paint, canvas, plaster, gesso; sand painting; black *or* Claude glass; sketchbook; atelier, studio; model; muller.

6, *(painting equipment)* brush, roller; drop cloth; latex, acrylic, *or* oil paint; flat, semigloss, *or* high-gloss paint, exterior *or* interior paint, enamel; varnish, lacquer, japan, stain, polyurethane.

7, painter, ARTIST, portrait *or* landscape painter, *etc.*; realist, surrealist, impressionist, cubist, pointillist, Postimpressionist, *etc.*; house painter.

Verbs—paint, design, limn, draw, sketch, pencil, scratch, shade, stipple, hatch, cross-hatch, hachure, dash off, block out, chalk out, square up; color, tint, dead-color; wash, varnish; illustrate; illuminate (see ORNAMENT); paint in oils; stencil; depict, represent; trace, copy. *Slang*, doodle.

Adjectives—pictorial, graphic, picturesque; painted; classic, romantic, realistic, impressionistic, *etc.*; pencil, oil, pastel, tempera, watercolor, *etc.*; freehand.

Quotations—Painting is silent poetry (*Simonides*), Good painters imitate nature, bad ones spew it up (*Cervantes*), You should not paint the chair, but only what someone has felt about it (*Edvard Munch*), It's with my brush that I make love (*Pierre Auguste Renoir*), Art does not reproduce the visible; rather, it makes visible (*Paul Klee*), Every time I paint a portrait I lose a friend (*John Singer Sargent*), [Abstract art is] a product of the untalented, sold by the unprincipled to the utterly bewildered (*Al Capp*), I try to apply colors like words that shape poems, like notes that shape music (*Joan Miró*).

Related categories, SCULPTURE, ENGRAVING.

---

pair, *n.* couple, duo, brace; mates; two of a kind. —*v.* match, mate, couple, suit, unite. See NUMERATION, SIMILARITY.

pajamas, *n.* pyjamas, PJs (*sl.*). See CLOTHING.

pal, *n.*, *slang,* [bosom *or* boon] companion, crony, comrade, mate; sidekick, buddy, chum. See FRIEND. *Ant.,* enemy.

palace, *n.* alcazar, château, mansion, great house, palazzo, palais; arena, pleasure dome, Crystal Palace. See ABODE.

palatable, *adj.* tasty, savory, toothsome, appetizing; pleasant, agreeable, easy to take. See TASTE, PLEASURE.

palatial, *adj.* sumptuous, luxurious; stately, majestic. See ORNAMENT, SIZE, BUILDING.

palaver, *n.* colloquy, conference, parley, CONVERSATION; babble, chatter; FLATTERY, soft soap (*inf.*); nonsense, absurdity. —*v.i.* converse, confer; dicker, BARTER; gossip, drivel, babble, chatter. See SPEECH, UNMEANINGNESS.

pale, *adj.* wan, waxen, ashy, ashen, colorless, bloodless; light, blond; faint, dim, vague; sickly. See COLORLESSNESS, DIMNESS. *Ant.,* colorful; ruddy. —*v.i.* whiten, blanch, blench; fade, dim. —*n.* stake, picket; border, boundary, LIMIT. —**beyond the pale,** out of bounds, overdone (see EXAGGERATION).

palisade, *n.* fence, paling; (*pl.*) cliffs, escarpment. See VERTICAL, ENCLOSURE.

pall, *v.* jade, weary; cloy, sicken, satiate. See WEARINESS, SUFFICIENCY. —*n.* murk, smoke, smog, coffin. See COVERING, INTERMENT.

pallet, *n.* palette; mattress, bed; platform. See PAINTING, SUPPORT.

palliate, *v.t.* extenuate, excuse; mitigate,

soften; relieve, ameliorate. See VINDI-
CATION, MODERATION, RELIEF.

pallid, *n.* pale, bloodless, wan, sallow,
white. See COLORLESSNESS. *Ant.*,
ruddy, healthy.

pallor, *n.* paleness, wanness, sallowless,
sickliness. See COLORLESSNESS. *Ant.*,
color.

palm, *n.* palmetto, palmyra; honor, prize,
reward, trophy, guerdon, laurel[s]. See
APPROBATION. —*v.* handle, TOUCH;
conceal, hide, cover; steal, pilfer; palm
off, impose *or* foist on, get rid of, deceive. See STEALING, DECEPTION.

palpable, *adj.* evident, plain, clear, manifest, obvious, apparent, unmistakable,
definite, unquestionable, distinct. See
FEELING, DISCLOSURE.

palpitate, *v.i.* beat, pulse, throb; vibrate;
quake, shake. See AGITATION, FEAR.

palsy, *n.* paralysis. See DISEASE.

palter, *v.i.* equivocate; haggle; trifle. See
BARTER, FALSEHOOD, UNIMPORTANCE.

paltry, *adj.* trifling, trivial, inconsequential, insignificant; mean, petty, worthless; contemptible, sorry, pitiable. See
UNIMPORTANCE, BADNESS, CHEAPNESS.

pamper, *v.t.* humor, indulge, spoil, pet,
coddle, gratify, overindulge. See LE-
NIENCY.

pamphlet, *n.* booklet, folder, brochure,
leaflet; monograph, manual. See PUBLI-
CATION.

pamphleteer, *n.* essayist, propagandist.
See WRITING.

pan, *n.* pot, kettle, saucepan; skillet, spider, grill; dishpan; utensil, vessel. See
RECEPTACLE.

panacea, *n.* universal REMEDY, cure-all.

pancake, *n.* hotcake, flapjack, battercake,
buckwheat cake, flannel cake, silver
dollar, griddlecake; crêpe [suzette, *etc.*];
fritter. See FOOD.

pandemic, *adj.* universal, epidemic. See
GENERALITY, DISEASE.

pandemonium, *n.* HELL, inferno, all hell
breaking loose (*inf.*); noise, racket,
din; EXCITEMENT, DISORDER, convulsion,
frenzy, bedlam, Babel, DISCORD. See
LOUDNESS.

pander, *v.* cater to; encourage (in bad
habits); pimp. —*n.* pimp, go-between.
See IMPURITY, SERVILITY.

Pandora's box, can of worms, hornets'
nest. See ADVERSITY.

pane, *n.* window[pane], light, skylight;
sheet glass, plate glass; side, face, section, surface. See TRANSPARENCY.

panegyric, *n.* praise; encomium, eulogy;
APPROBATION, laudation.

panel, *n.* jury, board of judges; board,
table. See ASSEMBLAGE, LAYER.

pang, *n.* PAIN, twinge, shoot, throe, ache.

panhandle, *v., slang,* beg, solicit, bum
(*sl.*), [make a] touch (*sl.*). See REQUEST.

panic, *n.* terror, fright, FEAR, consternation; stampede. —*v.* alarm, frighten;
stampede. See EXCITABILITY, FAILURE.
Ant., calm.

panicky, *adj.* panic-stricken *or* -struck (see
FEAR, EXCITABILITY). *Ant.*, calm, unruffled.

panoply, *n.* full armor, regalia, ARMS, arsenal, protection, shield; pageantry,
pomp, OSTENTATION; array, spread, assemblage.

panorama, *n.* vista, view, scene, perspective; representation, cyclorama, diorama. See PAINTING, INCLUSION.

panpipe, *n.* syrinx, Pan's pipes. See MUSIC.

pansy, *n., slang,* pantywaist, weakling;
homosexual. See WEAKNESS, MALE.
Ant., he-man.

pant, *v.i.* gasp, puff, blow; yearn *or* long
for. See DESIRE, WIND.

pantomime, *n.* mime, mimicry, chiron-
omy; dumbshow, tableau, charades,
silent film; gestures, gesticulation, hand
talk; puppet show. See DRAMA, INDICA-
TION.

pantry, *n.* STORE, cupboard, larder, kitchen,
scullery; galley, cuddy; buttery, butlery;
ewery, china closet. See RECEPTACLE.

pants, *n.pl.* trousers, breeches; slacks,
flannels, jeans, Levi's, dungarees; pantaloons, knickerbockers, knickers, plus-
fours; shorts, pedal-pushers, chinos,
jodhpurs; bloomers, briefs, panties. See
CLOTHING.

pap, *n.* spoon food, paste; teat, nipple;
slang, patronage, plum, pork. See SOFT-
NESS, CONVEXITY, INFLUENCE.

papacy, *n.* the Vatican, Holy See. See
CLERGY.

paparazzo, *n.* photographer (see PHOTOG-
RAPHY, NEWS).

paper, *n.* writing paper, wallpaper, newsprint, rag paper, pulp paper, foolscap, *etc.;* paper money, bill, banknote, folding money; certificate, deed, document; newspaper, journal; monograph, article, composition. See COVERING, MONEY, PUBLICATION, RECORD, NEWS.

paperback, *n.* pocket book, mass market *or* trade paperback; penny dreadful, dime novel. —*adj.* softcover. See PUBLICATION. *Ant.,* hardcover.

papers, *n.pl.* credentials; archives, records. See RECORD.

par, *n.* EQUALITY, equal footing; par *or* face value; level.

parable, *n.* allegory, analogy; fable, moral tale; comparison, similitude. See FIGURATIVE, DESCRIPTION.

parachute, *n.* chute, drogue, the silk (*inf.*); parafoil; paraglider; airdrop, free fall. —*v.i.* bail out, drop, jump, leap, hit the silk (*inf.*). See AVIATION.

parade, *n.* show, display, pageant[ry]; march, procession; OSTENTATION, pretension. —*v.* show, display; march; air, vent; flaunt, show off.

paradise, *n.* Eden, HEAVEN, Promised Land, Canaan, land of milk and honey; Utopia, Arcadia; never-never land; bliss, happiness; Elysian fields; Elysium; Shangri-la. *Ant.,* HELL.

paradox, *n.* inconsistency; oxymoron, ABSURDITY. See DIFFICULTY, UNINTELLIGIBILITY.

paradoxical, *adj.* self-contradictory, absurd. See ABSURDITY.

paragon, *n.* ideal, model, perfect example, pattern; nonesuch, nonpareil. See PERFECTION, GOODNESS.

paragraph, *n.* note, item; section, passage. See PART, GRAMMAR.

parallel, *n.* parallelism; coextension; analogy, comparison. —*adj.* coextensive, side by side; analogous, similar. See SIMILARITY, EQUALITY, SYMMETRY. *Ant.,* divergent.

paralysis, *n.* stroke, disablement, paraplegia, hemiplegia, malfunction. See DISEASE, IMPOTENCE.

paralyze, *v.* cripple; demoralize; disable; deaden; bring to a stop. See IMPOTENCE, INSENSIBILITY.

parameter, *n.* variable, term, contingency, condition. See QUALIFICATION.

paramount, *adj.* chief, first, supreme, all-important. See SUPERIORITY.

paramour, *n.* mistress, ladylove; lover. See LOVE, EVILDOER.

paranoid, *adj.* paranoiac; fearful, suspicious, distrustful. —*adj.* paranoiac; alarmist, pessimist. See INSANITY, FEAR.

parapet, *n.* wall, rampart, breastwork, embankment, DEFENSE; railing. See HINDRANCE.

paraphernalia, *n.pl.* apparatus, trappings, gear, equipment; belongings. See POSSESSION.

paraphrase, *n.* rendering, restatement, switch (*inf.*). —*v.* restate, alter, reword. See INTERPRETATION, IMITATION.

parasite, *n.* sycophant, fawner, hanger-on, freeloader (*inf.*); leech, bloodsucker; inquiline, commensal; symbiont, symbiotic. See SERVILITY, FLATTERY.

parasol, *n.* sunshade, umbrella. See COVERING.

paratrooper, *n.* [parachute] jumper, chutist (*inf.*). See COMBATANT.

parboil, *v.t.* brew, simmer, seethe, coddle, HEAT. See FOOD.

parcel, *n.* package, bundle, pack[et]; PART, portion, piece; land, lot, division, section. See ENCLOSURE.

parch, *v.* dry [up], shrivel; roast, scorch. See DRYNESS. *Ant.,* moisten, humidify.

parchment, *n.* vellum, sheepskin; pell, scroll; codex, document, diploma; bond paper, rag paper. See WRITING, MATERIALS.

pardon, *v.t.* forgive, excuse; release; overlook, tolerate. —*n.* excuse, release, FORGIVENESS; indulgence; remission; toleration.

pare, *v.t.* peel, trim, cut, shave, slice; reduce, shorten. See LAYER, CONTRACTION, DIVESTMENT, DEDUCTION, NARROWNESS.

parent, *n.* begetter, procreator, progenitor; forebear, ancestor, father, mother; foster parent; fount, source. See ANCESTRY.

parenthetical, *adj.* in parentheses; inserted, interpolated, incidental; disconnected, irrelevant. See BETWEEN, INSERTION.

par excellence, Fr., above all others. See SUPERIORITY.

pariah, *n.* outcast; untouchable, outcaste. See POPULACE, EXCLUSION.

parish, *n.* fold, church, LAITY, congregation, flock; parsonage, vicarage, manse; territory, REGION, area. See ABODE.

parishioner, *n.* layperson, churchman *or* -woman, brother, sister. See LAITY.

parity, *n.* EQUALITY, equal basis; similarity, equivalence; par.

park, *v.* leave, deposit, place. See LOCATION. —*n.* parkway; playground; public, botanical, *or* zoological gardens, ZOO; woodland, pleasance; grove; picnic grounds; village *or* bowling green, common; parking lot *or* space, parkade; amusement park, fairgrounds, fun fair, theme park. See AMUSEMENT.

parkway, *n.* boulevard, roadway. See PASSAGE.

parlance, *n.* language, manner of speaking. See SPEECH.

parlay, *v.* [re]bet (see CHANCE, INCREASE).

parley, *n.* conference, talk, discussion, CONVERSATION, council; palaver. —*v.* talk, confer, palaver, converse.

parliament, *n.* assembly, COUNCIL, convocation; assemblage, house.

parlor, *n.* living, front, *or* drawing room. See RECEPTACLE.

parochial, *adj.* provincial, local; narrow, illiberal; church-controlled, separate (*Canadian*). See REGION, RELIGION, NARROWNESS. *Ant.,* universal, Catholic.

parody, *n.* take-off, IMITATION, travesty, burlesque. See COPY, RIDICULE.

parole, *n.* pledge, PROMISE; custody, release, FREEDOM, probation. —*v.t.* free, liberate, let go, release, put on probation. See LIBERATION.

paroxysm, *n.* fit, seizure, spasm; convulsion, attack; outburst, frenzy. See AGITATION, VIOLENCE, PAIN.

parrot, *n.* polly, parakeet; prater, chatterbox; imitator, mimic. —*v.t.* imitate, echo, mime, repeat, say by rote, prate. See IMITATION, LOQUACITY.

parry, *v.* fend *or* ward off, avert, turn aside, deflect; evade; fence. See DEFENSE.

PARSIMONY
Excessive frugality

Nouns—1, parsimony, parsimoniousness, stinginess, miserliness; illiberality, avarice, greed (see DESIRE). See SELFISHNESS, ECONOMY.

2, miser, niggard, churl, skinflint, scrimp, lickpenny, curmudgeon, harpy; extortioner, usurer; scrooge. *Slang,* tightwad, cheapskate, penny-pincher, piker, muckworm.

Verbs—stint, [be]grudge, pinch, gripe, dole out, hold back, withhold, starve, live on nothing, pinch pennies, scrimp; drive a hard bargain; cheapen, beat down; have an itching palm, grasp, grab (see DESIRE).

Adjectives—parsimonious, penurious, stingy, miserly, mean, shabby, piddling, scrubby, pennywise, near, niggardly, close; close-, hard-, *or* tight-fisted, grasping; tight, sparing; chary; grudging, griping; illiberal, ungenerous; avaricious, greedy. *Informal,* skimping. *Slang,* grafty.

Antonyms, see GIVING, LIBERALITY.

---

parson, *n.* clergyman; pastor, minister, preacher. See CLERGY.

parsonage, *n.* manse, rectory. See TEMPLE.

part, *n.* piece, section (see PART); role, character (see DRAMA); voice, instrument (see MUSIC); concern, interest, PARTICIPATION, business, work.

PART·
Piece of a whole

Nouns—1, part, portion, sector, segment, fragment, fraction, item, particular, dose; aught, any; division, subdivision, section, ward, parcel, compartment, department, detachment, CLASS; county, REGION; partition, installment, interest, share (see APPORTIONMENT); chapter, verse, article, clause, paragraph; passage, excerpt, episode. See INCOMPLETENESS.

2, *(ingredient)* component *or* integral part, part and parcel; crux, kernel (see IMPORTANCE); element, factor, module, constituent, detail, ingredient, complement, material, specification, leaven; feature, principle, radicle. See COMPOSITION.

3, *(piece from a whole)* piece, lump, bit, chip, slab, chunk, dollop, slice, cut[ting]; shard, cob, crumb, flake, tatter; scale, lamina, LAYER; morsel, soupçon (see LITTLENESS); shred, snip, paring, shaving, scrap, remnant, sliver, splinter; pixel. *Informal,* hunk, smithereen.

4, *(body or plant part)* member, limb, organ, lobe, lobule, arm, wing, fin, flipper; joint, link, offshoot, ramification, appurtenance; scion, branch, bough, twig, bush, spray, leaf[let], stump.

5, *(discarded part)* debris, odds and ends, oddments, flinders, detritus, matchwood. See REMAINDER.

Verbs—part, divide, subdivide, break, disjoin (see DISJUNCTION); partition, share, parcel (see APPORTIONMENT); break up, disrupt, dismember, disconnect, disassociate, detach, terminate; chip, splinter, snip, snap, shred, tatter, flake; part company, separate.

Adjectives—1, part, partial, fractional, fragmentary, sectional, aliquot, incomplete; divided, cleft, multifid, separated, individual, in compartments; bipartite, tripartite, *etc.,* multipartite; broken, splintered, severed, disrupt[ed], scrappy; departmental; branch[y], branching, subsidiary.

2, component, constituent, INTRINSIC, integral; essential, inherent, innate; inclusive, comprehensive (see INCLUSION).

Adverbs—partly, in part, partially, piecemeal, part by part; by installments, by snatches, by inches, by driblets; in detail; bit by bit, inch by inch, foot by foot, drop by drop; in detail, in lots; somewhat.

Quotations—For now we see through a glass, darkly; but then face to face: now I know in part; but then I shall know even as I am known (*Bible*), What one beholds of a woman is the least part of her (*Ovid*), The beginning is the most important part of the work (*Plato*), No man is an island entire of itself; every man is a part of the continent, a part of the main (*John Donne*).

Antonyms, see WHOLE.

---

partake, *v.* share [in] (see PARTICIPATE); take (food or drink); receive (part of). See COOPERATION.

partial, *adj.* incomplete, fractional, unfinished, PART; biased, partisan, onesided, prejudiced; favoring. See INCOMPLETENESS, INEQUALITY, INJUSTICE.

participate, *v.i.* partake; share [in], come in for a share; prorate; go shares *or* halves; share and share alike, go Dutch (*inf.*), kick in (*sl.*), feed the kitty (*sl.*); have *or* own in common, possess *or* use jointly; join in; go in with, have a hand in; cooperate. See COOPERATION.

particle, *n.* speck, iota, jot, whit, bit; atom, molecule; suffix, prefix, conjunction, preposition, interjection. See LITTLENESS, GRAMMAR.

particular, *adj.* demanding, painstaking, meticulous; definite, specific; fussy, finicky, per[s]nickety, overnice; special, outstanding; personal; precise, exact. See TASTE, IMPORTANCE. —*n.* fact, specification, datum, detail. See DESCRIPTION, CARE. *Ant.,* general, nonspecific, unfussy.

particularize, *v.* specify, itemize, mention particularly, detail. See DESCRIPTION.

parting, *n.* leavetaking, DEPARTURE; farewell, severance, separation; partition, division. See DISJUNCTION. *Ant.,* ARRIVAL, welcoming.

partisan, *adj.* partial, onesided, pro, favoring, interested. —*n.* supporter, ally, follower, adherent; aide; champion; guerrilla, underground fighter. See AUXILIARY, FRIEND, COMBATANT.

partisanship, *n.* party spirit, loyalty; unfairness, bias, prejudice; clannishness, closeness; provincialism. See INJUSTICE.

partition, *n.* wall, screen, diaphragm, barrier; separation, severance, cutting-off; section, portion, division. See PART, APPORTIONMENT, BETWEEN.

partly, *adj.* in part, not wholly; incompletely, partially, in a way, not quite. See PART. *Ant.,* fully, completely.

partner, *n.* sharer, associate, co-owner, copartner, silent partner; spouse, mate; sidekick, pal, pardner, pard (*all inf.*). See ACCOMPANIMENT, MARRIAGE, AUXILIARY, FRIEND.

partnership, *n.* co-ownership, [BUSINESS] association; COOPERATION, alliance. See ACCOMPANIMENT.

part-time, *adj.* spare-time, after-hours, temporary, occasional, odd. See RARITY. *Ant.,* full-time.

party, *n.* organization (see PARTY); social gathering, festivity, reception, dance; participant, accomplice, partner. See SOCIALITY, PART.

PARTY
Body of persons

Nouns—1, party, faction, side; denomination, communion; community, body, fellowship, fraternity; confraternity; brotherhood, sisterhood; sodality; family, clan (see ANCESTRY).

2, (*social group*) gang, crew, band, clique, ring, set, camp, circle, coterie, club. See ASSEMBLAGE.

3, (*professional group*) guild; syndicate, cartel, trust; joint account. See BUSINESS.

4, (*political group*) society, association; institute, institution, foundation; union, trade union; league, alliance, Verein, Bund, Zollverein; lodge, den, chapter, post; COMBINATION, coalition, federation; confederation, confederacy; junta, cabal, bloc, machine; freemasonry; Republican, Democratic, Socialist, Communist, Fascist, Nazi, *or* Conservative Party, New Left *or* Right, Christian Right, reform *or* splinter party, majority *or* minority party, two-party system. See COOPERATION.

5, (*member of a party*) member, fellow, associate, cardholder, clubman *or* -woman, brother, sister, socius; politician, politico, activist, apparatchik, bedfellow, cadre, constituent, heeler, henchman, kingmaker, machine politician, mugwump, party boss *or* chairman, party hack, regular, precinct captain, state chairman; majority *or* minority leader, whip; Democrat, Republican, liberal, moderate, progressive, radical, reactionary, reformer, Dixiecrat; candidate, nominee, favorite son, dark horse, stalking-horse, standard-bearer. *Informal,* joiner, warhorse.

Verbs—become a member, join, go *or* come out for, sign up, enroll, affiliate with; be a member, belong; form a party, associate, league together.

Adjectives—in league, in partnership, in alliance; partisan, denominational; bonded, linked, *or* banded together; confederated, federative; joint, mutual; cliquish, clannish; factional, sectional; card-carrying.

Quotations—Party is organized opinion (*Benjamin Disraeli*), He knows nothing; and he thinks he knows everything. That points clearly to a political career (*G. B. Shaw*), If you want to succeed in politics, you must keep your conscience well under control (*David Lloyd George*), A politician is a statesman who places the nation at his service (*Georges Pompidou*).

Antonyms, see SECLUSION.

---

parvenu, *n.* pretender, newcomer, upstart, social climber, snob, Johnny-come-lately (*inf.*), pusher (*inf.*); nouveau riche. See NEWNESS, POPULACE.

pass, *n.* gap, gorge; way, opening, notch, defile, passage; free ticket; crisis, predicament, condition, CIRCUMSTANCE; leave [of absence]; *slang*, advance. See LOVE. —*v.* go through *or* by, bypass; get a passing mark, make the grade; do, pass muster; cross; hand over; admit, allow, tolerate; while away *or* spend; authorize, OK, sanction, permit (see PERMISSION). See PASSAGE, MOTION, PAST.

passable, *adj.* navigable, traversable; allowable, acceptable, tolerable; passing fair, good enough. See IMPERFECTION, MEDIOCRITY. *Ant.,* impassable, unacceptable.

passage, *n.* channel (see PASSAGE); voyage, journey; excerpt, phrase, movement, *etc.;* enactment, passing; lapse. See PROGRESSION, TRAVEL, NAVIGATION, PART.

PASSAGE
Means of passing

Nouns—1, *(passing through)* passage, transmission; permeation; penetration; interpenetration; transudation, infiltration; osmosis, endosmosis, exosmosis; intercurrence; access, INGRESS, EGRESS.

2, *(vehicle passage)* passageway, road, highway, thoroughfare, boulevard, avenue, street; byway, lane, pike, alley[way], trail; high road, the King's highway; roadway; turnpike, tollroad, tollway, skyway, speedway, thruway, expressway, interstate [highway], freeway, Autobahn, autoroute, autostrada, parkway, superhighway, dual *or* divided highway, limited-access highway; artery; beltway, ring road, bypass; cross, through, one-way, *or* stop street; back *or* side street, by-street, camino, carriageway, causeway; corniche, court, crescent; switchback, post road; cul-de-sac, dead end, driveway, frontage *or* service road; mew. *Informal,* main drag. See TRANSPORTATION.

3, *(walking passage)* esplanade, arcade, corridor, concourse, hall[way], way, aisle.

4, channel, gate, OPENING; way, path, footpath, thoroughfare; tube, pipe; vessel, tubule, canal, gutter, fistula; chimney, flue, tap, funnel, gully, tunnel, main; chute, artery; mine, pit, adit, shaft; gallery, alley, aisle.

Verbs—pass [through]; perforate, penetrate, permeate, tread, enfilade; go through *or* across; go over, pass by, bypass, pass over; cut across; ford, cross; work *or* make one's way through; thread *or* worm one's way through; force one's way; find a way; transmit, make way; clear the course *or* track; traverse, go over ground.

Adjectives—passing, elapsing, progressive; intercurrent; transient, portable, assignable; movable.

Adverbs—in passing, en passant, in transit, under way.

Quotations—Footfalls echo in the memory down the passage which we did not take towards the door we never opened into the rosegarden (*T. S. Eliot*).

Antonyms, see INACTIVITY, CLOSURE.

---

passé, *adj.* outmoded (see OLDNESS). *Ant.,* avant-garde, up-to-date.

passenger, *n.* rider, commuter, fare; hitchhiker, pickup, stowaway. See TRAVEL.

passe partout, Fr. universal pass; master *or* skeleton key, *etc.* See ENTRANCE.

passerby, *n.* man in the street, pedestrian, bystander, sidewalk superintendent (*sl.*). See PRESENCE, EVIDENCE.

passim, Lat., here and there. See DISPERSION.

passing, *adj.* cursory; fleeting. See TRANSIENTNESS, DISAPPEARANCE.

passion, *n.* LOVE; fervor, ardor, intensity, fever; infatuation, DESIRE; emotion, rage, anger, fury; EXCITEMENT; *informal,* predilection, preference. See FEELING, VIOLENCE.

passionate, *adj.* impassioned, vehement; irascible. See FEELING, EXCITABILITY, IRASCIBILITY. *Ant.,* disinterested, passive, dispassionate.

passive, *adj.* nonresistant; inactive, inert, quiet; unemotional, untouched, unstirred, indifferent. See LATENCY. *Ant.,* active.

passivity, *n.* passiveness, inaction, INACTIV-
ITY, inertness; nonresistance, quiescence;
indifference; neutrality, sluggishness,
SUBMISSION. See RESIGNATION.

passkey, *n.* master *or* skeleton key. See
OPENING.

passport, *n.* pass; safe-conduct. See PER-
MISSION, INSTRUMENTALITY.

password, *n.* countersign, shibboleth,
watchword. See INDICATION.

PAST
Gone by in time

Nouns—1, past, past tense, preterition; the past, yesterday; days of yore *or* of old; times
past *or* gone by; bygone days; olden times, the good old days, yesteryear, time immemorial; auld lang syne, eld; water over the dam *or* under the bridge. See PRIORITY,
OLDNESS.

2, *(historical periods)* antiquity, antiqueness; time immemorial; remote past; ar-
chaism, antiquarianism, medievalism, pre-Raphaelitism; Gay *or* Naughty Nineties,
Roaring Twenties, swingin' sixties; retrospection; looking back; MEMORY; ANCESTRY.
Informal, ancient history.

3, *(study of the past)* history, paleontology, paleography, paleology, archaeology, anthropology, dendrochronology, epigraphy, ethnology.

4, antiquary, antiquarian; paleologist, archaeologist, medievalist, anthropologist,
ethnologist.

5, ex. *Informal,* has-been.

Verbs—be past, have expired, have run its course, have had its day; pass; pass *or* go by,
go *or* pass away, pass off; lapse; blow over; look back, trace back; turn *or* put back
the clock; exhume, dig up.

Adjectives—past, gone, bygone, foregone; elapsed; lapsed, expired, no more, run out,
blown over, that has been, extinct, never to return, exploded, forgotten, irrecover-
able; obsolete (see OLDNESS); once, former, pristine, quondam, ci-devant, late; ancestral; foregoing; last, latter; recent, overgoing; perfect, preterite (see GRAMMAR);
looking back; retrospective, retroactive; archaeological, *etc. Informal,* ex-.

Adverbs—formerly; of old, of yore; erst, erstwhile, whilom, erewhile, time was, ago;
over; in the olden time; anciently, long ago, long since; a long time ago; yesterday; a
while back; last year, season, *or* month; ultimo; lately, retrospectively; before now;
hitherto, heretofore; no longer; at one time, once [upon a time]; from time immemorial, in the memory of man; time out of mind; already, yet, up to this time; ex post
facto.

Phrases—history is a fable agreed upon; history is fiction with the truth left out; history
repeats itself; what's done cannot be undone

Quotations—History . . . is, indeed, little more than the register of the crimes, follies,
and misfortunes of mankind (*Edward Gibbon*), History is a distillation of rumor
(*Thomas Carlyle*), History is more or less bunk (*Henry Ford*), But where are the
snows of yesteryear? (*François Villon*), O! call back yesterday, bid time return
(*Shakespeare*), The dark backward and abysm of time? (*Shakespeare*), Where is the
life that late I led? (*Shakespeare*), Those who cannot remember the past are condemned to repeat it (*George Santayana*), I tell you the past is a bucket of ashes (*Carl
Sandburg*), The past is a foreign country: they do things differently there (*L. P. Hart-
ley*), I believe in yesterday (*Lennon/McCartney*), In the carriages of the past you can't
go anywhere (*Maxim Gorky*), The past lies like a nightmare upon the present (*Karl
Marx*), We live in reference to past experience and not to future events, however inevitable (*H. G. Wells*).

Antonyms, see FUTURITY, PRESENT.

---

paste, *n.* cement, bond, binder, glue, adhesive, mucilage; rhinestones, glass; gaudery, trinkery, frippery. See COHERENCE, CONNECTION, ORNAMENT. —*v.t.* paste up, cement, stick, glue; *slang,* lambaste, clout, wallop, punch, slug, sock (*sl.*). See COHERENCE, IMPULSE.

pasteboard, *n.* card-, paper-, pulp-, *or* chipboard, Bristol board. See MATERIALS. —*adj.* fake, phony, stagy, theatrical, simulated, lifeless; flimsy, unsubstantial. See FALSENESS, INSUBSTANTIALITY.

pastel, *adj.* pale, light, soft, delicate; tinted, hued, shaded. See COLOR, PAINTING.

pasteurize, *v.t.* sterilize, disinfect. See CLEANNESS.

pastiche, *n.* medley, potpourri. See MIXTURE.

pastime, *n.* AMUSEMENT, recreation, entertainment, play, diversion.

pastor, *n.* clergyman, minister, *etc.* (see CLERGY).

pastoral, *adj.* clerical; rural, bucolic, idyllic; agrarian. See CLERGY, AGRICULTURE.

pastry, *n.* cake, crust, shell; pie, tart, strudel. See FOOD.

pasture, *n.* field, meadow, grassland; paddock, pasturage, range. See LAND, FOOD, VEGETABLE.

pasty, *adj.* doughy, soft; pallid, pale; gluey; viscid, glutinous. See COLORLESSNESS, SOFTNESS.

pat, *n.* caress, stroke; rap, tap; strike, beat, smack; patty. See ENDEARMENT, IMPULSE, DENSITY. —*adj.* apt, suitable, ready, appropriate, fitting; timely, fortuitous. See AGREEMENT.

patch, *n.* piece, segment, spot; repair, mend; field, lot. —*v.t.* repair, reconstruct, rebuild, revamp, adjust. See COMPROMISE, RESTORATION.

patent, *adj.* obvious, plain, clear, evident, apparent; noticeable; open. See VISIBILITY, DISCLOSURE. —*n. & v.* See PERMISSION.

paternal, *adj.* fatherly, patriarchal; ancestral, parental; indulgent, benign, benevolent; paternalistic, protective, autocratic; socialistic. See ANCESTRY. *Ant.,* maternal.

paternity, *n.* fatherhood, fathership, parentage. See ANCESTRY. *Ant.,* maternity.

pater noster, Lat., our father; the Lord's prayer. See WORSHIP.

path, *n.* pathway, trail, lane, road, footpath, route, way, course; lead, example. See DIRECTION, PASSAGE.

pathetic, *adj.* piteous, pitiable, saddening, touching; distressing, heartrending, sad; pitiful. See PAIN, BADNESS, PITY.

pathfinder, *n.* trailblazer, explorer, pioneer, frontiersman, scout, forerunner. See PREPARATION.

pathological, *adj.* unhealthy, infected, contaminated. See DISEASE.

pathos, *n.* passion, warmth; sentiment, FEELING.

patience, *adj.* LENIENCY, tolerance; perseverance, persistence; forbearance, long-suffering, SUBMISSION, endurance; solitaire. See INEXCITABILITY, RESIGNATION. *Ant.,* impatience.

patient, *n.* invalid, case, victim; out- *or* inpatient. See DISEASE. —*adj.* tolerant, indulgent, long-suffering. See LENIENCY, SUBMISSION. *Ant.,* impatient.

patina, *n.* verdigris, aerugo; polish, shine, finish; COVERING, coat[ing], veneer. See LAYER.

patio, *n.* courtyard, enclosure, court, atrium; yard; terrace, piazza, verandah. See ENCLOSURE.

patois, *n.* dialect, jargon, vernacular, lingo (*inf.*). See SPEECH.

patriarch, *n.* forefather, forebear, elder, graybeard; leader, headman, chief, master; priest, primate, ecclesiarch, hierarch. See ANCESTRY, CLERGY, AUTHORITY.

patrician, *adj.* noble, well-born, aristocratic. See NOBILITY. *Ant.,* commoner.

patrimony, *n.* heritage, estate. See POSSESSION.

patriot, *n.* chauvinist, flag-waver. See PRIDE.

patriotism, *n.* civic *or* national pride; loyalty, allegiance; love of country, civism, nationalism; chauvinism, jingoism, fascism; isolationism, provincialism, xenophobia. See PRIDE.

patrol, *n.* patrolman, guard, warden, ranger; lookout, sentinel, sentry; guardsman, picket; watch[man]; coast guard; vigilante, policeman *or* -woman. —*v.* guard, stand watch *or* guard, watch over, keep watch and ward; scout; walk the beat. See DEFENSE, SAFETY.

patrolman, patrolwoman, *n.* policeman *or* -woman, nightwatchman (see SAFETY).

patron, patroness, *n.* customer; benefactor, supporter; saint, defender, backer, angel. See PURCHASE, FRIEND.

patronage, *n.* condescension, favor; custom, interest, support, assistance; auspices. See AID, AUTHORITY, INFLUENCE, PURCHASE.

patronize, *v.t.* support, endorse, AID; deal *or* do business with; buy from, frequent, go to, shop at; look down upon, show contempt *or* condescension, condescend toward. See HUMILITY, AID, BARTER.

patsy, *n., slang,* dupe, gull. See CREDULITY.

patter, *v.i.* chatter, mumble, ramble, babble, jabber, mutter; tap, pitter-patter. — *n.* dialect, cant, chatter, babble. See LOQUACITY, SOUND.

pattern, *n.* form, original; mold, example; design, PLAN, last; model, ideal. See PERFECTION, CONFORMITY, ORNAMENT.

paucity, *n.* scantiness, fewness (see INSUFFICIENCY). *Ant.,* plenty.

paunch, *n.* stomach, abdomen, belly; fat. See CONVEXITY.

pauper, *n.* beggar, bankrupt, mendicant. See POVERTY. *Ant.,* rich person, nabob.

pause, *n.* cessation, rest, hesitation, INACTIVITY; lull, stop, DISCONTINUANCE, suspension. —*v.i.* desist, halt, stop, cease, break. See DOUBT, REPOSE.

pave, *v.t.* coat, cover, floor, cobble, surface, tar, macadamize, concrete, asphalt; prepare. See COVERING, SMOOTHNESS, PREPARATION.

pavement, *n.* paving; road, street, sidewalk; macadam, asphalt, cement, tar, concrete, tile, bricks, stone, flagging, cobbles, pavestone, paving blocks, flagstone. See COVERING.

pavilion, *n.* tent, canopy, canvas; kiosk; summerhouse. See COVERING, ABODE.

paw, *n.* forepaw; pad, mitt. —*v.* handle, TOUCH, finger; mishandle, rough up, maul; stamp, kick; feel, caress, stroke.

pawn, *v.t.* pledge, hock (*sl.*). See DEBT, SECURITY.

pawnshop, *n.* pawnbrokery, mont-de-piété, hockshop (*sl.*), spout (*sl.*), my uncle's (*sl.*). See DEBT.

pax vobiscum, Lat., peace be with you. See DEPARTURE, SOCIALITY.

pay, *v.* compensate; discharge, pay off; render, offer; be profitable, yield [a profit], show a profit, be worthwhile. —*n.* wages, salary; payment, compensation. See PAYMENT, SUCCESS, OFFER.

PAYMENT
Act of paying

Nouns—1, payment, defrayment; discharge, remission; acquittance, quittance; settlement, clearance, liquidation, satisfaction, reckoning, arrangement, restitution, repayment, reimbursement; down payment, part payment, deposit; retribution; refund. *Informal,* a pound of flesh, an arm and a leg. See PURCHASE, PRICE.

2, COMPENSATION, recompense, remuneration, bounty, reward, indemnity; expenditure, outlay; dividend; scholarship, fellowship, bursary, alimony, [child] support; welfare, relief, public assistance; starvation wages. *Slang,* palimony.

3, salary, stipend, wages, pay, paycheck, remuneration, emolument, allowance; minimum wage; bonus, premium, fee, retainer, honorarium, tip, baksheesh, scot, corkage, tribute, hire; bribe, blackmail, hush money; payday. *Slang,* kickback, giveback, rake-off, oil, backhander, dash, fix; the day the eagle screams *or* shits.

4, *(means of payment)* check, blank check, counter check, [bank] draft, money order; cash (see MONEY).

5, salaried worker, employee; dink, oink, sink.

Verbs—1, pay, defray, make payment; pay down, pay in advance; redeem; pay in kind; discharge, settle, quit, acquit oneself of; account, reckon, settle, be even *or* quits with; strike a balance; settle *or* square accounts with; wipe off old scores; satisfy; pay off, get even, pay in full; clear, liquidate; pay *or* put up.

2, pay one's way, pay the piper, pay the costs, pick up the check, do the needful; finance, set up; pay as one goes; ante up; expend; lay down; bribe (see PURCHASE). *Informal,* foot the bill, chip in, lay out, plunk down, lay *or* put on the line; go Dutch;

come across; see the color of one's money. *Slang,* kick *or* fork over, out, *or* up, tickle, oil, *or* grease the palm, dig down, cough up, kick in, shell out, rob Peter to pay Paul. 3, disgorge, make repayment, remit; expend, disburse; repay, refund, reimburse, retribute; reward, make compensation; spend money like water. *Slang,* pay through the nose, pay cash on the barrel-head *or* on the line; shoot one's wad; pay cold cash.

Adjectives—paying; paid, owing nothing, out of debt, quits, square.

Adverbs—to the tune of; on the nail; money down; in return.

Phrases—every man has his price; he who pays the piper calls the tune; they that dance must pay the fiddler; if you pay peanuts, you get monkeys; pay beforehand was never well served.

Quotations—He is well paid that is well satisfied (*Shakespeare*).

Antonyms, see NONPAYMENT, RECEIVING.

---

peace, *n.* peacetime; amity, friendship, harmony, concord; tranquillity, peace of mind, REPOSE, quiescence; truce; neutrality. See PACIFICATION, SILENCE, CONTENT, UNITY. *Ant.,* war, contention.

peaceful, *adj.* peaceable; quiet, tranquil; amicable. See REPOSE, PACIFICATION, FRIEND. *Ant.,* warlike, agitated.

peak, *n.* summit, top, apex, pinnacle; point, crag; crest, HEIGHT; climax. See SHARPNESS.

peaked, *adj.* wan, worn, pale, haggard, tired, weary, fatigued; ailing, unwell, unhealthy, ill, poorly, sickly; thin, gaunt, frail. See WEARINESS, DISEASE.

peal, *n.* reverberation, ring, outburst. — *v.i.* ring, toll, reverberate, sound. See LOUDNESS.

peanuts, *n., informal,* small change, petty cash, pin money. See MONEY.

pearl, *n.* margarite, nacre, mother-of-pearl; artificial *or* cultured pearl; gem, treasure, jewel; pearl beyond price. See ORNAMENT, GOODNESS.

pearly, *adj.* nacreous, silvery, grayish, whitish; lustrous. See COLOR.

peasant, *n.* countryman; peon, paisano, paisana, coolie, boor, muzhik, fellah; farmer, laborer, worker; rustic. See POPULACE, AGRICULTURE. *Ant.,* noble, aristocrat.

pebble, *n.* pebblestone, nugget, stone. See LAND, HARDNESS.

peck, *v.i.* nip, bite, pick, snip; tap, rap. See IMPULSE, FOOD.

peculiar, *adj.* individual, indigenous, idiosyncratic; idiomatic; strange, odd, unusual, queer; particular, especial. See UNCONFORMITY, SPECIALITY. *Ant.,* normal, usual.

pecuniary, *adj.* monetary (see MONEY).

pedagogical, *adj.* academic, educational, teacherly, professional, scholastic. See TEACHING.

pedal, *n.* treadle, lever. See INSTRUMENTALITY.

pedant, *n.* scholar, theorist, academician, doctrinaire; prig, bluestocking. See AFFECTATION.

pedantic, *adj.* precise, formal, narrow; bookish, stilted; affected, sophomoric. See AFFECTATION.

peddle, *v.* sell; canvass, hawk, retail. See SALE.

peddler, pedlar, *n.* hawker, huckster, colporteur, sutler, vendor, trader, dealer. See SALE.

pederast, *n.* child molester, pedophile. See IMPURITY.

pedestal, *n.* base, SUPPORT.

pedestrian, *n.* walker, ambler, stroller, peregrinator, hiker. See TRAVEL. —*adj.* prosaic, dull. See WEARINESS.

pedigree, *n.* genealogy, lineage, ANCESTRY, descent, family; background. See NOBILITY.

pedophile, *n.* child molester, pederast. See IMPURITY.

peek, *v.i.* peep, glance, look, watch; pry. See VISION, CURIOSITY.

peel, *v.t.* strip, divest, bare, uncover, skin, pare. See DIVESTMENT, LAYER. —*n.* See COVERING.

peep, *n.* chirp, cheep, chirrup; glimpse. — *v.i.* peer, peek, look; spy, pry. See VISION, CURIOSITY. —**peeping Tom,** voyeur (see CURIOSITY).

peer, peeress, *n.* equal; nobleman, noblewoman; lord, lady; match. See EQUALITY, NOBILITY. —*v.i.* squint, stare, peep, pry; gaze, scrutinize. See VISION.

peerage, *n.* aristocracy, NOBILITY, the upper class[es]. *Ant.*, commonalty, peasantry.

peerless, *adj.* unequaled, matchless, unbeatable, supreme, unrivaled; indomitable. See SUPERIORITY.

peevish, *adj.* irascible, fretful, cranky, cross, irritable, touchy. See IRASCIBILITY.

peg, *n.* pin; DEGREE. See SUPPORT.

pejorative, *adj.* disparaging, depreciating. See DETRACTION.

pellet, *n.* pill, tablet, capsule; missile, pebble, hailstone, bullet. See ARMS, ROTUNDITY.

pellmell, *adv.* madly, frantically; helter-skelter, every which way (*inf.*); hurry-scurry, breakneck, headlong, lickety-split (*sl.*). See DISORDER.

pelt, *n.* fur, hide, skin, peltry. See COVERING. —*v.* bombard, pepper, stone, strike; drive, beat; hurl, throw, pitch, fling. See IMPULSE, PROPULSION.

pen, *n.* stockade, ENCLOSURE, fold, stall, coop, cage, pound, corral, paddock; stylus, quill. —*v.t.* confine, jail, impound, enclose, restrain, cage, COOP; write, indite, inscribe. See RESTRAINT, ABODE, WRITING.

penalize, *v.t.* punish; fine, imprison, chastise, handicap, *etc.* See PUNISHMENT.

penalty, *n.* retribution, PUNISHMENT, rap (*sl.*); pain, penance, atonement; the devil to pay; penalization; handicap, fine, amercement; forfeit[ure], damages, confiscation.

penance, *n.* ATONEMENT, discipline, punishment; flagellation, fasting; price, suffering, repayment. See PENITENCE.

penchant, *n.* aptitude, leaning, inclination, flair, TENDENCY; predisposition, propensity, TASTE; DESIRE, longing, yearning, yen.

pencil, *n.* crayon, stylus, pastel, chalk. See WRITING, PAINTING.

pend, *v.i.* hang; depend, hang in the balance. See DOUBT, PENDENCY.

pendant, *n.* See PENDENCY, ORNAMENT.

PENDENCY
State of hanging

Nouns—1, pendency, dependency, dependence, pendulousness, pendulosity, pensility; droop[ing], sag[ging], suspension, hanging, overhang.

2, pendant, drop, earring, eardrop, lavaliere, necklace; pedicel, pedicle, peduncle; hanging, lobe, wattle, tail, train, flag, tag, bob, skirt, tassel, swag; pigtail, queue; bell rope; pendulum, chandelier; appendage, appendix, ADDITION; suspender, belt, garter, fastening, button; peg, knob, hook, hanger, nail, stud, ring, staple, pothook, tenterhook, spar; clothesline, clothespin; gallows.

Verbs—1, be pendent, hang, drape, depend, swing, dangle, droop, sag, draggle; bag; flap, trail, flow, overhang, project, jut.

2, suspend, pend, hang [up], sling, hook up, hitch, fasten to, append.

Adjectives—pendent, pendulous, pensile; hanging, pending, drooping, cernuous, flowing, loose; suspended, dependent; overhanging, projecting, jutting; pedunculate, tailed, caudate.

Antonyms, see SUPPORT.

---

pendent, *adj.* hanging (see PENDENCY); pending (see LATENESS).

pending, *adj.* open, up in the air, undecided; impending, contingent. See LATENESS, DOUBT.

pendulum, *n.* oscillator, swing, bob, pendant. See PENDENCY, OSCILLATION.

penetrate, *v.t.* bore, burrow, pierce, enter; cut, perforate; permeate, invade; discern, perceive, understand, uncover. See INGRESS, INTELLIGENCE, PASSAGE, INSERTION.

penetrating, *adj.* astute, discerning, piercing; sharp, subtle, acute, penetrative. See FEELING, INTELLIGENCE.

peninsula, *n.* projection, chersonese, neck, tongue of land. See LAND, CONVEXITY.

penis, *n.* phallus (see BODY).

PENITENCE
Contrition

Nouns—1, penitence, contrition, compunction, repentance, remorse, regret.

2, self-reproach, self-reproof, self-accusation, self-condemnation, self-humiliation; pangs, qualms, prickings, twinge, *or* voice of conscience; awakened conscience.

3, acknowledgment, confession (see DISCLOSURE); apology, penance, ATONEMENT; recantation.

4, penitent, Magdalene, prodigal son, a sadder and a wiser man.

Verbs—repent, be penitent, be sorry for; rue; regret, think better of; recant; plead guilty; sing miserere, sing de profundis; confess oneself in the wrong; acknowledge, confess (see DISCLOSURE); humble oneself; beg pardon, apologize, do penance (see ATONEMENT).

Adjectives—penitent, regretful, regretting, sorry, contrite; regrettable, lamentable.

Quotations—Remorse, the fatal egg by pleasure laid (*William Cowper*), To regret deeply is to live afresh (*Henry Thoreau*), Of all the means to regeneration Remorse is surely the most wasteful (*E. M. Forster*).

Antonyms, see IMPENITENCE.

---

penitentiary, *n.* PRISON, reformatory.

penmanship, *n.* chirography, handwriting. See WRITING.

pennant, *n.* banner, flag, streamer, pennon. See INDICATION.

penniless, *adj.* indigent, needy, bankrupt, impecunious, poor, broke (*sl.*). See POVERTY. *Ant.,* rich, wealthy.

pension, *n.* allowance, annuity, allotment, settlement; boardinghouse. See GIVING, ABODE.

pensive, *adj.* thoughtful, reflective, meditative, musing; melancholy, sad, dejected. See THOUGHT, DEJECTION.

pent-up, *adj.* held in, suppressed, repressed. See RESTRAINT.

penurious, *adj.* stingy, mean, miserly. See PARSIMONY.

penury, *n.* POVERTY, lack, indigence, destitution, pauperism.

peon, *n.* peasant, laborer (see SERVANT).

people, *n.* See HUMANITY, POPULACE.

pep, *n., slang,* peppiness; ENERGY, vitality, VIGOR, vim, dash, zest; liveliness, pungency, sharpness, gusto, go (*inf.*), zing (*inf.*), pepper (*sl.*).

pepper, *n.* cayenne, black *or* white pepper; bell, hot, *or* sweet pepper; *slang,* vim, VIGOR. See FOOD, PUNGENCY. —*v.t.* dot, stud; pelt; season. See DISPERSION, TASTE, ATTACK.

pep talk, exhortation (see ADVICE).

per, *prep.* by, as, by means *or* way of, through, via. See MEANS. —*adv., slang,* apiece, each, a head, per unit. See APPORTIONMENT.

per annum, Lat., annually. See TIME.

per capita, Lat., each. See APPORTIONMENT.

perceive, *v.t.* apprehend, discern; observe, notice, see; comprehend, know. See KNOWLEDGE.

percentage, *n.* compensation, commission, discount; fee; allowance. See PAYMENT.

perceptible, *adj.* appreciable, discernible, visible; tangible, observable, sensible; cognizable. See KNOWLEDGE.

perceptive, *adj.* knowledgeable, observant, understanding; aware, sympathetic; knowing, cognitive. See KNOWLEDGE, INTELLIGENCE, INTUITION, SENSIBILITY.

perch, *n.* rest, roost, nest, seat. —*v.i.* poise, place, roost, settle, alight, sit. See LOCATION, ABODE.

percolate, *v.i.* drip, trickle, permeate; ooze, filter. See EGRESS, WATER.

percussion, *n.* impact, IMPULSE; drums, cymbals, *etc.* (see MUSIC).

per diem, Lat., per day. See APPORTIONMENT, PAYMENT.

perdition, *n.* DESTRUCTION, downfall, ruin, LOSS, fall. See FAILURE.

peremptory, *adj.* commanding, arbitrary, tyrannical, dogmatic; compulsory, binding; absolute, decisive, conclusive. See AUTHORITY, COMPULSION, SEVERITY.

perennial, *adj.* enduring, lasting, endless, persistent; successive, consecutive. See CONTINUITY, DURABILITY.

PERFECTION
Flawlessness

Nouns—1, perfection, perfectness, indefectibility; impeccancy, impeccability, faultlessness, excellence. See GOODNESS, COMPLETION, IMPROVEMENT.

2, paragon; [beau] ideal, paradigm; nonpareil; pink *or* acme of perfection; ne plus ultra; summit, model, standard, pattern, mirror; masterpiece; transcendence, transcendency, SUPERIORITY; quintessence; a whole team and the dog under the wagon.

3, perfectionist, idealist.

Verbs—1, be perfect, transcend; bring to perfection, perfect, ripen, mature, consummate, complete, culminate.

2, perfect (see IMPROVEMENT, COMPLETION).

Adjectives—perfect, faultless; indefective, indeficient, indefectible; immaculate, spotless, impeccable; unblemished, sound, scatheless, unscathed, intact; right as rain; consummate, finished, best, model, standard, state-of-the-art; inimitable, unparalleled, nonpareil; superhuman, divine, fit for the gods; *sans peur et sans reproche.*

Adverbs—to perfection, to a fare-thee-well; perfectly, *etc.*; to a T, to a turn, to the letter.

Phrases—trifles make perfection, but perfection is no trifle; practice makes perfect.

Quotations—Faultless to a fault (*Robert Browning*), Perfection of means and confusion of goals seem, in my opinion, to characterize our age (*Albert Einstein*), What is so rare as a day in June? Then, if ever, come perfect days (*James Russell Lowell*), The seasons . . . are authentic; there is no mistake about them, they are what a symphony ought to be: four perfect movements in intimate harmony with one another (*Artur Rubinstein*), Nothing quite new is perfect (*Cicero*).

Antonyms, see IMPERFECTION.

---

perfidious, *adj.* treacherous, crooked, shifty, double-dealing, two-timing, double-crossing, like a snake in the grass; perjurious, lying, truthless; deceitful, insidious, snakelike. See IMPROBITY, FALSEHOOD. *Ant.,* faithful, loyal.

perforate, *v.t.* bore, drill, pierce, puncture, penetrate, prick; punch, riddle; tunnel. See OPENING, PASSAGE.

perforce, *adv.* compulsorily, by *or* of NECESSITY; against one's will, in spite of oneself. See COMPULSION.

perform, *v.* enact, play, execute; fulfill, achieve, discharge; act, render, do; operate, work, conduct. See ACTION, AGENCY, COMPLETION, DRAMA, MUSIC.

performance, *n.* ACTION, representation, achievement; rendition, execution, touch; efficiency. See EFFECT, DRAMA.

performing arts, *n.* MUSIC, DRAMA, DANCE, FILM.

perfume, *n.* fragrance, aroma; cologne, scent; sachet, attar, perfumery. See ODOR.

perfunctory, *adj.* formal, indifferent, careless; mechanical, crude; casual, superficial. See NEGLECT, INDIFFERENCE.

perhaps, *adv.* maybe, possibly, perchance, mayhap, conceivably. See CHANCE, POSSIBILITY, SUPPOSITION. *Ant.,* surely.

peril, *n.* DANGER, hazard, risk, chance, exposure. See THREAT.

perimeter, *n.* periphery, circumference, outline, contour; outside, border, boundary, limit; EDGE, rim, hem, margin, fringe. See CIRCUIT.

period, *n.* second, minute, hour; day, week, month; quarter, year, decade; lifetime, generation, TIME; century, age, millennium, era, epoch; [full] stop *or* pause, sentence; menstruation, monthlies, friend[s] (*sl.*), the curse (*sl.*). See END, REGULARITY.

periodic, *adj.* recurrent, cyclic, intermittent, epochal; periodical, seasonal. See DISCONTINUANCE. *Ant.,* continual, continuous.

periodical, *n.* magazine, journal, quarterly, weekly, monthly, zine (*sl.*). See PUBLICATION.

periodicity, *n.* REGULARITY, reoccurrence, cycle.

peripheral, *adj.* outer, EXTERIOR, neighboring; subsidiary, auxiliary, secondary, lesser; marginal. See LIMIT. *Ant.*, central.

perish, *v.i.* expire, die, crumble. See DEATH, DESTRUCTION, NONEXISTENCE.

perishable, *adj.* impermanent, destructible; temporal, mortal; unenduring. See TRANSIENTNESS.

perjury, *n.* false swearing, FALSEHOOD, perversion, forswearing, fraud.

perk, *v.* perk up, cheer [up], brighten, animate, liven, show signs of life; *informal,* bubble, percolate. See CHEERFULNESS, REFRESHMENT.

perky, *adj.* jaunty, pert, buoyant. See CHEERFULNESS. *Ant.,* dumpy, lethargic.

PERMANENCE
Fixed nature

Nouns—1, permanence, STABILITY, immutability, fixity; persistence, DURABILITY, duration; constancy, PERPETUITY, status quo; tenure, tenure-track.

2, PRESERVATION; conservatism, establishment; law of the Medes and the Persians; conservative, reactionary, stick-in-the-mud, diehard, fogy, right-winger, nonprogressive, Tory, Hunker, fixture. *Informal,* holdout, stand-patter. *Slang,* mossback, fuddy-duddy, troglodyte.

Verbs—persist, remain, stay; hold [out], hold on; last, endure, [a]bide, maintain, keep; stand [fast]; subsist, survive; hold one's ground, hold good, stand pat.

Adjectives—permanent, stable, fixed, standing, immovable, immutable, established, settled, steadfast; constant, eternal, lifelong, lasting, durable, persistent, unending, perpetual, monotonous; unfading, unfailing, *etc.*; invariable, indelible, indestructible, inextinguishable, intact, inviolate; conservative, reactionary, right-wing; stationary; rootbound.

Adverbs—in statu quo, as usual; at a standstill, permanently, finally, for good, forever. *Slang,* until hell freezes over.

Quotations—Men are mortal; but ideas are immortal (*Walter Lippman*), What's done cannot be undone (*Shakespeare*).

Antonyms, see CHANGE.

---

permanent, *adj.* lasting (see PERMANANCE). *Ant.,* temporary, ephemeral. —**permanent press,** drip-dry (see CLOTHING). — **permanent wave,** permanent, perm (*inf.*), set. See BEAUTY.

permeate, *v.t.* pervade, saturate, overspread, infiltrate, penetrate. See PASSAGE, PRESENCE, MIXTURE.

PERMISSION
Consent

Nouns—1, permission, leave; allowance, sufferance; tolerance, toleration; FREEDOM, liberty, law, license, concession, grace; indulgence, lenity, LENIENCY; favor, ASSENT, dispensation, EXEMPTION, release; connivance; open door.

2, authorization, warranty, accordance, admission, permit, warrant, brevet, precept, fiat, imprimatur, sanction, AUTHORITY, firman, go-ahead; free hand, pass, passport; furlough, license, carte blanche, ticket of leave; grant, charter, patent. *Informal,* green light, signal, okay, OK, blank check.

Verbs—1, permit; give permission, give power, entitle; let, allow, admit; suffer, bear with, tolerate, recognize; accord, vouchsafe, favor, humor, indulge, stretch a point; wink at, connive at, [let] pass; shut one's eyes to; give carte blanche; leave alone, leave to one's own devices, leave the door open; allow for, open the door to, open the floodgates, let loose; give the reins *or* free rein to. *Informal,* stand for.

2, grant, empower, character, enfranchise, confer a privilege, license, authorize, warrant; sanction; entrust, COMMISSION; sanctify, ordain, prescribe. *Informal,* okay, OK, write one's own ticket.

Adjectives—permitting, permissive, indulgent; permitted, permissible, allowable, lawful (see LEGALITY); unconditional.
Adverbs—permissibly, by leave, with leave, on leave; under favor of; ad libitum, freely; with no holds barred.
Quotations—No man is above the law and no man is below it; nor do we ask any man's permission when we require him to obey it (*Theodore Roosevelt*).
Antonyms, see PROHIBITION.

permutation, *n.* See INTERCHANGE, CHANGE.

pernicious, *adj.* malign, ruinous, poisonous, detrimental, injurious, harmful; wicked. See BADNESS.

peroration, *n.* epilogue, conclusion; harangue. See DIFFUSENESS, END, SPEECH.

perpendicular, *adj.* erect, upright; sheer, precipitous; VERTICAL, plumb. *Ant.*, parallel.

perpetrate, *v.t.* commit, inflict; perform, do, practice. See ACTION.

PERPETUITY
Endless duration

Nouns—perpetuity; everlastingness, unceasingness, *etc.*; eternity, INFINITY, aye, TIME without end, sempiternity; deathlessness, immortality, athanasia; incessance, CONTINUITY, DURABILITY, perpetuation, PRESERVATION. See STABILITY.
Verbs—last or endure forever, have no end, never end or die; perpetuate, eternalize, eternize, immortalize, continue, preserve.
Adjectives—perpetual, everlasting, unceasing, endless, ageless, unending, having no end; [co-]eternal, everliving, everflowing, sempiternal, continual, ceaseless, incessant, uninterrupted, interminable, infinite, neverending; unfailing, evergreen, amaranthine; deathless, immortal, undying, imperishable, perdurable; permanent, lasting, enduring, perennial, long-lived, dateless, illimitable, continued, constant.
Adverbs—perpetually, in perpetuity, always, ever[more], aye; forever, forevermore, for aye, forever and a day, forever and ever; in all ages, from age to age, without end, world without end, time without end; to the end of time, to the crack of doom; till death [do us part], till doomsday, till kingdom come; constantly. *Informal*, for keeps, for good [and all], until hell freezes over, till the cows come home.
Antonyms, see TRANSIENTNESS, TIME.

perplex, *v.* puzzle, bewilder, confuse, mystify, confound, nonplus; distract, disconcert. See DIFFICULTY, UNINTELLIGIBILITY, DOUBT.

perquisite, *n.* reward, bonus, gratuity, tip, perk (*sl.*); bribe; due. See ACQUISITION, GIVING, STEALING.

per se, *adv.* by itself, intrinsically, essentially; virtually, in the main; by nature, as a thing apart. See INTRINSIC, UNITY.

persecute, *v.t.* molest, oppress, maltreat, pursue, beset; abuse, injure; hound, annoy, trouble. See MALEVOLENCE, PAIN, BADNESS, WRONG.

perseverance, *n.* continuance, PERMANENCE; firmness, STABILITY; constancy, steadiness; TENACITY or singleness of purpose; persistence, plodding, patience; industry; pertinacity; gameness,

pluck, stamina, backbone; indefatigability; bulldog COURAGE, sand, grit; determination, stick-to-itiveness (*inf.*). See RESOLUTION, FREQUENCY.

persist, *v.i.* persevere, continue, remain, endure, stand, abide, plod. See PERMANENCE, FREQUENCY, CONTINUITY.

person, *n.* individual, body, somebody, anybody; man, woman, child; human. See HUMANITY.

personable, *adj.* presentable; charming, [con]genial. See BEAUTY.

personage, *n.* dignitary, official, celebrity, notable, figure, somebody, bigwig, VIP (*inf.*), big wheel (*inf.*). See IMPORTANCE, NOBILITY.

personal, *adj.* private, individual, intimate, own, special, particular; invidious (*of a remark*). See SPECIALITY.

personality, *n.* character, individuality, self, ego; *informal,* celebrity, notable. See REPUTE, SPECIALITY, IDENTITY.

persona non grata, *Lat.,* undesirable. See BADNESS, DISLIKE.

personify, *v.t.* embody, typify, symbolize, exemplify; represent, personate. See REPRESENTATION.

personnel, *n.* employees, workers, help, stable (*sl.*); faculty, hands, squad, crew, gang, staff, team, rank and file; staffers. See SERVANT.

perspective, *n.* view, angle, aspect, position, slant (*inf.*); field of view *or* vision, vista, prospect, scene, vantage [point]; outlook, viewpoint, scope, grasp, appreciation, comprehension, point of view, judgment; remove, DISTANCE; context, orientation, insight. See EXPECTATION, COLOR, APPEARANCE.

perspicacity, *n.* discernment, discrimination, acuteness, keenness; shrewdness; penetration, insight, acumen. See INTELLIGENCE.

perspicuity, *n.* intelligibility; manifestation; definiteness, definition; exactness. See INTELLIGENCE.

perspire, *v.* exude, sweat, exhale, excrete, swelter. See EXCRETION.

persuade, *v.t.* induce, prevail upon, win [over]; convince, satisfy, assure. See BELIEF, CAUSE, INFLUENCE.

persuasible, *adj.* docile, tractable, convincible; amenable, unresistant; persuadable. See INFLUENCE.

persuasion, *n.* argument, plea, exhortation; conviction; INFLUENCE, insistence. See BELIEF, CAUSE.

persuasive, *adj.* inducive; cogent, convincing, logical; winning. See BELIEF, CAUSE.

pert, *adj.* impudent, saucy, flippant, fresh, flip, sassy (*inf.*); forward, bold, perky. See DISCOURTESY, INSOLENCE.

pertain, *v.i.* apply, refer, bear upon; belong, relate; appertain, concern; affect. See RELATION.

pertinacious, *adj.* persevering, persistent; obstinate, unyielding, constant, resolute, firm. See RESOLUTION.

pertinent, *adj.* relevant, apposite, applicable, apt. See RELATION. *Ant.,* irrelevant.

perturbation, *n.* disturbance; disquiet, uneasiness, discomposure, apprehension, worry; trepidation, restlessness. See AGITATION, EXCITEMENT, FEAR.

peruse, *v.t.* read, con, study; examine. See INQUIRY, LEARNING.

pervade, *v.t.* fill, permeate, penetrate, imbue, overspread, impregnate, saturate; infiltrate. See PRESENCE, MIXTURE.

perverse, *adj.* contrary, stubborn, obstinate, self-willed; ungovernable, wayward; cross, petulant. See OBSTINACY, WRONG.

perversion, *n.* DISTORTION, misuse, misrepresentation, misconstruction; corruption, debasement. See DETERIORATION, IMPIETY, IMPURITY.

perversity, *n.* OBSTINACY, obduracy, perverseness, mulishness, cussedness (*sl.*); waywardness, unconformity; contumacy, wickedness. See IRASCIBILITY.

pervert, *v.t.* apostasize, distort, twist, garble, debase, misrepresent, corrupt, mislead, misinterpret, misstate; equivocate. See DISTORTION, FALSEHOOD.

pesky, *adj., informal,* troublesome, annoying. See DISCONTENT.

pessimism, *n.* DEJECTION; cynicism, morbidity. See HOPELESSNESS. *Ant.,* optimism.

pest, *n.* plague, pestilence, epidemic; parasite, infestation; nuisance, trouble; bane, scourge, curse. See BADNESS, DISEASE.

pester, *v.t.* plague, annoy, trouble, vex, irritate, displease. See DISCONTENT.

pesticide, *n.* insecticide, poison. See KILLING.

pestilence, *n.* DISEASE, plague, epidemic.

pet, *n.* favorite, beloved, love, dearest, darling. —*v.t.* cherish, fondle, caress, embrace, stroke, cuddle. See ENDEARMENT, LOVE, FLATTERY.

petal, *n.* perianth; corolla, calyx, corona. See VEGETABLE.

peter out, *v.i.* diminish, DECREASE.

petite, *adj.* small, mignon, diminutive, trim, tiny. See LITTLENESS.

petition, *n.* plea, REQUEST, entreaty, supplication, prayer; asking, address. —*v.t.* ask, beg, entreat, REQUEST, plead, appeal, implore.

petrify, *v.t.* calcify, turn to stone, lapidify, fossilize; stun, astonish; stupefy, shock; stiffen, harden, paralyze. See DENSITY, HARDNESS, FEAR, INORGANIC MATTER.

petroleum, *n.* OIL. See FUEL.

petticoat, *n.* slip, chemise, underskirt, crinoline, camisole, balmoral, half-slip. See CLOTHING.

petty, *adj.* trivial, unimportant, small, mean, trifling; contemptible, spiteful. See UNIMPORTANCE. *Ant.,* serious, major, important.

petulant, *adj.* fretful, irritable, complaining, peevish. See IRASCIBILITY.

phallic, *adj.* penile, genital. See BODY.

phantasm, *n.* apparition, specter; illusion. See IMAGINATION, DEMON.

phantom, *n.* specter, illusion, apparition, ghost, spirit, shade, shadow. See DEMON.

pharmacist, *n.* chemist, apothecary, druggist. See REMEDY.

phase, *n.* APPEARANCE, state, condition, situation, aspect; shape, FORM, angle. See CIRCUMSTANCE.

phenomenon, *n.* prodigy; marvel, WONDER; happening, OCCURRENCE.

philanderer, *n.* dallier, trifler, lecher, Romeo, Casanova, lover, rake, roué, libertine, playboy (*inf.*), sugar daddy (*sl.*), wolf (*sl.*). See ENDEARMENT, IMPURITY.

philanthropy, *n.* altruism, humanity, humanitarianism; BENEVOLENCE; generosity, LIBERALITY. See UNSELFISHNESS.

Philistine, *n.* vandal; bigot, yahoo, vulgarian, barbarian. See VULGARITY, MEDIOCRITY, MISJUDGMENT.

philosophical, *adj.* contemplative, deliberative, thoughtful, speculative; imperturbable, calm; wise, rational; stoical, Platonic, Socratic, Aristotelian. See KNOWLEDGE, THOUGHT.

phlegmatic, *adj.* stolid, dull, apathetic; calm, imperturbable, languid, unemotional, inert, cold. See INSENSIBILITY.

phobia, *n.* FEAR, dread, aversion, revulsion, repulsion, DISLIKE, antipathy; acrophobia, claustrophobia, *etc.* See INSANITY.

phone, *n. & v.* telephone (see COMMUNICATION).

phonetic, *adj.* phonetical, phonic, phonal, sonant; vocal, voiced, lingual, tonic, oral, spoken. See SOUND, SPEECH.

phonograph, *n.* Gramophone, Graphophone, Panatrope, Victrola, record player; pickup, playback, turntable; dictating machine. See RECORD.

phony, *adj., informal,* spurious, fraudulent, sham, mock, put-on (*sl.*), trumped-up, fake, forged; gimcrack, pasteboard; deceitful, false-hearted, lying; glib, canting, superficial. —*n., informal,* counterfeit, fraud; charlatan, quack, impostor, mountebank, fake, faker. See DECEPTION. *Ant.,* real, genuine.

photocopy, *v. & n.* COPY; photo-offset, Photostat.

PHOTOGRAPHY
Picture-taking

Nouns—1, photography, picture-taking; aerial, architectural, available-light, candid, digital, fashion, fine-art, infrared, laser, paper-negative, print, product, scenic, still, stereo-stroboscopic, tabletop, time-lapse, underwater, *or* wet-plate photography, black-and-white *or* color photography; silver-plate photography, daguerreotype; electron micrography; holography; photocopy[ing], xerography; photojournalism; portrait photography, portraiture; X-ray photography, radiography, skiagraphy; cinematography, motion-picture photography; photoengraving. See MOTION PICTURES, ENGRAVING, REPRESENTATION.

2, photograph, snapshot, picture, micrograph, tintype, ferrotype, photogram, hologram, collodion, calotype; X-ray, radiogram, radiography, skiagram; [photo]print, contact print, positive, negative, sepia; glossy, matte; contact *or* proof sheet; heat shot, closeup, mug shot, passport photo; photocopy, xerocopy, Xerox [copy], Photostat; blueprint; slide, transparency; enlargement, blowup; halation; photo CD. *Informal,* photo, shot.

3, camera, Kodak, Polaroid; aerial-reconnaissance, autofocus, box, folding, pinhole, single- *or* twin-lens reflex, *or* viewfinder camera; camera obscura *or* lucida; projector, magic lantern, slide projector *or* viewer; achromatic, anamorphic, anastigmatic, aplanatic, apochromatic, fisheye, fixed-focus, telephoto, wide-angle, *or* zoom lens, lens cap, lens shade; bellows, shutter, diaphragm, viewfinder, rangefinder, tripod, monopod, cable release; depth of field, angle of view, definition, contrast; flash, flash-gun, flashbulb, flashcube, strobe, snoot.

4, digital camera, digicam; charge coupled device (CCD) or CMOS (complementary metal-oxide semiconductor) sensor, digital signal processor (DSP); resolution, pixel; JPEG, FlashPIX.

5, color, black-and-white, orthochromatic, nonchromatic, panchromatic, *or* mono-chromatic film, microfilm, sheet film, emulsion, plate; filmholder, black back, cartridge, [film] pack, magazine; light *or* exposure meter; darkroom, safelight, enlarger, developer, fixative, stop bath. *Informal,* soup.

6, photographer, cameraman; daguerreotypist, calotypist; news photographer, photojournalist, paparazzo; radiographer, X-ray technician. *Informal,* shutterbug.

Verbs—photograph, take a picture (of); snap; X-ray, radiograph; develop, process, print, blow up, enlarge; project. *Informal,* shoot.

Adjectives—photographic; telephoto; photogenic; photosensitive.

Phrases—a picture is worth a thousand words.

Quotations—The camera is an instrument that teaches people how to see without a camera (*Dorothea Lange*); Photography is a moment of embarrassment and a lifetime of pleasure (*Tony Benn*).

---

phrase, *n.* expression; sentence, paragraph, clause; figure of speech, euphemism; idiom; locution; motto, maxim. —*v.t.* express, word, term, couch; voice. See FIGURATIVE, WRITING, GRAMMAR.

physic, *n.* laxative, cathartic, purgative; drug, medicine; pill, dose. —*v.t.* purge, drench; treat, doctor. See REMEDY.

physical, *adj.* bodily, anatomical; material, substantial. See SUBSTANCE.

physician, *n.* doctor, medic, medico, surgeon, specialist; [general] practitioner, GP; consultant, adviser, healer. See REMEDY.

physique, *n.* frame, body, FORM; appearance, size; build, musculature. See SUBSTANCE.

piano, *n.* pianoforte, fortepiano, spinet, pianette, upright; clavier, [clavi]cembalo, eighty-eight (*sl.*). See MUSIC.

piazza, *n.* square, place, street; porch, veranda, portico. See ABODE, RECEPTACLE.

picaresque, *adj.* roguish, swaggering, adventurous; episodic. See DESCRIPTION.

picayune, *adj.* trifling (see UNIMPORTANCE).

pick, *n.* best, cream, flower, elite; CHOICE; selection; pickax. See SHARPNESS. —*v.t.* select, choose; pluck, garner, gather; cull. See GOODNESS, APPROBATION.

picket, *n.* post, pale, fence; sentry, guard, sentinel, patrol; striker, protester, goon. See WARNING, RESTRAINT, DISOBEDI-

ENCE. —*v.* enclose, bar, fence; tether, restrain. See CIRCUMSCRIPTION.

pickle, *v.t.* preserve, salt, corn, brine, marinate. See PRESERVATION, SOURNESS.

pickpocket, *n.* thief, robber, cutpurse, dip (*sl.*). See STEALING.

pickup, *n.* pick-me-up, bracer, stimulant; acceleration, POWER; IMPROVEMENT, upturn, upswing; microphone; *slang,* date, one-night stand. See ENERGY, SOCIALITY.

picnic, *n.* excursion, junket, outing, festivity; cookout, barbecue, fish-fry, *etc.* See AMUSEMENT, FOOD.

pictorial, *adj.* delineatory, graphic, depicting; illustrated. See PAINTING, REPRESENTATION.

picture, *n.* image, likeness, counterpart; portrayal, REPRESENTATION, view, scene, tableau, setting; drawing, PAINTING, photograph, sketch, etching, ENGRAVING, canvas. See APPEARANCE.

picturesque, *adj.* artistic, graphic, attractive; vivid; quaint. See BEAUTY, VIGOR. *Ant.,* plain.

piddling, *adj.* trifling, petty, picayune. See UNIMPORTANCE.

pidgin, *n.* dialect, lingua franca, *bêche-de-mer.* See LANGUAGE.

pie, *n.* pastry, pasty, patisserie, tart; mud pie. See SWEETNESS, FOOD.

piece, *n.* scrap, morsel, bit; section, fragment, PART; *slang,* sex object, sexpot, BEAUTY, hunk. —*v.t.* unite, combine, patch, repair. See JUNCTION, DRAMA.

pièce de résistance, Fr., the main course. See GOODNESS, FOOD.

piecemeal, *adv.* one at a time, one by one; gradually, little by little, bit by bit, step by step, in drops; by stages *or* degrees, by dribs and drabs. See PART, DEGREE, SLOWNESS.

pied, *adj.* mottled, brindled, piebald, dappled. See VARIEGATION.

pied-à-terre, Fr., lodging. See ABODE.

pier, *n.* wharf, quay, mole, dock, breakwater; pillar, shaft, SUPPORT.

pierce, *v.t.* puncture, penetrate, perforate, bore, drill; stab, wound; affect; nip, chill. See OPENING.

piercing, *adj.* sharp, penetrating, keen, acute; discerning; cutting, biting; painful, affecting, chilling; high, shrill. See COLD, FEELING.

PIETY
Devoutness

Nouns—**1,** piety, piousness, devoutness; RELIGION, theism, faith, BELIEF; religiousness, holiness, saintliness; reverence, WORSHIP, veneration, devotion; grace, unction, edification; sanctity, sanctitude; consecration; theopathy; sanctum sanctorum. See VIRTUE.

2, *(act of piety)* beatification, canonization; sanctification; adoption, regeneration, palingenesis, conversion, justification, salvation, redemption; inspiration; pilgrimage (see TRAVEL); bread of life; body and blood of Christ.

3, *(pious person)* believer, convert, theist, Christian, devotee, pietist, pilgrim; revivalist, evangelist; the good, the righteous, the just, the believing, the elect; saint, Madonna, Sister Theresa; the children of God, the Kingdom of Light; born-again Christian. *Slang,* Jesus freak, Aunt Jane.

Verbs—**1,** be pious, have faith, believe, venerate, revere; be converted.

2, sanctify, beatify, canonize, inspire, hallow, bless, consecrate, enshrine, keep holy; convert, edify, redeem, save, regenerate.

Adjectives—pious, religious, devout, devoted, reverent, godly, humble, pure, holy, spiritual, pietistic; saintly, saintlike; seraphic, sacred, solemn; believing, faithful, Christian, Catholic; holier-than-thou; elected, adopted, justified, sanctified, beatified, canonized, regenerate[d], inspired, consecrated, converted, unearthly, inexpressible.

Quotations—With devotion's usage and pious action we do sugar o'er the devil himself (*Shakespeare*), Fear of death and fear of life both become piety (*H. L. Mencken*), And I could wish my days to be bound each to each by natural piety (*William Wordsworth*), My atheism . . . is true piety towards the universe and denies only gods fashioned by men in their own image, to be servants of their human interests (*George Santayana*).

Antonyms, see IMPIETY.

---

pig, *n.* hog, sow, boar, swine; piglet; glutton; sloven, slob. See ANIMAL, GLUTTONY, UNCLEANNESS.

pigeon, *n.* dove, homer, squab, pouter, turbit, tumbler, roler, fantail, nun; *slang,* dupe, easy mark, sitting duck, gull, sucker *(inf.),* chump *(inf.),* pushover *(sl.);* clay pigeon. See CREDULITY, ANIMAL.

pigeonhole, *n.* cubbyhole, niche, compartment. See RECEPTACLE.—*v.t.* file away, file and forget; postpone, put off, delay; classify. See LATENESS, CLASS.

piggish, *adj.* gluttonous; dirty, slovenly. See GLUTTONY, UNCLEANNESS.

piggyback, *adv.* pickaback. See SUPPORT.

pigheaded, *adj.* stubborn, tenacious, obstinate, entêté. See OBSTINACY.

pigment, *n.* COLOR, stain, dye, tint, paint, shade.

pigmy, *n.* See PYGMY.

pigsty, *n.* pigpen, sty; [rat]hole, dump *(inf.).* See ABODE, UNCLEANNESS.

pike, *n.* tip, point, spike; pikestaff, spear, lance, halberd, javelin. See ARMS, SHARPNESS.

piker, *n., slang,* pennypincher, tightwad, cheapskate, miser. See PARSIMONY.

pile, *n.* structure, building, edifice; nap; heap, mass, pyre; quantity. See ASSEM-

BLAGE. —*v.t.* accumulate, load, amass, furnish. See GREATNESS, COVERING, TEXTURE.

pile-up, *n.* collision, fender-bender (*inf.*). See IMPULSE.

pilfer, *v.* filch, rob, steal, plunder, thieve; shoplift. See STEALING.

pilgrim, *n.* wayfarer, traveler, migrant; settler, pioneer, newcomer; hadji, palmer, devotee. See TRAVEL, PIETY.

pilgrimage, *n.* journey, crusade, mission, quest, hadj, expedition; life, lifetime. See TRAVEL, UNDERTAKING.

pill, *n.* bolus, tablet, capsule, goofball (*sl.*); *slang,* trouble, pain-in-the-neck *or* -ass (*sl.*); *slang* baseball, softball, *etc.*; oral contraceptive, birth control pill. See REMEDY, DIFFICULTY, SPORTS, DRUGS, HINDRANCE.

pillage, *n.* spoliation, plunder, vandalism, theft, depredation. —*v.t.* plunder, rape, sack, thieve. See STEALING.

pillar, *n.* column, pedestal, SUPPORT, post, obelisk; mainstay. See STABILITY.

pillow, *n.* cushion, bolster, headrest, pad. See SUPPORT.

pilot, *n.* helmsman, steersman, guide; counselor; aviator, airman. See AVIATION, DIRECTION, INFORMATION, NAVIGATION.

pimp, *n.* procurer, solicitor, panderer, tout, hustler (*inf.*), cadet (*sl.*), fancy man (*sl.*); white slaver; whoremonger; maquereau. See EVILDOER.

pimple, *n.* pustule, boil, gathering, papule, pock, blackhead; blemish. See DISEASE, CONVEXITY.

pin, *n.* peg, spoke, dowel; fastener, bolt, toggle; needle, bodkin, skewer, style; brooch, scarf pin, fraternity pin, tie pin; badge. See ORNAMENT, SHARPNESS, MARRIAGE. —*v.t.* fasten, hold, bind, rivet, attach, secure; *informal,* engage. See JUNCTION, LOCATION.

pinch, *n.* stress, strain, pressure, emergency, DIFFICULTY, plight, predicament; pinching, nip; *slang,* arrest. See CIRCUMSTANCE, RESTRAINT. —*v.* nip, compress, tighten, squeeze; chill, bite, hurt. See CONTRACTION, PAIN.

pinch-hit, *v.i.* substitute (for), stand *or* fill in (for); relieve. See SUBSTITUTION.

pine, *v.i.* languish, long, crave; wither, droop. See DEJECTION, DISEASE, DESIRE.

pink slip, notice of dismissal, walking papers (*inf.*), the sack (*sl.*). See EJECTION.

pinnacle, *n.* summit, peak, spire, acme, crown. See HEIGHT.

pinpoint, *v.* locate, localize, place; pin down, nail. See LOCATION.

pinto, *adj.* mottled (see VARIEGATION).

pinup, *n.* cheesecake *or* beefcake [photograph], centerfold. See BEAUTY.

pioneer, *n.* forerunner, settler; originator. See PRECEDENCE.

pious, *adj.* devout (see PIETY). *Ant.,* impious.

pipe, *n.* PASSAGE, tube, main; briar, corncob, meerschaum; flute, fife, bagpipe, flageolet. See MUSIC, OPENING, CRY. —**pipe down,** *slang,* be quiet, shut up (*sl.*). See SILENCE. —**pipe dream,** vain hope, chimera, bubble. See DESIRE. —**pipe up,** *informal,* speak up (see SPEECH).

pipsqueak, *n., slang,* nobody, nonentity, cipher; shrimp, runt. See UNIMPORTANCE, LITTLENESS.

piquant, *adj.* pungent, flavorful, strong, sharp; tart; keen, stimulating. See FEELING, EXCITEMENT, PUNGENCY.

pique, *v.t.* sting, cut, nettle, irritate, vex, offend; prick, jab; intrigue, stimulate, arouse interest. See EXCITEMENT.

pirate, *n.* buccaneer, marauder, corsair, freebooter, sea robber, privateer; plagiarist. —*v.t.* plunder, picaroon, appropriate; plagiarize, steal. See STEALING.

pis aller, Fr., last resort. See SUBSTITUTION.

piss, *n., slang,* urine, piddle, number one, pee (*inf.*). —*v.i., slang,* urinate, piddle, make water, pee. See EXCRETION.

pistol, *n.* automatic, firearm, gun, derringer, revolver, shooting iron (*inf.*), gat (*sl.*), heater (*sl.*). See ARMS.

pit, *n.* hole, hollow, indentation, crater, excavation; abyss, HELL, Hades; mine, chasm; trap, snare. See CONCAVITY.

pitch, *n.* note, modulation, tone; roll, plunge, toss, dip, reel, lurch; slant, slope, drop; ascent, rise, grade, HEIGHT, range; resin, tar. —*v.t.* throw, toss; build, erect, set, establish; cast, heave. —*v.i.* roll, reel, plunge, toss; slope. See PROPULSION, SOUND, DEGREE.

pitcher, *n.* carafe, jug, jar, bottle, vessel, ewer, cruet, decanter; hurler, tosser, arm (*sl.*), chucker, spitballer, relief *or* starting pitcher, left- *or* right-hander, righty, lefty, portsider, southpaw. See RECEPTACLE, PROPULSION.

pitch in, *informal,* contribute; help out, participate. See AID.

piteous, *adj.* grievous, sorrowful; pitiable, pathetic; wretched, miserable. See PAIN, PITY.

pitfall, *n.* trap, snare, gin, pit; rocks, [coral] reefs, snags; [quick] sands, slippery ground; breakers, shoals, shallows; precipice. See DANGER.

pith, *n.* pulp, core, heart; essence, kernel, substance, gist. See MEANING, INTRINSIC, MIDDLE.

pithy, *adj.* concise; vigorous, forceful, powerful; meaningful; terse, brief, laconic. See MEANING.

pitiable, *adj.* miserable, paltry, wretched, deplorable; insignificant, woeful, pathetic. See BADNESS, PAIN, PITY, CONTEMPT.

pitiful, *adj.* compassionate (see PITY); deplorable, disreputable, pitiable, wretched; lamentable, piteous, paltry. See BADNESS, CONTEMPT, DISREPUTE.

pitiless, *n.* inclement, malevolent; merciless, cruel, unfeeling, ruthless. See SEVERITY. *Ant.,* kind, thoughtful.

pittance, *n.* bit, mite, driblet; dole; pension, alms, allowance. See INSUFFICIENCY.

pitted, *adj.* blemished, variolate; honeycombed, favose, pocked, dented; cratered. See CONCAVITY.

PITY
Feeling of compassion for another

Nouns—pity, compassion, commiseration, sympathy; LAMENTATION, condolence; empathy, fellow-feeling, tenderness, humanity, mercy, clemency; LENIENCY, charity, ruth, quarter, grace. See FEELING.

Verbs—1, pity; have, give, show, *or* take pity; commiserate, condole, sympathize, empathize; feel for, be sorry for; weep, melt, thaw, forbear, relax, relent, give quarter; give the coup de grâce, put out of one's misery; have mercy, have a heart, have one's heart go out to; be charitable; be lenient.

2, excite pity, touch, affect, soften; melt [the heart]; disarm; throw oneself at the feet of.

Adjectives—pitying, piteous, pitiful, pitiable; compassionate, sympathetic, affected, touched; merciful, clement, ruthful; humane; humanitarian, philanthropic, tenderhearted, softhearted, lenient; melting, weak.

Phrases—pity is akin to love.

Quotations—Then cherish pity, lest you drive an angel from your door (*William Blake*), Pity is the virtue of the law (*Shakespeare*), One cannot weep for the entire world. It is beyond human strength. One must choose (*Jean Anouilh*), No beast so fierce but knows some touch of pity (*Shakespeare*).

Antonyms, see SEVERITY.

---

pivot, *n.* axis, turning point; gudgeon; joint, axle, hinge; focus; jewel. See CAUSE, JUNCTION. —*v.i.* swivel, turn, whirl; roll; hinge. See ROTATION.

pivotal, *adj.* important, crucial, critical. See IMPORTANCE.

pixy, *n.* pixie, elf, sprite. See MYTHICAL DEITIES, DEMON.

placard, *n.* notice, poster, billboard, advertisement, bill. See PUBLICATION.

placate, *v.* soothe, quiet; pacify, conciliate; satisfy, give satisfaction, make it up; butter up, rub the right way. See PACIFICATION, FLATTERY.

place, *n.* lieu, spot, point; niche, nook, hole; premises, precinct, station; locality; somewhere, someplace, anyplace; situation. —*v.t.* locate, identify; arrange; put, repose; employ, engage. See ABODE, LOCATION, BUSINESS, CIRCUMSTANCE, ARRANGEMENT.

placid, *adj.* serene, unruffled; calm, cool, collected; gentle, peaceful, quiet, undisturbed. See INEXCITABILITY. *Ant.,* stormy.

plagiarize, *v.t.* pirate, infringe on, COPY, transcribe, pick one's brains, crib (*inf.*), lift (*inf.*); imitate, simulate, ape; forge, counterfeit. See STEALING.

plague, *n.* affliction, woe, visitation; nuisance, pest; bane, scourge, curse; pestilence, DISEASE, epidemic; bubonic plague, white *or* black death; cholera, tuberculosis, smallpox, typhoid, [Asian, *etc.*] flu. —*v.t.* annoy, tease, pester, molest, bother, get on one's nerves (*inf.*). See DISCONTENT.

plaid, *n.* plaidie, tartan, check; kilt, shawl. See VARIEGATION.

plain, *adj.* simple, unornamented (see SIMPLENESS); homely (see UGLINESS). —*n.* prairie, tableland, steppe, savanna, tundra, heath, pampas, mesa, llana; meadow, pasture, field. See LAND, HORIZONTAL. *Ant.,* fancy.

plainsong, *n.* [liturgical, Gregorian, *etc.*] chant. See MUSIC, RITE.

plain-spoken, *adj.* frank (see TRUTH).

plaintiff, *n.* litigant. See LAWSUIT, ACCUSATION.

plaintive, *adj.* mournful, wistful, sad, melancholy, sorrowful. See LAMENTATION.

PLAN
Formulated scheme for getting something done

Nouns—1, plan, scheme, design, project, UNDERTAKING; aim, INTENTION; proposal, proposition, suggestion; resolution, resolve, motion; precaution, provision, PREPARATION, calculation, meditation; operation, METHOD, way, setup, custom, modus operandi. See ORDER.

2, cartography, chorography, topography, hydrography.

3, *(drawn plan)* a. sketch, skeleton, outline, draft, diagram, blueprint, layout, schematic; architecture; delineation, pattern, format, representation, specifications, tabulation; chart, cartogram, chorograph, map, graph, atlas; bar graph, pie *or* circle chart, flip chart, flow chart, Gantt chart, bathtub curve; cylindrical *or* conic projection, equal-area projection, homolosine projection. b. graticule, great circle, grid, hachure, isobar, isobath, isoclinic line, isoglass, isogonic line.

4, *(written plan)* program, prospectus, syllabus, forecast, card, bill; protocol, order of the day, agenda; procedure, course, plank, platform; strategy, regime, line of CONDUCT, game plan, campaign; budget.

5, *(clever plan)* contrivance, invention, idea, conception, expedient, recipe, formula, nostrum; artifice, device, stratagem, ploy; trick (see CUNNING); alternative, loophole, makeshift; last resort, fall-back; ace in the hole, card up one's sleeve. *Informal,* dodge. *Slang,* gadget, gimmick, finagling, shtick. See INSTRUMENTALITY, IMAGINATION.

6, *(evil plan)* plot, intrigue, cabal, counterplot, countermine, conspiracy, machination, collusion. *Slang,* racket.

7, *(one who plans)* schemer, strategist, machinator, tactician; planner, architect, promoter, organizer, designer; conspirator, plotter, conniver, dreamer, Machiavelli; junto, cabal (see PARTY).

Verbs—1, plan, scheme; design, frame, diagram, sketch, map, lay off, delineate, figure, represent.

2, contrive, project, schedule, forecast, aim, propose, suggest, premeditate, spring a project; devise, invent, concoct; chalk, cut, lay, block, *or* map out, blueprint, lay down a plan; shape, mark, *or* set a course; [pre]concert, preestablish, prepare; study, calculate, formulate, work out, envision, contemplate, cogitate, digest, mature, resolve, intend, destine, provide, take steps *or* measures; [re]cast, systematize, organize, arrange; hatch [a plot], plot, brew, counterplot, intrigue; machinate, incubate, rig, conspire. *Informal,* cook up, have something on. *Slang,* wheel and deal.

Adjectives—1, planned, arranged, *etc.*; on the table, on the agenda, laid out, under consideration; premeditated, deliberate, purposed, meant, intended, intentional.

2, planning, strategic[al], systematic, schematic; conspiratorial, scheming, designing (see CUNNING); slated for. *Informal,* in the works, put-up.

Antonyms, see CHANCE.

---

plane, *n.* level, stratum, grade, surface; jointer, block, *or* jack plane. —*adj.* level, flat. —*v.t.* smooth, mill, even, traverse, shave, level. —*v.i.* glide. See AVIATION, HORIZONTAL, SMOOTHNESS.

planet, *n.* planetoid, asteroid. See UNIVERSE.

plank, *n.* board, timber; flooring, deck; gangplank *or* -board; platform, policy, PLAN, promise. See LAYER, MATERIALS.

plant, *n.* VEGETABLE, herb, organism, flower, seedling, shrub, sprout, shoot; machinery, factory, equipment; *slang,* hoax, trick, frameup. See DECEPTION. —*v.* implant, deposit, settle; colonize; sow, seed, engender. See AGRICULTURE, LOCATION.

plantation, *n.* outpost, colony, settlement; farm[stead], ranch, spread; nursery, orchard, grove, vineyard, stand. See AGRICULTURE, ABODE.

plaque, *n.* tablet, sign, nameplate, shingle (*inf.*). See INDICATION.

plaster, *n.* plaster of paris, mortar, parget, stucco, gesso; paste, lime; clay, adobe, mud; poultice, dressing, bandage. See MATERIALS, CONNECTION, REMEDY. —*v.t.* coat, cover, conceal, smear; caulk, repair, mend; stick up, paste. See COVERING.

plastered, *adj., slang,* drunk, tight (*sl.*), soused (*sl.*). See DRINKING. *Ant.,* sober.

plastic, *adj.* moldable, malleable, ductile, formable, pliant, impressionable, formative. See FORM, SOFTNESS. —*n.* thermoplastic, resin, cellulose, *etc.*; plastic money, credit, debit, *or* charge card. See MATERIALS, MONEY, PAYMENT.

plate, *n.* platter, dish, utensil, tray; slab, sheet, planch; coating, veneer, coat; denture. See RECEPTACLE, LAYER. —*v.t.* overlay, laminate; gild, silver, platinize; veneer; electroplate. See COVERING, LAYER.

plateau, *n.* plain, mesa; platform; highland, tableland. See HORIZONTAL.

platform, *n.* stand, dais, rostrum, pulpit, stage; foundation, base, basis; policy, PLAN. See SUPPORT, HORIZONTAL.

platitude, *n.* commonplace, cliché, truism, banality, MAXIM. See UNMEANINGNESS.

platonic, *adj.* idealistic, abstract, spiritual, intellectual; unsexual, uncarnal, chaste; pure, perfect. See THOUGHT, PURITY. *Ant.,* corporeal, sensual.

platter, *n.* trencher, tray, waiter, dish, plate. See RECEPTACLE, HORIZONTAL.

plaudit, *n.* acclaim, applause, encomium. See APPROBATION.

plausible, *adj.* credible, reasonable, believable; specious, colored; justifiable, defensible. See POSSIBILITY. *Ant.,* implausible.

play, *n.* sport, frolic, fun, AMUSEMENT, game, recreation; DRAMA, comedy, tragedy; scope, FREEDOM, latitude, sweep, range. —*v.* operate, wield, ply; act, perform; compete; pluck, bow, strike, beat; move, caper, gambol, dally, idle, disport. See INFLUENCE, EXERTION, SPACE, MUSIC, SPORTS.

playboy, *n., slang,* idler, do-nothing, loafer; voluptuary, sensualist, pleasure seeker, sybarite, epicurean, hedonist. See PLEASURE.

play down, depreciate, minimize, downplay. See DETRACTION. —**play down to,** *informal,* condescend, stoop (see PRIDE).

player, *n.* performer, actor, musician, instrumentalist; participant, competitor. See DRAMA, MUSIC, ARTIST.

playful, *adj.* frolicsome, mischievous, sportive, frisky; roguish, prankish; jolly, rollicking. See AMUSEMENT, CHEERFULNESS. *Ant.,* serious, staid.

playground, *n.* playing *or* athletic field. See AMUSEMENT, ARENA.

plaything, *n.* toy, doll, bauble; puzzle, kite, ball, top, *etc.*; bagatelle, trifle, trinket. See AMUSEMENT, UNIMPORTANCE.

playwright, *n.* playwriter, dramaturgist, dramatist, scenarist, librettist; farceur. See DRAMA, WRITING.

plaza, *n.* piazza, forum, marketplace. See RECEPTACLE.

plea, *n.* REQUEST, petition; assertion, allegation, advocation, advocacy; pretext, pretense, subterfuge, feint, blind; excuse, VINDICATION. See LAWSUIT.

plead, *v.* allege, assert, state; take one's stand upon; beg, petition, urge, REQUEST. See VINDICATION, LAWSUIT.

pleasant, *adj.* agreeable (see PLEASURE). *Ant.,* unpleasant.

pleasantry, *n.* WIT, jest, banter, chaff, chitchat, persiflage.

please, *adv.* if you please, pray; *s'il vous plaît, bitte, por favor, etc.*; kindly, do. See REQUEST. —*v.* gratify, satisfy, delight. See PLEASURE. *Ant.,* displease.

PLEASURE
Feeling of enjoyment

Nouns—1, pleasure, enjoyment, gratification; voluptuousness, sensuality; luxuriousness; GLUTTONY; titillation, gusto; creature comforts, comfort, ease, [lap of] luxury; purple and fine linen; bed of down *or* roses, life of Riley; velvet, clover; treat, music to one's ears; REFRESHMENT, feast, cakes and ale; AMUSEMENT; fleshpots, epicureanism, sybaritism, hedonism. See CONTENT, FEELING.

2, *(contentment)* delectation; relish, zest; satisfaction, contentment, complacency; well-being; good, snugness, comfort, cushion, sans souci, peace of mind.

3, *(great pleasure)* joy, gladness, delight, euphoria; CHEERFULNESS; happiness, felicity, bliss; beatitude, beatification; enchantment, transport, rapture, ravishment, ecstasy; summum bonum; HEAVEN; unalloyed happiness; Schadenfreude. *Informal,* one's cup of tea, forbidden fruit. *Slang,* bang, thrills, kicks, charge, jollies.

4, *(time of happiness)* honeymoon, palmy *or* halcyon days; golden age *or* time; Arcadia, Eden, Utopia, happy valley, time of one's life; prime, heyday. *Slang,* doll city, fat city.

5, *(quality of giving pleasure)* pleasurableness, pleasantness, agreeableness, delectability; sunny *or* bright side.

6, *(person who seeks or gives pleasure)* playboy, playgirl, voluptuary, sensualist, pleasure seeker, sybarite, epicure[an], hedonist; Doctor Feelgood. *Slang,* good-time Charlie *or* girl, sport, cutup.

Verbs—1, feel pleasure, be pleased, take pleasure in; revel, rejoice, *or* delight in, like, LOVE; enjoy oneself, give oneself up to; take to, take a fancy to; enjoy, relish, luxuriate in, riot in, bask in, swim in, wallow in; thrive *or* feast on; light up; gloat over, smack one's lips; be in clover, live on the fat of the land, walk on air, live in comfort, bask in the sunshine. *Informal,* live high off the hog; take the gravy train. *Slang,* have a ball, go into orbit; dig, get off (on), get a kick (from), lick one's chops, get one's jollies.

2, cause, give, *or* afford pleasure; please, charm, delight, beguile, enchant, entrance, enrapture, enthrall, transport, bewitch; [en]ravish; bless, beatify; satisfy, gratify; slake, satiate, quench; indulge, humor, flatter, tickle [the palate], regale, refresh; enliven; treat; amuse; strike *or* tickle one's fancy; warm the cockles of the heart; do one's heart good, do one good; attract, allure, stimulate, interest; thrill. *Informal,* hit the spot, tickle pink. *Slang,* send; give a kick, bang, *or* charge, blow one's mind.

Adjectives—1, pleased, glad[some]; pleased as Punch; happy as a king, as a lark, *or* as the day is long; thrice blest; in clover, in paradise, in raptures, on top of the world; overjoyed, entranced, *etc.*; ecstatic, beatific; unalloyed, cloudless. *Slang,* on cloud nine.

2, pleasing, pleasant, pleasurable; agreeable; grateful, gratifying, welcome [as the flowers in May], zaftig; to one's taste *or* liking, after one's own heart; sweet, delectable, nice, dainty; palatable; cozy, snug; sumptuous, sensuous, luxurious, voluptuous; empyrean, elysian, heavenly; palmy, halcyon; simpatico. *Informal,* up *or* down one's alley. *Slang,* scrumptious, hunky-dory, ducky.

Adverbs—with pleasure; happily, delightedly, *etc.*

Phrases—a good time was had by all.

Quotations—I never yet met a man that I didn't like (*Will Rogers*), I don't care anything about reasons, but I know what I like (*Henry James*), The art of pleasing consists in being pleased (*James Hazlitt*), Pleasure is nothing else but the intermission of pain (*John Selden*), Pleasure is a *thief* to business (*Daniel Defoe*), Great lords have their pleasures, but the people have fun (*Montesquieu*), One half of the world cannot understand the pleasures of the other (*Jane Austen*), All the things I really like to do are either illegal, immoral, or fattening (*Alexander Woollcott*), I seek the utmost pleasure and the least pain (*Plautus*).

Antonyms, see PAIN, ASCETICISM.

pleat, *n.* plait, corrugation, wrinkle; FOLD, plicature, ply; doubling. —*v.t.* crease, gather, flounce, ruffle; FOLD over, play, pucker; corrugate.

plebeian, *adj.* unrefined, ill-bred, common, vulgar; lowborn, obscure, proletarian. See POPULACE. *Ant.,* refined, noble, highborn.

plebiscite, *n.* referendum (see CHOICE).

pledge, *n.* PROMISE, SECURITY, gage, pawn, collateral, hostage, deposit; word, troth, vow, guarantee; bond, oath. See AFFIRMATION. —*v.t.* deposit, wage, pawn, hock (*sl.*), hypothecate, mortgage; vow, PROMISE, undertake, engage, honor; toast. See DEBT.

plenty, *n.* SUFFICIENCY, abundance, profusion, amplitude, copiousness; wealth, luxury. *Ant.,* scarcity, paucity.

pleonasm, *n.* redundance, verbosity, DIFFUSENESS, tautology, superfluity, circumlocution, wordiness.

plethora, *n.* superabundance (see SUFFICIENCY). *Ant.,* paucity.

pliable, *adj.* plastic, ductile, malleable; flexible, supple, limber, yielding; docile, tractable, obedient, compliant. See SOFTNESS, OBEDIENCE.

pliant, *adj.* pliable, supple, flexible, malleable, compliant, yielding. See SOFTNESS, OBEDIENCE. *Ant.,* unyielding, rigid.

pliers, *n.pl.* pincers, pinchers; grippers, nippers, tongs, grip, clamp, forceps; wire cutter, tooth extractor. See RETENTION, EXTRACTION.

plight, *n.* quandary, predicament, dilemma; trouble, DIFFICULTY, scrape, crisis; situation, condition; betrothal, PROMISE, engagement.

plod, *v.i.* persevere, persist; trudge, walk; labor, drudge, toil. See RESOLUTION, SLOWNESS, EXERTION.

plot, *n.* diagram, PLAN, outline; field, enclosure, paddock, lot; scheme, conspiracy, intrigue, collusion. See REGION. —*v.* conspire, machinate, scheme, intrigue; chart, PLAN, lay out. See CUNNING.

plow, plough, *v.* cultivate, dig, till, turn, break, FURROW. See AGRICULTURE.

ploy, *n.* maneuver, stratagem. See PLAN, CUNNING.

pluck, *n.* COURAGE, bravery, valor, stamina, endurance, grip, determination, WILL; twitch, tug, twang. See RESOLUTION. —*v.t.* pull, jerk; pick, twang; gather, garner; *slang,* rob, fleece. See TRACTION, STEALING, ACQUISITION.

plug, *n.* stopper, cork, dowel, plunger, tampon; quid, wad; wadding, padding, stopple, spigot. See CLOSURE.

plum, *n.* prune, sloe, damson; prize, haul, windfall, trophy; reward, patronage. See VEGETABLE, PAYMENT.

plumage, *n.* feathers, down, feathering. See COVERING, ORNAMENT.

plumb, *adj.* perpendicular, VERTICAL, erect; straight, true. —*adv., informal,* downright, utterly. See COMPLETION. —*v.t.* sound, fathom. See DEPTH.

plume, *n.* quill, feather, egret, panache, plumage. See COVERING, ORNAMENT.

plummet, *n.* weight, plumb, bob, lead. See VERTICAL. —*v.i.* fall, droop, plunge. See DESCENT.

plump, *adj.* corpulent, fat, chubby, stout, fleshy, buxom, pudgy, rotund; blunt, direct, unqualified. See SIZE. —*adv.* suddenly, directly. —*v.* fatten, fill, distend; blurt; fall; support, root (for); *informal,* plop [down]. See DESCENT, ROTUNDITY. *Ant.,* skinny.

plunder, *n.* pillage, loot, sack, spoil, booty; advantage, gain; spoliation, rapine. —*v.* devastate, harry, despoil, strip, rifle, loot, forage, pillage, ransack, maraud, rob, depredate. See STEALING, ACQUISITION.

plunge, *v.* dip, submerge; dive; sink, fall, drop; douse, go *or* put under water; gamble, bet heavily, go off the deep end (*inf.*); fling, jump. —*n.* dive, swim, dip; submersion; *informal,* venture. See WATER, HASTE.

plural, *adj.* See MULTITUDE. *Ant.,* singular.

plus, *adj., adv., & prep.* and; additional, extra, added (to). See ADDITION. *Ant.,* minus.

plush, *n.* pile, nap, hair; plushette; velvet, fluff. See MATERIALS. —*adj., informal,* plushy, nappy, velvety, piled, woolly; rich, luxurious, posh, swank[y], elegant, high-toned. See SOFTNESS, OSTENTATION. *Ant.,* plain, barebones.

plutocrat, *n.* man of means, [multi]millionaire, billionaire. See MONEY. *Ant.,* pauper.

ply, *v.t.* exert, urge, attack, apply; play, work; USE, exercise, manipulate, wield. See EXERTION. —*n.* See LAYER.

poach, *v.* steal, thieve, filch, pilfer; encroach, infringe, trespass; boil, parboil, coddle. See STEALING, HEAT.

pock, *n.* pustule, boil; pockmark, blemish. See CONVEXITY, DISEASE.

pocket, *n.* pouch, bin, purse; hollow, placket. See CONCAVITY, RECEPTACLE.

—*v.t.* appropriate, take, steal. See STEALING.

pocketbook, *n.* purse, wallet; [hand]bag; pouch, sporran, leather (*sl.*), kick (*sl.*). See RECEPTACLE.

pod, *n.* hull, husk, jacket, skin, shuck, shell, peapod; pouch; cabin. See COVERING.

podium, *n.* stand, dais, rostrum, platform. See SUPPORT.

POETRY
Expression in poems

Nouns—1, poetry, ars poetica, poesy, poeticism, poetics, metrics; balladry, the gay science; Muse, Calliope, Erato; versification, rhyming, prosody, orthometry, scansion. See WRITING, DESCRIPTION.

2, poem, ode, epode, idyl, lyric; accentual *or* quantitative verse; blank verse, free verse, vers libre; eclogue, pastoral, bucolic, georgic, dithyramb, anacreontic; carmen figuraturum; [Petrarchan *or* Shakespearean] sonnet, ode, monody, elegy, prothalamion, epithalamium; haiku, tanka; epic, epos, dramatic poetry, lyric poetry, melic poetry, concrete poetry; light verse, clerihew, comic verse, Hudibrastic verse, limerick, vers de société, occasional verse; flyting; nursery rhyme. See WRITING, DESCRIPTION.

3, (*poetry for music*) song, chanson [de geste], ballad, lay, roundelay, rondeau, rondo, roundel, ballade, villanelle, triolet, pantun, madrigal, canzonet, sirvente; lullaby; nursery rhymes; popular song. See MUSIC.

4, (*bad poetry*) doggerel, jingle, purple patches, macaronics.

5, (*poetic techniques*) canto, stanza, stich, verse, line; couplet, heroic couplets, elegiac, triplet, quatrain, octave, octet, passus, sestina; strophe, antistrophe; [masculine, feminine, single, double, *or* triple] rhyme, rime, assonance, alliteration; kenning; [common] meter, measure, foot, numbers, strain, [sprung, falling, *or* rising] rhythm; accentuation, stress, ictus, arsis, thesis; iamb[ic], dipody, trimeter, dactyl, spondee, trochee, anapest, pyrrhic; hexameter, pentameter, *etc.*

6, poet, poet laureate; bard, lyrist, skald, troubadour, trouvère, minstrel, minnesinger, meistersinger, goliard; versifier, poetaster; metaphrast. See MUSIC.

Verbs—poetize, sing, versify, make verses; rhyme; scan.

Adjectives—poetic[al], lyric; epic, heroic, bucolic, *etc.*; lofty, sublime, eloquent.

Quotations—Poetry is eloquent painting (*Simonides*), All poets are mad (*Robert Burton*), That willing suspension of disbelief for the moment, which constitutes poetic faith (*Samuel Taylor Coleridge*), Poets are the unacknowledged legislators of the world (*Percy Bysshe Shelley*), Poetry is the achievement of the synthesis of hyacinths and biscuits (*Carl Sandburg*), A poem should not mean but be (*Archibald MacLeish*), Writing a book of poetry is like dropping a rose petal down the Grand Canyon and waiting for the echo (*Don Marquis*), Genuine poetry can communicate before it is understood (*T. S. Eliot*), If poetry comes not as naturally as the leaves to a tree, it had better not come at all (*John Keats*).

Antonyms, see WRITING, DESCRIPTION.

---

pogrom, *n.* KILLING, massacre, carnage, butchery, slaughter, genocide, hecatomb, mass murder; persecution.

poignant, *adj.* painful, pungent, intense, piercing, sharp, keen, biting. See FEELING, PUNGENCY.

point, *n.* object, meaning, significance, intent, aim; speck, dot, spot; place, location; pin, needle, prick, spike, prong, tip, END; limit; goal, site. See IMPORTANCE, SHARPNESS, LITTLENESS. —*v.* aim; face, tend, lead, indicate. See

STRAIGHTNESS, DIRECTION, INDICATION.

point-blank, *adj.* close, straight, direct, undeviating; blunt, frank, candid, open. See STRAIGHTNESS.

pointed, *adj.* direct, concise, terse, pithy, brief; sharp, barbed, spiked. See SHARPNESS. *Ant.,* dull, roundabout, evasive.

point of view, viewpoint, outlook, angle, opinion, way of thinking. See BELIEF, JUDGMENT.

pointless, *adj.* meaningless, purposeless. See UNMEANINGNESS. *Ant.,* meaningful.

poise, *n.* equilibrium, balance, steadiness; bearing, self-possession, dignity, composure, imperturbability, coolness, nonchalance. See INEXCITABILITY.

poison, *n.* venom, toxicity, virus, bane. — *v.t.* corrupt, defile; intoxicate, drug, envenom; kill, murder. See DETERIORATION, KILLING.

poisonous, *adj.* venomous, toxic, deadly, virulent, noxious. See BADNESS. *Ant.,* benign, harmless.

poke, *v.* prod, nudge, stick, push; search, pry; dawdle; jab, punch. See IMPULSE, SLOWNESS, INQUIRY.

poker, *n.* fire iron, rod, branding iron, ramrod, salamander. See HEAT.

poker-faced, *adj., informal,* deadpan, frozen-faced, wooden, unrevealing, unreadable, secretive. See CONCEALMENT. *Ant.,* expressive, open.

poky, *adj.* slow, leisurely; boring. See SLOWNESS, WEARINESS. *Ant.,* quick, hasty.

polar, *adj.* extreme, ultimate, farthest, outermost; magnetic, attracting; polarized; COLD, frigid, icy, frozen. See OPPOSITION.

polarize, *v.* orient, align, concentrate, gather; split, separate, dichotomize, oppose. See OPPOSITION.

pole, *v.* push, jab, prod, thrust, punch, nudge. See IMPULSE. —*n.* shaft, staff, post, stick, beam, mast; terminal, axis, hub, pivot; extremity, North *or* South Pole. See OPPOSITION.

polemic, *adj.* polemical, controversial, disputatious, eristic[al], dialectical; quarrelsome, contentious. —*n.* polemics, debate, discussion, contention, dialectics. See DISCORD.

polestar, *n.* lodestar, Polaris; guide; magnet, cynosure. See ATTRACTION, DIRECTION.

police, *n.* police force, constabulary; vigilantes, posse; FBI, Royal Canadian Mounted Police, military police, MP, Sûreté, Scotland Yard, *etc.* See SAFETY.

policeman, policewoman, *n.* patrolman *or* -woman, officer (see SAFETY).

policy, *n.* CONDUCT, administration, management; tactics, strategy; art, wisdom; platform, PLAN.

polish, *n.* sheen, luster, shine, glaze, gloss; refinement, culture; COURTESY tact, suavity, diplomacy; discernment, discrimination. —*v.t.* shine, buff, burnish; scrub, scour, brighten; refine, perfect. See SMOOTHNESS, ELEGANCE, ORNAMENT, FRICTION.

polite, *adj.* mannerly, civil, courteous, gracious; gallant, courtly, polished, well-bred, refined. See COURTESY, FASHION. *Ant.,* impolite, surly.

politic, *adj.* discreet, expedient, artful, strategic; prudent, wise, judicious; wary, calculating, shrewd, crafty. See CAUTION, INTÉLLIGENCE, TASTE, CUNNING. *Ant.,* impolitic, indiscreet.

politician, *n.* office-holder *or* -seeker; legislator, senator, *etc.;* diplomat, machinator, Machiavellian, strategist, wire-puller. See CUNNING.

politics, *n.sing.* polity; government, political science, civics. See PARTY, CUNNING.

poll, *n.* election, ballot; register; pate, head, skull. See CHOICE. —*v.t.* cut, crop, top; survey, canvass, tabulate. See NUMERATION.

pollute, *v.t.* contaminate, foul, desecrate, taint, soil, defile, corrupt; demoralize. See IMPURITY, DETERIORATION, UNCLEANNESS. *Ant.,* clean (up).

poltergeist, *n.* ghost, specter, wraith, shade. See DEMON.

poltroon, *n.* cad; dastard, craven, coward. See COWARDICE.

polygamy, *n.* bigamy, trigamy; Mormonism; polyandry, polygyny. See MARRIAGE.

pomade, *n.* ointment, salve, unguent. See OIL.

pommel, *v.t.* See PUMMEL. —*n.* [saddle] horn. See SUPPORT.

pomp, *n.* grandeur, show, OSTENTATION, magnificence, display, splendor.

pompous, *adj.* self-important, ostentatious; high-flown, bombastic, stilted; haughty, vain, grandiose, puffed-up, arrogant, stuffy, snooty, stuffed-shirt (*inf.*). See BOASTING. *Ant.,* humble, unassuming.

pond, *n.* lake, pool, fishpond, millpond, tarn. See WATER.

ponder, *v.* think, muse, cogitate; reflect, meditate, weigh, deliberate, consider. See THOUGHT.

ponderous, *adj.* heavy, weighty, bulky, massive; tedious. See GRAVITY, INELEGANCE. *Ant.,* light, weightless.

pontiff, *n.* bishop, high priest; the pope. See CLERGY.

pontificate, *v.i.* declaim, state; preach, orate, lecture. See LOQUACITY, OSTENTATION.

pontoon, *n.* float, raft; boat, bladder, floater, buoy. See SHIP.

pony, *n.* scrub horse; cob, cow pony, cayuse; glass, half-jigger, dram; *slang,* translation, crib (*inf.*), trot (*inf.*), horse (*inf.*). See RECEPTACLE, INTERPRETATION.

pooch, *n., slang,* dog (see ANIMAL).

pool, *n.* association, amalgamation, fund; pond, puddle; reservoir, lake; swimming pool, natatorium. —*v.t.* combine, cooperate, share, contribute. See WATER, PARTY, CHANCE.

poop, *n., slang,* INFORMATION. —*v.t.* tire, exhaust. See WEARINESS.

poor, *adj.* indigent (see POVERTY); inferior, faulty, unsatisfactory, imperfect, defective; humble; weak, flimsy. See INSUFFICIENCY, IMPERFECTION, DISEASE. *Ant.,* rich, wealthy.

pop, *n.* bang, shot, burst, explosion; soda [pop]. See LOUDNESS, DRINKING. —*v.* burst; explode.

poppycock, *n.* nonsense, idle talk, foolishness. See ABSURDITY.

POPULACE
Common people

Nouns—1, populace; the people, MULTITUDE, crowd, masses; bourgeoisie; commonalty; democracy; common people, lower classes, hoi polloi, rank and file, the ruck, folk, proletariat, plebs, great unwashed, silent majority; the common touch. See HUMANITY, VULGARITY, SERVANT.

2, (*crowd*) mob, rabble, rout, hoi polloi, the many-headed monster; horde, canaille; dregs; scum of society *or* the earth; tag, rag and bobtail, riffraff; small fry.

3, (*common man*) commoner, man in the street, the average man, the little man, one of the people, democrat, plebeian, proletarian, republican, bourgeois; Mrs. Grundy, Philistine, Babbitt; Joe Blow, Joe Doakes, John *or* Jane Doe, John *or* Jane Q. Public.

4, (*country person*) peasant, countryman, boor, churl, lout, villein, curmudgeon; serf; dockwalloper, longshoreman, navvy; swain, clown, clod, clodhopper; hobnail, yokel, bumpkin; plowman, rustic, tiller of the soil; blue-collar man, woman, *or* worker; hewers of wood and drawers of water. *Informal,* hayseed, country mouse. *Slang,* hick, jay, rube.

5, (*city person*) city dweller. *Informal,* town mouse.

6, (*person of the street*) beggar, mudlark, sans culotte, raff, tatterdemalion, hobbledehoy, caitiff, ragamuffin, pariah; guttersnipe, urchin, street urchin *or* arab; tramp, hobo, knight of the road, vagabond, vagrant, bum, weary Willie. *Slang,* bindle stiff.

Adjectives—popular; plebeian, proletarian, common, democratic; homely, homespun; vulgar, lowborn, ignoble, illbred, baseborn, earthy; unknown to fame, obscure, untitled; rustic, countrified, provincial; loutish, boorish, clownish, churlish; barbarous, barbarian, barbaric.

Phrases—you can take the boy out of the country, but you can't take the country out of the boy; who builds upon the people, builds upon sand.

Quotations—In the common people there is no wisdom, no penetration, no power of judgment (*Cicero*), All the world over, I will back the masses against the classes

(*William Gladstone*), There is not a more mean, stupid, dastardly, pitiful, selfish, spiteful, envious, ungrateful animal than the public. It is the greatest of cowards, for it is afraid of itself (*William Hazlitt*), The people are a many-headed beast (*Horace*), The people are the only sure reliance for the preservation of our liberty (*Thomas Jefferson*), The people, and the people alone, are the motive force in the making of world history (*Mao Zedung*).

Antonyms, see NOBILITY.

---

popular, *adj.* common, public, plebeian; acceptable, cheap; approved, liked, praised; elect, chosen; desirable; admired, famous. See APPROBATION, REPUTE, POPULACE. *Ant.,* unpopular, aristocratic.

population, *n.* people, residents; nation. See INHABITANT.

populous, *adj.* well-populated, thickly settled; teeming. See MULTITUDE, ASSEMBLAGE. *Ant.,* thinly populated.

porcelain, *n.* china, ceramic. See MATERIALS.

porch, *n.* verandah, portico, piazza; entrance, portal; stoa. See OPENING, RECEPTACLE.

pore, *n.* breathing hole, skin hole, orifice; stoma, ostiole, porus; OPENING. —*v.i.* read, peruse, scan, scrutinize, examine closely; mull over, consider. See THOUGHT, INQUIRY, VISION.

pornography, *n.* erotica; prurience, sexuality; impudicity, obscenity, indecency, IMPURITY; VULGARITY, dirt, smut, filth, porn (*sl.*).

porous, *adj.* open; absorbent; perforated, honeycombed; sandy; permeable, loose, pervious. See OPENING. *Ant.,* impermeable.

porridge, *n.* pottage, stew, soup; gruel, mush, cereal, samp, pap, burgoo; stirabout, hasty pudding, pease porridge. See FOOD.

port, *n.* refuge, harbor, shelter, haven; OPENING, embrasure, porthole; APPEARANCE, bearing, deportment, demeanor; LEFT, larboard (*naut.*). See ARRIVAL.

portable, *adj.* portative, transportable, movable, carriable. See TRANSPORTATION.

portal, *n.* entrance, door, entry, doorway; portcullis. See OPENING.

portend, *v.t.* signify, presage, augur, forebode, foreshadow, omen, foretoken, mean. See PREDICTION, THREAT.

portent, *n.* wonder, marvel, phenomenon; sign, foreshadowing, foreboding, omen, token; importance, meaning. See PREDICTION, WARNING.

porter, portress, *n.* guard, gatekeeper, concierge, doorman, sentinel, warder; bearer, redcap (*inf.*). See TRANSPORTATION, SAFETY.

portfolio, *n.* briefcase, bag, portmanteau, attaché case; LIST, catalog. See RECEPTACLE.

portico, *n.* colonnade, stoa, verandah, porch. See RECEPTACLE.

portion, *n.* share, allotment, due, ration; PART, serving, morsel, fragment; fate, lot, destiny; dividend; section. —*v.t.* dower, apportion, divide, endow. See APPORTIONMENT, QUANTITY.

portly, *adj.* dignified, imposing, stately; fat, fleshy, stout, corpulent; bulky. See SIZE. *Ant.,* skinny, gaunt.

portmanteau, *n.* trunk, suitcase, valise; portfolio. See RECEPTACLE.

portrait, *n.* picture, likeness; depiction, DESCRIPTION; photograph, sketch. See PAINTING.

portray, *v.t.* picture, describe; enact, act out. See REPRESENTATION, DRAMA, DESCRIPTION.

pose, *n.* attitude, AFFECTATION; position, posture; aspect, figure. See FORM. —*v.* sit; attitudinize, affect; propound; question, puzzle, quiz, inquire, nonplus. See DIFFICULTY.

poser, *n.* puzzle[r], enigma; poseur, posturer. See UNINTELLIGIBILITY, AFFECTATION.

posh, *adj., informal,* luxurious; deluxe, sumptuous; exclusive. See OSTENTATION, EXCLUSION. *Ant.,* simple, unadorned.

posit, *v.t.* place, dispose; stipulate. See SUPPOSITION, LOCATION.

position, *n.* situation, placement, point, spot, place, LOCATION, site; billet, berth, post, station, office, rank, status; caste; incumbency; dignity, honor. See BUSINESS, CIRCUMSTANCE, REPUTE.

positive, *adj.* certain, decided, emphatic, unqualified, absolute; inescapable, peremptory, firm. See AFFIRMATION, CERTAINTY. *Ant.,* negative.

posse, *n.* deputation, deputies, vigilantes; riot squad. See ASSEMBLAGE.

possess, *v.t.* own (see POSSESSION); dominate, have power over. See SUPERIORITY.

POSSESSION
State of owning or the thing owned

Nouns—1, possession, ownership; proprietorship, lordship, fee, seigniorage, seigniory; empire, dominion (see AUTHORITY); interest, stake, estate, right, title, claim, demand, holding, blind trust; tenure; vested, contingent, beneficial, *or* equitable interest; USE, trust, benefit; fee simple *or* tail; occupancy, occupation; hold[ing]; tenure, tenancy, feudality, dependency; monopoly, corner, RETENTION; heritage, inheritance, heirship, reversion; bird in hand; nine points of the law. *Informal,* dibs.

2, *(possession passed on)* dower, dowry, dot; jointure, appanage; inheritance, heritage; patrimony; alimony; legacy (see GIVING).

3, *(belongings)* assets, belongings, MEANS, resources, circumstances; wealth, MONEY; credit; patent, copyright; landed property, real property, real estate, realty, land[s], grounds; tenements; hereditaments; territory, state, kingdom, principality, realm, empire; dependence; protectorate, sphere of influence; manor, domain, demesne; farm, plantation, hacienda; freehold, leasehold; fixtures, plant; easement. See ABODE.

4, *(smaller belongings)* personal property *or* effects; personalty, chattels, goods, effects, movables; stock in trade; things, traps, gear, paraphernalia; equipage; parcels, appurtenances; impedimenta; luggage, dunnage, baggage; bag and baggage; pelf; cargo, lading, freight; heirloom; endowment.

5, possessor, holder; occupant, occupier; tenant; renter, lodger, lessee; owner; proprietor, proprietress; trustee; master, mistress, lord; landholder, landowner, landlord, landlady, yeoman; lord of the manor, laird; legatee, devisee; heir[ess], inheritress, inheritrix. See INHABITANT.

Verbs—1, possess, have, hold, occupy, enjoy; be possessed of, have on one's hands, own, command; inherit, come to, come in for; stake a claim; acquire (see ACQUISITION); retain. *Slang,* have dibs on.

2, belong to, appertain to, pertain to; be in one's possession; vest in.

Adjectives—1, possessing, having; worth; possessed of, seized of, master of, in possession of; in fee simple; outright; endowed with, blessed with, fraught with; possessed; on hand, by one; in hand, in store, in stock; in one's hands, at one's command, to one's name, at one's disposal; one's own.

2, possessive, retentive, retaining, tenacious; reserved, entailed.

3, landed, manorial, allodial; freehold, leasehold; feudal.

Phrases—a bird in the hand is worth two in the bush; easy come easy go; you cannot lose what you never had; possession is nine points of the law.

Quotations—For we brought nothing into this world, and it is certain we can carry nothing out (*Bible*), Things are in the saddle, and ride mankind (*Emerson*), Property is organized robbery (*G. B. Shaw*), An ill-favored thing, sir, but mine own (*Shakespeare*).

Antonyms, see POVERTY, DEBT, ACQUISITION.

POSSIBILITY
Capability of being done

Nouns—possibility, potentiality, likelihood, LIABILITY; what may be, what is possible; compatibility (see AGREEMENT); reasonability; reasonableness (see REASONING); practicability, EXPEDIENCE, feasibility, potency, workability, workableness, accessibility, attainability; contingency, LATENCY, probability, CHANCE, hazard, outlook. *Informal*, toss-up, show, outside chance.

Verbs—be possible, stand a chance *or* show; admit of, bear; put in the way of; open up.

Adjectives—possible, potential, in *or* on the cards *or* dice, within the bounds of possibility, in posse; conceivable, imaginable, credible, thinkable, reasonable, plausible, presumable; compatible (see AGREEMENT); practicable, feasible, negotiable, workable, performable, achievable, accessible, superable, surmountable, attainable, obtainable, expedient, within reach; contingent, probably, likely; in the running; latent. *Informal*, liable, earthly.

Adverbs—possibly, by possibility; perhaps, perchance, peradventure; it may be, maybe, haply, mayhap; if [humanly] possible, [wind and] weather permitting, everything being equal, as luck may have it, God willing, Deo volente, DV. *Informal*, on the off-chance, could be.

Quotations—Certainly nothing is unnatural that is not physically impossible (*Richard Sheridan*), If it be possible, let this cup pass from me (*Bible*), With God all things are possible (*Bible*), Politics is the art of the possible, the attainable . . . the art of the next best (*Otto von Bismarck*), Politics is not the art of the possible. It consists in choosing between the disastrous and the unpalatable (*John Kenneth Galbraith*).

Antonyms, see IMPOSSIBILITY.

---

post, *n.* station, assignment, position; incumbency, place, office, mail; stake, picket, newel, pillar, pier. See BUSINESS, SUPPORT, COMMUNICATION, ACCOUNTING. —*v.* mail; inform, publish, RECORD, enter, transfer; speed, hurry. See LOCATION, VELOCITY, LIST.

postage, *n.* stamp, postmark, imprint. See COMMUNICATION.

poster, *n.* advertisement, placard, bill. See PUBLICATION.

posterior, *adj.* subsequent, later, succeeding, ensuing; postern, REAR, hindmost. See SEQUENCE. —*n.* buttocks, REAR. *Ant.*, FRONT.

POSTERITY
Future generations

Nouns—1, posterity, progeny, issue, fruit, seed, offspring, young, flesh and blood; brood, litter, farrow, spawn, spat, clutch, seed, product; [extended, institutional, *or* nuclear] family, children, grandchildren, heirs; younger, rising, *or* succeeding generation; empty nester. See FUTURITY.

2, child, son, daughter, grandchild, grandson, granddaughter, bantling, bairn, baby, infant; scion, shoot, sprout, sprit, [olive] branch, offshoot, offset, ramification; descendant, heir[ess]; heir apparent *or* presumptive; chip off the old block; foster child; stepchild, stepson, stepdaughter.

3, bastard, illegitimate *or* natural child, bantling, love-child, accident. *Informal*, incident. *Slang*, whoreson, bell-bastard, left-handed son, momzer, natural-child, off-girl, woods-colt, yard-child.

4, *(type of posterity)* straight descent, sonship, line, lineage, succession, filiation, primogeniture, heredity; origin, extraction; tribe, clan, sept, nationality; genealogy; generation gap. See ANCESTRY, HUMANITY.

Verbs—run in the family, come down; pass on.

Adjectives—filial, sonly, daughterly, family; lineal, hereditary; tribal, national; bastard, illegitimate, born out of wedlock, misbegotten, chance-born, adulterine, baseborn, of unknown birth.

Phrases—great oaks from little acorns grow; like father, like son; like mother, like daughter.

Quotations—The thing that impresses me most about America is the way parents obey their children (*Edward VIII*), Every generation revolts against its fathers and makes friends with its grandfathers (*Lewis Mumford*), Let us now praise famous men, and our fathers that begat us (*Bible*), As the generation of leaves, so is that of humanity (*Homer*), What has posterity ever done for me? (*Groucho Marx*).

Antonyms, see ANCESTRY.

---

posthaste, *adv.* speedily, hastily, at top speed, apace, expeditiously, swiftly. See RASHNESS, VELOCITY, HASTE. *Ant.*, slowly, at one's leisure.

posthumous, *adj.* post-obit, postmortem; late; postponed, delayed. See DEATH, SEQUENCE.

postman, *n.* mail carrier, mailman, courier, mail clerk. See COMMUNICATION.

postmortem, *adj.* See POSTHUMOUS. —*n.* autopsy, pathology, necropsy, necrotomy; *slang,* investigation, examination, INQUIRY, study, recapitulation.

postpone, *v.t.* procrastinate, delay, defer; shelve, adjourn, table. See LATENESS, NEGLECT.

postscript, *n.* ADDITION, appendix, afterthought; P.S., P.P.S.

postulate, *n.* proposition, axiom, SUPPOSITION; hypothesis, premise; fact, datum. —*v.* suppose, surmise, theorize, hypothesize.

posture, *n.* pose, attitude; bearing, position, carriage; mood, condition. See FORM, CIRCUMSTANCE.

pot, *n.* crock, jug, tankard; kettle, pan, vessel; mug; prize, pool. See WRITING.

potable, *adj.* drinkable (see CLEANNESS, WATER).

potboiler, *n.* trash, dime novel. See WRITING, PUBLICATION.

potent, *adj.* powerful, strong, mighty; intense, influential; effectual, effective, forceful; capable, able. See POWER, VIGOR. *Ant.,* impotent.

potentate, *n.* king, sovereign, ruler, monarch. See AUTHORITY.

potential, *adj.* dynamic, magnetic, charged; dormant, latent; unfulfilled, promising. See POWER, LATENCY, POSSIBILITY.

potion, *n.* potation; philter, elixir, brew, libation. See REMEDY, DRINKING.

potpourri, *n.* blend, medley, hodgepodge, miscellany, mélange; salmagundi, gallimaufry, pastiche. See MIXTURE, ODOR.

pottery, *n.* earthenware, china, porcelain, ceramics, ironstone; dishes, utensils. See MATERIALS.

pouch, *n.* bag, sack; purse, reticule, wallet; pocket, sac; marsupium. See RECEPTACLE.

poultry, *n.* chickens, ducks, geese, turkeys; fowl[s], hens, broilers, fryers, roosters; pigeons, squab. See ANIMAL.

pounce, *v.i.* spring, LEAP, jump; snatch, grasp, seize; ambush. See DESCENT.

pound, *v.* beat, thump, drum, bruise, tenderize; crush, pulverize. See POWDERINESS.

pour, *v.* flow, emerge; decant, fill; issue; rain, flood, shower. See EGRESS, WATER, SUFFICIENCY.

pout, *v.i.* sulk, grimace, moue. See DEJECTION, CONVEXITY.

POVERTY
Lack of money

Nouns—1, poverty, impecuniousness, indigence, penury, pauperism, destitution, want, poverty line *or* level; need, neediness; lack, NECESSITY, privation, distress, difficulties; bad, poor, *or* needy circumstances; reduced *or* straitened circumstances, extremity; slender means, straits, bottom dollar; hand-to-mouth existence; beggary; mendicancy, loss of fortune, bankruptcy, insolvency (see DEBT). *Slang,* dog's life, the bear, tap city. See ADVERSITY, INSUFFICIENCY, NONPAYMENT.

2, poor man, pauper, mendicant, beggar, starveling, homeless person, welfare mother; underclass, dangerous class, honest poor. *Informal,* street person. *Slang,* cracker, jim crow, latch, reliefer, bag lady *or* man, grate people, skell, mole people, zero-parent children, squeegee kid, driftwood, musher, bindle stiff, bum, hobo, tramp, vagrant, moocher, panhandler, ding, doxy, po' buckra, poorlander.

3, almshouse, poorhouse, workhouse, settlement house, flop[house]; public housing, slum clearance, favela, projects (see ABODE); welfare, workfare.

Verbs—1, want, lack, starve, live from hand to mouth, have seen better days, go down in the world, go to the dogs, go to wreck and ruin; not have a penny to one's name, be up against it; beg [one's bread]; tighten one's belt, keep body and soul together, keep the wolf from the door, scrape the barrel. *Slang,* go broke, lose one's shirt.

2, impoverish, reduce to poverty; pauperize, fleece, ruin, strip.

Adjectives—poor, indigent; poverty-stricken; economically disadvantaged, underprivileged; poor as a church mouse; poor as Job's turkey; penniless, impecunious; hard up; out at elbows *or* heels; seedy, shabby; beggarly, beggared, down and out; destitute, bereft, in want, needy, necessitous, distressed, pinched, straitened, strapped, wasted; unable to keep the wolf from the door, unable to make both ends meet; embarrassed, involved; insolvent, bankrupt, on one's uppers, on the rocks, on the beach. *Informal,* in the hole. *Slang,* broke, stony, stone-broke, flat [broke], down to the wire, looking for a handout, melted-out, on one's ear.

Phrases—poverty is not a crime; beggars can't be choosers; money isn't everything; you cannot get blood from a stone.

Quotations—The poor always ye have with you (*Bible*), The greatest of evils and the worst of crimes is poverty (*G. B. Shaw*), Anyone who has ever struggled with poverty knows how extremely expensive it is to be poor (*Alec Baldwin*), He is poor, and that's revenge enough (*Shakespeare*), Laziness travels so slowly that poverty soon overtakes it (*Benjamin Franklin*), Poverty is the parent of revolution and crime (*Aristotle*), There is something about poverty that smells like death (*Zora Neale Hurston*), If a free society cannot help the many who are poor, it cannot save the few who are rich (*J. F. Kennedy*), A hungry man is not a free man (*Adlai Stevenson*).

Antonyms, see MONEY, PROSPERITY.

POWDERINESS
Having consistency of fine, dry particles

Nouns—1, powderiness; grittiness, sandiness; efflorescence; friability. See VAPOR.

2, *(powdery substance)* powder, dust, sand, sawdust; grit; meal, bran, flour, farina; crumb, seed, grain; particle (see LITTLENESS); filings, debris, detritus, floc.

3, *(act of rendering powdery)* pulverization, grinding, comminution, attenuation, granulation, disintegration, trituration, levigation, abrasion, detrition, crystallization, limation; filing; erosion, corrosion (see DETERIORATION).

4, *(means of rendering powdery)* mill, grater, rasp, file, mortar and pestle, teeth, grinder, grindstone, quern. See FRICTION.

Verbs—pulverize, comminute, atomize, crystallize, granulate, triturate, levigate; scrape, file, abrade, rub down, grind, grate, rasp, pound, contuse, beat, crush, crunch, crumble; rust, shatter, disintegrate.

Adjectives—powdery, pulverulent, granular, ground, mealy, floury, farinaceous, branny, furfuraceous, flocculent, dusty, sandy; arenose, arenaceous; gritty; efflorescent; friable, crumbly, shivery; attrite; in pieces, shards, flinders, *etc.*

Quotations—Beauty is everlasting and dust is for a time (*Marianne Moore*).

Antonyms, see COHERENCE, SIZE.

POWER
Ability to act

Nouns—1, power, potence, potency, potentiality; puissance, might, force, ENERGY, VIGOR; dint; right hand *or* arm; ascendancy, sway, control; prepotency; almightiness, omnipotence, AUTHORITY, STRENGTH; irresistibility, invincibility, *etc. Informal,* steam. *Slang,* juice. See INTRINSIC.

2, *(power to act)* ability, ableness; efficiency, efficacy; validity, cogency; enablement; vantage ground; INFLUENCE; capability, MEANS, capacity; faculty, endowment, virtue, gift, property, qualification, susceptibility. *Slang,* the stuff, something on the ball, what it takes. See AGENCY.

3, *(power exerted)* pressure, gravity, electricity, magnetism, electromagnetism; ATTRACTION; force of inertia, dead force, living force; energy, hydroelectric power, waterpower; atomic power, horsepower; friction, suction; torque, thrust.

4, *(provider of power)* powerhouse; engine, motor, dynamo, generator; battery; [nuclear, fission, *or* fusion] reactor, tokamak; pump, mill, windmill; power plant; Diesel, gas, gasoline, internal combustion, *or* steam engine; reciprocating, rotary, Wankel, jet, *or* rocket engine; turbine.

Verbs—1, be powerful; be able; generate. *Slang,* pack a wallop *or* punch. See STRENGTH, ENERGY, VIGOR,

2, see INFLUENCE.

Adjectives—1, powerful, puissant; potent, potential; capable; able; equal to, up to; cogent, valid; effective, effectual; efficient, efficacious, adequate; strong, omnipotent, all-powerful, almighty; electric, magnetic, dynamic; attractive; mechanical; energetic, forcible, forceful, incisive, trenchant, electrifying; influential.

2, resistless, irresistible; invincible, indomitable, invulnerable, impregnable, unconquerable; overpowering, overwhelming.

Adverbs—powerfully, strongly, irresistibly, *etc.*

Phrases—might is right; power corrupts; the hand that rocks the cradle rules the world.

Quotations—Power tends to corrupt and absolute power corrupts absolutely (*Lord Acton*), Power is the great aphrodisiac (*Henry Kissinger*), A friend in power is a friend lost (*Henry Adams*), Political power is merely the organized power of one class to oppress another (*Karl Marx/Friedrich Engels*), The object of power is power (*George Orwell*).

Antonyms, see IMPOTENCE.

---

powerhouse, *n.* power plant, generating station; *informal,* tower of strength, muscle man. See POWER, STRENGTH. *Ant.,* weakling.

powerless, *n.* impotent; paralyzed, incapable, weak, disabled. See IMPOTENCE. *Ant.,* powerful.

powwow, *n.* conjurer, medicine man; *informal,* CONVERSATION, discussion. See SORCERY.

pox, *n.* smallpox, chicken pox, cow pox, variola, varicella, vaccinia; papules, maculas, vesicles, pustules; acne, eruption, breaking out; pocks, pockmarks; curse (see IMPRECATION). See DISEASE.

practicable, *adj.* possible, feasible; useful, practical; usable, workable, achievable.

See POSSIBILITY, UTILITY, FACILITY. *Ant.,* impracticable.

practical, *adj.* usable, useful; advisable; practicable, pragmatic, feasible, effective. See POSSIBILITY, UTILITY. *Ant.,* impractical.

practically, *adv.* actually, virtually; nearly, almost. See NEARNESS, INTRINSIC.

practice, *n.* training, drill, exercise; custom, HABIT; manner, METHOD, procedure. —*v.* exercise, apply; perform, act, do; drill, rehearse. See ACTION, TEACHING, USE, CONDUCT.

pragmatic, *adj.* practical, empirical; active, businesslike; materialistic, prosaic, pedantic, dogmatic, pedestrian. See UTILITY. *Ant.,* impractical.

prairie, *n.* plain, grassland, mesa, steppe, llano, savanna. See HORIZONTAL, LAND.

praise, *n.* commendation, acclaim, approval, applause; eulogy; homage; benediction, thanksgiving, grace. —*v.t.* acclaim, approve, commend, extol, eulogize, applaud; glorify, laud. See APPROBATION, GRATITUDE. *Ant.,* condemn, criticize.

praiseworthy, *adj.* commendable, laudable, meritorious, admirable. See APPROBATION. *Ant.,* condemnable.

prance, *v.i.* caper, cavort, spring, dance, slip; strut. See LEAP.

prank, *n.* caprice, frolic, caper, trick, jest, escapade. See AMUSEMENT.

prankster, *n.* trickster, joker, jokester, practical joker. See WIT.

prate, *v.i.* chatter, babble. See LOQUACITY.

prattle, *n.* chitchat, babbling, chatter. —*v.i.* murmur, chatter, babble, jabber. See LOQUACITY, SPEECH.

pray, *v.i.* implore, ask, beg, REQUEST, solicit, petition, entreat; WORSHIP.

preach, *v.* exhort, evangelize, lecture, sermonize, moralize, preachify (*inf.*). See RITE, TEACHING.

preacher, *n.* pastor; sermonizer (see CLERGY).

preamble, *n.* prologue, introduction, preface, prelude. See PRECEDENCE. *Ant.,* afterword, coda.

precarious, *adj.* dangerous, risky; critical; doubtful, uncertain, unsafe, insecure, unstable. See TRANSIENTNESS, DANGER. *Ant.,* safe.

precaution, *n.* CARE, CAUTION, warning; safeguard, PROVISION, protection; anticipation, forethought, foresight. See PREPARATION.

PRECEDENCE
Coming before

Nouns—1, precedence, coming before; SUPERIORITY, IMPORTANCE, preference; PRIORITY, preexistence; antecedence, precedency, antecedency, anteposition, anteriority, pecking order.

2, *(forward position)* precession, leading, heading, forerunning, going before; going *or* being first; the lead, the van (see FRONT).

3, *(something that precedes)* foreword, prelude, preamble, preface, prologue, prolusion, proem, prolepsis, prefix, introduction, heading, frontispiece, groundwork, PREPARATION; overture, voluntary, symphony. *Informal.* prequel.

Verbs—1, precede; come before, come first, antecede; introduce, usher in; set the fashion; take *or* have precedence; [out]rank; place before, prefix, premise, prelude, preface.

2, forerun; go before, go ahead, go in the van, go in advance; pioneer, herald, head, take the lead; lead [the way], get *or* have the start; steal a march; get before, get ahead, get in front of, outstrip. *Informal,* get in on the ground floor.

Adjectives—preceding, precedent, antecedent; anterior; prior, before; avant-garde; former, foregoing; above- *or* aforementioned, aforesaid, said; precursory, percursive, preliminary, prefatory, introductory; prelusive, prelusory, preludious, proemial, preparatory, forerunning.

Adverbs—in advance, before, ahead.

Phrases—we must learn to walk before we can run.

Quotations—For a successful technology, reality must take precedence over public relations, for Nature cannot be fooled (*Richard P. Feynman*).

Antonyms, see SEQUENCE.

---

precept, *n.* instruction, charge; prescript, prescription; recipe, receipt; golden rule; MAXIM, RULE, canon, law, code, act, statute, rubric, regulation; form, formula, formulary, order, COMMAND.

precinct, *n.* neighborhood, district, area; enclosure, boundary, LIMIT, environs. See REGION, ENVIRONMENT.

precious, *adj.* priceless, costly; precise, overrefined, overnice; beloved, dear.

See DEARNESS, AFFECTATION. *Ant.,* worthless, cheap.

precipice, *n.* cliff, drop, bluff, declivity. See VERTICAL, OBLIQUITY.

precipitate, *adj.* rash, hasty, hurried, headlong, impetuous. See RASHNESS. —*v.* CAUSE, foment; hasten, speed, expedite; separate (as a chemical solution); fall (as rain, snow, *etc.*). See HASTE, EARLINESS, DESCENT, DENSITY.

precipitous, *adj.* steep, abrupt, clifflike, sheer. See OBLIQUITY.

précis, *n.* summary, abstract. See SHORTNESS.

precise, *adj.* exact, accurate, definite, punctilious; fastidious; unbending, rigid; prim, precious. See RIGHTNESS, TRUTH. *Ant.,* imprecise.

preclude, *v.t.* prevent, stop, prohibit, obviate, check; forestall. See EXCLUSION, PROHIBITION.

precocious, *adj.* advanced, overforward, premature. See EARLINESS. *Ant.,* backward, slow.

preconception, *n.* anticipation, prejudgment; prejudice. See MISJUDGMENT.

precursor, *n.* forerunner (see PRIORITY).

predacious, predatory, *adj.* robbing, ravening, plundering. See STEALING.

predecessor, *n.* forerunner (see PRIORITY); ancestor, antecedent, progenitor. See ANCESTRY. *Ant.,* successor.

predestine, *v.t.* foredoom, predestinate, preordain, foreordain. See DESTINY, NECESSITY.

predetermine, *v.t.* premeditate, preresolve, preconcert, prearrange, stack the cards (*inf.*); foreordain, predestine, doom; plan. See DESTINY, INTENTION.

predicament, *n.* condition, quandary, fix, spot (*inf.*), corner, dilemma, mess, scrape, crisis, emergency. See CIRCUMSTANCE, DIFFICULTY.

predicate, *v.t.* assert, declare; base, found. See AFFIRMATION, SUPPOSITION.

PREDICTION
Foretelling the future

Nouns—1, prediction, announcement; premonition, WARNING; prophecy, vaticination, prognosis, prognostication, premonstration; augury, auguration; foreboding, presentiment, premonition, presage; ominousness; auspices, forecast; omen, horoscope, soothsaying; fortune-telling, crystal-gazing, chiromancy, palmistry, aleuromancy, augury, haruspication, necromancy, stargazing; divination, prophetic vision, auspice; necromancy (see SORCERY); spiritualism; clairvoyance (see INTUITION); astrology, horoscopy; prefiguration, prefigurement.

2, foresight, precognition, prescience, foreknowledge, anticipation, prevision, foretoken, forethought; providence, prudence, PREPARATION; clairvoyance, second sight; foreboding, premonition, presentiment; foretaste, preview; foreshadowing, foretelling, forecasting, prophecy, prophetic vision. See CAUTION, FUTURITY.

3, prophet, seer, augur, oracle, fortune-teller, soothsayer, crystal-gazer; weatherman *or* -woman; herald; Cassandra, sibyl, Delphic oracle, Sphinx; sorcerer, interpreter.

4, crystal ball, tea leaves, divining rod, *etc.*; Ouija board.

Verbs—1, predict, prognosticate, prophesy, forecast, divine, foretell, soothsay, augur, tell fortunes; cast a horoscope; presage, [fore]bode, foretoken, portend, foreshadow; herald, announce; call the turn *or* shot.

2, bid fair; promise; lead one to expect; be the precursor *or* forerunner.

3, foresee, anticipate, foreknow, presurmise, expect. See EXPECTATION.

Adjectives—predicting, predictive, prophetic, oracular, sibylline; ominous, portentous; auspicious; prescient, farsighted; minatory, monitory, premonitory.

Phrases—nothing is certain but the unforeseen; prevention is better than cure; look before you leap.

Quotations—The best laid schemes o' mice an' men gang aft a'gley (*Robert Burns*), You can only predict things after they've happened (*Eugène Ionesco*).

Antonyms, see CHANCE, SURPRISE.

predilection, *n.* partiality, preference, prejudice, bias. See TENDENCY, DESIRE. *Ant.,* dislike.

predisposed, *adj.* inclined, prone, partial; prepared, ready, willing. See INFLUENCE, TENDENCY.

predominant, *adj.* prevalent, controlling, ascendant, ruling, supreme. See INFLUENCE, SUPERIORITY. *Ant.,* subservient.

preeminent, *adj.* outstanding, notable, distinguished, renowned; foremost, paramount, superior, supreme. See REPUTE, SUPERIORITY.

preempt, *v.t.* commandeer, usurp, occupy, arrogate. See EARLINESS.

preen, *v.t.* groom, primp, prettify, doll up (*sl.*); strut. See VANITY.

prefabricated, *adj.* ready-built *or* -made, prefab (*inf.*). See PRODUCTION.

preface, *n.* foreword, prologue, preamble, introduction, prelude, preliminary. — *v.t.* introduce, open, premise, precede. See PRECEDENCE, BEGINNING.

prefect, *n.* magistrate; monitor, dean. See AUTHORITY, DIRECTOR.

prefer, *v.t.* select, fancy, choose, adopt; OFFER, promote, advance. See CHOICE, IMPROVEMENT.

preference, *n.* CHOICE, pick, desire, taste, liking, druthers (*inf.*). See PRECEDENCE.

preferment, *n.* promotion, advancement. See IMPROVEMENT.

prefigure, *v.t.* presage (see PREDICTION); imagine, envisage. See IMAGINATION.

pregnable, *adj.* vulnerable, assailable. See DANGER.

pregnant, *adj.* significant, weighty, potential; fertile, inventive; gravid, parturient; impregnated, big [with child], enceinte, in a family way (*inf.*). See IMPORTANCE, PRODUCTION.

prehistoric, *adj.* pristine, original; primeval, primal, primitive; archaic, lost to history, from before time; unrecorded, unwritten. See OLDNESS.

prejudge, *v.t.* presuppose, assume, presume. See MISJUDGMENT.

prejudice, *n.* partiality, bias, opinion; predilection, prepossession; detriment, injury; intolerance. —*v.t.* bias, INFLUENCE, color, jaundice. See MISJUDGMENT, INJUSTICE.

prelate, *n.* primate, bishop, cardinal. See CLERGY.

preliminary, *adj.* introductory, preparatory, prefatory. See PREPARATION, PRECEDENCE.

prelude, *n.* preface, foreword, prologue, introduction, precursor, overture. See MUSIC, PRECEDENCE. *Ant.,* postlude.

premature, *adj.* untimely, underripe, immature, overhasty, precocious, unprepared, incomplete; forward. See EARLINESS.

premeditate, *v.t.* calculate, PLAN, predesign, resolve, prearrange. See INTENTION.

premier, *adj.* chief, foremost; earliest. See PRIORITY, SUPERIORITY. —*n.* prime *or* first minister. See AUTHORITY.

premiere, *n.* opening, debut, first night, inauguration, bow. See BEGINNING.

premise, *n.* basis, assumption, hypothesis, proposition; (*pl.*) building, land, house, apartment, office, *etc.* See EVIDENCE, REASONING, REGION, LOCATION.

premium, *n.* reward, prize, PAYMENT, recompense, gift, bounty, fee, bonus. See COMPENSATION.

premonition, *n.* foreboding, presentiment. See WARNING, PREDICTION.

preoccupied, *adj.* inattentive, prepossessed, distracted; absorbed, engrossed, in a brown study (*inf.*). See INATTENTION. *Ant.,* attentive.

PREPARATION
Act of preparing

Nouns—1, preparation, preparing; providing; PROVISION, providence, prearrangement, anticipation, foresight, forethought; precaution, predisposition; PLAN; rehearsal; training, education (see TEACHING); inurement, HABIT; novitiate (see LEARNING). See SAFETY, PRECEDENCE, EARLINESS.

2, ARRANGEMENT; tuning, adjustment (see AGREEMENT); equipment, outfit.

3, (*preliminary work*) groundwork, keystone, cradle, stepping-stone; foundation.

4, (*types of preparation*) cuisine, cooking, cookery, culinary art (see FOOD); tilling, plowing, sowing, semination, cultivation; manufacture, PRODUCTION.

5, preparedness, readiness, ripeness, mellowness; maturity, EARLINESS.

6, *(model used in preparation for something)* prototype, original; model, pattern; precedent; standard, type; archetype; module, exemplary, example, paradigm; test, copy, design; drug, potion, *etc.*

7, preparer, trainer, teacher; pioneer, pathfinder, trailblazer; forerunner, advanceman.

Verbs—**1,** prepare; get *or* make ready; make preparations, settle preliminaries, get up, predispose; set *or* put in order (see ARRANGEMENT); forecast, concoct, PLAN; lay the foundations, basis, *or* groundwork, pave the way; roughhew; nurture (see AID). *Informal,* dust off. *Slang,* prep.

2, *(prepare something for a task)* equip, ready, set, prime, attune; adjust, put in working order, put in tune; pack; prepare for, train, teach, rehearse; make provision for; take steps, measures, *or* precautions; provide, provide against, set one's house in order; clear the decks for action, pave the way for; batten down the hatches, weatherize.

3, prepare oneself, get set, line up; serve an apprenticeship; get into harness, gird up one's loins, hold on to one's hat, buckle on one's armor; wind up, shoulder arms, get up steam, draw *or* take a long breath; save for a rainy day; keep one's powder dry. *Informal,* get one's ducks in a row, haul off. *Slang,* get one's ass in gear.

Adjectives—**1,** preparing, in preparation, in embryo, in hand; brewing, hatching, brooding; in store for, in reserve; precautionary, provident; preparative, preparatory; provisional; under revision; preliminary (see PRECEDENCE).

2, prepared, in readiness, at call, ready, handy, forthcoming; planned, strategic, schematic; in working order; of age, ripe; in practice; practiced, skilled; overqualified; in battle array, in war paint; armed to the teeth, sword in hand, armed at all points; booted and spurred, rough and ready; on alert, vigilant, *semper paratus;* at one's fingertips; turnkey. *Informal,* on the mark, all set, on tap, ready to roll, all systems go. *Slang,* loaded for bear.

Adverbs—in preparation, in anticipation of; against, for; under construction, afoot, afloat, under consideration, in the works, on foot. *Informal,* on the fire.

Phrases—for want of a nail the shoe was lost, for want of a shoe the horse was lost, and for want of a horse the man was lost; strike while the iron is hot; [hope for the best and] prepare for the worst; a stitch in time saves nine; look before you leap; think first and speak afterward.

Quotations—Watch therefore: for ye know not what hour your Lord doth come (*Bible*).

Antonyms, see NEGLECT, UNPREPAREDNESS.

---

preponderance, *n.* prevalence, predominance, supremacy, ascendancy. See INFLUENCE, SUPERIORITY.

prepossessing, *adj.* appealing, attractive; charming, winning, winsome, engaging. See BEAUTY. *Ant.,* ugly, unappealing.

preposterous, *adj.* ridiculous, absurd, nonsensical, idiotic; foolish, extravagant; improper, unsuitable. See ABSURDITY. *Ant.,* sensible, logical.

prerequisite, *n.* requirement, essential, necessity, must *(inf.),* proviso; stipulation, QUALIFICATION.

prerogative, *n.* franchise, right, privilege; birthright; liberty, advantage. See AUTHORITY.

presage, *n.* portent, prophecy, augury, forecast, omen; PREDICTION, precursor, harbinger, forerunner; inkling, promise.

preschool, *adj.* nursery school, kindergarten; playschool, day nursery, crèche. See SCHOOL.

prescribe, *v.* urge, suggest, advise; order, advocate, decree; appoint, institute; ordain. See ADVICE, COMMAND.

prescription, *n.* medicine; formula, recipe; mandate, decree, edict. See REMEDY, COMMAND, HABIT.

presence, *n.* attendance (see PRESENCE); vicinity, immediacy (see NEARNESS); demeanor, bearing, APPEARANCE; person of IMPORTANCE, VIP.

PRESENCE
Fact of being at a certain place

Nouns—1, presence, attendance; ASSEMBLAGE; occupancy, occupation, habitation, inhabitancy, residence; permeation, pervasion; diffusion, dissemination; ubiety, ubiquity, omnipresence, EXISTENCE.

2, spectator, beholder, observer, looker-on, onlooker, watcher, viewer, [eye]witness, bystander, passerby; sightseer, rubberneck, sidewalk superintendent; inspector; attender, patron; house, audience; the gallery, grandstand, *or* bleachers; Johnny-on-the-spot; kibitzer. See VISION, INHABITANT.

Verbs—1, be present, assist at; exist; look on, witness, watch; kibitz; attend, remain; find *or* present oneself, turn out; show one's face; lie, stand. *Informal*, show up. *Slang*, make the scene.

2, frequent, haunt; dwell, reside, stay; tenant. *Slang*, hang out. See ABODE, INHABITANT.

3, fill, pervade, permeate; infest; be diffused, be disseminated; overspread, overrun; run across.

Adjectives—present; occupying, inhabiting; moored; resident[ial]; domiciled, domiciliary; ubiquitous, omnipresent; peopled, populated, inhabited.

Adverbs—here, there, where, everywhere, aboard, on board, at home, afield; on the spot, at the kill, on hand, on deck; face-to-face; here, there, and everywhere (see SPACE); in the presence of, before, in person, to one's face; under the eyes of, under the nose of; in the face of. *Informal*, in the flesh; live (*radio and TV*).

Quotations—God is our refuge and strength, a very present help in trouble (*Bible*).

Antonyms, see ABSENCE.

---

present, *n.* PRESENT time; gift, favor, gratuity, offering, bonus, donation (see GIVING). —*adj.* here (see PRESENCE); now (see PRESENT). —*v.t.* award, endow, give, assign, deliver, proffer, tender, pass, bestow; introduce. See GIVING, OFFER.

PRESENT
Time now passing

Nouns—present time, day, moment, juncture, *or* occasion; the present, the times, the time being, the nonce; this day and age, existing times; nowadays; epoch, day, hour, age, TIME of life; now, the here and now, twentieth century; the spirit of the age; present tense, the historic[al] present (see GRAMMAR). See NEWNESS, CHRONOLOGY.

Verbs—seize the day, carpe diem.

Adjectives—present, actual, instant, current, existing, living, immediate; up-to-date, latter-day, present-day, modern, contemporary, topical.

Adverbs—1, at this time, at this moment, immediately (see INSTANTANEITY); at the present time, at present, now; at this time of day, today, nowadays; already, even now, but now, just now, as of now; on the present occasion; for the time being, for the nonce; on the spot; on the spur of the moment *or* occasion; until now, to this day, to the present day; in this day and age, in our time; forthwith, presently, soon, shortly, eventually (see FUTURITY).

2, to date, up to now, as yet, thus far, so far, hereunto.

Phrases—enjoy the present moment and don't plan for the future; today is the first day of the rest of your life.

Quotations—Sufficient unto the day is the evil thereof (*Bible*), We want to live in the present, and the only history that is worth a tinker's damn is the history we make today (*Henry Ford*), Tomorrow's life is too late. Live today (*Martial*), Let others praise ancient times. I am glad that I was born in these (*Ovid*), He who lives in the present lives in eternity (*Ludwig Wittgenstein*), The dogmas of the quiet past are inadequate to the stormy present (*Abraham Lincoln*), The word "now" is like a bomb through the window, and it ticks (*Arthur Miller*), Every day you wake up is a beautiful day (*John Wayne*).

Antonyms, see PRIORITY, SEQUENCE, FUTURITY, PAST.

---

presentable, *adj.* attractive, personable, engaging; decent; passable, tolerable, up to snuff *or* par. See BEAUTY, GOODNESS, MEDIOCRITY.

presentation, *n.* presenting, GIVING; exhibition, show (see DISCLOSURE).

presentiment, *n.* PREDICTION, foreboding, anticipation, premonition, apprehension; foretaste, prescience, omen.

presently, *adv.* soon, shortly, immediately, eventually. See EARLINESS.

PRESERVATION
Act of keeping alive or in good condition

Nouns—1, preservation, conservation, safekeeping (see SAFETY); maintenance, support; ECONOMY. See RETENTION.

2, *(methods of preservation)* embalming; curing, pickling, salting, smoking, canning; dehydration; tanning; refrigeration, freezing, quick-freezing, freeze-drying.

3, *(preservative substance)* preserver, conserver, preservative; brine, salt, formaldehyde, embalming fluid; lifesaver; reserve, reservation, park, preserve, sanctuary.

4, *(preserved food)* conserve, preserve, jelly, jam, marmalade. See FOOD.

Verbs—1, preserve, maintain, retain, keep, sustain, support; keep up, keep alive; bank up, nurse; save, rescue; make safe, take care of; guard, defend (see DEFENSE).

2, conserve; dry, cure, salt, pickle, corn, smoke; dehydrate, quick-freeze, freeze-dry; bottle, pot, tin, putting up, can; tan; husband; embalm, mummify; immortalize; lay by.

Adjectives—preserving, putting up; preservative; hygienic; preserved, unimpaired, unsinged, unmarred, unspoiled, safe and sound; intact, unscathed, with a whole skin.

Quotations—In wildness is the preservation of the world (*Henry David Thoreau*), Endure, and preserve yourselves for better things (*Virgil*).

Antonyms, see WASTE, DETERIORATION.

---

preside, *v.i.* supervise, superintend, control, rule, direct, manage; chair, head. See AUTHORITY.

president, *n.* head, chairperson, dean, principal, chief, ruler, prexy (*sl.*). See AUTHORITY.

press, *n.* crush, throng, crowd; pressure, urgency; closet, wardrobe, repository; ASSEMBLAGE; newspapers, news media, fifth estate. See PRINTING, PUBLICATION, COMMUNICATION, RECEPTACLE. —*v.* crush, push, iron, smooth; compel, force, urge, beg, persuade; conscript, draft; hug, embrace; squeeze, wring; solicit, entreat, importune. See COMPULSION, GRAVITY, SMOOTHNESS, HASTE.

pressing, *adj.* critical, important, urgent; exacting, demanding; persistent. See IMPORTANCE. *Ant.,* casual, unimportant.

pressure, *n.* strain, COMPULSION, stress; persuasion, coercion, persuasiveness; affliction, trouble; distress; heaviness, compression. See ADVERSITY, GRAVITY, IMPORTANCE, INFLUENCE, POWER.

prestige, *n.* REPUTE, reputation, dignity, fame, note, importance.

presto, *adv.* quickly, rapidly; immediately. See INSTANTANEITY, MUSIC.

presume, *v.* impose, venture; deduce, assume, infer, presuppose; infringe, take liberties. See SUPPOSITION, VANITY.

presumption, *n.* audacity, assurance, arrogance, haughtiness; impetuosity; deduction, conclusion, inference, guess, hypothesis. See INSOLENCE, BELIEF.

presuppose, *v.t.* assume, presume, imply. See SUPPOSITION.

pretend, *v.* sham, feign, dissemble, simulate; counterfeit, lie, fake; claim, aver. See FALSEHOOD.

pretender, *n.* claimant; impostor, fraud, humbug, hypocrite, deceiver. See DECEPTION.

pretense, *n.* show, pretension, AFFECTA-
TION, sham, IMITATION, OSTENTATION;
makeshift, simulation, excuse, pretext,
evasion. See FALSEHOOD, VANITY.

pretext, *n.* subterfuge, pretense, excuse,
justification, VINDICATION; cover,
cloak, blind, sham, evasion. See FALSE-
HOOD.

prettify, *v.t.*, *informal*, beautify, embellish
(see BEAUTY).

pretty, *adj.* attractive, comely, good-looking;
delicate, precise. See BEAUTY. —*adv.*,
informal, rather; moderately. See DE-
GREE. *Ant.*, ugly, unattractive.

prevail, *v.i.* preponderate, predominate,
rule, obtain; exist, be; overcome; succeed, induce, persuade. See EXISTENCE,
HABIT, SUCCESS.

prevalent, *adj.* customary, current; predominant, prominent, prevailing, preponderant; general, rife, current. See
HABIT, FREQUENCY, GENERALITY. *Ant.*,
rare, scarce.

prevaricate, *v.i.* lie, quibble, cavil, equivocate, palter. See FALSEHOOD.

prevent, *v.t.* preclude, hinder, stop, check,
impede, forestall, avert, restrain, prohibit. See PROHIBITION, HINDRANCE.

preview, *n.* sneak preview, advance screen-
ing; trailer. See EARLINESS, DRAMA.

previous, *adj.* antecedent, anterior; preceding, foregoing, former, prior. See
PRIORITY. *Ant.*, following.

prey, *n.* victim, quarry, game, kill; loot,
prize, spoil. —*v.i.* plunder, pillage, ravage; haunt, wear. See PURSUIT. *Ant.*,
hunter, pursuer.

PRICE
Something demanded in exchange

Nouns—1, price, amount, cost, expense, prime cost, charge, figure, demand; fare, hire, bill, tab, rental; overhead, carrying charge *or* cost; rent charge, rackrent, quitrent; expenditure, outlay (see PAYMENT). *Slang*, damage[s], score, bad news, nick, ante, setback, shakedown, tune.

2, *(price charged for a service)* dues, duty, toll, [income, sales, excise, *or* value added] tax, cess, levy, impost; poll *or* head tax; custom, excise, assessment, tithe, tenths, exaction, ransom, salvage, tariff; brokerage, wharfage, freightage, carriage.

3, *(price obtainable for something)* worth, rate, [face *or* book] value, valuation, appraisement, appraisal, estimate, evaluation, costliness; money's worth, pennyworth; current *or* market price, quotation, going rate, what it will fetch; pegged *or* fixed price, prix fixe, flat rate, package price. See DEARNESS, CHEAPNESS.

4, *(price for work)* recompense, pay (see PAYMENT).

5, price index, [price] ceiling *or* floor, floor *or* ceiling price; price controls, guidelines, *or* supports; price fixing; escalator clause; inflation index; bluebook.

Verbs—1, price; set, quote, fix, *or* peg a price; value, appraise, assess, estimate, rate, evaluate; charge, demand, ask, require, exact tax, levy, impose, apportion; have one's price.

2, amount to, come to, mount up to, fetch, sell for cost, bring in, yield, afford. *Informal*, stand one, stick for, set one back.

Adjectives—priced, appraised; taxable, dutiable; mercenary, venal.

Adverbs—to the tune of, at a price, for a consideration.

Phrases—every man has his price.

Quotations—Taxation without representation is tyranny (*James Otis*), Income tax has made more liars out of the American people than golf (*Will Rogers*), Only the little people pay taxes (*Leona Helmsley*), Read my lips: no new taxes (*George H. W. Bush*), Taxes are what we pay for civilized society (*Oliver Wendell Holmes*), Things are only worth what you make them worth (*Molière*), [A cynic:] a man who knows the price of everything and the value of nothing (*Oscar Wilde*).

Antonyms, see CHEAPNESS.

priceless, *adj.* invaluable, precious; expensive, costly. See DEARNESS. *Ant.,* cheap.

prick, *v.t.* puncture, pierce, stick; sting, wound; prod, urge, incite, goad, spur. See PAIN, SENSIBILITY, IMPULSE. —*n.* hole, wound, puncture; *slang,* penis. See OPENING, BODY.

prickly, *adj.* thorny, barbed, bristly, spiny, thistly, burry; stinging, tingling, smarting. See ROUGHNESS, SHARPNESS, PAIN. *Ant.,* smooth.

PRIDE
Sense of self-worth

Nouns—1, pride, hauteur; dignity, self-respect, self-esteem, self-sufficiency, reserve.

2, *(sympton of pride)* arrogance, INSOLENCE; OSTENTATION; VANITY, vainglory, crest, airs, high notions; condescension; purse-pride; BOASTING, conceit, self-complacency, self-exaltation, self-glorification, self-satisfaction, self-importance, self-admiration, self-love, amour-propre. *Slang,* swelled head, ego trip, vanity plate.

3, *(national pride)* patriotism, nationalism, civic *or* national pride; loyalty, allegiance; love of country, civism; chauvinism, jingoism, fascism; flag-waving.

4, proud man, highflier, peacock; fine gentleman *or* lady; boast, pride and joy; patriot, chauvinist, jingo[ist], fascist. *Slang,* swellhead.

Verbs—1, be proud, look one in the face, lift *or* hold up one's head, hold one's head high, perk oneself up; pride oneself on, glory in, take pride in, stand upon, be proud of.

2, be conceited; plume, preen, *or* hug oneself; put a good face on, carry with a high hand; boast, swagger, strut, presume, look big; set one's back up, bridle, toss one's head, give oneself airs; condescend, talk down to, patronize, stoop, lower oneself. *Informal,* get on one's high horse. *Slang,* put on side *or* airs, put on the dog, put on the ritz.

3, fill with pride, puff up, swell, inflate, turn one's head. *Informal,* give a big head.

Adjectives—1, proud, prideful, exalted, lordly, noble (see NOBILITY); mettlesome, [high] spirited; imposing, magnificent, splendid, majestic, grand.

2, arrogant (see INSOLENCE); vain, conceited (see VANITY); haughty, magisterial, puffed up, swollen, flushed, blown, vainglorious; supercilious, disdainful, contemptuous, presumptuous, condescending, cavalier; boastful, overweening, high and mighty; purse-proud; self-satisfied, self-confident, *etc.*; ego[t]istical; proud as a peacock *or* as Lucifer, bloated with pride, puffed up, too big for one's boots. *Informal,* uppish, uppity. *Slang,* high-hat.

3, stiff, formal, stiff-necked, starchy, prim, straitlaced; aristocratic (see NOBILITY); affected. *Informal,* stuck up.

4, patriotic, nationalistic, chauvinist[ic], jingo[ist], fascist.

Adverbs—proudly, haughtily; with dignity, with head erect, with nose in the air; in one's glory. *Informal,* on one's high horse.

Phrases—pride goes before a fall.

Quotations—Patriotism is the last refuge of a scoundrel (*Samuel Johnson*), Our country, right or wrong (*Stephen Decatur*), Ask not what your country can do for you— ask what you can do for your country (*J. F. Kennedy*), My family pride something inconceivable. I can't help it. I was born sneering (*W. S. Gilbert*), The Lord will destroy the house of the proud (*Bible*), Vanity is only being sensitive to what other people probably think of us (*Paul Valéry*), I have nothing to declare except my genius (*Oscar Wilde*), Small things make base men proud (*Shakespeare*).

Antonyms, see HUMILITY, MODESTY.

---

priest, priestess, *n.* father, clergyman, *etc.* See CLERGY.

priggish, *adj.* pedantic, affected; fastidious, prim, precious; conceited, egotistical. See AFFECTATION, VANITY.

prim, *adj.* precise, demure, formal, priggish; fussy, prudish. See AFFECTATION. *Ant.,* casual.

primacy, *n.* supremacy (see PRIORITY, SUPERIORITY).

prima donna, opera singer, leading lady, diva. See MUSIC, VANITY.

prima facie, Lat., at first sight. See EVIDENCE, VISION.

primal, *adj.* original, primeval; primary. See BEGINNING, CAUSE.

primary, *adj.* chief, original, initial, primal, first, elementary; immediate; primitive, prime, principal. See BEGINNING, CAUSE, IMPORTANCE. *Ant.,* secondary.

primate, *n.* chief, leader, head, master; bishop, archbishop, metropolitan, diocesan, suffragan, patriarch; man, ape, monkey, lemur, *etc.* See CLERGY, ANIMAL.

prime, *adj.* original, first, initial; primitive, primeval; chief, leading, main; choice, finest. See IMPORTANCE, OLDNESS, PREPARATION.

primer, *n.* abecedarium, grammar, reader. See LEARNING, BOOK.

primitive, *adj.* primeval, aboriginal, crude, unpolished, unrefined; basic, primal, primary; prime; old, antiquated. See OLDNESS, INTRINSIC, VULGARITY. *Ant.,* civilized, cultivated.

primness, *n.* prudery, prudishness, priggishness; formality; preciousness, stiffness. See AFFECTATION.

primp, *v.* prink, preen, groom, bedizen, prettify, freshen up, deck out (*inf.*), put one's face on (*inf.*), doll up (*sl.*). See ORNAMENT.

prince, *n.* monarch, ruler, sovereign; noble[man]; chief; *slang,* swell guy. See AUTHORITY, GOODNESS.

princely, *adj.* regal, royal, titled, noble; magnanimous, generous, munificent. See NOBILITY.

princess, *n.* crown princess, queen. See AUTHORITY.

principal, *n.* chief, leader, head; constituent, client; buyer, seller; capital, corpus. See MONEY. —*adj.* foremost, chief, prime, greatest, main, leading. See IMPORTANCE.

principality, *n.* principate, dominion, domain, sovereignty, rule; princedom, satrapy, country, province, REGION; duchy, palatinate, margraviate; sheikdom, imamate, emirate, caliphate, sultanate.

principle, *n.* tenet, code, doctrine, conviction; theory, premise; postulate; rule, law, precept; equity, integrity, probity, nature, origin, source, CAUSE. See BELIEF, PART, SUBSTANCE, INTRINSIC.

prink, *v.* dress up, adorn, deck out. See ORNAMENT, CLOTHING.

print, *n.* impression, imprint; seal, die; PUBLICATION. See CLOTHING. —*v.t.* impress, stamp; write in capitals. See PRINTING, ENGRAVING, WRITING.

PRINTING
Process of producing impressions

Nouns—1, printing; typography, stereotype, electrotype; block printing; lithography, chromolithography, planography, collotype; offset, letterpress, gravure, rotogravure, flexography, thermography, laser *or* dot-matrix printing; instant printing, Xerox; photoprinting, photoengraving, photocomposition, phototypography, reprography, Itek; intaglio; ENGRAVING; PUBLICATION; composition, typesetting, phototypesetting; Linotype, Monotype, Intertype, Multigraph, computer typesetting; Postscript, TrueType; imposition, pressrun; mat, matrix; reproduction; graphic arts. See COPY.

2, (*printing type*) type, case, lower *or* upper case, majuscule, minuscule, capital, small capitals; hot *or* cold type, hot metal; [soft] font; typeface, roman, italic, cursive, lightface, boldface, condensed, expanded; ligature; stick, stone; shank, serif, body, shoulder, beard, ascender, descender; point *or* set size; Baskerville, Bodoni, Caledonia, Caslon, Century, Cheltenham, Clarendon, Electra, English, Fraktur, Futura, Garamond, Gothic, Goudy, Helvetica, Janson, Old English, Optima, Palatino, Times Roman, Univers, oldstyle, modern, *etc.* type, dingbat; print; slug.

3, (*printing impression*) impression, proof, galley, galley proof, dummy, page proof, repro[duction] proof, revise, run, rerun; plate, replate, cliché.

4, (*printing machines and methods*) printing press, press, proof press; job press, flatbed press, cylinder press, rotary press, web press; laser, ink-jet, bubble-jet, *or* dot matrix printer, wax transfer; bed, chase, quoin, reglet, composing stick, form, galley, imposition, leading, linecasting; print shop.

5, printer, compositor, typographer, pressman, makeup man, proofreader, copyreader, copyholder; stone hand; printer's devil, proof boy.

Verbs—print, imprint, impress, run off; bleed; offset, laser print; compose, impose, set, make up, card out; proofread, revise, justify, kern; make ready; go to press.

Adjectives—printed; in type, in print; typographical; graphic; in black and white; condensed.

Quotations—The three great elements of modern civilization, Gunpowder, Printing, and the Protestant Religion (*Thomas Carlyle*), The printing press is either the greatest blessing or the greatest curse of modern times, one sometimes forgets which (*J. M. Barrie*).

Antonyms, see WRITING.

PRIORITY
Precedence in time

Nouns—**1,** priority, antecedence, anteriority, primogeniture; preexistence; precession; precursor, forerunner; PAST; premises. See PRECEDENCE, ANCESTRY, BEGINNING.

2, precursor, forerunner, antecedent, precedent, predecessor, forebears; bellwether, herald, harbinger, announcer; HABIT, standard, model; prototype; custom, practice, usage; prefigurement, PREDICTION, antecedent; head start. *Informal,* scoop.

3, prioritization, organization, triage, rank. See CLASS.

Verbs—**1,** precede, antecede, come *or* go before; lead; preexist; dawn; presage (see PREDICTION). *Informal,* beat one to it. *Slang,* get the jump on, beat to the punch *or* draw.

2, be beforehand, be early (see EARLINESS); steal a march upon, anticipate, forestall; have *or* gain a start; steal one's thunder, scoop. *Slang,* beat out, jump the gun.

3, prioritize, organize, triage, rank.

Adjectives—prior, previous; preceding, precedent; anterior, antecedent; forehanded; preexisting, preexistent; former, foregoing; aforementioned, abovementioned; aforesaid; said; introductory, precursory; preliminary; preparatory.

Adverbs—before, prior to; earlier; first[ly], first and foremost, in the first place; ere, heretofore, erstwhile, already, yet, beforehand; in advance, ahead; in the van *or* forefront; in front, foremost; on the eve of; antebellum; before Christ, B.C.; antediluvian, before the fact. *Informal,* first off.

Phrases—set the cart before the horse; don't count your chickens before they hatch; don't cross the bridge till you come to it; first come, first served; first things first.

Antonyms, see SEQUENCE.

---

prismatic, *adj.* prismal; sparkling, coruscant, colorful, chromatic; kaleidoscopic; spectral, rainbowlike. See VARIEGATION, COLOR. *Ant.,* monochromatic.

PRISON
Place of confinement

Nouns—**1,** prison, penitentiary; maximum, medium, *or* minimum security prison, jail, lockup, gaol, cage; coop, den, cell, oubliette; cell block; stronghold, fortress, keep, dungeon, Bastille; federal *or* state prison, city *or* county jail, tank, secure facility; Sing Sing, Dartmoor, Alcatraz, Bridewell, debtors' prison, prison farm, workhouse; guardroom, guardhouse; alimony jail; brig, hold; roundhouse, station house, station, police station; house of correction *or* detention, correctional institution, adjustment center, detention facility, quiet cell; reformatory, reform school, protectory; pen, fold, corral, pound; ENCLOSURE; penal colony *or* settlement; military prison, stockade; stocks, stone walls. *Informal,* lockup, cage of anger. *Slang,* jug, can, joint, calaboose, calabozo, hoosegow, pen, limbo, college, dog house, bucket, cow, crossbar [hotel], graystone college, city hotel, icebox, iron house, big house, stir, clink, cooler, slammer, school, gladiator farm or school, zoo, quad, pok[e]y, Club Fed. See RESTRAINT, PUNISHMENT.

2, concentration or detention camp, compound, stalag; extermination center, death camp; Auschwitz, Bergen-Belsen, Buchenwald, Dachau, Treblinka, Gulag; assembly center, relocation center.

3, shackles, bilboes, cangue, bastinado, flogging, rack, stocks, pillory, cat-o'-nine-tails; electric chair, firing squad, gas chamber, gibbet, guillotine, injection; [black] hole, solitary [confinement], drunk tank.

4, imprisonment, incarceration; mittimus; protective custody; prison term, time, commitment, confinement, lockdown, hitch, life sentence; death row; conjugal visit. *Informal,* short time. *Slang,* lag, time, nickel, dime, quarter.

5, prisoner, captive, felon; convict, inmate, détenu, detainee, jailbird; trusty, parolee; prisoner of war, POW; political prisoner, prisoner of conscience; ticket-of-leave man; chain gang. *Slang,* con, lifer, fish, punk.

6, warden, keeper, jailer, gaoler, turnkey, guard, warder. *Slang,* screw, roach, hack, the man, yard hack. See SAFETY.

Verbs—**1,** imprison, immure, incarcerate, confine, entomb, put in irons; arrest, detain, take into custody, capture, pick up, apprehend, take prisoner, run in, lead into captivity; send to prison, commit; give in custody, subjugate. *Informal,* nab; put away. *Slang,* collar, haul or pull in, haul up.

2, be imprisoned, serve time. *Slang,* do time, go the full distance.

Adjectives—imprisoned, pent-up, under lock and key, behind bars; condemned; in custody, laid by the heels, under arrest, in hand. *Informal,* in lockup, inside. *Slang,* in stir, in the can, sent up, on ice, up the river.

Quotations—Stone walls do not a prison make, nor iron bars a cage (*Richard Lovelace*), While there is a lower class, I am in it; while there is a criminal element, I am of it; while there is a soul in prison, I am not free (*Eugene Debs*), The thoughts of a prisoner—they're not free either. They keep returning to the same things (*Alexander Solzhenitsyn*).

Antonyms, see LIBERATION, FREEDOM.

---

prissy, *adj., informal,* priggish, prim; sissified, effeminate. See FEMALE.

pristine, *adj.* prime, first, dawnlike, primordial; fresh, dewy, pure, virginal, unspoiled. See BEGINNING, OLDNESS. *Ant.,* used, old.

private, *adj.* personal, secluded, intimate, sequestered; privy, confidential, unofficial; individual, special. See SECLUSION. *Ant.,* public.

privation, *n.* want, LOSS, POVERTY, indigence; deprivation, bereavement, dispossession.

privilege, *n.* option, franchise; prerogative, right; favor, EXEMPTION, exception, immunity, liberty. See RIGHTNESS.

privy, *adj.* personal, SECRET; privy to, apprised of, informed of, posted on, in on, on to (*inf.*), wise to (*inf.*). See CONCEALMENT, SPECIALITY. *Ant.,* public, impersonal.

prix fixe, *Fr.,* [at a] fixed PRICE.

prize, *n.* trophy, medal, award, decoration, laurel; premium, bonus, reward; advantage, privilege; pick, elite. —*v.t.* cherish, treasure, esteem, value. See APPROBATION, LOVE. *Ant.,* penalty.

probability, *n.* likelihood, POSSIBILITY; expectancy, CHANCE. *Ant.,* improbability.

probably, *adv.* likely, hopeful, to be expected, in the cards, in a fair way; plausible, ostensible, well-founded, reasonable, credible, believable, presumable, presumptive, apparent, prima facie. See CHANCE, BELIEF, POSSIBILITY, LIABILITY. *Ant.,* improbably, unlikely.

probe, *v.t.* prod, pierce, stab; sound, fathom; search, investigate, sift, explore; verify. See INQUIRY, MEASUREMENT.

PROBITY
Integrity

Nouns—1, probity, integrity, rectitude; uprightness, conscience; honesty, faith; honor; good faith, bona fides; clean hands; dignity, respectability; right, JUSTICE. See RE-PUTE, INNOCENCE, VIRTUE, RIGHTNESS, GOODNESS.

2, constancy; faithfulness, fidelity, loyalty; incorruption, incorruptibility; allegiance, devotion; trustworthiness, sincerity, candor, veracity. See TRUTH.

3, *(scruples)* punctilio, delicacy, nicety, conscientiousness; scrupulosity, scrupulous-ness, scruple, point of honor; punctuality, honor system.

4, UNSELFISHNESS, disinterestedness, sublimity, chivalry.

5, gentleman, man of honor, honest man, man of his word, fidus Achates, a gentle-man and a scholar; truepenny, straight arrow. *Informal,* square- *or* straight-shooter, brick. *Slang,* trump, regular fellow, good egg, right guy, ace [of spades].

Verbs—deal honorably, squarely, impartially, *or* fairly, play fair; speak *or* tell the truth, speak one's mind, call a spade a spade; do one's duty; keep one's promise *or* word; be as good as one's word; keep faith with; one's word is one's bond; carry the torch. *Informal,* be on the level; be on the up and up; level, shoot straight *or* square. *Slang,* tell it like it is; go straight.

Adjectives—1, upright; honest, veracious, truthful; virtuous, honorable, law-abiding; upstanding; fair, right, just, equitable, impartial, square; open and aboveboard; straightforward, frank, candid, forthright, openhearted, man-to-man, heart-to-heart, straight from the shoulder. *Slang,* on the level, on the up and up, straight [as a die], square-shooting, up-front, legit, kosher, stand-up.

2, constant, faithful, loyal, staunch; true, true-blue, true to the core; trusty, trustwor-thy; as good as one's word, reliable, dependable, to be depended on, steadfast, incor-ruptible, above suspicion. *Informal,* on the up and up, fair and square.

3, conscientious; disinterested, right-minded; high-principled, high-minded; scrupu-lous, religious, strict; nice, punctilious, correct, punctual; respectable, reputable, gen-tlemanly.

Adverbs—honorably, bona fide; on one's honor, on the square, from the heart, in good faith, honor bright, with clean hands.

Phrases—conscience gets a lot of credit that belongs to cold feet; let your conscience be your guide; honesty is the best policy; honesty is more praised than praticed; children and fools tell the truth; practice what you preach; there is honor among thieves.

Quotations—Conscience: the inner voice which warns us that someone may be looking (*H. L. Mencken*), A little sincerity is a dangerous thing, and a great deal of it is ab-solutely fatal (*Oscar Wilde*), The Christian ideal has not been tried and found want-ing. It has been found difficult; and left untried (*G. K. Chesterton*), Men should be what they seem (*Shakespeare*), This above all, to thine own self be true (*Shake-speare*), An honest man's word is as good as his bond (*Cervantes*), Being entirely hon-est with oneself is a good exercise (*Sigmund Freud*), The secret of success is sincerity. Once you can fake that, you've got it made (*Jean Giraudoux*), It's annoying to be honest for nothing (*Ovid*), Honesty is for the most part less profitable than dishon-esty (*Plato*).

Antonyms, see IMPROBITY, AFFECTATION.

---

problem, *n.* question, proposition, exer-cise; poser, puzzle, enigma, riddle; is-sue; query. See INQUIRY, SECRET.

problematical, *adj.* questionable, unset-tled, perplexing; uncertain, enigmatic. See DOUBT. *Ant.,* clear, unclouded.

pro bono publico, Lat., for the public good. See UTILITY.

proboscis, *n.* trunk, snout, nose. See CON-VEXITY.

procedure, *n.* process, METHOD, tactics,

proceeding, way, course; practice, CON-
DUCT; policy, ACTION, form. See PLAN.

proceed, *v.i.* continue, progress, advance;
move, arise; emanate, result, issue. See
PROGRESSION, EFFECT. *Ant.,* halt.

proceeding, *n.* ACTION, progress, move,
measure, step, procedure. See OCCUR-
RENCE, LAWSUIT.

proceeds, *n.pl.* balance, profit, gain, yield,
earnings, receipts, issue, outcome, results; income. See MONEY, RECEIVING,
EFFECT.

process, *n.* CONDUCT, METHOD, procedure, practice; course; outgrowth, protuberance, appendage, projection. See
ACTION.

procession, *n.* cavalcade, parade, train,
column, file; progression, sequence,
succession. See CONTINUITY, TRAVEL.

proclaim, *v.t.* announce, declare, broadcast, circulate, publish, herald. See PUB-
LICATION.

proclamation, *n.* announcement, public
statement *or* notice, declaration. See
PUBLICATION.

proclivity, *n.* inclination, TENDENCY,
propensity, proneness, predisposition.
Ant., disinclination.

procrastination, *n.* postponement, delay,
dilatoriness; negligence, omission. See
LATENESS, NEGLECT.

procreate, *v.* breed, reproduce, generate,
beget, give birth. See REPRODUCTION.

proctor, *n.* monitor, overseer, housemas-
ter; AGENT, steward. See DIRECTOR.

procure, *v.t.* acquire, PURCHASE, get, obtain; buy, hire; effect. See CAUSE.

procurer, procuress, *n.* pander, bawd,
pimp; obtainer. See EVILDOER, PUR-
CHASE, ACQUISITION.

prod, *v.t.* shove, goad, prick, spur, poke,
jab; motivate, impel, instigate, incite.
See IMPULSE.

prodigality, *n.* profligacy, WASTE; profusion, profuseness; extravagance, squan-
dering; excess, lavishness; LIBERALITY.
See SUFFICIENCY. *Ant.,* economy.

prodigious, *adj.* immense, enormous, vast,
gargantuan, huge; remarkable, wonderful; monstrous; astonishing. See
WONDER.

prodigy, *n.* phenomenon; WONDER, marvel, miracle; monster; curiosity, sight,
spectacle; precocious child, child
prodigy, boy *or* girl wonder, wiz kid
(*inf.*). See UNCONFORMITY, SKILL.

produce, *n.* goods, yield, harvest; fruit,
vegetables; stock, commodity, product.
See AGRICULTURE, SALE. —*v.* show, exhibit; create, originate, bear, breed,
hatch; make, fashion, manufacture. See
PRODUCTION, REPRODUCTION.

product, *n.* yield, output, produce; outcome, EFFECT, result. See PRODUCTION,
AGRICULTURE.

PRODUCTION
Making or bringing about

Nouns—**1,** production, creation, construction, formation, fabrication, manufacture;
building, erection, edification; coinage; organization; putting together, establishment;
workmanship, performance, operation; achievement, COMPLETION, authorship, PUB-
LICATION, works. See ACTION, PREPARATION.

2, *(something produced)* product, output; edifice, building, structure, fabric; invention, composition; WRITING, book, PAINTING, MUSIC; flower, fruit, work, handiwork;
chef d'œuvre, opus.

3, productiveness, fecundity, fertility, luxuriance; pregnancy, pullulation, fructification, multiplication; fertilization. See REPRODUCTION.

4, producer, creator, originator, inventor, author, founder, generator, mover, architect,
maker; contractor; construction worker, road gang, carpenter, *etc.*

5, *(act or process of producing)* manufacture, manufacturing, fabrication; mass production, assembly line; automation, robotics.

6, factory, plant, mill, foundry, works. See BUSINESS.

Verbs—produce, perform, operate, do, make, FORM, construct, fabricate, frame, contrive; mass-produce, hammer out, manufacture, turn out; weave, forge, coin, carve,
chisel; build, raise, rear, erect, put together; set up, run up, establish, constitute, com-

pose, organize, institute; achieve, accomplish, complete, perfect. *Slang,* churn out. See UTILITY.

Adjectives—produced, producing, productive; formative; fabricated, manufactured, synthetic, artificial, man-made, handmade *or* -crafted, machine-made, hand-built; technocentric.

Quotations—Cultured people are merely the glittering scum which floats upon the deep river of production (*Winston Churchill*).

Antonyms, see DESTRUCTION, USELESSNESS.

---

profane, *adj.* vulgar; sacrilegious, impious, unhallowed. —*v.t.* debase, desecrate, defile, pollute; abuse. See IMPIETY. *Ant.,* sacred.

profess, *n.* pretend, feign; teach, instruct; affirm, declare, avow; own, admit. See AFFIRMATION, FALSEHOOD.

profession, *n.* vocation, calling, occupation; sham, evasion, pretense; affectation, pretension; relief; acknowledgment, declaration, avowal. See AFFIRMATION, BUSINESS.

professor, *n.* academician, teacher, instructor, scholar, don, master, prof (*sl.*), doc (*sl.*). See TEACHING.

proffer, *v.t.* tender, OFFER.

proficient, *adj.* expert, adept, dext[e]rous, adroit; well-versed, practiced; masterly, skillful. See SKILL. *Ant.,* unskilled.

profile, *n.* outline, SIDE, shape, contour; sketch. See APPEARANCE, FORM.

profit, *n.* advantage, benefit, interest; gain, earnings, return. See INCREASE *Ant.,* loss. —*v.* benefit; improve; gain, line one's pockets. See MONEY, UTILITY.

profitable, *adj.* remunerative, lucrative, paying, gainful; advantageous, productive; serviceable, useful. See UTILITY. *Ant.,* unprofitable.

profiteer, *n.* extortionist, leech, highway robber (*inf.*). —*v.i.* overcharge, fleece, extort, hold up (*inf.*), skin (*inf.*), bleed (*inf.*), stick (*sl.*), sting (*sl.*). See STEALING.

profligate, *adj.* wanton, reckless, wild, intemperate; extravagant, wasteful. —*n.* roué, rake, libertine, lecher, reprobate; wastrel, spendthrift, squanderer, playboy. See WASTE, IMPURITY, EVILDOER. *Ant.,* economical.

pro forma, *Lat.,* as a matter of form. See CONFORMITY.

profound, *adj.* erudite, learned, abstruse; heavy, weighty, deep; heartfelt, intense; complete, thorough. See FEELING, GREATNESS, KNOWLEDGE, DEPTH. *Ant.,* shallow.

profusion, *n.* abundance, multiplicity; excess, waste, superfluity, extravagance; plenty. See MULTITUDE, SUFFICIENCY, DIFFUSION, LIBERALITY. *Ant.,* scarcity.

progenitor, *n.* forefather, ancestor; CAUSE. See ANCESTRY.

progeny, *n.* children, offspring, descendants. See POSTERITY.

prognosticate, *v.t.* prophesy, foretell, augur, predict. See PREDICTION.

program, *n.* playbill, prospectus, syllabus; agenda; forecast, draft, outline. See PLAN, CONDUCT.

progress, *n.* advance, growth; development, IMPROVEMENT. —*v.i.* proceed, advance; grow, develop. See PROGRESSION, IMPROVEMENT. *Ant.,* regression.

PROGRESSION
Moving forward

Nouns—progression, progress, progressiveness; MOTION; advance, advancing, advancement; ongoing, chain; floodtide, headway; march (see TRAVEL). See CONTINUITY, TIME.

Verbs—progress, advance, proceed; get on, get along, get under way; gain ground; go with the stream, current, *or* tide; hold *or* keep one's course; push *or* press on, forward, *or* ahead, go, move, go along, pass on; make one's way, work one's way; make progress *or* headway; make rapid strides; gain leeway. *Slang,* go great guns, get rolling, get cracking.

Adjectives—advancing, progressing, progressive, advanced.

Adverbs—progressively; forward, onward, along; forth, on, ahead; under way; en route, on one's way, on the move, on the [high] road; in progress.

Quotations—Men must walk at least before they dance (*Alexander Pope*), Belief in progress is a doctrine of idlers and Belgians. It is the individual relying upon his neighbors to do his work (*Charles Baudelaire*), All progress depends on the unreasonable man (*G. B. Shaw*), That's one small step for [a] man, one giant leap for mankind (*Neil Armstrong*), Is it progress if a cannibal uses a fork? (*Stanislaw J. Lec*).

Antonyms, see REGRESSION.

---

progressive, *adj.* enterprising, advanced, moving; improving, advancing; successive, continuing, continuous. See CONTINUITY, IMPROVEMENT, PROGRESSION. *Ant.,* regressive.

PROHIBITION
Act of forbidding

Nouns—prohibition, inhibition, forbiddance, disallowance, restriction (see RESTRAINT); veto, injunction, interdict[ion], proscription; preclusion, EXCLUSION; embargo, ban, taboo, gag order, no-no, forbidden fruit; prevention, stoppage, HINDRANCE; intemperance act, Volstead Act, Eighteenth Amendment, dry law. See ILLEGALITY, MODERATION.

Verbs—1, prohibit, inhibit, forbid, disallow; veto, kill, ban, interdict; put *or* place under an interdiction *or* ban; taboo, proscribe, enjoin, deny, [de]bar, forfend; preclude, prevent, hinder; set *or* put one's foot down, have none of. *Slang*, spike.

2, exclude, shut out, padlock, keep out; draw the color line, discriminate; shut *or* bolt the door; warn off; forbid the banns; disbar, unfrock.

Adjectives—1, prohibitive, prohibitory, prohibiting, forbidding, *etc.*

2, prohibited, forbidden, verboten, not permitted; unauthorized, unlicensed, illegal; banned, contraband, taboo; out of bounds, off limits.

Adverbs—on no account (see NEGATION).

Interjections—heaven forbid! hands off! keep off! keep out! hold! stop! avast! no thoroughfare! no trespassing!

Quotations—There is a charm about the forbidden that makes it unspeakably desirable (*Mark Twain*), Of course heaven forbids certain pleasures, but one finds means of compromise (*Molière*), I love to sail forbidden seas, and land on barbarous coasts (*Herman Melville*).

Antonyms, see PERMISSION.

---

project, *n.* PLAN, purpose, enterprise; endeavor. —*v.* protrude, bulge, jut; throw, hurl, pitch; devise, plan, scheme, intend. See CONVEXITY, PROPULSION, UNDERTAKING.

projectile, *n.* ball, pellet, bullet, missile, shell. See ARMS.

projection, *n.* extension, shelf; protuberance, protrusion; prominence, spur, eminence; transference, visualization. See CONVEXITY, ANGULARITY, OPTICAL INSTRUMENTS.

projector, *n.* magic lantern, stereopticon; slide projector; cinematograph. See OPTICAL INSTRUMENTS.

proletariat, *n.* working class, laborers, wage earners, labor force, POPULACE. *Ant.,* master.

proliferate, *v.i.* spread, multiply. See MULTITUDE, REPRODUCTION.

prolific, *adj.* fruitful, fecund, productive, fertile; lavish. See PRODUCTION, IMAGINATION. *Ant.,* unfruitful.

prolix, *adj.* lengthy, wordy, long-winded, discursive, verbose, diffuse; tedious. See DIFFUSENESS. *Ant.,* taciturn.

prologue, *n.* preface, introduction, proem, preamble, prelude. See DRAMA, PRECEDENCE.

prolong, *v.t.* extend, protract, hold; sustain, perpetuate, continue; lengthen. See LENGTH, DURABILITY. *Ant.,* shorten.

promenade, *n.* mall, alameda, boulevard, esplanade, boardwalk; promenade deck; stroll, outing, march; dance, ball. —*v.* walk, stroll, saunter. See TRAVEL, AMUSEMENT.

prominent, *adj.* notable, important, salient, memorable; convex, raised, protuberant, projecting, jutting; influential, distinguished, eminent; conspicuous, noticeable. See CONVEXITY, IMPORTANCE, REPUTE, ELEVATION, VISIBILITY. *Ant.,* unimportant.

promiscuous, *adj.* indiscriminate, mixed, miscellaneous, confused. See MIXTURE, DISORDER, IMPURITY.

promise, *n.* pledge, word. —*v.* give one's word; bid fair, show promise. See PROMISE, EXPECTATION, HOPE.

PROMISE
Pledge to do something

Nouns—1, promise, UNDERTAKING, word, troth, pledge, parole, word of honor, vow, avowal; oath (see AFFIRMATION); assurance, warranty, guarantee; insurance, obligation, mortgage; covenant, contract, compact, commitment; engagement, affiance (see MARRIAGE). See SECURITY, EVIDENCE, DUTY.

2, fiancé[e]; man of his word; promised land.

Verbs—1, promise; give *or* make a promise, undertake, engage; make *or* enter into an engagement; bind, pledge, *or* commit oneself; take upon oneself; vow; give, pledge, *or* plight one's word, swear; plight one's troth; betroth, plight faith, take an oath; assure, warrant, guarantee; covenant, attest (see EVIDENCE); contract an obligation; become bound to, become sponsor for; answer for, be answerable for; secure; give security; underwrite; promise the moon. *Informal,* cross one's heart, swear to God.

2, extract a promise, adjure, administer an oath, put to one's oath, swear a witness, swear in.

Adjectives—promising, promissory; votive; under hand and seal, upon *or* under oath; contractual; promised, affianced, pledged, bound; committed, compromised; in for it.

Interjections—so help me! cross my heart [and hope to die]!

Quotations—Politicians are the same all over. They promise to build bridges even when there are no rivers (*Nikita Khrushchev*), Men are all alike in their promises. It is only in their deeds that they differ (*Molière*), The woods are lovely, dark and deep, but I have promises to keep, and miles to go before I sleep (*Robert Frost*), We grew up founding our dreams on the infinite promise of American advertising (*Zelda Fitzgerald*).

Antonyms, see REFUSAL.

---

promising, *adj.* encouraging, auspicious. See HOPE. *Ant.,* hopeless.

promontory, *n.* spit, headland, cape. See HEIGHT, CONVEXITY.

promote, *v.t.* advance, further, AID; improve, dignify, elevate, raise; back, support, encourage. See IMPROVEMENT. *Ant.,* hinder.

promoter, *n.* founder, organizer, planner; backer, supporter, encourager. See PLAN.

prompt, *v.t.* incite, induce, motivate; actuate; remind, suggest, mention. See INFORMATION, MEMORY, CAUSE, INFLUENCE. —*adj.* immediate, ready, punctual, unretarded; alert, quick, active; instant, instantaneous; reasonable, early. See EARLINESS. *Ant.,* dilatory.

prompter, *n.* reminder; note, tickler, cue card, TelePrompTer; promptbook. See MEMORY.

promulgate, *v.t.* publish, disseminate, proclaim, sponsor, advocate. See PUBLICATION.

prone, *adj.* inclined, disposed, likely, predisposed; recumbent, flat, prostrate, HORIZONTAL. See POSSIBILITY.

prong, *n.* tine, point, pincer, spike, tooth, fang; extension. See SHARPNESS.

pronounce, *v.t.* speak, say, utter, enunciate, articulate; deliver, judge, conclude; affirm, assert. See AFFIRMATION, SPEECH.

pronto, *adv., informal,* at once, immediately. See INSTANTANEITY.

pronunciation, *n.* utterance, saying, voicing,

articulation, enunciation, orthoepy. See SPEECH.

proof, *n.* EVIDENCE, substantiation, verification, confirmation; conclusiveness; corroboration, ratification; trial, test; sample, impression. See DEMONSTRATION, EXPERIMENT. —*adj.* impenetrable, impervious; invulnerable. See STRENGTH.

prop, *n.* SUPPORT, brace, stay, pillar, underpin, shore, column, block, base; foundation; mainstay, assistant, helper, staff; fulcrum; truss; property. See DRAMA, PROPULSION. —*v.t.* SUPPORT, uphold, brace, encourage, back; truss; shore, underpin, underset.

propaganda, *n.* publicity; persuasion, proselytization, movement. See INFORMATION, TEACHING.

propagate, *v.* breed, generate, produce, disseminate; spread, broadcast, publish, increase; multiply. See PRODUCTION, PUBLICATION.

propel, *v.t.* push, force, impel, thrust, shove, drive. See PROPULSION, ROTATION.

propeller, *n.* propulsor, impeller, prop (*inf.*); rotor, blade, airfoil, screw. See PROPULSION, ROTATION.

propensity, *n.* TENDENCY, aptitude, inclination, talent, bent, proclivity, disposition.

proper, *adj.* correct, fastidious; suitable, becoming; decorous, demure, chaste, delicate; individual, special, limited, own, appropriate, pertinent, apropos, meet; seemly, befitting; equitable, fair, right, just. See RIGHTNESS, SPECIALITY, ELEGANCE, EXPEDIENCE, JUSTICE. *Ant.,* improper.

property, *n.* quality, characteristic; ownership; POSSESSION, real estate, LAND; (*pl.*) props, stage settings, stage furniture. See DRAMA, QUALIFICATION.

prophecy, *n.* PREDICTION, prognosis, forecast, augury, divination.

prophet, *n.* oracle, soothsayer, prognosticator, sibyl; predictor, seer, diviner. See PREDICTION.

prophylactic, *adj.* preventive, precautionary, preservative, protective. See HEALTH. —*n.* contraceptive, condom. See IMPOTENCY.

propinquity, *n.* NEARNESS; vicinity, proximity; adjacency; RELATION; juxtaposition. *Ant.,* DISTANCE.

propitiate, *v.t.* pacify, conciliate, reconcile; intercede, calm, mediate; atone. See ATONEMENT, PACIFICATION.

propitious, *adj.* encouraging, auspicious; gracious; fortunate, prosperous, favorable; timely, opportune; thriving. See HOPE, PROSPERITY, OCCASION. *Ant.,* inauspicious.

proponent, *n.* advocate, supporter; defender, champion, backer. See FRIEND, VINDICATION. *Ant.,* enemy.

proportion, *n.* dimension, ratio, extent; share, part, quota, distribution, allotment; adjustment, uniformity; magnitude. See APPORTIONMENT, SYMMETRY, RELATION, SIZE.

proportional, *adj.* proportionate, commensurable, measurable. See NUMBER, EQUALITY.

proportionate, *adj.* commensurate, proportionable, proportional, according. See AGREEMENT, RELATION. *Ant.,* incommensurate.

proposal, *n.* OFFER, statement, recommendation, proposition, motion, suggestion; REQUEST, overture, advance, PLAN.

propose, *v.* propound, advance, present, state; recommend, suggest; court, WOO; intend; proffer, nominate. See ENDEARMENT, SUPPOSITION, SUBMISSION.

proposition, *n.* OFFER, PLAN, project, proposal, undertaking; axiom, hypothesis, theorem, postulate, problem, thesis, predication. See REASONING. —*v.t.,* slang, solicit, hit on. See REQUEST, SEX.

propound, *v.t.* propose, state, suggest. See SUPPOSITION.

proprietary, *adj.* private, patented; possessive. See POSSESSION.

proprietor, proprietress, *n.* manager, owner; master, mistress, lord, lady. See POSSESSION.

propriety, *n.* decorum, conventionality, suitability; aptness, fitness; fastidiousness, becomingness, delicacy, decorum, seemliness; prudery. See AGREEMENT, EXPEDIENCE, FASHION.

PROPULSION
Driving forward

Nouns—1, propulsion, projection; push (see IMPULSE); ejaculation; EJECTION; throw, fling, toss, shot.

2, propeller, driver, turbine (see POWER); shooter, archer, bowman, rifleman, marksman, pitcher; good shot, crack shot, sharpshooter.

Verbs—propel, project, throw, fling, cast, pitch, chuck, toss, jerk, heave, shy, hurl; dart, lance, tilt; jet, squirt, spurt, ejaculate; fulminate, bolt, drive, sling, pitchfork; send; send, let, *or* fire off; discharge, shoot; launch, catapult, send forth; let fly; dash; put *or* set in motion; set going, start; give a start, give an impulse to; impel, expel, put to flight, send flying, put [a shot].

Adjectives—propelled, propelling, propulsive, projectile; self-propelled, automotive, automobile.

Antonyms, see TRACTION, REPULSION.

---

pro rata, *Lat.* in proportion. See RELATION.

prosaic, *adj.* unimaginative, dull, uninteresting, commonplace, prosy, plain, sober; unromantic. See WEARINESS, INSIPIDITY. *Ant.*, poetic.

proscribe, *v.t.* outlaw, forbid, interdict, prohibit, condemn; excommunicate, exile, curse. See PROHIBITION, CONDEMNATION. *Ant.*, permit.

prose, *n.* WRITING, style; fiction, nonfiction, prose poem, deathless prose (*inf.*); journalese, hack work.

prosecute, *v.* urge, pursue, follow, continue, press; arraign, sue, indict, charge. See LAWSUIT, PURSUIT, ACCUSATION.

proselyte, *n.* convert, follower, neophyte. See CHANGE, PIETY.

prosody, *n.* metrics, poetics, verse craft; rhyme, rhythm, meter. See POETRY.

prospect, *n.* view, outlook, scene, landscape, vista, sight; promise, probability, HOPE, EXPECTATION, foresight. See APPEARANCE, FUTURITY.

prospective, *adj.* probably, foreseen, expected; coming; imminent. See EXPECTATION.

prospector, *n.* miner, gold panner, placer miner, desert rat (*inf.*), sourdough (*inf.*), forty-niner (*inf.*). See INORGANIC MATTER.

prospectus, *n.* presentation, brochure, catalog; description, sketch; design, scheme. See LIST, PLAN.

PROSPERITY
Financial success

Nouns—1, prosperity, welfare, well-being; affluence, wealth, SUCCESS; thrift; good fortune, blessings, luck; sunshine; fair weather, fair wind; fat years, palmy days, halcyon days; boom, heyday; golden time, golden age; bed of roses, charmed life; lucky star; cornucopia, horn of plenty; fat of the land, milk and honey, good times; godsend, windfall, winning streak, manna from heaven; affluent society, American dream; Aladdin's cave. *Informal,* land-office business; lucky break, streak *or* run of luck, Lady Luck. *Slang,* fat city, high cotton. See MONEY, CHANCE.

2, rich person (see MONEY); Midas touch.

Verbs—1, prosper, grow, multiply, thrive, flourish; be prosperous; go well, smoothly, *or* swimmingly; flower, blow, burgeon, blossom, bloom, fructify, bear fruit, pay off; fatten, batten; live high off the hog. *Informal,* look like a million dollars. *Slang,* clean up.

2, rise [in the world], get on in the world; climb the ladder of success; make one's way *or* fortune; feather one's nest; bear *or* lead a charmed life; bask in the sunshine; have a run of luck, come on; have good fortune, have one's ship come in; take a favorable turn; live off the fat of the land, live in clover; win out, make a strike, make a hit, strike it rich, coin *or* make money. *Slang,* make one's pile, luck out, have it made, hit the jackpot, clock a grip.

Adjectives—prosperous; thriving; fruitful; well-to-do, in the chips, rich, wealthy, affluent; fortunate, lucky, in luck, in clover, in the lap of luxury, on easy street, in the clear; auspicious, propitious, providential; in the black; palmy, halcyon. *Slang,* in the chips *or* money, sitting pretty, chopping high, in the bacon.

Phrases—every dog has his day; sitting on top of the world; born with a silver spoon in one's mouth; be fruitful and multiply; have money to burn; the rich would have to eat money, but luckily the poor provide food.

Quotations—It is easier for a camel to go through the eye of a needle, than for a rich man to enter into the kingdom of God (*Bible*), Riches are for spending (*Francis Bacon*), The chief enjoyment of riches consists in the parade of riches (*Adam Smith*), To be clever enough to get all that money, one must be stupid enough to want it (*G. K. Chesterton*), The meek shall inherit the earth, but not the mineral rights (*J. P. Getty*), If you are poor today, you will always be poor. Only the rich acquire riches (*Martial*), Wealth . . . and poverty; . . . the one is the parent of luxury and indolence, and the other of meanness and viciousness, and both of discontent (*Plato*).

Antonyms, see ADVERSITY.

---

prostitute, *n.* whore, harlot, tart (see IMPURITY).

prostrate, *adj.* recumbent, prone, flat, supine; debased, abased, humbled; helpless, powerless, resigned. See HORIZONTAL. —*v.t.* debase, abase, flatten; bow, submit. See DEJECTION, LOWNESS, SERVILITY.

prosy, *adj.* See PROSAIC.

protagonist, *n.* lead, hero[ine], headliner. See DRAMA.

protect, *v.t.* defend, guard, shelter, shield, screen; preserve, save, champion, secure. See SAFETY.

protection, *n.* safeguard, DEFENSE, shelter, screen; championship, custody, care, guard; foil. See INFLUENCE, RESTRAINT, SAFETY.

protégé, protégée, *n.* ward, charge; pupil, trainee. See LEARNING, SUBJECTION.

pro tempore, Lat., for the time being. See TRANSIENTNESS.

protest, *n.* objection, complaint, remonstrance, contradiction, disapproval, expostulation, protestation. —*v.t.* object, remonstrate, complain, contradict, repudiate, default; declare (see AFFIRMATION). See DISSENT, DISAPPROBATION, NONPAYMENT, REFUSAL. *Ant.,* approve.

Protestant, *n.* non-Catholic, dissenter; Presbyterian, Baptist, Methodist, *etc.* See RELIGION, DISSENT.

protocol, *n.* draft, RECORD; customs, procedures. See CONFORMITY.

prototype, *n.* original; model, pattern; precedent; standard, type; archetype; module, exemplary, example, paradigm; test, copy design; keynote, die, mold; matrix, last. See CONFORMITY, PREPARATION.

protract, *v.t.* extend, lengthen; prolong, continue; postpone, defer, delay; chart. See LENGTH; DURABILITY.

protrude, *v.* jut, bulge, extend, project. See CONVEXITY.

protuberance, *n.* projection, bulge, jut, protuberancy, prominence, excrescence, lump, swelling. See CONVEXITY.

proud, *adj.* See PRIDE.

prove, *v.t.* confirm, verify, substantiate, show, demonstrate, document, check, try, test. See EVIDENCE, CERTAINTY, FEELING. *Ant.,* disprove.

provender, *n.* fodder, feed; FOOD, provisions.

proverb, *n.* MAXIM, axiom, adage, precept, saying.

provide, *v.* See PROVISION.

provided, *adv.* if, supposing, though. See CIRCUMSTANCE.

providential, *adj.* fortunate, lucky, fortuitous, timely, opportune, reasonable, auspicious. See PROSPERITY, OCCASION. *Ant.,* improvidential.

province, *n.* function, sphere; field, department, division, bailiwick, district; control; domain, jurisdiction. See BUSINESS, REGION.

provincial, *adj.* intolerant, illiberal; insular, narrow; local, rural, countrified; rustic. See NARROWNESS, MISJUDGMENT, ABODE. *Ant.,* urban, catholic.

provision, *n.* PREPARATION; proviso, condition; (*pl.*) stores, supplies. See QUALIFICATION, STORE.

PROVISION
Supplying with goods

Nouns—1, provision, purveyance, replenishment, reinforcement; subsidy, grant; stock, STORE; MEANS; equipment, furnishings, accoutrements, appurtenances, outfit, apparatus, gear, trappings; rig, tackle; matériel (see ARMS); grist [to the mill], FOOD, feed, fare, victuals, eatables, viands, nourishment, nutrition, provender.

2, PREPARATION, planning, arrangement, precaution, provident care.

3, provider, caterer, purveyor, supplier, commissary, commissariat, quartermaster, feeder, batman, victualer, grocer, merchant, steward, manciple, purser, innkeeper, restaurateur, sutler; breadwinner.

Verbs—1, provide, furnish, afford, supply, equip, fit out *or* up, gear, accouter; serve; arm; provision, victual, provender, cater, purvey, forage, feed, recruit, find; stock, lay in, come up with; make good, replenish, fill (up); outsource.

2, make provision for, take measures for, prepare *or* plan for; STORE, have in store, have in reserve; keep [handy *or* at hand]; have to fall back on, save for a rainy day.

3, provide for, make *or* earn a living, support, board; make one's way, make ends meet; manage. *Slang,* heel.

Adjectives—provided, prepared; well-stocked, -equipped, *etc. Slang,* well-heeled.

Phrases—take the goods the gods provide.

Antonyms, see WASTE, REFUSAL.

---

provisional, *adj.* conditional; temporary. See BETWEEN, QUALIFICATION. *Ant.,* unconditional.

proviso, *n.* condition[s], stipulation, clause, agreement; QUALIFICATION, reservation, covenant.

provisory, *adj.* provisional, conditional, dependent, subject. See QUALIFICATION.

provocation, *n.* aggravation, irritation, vexation, annoyance, indignity, affront. See DEFIANCE, EXCITEMENT.

provocative, *adj.* tantalizing, titillating; racy, piquant. See TASTE, ATTENTION, EXCITEMENT, ATTRACTION. *Ant.,* innocuous.

provoke, *v.t.* annoy, irritate, exasperate, nettle; excite, arouse; anger, incite, evoke, elicit; goad, vex. See CAUSE, EXCITEMENT, RESENTMENT.

prow, *n.* bow, FRONT, beak, nose, stem.

prowess, *n.* COURAGE, bravery, heroism; SKILL, competence.

prowl, *v.i.* ramble, wander, roam; lurk, slink, sneak; rove. See CONCEALMENT.

prowler, *n.* [sneak] thief, robber. See STEALING.

proximity, *n.* NEARNESS, vicinity, propinquity, neighborhood. *Ant.,* DISTANCE.

proxy, *n.* substitute, AGENT, delegate, representative; agency; procurator. See COMMISSION, SUBSTITUTION.

prude, *n.* formalist, puritan, prig. See AFFECTATION.

prudence, *n.* discretion, carefulness, CAUTION, circumspection, tact; policy, foresight; CARE, thoughtfulness, judiciousness. See VIRTUE. *Ant.,* imprudence.

prudent, *adj.* discreet, wary, circumspect, prudential, careful, heedful, chary, cautious; wise, politic. See CARE, CAUTION. *Ant.,* imprudent.

prudery, *n.* propriety; prudishness, stiffness, coyness, primness, preciousness. See AFFECTATION.

prudish, *adj.* prim, demure, precious, affected, precise. See AFFECTATION. *Ant.,* liberal, open.

prune, *v.t.* trim, abbreviate, thin, lop; remove. See DEDUCTION.

prurient, *adj.* lewd, obscene (see IMPURITY).

pry, *v.* examine, search, seek, peer, ransack, peek, reconnoiter; raise, force, prize, lever. See CURIOSITY, INQUIRY, VISION.

psalm, *n.* canticle, chorale (see MUSIC).

pseudo, *adj.* spurious, counterfeit, simulated, false, fake, mock. See IMITATION, SIMILARITY.

pseudonym, *n.* sobriquet, alias, nom de guerre; pen name, nom de plume; byname, nickname, epithet; disguise, incognito, John Doe, Richard Roe. See CONCEALMENT, NOMENCLATURE.

psych, *v.t.*, *slang* —**psych out**, outwit (see CUNNING); undo, demoralize (see FEAR). —**psych up**, prepare, prime, pump up. See PREPARATION. •

psyche, *n.* soul, pneuma, anima; self-personality, spirit, inner being, essence, essential nature, id, ego, and superego; INTELLECT.

psychiatrist, *n.* mental *or* mind doctor, [psycho]analyst *or* -therapist, alienist, psychiater (*archaic*), crazy *or* bug doctor (*sl.*), headshrinker (*sl.*), shrink (*sl.*). See INTELLECT.

psychic, *adj.* clairvoyant, prophetic, extrasensory, parapsychological, spiritualist, telepathic. —*n.* teleporter, mind reader, fortune-teller, seer, spiritualist,

mentalist, clairvoyant, medium. See INTELLECT.

psychopath, *n.* neurotic, psychotic, madman, psycho (*sl.*). See INSANITY.

psychosis, *n.* neuropsychosis, schizophrenia, dementia praecox, *etc.* See INSANITY.

psychotherapy, *n.* psychotherapeutics, psychiatry. See INTELLECT.

psychotic, *adj.* psychopathic, demented (see INSANITY).

pub, *n.* tavern, public house. See FOOD, DRINKING.

puberty, *n.* pubescence, adolescence, nubility, maturity. See YOUTH.

public, *adj.* popular, common, general; civic, political, national; notorious, known, published; communal, free. See PUBLICATION, POPULACE, HUMANITY. *Ant.*, private.

PUBLICATION
Act of publishing or disseminating

Nouns—1, publication, desktop publishing; announcement; NEWS, INFORMATION; promulgation, propagation, proclamation; circulation; bulletin, edition; hue and cry; banns; notification; divulgation, DISCLOSURE; publicity, notoriety, currency; VOX POPULI; report; newscast, broadcast, telecast, simulcast, radio; spotlight, limelight, white glare of publicity; public relations; blurb, plug, puff, write-up; press kit; author's tour. *Slang*, PR, promo. See WRITING, PRINTING, DISCLOSURE.

2, (*periodical media*) the press; newspaper, journal, gazette, paper, organ; scandal sheet, yellow sheet, tabloid; daily, weekly; magazine, review, periodical; serial; monthly, bimonthly, *etc.*; issue, number, album, portfolio; annual, journal. See NEWS.

3, volume, folio, tome, opus (see BOOK).

4, advertisement; press *or* publicity release; handout, placard, bill, broadside; poster; billboard, hoarding, sandwich board; flier, circular, brochure, circular letter, [bulk] mailing; manifesto; public notice, skywriting; negative advertising, push-polling. *Informal*, ad, want ad, classified ad; commercial, info[r]mercial, spot announcement; hitchhiker, cowcatcher; personal [ad], cross-posting, spamming, junk mail.

5, publisher, publicist, journalist, columnist, press agent; vanity *or* subsidy publisher; publicitor, sales rep[resentative], bookman; announcer, broadcaster, commentator, analyst; writer, author (see WRITING); printer, printer's devil. *Slang*, flack, PR man *or* woman.

6, bookstore, bookstall, bookseller; publishing house, small press, university *or* academic press, vanity press.

Verbs—1, publish; edit; put, get, *or* bring out; come out, appear, hit the stands. *Informal*, put to bed.

2, make public, make known, publicize, advertise, circularize; air; voice, broach, utter; circulate, promulgate, propagate; spread abroad; disseminate; issue; bandy about; bruit abroad; drag into the open; raise a hue and cry; spread the word *or* the Gospel; put on the wire; wash one's dirty linen in public; make a scene; wear one's heart on one's sleeve; get around *or* about, go the rounds.

3, report; proclaim, herald, blazon; trumpet forth; announce; beat the drum; shout *or* proclaim from the housetops; advertise, post; rumor, gossip, chatter, tattle; hang out one's shingle.

Adjectives—published, public, current, newsy, new, in circulation, afloat; notorious; flagrant, arrant, open; encyclical, promulgatory; broadcast; hardbound, paperbound.

Adverbs—publicly; in print, in public; in the air; on the air.

Phrases—it pays to advertise; any publicity is good publicity.

Quotations—Advertising may be described as the science of arresting human intelligence long enough to get money from it (*Stephen Leacock*), Society drives people crazy with lust and calls it advertising (*Bert Lahr*), Journalism largely consists in saying "Lord Jones Dead" to people who never knew that Lord Jones was alive (*G. K. Chesterton*), You can tell the ideals of a nation by its advertisements (*Norman Douglas*), Half the money I spend on advertising is wasted, and the trouble is, I don't know which half (*John Wanamaker*).

Antonyms, see SILENCE, CONCEALMENT.

publicity, *n.* notoriety, limelight; utterance, outlet, vent. See PUBLICATION.

pucker, *n.* wrinkle, crease, crinkle, ruffle, shirring. —*v.* contract; corrugate, crinkle, wrinkle, shirr, ruffle. See FOLD.

pudding, *n.* dessert, custard, junket. See FOOD.

puddle, *n.* pool, pond; mud puddle. See WATER, COHERENCE.

pudgy, *adj.* thickset, stocky, squat; plump, chubby, roly-poly. See SIZE.

puerile, *adj.* trivial, foolish, trifling, weak, nonsensical; childish, immature, boyish, juvenile. See YOUTH, IGNORANCE. *Ant.*, adult.

puff, *n.* swelling; blow, breath, cloud, wind, breeze; *informal*, gesture, praise. —*v.* brag, boast, praise, commend; blow, pant, gasp; inflate. See APPROBATION, BOASTING, INCREASE, FLATTERY.

pugilism, *n.* boxing, fisticuffs. See CONTENTION.

pugnacious, *adj.* combative, quarrelsome, militant, belligerent, contentious, bellicose. See CONTENTION, IRASCIBILITY. *Ant.*, pacific.

puke, *v.*, *vulgar*, vomit, retch, gag. See EJECTION.

pull, *n.* power, sway; jerk, wrench, tug; magnetism, gravity, ATTRACTION; *slang*, INFLUENCE. —*v.* tug, wrench, haul, drag, draw; extract; row, paddle; tow. See EXTRACTION, EXERTION, TRACTION.

pulp, *n.* paste, dough; curd; pap; jam, pudding; poultice; mush. See SOFTNESS.

pulpit, *n.* platform, rostrum, desk; priesthood, ministry. See TEMPLE.

pulsate, *v.i.* beat, throb; drum, palpitate. See OSCILLATION.

pulse, *v.i.* throb, beat, quiver, palpitate; thump; shudder, tremble; pulsate, vibrate. See OSCILLATION, AGITATION, REGULARITY.

pulverize, *adj.* crush, powder, crumble. See POWDERINESS.

pummel, *v.t.* pommel, beat, belabor. See IMPULSE, PUNISHMENT.

pump, *v.t.* draw, suck [out]; interrogate, question, catechize; inflate, puff up. See INQUIRY, WIND, EXTRACTION.

pun, *n.* wordplay, paronomasia, pundigrion, calembour, equivoque; quip, joke, double entendre; paragram. See WIT, SIMILARITY.

punch, *v.t.* strike, hit, poke, beat, knock; puncture, perforate, pierce. See IMPULSE, OPENING.

punchy, *adj.*, *informal*, dazed, confused; punch-drunk. See INSENSIBILITY.

punctilious, *adj.* conscientious, scrupulous; exact, precise; formal, ceremonious; severe, strict. See OSTENTATION.

punctual, *adj.* prompt, regular, precise, punctilious; periodical; early, timely. See EARLINESS, REGULARITY.

punctuate, *v.t.* point, interpoint, interpunctuate; accentuate; interrupt. See GRAMMAR, IMPORTANCE.

puncture, *n.* perforation, hole, pinprick, OPENING. —*v.t.* pierce, jab, perforate, prick.

pundit, *n.* wise man, sage, savant, know-it-all, wise guy (*sl.*). See KNOWLEDGE, TEACHING, CLERGY.

PUNGENCY
Caustic nature

Nouns—1, pungency, piquancy, poignancy, tang, raciness, *haut goût*, strong TASTE; sharpness, keenness, acrimony, acritude, acridity, astringency, acerbity, SOURNESS, gaminess; tartness, spiciness, heat, acidity, causticity, bite, tang. *Informal,* zip, nip, punch, ginger. See ODOR, MALODOROUSNESS.

2, mustard, cayenne, pepper, salt, brine, mace, onion, garlic, pickle, ginger, caviar; seasoning, spice, relish, condiment, catsup, curry, vinegar, sauce piquante; ammonia, smelling salts, niter. See FOOD.

3, nicotine, tobacco, snuff, quid; cigarette, smoke, regular, king-size, long[-size], plain, oval, cork tip, filter tip, 100; cigar, cheroot, stogie, panatela, perfecto, corona, belvedere; cigarillo; smokeless tobacco. *Slang,* coffin nail, cig, fag, butt, gasper, tube, weed, reefer, peewee, slim, square, cancer stick.

Verbs—be pungent, bite the tongue, sting; season, [be]spice, salt, pepper, pickle, curry, brine, devil; smoke, puff, chain smoke; chew, take snuff.

Adjectives—pungent, piquant, poignant, tangy, racy; sharp, keen, acrid, acerb, acrimonious, astringent, bitter; sour (see SOURNESS); unsavory (see TASTE); gamy, high, strong, high- *or* full-flavored, high-tasted; biting, stinging, mordant, caustic, pyrotic, burning, acid; odiferous (see ODOR); piercing, pricking, penetrating, stimulating, appetizing; tart, spicy, spiced, seasoned, peppery, hot [as pepper]; salt[y], saline, brackish, briny; nutty, zesty. *Informal,* zippy, snappy.

Quotations—He who lives without tobacco is not worthy to live (*Molière*), What this country needs is a really good 5-cent cigar (*Thomas Marshall*), I smoked my first cigarette and kissed my first woman on the same day. I have never had time for tobacco since (*Arturo Toscanini*), A woman is only a woman, but a good cigar is a smoke (*Rudyard Kipling*), I have never smoked in my life and look forward to a time when the world will look back in amazement and disgust to a practice so unnatural and disgusting (*G. B. Shaw*).

Antonyms, see INSIPIDITY, ODORLESSNESS.

PUNISHMENT
Applying a penalty for an offense

Nouns—1, punishment; chastisement, chastening; correction, castigation; discipline, infliction, trial; judgment, penalty; retribution; thunderbolt, nemesis; requital, RETALIATION; penology. See PAIN, KILLING.

2, *(modes of punishment)* capital punishment, execution, electrocution, hanging, gassing, firing squad, decapitation, crucifixion, lynching, stoning; imprisonment (see PRISON, RESTRAINT); torture, rack, thumbscrew, question; transportation, banishment, expulsion, exile, ostracism, Coventry (see EJECTION); stocks, pillory, cucking stool; penal servitude, hard labor, solitary confinement; galleys; beating, hiding, rawhiding, flagellation, the lash, gauntlet, whipping post; rap on the knuckles, spanking, thrashing, box on the ear; blow (see IMPULSE); walking the plank, keelhauling; picket[ing]; martyrdom, auto-da-fé; harakiri, tarring and feathering, riding on a rail; fine, forfeit. *Informal,* the chair. *Slang,* hot seat, rope necktie, necktie party, kangaroo court, Judge Lynch, Jack Ketch.

3, *(implements of punishment)* scourge, whip, lash [of scorpions], *etc.*, drop, gallows, gibbet, scaffold, rope, noose, halter; block, ax; stake, cross; guillotine, electric chair, gas chamber.

Verbs—1, punish, penalize, chastise, chasten; fine, dock; castigate, correct, inflict punishment; retaliate, administer correction, deal out justice; visit upon; pay; make short work of, give short shrift, give a lesson to, serve one right, let one have it, give it to, make an example of; thrash, flog, spank, cane, whale away, whip; beat *or* mess up. *Informal,* give one his comeuppance; paddle; lower the boom; tan one's hide, skin alive; settle one's hash, throw the book at. *Slang,* give what for, give hell, make it hot for, work over, kick ass.

2, strike, hit, *etc.* (see IMPULSE).

3, execute, electrocute; behead, decapitate, guillotine; hang, gibbet, bowstring; shoot; decimate; burn at the stake; boil in oil; break on the wheel; crucify; tar and feather; impale, flay; lynch; torture, put on the rack, picket. *Informal,* string up. *Slang,* burn, fry. See KILLING.

4, banish, exile, transport, expel, ostracize; rusticate; drum out; dismiss, disbar, disbench; demote; strike off the roll, unfrock; post. See EJECTION.

5, suffer punishment; take one's medicine, face the music; pay the piper, the fiddler, or the price. *Slang,* take it, take the rap.

Adjectives—punishing, penal, punitory, punitive; castigatory; capital.

Phrases—spare the rod and spoil the child; if you can't do the time, don't do the crime.

Quotations—Men are not hanged for stealing horses, but that horses may not be stolen (*Lord Halifax*), Let the punishment fit the crime (*W. S. Gilbert*), Punishment brings wisdom. It is the healing art of wickedness (*Plato*), The reformative effect of punishment is a belief that dies hard, chiefly, I think, because it is so satisfying to our sadistic impulses (*Bertrand Russell*).

Antonyms, see COMPENSATION.

---

punk, *n., slang,* hood, mug; henchman; kid, delinquent, snotnose [kid]. See YOUTH, EVILDOER.

puny, *adj.* small, underdeveloped, undersized, tiny; stunted. See LITTLENESS. *Ant.,* substantial.

pup, *n.* See PUPPY.

pupil, *n.* student, schoolchild, schoolgirl, schoolboy; learner, tyro, scholar. See LEARNING, SCHOOL.

puppet, *n.* marionette; manikin, doll; figure, tool, cat's-paw, hireling, henchman, vassal. See REPRESENTATION, AMUSEMENT, SERVANT.

puppy, *n.* pup, whelp, cub, youngling; child, tad, *etc.* See YOUTH.

purblind, *adj.* obtuse, dull, stupid; mole-eyed. See VISION.

PURCHASE
Act of buying

Nouns—**1,** purchase, buying, emption; purchasing power; bargain (see CHEAPNESS); installment buying *or* plan, time purchase plan, buying on time, deferred payment, layaway plan, revolving charge plan, hire-purchase (*Brit.*); ACQUISITION, acquirement, procurement, expenditure, conspicuous consumption; PAYMENT; buyout; bribery, bribe, dealing. *Informal,* buy. See OFFER.

2, purchaser, buyer, procurer, emptor, vendee; shopper, marketer, patron, employer; client, customer, consumer; constituency; trafficker; clientry, clientele, patronage. *Slang,* rough trade. See BUSINESS.

Verbs—purchase, buy, invest in, procure, acquire; shop, market, go shopping, bargain for; rent, hire (see BORROWING); repurchase, redeem; buy in; pay (for), spend; make *or* complete a purchase; buy over *or* under the counter; buy out; be in the market for; keep in one's pay, bribe, buy off, suborn. *Slang,* cop.

Adjectives—purchased; purchasable, buyable, available, obtainable; bribable, venal, commercial.

Phrases—caveat emptor, let the buyer beware; the customer is always right; there are more foolish buyers than foolish sellers; I shop, therefore I am.

Quotations—He who findeth fault, meaneth to buy (*Thomas Fuller*).

Antonyms, see SALE.

pure, *adj.* clean, pollution-free; chaste, sinless, immaculate; genuine, sincere; sheer, simple. See PURITY, VIRTUE, INNOCENCE, CLEANNESS, SIMPLENESS. *Ant.,* impure, polluted.

purgative, *n.* cathartic, emetic, laxative, physic, aperient. —*adj.* purifying, cleansing; abstergent, evacuant, cathartic, expulsive, emetic, aperient, physic, laxative; restorative. See CLEANNESS.

purgatory, *n.* limbo, netherworld, underworld; ATONEMENT. See HELL.

purge, *v.t.* cleanse, clarify; flush, wash, clear; atone; pardon, absolve, acquit; expiate; evacuate, remove; liquidate, kill. See ATONEMENT, CLEANNESS, PURITY, KILLING.

purify, *v.t.* refine, distill; cleanse. See PURITY.

puritanical, *adj.* strict, prudish, prim, severe, rigid. See ASCETICISM.

purity, *n.* refinement (see PURITY); sincerity, honesty; abstraction; simplicity. See PROBITY, SIMPLENESS, INNOCENCE, VIRTUE, CLEANNESS. *Ant.,* dishonesty.

PURITY
Freedom from pollution

Nouns—1, purity, pureness, cleanness, *etc.* (see *Adjectives*); refinement, purification, clarification, cleansing; defecation, depilation; filtering, filtration; sublimation, distillation; percolation, leaching, lixiviation; elutriation; strain, sieve. See CLEANNESS.

2, refinery; cleanser, clarifier, defecator, *etc.;* filter, sieve, colander, strainer, screen.

Verbs—purify, make pure, free from impurity, decrassify; clear, clarify, clean, wash, cleanse; rectify; refine, purge, defecate, depurate, expurgate, sublimate; distill; strain (see CLEANNESS).

Adjectives—pure, unadulterated, unalloyed, unmixed, unpolluted, undefiled, untainted, uncorrupted; refined; genuine, real, true, simple, perfect, clear; fine; full-blooded, thoroughbred; clean, unspoiled, unblemished, untarnished, unviolated, wholesome.

Antonyms, see IMPURITY.

purlieus, *n. pl.* neighborhood, environs, surroundings, outskirts, limits, bounds, confines. See NEARNESS.

purple, *adj. & n.* See COLOR.

purport, *n.* MEANING, significance, import, sense.

purpose, *n.* INTENTION, determination, resolution, resolve; END, aim, view.

purposeful, *adj.* determined, resolved; intentional. See RESOLUTION, INTENTION. *Ant.,* irresolute.

purse, *n.* handbag, reticule, pocketbook, wallet, moneybag, fanny pack (*sl.*); MONEY, exchequer, funds; prize.

pursuant, *adj.* following; according. See INTENTION.

pursue, *v.t.* follow (see PURSUIT); continue; seek after; be engaged in, undertake. See INQUIRY, UNDERTAKING, BUSINESS.

PURSUIT
Act of following

Nouns—1, pursuit; pursuing, prosecution; pursuance; enterprise (see UNDERTAKING, BUSINESS); adventure, quest, INQUIRY; hue and cry; game, hobby. *Slang,* headhunting. See SEQUENCE, SEX.

2, night hunting, shining, jack-lighting, spotlighting.

3, chase, hunt, steeplechase, coursing; safari; venery; foxhunt.

4, pursuer, hunter, huntsman, sportsman, Nimrod; hound, bloodhound; fisher, angler, fisherman *or* -woman; stalker.

Verbs—1, pursue, prosecute, follow, go after, go for; run, take, make, *or* chase after; gun for; carry on, engage in, undertake, set about; endeavor, court, REQUEST; seek, aim at, fish for; press on.

2, chase, give chase, chase or run after, course, dog, hunt [down], hound; track down; tread or follow on the heels of; follow the hounds; run down; trail, shadow, dog; stalk. *Informal,* breathe down one's neck, doorstep, cruise. *Slang,* tail.

Adjectives—pursuing, in search or quest of, in pursuit, in full cry, in hot pursuit; on the trail, track, or scent.

Adverbs—in pursuance of; at one's heels; after. *Informal,* on the prowl.

Phrases—seek and ye shall find; set a thief to catch a thief.

Quotations—The English country gentleman galloping after a fox—the unspeakable in full pursuit of the uneatable (*Oscar Wilde*), When a man wants to murder a tiger he calls it sport; when a tiger wants to murder him, he calls it ferocity (*G. B. Shaw*).

Antonyms, see AVOIDANCE.

---

purvey, *v.t.* deliver, yield, hand, give; provide, furnish, cater, PROVISION.

purview, *n.* scope, extent, range (see DISTANCE).

pus, *n.* matter, suppuration, purulence. See UNCLEANNESS.

push, *n.* nudge, thrust, shove; pressure, exigency; crisis, pinch; *informal,* endeavor, effort, drive, determination, perseverance, persistence, aggressiveness. See CIRCUMSTANCE. —*v.t.* drive, urge, force; propel, advance, impel; shove, encourage, hearten; prosecute. See IMPULSE, PROPULSION. *Ant.,* pull.

pushover, *n., slang,* easy mark, cinch (*inf.*), sucker (*inf.*), duck soup (*sl.*), set up (*sl.*). See FACILITY.

pushy, *adj.* aggressive. See ATTACK.

pusillanimous, *adj.* cowardly, mean-spirited. See COWARDICE. *Ant.,* courageous.

pussy-foot, *v.t.* tiptoe, walk on eggs; beat around the bush, hedge. See AVOIDANCE, CAUTION.

put, *v.t.* place, locate, set, deposit, plant, fix, lay; cast, throw; thrust; impose, rest, stick. See LOCATION, PROPULSION. —**put down,** attribute; inscribe, write down; *slang,* suppress, smash; *slang,* snub. See ATTRIBUTION, WRITING, RESTRAINT, CONTEMPT. —**put forward,** propose, suggest (see SUBMISSION. — **put off,** postpone, delay; avoid. See LATENESS, AVOIDANCE. —**put out,** vex, offend; inconvenience, discommode,

impose on; extinguish, douse; expel; expend, spend. See DISCONTENT, INEXPEDIENCE, DESTRUCTION, EXPULSION, PAYMENT. —**put up with,** suffer, tolerate. See LENIENCY.

putative, *adj.* thought, alleged, considered, supposed, reputed, presumed. See SUPPOSITION.

putdown, *n., slang,* insult, slight, rejection. See DETRACTION.

putrefy, *v.i.* rot, decay, decompose. See UNCLEANNESS.

putrid, *adj.* decomposed, decayed, rank, foul, rotten, corrupt. See UNCLEANNESS, BADNESS.

putter, *v.i.* dabble, dawdle, idle, loaf, tinker, fiddle (*inf.*), monkey (*inf.*). See INACTIVITY, UNIMPORTANCE.

puzzle, *n.* riddle, conundrum, poser, enigma; mystification, perplexity, complication; dilemma, bewilderment, confusion. —*v.t.* confound, perplex, bewilder, confuse, mystify. See DIFFICULTY, UNINTELLIGIBILITY, SECRET.

pygmy, *n.* pigmy, dwarf, midget, atomy; Lilliputian. See LITTLENESS. *Ant.,* giant.

pyramid, *n.* pyramidion, polyhedron; progression, pile, accumulation, snowball. See INTERMENT, ANGULARITY, SHARPNESS, INCREASE.

pyromaniac, *n.* arsonist, firebug (*inf.*). See HEAT.

Q

quack, *n.* charlatan, quacksalver, mountebank. See DECEPTION, FALSEHOOD, UNSKILLFULNESS.

quadrangle, *n.* rectangle, square, quad, quadrilateral; yard, compound, court [yard], ENCLOSURE. See ANGULARITY, ABODE.

quaff, *v.t.* drink; swill, guzzle. See DRINKING.

quagmire, *n.* quag, quicksand, marsh [land], mire, fen, morass, bog, slough; dilemma, problem, DIFFICULTY. See MOISTURE.

quail, *v.i.* shrink, cower, RECOIL, flinch. See FEAR, COWARDICE. *Ant.*, stand firm.

quaint, *adj.* old-fashioned, picturesque. See UNCONFORMITY.

quake, *v.i.* tremble, quiver, shake, shudder. See AGITATION, FEAR, COLD.

qualification, *n.* modification, restriction (see QUALIFICATION); ABILITY, REPUTE, SKILL.

QUALIFICATION
Act of limiting

Nouns—qualification, limitation, modification, restriction, coloring, leavening; allowance, consideration, extenuating circumstances; condition, proviso, provision, exception (see EXEMPTION); prerequisite, stipulation, specification, saving clause. See SUPPOSITION.

Verbs—qualify, LIMIT, modify, leaven, allow for, make allowance for, take into account *or* consideration, consider, discount; take with a grain of salt.

Adjectives—qualifying, conditional, provisional, provisory; qualified, restrictive, contingent.

Adverbs—conditionally, admitting, admittedly, provided, if, unless, but, yet; nevertheless; according as; supposing; with the understanding, even, although, though, for all that, after all, at all events; with a grain of salt; wind and weather permitting; if possible; subject to; with this proviso, on condition that.

Prepositions—except for, but for.

Phrases—the exception proves the rule.

Quotations—The condition upon which God has given liberty to man is eternal vigilance (*John Philpot Curran*).

Antonyms, see CERTAINTY.

---

qualified, *adj.* competent, fit; limited, restricted. See QUALIFICATION, JUSTICE, PREPARATION. *Ant.*, unqualified, inapt.

quality, *n.* attribute, property; excellence; trait, characteristic; status, brand, grade; NOBILITY, gentility. See ATTRIBUTION, FEELING, INTRINSIC, SPECIALITY.

qualm, *n.* twinge, pang, throe; misgiving, compunction, uneasiness, remorse. See FEAR, PENITENCE.

quandary, *n.* dilemma, plight, perplexity, bewilderment. See DOUBT, DIFFICULTY.

QUANTITY
Amount

Nouns—1, quantity, magnitude, amplitude; numbers, amount; content, mass, bulk, weight; sum, aggregate; MEASUREMENT; number, quantifier; MULTITUDE. See ASSEMBLAGE.

2, portion (see APPORTIONMENT); quantum; handful, armful, pocketful, mouthful, spoonful, *etc.;* batch, lot, stock, supply, STORE; some[what], aught, any, so much, so many.

Verbs—quantify, measure (see MEASUREMENT); count (see NUMERATION).

Adjectives—quantitative, quantitive, numerical, metrical; counted, weighed, figured, calculated, estimated; measurable, weighable, estimable; in bulk, mass, *or* quantity; certain; some, any, more, less; more *or* better than, more *or* less. *Informal,* to the tune of.

Adverbs—in all sizes and shapes.

Phrases—the more the merrier; there is safety in numbers.

Quotations—It is our national joy to mistake for the first-rate, the fecund rate (*Dorothy Parker*).

Antonyms, see UNITY.

---

quantum, *n.* QUANTITY, amount; substance, mass; particle, photon, phonon, magneton, light quantum, ENERGY. See APPORTIONMENT.

quarantine, *n.* detention, detainment, RESTRAINT, confinement, SECLUSION, segregation, sequestration, isolation; cordon sanitaire. —*v.t.* detain, segregate, separate, isolate, sequester. See EXCLUSION.

quarrel, *n.* altercation, wrangle, squabble, spat (*inf.*); dispute, controversy, feud. —*v.i.* dispute, disagree, wrangle, squabble; find fault. See DISCORD, DISAPPROBATION.

quarrelsome, *adj.* contentious, disputatious, pugnacious, combative. See IRASCIBILITY, CONTENTION.

quarry, *n.* prey, game; catch, bag, take; target, pursuit; lode, bed, [stone]pit, mine; STORE, source.

quarter, *n.* one-fourth; trimester; district, REGION, DIRECTION; lodging, billet; mercy; two bits (*inf.*). See SIDE, PITY, LENIENCY, ABODE. —*v.t.* quadrisect; divide, cut up; billet, station. See LOCATION, NUMERATION.

quarters, *n.pl.* ABODE, lodgings, residence; billet, barracks.

quartet, *n.* foursome, quadruplet, tetrad. See NUMERATION.

quash, *v.t.* suppress, subdue, crush; set aside, annul, void. See NULLIFICATION, RESTRAINT.

quasi, *adj.* apparent, seeming, so-called,

pseudo, IMITATION, near, approximate. —*adv.* almost, in a sense, nearly, not quite; as though, as if, as it were, so to speak, seemingly. See SIMILARITY, SUPPOSITION.

quaver, *v.i.* quiver, shake, tremble; tremolo, warble, trill. See OSCILLATION, AGITATION.

quay, *n.* wharf, dock, pier, mole, levee. See ABODE.

queasy, *adj.* nauseated; squeamish, uneasy; timid, fearful, apprehensive; finicky, skittish, jittery. See DISEASE, FEAR. *Ant.,* fearless, confident.

queen, *n.* ruler, mistress; belle. See AUTHORITY, BEAUTY.

queer, *adj.* odd, singular, strange; eccentric, deranged (*inf.*); giddy, faint; *slang,* shady, counterfeit; *slang,* gay, homosexual. See UNCONFORMITY, MALE, FEMALE. *Ant.,* usual, normal, straight.

quell, *v.t.* subdue, suppress, crush; quiet, allay. See DESTRUCTION, MODERATION.

quench, *v.t.* put *or* snuff out; extinguish; still; damp, chill; slake, sate, satisfy. See INCOMBUSTIBILITY, DISSUASION, PLEASURE.

querulous, *adj.* whining, complaining, fretful, petulant, peevish. See LAMENTATION, DISCONTENT.

query, *n.* INQUIRY, question, DOUBT.

quest, *n.* search, PURSUIT; probe, investigation, INQUIRY; adventure, mission, expedition; aim, goal, objective, desire.

question, *n.* problem, subject; query, interrogation; DOUBT, dispute. See INQUIRY.
—*v.t.* interrogate, examine, cross-examine, quiz; dispute, challenge, DOUBT.

questionable, *adj.* doubtful, uncertain, debatable, fishy (*inf.*). See DOUBT, IMPROBITY.

questionnaire, *n.* form, blank; examination, interrogation; INQUIRY, survey, canvass, poll.

queue, *n.* cue, pigtail; line[up], file, rank.
—*v.i.* line *or* queue up, form a line, fall in, wait. See CONTINUITY, SEQUENCE.

quibble, *n.* evasion, equivocation, sophism, cavil. See AVOIDANCE, DISSENT, FALSEHOOD.

quick, *adj.* rapid, swift, brief; prompt, alert; ready, unhesitating; hasty, irascible; sensitive, keen; alive, living, sentient. See VELOCITY, ACTIVITY, FEELING, IRASCIBILITY, INTELLIGENCE. *Ant.,* slow, sluggish.

quicken, *v.t.* revive, refresh, arouse, animate; hasten, speed, accelerate. See VELOCITY, AGENCY, HASTE. *Ant.,* retard, slow.

quicksand, *n.* quagmire, mire, morass, bog, slough. See MOISTURE.

quick-tempered, *adj.* impetuous, hotheaded, irascible, hot, peppery. See IRASCIBILITY. *Ant.,* coolheaded, slow to anger.

quiddity, *n.* essence; quintessence, substance, kernel, pith; equivocation, quibble, hairsplitting. See INTRINSIC, WIT.

quid pro quo, *Lat.,* give-and-take, tradeoff, equivalent. See COMPENSATION, RETALIATION, SUBSTITUTION, INTERCHANGE.

quiescent, *adj.* still, motionless, moveless, fixed, stationary; stagnant, becalmed, quiet; tranquil, unmoved, undisturbed, unruffled; calm, restful; sleeping, silent. See INACTIVITY, REPOSE, LATENCY.

quiet, *adj.* peaceful, tranquil, serene; hushed, silent; modest, restrained, subdued; gentle, calm; unostentatious. See REPOSE. —*n.* quietude, peacefulness,

calm; SILENCE, hush. See MODERATION, INEXCITABILITY. *Ant.,* loud, talkative.

quill, *n.* feather; plume; pen; spine, bristle, seta, barb, spike, needle; pick, plectrum. See ROUGHNESS, SHARPNESS.

quilt, *n.* coverlet, patchquilt, comforter, goosedown, quilting. See COVERING.

quintessence, *n.* ideal, PERFECTION.

quintet, *n.* fivesome, quintuplet, pentad. See NUMERATION.

quip, *n.* joke, witticism, retort, repartee, [wise]crack (*sl.*). See WIT.

quirk, *n.* flourish; quip, taunt, jibe; quibble, deviation, evasion; peculiarity, trick, eccentricity. See WIT, INSANITY.

quisling, *n.* traitor (see EVILDOER).

quit, *v.* satisfy, requite; resign, abandon, relinquish, leave; cease, stop, desist. See PAYMENT, RELINQUISHMENT, DISCONTINUANCE, ACQUITTAL, RESIGNATION.

quite, *adv.* entirely, utterly, wholly; really, actually; *informal,* rather, somewhat, very. See COMPLETION.

quittance, *n.* ACQUITTAL, freedom; receipt, quitclaim, relinquishment; retaliation, vindication, ATONEMENT; PAYMENT, recompense.

quitter, *n., informal,* shirker, evader, avoider, slacker (*sl.*), welsher (*sl.*). See AVOIDANCE.

quiver, *v.i.* tremble, shudder, shiver, flutter, vibrate, shake, quaver. See AGITATION.

qui vive, *Fr.,* alertness. See CAUTION, EXCITEMENT.

quixotic, *adj.* visionary, unrealistic, whimsical; foolish, crazy. See RASHNESS.

quiz, *v.t.* interrogate, question, examine; tease, banter. See INQUIRY.

quizzical, *adj.* bantering, teasing; odd, comical. See WIT, ABSURDITY.

quorum, *n.* plenum, SUFFICIENCY, majority.

quota, *n.* allotment, share, proportion, percentage. See APPORTIONMENT.

quotation, *n.* citation, excerpt, REPETITION; PRICE.

quote, *v.t.* repeat, cite, instance, refer to, abstract. See EVIDENCE, REPETITION, PRICE.

R

rabbi, *n.* master, teacher; rabbin, rabbinist. See CLERGY.

rabble, *n.* crowd, proletariat, POPULACE, common herd, hoi polloi; mob, canaille, riffraff, scum. See ASSEMBLAGE.

rabblerouser, *n.* demagogue, agitator, troublemaker. See CAUSE.

rabid, *adj.* mad, furious; fanatical, over-zealous. See FEELING, EXCITEMENT, EXCITABILITY.

rabies, *n.* hydrophobia, lyssa; foaming at the mouth. See DISEASE, INSANITY.

race, *n.* onrush, advance; competition; sprint, dash; stream; channel, millrace, tide, river; career; family, clan, tribe; people, ethnic group. —*v.* rush, career; hasten; compete; speed. See VELOCITY, ANCESTRY, CONTENTION, HUMANITY, OPPOSITION.

raceway, *n.* [race]track, racecourse, oval, turf. See AMUSEMENT, ARENA.

racial, *adj.* tribal, family; hereditary, ancestral. See HUMANITY.

racism, *n.* prejudice, bigotry; segregation, color line, apartheid, Jim Crow (*inf.*); white *or* black supremacy, black nationalism; genocide. See INJUSTICE, MISJUDGMENT.

rack, *v.t.* strain, exert; torture, distress, torment, agonize. See THOUGHT, PAIN. —*n.* single-foot, pace; frame[work]; wheel, iron maiden; scud, broken clouds. See MOTION, CLOUDINESS, SUPPORT.

racket, *n.* uproar, din, clatter, hubbub; frolic, carouse, rumpus, hurly-burly; battledore. See AMUSEMENT, LOUDNESS.

racketeer, *n.* mobster, gangster, hoodlum. See EVILDOER.

raconteur, *n.* narrator, storyteller (see DESCRIPTION).

racy, *adj.* spirited, lively; piquant; *informal,* risqué, suggestive. See VIGOR, PUNGENCY, FEELING. *Ant.,* tame, dull.

radial, *adj.* spoked, radiating. See CIRCULARITY.

radiant, *adj.* shining, sparkling, glowing; splendid, resplendent, glorious. See LIGHT, BEAUTY.

radiation, *n.* DISPERSION, diffusion, emission, emanation; radiance, illumination. See LIGHT.

radical, *adj.* fundamental, INTRINSIC; extreme, drastic, thorough; sweeping, revolutionary. See COMPLETION. —*n.* liberal, leftist, left-winger (see CHANGE); reformer, rebel, revolutionary; anarchist, nihilist, Communist, Bolshevik, red (*inf.*), [parlor] pink (*inf.*), fellow-traveler (*inf.*), Commie (*sl.*), pinko (*sl.*). See REVOLUTION. *Ant.,* superficial; middle-of-the-road.

radio, *n.* wireless, radio telegraphy, radio telephony; radiogram. See COMMUNICATION.

radioactive, *adj.* charged, hot, irradiated; contaminated. See POWER, UNCLEANNESS.

radiology, *n.* X-ray imaging, radioscopy; fluoroscopy, mammography, *etc.*; magnetic resonance imaging, MRI. See INQUIRY.

radius, *n.* half-diameter; spoke; range, scope, sphere, LENGTH. See BREADTH.

raffish, *adj.* rowdy (see VULGARITY).

raffle, *n.* drawing, door prize, lottery, sweepstake[s]. See CHANCE.

raft, *n.* flatboat, barge; float, pontoon; *informal,* MULTITUDE. See SHIP.

rafter, *n.* beam, timber, crosspiece, joist. See SUPPORT.

rag, *n.* shred, tatter, scrap, remnant; ragtime; (*pl.*) castoffs, hand-me-downs. See CLOTHING, MUSIC. —*v.,* *slang,* tease, rib, kid, RIDICULE.

ragamuffin, *n.* tatterdemalion (see DETERIORATION).

rage, *n.* fury, frenzy, wrath, VIOLENCE; FASHION, fad, craze. See DESIRE. —*v.i.* storm, rave, bluster. See EXCITEMENT, EXCITABILITY.

ragged, *adj.* tattered, frayed, shabby,

seedy, worn; in shreds; in patches; patched, torn, rough; tatterdemalion, ragamuffin; dog-eared. See DETERIORATION, DIVESTMENT.

raid, *n.* ATTACK, invasion, onset, incursion; foray. See STEALING. —*v.t.* ATTACK, invade; pounce upon.

rail, *v.* rant, scold, chide; inveigh, carry on, harangue. See DISAPPROBATION.

railing, *n.* fence, barrier, balustrade. See ENCLOSURE.

raillery, *n.* banter, badinage, persiflage, quizzing, kidding, ribbing. See RIDICULE.

railroad, *n.* railway; main *or* trunk line, spur; model railroad; tramline, tramway, trolley *or* streetcar line, street railway, subway. See TRANSPORTATION. —*v., informal,* rush *or* push through, expedite; *slang,* frame, jail. See INJUSTICE.

raiment, *n.* CLOTHING, apparel, attire, vesture, garb.

rain, *n.* shower, precipitation, rainstorm, downpour. —*v.* shower, pour, drizzle; bestow, lavish, shower upon. See WATER.

rainbow, *n.* arc, *arc-en-ciel;* spectrum. See VARIEGATION, COLOR.

rain check, delay, postponement; standing invitation. See LATENESS.

raincoat, *n.* slicker, oilskin, poncho, mackintosh, trenchcoat, rainproof, plastic raincoat. See CLOTHING.

raise, *v.t.* lift, elevate; [a]rouse, stir up, incite; muster, collect; resurrect; erect, build, exalt, honor; INCREASE; cultivate, breed. See ELEVATION, EXCITEMENT, CONVEXITY.

raison d'être, Fr., reason for being *or* living, justification. See INTENTION.

rake, *v.t.* gather, collect; comb, ransack, search, rummage; enfilade, spray with bullets; incline, slope. See ASSEMBLAGE. —*n.* libertine, roué, rakehell; slope, ramp. See CLEANNESS, OBLIQUITY, AGRICULTURE.

rake-off, *n., slang,* rebate, refund, PAYMENT, return, kickback, payoff; payola, share, cut, percentage; bribe; extortion.

rally, *v.* muster, marshal, call together; revive, restore, rouse, encourage; banter, chaff. See COURAGE, ASSEMBLAGE.

ram, *v.t.* butt, batter, bump; pound, drive, tamp; cram, stuff. See IMPULSE.

ramble, *v.i.* stroll, saunter, stray, rove, wander; digress, maunder. See TRAVEL, LOQUACITY, DEVIATION, DIFFUSENESS.

rambunctious, *adj.* boisterous, pugnacious, quarrelsome. See IRASCIBILITY.

ramification, *n.* divergence, division, branching; PART, offshoot, spur. See DEVIATION.

ramp, *n.* incline, slant, slope. See OBLIQUITY.

rampage, *v.i.* ramp, rage, go berserk, run amuck, go crazy. —*n.* tantrum, VIOLENCE, disturbance, frenzy, turmoil.

rampant, *adj.* rife, widespread, raging, epidemic; luxurious, lush; wild, unrestrained, unchecked; turbulent, tempestuous. See FREEDOM, VIOLENCE. *Ant.,* rare, local.

rampart, *n.* parapet, fortification, wall, bulwark, embankment. See DEFENSE.

ramrod, *n.* ram[mer], stick, rod, poker, iron. See HARDNESS, STRAIGHTNESS.

ramshackle, *adj.* dilapidated, tumbledown, rickety. See DETERIORATION.

ranch, *n.* range, farm, grange, spread. See ABODE, AGRICULTURE.

rancid, *adj.* rank, stale, putrid, malodorous. See MALODOROUSNESS, SOURNESS. *Ant.,* fresh, sweet-smelling.

rancor, *n.* spite, malice, bitterness, vengefulness, vindictiveness, MALEVOLENCE, hatred. *Ant.,* goodwill, LOVE.

random, *adj.* haphazard, casual, CHANCE, fortuitous, aimless. *Ant.,* planned, expected, foreseen.

randy, *adj.* vulgar, bawdy; *slang,* lascivious, horny (*sl.*). See VULGARITY, DESIRE.

range, *n.* row, series, chain; scope, extent; habitat; limit, span, latitude; compass, register; DISTANCE; stove[top], cooktop. See CONTINUITY, SPACE, BUSINESS, FREEDOM, DIRECTION, DEGREE.

rangy, *adj.* slender, slim, lanky; spacious, roomy. See HEIGHT, SPACE.

rank, *adj.* lush, luxuriant, vigorous; coarse; malodorous, fetid, rancid, offensive; arrant, extreme, gross. —*n.* row, line; position, caste, quality; status, grade, standing, footing. See REPUTE, BADNESS, CLASS, HORIZONTAL, CONTINUITY.

rankle, *v.i.* fester, irritate, gall, PAIN.

ransack, *v.t.* rummage, scour, search diligently; rifle, loot, pillage. See INQUIRY, STEALING.

ransom, *v.t.* redeem. —*n.* redemption, release, LIBERATION. See ATONEMENT, PAYMENT, PRICE.

rant, *v.i.* rage, rave, scold, nag; harangue. See EXCITABILITY, SPEECH.

rap, *v.* tap, knock, blow, cuff, box, clout, sock, swat; criticize; *informal,* converse. See IMPULSE, DISAPPROBATION, CONVERSATION. —*n., informal,* penalty, sentence, PUNISHMENT; blow, tap; bit, trifle, a damn (*sl.*). IMPULSE, LITTLENESS, MUSIC.

rapacious, *n.* greedy, ravenous, voracious. See DESIRE, GLUTTONY. *Ant.,* generous.

rape, *v.t.* seize, plunder; seduce, debauch, ravish. See IMPURITY, STEALING.

rapid, *adj.* swift, speedy, fleet, prompt, quick, rapid-fire. See VELOCITY. —*n.* (*pl.*) white water, chute, shoot. See WATER. *Ant.,* slow, sluggish. —**rapid tran-**sit, subway *or* elevated train. See TRANSPORTATION.

rapier, *n.* sword (see ARMS).

rapine, *n.* plunder (see STEALING).

rapport, *n.* touch, sympathy, understanding, communication; affinity, empathy, compatibility. See RELATION, AGREEMENT.

rapt, *adj.* ecstatic, enraptured, transported; absorbed, engrossed. See ATTENTION, THOUGHT, FEELING. *Ant.,* unmoved, uninterested.

rapture, *n.* ecstasy, transport, bliss, joy, delight. See PLEASURE.

rara avis, *Lat.,* rare bird; unusual thing. See UNCONFORMITY, GOODNESS.

rare, *adj.* scarce, sparse; unusual, choice, remarkable; tenuous (see RARITY); underdone, half-done, half-cooked, raw (see UNPREPAREDNESS). *Ant.,* plenteous, ubiquitous; well-done.

RARITY
Sparseness

Nouns—1, rarity, tenuity, subtlety, thinness, lightness, compressibility; rarefaction, attenuation, dilatation, inflation. See VAPOR.

2, rareness, scarcity, uncommonness, infrequency, infrequence; collector's item. See UNCONFORMITY.

Verbs—rarefy, expand, dilate, attenuate, thin out.

Adjectives—1, rare, subtle, thin, fine, tenuous, compressible, slight, light, ethereal; rarefied, unsubstantial.

2, scarce, unusual, infrequent, uncommon, few [and far between], scant, sporadic, occasional; part-time; unprecedented, unheard-of; odd, curious, singular.

Adverbs—rarely, infrequently, *etc.*; seldom, scarcely *or* hardly ever; once in a [great] while, once in a blue moon; now and then *or* again, from time to time, at times; once and for all.

Quotations—A well-written life is almost as rare as a well-spent one (*Thomas Carlyle*), A lucky man is rarer than a white cow (*Juvenal*), What is so rare as a day in June? Then, if ever, come perfect days (*James Russell Lowell*), Simplicity, most rare in our age (*Ovid*), Truth is rarely pure and never simple (*Oscar Wilde*).

Antonyms, see DENSITY, FREQUENCY, MULTITUDE.

---

rascal, *n.* scoundrel, knave, rogue, reprobate, blackguard; imp, scamp. See EVILDOER.

rascality, *n.* knavery, villainy, roguery, blackguardism. See IMPROBITY.

rash, *adj.* reckless (see RASHNESS). —*n.* eruption, breaking out (see DISEASE).

RASHNESS
Hastiness

Nouns—1, rashness, temerity, incautiousness, imprudence, indiscretion, recklessness, FOLLY; overconfidence, audacity, COURAGE, sporting blood; precipitancy, precipitation, impetuosity, foolhardiness, heedlessness, thoughtlessness, NEGLECT; desperation, quixoticism; DEFIANCE; gaming, gambling; blind bargain, leap in the dark, fool's paradise. See DANGER.

2, desperado, hotspur, madcap, daredevil, fire-eater, bully, bravo, scapegrace, Don Quixote, adventurer; gambler, gamester; stunter, stuntman; speeder. *Slang,* speed demon, cowboy.

Verbs—be rash, stick at nothing, play a desperate game, play with fire, walk on thin ice, go out of one's depth, ride for a fall, take a leap in the dark, buy a pig in a poke, tempt Providence, clutch at straws, lean on a broken reed; run the gauntlet; dare, risk, hazard, gamble, throw caution *or* discretion to the winds, daresay, throw one's cap over the windmill, take the bull by the horns; put all one's eggs in one basket. *Slang,* take a flyer, go for broke, burn some wheels.

Adjectives—rash, daring, incautious, indiscreet, imprudent, improvident, temerarious, heedless, careless, reckless, giddy, wild; madcap, desperate, devil-may-care, hotblooded, hotheaded, headlong, headstrong, breakneck; foolhardy, harebrained, precipitate, overconfident, adventurous, venturesome, quixotic, free-and-easy; risky, hazardous. *Informal,* quick on the trigger, trigger-happy. *Slang,* half-assed.

Adverbs—rashly, recklessly, *etc.;* hotfoot, headlong, posthaste, head over heels, headforemost; at all costs, at all hazards.

Quotations—Take calculated risks. That is quite different from being rash (*George S. Patton*), Fortune sides with him who dares (*Virgil*), Boldness be my friend! Arm me, audacity (*Shakespeare*).

Antonyms, see CARE, CAUTION, SAFETY.

---

rasp, *v.* scrape, file, grate; chafe, nag, worry, abrade. See FRICTION. —*n.* file, scraper, rasper, abrasive; hoarseness, huskiness. See ROUGHNESS.

rat, *n., slang,* sneak, polecat, skunk; traitor, turncoat, renegade; welsher, liar, informer, nark (*sl.*). See EVILDOER. —*v.i.,* *slang,* betray, inform, spill the beans, squeal (*sl.*); desert, bolt, sell out. See INFORMATION, IMPROBITY.

rate, *n.* ratio, percent, DEGREE, proportion; rank, CLASS; PRICE, value; VELOCITY. See JUDGMENT.

rather, *adv.* somewhat, passably, preferably, more correctly, sooner; considerably. See LITTLENESS, CHOICE, DEGREE, COMPENSATION.

ratify, *v.t.* approve, confirm, validate; endorse, verify, OK (*inf.*). See EVIDENCE, ASSENT. *Ant.,* veto.

rating, *n.* appraisal, evaluation, standing; scolding, vilification. See DEGREE, JUDGMENT, DISAPPROBATION.

ratio, *n.* proportion, rate, percentage, value. See DEGREE, RELATION.

ration, *v.t.* apportion, allocate, allot, dole out; limit, restrict, withhold. See APPORTIONMENT, FOOD.

rational, *adj.* sound, sane, logical, sensible, reasonable. See REASONING, INTELLECT, SANITY. *Ant.,* irrational, insane.

rationale, *n.* theory, explanation, raison d'être, justification; METHOD, philosophy, principle.

rationalize, *v.* explain away, justify; organize. See INTERPRETATION, CAUSE.

rat race, *n.* drudgery, treadmill; futility. See WEARINESS, USELESSNESS.

rattle, *v.* clatter, chatter, clack; babble, prattle, gabble, jabber; fluster, befuddle, upset. See LOUDNESS, MUSIC, INATTENTION.

ratty, *adj.* seedy, rundown (see DETERIORATION). *Ant.,* fancy, deluxe.

raucous, *adj.* harsh, grating, rasping, hoarse, strident. See LOUDNESS. *Ant.,* quiet, smooth-talking.

raunchy, *adj., slang,* obscene, indecent; lustful. See IMPURITY. *Ant.,* proper, G-rated.

ravage, *v.t.* lay waste, pillage, plunder, sack, devastate. See DESTRUCTION.

rave, *v.i.* bluster, storm, rant, tear; ramble, wander. See EXCITEMENT, INSANITY, EXCITABILITY. —*n., informal,* praise, good review. See APPROBATION. *Ant.,* pan.

ravel, *v.* entangle, involve, unravel, fray, untangle, disentangle, separate. See DIFFICULTY, DISORDER.

ravenous, *adj.* rapacious, hungry, greedy, voracious, gluttonous. See DESIRE, GLUTTONY.

ravine, *n.* gorge, gulf, canyon, gully, coulee, gap, notch. See INTERVAL.

ravish, *v.t.* charm, captivate, enchant, enthrall; carry off, deflower, rape, violate. See PLEASURE, IMPURITY.

raw, *adj.* crude; unprepared, uncooked; undisciplined, unexperienced; skinned, scraped, abraded; bleak, piercing; harsh; naked; untrained; unpolished, boorish. See COLD, UNSKILLFULNESS, NEWNESS, UNPREPAREDNESS. *Ant.,* refined; cooked.

ray, *n.* skate; beam, gleam, radiation; stripe. See ANIMAL, LIGHT.

raze, *v.t.* demolish, level, tear down, obliterate. See DESTRUCTION.

razz, *v.* RIDICULE, heckle, scoff (at), jeer (at); *informal,* tease.

razzle-dazzle, *n., slang,* flash, panache, flamboyance, glitz. See OSTENTATION.

reach, *v.* touch, attain, gain, get to, arrive at, pass, influence; stretch, extend; strive; hand over, deliver. See DISTANCE, TRANSPORTATION. —*n.* stretch, span, range, expanse, DISTANCE, scope. See ARRIVAL.

reaction, *n.* response, revulsion, reflex, RECOIL. See COMPENSATION.

reactionary, *n.* conservative, right-winger, recalcitrant, Tory, [John] Bircher, standpatter, diehard, fogy. See PERMANENCE.

reactor, *n.* nuclear reactor *or* pile, atom smasher; breeder. See POWER.

read, *v.* peruse, con; interpret, decipher, predict; pronounce; study; teach, admonish. See INTERPRETATION.

reader, *n.* peruser; critic; elocutionist; proofreader; lecturer, prelector; textbook, anthology. See PRINTING, TEACHING.

readily, *adv.* willingly; easily, promptly. See WILL, FACILITY. *Ant.,* with difficulty, reluctantly.

ready, *adj.* prepared, available, handy; prompt, quick; apt, ingenious; alert; ripe. See UTILITY, PREPARATION, SKILL, EARLINESS, EXPECTATION. *Ant.,* unprepared, slow.

ready-made, *adj.* ready-to-wear, prefabricated, ready-built, oven-ready, instant, precooked; unoriginal, cut and dried, derivative. See PREPARATION, PRODUCTION.

real, *adj.* actual, veritable, true, genuine; certain, sure, authentic. See EXISTENCE, TRUTH.

realism, *n.* actuality, naturalism, genre, verity. See PAINTING.

realistic, *adj.* lifelike, faithful, graphic. See SIMILARITY, CONFORMITY. *Ant.,* unrealistic.

reality, *n.* TRUTH, actuality, verity, factuality, fact. See EXISTENCE, SUBSTANCE. *Ant.,* unreality, FALSEHOOD.

realize, *v.t.* comprehend, appreciate, understand; objectify, imagine; gain, net; produce, bring in; fulfill, attain, achieve. See KNOWLEDGE, COMPLETION, ACQUISITION, SALE, IMAGINATION.

really, *adv.* surely, indeed, truly, honestly, certainly, positively, absolutely; very, emphatically; genuinely, actually. See TRUTH.

realm, *n.* kingdom, empire, domain; sphere, bailiwick, province; land, REGION, AUTHORITY.

realty, *n.* real estate, property. See POSSESSION.

ream, *v.t.* gouge, bore, drill. See OPENING.

reap, *v.t.* mow, cut, gather, harvest; acquire. See AGRICULTURE, ACQUISITION, SHORTNESS.

reappearance, *n.* reincarnation, revival; rebirth, resurgence, return, comeback; rerun, reprint. See REGULARITY.

rear, *n.* See REAR. —*v.* erect, construct, establish; raise, elevate; foster, nurture, bring up; breed. See DOMESTICATION, TEACHING.

REAR
Back part

Nouns—1, rear, back, posteriority; rear guard; background, hinterland, back door; postern; rumble seat; reverse; END. See INVERSION, SEQUENCE.

2, *(rear of body)* nape, chine, heels, tail, tail *or* rear end, rump, croup, buttocks, posterior, backside; breech, loin, dorsal region, lumbar *or* gluteal region, hindquarters; derriere. *Informal,* fanny, bottom. *Slang,* duff, ass, behind, bim, bum, buns, butt, caboose, can, cheeks, chuff, culo, dish, dock, duster, fun, gazonga, hams, heinie, jibs, keel, keester, moon, patootie, prats, rump, scut, seat, stern, tokus, tush[ie]. See BODY.

3, *(rear of thing)* stern, poop, afterpart, heelpiece, crupper, tail; wake, train; straggler.

Verbs—be behind, fall astern, bend backward, straggle, bring up the rear, follow, heel; END, tail off; back [up], reverse. *Slang,* moon, gaucho.

Adjectives—back, rear, hind, hindmost, hindermost, postern, dorsal, after, caudal, lumbar, posterior, aftermost, aft.

Adverbs—behind, in the rear, in the background, behind one's back, back to back, backward, rearward, rearmost; after, aft, abaft, astern, aback.

Prepositions—[in] back of, behind.

Antonyms, see FRONT.

---

reason, *n.* SANITY, INTELLECT, common sense, JUDGMENT, explanation; ground, CAUSE. See REASONING.

reasonable, *adj.* sound, sensible; fair, moderate; rational, logical. See CHEAPNESS, MODERATION, SANITY. *Ant.,* unreasonable, irrational.

REASONING
Process of understanding

Nouns—1, reasoning, ratiocination, rationalism, deduction, dialectics, induction, generalization, logic, synthesis, syncretism, analysis, rationalization, discursive *or* circular reasoning; fuzzy logic; sophistry. See INTELLECT, SANITY, THOUGHT.

2, *(reasoned process)* debate, polemics, discussion, INQUIRY; apologia, clarification; DISSERTATION, exposition, explanation (see INTERPRETATION). See DISCORD.

3, *(basis for reasoning)* argument, case, proposition, terms, premise, postulate, data, principle, inference, analogy, syllogism, hypothesis (see SUPPOSITION).

4, reasoner, logician, dialectician, disputant, controversialist, debater, polemicist, polemist, casuist, rationalist, rationalizer.

Verbs—reason, deduce, induce, infer, derive; allege, adduce; argue, discuss, debate, philosophize, consider; stand to reason, make sense; talk over, work out, brainstorm.

Adjectives—1, reasoning, thinking, sapient; rationalistic; argumentative, controversial, dialectic, polemical, discursive; disputatious, forensic.

2, logical, relevant, rational; inductive, deductive, syllogistic; a priori, a posteriori.

Adverbs—for, because, hence, seeing that, since, so, inasmuch as, whereas, in consideration of; therefore, consequently, ergo, accordingly, a fortiori; QED, quod erat demonstrandum; reductio ad absurdum; in reason.

Quotations—Reason is the ruler and queen of all things (*Cicero*), If everything on earth were rational, nothing would happen (*Feodor Dostoevski*), Reason is God's crowning gift to man (*Sophocles*), Passion and prejudice govern the world, only under the name of reason (*John Wesley*), Every man's own reason must be his oracle (*Thomas Jefferson*).

Antonyms, see INTUITION.

---

reassure, *v.* comfort, placate, set at rest, content; encourage. See COURAGE.

rebate, *n.* discount, refund, repayment, DEDUCTION.

rebel, *v.i.* revolt, resist, mutiny, rise up. See DISOBEDIENCE.

rebellion, *n.* revolt, uprising, insurrection, insurgence, mutiny, sedition, REVOLUTION. See DISOBEDIENCE, DEFIANCE.

rebirth, *n.* resurrection, reincarnation, renascence, renaissance, revival; resurgence, upsurge; salvation, redemption; new life. See CHANGE, RESTORATION.

rebound, *v.i.* bounce, ricochet, react, bound back, RECOIL. See ELASTICITY.

rebuff, *n.* snub, slight, cut; repulse, rout, check. See FAILURE. —*v.t.* repel, repulse; snub, cut, slight, high-hat (*sl.*), cold-shoulder (*sl.*). See REJECTION, REPULSION.

rebuild, *v.t.* re-create, refashion, re-form, restore. See RESTORATION.

rebuke, *n.* reproof, reprimand, admonition. —*v.t.* reprove, reprimand, chide, admonish, upbraid. See DISAPPROBATION.

rebus, *n.* picture puzzle, hieroglyphic, pictograph *or* -gram; charade. See SECRET.

rebut, *v.t.* ANSWER, contradict, oppose, refute. See NEGATION, CONFUTATION.

rebuttal, *n.* refutation, rejoinder, retort, ANSWER, defense, clincher, crusher (*inf.*), the perfect squelch (*inf.*); counterstatement, NEGATION, disclaimer.

recalcitrant, *adj.* refractory, stubborn, difficult, intractable; balky, mulish, cussed (*inf.*), cantankerous (*inf.*). See DISOBEDIENCE, OBSTINACY, RESISTANCE. *Ant.*, obedient, cooperative.

recall, *v.t.* recollect, remember; revoke, annul, withdraw; retract, countermand; revive, restore. See MEMORY, NULLIFICATION.

recant, *v.t.* withdraw, take back, renounce, retract, disavow, repudiate. See PENITENCE., NULLIFICATION

recapitulate, *v.t.* summarize, restate, review, rehearse, recap (*inf.*). See REPETITION, DESCRIPTION.

recast, *v.t.* recompose, reconstruct, refashion; remold; recompute. See REVOLUTION, CHANGE.

recede, *v.i.* retrograde, retrogress, retrocede; go, retire, withdraw; shrink, ebb, wane; move *or* drift away, move off, sheer off, fall back, depart, retreat, run away. See REGRESSION. *Ant.,* advance.

receipt, *n.* recipiency, reception, RECEIVING; recipe. See RULE.

RECEIVING
Getting by transfer

Nouns—1, receiving, reception, receipt, recipiency, ACQUISITION, acceptance, admission; absorbency, absorption.

2, *(money received)* receipts, share; income, revenue, intake, proceeds, return, net profits, yield, earnings, dividends; box office; salary, wages, remuneration (see PAYMENT); rent; pension; alimony, allowance; inheritance, legacy, bequest, patrimony, birthright, heritage. *Slang,* split, take, gate.

3, *(written acknowledgment)* sales check *or* slip, stub, acknowledgment, voucher, quittance, discharge, release.

4, *(one who receives)* recipient, receiver, donee, grantee, lessee, beneficiary, assign[ee], devisee, pensioner, stipendiary; payee, endorsee; legatee, heir (see POSSESSION).

Verbs—1, receive, take, get, acquire, take in, catch, pocket, put into one's pocket, derive, come in for; throw open; come into one's own; accept, admit, take off one's hands, open doors to; absorb, inspire, suck in; download.

2, be received, come in, come to hand, go into one's pocket, fall to one's lot, accrue; yield, pay, return, bear.

Adjectives—receiving, recipient, receptive, pensionary; absorbent.

Quotations—It is more blessed to give than to receive (*Bible*).

Antonyms, see GIVING, PAYMENT, EXCLUSION.

---

recent, *adj.* late, new, fresh, modern; newly come, just arrived *or* in; former, erstwhile, onetime. See NEWNESS, PAST. *Ant.,* distant.

RECEPTACLE
Container

Nouns—1, receptacle, recipient, receiver; compartment, cell, follicle, hole, corner, niche, recess, nook, crypt, booth, stall, pigeonhole, cubbyhole, cove, bay, alcove. See BUILDING, INTERMENT.

2, *(flexible container)* capsule, vesicle, cyst, pod, calyx, utricle, arc; blister. See COVERING.

3, *(bodily container)* stomach, abdomen, paunch, ventricle, crop, craw, maw, gizzard, mouth, gullet, sac, bladder.

4, *(carrying case)* pocket, pouch, fob, sheath, scabbard, socket, folder, bag, sack, purse, reticule, wallet, tote bag, portfolio, pocketbook, evening bag, clutch, scrip, poke; carryall, holdall, carry-on bag, flight bag, garment bag, grip[sack], gunny sack; case, knapsack, rucksack, musette bag, backpack, packsack, bindle, boot, bridget, tucker bag, gamebag, shoulder bag, bridget, haversack, club bag, kit bag, carpetbag, kit, briefcase, attaché case, valise, fanny pack, cosmetic bag, housewife, disco bag; impedimenta, kit, luggage, baggage, barracks bag, suitcase, overnight case, traveling bag *or* case, pullman case, trunk, Saratoga trunk, wardrobe [trunk]; Dorothy bag, Boston bag, Gladstone bag; handbag, Bermuda bag, portmanteau, satchel, bandbox, hat box, ditty bag, gym bag, toilet kit, vanity bag; etui, reticule; quiver, golf *or* caddie bag; duffel bag, schoolbag, seabag; saddlebag, alforja, aparejo; monstrance, ostensorium. *Informal,* grip. *Slang,* kick, coffee-bag, hussy, hide, mouse.

5, *(boxlike container)* chest, box, carton, coffer, caddy, case, casket, caisson, lockbox, safe, bandbox, cage, manger, rack, snuffbox, vanity case, cedar chest, [foot]locker, lunchpail, vasculum.

6, *(open container)* vessel, bushel, barrel, kilderkin, kibble, canister, ginger jar, krater, basket, corbeil, dosser, frail, mocock, punnet, skep, trug, pannier, hopper, creel, crate, cradle, bassinet, hamper, tray, hod, scuttle, utensil, carrier, billycan, Tupperware, pot (see FOOD). *Slang,* chillum.

7, *(container for liquid)* vat, caldron, tank, olla, cistern, washstand, font; cask, puncheon, keg, rundlet, tun, butt, botta bag; firkin, jemcan; carboy, amphora, gallipot; bottle, jar, potiche, decanter, pitcher, ewer, cruse, vase, carafe, crock, flagon, magnum, jeroboam, rehoboam, demijohn, flask, breaker, stoup, jigger, noggin, pony; vial, phial, flacon, canteen; cruet; urn, tub, bucket, pail, lota; pot, pipkin, pan, tankard, jug, pitcher, mug; retort, alembic, test tube; tin, can, cannikin, kettle, bowl, basin, punchbowl, cup, goblet, chalice, tumbler, glass, flagon, tankard, stoup; saucepan, skillet, tureen; vacuum bottle *or* jug, thermos; chamber pot. *Slang,* piggin, puppy, gash-bucket, glory hole, mingo, growler.

8, *(flat container)* plate, platter, dish, trencher, porringer, saucer, crucible.

9, *(spoonlike container)* shovel, trowel, spoon, spatula, ladle, dipper, scoop.

10, *(furniture)* closet, garderobe, commode, cupboard, cellaret, locker, chiffonier, bin, bunker, buffet, press, safe, showcase, whatnot, sideboard, desk, dresser, bureau, wardrobe, secretary, till, bookcase, cabinet, console.

11, *(room)* chamber, apartment, room, cabin, office, court, hall; suite, flat, salon, parlor; dining, living, waiting, sitting, *or* drawing room; antechamber; stateroom; gallery, pew, box; boudoir, sanctum, bedroom, dormitory, refectory, playroom, nursery, schoolroom, library, study, studio; bathroom, lavatory, smoking room, den, lounge; rumpus room. See ABODE.

12, *(storage room)* attic, loft, garret; cellar, basement, vault, hold; cockpit; kitchen, pantry, scullery, buttery; storeroom; dairy; laundry, bathroom, lavatory, outhouse; penthouse; lean-to, garage, hangar, shed, toolhouse, roundhouse.

13, *(covered room)* portico, porch, verandah, lobby, court, hall, vestibule, foyer, corridor, PASSAGE.

14, *(container for plants)* conservatory, greenhouse, summerhouse, hothouse, alcove, grotto, arbor, bower; hermitage.

15, *(open area)* plaza, forum, piazza, place; market[place], agora; court[yard], square, quadrangle, campo.

16, *(transporting vehicle)* carryall, bus, coach; delivery *or* trailer truck, dray, dump truck, flatbed, garbage truck, moving van, pantechnicon; baggage car, coal car, boxcar, stock car, gondola, dump car, flatcar, platform car, produce *or* refrigerator car, tender car, rack car, freight car, hopper car; Dumpster. *Slang,* crate, jimmy, reefer. See TRANSPORTATION, VEHICLE.

---

reception, *n.* admission, admittance, entrée, entrance; importation; introduction, taking; party, affair. See RECEIVING, SOCIALITY.

receptionist, *n.* host[ess], greeter. See SOCIALITY.

receptive, *adj.* open-minded; impressionable. See LIBERALITY, TEACHING.

recess, *n.* alcove, niche, nook, bay; intermission, pause, interim, rest, break, breathing spell, coffee *or* lunch break. See RECEPTACLE, ANGULARITY, REPOSE.

RECESSION
Withdrawing

Nouns—1, *(physical withdrawal)* recession, receding, retirement, withdrawal, retrocession, DEPARTURE; retreat, flight (see ESCAPE); REGRESSION, regress, RECOIL.

2, *(financial slowdown)* depression, slowdown, temporary setback, hard times, decline, shakeout, bear market. *Informal,* slump. See DETERIORATION.

Verbs—1, recede, retrocede, regress, retire, withdraw; go [back]; move back, away, from, *or* off, sheer off; avoid; shrink, ebb, wane; drift *or* fade away, stand aside; fall back, RECOIL; retreat, run away, flee.

2, decline, slow down. *Informal,* slump.

Adjectives—recessive, receding, recedent; retiring, in retreat, retreating; ebbing, waning.

Quotations—Recession is when your neighbor loses his job; depression is when you lose yours (*Anon.*).

Antonyms, see APPROACH, PROGRESSION.

---

recherché, *adj.* uncommon, out of the ordinary, rare; esoteric, obscure; elegant, choice, refined. See FASHION.

recidivism, *n.* relapse, reversion, regression, backslide. See REVERSION.

recipe, *n.* receipt, formula, instructions, directions, method, prescription, ingredients. See MAXIM, RULE, REMEDY.

recipient, *n.* See RECEIVING.

reciprocal, *adj.* mutual, complementary, interchangeable, alternative, correlative. See RELATION, INTERCHANGE.

reciprocation, *n.* repayment, INTERCHANGE, exchange, reciprocity, alternation. See OSCILLATION, RETALIATION.

recital, *n.* telling, narration, rehearsal; account, recapitulation; concert, musicale. See MUSIC, DESCRIPTION.

recitation, *n.* declamation, elocution; recital, lesson. See SPEECH.

recite, *v.* rehearse, relate, repeat, declaim,

detail, recapitulate. See SPEECH, DESCRIPTION.

reckless, *adj.* careless, foolhardy, incautious, heedless, rash, devil-may-care, daring. See RASHNESS.

reckon, *v.* calculate, count, compute, estimate; esteem, consider, believe; rely, depend; *informal,* think, suppose, guess. See PAYMENT, EXPECTATION, SUPPOSITION, NUMERATION.

reckoning, *n.* calculation, computation, count; accounting, settlement; bill, tally, score. See PAYMENT, NUMERATION, EXPECTATION.

reclaim, *v.t.* redeem, restore, reform, recover, retrieve; tame. See RESTORATION, ATONEMENT.

recline, *v.i.* lie, rest, couch, REPOSE, loll. See HORIZONTAL.

recluse, *n.* hermit, anchorite, ascetic, eremite. See SECLUSION, ASCETICISM.

recognize, *v.t.* acknowledge, concede, remember; perceive, realize, know, distinguish; salute, greet; commend, appreciate. See VISION, KNOWLEDGE, MEMORY, PERMISSION, GRATITUDE, ASSENT, COURTESY.

RECOIL
Springing back

Nouns—recoil, reaction, retroaction, revulsion, rebound, ricochet, bounce, boomerang, kick, backlash, repercussion, reflex, return, repulse, REPULSION, reverberation, echo; reactionary, reactionist. See REVERSION, REGRESSION, LEAP.

Verbs—1, recoil, react, rebound, reverberate, echo, spring *or* fly back, kick, ricochet, reflect, boomerang, carom, bounce, shy; backfire. *Slang,* knee-jerk.

2, cringe, cower, wince, flinch, quail, shrink; draw, fade, fall, *or* drop back, retreat (see RECESSION).

Adjectives—recoiling, refluent, repercussive, recalcitrant, reactionary; flinching, cowering, *etc.*

Quotations—To every action there is always opposed an equal reaction (*Isaac Newton*).

Antonyms, see IMPULSE.

recollection, *n.* remembrance, reminiscence, MEMORY, retrospection.

recommend, *v.t.* commend, advise, suggest; commit, entrust; urge, advocate. See ADVICE, APPROBATION.

recompense, *n.* reward, COMPENSATION, PAYMENT, requital. —*v.t.* requite, reward, repay, remunerate, indemnify, atone.

reconcile, *v.t.* conciliate, propitiate, placate, appease; harmonize, accord; settle. See PACIFICATION, AGREEMENT, COMPROMISE.

recondite, *adj.* mysterious, obscure, SECRET, abstruse, profound, esoteric, cryptic. See CONCEALMENT.

recondition, *v.t.* repair, renew, overhaul, renovate, restore, regenerate, rejuvenate. See RESTORATION.

reconnaissance, *n.* survey, surveillance, espionage, observation, inspection, INQUIRY; aerial reconnaissance. See VISION.

reconnoiter, *v.* investigate, survey, spy out, scout, case (*sl.*). See VISION.

reconsider, *v.* reexamine, review, think over *or* again, change one's mind, tergiversate. See THOUGHT, CHANGE.

reconstruct, *v.t.* rebuild; make over, redo, restore, renovate, recondition; overhaul; piece together, project. See REPRODUCTION, RESTORATION.

RECORD
Keeping as evidence

Nouns—1, record, note, minute; register, poll, diptych, entry, memorandum, COPY, duplicate, docket; muniment, deed; document, chart, matter of record; testimony, deposition, affidavit, certificate; coupon, receipt (see RECEIVING); notebook, statistic; registry, registration, enrollment; rap sheet; tabulation, transcript, transcription, entry, booking, signature. See LIST, INDICATION, EVIDENCE, WRITING.

2, *(printed record)* gazette, newspaper, magazine; almanac, calendar; diary, memoir, log, journal, daybook, album, ledger, Web log; yearbook, annual; archive, scroll, chronicle, annals; legend, history, biography. *Informal,* blog. See PUBLICATION, NEWS.

3, *(solid monument)* monument, hatchment, slab, tablet, trophy, obelisk, pillar, column, monolith; memorial; memento, testimonial, medal; commemoration. See MEMORY.

4, *(remains)* trace, vestige, relic, remains, scar, footstep, footprint, track, mark, wake, trail, spoor, scent.

5, *(electric record)* phonograph record, extended-play record, EP, 45, long-playing record, LP, 78; videodisc, DVD, Laserdisc, compact disc, CD, digital *or* analog record[ing], optical disk; floppy disk, diskette, hard disk, CD-ROM, WORM; wire *or* tape recording, transcription, digital audio tape, DAT; disk, disc, waxing, platter; track, sector, field, record, groove; database.

6, *(person who records)* recorder, registrar, register, notary, prothonotary, clerk, amanuensis, secretary, stenographer, scribe, bookkeeper; editor, author, journalist; annalist, historian, chronicler, biographer, antiquary, antiquarian, archivist; scorekeeper, scorer, timekeeper, timer.

7, *(recording machine)* recording instrument, recorder, ticker, ticker tape; tracer; timer, dater, stopwatch, speedometer (see MEASUREMENT, CHRONOMETRY); log, turnstile; seismograph; phonograph, record player, turntable; tape *or* wire recorder, dictating machine; adding machine, cash register (see NUMERATION); video[tape *or* -cassette] recorder, VTR, VCR.

Verbs—record, put on record, chronicle, set down, hand down to posterity, commemorate, write, put in writing, take down; jot down, note, make a note; enter, book; post, make an entry of, enroll, register; check off, check in *or* out, sign in; notarize; make out; mark, sign, attest, file; wax, tape, transcribe; go down in history *or* records. *Informal,* chalk up.

Adjectives—recorded, recording; on record *or* file, on the books; documentary, in writing *or* print, in black and white.

Quotations—A memorandum is written not to inform the reader, but to protect the writer (*Dean Acheson*), Poetry is the record of the best and happiest moments of the happiest and best minds (*Percy Bysshe Shelley*), Writing may be either the record of a deed or a deed. It is nobler when it is a deed (*Henry David Thoreau*), Nothing has really happened until it has been recorded (*Virginia Woolf*).

Antonyms, see OBLIVION.

---

recount, *v.t.* tell, recite, repeat, rehearse, relate, narrate, enumerate; recapitulate. See DESCRIPTION, NUMERATION.

recoup, *v.t.* regain, retrieve, indemnify, reimburse. See RESTORATION.

recourse, *n.* appeal, resort, resource, expedient; aid. See USE.

recover, *v.* regain, get back, redeem, retrieve, reclaim, salvage; get well, recuperate. See RESTORATION, IMPROVEMENT.

recreant, *adj.* cowardly, craven, dastardly, disloyal, false, treacherous; apostate, renegade. See COWARDICE, EVILDOER.

recreation, *n.* diversion, sport, pastime, REFRESHMENT. See AMUSEMENT.

recrimination, *n.* countercharge, RETALIATION, tu quoque, rejoinder, reply in kind; name calling, bickering. See ACCUSATION.

recruit, *v.t.* enlist, raise, furnish, supply, replenish; restore, renew. —*n.* conscript, draftee; newcomer, novice, tyro, rookie, boot (*sl.*). See COMBATANT, COMMISSION.

rectangular, *adj.* orthogonal, oblong, foursquare, square. See ANGULARITY.

rectify, *v.t.* correct, improve, repair, purify,

redress, amend. See IMPROVEMENT, STRAIGHTNESS.

rectitude, *n.* uprightness, integrity, righteousness, goodness, VIRTUE, honesty. See PROBITY.

rector, rectress, *n.* pastor, parson; DIRECTOR, monitor, prefect. See CLERGY.

rectory, *n.* manse, parsonage, vicarage, parish house, deanery, presbytery; benefice. See ABODE, TEMPLE.

recumbent, *adj.* lying, reclining, leaning. See OBLIQUITY, HORIZONTAL.

recuperation, *n.* recovery, IMPROVEMENT, convalescence. See RESTORATION.

recur, *v.* return, come back, reoccur, repeat, intermit, revert. See REPETITION.

recusant, *n.* nonconformist, dissenter, schismatic, sectarian, Protestant; separatist, apostate. —*adj.* rebellious, dissenting, apostate, disobedient. See DISSENT, IMPENITENCE.

red, *n.* crimson, scarlet, *etc.;* radical, revolutionary. See COLOR, REVOLUTION, CHANGE.

redden, *v.* encrimson, incarmine; blush, flush, glow; bloody. See COLOR, MODESTY, RESENTMENT.

redecorate, *v.* renovate, refurbish, restore, remodel, do over. See RESTORATION.

redeem, *v.t.* ransom, recover, rescue, restore, liberate, deliver, convert, fulfill, perform. See RESTORATION, ATONEMENT, PIETY, PAYMENT.

redeemer, *n.* savio[u]r, Messiah, Christ, the Lord, *etc.*; emancipator. See LIBERATION.

redemption, *n.* salvation; deliverance; rescue; recovery. See RESTORATION, LIBERATION, ATONEMENT, PIETY.

redhanded, *adj.* in the act, in flagrante delicto. See GUILT.

red herring, ruse, artifice, dodge. See DECEPTION.

red-hot, *adj.* intense; violent; fresh, new. See HEAT, NEWNESS.

redneck, *n.* rowdy, ruffian, lout. See VULGARITY.

redo, *v.t.* repeat, revise, redecorate, *etc.* See RESTORATION.

redolent, *adj.* fragrant, odorous, aromatic, perfumed; heady, musky; reminiscent, remindful, having an aura (of). See ODOR.

redoubtable, *adj.* formidable. See FEAR.

redound, *v.* bounce back, rebound; do credit (to), accrue. See REPUTE, RECOIL, TENDENCY.

redress, *v.t.* right, correct, repair, reform, relieve, remedy. —*n.* amends, restitution, reparation, requital, COMPENSATION, relief. See RESTORATION, ATONEMENT.

redskin, *n., offensive,* [American] Indian, Native American. See HUMANITY.

red tape, bureaucracy, officialdom; paperwork; delay, HINDRANCE.

reduce, *v.* diminish, lessen, curtail, lower; allay, alleviate; set (a fracture); demote, abase, subjugate, subdue; diet, slenderize. See DECREASE, CONTRACTION, NARROWNESS.

redundance, *n.* redundancy; REPETITION, tautology; superabundance, superfluity, superfluence; profuseness, profusion, repletion, plethora; surfeit, surplus, surplusage; coals to Newcastle. See SUFFICIENCY.

reed, *n.* stem, stalk, straw, rush; pastoral pipe. See MUSIC.

reef, *n.* sandbar, shoal, bank, ledge. See CONVEXITY, SHALLOWNESS.

reek, *n.* vapor, fumes, ODOR; stench, stink, malodor, fetor, miasma. —*v.* stink, smell; give off, exude; sweat, perspire. See MALODOROUSNESS.

reel, *v.i.* sway, stagger, waver; spin, wheel. See AGITATION, ROTATION. —reel off, rattle off, repeat. See REPETITION.

reentry, *n.* return, insertion, splashdown. See REVERSION.

reestablish, *v.t.* restore, renew, revive, refound. See RESTORATION.

refashion, *v.t.* make over, remake, remodel, revolutionize. See REVOLUTION, CHANGE.

refer, *v.t.* submit, commit, send, direct, assign, ascribe, attribute. See EVIDENCE. —*v.i.* allude, advert, apply, concern, appeal. See RELATION, ATTRIBUTION.

referee, *n.* arbiter, arbitrator, umpire, mediator, moderator, judge, ref (*inf.*), ump (*inf.*). See JUDGMENT.

reference, *n.* citation, allusion; testimonial, credentials; consultation; bearing, concern, applicability; reference book, dictionary, encyclopedia, yearbook, atlas, almanac, catalog, concordance, thesaurus. See RELATION, EVIDENCE, PUBLICATION.

referendum, *n.* vote, plebiscite, initiative, vox populi. See CHOICE.

refill, *v.t.* See REPLENISH.

refine, *v.t.* purify, cleanse, educate, improve, polish, cultivate, elaborate. See PURITY, IMPROVEMENT.

refined, *adj.* well-bred, cultivated, polished; pure; subtle. See ELEGANCE, COURTESY, TASTE, PURITY.

reflect, *v.* throw back, cast back, mirror, imitate, reproduce, echo; meditate, ponder, muse, ruminate. See THOUGHT, LIGHT, DISAPPROBATION, COPY.

reflection, *n.* refraction, image, echo, duplication, counterpart, COPY; meditation, rumination, retrospection; comment; slur, insinuation, innuendo. See LIGHT, THOUGHT, DISAPPROBATION.

reflex, *n.* reaction, instinct, repercussion, RECOIL, rebound. —*adj.* reflective; involuntary, reactive, automatic, conditioned. See COPY, NECESSITY.

reflux, *n.* ebb, refluence, subsidence, backwater. See DECREASE, REGRESSION.

reform, *v.t.* better, reclaim, restore, improve, redeem, regenerate, convert. See CHANGE. —*n.* IMPROVEMENT, amendment, regeneration, reformation; crusade.

reformation, *n.* reform, IMPROVEMENT, betterment, correction; regeneration. See CHANGE, PIETY.

reformatory, *n.* reform school, juvenile detention ward, juvenile PRISON.

reformer, *n.* altruist, crusader, zealot, missionary. See IMPROVEMENT.

refraction, *n.* bending, deflection. See DEVIATION, VISION.

refractory, *adj.* unruly, unmanageable, obstinate, stubborn, intractable. See DISOBEDIENCE.

refrain, *v.t.* abstain, cease, desist, forbear. See AVOIDANCE. —*n.* chorus, burden, repetend. See REPETITION.

refresh, *v.* invigorate, stimulate; renew, recharge, re-create. See REFRESHMENT, COMPUTERS.

REFRESHMENT
Invigoration

Nouns—refreshment, invigoration, recuperation (see RESTORATION); ventilation; recreation, diversion, regalement, repast, FOOD, nourishment. *Informal,* pick-me-up, bracer. See RELIEF, PLEASURE.

Verbs—1, refresh, brace, strengthen, invigorate, stimulate; brisken, freshen (up), recruit, enliven; renew, revive, revivify, [re]animate; regale, cheer, cool, fan, ventilate, AIR, slake. *Informal,* give a new lease on life, buck up.

2, breathe, respire, take a long breath; recuperate, revive, regain one's strength, come to oneself, perk (up).

Adjectives—refreshing, *etc.*; brisk, cool, restorative, recuperative, restful, pleasant, comfortable; refreshed, fresh, untired, unwearied.

Antonyms, see WEAKNESS, WEARINESS.

refrigerant, *n.* coolant; Freon, liquid nitrogen, *etc.*

refrigerate, *v.* cool, ice, freeze, infrigidate; benumb, chill [to the marrow]; quick-freeze. See COLD.

refuge, *n.* asylum, sanctuary; hideout, hideaway; safe harbor; any port in a storm; last resort; support, seclusion; anchor[age]; home, hospital; retreat, den, lair. See SAFETY.

refugee, *n.* fugitive, misplaced person, evacuee, escapee, runaway. See ESCAPE, AVOIDANCE, DISPLACEMENT.

refund, *v.t.* return, give back, pay back, repay, reimburse. See PAYMENT, RESTORATION.

refurbish, *v.* redecorate, renovate (see RESTORATION).

REFUSAL
Declining to do or accept

Nouns—refusal; nonacceptance, denial, declining, declination, rejection; disclaimer, repudiation; negation, contradiction; rebuff, repulse, snub. *Informal,* thumbs-down. See REJECTION, EXCLUSION, RESISTANCE, REPULSION, DISSENT, NEGATION, UNWILLINGNESS.

Verbs—refuse, reject, repudiate, deny, decline; negate; rebuff, repulse, snub; [be]grudge, be deaf to; turn a deaf ear to, turn one's back on; discountenance, not hear of, turn [thumbs] down, vote down; wash one's hands of, stand aloof; pass up.

Adjectives—1, refusing, recusant; uncomplying, unaccommodating, unconsenting, deaf to; unwilling.

2, refused, rejected, ungranted, out of the question, not to be thought of, impossible.

Adverbs—no, on no account, never, by no [manner of] means.

Phrases—not for the world; no, thank you; out of the question. *Informal,* not a chance; not on your life; no way; nothing doing; over my dead body. *Slang,* no soap; no deal; no dice; no go; no sale; no way, José; in a pig's eye *or* ass.

Quotations—I'll make him an offer he can't refuse (*Mario Puzo*), Wars will cease when men refuse to fight (*Anon.*).

Antonyms, see CONSENT.

refuse, *n*. trash, truck, rubbish, waste, leavings, garbage. See USELESSNESS. —*v*. See REFUSAL.

refute, *v.t.* confute, controvert, disprove, deny, dispute. See NEGATION, CONFUTATION.

regain, *v.t.* recover, retrieve, get back [to]. See RESTORATION.

regal, *adj*. royal, splendid, stately, majestic; kingly, autocratic. See AUTHORITY.

regale, *v.t.* entertain, feast, wine and dine, treat; give PLEASURE. See FOOD.

regalia, *n.pl.* emblems, decorations, insignia; finery. See INDICATION.

regard, *v.t.* consider, deem, observe, mark, note; RESPECT, REPUTE, esteem; concern. —*n*. reference, concern, gaze, scrutiny, ATTENTION, deference, esteem. See RELATION, VISION.

regarding, *prep*. respecting, concerning. See RELATION.

regardless, *adj*. heedless, careless, indifferent, negligent. See INATTENTION, NEGLECT. —*adv*. notwithstanding, anyhow. See COMPENSATION.

regenerate, *adj*. reformed, reborn, converted. —*v.t.* make over, revivify; reform, convert. See RESTORATION, PIETY.

regent, *n*. viceroy, deputy, ruler, trustee. See AUTHORITY.

regime, *n*. rule, reign, sovereignty; rulers, incumbents; policy, program, PLAN, regimen. See AUTHORITY.

regimen, *n*. course, METHOD, prescription, program, procedure, schedule; drill, training; diet[etics]. See FOOD, REMEDY.

regiment, *n*. corps, troop[s], army, company; multitude, assemblage. See COMBATANT. —*v.t.* muster, enlist; organize, systematize, train, drill, discipline; harness, enslave. See RESTRAINT, ARRANGEMENT.

REGION
Area of indefinite extent

Nouns—1, region, sphere, ground, soil, area, hemisphere, latitude, meridian, zone, clime, climate; quarter, district, beat, orb, circuit, circle; vicinity, neighborhood, premises, precinct, pale, department, domain, bailiwick, dominion, section, tract, territory. *Slang*, turf.

2, country, state, canton, county, shire, province, city, conurbation, arrondissement, parish, township, borough, hundred, riding, principality, duchy, realm, kingdom, empire.

3, Bible Belt, corn belt, green belt, Pacific Rim, rust belt, sun belt.

4, arena, march; patch, plot, enclosure, enclave, field, court.

5, a. [North] American, northerner, southerner, easterner, westerner. *Slang*, John Q. Public, Joe Sixpack, Joe Blow. b. Australian, down under. *Slang*, Oz. c. Canadian. *Slang*, hoser, canuck. d. Dutchman, Netherlander. *Slang*, nic frog, Dutcher. e. Frenchman. *Slang*, frog[-eater], parleyvoo. f. German [American]. *Slang*, jerry, gerry, heinie, kraut[head], hun, Dutcher, flapdragon, limburger. g. Hungarian [American]. *Slang*, hunkie. h. [American] Indian, Native American, Amerind[ian]; Eskimo, Inuit. *Slang*, siwash. i. Irish [American]. *Slang*, flannel mouth, Greek, harp, paddy, mick[ey]. j. Italian [American]. *Slang*, dino, dago, eytie, greaser, organ-grinder, Guinea, spaghetti, spic, wop, chawmouth, ghin, gingo, pizza man, ringtail, salt-water turkey, sky, spill. k. Indian, Pakistani. *Slang*, dothead, Packie. l. Polish [American]. *Slang*, polack, poski, pscrew, yak, lock. m. Scandinavian. *Slang*, dumbsocks, herring-choker. n. Spanish American, Hispanic, Mexican [American], Puerto Rican, Cuban, chicano. *Slang*, beaner, dago, chicano, greaseball, Mick[ey], greaser, mex, oiler, paisano, chili-eater, spic, parakeet, taco[-bender], tio taco, tamale, wetback, pepper[-belly]. See INHABITANT.

Adjectives—regional, sectional, territorial, local, parochial, vicinal, provincial, topographical.

Related categories, see LOCATION, SPACE, ABODE, PART.

register, *n.* RECORD, roll, LIST; registra- tion, enrollment. —*v.t.* enroll, LIST; mark, RECORD; express, indicate. See ARRANGEMENT.

REGRESSION
Passage back

Nouns—1, regression, retrogression, retrogradation, retroaction, retreat, return, RE- VERSION; relapse, RECESSION, recess; recidivism, backsliding, fall, DETERIORATION. See FAILURE.

2, reflux, refluence, backwater, regurgitation, ebb; resilience, reflection, RECOIL.

Verbs—1, regress, retrogress, recede, return, revert, retreat, retrograde; [re]lapse; back down, off, *or* out, rebound; lose ground, fall astern, back water, put about, wheel, countermarch; turn, turn tail, about-face, turn around, turn one's back upon; retrace one's steps, beat a retreat, go home; backslide; pull *or* draw in one's horns.

2, ebb, flow back, regurgitate.

Adjectives—1, regressive, retrograde; retrogressive, refluent, reflex, recidivous, crablike, reactionary, recessive, receding.

2, relapsing, backsliding, recrudescent; reversionary, atavistic.

Adverbs—back, backward[s], reflexively, in retreat, on the run, behind.

Antonyms, see PROGRESSION.

REGRET
Looking back with sorrow

Nouns—regret, remorse, qualms, compunction, contrition, attrition, repentance, PENI- TENCE; LAMENTATION, mourning; heartache, sorrow, grief, bitterness, DISAPPOINT- MENT, DISCONTENT; repining, homesickness, nostalgia, *mal du pays.*

Verbs—regret, deplore, feel sorry *or* contrite, think better of; sorrow, grieve, repent, re- pine, rue [the day]; weigh *or* prey on the mind, leave an aching void. *Informal,* kick oneself.

Adjectives—1, regretting, regretful, sorry, contrite, remorseful, rueful, mournful, peni- tent, ashamed; repining, homesick, nostalgic.

2, regretted, regrettable, deplorable, unfortunate, lamentable; culpable, blamewor- thy, opprobrious.

Interjections—what a pity! what a shame! too bad! *Slang,* tough luck!

Quotations—For of all sad words of tongue or pen, the saddest are these: "It might have been" (*John Greenleaf Whittier*), We have left undone those things which we ought to have done; and we have done those things which we ought not to have done; and there is no health in us (*Book of Common Prayer*), To regret deeply is to live afresh (*Henry David Thoreau*), Tribe follows tribe, and nation follows nation, and regret is useless (*Seattle*).

Antonyms, see CONTENT, REJOICING.

---

regroup, *v.* reform, realign, reorganize. See ORDER.

regular, *adj.* steady, rhythmical (see REGU- LARITY); normal, customary, according to RULE. See ORDER, HABIT, SYMMETRY.

REGULARITY
Periodicity

Nouns—1, regularity, periodicity; evenness, steadiness, constancy, consistency, invari- ability, punctuality; nonchaotic attractor; biorhythm; intermittence, alternation (see OSCILLATION); beat, pulse, pulsation, cadence, swing, rhythm. See REPETITION.

2, (*recurring cycle*) round, bout, turn, period, CIRCUIT, cycle, routine; monthly bills, payments, *etc.*; period, menstruation, menses, catamenia, female disorder. *Slang,* floods, courses, little friend, monthlies, the curse, visitor, red mary.

3, a. anniversary, jubilee; diamond, golden, silver, wooden, paper, *etc.* anniversary; holiday; spring, winter, *etc.* break; centennial, biennial, *etc.;* feast, festival, CELEBRATION, fast day, birthday, saint's day, holy day. **b.** Christmas, Easter, Thanksgiving, New Year's Day, Independence Day, Fourth of July, Memorial Day, Columbus Day, St. Patrick's Day, Labor Day, Groundhog Day, St. Valentine's Day, April Fool's Day, Halloween, All Hallows' *or* All Saints' Day, Dominion Day, Boxing Day; Washington's, Lincoln's, *etc.* Birthday, Martin Luther King Jr. Day, Veterans Day, Armistice Day, Presidents' Day; Admission Day, American Indian Day, Anzac Day, Arbor Day, Armed Forces Day, Armistice *or* Veterans Day, Pan American Day, Father's *or* Mother's Day, Human Rights Day, Robert E. Lee's Birthday, Sadie Hawkins Day, World Health Day, Jefferson Davis's Birthday. **c.** Hanukkah, Passover, High Holy Day, Rosh Hashanah, Yom Kippur, Purim, Sukkoth. **d.** Kwanza, junkanoo, Pinkster Day; Chinese New Year, Bairam, Bastille Day, Bon, Moharram, Peach Festival, Ramadan, Omisoka, Canada *or* Dominion Day, Simon Bolivar's Birthday, Spring Bank Holiday, Tet, Cinco de Mayo, Commonwealth Day, Diwali, Kenyatta Day, Flower Festival, Guy Fawkes Day.

Verbs—recur, return, reappear, come again, come [a]round, come in its turn, revolve, circle; beat, pulsate, throb, alternate, intermit, oscillate; come and go. *Informal,* roll around.

Adjectives—**1**, regular, steady, constant, uniform, even, symmetrical, consistent, punctual, systematic, methodical, orderly, unvarying, congruous; periodic[al], serial, recurrent, cyclical, seasonal, rhythmic[al], intermittent, remittent, alternate, every other; fixed, established, settled, continued, permanent; normal, natural, customary, habitual, usual, conventional, ordinary, typical, correct.

2, hourly, diurnal, daily, quotidian, tertian, weekly, biweekly, fortnightly, monthly, yearly; annual, biennial, triennial, centennial; secular, paschal, lenten; menstrual, catamenial.

Adverbs—regularly, normally, periodically, constantly, punctually; at regular intervals, like clockwork, at fixed periods, at stated times, from day to day, day by day; by turns, in turn, in rotation, alternately, every other day, off and on, round and round, year after year.

Antonyms, see IRREGULARITY.

---

regulate, *v.t.* ORDER, manage, legislate, rule, direct; adjust, rectify, fix, organize, systematize, tranquilize, moderate. See CONFORMITY, ARRANGEMENT, AGREEMENT, AUTHORITY.

regulation, *n.* adjustment (see REGULATE); law, RULE, order, ordinance. See LEGALITY.

regurgitate, *v.t.* vomit, disgorge; ebb. See EJECTION, REGRESSION.

rehabilitate, *v.t.* restore, reinstate, reestablish. See RESTORATION.

rehash, *v.t.* review, repeat, restate, chew one's cud (*inf.*); summarize, recapitulate, sum up, recap (*inf.*). See REPETITION.

rehearse, *v.t.* repeat, recite, enumerate; drill, practice, prepare. See REPETITION, PREPARATION, DESCRIPTION, DRAMA, MUSIC.

reign, *v.i.* rule, govern, command, hold sway. —*n.* rude, sway; currency, prevalence; INFLUENCE. See AUTHORITY, GENERALITY.

reimburse, *v.t.* repay, compensate, indemnify, restore, refund. See PAYMENT, RESTORATION.

rein, *n.* curb, check, control; (*pl.*) lines, RESTRAINT, guidance.

reincarnation, *n.* rebirth, resurrection. See RESTORATION.

reinforce, *v.t.* strengthen, support, buttress, replenish. See STRENGTH.

reinforcements, *n.pl.* replenishment, AID, recruits, auxiliaries. See PROVISION.

reinstate, *v.t.* restore, put back, reinstall, rehabilitate. See RESTORATION.

reiterate, *v.t.* repeat, iterate (see REPETITION).

reject, *v.t.* throw away, discard (see REJECTION); decline; deny (see REFUSAL).

REJECTION
Throwing away

Nouns—rejection, repudiation, EXCLUSION, REPULSION, rebuff; REFUSAL, declination; disallowance, disavowal; veto; disbelief (see DOUBT); ostracism (see EXCLUSION); relegation, dismissal, discard (see DISUSE). *Informal,* kick in the pants *or* teeth. *Slang,* brush-off, cold shoulder. See RELINQUISHMENT.

Verbs—1, reject, repudiate, abandon, renounce, exclude, except, repulse, repel, rebuff, scorn, spurn, slight; set *or* lay aside, pass over, give up, cast off, dump, discard, cast behind one, cast to the winds, set at naught, throw to the dogs, toss overboard, throw away, wash one's hands of, have done with; scrap, dismiss, cashier, deport, eject, relegate, resist; jilt. *Informal,* brush off; opt out.

2, refuse, disallow, disapprove, disclaim, overrule, abnegate, abjure; veto, be deaf to.

Adjectives—rejected, repudiated, refused, not chosen, not granted, out of the question, impossible; unaccepted, unloved, unwelcome, discarded, castaway, excluded, jilted; rejective, repudiative.

Antonyms, see APPROBATION, CHOICE.

REJOICING
Feeling of joy

Nouns—1, rejoicing, exultation, triumph, jubilation, joy, revelry, reveling, merrymaking, festivity, jubilee, CELEBRATION, paean, acclamation, thanksgiving, CONGRATULATION.

2, *(expression of pleasure)* smile, simper, smirk, gloat, grin; laughter, giggle, titter, snigger, snicker, crow, chuckle, horse laugh; fit, shout, roar, gale, *or* peal of laughter; risibility; laugh track. *Informal,* canned laughter.

3, *(expression of pleasure at success)* cheer, hurrah, hooray, shout, yell, hallelujah.

Verbs—1, rejoice, thank one's [lucky] stars, congratulate oneself, clap one's hands, fling up one's cap; dance, skip; sing, chirrup, hurrah; cry *or* leap for joy, leap with joy, exult, glory, triumph, celebrate; be tickled.

2, make merry, smile, simper, smirk, grin, laugh, giggle, titter, snigger, crow, snicker, chortle, chuckle, cackle; cheer; hurrah, yell, shout, roar, split one's sides. *Informal,* crack a smile, break up, hoot.

3, enjoy, revel in, delight in, be glad.

Adjectives—rejoicing, jubilant, exultant, triumphant, flushed, glad, gladsome, elated, laughing, bursting *or* convulsed with laughter; risible, laughable. *Informal,* in stitches.

Interjections—hurrah! hooray! three cheers! hail! Heaven be praised! *Slang,* swell! great! oh, boy!

Phrases—he laughs best who laughs longest.

Quotations—Weeping may endure for a night, but joy cometh in the morning (*Bible*), The secret of happiness is to face the fact that the world is horrible, horrible, *horrible* (*Bertrand Russell*), My heart is like a feather and my spirits are dancing (*Abigail Adams*).

Antonyms, see LAMENTATION.

---

rejoin, *v.t.* reply, retort, respond; reunite, reassemble. See ANSWER, ASSEMBLAGE.

rejoinder, *n.* ANSWER, reply, retort, response.

rejuvenate, *v.* renew, refresh, reinvigorate. See YOUTH, RESTORATION.

relapse, *n.* recurrence (of illness *or* behavior); DETERIORATION, backsliding; REGRESSION. —*v.i.* lapse, fall back, backslide.

relate, *v.t.* tell, recount, report, narrate; connect, associate (see RELATION). See DESCRIPTION.

relation, *n.* bearing, close connection; narration, narrative, storytelling; kinship, family tie; kinsman, relative; reference; proportion, ratio. See RELATION, DESCRIPTION, POSTERITY.

RELATION
Close connection
Nouns—1, relation, relationship, bearing, reference, connection, concern, dependence, cognation; correlation, analogy, SIMILARITY, affinity, reference; kinship, consanguinity, common descent, blood [tie], brotherhood, sisterhood; parentage, paternity, maternity (see ANCESTRY); alliance, homogeneity, association, fraternization, approximation, affiliation, interest, relevancy; propinquity; comparison, ratio, proportion, link, tie, bond of union. See INTERCHANGE, DEGREE.

2, kin, kinfolk, kinsman, kinswoman, relation[s]; agnate, enate, blood relation; distaff *or* spindle side, spear side; [nuclear] family, ilk, breed, bloodline, extended family; stock, strain; lineage, line; root, branch, tree; tribe, clan; generation; offspring, children, progeny (see POSTERITY); house[hold], kith [and kin].

3, aunt, uncle; [blood] brother *or* sister, sibling, brother- *or* sister-in-law, half brother *or* sister, kid brother *or* sister; child, son, daughter; cousin, cousin-german; son *or* daughter[-in-law], mother *or* father[-in-law]; husband, wife, spouse; maternal *or* paternal grandmother *or* grandfather; stepbrother, -sister, -child, -son, -daughter, -father, *or* -mother; grandaunt, -child, -daughter, -son, -father, -mother, -nephew, -niece, -parent, *or* -uncle. *Informal,* auntie, unc, bro, sis, grandpa, grampa, gramps, grandma, gammer, grammy, granny, nana.

Verbs—1, be related, relate to, refer to, bear upon, regard, concern, touch, affect, have to do with; pertain *or* belong to *or* with, interest; correspond.

2, relate, bring into relation with, bring to bear upon, connect, associate, fraternize, ally, draw a parallel, link, compare; allude to, refer to, speak of, deal with; correlate, interrelate, TOUCH.

Adjectives—1, relative, correlative, cognate, relating, referable; belonging, appurtenant.

2, related, connected, implicated, associated, affiliated, allied to; akin, like, similar; relevant, pertinent, germane; reciprocal; mutual, common, correspondent, interchangeable, alternate.

3, approximating, proportionate, proportional, allusive, comparable.

Adverbs—relatively, pertinently, comparatively; en rapport, in touch with; for that matter.

Prepositions—as to, as for, as regards, regarding, about, concerning, anent, relating to, relative to, with relation to, touching, with reference to, with regard to, apropos of, on the score of; under the head of, in the matter of, in re, re; compared to, alongside; cum.

Phrases—blood is thicker than water.

Quotations—It is a melancholy truth that even great men have their poor relations (*Charles Dickens*), My closest relation is myself (*Terence*).

Antonyms, see DISAGREEMENT, DIFFERENCE.

---

relative, *n.* RELATION, kinsman; comparative, dependent.

relax, *v.* rest, relent, slacken, loosen, unbend, abate, relieve, ease, mitigate. See SOFTNESS, PITY, REPOSE, MODERATION.

relaxation, *n.* ease, REPOSE, diversion, recreation; abatement, loosening. See AMUSEMENT, MODERATION.

relaxed, *adj.* loose, slack; not tense, at ease. See REPOSE.

relay, *n.* replacement, substitute, shift; intermediary, medium, go-between, agent, agency. —*v.* forward, advance, transmit. See SUBSTITUTION, TRANSPORTATION.

release, *v.t.* free, liberate, give out, relinquish. See LIBERATION, ACQUITTAL. —*n.* EXEMPTION; DEATH.

relegate, *v.t.* consign, commit, assign, refer, banish. See EJECTION, EXCLUSION.

relent, *v.i.* soften, yield, submit. See SOFTNESS, PITY.

relentless, *adj.* pitiless, merciless, implacable, remorseless; inexorable, indefatigable. See RESOLUTION, RETALIATION, SEVERITY.

relevant, *adj.* pertinent, fitting, apposite, applicable, apropos, germane, appropriate. See RELATION.

reliable, *adj.* trustworthy, dependable, trusty, responsible. See CERTAINTY, PROBITY.

reliance, *n.* dependence, trust, confidence, faith, credence. See BELIEF.

relic, *n.* memento, souvenir, keepsake, to-ken, antique, remains. See MEMORY, RECORD, REMAINDER, OLDNESS, RITE.

relief, *n.* comfort, alleviation (see RELIEF); assistance, welfare, AID; SUBSTITUTION; substitute; projection, CONVEXITY.

RELIEF
Alleviation

Nouns—1, relief, deliverance, easement, softening, alleviation, mitigation, MODERA-TION, palliation, soothing, assuagement, slaking. See REFRESHMENT, IMPROVEMENT, RESTORATION.

2, solace, consolation, comfort. See AID, CONTENT.

3, lenitive, restorative, palliative, alleviative, anodyne, tranquilizer, painkiller, analgesic; cushion, oasis. See LENIENCY, REMEDY.

Verbs—1, relieve, ease, alleviate, mitigate, palliate, soothe, salve, soften, mollify; poultice; spell (see SUBSTITUTION); assuage, allay, disburden, lighten; quench, slake.

2, cheer, comfort, solace; REMEDY, cure, refresh.

3, be relieved, breathe more freely, take comfort, breathe a sigh [of relief].

Adjectives—1, relieving, consolatory, comforting, soothing, assuaging, assuasive, balmy, lenitive, palliative, remedial, curative.

2, at [one's] ease, comfortable, CONTENT, contented; relaxed.

Quotations—Diseases desperate grown by desperate appliance are relieved, or not at all (*Shakespeare*), Time eases all things (*Sophocles*).

Antonyms, see INCREASE.

RELIGION
System of faith

Nouns—1, religion, faith; theology, isagogics, divinity, deism, theism, monotheism, ditheism, polytheism, pantheism; liberation theology; scientific creationism; hagiology; BELIEF, truth, creed, doctrine, dogma; cult; canonicity; declaration, profession, or confession of faith; articles of faith; conformity, orthodoxy, strictness. See PIETY.

2, *(religions)* a. Christianity; Catholicism, Roman Catholicism, Roman Catholic Church, Church of Rome, Orthodox Eastern Church, Russian or Greek Orthodox Church, Uniates; Protestantism, Presbyterianism, Quakerism, [Society of] Friends, Mormonism, Church of Jesus Christ of Latter-day Saints, Christian Science, Church of Christ Scientist, African Methodist Episcopal, A.M.E., Amish, Anabaptist, Anglican, Church of England, Armenian Apostolic, Pentecostal, Assemblies of God, Baptist, Brethren, Calvinist, Church of Christ, Church of God, Church of the Brethren, Dunkers, Church of the New Jerusalem, Ethical Culturalism, Swedenborgian, Congregational, Coptic, Episcopal, Hare Krishna, Huguenots, International Church of the Four-Square Gospel, Jehovah's Witnesses, Lutheran, Mennonite, Methodism, Metropolitan [Community] Church, Millenial Church, Shakers, Moravians, New Light Presbyterianism, New Thought, Puritans, Reformed Church, Rosicrucians, Russellites, Schwenkfelders, Scientology, Seventh Day Adventists, Transcendentalism, Unitarianism[-Universalism], United Church of Christ, Universalism, Zwinglianism; Gnosticism; Moral Majority, Christian Right, Christian Coalition, 700 Club. *Slang,* Scarlet Woman, Holy Rollers. b. Judaism, Druze. c. Mohammedanism, Moslemism, Islam; Nation of Islam. d. Buddhism, Zen, Shintoism, Confucianism, Hinduism, Brahmanism, Sikhism, Jainism, Mazdaism, Zoroastrianism, Lamaism, Shinto, Taoism. e. Baha'i, Theosophical Society. f. Rastafarianism. g. voodoo, hoodoo, vodun, brujera.

3, the Church, Holy Church, Established Church; temple of the Holy Ghost, Universal Church, Apostolic Church, muscular Christianity; native or indigenous religion, faith healing, love feast; Bible Belt.

4, true believer, Christendom, Christians; Islam; Jewry; Christian, Catholic, Protestant (Presbyterian, Christian Scientist, Swedenborgian, Moravian, *etc.*), Quaker, Friend, Mormon; Jew; Moslem; Buddhist; Brahman, Hindu, *etc. Slang,* bead-puller, fish-eater, mackerel-snapper, mick[ey], poper, papist; Jesus-screamer *or* -shouter, Jesus freak, God squad; white Anglo-Saxon Protestant, WASP, proddo, bible-belter, blueskin, congo, dipper, metho, presbo; Moonie; five and two, fiver, Ike, bagel-bender, Red Sea pedestrian, sheeny, skid, heeb, kike, mocky, porker, reef, lid, yid; rasta, ganza, dreadlocks.

5, *(religious writings)* scriptures, canons, SACRED WRITINGS; catechism; Apostles' Creed, Nicene Creed, Athanasian Creed; Articles of Religion.

6, WORSHIP, prayer, hymn, hymnody, psalmody; sacrifice, oblation, incense, libation, offering, offertory; disciple, fasting, asceticism; RITE, divine service, office, duty, Mass, matins, evensong, vespers.

7, CLERGY, clergyman; theologian, theist, monotheist; churchwarden, altar boy, acolyte, chorister; congregation, flock, worshiper, communicant, celebrant; presbyter, elder, vestryman, usher.

Verbs—WORSHIP, pray, invoke, supplicate, say one's prayers, tell one's beads; return thanks, say grace; praise, glorify, magnify; bless, give benediction; attend services, attend Mass, go to church; communicate, take communion.

Adjectives—religious, God-fearing; reverential (see RESPECT); orthodox, sound, strict, canonical, authentic, faithful, Catholic; theological; doctrinal, dogmatic, denominational, sectarian; Christian, Catholic, Protestant, Lutheran, Calvinistic, *etc.*; evangelical, scriptural; divine, true (see DEITY); Jewish, Judaic, Hebrew, Hindu, Mohammedan, *etc.*; born-again, charismatic.

Phrases—a church is God between four walls; you can't build a church with stumbling blocks; man's extremity is God's opportunity; the Church is an anvil that has worn out many hammers.

Quotations—Religion is by no means a proper subject of conversation in mixed company (*Lord Chesterfield*), I count religion but a childish toy (*Christopher Marlowe*), We have just enough religion to make us hate, but not enough to make us love one another (*Jonathan Swift*), Religion's in the heart, not in the knees (*Douglas Jerrold*), Religion . . . is the opium of the people (*Karl Marx*), There is only one religion, though there are a hundred versions of it (*G. B. Shaw*), Science without religion is lame, religion without science is blind (*Albert Einstein*), To die for a religion is easier than to live it absolutely (*Jorge Luis Borges*), One religion is as true as another (*Robert Burton*), Religion is an illusion, and it derives its strength from the fact that it falls in with our instinctual desires (*Sigmund Freud*), Religion is a monumental chapter in the history of human egotism (*William James*), Men despise religion; they hate it, and they fear it is true (*Pascal*), If you really want to make a million, the quickest way is to start your own religion (*L. Ron Hubbard*).

Antonyms, see IRRELIGION, IDOLATRY, HETERODOXY, LAITY.

RELINQUISHMENT
Giving up

Nouns—**1,** *(of an object)* relinquishment, abandonment, expropriation, dereliction; cession, surrender, dispensation; RESIGNATION, abdication; abnegation, REJECTION; riddance. See DISCONTINUANCE, DISUSE.

2, *(of a person)* desertion, defection, secession, withdrawal. *Slang,* granny dumping.

3, derelict, foundling, outcast, castaway; deserter, defector; flotsam, jetsam, rubbish, trash, refuse, waste.

Verbs—**1,** relinquish, give up, surrender, release, yield, abnegate, cede, let go, spare, drop, resign, forgo, renounce, abandon, give away, dispose of, part with, lay aside, lay on the shelf, lay down, throw up *or* over, discard, cast off, dismiss, get rid of, eject, divest oneself of, wash one's hands of, throw overboard, throw to the winds; sweep away, jettison, maroon; defect. *Slang,* un-ass.

2, desert, forsake, leave in the lurch, depart from, secede from, renege, withdraw from, back out of, turn one's back on, walk out on, take leave of, walk out on, leave holding the bag, leave, quit, vacate. *Informal,* leave flat. *Slang,* ditch, give the gate, rat out on.

3, be relinquished, go by the board.

Adjectives—1, relinquished, abandoned, cast off, high and dry, out in the cold; derelict, forlorn, unowned, unappropriated, left; dropped.

2, renunciatory, abjuratory, abdicant; relinquishing, *etc.*

Quotations—All hope abandon, ye who enter here (*Dante*), When all the desires that enter one's heart are abandoned, then does the mortal become immortal (*Brihadaranyaka Upanishad*), My God, my God, why hast thou forsaken me? (*Bible*).

Antonyms, see POSSESSION, ACQUISITION.

---

relish, *n.* zest, gusto; flavor, TASTE; spice, condiment, appetizer; liking, fondness. See PLEASURE, DESIRE, PUNGENCY.

relocate, *v.* move (see TRANSPORTATION).

reluctance, *n.* UNWILLINGNESS, hesitation, aversion, disinclination, DISLIKE.

rely, *v.i.* trust, depend (on), count (on). See BELIEF.

remain, *v.i.* stay; endure, last; continue. See REMAINDER, DURABILITY, CONTINUITY, ABODE.

REMAINDER
Anything left over

Nouns—1, remainder, residue, hangover, result; remains, remnant, vestige, rest, relic, leavings, crumbs, heeltap, odds and ends, leftovers, debris, cheese parings, orts, residuum, dregs, lees, grounds, silt, sediment, slag, refuse, chaff, stubble, fag end, ruins, wreck, butt, rump, carcass, skeleton, stump, alluvium, deposit; precipitate; dross, cinder, ash, clinker. *Informal,* shank. *Slang,* cremains. See UNCLEANNESS.

2, surplus, surplusage, overplus, excess, balance, superfluity, survival. *Informal,* money to burn. *Slang,* fifth wheel, broadus, jibba.

Verbs—remain, be left, be left over, exceed, survive.

Adjectives—remaining, left; left over, left behind, residual, residuary, over, odd, unconsumed, sedimentary, surviving; net, exceeding, over and above; superfluous.

Quotations—When men grow virtuous in their old age, they only make a sacrifice to God of the devil's leavings (*Alexander Pope*), When you have eliminated the impossible, whatever remains, *however improbable,* must be the truth (*A. Conan Doyle*).

Antonyms, see COMPLETION, END, DECREASE.

---

remand, *v.* send *or* order back, recommit, recall, return to custody. See COMMAND.

remark, *v.t.* note, observe; comment on, mention. See ATTENTION. —*n.* observation, statement, comment. See SPEECH.

remarkable, *adj.* noteworthy, notable, extraordinary, striking, unusual, singular, uncommon. See UNCONFORMITY, WONDER.

REMEDY
Something that cures or counteracts

Nouns—1, remedy, help, redress, RESTORATION; antidote, counterpoison, counterirritant, counteragent, antitoxin, antibody, prophylactic, antiseptic, corrective, restorative, sedative, palliative, febrifuge; germicide, specific, emetic, cathartic, carminative; narcotic, sedation (see INSENSIBILITY, DRUGS). *Slang,* jollop. See RELIEF.

2, a. antibiosis; antibiotic, germicide, wonder drug, miracle drug; toxin, antitoxin, penicillin, gramicidin; bacitracin, Chloromycetin, Aureomycin, bactericide, bacteriostat, cyclosporin, dihydrostreptomycin, erythromycin, gumagillin, magnamycin, neomycin, polymycin, streptomycin, Terramycin, tetracycline; sulfa, sulfonamide, sulfadiazine, sulfanilamide, sulfapyridine, sulfathiazole. **b.** medication; anticoagulant, anticonvulsant, antidepressant, antidiuretic, antiemetic, antihistamine, antipruritic, antipyretic, antiserum, antispasmodic, antitoxin, antitussive, antivenin; antidote; analgesic, painkiller, acetaminophen, aspirin, phenacetin, acetylsalicylic acid, ibuprofen, Anacin, Bufferin, Bayer, Darvon, Tylenol, Vioxx; adrenaline, epinephrine; antacid, Brioschi, Alka-Seltzer, Bromo-Seltzer, Rolaids, Maalox, Milk of Magnesia, Tums, Zantac; astringent; [local *or* general] anesthetic, benzocaine, clove oil, counterirritant, ether, laudanum, lidocaine, Novocaine, procaine, Nupercaine; beta blocker; bronchodilator; camphor; laxative, purgative, castor oil, glycerin, mineral oil, senna; hormone, cortisone, ephedrine, epinephrine, estrogen, progesterone, fertility drug, insulin, testosterone; cough suppressant, cough syrup, expectorant; anticoagulant, Coumadin, dicoumarin; antiseptic, cresol; relaxant, curare; nitroglycerin; sanative, curative; decongestant, inhalant; febrifuge; elixir, electuary; paregoric; quinine; [anabolic] steroid; vaccine, toxoid; sleeping pill, soporific; tolbutamide; vasoconstrictor, vasodilator.

3, *(general remedy)* physic, palliative, medicine, medication, simples, drug, potion, draught, draft, dose, pill, caplet, capsule, troche, lozenge, bolus, tincture, medicament.

4, *(unproved remedy)* nostrum, receipt, recipe, prescription; panacea, sovereign remedy, cure[-all], catholicon, miracle drug, elixir, elixir vitae, philosopher's stone, balm, balsam, cordial, ptisan, tisane, patent medicine; herb, borage, heartleaf, hog hoof tea, horse-mint tea.

5, salve, balm, balsam, ointment, OIL, lenitive, [calamine] lotion, cosmetic, emollient, demulcent, embrocation, liniment, depilatory, glycerin, glycerol, mustard plaster, ointment, unguent, poultice, rubefacient, salve; petrolatum, petroleum jelly, Vaseline; sitz bath, Epsom salts; eyewash; antiseptic, iodine, Mercurochrome, thimerosal, Merthiolate.

6, bandage, binder, poultice, plaster, gauze, dressing, Band-Aid, compress, stupe, Ace *or* elastic bandage, tourniquet, surgical dressing; sling, splint, support; brace; cotton ball *or* swab; artificial limb, prosthesis, prosthetic device.

7, *(medical action)* hospitalization; treatment, therapy, regimen, first aid; physical examination; diet, dietetics; appliance; cosmetic, exploratory, laser, major *or* minor, noninvasive, open-heart, oral, plastic, *or* reconstructive surgery; ablation, abortion, abscission, acupressure, acupuncture, amniocentesis, amputation, angiography, appendectomy, arthroscopy, artificial insemination, aspiration, auscultation, aversion therapy, autopsy, behavior modification, biofeedback, biopsy, bleeding, bloodletting, phlebotomy, bypass, cesarean section, cardiopulmonary resuscitation, CPR, cautery, chemotherapy, cholecystectomy, circumcision, colonic irrigation, colostomy, cordotomy, cosmetic surgery, couching, cryosurgery, cupping, debridement, decompression, desensitization, detoxification, dialysis, diathermy, dilation and evacuation, echography, electrocardiogram, electrocautery, electroencephalogram, electrophoresis, electrosurgery, enema, enterostomy, episiotomy, ergotherapy, euthanasia, mercy killing, excision, extraction, fenestration, fluoroscopy, gastrectomy, graft, Heimlich maneuver, hemodialysis, hepatectomy, hydrotherapy, hypnosis, hysterectomy, ileostomy, incision, injection, inoculation, intubation, irradiation, keratoplasty, corneal transplant, laparoscopy, laparotomy, laryngectomy, lavage, leeches; surgery, leeching, life care, liposuction, lithotripsy, lobotomy, magnetic resonance imaging, MRI, mammography, mastectomy, microsurgery, nephrectomy, nephrolithotomy, neurotomy, operation, organ transplant, orthodontics, ostectomy, osteoclasis, palpation, Pap test, patch test, percussion, perfusion, periodontics, phlebotomy, phototherapy, physiotherapy, plastic surgery, prophylaxis, prosthesis, pyelography, resection, rhinoplasty, rhizotomy, salpingectomy, scratch test, section, shock treatment, stress test, tomography, tonsillectomy, tracheotomy, traction, tubal ligation, urinalysis, uroscopy, vasectomy, venesection, venipuncture, ventilation.

8, *(areas of medical specialization)* aerospace, behavioral, clinical, community, emergency, environmental, general, holistic, industrial, internal, laboratory, nuclear, occupational, physical, preventive, space, sports, tropical, *or* veterinary medicine; allopathy, anesthesiology, audiology, bacteriology, biomedicine, cariology, chemotherapy, chiropody, chiropractic, cosmetic surgery, crisis intervention, dentistry, dermatology, embryology, endocrinology, endodontics, epidemiology, etiology, forensic pathology, gastroenterology, geriatrics, gerontology, gynecology, hematology, histology, homeopathy, hydrotherapy, hypnotherapy, immunology, lomilomi, massage therapy, mental hygiene, midwifery, myotherapy, naturopathy, neonatology, nephrology, neurology, neurosurgery, obstetrics, oncology, ophthalmology, optometry, oral surgery, orthodontics, orthopedics, osteopathy, otolaryngology, otorhinolaryngology, parasitology, pathology, pediatrics, pedodontics, perinatology, periodontics, pharmaceutics, pharmacology, pharmacy, plastic surgery, podiatry, proctology, prosthodontics, psychiatry, psychoanalysis, psychology, public health, radiology, radiotherapy, rheumatology, serology, surgery, symptomatology, tertology, therapeutics, tocology, toxicology, urology, virology.

9, [backup, base, children's, convalescent, cooperative, county *or* city, day, maternity, mental, private, teaching, *or* veterans] hospital, facility, medical center, infirmary, pesthouse, lazaretto, dispensary, clinic, sanitarium, sanatorium, asylum, spa, halfway house, rest home, hospice, field hospital; emergeny room, examining room, intensive care unit, isolation ward, operating room, recovery room, sick bay, sickroom, trauma center, waiting room, ward; Red Cross, World Health Organization, Public Health Service; managed care, health management organization, HMO, Blue Cross, Blue Shield, universal health care, Medicare, Medicaid, gatekeeper, preferred provider organization, PPO, primary care network; socialized medicine; primary, secondary, *or* tertiary care; self-care. *Slang,* doc-box.

10, doctor, physician; dentist; surgeon, general practitioner, caregiver; neurologist, pathologist, psychiatrist, oculist; allergist, allopath, anesthesiologist, anesthetist, apothecary, pharmacist, chemist, druggist, pharmacologist, chiropractor, clinician, coroner, medical examiner, dental hygienist *or* technician, dentist, orthodontist, orthopedic surgeon, dietitian, nutritionist, faith healer, family doctor *or* practitioner, GP, homeopath, internist, medic, medicine man, shaman, midwife, accoucheur, accoucheuse, naturopathic doctor, nurse practitioner, nurse's aide, nutritionist, oculist, ophthalmologist, optician, optometrist, orderly, orthopedic surgeon, bonesetter, osteopath, otologist, aurist, paramedic, physical therapist, physiotherapist, provider, psychiatrist, psychotherapist (see INSANITY), radiographer, radiologist, radiotherapist, specialist, technician. *Informal,* candy-striper. *Slang,* doc, sawbones, bone crusher, pill pusher, quack, bolus, plumber, gasser, croaker, doctorine, femme D, mediciner, medico, Doctor Feelgood, rear admiral; gumdigger, tooth-doctor.

11, patient (see DISEASE). *Slang,* gomer.

Verbs—remedy, doctor, dose, physic, nurse, operate, minister to, treat, attend; dress the wounds, plaster; prevent, relieve, cure, heal, clear up, palliate, restore (see RESTORATION); bleed; respond to treatment.

Adjectives—remedial, restorative, corrective, curative, palliative, healing, sanatory, sanative; cathartic; antitoxic, antiseptic, prophylactic, medical, medicinal, surgical, therapeutic, tonic, analeptic, balsamic, anodyne, hypnotic, neurotic, narcotic, sedative, lenitive, demulcent, emollient, detergent; antibiotic, bactericidal, bacteriostatic; disinfectant, febrifugal, laxative, dietetic, alimentary, nutritious, nutritive, peptic; curable, remediable. *Informal,* touchy-feely.

Phrases—an apple a day keeps the doctor away; medicine can prolong life, but death will seize the doctor, too; illness tells us what we are; feed a cold, starve a fever; time is a great healer.

Quotations—The remedy is worse than the disease (*Francis Bacon*), Death is the cure of all diseases (*Thomas Browne*), If a lot of cures are suggested for a disease, it means that the disease is incurable (*Anton Chekhov*), God heals and the doctor takes the fees (*Benjamin Franklin*), Natural forces within us are the true healers of disease (*Hippocrates*), Nearly all men die of their medicines, and not of their illnesses (*Molière*), There are some remedies worse than the disease (*Publilius Syrus*).

Antonyms, see DISEASE.

---

remember, *v.t.* recollect (see MEMORY); observe, acknowledge.

remind, *v.t.* prompt (see MEMORY).

reminiscent, *adj.* retrospective, suggestive. See MEMORY.

remiss, *adj.* lax, slack, neglectful, dilatory. See NEGLECT.

remission, *n.* annulment, cancellation; pardon, FORGIVENESS; suspension, respite, abatement. See PAYMENT.

remit, *v.t.* forgive, pardon, excuse, exempt, relax, slacken; restore, replace; discharge, pay, send. See FORGIVENESS, RESTORATION, PAYMENT.

remnant, *n.* REMAINDER, residue, fragment, scrap, vestige.

remodel, *v.t.* rearrange, rebuild, modernize; renovate, rehabilitate, refurbish, make over, recondition. See NEWNESS, RESTORATION, CHANGE.

remonstrance, *n.* protest, objection; reproof, expostulation. See DISSUASION, DISAPPROBATION.

remorse, *n.* self-reproach, REGRET, compunction, contrition, PENITENCE.

remorseless, *adj.* impenitent, hardened, callous, obdurate; hard, cold, ruthless. See IMPENITENCE.

remote, *adj.* distant, secluded, alien; slight, inconsiderable. See DISTANCE, SECLUSION.

remove, *v.* depart, go away, move; displace, excise, shift, eliminate, take off, discharge, evict. See EJECTION, DEPARTURE, DEDUCTION, EXTRACTION, TRANSFER, TRANSPORTATION, DISPLACEMENT.

remunerate, *v.t.* pay, reimburse, recompense, requite, reward. See PAYMENT.

remunerative, *adj.* profitable, paying, rewarding, compensatory, gainful, lucrative; worthwhile. See UTILITY.

renaissance, *n.* renascence, rebirth, revival. See RESTORATION.

rend, *v.t.* tear, shred, rip, rive, split; harrow, cut, cleave. See DISJUNCTION.

render, *v.t.* give, pay, deliver, furnish, supply, yield, produce, perform; express, translate, interpret; reduce, melt; return, present. See GIVING, INTERPRETATION.

rendezvous, *n.* tryst, appointment, date, meeting, assignation. See SOCIALITY, ASSEMBLAGE.

rendition, *n.* rendering; execution, performance, REPRESENTATION; view, version, INTERPRETATION, reading, paraphrase.

renegade, *n.* traitor, turncoat, apostate, defector; mutineer. See EVILDOER. —*adj.* treacherous, disloyal; rebellious, mutinous. See IMPROBITY.

renege, *v.,* *informal,* break one's word or promise, disavow, disclaim, take back, go back (on), cancel, back out. See NULLIFICATION, NEGATION, NONPAYMENT.

renew, *v.t.* revive, restore; resume, continue; replace, renovate, replenish. See RESTORATION, NEWNESS.

renounce, *v.t.* abjure, disclaim, disown, repudiate, reject, give up, abandon, surrender. See REJECTION.

renovate, *v.t.* renew, restore, repair, freshen, purify. See RESTORATION.

renown, *n.* REPUTE, fame, reputation, glory, distinction, kudos.

rent, *n.* tear, slit, fissure; split, division, rupture, schism; payment, return, rental. See INTERVAL.

reorganize, *v.t.* resystematize, remodel, reform, rehabilitate, reestablish. See CHANGE, RESTORATION.

repair, *v.* betake oneself, go; mend, renovate, restore; amend, remedy. See TRAVEL. —*n.* RESTORATION, renovation, mending, redress. See ATONEMENT.

reparation, *n.* amends, redress, restitution, indemnity. See ATONEMENT.

reparative, *adj.* mending, restorative, remedial, corrective, compensatory. See COMPENSATION, RESTORATION, RETALIATION.

repartee, *n.* [witty] retort, [clever] rejoinder, [snappy] comeback (*sl.*); sally, persiflage, banter. See ANSWER, WIT.

repast, *n.* meal, collation, snack; feast, banquet, spread. See FOOD.

repay, *v.t.* reimburse, indemnify, refund; recompense, requite. See PAYMENT, RETALIATION.

repeal, *v.t.* revoke, recall, annul, nullify, vacate, abrogate. See NULLIFICATION.

repeat, *v.t.* iterate, quote, recite; redo, duplicate. See REPETITION, COPY, SIMILARITY.

repel, *v.t.* repulse, resist, reject, scatter, drive apart; disgust, revolt. See PAIN, DISLIKE.

repellent, *adj.* repulsive, resistant, forbidding, distasteful. See RESISTANCE, UGLINESS.

repent, *v.* rue, REGRET. See PENITENCE.

repercussion, *n.* rebound, RECOIL, impact, reverberation, kick; result, EFFECT.

repertory, *n.* repertoire; LIST, catalog, collection, store, stock; acts, routines, bag of tricks (*inf.*), one's paces (*inf.*). See DRAMA.

REPETITION
Act of repeating

Nouns—1, repetition, reiteration, harping; recurrence, reappearance; résumé, recapitulation, run; tautology, monotony, rhythm, periodicity, redundance, alliteration; DIFFUSENESS. See REGULARITY, FREQUENCY, IDENTITY, HABIT.

2, echo, burden of a song, refrain, repetend, encore, rehearsal; drone, monotone; reverberation, reverb, drumming, chimes; twice-told tale, old story, second edition; loop; double duty; old wine in new bottles. *Slang,* chestnut. See MEMORY.

3, reproduction, duplication, reduplication; retake; COPY; SIMILARITY.

Verbs—1, repeat, [re]iterate, reproduce, duplicate, retake, refilm, retape, renew, echo, reecho, drum, pulsate, harp upon, keep after, dwell (upon), drill, hammer, redouble. *Informal,* beat into one's head. *Slang,* rub it in, ding.

2, recur, revert, return, reappear, redound, resume, rehearse, retell, go over the same ground, rehash, return to, [re]capitulate, reword; chew one's cabbage twice, repeat oneself, ring the changes. *Informal,* double in brass.

Adjectives—repeated, repetitive, repetitious, recurrent, recurring, frequent, incessant; monotonous, harping, iterative, chiming, retold, aforesaid, above-mentioned, habitual.

Adverbs—repeatedly, often, again, anew, over again, afresh, once more, ditto, encore, over [and over], time after time, time and [time] again, frequently; da capo.

Interjections—come again? bis!

Phrases—lightning never strikes twice in the same place; history repeats itself; opportunity never knocks twice [at any man's door].

Quotations—Man is a history-making creature who can neither repeat his past nor leave it behind (*W. H. Auden*), There are only two or three human stories, and they go on repeating themselves as fiercely as if they had never happened before (*Willa Cather*), Those who cannot remember the past are condemned to repeat it (*George Santayana*).

Antonyms, see END.

---

repine, *v.i.* fret, complain, mope, grieve, despond. See DISCONTENT, DEJECTION.

replace, *v.t.* put back; supplant, succeed, supersede; substitute; restore, return; move. See SUBSTITUTION.

replay, *n.* repeat, reprise, encore, rebroadcast, instant replay. See REPETITION.

replenish, *v.t.* refill, restock, renew; stock up. See PROVISION, SUFFICIENCY.

repletion, *n.* surfeit, satiety, overfullness, glut, engorgement. See SUFFICIENCY.

replica, *n.* image, double, twin, likeness; facsimile, COPY, reproduction, imitation, duplicate, model; photostat, print, transfer, impression.

replicate, *v.t.* FOLD back; reproduce, COPY.

reply, *n.* ANSWER, response, retort, rejoinder; countermove.

report, *v.t.* state, review; rehearse, give tidings, announce, give notice of, proclaim. See INFORMATION, PUBLICATION. —*n.* record, account, statement; news; rumor; hearsay; fame, repute; bang, blast, detonation. See INFORMATION, NEWS.

reporter, *n.* news gatherer, journalist, newspaperman, leg man (*sl.*), newshound (*sl.*), newshawk (*sl.*). See NEWS, COMMUNICATION.

repose, *v.* rest (see REPOSE); lay, place, entrust, deposit, put. See SUPPORT, LOCATION.

REPOSE
State of rest

Nouns—1, repose, rest, INACTIVITY, relaxation, breathing time *or* spell, letup, halt, pause, respite, breather.

2, (*sleep*) sleep, slumber, somnolence, sound *or* heavy sleep, the land of Nod; Morpheus; coma, swoon, trance; catalepsy; dream; hibernation, estivation; nap, catnap, doze, siesta; land of nod; beauty sleep. *Informal,* forty winks, snooze, shut-eye.

3, (*relaxation*) day of rest, Sabbath, Sunday, Lord's day, holiday, vacation, recess, playtime, liberty, leave [of absence], interlude, getaway, furlough, free time, escape, break, breather, day off, downtime, time off; pause, lull; busman's holiday; leisure, spare time, idleness, ease; coffee break; time out, shore leave; rest and recreation, R and R.

4, (*quiet repose*) quiescence, quiet, stillness, tranquillity, calm, peace, composure; stagnation, stagnancy, immobility.

5, (*relaxing drug*) sedative, tranquilizer, sleeping draft *or* pill, soporific, opiate (see REMEDY, DRUGS). *Slang,* knockout drops.

6, bed, pallet, futon; sleeping bag. *Slang,* fart-sack.

7, [heavy *or* light] sleeper, slumberer, sleepyhead, layabed, dormouse. *Informal,* couch potato.

Verbs—1, (*sleep*) repose, rest, take one's ease, recline, lie down, go to bed, turn in, go to sleep, sleep, slumber, sleep a wink; snore; put to bed; hibernate; oversleep; sleep like a top *or* log; doze, drowse, snooze, nap; dream; snore; nod, yawn. *Informal,* drop off. *Slang,* saw wood, count sheep, conk out, flop, sack out *or* in, hit the hay *or* sack, pound the ear, bag *or* cop some z's, spaniel, kip, rack out, flake out.

2, (*relax*) relax, unbend, slacken, take breath, rest upon one's oars, pause; loaf, idle, while away the time, take a holiday, shut up shop. *Informal,* take it easy, let down, let go, take a breather, take time out, kill time; let one's hair down, catch one's breath. *Slang,* chill [out], cut one a little slack, hang loose, keep cool, lighten up, mellow [out]; knock off.

Adjectives—1, asleep, sleeping, comatose; in the arms of Morpheus; sleepy, drowsy, somnolent; napping, dozing; laid-back. *Informal,* out like a light, dead to the world.

2, reposing, reposed, reposeful, calm, quiet, restful, relaxed, unstrained, tranquil; quiescent, dormant; quiet; leisurely, slow, unhurried, calm; type B.

Adverbs—at rest, at ease, calmly, peacefully; at a standstill; at [one's] leisure, unhurriedly.

Phrases—all work and no play makes Jack a dull boy; some sleep five hours—nature requires seven, laziness nine, and wickedness eleven; the beginning of health is sleep; a change is as good as a rest; idle people have the least leisure.

Quotations—Sleep that knits up the raveled sleeve of care (*Shakespeare*), What hath night to do with sleep? (*John Milton*), Early to rise and early to bed makes a male healthy and wealthy and dead (*James Thurber*), I love sleep because it is both pleasant and safe to use (*Fran Lebowitz*), Rest is for the dead (*Thomas Carlyle*), Too much rest itself becomes a pain (*Homer*), Sleep is the twin of death (*Homer*), Certainty generally is an illusion, and repose is not the destiny of man (*Oliver Wendell Holmes*).

Antonyms, see EXERTION, MOTION, ACTIVITY.

repository, *n.* vault, warehouse, museum. See STORE.

repossess, *v.t.* reclaim, take back, repo (*inf.*). See POSSESSION, TAKING.

reprehensible, *adj.* blameworthy, censurable. See DISAPPROBATION.

represent, *v.t.* portray (see REPRESENTATION); denote, symbolize, stand for; substitute for, replace, represent; set forth, assert; consist in, be composed of. See INDICATION, SUBSTITUTION, AGENCY, AFFIRMATION, COMPOSITION.

REPRESENTATION
Portrayal

Nouns—1, representation, IMITATION, illustration, delineation, depiction, depictment, imagery, portraiture, design, designing, art, fine arts, PAINTING, drawing, SCULPTURE, ENGRAVING, PHOTOGRAPHY, holography; collage, montage; expression. See DESCRIPTION.

2, personation, personification, impersonation; rendition; motion picture, movie, *etc.* See DRAMA.

3, *(graphic portrayal)* picture, drawing, sketch, draft, tracing, COPY, photograph, daguerreotype; hologram; image, likeness, icon, portrait, effigy, facsimile; enlargement, blowup; bitmap, golliwog, sprite; clip art, dingbat; dithering; fractal. See COMPUTERS.

4, *(statue)* figure, puppet, marionette, doll, figurine, action figure, manikin, model, dummy, waxwork, bust, statue, statuette, figurehead, effigy. See SCULPTURE.

5, map, plan, chart, graph, ground plan, blueprint, projection, elevation; diagram, cartography, atlas, outline, view.

6, ARTIST, designer, sculptor, draftsman, delineator.

Verbs—1, represent, delineate, depict, portray; photograph, figure, picture, describe, draw, sketch, trace, graph, COPY, mold, illustrate, symbolize, paint, carve, engrave, *etc.*

2, personate, personify, impersonate, embody, pose as, act [out], play, mimic, imitate.

Adjectives—representative, representing, depictive, illustrative, imitative, figurative, like, graphic, descriptive.

Phrases—all arts are brothers—each is a light to the other.

Quotations—Art is a jealous mistress (*Emerson*), We all know that Art is not truth. Art is a lie that makes us realize truth (*Pablo Picasso*), One picture is worth a thousand words (*Fred Barnard*), A picture is a model of reality (*Ludwig Wittgenstein*)

Antonyms, see DISTORTION.

---

representative, *adj.* typical, characteristic, illustrative, descriptive, exemplary; democratic, legislative, popular, republican. —*n.* delegate, nominee, agent, deputy; congressman, assemblyman, legislator, Member of Congress *or* Parliament, M.P. See AGENT, SUBSTITUTION, AUTHORITY.

repress, *v.t.* suppress, restrain, curb, control, quell, stifle, smother, crush. See RESTRAINT.

reprieve, *n.* delay, stay, respite, suspension; pardon. See LATENESS, FORGIVENESS, ACQUITTAL.

reprimand, *n.* reproof, rebuke, censure,

admonition, reprehension. See DISAPPROBATION.

reprint, *n.* reissue, new edition, revision; COPY, replica. See PUBLICATION.

reprisal, *n.* RETALIATION, revenge, requital, indemnity.

reproach, *v.t.* blame, rebuke, upbraid, censure; stigmatize. —*n.* reproof, blame, disgrace, discredit, dishonor. See DISAPPROBATION, DISREPUTE, ACCUSATION.

reprobate, *n.* sinner, scoundrel; rogue, blackguard. See IMPIETY.

reproduce, *v.* COPY, duplicate; procreate, beget. See REPRODUCTION.

REPRODUCTION
Procreation

Nouns—1, reproduction, sexual reproduction; [re]generation, propagation, multiplication, reenactment, REPETITION, procreation, fructification, breeding, begetting; ontogeny, oogamy; baby boom, blessed event. See RESTORATION.

2, **a.** bringing forth, parturition, birth, childbirth, delivery, confinement, travail, labor, midwifery, obstetrics; gestation, evolution, development, growth; genesis, generation, procreation, progeneration, propagation; fecundation, impregnation; parthenogenesis, spontaneous generation; biogenesis, abiogenesis. See SEX. **b.** oocyte, myoblast, amnion, blastula, germ cell, gamete, egg, meso-, endo-, *or* ectoderm, embryo, estrus, fetus. **c.** spermatozoon, semen, sperm, sex hormone, testosterone. **d.** lacteinizing hormone, LH, androgen, estradiol, estriol, estrogen, FSH, progesterone, somatotropin, growth hormone, GH, prolactin.

3, fecundity, fertility; pregnancy, delicate condition; multiplication; fertilization; pseudopregnancy, false pregnancy. *Informal,* family *or* familiar way.

4, reconstruction, REPRESENTATION, IMITATION, offprint, illustration.

5, pregnant woman, gravida. *Slang,* lady in waiting, light bulb.

Verbs—1, reproduce, reconstruct; multiply, propagate, procreate, revivify, breed, populate, crop up; produce, flower, bear fruit, fructify; teem, yean, farrow, drop, whelp, pup, kitten, find; bear, lay, bring forth, give birth to, lie in, be delivered of; evolve, pullulate, usher into the world. *Slang,* stork.

2, create; mother, father, beget, get, generate, fecundate, impregnate; proliferate, progenerate, fertilize, spermatize, conceive; bud, bloom, blossom, burgeon; engender. *Informal,* get with child. *Slang,* jazz up, knock up, cock up, do the trick, seal, spermatize.

3, become pregnant. *Slang,* blow up, have one in the oven; sprain an ankle, break one's neck, *etc.*

4, COPY, portray, duplicate, repeat, reprint, transcribe.

Adjectives—1, reproductive, reproduced, recreative, procreative, generative.

2, fertile, fecund, creative; genetic, genital; pregnant, expecting, anticipating, enceinte, big with child, with young, parturient; teeming, parturient, puerperal; in vitro, in utero. *Informal,* expectant, in the family way, in an interesting condition *or* situation, that way. *Slang,* bagged, fragrant, knocked up, preggers.

Quotations—We want better reasons for having children than not knowing how to prevent them (*Dora Russell*), Death and taxes and childbirth! There's never any convenient time for any of them (*Margaret Mitchell*), If men could get pregnant, abortion would be a sacrament (*Florynce Kennedy*).

Antonyms, see IMPOTENCE, CELIBACY, HINDRANCE.

---

reprove, *v.t.* admonish, censure, rebuke, chide, criticize. See DISAPPROBATION.

reptile, *n.* saurian, crocodilian, serpent, lizard, *etc.;* toady, bootlicker. See ANIMAL, SERVILITY.

republic, *n.* democracy, free state, commonwealth, res publica; self-government, vox populi; people's republic, soviet; country. See HUMANITY, AUTHORITY.

repudiate, *v.t.* renounce, disavow, disclaim, disown, divorce, deny. See DIS-

SENT, NEGATION, NONPAYMENT, REJECTION.

repugnance, *n.* DISLIKE, aversion, antipathy, disgust; inconsistency, contradictoriness; OPPOSITION. See HATE.

repugnant, *adj.* distasteful, repulsive; incompatible, contrary, antagonistic. See DISAGREEMENT, DISLIKE.

repulse, *v.t.* drive back, repel (see REPULSION); refuse, reject (see REFUSAL, REJECTION).

REPULSION
Driving back

Nouns—1, repulsion, repulse, repellency; REJECTION, rebuff, spurning; diamagnetism; RESISTANCE.

2, revulsion, abhorrence, aversion (see DISLIKE).

Verbs—1, repulse, repel, drive from, beat back; push *or* send away; send, ward, beat, fend, fight, *or* drive off; fling *or* throw back; chase, dispel, scatter, rout, disperse.

2, rebuff, reject, refuse, discard, snub, spurn, kick aside; keep at arm's length, turn one's back upon, give the cold shoulder to. *Informal,* cold shoulder. *Slang,* freeze.

Adjectives—repulsive, repelling, repellent, abhorrent, repugnant, loathsome, odious, offensive, mawkish, nauseating, revolting; diamagnetic. See UGLINESS.

Antonyms, see ATTRACTION.

REPUTE
Reputation

Nouns—1, repute, reputation, distinction, mark, name, figure; note, notability, celebrity, fame, famousness, renown, popularity, credit, prestige, glory, honor; luster, illustriousness, account, regard, face, reputableness, respectability, good *or* fair name. See PROBITY.

2, dignity, GREATNESS, IMPORTANCE, eminence, preeminence.

3, rank, standing, station (see CLASS).

4, elevation, ascent, exaltation, dignification, aggrandizement; dedication, consecration, enthronement, canonization, celebration, enshrinement, glorification.

5, hero, man of mark, celebrity; lion, luminary, notability, somebody, pillar of the church *or* the community; chief, first fiddle, flower, pink, pearl, paragon, star, glitterati; the great and the good; visiting fireman. *Informal,* personality, a legend in one's own lifetime, nine days' wonder. *Slang,* VIP, big wheel.

6, *(sign of good repute)* ornament, honor, feather in one's cap, halo, aureole, nimbus, blaze of glory, laurels.

7, MEMORY, posthumous *or* lasting fame, immortality, immortal name.

Verbs—1, *(make a reputation)* shine [forth], figure, cut a figure, [make a] splash, live, flourish, glitter, gain honor, play first fiddle, take precedence, win laurels, win [one's] spurs, leave one's mark, star, come into vogue, look to *or* rest on one's laurels.

2, *(rival the repute of)* rival, surpass, outshine, outrival, outvie, emulate, eclipse, cast into the shade, overshadow.

3, *(assign repute to)* enthrone, immortalize, deify, exalt; consecrate, dedicate, enshrine, lionize, crown with laurel; honor, confer honor, do honor *or* credit to, accredit, dignify, glorify, look up to, aggrandize, elevate. *Informal,* do proud, put on the map. *Slang,* build up.

Adjectives—1, *(of good repute)* reputable, creditable, honorable, respectable, decent, in good order, in high favor.

2, *(famous)* distinguished, distingué, noted, of note, honored, popular; fashionable; remarkable, notable, celebrated, renowned, talked of, famous, famed, legendary, conspicuous, foremost, in the ascendant; illustrious, glorious, splendid, brilliant, radiant, bright; eminent, prominent, lofty; peerless, superior, preeminent; great, dignified.

3, *(having lasting repute)* imperishable, deathless, immortal, never-fading, time-honored, sacrosanct.

Phrases—character is what we are—reputation is what others think we are; a good reputation stands still—a bad one runs.

Quotations—The celebrity is a person who is known for his well-knownness (*Daniel Boorstin*), A good name is rather to be chosen than great riches (*Bible*), The purest treasure mortal times afford is spotless reputation (*Shakespeare*), Reputation, like a face, is the symbol of its possessor and creator, and another can use it only as a mask (*Learned Hand*), One who has a reputation for rising early can sleep until noon (*Alphonse Daudet*).

Antonyms, see DISREPUTE.

REQUEST
Asking for

Nouns—1, request, requisition, petition, plea, suit, prayer; motion, overture, application, proposition, proposal, OFFER, canvass, address, appeal, apostrophe, orison, incantation; prayer (see WORSHIP). *Slang,* touch, shakedown, bite. See PURSUIT, INQUIRY.

2, *(ways of asking for money)* mendicancy; asking, begging, postulation, solicitation, invitation, entreaty, importunity, beseechment, supplication, imploration, obtestation, invocation, interpellation; fund raising, telethon, radiothon; charity case. *Slang,* sponging.

3, *(one who asks for money)* requester, petitioner, cadger, beggar, solicitor, canvasser, door-to-door salesman; applicant, supplicant, suitor, demander, importuner; bidder, asker. *Informal,* sponger. *Slang,* moocher, freeloader, panhandler, schnorrer.

Verbs—1, request, ask, beg, crave; sue, pray, petition, solicit; invite, beg, beg leave, crave *or* ask a boon; speak for, apply to, call upon, call for, commandeer, enlist, requisition, ask a favor; coax (see FLATTERY).

2, entreat, beseech, plead, conjure, supplicate, implore, adjure, cry to, kneel to, appeal to; invoke, ply, press, urge, beset, importune, dun, cry for help; raise money; hound; whistle for. *Informal,* buttonhole. *Slang,* put the bite, sting, *or* touch on; fly a kite, spange, hit on.

3, *(ways of asking for money)* beg from door to door, go a-begging, cadge, pass the hat. *Informal,* sponge. *Slang,* mooch, panhandle, freeload.

Adjectives—1, requesting, precatory, suppliant, supplicant, supplicatory.

2, importunate, clamorous, urgent, cap in hand, on bended knee, on one's knees.

Adverbs—prithee, do, please, pray, be so good as, be good enough, if you please, for the asking.

Quotations—Ask, and it shall be given you; seek, and ye shall find; knock, and it shall be opened unto you (*Bible*), In an examination those who do not wish to know ask questions of those who cannot tell (*Sir Walter Raleigh*), Animals are such agreeable friends—they ask no questions, they pass no criticisms (*George Eliot*), Ask not what your country can do for you, ask what you can do for your country (*John F. Kennedy*).

Antonyms, see OFFER.

---

requiescat in pace, *Lat.,* [may he] rest in peace. See INTERMENT.

requirement, *n.* want, NECESSITY; the necessary *or* requisite; requisition, demand; needfulness, essentiality, indispensability; urgency, exigency, sine qua non, matter of life and death. See COMPULSION, COMMAND.

requisite, *adj.* necessary, required; imperative, essential, indispensable, urgent, pressing. See NECESSITY.

requisition, *n.* demand, order, claim, exaction, REQUEST. See COMMAND.

requite, *v.t.* retaliate, avenge; repay, indemnify, make amends, reward. See RETALIATION, GRATITUDE.

rescind, *v.t.* revoke, repeal, recall, abrogate, annul. See NULLIFICATION.

rescue, *v.t.* liberate, set free, deliver, save; recover, reclaim. See LIBERATION.

research, *n.* INQUIRY, investigation, study, exploration.

resemblance, *n.* SIMILARITY, likeness, similitude.

RESENTMENT
Feeling of having been affronted

Nouns—1, resentment, displeasure, animosity, anger, wrath, indignation, exasperation; pique, umbrage, huff, miff, soreness, dudgeon, acerbity, virulence, bitterness, acrimony, asperity, spleen, gall [and wormwood], rankling; ill humor, temper (see IRASCIBILITY); HATE, irritation, bile, choler, ire, fume, dander, ferment, ebullition, pet, tiff, slow burn, passion, fit, tantrum. See MALEVOLENCE, JEALOUSY, DISCONTENT.

2, sullenness, moroseness, sulks, black looks, scowl, chip on one's shoulder, hard feelings.

Verbs—1, resent, take amiss, take to heart, take offense, take in bad part, fly into a rage, bridle, bristle, flare up; sulk, pout, frown, scowl, simmer, lower, glower, snarl, growl, gnarl, gnash, snap, look daggers, grind one's teeth; chafe, fume, kindle, seethe, boil [with indignation], get one's back *or* dander up, rage, storm, have a fit, foam [at the mouth], vent one's spleen, take it out on, lose one's temper, quiver with rage; burst with anger. *Informal,* blow one's top, a fuse, a gasket, *or* one's stack, take hard, fly off the handle, see red, burn up. *Slang,* flip one's lid *or* wig, hit *or* go through the ceiling *or* roof, go into orbit.

2, anger, affront, offend, displease, give umbrage, hurt the feelings, tread *or* step on one's toes, insult, fret, ruffle, frazzle, nettle, chafe, wound, incense, inflame, enrage, aggravate, envenom, embitter, exasperate, get one's goat, infuriate, rankle, rub [up] the wrong way, put out of humor, put one's nose out of joint, raise one's dander, make a person's hackles rise, put a person's back up, make one's blood boil, drive one mad. *Slang,* get a rise out of, piss off, jerk someone around, jerk one's chain, rattle one's cage.

3, have a chip on one's shoulder. *Slang,* have one's ass in a sling.

Adjectives—1, resentful, offended, sullen; wrought up, worked up, indignant, hurt. *Informal,* sore, bitchy, on the rag.

2, angry, irate; wrathful, wroth, cross, sulky, bitter, virulent; acrimonious, warm, burning; boiling, fuming, raging; foaming at the mouth; convulsed with rage; in a stew, fierce, wild, rageful, furious, mad with rage, fiery, rabid, savage; flushed with anger, in a huff, in a passion, up in arms, in high dudgeon. *Informal,* hot under the collar, steamed up, blue in the face, fit to be tied, mad as a hornet *or* wet hen, on the warpath, teed off, bent out of shape, rigid. *Slang,* hacked-, pissed-, *or* cheesed-off, loaded for bear.

Adverbs—resentfully, angrily, *etc.;* in the heat of passion, in the heat of the moment.

Phrases—anger improves nothing but the arch of a cat's back; a little pot is soon hot; hell hath no fury like a woman scorned.

Quotations—Envy and wrath shorten the life (*Bible*), People don't resent having nothing nearly as much as too little (*Ivy Compton-Burnett*).

Antonyms, see GRATITUDE.

---

reservation, *n.* exception, QUALIFICATION, misgiving; booking, engagement. See COMMISSION.

reserve, *n.* restriction, qualification; restraint, caution, reticence, dignity; STORE, stock. See SILENCE, MODESTY, ECONOMY, TACITURNITY.

reserved, *adj.* undemonstrative, diffident, distant, reticent; set aside. See MODESTY, SILENCE, STORE.

reservoir, *n.* cistern, reserve, source, supply. See STORE.

res gestae, *Lat.,* exploits; EVIDENCE. See COMPLETION, PRODUCTION.

reside, *v.i.* live, dwell, abide, sojourn, lodge. See ABODE, INHABITANT.

residual, *adj.* left over, extra, surplus; future, continuing. See REMAINDER.

residue, *n.* REMAINDER, rest, remnant, leavings.

RESIGNATION
Giving up

Nouns—1, resignation, demission, retirement, abdication, withdrawal, surrender, quitting; RELINQUISHMENT. See SUBMISSION.

2, resignedness, patience, forbearance, long-suffering, sufferance, acquiescence; passiveness, meekness, stoicism. See INEXCITABILITY.

Verbs—1, resign, withdraw, demit, yield, surrender, resign oneself, grin and bear it, submit, desert, retire, tender one's resignation, lie down, give up, throw in the towel *or* sponge, quit, take it on the chin; make a virtue of necessity.

2, abrogate, abdicate, vacate, step down; walk the plank.

Adjectives—1, resigning, renunciatory, abjuratory, abdicant; retired, in retirement. *Informal*, out to pasture.

2, resigned, submissive, patient, long-suffering, acquiescent, unresisting, complying, yielding, uncomplaining, reconciled, philosophical, stoical.

Quotations—Better to accept whatever happens (*Horace*), A calm despair, without angry convulsion or reproaches directed to heaven, is the essence of wisdom (*Alfred de Vigny*), Hear me, my chiefs, I am tired; my heart is sick and sad. From where the sun now stands, I will fight no more forever (*Chief Joseph*), What is called resignation is confirmed desperation (*Henry David Thoreau*).

Antonyms, see OBSTINACY.

---

resilient, *adj.* elastic, pliable, rubbery, tensile, ductile, malleable; recuperative, tough, rugged; irrepressible, indestructible; resistant, renitent; buoyant, youthful. See ELASTICITY.

resin, *n.* rosin, gum, lac, sealing wax, amber; bitumen, pitch, tar, asphalt, asphaltum; varnish, copal, mastic, lacquer, japan. See COHERENCE.

resistance, *n.* recalcitrance (see RESISTANCE); impedance (see HINDRANCE, ELECTRONICS).

RESISTANCE
Active opposition

Nouns—1, resistance, OPPOSITION, oppugnance, renitence, stand, front; recalcitrance, OBSTINACY; impeding, kicking, parrying, imperviousness, endurance, fastness, immunity, immovability; REPULSION, REFUSAL; impedance; FRICTION. See UNWILLINGNESS, DURABILITY.

2, strike, turnout, lockout, walkout, job action, [work] stoppage; tie-up, slowdown, work-to-rule; boycott; sit-down strike, passive resistance, [civil] DISOBEDIENCE. See REVOLUTION.

3, striker, picket; strikebreaker. *Slang,* scab, rat.

Verbs—1, resist, withstand, stand [firm], stand one's ground, hold one's own, stick to one's own guns, hold out, make a stand, take one's stand, show a bold front. *Informal,* stick it out.

2, oppose, defy, face, confront, stand up against, strive against, bear up against; balk, kick (against), grapple with, keep at bay; obstruct, impede (see HINDRANCE).

3, fight, struggle, put up a fight, attack, defend, persevere, die hard, sell one's life dearly, fight to the last ditch. See TENACITY.

4, [go on] strike, walk [out], turn out, boycott, picket, remonstrate, disobey, sabotage; riot, rebel, revolt; lock out.

Adjectives—resisting, resistant, renitent, resistive, refractory, recalcitrant, disobedient; repellent, repulsive, proof against, up in arms; unconquerable, irresistible, resistless, indomitable, unyielding, invincible; stubborn, obstinate, obdurate, dogged, firm, uncompromising.

Quotations—It is better to die on your feet than live on your knees! (*Dolores Ibarruri*), There is a price which is too great to pay for peace, and that price can be put in one word. One cannot pay the price of self-respect (*Woodrow Wilson*), We are determined to defend our lands, and if it is His will, our bones shall whiten upon them, but we will never give them up (*Tecumseh*).

Antonyms, see OBEDIENCE, SUBMISSION.

RESOLUTION
Determination

Nouns—1, resolution, resoluteness, determination, WILL, decision, strength of mind, resolve, firmness, steadfastness, ENERGY, pluck, grit, backbone, morale, gumption, COURAGE, devotion, devotedness.

2, mastery over self, self-control, self-command, self-possession, self-reliance, moral courage, perseverance, TENACITY, OBSTINACY, doggedness. See INTENTION, STRENGTH.

Verbs—1, resolve, determine, have determination, be resolved, make up one's mind, WILL, decide, form a resolve; conclude; devote oneself to, set one's teeth, put one's foot down, take one's stand; stand firm, steel oneself, stand no nonsense; put one's heart into, take the bull by the horns, go in for, insist upon, make a point of, set one's heart upon; stick at nothing, go the limit, burn one's boats, do or die. *Informal,* go all out, go the whole hog, stick to one's guns, make no bones about.

2, persevere, persist; apply oneself; stick with, stick it out, see it through, leave no stone unturned, move heaven and earth, see out, bear up, hold out, hang on, die hard, fight, insist, never say die. *Informal,* mean business, hang in [there].

Adjectives—resolute, resolved, determined, strong-willed, grim, self-possessed, decided, decisive, definitive, pertinacious, peremptory, unhesitating, unflinching, firm, indomitable, game, inexorable, do-or-die; tireless, untiring, indefatigable, unwearied; relentless, unshakable, inflexible, obstinate, steady, persevering, steadfast. *Informal,* together.

Adverbs—resolutely, in earnest, seriously, earnestly, heart and soul, at any risk, at any price, cost what it may, all or nothing, rain or shine, sink or swim, come hell or high water, through thick and thin.

Phrases—if at first you don't succeed, try, try again; little strokes fell great oaks; *nil carborundum illegitimi* (don't let the bastards grind you down); the show must go on; slow and steady wins the race; we shall overcome; where there's a will there's a way.

Quotations—The best way out is always through (*Robert Frost*), Great works are performed not by strength, but by perseverance (*Samuel Johnson*), Perseverance is the hard work you do after you get tired of doing the hard work you already did (*Newt Gingrich*).

Antonyms, see DOUBT.

---

resolve, *n.* determination, commitment, intention, steadfastness, RESOLUTION. —*v.* determine, decide; separate, solve; elucidate, clear up, explain. See INQUIRY, CHANGE, JUDGMENT, ANSWER.

RESONANCE
Capability to produce vibrations

Nouns—1, vibration; reverberation, resounding, rebound; reflection, echo, reecho; ringing, tintinnabulation; ring, boom, rumble. See LOUDNESS, SOUND.

2, bell, gong, tamtam; triangle, crotales; chime, set of bells, handbell; cowbell; doorbell, school bell, *etc.;* resonator, echo chamber, soundbox, soundboard.

Verbs—resonate, vibrate, reverberate, resound, rebound, reflect, echo, reecho; ring, peal, tintinnabulate, jingle, jangle, tinkle; boom, rumble.

Adjectives—resonant, vibrant, reverberant, resounding, sonorous; ringing, pealing, jingling, jangling, tinkling; booming, rumbling.

Quotations—Every suppressed or expunged word reverberates through the earth from side to side (*Emerson*).

---

resort, *v.i.* gather, flock, frequent; turn to; have recourse to. —*n.* haunt, meeting place; refuge, resource. See USE, ABODE, AMUSEMENT.

resound, *v.i.* echo, reecho, ring, reverberate, peal. See LOUDNESS, SOUND.

resourceful, *adj.* ingenious, inventive, imaginative, versatile, skillful; adaptable, resilient, prepared; devious, CUNNING. See SKILL.

resources, *n.pl.* assets, wealth, PROSPERITY; ingenuity, expedients. See MONEY, MEANS.

respect, *v.t.* heed, regard; relate to, refer to. —*n.* esteem; feature, particular; (*pl.*) compliments. See RESPECT, RELATION, COURTESY.

RESPECT
High esteem

Nouns—1, respect, regard, consideration, COURTESY, ATTENTION, deference, reverence, honor, esteem, estimation, veneration, admiration; APPROBATION, devotion, homage. See WORSHIP, OBEDIENCE.

2, homage, fealty, obeisance, genuflection, genuflexion, kneeling, prostration, obsequiousness, salaam, kowtow, bow, salute. See RELIGION.

3, respects, regards (see COURTESY); duty, devoirs; feather in one's cap.

Verbs—1, respect, regard, admire, consider; think a great deal, a lot, *or* much of, revere, reverence, hold in reverence, honor, venerate, esteem, think much of, look up to, defer to, pay attention to, do honor, hail, salute, pay tribute to, take one's hat off to; kneel to, bow to, bend the knee to, prostrate oneself, WORSHIP.

2, command *or* inspire respect; awe, overawe; dazzle; impress.

Adjectives—1, respectful, deferential, decorous; reverent, reverential, worshipful, obsequious, ceremonious.

2, respected, respectable, worthy, estimable, in high esteem, on a pedestal, time-honored, venerable, emeritus; creditable.

Adverbs—deferentially, *etc.*; with due respect, in honor (of), in homage (to).

Phrases—a prophet is not without honor save in his own country.

Quotations—God is no respecter of persons (*Bible*), We must never forget that the only real source of power that we as judges can tap is the respect of the people (*Thurgood Marshall*), He that will have his son have respect for him and his orders, must himself have a great reverence for his son (*John Locke*), We must respect the other fellow's religion, but only in the sense and to the extent that we respect his theory that his wife is beautiful and his children smart (*H. L. Mencken*), A youth is to be regarded with respect. How do you know that his future will not be equal to our present? (*Confucius*).

Antonyms, see DISRESPECT.

---

respectable, *adj.* worthy, reputable, estimable; moderate, fairly good, decent. See REPUTE.

respective, *adj.* particular, individual, several. See SPECIALITY, APPORTIONMENT.

respectively, *adv.* severally, one by one, each to each; in order. See APPORTIONMENT.

respire, *v.i.* breathe (see WIND).

respite, *n.* postponement, pause, reprieve,

cessation, intermission. See LATENESS, REPOSE.

resplendent, *adj.* shining, lustrous, radiant, splendid, gleaming. See LIGHT, BEAUTY.

response, *n.* ANSWER, reply, rejoinder; reaction; responsory. See MUSIC, FEELING.

responsible, *adj.* trustworthy, dependable; answerable, accountable, liable, chargeable; solvent. See DUTY, LIABILITY.

responsive, *adj.* sympathetic, sensitive, receptive, adaptable; antiphonal. See SOFTNESS, ANSWER.

rest, *n.* REMAINDER, remains, balance, residuum; REPOSE; DEATH. See MUSIC.

restaurant, *n.* café, eating house, coffeehouse, roadhouse, cafeteria, diner, Automat, canteen, grill. See FOOD.

restful, *adj.* soothing, quiet, reposeful, tranquil. See REPOSE.

restitution, *n.* RESTORATION, reparation, amends, *amende honorable;* atonement, redemption; remuneration; recovery, repossession; return, compensation; making good; rehabilitation; indemnification; retrieval; repair. See PAYMENT.

restive, *adj.* nervous, skittish, balky; refractory, disobedient, unruly; uneasy, impatient; restless. See AGITATION, DISOBEDIENCE.

restless, *adj.* nervous, restive, impatient; fidgety, skittish, jumpy, unquiet, disturbed. See AGITATION, CHANGEABLENESS, FEAR.

RESTORATION
Bringing back to a former state

Nouns—1, restoration, reinstatement, replacement, rehabilitation, reestablishment, reconstruction, renovation, renewal, revival, REFRESHMENT, resuscitation, reanimation, revivification, second wind *or* breath; reorganization, perestroika. See IMPROVEMENT, NEWNESS.

2, *(rebirth)* renaissance, renascence, second youth, rejuvenescence, resurrection, resurgence, rebirth, recrudescence, new birth; regeneration, regeneracy, reconversion; comeback; reincarnation.

3, recovery, convalescence, recuperation, cure, repair, reparation, reclamation, retrieval, RELIEF, healing, rectification, cicatrization. See REMEDY.

4, restitution, return, rendition, redemption, reinvestment, ATONEMENT; redress, replevin, REVERSION; status quo ante. *Informal,* giveback.

5, *(someone or something that restores)* restorer, refinisher; repairer, repairman *or* -woman, mechanic; adjuster; service station; halfway house, convalescent home.

Verbs—1, restore, put back, reinstate, rehabilitate, reestablish, reinstall, reconstruct, rebuild, reorganize, reconstitute, reconvert; renew, renovate, regenerate; redecorate, remodel; make *or* do over.

2, recover, rally, convalesce, revive, come to, come around, pull through, be oneself again, come to one's senses, get well, rise from the grave, survive, live again, get over. *Informal,* snap out of it.

3, redeem, reclaim, recover, retrieve, rescue, salvage.

4, *(revive)* redress, cure, heal, REMEDY, doctor, physic, medicate; bring [a]round, set on one's legs; resuscitate, bring to, reanimate, revivify, resurrect, reinvigorate, refresh, freshen, strengthen, pick up; make whole, recoup, make good, make all square, rectify, put to rights, clear up, set straight, correct, put in order, put one's house in order; refit, recruit, reinforce.

5, *(restore to former state)* repair, mend, fix, retouch, touch up, recondition, overhaul, [re]vamp, tinker, patch [up], darn, stop a gap, staunch, caulk, splice, bind up wounds.

6, return, give back, bring back, render up, give up, let go, disgorge, reimburse, refund, remit; get back, revert. *Slang,* cough up, kick back. See RELINQUISHMENT.

Adjectives—1, restored, renewed, convalescent, on the mend, none the worse, on one's feet, all better; refreshed.

2, restoring, restorative, recuperative, sanative, curative, remedial, sanatory, salubrious (see HEALTH); refreshing, bracing.

3, restorable, recoverable, retrievable, curable.

Antonyms, see DESTRUCTION, ACQUISITION.

RESTRAINT
Act of holding back

Nouns—1, restraint, inhibition, repression, discipline, control, check, curb, rein; limitation, restriction; PROHIBITION; monopoly. See CIRCUMSCRIPTION, LIMIT, SUBJECTION, RETENTION, PUNISHMENT, DISSUASION.

2, HINDRANCE, confinement, durance, duress; imprisonment, incarceration, solitary confinement; isolation ward, quarantine; entombment; limbo; captivity; embargo, blockade, siege, besiegement, beleaguerment.

3, arrest, custody, keep, CARE, charge, ward, protection.

4, bond[s], irons, chains, pinions, gyves, fetters, shackles, manacles, handcuffs, bracelets; straitjacket; seat, shoulder, *or* lap belt, car seat, air bag, passive restraint; muzzle, gag, yoke, collar, halter, harness, reins; bit, brake, curb, snaffle, bridle, seine; martingale, lead; tether, hobble, picket, band, leash; bolt, bar, lock, latch; bars, PRISON. See CLOSURE.

5, detainee; prisoner (see PRISON).

Verbs—1, restrain, check, put under restraint, enthrall, enslave, restrict, contain, debar, hinder, clip one's wings; curb, control, govern, hold back, hold in, put down, hold in check *or* leash, harness; withhold, keep under, keep *or* clamp down, repress, suppress, smother, burke, pull *or* rein in; prohibit, inhibit, dissuade. *Informal,* hold one's horses, cramp one's style.

2, enchain, fasten, fetter, shackle, trammel; tie one's hands; bridle, gag, pinion, manacle, handcuff, hobble, bind, pin down, tether, picket, tie up *or* down, secure; moor, anchor, belay. *Informal,* hogtie.

3, arrest; confine; shut up, lock up, box, bottle up, cork up, seal up, hem in, bolt in, wall in, rail in; trap, bring to bay, corner; impound, pen, coop, enclose, cage; snow in. *Slang,* flake, roust, send up. See ENCLOSURE.

Adjectives—1, restrained, in check, constrained, pent up, jammed in, wedged in; bound; muscle-bound; icebound, snowbound, flood bank.

2, stiff, restringent, straitlaced, hidebound, reserved.

Quotations—Judicial decrees may not change the heart, but they can restrain the heartless (*Martin Luther King*).

Antonyms, see FREEDOM.

---

restrict, *v.t.* check, LIMIT, confine, restrain, circumscribe, hinder, impede. See CIRCUMSCRIPTION, HINDRANCE, RESTRAINT.

result, *n.* consequence, conclusion, outcome, upshot, fruit, EFFECT, product. See JUDGMENT.

resume, *v.t.* recommence, reoccupy, retake, reassume; continue. See REPETITION, CONTINUITY.

résumé, *n.* abstract, summary, compendium, condensation, digest, brief, précis, outline, review, synopsis; job summary, [curriculum] vitae. See REPETITION, SHORTNESS.

resurgence, *n.* reappearance, renewal, revival; recovery, refreshment, RESTORATION; improvement, growth, increase, rise, surge.

resurrect, *v.t.* restore, revive, rebuild, reestablish, renew, rehabilitate; reanimate; disinter. See RESTORATION.

resuscitate, *v.t.* revive, restore, reanimate; refresh, revivify. See RESTORATION.

retail, *v.t.* sell, dispense, vend, peddle, spread (gossip). See SALE, INFORMATION.

retain, *v.t.* See RETENTION.

retainer, *n.* emolument, remuneration, PAYMENT; adherent, SERVANT; hireling, henchman; guardian, bodyguard; (*pl.*) household, retinue. See ACCOMPANIMENT.

retake, *v.t.* resume; recover, recapture, retrieve; refilm. See REPETITION.

RETALIATION
Returning like for like

Nouns—1, retaliation, reprisal, requital, counterstroke, retribution, COMPENSATION, reciprocation, reciprocity, retort, counterattack, recrimination, tit for tat, give and take, blow for blow, quid pro quo, measure for measure, the biter bit, comeuppance, just deserts. *Slang,* the hair of the dog [that bit one]. See PUNISHMENT.

2, *(retaliation for a wrong)* revenge, vengeance, avengement; vendetta, feud, grudge fight; an eye for an eye, a Roland for an Oliver, quid pro quo, a dose of one's own medicine.

3, vengefulness, vindictiveness, implacability; spite, rancor (see RESENTMENT).

4, avenger, vindicator, Nemesis, Eumenides, Furies, Erinyes.

Verbs—1, retaliate, strike back, retort, requite, repay, turn upon, pay back, return in kind, pay in the same coin, cap, reciprocate, turn the tables upon, return the compliment, give as good as one gets, give and take, scratch one's back, be quits, be even with, pay off old scores; call *or* make it quits. *Informal,* give one a dose of his own medicine.

2, *(retaliate for a wrong)* revenge, avenge, take one's revenge, get even, get back at, settle the score, square *or* settle accounts, wreak vengeance; feud with.

3, *(have something to retaliate for)* have a bone to pick, harbor a grudge, bear malice, rankle in the breast. *Informal,* have it in for.

4, *(be retaliated against)* get what's coming to one, have it coming.

Adjectives—1, retaliative, retaliatory, recriminatory, retributive.

2, revengeful, vengeful, vindictive, rancorous, ruthless, unforgiving, implacable, relentless.

Phrases—don't cut off your nose to spite your face; he who laughs last laughs best; revenge is a dish best eaten cold; revenge is sweet.

Quotations—Vengeance is mine; I will repay, saith the Lord (*Bible*), Indeed, revenge is always the pleasure of a paltry, feeble, tiny mind (*Juvenal*), Cry "Havoc!" and let slip the dogs of war (*Shakespeare*), Heaven has no rage . . . nor Hell a fury, like a woman scorned (*William Congreve*), In taking revenge, a man is but even with his enemy; but in passing it over, he is superior (*Francis Bacon*), Don't get mad, get even (*Joseph Kennedy*).

Antonyms, see FORGIVENESS.

---

retard, *v.t.* delay, slow down, check, hinder, impede, postpone, hold up. See SLOWNESS, HINDRANCE.

retarded, *adj.* delayed; mentally deficient or handicapped, brain-damaged, moronic; backward, slow. See SLOWNESS, INSANITY.

retch, *v.i.* vomit (see EJECTION).

RETENTION
Keeping in possession

Nouns—1, retention, retaining, holding, keeping, custody, maintenance, PRESERVATION; hold, grasp, gripe, grip, clutch[es]; snare, trap. See POSSESSION, RESTRAINT, TENACITY.

2, retentiveness, retentivity, MEMORY.

3, *(that which retains)* fangs, teeth, claws, talons, nails, hooks, tentacles, nipper, pincer, tusk; paw, hand, finger, digit, fist, jaws; tongs, forceps, tweezers, pincers, nippers, pliers, pucellas, clasp, dog, wrench, cramp, clamp, press, chuck, vise, hand screw, pinchcock, Vise-Grip; grapnel, grappling iron *or* hook.

Verbs—1, retain, hold, keep, maintain, restrain, hold fast *or* tight, hold one's own; clinch, clench, grasp, grip, gripe, hug, hand *or* hold on to; save, preserve, secure, husband, reserve, STORE, withhold, hold *or* keep back, keep close, have a firm hold on, have in stock; keep on; entail, tie up, settle.

2, remember, recall, recollect, bear in mind (see MEMORY).

Adjectives—retentive, retaining, keeping, holding, prehensile; unforfeited, undeprived, undisposed, incommunicable, uncommunicated, inalienable; unforgetting, dependable, tenacious, of good memory.

Antonyms, see RELINQUISHMENT, LOSS.

reticence, *n.* reserve, TACITURNITY, muteness. See CONCEALMENT.

retinue, *n.* train, following, suite, cortege, attendants, retainers. See ACCOMPANIMENT, CONTINUITY, SERVANT.

retire, *v.* withdraw, retreat, leave, resign, rusticate, lie low, keep aloof; put out [to pasture]; go to bed. See SECLUSION, DEPARTURE, RECESSION, RESIGNATION, REPOSE.

retiring, *adj.* modest, unassuming, self-effacing, bashful, withdrawn, shy, diffident. See MODESTY, HUMILITY.

retort, *n.* reply, rejoinder, witticism, sally, comeback (*sl.*); alembic. See ANSWER, WIT, RETALIATION.

retouch, *v.t.* touch up; repaint, polish, *etc.* See RESTORATION.

retract, *v.t.* withdraw, recall, take back, recant, disavow, repudiate, revoke. See NULLIFICATION, NEGATION.

retreat, *n.* withdrawal, retirement; seclusion; shelter, asylum; refuge, resort. See ABODE. —*v.i.* withdraw, retire, fall back. See REGRESSION, DEPARTURE, ESCAPE.

retrench, *v.* cut [down], reduce, decrease, curtail; economize; cut back. See ECONOMY, DEDUCTION.

retribution, *n.* compensation, redress, reparation, reprisal, reciprocation; nemesis; amends. See RETALIATION, PAYMENT.

retrieve, *v.t.* recover, regain, reclaim, repair, restore, make amends, fetch. See RESTORATION, LIBERATION, TRANSPORTATION.

retroactive, *adj.* retrospective, regressive, ex post facto. See PAST.

retrograde, *adj.* retreating, retrogressive, reversed, deteriorating, degenerate, decadent. See REGRESSION.

retrogress, *v.i.* revert, decline. See REVERSION, REGRESSION, DETERIORATION.

retrospect, *n.* reminiscence, remembrance, retrospection, review. See MEMORY.

retrospective, *adj.* looking backward, reminiscent; retroactive. See PAST. —*n.* exhibition, showing. See PAINTING.

return, *v.* restore, put back, bring back, echo, yield, render, reply, ANSWER, reciprocate; nominate, elect; come back, recur, reappear, revert. See RESTORATION. —*n.* ARRIVAL, homecoming, REVERSION, recurrence, reappearance, rebound, ANSWER, reply, recovery, RETALIATION, restitution, compensation; profit, yield. See REPETITION, RECOIL, REGULARITY.

reunion, *n.* gathering, assembling, convention; reconciliation. See SOCIALITY, RESTORATION.

revamp, *v.t.* do *or* make over; recast, rework, rewrite; rehash, remodel, redesign, modernize, improve. See CHANGE, RESTORATION.

reveal, *v.t.* disclose, show, divulge, announce, display, exhibit, expose, bare. See DISCLOSURE, VISIBILITY.

revel, *v.i.* disport, gambol, romp, carouse; delight in, enjoy. See PLEASURE. —*n.* lark, spree, carouse. See AMUSEMENT, REJOICING.

revelation, *n.* DISCLOSURE, manifestation, exposition, revealment; Bible. See SACRED WRITINGS.

revelry, *n.* merrymaking, festivity, conviviality, jollification. See AMUSEMENT, REJOICING.

revenge, *n. & v.* See RETALIATION.

revenue, *n.* income, receipts; earnings, profits, net, yield, dividends; taxes, tariff, customs, duties. See RECEIVING.

reverberate, *v.i.* reecho, respond, be reflected. See SOUND, LOUDNESS, RECOIL.

revere, *v.t.* venerate, honor, RESPECT, esteem, admire; WORSHIP. See LOVE, PIETY.

reverend, *adj.* venerable, worshipful. See RESPECT, CLERGY.

reverent, *adj.* respectful; devout, reverential. See RESPECT, PIETY.

reverie, *n.* daydream, musing, fancy, brown study, woolgathering. See IMAGINATION, INATTENTION.

reversal, *n.* setback; turnabout, tit-for-tat; INVERSION; repeal; upset; abrogation. See CHANGE, REVERSION.

reverse, *n.* antithesis, converse, opposite; misfortune, setback, comedown, defeat; tail, back (of coin), about-face, right- about. See OPPOSITION. —*v.t.* transpose, invert, evert, turn around; back; revoke, annul, set aside. See NULLIFICATION.

REVERSION
Return to a former state

Nouns—1, reversion, reverse, reversal, return[ing], reconversion; atavism, reversion to type; turning point, turn of the tide; REGRESSION, relapse, recurrence; RESTORATION; INVERSION; RECOIL, reaction, backlash. See TRANSFER.

2, throwback, revenant, atavist; repeater, recidivist; backslider; escheat, lapse, succession; reversionist.

Verbs—revert, return, reverse; turn, hark, *or* go back; recur, recidivate, recrudesce, relapse; restore; retreat, RECOIL; turn the tide *or* scale[s]; regress, retrogress, backslide, escheat, lapse; do an about face *or* a 180.

Adjectives—reversionary, reversive, reversional, regressive, retrogressive, recidivist; reactionary; atavistic; reversionable.

Quotations—Trust, like the soul, never returns once it is gone (*Publilius Syrus*), Oh, call back yesterday, bid time return (*Shakespeare*), For all at last returns to the sea (*Rachel Carson*).

Antonyms, see CHANGE.

review, *v.t.* reexamine, reconsider, revise, recall, rehearse, criticize, inspect. See INQUIRY, MEMORY, ATTENTION. —*n.* retrospection, recollection; critique, criticism; inspection, parade; résumé, recapitulation, summary. See DRAMA, REPETITION, THOUGHT, JUDGMENT.

revile, *v.t.* abuse, vilify, malign, asperse, calumniate, deride. See CONTEMPT, DETRACTION.

revise, *v.t.* alter, correct, reconsider, edit, amend, rewrite. See IMPROVEMENT.

revision, *n.* redaction; emendation, IMPROVEMENT; new version, remake, rewrite, new edition; old wine in new bottles; innovation, enlargement.

revival, *n.* resuscitation, revivification, reanimation; WORSHIP, camp meeting; reestablishment, reintroduction. See RESTORATION.

revivalist, *n.* evangelist, gospel shouter, jubilee singer. See PIETY.

revive, *v.* reanimate, revivify; refresh; bring back, reestablish; rally, perk up. See RESTORATION.

revoke, *v.t.* recall, repeal, annul, rescind, withdraw, abrogate; recant, repudiate, disavow. See NULLIFICATION.

revolt, *n.* uprising, rebellion, insurgence, insurrection, mutiny, sedition; demonstration. See DISOBEDIENCE, REVOLUTION.

revolting, *adj.* disgusting, repellent, loathsome, repulsive. See UNCLEANNESS.

revolution, *n.* uprising (see REVOLUTION); ROTATION; cycle. See CIRCUIT.

REVOLUTION
Radical change

Nouns—1, revolution, radical *or* sweeping CHANGE, clean sweep, foquismo; coup, coup d'état, uprising, counterrevolution, shakeup, breakup, upset, overthrow, putsch, reversal, debacle, cataclysm, upheaval, groundswell, convulsion, revulsion. See DESTRUCTION.

2, insurrection, rebellion, revolt, insurgence, insurgency, mutiny; RETALIATION; riot, uprising, DISORDER, sabotage; civil disobedience *or* disorder, strike, boycott, direct action; demonstration. See RESISTANCE, WARFARE.

3, revolutionary, rabblerouser, rebel, guerrilla, incendiary, young Turk, freedom fighter, urban guerrilla; anarchist, destructionist; Intifada; red, Bolshevik, Jacobin, Fenian, Luddite, *etc.*; fifth column, popular front; cell, foco.

Verbs—1, revolutionize, change radically, remodel, recast, refashion, reform, change the face of, break with the past.

2, rebel, revolt. *Slang,* kick over the traces.

Adjectives—revolutionary, anarchic, rebellious, insurgent, radical, antiestablishment, revulsionary, cataclysmic; Bolshevist, Fenian; card-carrying.

Phrases—every revolution was first a thought in one man's mind; rebellion to tyrants is obedience to God.

Quotations—A desperate disease requires a dangerous remedy (*Guy Fawkes*), When people contend for their liberty, they seldom get anything by their victory but new masters (*Lord Halifax*), *Après nous le déluge* (*Mme. de Pompadour*), A little rebellion now and then is a good thing (*Thomas Jefferson*), Anarchism is a game at which the police can beat you (*G. B. Shaw*), Those who make peaceful revolution impossible will make violent revolution inevitable (*J. F. Kennedy*), What is a rebel? A man who says no (*Albert Camus*), A great revolution is never the fault of the people, but of the government (*Goethe*), Revolution is the proper occupation of the masses (*Mao Zedong*), A revolution is like a forest fire. It burns everything in its path (*Malcolm X*).

Antonyms, see INACTIVITY, PERMANENCE.

---

revolve, *v.* rotate, roll, circle, spin, recur. See ROTATION.

revolver, *n.* handgun, pistol, repeater, six-shooter, six-gun. See ARMS.

revue, *n.* review, vaudeville; Follies, New Faces, *etc.* See DRAMA.

revulsion, *n.* DISLIKE, distaste, aversion, repugnance, disgust, repulsion.

reward, *n.* reward, recompense, remuneration, meed, prize, guerdon; indemnity, indemnification; quittance; compensation, reparation, redress (see RESTORATION); perquisite; spoils; salary, pay, PAYMENT; tribute, bonus, tip, premium, fee, honorarium, jackpot, payoff. —*v.* recompense, repay, requite, remunerate, compensate; enrich, indemnify, satisfy; pay off.

rhapsody, *n.* ecstasy, exaltation, transport, rapture; effusion, tribute, eulogy, panegyric, lyricism. See PLEASURE, POETRY.

rhetoric, *n.* oratory, eloquence, elocution, declamation, floridity. See SPEECH.

rheumatism, *n.* inflammation; ache; rheumatoid arthritis, sciatica, gout, bursitis, lumbago, backache; neuritis, rheumatic fever, rheumatics, the rheumatiz (*inf.*), the misery (*inf.*). See DISEASE.

rhyme, *n.* alliteration, assonance; verse, poesy, doggerel; agreement, harmony, concord, SIMILARITY. See POETRY.

rhythmic, *adj.* metrical, pulsating, periodic, recurrent. See REGULARITY.

rib, *v.t., informal,* tease, kid, razz (*inf.*), roast (*inf.*). See WIT.

ribald, *adj.* coarse, low, broad, vulgar; profane, blasphemous. See IMPURITY, VULGARITY.

ribbon, *n.* riband, strip; badge; (*pl.*) shreds, tatters. See FILAMENT, REPUTE, DISJUNCTION.

rich, *adj.* wealthy, affluent, opulent; fruitful, fertile, luxuriant; vivid; fattening; abundant, bountiful; sumptuous; gorgeous; sonorous, mellow. See MONEY, ORNAMENT.

riches, *n.pl.* wealth, possession, fortune, affluence, opulence. See MONEY.

rich man, Croesus, Midas, Dives, [multi] millionaire, capitalist, moneybags. See MONEY.

rickety, *adj.* shaky, infirm, weak, ramshackle; rachitic. See WEAKNESS, DISEASE.

ricochet, *n.* bounce, rebound, carom, RECOIL. —*v.i.* bounce off, carom, cannon (*Brit.*), glance off, deflect, reflect, skim, RECOIL.

rid, *v.t.* free, disburden, disencumber. See EJECTION, LIBERATION, LOSS.

riddle, *n.* conundrum, enigma, puzzle; problem, poser. See SECRET, DIFFICULTY, UNINTELLIGIBILITY.

ride, *v.i.* drive, tour, journey, travel; jog, gallop, trot, *etc.*; cycle, pedal. —*v.t.* be borne; sit (a horse); mount, straddle; tease, harass. See SUPPORT, TRAVEL, RIDICULE.

rider, *n.* postscript, codicil, ADDITION; horseman, cyclist, passenger, *etc.* See TRAVEL.

ridge, *n.* fold, welt, wrinkle, flange; arete, spine, esker. See HEIGHT.

RIDICULE
Derision

Nouns—1, ridicule, derision, scoffing, mockery, quiz, banter, irony, persiflage, raillery, chaff, badinage. See CONTEMPT.

2, parody, burlesque, travesty, farce, caricature, camp; buffoonery, practical joke. See WIT.

3, ridiculousness, *etc.* (see ABSURDITY).

4, sarcasm; squib, lampoon, satire, skit, quip, grin, leer; insult. *Slang*, Bronx cheer.

5, laughingstock, fool, object of ridicule, fair game, April fool, jest, joke, queer *or* odd fish, mockery, monkey, buffoon, caution. *Slang*, goat, gag. See FOLLY.

Verbs—1, ridicule, deride, jeer; laugh, grin, *or* smile at, tease; snigger, snicker, scoff, banter, rally, chaff, joke, twit, gibe, rag, mock, tease, poke fun at, play tricks on, fool, show up; satirize, parody, caricature, lampoon, burlesque, travesty, make fun of, make game of, make a fool of. *Informal,* give a bad time. *Slang,* roast.

2, be ridiculous, play the fool, make a fool of oneself, commit an absurdity, raise a laugh. *Slang,* camp it up.

Adjectives—derisive, derisory, mock; sarcastic, cutting, facetious; ironical, quizzical, burlesque, satirical, scurrilous, base.

Quotations—He jests at scars that never felt a wound (*Shakespeare*), There is nothing so ridiculous but some philosopher has said it (*Cicero*), Ridicule is the best test of truth (*Lord Chesterfield*).

Antonyms, see RESPECT.

---

ridiculous, *adj.* laughable, absurd, preposterous. See ABSURDITY.

riding, *n.* horsemanship, motoring; district, bailiwick (*both Brit.*). See TRAVEL, REGION.

rife, *adj.* prevalent, current, widespread, epidemic; abundant, plentiful, profuse, teeming. See NEWS, GENERALITY.

riffraff, *n.* rabble, canaille, dregs of society. See POPULACE.

rifle, *n.* gun, firearm; piece, carbine, automatic rifle; [sub]machine gun; chasse-pot, culverine, needle gun; flintlock, wheel lock, matchlock. See ARMS.

rift, *n.* crack, cleft, crevice, fissure; schism, breach. See INTERVAL.

rig, *v.* equip, furnish, fit out; improvise, jury-rig; appoint; scheme, manipulate, maneuver, fix (*inf.*), frame (*inf.*); clothe, outfit. —*n.* rigging, ropes, ropework, cordage, ratlines, shrouds, stays, wires; equipment, outfit, fittings, furnishings; VEHICLE; apparatus, machinery, pump, derrick, well. See PLAN, PROVISION.

RIGHT
Pertaining to the right side

Nouns—1, right; rightness, dextrality; right hand *or* side, dexter, starboard (*naut.*), recto, decanal side, off side. See SIDE.

2, conservativism, reactionarism, Toryism, *etc.* (see PERMANENCE).

3, conservative, reactionary, Tory; right-hander; moral majority.

Verbs—turn [to the] right. *Slang,* hang a louie.

Adjectives—1, right, dextral, dexter, off [side], starboard, recto.

2, rightist, conservative, right-wing, Tory, antileftist, reactionary; right-handed; clockwise.

Adverbs—rightward[s], right-handedly, starboard.

Antonyms, see LEFT.

RIGHTNESS
Conformity with reason or justice

Nouns—1, rightness, right, what ought to be, what should be, fitness, propriety; due[ness], rightfulness; morality, PROBITY, honor, VIRTUE, lawfulness; dictate of conscience. See AGREEMENT.

2, right, privilege, prerogative, title, claim, grant; franchise, license; human *or* civil rights, bill of rights; suffrage, woman's rights, feminism; affirmative action; executive privilege; states' rights; right to life, right to die, right to work, *etc.* See PERMISSION, POSSESSION, FREEDOM.

3, [civil, women's, *etc.* rights] activist; suffragist, feminist, suffragette (*archaic*).

4, correctness, accuracy, precision; exactness, TRUTH.

Verbs—1, be right *or* just, stand to reason.

2, right, make right, correct, remedy, see justice done, play fair, do justice to, recompense, hold the scales even, give everyone his due.

Adjectives—1, right, upright, good; rightful, just, equitable, due, square, fit[ting], meet, seemly, reasonable, suitable, becoming; decorous, creditable; allowable, lawful, legal, legitimate, licit, in the right.

2, right, correct, proper, precise, exact, accurate, true. *Slang,* right on, on the nose.

Adverbs—rightly, justly, fairly, correctly; in justice, in equity, in reason, without distinction of persons, on even terms; just so.

Phrases—a right sometimes sleeps, but it never dies; rights are lost by disuse; two wrongs don't make a right.

Quotations—I had rather be right than be president (*Henry Clay*), Natural rights is simple nonsense (*Jeremy Bentham*), We hold these truths to be self-evident, that all men are created equal (*Thomas Jefferson and others*), There is no such thing as rights anyhow. It is a question of whether you can put it over. In any legal sense or practical sense, whatever is, is "a right" (*Clarence Darrow*).

Antonyms, see WRONG, INJUSTICE.

---

righteous, *adj.* godly, upright, just, moral, good; puritanical; devout, virtuous. See VIRTUE.

rightful, *adj.* See RIGHTNESS.

rigid, *adj.* stiff, inflexible, unyielding; set, firm, obdurate, strict; rigorous, clean-cut. See HARDNESS, SEVERITY, OBSTINACY.

rigor, *n.* harshness, hardness, austerity, SEVERITY, stringency, rigorousness, strictness, rigidity, inflexibility, sternness.

rigor mortis, *Lat.,* the stiffness of DEATH.

rile, *v.t., informal,* annoy, vex. See DISCONTENT.

rill, *n.* brook, stream. See WATER.

rim, *n.* EDGE, border, margin, curb, brink.

rime, *n.* ice, [hoar]frost. See COLD.

rind, *n.* skin, peel, epicarp, integument. See COVERING.

ring, *v.* encircle, girdle, environ, encompass, hem in; toll, chime, clang, peal, tinkle; resound, reverberate, reecho. See SOUND. —*n.* circlet, circle, annulet,

hoop, signet, girdle; machine, gang, clique; ARENA; ringing, peal, chime. See PARTY, CIRCULARITY.

ringer, *n., slang,* dead ringer, double, look-alike; substitute; pretender, fraud, poseur. See SIMILARITY, DECEPTION, SUBSTITUTION.

ringleader, *n.* rabble-rouser, demagogue. See CAUSE.

rink, *n.* course, drome, skating palace; ice-drome, rollerdrome. See ARENA, AMUSEMENT.

rinky-dink, *adj., slang,* cheap, shabby (see CHEAPNESS).

rinse, *v.* rewash, dip, splash; tint, color, touch up. See CLEANNESS. —*n.* conditioner, hairdressing, hair rinse.

riot, *n.* brawl, uprising; DISORDER, row, fracas, uproar, tumult. See DISOBEDIENCE, VIOLENCE.

rip, *v.t.* tear, split, rend, slit, sever, part. See DISJUNCTION.

ripe, *adj.* mature[d], perfect[ed], com-

plete, mellow, consummate, ready. See
PREPARATION, AGE, COMPLETION.

ripen, *v.t.* mature, prepare, perfect, mellow, season, temper. See CHANGE, COMPLETION.

ripoff, *n.,* *slang,* DECEPTION, swindle.

riposte, *n.* thrust, counterthrust *or* -stroke, parry, stroke; repartee, witticism, mot, [wise]crack. See WIT, ANSWER.

ripple, *v.i.* gurgle, babble, purl. —*n.* riffle, wavelet. See AGITATION, WATER.

rise, *v.i.* arise, ascend, soar; slope upward; loom, appear; INCREASE, augment; orig-

inate, spring from; get up; prosper; revolt, rebel. —*n.* ASCENT; acclivity, slope; origin, source; appreciation, INCREASE; promotion, advancement; revolt; *slang,* reaction. See OBLIQUITY, BEGINNING, CAUSE, PROGRESSION, DISOBEDIENCE.

risible, *adj.* laughable; jovial, merry. See CHEERFULNESS, ABSURDITY.

risk, *v.t.* CHANCE, venture, hazard, gamble, jeopardize; invest. See DANGER, RASHNESS.

risqué, *adj.* suggestive, indelicate, off-color, racy, spicy, sexy, daring. See IMPURITY.

RITE
Solemn observance

Nouns—1, rite, ceremony, ceremonial, ordinance, observance, CELEBRATION, duty, form, function, office, solemnity, sacrament; service. See RELIGION, WORSHIP, OSTENTATION.

2, *(religious teaching)* ministration, preaching, sermon, homily, preachment. See TEACHING.

3, *(church sacraments)* seven sacraments: baptism, christening, immersion; confirmation, laying on of hands; Eucharist, Lord's supper, communion, consecration, transubstantiation, consubstantiation, Mass; penance, ATONEMENT, repentance, confession; extreme unction, last rites; holy orders, ordination; matrimony, MARRIAGE.

4, *(church rites)* canonization, transfiguration, telling of beads, processional, purification, incense, holy water, aspersion, offertory, burial, excommunication; ablution, absolution, benediction, blessing, benison, confession, consecration, faith healing, lustration, oblation.

5, *(religious objects)* relics, rosary, beads, reliquary, host, cross, crucifix, pax, pyx, agnus Dei, censer, thurible, rood, chrys[o]m, chalice, Eucharistic cup, aspergillum, aspersorium, chrism, chrisom, ciborium, crosier, stoup; shofar, tefillin, yarmulke, phylactery.

6, *(service materials)* ritual, rubric, canon, ordinal, liturgy, prayer book, Book of Common Prayer, litany, lectionary, missal, breviary, Mass book; psalter, hymn book, hymnal, psalmody, chant.

7, ritualism, ceremonialism, Sabbatarianism; ritualist, Sabbatarian.

8, holy day, feast, fast, Sabbath, Passover (see REGULARITY).

9, *(magic rites)* incantation, mumbo jumbo, abracadabra, black art, cabala, calling up of spirits, haruspication, idolatry, levitation, mysteries, spirit rapping *or* writing, sun dance.

Verbs—perform service, celebrate [the mass], minister, officiate, baptize, christen, confirm, lay hands on, administer *or* receive the sacrament; administer *or* receive extreme unction, anoint, anele; preach, sermonize, lecture, deliver a sermon, homily, *etc.*

Adjectives—ritual, ritualistic, ceremonial, liturgical, baptismal, eucharistical, sacramental.

---

ritzy, *adj., slang,* classy, swell, swank[y], plush, posh. See OSTENTATION.

rival, *n.* competitor, contender, antagonist, emulator. —*v.t.* vie *or* cope with; emulate; exceed, excel. See OPPOSITION, CONTENTION, REPUTE.

river, *n.* waterway (see WATER).

rivet, *n.* pin, bolt. —*v.t.* fasten, bolt, pin; arrest *or* engage the ATTENTION. See CONNECTION.

riveting, *adj.* fascinating, engrossing (see ATTENTION).

road, *n.* way, path, track, PASSAGE, highway, roadway, thoroughfare, trail; anchorage. See ABODE.

roam, *v.i.* wander, range, ramble, rove, stray, stroll. See DEVIATION, TRAVEL.

roar, *v.i.* shout, bellow, howl, bawl; resound, roll, rumble, thunder; guffaw. —*n.* uproar, vociferation; roll, rumble, boom, rote; guffaw. See LOUDNESS, CRY, LAMENTATION, REJOICING.

roast, *v.t.* grill, barbecue, broil, bake, toast, parch; *slang,* tease, RIDICULE. See HEAT, FOOD.

rob, *v.t.* plunder, rifle, pillage, steal, purloin, burglarize; defraud. See STEALING.

robe, *n.* cloak, mantle, gown, vestment, robe of state; purple. See CLOTHING.

robot, *n.* automaton, golem, mechanical man, cybernaut; slave, drudge, worker; pawn, cat's-paw, puppet, dummy. See SERVANT, INSTRUMENTALITY, NECESSITY.

robust, *adj.* vigorous, healthy, lusty, strong, sturdy, stalwart; rude, boisterous, rough. See HEALTH, STRENGTH.

rock, *v.i.* swing, sway, oscillate, teeter. See OSCILLATION. —*n.* crag, boulder, cliff, stone; refuge, haven, support, defense; *slang,* diamond, jewel, gem. See LAND, STABILITY.

rock-bottom, *adj.* basic, fundamental. See LOWNESS, SUPPORT.

rocket, *n.* projectile, missile; propulsor; rocket *or* space ship; skyrocket, firework. See ASTRONAUTICS, ARMS, VELOCITY.

rocky, *adj.* rugged, stony, hard; unfeeling; dizzy, shaky. See ROUGHNESS.

rod, *n.* wand, pole, staff, switch, scepter, caduceus; *slang,* pistol, gat. See SUPPORT, ARMS.

rogue, *n.* vagabond, scoundrel, cheat, scamp; imp. See EVILDOER.

roguery, *n.* knavishness, rascality, mischief. See IMPROBITY, BADNESS.

roguish, *adj.* dishonest; mischievous, prankish, waggish. See AMUSEMENT, IMPROBITY.

roil, *v.t.* disturb, vex, annoy. See DISCONTENT.

roister, *v.i.* bluster, swagger, bully; rollick, frolic, make merry, riot; rejoice, celebrate, paint the town [red], carry on, raise hell (*sl.*). See BOASTING, AMUSEMENT.

role, *n.* PART, character, career, function, business. See CONDUCT, DRAMA. —**role model,** standard, example (see CONFORMITY).

roll, *n.* drumming, rumble, rattle, clatter, patter, toll; trill, chime, beat; reverberation, echoing, thunder; tattoo, rat-a-tat, rub-a-dub, pitter-patter, dingdong, ticktock, charivari, quaver, peal of bells; biscuit, bun, muffin, gem, popover,

scone (see FOOD). —*v.* drum, rumble (see *n.*); reverberate, reecho, resound; whirl, twirl. See SOUND, LOUDNESS, ROTATION, CONVOLUTION, ROTUNDITY.

rollback, *n.* reduction, retrenchment. See DECREASE, REGRESSION.

roller, *n.* cylinder, wheel, roll, rouleau, platen, mill; breaker. See ROTATION, ROTUNDITY, WATER.

roly-poly, *adj.* pudgy, tubby, stout, obese; round. See ROTUNDITY.

romance, *n.* novel, love story; exaggeration, fiction, tall story; love affair, gest, fantasy. See DESCRIPTION, IMAGINATION, FALSEHOOD.

romantic, *adj.* sentimental, heroic, picturesque, idealistic; dreamy, poetic, fantastic, visionary, quixotic, fanciful. See IMAGINATION, SENSIBILITY.

romp, *v.i.* frolic, caper, cavort, gambol, frisk. See AMUSEMENT.

roof, *n.* COVERING, housetop, rooftop, shelter, ceiling; home, rooftree; top, summit. See ABODE, HEIGHT.

rook, *v.* cheat, fleece (see STEALING).

rookie, *n., slang,* beginner, novice, greenhorn, tenderfoot. See BEGINNING.

room, *n.* chamber, hall, apartment; SPACE, capacity, elbow room; lodging. RECEPTACLE, ABODE. —*v.* lodge, put up (see ABODE).

roomer, *n.* tenant, lodger, occupant, boarder, INHABITANT.

roommate, *n.* berth *or* bunk mate, bunkie (*inf.*), roomie (*sl.*). See FRIEND.

roomy, *adj.* spacious, commodious, capacious, ample. See SPACE.

roost, *n.* perch, foothold, limb, branch; nest, rookery; *informal,* ABODE, residence, refuge, place, berth, bunk, niche. —*v.i.* alight, land, perch on; stay, remain, settle, nestle, bed down; *informal,* lodge, inhabit. See LOCATION.

root, *n.* rootlet, radicle, radicel, taproot; radical; base, origin, essence, source; etymon. See NUMERATION, CAUSE. —*v.* plant, implant, fix; eradicate, extirpate; take root; *informal,* acclaim, cheer. See LOCATION, ABODE, APPROBATION.

rope, *n.* cord, line; hawser, painter, lanyard; lasso, riata; hangman's noose, execution; string, twist. See FILAMENT.

rosary, *n.* beads, beadroll; garland, bed of roses. See RITE.

roseate, *adj.* rosy, blooming; optimistic, promising, propitious. See COLOR, HOPE.

roster, *n.* LIST, register, roll call, muster; membership; schedule, program; census, count, tally, record, catalog, slate. See PLAN, PREPARATION.

rostrum, *n.* platform, dais, podium, stand, floor, pulpit, lectern. See SUPPORT.

rosy, *adj.* blushing, blooming, bright, promising, hopeful. See COLOR, HOPE.

rot, *v.i.* decay, decompose, putrefy; degenerate, waste. See DETERIORATION. —*n.* decay, decomposition, putrefaction; *slang,* nonsense, twaddle (see UNMEANINGNESS).

rotary, *adj.* turning, rotational (see ROTATION).

rotate, *v.* revolve, turn round, pivot; alternate. See ROTATION, OSCILLATION.

ROTATION
Motion around a center axis

Nouns—1, rotation, revolution, gyration, turning, circulation, roll; circumrotation, circumvolution, circumgyration, turbination, CONVOLUTION.

2, whir, whirl, turn, pirouette, eddy, vortex, whirlpool, cyclone, tornado; vertigo; maelstrom; stadium effect.

3, *(object that rotates)* wheel, screw, whirligig, windmill, propeller, top, roller, flywheel; caster; axis, axle, spindle, pivot, pin, hinge, pole, swivel, bobbin, mandrel, reel; turbine; carousel, merry-go-round; rotor, arbor; crank; capstan.

Verbs—rotate, roll, revolve, spin, turn, turn around, swivel, circulate, gyrate, wheel, whirl, twirl, eddy, trundle, bowl, roll up, furl, spin like a top; whirl like a dervish; pivot; crank; turn on one's heel, turn on a dime.

Adjectives—rotary, rotating, rotatory, rotational, rotative, whirling, circumrotatory, trochilic, dizzying, vertiginous, gyratory, vortical; centrifugal, centripetal.

Antonyms, see DIRECTION, STRAIGHTNESS.

---

rote, *n.* —**by rote,** by MEMORY, memorized.

rotten, *adj.* decomposed, putrefied, putrid; unsound, treacherous; corrupt; dishonest; offensive, disgusting. See UNCLEANNESS, DETERIORATION, BADNESS.

ROTUNDITY
Rounded-out quality

Nouns—1, rotundity, roundness, cylindricity, sphericity, spheroidicity, orbicularity, globosity, globularity. See CIRCULARITY, CURVATURE.

2, *(spherical object)* cylinder, cylindroid, barrel, drum, roll, rouleau, roller, column, rundle; sphere, globe, ball, spheroid, ellipsoid, drop, spherule, globule, blob, bubble, vesicle, bulb, bullet, pellet, bead, pill, BB shot, marble, pea, knob, pommel; cone, conoid, funnel, cornet; pear-, egg-, *or* bell-shape; bubo.

3, corpulence, obesity, embonpoint, stoutness, plumpness; middle, midsection, abdomen. *Informal,* bay window, breadbasket, belly, middle-age spread, spare tire, brisket, love handles, front porches, epigastrium, tummy, venter. *Slang,* fat city; bazoo, guts, table-muscle, puzzle-gut, bubble butt. See CONVEXITY, SIZE.

4, fat *or* obese person. *Informal,* fatty. *Slang,* chubbette, lardo, lard-ass, lard-bucket, porker, oinker, buffalo.

Verbs—round [out], fill out, sphere, form into a sphere, ball, roll into a ball; snowball, bead; round off.

Adjectives—1, rotund[ate], round, circular; cylindric[al], columnar; conic[al], funnelshaped, infundibular; spherical, orbicular, globular, global, globous, gibbous; beadlike, moniliform; pear-shaped, pyriform; egg-shaped, oval, ovoid, oviform, elliptical; bulbous, fungilliform; bell-shaped, campanulate, campaniform; eccentric.

2, corpulent, obese, fat, stout, plump, chubby, beefy, barrel-chested, adipose, ample, dumpy, fleshy, hunky, lumpish, meaty, overstuffed, paunchy, porcine, portly, potbellied, pudgy, tubby, thickset, stocky, full-fleshed, well-padded, callipygian, callipygous, roly-poly, differently sized; buxom, full[-figured], top-heavy, curvaceous, voluptuous, zaftig. *Slang*, stacked, built [like a brick shithouse].

3, resonant, sonorous, rounded, grandiloquent, magniloquent (see LOUDNESS).

Quotations—Has it ever struck you that there's a thin man inside every fat man? (*George Orwell*), The opera ain't over till the fat lady sings (*Anon.*), Guns will make us powerful; butter will only make us fat (*Hermann Goering*), Fat is a feminist issue (*Susie Orbach*).

Antonyms, see ANGULARITY, LAYER.

---

roué, *n.* rake, libertine. See IMPURITY.
roughage, *n.* fodder, bulk (see FOOD).
roughhouse, *n.* rowdiness, horseplay. See AMUSEMENT.

roughly, *adv.* approximately, about, circa, nearly. See NEARNESS.
roughneck, *n.* boor, rowdy. See VULGARITY, EVILDOER.

ROUGHNESS
Quality of not being smooth or even

Nouns—**1,** roughness, unevenness, ruggedness, asperity, rugosity, corrugation, nodosity, nodulation, hairiness, arborescence, tooth, grain, TEXTURE, ripple.

2, *(hairlike roughness)* brush, HAIR, beard, shag, mane, whiskers; plumage, plumosity, bristle, plume, crest, feather, tuft, fringe; hair shirt.

3, *(soft roughness)* plush, corduroy, nap, pile, floss, fur, down, moss, bur. See SOFTNESS.

4, raspiness, harshness, *etc.* (see *Adjectives*); rasp.

Verbs—rough[en], ruffle, crisp, crumple, corrugate, make one's hackles stand up; rub the wrong way; rumple; go against the grain; grate, rasp, grate [on the ears]; scrabble. See FRICTION.

Adjectives—**1,** rough, uneven, scabrous, knotted, rugged, angular, irregular, crisp, gnarled, unpolished, unsmooth, roughhewn, craggy, cragged, scraggy; prickly, bristling, sharp; lumpy, bumpy, knobbed, ribbed, corduroy.

2, feathery, plumose, tufted, hairy, ciliated, filamentous, hirsute; bushy, leafy, whiskery, bearded, pilous, pilose, filar, shaggy, shagged, fringed, setaceous, bristly.

3, raspy, harsh, coarse, hoarse, husky, throaty, guttural, raucous, croaking.

Antonyms, see SMOOTHNESS.

---

round, *adj.* circular, annular, spherical, globular, cylindrical; approximate. See CIRCULARITY, ROTUNDITY, NUMERATION. —*n.* revolution, cycle; CIRCUIT, ambit, course, itinerary; beat; series, catch, rondeau; routine, rut. See CONTINUITY, ROTATION, BUSINESS.
roundabout, *adj.* circuitous, indirect. See CIRCUITY, DEVIATION, DIFFUSENESS.
roundly, *adv.* vigorously, earnestly. See COMPLETION.
roundup, *n.* gathering; summation. See ASSEMBLAGE.
rouse, *v.* waken, arouse, animate, stir, stimulate, excite, incite, inflame. See CAUSE.

roustabout, *n.* longshoreman (see STEVEDORE); circus hand, ranch hand, odd-job man. See EXERTION.
rout, *v.t.* stampede, panic; discomfit, defeat, repulse. See SUCCESS, FAILURE, POPULACE.
route, *n.* path, road, way, course, passage, track, itinerary. See CIRCUIT, TRAVEL.
routine, *n.* practice, procedure, system, HABIT, round, rut. See BUSINESS, METHOD.
rove, *v.i.* wander, ramble, meander. See DEVIATION, TRAVEL.
roving, *adj.* vagrant, restless, vacillating. See CHANGEABLENESS, TRAVEL.
row, *v.* paddle, scull, oar. See NAVIGATION.

—*n.* rank, file, tier, range; quarrel, brawl, rumpus, melée. See CONTINUITY, LENGTH, DISORDER, CONTENTION.

rowboat, *n.* skiff, dinghy, dory, longboat, whaleboat, shell, punt, gig. See SHIP.

rowdy, *n.* RUFFIAN, tough, hoodlum, bully, thug. See EVILDOER, VULGARITY.

rower, *n.* oarsman, oar, sculler, galley slave, waterman, gondolier. See NAVIGATION.

royal, *adj.* regal, imperial, princely, magnificent. See AUTHORITY, NOBILITY.

rub, *v.t.* buff, abrade, scour, polish; chafe, massage, stroke, graze; annoy, disturb. See FRICTION, SMOOTHNESS, DISCONTENT.

rubber, *n.* eraser, eradicator; latex, Lastex, gum arabic, buna, neoprene, caoutchouc, foam rubber; vulcanite; overshoe, galosh, arctic boot, wader, hipboot; rubber band; session, game, series. See MATERIALS, CLOTHING, ELASTICITY.

rubberneck, *n., slang,* sightseer, busybody. See CURIOSITY, VISION.

rubbish, *n.* trash, waste, debris, litter, junk. See USELESSNESS.

rubble, *n.* rubbish, litter, trash, refuse, waste; ruins, debris, remains, detritus, wreckage, shards, pieces. See HARDNESS, USELESSNESS, REMAINDER.

rubdown, *n.* massage (see FRICTION).

rube, *n., slang,* countryman, rustic, hick. See POPULACE.

rub out, *slang,* murder, assassinate (see KILLING).

ruckus, *n., slang,* uproar, commotion, racket. See AGITATION, EXCITEMENT.

ruddy, *adj.* red, florid (see COLOR).

rude, *adj.* barbarous, crude, primitive, rough, rustic; harsh, rugged; coarse, uncouth; discourteous, uncivil, insolent. See VULGARITY, COURTESY, INELEGANCE, FORMLESSNESS.

rudiment, *n.* element, germ, embryo, root. See CAUSE, BEGINNING.

rudimentary, *adj.* elementary, abecedarian; embryonic, undeveloped, imperfect, vestigial. See BEGINNING, UNPREPAREDNESS.

rueful, *adj.* sorrowful, regretful, doleful; pitiable, deplorable, pathetic. See DEJECTION, PAIN, REGRET.

ruffian, *n.* rowdy, bully, tough, thug. See EVILDOER.

ruffle, *v.t.* gather, shirr, crinkle, corrugate, plait; agitate, ripple, tousle, rumple, disarrange; vex, irritate. See AGITATION, EXCITEMENT, DISORDER, ROUGHNESS, FOLD.

rug, *n.* mat, drugget, shag [rug], throw [rug]; carpet[ing]; lap robe; *slang,* wig, hairpiece, toupee. See COVERING.

rugged, *adj.* craggy; shaggy, rough, unkempt; harsh, stern, austere; hilly, uneven; unpolished, uncultivated; fierce, tempestuous; *informal,* robust, hale. See ROUGHNESS, FORMLESSNESS, VIOLENCE, SEVERITY.

ruin, *n.* DESTRUCTION, downfall, perdition; wreck, remains, relic. See FAILURE, REMAINDER. —*v.t.* wreck, raze, demolish; impoverish, seduce, *etc.* See IMPURITY, POVERTY.

ruinous, *adj.* dilapidated, rundown; disastrous, calamitous, desolating, tragic. See DETERIORATION, PAIN, ADVERSITY.

rule, *n.* law, regulation; government, AUTHORITY; ruler. See RULE, MEASUREMENT.

RULE
Regulation for standard procedure

Nouns—1, rule, law, ordinance, regulation, canon, code, act, measure, statute; decision, ruling (see JUDGMENT); commandment, COMMAND; guide, gospel, formula, form, standard, model, precept, convention; MAXIM, aphorism, axiom; natural *or* normal state, normality, average (see MEAN); order of things; standing order, parliamentary law, Procrustean law, law of the Medes and the Persians, hard and fast rule; dead letter.

2, REGULARITY, uniformity, constancy, consistency, CONFORMITY; punctuality, exactness; routine, custom, HABIT, system, METHOD.

3, *(traditional rules)* rule of thumb, Murphy's law, benchmark.

Verbs—settle, fix, establish, determine, decide, adjudicate, judge (see JUDGMENT).

Adjectives—1, regular, uniform, symmetrical, constant, steady, systematic, methodical, according to rule; customary, conformable, natural, habitual, normal.
2, conventional, formalistic, rigid, legalistic, ceremonious. See CONFORMITY.
Adverbs—by the rule, by the book; as a rule; normally, usually.
Phrases—the exception proves the rule; there is an exception to every rule.
Quotations—If you like laws and sausage, you should never watch either being made (*Otto von Bismarck*), The people's good is the highest law (*Cicero*), Good people must not obey the laws too well (*Emerson*), The execution of the laws is more important than the making of them (*Thomas Jefferson*), Useless laws weaken the necessary laws (*Montesquieu*).

Antonyms, see DISOBEDIENCE.

---

ruler, *n.* sovereign (see AUTHORITY); rule, straightedge, folding rule, slide rule. See MEASUREMENT.

rumble, *n.* roll, hollow roar, reverberation. See LOUDNESS.

ruminate, *v.i.* meditate, ponder; chew, chew the cud. See FOOD, THOUGHT.

rummage, *v.* hunt, ransack; junk, odds and ends. See INQUIRY, USELESSNESS.

rumor, *n.* report, hearsay, gossip, common talk. See INFORMATION, NEWS.

rump, *n.* croup, buttocks; REMAINDER, fag, end; steak. See REAR, FOOD.

rumple, *v.t.* muss, dishevel, tousle, wrinkle, crumple. See ROUGHNESS, DISORDER.

rumpus, *n., informal,* brawl, commotion, disturbance. See VIOLENCE, AGITATION.

run, *v.* scurry, hasten, travel, abscond; ply, flow; liquefy; act, function, extend, complete, pass into, continue, elapse; operate, work; ravel; thrust, compete; smuggle; *informal,* streak. See MOTION, VELOCITY, ILLEGALITY. —*n.* swift pace, race; trip, current, flow; TENDENCY; sequence, course, progress; demand; yard; brook, rill. See PROGRESSION, WATER.

runaway, *n.* fugitive, escapee, truant, renegade; refugee, turntail, fly-by-night, hit and run, lam[mi]ster (*sl.*); landslide, no contest, walkover (*inf.*), white wash (*inf.*). See COWARDICE, ESCAPE, SUCCESS. —*adj.* fugitive; uncontrollable, wild, speeding. See AVOIDANCE, VELOCITY, FREEDOM.

run-down, *adj.* dilapidated, broken-down, tumbledown; weakened, weary, debilitated, done up, used up, in a bad way. See DETERIORATION. —*n., informal,* narrative, DESCRIPTION.

run down, *v.t.* disparage, criticize; enumerate, list; unwind. See DETRACTION, LIST, END.

rung, *n.* rundle, round, spoke; step, degree. See SUPPORT.

run in, arrest, imprison. See HINDRANCE, PRISON.

runner, *n.* race horse, racer, sprinter; messenger, courier, solicitor; blade, skid; rotor; rug, mat, scarf; operator; sarmentum; tackle. See CONTENTION, COMMUNICATION, SMOOTHNESS, COVERING.

runt, *n.* dwarf, pigmy. —*adj.* stunted, underdeveloped, tiny, wee. See LITTLENESS.

run-through, *n.* rehearsal; recapitulation, recap (*inf.*). See SHORTNESS.

runway, *n.* channel; course; landing strip, airstrip, taxiway. See AVIATION, PASSAGE.

rupture, *n.* DISCORD, schism, split, falling-out; break, rift, breach; hernia. See DISJUNCTION, DISEASE.

rural, *adj.* rustic, provincial, countrified, bucolic, pastoral, arcadian, agrarian. See AGRICULTURE, POPULACE.

ruse, *n.* trick, stratagem, artifice, wile, subterfuge. See CUNNING.

rush, *v.* hurry, scurry, dash, speed, gush, surge; hasten, expedite, precipitate, urge, drive; assault, attack; advance; *informal,* court, woo (see LOVE); *informal,* pledge, recruit. —*n.* HASTE, run, dash, precipitation; surge, gush, onrush; stampede. See VELOCITY, EXCITEMENT.

rust, *v.* corrode, oxidize; deteriorate. See DETERIORATION, COLOR.

rustic, *adj.* rural, countrified, bucolic; artless, unsophisticated; unpolished, rude, backwoods. See UNSKILLFULNESS. —*n.*

peasant, farmer, bumpkin, boor. See POPULACE, AGRICULTURE.

rustle, *v.i.* crackle, swish, whisk, whisper; *informal,* steal (cattle). See SOFTNESS, STEALING.

rusty, *adj.* reddish-brown; timeworn, frowsy, antiquated; out of practice. See INACTIVITY, DETERIORATION, UNSKILL-FULNESS.

rut, *n.* groove, beaten path, track, FURROW; HABIT, routine; heat (see FEMALE).

ruthless, *adj.* relentless, merciless, inexorable, cruel. See SEVERITY.

S

Sabbath, *n.* day of rest, Lord's Day; Sunday, Saturday; First Day. See RITE.

sabbatical, *n.* sabbatical year *or* leave, vacation. See REPOSE.

saber, *n.* sabre; sword, scimitar, broadsword, cutlass. See ARMS.

sabotage, *n.* DESTRUCTION, vandalism;
subversion. —*v.t.* destroy, cripple, disable, undermine, scuttle, throw a monkey wrench in the works (*inf.*). See
HINDRANCE.

sac, *n.* pouch, pocket, cyst; vesicle; sound,
bladder. See RECEPTACLE.

saccharine, *adj.* sweet, sickening, cloying,
sugary, fulsome. See SWEETNESS.

sack, *n.* bag; destruction, pillage; wine.
—*v.t.* ravage, plunder, pillage, despoil;
slang, discharge, fire. See STEALING, RE-
CEPTACLE, EJECTION. —sack out, sleep,
snooze (*inf.*). See REPOSE.

sacrament, *n.* RITE, ceremony; host, consecrated bread *or* wine.

sacred, *adj.* hallowed, sanctified, sacrosanct, holy; consecrated, dedicated, inviolable. See DEITY, PIETY. *Ant.,* profane.
—sacred cow, *n.* idol, god; tradition;
taboo, superstition. See IDOLATRY.

SACRED WRITINGS
Scriptures

Nouns—1, a. scripture, the Scriptures, the Bible, the Book, the Good Book, Holy Writ,
Holy Scriptures; Gospel; revelation, inspiration; text; King James Bible, Douay Bible,
Vulgate; Talmud, Oral Law, Midrash, Mishnah, Masorah, Torah, megillah,
mezuzah; Haggadah, Halakah; exegesis (see INTERPRETATION); Authorized *or* King
James Version, [Revised *or* American] Standard Version; Breeches, Geneva, Treacle,
Printers', Gutenberg, *or* Wicked Bible; Book of Common Prayer, missal; Dead
Sea Scrolls; pseudoepigrapha. b. Old Testament, Septuagint, Pentateuch, Zohar;
Octateuch, the Law, Jewish Law, the Prophets; major *or* minor Prophets; Ha-
giographa, Ketuvim, the Writings, Hagiology; Hierographa, Apocrypha. c. New Tes-
tament; [Synoptic] Gospels, Evangelists, Acts, Epistles, Apocalypse, Revelation.
d. (*Muhammedism*) Koran, Alcoran, Qur'an. e. (*Hinduism*) Veda: Atharva-Veda,
Rig-Veda, Sama-Veda, Yajur-Veda; Upanishad, Bhagavad-Gita, Mahabharata, Brah-
mana, Kama Sutra, Ramayana, Tantra. f. (*Buddhism*) Pali Canon, Tripitaka: Abhid-
hamma Pitaka, Sutta Pitaka, Vinaya Pitaka; Dhammapada, Jataka. g. (*Sikhism*)
Adigranth, Granth. h. (*Confucianism*) Analects; Five Classics: I Ching, Book of Rites,
Book of History, Book of Songs, Spring and Autumn Annals. i. (*Other*) Angas; Book
of the Dead; Zend-Avesta; Book of Mormon; the Eddas.

2, prophet (see PREDICTION); evangelist, apostle, disciple, saint; the Apostolic Fathers; Holy Man; Gautama Buddha, Zoroaster, Lao-tse, Mohammed, Confucius,
Joseph Smith.

Adjectives—scriptural, biblical, sacred, prophetic; evangelical, evangelistic, apostolic,
inspired, apocalyptic, ecclesiastical, canonical, textuary; exegetic, Masoretic, Talmudic; apocryphal.

Quotations—The devil can cite Scripture for his purpose (*Shakespeare*), What I know
of the divine science and Holy Scripture I learnt in woods and fields (*St. Bernard*), An
apology for the Devil: It must be remembered that we have only heard one side of the
case. God has written all the books (*Samuel Butler*), I know of no book which has

been a source of brutality and sadistic conduct, both public and private, that can compare with the Bible (*Reginald Paget*), We have used the Bible as if it was a constable's handbook—an opium-dose for keeping beasts of burden patient while they are being overloaded (*Charles Kingsley*).

Antonyms, see IMPIETY.

sacrifice, *n.* oblation, offering, hecatomb, holocaust; immolation, self-denial. —*v.t.* renounce, give up; immolate. See GIVING, IDOLATRY, ATONEMENT, DESTRUCTION.

sacrilege, *n.* desecration, profanation, blasphemy, IMPIETY, irreverence, disrespect; defilement; sin, trespass, transgression; vandalism.

sacrosanct, *adj.* hallowed (see SACRED); saintly, snow-white; sanctimonious, lily-white (*sl.*). See DEITY. *Ant.,* unholy, unblessed.

sad, *adj.* sorrowful, downcast, dejected, unhappy, woeful, woebegone, depressed, disconsolate, blue (*inf.*), down (*inf.*); melancholy, gloomy, cheerless, somber, dismal; heavy[-hearted]; regrettable, shameful. See DEJECTION, PAIN, BADNESS. *Ant.,* happy, joyful.

saddle, *n.* seat, pad; packsaddle, panel, pillion, pommel, cantle; back, joint, ridge, hump, crest; *slang,* rig, hull. See SUPPORT. —*v.t.* harness; load, encumber, embarrass; blame, accuse. See DUTY, DIFFICULTY.

sadistic, *adj.* cruel, brutal, fiendish; malicious, pernicious. See MALEVOLENCE. *Ant.,* gentle, kind.

safari, *n.* journey, expedition, trek; caravan. See TRAVEL, PURSUIT.

safe, *adj.* secure, protected; unharmed, intact; trustworthy. See SAFETY, SECURITY, TRUST. *Ant.,* dangerous. —*n.* repository, strongbox, locker, vault; *slang,* condom. See STORE, SAFETY, HINDRANCE.

safeguard, *n.* DEFENSE, protection, shield, egis; passport, safe-conduct, convoy. See SAFETY.

safekeeping, *n.* care, custody, guardianship, protection. See SAFETY.

SAFETY
Secure condition

Nouns—**1,** safety, safeness, SECURITY, surety, assurance; impregnability, invulnerability, invulnerableness; ESCAPE, safety valve; safeguard, passport, safe conduct; confidence (see HOPE).

2, *(protection)* guardianship, wardship, wardenship; tutelage, [protective] custody, safekeeping; PRESERVATION, protection, auspices, egis.

3, protector, guardian; keeper, warden, warder; preserver, custodian; duenna, chaperon; escort, convoy; guard, shield (see DEFENSE); guardian angel, tutelary saint; watchman, company *or* yard bull; mother, father; janitor, sentinel, sentry, ranger, scout (see WARNING); garrison, watchdog; Cerberus, doorman, doorkeeper. *Slang,* rentacop, shamus.

4, policeman *or* -woman, patrolman *or* -woman, officer; peace officer, traffic *or* motorcycle officer; constable, sheriff, deputy, state trooper; detective, plainclothesman; mountie, gendarme, bobby; police *or* riot squad, SWAT [team], special weapons attack team; shore patrol. *Informal,* long arm of the law. *Slang,* cop, copess, copper, bluecoat, heat, flatfoot, dick, Mountie, bull, bear, flic, Smokey [the bear], fuzz, pig, the Man, nark, Fed, fink, jack, fly, goon squad, gumshoe, snatcher, lard, leather-head, lobster, pavement-pounder, pork, roach, Sam and Dave; peeper; choirboy.

5, *(police procedures)* all-points bulletin, APB, citizen's arrest, false arrest, dragnet, crackdown, manhunt, posse, search and seizure, frisk, search warrant, stakeout, sweep; forensics, fingerprinting, ballistics, crime lab, detection, detention; lie detector, polygraph, lineup, Miranda rule, moulage, mug shot, voiceprint; handcuffs (see RESTRAINT).

6, life preserver, personal flotation device, lifeline; fender, bumper, buffer; safety zone, island, *etc. Informal,* security blanket.

7, refuge, asylum, sanctuary; hideout, hideaway; haven, hospice, shelter, safe harbor; safe house; any port in a storm; last resort; anchor[age]; home, hospital; retreat, den, lair; precaution (see PREPARATION); quarantine, cordon sanitaire; police station, precinct [house]; police *or* squad car. *Informal,* paddy wagon. *Slang,* pig heaven; pig-mobile, roller.

Verbs—1, be safe; ride out *or* weather the storm; land upon one's feet; bear *or* live a charmed life; fall back on; ESCAPE. *Informal,* be over the hump. *Slang,* save one's bacon.

2, safeguard, protect; take care *or* charge of (see CARE); preserve, cover, screen, shelter, shroud, flank, ward; ensure; guard (see DEFENSE); escort, convoy, ride herd on; garrison; stand over, watch, mount guard, patrol; take precautions (see PREPARATION); take shelter *or* refuge. *Slang,* hole up, cover one's ass *or* tail.

Adjectives—1, safe, secure; in safety *or* security; on the safe side; under the shield *or* aegis of; under the wing of; under cover, under lock and key; out of danger, out of harm's way; on sure ground, at anchor, high and dry, above water; unthreatened, unmolested; protected; safe and sound; scatheless, unscathed; out of danger, in the clear.

2, snug, seaworthy; weatherproof, waterproof, fireproof, bulletproof, bombproof; defensible, tenable, proof (against), invulnerable; unassailable, unattackable, impregnable, inexpugnable.

3, harmless (see GOOD); not dangerous; protecting, guardian, tutelary, custodial; preservative; trustworthy.

Adverbs—safely, with safety, with impunity, without risk.

Phrases—the Mounties always get their man; Heaven protects children, sailors, and drunken men; a barking dog never bites; better [be] safe than sorry; he who fights and runs away may live to fight another day.

Quotations—All the security around the American president is just to make sure the man who shoots him gets caught (*Norman Mailer*), The policeman's lot is not a happy one (*W. S. Gilbert*).

Antonyms, see DANGER.

---

sag, *v.* droop, buckle, warp, curve; slouch, slump; weaken, wilt; decline, languish; lapse, fall off. See OBLIQUITY, PENDENCY, CURVATURE.

saga, *n.* epic, prose narrative. See DESCRIPTION.

sagacious, *adj.* penetrating, shrewd, astute. See INTELLIGENCE. *Ant.,* ignorant.

sage, *n. & adj.* See KNOWLEDGE.

sail, *v.* cruise, voyage; set sail; navigate, traverse. See NAVIGATION. —*n.* canvas; moonsail, moonraker; jib, foresail, lateen, lug, mainsail, mizzen, spanker, topsail. See SHIP.

sailboat, *n.* See SHIP.

sailor, *n.* seaman, mariner (see NAVIGATION).

saint, *n.* hallow, pietist, apostle; votary; saintess, patroness; martyr; pir; saintling, saint-errant, angel (*inf.*), paragon (*inf.*). See PIETY, INNOCENCE, VIRTUE. *Ant.,* devil, DEMON.

sainted, *adj.* saintly; hallowed, sacred. See PIETY, VIRTUE.

sake, *n.* purpose, motive, reason; behalf, regard, good. See INTENTION.

salaam, *n.* obeisance, curtsy, bow. See COURTESY.

salad, *n.* greens, herb, lettuce; tossed salad, cole slaw, aspic. See FOOD. —**salad days,** YOUTH.

salary, *n.* stipend, pay, remuneration, wage[s], hire, compensation, PAYMENT. See RECEIVING.

SALE
Transfer for money

Nouns—1, sale, selling, disposal, merchandising, deaccession; telemarketing; auction, vendue, market, custom, BARTER; BUSINESS; salesmanship; vendibility, vendibleness, salability; sales talk; bill of sale; catalog sales. See PURCHASE.

2, *(sale at reduced price)* clearance sale, liquidation, white sale, end-of-month sale; bargain basement *or* counter; closeout, fire sale, case sale; black market, gray market; garage, yard, *or* tag sale, flea market; close-out sale, going-out-of-business sale; land-office business. See CHEAPNESS.

3, *(items to be sold)* consumer goods *or* items, merchandise, wares, commodities; durable *or* nondurable goods, hard *or* soft goods; ego goods; effects; goods, articles; stock [in trade]; supplies, stores, cargo; produce, *etc.*

4, seller, vendor, vender, retailer; merchant, trader, dealer, tradesman, négociant, merchandiser; shopkeeper, storekeeper; businessman *or* -woman; retailer, wholesaler, middleman, jobber; salesperson, -woman, -girl, -lady, *or* -man, [sales] clerk, monger, solicitor, huckster, hawker, peddler, pedlar; sutler, costermonger, fishmonger; canvasser, agent, door-to-door salesman; traveling salesman, roadman, sales agent; cashier; auctioneer; sales force. *Slang,* scalper, schlockmeister, quizmaster, shonky; rainmaker. See AGENT.

5, *(provider of goods)* purveyor, supplier, caterer, commissary, sutler; grocer, druggist, soda jerk, *etc.*; quartermaster; batman, steward, purser, supercargo (see PROVISION).

6, *(sales location)* marketplace; shopping center, mall; store, general store, department store, supermarket, flagship *or* chain store, shop, five-and-dime, army-navy store, mart, bodega, variety store, market, emporium, commissary, company store, convenience store, galleria, bazaar, fair, booth, kiosk; vending machine; package store (see DRINKING); surplus store, thrift shop, bargain basement, factory outlet, discount house (see CHEAPNESS); online *or* Web merchant; Automat (see FOOD).

7, client (see PURCHASE).

Verbs—sell, vend, dispose of, deaccession, effect a sale; trade, merchandise, market, OFFER, BARTER, distribute, dispense, wholesale, retail; deal in, handle; traffic (in); liquidate, turn into money, realize, auction (off); bring under the hammer; put up [at auction *or* for sale]; hawk, peddle, bring to market; undersell; flood the market; sell out; make *or* drive a bargain. *Slang,* flog. See SUCCESS.

Adjectives—salable, marketable, vendible; unsalable, unpurchased, unbought; commercial; cut-rate, bargain-counter.

Adverbs—for sale, on sale, on the market, over *or* under the counter; marked up *or* down, under the hammer, on the [auction] block; in *or* on the market.

Phrases—the customer is always right.

Quotations—Buying and selling is essentially antisocial (*Edward Bellamy*), Thou, O God, dost sell us all good things at the price of labor (*Leonardo da Vinci*), When a man sells eleven ounces for twelve, he makes a compact with the devil, and sells himself for the value of an ounce (*Henry Ward Beecher*).

Antonyms, see PURCHASE.

---

salient, *adj.* outstanding, prominent, striking, conspicuous; notable, momentous, signal. See IMPORTANCE, ANGULARITY, CONVEXITY.

saliva, *n.* spit, spittle, sputum. See EXCRETION.

salivate, *v.i.* drool, slaver. See EXCRETION.

sallow, *adj.* yellow, muddy; sickly, pallid, wan, jaundiced. See COLOR, COLORLESSNESS. *Ant.,* ruddy, colorful.

sally, *n.* sortie, raid, foray, ATTACK; excursion, expedition, trip; outburst, outbreak; banter, riposte, repartee. See WIT, DEPARTURE.

salmon, *n.* kipper, lox; alevin, parr, smolt, samlet, *etc.* See FOOD, ANIMAL.

salon, *n.* drawing room, parlor, ballroom; gathering, reception, exhibition; gallery, studio, atelier, workshop, showroom; beauty parlor. See SOCIALITY, RECEPTACLE, BEAUTY.

saloon, *n.* bar, tavern, taproom, bistro, oasis (*sl.*); hall, dining room, main cabin; sedan, four-door. See DRINKING, FOOD, VEHICLE.

salt, *v.t.* salinize; season; pickle, brine, drysalt, preserve, souse. See PRESERVATION, STORE. —**salt away,** *informal,* invest, bank, save. See ECONOMY.

salty, *adj.* briny, brackish, saline; corned, salted; racy, pungent. See TASTE, PUNGENCY.

salubrity, *n.* healthfulness, wholesomeness. See HEALTH.

salutary, *adj.* healthful, salubrious, wholesome; healing, medicinal, sanatory; tonic; beneficial, good. See HEALTH, GOODNESS. *Ant.,* insalubrious, unhealthful.

salutation, *n.* salute, address, greeting, welcome; reception, respects, salvo; salaam, bow, curtsy. See COURTESY.

salute, *v.* welcome, greet, hail; uncover, bow, curtsy, present arms, dip colors. See COURTESY, CONGRATULATION, RESPECT.

salvage, *n.* salvation, rescue, retrieval, recovery, reclamation; flotsam, jetsam. —*v.t.* rescue, save, recover, retrieve, redeem, reclaim, rehabilitate; snatch from the jaws of death. See RESTORATION, LIBERATION.

salvation, *n.* redemption, deliverance, reclamation, salvage. See PIETY, RESTORATION. *Ant.,* damnation.

salve, *n.* ointment, balm, unguent; REMEDY, lenitive, emollient.

salvo, *n.* volley, gunfire, burst; discharge, broadside, fusillade, rafale; strafing, shellfire; peppering, riddling; fanfare, salute; proviso, QUALIFICATION. See ATTACK, CELEBRATION.

same, *adj.* identical, selfsame, interchangeable, alike, equivalent; monotonous. See IDENTITY, WEARINESS. *Ant.,* different.

sample, *n.* specimen, example, exemplar, pattern; prototype, archetype; trial, portion, TASTE, teaser. See CONFORMITY.

sanatorium, *n.* sanitarium, health resort, retreat, hospital, rest home. See REMEDY, INSANITY, ABODE.

sanctify, *v.t.* consecrate, bless, hallow, purify, beatify; sanction, authorize. See DEITY, PIETY, PERMISSION. *Ant.,* damn, curse.

sanctimonious, *adj.* pietistic, sacrosanct; self-righteous, holier-than-thou; hypocritical, goody-goody (*inf.*). See IMPIETY.

sanction, *n.* PERMISSION, confirmation, ratification; approval, APPROBATION; interdiction, penalty, punishment. See LEGALITY.

sanctuary, *n.* chancel; refuge, asylum, immunity. See TEMPLE, ABODE.

sanctum, *n.* retreat; sacred place, sanctum sanctorum, holy of holies. See SAFETY, PIETY, ESCAPE.

sand, *n.* grit, granules; particle, grain, speck; beach, strand, desert, dune; abrasive; silica, otolith; COURAGE, pluck, spunk. See LAND, POWDERINESS. —*v.* sprinkle, dust, powder; smooth, polish, abrade, sandpaper. See SMOOTHNESS, FRICTION.

sandal, *n.* slipper; thong, flip-flop; loafer. See CLOTHING.

sandwich, *n.* combination, club, deli, hero, *etc.* sandwich; lamination. —*v.t.* insert; laminate. See FOOD, BETWEEN.

sandy, *adj.* gritty, granular, grainy, arenaceous. See POWDERINESS.

sane, *adj.* rational (see SANITY). *Ant.,* insane.

sang-froid, *Fr.,* cold blood; calmness; composure. See INEXCITABILITY, CAUTION.

sanguinary, *adj.* sanguineous, gory, bloody; bloodthirsty, murderous, savage, cruel. See KILLING.

sanguine, *adj.* cheerful, confident, hopeful; ruddy. See HOPE, CHEERFULNESS, HEALTH. *Ant.,* hopeless, pessimistic.

sanitarium, *n.* See SANATORIUM.

sanitary, *adj.* hygienic, clean, sterilized, germ-free, safe, aseptic, antiseptic. See CLEANNESS, HEALTH. *Ant.,* unsanitary, infected.

SANITY
Mental soundness

Nouns—sanity, saneness, soundness, reason; rationality, normality, sobriety; lucidity; senses, sound mind, mens sana [in corpore sano]. See INTELLECT.

Verbs—be sane, keep one's senses *or* reason, have it all together; come to one's senses, sober up; bring to one's senses. *Slang,* have all one's marbles *or* buttons.

Adjectives—sane, rational, reasonable, compos mentis, of sound mind; self-possessed; sober, in one's right mind; in possession of one's faculties. *Informal,* all there *or* here, hitting on all cylinders.

Adverbs—sanely, reasonably, *etc.*; in reason, within reason.

Quotations—Sanity is very rare (*Emerson*), Sanity is madness put to good uses (*George Santayana*), Sanity is like a clearing in the jungle where the humans agree to meet from time to time and behave in certain fixed ways that even a baboon could master (*Wilfrid Sheed*).

Antonyms, see INSANITY.

sans souci, *Fr.*, without care. See CON-
TENT, INSENSIBILITY, PLEASURE. *Ant.*,
concerned.

sap, *n.* plant juice, lifeblood; vigor, vitality; trench, furrow; *slang*, fool (see IG-
NORANCE). See FLUIDITY, INTRINSIC.
—*v.t.* undermine; tunnel; enfeeble, debilitate, devitalize. See CONCAVITY, DE-
TERIORATION, WEAKNESS.

sapid, *adj.* savory (see TASTE).

sapling, *n.* seedling, treelet, treeling;
stripling, youngster. See YOUTH.

sappy, *adj.* vital; *slang*, foolish, silly. See
ENERGY, FOLLY.

sarcastic, *adj.* scornful, contemptuous,
withering, cynical, satiric, ironical, sardonic. See RIDICULE, DISRESPECT.

sardonic, *adj.* scornful, derisive; caustic,
malicious, twisted. See DISAPPROBATION.

sash, *n.* casement, casing; waistband, cummerbund, scarf; obi, baldric. See CLOTH-
ING, SUPPORT, CIRCUMSCRIPTION.

sass, *n.*, *slang*, sauce, INSOLENCE.

Satan, *n.*, satanic, *adj.* See DEMON.

satchel, *n.* bag, carpetbag, schoolbag. See
RECEPTACLE.

sate, *v.t.* satisfy; fill. See SUFFICIENCY.

satellite, *n.* hireling, dummy, puppet;
moon; artificial satellite, space station;
slave state. See ASTRONAUTICS, UNI-
VERSE, ACCOMPANIMENT, AUXILIARY.

satiate, *v.* sate, satisfy; cloy, jade, make
blasé; quench, slake, pall; glut, gorge,
surfeit, bore; spoil. See SUFFICIENCY.
Ant., leave wanting, disappoint.

satire, *n.* RIDICULE, sarcasm, irony, mockery, travesty, burlesque.

satirical, *adj.* cutting, bitter, sarcastic, wry,
ironic, sardonic, lampooning, cynical.
See DISAPPROBATION.

satisfaction, *n.* COMPENSATION, gratification, enjoyment, CONTENT, contentment; ATONEMENT, reparation, redress,
amends; fulfillment. See PLEASURE, PAY-
MENT, SUFFICIENCY. *Ant.*, dissatisfaction.

satisfy, *v.t.* CONTENT; set at ease; gratify,
sate, appease; convince, assure; pay,
liquidate, discharge; fulfill, meet; suffice, do, ANSWER. See PLEASURE, BELIEF,
PAYMENT, SUFFICIENCY. *Ant.*, dissatisfy, disappoint.

saturate, *v.t.* soak, fill, drench, impregnate, imbue. See COMPLETION, MOIS-
TURE, SUFFICIENCY.

saturnalia, *n.* festival, carnival; revel[ry],
rejoicing, celebration. See AMUSEMENT.

saturnine, *adj.* morose, phlegmatic. See
DEJECTION.

satyr, *n.* faun, goat-man, panisc, demigod,
godling; sensualist, lecher, rake, roué,
wanton. See MYTHICAL DEITIES, IMPU-
RITY, DEMON.

sauce, *n.* dressing, dip, gravy; compote; fillip, flavor, zest, TASTE; *slang*, liquor; *informal*, INSOLENCE. See FOOD, DRINKING.

saucy, *adj.* pert, impertinent, impudent,
bold; smart, chic, piquant. See INSO-
LENCE.

saunter, *v.i.* stroll, loiter, amble, meander,
ramble. See TRAVEL, SLOWNESS.

sausage, *n.* frankfurter, frank (*sl.*), hot
dog, (*inf.*), wienie (*inf.*), Wurst, kielbasa, salami, pepperoni; liverwurst,
bratwurst, *etc.* See FOOD.

sauté, *v.t.* pan-fry, sear, blacken, brown
(see FOOD).

savage, *adj.* wild, untamed, uncivilized,
uncultivated; barbarous, ferocious,
fierce, feral, cruel, rude; angry, enraged.
See VIOLENCE, MALEVOLENCE, EVIL-
DOER. *Ant.*, civilized, gentle.

save, *v.t.* rescue, deliver, preserve, salvage,
safeguard; STORE, lay up, keep, hoard;
redeem, convert; spare, avoid; economize, conserve. See PRESERVATION,
PIETY. —*prep.* saving, except[ing], barring, but, excluding. See EXCLUSION,
LIBERATION. *Ant.*, lose, squander.

savings, *n.pl.* backlog, reserves, nest egg,
bank account. See STORE, ECONOMY.

savior, *n.* rescuer, liberator; Saviour,
Christ, Jesus [of Nazareth], Messiah,
the [Lord's] Anointed, Redeemer, Son
of God, [our] Lord. See LIBERATION,
DEITY. *Ant.*, nemesis.

savoir-faire, *Fr.*, know-how; poise. See
KNOWLEDGE, SKILL.

savory, *adj.* tasty (see TASTE).

savvy, *n.*, *informal*, understanding, acuity,
smarts (*inf.*). See KNOWLEDGE, SKILL.

saw, *n.* proverb, MAXIM; blade, handsaw,
hacksaw, ripsaw, *etc.*; serration. See
SHARPNESS. —*v.t.* cut, kerf; scratch,
scrape, rasp, grate. See DISJUNCTION,
FRICTION.

say, *v.t.* speak, tell, declare, state, aver, affirm, mention, allege, recite; decide. See
SPEECH, AFFIRMATION.

saying, *n.* saw, MAXIM, proverb, adage, epigram, dictum, ipse dixit. See AFFIRMATION.

say-so, *n., informal,* assertion, statement; AUTHORITY. See CERTAINTY.

scab, *n.* crust, cicatrice, eschar, incrustation; strikebreaker, fink (*sl.*). See COVERING.

scabbard, *n.* sheath, case. See COVERING.

scabrous, *adj.* scabby, scaly; difficult, thorny; risqué, salacious. See LAYER, DIFFICULTY, IMPURITY.

scaffold, *n.* framework, scaffolding, platform; gallows, gibbet. See SUPPORT.

scald, *v.* [par]boil, steam, broil, stew, cook; burn, scorch, scathe, sear, seethe, simmer. See HEAT.

scale, *n.* balance, steelyard; lamina, flake, scab, incrustation, horny plate, squama, lamella, eschar; degree, graduation, table, ratio, proportion; gamut. See MEASUREMENT, LAYER, COVERING, MUSIC, CONTINUITY, GRAVITY. —*v.* weigh; peel, husk, exfoliate, flake; climb, surmount. See DIVESTMENT, ASCENT.

scalp, *n.* hair, epicranium. See COVERING. —*v.t.* strip, flay; fleece, gouge, overcharge. See DIVESTMENT.

scam, *n., slang,* swindle, scheme, con (*sl.*), DECEPTION.

scamp, *n.* good-for-nothing, rogue, rascal, scalawag. See EVILDOER. —*v.t.* skimp, scrimp; slight, botch, work carelessly. See NEGLECT.

scamper, *v.i.* run, scurry, scuttle, skitter, scoot, flit, dash, dart, skip (*inf.*), hotfoot (*inf.*), skiddoo (*sl.*). See VELOCITY.

scan, *v.t.* examine, study, scrutinize, give the once-over (*sl.*); look over, peruse, survey; contemplate; take a gander at (*sl.*). See VISION, INQUIRY, POETRY.

scandal, *n.* disgrace, infamy, shame, humiliation, stigma; defamation, slander, backbiting, calumny; gossip. See DISREPUTE, DETRACTION, INFORMATION, NEWS.

scandalize, *v.* insult, defame, calumniate, stigmatize; horrify, shock, appall, outrage. See DISAPPROBATION, WRONG.

scant, *adj.* scanty, limited, meager, inadequate, sparse. See INSUFFICIENCY. *Ant.,* plenteous.

scapegoat, *n.* goat, whipping boy; butt, tool, victim, dupe. See SUBSTITUTION.

scar, *n.* blemish, flaw, cicatrix, pock; scab, crust; precipice, rock, crag, cliff. See RECORD. —*v.* cicatrize, mark, pit, scarify, blemish, disfigure, deface, mutilate; mar, damage, dent, scratch. See INTERVAL, INDICATION, DETERIORATION.

scarce, *adj.* rare, uncommon, deficient, scanty, few. See INSUFFICIENCY, RARITY. *Ant.,* plenteous, common.

scarcely, *adv.* hardly, barely. See RARITY, LITTLENESS.

scare, *v.t.* frighten, alarm. See FEAR.

scarf, *n.* muffler, neckerchief, shawl; boa; sash, cornet, fichu, choker, veil, stole; cravat; snood, wimple, babushka; prayer shawl, talith. See CLOTHING.

scarify, *v.t.* scratch; lacerate, harass. See FRICTION, FURROW, DISCONTENT.

scathe, *v.t.* injure, harm, hurt, scorch; castigate, denounce, tear apart (*inf.*), lash into (*inf.*), lambaste (*sl.*). See DETERIORATION.

scatter, *v.t.* strew, disperse, disseminate, dispel, dissipate. See DISPERSION.

scatterbrained, *adj.* absentminded, flighty, harebrained, daft, dizzy (*inf.*), daffy (*inf.*), barmy (*Brit. sl.*). See FOLLY. *Ant.,* organized, levelheaded.

scavenge, *v.* look (for), comb, pick, sift, hunt, cull, ransack, glean, scrounge (*sl.*); dig, grub, root, scratch. See INQUIRY.

scenario, *n.* plot, script, text, book, libretto; summary, skeleton, screenplay, photoplay; typescript. See DRAMA, WRITING.

scene, *n.* view, vista, landscape, panorama; site, location, setting; episode, event; outburst, tantrum; picture, tableau, pageant. See APPEARANCE, DRAMA.

scenery, *n.* prospect, landscape, view, scene; mise en scène, setting, backdrop, wings, borders, *etc.* See APPEARANCE, DRAMA.

scenic, *adj.* picturesque, theatrical, dramatic, stagy. See DRAMA, APPEARANCE.

scent, *v.t.* smell, detect; perfume. —*n.* ODOR, fragrance, aroma; sachet, perfume; track, trail, spoor.

scepter, *n.* staff, mace, rod, baton, wand; rod of empire; insignia of AUTHORITY.

schedule, *n.* LIST, catalog, inventory, record, docket; agenda, outline, register; timetable, calendar, time sheet. —*v.t.* PLAN, order, program, slate, book, TIME, docket, designate, appoint.

schema, *n.* scheme, diagram, PLAN.

scheme, *n.* PLAN, plot, project, design, intrigue; system, METHOD; CUNNING.

schism, *n.* DISJUNCTION, division, DISSENT, separation, split; HETERODOXY; factionalism, faction, sect, subdivision.

scholar, *n.* savant, sage (see KNOWLEDGE); bookworm; man of learning, letters, *or* education; pedant, pedagogue; student. See SCHOOL, LEARNING.

scholarship, *n.* learning, erudition, KNOWLEDGE; scholastic *or* financial AID, fellowship, bursary.

school, *n.* See SCHOOL, ASSEMBLAGE.

SCHOOL
Educational institution

Nouns—1, school, academy, university, alma mater, college, multiversity, land-grant college, cluster college, junior college, community college, siwash, seminary, yeshiva, lyceum, lycée, école, palestra; institute, institution, institution of [higher] learning *or* education; child care; gymnasium; class, semester; [groves of] academe, ivy halls *or* tower; accreditation.

2, *(types of schools)* day, boarding, primary, elementary, grammar, grade, secondary, junior high, high, summer, [college] preparatory, *or* graduate school, country day school, Latin school, night school; adult school, continuing education, storefront school; alternative school; Bible, Hebrew, *or* church school; parochial, separate, denominational, consolidated, continuation, magnet, public, independent, *or* private school; kindergarten, nursery school, day nursery; crèche, preschool; reformatory, reform school; law *or* medical school; teachers' college, dental college; normal school; correspondence *or* night school; extension school; female academy *or* seminary; vocational, technical, trade, business, secretarial, finishing, *or* music school, conservatory; art, dramatic, *or* dancing school; Montessori school; divinity school, seminary; military school *or* academy. *Informal,* prep school. *Slang,* cow college.

3, *(school grounds)* campus, quadrangle, grounds.

4, *(school terms)* academic year; matriculation, graduation, commencement; open admissions, open classroom, study hall; curriculum, course, elective, quadrivium; tuition; catalog; class, form, grade, seminar, proseminar, colloquium, master class; classroom, lecture room *or* hall, homeroom; language lab[oratory]; grade-point average, honor roll, pass-fail grading, nonpass, NP; schoolwork, homework, lesson plan; desk, blackboard; textbook, schoolbook; slate, chalk, eraser; three Rs, ABCs; [audio]visual aids, flashcard; advanced degree, baccalaureate, certificate, diploma, doctorate, postdoctoral, postgraduate; tenure, sabbatical.

5, *(school personnel)* learner, student (see LEARNING); undergraduate, freshman, sophomore, junior, senior, plebe, yearling, collegian, upperclassman; graduate, alumnus, alumna; bachelor, doctor; faculty, professorship, chair, fellowship; master, proctor; teacher, instructor (see TEACHING); provost, dean, bursar, headmaster *or* -mistress, head of school, regent. *Slang,* preppie.

6, subject, course; reading, writing, arithmetic, the three Rs. See TEACHING, LEARNING, KNOWLEDGE.

Verbs—go to school, attend, pursue a degree, enter a degree program; matriculate, enroll, register; graduate, be graduated, earn a degree; teach, learn.

Adjectives—scholastic, academic, collegiate, collegial; educational, curricular, extracurricular; accredited; schooled, educated (see KNOWLEDGE).

Phrases—schooldays are the best days of your life.

Quotations—Public schools are the nurseries of all vice and immorality (*Henry Fielding*), A whale ship was my Yale College and my Harvard (*Herman Melville*), A University should be a place of light, of liberty, and of learning (*Benjamin Disraeli*), The true University of these days is a collection of books (*Thomas Carlyle*), You can't expect a boy to be depraved until he has been to a good school (*Saki*), The founding fathers in their wisdom decided that children were an unnatural strain on parents. So they provided jails called schools, equipped with torture called education (*John Updike*).

Related categories, see TEACHING, LEARNING.

---

schooling, *n.* education, LEARNING.

science, *n.* KNOWLEDGE, SKILL, efficiency, technology.

scientific, *adj.* systematic, accurate, exact, sound. See KNOWLEDGE.

scintillate, *v.* glisten, twinkle, sparkle, glitter, coruscate, shine; be charming *or* witty, effervesce, turn on the charm (*sl.*). See LIGHT, INTELLIGENCE, WIT.

scion, *n.* sprout, shoot, twig, cutting, graft; heir, descendant. See POSTERITY.

scissors, *n.pl.* shears, trimmer, cutter, clipper, secateur. See SHARPNESS.

scoff, *v.t.* jeer, be contemptuous *or* derisive (of), flout, laugh (at). See CONTEMPT, DISRESPECT. *Ant.,* encourage.

scold, *v.* reprove, rebuke, rate, chide, berate, tongue-lash, bawl out (*sl.*). See DISAPPROBATION. *Ant.,* praise.

scoop, *n.* scooper, ladle, dipper, spoon; *slang,* NEWS, story, beat, lead, exclusive, dope (*sl.*). —*v.* dig out, lade, hollow, rout, gouge, excavate; *slang,* beat out. See CONCAVITY.

scoot, *v.i., informal,* dash, run, dart, scurry, scamper; leave, depart, go, decamp, exit, beat it (*sl.*), scram (*sl.*), vamoose (*sl.*), get lost (*sl.*). See VELOCITY.

scope, *n.* extent, range, sweep, compass, SPACE, sphere, field. See BREADTH, DEGREE, FREEDOM.

scorch, *v.t.* char, singe, brown, blacken, toast, roast, parch, shrivel, wither; denounce, upbraid; *informal,* speed, burn up the road. See DRYNESS, HEAT.

score, *n.* account, reckoning, tally, record; reason; twenty; music, orchestration, arrangement, chart (*sl.*); notch, scratch. See DEBT, MUSIC, CREDIT, FURROW.

scorn, *n.* CONTEMPT, disdain, superciliousness; derision, ridicule. —*v.t.* despise, disdain, contemn, spurn, neglect. See REJECTION, DISRESPECT. *Ant.,* respect.

scot-free, *adj.* clear, free (see FREEDOM).

scoundrel, *n.* knave, villain, rascal, rogue, blackguard. See EVILDOER. *Ant.,* angel, good person.

scour, *v.t.* scrub, abrade, polish, cleanse; search, range. See FRICTION, CLEANNESS, INQUIRY.

scourge, *n.* whip, strap, belt, lash, horsewhip; PUNISHMENT, curse, affliction, bane, nuisance, plague. —*v.t.* whip, lash, flay, beat; punish, afflict, plague. See EVIL, BADNESS.

scout, *n.* spy, observer, spotter, outrider, reconnoiterer, forerunner. See PRECEDENCE, INQUIRY.

scowl, *v.i.* frown; lower, glower. See DISAPPROBATION. *Ant.,* smile, grin.

scraggly, *adj.* irregular, ragged. See ROUGHNESS.

scram, *v.i., slang,* go away, leave (see DEPARTURE).

scramble, *v.i.* clamber, swarm, struggle, scrabble, tussle, scuffle. See CONTENTION, DISORDER, HASTE.

scrap, *n.* bit, crumb, morsel; splinter, fragment, chip; whit, tittle, jot, speck; *slang,* fight, bout, tussle. See LITTLENESS, CONTENTION.

scrapbook, *n.* album, looseleaf. See RECORD.

scrape, *v.* graze, brush; scratch, rasp, abrade, grind; grate; curtsy, bow. See FRICTION. —*n.* abrasion, scratch; DIFFICULTY, plight, predicament.

scrappy, *adj., slang,* pugnacious, contentious, argumentative. See CONTENTION.

scratch, *v.* score, gash, scrape, rasp, wound, lacerate, deface; erase, withdraw, reject; scribble, scrawl; irritate; sputter. See FRICTION, WRITING, FURROW, SHALLOWNESS.

scrawl, *v.t.* scribble, scratch. See WRITING.

scrawny, *adj.* underweight, puny, rawboned, bony, meager, lean. See NARROWNESS. *Ant.,* plump, overweight.

scream, *v.i.* shriek, screech, shrill, yell, CRY. See LOUDNESS.

screen, *n.* partition, curtain, shield, mask, protection, shelter; netting, mesh; sieve, sifter, bolter; cinema, MOTION PICTURES, silver screen. —*v.t.* shelter, shield, protect, hide, conceal, veil, shroud; sift, sort; film, exhibit. See DEFENSE, CONCEALMENT, CLASS, CLEANNESS, CHOICE, DRAMA.

screw, *n.* spiral, helix, volute; twist; propeller, prop, jack; pressure, coercion; extortionist, niggard, skinflint; *slang,* jailer, turnkey. See ROTATION, CONNECTION, PRISON. —**screw up,** *v.t. slang,* bungle, botch (see ERROR, UNSKILLFULNESS).

screwy, *adj.* twisted, tortuous, spiral; *slang,* crazy, eccentric. See CONVOLUTION, UNCONFORMITY.

scribble, *v.* scrawl, scratch. —*n.* scrawl, hen tracks. See WRITING.

scribe, *n.* scrivener, secretary, amanuensis, clerk, copyist; writer, author. See WRITING.

scrimmage, *n.* free-for-all, fracas, scuffle, tussle, brawl. See CONTENTION.

scrimp, *v.* curtail, limit, pinch, tighten, reduce; economize, skimp, stint, save, niggardize. See ECONOMY, PARSIMONY. *Ant.,* squander, spend.

script, *n.* handwriting, penmanship, calligraphy, cursive, round hand; scenario, libretto, book, screenplay, dialogue. See WRITING, DRAMA.

scriptural, *adj.* biblical, sacred; prophetic, evangelical, evangelistic, apostolic, inspired, apocalyptic, ecclesiastical. See SACRED WRITINGS.

Scriptures, *n.pl.* See SACRED WRITINGS.

scroll, *n.* roll, list, memorial; volute, flourish. See ORNAMENT, WRITING.

scrounge, *v.* pilfer, sponge. See STEALING.

scrub, *v.t.* rub, scour, holystone, swab, mop. See FRICTION, CLEANNESS.

scrubby, *adj.* wretched, shabby; undersize, stunted. See SHORTNESS, UNIMPORTANCE.

scruffy, *adj.* unkempt, shabby. See UNCLEANNESS.

scrumptious, *adj., informal,* first-rate; delicious, tasty. See TASTE, GOODNESS. *Ant.,* bad-tasting.

scruple, *n.* DOUBT, perplexity, misgiving, reluctance, UNWILLINGNESS, qualm, conscience. See PROBITY.

scrupulous, *adj.* exact, careful; fastidious, meticulous, punctilious; conscientious; upright, moral. See PROBITY. *Ant.,* careless, sloppy.

scrutiny, *n.* examination, inspection, investigation, INQUIRY.

scuff, *v.t.* scratch, abrade, scrape; disfigure. See FRICTION.

scuffle, *n.* strife, tussle, struggle, contest, CONTENTION, fray, fracas, brawl; shuffle.

SCULPTURE
Art of carving or sculpting

Nouns—1, sculpture, sculpting, sandblasting; plastic arts; [stone *or* wood] carving; installation.

2, statuary, statue, colossal; statuette, bust, head (see REPRESENTATION); cast (see FORM); relief, relievo; high *or* low relief, bas relief, mezzo-relievo; intaglio, cameo; anaglyph; medal, medallion; akrolith, anaglyph, assemblage, collage; ice sculpture; mobile, stabile; totem; video sculpture.

3, *(sculpture tools, techniques, and materials)* **a.** matrix; marble, grounding, dead stone, alabaster, soapstone; terra-cotta, clay; ceramics, ceramic ware, pottery, porcelain, china, earthenware; acrylic resin, Plasticine; bronze, electrum, niello; damascene. **b.** boucharde, chisel, file, gouge, gradine, hammer, lathe, mallet, peen, pick, pointing device, rasp, sander. **c.** casing, casting; cire perdu, lost-wax process, moulage, mantle, maquette, piece mold.

4, sculptor, sculptress, carver, chiseler, modeler. See ARTIST, ENGRAVING.

Verbs—sculpture, carve, grave, chase, cut, emboss, chisel, model, FORM, mould, turn; fabricate; cast; anodize, charge, chase, galvanize, temper.

Adjectives—sculptured; carven, graven; in relief; ceramic, marble, marmoreal, anaglyptic, plastic.

scum, *n.* froth, foam; slag, dross; mother (in fermentation); riff-raff. See UN-CLEANNESS, POPULACE, LAYER.

scurfy, *adj.* flaky, scabby, squamous, flocculent, furfuraceous. See LAYER.

scurrilous, *adj.* abusive, foul-mouthed, vituperative, insulting, offensive, coarse, vulgar, opprobrious. See DETRACTION, DISRESPECT.

scurry, *v.i.* hasten, dash, scuttle, scoot. See HASTE.

scurvy, *n.* scorbutus, scurf, Werlhof's *or* Barlow's disease. —*adj.* scorbutic, scurfy; villainous, mean, low, nasty, vile. See DISEASE, IMPROBITY.

scuttle, *n.* hod, RECEPTACLE, pail, bucket; scoop, shovel; hatch[way], hole, OPENING. —*v.i.* flee, escape, run, scurry. —*v.t.* sink, scupper, swamp, destroy, sabotage; demolish, overthrow, suppress. See DESTRUCTION, VELOCITY, HASTE.

scuttlebutt, *n.* cask; *slang,* gossip, rumor, hearsay. See INFORMATION.

sea, *n.* ocean, main, lake; wave, billow, swell; profusion, MULTITUDE. See WATER.

seacoast, *n.* seashore, seaside, seaboard. See LAND.

seafood, *n.* shellfish, FISH.

seal, *n.* die, stamp, signet; embossment, wafer, stamp; guarantee, confirmation; safeguard, stopper. —*v.t.* stamp, ratify, confirm; fasten, secure, occlude; close, confine. See COMPLETION, CLOSURE.

seam, *n.* ridge, JUNCTION; scar, wrinkle, FURROW; stratum, bed, LAYER.

seaman, *n.* mariner, sailor, salt, tar, gob (*sl.*), seadog, seafarer. See NAVIGATION.

seamster, seamstress, *n.* sewer, stitcher; dressmaker, tailor[ess]. See CLOTHING.

seamy, *adj.* sordid, worst. See UNCLEANNESS.

séance, *n.* session, gathering, sitting, COUNCIL; spiritualism, spirit-rapping. See ASSEMBLAGE.

seaplane, *n.* flying boat; hydroplane, amphibian, water plane, aeroboat, supermarine. See AVIATION.

sear, *adj.* sere, dry, arid, desiccated, waterless, dry-as-dust; barren, sterile, effete; yellow, pale, colorless. See DRYNESS, USELESSNESS. —*v.* dry, dehydrate, dessicate; singe, burn, scorch; brand, cauterize; wither, blast; fade, yellow. See HEAT, DRYNESS.

search, *v.t.* hunt, seek, look for; explore, examine, penetrate; probe; test. —*n.* quest, pursuit; INQUIRY, examination, investigation, scrutiny, exploration.

searching, *adj.* penetrating, keen, sharp; rigorous, unsparing. See SEVERITY. *Ant.,* superficial.

seashore, *n.* seaside, shore, strand, beach; [sea]coast, littoral, coastline, waterfront. See LAND.

seasickness, *n.* mal de mer, naupathia; nausea, queasiness, qualm. See DISEASE.

season, *n.* period, TIME, spell, interval. —*v.t.* harden, acclimate, habituate, inure, accustom; prepare, AGE, cure, ripen, dry out; imbue; spice, flavor. See HABIT, PUNGENCY, CHRONOMETRY.

seasonable, *adj.* suitable, opportune, timely. See EXPEDIENCE, AGREEMENT.

seasoning, *n.* relish, condiment, flavor[ing]. See TASTE.

seat, *n.* chair, bench, howdah, *etc.* (see SUPPORT); site, location, ABODE; villa, estate; membership; *informal,* buttocks, rump (see REAR).

seaweed, *n.* algae, fucus, kelp, conferva, carrageen. See VEGETABLE.

secede, *v.i.* withdraw, separate, bolt. See RELINQUISHMENT.

SECLUSION
Shutting away

Nouns—1, seclusion, privacy; retirement; reclusion, recess; rustication, *rus in urbe*; solitude; solitariness, isolation; loneness, withdrawal, hermitism, ermitism, anchoritism, voluntary exile, aloofness; inhospitality, inhospitableness; unsociability; quarantine; domesticity. *Slang,* monking. See OBSCURITY, CONCEALMENT, UNITY, ASCETICISM.

2, *(isolated place)* cell, hermitage; cloister, convent; holy of holies, Most Holy Place, sanctum sanctorum; depopulation, desertion, desolation; desert, wilderness; retreat, refuge (see SAFETY). See ABODE.

3, recluse, hermit, cenobite, eremite, anchoret, anchorite; St. Anthony; Simeon Stylites; Timon of Athens; solitaire, ruralist, cynic, Diogenes. *Informal,* lone wolf, loner. See ASCETICISM.

Verbs—be secluded, keep aloof, stand in the background; shut oneself up, creep into a corner, keep to oneself, keep one's own counsel, withdraw; rusticate; sequester, seclude, retire; take the veil, take orders. *Slang,* go it alone.

Adjectives—secluded, sequestered, retired, private; conventual, cloistered, out of the world; remote, inaccessible, out of the way; snug, domestic, stay at home; unsociable, unsocial, antisocial; inhospitable, solitary; lone, lonely, lonesome; isolated, single; unfrequented, uninhabited, uninhabitable; tenantless; abandoned.

Adverbs—by oneself; in private; in one's shell; in a world of one's own.

Quotations—God created man and, finding him not sufficiently alone, gave him a companion to make him feel his solitude more keenly (*Paul Valéry*), My heart is a lonely hunter that hunts on a lonely hill (*Fiona McLeod*), We live, as we dream—alone (*Joseph Conrad*), I want to be alone (*Greta Garbo*), We're all of us sentenced to solitary confinement inside our own skins, for life! (*Tennessee Williams*), The loneliness of the long-distance runner (*Alan Silitoe*), All the lonely people, where do they all come from? (*Lennon/McCartney*).

Antonyms, see SOCIALITY.

---

second, *n.* moment, instant, trice, twinkling; backer, supporter, assistant. See INSTANTANEITY, AUXILIARY.

secondary, *adj.* subordinate, minor, inferior, second-rate; resultant, consequent. See INFERIORITY, EFFECT.

second-guess, *v.t.* anticipate, predict. See EXPECTATION.

secondhand, *adj.* used, hand-me-down; indirect, hearsay, unoriginal. See OLDNESS. *Ant.,* brand-new, unused.

second nature, HABIT.

second-rate, *adj.* inferior, lesser, secondary, next best; mediocre, second-class, also-ran (*inf.*). See INFERIORITY, MEDIOCRITY. *Ant.,* first-rate, best.

second sight, clairvoyance (see PREDICTION)

second thought, reconsideration, afterthought, CHANGE of mind. See THOUGHT.

SECRET
Kept private

Nouns—secret; dead secret, profound secret; mystery; sealed *or* closed book; skeleton in the closet; confidence; hidden agenda; problem, enigma, riddle, puzzle, crossword puzzle, [double] acrostic, jigsaw puzzle, nut to crack, conundrum, charade, rebus, logograph, anagram (see DIFFICULTY); Sphinx, riddle of the Sphinx, milk in the coconut, skeleton in the closet; covert action, inside information; grapevine; labyrinth; UNINTELLIGIBILITY; terra incognita; arcanum, esotery, esotericism, occult, occultism; encryption, password. See CONCEALMENT, WONDER, SORCERY, LATENCY.

Verbs—secrete, hide, conceal, disguise; classify; keep to oneself, keep under one's hat, hush up. *Informal,* sit on. *Slang,* softshoe.

Adjectives—1, secret, concealed, clandestine, underhand[ed], arcane, enigmatical, recondite, privy, mysterious, puzzling, labyrinthine, veiled, hidden, problematical, paradoxical, inscrutable, unintelligible; esoteric, occult, mystic. *Informal,* hush-hush, under the counter, hugger-mugger. *Slang,* closet.

2, classified; restricted, confidential, secret, top secret, most secret, eyes only.

3, secretive, evasive; uncommunicative, poker-faced, reticent (see TACITURNITY).

Adverbs—secretly, on the sly, like a thief in the night; under one's breath; sub rosa, between you and me [and the bedpost]. *Informal,* on the q.t. See CONCEALMENT.

Phrases—little pitchers have large ears; never tell tales out of school; a secret is either too good to keep or too bad not to tell; there are tricks in every trade.

Quotations—I know that's a secret, for it's whispered everywhere (*William Congreve*), We dance round in a ring and suppose, but the Secret sits in the middle and knows (*Robert Frost*), Once the toothpaste is out of the tube, it is awfully hard to get it back in (*H. R. Haldeman*), Digestion is the great secret of life (*Rev. Sydney Smith*), It is good to keep close the secret of a king (*Bible*).

Antonyms, see DISCLOSURE, INFORMATION.

---

secretary, *n.* amanuensis, clerk; minister, administrator; desk, escritoire. See WRITING, RECEPTACLE, AUXILIARY, SERVANT.

secrete, *v.t.* hide, conceal, mask; separate, prepare, excrete. See CONCEALMENT, EXCRETION.

sect, *n.* denomination, faction, following, school, fellowship. See CLASS, HETERODOXY.

sectarian, *adj.* denominational; nonconformist, unorthodox, heterodox, heretical; dissident, schismatic, recusant, iconoclastic. See DISSENT, HETERODOXY.

section, *n.* separation, DISJUNCTION, division; segment, PART, portion, cross section; book, chapter; land, subdivision, sector, REGION; subdivision, subgenus, group, CLASS. —*v.t.* disjoin, divide, separate, bisect, slice, dismember, partition, distribute.

sector, *n.* pie section; area, REGION.

secular, *adj.* lay, temporal, profane, mundane, worldly, earthly. See IRRELIGION, LAITY. *Ant.,* religious, sacred.

secure, *adj.* safe; firm, stable; certain. —*v.t.* make safe; obtain (see ACQUISITION); fasten (see CONNECTION). See SECURITY, JUSTICE. *Ant.,* insecure.

SECURITY
Guaranty

Nouns—1, security, guaranty, guarantee; gage, warranty, bond, tie, pledge, plight, mortgage, debenture, hypothecation, bill of sale, lien, pawn; stake, deposit, earnest, collateral. See PROMISE.

2, *(record of security)* promissory note; bill [of exchange]; IOU; covenant, acceptance, endorsement, signature; execution, stamp, seal; sponsor, sponsorship; surety, bail; hostage; recognizance; indemnity; authentication, verification, warrant, certificate, voucher, RECORD; probate, attested copy; receipt, acquittance; discharge, release.

3, *(certificate)* title deed, instrument; deed, deed poll; assurance, insurance, indenture; charter, compact; paper, parchment, settlement, will, testament, last will and testament; codicil.

4, *(types of insurance)* no-fault, personal injury, mortgage, [major] medical, liability, life, disability, disaster, health, fire, group, malpractice, term [life], *or* unemployment insurance; Social Security, workmen's compensation.

5, *(insurance terms)* mortality table, premium, adjustor, actuary, agent, carrier; insured, policyholder; insurer, underwriter.

Verbs—secure; give security, give bail, go bail; put up, deposit, pawn, mortgage, hypothecate; guarantee, pledge, ensure, warrant, assure; accept, endorse, underwrite, insure; execute, stamp; sign, seal.

Adjectives—secure, guaranteed, warrantied, bonded, pledged. *Slang,* in the bag.

Quotations—Who will guard the guardians themselves? (*Juvenal*), Security is like liberty in that many are the crimes that are committed in its name (*Robert H. Jackson*).

Antonyms, see DANGER.

---

sedan, *n.* VEHICLE, automobile, limousine, landau[let], closed *or* touring car; litter, palanquin, palkee. See SUPPORT.

sedate, *adj.* staid, calm, inexcitable, serious, dignified, serene, demure, decorous, composed. See INEXCITABILITY. *Ant.,* agitated, excitable.

sedation, *n.* alleviation; narcosis, hypnosis; sedative. See REMEDY.

sedative, *n.* sedation; tranquilizer, bromide, calmant; sleeping pill; drug, narcotic, opiate, morphine; hypnotic; painkiller, barbiturate, analgesic, downer (*sl.*), goofball (*sl.*); Demerol, Nembutal. See

REMEDY, INACTIVITY, MODERATION, DRUGS. *Ant.*, stimulant, antidepressive, upper (*sl.*).

sedentary, *adj.* stationary, seated; inactive, sluggish, passive; nonmigratory, white-collar, desk, office, stay-at-home (*inf.*). See INACTIVITY.

sediment, *n.* alluvium, silt, settlings, precipitate, lees, dregs, heeltap. See REMAINDER, UNCLEANNESS.

sedition, *n.* incitement, insurgence, disloyalty. See DISOBEDIENCE.

seduce, *v.t.* lead astray, lure, entice, corrupt, inveigle; debauch, betray. See IMPURITY, ATTRACTION.

sedulous, *adj.* diligent, industrious, assiduous, persevering, persistent. See ACTIVITY, TENACITY.

see, *v.* view, descry, behold; discern, perceive, comprehend; observe, note; know, experience; ascertain, make sure; consider; meet; escort, attend. See VISION, KNOWLEDGE.

seed, *n.* germ, ovule, semen, milt; CAUSE, origin; offspring, children, descendants; grain, corn. See BEGINNING, ORGANIC MATTER, POSTERITY.

seedy, *adj.* gone to seed *or* to pot; shabby, rundown, shoddy, grubby (*inf.*), grimy (*inf.*); broken-down, ramshackle; poor, indigent. See DETERIORATION, POVERTY, DISEASE.

seek, *v.t.* search for, hunt, pursue; request, solicit; try, attempt, endeavor. See INQUIRY, PURSUIT.

seem, *v.i.* appear, look. See APPEARANCE.

seemly, *adj.* decorous, proper, becoming, decent, fitting. See EXPEDIENCE, BEAUTY. *Ant.*, unseemly, improper.

seep, *v.* leak, ooze, drain, drip, exude; trickle. See EGRESS.

seer, seeress, *n.* prophet, crystal gazer, clairvoyant; soothsayer, oracle. See PREDICTION.

seesaw, *v.i.* teeter[-totter]; waver, vacillate, dilly-dally; crossruff. See OSCILLATION.

seethe, *v.* boil, stew, simmer; steep, soak; fume, chafe. See HEAT, RESENTMENT, AGITATION, EXCITABILITY.

segment, *n.* slice, portion; component, member, branch, PART.

segregate, *v.t.* separate, set *or* keep apart, single out, discriminate; quarantine, isolate; exclude. See EXCLUSION, DISJUNCTION. *Ant.*, desegregate, unite.

seize, *v.t.* grasp, clutch; capture, arrest, appropriate, confiscate; afflict; attach, distrain; comprehend, understand. See STEALING, INTELLIGENCE, ACQUISITION.

seizure, *n.* confiscation, appropriation, arrest, capture; attack, fit, spell, stroke. See ACQUISITION, DISEASE, RESTRAINT.

seldom, *adv.* rarely, not often, infrequently. See RARITY. *Ant.*, often, frequently.

select, *v.t.* choose, pick, prefer, elect, opt, specify, designate. See CHOICE.

self, *n.* ego, I; being, essence; personality, IDENTITY, individuality, persona; mind, soul, spirit, self-esteem; inner self *or* being, inner man *or* woman.

self-centered, *adj.* egotistic; selfish. See SELFISHNESS, VANITY. *Ant.*, selfless.

self-confident, *adj.* self-reliant *or* -assured, sure of oneself, poised, cocky, cocksure, smug. See CERTAINTY, INEXCITABILITY.

self-conscious, *adj.* self-aware, introspective; shy, embarrassed; unsure, hesitant; unnatural, stylized, theatrical. See AFFECTATION.

self-control, *n.* self-discipline, -possession, *or* -restraint; poise, composure; reserve. See RESOLUTION.

self-defense, *n.* self-preservation; martial arts, karate, judo, *etc.* See DEFENSE.

self-denial, *n.* self-sacrifice, abnegation, renunciation, asceticism. See UNSELFISHNESS.

self-effacing, *adj.* diffident, modest. See MODESTY. *Ant.*, self-centered, vain.

self-esteem, *n.* PRIDE, self-respect; egotism, conceit, VANITY.

self-governing, *adj.* autonomous, independent, sovereign. See AUTHORITY.

self-indulgent, *adj.* unrestrained, selfish, sensual, voluptuous, unbridled, sybaritic. See SELFISHNESS.

SELFISHNESS
Devotion to oneself

Nouns—1, selfishness, self-indulgence, self-interest; egotism, egoism; VANITY; nepotism; worldliness; egomania, megalomania; illiberality; meanness, PARSIMONY. See MALEVOLENCE.

2, self-seeker, fortune-hunter, worldling; egotist, egoist, monopolist, nepotist; dog in the manger; spoiled child *or* brat.

Verbs—be selfish; indulge oneself; look after one's own interests; feather one's nest; take care of number one; have an eye to the main chance; know on which side one's bread is buttered; give an inch and take an ell; cultivate one's garden; sell oneself to the Devil.

Adjectives—selfish, self-seeking, self-indulgent, self-interested, self-centered; egotistic, egotistical; mean, mercenary, venal; earthly, mundane; worldly, materialistic, worldly-wise.

Adverbs—selfishly, ungenerously.

Phrases—every man for himself, and the Devil take the hindmost; if you want a thing done well, do it yourself; I'm all right, Jack.

Quotations—Manifest plainness, embrace simplicity, reduce selfishness, have few desires (*Lao-tzu*).

Antonyms, see UNSELFISHNESS, LIBERALITY.

---

selfless, *adj.* See UNSELFISHNESS. *Ant.,* self-centered.

self-made, *adj.* autogenous, spontaneous; self-educated, self-taught, autodidactic; raised up by one's own bootstraps. See PRODUCTION, KNOWLEDGE.

self-righteous, *adj.* smug, priggish; supercilious; sacrosanct, sanctimonious; hypocritical, holier than thou. See IMPIETY.

sell, *v.* See SALE.

sellout, *n., informal,* deception, betrayal, treachery, double-dealing; depletion, exhaustion; clearance, liquidation, closeout, fire sale; SUCCESS, hit, smash, full house, standing room only, SRO. See SALE.

semblance, *n.* likeness, resemblance, aspect; counterfeit, COPY, IMITATION; APPEARANCE, seeming, similitude, show, pretext. See SIMILARITY.

semen, *n.* sperm, seed, jism (*sl.*), come (*sl.*). See EXCRETION.

semiliquidity, *n.* stickiness, viscidity, viscosity; glutinosity; adhesiveness; inspissation, incrassation; thickening, gelatinousness; muddiness, miriness, slushiness. See COHERENCE, SOFTNESS.

seminal, *adj.* germinal; rudimentary, fundamental; productive, creative, catalytic, far-reaching. See CAUSE, ORGANIC MATTER.

seminar, *n.* study group, tutorial. See SCHOOL.

seminary, *n.* SCHOOL, academy; theological school; seminar.

semper fidelis, *Lat.,* ever faithful. See PROBITY.

semper paratus, *Lat.,* ever ready. See PREPARATION.

senator, *n.* legislator, congressman *or* -woman; solon, lawgiver, statesman. See COUNCIL.

send, *v.t.* dispatch, forward, transmit, broadcast; impel, drive; *slang,* excite, move (see EXCITEMENT). See TRANSFER, PROPULSION.

send-off, *n.* farewell, good-bye; outset, BEGINNING. See DEPARTURE.

send-up, *n., slang,* parody, RIDICULE.

senility, *n.* dotage, second childhood, superannuation, old age, degeneration, decrepitude. See AGE, INSANITY, WEAKNESS. *Ant.,* juvenility, puerility.

senior, *adj.* elder, older; superior, top-ranking. See AGE. *Ant.,* junior. —**senior citizen,** elderly person, old person, golden-ager, geezer (*inf.*). See AGE.

seniority, *n.* AGE, primogeniture; PRECEDENCE, PRIORITY.

sensation, *n.* FEELING, perception, consciousness, impression; furor. See SENSIBILITY.

sensational, *adj.* melodramatic, thrilling, startling; lurid, yellow. See EXCITEMENT.

sense, *n.* MEANING, import; perception, feeling; judgment, appreciation; opinion, consensus. See INTELLECT, INTUITION, SENSIBILITY.

senseless, *adj.* unconscious; foolish, stupid, dull; meaningless, unreasonable, absurd. See INSENSIBILITY, ABSURDITY. *Ant.,* sensible, sensual.

SENSIBILITY
Receptivity

Nouns—1, sensibility, sensitivity, sensitiveness; FEELING, perceptivity, esthetics; sensation, impression; consciousness (see KNOWLEDGE); sensorium.

2, *(mental sensibility)* sensibleness, impressionableness, affectibility; susceptibleness, susceptibility, susceptivity; tenderness, softness; sentimentality, sentimentalism. *Slang,* mush, corn, schmaltz. See IRASCIBILITY, EXCITABILITY.

3, *(physical sensibility)* sensation, tickle, tickling, titillation, itch[iness], itching; formication; aura; tingling, prickling; pins and needles; sore spot *or* point; allergy; the five senses. See TOUCH, TASTE, ODOR, HEARING, VISION.

Verbs—1, be sensible of; feel, perceive; sharpen, cultivate, tutor; impress. See TOUCH.

2, have a tender, warm, *or* sensitive heart, be sensitive; take to, treasure; shrink; touch to the quick, touch the heart.

3, itch, tingle, creep, thrill, sting; prick[le], formicate; tickle, titillate.

Adjectives—sensible, sensitive, sensuous; aesthetic, perceptive, sentient; conscious; acute, sharp, keen, vivid, lively, impressive; impressionable; susceptive, susceptible; alive to; gushing; warmhearted, tenderhearted, softhearted; tender, soft, sentimental, romantic; enthusiastic, high-flying, spirited, mettlesome, vivacious, lively, expressive, mobile, excitable; oversensitive, thin-skinned; fastidious; alert, aware. *Slang,* corny, cornball, mushy, sappy.

Quotations—O for a life of sensations rather than of thoughts! (*John Keats*), Whatever withdraws us from the power of our senses; whatever makes the past, the distant, or the future predominate over the present, advances us in the dignity of thinking beings (*Samuel Johnson*).

Antonyms, see INSENSIBILITY.

sensitive, *adj.* perceptive, conscious, impressionable, tender, susceptible, sentient; alert, aware; sentimental. See SENSIBILITY. *Ant.,* insensitive, unfeeling.

sensual, *adj.* voluptuous, carnal; salacious, lewd; sybaritic, epicurean. See INTEMPERANCE, PLEASURE.

sensualist, *n.* voluptuary; epicure; libertine. See INTEMPERANCE, PLEASURE.

sensuous, *adj.* sensitive, aesthetic, hedonistic; emotional, pleasurable. See SENSIBILITY, PLEASURE.

sentence, *n.* statement, expression; JUDGMENT, decision, penalty. See SPEECH, CONDEMNATION, WRITING.

sententious, *adj.* terse, laconic, pithy, succinct, curt; didactic. See MAXIM, TACITURNITY.

sentient, *adj.* perceptive, sensitive, feeling, responsive, alive. See SENSIBILITY, FEELING. *Ant.,* insentient.

sentiment, *n.* opinion, FEELING; sensitivity, delicacy, sympathy; motto, toast. See BELIEF, SENSIBILITY.

sentimental, *adj.* emotional, romantic, simpering, maudlin, mawkish. See SENSIBILITY. *Ant.,* unsentimental, cool.

sentinel, sentry, *n.* watchman, guard, lookout, picket. See DEFENSE.

separate, *v.* divide, disunite, disconnect, part, detach, sever, keep apart, isolate, segregate, sift, screen; part company. *Ant.,* unite, connect.—*adj.* disconnected, distinct, alone, isolate, unconnected, individual. See DISJUNCTION, DIVORCE, EXCLUSION, INTERVAL. *Ant.,* united, connected.

sepulcher, *n.* tomb, vault, crypt, mausoleum, sarcophagus. See INTERMENT.

sequel, *n.* upshot, outcome, continuation; consequence, appendix, postscript; epilogue, afterword. See SEQUENCE.

SEQUENCE
Order of succession

Nouns—1, sequence, coming after; going after, following, consecutiveness, succession, extension, continuation, order of succession, successiveness; flow chart; CONTINUITY. See REAR, PURSUIT, ACCOMPANIMENT.

2, successor, sequel, continuance; FUTURITY, posteriority.

Verbs—1, succeed; come after, come on, come next; follow (up), ensue, step into the shoes of; alternate; place after, suffix, append (see ADDITION).

2, pursue, go after, fly after; attend, beset, dance attendance on, dog; hang on the skirts of; tread on the heels of; lag, get behind.

Adjectives—1, succeeding, successive; sequent, subsequent, consequent; ensuing, proximate, next; consecutive, alternate; latter, posterior; chronological (see CHRONOLOGY).

2, following, attendant, trailing, in line, in sequence. *Slang*, hand running.

Adverbs—after, subsequently; behind, in the rear of, in the wake of; successively; sequentially, consequentially, consequently; after which, whereupon; as follows, next; as soon as; seriatim.

Antonyms, see PRIORITY, PRECEDENCE.

---

sequester, *v.* seclude, isolate, separate; cloister, shut up *or* away, immure, confine; confiscate, commandeer, expropriate. See SECLUSION.

sequin, *n.* spangle (see ORNAMENT).

seraph, *n.* ANGEL.

sere, *adj.* withered, dry. See DRYNESS.

serenade, *n.* serenata, cassation, nocturne, shivaree. See MUSIC. —*v.* sing to, entertain, perform for; court, woo. See ENDEARMENT.

serendipity, *n.* happy CHANCE, good luck; discovery, fortuity.

serene, *adj.* calm, placid, tranquil, unperturbed; clear, unclouded. See INEXCITABILITY, CONTENT. *Ant.*, agitated, ruffled.

serf, *n.* bondman, esne, villein, vassal; peasant. See SERVANT, POPULACE, SUBJECTION. *Ant.*, lord, master.

sergeant, *n.* noncommissioned officer, NCO; staff sergeant, sergeant major, top sergeant, top [kick] (*sl.*), gunny (*sl.*), *etc.* See COMBATANT.

serial, *adj.* seriatim; sequential, continuous, ordered, ranked, episodic; consecutive; to be continued. See CONTINUITY, PART, REGULARITY.

series, *n.* sequence, set, succession, chain, progression, cycle. See CONTINUITY.

serious, *adj.* grave, momentous, solemn; earnest, resolute; important, weighty; alarming, critical. See IMPORTANCE. *Ant.*, lightweight, insignificant.

sermon, *n.* homily, lecture, discourse, DISSERTATION, exhortation. See RITE, TEACHING, DISAPPROBATION, SPEECH.

serpentine, *adj.* snaky, reptilian, herpetic; sinuous, slithery; winding, tortuous, snaking; cunning, wily, venomous, cold-blooded. See CONVOLUTION. *Ant.*, straight[forward].

serrate, *adj.* serrated, saw-edged *or* -toothed, dentate; jagged; crenulate, scalloped. See SHARPNESS.

serried, *adj.* crowded, packed, dense. See DENSITY.

serum, *n.* antitoxin, vaccine; antigen, agglutinin; plasma; whey, WATER. See FLUIDITY.

SERVANT
One who serves another

Nouns—1, servant, servitor, domestic, menial, help; retainer, follower, henchman, subject, liegeman; retinue, suite, cortege, staff, entourage, court; majordomo, chamberlain. See AUXILIARY, ACCOMPANIMENT.

2, employee, staff, personnel, manpower, workforce, human resources; secretary; clerk; subsidiary; AGENT.

3, (*male servant*) attendant, servitor, squire, usher, page; waiter, waitron, garçon, waitperson, butler, household administrator, steward; livery servant, lackey, footman, flunky, factotum, bellboy, valet, valet de chambre; man; equerry, groom; jockey, hostler; orderly, batman, messenger; [hired] hand. *Informal,* droid. *Slang,* jack, slavey, record changer, bedbug, fart-catcher.

4, *(female servant)* maid[servant], handmaid[en]; lady's maid, nurse, bonne, ayah, wet nurse, nursemaid, housemaid, parlor maid, waiting maid, chambermaid, kitchen maid, scullery maid; femme *or* fille de chambre, abigail, girl; chef de cuisine, cook, scullion; maid of all work, hired hand, laundress, charwoman; [baby-]sitter; bar girl, barmaid, waitress, waitperson. *Slang,* fancy girl, B-girl.

5, *(lowly servant)* serf, vassal, slave, minion, bondsman *or* -woman; bondslave; villein; pensioner, dependent; hanger-on, satellite; parasite (see SERVILITY); protégé[e], ward; hireling, underling, mercenary, puppet, creature, henchman, cat's-paw, myrmidon, errand *or* office boy *or* girl; batman, dog robber. *Slang,* shit-kicker.

Verbs—serve, work for, tend, minister to; wait at *or* on table, wait on, attend (upon), squire (see OBEDIENCE).

Adjectives—serving, ministering, tending; in the train of, in one's pay *or* employ, on the payroll; at one's call (see OBEDIENCE); in bondage; unliberated.

Quotations—Modern science was largely conceived of as an answer to the servant problem (*Fran Lebowitz*), The one point on which all women are in furious secret rebellion against the existing law is the saddling of the right to a child with the obligation to become the servant of a man (*G. B. Shaw*), Living? The servants will do that for us (*Philippe-Auguste Villiers de L'Isle-Adam*), When domestic servants are treated as human beings it is not worth while to keep them (*G. B. Shaw*).

Antonyms, see AUTHORITY, DIRECTOR.

---

serve, *v.* attend, wait on (see SERVANT); replace; AID; avail, be of use; supply; suffice. See UTILITY, PROVISION, SUFFICIENCY.

service, *n.* aid, help, duty; servitude, ministration, employment; worship, ritual, armed forces; wear, usefulness, USE; set, equipment; serving, helping. See BUSINESS, UTILITY, RITE.

serviceable, *adj.* useful, functional (see USE). *Ant.,* useless, out of service.

serviceman, servicewoman, *n.* See COMBATANT.

SERVILITY
Obsequiousness

Nouns—1, servility, obsequiousness, subserviency; abasement (see HUMILITY); prostration, genuflection; fawning, ingratiation; tuft-hunting, time-serving, flunkyism; sycophancy, FLATTERY. *Slang,* apple-polishing.

2, sycophant, parasite; toady, freeloader, tuft-hunter; snob, flunky, slavey, lapdog; hanger-on, leech, sponger; clinging vine; time-server, fortune-hunter; flatterer, lickspittle; henchman, hireling, tool, cat's-paw; courtier. *Slang,* yesman, handshaker, baby-kisser, back-slapper, apple-polisher, Uncle Tom, Aunt Jemima, latch, pancake. See SERVANT.

Verbs—1, cringe, bow, stoop, kneel, bend the knee; sneak, crawl, crouch, cower; truckle to, curry favor with; grovel, fawn, lick the feet of, kiss the hem of one's garment, throw oneself at the feet of; freeload.

2, pay court to, make up to; dance attendance on, wait on hand and foot, hang on the sleeve of, fetch and carry, do the dirty work of. *Informal,* sponge. *Slang,* polish the apple, play up to, kiss ass.

Adjectives—servile, obsequious, abject; soapy, oily, unctuous; flattering, adulatory, fulsome; pliant, cringing, subservient, fawning, slavish, groveling, sniveling, mealy-mouthed; beggarly, sycophantic, parasitical; base, mean, sneaking, skulking.

Adverbs—servilely, abjectly, *etc.*; with hat in hand; abased.

Antonyms, see INSOLENCE.

servitude, *n.* slavery, SUBJECTION.

session, *n.* sitting, meeting; period, term, semester; conference, hearing, convocation. See ASSEMBLAGE, COUNCIL.

set, *v.* place, put, station; arrange, prepare; establish; mount; adjust, regulate; fix, assign, appoint; plant, set out; overthrow, unsettle; sink, go down; solidify, jell, harden; start out. See LOCATION, COMMAND, DESCENT, DENSITY. —*n.* clique, coterie, group; collection, series, outfit; TENDENCY, trend, drift; carriage, posture; agglutination, solidification; scenery. See COHERENCE, DIRECTION, PARTY, ASSEMBLAGE, CLASS, FORM, DRAMA.

setback, *n.* backslide; relapse, reverse, reversion, regression; defeat, LOSS, upset, check, discouragement.

settee, n. seat, settle, bench, form, sofa, lounge. See SUPPORT.

setting, *n.* background, backdrop; LOCATION, place[ment], site, locale, scene, ENVIRONMENT, milieu, region; mounting, base, frame, monture, collet, chape. See APPEARANCE.

settle, *v.* define, fix, confirm, appoint; agree upon; resolve, determine, decide, conclude; tranquilize, calm; reconcile, adjust, compose; discharge, square, pay, set at rest; place, establish; people, colonize, defeat, outwit; locate, settle down, take residence; sink, subside, sag, solidify; precipitate; alight; arrange, agree. See STABILITY, AGREEMENT, PAYMENT, ABODE, CERTAINTY, DESCENT.

settlement, *n.* arrangement; disposition, reconciliation, COMPROMISE, agreement, JUDGMENT; colony, base, outpost, LOCATION; bestowal, PAYMENT, discharge, award.

settler, *n.* colonist, pioneer, emigrant, homesteader. See INHABITANT.

set-to, *n., informal,* fight, brawl. See CONTENTION.

setup, *n.* arrangement, situation, facilities, plant, layout; makeup, PLAN, COMPOSITION, rig; *slang,* gull, fall guy; *slang,* frame-up, fix.

sever, *v.t.* cut off, cleave, separate, sunder, part; disjoin, dissolve. See DISJUNCTION. *Ant.,* connect, join.

several, *adj.* individual, distinct, separate, particular; different, various; few, sundry. See MULTITUDE, DISJUNCTION.

severance, *n.* SEPARATION; dissolution, DISJUNCTION; severance pay, payoff. See PAYMENT.

severe, *adj.* austerity, serious, earnest; rigorous, trying; harsh, strict; sharp, distressing, extreme. See SEVERITY, IMPORTANCE, ADVERSITY. *Ant.,* relaxed, laissez-faire.

SEVERITY
Strictness

Nouns—1, severity; strictness, harshness, rigor, stringency, austerity, straight face; ill treatment; inclemency, pitilessness, arrogance. See INSOLENCE, VIOLENCE, AUTHORITY.

2, *(strict rule)* arbitrary power, absolutism, despotism; dictatorship, autocracy, tyranny, domineering, oppression; inquisition, reign of terror, martial law; iron heel *or* hand; brute force *or* strength; coercion, COMPULSION; strong hand.

3, *(strict ruler)* tyrant, dictator, disciplinarian, martinet, stickler, despot, taskmaster, hard master, Draco, oppressor, inquisitor, extortioner, harpy, vulture, Simon Legree, slavedriver, drillmaster. *Slang,* prick, hard-ass.

Verbs—be severe, give no quarter, domineer, bully, tyrannize; rack, put the screws on, be hard on, mistreat; come down on; ill-treat; rule with a rod of iron; oppress, override; trample [under foot], tread upon, crush under an iron heel, crack the whip, crack down, ride roughshod over; keep a tight rein; work in a sweatshop. *Slang,* play hardball.

Adjectives—severe, strict, hard, harsh, astringent, tough, dour, rigid, stiff, stern, rigorous, uncompromising, unyielding, heavy-handed, exacting, exigent, inexorable, inflexible, obdurate, hard-boiled, hard-as-nails, austere, relentless, merciless, pitiless, unforgiving, Draconian, Spartan, stringent, straitlaced, searching, unsparing, hardfisted, ironhanded, peremptory, high-handed, absolute, positive, imperative; hard-

and-fast, coercive, puritanical, dictatorial, tyrannical, extortionate, grinding, withering, oppressive, inquisitorial; inclement, ruthless, cruel, grueling; cutthroat; haughty, arrogant. *Slang,* hard-nosed, hard-line.

Adverbs—severely, *etc.*; with a high *or* heavy hand; at sword's point.

Quotations—Government by a tyrant is the worst form of rule (*St. Thomas Aquinas*), The face of tyranny is always mild at first (*Racine*), Kindness effects more than severity (*Aesop*), Severity breedeth fear (*Francis Bacon*).

Antonyms, see MODERATION, NEGLECT, PITY.

---

sew, *v.t.* stitch, mend, baste, seam. See JUNCTION.

sewage, *n.* refuse, garbage, rubbish, waste, offal; drainage. See UNCLEANNESS.

sewer, *n.* seamstress; drain, cloaca, culvert, conduit, PASSAGE, sluice. See CLEANNESS.

SEX
Interaction between the sexes

Nouns—1, gender; sexuality; eroticism, sensuality; MALE, FEMALE, masculine, feminine; free love, promiscuity; facts of life, birds and the bees; conjugal rights; Kinsey scale; red-light district, adult entertainment zone, combat zone; sexual prejudice, sexism, heterosexism; sexual revolution. *Slang,* queer-bashing. See CLASS, ENDEARMENT, LOVE.

2, sex appeal, [animal] magnetism, machismo; aphrodisiac, love potion, philter, Spanish fly.

3, sexual orientation *or* preference; heterosexuality; homosexuality, homoeroticism, ephebophobia, androphilia; sexual orientation disturbance, SOD; gay power, gay pride, gay subculture; sodomy, pederasty; bisexuality; lesbianism, sapphism, lesbian separatism, tribadism. *Slang,* faggotry, concubitus, Greek love, pedication.

4, erotica, pornography, erotology, curiosa, facetiae, obscenity; centerfold; blue film, pornographic movie. *Informal,* beefcake, cheesecake. *Slang,* skin flick, porn flick, snuff film.

5, libido, sexual *or* carnal desire, lust, concupiscence, craving, DESIRE, passion, prurience; estrus, heat, must[h], rutting; lechery, lubricity, lewdness, lustfulness; nymphomania, satyriasis. *Slang,* hots, itch, urge to merge, blue balls.

6, a. [sexual] foreplay, necking, frisking, dalliance, feel; cybersex, chat room, cyberporn, computer sex; phone sex; doctors and nurses, spin the bottle. *Slang,* grab-ass, touchy-feely, outercourse. b. sex, sex act, [sexual] intercourse, [sexual] relations, [sexual] union, penetration, lovemaking, coition, coitus, [sexual] congress, carnal knowledge, conjugal relations, consummation, copulation, fornication, action, act of love; anal intercourse; oral sex, cunnilingus, anilingus, penilingus, fellatio, irrumation, blow job; masturbation, autoeroticism, onanism, self-abuse *or* -pollution; safe sex; rape (see IMPURITY); procreation (see REPRODUCTION). *Informal,* quickie. *Slang,* fucking, funch, nooner, action, all the way, fun and games, bone dance, vanilla sex, ass, bareback, between the sheets, nooky; slam bang, poontang; sixty-nine, minetting, blow job, lip service, box lunch, mouth-music, hair pie, head; buggery, rim job; hand job, circle jerk; dry fuck. c. missionary position, matrimonial position. *Slang,* dog-style. d. orgasm, climax, clitoral *or* vaginal orgasm, ejaculation; wet dream. e. sexual deviation, perversion, crime against nature, deviance, unnatural act; sadism, algolagnia, bestiality, bondage, child abuse, coprophilia, dominance, exhibitionism, exploitation, fetish, flagellation, flashing, frottage, golden shower, orgy, group grope, homeovestism, incest, indecent exposure, public nudity, masochism, molestation, mooning, necrophilia, nymphomania, paraphilia, pedophilia, sadomasochism, S&M, English guidance, satyriasis, scopophilia, sodomy, Greek arts, streaking, submission, swinging, transsexuality, transvestism, urolagnia, voyeurism, water sports, wife swapping, zooerasty, zoophilia. f. group sex, orgy. *Slang,* circle-jerk, club sandwich, daisy chain, gang-bang, petting-party, three-way, everythingathon.

7, sex *or* reproductive organs (see BODY).

8, asexuality, sexlessness; IMPOTENCE.

9, sex toy *or* aid, marital aid *or* device, dildo, vibrator; sex clinic; brothel (see IMPURITY).

10, a. sex object, sex symbol; sex fiend, libertine, voluptuary, sybarite, satyr; dirty old man; nymphet, sex goddess; sex surrogate; homophile, lesbian; catamite, gunsel. *Informal,* sex kitten, sexpot. *Slang,* fox, hot number, hunk, letch, masher, fag hag, feigele. See MALE, FEMALE. **b.** sexual pervert *or* deviant, pederast, sodomist, catamite. *Slang,* angel, backdoor man, birdie, bugger, capon, inserter, jockey, joey, mason, reamer, sodomite, turk, uncle, usher; bimbo, bitch, boxer, boy, gal-boy, gash, hump, ingle, kife, lamb, male varlet, pansy, pink pants, receiver, wife. **c.** cunnilingist, penilingist, fellator, fellatrice. *Slang,* cannibal, cocksucker, diver, lapper, nibbler, punk, smoker, stand, maneater, mantrap. **d.** masturbator, onanist. *Slang,* jacker, jerk-off, jerkwad, milkman *or* -woman, whanker, fricatrix.

Verbs—**1,** make love, neck, fool around, spoon, make out, neck, pet, park. *Slang,* feel up, clitorize, cop a feel, dally, diddle, feel up, finger, futz around, love up, mess about, paw, play grab-ass, stroke, toy. See ENDEARMENT.

2, make love (to), know, lie with, cohabit with, be familiar with, go to bed with, sleep with, shack up with, mate (with), mount, seduce; make the beast with two backs, have the earth move, make music together, roll in the hay. *Slang,* have sex, make babies, couple, fuck, adamize, ball, bang, boff, boink, bonk, bury the weenie, diddle, dip the wick, do it, do the nasty, drill, firk, frig, get down, get it on *or* up, go all the way; conjugate, get into her pants, get it on, get laid, get off, get some ass *or* action, goose, hide the salami, hose, hump, impale, jump [his *or* her bones], lay, make, make one's love come down, play hospital, pop, pork, pump, put out, ream, roger, romp, rut, score, screw, service, shtup, slam, stab, swive (*archaic*), thump, twiddle; fingerfuck, fist; cornhole, rim; blow, eat, give head, go down on, suck; deflower; pull a train.

3, masturbate, abuse oneself, waste time; have an erection. *Slang,* beat, jack *or* jill off, pound, wank, whack, *or* jerk off; choke the chicken, chuff, flog, get one's nuts off, hand-jive, beat the bishop, play with *or* touch oneself, whank, yank; get it up.

4, have an orgasm. *Slang,* come, cum, cream, get one's rocks off, drop one's load.

5, be homosexual, bisexual, *or* heterosexual; be transsexual, crossdress. *Slang,* go *or* swing both ways; come out.

Adjectives—**1,** sensual, erogenous, erotogenic, carnal, erotic, racy, raunchy, obscene, risqué, [sexually] explicit, sexually oriented, steamy, scabrous, lascivious, lewd.

2, lustful, ruttish, salacious; liberated; ithyphallic; oversexed; easy, fast; amative, amorous, in the mood. *Slang,* horny, hot [and bothered], hot to trot, foxy, affy, brimming, dripping, frisky, fuckish, gamy, hairy, in season, itching, juicy, rammish, randy, ruttish, sexed-up, turned on, wet; in the saddle.

3, sexually active; bisexual, epicene, gynandrous, transsexual, homosexual, in *or* out of the closet, age- *or* gender-differentiated, heterosexual, straight, unisexual; hermaphrodite, androgynous, sexually otherwise. *Slang,* AC/DC, ambidextrous, bi, kiki, double-gaited.

4, undersexed, unsexual, cold, asexual, unresponsive, frigid, impotent.

Phrases—wham bam, thank you, ma'am; the love that dare not speak its name.

Quotations—Give me chastity and continence—but not yet! (*St. Augustine of Hippo*), Is it not strange that desire should so many years outlive performance? (*Shakespeare*), The pleasure is momentary, the position ridiculous, and the expense damnable (*Lord Chesterfield*), Give a man a free hand and he'll try to put it all over you (*Mae West*), Personally I know nothing about sex because I've always been married (*Zsa Zsa Gabor*).

sexism, *n.* sexual discrimination; machismo. See INJUSTICE.

sexless, *adj.* neuter, asexual; gelded, castrated, emasculated, spayed, altered, fixed; impotent; cold, frigid, passionless. See IMPOTENCE.

sexton, *n.* sacristan, verger; vestryman, beadle. See CLERGY.

sexual, *adj.* carnal, sensual; erotic. See DESIRE, MALE, FEMALE, IMPURITY, SEX.

sexy, *adj., slang,* voluptuous, seductive, erotic; lewd, lascivious; wanton, sensational, bold; pornographic, X-rated. See IMPURITY. *Ant.,* unsexy, sexless

shabby, *adj.* dilapidated, seedy, rundown, threadbare; mean, sorry, pitiful, contemptible. See DETERIORATION, UNIMPORTANCE. *Ant.,* impeccable, fancy.

shack, *n.* hut, shanty, shed, hovel. See ABODE.

shackle, *n.* fetter, hobble, manacle, gyve, handcuff, bond; check, curb. —*v.t.* bind, restrain; handcuff, manacle, chain. See RESTRAINT.

shade, *n.* shadiness, shadow, umbrage, gloom, gloaming, DIMNESS, DARKNESS; OBSCURITY; duskiness; shading, tone; curtain, veil, film, haziness, haze, misti[ness], CLOUDINESS; COLOR, hue, tint; nuance, DEGREE; blind, curtain, shutter, Venetian blind; spirit, ghost, phantom, specter, apparition, haunt (see DEMON). —*v.t.* hide, conceal; darken, shadow; cover, veil; COLOR, tinge, tint. See COVERING, CONCEALMENT.

shadow, *n.* umbra, silhouette, shade; spy, follower; reflection; shelter, protection; trace, suggestion; ghost, tail (*sl.*); See ACCOMPANIMENT, IMAGINATION. —*v.t.* overcast, darken, shade; foreshadow, adumbrate; trail, dog, tail (*sl.*). See PURSUIT, DARKNESS, CLOUDINESS, COPY, DIMNESS.

shady, *adj.* shadowy, indistinct; *informal,* uncertain, questionable, sinister. See CLOUDINESS, IMPROBITY.

shaft, *n.* arrow, spear; beam, ray; handle; bar, axle; thill; column, pillar; well, pit. See ARMS, DEPTH, SUPPORT.

shaggy, *adj.* nappy, fuzzy, wooly; unkempt, scragg[l]y, stubbly, bearded, hirsute; matted, tangled; rough[hewn], crude. See ROUGHNESS.

shake, *v.* vibrate, agitate, shiver, brandish, flourish, rock, sway, wave, rattle, jolt, worry, jar; unsettle, disillusion, impair, unnerve; tremble, quiver, quaver, quake, shudder, flutter, vibrate. See AGITATION, EXCITEMENT, FEAR, OSCILLATION, WEAKNESS.

shakedown, *n., slang,* extortion (see STEALING).

shake-up, *n.* agitation, disturbance; reorganization, overhaul, REVOLUTION, change, reformation, rearrangement, reconstruction.

shaky, *adj.* trembling, wavering, unsteady; insecure, unstable. See AGITATION, OSCILLATION, FEAR, UNCERTAINTY. *Ant.,* steady, secure.

SHALLOWNESS
Lack of depth, superficiality

Nouns—1, shallowness, shoalness, flatness; superficiality; inanity, FOLLY; banality, insipidity, dullness, vapidity; IGNORANCE; triviality, frivolity. See UNIMPORTANCE.

2, shallow, shoal, flat, shelf, sandbank, bar, [coral] reef, ford; facade, gloss, veneer, scratch, pinprick; surface *or* flesh wound; trivia.

Verbs—scratch the surface, skim over, touch upon.

Adjectives—shallow, shoal[y], depthless, flat; empty, superficial, cursory; skin-, angle-, *or* knee-deep; flighty, silly, slight, unintelligent, simple, foolish, ignorant; banal, fatuous, inane, insipid, puerile, jejune, vapid; trivial, frivolous, trifling, flimsy, obvious, dull.

Quotations—It is only shallow people who do not judge by appearances. The true mystery of the world is the visible, not the invisible (*Oscar Wilde*), There is a tide in the affairs of men which, taken at the flood, leads on to fortune; omitted, all the voyage of their life is bound in shallows and in miseries (*Shakespeare*).

Antonyms, see DEPTH, IMPORTANCE.

shalom aleichem, Hebrew, peace be with you. See DEPARTURE.

sham, *n.* counterfeit, IMITATION, fake; pretense, dissimulation; humbug; imposture. —*adj.* make-believe, spurious, bogus, fake. See DECEPTION, FALSEHOOD, AFFECTATION.

shambles, *n.pl.* slaughterhouse, abattoir (see KILLING); wreck, chaos, mess. See DISORDER.

shame, *n.* humiliation, mortification, abashment; ignominy, reproach, disgrace, dishonor. —*v.t.* humiliate, mortify, abash, disgrace. See DISREPUTE, IMPURITY, WRONG. *Ant.,* PRIDE, honor.

shameful, *adj.* disgraceful, deplorable (see DISREPUTE).

shameless, *adj.* brazen, barefaced, unblushing, graceless, wanton, immodest. See INSOLENCE, IMPURITY.

shamefaced, *adj.* ashamed, humiliated, mortified (see DISREPUTE).

shanghai, *v.t.* abduct, kidnap, impress, commandeer. See COMPULSION.

shank, *n.* leg, shin; shaft, stem; handle; *informal,* END, REMAINDER. See SUPPORT.

shanty, *n.* shack, shed; hovel, tumbledown; hutch, bungalow. See ABODE.

shape, *n.* FORM, figure, contour; pattern, mold; state, condition.

shapeless, *adj.* amorphous, vague, ill-defined; disorganized; misshapen, distorted; unshapely, blobby. See FORMLESSNESS. *Ant.,* shapely.

shapely, *adj.* well-built, -proportioned, *or* -developed, curvaceous, chesty (*inf.*), busty (*inf.*), stacked (*sl.*); handsome, beautiful, gainly, svelte, lissome, lithe; buxom, voluptuous. See BEAUTY, SYMMETRY. *Ant.,* shapeless, flat (*inf.*).

shard, *n.* potsherd; fragment, piece, splinter. See PART.

share, *n.* portion, part, allotment, quota, dole, cut (*sl.*). —*v.* apportion, allot, assign, mete; partake, participate. See APPORTIONMENT.

shark, *n.* dogfish, hammerhead, *etc;* sharper, swindler; *slang,* expert. See ANIMAL, STEALING.

sharp, *adj.* cutting (see SHARPNESS); distinct, well-defined; abrupt, angular; pungent, penetrating; acute, keen; alert, smart, quick; elegant, smart. See VISIBILITY, PUNGENCY, WIT, ELEGANCE. *Ant.,* dull.—*n.* needle (see SHARPNESS); sharper, con man, shark; *informal,* expert, ace. See SKILL, DECEPTION.

sharper, *n.* cardsharp, slicker, cheat[er], swindler, chiseler, crook, con man, gyp; shark, mechanic. See DECEPTION.

SHARPNESS
Fine cutting edge or point

Nouns—1, sharpness, acuity, acumination; spinosity.

2, *(small pointed item)* point, spike, spine, spiculum; needle, pin; prick, prickle; spur, rowel; barb, barbed wire; spit, cusp; horn, antler; snag, thorn, briar, bramble, thistle; bristle; tine, prong; nib, tooth, tusk, fang; spoke, cog, ratchet. See DRUGS.

3, *(pointed building or natural object)* crag, crest, arête, cone, peak, sugarloaf, pike; spire, pyramid, steeple.

4, *(pointed implement)* wedge; knife, blade, edge, point, steel, carving knife; snickersnee; dagger, poniard, dirk, bodkin, stiletto; jackknife; scalpel, lancet; cutting edge, blade, razor; probe; plowshare; hatchet, ax, pickax, mattock, pick, adz, bill; billhook, cleaver, slicer, cutter; scythe, sickle, scissors, shears; sword (see ARMS); perforator; saw; iron maiden. *Slang,* shiv, toothpick, shank. See ARMS, ANGULARITY.

5, sharpener, hone, strop; grindstone, whetstone, steel; abrasive.

Verbs—be sharp, have a point; bristle with; sharpen, point, aculeate, whet, barb, spiculate, set, strop, grind; cut (see DISJUNCTION).

Adjectives—sharp, keen, cutting; acute, acicular, aciform; aculeate[d], acuminated; pointed; tapering; conical, pyramidal; spiked, spiky, ensiform, peaked, salient; cusped, cuspidate, cornute; prickly, spiny, spinous; thorny; bristling; studded; thistly, briary; craggy, rough, snaggy; digitated, two-edged, fusiform; dentiform; toothed, odontoid; starlike, stellate; arrow-headed; arrowy, barbed, spurred; cutting; sharp-edged, knife-edged; sharpened.

Quotations—How sharper than a serpent's tooth it is to have a thankless child (*Shakespeare*), A mind all logic is like a knife all blade. It makes the hand bleed that uses it (*Rabindranath Tagore*), Satire should, like a polished razor keen, wound with a touch that's scarcely felt or seen (*Lady Mary Wortley Montagu*).

Antonyms, see BLUNTNESS.

sharpshooter, *n.* marksman *or* -woman, crack shot; sniper. See COMBATANT, ARMS.

shatter, *v.* splinter, shiver, smash, disintegrate; destroy; madden, craze; crash, shatter. See BRITTLENESS, DISJUNCTION, INSANITY, DESTRUCTION.

shave, *v.t.* pare, plane, crop; skim, graze; cheapen, mark down, trim. See DEDUCTION, LAYER, NARROWNESS, SHORTNESS.

shaving, *n.* slice, paring, scale, LAYER. See PART, FILAMENT.

shawl, *n.* scarf, stole, mantle, serape, mantilla, wrap; tallith. See CLOTHING.

sheaf, *n.* bundle, fagot; cluster, batch, bunch; quiver; fascicle, packet, bale. —*v.t.* sheave; bundle, tie, bind; gather. See ASSEMBLAGE.

shear, *v.* clip, scissor; cut, lop, snip, trim, prune; shave, mow, fleece; despoil, strip, denude, rob of. See DIVESTMENT, SHARPNESS, SHORTNESS.

shears, *n.pl.* scissors, clippers. See SHARPNESS.

sheath, *n.* scabbard, sheathing, case, envelope, casing; involucre, capsule, fascia, lorica. See COVERING, RECEPTACLE.

shed, *n.* shelter, lean-to; shack, shanty, hangar, train shed. See ABODE. —*v.t.* spill, pour out; drop, cast off; molt, slough off; spread, diffuse, scatter. See DIVESTMENT, EJECTION, DISPERSION.

sheen, *n.* LIGHT, gleam, luster, shine, glow, shimmer, splendor. See SMOOTHNESS.

sheep, *n.* ram, ewe, lamb; bighorn, karakul; mutton; congregation, parish; follower. See ANIMAL, LAITY, MODESTY.

sheepish, *adj.* shamefaced, blushing, downcast, coy. See MODESTY. *Ant.*, brazen, wolfish.

sheer, *adj.* utter, absolute; mere, simple; thin, diaphanous; perpendicular, precipitous, VERTICAL, steep. See TRANSPARENCY, SIMPLENESS.

sheet, *n.* bedsheet; shroud, winding sheet, cerement; page, leaf, folio; plane, surface, plate, lamina, LAYER, membrane; rope, mainsheet. See COVERING, HORIZONTAL, INTERMENT, NAVIGATION.

shelf, *n.* ledge, mantel, mantelpiece; sandbank, reef. See SUPPORT.

shell, *v.t.* bomb, bombard, cannonade, strafe, pepper; shuck, strip, pod, hull. See ATTACK, DIVESTMENT. —*n.* case; carapace; husk, seashell; bomb, grenade, explosive, shrapnel, torpedo; boat, cockleshell, racing boat. See COVERING, DEFENSE. —shell out, *v.t. informal,* hand over, pay (see PAYMENT). —shell shock, *n.* combat fatigue; psychosis, neurosis; amnesia. See INSANITY, FEAR.

shellac, *n.* varnish. —*v.t.* varnish; *slang,* defeat, clobber. See COVERING, SUCCESS.

shelter, *n.* refuge, retreat, sanctuary, asylum; cover, security, protection, SAFETY. See COVERING, DEFENSE.

shelve, *v.t.* put aside *or* off, postpone. See DISUSE, LATENESS.

shenanigans, *n.pl.* foolery, pranks, horseplay. See AMUSEMENT.

shepherd, *n.* herder, sheepherder, herdsman; pastor, clergyman; Good Shepherd. See DOMESTICATION, CLERGY, DEITY.

sherbet, *n.* ice, sorbet, granita. See SWEETNESS.

sheriff, *n.* peace officer, marshal. See SAFETY.

shield, *n.* armor, safeguard, screen; protection, protector, aegis; arms, escutcheon. See DEFENSE, COVERING, INDICATION.

shift, *v.* veer, vary, CHANGE; equivocate; contrive, get along; transfer; substitute. —*n.* CHANGE, SUBSTITUTION, dislocation; expedient, subterfuge, trick. See DEVIATION, CUNNING.

shiftless, *adj.* lazy, indolent, improvident, thriftless, negligent. See INACTIVITY, UNPREPAREDNESS.

shifty, *adj.* unreliable, tricky; CUNNING; evasive, slippery; alert, resourceful. See AVOIDANCE.

shill, *n., slang,* accomplice; decoy, plant. See AID, DECEPTION.

shillelagh, *n.* cudgel (see ARMS).

shilly-shally, *v.i.* vacillate, waver; dawdle, loiter. See UNCERTAINTY, INACTIVITY.

shimmer, *n.* flicker, glimmer, gleam, sheen, glint, twinkle. See LIGHT.

shin, *n.* shinbone, tibia, shank, leg. See PART. —*v.* climb, creep up, clamber, scale, shinny (*inf.*); kick. See ASCENT.

shindig, *n., slang,* party, gala, affair, cele-bration, spree, shindy. See SOCIABILITY, AMUSEMENT.

shine, *v.* glow, gleam, scintillate; excel; polish, wax, burnish. See LIGHT, RE-PUTE. —**take a shine to,** *informal,* like, fancy (see LOVE).

shingle, *n.* roof *or* wall slate; signboard; beach gravel; bob. See COVERING, MA-TERIALS.

SHIP
Vehicle for navigation on water

*Nouns—*1, ship, vessel, sail; craft, bottom; airship (see AVIATION). See NAVIGATION.

2, *(naval organization)* navy, marine, fleet, flotilla, argosy; shipping, merchant marine; coast guard.

3, transport, tender, storeship; freighter, merchant ship, merchantman; packet; whaler, slaver, collier, coaster, lighter; fishing *or* pilot boat; dragger, drogher, trawler; hulk; yacht; liner; tanker, oiler; barge, scow; steamer, steamboat, steamship; paddle steamer; icebreaker; tug, tugboat; hovercraft, hydrofoil, hydroplane, airboat; bathyscaphe, bathysphere (see DEPTH).

4, *(sailing ship)* sailer, sailing vessel, fore-and-after, bark, barque, brig, brigantine, barkantine; schooner; sloop, cutter, corvette, clipper, yawl, ketch, sharpie, smack, dogger, lugger, nickey; cat[boat], carvel, caravel; bireme, trireme; galley, dromond, hooker, argosy, carrack; galleass, galleon, galiot; hoy, jangada, junk, lorcha, nuggar, moleta, praam, proa, prahu, saic, sampan, xebec, dhow; dahabeah; knockabout; iceboat.

5, boat, pinnacle, launch; rowboat, shallop, johnboat; lifeboat, longboat, jollyboat; bumboat, flyboat, cockboat, canalboat, ferryboat; shallop, gig, skiff, dinghy, scow; cockleshell, wherry, nobby, punt, outrigger; float, raft, pontoon; fireboat, motorboat; cabin cruiser; houseboat; class boat; catamaran, coracle, gondola, felucca, caique, gufa; dugout, canoe; kayak, faltboat.

6, marine, navy, naval forces, fleet, flotilla, armada, squadron; man-of-war, ship of the line, ironclad, warship, frigate, gunboat, flagship, cruiser; minesweeper; privateer; troopship, transport, corvette, torpedo boat, submarine, battleship, scout, dreadnought, aircraft carrier, flattop, destroyer. *Slang,* gob, gyrene.

7, *(parts of a ship or boat)* oar, paddle, scull, screw, sail, course, crossjack, foresail, headsail, mizzen, moonraker, jigger, kite, lateen, lugsail, mainmast, mainsail, square sail, staysail, studding sail, topgallant, royal sail, skysail, spanker, topsail, gennaker, pennant, gaff, canvas, fish's tail; paddle wheel, side, *or* stern wheel; rudder, leeboards, rigging, sail, sheet, line, rope, mainsheet; mast, aftermast, foremast, boom, pole, bibb, jib, sprit, genoa, crosstree, yard, yardarm; beam; keep; deck, quarterdeck, forecastle, fo'c'sle; spar, bowsprit; alleyway, hatchway, booby hatch, gangplank, gangway; anchor, bower, fluke, hook, barb, shank, grapnel, kedge, sea anchor, anchor chock; backstay, becket, bight, block, bobstay, buntline, hawser, halyard, heaving line, spring line, lanyard, ratline, mainstay, vang, warp, shroud, burton, capstan, cleat; batten, ballast, carlings, davit, derrick; berth; after, fore, boat, poop, orlop, flight, *etc.* deck, quarterdeck, bridge, brig; boiler room, engine room, cabin, stateroom, galley, head, hold, sick bay; bow, stern, bilge, bulkhead, bulwark, buttock, cuddy, cutwater, fantail, fidley, futtock, strake, garboard, gunwale, hull, keel, keelson, paravane, porthole, scupper, skeg; compass, gimbal, pelorus, sextant, helm, wheel, rudder.

*Verbs—*sail, cruise, steam, drift, navigate (see NAVIGATION).

*Adjectives—*full-rigged, square-rigged; fore-and-aft; abeam; fore, aft, midship, outboard.

*Adverbs—*afloat, aboard, on board, aboardship, on shipboard, amidship(s), athwartships, belowdecks.

Quotations—Don't give up the ship (*James Lawrence*), The human heart is like a ship on a stormy sea driven about by winds blowing from all four corners of heaven (*Martin Luther*), Ships that pass in the night, and speak to each other in passing (*Wordsworth*), They that go down to the sea in ships, that do business in great waters; these see the works of the Lord, and his wonders in the deep (*Bible*), What is a ship but a prison? (*Robert Burton*), His heart was mailed with oak and triple brass who first committed a frail ship to the wild seas (*Horace*), Being in a ship is being in jail, with the chance of being drowned (*Samuel Johnson*), Ships at a distance have every man's wish on board (*Zora Neale Hurston*).

shipment, *n.* delivery, conveyance, carriage, truckage; load, cargo, freight, lading; order, consignment. See TRANSPORTATION.

shipshape, *adj.* trim, tidy, neat, orderly, spruce; prepared, set; methodical; taut, seaworthy; tiptop, in the pink, perfect. See ORDER.

shipwreck, *n.* derelict, castaway, wreckage, flotsam, hulk; ruin, bankruptcy, *etc.*—*v.* wreck, ruin, scuttle, sink, capsize, run ashore; ground; shatter, destroy, fail. See DESTRUCTION.

shirk, *v.* evade, shun, neglect; slack, soldier, malinger, goldbrick (*sl.*). See AVOIDANCE.

shirt, *n.* blouse, chamise[tte], camisole, shift, plastron. See CLOTHING.

shiver, *v.i.* tremble, shudder, quiver, shake; shatter, splinter, burst. See AGITATION, BRITTLENESS, COLD, DISJUNCTION, FEAR.

shoal, *n.* school, multitude, host, horde; shallow, sandbar. See ASSEMBLAGE, LOWNESS.

shock, *v.t.* shake, jar, jolt; startle, surprise, horrify, scandalize, disgust; paralyze, stun; galvanize, electrify. —*n.* concussion, jar, impact; brunt, onset, assault; earthquake, temblor; prostration, stroke, paralysis, shellshock, apoplexy; ordeal, calamity; stack, stook; crop, thatch, mop (of hair). See DISEASE, ASSEMBLAGE, PAIN, VIOLENCE, SURPRISE, DISAPPROBATION, IMPULSE.

shocking, *adj.* distressing, horrible, abominable, odious, opprobrious, ghastly, indecent, dire, frightful, fearful, appalling, horrendous. See FEAR, DISREPUTE, VULGARITY.

shoddy, *adj.* inferior, low-grade, shabby; tawdry, gimcrack; sham, vulgar, common; low, mean, ignoble. See VULGARITY. *Ant.,* high-grade, superior.

shoe, *n.* footwear; footgear; sandal, espadrille, boot, loafer, casual, sneaker; runner, [tire] casing; [brake] lining. See CLOTHING.

shoemaker, *n.* cobbler, bootmaker. See PRODUCTION.

shoestring, *n.* —**on a shoestring,** economically, cheaply (see ECONOMY). *Ant.,* lavishly.

shoo, *v.t.* chase, disperse, scatter, dispel. —*interj.* scat! get away! get out! go away! scram! beat it! blow! (*sl.*) See DEPARTURE.

shoot, *v.* rush, dart; sprout, burgeon, grow; fire, discharge; detonate, explode; kill, wound, hit; propel, drive, emit. See VELOCITY, PROPULSION.

shop, *n.* mart, market, store, bazaar, emporium; office, workshop, shoppe, works, factory, mill. See BUSINESS.

shopkeeper, *n.* tradesman, merchant, dealer, retailer. See SALE.

shoplifter, *n.* thief, kleptomaniac. See STEALING.

shore, *n.* coast, beach, coastline; bank, strand, shingle, seaside. See LAND.

short, *adj.* brief, concise, curt; deficient, failing; compact, stubby. See INSUFFICIENCY, SHORTNESS, LITTLENESS.

shortage, *n.* deficiency, shortcoming. See INSUFFICIENCY. *Ant.,* abundance, overstock.

short-change, *v.t., informal,* cheat, gyp. See DECEPTION.

shortcoming, *n.* failing, foible, weakness, fault; deficiency, defect, default; delinquency, failure, inadequacy, INSUFFICIENCY, shortage, lack. See IMPERFECTION.

shortening, *n.* fat, lard, butter, suet, [oleo]margarine, OIL.

shortfall, *n.* deficiency, deficit (see INSUFFICIENCY). *Ant.,* excess.

shorthand, *n.* stenography, phonography, stenotypy, stenology; Pitman, Gregg, Speedwriting. See WRITING.

shorthanded, *adj.* understaffed, short. See INSUFFICIENCY.

short-lived, *adj.* transitory, impermanent, mortal, perishable, ephemeral, fugitive, evanescent; doomed. See TRANSIENTNESS. *Ant.,* longlived, permanent.

shortly, *adv.* soon; briefly, concisely, curtly. See EARLINESS, SHORTNESS.

SHORTNESS
Lack of length

Nouns—1, shortness, brevity, briefness, conciseness; shortening, abbreviation, abridgement, retrenchment, curtailment; compression, condensation, initialism, CONTRACTION; reduction, epitome, digest, synopsis, compendium; butt, stub; logogram; short cut. *Informal,* short haul.

2, abridger, cutter, editor, condenser, shortener.

Verbs—be short, shorten, curtail, abridge, boil down, abstract, condense, digest, abbreviate, take in, reduce; compress, contract; epitomize; retrench, cut short, scrimp, cut, chop up, hack, hew; cut down; clip, dock, lop, prune, bob; take up; cut corners; shear, shave; mow, reap, crop; snub; truncate, stunt, nip in the bud, check the growth of; foreshorten; come to the point.

Adjectives—short, brief, curt, succinct, short and sweet, crisp, epitomized, compendious, compact, concise, summary, stubby, shorn, stubbed; stumpy, thickset, pug; squat, dumpy; dwarfed, dwarfish, little; oblate; sawed-off. *Informal,* vertically challenged.

Adverbs—shortly, in short; for short, concisely, in brief, in fine, in a nutshell, in a word, in a few words; to come to the point, to make a long story short, to be brief; abruptly.

Phrases—brevity is the soul of wit; less is more.

Quotations—If the nose of Cleopatra had been a little shorter, the whole face of the world would have been changed (*Pascal*), I have made this letter longer than usual, because I lack the time to make it short (*Pascal*), Wickedness is always easier than virtue; for it takes the short cut to everything (*Samuel Johnson*), If there are obstacles, the shortest line between two points may be the crooked line (*Bertolt Brecht*).

Antonyms, see LENGTH, LOQUACITY.

---

shortsighted, *adj.* myopic, nearsighted; improvident, unimaginative, lacking foresight. See VISION. *Ant.,* farsighted, imaginative.

short-term, *adj.* brief, temporary. See TRANSIENTNESS. *Ant.,* long-term.

short-winded, *adj.* dyspn[o]eic, broken-winded, asthmatic, wheezy. See WEARINESS.

shot, *adj.* propelled, struck (see PROPULSION); interspersed, interwoven. —*n.* bullet, ball, pellet; discharge, stroke, attempt; *slang,* injection, inoculation, hypodermic, hypo. See ARMS, REMEDY.

shoulder, *n.* scapula; projection, abutment. See ANGULARITY, CONVEXITY. —*v.* assume, bear, carry; sustain, maintain, SUPPORT; jostle, poke (see IMPULSE).

shout, *v. & n.* scream, call, bawl, bellow, yell; whoop, cheer, roar. See CRY, REJOICING, LOUDNESS. *Ant.,* whisper.

shove, *v.* push, hustle; urge, thrust, force; crowd, cram, wedge; shoulder, jostle, jog, jar, elbow, nudge. See IMPULSE.

shovel, *n.* spade, digger; scoop[er], excavator, trowel, scuttle. —*v.* dig, excavate, unearth; ladle, dip. See CONCAVITY.

show, *v.* exhibit, display; explain, teach; demonstrate, prove, guide, escort; appear, stand out. See EVIDENCE, DISCLOSURE. —*n.* display, exhibition, play, entertainment, pageant, spectacle; pomp, OSTENTATION; semblance, APPEARANCE, pretext. See DRAMA, VISIBILITY, DEMONSTRATION. —**show business,** *n.* entertainment industry (see AMUSEMENT, DRAMA).

showboat, *v.i.* show off, parade, grandstand (see OSTENTATION).

showcase, *n.* display case *or* window; vitrine, étalage; exhibition; repository, reliquary; étagère, whatnot, mantelpiece. See RECEPTACLE.

showdown, *n.* confrontation, face-off; climax, denouement; settling of accounts, putting one's cards on the table, show of hands. See OPPOSITION, DISCLOSURE.

shower, *n.* rain, sprinkle, drizzle; spate; volley; fall. See WATER, ASSEMBLAGE, CLEANNESS.

showing, *n.* performance; display, exhibition. See DISCLOSURE, OSTENTATION.

showman, *n.* exhibitor, impresario, producer. See DRAMA, OSTENTATION.

showmanship, *n.* skill, stagecraft; dramaturgy, histrionics; OSTENTATION, style, garishness, exhibitionism, fanfare, pageantry, display, theatricality. See DRAMA.

show-off, *n.* display, OSTENTATION; exhibitionist, peacock, hotshot (*sl.*), ham (*inf.*). *Ant.,* shrinking violet (*inf.*).

showpiece, *n.* [display] model; paradigm, classic. See PERFECTION, SUPERIORITY.

show up, *v.t.* appear, arrive; eclipse, overshadow, put to shame. See APPEARANCE, SUPERIORITY.

showy, *adj.* conspicuous, colorful; ornate, florid, flashy, gaudy, pretentious, ostentatious, imposing. See COLOR, VULGARITY, OSTENTATION.

shred, *n.* strip, tatter, remnant, snippet, scrap; modicum, bit, particle, speck; trace, vestiges. —*v.t.* grate; macerate, mangle, lacerate; tear, rip. See PART, FILAMENT, DISJUNCTION.

shrew, *n.* termagant, scold, virago, vixen, fishwife, henpecker, beldame. See EVILDOER, FEMALE.

shrewd, *adj.* clever, keen, farsighted, astute; CUNNING, wily, artful; sharp, acute, piercing. See SKILL. *Ant.,* slow, unimaginative.

shriek, *v.i.* scream, screech, shrill, squeal. See CRY.

shrill, *adj.* sharp, piercing, strident, high-pitched, piping, penetrating, poignant. See LOUDNESS, CRY.

shrine, *n.* altar, TEMPLE; RECEPTACLE (for sacred objects), reliquary; tomb.

shrink, *v.* contract, shrivel, diminish, wizen; flinch, draw back, RECOIL, wince, quail, cower; compress, reduce, DECREASE. See CONTRACTION, FEAR.

shrivel, *v.* shrink, wrinkle, wizen, pucker; wither, sear. See CONTRACTION, FOLD.

shroud, *n.* winding sheet, graveclothes; pall; screen, cloak, veil. See INTERMENT, CONCEALMENT.

shrub, *n.* shrubbery; scrub, bush, arbuscle, hedge, treelet. See VEGETABLE.

shrug, *v.* raise the shoulders. See INDICATION, DISAPPROBATION, DISLIKE.

shudder, *v.i.* tremble, quake, quiver, shiver, vibrate. See COLD, FEAR.

shuffle, *v.* rearrange, switch, shift, mix, intermingle, jumble; scuff, drag; fidget; scuffle, shamble, slouch; equivocate, quibble, evade. See INTERCHANGE, SLOWNESS, CHANGEABLENESS.

shun, *v.t.* avoid, elude, evade, eschew; cut, ignore; steer clear of. See AVOIDANCE.

shunt, *v.t.* turn aside, sidetrack, get rid of. See DEVIATION.

shut, *v.t.* close, fold; imprison, confine; silence; cease operations, terminate; bar, exclude, blockade. See CLOSURE. *Ant.,* open.

shutdown, *n.* stoppage, cessation, end, termination, halt; layoff, sitdown strike, closing, foreclosure; lockout, walkout; CLOSURE. See DISCONTINUANCE.

shut-in, *n.* invalid (see DISEASE).

shutter, *n.* blind[s], louver, persiennes; screen, grille. See CONCEALMENT.

shuttle, *n.* See OSCILLATION, TRANSPORTATION.

shy, *adj.* bashful, reserved, retiring, demure; cautious, suspicious, wary; timid, skittish, fearful; short, lacking. See MODESTY, FEAR, INCOMPLETENESS. *Ant.,* forward, brash, incautious. —*v.* start, RECOIL. See DEVIATION, FEAR.

shyster, *n.* See LAWSUIT, DECEPTION.

sibilant, *adj. & n.* hissing; whispering; whistling. See SOUND.

sibling, *n.* kinsman; brother, sister, sib. See RELATION.

sick, *adj.* ill, ailing, diseased; nauseated; disgusted, fed up (*sl.*); bored. See DISEASE, DISLIKE. *Ant.,* healthy, well.

sicken, *v.* ail; languish, droop, waste away; cloy, weary; make ill, afflict; nauseate, revolt. See DISEASE, PAIN, DISLIKE.

sickly, *adj.* invalid, ailing, unwell; debilitated, languid, peaked; wan, pale, washed out, faint; mawkish, nauseating. See DISEASE, WEAKNESS, COLORLESSNESS. *Ant.,* healthy.

side, *n.* surface, flank; aspect, point of view. See SIDE, RIGHT, LEFT, PARTY. —*v.i.* ally oneself (with) (see AID).

SIDE
Terminal surface

Nouns—side, flank, quarter, lee, leeward, weather, windward; skirt, EDGE; hand; cheek, jowl; wing; profile; temple; loin, haunch, hip; laterality; gable[-end]; broadside; outside, inside (see EXTERIOR, INTERIOR); east, west (see DIRECTION); orientation, aspect; unilateralism, bilateralism, trilateralism.

Verbs—be on one side, flank, outflank; sidle; skirt, border.

Adjectives—1, side, lateral, sidelong; collateral; parietal, flanking, skirting; flanked; bordering; lee[ward], weather, windward; askance; shoulder-to-shoulder. See NEARNESS. 2, onesided, many-sided, multilateral; bilateral, trilateral, quadrilateral.

Adverbs—sideways, sidewise, sidelong; laterally; broadside on; on one side, abreast, abeam, alongside, beside, aside; by, by the side of; side by side; cheek by jowl; to windward, to leeward; right and left.

Antonyms, see MIDDLE.

side effect, reaction (see EFFECT, ACCOMPANIMENT).

sidekick, *n., informal,* buddy, partner. See FRIEND, ACCOMPANIMENT.

sideline, *n.* hobby, avocation, pastime. See AMUSEMENT, BUSINESS.

sidestep, *v.* avoid, circumvent, evade; jockey, parry; equivocate. See AVOIDANCE.

sideswipe, *v.t.* graze, carom, skirt. See NEARNESS.

sidetrack, *v.t.* divert, distract. See DEVIATION, INATTENTION.

sidewalk, *n.* walk, footwalk, crosswalk, pavement; footpath, footway, banquette; boardwalk, trottoir, promenade, mall. See PASSAGE.

sideways, *adv.* laterally, edgeways, crabwise. See SIDE.

siding, *n.* sidetrack, [track] spur; paneling, boarding. See COVERING, DEVIATION.

sidle, *v.* EDGE, crab; sidestep, skirt, flank; slither. See DEVIATION, OBLIQUITY, SIDE.

siege, *n.* investment, encirclement; besiegement, blockade, beleaguerment; period, long spell. See ATTACK, RESTRAINT.

siesta, *n.* nap, snooze, doze, rest. See REPOSE.

sieve, *n.* riddle, colander, sifter, screen, strainer, bolter. See OPENING.

sift, *v.t.* separate, bolt, screen, sort; examine, scrutinize, segregate, eliminate. See CHOICE, CLEANNESS, TASTE.

sigh, *v.i.* suspire, sough, moan; long, yearn, *or* grieve (for). See WIND, DESIRE, LAMENTATION.

sight, *n.* VISION, eyesight; view, vista, scene; APPEARANCE, aspect, look; spectacle, display; visibility; aim, observation; eyesore (see UGLINESS). —at sight, immediately (see IMMEDIACY).

sightless, *adj.* blind, eyeless, unseeing; amaurotic; invisible, imperceptible. See BLINDNESS, INVISIBILITY. *Ant.,* sighted, seeing.

sightseeing, *n.* tour[ing], tourism; excursion, expedition; globetrotting, vacationing, rubbernecking (*sl.*). See CURIOSITY, TRAVEL.

sign, *n.* omen, portent; INDICATION, symptom, token, mark; symbol, emblem; gesture, signal; trace, vestige; signboard, shingle; guidepost. See INDICATION, DIRECTION.

signal, *n.* sign, watchword, cue; alarm, WARNING, direction, order; traffic light, beacon, foghorn, wigwag; trace, vestige. See INDICATION. —adj. memorable, conspicuous, momentous. See IMPORTANCE. —v.t. signalize, speak, hail, call, beckon, gesticulate; semaphore, wigwag; radio, broadcast, beam. See INDICATION.

signalize, *v.* indicate, point out; celebrate. See INDICATION, CELEBRATION.

signatory, *n.* signer, signator; witness, testifier; subscriber, party, under writer, endorser, co-signer, co-maker. See ASSENT.

signature, *n.* autograph, hand, fist (*sl.*), John Hancock (*inf.*), John Henry (*inf.*); sign manual; subscription; mark, endorsement; identifying theme, music, letters, *etc.*; identification; attestation. See INDICATION, NOMENCLATURE.

significant, *adj.* important, consequential; meaningful, expressive. See IMPORTANCE, MEANING. *Ant.,* insignificant. —**significant other,** *n. informal,* spouse, live-in [lover]. See MARRIAGE.

signify, *v.t.* show; declare, portend; mean, denote, express, connote, indicate. See MEANING, IMPORTANCE.

sign up, enlist, enroll (see LIST).

SILENCE
Absence of sound

Nouns—1, silence; stillness, quiet, peace, hush; inaudibility.

2, *(reluctance or inability to speak)* muteness, dumbness, aphony, voicelessness; TACITURNITY, reticence; deadness, dullness.

3, silencer, muffler, damper, mute; gag, muzzle.

4, mute, deafmute.

Verbs—1, silence, baffle, strike dumb, quiet, still, hush (up); stifle, muffle, stop, cut one short, cut off; drown (out); smother, muzzle, mute, gag, put to silence; dampen, deaden. *Informal,* shush, squelch. *Slang,* shut up, slap down, put the kibosh on, soft-pedal.

2, hold one's tongue, speak softly, whisper. *Informal,* save one's breath, keep one's mouth shut. *Slang,* button *or* zip one's lip, clam up, save it, put a sock in it.

Adjectives—1, silent; still, stilly; quiet [as a mouse], noiseless, soundless; hushed, soft, solemn, awful, tomblike, deathlike, silent as the tomb *or* grave; inaudible, faint; soundproof, muted, muffled, noiseproof.

2, mute, dumb, mum, tongue-tied, tongueless, voiceless, speechless; aphonic; tacit; unspoken; silent, gagged, muzzled; inarticulate; taciturn (see TACITURNITY).

Adverbs—silently, mutely, *etc.*; with bated breath, under one's breath, sotto voce; tacet. *Slang,* on the q.t.

Interjections—hush! silence! shut up! cat got your tongue? mum's the word! *Slang,* dry up! belay that! stow it!

Phrases—silence is a still noise; [speech is silver, but] silence is golden; a shut mouth catches no flies; children should be seen and not heard; see no evil, hear no evil, speak no evil; the silent dog is the first to bite.

Quotations—Silence is the virtue of fools (*Francis Bacon*), No voice; but oh! the silence sank like music on my heart (*Coleridge*), Thou still unravished bride of quietness, thou foster-child of silence and slow time (*John Keats*), Drawing on my fine command of language, I said nothing (*Robert Benchley*), Do you wish people to believe good of you? Don't speak (*Pascal*), God is the friend of silence (*Mother Teresa*), Try as we may to make a silence, we cannot (*John Cage*).

Antonyms, see SOUND, LOUDNESS.

silhouette, *n.* shadow [figure], shadowgram, skiagraph *or* -gram; outline, profile, cutout, cameo. See FORM.

silky, *adj.* silken, sericeous; satiny, lustrous; flossy, sleek, smooth, luxurious; suave, mellifluous. See SMOOTHNESS, SOFTNESS. *Ant.,* rough, coarse.

sill, *n.* windowsill, ledge, shelf; threshold, base, SUPPORT; frame, beam.

silly, *adj.* witless, foolish, stupid, childish; fatuous, inane; senseless, absurd, ridiculous; stunned. See ABSURDITY, CREDULITY, FOLLY.

silo, *n.* grainery, granary, grain elevator; crib, bin; storehouse (see STORE).

silt, *n.* sediment, deposit, alluvium, loess, clay. See UNCLEANNESS, REMAINDER.

silver, *n.* argentum, sterling, silver plate; [small *or* loose] change, cash; pin *or* hard money; silverware. —*adj.* argent[al]; silvery, silver gray; eloquent, silver-tongued, mellisonant. See MINERAL, COLOR.

s'il vous plaît, *Fr.,* if you please. See REQUEST.

SIMILARITY
Resemblance

Nouns—1, similarity, resemblance, likeness, similitude, semblance; affinity, approximation, parallelism; AGREEMENT; analogy; family likeness; alliteration, rhyme, pun. See IMITATION, NEARNESS, CONFORMITY.

2, REPETITION; sameness, IDENTITY; uniformity, EQUALITY; parallel; simile, [spitting] image; counterpart; striking, speaking, *or* faithful likeness; double, twin, picture. *Informal*, chip off the old block. *Slang*, [dead] ringer, spit and image. See COPY.

Verbs—1, look like, look alike, resemble; bear resemblance; smack of; approximate, partake of; parallel, match; take after; imitate; assimilate.

2, compare, identify, parallel, relate. See RELATION.

Adjectives—similar; resembling, like, alike; twin, analogous, analogical; parallel, of a piece; so; much the same; near, close, something like; comparable; akin; mock, pseudo, simulating, representing; exact, lifelike, faithful; true to nature, true to life, the very image, the very picture of; like [as] two peas in a pod, cast in the same mold, in the same boat.

Adverbs—similarly, as if, so to speak, as it were, quasi, just as, à la; such as.

Phrases—all cats are gray in the dark; birds of a feather flock together; like breeds like; comparisons are odious; great minds think alike.

Quotations—The road up and the road down are one and the same (*Heraclitus*), Comparisons are odorous (*Shakespeare*), Shall I compare thee to a summer's day? (*Shakespeare*).

Antonyms, see DIFFERENCE, DEVIATION.

---

simile, *n.* figure of speech, comparison. See FIGURATIVE.

simmer, *v.* boil, cook, bubble, parboil; effervesce, fizz; fume, chafe, brood, fret, ferment. See HEAT, RESENTMENT.

Simon Legree, slave driver, martinet (see SEVERITY).

simony, *n.* See IMPIETY.

simpatico, *adj.* congenial, amiable. See SOCIALITY.

simper, *v.i.* smile, smirk; strut, prance. See AFFECTATION, REJOICING.

simple, *adj.* elementary, uncomplicated; plain, common; unassuming, humble, unaffected; pure, absolute; gullible, silly. See SIMPLENESS, HUMILITY, FOLLY, PURITY. *Ant.*, complex, complicated, difficult.

SIMPLENESS
Lack of complication

Nouns—1, simpleness, classicism; PURITY, homogeneity; CLEANNESS.

2, simplicity, artlessness, INNOCENCE; plainness, homeliness; undress; chastity, SEVERITY; ELEGANCE. See CREDULITY.

Verbs—simplify; clear, purify, clean; disentangle (see DISJUNCTION); come down to earth; call a spade a spade, lay on the line.

Adjectives—1, simple, homogeneous, single, pure, clear, sheer, neat, mere; bare, austere; classic; unmixed, uncomplex; simplistic, oversimplified; elementary; unadulterated, unsophisticated, unalloyed; pure and simple; free from, exempt from; exclusive; no-frills, severe, chaste; naive.

2, plain, homely, homespun; Anglo-Saxon; dry, unvaried, monotonous; earthy; down-to-earth; ordinary; bald, flat; dull, artless, ingenuous, unaffected, free from affectation *or* ornament; chaste, severe; unadorned, unornamented, ungarnished, unvarnished, unarranged, untrimmed. *Informal*, [plain] vanilla. *Slang*, down-home, no-frills, raw.

3, outspoken, blunt, direct, forthright, straight from the shoulder, down to brass tacks; in plain words, in plain English.

Adverbs—simply, purely; solely, only; unadornedly, in the raw; in plain terms, words, English, *etc.*, in words of one syllable, in no uncertain terms; bluntly, point-blank, right out, straight. *Informal*, flat-out.

Phrases—less is more.

Quotations—Everything should be made as simple as possible, but not simpler (*Albert Einstein*), Beauty of style and harmony and grace and good rhythm depend on simplicity (*Plato*), Our life is frittered away by detail . . . Simplify, simplify (*Henry David Thoreau*).

Antonyms, see ORNAMENT, DISORDER, AFFECTATION, LOQUACITY.

---

simple-minded, *adj.* foolish, ingenuous; simple, moronic, imbecilic. See FOLLY, IGNORANCE.

simpleton, *n.* dunce, blockhead, moron, ninny, nincompoop, innocent, fool, nitwit, dope (*sl.*), jerk (*sl.*). See FOLLY, IGNORANCE. *Ant.,* sage.

simplistic, *adj.* naive; oversimplified. See SIMPLENESS, IGNORANCE.

simulate, *v.t.* imitate, resemble, mimic; feign, counterfeit, pretend. See FALSEHOOD, IMITATION.

simultaneous, *adj.* coincident, concurrent, contemporaneous, in concert, in unison, synchronous. See TIME, SYNCHRONISM.

sin, *n.* IMPIETY, sacrilege, transgression, wickedness, IMPURITY, iniquity, vice; offense, crime, fault, error, peccadillo. —*v.i.* transgress, err, offend. See GUILT, WRONG, BADNESS, EVIL.

since, *adv.* ago, later, subsequently, afterwards. —*conj.* because, inasmuch as; after. See CAUSE, ATTRIBUTION, CIRCUMSTANCE, REASONING.

sincere, *adj.* honest, genuine; ingenuous, forthright, unreserved, candid; cordial, hearty, earnest. See TRUTH, FEELING, PROBITY. *Ant.,* insincere, feigned.

sinecure, *n.* easy job, snap, cinch, gravy (*sl.*). See FACILITY.

sine qua non, Lat., [pre]requisite, NECESSITY. See IMPORTANCE.

sinewy, *adj.* fibrous, wiry, stringy; strong, well-knit. See STRENGTH.

sinful, *adj.* iniquitous, wicked; ungodly, impious. See WRONG. *Ant.,* sinless.

sing, *v.* troll; chant, carol, intone, warble; laud, praise; vocalize; yodel; versify; hum, whistle. See MUSIC, POETRY, DISCLOSURE.

singe, *v.t.* scorch, sear. See HEAT.

singer, *n.* vocalist, songster (see MUSIC).

single, *adj.* one, separate, solitary, individual; unmarried; unique, sole; detached,

alone; sincere, honest, unequivocal. See CELIBACY, UNITY, SECLUSION.

single-handed, *adj.* alone, solo; by oneself, independent, unassisted, one-man; with one hand tied behind one's back. See UNITY.

single-minded, *adj.* one-track, narrow [-minded]; resolute, stubborn, determined; obsessive, monomaniacal; undeviating. See RESOLUTION.

singular, *adj.* unique, individual; peculiar, unusual, odd, eccentric; exceptional, rare; extraordinary. See UNCONFORMITY, SPECIALITY. *Ant.,* common, multiple.

sinister, *adj.* ominous, unlucky, portentous; LEFT; evil, bad; unpropitious, baleful, injurious; ill-starred; malicious, harmful, corrupt. See BADNESS.

sink, *v.* founder, drown, go down; ebb, wane, decline, lapse, settle, subside, precipitate; retrograde, go downhill; languish, droop, flag; despond; fail, deepen, dig, lower; debase, abase, bring low; suppress, overwhelm; submerge, immerse, bury; discourage, dampen; invest, risk, venture. See DEPTH, DESCENT, DETERIORATION, DEJECTION, FAILURE.

sinless, *adj.* impeccable, virtuous, innocent, immaculate; absolved, shriven, purified, forgiven; unfallen, prelapsarian. See PURITY, INNOCENCE. *Ant.,* sinful.

sinuous, *adj.* winding, curvy; devious, convoluted. See CIRCUITY, DEVIATION, DECEPTION. *Ant.,* straight[forward].

sip, *v.* drink, imbibe, taste; siphon, suck. —*n.* taste, soupçon, sampling; drink, draft; modicum. See FOOD, DRINKING.

sire, *v.* beget, father. See ANCESTRY.

siren, *n.* water nymph, temptress, vamp, vampire, gold digger (*sl.*), Circe, Lorelei, Delilah, Jezebel; alarm, warning, signal. See DEMON, ATTRACTION, FEMALE.

sissy, *n., informal,* weakling, milksop, milquetoast, mama's boy, mollycoddle, chicken (*sl.*), scaredy-cat (*sl.*); effeminate, transvestite. See WEAKNESS, COWARDICE. *Ant.*, he-man, hero.

sister, *n.* kinswoman; nun, sister of mercy, religieuse; associate, soror, fellow; nurse; counterpart. See CLERGY, SIMILARITY, RELATION.

sit, *v.i.* sit down, perch; pose; hold session, convene; fit, suit; brood; be situated. See LOCATION.

site, *n.* position, LOCATION.

sitting, *n.* session; séance. See ASSEMBLAGE.

situate, *v.* place, locate; set, station, put; lie, be situated. See LOCATION.

situation, *n.* place, LOCATION; position, site; state, predicament, plight, case, CIRCUMSTANCE; job, office, post, station, employment. See BUSINESS.

SIZE
Ample dimensions

Nouns—1, size, magnitude, dimension, bulk, volume; largeness, GREATNESS; expanse, SPACE; extent, scope (see DEGREE); AMPLITUDE; mass, DENSITY; proportions, MEASUREMENT; capacity, tonnage, caliber; corpulence, obesity, plumpness, fatness, embonpoint, avoirdupois, girth, corporation; hugeness, enormousness, immensity, monstrosity. See EXPANSION, ROTUNDITY.

2, giant, titan, Brobdingnagian, Antaeus, Goliath, Anak, Gog and Magog, Gargantua, Cyclops, Fasolt and Fafner, Gigantes, Gorgons, Grendel, Baba Yaga, Chimera; monster, mammoth, dragon, griffin, Loch Ness monster; whale, porpoise, behemoth, leviathan, elephant, hippopotamus, mastodon; colossus. *Informal,* whopper, bumper, lollapalooza.

Verbs—expand, enlarge; grade, assort, graduate (see DEGREE).

Adjectives—1, sizable, large, big, great; considerable, goodly, hefty, bulky, voluminous, ample, massive, mammoth, massy; capacious, comprehensive, vast; spacious, towering, magnificent; tremendous, huge, immense, enormous, mighty; monstrous, bull-necked, mesomorphic, prodigious, titanic, gigantic, elephantine, mastodonic, jumbo; giant, stupendous, colossal; Cyclopean, Brobdingnagian, Gargantuan, amazon, Antaean, Herculean, Junoesque; gross; life-size, big *or* large as life. *Informal,* humongous, bodacious.

2, corpulent, stout, fat, plump (see ROTUNDITY); full, lusty, strapping, bouncing; portly, burly, well-fed, full-grown; stalwart, brawny, fleshy; goodly; lumbering, unwieldy; whopping, thumping, thundering, hulking; overgrown, bloated; big as a house. *Informal,* queen- *or* king-size.

Phrases—great oaks from little acorns grow; the bigger they are, the harder they fall.

Quotations—Women have served all these centuries as looking-glasses possessing the magic and delicious power of reflecting the figure of man at twice its natural size (*Virginia Woolf*), No one loves his country for its size or eminence, but because it is his own (*Seneca*), God is ordinarily for the big battalions against the little ones (*Count Bussy-Rabutin*), [Of Chicago:] Stormy, husky, brawling, city of the big shoulders (*Carl Sandburg*), A government that is big enough to give you all you want is big enough to take it all away (*Barry Goldwater*), Very big, China (*Noël Coward*).

Antonyms, see LITTLENESS.

---

sizzle, *v.* crepitate, fizz, crackle, sp[l]utter; scorch, broil, fry, sear; burn, swelter. See HEAT.

skein, *n.* coil; tangle, twist, snarl. See CONVOLUTION.

skeleton, *n.* frame[work]; outline, diagram; bones, bony structure. See SUPPORT, PLAN, REMAINDER.

skeptic, *n.* doubter, agnostic, freethinker, doubting Thomas, questioner; infidel; unbeliever. See IRRELIGION, DOUBT. *Ant.,* believer.

sketch, *v.t.* draw, outline, block out, rough in; state briefly; draft, chart, map. See REPRESENTATION, FORM, PAINTING, PLAN.

skew, *adj.* oblique, distorted. See OBLIQUITY.

skewer, *n.* spit, pin. See JUNCTION.

skid, *n.* sideslip; incline; runner, check, curb, brake; skidway, travois; (*pl.*) *slang,* skid row, downfall, bankruptcy. —*v.* slide, [side]slip; spin; swerve; grip, brake, lock. See DESCENT, SIDE, DEBT, POVERTY. —**skid row,** slum, tenderloin, Bowery. See POVERTY.

SKILL
Expertness

Nouns—**1,** skill, skillfulness, address; dexterity, dexterousness; adroitness, expertise, proficiency, adequacy, competence, handicraft, finesse, savoir-faire, FACILITY, knack; mastery, mastership; professionalism; excellence, ambidexterity, versatility, virtuosity, prowess; artistry, wizardry.

2, (*result of skill*) accomplishment, acquirement, endowment, attainment (see SUCCESS); art, science, touch, flair; technicality, technology; KNOWLEDGE, experience; discretion, [quiet, shuttle, *etc.*] diplomacy; delicacy; craftiness, CUNNING; management. See LEARNING.

3, (*talent*) cleverness, talent, ability, ingenuity, capacity, parts, faculty, endowment, forte, turn, gift, genius; INTELLIGENCE, sharpness; aptness, aptitude; capability, qualification; trick of the trade. *Informal,* know-how. *Slang,* the goods, what it takes.

4, (*skillful action*) masterpiece, master stroke, coup, coup de maître, chef d'œuvre, tour de force; trump card.

5, expert, adept, connoisseur, virtuoso, master; man of arts; artisan; master hand, top sawyer (*Brit.*), prima donna, first fiddle, old hand; armchair general, Monday-morning quarterback; practiced eye, marksman, crack; conjuror; veteran, champion, ace; old stager *or* campaigner; handyman; genius, mastermind, tactician, strategist, diplomat; Sherpa. *Informal,* techie. *Slang,* sharp, shark, wizard, whiz, jack-leg mechanic, preacher, top gun, butt-kicker.

Verbs—be skillful, excel in, be master of; have a turn for, play one's cards well *or* right, hit the nail on the head; have all one's wits about one; have one's hand in; have a lot on the ball. *Slang,* know one's stuff; have been around; take care of business.

Adjectives—**1,** skillful, dexterous; adroit, expert, apt, handy, quick, deft, ready, smart, proficient, good at, up to, at home in, master of, a good hand at; masterly, crack, accomplished, versed in, conversant (see KNOWLEDGE); versatile; sophisticated, experienced, practiced, skilled, [well] up in, dry behind the ears; in practice; competent, efficient, qualified, capable, fitted for, up to the mark, trained, initiated, prepared, primed, finished. *Slang,* ginchy, been there[, done that].

2, clever, able, ingenious, felicitous, gifted, talented, endowed; inventive, shrewd, sharp, intelligent; ambidextrous, surefooted; artistic, workmanlike, businesslike, statesmanlike.

Adverbs—skillfully, handily, well, artistically; with skill.

Phrases—he who can, does—he who cannot, teaches.

Quotations—Experience is the name which every one gives to their mistakes (*Oscar Wilde*), Any sufficiently advanced technology is indistinguishable from magic (*Arthur Clarke*), An expert is one who knows more and more about less and less (*Nicholas Butler*), One thorn of experience is worth a whole wilderness of warning (*James Russell Lowell*), Though this be madness, yet there is method in it (*Shakespeare*).

Antonyms, see UNSKILLFULNESS.

---

skillet, *n.* frying pan, frypan, spider; saucepan, casserole. See RECEPTACLE.

skim, *v.* scum; strain, cream, separate; scan, thumb through; glide, skip, skid, graze, brush, TOUCH. See VELOCITY.

skimp, *v.* scrimp, stinge, stint; economize. See ECONOMY, NEGLECT. *Ant.,* spend, squander.

skimpy, *adj.* meager, scanty (see INSUFFICIENCY).

skin, *v.t.* flay, peel, decorticate; *Slang,* fleece, cheat. See DIVESTMENT, STEAL-

ING. —*n.* integument, cuticle, dermis, epidermis; pelt, hide; rind; veneer, plating, lamina; parchment. See COVERING.

skinflint, *n.* niggard, scrimp, hoarder, tightwad. See PARSIMONY. *Ant.,* philanthropist.

skinny, *adj.* thin, lean, slim, slender. See NARROWNESS. *Ant.,* fat, plump.

skip, *v.* caper, spring, LEAP, hop, trip, frisk, gambol, frolic; omit, pass over, stay away; ricochet; *slang,* decamp, play truant. See NEGLECT, ABSENCE.

skipper, *n.* captain, master, pilot; commodore, commander. See NAVIGATION, AUTHORITY.

skirmish, *n.* clash, brush, tilt, encounter, engagement. See CONTENTION.

skirt, *n.* overskirt, kilt, petticoat, farthingale, coattail; purlieu, borderland, EDGE, margin, outskirts; *slang,* woman, girl. See CLOTHING, FEMALE.

skit, *n.* burlesque, satire, parody, lampoon, pasquinade; sketch, playlet, vignette, tableau. See RIDICULE, DRAMA.

skittish, *adj.* lively, frisky, spirited; excitable, restive, nervous, jittery; timorous, fearful; coy, bashful; capricious, fickle. See EXCITABILITY.

skulduggery, *n.* trickery, DECEPTION.

skulk, *v.i.* lurk, sneak, slink, malinger, steal, hide; cower. See CONCEALMENT, COWARDICE.

sky, *n.* firmament, heavens, HEAVEN, welkin. See AIR.

skyline, *n.* horizon (see HORIZONTAL).

skyrocket, *v.i.* leap, shoot (up). See ASCENT, IMPROVEMENT.

skyscraper, *n.* high-rise, tower. See ABODE.

slab, *n.* slice, wedge, section, piece, cut, hunk, chunk; plate, board, plank, shingle; tablet, gravestone. See PART, INTERMENT, HORIZONTAL, LAYER.

slack, *adj.* careless, lax, negligent, remiss; loose, limp, flaccid, relaxed; sluggish, stagnant; dull, slow, not busy, light. See NEGLECT, INACTIVITY, SOFTNESS, INSUFFICIENCY. *Ant.,* tight, taut.

slacken, *v.* retard, diminish, lessen; loosen, relax; abate; languish, decline; ease up, dwindle. See MODERATION, REPOSE, SLOWNESS, DECREASE. *Ant.,* tighten, INCREASE.

slacker, *n.* shirker, quitter, evader. See AVOIDANCE.

slake, *v.t.* quench, satisfy, appease, allay, abate, sate. See PLEASURE, REFRESHMENT, RELIEF.

slam, *v.* shut, close; swat, pound, batter, bash, slug. —*n.* impact, closing, crash, clang; buffet. See IMPULSE.

slammer, *n., slang,* PRISON.

slander, *n.* scandal, aspersion, defamation, calumny, disparagement. See DETRACTION.

slang, *n.* argot, jargon, cant, lingo, patois, vernacular; dialect; colloquialism, neologism, vulgarism. See SPEECH.

slant, *n.* OBLIQUITY, slope, inclination, declination, tilt, pitch; bias, leaning, TENDENCY.

slap, *v.t. & n.* hit, smack, swat, cuff; insult. See IMPULSE, RIDICULE, PUNISHMENT.

slapdash, *adj.* precipitate, hasty, careless, hit *or* miss; superficial, sketchy, rough, hack, sloppy. See HASTE. *Ant.,* careful, methodical.

slaphappy, *adj., slang,* dazed, groggy; silly, foolish. See INSANITY, INATTENTION.

slapstick, *n.* buffoonery, farce, burlesque. See AMUSEMENT.

slash, *v.* hack, cut, gash, cleave, sever, sunder, slice, carve; whip, scourge; mark down, reduce, lower. See DISJUNCTION, DECREASE.

slat, *n.* lath, strip. See NARROWNESS, FILAMENT, LAYER, MATERIALS.

slate, *n.* LIST, ballot, ticket; blackboard; slab, rock, roof. See MATERIALS.

slattern, *n.* sloven; slut, trollop. See UNCLEANNESS.

slaughter, *n.* butchering; butchery, massacre, carnage, murder. See KILLING.

slaughterhouse, *n.* abattoir, shambles, butchery. See KILLING.

slave, *n.* bondsman, bond servant, thrall, serf; drudge, peon, vassal, menial; addict, victim. See SERVANT. —*v.i.* toil, drudge; overwork. See EXERTION. *Ant.,* master, owner.

slaver, *v.i.* slobber, drivel; fawn. See EXCRETION, SERVILITY.

slavery, *n.* bondage; forced labor; servitude, chains, captivity; drudgery, toil; addiction, submission. See SUBJECTION.

slay, *v.t.* kill, slaughter, dispatch; murder, assassinate. See KILLING.

sleazy, *adj.* flimsy, gauzy; shabby; shoddy, cheap, unsubstantial. See WEAKNESS, INSUBSTANTIALITY. *Ant.,* sturdy, high-quality.

sled, *n.* sledge, sleigh; bobsled; dogsled; skid, cutter, pung. See VEHICLE.

sleek, *adj.* slick, oily, smooth, glossy; well-groomed; chic, soigné, elegant, suave, urbane, skillful, adroit. See SMOOTH-NESS.

sleep, *n.* slumber, somnolence, nap, doze, drowse, rest, REPOSE; coma; hypnosis. —*v.i.* slumber, repose, doze, nap; be dead *or* dormant.

sleeping pill, barbiturate, opiate, goof ball (*sl.*); tranquilizer, sedative. See DRUGS.

sleepless, *adj.* wakeful, insomniac, restless; alert, vigilant. See CARE, ACTIVITY. *Ant.,* somnolent.

sleepwalker, *n.* somnambulist, noctambulist, nightwalker. See TRAVEL.

sleepy, *adj.* drowsy; languid; lethargic. See REPOSE, INACTIVITY. *Ant.,* [wide-] awake, alert.

sleet, *n.* frozen *or* freezing rain, hail; ice storm. See COLD.

sleeve, *n.* COVERING, envelope, pipe; mandrel, quill, bushing, coupling, union.

sleigh, *n.* See SLED.

slender, *adj.* slim, thin, skinny, attenuated; tenuous, slight, meager; scanty, weak. See NARROWNESS. *Ant.,* wide, fat, thick.

sleuth, *n.* bloodhound; detective, hawkshaw, gumshoe; plainclothesman; shadow, operative, [private] investigator, dick (*sl.*), private eye, shamus, op (*sl.*). See CONCEALMENT.

slew, *v.i.* veer, twist (see DEVIATION). —*n., informal,* throng, crowd, host (see MULTITUDE).

slice, *v.t.* cut, slash, carve, shave, skive. See LAYER.

slick, *adj.* glossy, shiny, polished; oily, slippery, greasy; unctuous, obsequious; sophisticated, urbane; *informal,* crooked, cheap, glib; sly, ingenious, CUNNING, tricky. See SMOOTHNESS, OIL, KNOWLEDGE.

slicker, *n.* raincoat, waterproof, poncho, oilcoat, oilskin; *informal,* swindler. See CLOTHING.

slide, *v.i.* glide, slip, coast, skim; steal, pass. See MOTION, DESCENT.

slight, *adj.* slender, slim, frail, delicate; trivial; meager, scant. See UNIMPORTANCE. —*v.t.* ignore, cut, snub, rebuff; scamp, NEGLECT, disdain. —*n.* snub, rebuff, cut. See CONTEMPT.

slim, *adj.* slender, thin, slight; frail, weak, meager. See NARROWNESS.

slime, *n.* ooze, mire, sludge, mud, muck; primordial slime; filth. See UNCLEANNESS.

sling, *v.t.* propel, fling, catapult, chuck (*inf.*), peg (*inf.*); shoot, pitch; hang, fasten up, suspend. See PROPULSION, PENDENCY. —*n.* slingshot, catapult, perrier, ballista; bandage, strap, suspensory, SUPPORT. See ARMS.

slink, *v.i.* sneak, steal, skulk, slither; creep, snoop. See CONCEALMENT, COWARDICE.

slip, *v.* glide, slide; misstep; steal; ESCAPE, elapse; blunder, err; don. —*n.* misstep, slide; blunder, ERROR; scion, graft; faux pas, indiscretion; undergarment; pillowcase; dock; strip, sheet; chit, girl; ceramic, cement. See DESCENT, CLOTHING, TRAVEL.

slippery, *adj.* slimy, greasy, slick, glassy, shifty, elusive, unreliable; sly, insecure. See SMOOTHNESS, DANGER.

slipshod, *adj.* negligent, slovenly, careless. See NEGLECT, DISORDER.

slit, *v. & n.* cut, gash, slash, slice. See INTERVAL, FURROW.

slither, *v.* slink, sinuate, worm; crawl, creep; slide, slip. See SMOOTHNESS, DESCENT.

sliver, *n.* splinter, shive; slice, chip, shaving; shard, fragment. See PART, FILAMENT.

slob, *n., slang,* sloven, slattern; pig, slovenly Peter. See UNCLEANNESS.

slobber, *v.i.* slaver, drivel, dribble, drool. See EXCRETION, MOISTURE.

slog, *v.i.* plod, trudge (see SLOWNESS).

slogan, *n.* watchword, shibboleth, password, byword, motto, MAXIM.

slop, *n.* spillage, muck, slush, slime; spillings, refuse, garbage, swill, waste, sewage; puddle; *slang,* chow, FOOD; *slang,* gush, sloppiness, schmaltz. —*v.* spill, overflow, splash. See UNCLEANNESS, MOISTURE.

slope, *n.* slant, tilt, pitch, inclination; incline, grade, gradient, ramp, ascent, rise. See OBLIQUITY.

sloppy, *adj.* untidy, messy; maudlin;

slovenly. See DISORDER, NEGLECT, FEELING. *Ant.*, neat, unsentimental.

slosh, *v.* splash, slop, spill. See WATER, MOISTURE.

slot, *n.* aperture, slit, OPENING; groove, notch, nick, channel, PASSAGE. —**slot machine,** vending machine; one-armed bandit. See SALE, CHANCE.

sloth, *n.* laziness, idleness, INACTIVITY, inertia; slowness, sluggishness, indolence. *Ant.*, ACTIVITY, energy.

slouch, *v.* droop, flag, slump, sag, bend; shamble, shuffle, lounge, loll. See SLOWNESS, INACTION, DEPRESSION.

slovenly, *adj.* slatternly, sluttish; untidy, unkempt, disorderly, sloppy, tacky (*inf.*); slipshod, lax. See DISORDER, UNCLEANNESS, NEGLECT. *Ant.*, neat, clean.

slow, *adj.* time-consuming; dull-witted, dense (*sl.*); tardy, sluggish; slack, leisurely; tedious, boring. See SLOWNESS, IGNORANCE, LATENESS, WEARINESS. *Ant.*, fast, quick-witted, bright. —*v.* slacken, moderate, relax; decelerate; arrest, check, hold back. See HINDRANCE, MODERATION. *Ant.*, speed [up], accelerate.

SLOWNESS
Quality of taking a relatively long time

Nouns—1, slowness, languor, INACTIVITY; leisureliness; retardation; slackening; delay, LATENESS; walk, stroll, saunter, snail's pace, jog-trot, dog-trot; slow motion, slowdown. *Informal,* slowup.

2, dullness, flatness, monotony, boredom. See WEARINESS.

3, laggard, lingerer, loiterer, sluggard, tortoise, plodder; snail; dawdler. *Slang,* slowpoke.

Verbs—1, move slowly, creep, crawl, lag, linger, loiter, straggle, stroll, saunter, walk, plod, trudge, inch, stump along, lumber; trail, drag; dawdle, worm one's way, steal along; toddle, waddle, slouch, shuffle, halt, hobble, limp, shamble; flag, falter, totter, stagger; take one's time; hang fire (see LATENESS). *Informal,* take one's own sweet time, laze along. *Slang,* get no place fast, mosey along, hold one's horses.

2, slow, retard, relax; slacken, check, moderate, rein in, fall behind, slow down, curb; reef; strike, shorten, *or* take in sail; set back; put on the drag, brake, apply the brake; clip the wings; reduce the speed; slacken speed *or* one's pace; lose ground; slack off *or* down; step down.

Adjectives—slow, slack; tardy; dilatory, inactive, gentle, easy, leisurely; deliberate, gradual; dull, uninteresting; languid, sluggish, snail- *or* slow-paced, snaillike, creeping; slow but sure. *Informal,* slow as molasses.

Adverbs—slowly, leisurely; at half speed, under easy sail; at a snail's pace; in slow time; in slow motion; gradually, by degrees *or* inches, step by step, drop by drop, inch by inch, bit by bit, little by little.

Phrases—festina lente (hasten slowly).

Quotations—Wisely and slow. They stumble that run fast (*Shakespeare*), Slow and steady wins the race (*Aesop*), The march of the human mind is slow (*Edmund Burke*), Though the mills of God grind slowly, yet they grind exceedingly small (*Friedrich von Logau*), Jupiter is slow looking into his notebook, but he always looks (*Zenobius*), Justice is not to be taken by storm. She is to be wooed by slow advances (*Benjamin N. Cardozo*).

Antonyms, see VELOCITY, HASTE.

sludge, *n.* mud, mire, filth; ooze, slime, slush; slag; sewage. See UNCLEANNESS.

slug, *v.* hit, swat, belt; bash, smash, whale. See IMPULSE.

sluggish, *adj.* inactive, stagnant, torpid, slow; lazy, slothful, dull, indolent; languid, apathetic, lethargic. See INACTIVITY, SLOWNESS. *Ant.*, energetic, active.

sluice, *n.* channel (see EGRESS, CONDUIT).

slum, *n.* tenements, skid row, wrong side of the tracks; ghetto. See ABODE, POVERTY, UNCLEANNESS.

slumber, *n.* sleep, nap, doze, quiescence. See REPOSE.

slump, *v.i.* fall, settle, sink, drop; slouch, lounge, sprawl; sag, droop; decline, di-

minish, wane, languish; fail, collapse.
—*n.* decline; setback, depression, RE-
CESSION, regression, reversion, comedown, collapse, failure; *informal,*
slowdown, slack season.

slur, *v.t.* slight, disparage, calumniate, traduce, asperse; skim, skip, gloss over; ignore; elide. See DISREPUTE, NEGLECT.

slush, *n.* slosh, sludge, slop; gush, effu-
siveness, drivel; bribery. See COHER-
ENCE, SENSIBILITY.

slut, *n.* sloven, slattern, slob; prostitute,
doxy (*sl.*), chippy (*sl.*). See IMPURITY.

sly, *adj.* CUNNING, furtive, wily; crafty, deceitful, stealthy, underhand; roguish,
mischievous. See CONCEALMENT. *Ant.,*
artless.

smack, *n.* clap, whack, slap; kiss, buss; savor, tastiness, flavor, gusto, relish,
TASTE. See IMPULSE, ENDEARMENT. —*v.*
slap, strike, smite, whack; TASTE, savor;
smack of, recall, call to mind. See SIMI-
LARITY, MEMORY.

small, *adj.* little, tiny, short, wee; dwarfish,
undersized, stunted; lowercase; humble;
minute, infinitesimal; dainty, petite; trivial, unimportant, petty, small-minded;
puny, slight, weak; mean, paltry, unworthy; pygmy, Lilliputian, minikin. See LIT-
TLENESS, HUMILITY, UNIMPORTANCE.
Ant., large, substantial, important.

small-time, *adj., slang,* minor, unimportant, trivial, petty; one-horse, jerkwater,
tinhorn, minor-league. See UNIMPOR-
TANCE. *Ant.,* major[-league], important.

smart, *adj.* chic, stylish, jaunty, dapper;
severe, sharp, keen; witty, pert,
sparkling; brisk, energetic, fresh;
shrewd, clever. See SKILL, FEELING, WIT.
Ant., stupid, slow[witted], unstylish.
—*v.i.* sting, PAIN, rankle. —smart aleck,
n. know-it-all, braggart. See VANITY.

smash, *v.t.* shatter, crush; hit, strike; ruin,
destroy, disintegrate. See DESTRUCTION,
SUCCESS.

smash-up, *n.* crash, collision, wreck,
crackup, pileup; accident; calamity, catastrophe, disaster. See IMPULSE.

smattering, *n.* superficiality, sciolism. See
IGNORANCE.

smear, *v.t.* [be]daub, besmirch, smudge;
grease, anoint, defame; slander; soil,
sully. See COVERING.

smell, *v.* scent; stink; sniff, snuff, inhale;
detect, nose out. See ODOR, MALODOR-
OUSNESS.

smelly, *adj.* [mal]odorous, foul-smelling,
fetid (see MALODOROUSNESS). *Ant.,*
odorless.

smile, *v.i.* grin, simper, smirk; beam, look
with favor; sneer, RIDICULE. See RE-
JOICING. *Ant.,* frown, grimace.

smirk, *n.* simper, grin, leer; smug look, grimace. See REJOICING, RIDICULE.

smite, *v.t.* strike, hit, cuff, pummel; affect,
captivate, enamor, entrance; afflict. See
IMPULSE, FEELING.

smith, *n.* blacksmith, tinsmith, tinker. See
EXERTION.

smock, *n.* blouse, housecoat, housedress;
coverall, apron. See CLOTHING.

smog, *n., informal,* [weather] inversion.
See CLOUDINESS.

smoke, *v.* reek, fume, smolder; steam;
puff, inhale, chain-smoke; smoke-dry,
cure; fumigate; begrime, pollute. See
DRYNESS, UNCLEANNESS, PUNGENCY,
PRESERVATION.

smoky, *adj.* hazy, cloudy. See OBSCURITY.

smolder, *v.i.* reek, fume, smoke; hang fire,
be latent, lurk. See HEAT, LATENCY.

smooch, *v.i., slang,* kiss, peck. See EN-
DEARMENT.

SMOOTHNESS
Evenness of surface

Nouns—1, smoothness, polish, gloss, glaze, sheen; slickness, slipperiness; blandness;
evenness. See TEXTURE, FRICTION.

2, (*evenness*) level, velvet, silk, satin; glass, ice; flatness. See HORIZONTAL.

3, (*smoothing element*) plane, roller, steamroller; sandpaper, abrasive, hone; buffer,
burnisher, polisher; wax, varnish; iron, mangle; Teflon, graphite; OIL.

Verbs—1, smooth, plane; file; mow, shave; level, roll; unroll, unfurl; pave; polish, rub,
shine, buff, burnish, calender, glaze; varnish, wax; iron, press; lubricate; sand.

2, slip, slide, glide (see TRAVEL, DESCENT).

Adjectives—1, smooth; polished, even; level; plane, flat, HORIZONTAL; sleek, glossy; silken, silky; downy, velvet[y]; slippery, glassy; greasy, oily; soft, unwrinkled; smooth as glass, silk, ice, *or* velvet; slippery as an eel; bald [as an egg *or* billiard ball].

2, slippery, greasy, oily, slick, unctuous, lubricating.

Antonyms, see ROUGHNESS.

---

smother, *v.t.* suffocate, stifle; suppress, repress; extinguish, deaden. See KILLING, RESTRAINT, DEATH.

smudge, *n.* soot, grime, dirt, blotch, smear, blot, smutch; smolder. —*v.* soil, smear, mark, daub, dirty; stain, blacken. See HEAT, UNCLEANNESS.

smug, *adj.* sleek, trim, neat; self-satisfied, complacent; priggish, conceited. See AFFECTATION, VANITY. *Ant.,* modest.

smuggler, *n.* contrabandist, bootlegger, runner. See ILLEGALITY.

smut, *n.* soot, smudge, spot, blemish; dirt, filth, pornography; fungus, rot, mildew. See IMPURITY. —*v.* blacken, sully, smudge. See UNCLEANNESS.

snack, *n.* repast, collation, refreshment, coffee break. See FOOD.

snag, *n.* catch, detent, snaggle-tooth; HINDRANCE, difficulty. —*v.* catch, fix, entangle; snarl, impede, hamper, hinder. See IMPERFECTION.

snake, *n.* serpent, reptile, ophidian; snake in the grass, deceiver, double dealer. See ANIMAL, DECEPTION.

snap, *n.* crackle, rapping, pop, crack, report, clap, smack; vigor, pep, verve, dash, élan; smartness, spruceness, crispness; spell (of weather); *informal,* sinecure, cinch, soft job. —*v.* break, crack, crackle; knock, rap, tap; snarl, bark, scold; bite, nip. See DISJUNCTION, DISCOURTESY, SOUND, BRITTLENESS.

snappy, *adj.* brisk, COLD; *informal,* smart, quick, crisp. See FASHION.

snapshot, *n.* photo[graph], picture (see PHOTOGRAPHY).

snare, *n.* trap, springe, gin; artifice, pitfall, ambush. See DECEPTION, RETENTION.

snarl, *v.i.* growl, gnarl, grumble; entangle. See DISCOURTESY, THREAT.

snatch, *v.t.* grab, seize, grasp, clutch, jerk; twitch, pluck, wrench; steal; *slang,* kidnap. See STEALING.

sneak, *v.i.* slink, skulk, crawl, steal. —*n.* skulker, sneak thief; coward. See COWARDICE, DECEPTION, SLOWNESS.

sneaky, *adj.* furtive, sly, underhanded. See SECRET, DECEPTION. *Ant.,* open, aboveboard.

sneer, *v.* smile, jeer, taunt, scoff; flout, deride. See CONTEMPT.

sneeze, *n.* sternutation. See WIND.

snicker, *v.i.* snigger, titter, laugh, giggle, chuckle; RIDICULE.

snide, *adj.* spiteful, malicious, sarcastic, cynical, derogatory; mean, invidious. See DISREPUTE, BADNESS.

sniff, *v.* sniffle; smell, scent; breathe, inhale, detect. See ODOR, WIND.

snip, *v.* cut, slice, shear, scissor; prune, trim, lop. See DISJUNCTION.

sniper, *n.* marksman, sharpshooter; critic. See COMBATANT, DISAPPROBATION.

snit, *n.* fret, dither (see AGITATION).

snitch, *v., slang,* swipe, filch; inform. See STEALING, INFORMATION.

snivel, *v.i.* snuffle, sniff, blubber; whimper, cry, weep; cower, grovel, crawl, cringe. See LAMENTATION.

snob, *n.* sycophant, toady, fawner, bounder, upstart; parvenu, social climber. See SERVILITY, VULGARITY. *Ant.,* aristocrat, democrat.

snoop, *v.i., informal,* pry; investigate, probe; meddle; play detective. —*n.* snooper, pry; meddler, busybody. See CURIOSITY.

snooze, *n.* nap, doze, sleep, forty winks. See INACTIVITY.

snore, *n.* stertor, wheeze, rhoncus, rale, zzz. See SOUND, LOUDNESS.

snort, *v.* grunt, snortle, guffaw. See CRY. —*n.* grunt, laugh; drink, draft, dram, jigger, shot (*inf.*). See DRINKING.

snotty, *adj.* snobbish, priggish; impudent, scornful. See IMPUDENCE, VANITY.

snout, *n.* nose, nostrils, muzzle, beak, bill, trunk. See CONVEXITY.

snow, *n.* snowfall, snowflake, flurry; snowstorm, blizzard; snowslide, drift, avalanche; hail, sleet. —*v.* snow in *or* under; swamp, flood, inundate; *slang,* impress, flatter, do a snow job on. See COLD, FLATTERY.

snowball, *v.i., informal,* accelerate, gain momentum, pick up speed. See IN-CREASE.

snow job, *slang,* FLATTERY.

snub, *v.t.* cut, ignore, slight, rebuff, cold-shoulder; check, curb, halt. —*n.* rebuff, slight, cut. —*adj.* turned-up, blunt, retroussé. See CONTEMPT, REPULSION.

snuff, *v.t.* extinguish, put out; sniff, inhale; smell, scent; snuffle, sniffle. See WIND, ODOR, INCOMBUSTIBILITY.

snug, *adj.* cozy, comfortable; sheltered; trim, compact, neat. See PLEASURE, CLOSURE, CONTENT, SAFETY. *Ant.,* uncomfortable, drafty.

snuggle, *v.i.* nestle, cuddle, lie snug. See ENDEARMENT.

soak, *v.t.* wet, drench, saturate, steep; absorb; permeate; drink, tipple; *slang,* overcharge, bleed. See WATER, MOISTURE, DRYNESS, DRINKING, DEARNESS.

soap, *n.* cleanser, cleansing agent; lather; detergent; shampoo; *slang,* softsoap, corniness, sentimentality. See CLEANNESS, SENSIBILITY.

soapbox, *n.* podium, rostrum (see SUPPORT).

soar, *v.i.* fly, fly high; tower; glide. See AVIATION, HEIGHT, ASCENT.

sob, *v.i.* weep, cry, sigh; moan. See LAMENTATION.

sober, *adj.* grave, quiet, sedate, staid, serious; abstemious; drab, plain, severe, unadorned; calm, moderate; thoughtful; subdued; inconspicuous; demure; earnest; solemn, somber. See MODERATION, INEXCITABILITY, DEJECTION, SANITY. *Ant.,* intoxicated, drunk, flighty.

sobriquet, *n.* nickname. See NOMENCLATURE.

sob story, *n., slang,* tearjerker, melodrama, human interest, mush (*sl.*), schmaltz (*sl.*); tale of woe, hard-luck story. See FEELING.

sociable, *adj.* gregarious, friendly, amiable. See SOCIALITY. *Ant.,* unfriendly, unsocial.

social, *adj.* gregarious, friendly; fashionable; communal, public. —*n.* social gathering, get-together, party. See SOCIALITY, PARTY, HUMANITY.

socialism, *n.* public ownership, communism, collectivism; communalism. See AUTHORITY, LEFT.

socialite, *n.* jet-setter. See FASHION.

SOCIALITY
Association with others

Nouns—1, sociality, sociability, sociableness, friendship, bonhomie; social intercourse, community; fellowship, fraternity, companionship, camaraderie; familiarity, intimacy; association, brotherhood; communion; gregariousness. See CONVERSATION, AMUSEMENT.

2, *(social pleasure)* conviviality, good fellowship, joviality, jollity, savoir vivre, festive board.

3, *(courteous reception)* hospitality, cheer; welcome, greeting; hearty *or* warm welcome *or* reception; urbanity (see COURTESY).

4, *(social gathering)* social circle, sewing circle, family circle; coterie, society; club; social [gathering], box social, assembly (see ASSEMBLAGE); party, affair, function, get-together, entertainment, reception, salon, levee, at home, *conversazione,* soirée; garden party; housewarming; houseparty, reunion; [high *or* afternoon] tea, tea party, *thé dansant,* coffee *or* happy hour, coffee klatsch; banquet, luau, clambake, DANCE; cocktail party, debut, visit[ing]; call; powwow, potlatch, corroboree, extravaganza, bonfire, roast; video visit; affair; appointment, tryst, date. *Informal,* get-together, hen party, stag party, coming-out party, mixer, be-in, shindig, shindy. *Slang,* boink, face-time.

5, social person, good company, companion, crony, bon vivant; host, maven. *Informal,* joiner; good mixer, back-slapper, hand-shaker, hail-fellow-well-met. *Slang,* good egg *or* scout.

Verbs—1, be sociable, know; be acquainted, associate with, keep company with, club together, consort, bear one company, join; make acquaintance with; make advances, fraternize, socialize, tie up with, take up with, rub shoulders *or* elbows, hobnob, mix with, mingle with; embrace; be, feel, *or* make oneself at home with; date, double-date; make free with; be hospitable; roll out the red carpet; shake hands. *Informal,* throw a party; fix someone up with. *Slang,* give one some skin, press the flesh.

2, visit, pay a visit; call [up]on, drop in, look in on; look one up; entertain, give a party, hold court, be at home, keep open house, do the honors, receive with open arms, welcome, bid one welcome, give a warm reception to; kill the fatted calf; see one's friends, drop by *or* around, stop by.

Adjectives—sociable, companionable, friendly; conversable, cozy, chatty, conversational; social, neighborly, gregarious, affable; convivial, festive, festal; jovial, jolly, hospitable; welcome; free and easy. *Informal,* clubby, chummy.

Adverbs—socially, companionably, intimately, *etc.*

Phrases—the company makes the feast; food without hospitality is medicine; there isn't much to talk about at some parties until one or two couples leave.

Quotations—At a dinner party one should eat wisely but not too well, and talk well but not too wisely (*W. Somerset Maugham*), Small cheer and great welcome makes a merry feast (*Shakespeare*), One cannot have too large a party (*Jane Austen*), I hate cocktail parties. They're for people who're not good enough to invite for dinner—then they *stay* to dinner (*Elsa Maxwell*).

Antonyms, see SECLUSION.

---

socialize, *v.i.* be sociable (see SOCIALITY). —*v.t.* communalize, collectivize, nationalize. See ACQUISITION.

society, *n.* HUMANITY, mankind, folk; culture, civilization, group; community; companionship, fellowship; bon ton, elite, aristocracy; sodality, solidarity, association, league, union, alliance; parish, congregation. See SOCIALITY, PARTY, FASHION.

sociopath, *n.* psychopath (see INSANITY).

sock, *n.* [half] hose, anklet, stocking; *slang,* slug, punch, clout, wallop, jab. —*v.t., slang,* strike, slug, *etc.* See CLOTHING, IMPULSE.

socket, *n.* holder, cup, RECEPTACLE, CONCAVITY, hole, pit.

sod, *n.* turf, sward, glebe; clod, divot. See VEGETABLE, LAND.

soda, *n.* carbonated water, [soda] pop, seltzer, fizz, mineral water. See DRINKING.

sodality, *n.* association, society; fellowship, comradeship. See PARTY, SOCIALITY.

sodden, *adj.* soaked, saturated, soggy, doughy, dull; drunken, befuddled, bloated. See MOISTURE, DRINKING.

sodomy, *n.* anal intercourse, buggery (*sl.*). See SEX.

sofa, *n.* couch, seat, lounge, divan, settee, love seat. See SUPPORT.

soft, *adj.* supple, pliant; faint, low; kind, lenient; easy. See SOFTNESS, FAINTNESS, LENIENCY, FACILITY.

softhearted, *adj.* sympathetic, compassionate. See PITY, BENEVOLENCE. *Ant.,* hardhearted.

SOFTNESS
Quality of yielding readily to pressure

Nouns—**1,** softness, pliableness, pliancy, pliability, flexibility; malleability; ductility, tractility; extendability, extensibility; plasticity; flaccidity, flabbiness, laxity; sensitivity, responsiveness, susceptibility (see SENSIBILITY).

2, clay, wax, butter, dough, pudding; cushion, pillow, featherbed, down, padding, wadding; foam rubber.

3, softening, modification; mellowness, relaxation (see MODERATION).

Verbs—soften, mollify, mellow, relax, temper; mash, knead, squash; melt, liquefy; bend, yield, relent, give.

Adjectives—soft, tender, supple, pliant, pliable; flexible, flexile; sensitive, responsive, susceptible; lithe[some], lissom, limber, plastic; ductile; tractile, tractable; malleable, extensile; yielding, flabby, limp, flimsy; flaccid, flocculent, downy, feathery, fleecy, spongy, doughy; mellow, velvet[y], silky, satiny.

Adverbs—soft as butter, soft as down, soft as silk; yielding as wax.
Quotations—Music has charms to soothe a savage breast, to soften rocks, or bend a
knotted oak (*William Congreve*).

Antonyms, see HARDNESS, INELASTICITY.

---

soft-pedal, *v.t.* tone down, suppress (see MODERATION, SUPPRESSION).

soft-soap, *v.t., informal,* flatter, feed a line to, snow (*sl.*). See FLATTERY.

soft-spoken, *adj.* unassertive, quiet, gentle, kindly. See COURTESY. *Ant.,* loud, assertive.

software, *n.* program, code, instructions (see COMPUTERS).

softy, *n., informal,* weakling, wimp (see WEAKNESS).

soggy, *adj.* saturated, soaked, soppy; sodden, doughy. See MOISTURE.

soi-disant, *Fr.,* self-styled. See BOASTING.

soil, *n.* loam, earth, sod, topsoil, dirt, mold, ground; stain, blotch, smudge, smear, filth. —*v.t.* besmear, dirty, daub, stain; defile, sully. See LAND, REGION, UNCLEANNESS.

soirée, *n.* reception, affair, salon, social. See SOCIALITY.

sojourn, *v.i.* tarry, abide, stay, lodge, stop over, visit. See ABODE.

solace, *n.* comfort, consolation, RELIEF. —*v.t.* soothe, calm, comfort; cheer, console; assuage, mitigate.

solder, *v.* spelter, fuse, braze, weld; bond, cement, mend. See JUNCTION, COHERENCE, CONNECTION.

soldier, *n.* warrior, fighting man. See COMBATANT.

soldierly, *adj.* military, martial; brave, courageous; gallant, snappy, spruce; erect. See WARFARE.

sole, *adj.* only, one, single, unique, exclusive, individual. See UNITY, EXCLUSION.

solecism, *n.* ERROR, lapse, slip, blunder; grammatical error; barbarism, faux pas, social error, impropriety; incongruity, mistake. See INELEGANCE.

solemn, *adj.* awesome, impressive; grave, serious, dignified; sober; formal, ceremonious; reverent, ritualistic. See IMPORTANCE, DEJECTION, PIETY, OSTENTATION. *Ant.,* light[weight], flippant.

solemnize, *v.t.* celebrate, perform, observe. See CELEBRATION, RITE.

solicit, *v.t.* REQUEST, invite, ask, entreat, importune, beg, canvass, petition.

solicitous, *adj.* considerate; anxious, concerned; eager, careful. See CARE. *Ant.,* uncaring, inconsiderate.

solicitude, *n.* CARE, concern, anxiety; consideration; uneasiness. See DESIRE, FEAR.

solid, *adj.* dense, compact, hard, firm, rigid; substantial; united, unanimous, reliable; unbroken, undivided, whole, intact; sound, valid; stable, solvent; genuine, real. See DENSITY, SUBSTANCE, CERTAINTY, TRUTH. *Ant.,* liquid, soft, broken, instable.

solidarity, *n.* union, fellowship. See UNITY.

solidify, *v.* set, cohere, congeal; coalesce, come together. See DENSITY, COMBINATION.

soliloquy, *n.* monologue; apostrophe, aside. See SPEECH.

solitaire, *n.* patience (see AMUSEMENT).

solitary, *adj.* alone, lonesome; sole, single, individual, lone; deserted, remote, unfrequented; unsocial, retiring. See SECLUSION.

solitude, *n.* SECLUSION, privacy, isolation; remoteness; loneliness; wilderness.

solo, *n.* single; aria, arietta; recital, solo flight. —*adj.* lone, single, singlehanded; one-man; unaided. See UNITY.

soluble, *adj.* dissolvable (see LIQUEFACTION). *Ant.,* insoluble.

solution, *n.* ANSWER, explanation, INTERPRETATION, key, clue; disintegration, dissolution; lixivium, decoction; LIQUEFACTION.

solve, *v.t.* explain, interpret; ANSWER; resolve, clear up; decipher, decode. See DISCLOSURE.

solvent, *adj.* financially sound, moneyed; responsible, reliable; soluble, separative, dissolvent, diluent. —*n.* dissolvent, dissolver, liquefier. See LIQUEFACTION, MONEY. *Ant.,* insolvent, unsound, broke.

somber, *adj.* gloomy, dark, overcast, dull; sad, dismal, leaden, depressing, funereal. See DARKNESS, DEJECTION. *Ant.,* bright, cheerful.

some, *adj.* several, [a] few, a number of; one, any; certain, divers, various, sundry; *informal,* what a, quite a.

—*pron.* any, a few, one *or* more, someone, somebody. —*adv.* about, around, approximately, nearly, almost, in a way; to a degree. See QUANTITY.

somebody, *n.* one, someone; person, individual; bigwig, personage. See IMPORTANCE.

somehow, *adv.* some way, by some means. See METHOD.

somersault, *n.* See INVERSION.

something, *n.* thing, object, anything; matter, part; affair, event. See SUBSTANCE.

sometimes, *adv.* occasionally, now and then. See OCCASION, FREQUENCY.

somewhat, *adv.* to some extent, to a degree, partially. See QUALIFICATION.

somewhere, *adv.* someplace; anywhere, somewhere about; approximately. See LOCATION.

somnolent, *adj.* sleepy, drowsy, slumb[e]rous; dozing; lethargic. See INACTIVITY.

son, *n.* male child, boy, offspring; descendant, inheritor. See POSTERITY.

song, *n.* lyric, ballad, popular song; aria, chanson, cavatina; carol, lilt, madrigal, glee, ditty; minstrelsy, poem, chanty, lay, birdsong, folksong, spiritual, *etc.* See MUSIC, POETRY.

sonorous, *adj.* resonant, deep-toned, rich, majestic; grandiloquent, high-flown. See LOUDNESS, SOUND. *Ant.,* tinny.

soon, *adv.* anon, presently; promptly, quickly; readily, willingly. See EARLINESS.

soot, *n.* smoke, carbon dust, smut, grit, coal dust; lampblack; smog, smaze. See UNCLEANNESS.

soothe, *v.t.* calm, quiet, tranquilize; relieve, assuage, mitigate, allay, console, comfort. See MODERATION, RELIEF, CONTENT, FLATTERY.

sop, *n.* morsel, pacifier; bribe, inducement, compensation, propitiation, token; milksop. See PAYMENT, MODERATION. —*v.* steep, dunk, dip, soak; wet, moisten. See MOISTURE.

sophisticate, *n.* worldling; cosmopolitan, man about town, man of the world. See SKILL, KNOWLEDGE.

sophistication, *n.* AFFECTATION; worldliness, veneer. See SKILL, KNOWLEDGE. *Ant.,* naiveté.

sophistry, *n.* sophism; false *or* specious reasoning; casuistry; fallaciousness, paralogism; shift, subterfuge, equivocation; absurdity, inconsistency; hair-splitting. See FALSEHOOD.

sophomoric, *adj.* immature, callow; inane, foolish. See FOLLY.

soporific, *adj.* sedative, narcose, soothing; lethargic, torpid, dull, slow, sluggish; tedious, wearisome. See REPOSE, WEARINESS.

soppy, *adj.* soaked, drenched; rainy, wet; *slang,* mawkish, sentimental. See WATER, FEELING.

SORCERY
Magic

Nouns—**1,** sorcery; the occult; magic, the black art, necromancy, theurgy, thaumaturgy; demonology, diablerie, bedevilment, devil worship, diabolism; voodoo, obeah, hoodoo, macumba, santeria; witchcraft, wicca, witchery; alchemy; white *or* black magic; black Mass; fetishism, vampirism; conjuration; bewitchery, enchantment, mysticism, second sight, mesmerism, animal magnetism; od *or* odylic force; clairvoyance (see INTUITION); spiritualism, spirit-rapping, table-turning, ancestor worship, palmistry, chiromancy, numerology, oneiromancy; divination (see PREDICTION); sortilege, hocus-pocus (see DECEPTION). See SECRET.

2, spell, charms, hex, incantation, cabala, runes, abracadabra, open sesame, mumbo jumbo, evil eye, door sign. *Informal,* jinx, Indian sign, hand.

3, exorcism; countercharm; conjuring potion, essence of St. Michael, fast luck oil, fast scrubbing essence; bell, book, and candle; talisman, amulet, mojo, toby, periapt, phylactery, philter; fetish, agnus Dei; esbat. *Slang,* lucky dog, water notre dame, gris-gris.

4, *(tools of sorcery)* wand, caduceus, rod, divining rod, magic lamp *or* ring, wishing cap, Fortunatus' cap, magic carpet; philosophers' stone; hoodoo animal, moonack, familiar; goofer bag. *Slang,* moonack.

5, sorcerer, magician; adept; thaumaturgist, theurgist; conjuror, voodooist, necromancer, seer, wizard, witch, archimage; lamia, hag, warlock, charmer; medicine man; alchemist; shaman, witch doctor, medium, clairvoyant, mesmerist; deus ex machina; soothsayer, oracle; Cagliostro, Mesmer; Circe, siren, weird sisters. *Slang*, night hag. See DEMON.

Verbs—practice sorcery, conjure, charm, enchant; bewitch, bedevil; entrance, mesmerize, magnetize; exorcise; fascinate; taboo; wave a wand; rub the ring *or* lamp; cast a chart; cast a spell; hold a séance, call up spirits, raise spirits from the dead. *Informal*, jinx. *Slang*, hoodoo, goober.

Adjectives—magic, magical; occult; SECRET, mystic, weird, cabalistic, talismanic, phylacteric, incantatory, apotropaic; charmed, bewitched; spellbound, haunted.

Quotations—To deny the possibility, nay, the actual existence of witchcraft and sorcery is flatly to contradict the revealed word of God (*William Blackstone*), Nature has given us astrology as an adjunct and ally to astronomy (*Johannes Kepler*), Astrology is framed by the devil (*Martin Luther*), Belief in magic is older than writing (*Zora Neale Hurston*), May the Force be with you (*George Lucas*).
Antonyms, see RELIGION.

---

sordid, *adj.* mean, base, ignoble; covetous, niggardly; mercenary, self-seeking; squalid, dirty, foul. See PARSIMONY, UNCLEANNESS.

sore, *adj.* painful, tender, sensitive; grieved, distressed; harsh, severe, intense, dire; *slang,* aggrieved, resentful, disgruntled. See PAIN, DISCONTENT, RESENTMENT. —*n.* wound, abrasion, ulcer, chancroid, sore spot. See DISEASE.

sorrow, *n.* grief, sadness, dolor, distress; contrition, remorse, penitence; affliction, woe. See DEJECTION. *Ant.,* joy, happiness.

sorry, *adj.* rueful, regretful, penitent; sympathetic, sorrowful; pitiful, deplorable; shabby, paltry, wretched, mean. See PENITENCE. *Ant.,* impenitent, unsympathetic.

sort, *n.* CLASS, kind, variety, group, category, description. —*v.t.* segregate, separate, isolate; size, grade, group, match; assort, arrange, classify; sift, screen. See ARRANGEMENT.

sortie, *n.* sally, mission, ATTACK.

so-so, *adj.* passable, fair; *comme ci, comme ça.* See MEDIOCRITY.

sot, *n.* drunkard (see DRINKING).

sotto voce, *Ital.,* under one's breath, softly. See SOFTNESS, CONCEALMENT, SILENCE.

soubrette, *n.* actress, ingenue, comedienne; coquette, flirt. See DRAMA.

soul, *n.* psyche, spirit, mind; vital principle; essence; person, mortal, individual; ego; nobility, courage, heart, fire, élan; genius. See HUMANITY, INTELLECT.

soulful, *adj.* emotional, affective. See FEELING. *Ant.,* soulless, unfeeling.

soul-searching, *n.* self-examination *or* -analysis, crisis of conscience. See INQUIRY, DOUBT.

sound, *adj.* whole, undamaged; healthy, robust; logical, true, valid, reliable, honorable, trustworthy; solvent; strong, firm; thorough; unbroken. See PERFECTION, HEALTH, STABILITY. *Ant.,* unsound, unhealthy, illogical, insolvent. —*n.* inlet, channel, bay, gulf; noise (see SOUND). —*v.* fathom, plumb, measure; probe; investigate, examine; utter; investigate. See DEPTH, INQUIRY.

SOUND
Vibrations sensed by the ear

Nouns—1, sound, noise, strain; accent, twang, intonation, tone; cadence; sonorousness, resonance, audibility (see HEARING); resonance, voice; sound effects; sine, square, sawtooth, *etc.* wave, sound wave, white noise; ultrasound; cacophony, euphony, harmony; decibel, phon, hertz. See SPEECH.

2, (*study of sound*) acoustics, phonics, phonetics, phonology, phonography; diacoustics, diaphonics, telephonics, radiophony; acoustician, acoustical engineer.

3, (*sound color*) tone, tonality, intonation, inflection, modulation; pitch, key, timbre, tone color; monotone; overtone, fundamental; homophony, polyphony.

4, (*type of sound*) a. vociferation, roar, CRY, utterance, voice. b. snap, crash, bang, boom, roll, clatter, detonation, explosion; sonic boom. See LOUDNESS. **c.** belch, gargle, gobble, gulp, gurgle, rattle, rumble, sneeze, sniff[le], snivel, snore, snuffle, sob, wheeze. *Slang*, fart. **d.** boing, chink, clang, clank, clink, ding[-dong], gong, ring, tink[-a-ling], bang, bong, chime, clangor, jangle, jingle, tinkle, tintinnabulate.

5, *(producer of sound)* sound *or* audio system, high-fidelity system; amplifier, record, tape, *or* compact disc player, cartridge, tone arm, needle; monophonic, stereophonic *or* quadraphonic system; tape recorder *or* player, recording *or* playback head, multitrack, digital audio tape, DAT; public-address *or* PA system, intercom; microphone; [loud]speaker, tweeter, woofer, headphone, headset, earphone; jukebox.

Verbs—**1,** sound, ring, resound; make a noise; give out *or* emit sound.

2, speak (see SPEECH); snap, roll, reverberate, detonate, *etc.*; buzz. See LOUDNESS.

3, listen, hear, attend (see HEARING).

Adjectives—sounding; soniferous, sonorous, resonant; audible, distinct; sonant, stertorous; sonic, sub- *or* supersonic; phonetic; acoustic, phonic; sibilant.

Quotations—I neglect God and his Angels for the noise of a fly, for the rattling of a coach, for the whining of a door (*John Donne*).

Antonyms, see SILENCE.

---

sound bite, *n.* [sound] clip, excerpt. See PART.

soundless, *adj.* silent (see SILENCE).

soundly, *adv.* completely, thoroughly. See COMPLETION.

soundproof, *adj.* insulated, sound-absorbing; muted, muffled, noiseproof; noiseless, quiet, silent. See SILENCE.

soup, *n.* stock, broth, bouillon, consommé; potage, purée, bisque, chowder. See FOOD. **—soup up,** *v.t.* slang, enliven, rev up (*inf.*). See INCREASE.

soupçon, *n.* hint, trace (see LITTLENESS).

soupy, *adj.* thick, dense (see DENSITY).

sour, *adj.* acid, tart, bitter; fermented, unpleasant; morose, testy, touchy. See SOURNESS, IRASCIBILITY, UNSAVORINESS. *Ant.,* sweet, good-humored.

source, *n.* CAUSE, origin, fountainhead, fount, derivation. See BEGINNING.

SOURNESS
Acid taste

Nouns—**1,** sourness, acid[ity], acerbity, acridity, astringency, tartness, rancidness, UNSAVORINESS. See TASTE, PUNGENCY, DISCORD.

2, *(sour substance)* vinegar, acetum, verjuice, acetic acid, alum; lemon, lime, crab, pickle, sauerkraut; sour milk *or* cream, buttermilk, crème fraîche, yogurt; sour grapes.

Verbs—sour, turn sour, ferment, set the teeth on edge; acidify, acidulate, curdle, clabber, turn.

Adjectives—sour, acid, subacid, acidulous; acetic, acerbic, astringent, acrid, acetous, acetose; tart, crabbed, vinegary; sourish, sour as vinegar, sour as a pickle *or* lemon; green, unripe; styptic, hard, rough, caustic, bitter; distasteful; soured, rancid, curdled, coagulated, turned, spoiled, musty, bad.

Antonyms, see SWEETNESS.

---

southern, *adj.* southerly, austral. See DIRECTION. *Ant.,* northern, boreal.

souvenir, *n.* memento, keepsake, relic. See MEMORY.

sovereign, *n.* monarch, ruler; potentate; king, queen, emperor, empress. See AUTHORITY, SUPERIORITY.

sow, *v.t.* strew, scatter, disseminate, broadcast; plant, seed. See AGRICULTURE, DISPERSION.

spa, *n.* mineral spring, watering place, thermal spring, mudbaths, balneum, hydro, Bad, waters; health club; resort. See REMEDY.

space, *n.* expanse (see SPACE); outer space, interplanetary, intergalactic, *etc.* space (see UNIVERSE). **—***v.t.* space out, separate, DISTANCE.

SPACE
Expanse in all directions

Nouns—1, space, extension, extent, superficial extent, area, expanse; sphere, range, latitude, field, way, EXPANSION, compass, gamut, sweep, play, swing, spread, capacity, stretch; open *or* free space; void, emptiness; waste, wild, wilderness, wide open spaces; moor, prairie, campagna, champaign; abyss, unlimited space, INFINITY, UNIVERSE, creation; space-time [continuum] (see TIME); heavens, sky; interplanetary space; length and breadth of the land.

2, room, scope, spare room, elbow room; margin; leeway, headway. *Slang,* room to swing a cat.

3, proportions, dimensions, acreage, acres, BREADTH, width; square inches, feet, yards, *etc.* See LENGTH, MEASUREMENT, SIZE, TIME.

Verbs—extend, reach, stretch, cover, spread, sweep, range; give *or* make room *or* way, open up [on].

Adjectives—spatial; spacious, roomy, commodious, extensive, expansive, capacious, ample; widespread, vast, worldwide, uncircumscribed; unlimited, endless; infinite, universal; boundless, unbounded, shoreless, trackless, pathless, bottomless.

Adverbs—extensively, wherever; everywhere; far and near, far and wide, right and left, all over, all the world over; throughout the world; under the sun, in every quarter, in all quarters, in all lands; here, there, and everywhere; from pole to pole, from end to end; on the face of the earth, in the wide world, from all points of the compass, to the four winds, to the uttermost parts of the earth; infinitely, ad infinitum.

Quotations—Space is the stature of God (*Joseph Joubert*), Nothing exists except atoms and empty space; everything else is opinion (*Democritus*), Nothing puzzles me more than time and space; and yet nothing troubles me less as I never think about them (*Charles Lamb*), Time and space—time to be alone, space to move about—these may well be the greatest scarcities of tomorrow (*Edwin Way Teale*).

Antonyms, see CIRCUMSCRIPTION, RESTRAINT.

---

space-age, *adj.* twentieth-century, modern, contemporary. See NEWNESS.

spacecraft, *n.* spaceship, rocket, transport (see ASTRONAUTICS).

spaced-out, *adj., slang,* confused, dazed, spacey. See UNINTELLIGIBILITY.

spacious, *adj.* roomy, capacious, vast (see SIZE, SPACE). *Ant.,* cramped.

spade, *n.* shovel, spud. —*v.* dig, delve, shovel, excavate. See CONCAVITY.

span, *v.t.* measure; encircle; stretch over, bridge. —*n.* bridge; extent; period; lifetime; nine-inch spread; team, yoke. See MEASUREMENT, SPACE, JUNCTION, DISTANCE, LENGTH, TIME.

spangle, *n.* sequin, paillette, ORNAMENT, bead, gem, stud, bauble, trinket, sparkler. —*v.t.* bespangle, jewel, stud, ORNAMENT, decorate. —*v.i.* sparkle, glitter, glisten, scintillate, coruscate. See LIGHT.

spank, *v.t.* slap, paddle, wallop; punish, chastise. See PUNISHMENT.

spanking, *adj.* brisk, lively, fresh; exceptional. See ACTIVITY, GREATNESS. —*n.* PUNISHMENT, hiding, thrashing.

spar, *v.i.* box; stall, play for time; bandy words, argue, bicker, wrangle, dispute. See CONTENTION. —*n.* mast, pole, gaff, boom, sprit, yard, bowsprit; varnish. See SHIP.

spare, *v.t.* be lenient; save; refrain, abstain, forbear, withhold; exempt; give up, surrender, forgo, relinquish. See LENIENCY, EXEMPTION, STORE, RELINQUISHMENT. *Ant.* condemn, keep. —*adj.* lean, gaunt, bony; meager; extra, reserve; frugal. See NARROWNESS, DISUSE, ECONOMY. *Ant.,* meaty, plump, generous.

spark, *n.* flash; inspiration; iota, jot; *informal,* beau, swain, gallant. See HEAT, LOVE.

sparkle, *v.i.* glisten, spark, twinkle, flash, glitter, scintillate; effervesce, bubble. See LIGHT, CHEERFULNESS.

sparse, *adj.* scattered, sporadic; thin, few,

meager, scanty. See RARITY. *Ant.*, many, frequent.

Spartan, *adj.* simple, unadorned, stark; strict, severe, disciplined. See SEVERITY, SIMPLENESS.

spasm, *n.* throe, paroxysm, convulsion, seizure; fit, furor. See AGITATION, IRREGULARITY, PAIN, VIOLENCE, DISCONTINUANCE.

spastic, *adj.* spasmodic, convulsive, jerky. See IRREGULARITY, DISCONTINUANCE.

spat, *n.* quarrel, dispute; slap, smack; gaiter. See DISCORD, IMPULSE, CLOTHING.

spate, *n.* freshet, storm. See WATER.

spatial, *adj.* dimensional. See SPACE.

spatter, *v.t.* splash, sprinkle; besprinkle, bedraggle, bespatter; sully, soil. See UNCLEANNESS.

spawn, *v.* deposit, lay; propagate, breed, beget; produce, bring forth, give birth to, engender. —*n.* eggs, roe, ova; products, handiwork; offspring, scions, progeny, brood. See POSTERITY, REPRODUCTION.

speak, *v.* talk, converse; lecture, discourse, orate; say, utter, pronounce; express, communicate. See SPEECH.

speaker, *n.* presiding officer, chairperson, orator, spokesman; loudspeaker, reproducer. See SPEECH, AUTHORITY.

spear, *n.* lance, pike, javelin, blade; shoot. See ARMS, VEGETABLE.

special, *adj.* particular, certain, singular; unusual, exceptional. See SPECIALITY, UNCONFORMITY.

SPECIALITY
Particular skill, etc.

Nouns—1, speciality, individuality, originality, particularity, peculiarity, distinction; state, trait, feature, mark, stamp, property, attribute (see ATTRIBUTION); IDENTITY, character (see INTRINSIC); personality, characteristic, hallmark, TENDENCY, mannerism, trick, idiosyncrasy, the nature of the beast, je ne sais quoi; fingerprint, voice print; aroma, mystique, aura, charisma; technicality, singularity (see UNCONFORMITY). See DIFFERENCE, UNITY.

2, specialty, specialization; hobby, métier; specialist. *Informal,* keynote, bit.

3, particulars, details, items, counts, circumstances, ins and outs.

4, I, self, I myself, me, ego, psyche. *Informal,* number one. See IDENTITY.

Verbs—specialize, specify, be specific, particularize, individualize, individuate, realize; pick out, designate, lay *or* put one's finger on, name, detail, earmark, show clearly, clarify; give particulars, go into detail, come to the point. *Informal,* get down to cases *or* brass tacks.

Adjectives—special, particular, individual, specific, singular, exceptional, extraordinary, original, unique, uncommon, unlike, picked, marked, distinct, distinctive, sui generis; proper, own, personal, private, privy, partial, party; respective, certain, definite, express, determinate, detailed, diagnostic; especial, esoteric, endemic, idiomatic, idiosyncratic, characteristic, charismatic; in character, true to form, appropriate, typical, exclusive, several; tailor-made, made to measure *or* order. See EXCLUSION.

Adverbs—specially, in particular, on *or* for my part, personally, ad hominem; each, apiece, one by one, severally, individually, respectively, each to each; seriatim, in detail, bit by bit; namely, that is to say, videlicet, viz., to wit.

Phrases—the devil is in the details; there are tricks in every trade.

Quotations—We can't all do everything (*Virgil*), Little things affect little minds (*Benjamin Disraeli*), Men who love wisdom should acquaint themselves with a great many particulars (*Heraclitus*), Each man for himself (*Geoffrey Chaucer*).

Antonyms, see GENERALITY.

species, *n.* variety, sort, CLASS, category.

specific, *adj.* special, distinct (see SPECIALITY); limited, exact, precise, absolute, unequivocal, right; explicit, definite.

Ant., general, vague. —*n.* REMEDY, medicine, medicament, cure, treatment. See CIRCUMSTANCE.

specification, *n.* particular, requirement, QUALIFICATION.

specify, *v.* name, mention, identify, enumerate, indicate, stipulate, define, state, itemize, detail; order, request. See SPECIALITY, INDICATION, DESCRIPTION, QUALIFICATION.

specimen, *n.* sample, example, representative, instance, pattern, taster. See CONFORMITY.

specious, *adj.* plausible, ostensible, apparent, casuistic, insincere; deceptive. See FALSEHOOD, IMAGINATION. *Ant.,* logical, sincere.

speck, *n.* blemish, speckle, spot, macula; particle, iota, mite, mote, dot. See LITTLENESS.

speckle, *v.t.* spot, sp[l]atter, speck. See LITTLENESS, IMPERFECTION.

spectacle, *n.* sight, phenomenon, pageant, parade, show; exhibition, scene, display. See APPEARANCE, OSTENTATION, DRAMA.

spectacles, *n.pl.* [eye]glasses, goggles; lorgnette, specs (*sl.*), cheaters (*sl.*). See OPTICAL INSTRUMENTS.

spectator, *n.* observer, onlooker (see PRESENCE).

specter, *n.* ghost, spirit, apparition, vision, shadow, shade; wraith, phantom, phantasm, haunt, spook; aura, emanation, materialization, reincarnation, illusion, delusion, hallucination. See DEMON, IMAGINATION.

spectrum, *n.* rainbow; color gamut. See COLOR, VARIEGATION.

speculate, *v.i.* ponder, contemplate, meditate, theorize, conjecture, surmise; gamble, play the market. See THOUGHT, CHANCE, BARTER.

SPEECH
Oral communication

Nouns—1, speech, talk, faculty of speech; locution, parlance, expression, vernacular, oral COMMUNICATION, word of mouth, parole, palaver, prattle; effusion, discourse; soliloquy; interlocution, CONVERSATION; LOQUACITY. *Informal,* gab, confab, powwow, corroboree. See SOUND, LANGUAGE.

2, *(formal speaking)* a. speechifying, oration, recitation, delivery, peroration, valedictory, monologue, sales talk; oratory, elocution, eloquence; rhetoric, declamation; bombast, grandiloquence; burst of eloquence; fecundity; flow *or* command of language; power of speech, gift of gab, blarney. *Slang,* spiel, line, earful, pep talk. b. allocution, exhortation, appeal, harangue, lecture, sermon, tirade, diatribe, invocation.

3, *(speech mechanism)* vocalization, enunciation, articulation, delivery; expression, utterance; vociferation, exclamation, ejaculation; clearness, distinctness; whisper, stage whisper; ventriloquism, ventriloquy. See CRY.

4, [public] speaker, spokesman; prolocutor, interlocutor; mouthpiece, orator; Demosthenes, Cicero; rhetorician; stump *or* platform orator; speechmaker, patterer, improvisator, monologist; gossip; singer (see MUSIC). *Slang,* talkmaster, flannel mouth.

5, *(speech characteristics)* accent, accentuation; inflection, intonation; tone of voice; emphasis, stress; brogue, burr; pronunciation, euphony.

6, *(instrument of speech)* voice, vocality; speaking *or* singing voice; larynx, voice box, glottis, vocal cords; voice print (see SPECIALITY); lung power.

7, pronunciation; orthoepy, phonetics, phonology; sound spectrogram *or* spectrograph; alveolar, dental, *etc.* sound (see *Adjectives*); click, suction stop, consonant, continuant, plosive, stop; flap, click; schwa; primary *or* secondary accent *or* stress; monophthong, diphthong, tripthong, cardinal vowel, aspirate, short *or* long vowel; inflection, intonation, modulation; bilabial; brogue; accent.

Verbs—1, speak, talk, speak of; say, utter, pronounce, deliver, comment, remark, recite, voice, give utterance to, vocalize; breathe, let fall, come out with; rap out, blurt out; chatter, open one's mouth; lift *or* raise one's voice; speak one's mind; state, assert, declare announce, annunciate. *Informal,* go, gab, shoot one's mouth off, shoot the breeze, talk a blue streak. *Slang,* flap one's gums.

2, *(deliver a speech)* hold forth; make *or* deliver a speech, speechify, orate, declaim, stump, flourish, spout, rant, recite, discourse, have *or* say one's say, say *or* speak one's piece; expatiate, be eloquent, have the gift of gab; allocute, exhort, appeal, harangue, lecture, preach, invoke, sermonize.

3, *(communicate through speech)* soliloquize, apostrophize, talk to oneself; tell, impart, inform (see INFORMATION); converse, speak to, talk together; communicate; divulge (see DISCLOSURE); express, phrase, put into words; translate, interpret.

4, enunciate, pronounce, articulate, verbalize, emit, give voice, let out, mention, bring up, expound, spell [out]; accentuate, aspirate; express oneself, think out loud *or* aloud, exclaim, ejaculate, CRY; shout, yell, mouth. *Informal,* pipe up.

Adjectives—1, speaking, spoken; vocal, oral, lingual, phonetic, outspoken; eloquent, elocutionary; oratorical, rhetorical, flamboyant; declamatory, bombastic, grandiloquent; talkative (see LOQUACITY).

2, alveolar, dental, dorsal, labial, labiodental, laminal, mouillé, nasal, uvular, voiced, voiceless, palatal, pharyngeal, obstruent, laryngeal, retroflex, glottal, guttural, sibilant, sonant, implosive, ingressive, interdental, egressive, ejective, fricative, spirant.

Adverbs—orally; vocally; by word of mouth, viva voce, from the lips of; loudly, out loud, aloud; softly, sotto voce.

Phrases—talk is cheap; think first and speak afterward.

Quotations—A word fitly spoken is like apples of gold in pictures of silver (*Bible*), The tongue can no man tame; it is an unruly evil (*Bible*), Speech is the small change of silence (*George Meredith*), I don't want to talk grammar, I want to talk like a lady (*G. B. Shaw*), Refrain not to speak, when there is occasion to do good (*Bible*), Speech is a mirror of the soul; as a man speaks so he is (*Publilius Syrus*), Talkativeness is one thing, speaking well another (*Sophocles*), Great talkers, little doers (*Benjamin Franklin*), Here comes the orator! with his flood of words, and his drop of reason (*Benjamin Franklin*), If you don't say anything, you won't be called on to repeat it (*Calvin Coolidge*).

Antonyms, see SILENCE, WRITING.

---

speechless, *adj.* aphonic, mute, dumb. See SILENCE, TACITURNITY. *Ant.,* talkative.

speed, *v.i.* HASTE, hasten, hurry, accelerate. —*n.* VELOCITY, dispatch, expedition, swiftness.

speedway, *n.* expressway, superhighway; racecourse, track, drag strip. See PASSAGE, CONTENTION.

speedy, *adj.* rapid, quick; prompt, expeditious. See VELOCITY, HASTE. *Ant.,* slow, plodding.

spell, *n.* charm, trance; talisman; incantation, SORCERY, magic; witchery, allure, glamour; enchantment; spellbinding; term, period, interval; TIME; turn, stretch; breathing spell, respite. See SUBSTITUTION, REPOSE.

spellbound, *adj.* entranced, fascinated, enchanted. See SORCERY, ATTENTION.

spend, *v.t.* disburse, pay out, expend; consume, exhaust; pass, employ. See EJECTION, WASTE.

spendthrift, *n.* wastrel, prodigal, profligate, squanderer. See WASTE.

spent, *adj.* used up, exhausted, fatigued,

dead-tired, fagged; effete, worn-out, impotent. See WEARINESS.

sperm, *n.* semen, seed, germ, jism (*sl.*). See REPRODUCTION.

spew, *v.* vomit, regurgitate, retch, throw up; gush, shoot, spout, eject, emit, expel; spit; discharge. See EJECTION.

sphere, *n.* orb, globe, ball; environment, province, status, field, range. See BUSINESS, REGION, ROTUNDITY, SPACE.

sphinx, *n.* prophetess; enigma, riddle. See PREDICTION, SECRET.

spice, *v.t.* season, flavor; make piquant. See EXCITEMENT, TASTE, ODOR, PUNGENCY.

spiel, *n., slang,* sales pitch, patter. See SALE, SPEECH.

spiffy, *adj., slang,* smart, fashionable, chic. See FASHION.

spigot, *n.* faucet. See PASSAGE.

spike, *n.* cleat, skewer, spindle; projection; goad, prod. See SHARPNESS. —*v.* pierce, gore; nail, rivet, impale, transpierce; *slang,* lace (with); needle. See CONNECTION, OPENING, DRINKING.

spill, *v.* overturn, upset; splash; brim over, slop, pour out; *slang,* tell, let slip. See EJECTION, DISCLOSURE, DESCENT, WATER.

spin, *v.* twirl, whirl, rotate; protract, draw out; gyrate, swirl, reel, eddy; fabricate. See ROTATION, LOQUACITY, IMAGINATION.

spindle, *n.* axis, axle, shaft; stick, spike, mandrel, arbor; stalk, stem. See ROTATION.

spindly, *adj.* spindling, gangling. See HEIGHT, NARROWNESS.

spine, *n.* backbone; ridge, arête; thorn, prickle, spike, spiculum, quill, barb. See SHARPNESS.

spineless, *adj.* invertebrate, boneless; pliant, limp, flabby; irresolute, cowardly, craven, gutless (*sl.*), yellow (*sl.*). See COWARDICE. *Ant.*, vertebrate, brave.

spin-off, *n.* derivative, offshoot. See EXTRACTION.

spinster, *n.* maid[en], old maid; spinner. See CELIBACY.

spiny, *adj.* spined, acanthous, hispid. See SHARPNESS.

spiral, *adj.* coiled, winding, helical, turbinate, cochlear. See CONVOLUTION.

spire, *n.* steeple, minaret; flèche; point, pinnacle, peak; pyramid, obelisk; epi, finial, aiguille. See HEIGHT, SHARPNESS.

spirit, *n.* vitalness, essence; soul; ghost, fairy, ANGEL, DEMON; disposition, temper, mood, humor; energy, vivacity, élan, verve, intrepidity, enthusiasm, dash, gallantry, intent; (*pl.*) [hard] liquor. See MEANING, ACTIVITY, VIGOR, FEELING, CHEERFULNESS, DRINKING, INTELLECT.

spirited, *adj.* animated, lively, mettlesome, bold, ardent; blithe, debonair, jaunty, sparkling, racy. See ACTIVITY, CHEERFULNESS. *Ant.*, spiritless, lethargic.

spiritual, *adj.* immaterial, incorporeal, insubstantial, fleshless; divine, exalted, celestial, holy, sacred; religious; inspired, supernatural, virtuous, platonic; occult. See INSUBSTANTIALITY, PIETY, VIRTUE.

spit, *v.* impale, transfix, pierce, stab; sprinkle, drizzle, discharge (bullets); sputter, expectorate, hiss. —*n.* saliva, spittle. See OPENING, EXCRETION.

spite, *n.* malice, ill will, grudge, malignity, MALEVOLENCE.

spitfire, *n.* firebrand, hothead, tigress, hellcat. See IRASCIBILITY.

splash, *v.* splatter, [be]spatter; dash, plop, spill; slop, splash, dabble, paddle. See WATER, UNCLEANNESS, OSTENTATION.

splay, *v.* spread out, fan out, diverge. See EXPANSION.

spleen, *n.* RESENTMENT, wrath, choler; anger, malice, spite, MALEVOLENCE.

splendid, *adj.* gorgeous, magnificent; heroic, glorious; resplendent; admirable, grand, excellent. See BEAUTY, REPUTE.

splice, *v.t.* join, unite, interweave; *slang,* marry. See JUNCTION, MARRIAGE.

splint, *n.* splinter; slat, strip; support, cast, brace, bracket. See REMEDY.

splinter, *n.* splint; shard, sliver, shaving, shive; fragment, particle, toothpick, matchwood. See PART, LITTLENESS. —*v.* sliver, rend, smash, fragmentize, fracture. See DISJUNCTION, BRITTLENESS, FILAMENT.

split, *v.t.* rive, rend, cleave, splinter; divide, separate, disunite, divorce; apportion; *slang,* leave, depart. See DISJUNCTION, BRITTLENESS, DEPARTURE.

splurge, *n., informal,* extravagance, waste, expense. —*v., informal,* indulge (oneself), extravagate, lavish, shoot the works (*inf.*), go [the] whole hog (*sl.*). See OSTENTATION.

spoil, *v.* damage, ruin, impair; overindulge, humor; despoil, plunder, sack, pillage, rob; decay, putrefy, rot, mold, ferment. See DETERIORATION. —*n.* plunder, loot, booty, spoliation. See ACQUISITION.

spoilsport, *n.* party pooper, wet blanket. See DEJECTION.

spoke, *n.* ray; rung, rundel, stave. See SUPPORT.

spoken, *adj.* oral, vocal; verbal. See SPEECH.

spokesperson, spokesman, spokeswoman, *n.* voice, mouthpiece; front, figurehead; representative, go-between, proxy, AGENT, delegate, advocate. See SPEECH.

sponge, *n.* swab, blotter, dryer; *informal,* hanger-on, parasite, leech, dependent, moocher (*sl.*), scrounge (*sl.*), freeloader (*sl.*). See CLEANNESS, SERVILITY, DRINKING. —*v.* sop, soak up, mop, swab, blot, absorb, dry, suck in, drink up; *informal,* touch, live off, scrounge (*sl.*), mooch (*sl.*), freeload (*sl.*). See DRYNESS, MOISTURE.

sponsor, *n.* patron, backer; surety, guarantor; godparent; advertiser. See SECURITY.

spontaneous, *adj.* instinctive, automatic, involuntary; extemporaneous, uninhibited, unforced, natural. See IMPULSE, WILL, FREEDOM.

spoof, *n., slang,* jest, joke, banter, hoax; satire, burlesque, parody, takeoff, caricature, lampoon. —*v., slang,* deceive, hoodwink, fool; needle, josh, kid; lampoon, parody, satirize. See DECEPTION, COPY.

spook, *v.* frighten. —*n., informal,* ghost, specter. See DEMON, FEAR.

spool, *n.* spindle, bobbin, reel. See CIRCULARITY.

spoon, *v.* ladle, dip; *informal,* pet, make love. See TRANSFER, ENDEARMENT.

sporadic, *adj.* occasional; irregular. See RARITY, IRREGULARITY. *Ant.,* frequent, constant.

sport, *n.* recreation, athletics, SPORTS; jesting, merriment, fun, diversion; mockery, ridicule; freak, mutant; gamester, gambler, spender; dandy, fop. See AMUSEMENT, EXERTION, FASHION.

SPORTS
Athletic pastime

Nouns—**1,** sports, recreation, athletics, pastime; angling, hunting, chase (see PURSUIT); sportsmanship, fair play (see JUSTICE); sportswear (see CLOTHING).

2, sportsman, sportswoman, Nimrod, hunter, angler; athlete, ballplayer, golfer, *etc.*; benchwarmer, free agent.

3, a. baseball, national pastime; major *or* minor league, big league, National *or* American League; farm team *or* system; ballpark, home plate, [first, second, *or* third] base, infield, outfield, pitcher's mound; battery, pitcher, catcher, shortstop, infielder, outfielder, manager, coach; umpire; home run, homer, single, double, triple, pop fly, fly ball, line drive, liner, ground ball, grounder, foul ball; strike, walk, base on balls, out; base runner, batter; pitch, fast ball, change-up, curve, slider, spitball, knuckle ball; inning; World Series, playoffs, wildcard team. **b.** football, National *or* American Football League, division; college football, conference, Rose Bowl, Cotton Bowl, Orange Bowl, *etc.*; stadium, field, gridiron, line, end zone, goal line, yard line; lineman, end, tackle, guard, center, fullback, halfback, quarterback, receiver, punter; line, backfield; official, judge, linesman; [lateral *or* forward] pass, kick, handoff, rush; touchdown, conversion; period, quarter, half. **c.** basketball, hoop; court, fore-, mid-, *or* backcourt, sideline, basket, backboard, free throw line, foul line; basketball player, basketballer, forward, guard, center, playmaker; official, referee, jump ball, dribble; screen, one-on-one, zone; basket, field goal, shot, lay-up, [slam] dunk, tip-in. **d.** [lawn] tennis, singles, doubles; ball, racket; hard surface, clay court, grass court, composite court; service, ace; love, deuce, tiebreaker, set point, match point; volley, forehand, backhand, overhead, smash, groundstroke, drop shot, lob. **e.** soccer, association football; forward, striker, lineman, defender, goalie; penalty kick, free kick; goal. *Slang,* kicking the bladder. **f.** bowling, kegling, tenpin, candlepin, duckpin, *or* fivepin bowling, lawn bowling, bowls; alley, lane, gutter; pin, pinspotter, bowling ball; string, frame, strike, spare, split; perfect game. **g.** hockey, ice, roller, deck, street, floor, *or* field hockey, banty, shinty, hurling; bench, squad, defense, wingman, line, goalie; pass, [body, hip, poke, *or* stick] check, [slap *or* wrist] shot, flip, power play, shoot-out; cross checking, high-sticking. **h.** boxing, the noble art of self-defense, [prize]fighting, pugilism, the ring; canvas, prize ring, corner; boxer, fighter, slugger, manager, trainer, handler, corner man; match, bout; referee, official; punch, chop, cross, jab, hook, haymaker, rabbit punch, uppercut; lightweight, bantamweight, featherweight, welterweight, heavyweight; knockout, KO, technical knockout, TKO, split decision; round, bell. **i.** horse racing, sport of kings; jockey, rider, owner, trainer, breeder; racehorse (see ANIMAL); favorite, pacesetter, nag; backstretch, post, turn, straightaway. j. cricket, batsman, wicket, bail, bowler, run, out, century; test match. k. golf; golf course, fairway, dogleg, tee, rough, green, cup; golfer, duffer; hole-in-one, par [for the course].

4, gymnastics, rings, balance beam, [parallel or unparallel] bars, horse, tumbling, floor exercises, pommel horse; track and field, discus [throw], hammer throw, high jump, long jump, pole vault, shot put, javelin throw, decathlon, triathlon, biathlon; bicycle racing, motocross; target shooting, archery, skeet or trap shooting; weightlifting, bodybuilding.

5, martial arts; aikido, boxing, capoeira, Greco-Roman wrestling, jujitsu, judo, karate, kung-fu, tae kwon do, kick boxing, wrestling, wu shu.

6, (animal sports) rodeo, bronco riding, calf roping, steer roping, steer wrestling, bull riding; bullfighting, bullfighter, toreador, picador, matador; cockfighting; dog or greyhound racing; harness racing; polo; steeplechase.

7, (water sports) swimming, [Australian] crawl, sidestroke, breaststroke, backstroke, dogpaddle, butterfly; scuba diving, snorkeling, deep-sea diving; surfing; synchronized swimming; water polo; windsurfing, sailboarding; canoeing, kayaking, boating, rowing, yachting; fishing (see PURSUIT).

8, hang gliding, parachuting, parasailing, sky-diving, bungee jumping, ballooning. See AVIATION.

9, (winter sports) a. skiing, Alpine, downhill, or cross-country skiing, skijoring, ski jumping, extreme skiing, ski lift, rope tow, chair lift, slalom, ski jump, downhill, christie, herringbone, Telemark, snowplow, wideln, wedge, stem, tuck, bathtub, bunny, hot dog, langlauf, mogul, [off-]piste, schuss. b. skating, figure skating, ice dancing, free skating, long or short program; jump, axel, butterfly, [camel, layback or sit] spin, choctaw, school or compulsory figure, death spiral, double or triple jump, Lutz, mohawk, Salchow, spiral, spread eagle, [toe] loop, Walley. c. sledding, tobogganing, snow tubing, snowboarding, luge. d. ice hockey (see 3, g. above); curling; ice boating or sailing; skier, snowboarder. Informal, shredder.

Verbs—play sports, compete; take it on the chin, throw in the sponge or towel.

Adjectives—sportive, sporting; sportsmanlike; on the ropes, up to scratch, down for the count.

Phrases—nice guys finish last.

Quotations—The only athletic sport I ever mastered was backgammon (Douglas Jerrold), To play billiards well is the sign of an ill-spent youth (Charles Roupell), Golf is a good walk spoiled (Mark Twain), [Of sports:] I used to think the only use for it was to give small boys something else to kick besides me (Katharine Whitehorn), The trouble with referees is that they just don't care which side wins (Tom Canterbury), Boxing's just show business with blood (Frank Bruno), Baseball is very big with my people. It figures. It's the only way we can get to shake a bat at a white man without starting a riot (Dick Gregory), In America, it is sport that is the opiate of the masses (Russell Baker).

---

sporty, adj. sporting; flashy, dressy; casual. See SPORTS, OSTENTATION, CLOTHING.

spot, n. place, locality, site; blotch, dapple, speckle, macula; smear, spatter, daub, blot; blemish, flaw, stain, stigma. See LOCATION, DISREPUTE. —**on the spot,** adv. handy, convenient; in a bind, behind the eight ball (sl.). See UTILITY, DIFFICULTY.

spotless, adj. clean, unsullied, immaculate; pure, unblemished, impeccable. See PERFECTION, CLEANNESS, INNOCENCE.

spotlight, n. limelight, spot[lamp], searchlight, beacon, headlamp; notoriety, attention. —v.t. feature, star, play up. See PUBLICATION, DRAMA, LIGHT.

spotty, adj. irregular, discontinuous, sporadic, intermittent. See DISCONTINUITY, IRREGULARITY.

spouse, n. mate, husband, wife, consort. See MARRIAGE, ACCOMPANIMENT.

spout, n. tube, pipe, trough, nozzle, rainspout, gargoyle; jet, spurt, geyser, waterspout. See EGRESS, WATER.

sprain, *v.t.* wrench, strain, twist. See EXERTION.

sprawl, *v.* spread, extend, slump, slouch, lounge, loll. See LENGTH, HORIZONTAL.

spray, *n.* spindrift, spume, scud; fusillade, barrage; sprinkler, atomizer; sprig. —*v.t.* sprinkle, atomize; pepper, riddle (with bullets). See VAPOR, VEGETABLE, DISPERSION.

spread, *v.* scatter, strew; disseminate, diffuse, circulate; cover; unfold, stretch; part, separate; show, display; expand, disperse, deploy. —*n.* diffusion, EXPANSION; extent, expanse; bedspread, coverlet; meal, banquet, collation; layout; ranch. See COVERING, FOOD, INCREASE, PUBLICATION.

spreadsheet, *n.* worksheet, columnar pad. See ACCOUNTING.

spree, *n.* frolic, lark, escapade, fling, revel; carousal, saturnalia; souse, jag, toot, binge, bat, bust (*all sl.*). See AMUSEMENT, DRINKING.

sprig, *n.* branch, shoot, spray. See VEGETABLE, PART.

sprightly, *adj.* gay, brisk, vivacious, animated; scintillating, smart. See CHEERFULNESS, WIT.

spring, *v.* LEAP, bound, dart, start; bounce, RECOIL, rebound; arise, rise; result *or* derive from; release; detonate; reveal, disclose; bend, twist; *slang,* release, bail. See LIBERATION. —*n.* LEAP, bound; ELASTICITY, RECOIL; well, fount, origin, source; coil. See CAUSE.

sprinkle, *v.* scatter, spread, sow; spray, wet; speckle, mottle, powder; drizzle, shower. See WATER, DISPERSION, MOISTURE.

sprint, *n.* run, dash; speed, rush; bolt, dart, tear, hotfoot (*inf.*). See VELOCITY, CONTENTION.

sprite, *n.* elf, fairy. See DEMON, MYTHICAL DEITIES.

sprout, *v.i.* germinate, shoot, bud, burgeon. See INCREASE, EXPANSION.

spruce, *adj.* trim, neat, tidy, shipshape; smart, dapper, chic. See CLEANNESS.

spry, *adj.* lively, alert, athletic, nimble, agile. See ACTIVITY. *Ant.,* sluggish, lethargic.

spunky, *adj., informal,* plucky, mettlesome, brave, intrepid. See COURAGE, RESOLUTION.

spur, *n.* spine; rowel; incentive, goad, stimulus; projection, headland, siding. See SHARPNESS, CAUSE. —*v.t.* goad, incite. See CAUSE.—**spur of the moment,** impromptu, ad hoc. See UNPREPAREDNESS, INSTANTANEITY.

spurious, *adj.* false, counterfeit, sham, specious; bastard, illegitimate. See DECEPTION, ERROR, FALSEHOOD. *Ant.,* accurate, true.

spurn, *v.t.* flout, scout, reject, repudiate, repel, contemn, scorn, disdain; kick. See CONTEMPT, DISRESPECT.

spurt, *v.i.* gush, squirt, spray; burst. See WATER, HASTE, REPULSION, EJECTION, TRANSIENTNESS.

sputter, *v.* spit, spew, splutter, spatter, eject, splash; blurt, babble, jabber, stammer; misfire, fizzle. See STAMMERING, ACTIVITY, AGITATION.

spy, *n.* secret agent, scout, undercover man, informer, stool pigeon, mole (*sl.*). See INFORMATION, CONCEALMENT.

spyglass, *n.* telescope. See OPTICAL INSTRUMENTS.

squabble, *v.i.* quarrel, bicker, altercate, fall out. —*n.* falling out, quarrel, dispute, wrangle, spat, argument. See CONTENTION, DISCORD.

squad, *n.* band, patrol; squadron, wing, unit; crew, team. See ASSEMBLAGE, COMBATANT.

squalid, *adj.* filthy, dirty, foul, sordid, repulsive, wretched, degraded. See UNCLEANNESS, UGLINESS.

squall, *n.* gust, blow, blast; turmoil; scream, CRY. —*v.i.* blow, bluster; scream, bawl, wail. See WIND, VIOLENCE.

squalor, *n.* dirt, filth, decay, UNCLEANNESS, misery, poverty. See DISORDER.

squander, *v.t.* WASTE, lavish, dissipate. *Ant.,* save.

square, *n.* tetragon, quadrilateral, equilateral rectangle; block; quadrangle; plaza, court; T square; *slang,* misfit, fogy. See NUMERATION, MEASUREMENT, ANGULARITY, PERMANENCE. —*v.t.* quadrate; balance, settle, reconcile; set, adjust. See AGREEMENT, VERTICAL.

squash, *v.t.* crush, mash, squeeze, flatten; squelch; *informal,* suppress, SILENCE. See DESTRUCTION.

squat, *adj.* dumpy, stocky, pudgy. See SHORTNESS, LOWNESS. *Ant.,* tall, lanky.

squawk, *v.* CRY, call, scream, screech; *informal,* complain, kick (*sl.*), gripe (*sl.*), grouse (*sl.*). —*n.* outcry, squeak, croak, caw, screech. See DISCONTENT.

squeak, *v.* creak, CRY; *informal,* squeak by, just make it, pull through. See ESCAPE.

squeal, *v.* yell, CRY, yelp, shriek, screech; *slang,* confess, inform, blab, tattle, tell (on), spill [the beans], stool (*sl.*), sing (*sl.*). See DISCLOSURE.

squeamish, *adj.* queasy, qualmish, nauseated; fearful, skittish, nervous; fastidious, picky; hypercritical. See UNWILLINGNESS, TASTE. *Ant.,* fearless, all-consuming.

squeeze, *v.t.* press, compress; express, extract; stuff, cram; exact, extort, blackmail. See EXTRACTION, CONTRACTION.

squelch, *v.t.* disconcert, discomfit, rout, crush; silence, stifle, muffle. See DESTRUCTION.

squint, *n.* cross-eye, strabismus; peek, peering, glance. See VISION.

squire, *n.* landed gentleman; esquire; attendant, escort. —*v.t.* attend, escort. See ACCOMPANIMENT, NOBILITY.

squirm, *v.i.* twist, turn, thrash (about); wriggle, writhe. See AGITATION, EXCITEMENT.

squirt, *v.* spray, jet, douche, hose, spatter. See EJECTION. —*n.* spurt, jet, stream[let]; syringe, spray[er], atomizer; *informal,* upstart, runt, shrimp, imp, half pint (*sl.*), snotnose (*sl.*). See UNIMPORTANCE.

stab, *v.t.* pierce, puncture, perforate, stick, prick, pink; distress, hurt. See OPENING, PAIN, ATTACK.

STABILITY
Permanence

Nouns—1, stability; immutability, unchangeableness, constancy, firmness, equilibrium, immobility, soundness, vitality, stiffness, solidity, aplomb; establishment, fixture; homeostasis; PERMANENCE; obstinacy, RESOLUTION. See DURABILITY.

2, rock, pillar, tower, foundation, leopard's spots; rock of Gibraltar; zero population growth, ZPG.

Verbs—1, be *or* stand firm; stick fast; weather the storm, hold up; settle down, take root; entrench oneself, hold the line, stand pat, stay put; hold *or* stand one's ground, hold one's own. *Informal,* hold the fort.

2, establish, settle, fix, set, retain, keep *or* take hold, pin down; make good *or* sure; perpetuate (see PERPETUITY); mark time.

Adjectives—1, stable, fixed, steadfast, firm, fast, steady, balanced; confirmed, valid, immovable, irremovable, riveted, rooted; settled, established, vested; incontrovertible; tethered, anchored, moored; firm as a rock; firmly seated *or* established; deep-rooted, ineradicable; inveterate; stuck fast, aground, high and dry, stranded. See OBSTINACY.

2, unchangeable, immutable; unaltered, unalterable; changeless, constant, permanent; invariable, undeviating; durable, perennial.

3, conservative, Tory, reactionary, diehard (see PERMANENCE).

Adverbs—in status quo; at a standstill; as is.

Quotations—The law must be stable, but it must not stand still (*Roscoe Pound*), There is nothing stable in the world—uproar's your only music (*John Keats*).

Antonyms, see CHANGEABLENESS, MOTION.

---

stable, *n.* barn, stall, mews. See ABODE. —*adj.* See STABILITY.

stack, *n.* pile[s], heap[s], mound, lots (*inf.*); rick, sheaf, faggot; chimney, flue. See ASSEMBLAGE, MULTITUDE. —*v.* pile, heap, bundle; doctor, rig, prearrange; fix, load. See DECEPTION.

stadium, *n.* See ARENA.

staff, *n.* walking stick, cane, cudgel; scepter, wand, baton, truncheon, crosier; flagpole; assistants, crew, aides, associates,

personnel, force. See SUPPORT, SERVANT, ARMS.

stage, *n.* platform, rostrum, scaffold; DRAMA, theater; ARENA, field, scene; degree, step, phase; period, stretch, interval, span; stagecoach, diligence, omnibus. See SUPPORT, VEHICLE, LAYER. —*v.t.* produce, present, put on; dramatize. See DRAMA, PREPARATION.

stagger, *v.* reel, sway, falter, totter, lurch; waver, hesitate; surprise, stun, jar, shock, startle, take aback; alternate. See AGITATION, OSCILLATION.

staggering, *adj.* amazing, astounding, astonishing. See SURPRISE.

staging, *n.* direction, mise en scène, production; scaffolding. See DRAMA, SUPPORT.

stagnant, *adj.* static, inert; foul; sluggish, dull, torpid. See INACTIVITY, REPOSE. *Ant.,* active.

stagy, *adj.* theatrical, artificial. See AFFECTATION. *Ant.,* natural, lifelike.

staid, *adj.* demure, serious, sedate, settled, inexcitable, sober. See INEXCITABILITY, MODERATION. *Ant.,* lively.

stain, *n.* COLOR, dye, dyestuff; discoloration; blotch, blot, smear, smudge; blemish, tarnish; stigma, taint, brand. See UNCLEANNESS, DISREPUTE.

stairway, *n.* stairs, steps, staircase; moving stairway, escalator; companionway, ladder. See ASCENT.

stake, *n.* post, peg, pile; palisade; burning, execution; wager, bet, ante, pot; SECURITY, earnest, deposit; interest, claim, holding; prize, reward. See CHANCE, PROPERTY. —**stake out,** lay claim to,

stake; observe, keep under surveillance. See POSSESSION, CARE.

stale, *adj.* passé; rancid, dried up, tasteless, insipid, flat, vapid; trite, dull, banal, old hat (*inf.*). See INSIPIDITY, WEARINESS. *Ant.,* fresh.

stalemate, *n.* draw, deadlock, standoff, tie; stall; RESISTANCE, opposition; impasse, standstill; check, hindrance, bottleneck, jam. See DIFFICULTY.

stalk, *n.* stem, pedicle, petiole. See SUPPORT. —*v.t.* follow, pursue. See PURSUIT.

stall, *n.* stable, manger; ENCLOSURE, chamber; booth, concession, kiosk; alcove, niche; *informal,* pretext, evasion. See RECEPTACLE, AVOIDANCE. —*v.* stick, stand still, bog down; fail, go dead; *informal,* delay, dodge, play for time, put *or* hold off, stave off.

stallion, *n.* stud[horse], entire [horse]. See ANIMAL.

stalwart, *adj.* strong, brawny, husky; dauntless, steadfast. See STRENGTH, SIZE.

stamina, *n.* staying power, hardiness, force, VIGOR; vitality, STRENGTH; grit, pluck, backbone; endurance, durability, resilience.

STAMMERING
Speech defect

Nouns—stammering, stuttering, *etc.*; hesitancy, broken voice; speech impediment; lisp, drawl; mispronunciation, slip of the tongue, lapsus linguae.

Verbs—stammer, stutter, falter, sputter, splutter, stumble, halt, hesitate, pause, balbutiate, hem and haw, trip over one's tongue, be unable to put two words together; mumble, mutter, dither; lisp, speak thickly, swallow one's words, mispronounce, missay. *Informal,* mushmouth.

Adjectives—inarticulate, indistinct, hesitant, halting; guttural, nasal, husky, throaty, tremulous, tongue-tied.

Antonyms, see SPEECH.

---

stamp, *n.* impression, symbol, device, seal, trademark, brand; authorization, certification, approval, assent; postage; die, rubber stamp; certificate, wafer, label; kind, sort, quality. See INDICATION, FORM, CLASS, SPECIALITY.

stampede, *n.* flight, charge, rampage, onrush. —*v.* panic, rout, scare, alarm, incite, inflame. See FEAR.

stance, *n.* foothold, placement, post, station; posture, carriage, bearing; pose, form, appearance; standpoint, view[point], slant (*inf.*). See SUPPORT, LOCATION, VISION.

stanch, *v.* stem flow of.

stand, *v.* abide, tolerate, endure, SUPPORT; last, persist; remain upright; pause, halt, stop; be, remain; stagnate; be valid; put, place; bear, undergo; stand for, represent, mean. See DURABILITY, INDICATION, EXISTENCE, PERFECTION, RESISTANCE. *Ant.,* reject, sit.

standard, *n.* emblem, ensign; criterion, measure, grade, exemplar, norm, canon, prototype, ethics. —*adj.* regulation, normal, conventional. See CONFORMITY, RULE, MEASUREMENT, DEGREE. *Ant.,* nonstandard, substandard, unconventional.

standby, *n.* mainstay, ally, supporter; staple; alternate, replacement, substitute. See AUXILIARY.

stand-in, *n.* substitute (see SUBSTITUTION).

standing, *n.* station, rank, REPUTE; duration, continuance; status, rating. See DURABILITY, CIRCUMSTANCE. —*adj.* continuing, permanent. See PERMANENCE.

standoff, *n.* tie, draw; stalemate. See EQUALITY.

standpoint, *n.* vantage [point]; viewpoint, point of view. See LOCATION, VISION.

standstill, *n.* full *or* dead stop, halt, suspension, impasse. See DISCONTINUANCE, REPOSE.

stanza, *n.* verse, stave, strophe. See POETRY.

staple, *adj.* chief, principal; stable, established, regular; marketable, popular. See CONNECTION. —*n.* commodity, raw material (see MATERIALS).

star, *n.* sun, celestial body; pentagram, asterisk; prima donna, primo uomo, leading man *or* lady, chief performer; DESTINY; planet. See INDICATION, DRAMA, REPUTE.

stare, *v.i.* gaze, gape, gawk; stand out. See VISION, CURIOSITY.

stark, *adj.* sheer, downright; rigid; desolate, naked. See COMPLETION, HARDNESS, DIVESTMENT.

starry, *adj.* spangled, stellar, stellate, star-studded; starlit; shiny, glittering. See UNIVERSE.

start, *v.* begin, commence, set out; jerk, jump, shy; loosen, crack; originate; get going; startle, rouse. See BEGINNING, PROPULSION, IMPULSE, DEPARTURE, FEAR.

startle, *v.t.* start, alarm, frighten, shock, surprise, amaze. See SURPRISE, DOUBT, FEAR.

starve, *v.* hunger, famish, fast; pine; pinch, scrimp, deny. See PARSIMONY, POVERTY. *Ant.,* feed.

stash, *v.t., slang,* put away, hide. See CONCEALMENT.

state, *n.* condition, shape (*inf.*), kilter (*inf.*), category, estate, lot, makeup (*inf.*); case, mood, disposition, temper; pickle, contretemps, quandary, dilemma, plight; aspect, appearance; constitution, habitude, frame; pomp, dignity, formality, CIRCUMSTANCE; mode, modality; form, tone, tenor, turn; fashion, style, character, rank, situation, position, status; nation, country, government; commonwealth. —*v.* allege, say, assert, declare, avow, aver, express, make a statement. See AFFIRMATION, OSTENTATION.

stately, *adj.* impressive, imposing, grand; dignified, noble, lofty. See OSTENTATION, PRIDE, NOBILITY. *Ant.,* unimposing, small.

statement, *n.* assertion, declaration, AFFIRMATION; report; bill, account. See ACCOUNTING, SPEECH.

state-of-the-art, *adj.* latest, newest, up-to-date. See NEWNESS. *Ant.,* out-of-date, obsolete.

statesman, stateswoman, *n.* legislator, diplomat, solon, Draco; politician. See DIRECTOR.

static, *adj.* immobile, motionless, inert, passive, inactive; unchanging, the same, conservative; fixed, stationary, stagnant. See REPOSE. *Ant.,* active, in motion. —*n.* interference, noise; crackling, snow, ghosts, jamming. See COMMUNICATION.

station, *n.* place, position; office, situation, rank, standing; depot, terminal; headquarters, stopping place, post. See LOCATION, REPUTE, BUSINESS, CLASS. —*v.t.* set, place, assign, post. See LOCATION.

stationary, *adj.* fixed, rooted, planted, immovable; constant, unchanging, static. See PERMANENCE, INACTIVITY. *Ant.,* moving, movable, changing.

stationery, *n.* writing materials, office products; paper, stock, *etc.* See MATERIALS, WRITING.

statistics, *n.sing.* data, charts, computations, graphs. See NUMERATION.

statue, *n.* SCULPTURE, effigy, image, statuette. See APPROBATION.

statuesque, *adj.* monumental, marmoreal; dignified, majestic, tall, well-proportioned. See BEAUTY, SCULPTURE.

stature, *n.* size, HEIGHT, form; standing, rank, status, importance, repute.

status, *n.* position, rank, standing; state, condition. See CIRCUMSTANCE, CLASS. —**status quo,** existing condition, as things stand. See STABILITY, PERMANENCE.

statute, *n.* law, ordinance, enactment; RULE. See LEGALITY.

statutory, *adj.* legal, official (see AUTHORITY).

staunch, *adj.* loyal, reliable, faithful, constant, steadfast; seaworthy, strong. See PROBITY.

stave, *n.* slat, strip. See MATERIALS, SUPPORT, MUSIC. —*v.t.* break (up), penetrate, puncture, pierce; stave *or* fend off, hold off *or* back, avert. See OPENING, DEFENSE, CONTENTION.

stay, *v.* check, halt, stop; restrain, detain, delay; suspend, defer; support, brace; appease; outlast; linger, tarry, remain; endure, last; dwell, sojourn; stick, stay put; continue. See HINDRANCE, PRESENCE, ABODE, PERMANENCE, RESTRAINT. *Ant.,* go, leave.

steadfast, *adj.* firm, unswerving, constant, stanch, resolute, industrious. See RESOLUTION, PERMANENCE, PROBITY, STABILITY. *Ant.,* inconstant, irresolute, changeable.

steady, *adj.* firm, secure, stable; constant, unvarying, uniform; regular, habitual; trustworthy. See STABILITY, REGULARITY. *Ant.,* unsteady, unstable.

steak, *n.* beefsteak; club, flank, tenderloin, Swiss, New York, porterhouse, *etc.* steak, filet mignon. See FOOD.

steal, *v.* rob (see STEALING); sneak, tiptoe, creep (see SECRET, TRAVEL). —*n.,* *informal,* bargain, good buy (see CHEAPNESS).

STEALING
Taking dishonestly

Nouns—**1,** stealing, theft, thievery, robbery; abduction, kidnapping; abstraction, appropriation; plagiarism; rape, depredation, poaching, raid; spoliation, plunder, pillage, sack, rapine, brigandage, foray; extortion, blackmail; graft; piracy, privateering, buccaneering; burglary; housebreaking; peculation, pilfering, embezzlement; fraud, swindle (see DECEPTION); identity theft; kleptomania; grand *or* petty larceny; pickpocketing, shoplifting, highway robbery; holdup, stick-up, mugging, hijacking; cybercrime. *Informal,* haul, inventory leakage, social engineering. *Slang,* make, heist, snatch, snitch, touch, inside job, score, rip-off, Black Power dance, hustle.

2, thief, robber, bandit, crook, sneak thief, pickpocket, hook, cracksman, safe cracker, peterman, pilferer; swindler, confidence man; shoplifter, housebreaker, kleptomaniac; stealer, pirate, purloiner, filcher; highwayman, brigand, cateran, gentleman of the road; [cat] burglar, second-story man, *etc.*; horse thief, rustler; poacher; looter; cyberthief; white-collar criminal. *Slang,* apache, cat bandit, dip, stickup artist, yegg, big juice, flimp, gonif, perp, alley rat, ham-snatcher, dipster, ice man, rip-off artist. See EVILDOER.

3, stolen goods, booty. *Slang,* five-finger discount, hot roller, merch, swag, loot, smoker.

Verbs—**1,** steal, thieve; rob, purloin, pilfer, filch, cop, crib, palm; scrounge, sponge; abstract, appropriate, plagiarize; abduct, kidnap; make, walk, *or* run off *or* away with; seize, take, help oneself to; spirit away; plunder, pillage, rifle, sack, loot, ransack; mug; prey on; spoil, spoliate, despoil, strip, sweep, gut, forage; blackmail, pirate, maraud, poach, smuggle, run; hold up, stick up, hijack, skyjack. *Informal,* swipe, do out of, rob the till, have one's hand in the till. *Slang,* heist, rip off, knock off *or* over, snitch, take to the cleaners, roll, dip, jostle, liberate, skim, boost, nick.

2, swindle, peculate, embezzle, extort; sponge, mulct, rook, bilk, milk, pluck, fleece, defraud; obtain under false pretenses; live by one's wits; rob Peter to pay Paul; set a thief to catch a thief. *Informal,* rook, gouge, shake down, bleed white. *Slang,* wrangle, hustle, cuff, murphy.

3, be stolen. *Informal,* fall off the back of a truck.

Adjectives—stealing, thieving, thievish, sticky- *or* light-fingered, furtive; piratical, predaceous, predacious, predatory; stolen. *Slang,* hot.

Interjections—reach for the sky! stick 'em up! stand and deliver! your money or your life! *Slang,* break yourself!

Phrases—the rich rob the poor, and the poor rob each other; set a thief to catch a thief; rob Peter to pay Paul.

Quotations—Opportunity makes a thief (*Francis Bacon*), Once in the racket you're always in it (*Al Capone*), Crime isn't a disease, it's a symptom. Cops are like a doctor that gives you aspirin for a brain tumor (*Raymond Chandler*), If you steal from one author, it's plagiarism; if you steal from many, it's research (*Wilson Mizner*), The robber that smiles steals something from the thief (*Shakespeare*), Why do you rob banks? Because that's where the money is (*Willie Sutton*).

Antonyms, see PROBITY, RESTORATION.

---

stealth, n. furtiveness, secrecy, skulking, stalking. See CONCEALMENT.

steam, n. VAPOR, water vapor, mist, fog, gas, evaporation. —v. cook, boil, simmer; soften, moisten; clean, renovate; progress, speed. See HEAT.

steamer, n. riverboat, steamboat, steamship, launch, liner, packet boat, side wheeler, stern-wheeler, paddle-wheeler. See SHIP.

steed, n. horse, mount, charger. See TRANSPORTATION.

steel, v.t. plate, armor, coat; temper, anneal, case-harden; harden, inure, strengthen, toughen; brace, gird, fortify. See HARDNESS, STRENGTH.

steep, v.t. soak, saturate, macerate. See WATER. —adj. precipitous, abrupt, sheer, declivitous; VERTICAL; informal, expensive (see DEARNESS).

steeple, n. spire, finial, flèche, belfry, campanile. See HEIGHT, TEMPLE, SHARPNESS.

steer, v.t. guide, pilot, control; manage, direct; follow (a course). See DIRECTION.

stellar, adj. starry, astral, celestial; radiant, glorious; feature[d], top, star[ring]. See UNIVERSE, GOODNESS.

stem, n. tree trunk, stalk, petiole, pedicle; tube, shaft; cutwater, prow; lineage, extraction, derivation. See ANCESTRY, FRONT.

stench, n. fetor, stink, mephitis, fetidness, malodor, (strong) smell. See MALODOROUSNESS.

stenography, n. See SHORTHAND.

step, n. pace, stride, football; footprint; gait, tread; stair, rung; interval, gradation; (pl.) measures, action. See DEGREE, AGENCY, NEARNESS, TRAVEL.

stepping-stone, n. rung [of the ladder], stage, MEANS [to an end].

stereotype, n. plate, mold (see PRINTING); pattern, type; cliché, convention; preconception. —v.t. reproduce, print, copy; stylize, type, conventionalize, conform. See CONFORMITY.

sterile, adj. barren, unproductive, unfruit-

ful, unfertile; aseptic, germ-free. See USELESSNESS, CLEANNESS. Ant., fertile, fruitful, unsterile.

sterling, adj. genuine, unalloyed, pure; noble, excellent, exemplary; silver. See TRUTH, VIRTUE.

stern, adj. rigorous, austere; forbidding, grim; strict, harsh, uncompromising. See SEVERITY. Ant., moderate, lenient. —n. poop, counter, REAR. Ant., bow.

stevedore, n. longshoreman, roustabout; lader, stower, docker, navvy, loader, dockman, dockwalloper. See EXERTION, TRANSPORTATION.

stew, v. simmer, seethe, [pressure-]cook, steam; informal, worry, fret, fume, stew in one's own juice. —n. pepperpot, ragout, goulash, fricassee, bouillabaisse; informal, agitation, dither, sweat, tizzy. See FOOD, DIFFICULTY, EXCITEMENT.

steward, n. agent, manager, trustee; provider, caterer; SERVANT, waiter. See STORE, DIFFICULTY.

stick, v.t. stab, puncture, prick; put, place, thrust; glue; transfix, impale; informal, puzzle, stump. See OPENING, COHERENCE, DIFFICULTY. —v.i. adhere, cling; stay, remain, tarry; stall, freeze, be immobile. See COHERENCE, STABILITY. —n. piece, branch; cane, staff, cudgel, rod, baton; (pl.) informal, suburbs, country. See SUPPORT, REGION.

stickler, n. purist, pedant, quibbler; puritan, prig; perfectionist; poser, puzzle, enigma, baffler. See OBSTINACY, SEVERITY, DIFFICULTY. Ant., libertarian.

sticky, adj. adhesive, mucilaginous, glutinous, viscous, tenacious; humid, muggy; sweaty; tacky. See COHERENCE.

stiff, adj. rigid, inflexible, firm, nonfluid; strong, brisk; difficult, hard; severe, excessive; formal, unreserved; awkward, stilted. See HARDNESS, SEVERITY, AFFECTATION, INELEGANCE, RESTRAINT, PRIDE. Ant., flexible, pliant.

stifle, v.t. smother, suffocate; extinguish,

put down, suppress; repress, check. See KILLING, CONCEALMENT, SILENCE.

stigma, *n.* blemish, birthmark; brand, blot, stain, reproach. See DISREPUTE, IMPERFECTION.

stigmatize, *v.t.* denounce, reproach, brand, vilify. See DISREPUTE.

stiletto, *n.* dagger, dirk. See ARMS.

still, *adj.* silent, quiet, hushed; calm, peaceful, tranquil; motionless, at rest, stationary. See SILENCE. *Ant.,* active, in motion, agitated. —*adv.* yet, nevertheless. See COMPENSATION.

stilted, *adj.* formal, stiff; unnatural, affected, mannered, prim, stuffy; inflated, florid, flowery, pedantic. See AFFECTATION, INELEGANCE. *Ant.,* informal, natural.

stimulant, *n.* excitant, stimulus, bracer, tonic, spur; liquor. See ENERGY, DRUGS. *Ant.,* depressant, sedative.

stimulate, *v.t.* excite, rouse, animate, stir, spur, invigorate, exhilarate. See EXCITEMENT, CAUSE, REFRESHMENT, STRENGTH.

stimulus, *n.* prick, goad, incentive; exciter. See CAUSE, EXCITEMENT.

sting, *v.* smart, tingle; irritate, trouble, PAIN; bite, wound, nettle, gall, goad. See RESENTMENT. —*n.* wound, prickle, smart, irritation; stimulus, goad; stinger, prickle, nettle. See PAIN, PUNGENCY, SENSIBILITY.

stingy, *adj.* penurious, miserly, niggardly, near, tight, close; scanty, meager. See PARSIMONY. *Ant.,* generous.

stink, *n. & v.* See MALODOROUSNESS.

stint, *v.* restrain, restrict, LIMIT; scrimp, skimp, economize. —*n.* RESTRAINT, LIMIT; turn, shift, bout; task, chore, job. See PARSIMONY.

stipend, *n.* compensation, wage, pay, salary. See PAYMENT.

stipple, *v.* mottle, speckle, pepper; splatter, dapple. See VARIEGATION.

stipulate, *v.t.* specify, demand, insist upon, require, negotiate. See QUALIFICATION.

stir, *v.t.* move, budge, circulate; agitate, incite, arouse; animate, stimulate, provoke. See AGITATION, MOTION, EXCITEMENT.

stitch, *n.* seam, suture. —*v.t.* sew; knit, crotchet, tack, smock, overcast; staple; darn, mend. See JUNCTION.

stock, *n.* stem, bole, trunk; race, family; livestock, cattle; [gun] butt; capital;

broth; merchandise, goods; raw MATERIALS; repertory; *informal,* BELIEF. See ANCESTRY, STORE, DRAMA, PROVISION, QUANTITY.

stockade, *n.* palisade, palings, ENCLOSURE; wall, barrier, barricade, fort, fortification; pen, compound, PRISON.

stockpile, *n.* reserve, STORE; hoard, cache; materials, surplus.

stocky, *adj.* thickset, sturdy, chunky, squat. See SHORTNESS. *Ant.,* lanky.

stodgy, *adj.* short, thickset, stocky; sluggish, slow, obstinate, stolid; tedious, dull, unimaginative; backward, old-fashioned. See PERMANENCE, WEARINESS.

stoic, *adj.* stoical; self-controlled, impassive, unfeeling; long-suffering, ascetic. See INEXCITABILITY, RESIGNATION.

stoke, *v.* tend, poke, prod, stir; FUEL, fire, feed. See HEAT.

stole, *n.* scarf, cape, mantle, fur piece; surplice. See CLOTHING.

stolid, *adj.* inexcitable, impassive, dull, lethargic, sluggish. See IGNORANCE, INEXCITABILITY. *Ant.,* energetic, excitable.

stomach, *n.* appetite, hunger; DESIRE, craving, inclination; maw, craw; *informal,* belly, paunch, corporation. See RECEPTACLE.

stomachache, *n.* colic, gastralgia, gripe. See PAIN.

stone, *n.* coblestone, pebble; mineral; gem, jewel; gravestone, tombstone, millstone, whetstone, hearthstone, flagstone, *etc.*; pit, endocarp, pyrene; concretion, calculus. See DENSITY, ORNAMENT.

stoned, *adj., slang,* intoxicated, high *(inf.).* See DRINKING.

stonewall, *v.i., informal,* obstruct, drag one's feet, delay. See LATENESS, OBSTINACY.

stooge, *n., informal,* dupe, butt; tool; sucker, fall guy *(sl.),* patsy *(sl.);* straight man, yes-man; SERVANT, henchman, sidekick *(inf.),* lackey. See SERVILITY, MEANS, AGENT.

stool, *n.* cricket, hassock; seat; footrest, footstool; prie-dieu, kneeling stool; piano stool, milking stool, ducking stool. See SUPPORT.

stool pigeon, *slang,* decoy, informer, betrayer. See INFORMATION.

stoop, *v.i.* bend, bow, crouch; condescend, deign; submit. See SERVILITY, HUMILITY, SUBMISSION.

stop, *v.* close; obstruct; stanch; arrest, halt, impede; inhibit; delay, hold up, detain; discontinue, suspend; END, terminate, conclude; cease, desist. *Ant.*, go, continue, encourage. —*n.* halt, standstill, pause; DISCONTINUANCE, stoppage; stay, sojourn; stopping place, station; period, punctuation mark; brake, catch, skid, detent, curb. —*interj.* halt! belay! avast! stay! cease! See END, CLOSURE, LATENESS.

stopgap, *n.* expedient, makeshift; substitute. See SUBSTITUTION.

stoplight, *n.* traffic signal *or* light, wigwag signal. See INDICATION.

stopper, *n.* plug, cork (see CLOSURE).

stopple, *n.* stopper, plug, cork. See CLOSURE.

stopwatch, *n.* timer, chronograph. See CHRONOMETRY.

storage, *n.* safekeeping (see STORE).

STORE
Place for storage

Nouns—1, store, accumulation, hoard; mine, vein, lode, quarry; spring, wellspring; treasure, reserve, savings, nest egg; fund, savings bond, stamp, account, *etc.*; stock [in trade], merchandise; supply, heap (see ASSEMBLAGE); crop, harvest, vintage; supplies, provisions. See PROPERTY, PROVISION, MEANS, ACQUISITION, QUANTITY.

2, storage, conservation; storehouse, storeroom, depository; depot, warehouse, cache, repository, magazine, arsenal, armory; buttery, larder, pantry, closet; garage; stockpile; bank, vault, safe-deposit box, treasury, piggy bank; museum, gallery, conservatory; silo, grain elevator, granary; menagerie; zoo; reservoir, tank, cistern, pond, millpond; data storage (see COMPUTERS). See RETENTION.

Verbs—store; put, set, *or* lay by, lay *or* stow away, set *or* lay aside; store, lay, heap, put, *or* save up, accumulate, amass, hoard, garner, save; reserve, keep *or* hold back; save, bank, deposit; husband [one's resources] (see ECONOMY); stow, stack, load; harvest; heap, collect, stockpile, stock up, lay in store, keep, file; lay in, provide; preserve. *Informal,* salt away. *Slang,* stash.

Adjectives—stored, in store, in reserve; on hand, in stock (see PRESENCE); spare, supernumerary; extra.

Phrases—a penny saved is a penny earned; waste not, want not.

Quotations—A library is thought in cold storage (*Lord Samuel*).

Antonyms, see WASTE, POVERTY.

---

store, *n.* supply (see STORE); market, shop, boutique (see SALE). —**set store by,** *n. & v.i.* esteem (see REPUTE).

storehouse, *n.* See STORE.

storied, *adj.* celebrated (see REPUTE).

storm, *n.* hurricane, tempest, tornado; spate, flood; cloudburst, blizzard; outburst, commotion; assault, onslaught, ATTACK. —*v.* assault, assail, ATTACK; rage, rant; bluster; blow violently, pour, rain, snow. See RESENTMENT, WIND, VIOLENCE.

stormy, *adj.* turbulent, tempestuous. See VIOLENCE, WIND.

story, *n.* tale, narrative, yarn; report, account, news article; plot; floor, stage, level. See DESCRIPTION, NEWS, LAYER.

stout, *adj.* stalwart, robust, brawny, firm; doughty, bold, dauntless, resolute, stouthearted; determined, stubborn; stocky,

thickset, portly. See COURAGE, SIZE, ROTUNDITY, STRENGTH. *Ant.*, slim, timid, weak.

stove, *n.* oven, range[tte], cookstove, cooker; heater, furnace; kiln, etna, hot plate, rotisserie. See HEAT.

stow, *v.t.* put away, conceal, stash, STORE; fill, cram, park; chuck, can, junk; *slang,* stop, leave off. See LOCATION, CONCEALMENT.

straddle, *v.t.* bestride, bestraddle; equivocate; be neutral, sit on the fence. See SUPPORT.

strafe, *v.* ATTACK, fusillade, pepper, riddle; castigate, assail, chasten, chastise. See DISAPPROBATION.

straggle, *v.* drag, dawdle, bring up the rear, trail, drag one's feet; disperse; meander, wander, rove, stray. See SLOWNESS, DEVIATION.

straight, *adj.* unbent (see STRAIGHTNESS); upright, honorable; honest, straightforward; regular, undiluted, unmodified; consecutive, seriatim; proper, correct; *informal,* heterosexual. See PROBITY, PURITY, SEQUENCE, SEX. *Ant.,* curved, crooked, dishonest; gay, lesbian, bisexual. —*adv.* at once, directly. See INSTANTANEITY.

STRAIGHTNESS
Absence of bending

Nouns—1, straightness, directness (see *adjectives*); rectilinearity, alignment, truing; straight, direct, *or* right line, straight angle; beeline, short cut; inflexibility, stiffness (see INELASTICITY); verticality, perpendicularity (see VERTICAL).

2, straightedge, ruler, yardstick; T square, carpenter's square; straightaway; chalk line; straightener, hot comb.

Verbs—be straight, not turn, not bend, *etc.*; go straight, steer for, aim for, head for (see DIRECTION); sit up, straighten, rectify, set straight; line, align, true, level; unbend, uncurl, unravel, unfold, unwrap.

Adjectives—straight, rectilinear, rectilineal; direct, even, right, true, near, short; linear, in a line, straightaway, straightforward, straight as an arrow *or* a die, point-blank; unbent, invariable, inflexible, unbroken; VERTICAL, perpendicular.

Adverbs—straight[way], straightforward[s], in line, in a straight line, as the crow flies; continuously, through; correctly, rightly, bluntly, point-blank; upright.

Quotations—Out of the crooked timber of humanity no straight thing ever can be made (*Immanuel Kant*).

Antonyms, see CURVATURE.

---

strain, *v.t.* stretch, make taut; strive, exert; sprain; overtax, overstretch; filter, percolate. See CLEANNESS, EGRESS, EXAGGERATION. —*n.* effort, EXERTION; pressure; line of descent, stock, ANCESTRY; streak, trace; sprain; section, passage (see MUSIC, POETRY).

strainer, *n.* sieve, sifter, colander, screen, filter, percolator; cheesecloth, tamis, riddle. See PURITY, CLEANNESS.

strait, *n.* straits, narrows; DIFFICULTY. See NARROWNESS.

straitlaced, *adj.* severe, stern, dour, stiff; proper, formal, self-righteous; prim, prudish, fastidious; strict, puritanical. *Informal,* bluenosed. See SEVERITY. *Ant.,* relaxed, liberal.

strand, *n.* thread, string, fiber, rope, FILAMENT. See LAND.

stranded, *adj.* aground, stuck, left high and dry, grounded; embarrassed, penniless. See STABILITY, DIFFICULTY.

strange, *adj.* unusual, odd, unfamiliar; queer, fantastic; alien, foreign, extraneous, outlandish, exotic; eccentric, mysterious. See UNCONFORMITY. *Ant.,* normal, usual, common.

stranger, *n.* newcomer, foreigner, alien, outsider. See EXTRINSIC.

strangle, *v.t.* choke, garrotte, stifle, suffocate; suppress, repress; squeeze, constrict, strangulate. See KILLING, CLOSURE.

strap, *n.* band, bond, strip, tape, tether; strop, thong, rope; rein; cinch, girdle. —*v.t.* secure, tether, fasten, tie, support, lash; thrash, flagellate; strop, hone. See FILAMENT, CONNECTION, PUNISHMENT.

strapping, *adj.* robust, sturdy. See STRENGTH.

stratagem, *n.* trick, subterfuge, artifice, ploy, ruse, guile, wile. See DECEPTION, CUNNING.

strategy, *n.* generalship, maneuvering, CONDUCT, warcraft, artifice. See WARFARE, METHOD, PLAN.

stratum, *n.* LAYER, bed; lamella; social status, CLASS.

stray, *v.i.* wander, straggle, roam, rove, ramble; digress; deviate, err. See DEVIATION, ERROR.

streak, *n.* band, stripe, smear; vein, layer; disposition; run; trait, idiosyncrasy. See NARROWNESS, INTRINSIC, VELOCITY, INDICATION, LENGTH.

stream, *n.* river, streamlet, rivulet, rill; gush; trickle; creek, brook, runnel, runlet; current, flow, flux, course, flood, tide, race; shower, outpouring, downpouring. —*v.i.* issue; pour out, forth, *or* down; flow, run, rush; shed; blow, extent, run across *or* along; drift, tend;

jet, spurt, gush. See WATER, MOTION, WIND, LIGHT, PASSAGE.

streamer, *n.* pennant, banner, bunting; banner headline. See INDICATION.

streamlined, *adj.* efficient, simplified; smooth, fast, speedy; trim, tapering; up-to-date, modernized. See NEWNESS, SIMPLENESS.

street, *n.* thoroughfare, avenue, boulevard, alley; roadway. See PASSAGE.

streetcar, *n.* tram[car], tramway, trolley, street railway. See TRANSPORTATION, VEHICLE.

street person, *n. informal,* homeless person, bag lady *or* man; vagrant, beggar. See POVERTY, DISPLACEMENT.

streetwalker, *n.* prostitute (see IMPURITY).

streetwise, *adj., informal,* savvy, experienced. See KNOWLEDGE.

strength, *n.* POWER, vigor (see STRENGTH); potency, efficacy; HARDNESS, resistance; strength of purpose, RESOLUTION, TENACITY, COURAGE.

STRENGTH
Power of exertion

Nouns—**1,** strength, POWER, ENERGY, VIGOR; might, main [force], physical *or* brute force, manpower, horsepower; spring, ELASTICITY, tone, tonicity, tension; stamina; brawn, muscle, muscularity, sinew, gristle, thews and sinews, pith[iness], physique; HEALTH, virility, vitality. *Slang,* beef, grit. See REFRESHMENT, RESTORATION.

2, strong man *or* woman, tower of strength, powerhouse; athlete, gymnast, acrobat, equilibrist; Atlas, Hercules, Antaeus, Samson, Cyclops, Goliath; amazon; horse, ox; oak, rock; iron, steel, nails; iron grip, grit, bone, horn; feats of strength, athletics, athleticism, gymnastics, calisthenics. *Informal,* he-man, muscleman.

Verbs—strengthen, fortify, harden, case-harden, steel, toughen, indurate, roborate, brace, nerve, gird, train; set on one's legs, gird up one's loins; build (up), reinforce, restore, consolidate; confirm, corroborate (see DEMONSTRATION); invigorate, vitalize, stimulate, enliven, energize, animate, encourage, lift, reman; enhance, heighten, brighten, intensify; regain strength, rally, grow, wax (see INCREASE). *Informal,* beef up. *Slang,* give a shot in the arm, pep up.

Adjectives—**1,** strong, powerful; robust, stout, stalwart, strapping, hardy, burly, husky, leathery, brawny, thewy, sturdy, sinewy, virile, muscular, wiry, limber, hale, hearty, healthy, vibrant; hard as nails, hard-fisted; athletic, gymnastic, able-bodied, broad-shouldered, well-built, -knit, *or* -developed, strong as a lion, horse, *or* ox; titanic, gigantic, Herculean; mettlesome, in fine feather *or* fettle. *Slang,* beefy.

2, strengthening, refreshing, bracing, tonic, roborant.

3, irresistible, invincible, impregnable, unconquerable, indomitable, more than a match for, heavy-duty; proof; airtight, waterproof, *etc.*; foolproof, fail-safe.

Adverbs—by [main] force, by main strength, with might and main.

Phrases—a reed before the wind lives on, while mighty oaks do fall; when the going gets tough, the tough get going.

Quotations—The gods are on the side of the stronger (*Tacitus*), The strongest man in the world is the man who stands most alone (*Henrik Ibsen*), The weak are strong because they are reckless. The strong are weak because they have scruples (*Otto von Bismarck*), I am strong as a bull moose and you can use me to the limit (*Theodore Roosevelt*).

Antonyms, see WEAKNESS.

---

strenuous, *adj.* vigorous, energetic, dynamic; arduous, exhausting, straining, laborious. See EXERTION. *Ant.,* easy, unstrenuous.

stress, *n.* pressure, strain, compulsion; emphasis, urgency, IMPORTANCE; accent. See NECESSITY.

stretch, *v.* extend, lengthen, spread, expand, INCREASE; stretch out, sprawl; *informal,* exaggerate, strain, force. —*n.* EXPANSION, reach, range; LENGTH, field, expanse; ELASTICITY; long run, distance, home- *or* backstretch; overstatement, EXAGGERATION; *slang,* sentence, hitch. See EXERTION, PUNISHMENT.

stretcher, *n.* litter, carrier; frame, brace. See SUPPORT, TRANSPORTATION.

strew, *v.* scatter, disperse, disseminate; throw to the winds. See DISPERSION.

stricken, *adj.* hurt, ill, disabled; knocked out, afflicted, beset. See PAIN.

strict, *adj.* exact, precise; rigid; accurate, meticulous, scrupulous, punctilious, conscientious, nice; stringent, exacting; straitlaced, puritanical. See TRUTH, SEVERITY. *Ant.*, lenient.

stricture, *n.* censure, criticism, blame, reprehension, restraint; compression, constriction, contraction. See DISAPPROBATION, DISTANCE, HINDRANCE.

stride, *n.* step, pace; progress, improvement. —*v.* walk, march, step; straddle. See TRAVEL, MOTION.

stridency, *n.* stridulation; shrillness, harshness; DISCORD, dissonance, LOUDNESS, roughness, sharpness; noise, noisiness, raucousness, cacophony; clangor, clamor.

strife, *n.* CONTENTION, emulation, rivalry; altercation; dissension, discord, dispute, quarrel; war, warfare; struggle, conflict. *Ant.*, peace, calm.

strike, *v.* hit, smite, beat, thump; give, deliver, deal; affect, TOUCH, impress, occur to; blast; lower, take down; collide, bump; conclude, agree upon; ATTACK; collide; walk out, quit, rebel, cancel; print. See IMPULSE, EXCITEMENT, AGENCY, RESISTANCE, SUCCESS, NULLIFICATION.

strikebreaker, *n.* scab, fink, rat (*all inf.*). See DISOBEDIENCE.

striking, *adj.* impressive, remarkable; attractive; dramatic. See WONDER, EXCITEMENT.

string, *n.* twine, thread, cord; catgut; series, row, line, chain; set, stud of horse. See FILAMENT, CONTINUITY, MUSIC, LENGTH.

stringent, *adj.* severe, strict, stern. See COMPULSION, SEVERITY.

strip, *v.* divest, denude, decorticate, peel, skin, pull off; dismantle; plunder, fleece; dispossess, deprive; disrobe, undress; cut in strips. See STEALING, DIVESTMENT. —*n.* hue, stripe, bend, fillet, shred; lath, ribbon; *slang,* comic [strip]. See FILAMENT, NARROWNESS, WIT.

stripe, *n.* line, band, streak, belt, hash mark; CLASS, ilk. See LENGTH, VARIEGATION.

stripling, *n.* lad, boy, teenager, YOUTH.

strive, *v.i.* endeavor, strain, ESSAY; struggle, contend; quarrel. See CONTENTION, EXERTION.

stroke, *n.* blow, impact, beat, throb, pulsation, bolt, blast, coup; seizure, apoplexy, shock; feat, exploit, coup; mark, flourish; caress. See DISEASE, TOUCH, ENDEARMENT.

stroll, *n.* ramble, saunter, promenade, walk, constitutional (*inf.*). See TRAVEL, SLOWNESS.

strong, *adj.* powerful (see STRENGTH); strong-smelling, pungent, piquant, *etc.* (see ODOR); intense, concentrated, brilliant, bright, vivid, dazzling, *etc.*; alcoholic, spirituous, hard, bodied, heady, proof (see DRINKING). *Ant.*, weak.

strong-arm, *v.t.* coerce, force, muscle (*inf.*). See COMPULSION.

strongbox, *n.* chest, coffer, safe. See RECEPTACLE.

stronghold, *n.* refuge; fort[ress], citadel; blockhouse; fastness, bulwark. See DEFENSE, PRISON.

structure, *n.* BUILDING, edifice, construction, fabrication; framework, makeup, arrangement, COMPOSITION, anatomy, constitution. See FORM, ARCHITECTURE.

struggle, *v.i.* strive, strain, endeavor, contend, labor; flounder, writhe, squirm; fight, battle. —*n.* endeavor, effort, CONTENTION, essay; fight, conflict, warfare. See EXERTION.

strut, *v.* swagger; stalk, peacock. See VANITY, OSTENTATION, TRAVEL.

stub, *n.* stump, end, stubble; receipt, record; butt. See SHORTNESS, RECEIVING, REMAINDER. —*v.t.* bump, hit, strike. See IMPULSE.

stubble, *n.* stumps, stalks, stubs, remnants; beard, bristles. See REMAINDER, ROUGHNESS, HAIR.

stubborn, *adj.* perverse, obstinate; dogged, persistent; intractable, unyielding; tough. See OBSTINACY, HARDNESS. *Ant.*, cooperative, tractable.

stubby, *adj.* thickset; bristly. See SHORTNESS, ROUGHNESS.

stuck-up, *adj.* vain, conceited, aloof, snooty. See VANITY. *Ant.*, modest.

stud, *n.* boss, knob, projection, jewel; timber, SUPPORT; studhorse, breeder; *slang*, hunk (*inf.*) (see SEX). —*v.t.* bestud, ORNAMENT, bejewel, spangle; dot, scatter. See DISPERSION, REPRODUCTION, CONVEXITY.

student, *n.* learner, pupil, apprentice, schoolboy *or* -girl; scholar, schoolman *or* -woman, pedant. See SCHOOL, LEARNING.

studied, *adj.* deliberate, careful. See CARE, INTENTION.

studio, *n.* atelier, salon, workshop; study; station. See BUSINESS.

studious, *adj.* scholarly, thoughtful, speculative, contemplative, bookish. See THOUGHT, LEARNING.

study, *n.* meditation, research, examination, investigation; library, atelier, den; PLAN; sketch, cartoon; étude. —*v.* investigate, weigh, consider, examine; scrutinize; con; memorize; ponder; hit the books (*inf.*), grind (*inf.*). See THOUGHT, INQUIRY, ATTENTION, REPRESENTATION, LEARNING, PAINTING.

stuff, *v.* cram, pack, jam, fill; pad, wad; plug, block; gormandize, gorge, overeat. See GLUTTONY, EXPANSION. —*n.* fabric, cloth, material; nonsense; SUBSTANCE; rubbish. —the stuff, *slang*, the goods, the ability.

stuffing, *n.* dressing, filling, forcemeat, farce; contents. See COMPOSITION.

stuffy, *adj.* ill-ventilated, close, stifling, airless; sultry, oppressive, musty; dull, stiff, stodgy. See DENSITY, HEAT, PERMANENCE.

stumble, *v.i.* trip, stub one's toe; hobble, stagger, lumber; blunder, flounder, stammer; err, slip, backslide. See DESCENT, AGITATION, ERROR, STAMMERING. —stumbling block, *n.* obstacle, HINDRANCE.

stump, *n.* stub, butt, snag, remnant, fag end; rostrum, pulpit; hobble, heavy tread. See REMAINDER, SHORTNESS. —*v.* confound, puzzle, nonplus; *informal*, electioneer. See DOUBT.

stun, *v.t.* benumb, deaden, daze, stupefy; dizzy; dumbfound, astound, astonish, bewilder. See INSENSIBILITY, SURPRISE.

stunning, *adj., informal*, striking, lovely. See BEAUTY.

stunt, *v.* dwarf; cramp, retard, check; perform feats, do tricks, grandstand. See SHORTNESS, CONTRACTION. —*n.* trick, feat, daredevil[t]ry, tour de force. See ACTION.

stupefy, *v.t.* deaden, dull, numb, narcotize; stun, astound, daze, dumbfound. See INSENSIBILITY, SURPRISE.

stupendous, *adj.* prodigious, enormous, astounding, amazing, wonderful, immense, vast, colossal, overwhelming. See WONDER.

stupid, *adj.* slow-witted, dull, obtuse; benumbed, bemused; absurd, inane; banal, tiresome, tedious, dull. See IGNORANCE, CREDULITY, FOLLY. *Ant.*, smart, witty.

stupor, *n.* lethargy, torpor, apathy, coma, daze. See INSENSIBILITY, WONDER.

sturdy, *adj.* stalwart, hardy, husky, robust; durable, long-wearing; firm; stubborn, unyielding. See STRENGTH. *Ant.*, weak.

stutter, *v.i.* See STAMMERING.

sty, *n.* pigpen, pigsty; pen; hovel, shed; stable. See ENCLOSURE, UNCLEANNESS, ABODE.

style, *n.* form, manner, METHOD, way; FASHION; smartness, vogue, mode, chic; craze, fad, rage, last word; practice, habit, [characteristic] behavior, air; diction, phraseology, wording, rhetoric; distinction, ELEGANCE. See GRAMMAR.

stymie, *v.* hinder, obstruct, impede; thwart, frustrate, puzzle, perplex, put at a loss, baffle, throw (*inf.*), floor (*inf.*). See HINDRANCE.

suave, *n.* urbane, bland, courteous, gracious; oily, smooth, ingratiating. See COURTESY, FASHION. *Ant.*, unsophisticated, awkward.

subconscious, *adj.* subliminal, nonconscious, unconscious, automatic. —*n.* subliminal self, id, unconscious. See INTELLECT. *Ant.*, conscious.

subdue, *v.t.* tame, overcome, master; vanquish, conquer; repress; restrain; soften, tone down. See MODERATION.

subject, *n.* topic, theme; matter; liege, vassal, citizen. See GRAMMAR, THOUGHT, SERVANT, TEACHING. —*v.t.* reduce, control, restrain, tame; treat, expose. See SUBJECTION, THOUGHT. —*adj.* liable, conditioned (upon). See LIABILITY.

SUBJECTION
Position under the power of another

Nouns—1, subjection; dependence, dependency; subordination; thrall, thraldom, enthralment, subjugation, oppression, bondage, serfdom; feudalism, vassalage, villeinage; slavery, enslavement, servitude; constraint, yoke, RESTRAINT; OBEDIENCE. See SUCCESS, SUBMISSION.

2, subject, citizen; serf, slave (see SERVANT); client state.

Verbs—1, be subject, be at the mercy of; depend, lean, *or* hang upon; fall a prey to, fall under, not dare to call one's soul one's own; drag a chain; serve (see SERVANT); obey, comply, submit.

2, subject, subjugate, hold down, bring to terms, break in, tame; master; tread down, tread under foot; enthrall, enslave, take captive; take into custody; rule (see AUTHORITY); drive into a corner, hold at sword's point; keep under; hold in bondage; tie to one's apron strings.

Adjectives—subject, dependent, subordinate; feudal, feudatory, in harness; subjected, enslaved, constrained, downtrodden, under the lash, led by the nose; henpecked; the puppet *or* plaything of; under orders *or* command; under one's thumb; a slave to; in the toils; in the power, hands, *or* clutches of, at the mercy of; over a barrel; at the feet of; at one's beck and call (see OBEDIENCE). *Slang,* pussy-whipped.

Quotations—Where slavery is, there liberty cannot be; and where liberty is, there slavery cannot be (*Charles Sumner*). Better to die than to live in slavery (*Emmeline Pankhurst*), All socialism involves slavery (*Herbert Spencer*).

Antonyms, see FREEDOM, LIBERATION.

---

subjective, *adj.* nonobjective; personal, individual, selfish; introspective, introverted. See INTRINSIC.

sub judice, *Lat.,* before the court; under consideration. See LAWSUIT.

subjugate, *v.t.* conquer, vanquish, master, subdue; overthrow; enslave. See SUBJECTION.

sublimate, *v.t.* elevate, exalt; vaporize; divert, channel, transform, convert. See GREATNESS, PURITY, LEVITY.

sublime, *adj.* inspiring, impressive; noble, lofty, exalted, elevated; superb, magnificent, glorious. See BEAUTY, GREATNESS, PLEASURE. *Ant.,* common, lowly.

submarine, *adj.* suboceanic, undersea *or* -water. —*n.* torpedo boat; U-boat, submersible, sub (*inf.*), pigboat (*sl.*). See DEPTH, SHIP.

submerge, *v.* drown, sink, plunge, dive, submerse, immerse, engulf, inundate; be overshadowed, subordinate to, play second fiddle to. See WATER, DEPTH, INFERIORITY.

SUBMISSION
Yielding

Nouns—1, submission, submissiveness, OBEDIENCE, RESIGNATION, patience, HUMILITY, self-abasement, compliance, pliancy, docility, passivity, acquiescence, sufferance, conformity, SUBJECTION; capitulation, surrender, cession, yielding. See INEXCITABILITY, SERVILITY.

2, obeisance, homage, kneeling, curtsy, kowtow, salaam; white flag.

Verbs—1, submit, succumb, yield, comply, acquiesce, accede, resign, bend, stoop, obey, defer to, be subject, be submissive.

2, capitulate, surrender, cede, come to terms, retreat, lay down *or* deliver up one's arms, lower, haul down *or* strike one's flag *or* colors; show the white flag; give up *or* in, give up the ship, give way, lie down, give ground, cave in, bend before the storm; throw up one's hands; knuckle down *or* under. *Informal,* throw in the towel *or* sponge. *Slang,* say uncle.

3, be submissive, eat dirt, humble pie, *or* crow; bite *or* lick the dust; throw oneself at the feet of, be *or* fall at one's feet, swallow the pill, kiss the rod, turn the other cheek;

crouch before, kneel to, bow to, pay homage to, cringe to; truckle to, bend the neck *or* knee; kneel, fall on one's knees, curtsy, kowtow, salaam, make an obeisance, bow submission, bow and scrape; lick one's boots. *Slang,* eat one's dust, take it [lying down].
4, endure, tolerate, put up with, bear with, be reconciled to, resign oneself, swallow the insult, pocket the affront, grin and bear it, submit with a good grace.

Adjectives—submissive, subdued, yielding, unresisting, tractable, compliant, dutiful, long-suffering, patient, passive, acquiescent, unassertive, manageable, governable, docile, agreeable; obsequious, slavish, servile, fawning, deferential, defeatist, self-abasing, lowly; prostrate, crouching, downtrodden, on bended knee, down on one's legs.

Quotations—A woman dictates before marriage in order that she may have an appetite for submission afterwards (*George Eliot*).

Antonyms, see DEFIANCE, RESISTANCE.

---

submit, *v.* yield (see SUBMISSION); propose, state; refer. See SUPPOSITION, OFFER.

subnormal, *adj.* below average *or* par, substandard; abnormal. See INFERIORITY, UNCONFORMITY. *Ant.,* normal, standard.

subordinate, *adj.* lower, inferior, secondary; dependent, subservient. See INFERIORITY, UNIMPORTANCE, SUBJECTION.

suborn, *v.t.* bribe, induce (see CAUSE, PAYMENT).

subpoena, *n.* summons, writ, order, monition, citation. See COMMAND.

sub rosa, Lat., secretly. See SECRET, CONCEALMENT.

subscribe, *v.* sign, endorse, contribute; ASSENT, AID, abet, back, patronize; undertake, contract.

subsequent, *adj.* succeeding, following, sequent, later, ensuing, consequent. See SEQUENCE.

subservient, *adj.* servile, submissive, obsequious, cringing, abject; subordinate, contributory, instrumental, subsidiary. See SERVILITY, INSTRUMENTALITY. *Ant.,* controlling, in charge.

subside, *v.i.* sink, fall, ebb, lower; abate, lessen; settle, precipitate. See DESCENT, DECREASE.

subsidiary, *adj.* branch, incidental; helpful; supplementary; secondary. See PART, AID, AUXILIARY.

subsidize, *v.t.* AID, support, promote; patronize, finance, underwrite, back, pay for, subscribe to; endow, invest in; encourage. See PROVISION.

subsist, *v.i.* exist, live, be, continue, survive, abide; eke out a living. See EXISTENCE, PERMANENCE, SUBSTANCE.

subsistence, *n.* EXISTENCE, being, continuance; maintenance, livelihood, sustenance. See FOOD.

substance, *n.* material (see SUBSTANCE); subject [matter], MEANING, gist; wealth (see MONEY).

SUBSTANCE
Material existence

Nouns—**1,** substance, matter; corpus, frame, protoplasm, principle; person, thing, object, article; incarnation, embodiment, avatar; something, a being, an existence, entity; creature, body, stuff, clay. See HUMANITY, TEXTURE.

2, *(material nature)* substantiality, materiality, materialness, essence, reality, corporeality; tangibility; flesh and blood.

3, *(study of material existence)* physics, physical science, quantum mechanics; somatology, somatics; materialism; materialist, physicist.

Verbs—embody, incorporate, incarnate, actualize, materialize, subsist, be; substantiate.

Adjectives—substantive, substantial; concrete, sound, solid; personal; bodily, tangible, corporeal, real, material; appreciable.

Adverbs—substantially, bodily, essentially, *etc.*; on solid ground; in the flesh.

Quotations—Anybody who is not shocked by this subject [quantum mechanics] has failed to understand it (*Niels Bohr*).

Antonyms, see INSUBSTANTIALITY.

substandard, *adj.* below par *or* average, not up to snuff. See INFERIORITY. *Ant.,* standard, above average.

substantiate, *v.t.* embody (see SUBSTANCE);

evidence, CORROBORATE, verify, bear out, demonstrate, confirm, support. See DEMONSTRATION, TRUTH.

SUBSTITUTION
Serving in place of another

Nouns—1, substitution, commutation; supplanting, supersedure, supersession, replacement; metonymy (see FIGURATIVE); INTERCHANGE; TRANSFER.

2, *(substitute object or action)* makeshift, pis aller, stopgap, expedient, jury mast, locum tenens; palimpsest; quid pro quo, alternative; backup; [make]shift, apology *or* excuse for.

3, *(substitute person)* substitute, understudy, replacement, delegate, deputy, AGENT; surrogate, alternate, representative; viceroy, viceregent, vicegerent; dummy, scapegoat, whipping boy; double; changeling; supplanter; alternate; backup, understudy, cover, stand-in, pinch-hitter, bench-warmer, ghost writer. *Informal,* sub. *Slang,* patsy, ringer, fall guy, goat.

Verbs—1, substitute, put in the place of, change for; deputize; make way for, give place *or* way to. *Informal,* let George do it.

2, substitute *or* be deputy for; represent; stand for, appear *or* answer for; fill, step into, *or* stand in the shoes of, fill in for, do duty for; take the place of, supplant, supersede, replace, cut out; rob Peter to pay Paul; baby-sit, house-sit. *Informal,* pinch-hit. *Slang,* cover up for; be the goat; ghostwrite.

Adjectives—substitutive, substituted, vicarious, temporary, deputy, acting; vice, viceregal; jury (*naut.*).

Adverbs—instead; in the place of, on behalf of, in lieu of, in the stead of, in one's shoes *or* boots, in loco parentis; faute de mieux, by proxy; for want of something better.

Quotations—In war there is no substitute for victory (*General Douglas MacArthur*), There is no substitute for hard work (*Thomas Alva Edison*), Books are good enough in their own way, but they are a mighty bloodless substitute for life (*Robert Louis Stevenson*), Democracy substitutes election by the incompetent many for appointment by the corrupt few (*G. B. Shaw*), Faith in a holy cause is to a considerable extent a substitute for the lost faith in ourselves (*Eric Hoffer*), The work of science is to substitute facts for appearances, and demonstration for impressions (*John Ruskin*).

Antonyms, see IDENTITY.

---

subterfuge, *n.* ruse, shift, pretext, artifice, device, stratagem, CUNNING; evasion. See AVOIDANCE.

subterranean, *adj.* underground; infernal, Stygian, nether; hidden. See DEPTH.

subtext, *n.* MEANING. See SECRET.

subtle, *adj.* sly, artful, crafty, wily, CUNNING; discerning, acute, penetrating; elusive, unobvious, abstruse, delicate; dainty, fragile, rarefied, ethereal, unsubstantial. See INTELLIGENCE, RARITY. *Ant.,* blatant, obvious.

subtract, *v.* deduct, take away; remove, detract. See DEDUCTION.

suburban, *adj.* out-of-town, rural, provincial. See ABODE, REGION.

suburbs, *n.* suburbia, outskirts, environs, purlieus. See NEARNESS, ABODE, ENVIRONMENT.

subversion, *n.* overthrow, defeat, disruption, disorder, mutiny, rebellion. See REVOLUTION.

subvert, *v.i.* overthrow, overturn, upset; ruin, fell, raze. See DESTRUCTION.

subway, *n.* underground, subrailway, Métropolitain, tube, Métro (*inf.*); underpass. See VEHICLE.

succeed, *v.* follow, come after; displace, supplant; thrive (see SUCCESS). See SEQUENCE. *Ant.,* fail, precede.

SUCCESS
Favorable termination

Nouns—1, success, successfulness; good fortune, luck, run of luck; PROSPERITY; accomplishment (see COMPLETION); one's finest hour.

2, *(financial success)* great success, land-office business; hit, stroke [of luck], breakthrough, windfall; [lucky] strike; master stroke, coup de maître; all-time high; checkmate; half the battle, prize; trump card. *Informal,* smash [hit]; sleeper, dark horse; fast track; cash cow.

3, *(other success)* victory, triumph, advantage; landslide, runaway, sweep; upper *or* whip hand; ascendance, ascendancy, SUPERIORITY; expugnation, conquest, subjugation, SUBJECTION.

4, winner, champion; conqueror, conquistador, victor; master of the situation, king of the mountain. *Slang,* boss player, roller.

Verbs—1, succeed; be successful, gain one's end *or* ends, make the grade; crown with success; gain, carry, *or* win a point; manage to, contrive to; accomplish, effect (see COMPLETION); do *or* work wonders; score a success, make one's mark, win one's laurels *or* spurs, get to first base; deliver the goods. *Informal,* pan out, click, make a go of, cut the mustard, pull off, come off, go over, make out, bring home the bacon. *Slang,* set the world on fire, get on like a house on fire, hack it, go great guns.

2, *(succeed financially)* make progress, advance, get ahead, go places, go to town; win, make, *or* find one's way; prosper (see PROSPERITY); reap the fruits *or* benefit of; reap *or* gather the harvest; make one's fortune, turn to good account. *Informal,* hit one's stride, do a land-office business, cook on the front burner. *Slang,* sell like hotcakes; wow them, knock 'em dead.

3, *(succeed in contest)* win, prevail, triumph, be triumphant; gain *or* obtain a victory *or* advantage; master; get *or* have the best *or* better of; get *or* have the upper hand, ascendancy, *or* whip hand; distance, surpass (see SUPERIORITY); come off well, rise to the occasion, come off with flying colors; make short work of; take *or* carry by storm; win out; win one's spurs; win the battle; win *or* carry the day, win *or* gain the prize *or* palm; have the best of it, have it all one's own way, call the turn, set the pace, have the world at one's feet; carry all before one, remain in possession of the field; bear *or* carry off the palm. *Informal,* come through. *Slang,* win in a walk; romp home; score standing up, walk off with, bat a thousand.

4, *(overcome an opponent)* defeat, conquer, vanquish, discomfit; overcome, overthrow, overpower, overmaster, overmatch, overset, override, overreach; outwit, outdo, outflank, outmaneuver, outgeneral, outvote; take the wind out of one's sails; beat, rout, lick, drub, floor, best, worst, dispose of; put down, put to flight *or* rout, run into the ground, pin one's ears back; shout down; bring to terms (see SUBMISSION); edge out; snow under. *Informal,* nose out, polish off. *Slang,* whip, trash, beat all hollow, clobber, mop the floor with, ace out.

5, *(overcome a problem)* surmount *or* overcome a difficulty *or* obstacle; make headway against; stem the torrent, tide, *or* current; weather the storm; turn a corner, keep one's head above water, tide over.

6, *(succeed in solving a problem)* answer [the purpose], avail, take effect, do, turn out well, work well, take, tell, bear fruit; hit the mark, hit the nail on the head; turn up trumps, make a hit; find one's account in. *Informal,* do *or* turn the trick, bring down the house, kill two birds with one stone. *Slang,* take the cake.

Adjectives—succeeding, successful, fortunate; prosperous (see PROSPERITY); triumphant; flushed *or* crowned with success, at the top of the tree, on the crest of the wave; victorious; set up, in the ascendant; unbeaten; felicitous, effective. *Informal,* in like Flynn. *Slang,* like a mojo, cooking [with gas], on a roll.

Adverbs—successfully, with flying colors, in triumph, swimmingly.

Phrases—he that will thrive must first ask his wife; nothing succeeds like success; the only place where success comes before work is in a dictionary; a rising tide lifts all boats; if you can't beat 'em, join 'em; win a few, lose a few.

Quotations—The desire accomplished is sweet to the soul (*Bible*), I shall be like that tree, I shall die at the top (*Jonathan Swift*), I have climbed to the top of the greasy pole (*Benjamin Disraeli*), Success is a science; if you have the conditions, you get the result (*Oscar Wilde*), All you need in this life is ignorance and confidence; then success is sure (*Mark Twain*), Success is relative: it is what we can make of the mess we have made of things (*T. S. Eliot*), If A is a success in life, then A equals X plus Y plus Z. Work is X; Y is play; and Z is keeping your mouth shut (*Albert Einstein*), Whenever a friend succeeds, a little something in me dies (*Gore Vidal*), In war there is no substitute for victory (*General Douglas MacArthur*), All's well that ends well (*Shakespeare*).

Antonyms, see FAILURE.

---

succession, *n.* series; SEQUENCE, progression; heirship, inheritance, heritage, primogeniture, REVERSION; lineage, family. See POSTERITY.

successor, *n.* follower; heir[ess]; replacement. See SEQUENCE. *Ant.*, predecessor.

succinct, *adj.* terse, concise, brief, crisp, laconic, meaty, pithy, sententious. See SHORTNESS.

succor, *v.t.* help, AID, assist, serve, comfort.

succulent, *adj.* juicy, succulous, fleshy, tender; savory, tasty, toothsome; wet, watery, moist; interesting, spicy, piquant. See TASTE, FLUIDITY.

succumb, *v.* give in, yield, submit, surrender, assent; die, expire, give up the ghost. See WEAKNESS, SUBMISSION, FAILURE, DEATH.

such, *adj.* like, suchlike, similar, of the same kind; such and such, aforementioned; such a, some, one who. —*adv.*, *informal,* so, thus, that; very; such as, like, resembling. See SIMILARITY.

suck, *v.* draw, extract, absorb, pull in, sponge up; pump; nurse, suckle; drain, leech, bleed, extort; suck in, seduce, lure; inhale. See EXTRACTION, RECEIVING.

sucker, *n.*, *informal,* lollipop, all-day sucker, sourball; *slang,* dupe, gull, pushover, [easy] mark, soft touch. See CREDULITY, SWEETNESS.

suckle, *v.* give suck, nurse, nurture; wet-nurse, breast-feed. See FOOD.

suction, *n.* inhalation, EXTRACTION; absorption, siphonage, capillarity.

sudden, *adj.* abrupt, unexpected; hasty, quick, unpremeditated; instantaneous; precipitate; hot-tempered, rash. See SURPRISE, INSTANTANEITY. *Ant.*, expected, considered.

suds, *n.* lather, foam, bubbles, froth, spume. See AGITATION.

sue, *v.* prosecute, bring suit, petition; beg, solicit, REQUEST; court, WOO. See LAWSUIT, ENDEARMENT.

suffer, *v.t.* endure, encounter, undergo, experience, sustain; allow, permit, tolerate. See FEELING, PERMISSION. —*v.i.* endure pain, be troubled, ache; ail, be ill. See PAIN, DISEASE.

SUFFICIENCY
Adequacy

Nouns—**1,** sufficiency, adequacy, enough, satisfaction, competence, *basta*; MEDIOCRITY; fill, fullness, completeness; plenitude, plenty; critical mass.

2, abundance, copiousness; amplitude, profusion, prodigality; full measure; luxuriance, affluence (see PROSPERITY); quorum; outpouring; flood. *Informal,* lots, oodles, rafts, God's amount. *Slang,* scads, loads.

3, *(oversupply)* satiety, satiation, saturation, repletion, glut, excess, surfeit, superfluity (see REMAINDER); feast, deluge, overkill; too much of a good thing, a drug on the market, *embarras de richesses.*

Verbs—**1,** suffice, do, just do, satisfy, pass muster, make the grade; make ends meet, have enough to go around, make do, get by, manage, get along; eat, drink, *or* have one's fill, sate, be satiated, have enough; fill, charge, load, saturate, replenish, piece *or* eke out. *Informal,* gas up.

2, run over, burst at the seams; roll, wallow, *or* swim in; abound, exuberate, teem, flow, stream, rain, shower down; pour [in]; swarm, bristle with; cloy; run into the ground; gild the lily.

Adjectives—1, sufficient, enough, adequate, up to the mark, commensurate, competent, satisfactory, full, complete; ample, plenty, plentiful, plenteous; copious, abundant, abounding, replete, enough and to spare, flush; chock-full, well-stocked, well-provided; liberal; unstinted, unstinting; stintless; without stint; all kinds of; unsparing, unmeasured, lavish, wholesale; rich; luxuriant; affluent, wealthy; big with, pregnant.

2, satiated, sated, gorged; blasé, jaded; sick (of), fed up; de trop.

Adverbs—sufficiently, amply, full, galore, in abundance, in full measure; to one's heart's content; ad libitum, without stint; enough is enough, enough said; to a fault. *Informal,* enough already.

Phrases—enough is as good as a feast; half a loaf is better than no bread; less is more; it never rains but it pours; man cannot live by bread alone; you can[not] have too much of a good thing.

Quotations—As long as I have a want, I have a reason for living. Satisfaction is death (*G. B. Shaw*), Too much of a good thing can be wonderful (*Mae West*).

Antonyms, see INSUFFICIENCY.

---

suffix, *n.* affix, addition, ending. See ADDITION, END.

suffocate, *n.* smother, stifle, asphyxiate; choke; extinguish; strangle. See KILLING, DEATH.

suffrage, *n.* franchise, right to vote; [the] vote, ballot. See CHOICE, RIGHTNESS.

suffuse, *v.* spread [out], overspread, pervade; permeate, imbue; wash, dye, tinge. See COLOR, MIXTURE.

sugar, *n.* sweetening, sucrose, lactose, glucose, dextrose, maltose, fructose, *etc.* See SWEETNESS. —**sugar daddy,** *informal,* angel, benefactor (see GIVING).

sugarcoat, *v.t.* sweeten, glaze. See SWEETNESS, MODERATION.

suggest, *v.t.* intimate, hint, insinuate; propose, submit; imply, connote; recommend, advise, advocate. See INFORMATION, ADVICE, OFFER.

suggestible, *adj.* malleable, easily influenced (see CREDULITY, INFLUENCE).

suggestive, *adj.* indicative, expressive; thought-provoking, stimulating; remindful, mnemonic; risqué, indecent. See MEANING, SUPPOSITION.

suicide, *n.* self-destruction, self-ruin; felo-de-se, harakiri. See KILLING.

sui generis, Lat., one of a kind; unique. See UNCONFORMITY, SPECIALITY.

suit, *n.* petition, appeal, prayer; courtship, wooing; suite, retinue, train; outfit, set, group, sequence; LAWSUIT, action, litigation. See REQUEST, ENDEARMENT, CLOTHING, CONTINUITY, CLASS. —*v.t.*

satisfy, please; become, befit; fit, adapt. See AGREEMENT.

suitable, *adj.* fitting, appropriate, proper, convenient, apropos, becoming, fit[ted], compatible. See AGREEMENT, EXPEDIENCE. *Ant.,* unsuitable, inapt.

suitcase, *n.* bag, valise, grip; (*pl.*) luggage, baggage. See RECEPTACLE.

suite, *n.* company, train, retinue, following, escort; set, series, group; apartment. See CONTINUITY, RECEPTACLE.

suitor, *n.* lover, wooer, beau, swain, admirer, boyfriend. See LOVE.

sulk, *v.i.* be sullen, pout, mope; grumble, gripe, grouch. See IRASCIBILITY, REJECTION.

sullen, *adj.* sulky; ill-tempered, ill-humored; out of sorts, temper, *or* humor; crusty, crabbed; sour, surly, discourteous; moody; spleenish, splenetic; resentful; cross[-grained]; perverse, wayward, forward; dogged, stubborn; grumpy, glum, grim, morose; scowling, glowering, growling; peevish, irascible. See DISCOURTESY, RESENTMENT. *Ant.,* good-humored, cheerful.

sully, *v.* soil, stain, tarnish, smear; defile, dishonor, blemish, stigmatize. See UNCLEANNESS, DISREPUTE.

sultan, *n.* caliph, imam, khan, emir. See AUTHORITY.

sultry, *adj.* hot, oppressive, sweltering, humid, muggy, stifling, close; voluptuous, sensual, sexy. See HEAT, IMPURITY.

sum, *n.* QUANTITY, amount; total, aggregate, sum total; substance, gist; problem; summary. See WHOLE, MONEY.

summary, *n.* compendium, abridgment,
abstract, brief, epitome, résumé, digest.
—*adj.* prompt, expeditious, speedy,
fast, immediate; brief, concise, compact, condensed. See TRANSIENTNESS,
SHORTNESS, DESCRIPTION, ILLEGALITY.

summer, *n.* summertime, summer tide;
high point, zenith, acme, *etc.* See
CHRONOMETRY.

summit, *n.* top (see HEIGHT); maximum,
climax; culminating, high, crowning, *or*
turning point; tiptop; extremity. See
PERFECTION, SUPERIORITY.

summon, *v.t.* call [for], send for; cite, arraign, subpoena; convoke; rouse, invoke, evoke. See COMMAND, LAWSUIT,
EXTRACTION. —*n.* subpoena, warrant,
writ; call, invitation. See LAWSUIT, RE-
QUEST.

sumptuous, *adj.* lavish, luxurious, splendid, imposing, grand; costly. See OS-
TENTATION.

sun, *n.* daystar, Sol; sunshine, sunlight;
prosperity, happiness; star. See UNIVERSE.

Sunday, *n.* day of rest, Lord's Day, holy
day, Sabbath; day off, holiday. See RE-
POSE, RELIGION.

sunder, *v.t.* break, separate, sever, dissever, divide. See DISJUNCTION, PART.

sundial, *n.* sun-clock, solarium, dial; gnomon, style. See CHRONOMETRY.

sundown, *n.* dusk, nightfall, twilight. See
CHRONOMETRY.

sundry, *adj.* various, divers; several, numerous; (*n. pl.*) notions, knickknacks,
toiletries, cosmetics, *etc.* See MULTITUDE,
SALE.

sunny, *adj.* warm, bright, sunshiny; cheerful, cheery, blithe; prosperous, palmy,

halcyon. See HEAT, CHEERFULNESS.
Ant., cloudy, morose.

sunrise, *n.* dawn, prime, daybreak,
dayspring, aurora, cockcrow, sunup.
See CHRONOMETRY.

sunset, *n.* twilight, sundown, dusk, nightfall, curfew, eventide. See CHRONOME-
TRY.

sunshade, *n.* parasol, umbrella; awning;
sunscreen. See COVERING.

sunstroke, *n.* insolation, heatstroke, prostration; siriasis, heliosis. See DISEASE.

superb, *adj.* magnificent, impressive, stately;
admirable, excellent; costly, rich, gorgeous, sumptuous. See BEAUTY, OSTENTA-
TION.

supercilious, *adj.* disdainful, contemptuous, scornful; arrogant, cavalier. See IN-
SOLENCE, CONTEMPT.

superficial, *adj.* shallow, cursory, dilettante,
slight, slender, trivial, inane; surface,
skin-deep. See EXTERIOR, SHALLOWNESS,
IGNORANCE. *Ant.*, in-depth, serious.

superfluous, *adj.* unnecessary, needless;
excessive, overmuch. See REMAINDER.
Ant., necessary.

superhighway, *n.* interstate [highway], autoroute, divided highway, turnpike. See
PASSAGE.

superhuman, *adj.* sublime, divine; Olympian, Jovian; herculean, preterhuman,
phenomenal, extraordinary. See UN-
CONFORMITY, SUPERIORITY. *Ant.*, human, subhuman, normal.

superimpose, *v.* superpose, stratify, overlay, cover. See COVERING, ADDITION.

superintend, *v.t.* oversee, direct, control;
boss, manage. See AUTHORITY.

superior, *adj.* better (see SUPERIORITY);
higher-ranking; proud. —*n.* higher AU-
THORITY; mother *or* father superior. See
ASCETICISM.

SUPERIORITY
Greater excellence

Nouns—1, superiority; excellence (see GOODNESS); majority, plurality; advantage; preponderance, preponderation; vantage point *or* ground, prevalence, partiality; lead,
gain; NOBILITY. *Informal,* edge, inside track. See INEQUALITY, OVERRUNNING.

2, supremacy, primacy, preeminence, PRECEDENCE; whip *or* upper hand; victory, triumph (see SUCCESS); championship; maximum; climax; catbird seat; culmination,
summit, transcendence, transcendency, prepotence, ne plus ultra; lion's share, excess,
surplus; PERFECTION, sovereignty (see AUTHORITY).

3, cream of the crop, number one; ace; elite; overachiever. *Informal,* first string,
chairman. *Slang,* class act, mammy jammer.

Verbs—excel, exceed, transcend; outdo, better, outbalance, outweigh, outrival; pass, surpass, get ahead of; overtop, override, overpass, overbalance, overweigh, overmatch; top, cap, beat, cut out, steal a march on, upstage; beat hollow; outstrip, eclipse, throw into the shade, run circles around, put one's nose out of joint; have the upper hand, have the whip hand, have the advantage, hold all the trumps; have at one's feet (see SUBMISSION); turn the scale, play first fiddle (see IMPORTANCE); preponderate, predominate, prevail; precede, take precedence, come first; come to a head, culminate; beat all others, bear the palm, break the record. *Informal,* get the drop on, have it [all] over (someone), have an edge on, have the last laugh. *Slang,* pull rank; have something going for one, one-up, kick ass *or* butt.

Adjectives—1, superior, greater, major, higher, premier; exceeding; great, distinguished, ultra; vaulting; more than a match for; supreme, greatest, utmost, paramount, preeminent, foremost, crowning; first-rate, first-class, world-class, top-notch, important, excellent; increased, enlarged; one up. *Informal,* of the first water; ahead of the game. *Slang,* tops, top-drawer, far-out, killer[-diller], out of sight, pukka, something else. 2, superlative, inimitable, incomparable, sovereign, without parallel, ne plus ultra; unrivaled, peerless, matchless; champion, second to none, nonpareil; unparalleled, unequaled, unapproached, unsurpassed; beyond compare *or* comparison; culminating, topmost; transcendent; superhuman.

Adverbs—beyond, more, over; over *or* above the mark; above par, at the top of the scale, on top, at its height; eminently, preeminently, surpassing, prominently, superlatively, supremely, above all, par excellence, [summa] cum laude, exceedingly, principally, especially, particularly, peculiarly, even, yea, still more.

Quotations—If a man write a better book, preach a better sermon, or make a better mousetrap than his neighbor . . . the world will make a beaten path to his door (*Emerson*), You're a better man than I am, Gunga Din! (*Rudyard Kipling*), Nature made him and then broke the mould (*Ariosto*), I don't want to belong to any club that would accept me as a member (*Groucho Marx*).

Antonyms, see INFERIORITY.

---

superlative, *adj.* See SUPERIORITY.

supernatural, *adj.* miraculous, preternatural; abnormal, unearthly, superhuman, occult. See DEMON, UNIVERSE. *Ant.,* earthly, worldly.

supernumerary, *n.* bit [player], subordinate, walk-on, stand-in, extra, super (*inf.*). See DRAMA, SUBSTITUTION.

supersede, *v.t.* replace, displace, supplant, succeed. See SUBSTITUTION, DISUSE.

superstar, *n.* prodigy, virtuoso, luminary. See REPUTE.

superstition, *n.* irrationality, CREDULITY; fear, phobia; paganism, witchcraft, animism; old wives' tale, fairy tale, folklore. See HETERODOXY.

supervision, *n.* oversight, surveillance, superintendence. See AUTHORITY, DIRECTOR.

supine, *adj.* recumbent, reclining, prostrate; apathetic, sluggish, torpid; indifferent, passive. See INACTIVITY, INSENSIBILITY, HORIZONTAL. *Ant.,* standing, upright, energetic.

supper, *n.* meal, repast, refection; banquet, feast, entertainment. See FOOD.

supplant, *v.* supersede, succeed, replace (see SUBSTITUTION).

supple, *adj.* limber, lithe, pliant, flexible; yielding, compliant, adaptable; fawning, servile. See SOFTNESS. *Ant.,* inflexible, rigid, stiff.

supplement, *n.* adjunct, ADDITION, addendum, appendix, complement, conclusion. See AUXILIARY.

supplicate, *v.t.* entreat, petition, pray, beg, beseech. See REQUEST, WORSHIP.

supply, *v.t.* provide, furnish, give, afford, present, contribute. See PROVISION, STORE, QUANTITY.

SUPPORT
Maintenance

Nouns—1, *(financial support)* support, maintenance, upkeep, sustenance. See AID.

2, *(foundation)* ground, foundation, groundwork, substratum, base, basis; terra firma; purchase, grip, footing, hold, foothold, toehold, handhold; landing, landing stage, landing place; stage, platform; block; rest, resting place, basement, supporter, prop, stand; anvil, bearing; fulcrum, rowlock, oarlock; stay, shore, skid, rib, lap; bar, rod, boom, sprit, outrigger. See STABILITY.

3, *(walking support)* staff, stick, crutch, alpenstock, baton, walking stick; handle, heft.

4, *(postlike support)* post, pillar, shaft, column, pilaster, stud, sash, pier, atlas, atlantes *(pl.)*, caryatid; pediment, pedicle, stalk; prop; pedestal; plinth, shank, leg, foot; [flying] buttress, jamb, mullion, abutment; baluster, banister, stanchion; balustrade, railing; bracket.

5, *(supporting framework)* frame, framework, gantry, trellis; scaffold[ing], skeleton, beam, rafter, girder, lintel, joist, travis, trave, cornerstone, summer, transom; spoke, rung, round, step, sill, tholepin.

6, *(central support)* backbone; keystone; axle[tree]; axis; arch, mainstay.

7, *(supporting ledge)* board, ledge, shelf, hob, bracket, trevet, trivet, arbor, rack; mantel, mantelpiece; mantelshelf; slab, console; counter, dresser; seat, saddle, pommel, cantle; flange, corbel; table, trestle; shoulder; perch; stand, [saw]horse; easel, desk; box spring. See FURNITURE.

8, brassière, corset, support hose (see CLOTHING).

9, Atlas, Persides, Hercules.

Verbs—1, lie, sit, recline, lean, loll, rest, stand, step, repose about, bear *or* be based on; have at one's back.

2, support, bear, carry, hold (up), sustain, shoulder; hold, back, bolster, shore up, buttress; uphold, prop; underpin; bandage, tape, brace.

3, found, base, ground, imbed, embed.

4, maintain, keep on foot.

Adjectives—supporting, supported, braced, propped, bolstered; founded, based, basic, grounded, built on; fundamental, bottom, undermost; pickaback, piggyback.

Adverbs—astride, astraddle.

Antonyms, see PENDENCY.

---

supporter, *n.* advocate, champion, backer. See AID.

supportable, *adj.* tolerable, bearable. See DURABILITY.

SUPPOSITION
Assumption

Nouns—1, supposition, assumption, postulation, condition (see QUALIFICATION); presupposition, hypothesis, postulate, theory, data; proposition, position; thesis, theorem; proposal; conceit; conjecture, cast; guess[work], rough guess, shot [in the dark]; surmise, suspicion, inkling, notion, suggestion, association of ideas; presumption (see BELIEF); divination, speculation. *Informal,* hunch. See REASONING.

2, theorist, theoretician, hypothesist, speculator, conjecturer.

Verbs—1, suppose, conjecture, gather, surmise, suspect, guess, divine; theorize; presume, presuppose; assume, beg the question, fancy, take it; give a guess, speculate, believe, daresay, take it into one's head, take for granted.

2, put forth, propound, propose; start, put *or* give a case, move, make a motion; hazard a suggestion *or* conjecture; put forward a suggestion; submit; allude to, suggest, hint, put it into one's head.

Adjectives—supposing, supposed, given, postulatory; assumed, suppositive, supposititious; speculative, conjectural, hypothetical, theoretical, supposable, presumptive, putative, academic, gratuitous; impractical; suggestive.

Adverbs—supposedly, theoretically, on paper, seemingly, if, if so be; on the supposition of, in case of, in the event of; quasi, as if, provided; perhaps; for all one knows; for the sake of argument.

Quotations—How seldom is it that theories stand the wear and tear of practice! (*Anthony Trollope*), The great tragedy of Science—the slaying of a beautiful hypothesis by an ugly fact (*Aldous Huxley*), All theory, dear friend, is grey, but the golden tree of actual life springs ever green (*Goethe*).

Antonyms, see KNOWLEDGE, CERTAINTY.

---

suppress, *v.t.* put down, quell, subdue; repress, restrain; conceal; quash; withhold; abolish, ban; stanch, check. See RESTRAINT, CONCEALMENT.

suppurate, *v.i.* run, fester, putrefy, rankle; pustulate, ulcerate. See EXCRETION.

supremacy, *n.* mastery, SUPERIORITY, ascendancy, AUTHORITY.

supreme, *adj.* highest, utmost, paramount, prime, chief, dominant. See SUPERIORITY.

sure, *adj.* certain, positive; dependable, trustworthy; safe, secure; confident, convinced; unfailing, infallible, surefire (*inf.*). See CERTAINTY, SAFETY. *Ant.,* uncertain, unsure.

surf, *n.* sea, waves, breakers, rollers, whitecaps, white horses, billows, surge, spume, sea-foam, froth, spindrift, spray. See WATER, AGITATION.

surface, *n.* outside, EXTERIOR, superficies.

surfeit, *n.* excess, glut, superfluity, superabundance, plethora; satiety, repletion, engorgement. See SUFFICIENCY. *Ant.,* lack, dearth.

surge, *v.i.* rise, swell, billow, seethe, swirl; sweep, rush, stream, gush. See WATER, ASSEMBLAGE.

surgeon, *n.* chirurgeon (*archaic*), sawbones (*sl.*), medic (*sl.*), knife man (*sl.*). See REMEDY.

surly, *adj.* sullen, morose, churlish, gruff, uncivil. See DISCOURTESY. *Ant.,* courteous, civil.

surmise, *v.t.* guess, conjecture, suppose, suspect, presume. See BELIEF, SUPPOSITION.

surmount, *v.t.* overtop, rise above; master, surpass, transcend; crown, cap, top; scale, climb over; overcome, conquer. See HEIGHT, ASCENT, SUCCESS.

surname, *n.* family name, cognomen, patronymic. See NOMENCLATURE.

surpass, *v.t.* exceed, excel, overtop, outshine, outdo, outclass, eclipse, outstrip. See SUPERIORITY, REPUTE. *Ant.,* fall behind.

surplus, *n.* surplusage; excess, oversupply, glut; REMAINDER, overage; profit, balance. See SUFFICIENCY. *Ant.,* shortfall.

SURPRISE
Unexpectedness

Nouns—surprise, nonexpectation, unexpectedness, the unforeseen, unforeseen contingency *or* circumstances, miscalculation, astonishment, WONDER, thunderclap, turn, blow, shock, bolt from the blue, eye-opener. *Informal,* one for the book. See INATTENTION. See FEAR, UNPREPAREDNESS.

Verbs—1, not expect, be taken by surprise, miscalculate, not bargain for. *Informal,* do a double take, sit up and take notice. *Slang,* fall out.

2, burst, steal, creep, *or* sneak up on one, be unexpected, come unawares, turn *or* pop up, drop from the clouds, take by surprise, take unawares, catch napping, catch with one's pants down, boggle the mind, beat all, beat the Dutch. *Slang,* come from left field, blaze on.

3, surprise, astonish, amaze, astound; dumbfound, startle, dazzle; strike with WONDER *or* awe; raise eyebrows, daze; stun, stagger, strike dumb, stupefy, flabbergast, turn the head, make one's heart skip a beat, hit between the eyes, knock off one's feet, make one's jaw drop, take away one's breath; make one's hair stand on end, make one's eyes pop, take by surprise, set one back on one's heels; ambush, waylay. *Informal,* bowl over, explode *or* drop a bombshell, astonish the natives. *Slang,* knock *or* throw for a loop, throw a curve, goose, sandbag.

Adjectives—1, surprised, nonexpectant, unsuspecting, unwarned, off one's guard, inattentive. *Slang,* caught with one's pants down. See WONDER.

2, surprising, unexpected, unlooked for, unforeseen, unhoped for, beyond expectation, unheard of, startling, sudden, breathtaking. *Slang,* mind-blowing.

Adverbs—surprisingly, unexpectedly, abruptly, plump, pop, unawares, without warning, out of a clear [blue] sky, out of nowhere, like a bolt from the blue, out of the blue, suddenly. *Informal,* smack.

Interjections—dear me! do tell! you don't say! for crying out loud!

Phrases—the unexpected always happens; will wonders never cease; you could have knocked me down with a feather.

Quotations—Surprises are foolish things. The pleasure is not enhanced, and the inconvenience is often considerable (*Jane Austen*), Since a politician never believes what he says, he is surprised when others believe him (*Charles de Gaulle*), A sudden, bold, and unexpected question doth many times surprise a man and lay him open (*Francis Bacon*).

Antonyms, see EXPECTATION.

---

surreal, *adj.* singular, absurd, queer. See UNCONFORMITY.

surrender, *n.* capitulation, cession; RELINQUISHMENT, abandonment, SUBMISSION. —*v.* capitulate, yield, give up; cede, renounce, relinquish. See RESIGNATION.

surreptitious, *adj.* stealthy, clandestine. See CONCEALMENT. *Ant.,* overt.

surrogate, *n.* deputy, substitute, alternate, proxy. See SUBSTITUTION, AGENT.

surround, *v.t.* encompass, enclose, hem in, encircle; ring; circumscribe; environ; invest, besiege; embrace. See CIRCUMSCRIPTION, ENVIRONMENT.

surveillance, *n.* watch, observation, scrutiny, vigilance, CARE, attention; oversight, supervision, superintendence, keeping tabs on (*inf.*); lookout, patrol, guardianship; espionage, reconnaissance, stakeout (*sl.*), watch and ward. See VISION.

survey, *v.* view, examine, inspect, appraise; measure, lay out, plot. See VISION, MEASUREMENT.

survive, *v.* outlive, outlast; live; escape [with one's life]; continue, persist, remain, endure, abide, last. See DURABILITY, PERMANENCE. *Ant.,* succumb, pass.

susceptible, *n.* liable; allergic; vulnerable, impressionable, sensitive. See LIABILITY, SENSIBILITY, TENDENCY. *Ant.,* invulnerable, unsusceptible.

suspect, *v.t.* surmise, infer, conjecture, imagine, suppose, believe; mistrust, DOUBT. See SUPPOSITION.

suspend, *v.t.* hang, dangle; defer, postpone, stave off; adjourn, recess, intermit, prorogue, interrupt; debar, exclude. See LATENESS, DISCONTINUANCE, LATENCY, PENDENCY.

suspenders, *n.pl.* braces, garters, elastics, galluses. See PENDENCY.

suspense, *n.* anxiety, apprehension; uncertainty, indecision, hesitation; DISCONTINUANCE, interruption, pause; inaction, abeyance. See EXPECTATION, LATENCY.

suspicion, *n.* mistrust, distrust, apprehension; DOUBT, misgiving, JEALOUSY; SUPPOSITION, inkling, intimation, hint; trace, touch, shade, modicum. See LITTLENESS, FEAR, FEELING.

sustain, *v.t.* bear up, SUPPORT; endure; maintain, prolong, protract; nourish; corroborate, confirm, ratify, substantiate; assist. See AID, AGENCY.

sustenance, *n.* FOOD, nourishment; SUPPORT, maintenance, subsistence.

svelte, *adj.* slim, narrow-waisted; lithe. See NARROWNESS, BEAUTY.

swab, *n.* mop; swab stick, applicator, Q-tip; sponge. —*v.* mop, scrub, cleanse; wipe, dab, daub. See CLEANNESS.

swaddle, *v.t.* wrap, envelop (see COVERING).

swagger, *v.i.* strut, stalk, bluster, boast,

bully. —*n.* arrogance, braggadocio, pomposity, swank (*inf.*), side (*inf.*). See VANITY, BOASTING.

swallow, *v.t.* ingest, gulp, devour, consume; absorb, engulf, assimilate, envelop; retract; bear, endure, submit to; believe, accept. See FOOD, CREDULITY, RECEIVING.

swamp, *n.* swampland, marsh, bog, wetland, moor, slough, fen, morass, quagmire. —*v.t.* submerge, sink, flood, inundate, immerse, drench, deluge; overwhelm, snow under. See MOISTURE, WATER.

swanky, *adj., slang,* showy, ostentatious, smart, elegant, fancy, posh (*inf.*), plush (*inf.*), swell (*sl.*), ritzy (*sl.*), classy (*sl.*). See OSTENTATION.

swap, *n. & v.* exchange, BARTER. See INTERCHANGE.

swarm, *n.* group, crowd, MULTITUDE, horde, colony, hive. See ASSEMBLAGE, SUFFICIENCY.

swarthy, *adj.* dark, swart, dusky; dark-complexioned. See DARKNESS, COLOR.

swashbuckler, *n.* adventurer, daredevil; bully, swaggerer. See BOASTING, RASHNESS.

swastika, *n.* fylfot, gammadion. See CROSSING.

swat, *v.t., informal,* slap, clip, slug. See IMPULSE.

swatch, *n.* sample (see CONFORMITY).

swath, *n.* strip, belt; window. See CONTINUITY, FILAMENT.

sway, *v.* swing, rock; INFLUENCE, direct, control, rule, bias, prejudice, warp; lurch, rock, roll, reel, dangle. See

CAUSE, AGITATION. —*n.* domination, rule; INFLUENCE; OSCILLATION. See AUTHORITY, POWER.

swear, *v.i.* affirm, depose, depone, vow; testify, witness; blaspheme, curse. See AFFIRMATION, IMPRECATION.

sweat, *v.* perspire; run, exude, secrete, ooze, drip; bead, dew, wet; *informal,* drudge, overwork; suffer, extract; force out; exploit. —*n.* perspiration, sudor, exudation; *informal,* EXERTION, toil, sweat of one's brow, AGITATION, stew, excitement. See EXCRETION.

sweater, *n.* knitwear, jersey, guernsey, pullover, cardigan. See CLOTHING.

sweep, *v.* brush, clean, vacuum; push, drive, blow, impel; trail; scan; strum; bend, curve; stream, glide, skim. See CLEANNESS, CURVATURE, MOTION, VELOCITY, SPACE.

sweeping, *adj.* comprehensive; extensive, wide-ranging. See INCLUSION, GENERALITY.

sweepstakes, *n.* lottery, draw, raffle, CHANCE; winner-take-all; contest.

sweet, *adj.* sugary (see SWEETNESS); pleasing; amiable; dear, precious; fragrant, sweet-smelling. *Ant.,* sour, unpleasant, foul-smelling. —*n.* candy, bonbon, dessert, *etc.* See PLEASURE, COURTESY, DEARNESS, ODOR.

sweetheart, *n.* lover, love, suitor, beloved, truelove, sweetie (*inf.*), flame, steady (*sl.*); beau, swain, boy friend; ladylove, [best] girl, gal (*sl.*). See LOVE, ENDEARMENT.

SWEETNESS
Sugary taste

Nouns—1, sweetness, sugariness, saccharinity; sweetening, [barley, brown, cane, caramel, confectioner's, cube, granulated, icing, light *or* dark brown, powdered, raw, spun, *or* superfine] sugar, molasses, honey, sirup, syrup; saccharin, aspartame, sugar substitute, artificial sweetener, corn syrup, fructose; nectar; breath sweetener, cachou.
2, a. sweets, confection, confectionery, confectionary; fondant; icing, frosting; conserve, preserve, confiture, marmalade, jam, julep; licorice, jujube; caramel, candy, candy bar, candy cane, rock candy, saltwater taffy, cotton candy; nougat, nonpareil; lollipop, lemon drop, jawbreaker, jelly bean; chewing gum, chicle; sugarplum, bonbon, comfit, sweetmeat; halvah; taffy, butterscotch, bark, brittle; mint, spearmint, peppermint; marzipan, marchpane; chocolate, fudge, penuche, *etc. Informal,* sucker.
b. nectar, mead, liqueur, cordial, sweet wine, punch, soda [water *or* pop], lemonade, carbonated drink (see DRINKING). **c.** dessert, pastry, pie, tart, cake, torte, cream puff,

custard, pudding, *etc.*; ice cream, sherbet, frozen custard; zabaglione, gelato. See
FOOD.
3, lover of sweets. *Informal,* chocaholic.
Verbs—sweeten, sugar[-coat], candy, mull.
Adjectives—sweet, saccharine; dulcet, candied, honeyed; luscious, lush; sweetened;
sweet as sugar, honey, *or* candy; sugar-coated, sirupy.

Antonyms, see SOURNESS.

---

swell, *v.i.* expand, dilate, bulge, protrude; billow; INCREASE, grow, surge. See WATER, FEELING, PRIDE. —*n.* swelling, INCREASE; billow, wave, groundswell, sea, roller; rise, slope, knoll. See CONVEXITY, EXPANSION, NOBILITY.

swelter, *v.i.* perspire, sweat. See HEAT, EXCRETION.

swerve, *v.i.* turn aside, deviate, shift, sheer, veer, yaw; dodge. See DEVIATION, CHANGE.

swift, *adj.* quick, rapid, fast, fleet, speedy; expeditious. See VELOCITY, HASTE.

swig, *v.t., informal,* guzzle, toss off *or* down, chug-a-lug (*sl.*). See DRINKING.

swill, *v.* flood, drench, swamp, soak, slosh; wash, rinse; guzzle, swizzle, swallow, swig (*inf.*). —*n.* garbage, refuse, waste, slop[s], mess, filth; eyewash, hogwash. See UNCLEANNESS, DRINKING.

swim, *v.* paddle, crawl, stroke, float, kick, tread water; feel dizzy, faint, swoon, reel, whirl; soak, be saturated, steep. See WATER. —**swimsuit,** *n.* bathing suit, bikini, two- *or* one-piece [suit]. See CLOTHING.

swimmingly, *adv.* easily; prosperously. See FACILITY, SUCCESS.

swindle, *v.t.* defraud, hoax, cheat, fleece, victimize, trick, gyp (*sl.*). See STEALING, DECEPTION.

swine, *n.* pig, hog, porker, sow, boar; scoundrel, sloven, wretch. See ANIMAL, EVILDOER.

swing, *v.i.* oscillate, sway, wag; depend, dangle; pivot, turn; *informal,* be hanged; *slang,* [wife- *or* husband-]swap. See OSCILLATION, PUNISHMENT, IMPURITY, SEX. —*n.* sweep, sway, OSCILLATION; rhythm, lilt, scope, range, latitude, FREEDOM; REGULARITY, PENDENCY.

swipe, *v.* strike, hit, thwack; *informal,* steal, grap, snatch, pilfer, snitch (*sl.*),

lift, filch, cop, borrow. See IMPULSE, STEALING.

swirl, *v.* whirl, eddy, twist. See ROTATION.

swish, *v.* whisk, flourish; rustle. See SOFTNESS, AGITATION.

switch, *n.* twig, sprig, spray; rod, cane, birch; shunt; paraphrase; CHANGE, new version. —*v.t.* cane, whip, lash; shunt, deflect, turn, shift; paraphrase, modify, CHANGE; transpose. See INTERCHANGE, VEGETABLE, PUNISHMENT.

swivel, *v.* turn, pivot, rotate, wheel, veer, swing. See ROTATION.

swoon, *v.i.* faint (see WEAKNESS).

swoop, *v.* sweep up, catch up, clutch, carry off; pounce, hawk, souse, fly, fall on, descend, sweep down, dive. See DESCENT, ACQUISITION.

sword, *n.* blade, broadsword, falchion, glaive; rapier, foil, épée, saber, cutlass, *etc.*; war, vengeance, DESTRUCTION. See ARMS, WARFARE.

sybarite, *n.* sensualist, voluptuary, hedonist. See PLEASURE.

sycophant, *n.* parasite, toady, bootlicker, lickspittle, flatterer, fawner, truckler. See SERVILITY, FLATTERY.

syllable, *n.* sonant; phone; tone, accent, inflection. See SPEECH.

syllabus, *n.* outline, schedule, PLAN, calendar; prospectus; abstract, compendium. See PUBLICATION.

sylvan, *adj.* forest, wooded, wood[s]y, arboreous; rural, bucolic. See VEGETATION. *Ant.,* urban.

symbiosis, *n.* coexistence, COOPERATION.

symbol, *n.* token, emblem, mark, badge, device, character, letter. See INDICATION, FIGURATIVE, NUMERATION.

symbolize, *v.t.* represent, indicate, signify, typify, mean, betoken, express, imply. See INDICATION.

SYMMETRY
Regularity of form

Nouns—symmetry, proportion, balance, parallelism; uniformity, correspondence, congruity, REGULARITY, regular ARRANGEMENT; ORDER, harmony, eurythmy; shapeliness, FORM, BEAUTY, eurythmics.

Verbs—symmetrize, make symmetrical, balance, proportion, regularize, harmonize, coordinate, equalize.

Adjectives—symmetric[al], proportional, balanced, bilateral, parallel, coextensive; corresponding, congruent, consistent, coordinate, equal (see EQUALITY); even, regular, uniform, orderly, harmonious, eurythmic; shapely, well-set, well-formed, finished, beautiful, classic.

Quotations—Tiger! Tiger! burning bright in the forests of the night, what immortal hand or eye could frame thy fearful symmetry? (*William Blake*).

Antonyms, see DISTORTION, IRREGULARITY.

---

sympathize, *v.i.* feel for, sorrow for; condole; understand; feel sorry for, commiserate. See PITY, BENEVOLENCE.

sympathizer, *n.* upholder, supporter, advocate, champion, well-wisher; commiserator, condoler, FRIEND. See PITY, AUXILIARY.

sympathy, *n.* agreement, understanding, accord; compassion, PITY, condolence, commiseration, fellow-feeling; empathy. See FEELING, BENEVOLENCE.

symphony, *n.* consonance, harmony, concert, concord; sinfonia, sinfonietta, symphony orchestra, philharmonic. See MUSIC.

symposium, *n.* banquet, collation, feast; panel [discussion], colloquium, colloquy, round table, forum; gathering, social. See ASSEMBLAGE, COUNCIL, CONVERSATION.

symptom, *n.* sign, INDICATION, token, mark. See WARNING.

synagogue, *n.* tabernacle, TEMPLE.

SYNCHRONISM
Occurrence at the same time

Nouns—synchronism, synchronization, coexistence, coincidence, concurrence; simultaneity, coinstantaneity, concomitance, unity of TIME, isochronism; simulcast.

Verbs—synchronize, agree in time, be simultaneous; coexist; coincide, agree, concur, match, correspond, harmonize, mesh, dovetail, work together, accompany, go hand in hand, keep pace with; cooperate, coordinate, intermesh, interlock, interact; syncromesh, synthesize, synthetize, syncretize, contemporize. *Informal,* gee, sync, jibe, fit to a T.

Adjectives—synchronous, synchronal, synchronical, synchronistical; simultaneous, coinstantaneous, coexistent, coexisting, coincident, concomitant, concurrent; coeval, contemporary, contemporaneous, coetaneous; coeternal; isochronous.

Adverbs—at the same time, at *or* in one fell swoop, at a time, at once, at one time, simultaneously, contemporaneously, during the same time, in concert, together, in the same breath; at the very moment.

Antonyms, see DISAGREEMENT.

---

syncopation, *n.* syncope; jazz, blues, ragtime. See MUSIC.

syndicate, *n.* cartel, combine, pool, monopoly, trust; directorate. See PARTY, COMBINATION, COUNCIL.

syndrome, *n.* characteristics (see INDICATION, SPECIALITY).

synergy, *n.* synergism, symbiosis, collaboration, COOPERATION.

synod, *n.* council, convocation, congregation, conclave. See ASSEMBLAGE, CLERGY.

synonymous, *adj.* similar, equivalent, analogous. See IDENTITY, MEANING. *Ant.,* differing.

synopsis, *n.* condensation, abridgment, digest. See SHORTNESS.

synthesis, *n.* COMBINATION, composite,

amalgamation, unity; construct, fabrication; blend, marriage; syncretism.

synthetic, *adj.* artificial, manmade, unnatural. See PRODUCTION. *Ant.,* natural.

syringe, *n.* sprinkler, atomizer, spray[er]; enema, clysma, clyster, douche; needle, hypodermic; syringium. See WATER, CLEANNESS, DRUGS.

syrup, *n.* concentrate, extract, elixir; glucose, sugar water; sorghum, molasses, treacle. See SWEETNESS, COHERENCE.

system, *n.* coordination, organization, routine, ARRANGEMENT, METHOD, scheme, plan; classification; complex. See ORDER, REGULARITY.

systematic, *adj.* methodic[al], orderly. See ORDER, REGULARITY. *Ant.,* unsystematic, random.

T

tab, *n.* flap, tag, strip, lug, label; earmark, ticket; tabulation, bill, check, charge, reckoning. —*v.t., informal,* appoint, select, designate, nominate, choose, pick [out], finger (*sl.*). See INDICATION, ADDITION.

tabernacle, *n.* synagogue, TEMPLE.

table, *n.* board, slab; desk, counter; FOOD, diet, fare, cuisine, menu; index, compendium, catalog, chart, tabulation, LIST, schedule; tableland, plateau, mesa. See HORIZONTAL.

tableau, *n.* group; picture, scene, backdrop, set, diorama; *tableau vivant*; arrangement, array. See DRAMA, PAINTING, APPEARANCE, REPRESENTATION.

tablet, *n.* slab, stone, memorial; slate, plaque, signboard; pad, booklet; pill, lozenge, pastille, wafer. See HORIZONTAL, RECORD.

table tennis, *n.* Ping-Pong (see SPORTS).

tabloid, *n.* yellow journal, scandal sheet, tattler, rag (*sl.*), blat (*sl.*). See PUBLICATION.

taboo, *n.* tabu, PROHIBITION, interdiction, forbiddance. —*v.t.* forbid, prohibit, keep inviolate. —*adj.* forbidden; untouchable, unprofanable, inviolate.

tabulate, *v.t.* chart, graph; LIST, catalog; calculate, figure, enumerate, tally; enroll, RECORD. See ARRANGEMENT.

tacit, *adj.* unspoken, unexpressed; silent, mute; implied, understood. See SILENCE, TACITURNITY.

TACITURNITY
Reserve in speaking

Nouns—1, taciturnity, uncommunicativeness, reticence, reserve, closeness, curtness; SILENCE, muteness, pauciloquy, laconicism; secrecy, CONCEALMENT.

2, man *or* woman of few words, mouse. *Slang,* oyster, clam.

Verbs—be taciturn *or* silent, keep SILENCE, not speak, say nothing; hold *or* put a bridle on one's tongue, hold one's peace, bottle up, seal the lips, close the mouth, keep one's tongue between one's teeth, lose one's tongue, lay a finger on the lips, not let a word escape one, make no sign, keep a secret, not have a word to say, cat's got one's tongue. *Slang,* pipe down, clam up.

Adjectives—taciturn, uncommunicative, reticent, reserved, close, closemouthed *or* -tongued, tight-lipped, short-spoken, unconversable, unsociable, short, curt, laconic, sparing of words, mousy; silent, still, mute, speechless; pauciloquent, concise, terse, sententious; secretive.

Quotations—Men of few words are the best men (*Shakespeare*), Whereof one cannot speak, thereof one must be silent (*Ludwig Wittgenstein*), Blessed is the man who, having nothing to say, abstains from giving in words evidence of the fact (*George Eliot*).

Antonyms, see LOQUACITY.

---

tack, *n.* thumbtack, carpet tack, *etc.*; nail; change of course, yaw, veer; route, course, path; FOOD, fare. —*v.* change course *or* direction; yaw; zigzag; baste. See CONNECTION, DIRECTION, DEVIATION.

tackle, *n.* pulley; gear, equipment, apparatus, instruments; luggage. —*v.t.* grasp, grapple with; seize; address, attach; attempt, try, undertake. See UNDERTAKING, PROVISION.

tacky, *adj., informal,* shabby, shoddy, seedy, cheap, tawdry, sleazy, cheesy (*sl.*), in poor taste; sticky, adhesive. See CO-HERENCE, DETERIORATION.

tact, *n.* diplomacy, finesse, discretion, consideration. See TASTE, CONDUCT.

tactics, *n.pl.* strategy, generalship, CONDUCT; maneuvering; policy, diplomacy; mode, METHOD. See WARFARE.

tactile, *adj.* tangible; tactual. See TOUCH.

tactless, *adj.* thoughtless, insensitive, inconsiderate; callous, unfeeling, blunt, direct. See INDIFFERENCE.

tad, *n.* dab, speck, dot (see LITTLENESS).

tag, *n.* stub, tab, flap; tail, tassel, pendant; slogan, phrase, name, catchword; tatter, shred, rag. See ADDITION, END, INDICATION.

tail, *n.* appendage, END; cauda; tip, extremity; REAR, rudder, queue, pigtail, train; *slang,* shadow. See PENDENCY, PURSUIT.

tailor, *n.* sartor, clothier, costumier, dressmaker, seamstress. —*v.* fit, design, make, cut, trim, alter; sew, stitch, style, fashion, shape, drape, hand-tailor, finish. See CLOTHING, FORM, AGREEMENT.

taint, *v.* corrupt, spoil, poison; tarnish, stain, sully; pollute, infect, contaminate. —*n.* corruption; spoilage; stigma, dishonor, defilement; fault, flaw, blemish; contamination. See DISEASE, DISREPUTE, IMPERFECTION, BADNESS, DETERIORATION.

take, *v.* catch, capture (see ACQUISITION); plagiarize, pirate (see STEALING); take by storm; snap *or* pick up; do; work, be effective; snap a picture. —*n.* taking; *informal,* receipts, haul (*inf.*), gate (*sl.*), swag (*sl.*). See RECEIVING. —**take back,** retract, recant (see NULLIFICATION). —**take over,** take charge, appropriate, buy out. See ACQUISITION, AUTHORITY.

takeoff, *n.* liftoff; *informal,* IMITATION, parody, satire, burlesque, skit. See ASCENT.

taking, *n.* reception, RECEIVING; appropriation (see ACQUISITION); extortion, theft (see STEALING). —*adj.* fetching, winning, endearing. See PLEASURE, BEAUTY.

tale, *n.* story, account, recital; count[ing], tally; report; fable, yarn, legend; rumor. See DESCRIPTION, INFORMATION.

talent, *n.* gift, faculty, ability, power; turn, knack, aptitude; genius. See SKILL.

talisman, *n.* lucky piece; charm, amulet, fetish. See SORCERY.

talk, *n.* CONVERSATION; chatter, chat, gossip; SPEECH, lecture, discourse; rumor, hearsay. —*v.* say, speak, chat, converse, gossip. See NEWS, INFORMATION. —**talk into,** persuade, convince, sway. See BELIEF.

talkative, *adj.* talky, verbose (see LOQUACITY).

tall, *adj.* high, lofty, towering; long, long-limbed; *informal,* exaggerated. See HEIGHT, EXAGGERATION.

tally, *n.* count, tale, counting; score, check; tag, label; match[ing]; roll call. —*v.* count, tell; record, register, score; tag; suit, correspond, agree, harmonize; check. See LIST, NUMERATION, INDICATION, AGREEMENT, CREDIT.

tame, *adj.* tamed, domestic, domesticated; broken, subdued; meek, gentle; docile, tractable; dull, insipid; flat; spiritless, feeble. —*v.t.* subdue, cow, break; harness; domesticate. See DOMESTICATION, SUBJECTION, INSIPIDITY.

tamp, *v.t.* punch, pound, stamp. See IMPULSE.

tamper, *v.i.* meddle, intermeddle, interfere; bribe, seduce, corrupt, taint; CHANGE, alter, doctor (*inf.*), monkey (with) (*inf.*). See DETERIORATION.

tan, *v.t.* prepare, cure; brown, sunbathe; *informal,* thrash, whip. See PREPARATION, COLOR, PUNISHMENT.

tang, *n.* savor, flavor, TASTE, zest; sharpness, PUNGENCY, tanginess; bite, nip, twang, snappiness.

tangent, *n.* divergence, DEVIATION. —*adj.* touching (see CONTACT).

tangible, *adj.* material, real; touchable, palpable; concrete, perceptible. See FEELING, SUBSTANCE, TOUCH.

tangle, *n.* snarl, mix-up, jumble, mattedness; complication, involvement. —*v.* mat, snarl; knot, mix inextricably; snare, trap, enmesh; catch, perplex; embroil, complicate. See DISORDER, DIFFICULTY.

tank, *n.* reservoir, cistern; boiler; panzer; pond, swimming pool; (*pl.*) armor. See STORE, ARMS. —**tank up,** *v.* drink *or* fill up (see DRINKING).

tankard, *n.* cup, mug. See RECEPTACLE.

tantalize, *v.* tease, tempt, excite, provoke; balk. See DESIRE.

tantamount, *adj.* equivalent (see EQUALITY).

tantrum, *n.* fit, outburst; display (of ill

temper); rage, frenzy, paroxysm. See RESENTMENT, VIOLENCE.

tap, *n.* spigot, faucet, valve; plug, bung, stopper; outlet; knock, rap; tapping, tap dance, soft shoe; taproom, bar, saloon. —*v.* knock, rap, pat, strike, TOUCH; tap-dance; broach, draw off (liquor, *etc.*); wiretap; draw upon, nominate. See IMPULSE, OPENING, EGRESS, CHOICE.

tape, *n.* band, strip, ribbon; cellophane, Scotch, masking, electrical, *or* friction tape; tapeline. See MEASUREMENT. —*v.* bind, bandage, swaddle, mummify; *informal,* tape-record, copy. See FILAMENT.

taper, *v.* narrow; come to a point; lessen, slacken, slack off, diminish. —*n.* candle, LIGHT; pyramid, cone, spire, *etc.* See NARROWNESS.

tapestry, *n.* weaving, rug; mosaic, montage. See COVERING, REPRESENTATION.

tar, *n.* asphalt, pitch, resin, bitumen; goo, sludge. —*v.* besmirch, stain, blacken, defame; tar and feather. See NAVIGATION, COVERING, PUNISHMENT.

tardy, *adj.* overdue, late, behind-time; slow, slack, dilatory, sluggish. See LATENESS, LATENCY.

target, *n.* aim, mark; goal; bull's-eye; quarry, object; butt. See INTENTION.

tariff, *n.* duty, customs, impost; price list; PRICE, cost. See PAYMENT.

tarnish, *v.* smirch, taint; dishonor; stain, sully, besmirch; defame; dull, smudge, dim, spot, blemish; discolor. See DISREPUTE, UNCLEANNESS.

tarpaulin, *n.* tarp, canvas, oilcloth, tent; poncho, slicker. See COVERING.

tarry, *v.i.* linger, stay, wait; idle, dawdle; visit (with); bide a while, sojourn; delay, dally. See LATENESS, DURABILITY.

tart, *adj.* acid, sour; sarcastic, acerbic, snappy, sharp, astringent. —*n.* pie; *slang,* strumpet. See SOURNESS, DISCOURTESY, PUNGENCY, IMPURITY.

tartan, *n.* plaid, check; kilt, trews, filibeg. See VARIEGATION.

task, *n.* work, stint, job, labor; lesson, assignment, charge, DUTY, chore; drudgery, burden. —*v.t.* strain, tax, overburden, overwork; impose, assign, charge. See EXERTION, COMMISSION, COMMAND, BUSINESS.

taskmaster, *n.* overseer, martinet, slave-driver. See SEVERITY.

tassel, *n.* fringe (see EDGE).

taste, *v.* savor; sample. —*n.* flavor; tasting, morsel, sample; predilection, relish, preference; JUDGMENT. See TASTE, CHOICE.

TASTE
Sense of flavor

Nouns—1, taste, tastefulness; good *or* cultivated taste; delicacy, refinement, tact, finesse, flair; nicety, discrimination; distinction, polish, ELEGANCE; virtu, connoisseurship, dilettantism; fine art; culture, cultivation, fastidiousness; esthetics. See FASHION, INTELLIGENCE, JUDGMENT.

2, *(something tasted)* sample; tinge, bit, trace, scrap, soupçon; tasting, gustation, degustation; palate, tongue, tooth, stomach. See PART, LITTLENESS.

3, *(taste quality)* flavor, gusto, savor, zest; sapor, sapidity, aftertaste, tang; savoriness, tastiness, palatability; unsavoriness, unpalatability, austerity, INSIPIDITY; SWEETNESS; SOURNESS, acidity, acerbity; PUNGENCY.

4, seasoning, condiment; spice, relish; tidbit, dainty, delicacy, morsel, appetizer, hors d'oeuvres, antipasto, delicatessen; sauce; ambrosia; nectar; rue, hemlock, myrrh, aloes, gall and wormwood. See FOOD.

5, man of taste, connoisseur; epicure, gourmet; judge, critic, virtuoso; amateur, dilettante. See JUDGMENT.

Verbs—1, have good taste, appreciate, have an eye for; judge, criticize, discriminate, distinguish, particularize; single out, draw the line, sift, estimate, weigh, consider, diagnose; pick and choose, split hairs, know which is which.

2, savor, taste, sample; relish, like, enjoy, smack the lips; tickle the palate; turn the stomach, disgust; pall, stale, spoil; sour, curdle, ferment, turn.

3, season, spice, garnish.

Adjectives—1, in good taste; tasteful, unaffected, pure, chaste, classical, cultivated, refined; dainty, delicate, aesthetic, artistic; meticulous, precise, exact, precious; elegant;

euphemistic; choosy, fussy; astute, keen; fastidious, finicky, finical, crotchety, per[s]nickety, squeamish; [over]nice, particular, discriminating, discriminative, discerning, perceptive; to one's taste, after one's fancy; comme il faut, de rigueur. *Informal,* picky.

2, tasty, flavorful, toothsome, sapid, saporific; palatable, gustable, gustatory, tastable; pungent, strong; flavored, spicy, hot; sweet, sour, salt[y], bitter, nutty; savory, unsavory.

Adverbs—tastefully, elegantly; purely, aesthetically, *etc.*

Phrases—every man to his [own] taste; the style is the man; there is no accounting for tastes.

Quotation—They never taste who always drink (*Matthew Prior*).

  Antonyms, see VULGARITY, INSIPIDITY, NEGLECT, DISORDER.

---

tasteless, *adj.* insipid, flat; inelegant; inept, clumsy, vulgar, savorless, unappetizing. See INSIPIDITY, VULGARITY, INELEGANCE.

tatters, *n.pl.* rags, odds and ends, fragments. See PART.

tattle, *v.* prattle, prate; chat[ter]; jabber, talk, gossip; reveal (a secret), inform, peach (*inf.*), tell on, tell tales, blab (*sl.*), spill the beans (*sl.*). See ACCUSATION, DISCLOSURE.

tattletale, *n.* gossip, blabbermouth; informer, snitch. See LOQUACITY, DISCLOSURE.

taunt, *v.* RIDICULE, scoff, jeer, twit; provoke, mock, flout, deride. See ACCUSATION.

taut, *adj.* tight, stretched, tense, strained; keyed up, on edge; snug, tidy, shipshape, neat. See HARDNESS, ORDER.

tautology, *n.* REPETITION, reiteration, redundancy, verbosity.

tavern, *n.* inn, hostel, restaurant, café; saloon, bar. See FOOD, DRINKING.

tawdry, *adj.* cheap, showy, flashy; loud, garish; tinsel, gimcrack. See VULGARITY, OSTENTATION.

tax, *n.* assessment, levy, duty, tariff, excise, toll, tithe; impost, custom; rate, income tax, internal revenue; *informal,* charge. See PAYMENT. —*v.* assess, rate, COMMAND; charge, accuse; take to task; strain, overwork, burden, fatigue. See ACCUSATION, COMPULSION, EXERTION.

taxi, *n.* taximeter cab, taxicab; hack[ney], jitney; taxiplane; fiacre, droshky, [jin]rickshaw, pedicab. See VEHICLE, TRANSPORTATION.

tea, *n.* pekoe, souchong, oolong, herb[al], *etc.* tea; beef tea, broth, bouillon; collation, afternoon *or* five o'clock tea, high tea, snack. See DRINKING.

TEACHING
Instruction

Nouns—1, teaching, instruction, edification, education, tuition; tutorship, tutelage; DIRECTION, guidance; PREPARATION, training, upbringing, schooling; outreach; discipline; exercise, drill, practice; learning process; indoctrination, inculcation, inoculation; explanation, INTERPRETATION. See SCHOOL, LEARNING.

2, lesson, catechism; lecture, sermon; apologue, parable; discourse, prelection, preachment; exercise, task; master class.

3, [school]teacher, educator, educationist, [privat]docent, preceptor, trainer, instructor, master, tutor, director, coach, disciplinarian; [full, associate, *or* assistant] professor, lecturer, reader, prelector, prolocutor; preacher, pastor (see CLERGY); schoolmaster, dominie, pedagogue, abecedarian; substitute, practice *or* student teacher, teaching assistant, TA, teaching fellow, teacher's aide, monitor, prefect, proctor; schoolmistress, governess; expositor, interpreter; preceptor, guide, mentor, sherpa, mullah, pundit; adviser (see ADVICE); exponent; pioneer, apostle, missionary, propagandist; faculty, professoriate. *Informal,* schoolmarm. *Slang,* teach, scrag.

Verbs—1, teach [a lesson], instruct, edify, school, tutor; cram, prime, coach; enlighten, inform; inculcate, indoctrinate, inoculate, infuse, instill, infiltrate; imbue, impregnate, implant; graft, sow the seeds of, disseminate; give an idea of; put up to, set right, sharpen the wits, broaden one's horizon, open the eyes, bring forward, improve; direct, guide; direct attention to, impress upon the mind *or* memory; convince (see BELIEF). *Informal,* beat into [the head].

2, *(give a lecture)* expound, set forth, develop; interpret, lecture, editorialize, hold forth, preach; sermonize, moralize.

3, train, discipline; bring up, educate, form, ground, prepare, qualify, drill, exercise, practice; nurture, breed, rear, take in hand; break [in]; tame; preinstruct; initiate, inure, habituate; brainwash (see DECEPTION). *Informal,* show the ropes.

Adjectives—teaching, taught, educational; scholastic, academic, doctrinal; disciplinal, disciplinary; teachable, receptive; instructive, didactic, homiletic; consciousness-raising; professorial, pedagogical, donnish.

Phrases—education doesn't come by bumping your head against the school house; experience is the best teacher; you can't teach an old dog new tricks.

Quotations—Even while they teach, men learn (*Seneca*), He who can, does. He who cannot, teaches (*G. B. Shaw*), A teacher affects eternity; he can never tell where his influence ends (*Henry Adams*).

Antonyms, see LEARNING.

---

team, *n.* crew, side, aggregation; nine, five, eleven (*baseball, basketball, and football teams*); rig, span (of horses); combat team, group; brace, pair, foursome, *etc.* See COÖPERATION, NUMERATION.

teamster, *n.* wagonmaster, muleteer; carter, drayman, wagoner; truck driver, truckman, trucker, vanman, carrier. See TRANSPORTATION.

teamwork, *n.* coordination, collaboration, COOPERATION.

tear, *v.* rip, rend, lacerate, tatter, shred; split, burst, break, part, separate, remove, raze, wrench; give; snatch, race; speed, dash, fly. —*n.* break, rent, split; wound; crack, fissure, gap; (*pl.*) teardrops, weeping, crying, LAMENTATION; *slang,* spree, binge, toot, bender, jag. See DISJUNCTION, PART, VELOCITY, INTEMPERANCE. —tear down, raze, wreck, demolish; dismantle. See DESTRUCTION.

tearful, teary, *adj.* weeping, sorrowful. See DEJECTION, LAMENTATION.

tease, *v.* plague, annoy, vex, harass; taunt, mock; beg; tantalize; titillate, excite. See RIDICULE, MALEVOLENCE.

technical, *adj.* scientific, technological; professional, skilled. See KNOWLEDGE, BUSINESS, SKILL.

technicality, *n.* fine point, minutiae (*pl.*); nuance, detail, subtlety, formality; law, rule, rubric; loophole, letter of the law; procedure, problem. See SKILL.

technique, *n.* technic, execution, style, METHOD.

technology, *n.* technics; knowledge, information, craft, science, engineering, mechanics; SKILL, practice, know-how (*inf.*); automation, mechanization.

tedious, *adj.* wearisome, wearing, dry, dry-as-dust, boring, tiresome, irksome, dull, monotonous, prosy, uninteresting. See WEARINESS.

teem, *v.i.* swarm, abound; multiply, pullulate; rain heavily, pour; bear, generate, produce. See PRODUCTION, SUFFICIENCY.

teeming, *adj.* swarming, abounding, abundant, plentiful; crowded, chock-full, jam-packed; replete, fraught, full, pullulating; raining. See MULTITUDE.

teenager, *n.* YOUTH, adolescent, bobby-soxer, teen, teeny-bopper (*sl.*).

teepee, *n.* wigwam, hut, lodge. See ABODE.

teeter, *v.i.* seesaw, rock, sway, totter, tremble; hesitate, vacillate. See OSCILLATION, DOUBT.

teetotal, *adj.* absolute, entire; abstinent; dry, prohibitionist; *informal,* all, entire, whole. See WHOLE, MODERATION.

telegram, *n.* message, wire, cable. See COMMUNICATION.

telegraph, *n.* telegram; wireless, Morse, wire, cable[gram], semaphore, heliograph, pantelograph, phototelegraph. —*v.t.* signal, wire, radio, cable; *informal,* betray, disclose, reveal. See COMMUNICATION, INDICATION.

telepathy, *n.* psychic COMMUNICATION, thought transference, extrasensory perception, ESP; psi.

telephone, *v.* call [up], phone, dial, get through to. See COMMUNICATION.

telescope, *n.* glass, field glass, spyglass. — *v.* collapse, fold; [fore]shorten, condense, abridge. See OPTICAL INSTRUMENTS, DISTANCE.

television, *n.* video, TV; telefilm, kinescope; [video]tape; station, studio, channel, network, syndicate; closed-circuit, cable, *or* pay television; telecast; CATV. See COMMUNICATION.

tell, *v.* recount, relate, narrate; inform, apprise, acquaint; explain; weigh, matter, influence; reveal, disclose, own, confess, acknowledge; discern, distinguish, make out, see, recognize; count, number, reckon, rally; speak, state, declare. See INFORMATION, DESCRIPTION, DISCLOSURE, SPEECH, INFLUENCE.

teller, *n.* bank clerk, cashier. See STORE.

telling, *adj.* effective, striking. See EFFECT, POWER, IMPORTANCE.

telltale, *adj.* significant, revealing. —*n.* tattler, talebearer. See INFORMATION.

temerity, *n.* RASHNESS, boldness, audacity, recklessness, daring, nerve, gall, brass (*sl.*), cheek (*sl.*).

temper, *n.* temperament, nature, disposition; mood, humor, tone; tantrum, passion, rage; mettle, quality; calmness, composure, equanimity. See IRASCIBILITY, FEELING, INTRINSIC. —*v.t.* moderate, soften; harden, anneal, toughen. See HARDNESS, SOFTNESS, CHANGE.

temperament, n. constitution, disposition, nature, humor. See FEELING, SENSIBILITY.

temperamental, *adj.* irritable, sensitive; constitutional, innate. See IRASCIBILITY, INTRINSIC.

temperance, *n.* See MODERATION.

temperate, *adj.* moderate, ascetic, cautious, mild, sober, abstemious, abstinent, continent; Pythagorean; vegetarian. See MODERATION.

temperature, *n.* HEAT, fever; COLD. See DISEASE.

tempest, *n.* storm, gale, hurricane, squall, blizzard; excitement, tumult, disturbance; maelstrom. See WIND, VIOLENCE.

tempestuous, *adj.* stormy, raging, furious; gusty, blowy, squally; violent, tumultuous, turbulent. See WIND, VIOLENCE.

template, *n.* templet, guide, pattern. See PLAN.

TEMPLE
Edifice for worship

Nouns—1, temple, place of worship; house of God, house of prayer, sanctum.

2, cathedral, minster, church, kirk, bethel, fane, chapel, meetinghouse, mission, tabernacle, basilica, holy place, chantry, oratory; conjuring lodge; synagogue, shul; mosque; marabout; pantheon; mandira; pagoda; shrine, naos. *Slang,* glory hole. See ABODE.

3, *(part of a temple)* altar, bema, shrine, sanctuary, Holy of Holies, sanctum sanctorum, communion table; pyx; baptistery, font; sedilia; reredos; rood-loft, rood-screen, jube; chancel, nave, aisle, transept, vestry, sacristy, crypt, cloisters, misericord, churchyard, golgotha, calvary; stall, pew; pulpit, ambo, lectern, reading-desk, confessional; apse, oriel, belfry, steeple; chancery; dagoba; mihrab, tope. *Slang,* amen corner *or* bench.

4, *(living place for clergy)* parsonage, parish house, rectory, vicarage, manse, deanery, presbytery, Vatican, bishop's palace.

5, *(living place for monastic life)* monastery, priory, abbey, friary, convent, nunnery, cloister; sanctuary.

Adjectives—churchly, claustral, cloistral, cloistered; monastic, conventual.

Quotations—A Church is God between four walls (*Victor Hugo*).

---

tempo, *n.* time, beat, rate, pace, rhythm. See MUSIC.

temporal, *adj.* worldly, mundane, secular; civil, political, profane, unsacred; temporary, ephemeral, impermanent. See TRANSIENTNESS.

temporary, *adj.* impermanent, irregular, seasonal, provisional, momentary, brief, fleeting, transitory; stopgap, makeshift, ersatz. See TRANSIENTNESS.

temporize, *v.i.* adapt oneself, maneuver; vacillate, procrastinate, stall, delay, hedge, blow hot and cold, play for time. See LATENESS, DURABILITY.

tempt, *v.t.* entice, cajole, fascinate, lure, decoy, seduce; provoke, defy, incite, appeal, attract. See DESIRE, ATTRACTION.

temptation, *n.* ATTRACTION, enticement, allurement; bait; siren song; provocativeness. See DESIRE.

TENACITY
Persistence

Nouns—tenacity, cohesion, COHERENCE; holding, STRENGTH; viscidity, viscosity; pertinacity, perseverance, persistence, RESOLUTION, patience; OBSTINACY, RESISTANCE, constancy, RETENTION. *Informal,* stick-to-itiveness, trucking.

Verbs—adhere (to), stick (to), cling (to); persevere, persist, hold on *or* out, never say die, fight to the last ditch, be in at the death, stick to one's guns; keep on, hold one's course *or* ground, bear *or* keep up, continue, plod, follow through *or* up. *Informal,* stick it out, muddle through, see it through, hang on for dear life, keep a stiff upper lip, keep one's chin up.

Adjectives—tenacious, cohesive, adhesive, clinging, holding, fast, resisting, strong; sticky, gummy, tacky, waxy, glutinous, viscous, viscid; pertinacious, persistent, persevering, dogged, determined, unyielding, uncompromising, unwavering, unfaltering; obstinate, stubborn, intransigent, opinionated, positive, single-minded; steady, steadfast, firm, resolute, constant, purposeful, relentless; retentive. *Informal,* pigheaded, never-say-die.

Adverbs—tenaciously, *etc.*; through thick and thin, rain or shine.

Quotations—To persevere, trusting in what hopes he has, is courage in a man (*Euripides*), Great works are performed not by strength, but by perseverance (*Samuel Johnson*), Perseverance is more prevailing than violence (*Plutarch*).

Antonyms, see WEAKNESS, SUBMISSION.

---

tenant, *n.* occupant, occupier, resident, INHABITANT, renter; inmate. See POSSESSION, ABODE.

tend, *v.* mind, watch, care for, guard, keep; attend, serve, wait on, incline, bend, bear toward, lean, gravitate. See SERVANT, TENDENCY, UTILITY.

TENDENCY
Disposition to act in a particular way

Nouns—tendency; aptness, aptitude; proneness, proclivity, predilection, bent, turn, tone, tenor, bias, set, leaning, penchant, [pre]disposition, inclination, propensity, susceptibility; likelihood, LIABILITY; nature, temperament; idiosyncrasy; cast, vein, grain; humor, mood; trend, drift, the way the wind blows; conduciveness, conducement; applicability. *Informal,* tendency. See SPECIALITY, INTRINSIC, DIRECTION.

Verbs—tend, contribute, conduce, lead, dispose, incline, verge, lean, bend to, trend, affect, carry, redound to, bid fair to, gravitate toward; be liable.

Adjectives—tending, conducive, working toward, in a fair way to, calculated to; liable, prone; useful, subsidiary.

Quotations—As natural selection works solely by and for the good of each being, all corporeal and mental endowments will tend to progress toward perfection (*Charles Darwin*), In a hierarchy, every employee tends to rise to his level of incompetence (*Laurence J. Peter*), The forces of a capitalist society, if left unchecked, tend to make the rich richer and the poor poorer (*Jawaharlal Nehru*).

Antonyms, see OPPOSITION.

tender, *v.t.* present, OFFER, proffer, hold out; propose, suggest; volunteer. —*adj.* gentle, kind; sentimental; affectionate, tenderhearted, loving, amorous; immature; sympathetic, soft; humane, merciful; young; fragile, delicate; pathetic, touching; painful, sore. See BENEVOLENCE, LOVE, SOFTNESS, FEELING, PITY, YOUTH. —*n.* MONEY; supply ship; supply car, coal car. See SHIP, VEHICLE.

tenderfoot, *n.* newcomer, recruit, novice, greenhorn (*inf.*). See BEGINNING.

tenderhearted, *adj.* kind, sympathetic. See CARE.

tenebrous, *adj.* dark, gloomy. See DARKNESS.

tenement, *n.* apartment house; flat, dwelling, ABODE; slum.

tenet, *n.* dogma, BELIEF, opinion, creed, doctrine.

tenor, *n.* drift, purport, TENDENCY, import, MEANING, significance; gist, sense; course, manner, nature, mood; DIRECTION. See MUSIC.

tense, *adj.* taut, rigid; intent; excited; highstrung, nervous, strained. See HARDNESS. —*n.* time, verb form, inflection. See GRAMMAR.

tensile, *adj.* stretchable, ductile, flexile; resilient, pliable. See ELASTICITY.

tension, *n.* strain, pressure, tensity, tenseness; stretching; anxiety, nervousness. See LENGTH, TRACTION, HARDNESS, FEAR.

tent, *n.* canvas, wigwam, teepee, pavilion, shelter. See COVERING, ABODE.

tentacle, *n.* process, feeler, palp; power, grasp. See RETENTION.

tentative, *adj.* experimental, provisional, conditional, temporary, makeshift. See EXPEDIENCE, EXPERIMENT.

tenuous, *adj.* unsubstantial, flimsy; thin, slender; rarefied. See NARROWNESS, RARITY.

tenure, *n.* holding, tenancy, occupancy, occupation, habitation, POSSESSION.

tepid, *adj.* lukewarm, mild; indifferent. See HEAT, INDIFFERENCE.

term, *n.* word, expression, locution; LIMIT, bound; period, TIME, tenure, duration; semester. See NOMENCLATURE.

terminal, *adj.* final; closing, concluding. See END. —*n.* station, terminus. See LOCATION, ARRIVAL.

termination, *n.* END, ending, conclusion; LIMIT, bound; result, outcome, consequence, completion; suffix.

terminology, *n.* See NOMENCLATURE.

terms, *n.pl.* provisions, limitations, stipulations, conditions, agreement; relationship, footing. See COMMAND, QUALIFICATION.

terrace, *n.* level, plateau, plane; parterre, esplanade, promenade; porch, patio, balcony, embankment. See HORIZONTAL.

terra firma, *Lat.*, solid ground; LAND, SUPPORT.

terrain, *n.* LAND, tract, ground, field.

terra incognita, *Lat.*, unknown territory. See IGNORANCE, SECRET.

terrestrial, *adj.* earthly; worldly, mundane, secular, temporal. See LAND.

terrible, *adj.* terrifying, dreadful; awesome, appalling, frightful, horrible, shocking, fearful, alarming; *informal,* excessive. See FEAR.

terrific, *adj.* terrible (see FEAR); *informal,* sensational, wonderful, fabulous, stupendous, out of this world. See GREATNESS.

terrify, *v.t.* terrorize, frighten, alarm; appall, dismay; cow, intimidate; panic, stampede. See FEAR.

territory, *n.* REGION, district; possession; kingdom, state, realm, province; jurisdiction; field, ground. See KNOWLEDGE.

terror, *n.* FEAR, dread; fright, alarm; dismay, horror; panic.

terrorism, *n.* oppression, tyranny, anarchy, revolution, bolshevism, nihilism; VIOLENCE, destruction, sabotage, intimidation, agitation. See FEAR, THREAT.

terse, *adj.* concise, brief, curt; pithy, laconic, succinct; short, compact. See MAXIM, SHORTNESS.

test, *n.* examination; trial, essay; criterion; EXPERIMENT.

testament, *n.* will, last will and testament, probate; covenant, AGREEMENT. See GIVING.

testicles, *n.pl.* testes, balls (*sl.*). See BODY.

testify, *v.* affirm, declare, state, depose; swear, avow, witness. See EVIDENCE.

testimonial, *n.* recommendation, reference; certificate. See RECORD, APPROBATION, EVIDENCE.

testimony, *n.* declaration, affirmation, profession, attestation; witness, EVIDENCE; Scriptures.

testy, *adj.* irritable, irascible, petulant, cross; ornery (*inf.*), tetchy (*dial.*). See IRASCIBILITY.

tête-à-tête, *Fr.*, private CONVERSATION, chat.

tether, *v.t.* picket, stake, tie, fasten. See RESTRAINT.

text, *n.* composition; matter; textbook; topic, subject, theme. See WRITING, PUBLICATION, TEACHING.

textile, *n.* cloth, fabric. See MATERIALS.

TEXTURE
Surface characteristics

Nouns—1, texture, quality, fabric, surface, fiber, nap, tooth, tissue, weave, warp and woof, weft, grain, fineness *or* coarseness of grain; SMOOTHNESS, ROUGHNESS. See ORNAMENT. 2, SUBSTANCE, stuff, staple (see MATERIALS); mat, web[bing], braid, plait, trellis, mesh, lattice[work], tissue. See CROSSING.

Verb—texture; braid, plait, *etc.*; coarsen, grain.

Adjectives—textured, textural, textile, woven; structural, anatomic[al], organic; coarse, grainy, coarse-grained, homespun; shaggy, nappy; fine, fine-grained; delicate, subtle, filmy, downy, gossamery, smooth.

Antonyms, see SMOOTHNESS.

---

thank, *v.t.* express GRATITUDE to; acknowledge, recognize, credit.

thankful, *adj.* grateful, appreciative; much obliged. See GRATITUDE.

thankless, *adj.* ungrateful, unthankful, unappreciative, ingrate, ungracious; unrewarding, unpleasant. See INGRATITUDE, DISCONTENT.

thanks, *n.pl.* GRATITUDE; acknowledgment, appreciation; thank you; grace.

thanksgiving, *n.* grace, prayer, praise. See GRATITUDE.

thaw, *v.* melt, dissolve, liquefy; soften, unbend. See HEAT, LIQUEFACTION.

theater, *n.* stage, ARENA, field [of action]; DRAMA; playhouse, motion-picture house, studio. See AMUSEMENT.

theatrical, *adj.* dramatic, melodramatic; histrionic; scenic; showy, stagy, affected; vivid, moving. See AFFECTATION, DRAMA, OSTENTATION.

theft, *n.* larceny, STEALING.

theme, *n.* subject, topic, text; essay, thesis, treatise, DISSERTATION; composition; melody, motif. See MUSIC, THOUGHT.

then, *adv.* soon, next, immediately; consequently, therefore, evidently, again; afterward. See CIRCUMSTANCE, SEQUENCE.

theology, *n.* RELIGION; creed, BELIEF; doctrine, dogma.

theoretical, *adj.* speculative, hypothetical, conjectural; unapplied; pure, abstract. See SUPPOSITION.

theory, *n.* speculation, surmise, conjecture; contemplation; principle, philosophy, doctrine; hypothesis; guess, idea, plan. See SUPPOSITION.

therapy, *n.* therapeutics, REMEDY, healing, cure; rehabilitation, RESTORATION; physical therapy, psychotherapy, *etc.*

thereafter, *adv.* after[ward], after that; subsequently, [t]henceforth, from that moment; after which; later, in the future. See SEQUENCE.

therefore, *adv.* consequently, ergo, hence, wherefore, so, accordingly. See REASONING, ATTRIBUTION, CIRCUMSTANCE, EFFECT.

thermal, *adj.* warm[ing] (see HEAT).

thermometer, *n.* thermostat, pyrometer, calorimeter; mercury, glass. See MEASUREMENT, HEAT.

thermonuclear, *adj.* See POWER.

thesaurus, *n.* treasury; repository, lexicon, dictionary. See PUBLICATION.

thesis, *n.* proposition, topic, argument; affirmation; postulate; statement; composition, treatise, DISSERTATION. See THOUGHT.

thick, *adj.* broad, wide, massive, thickset, stout, fat; dense, solid; populous, crowded; heavy, viscous, creamy, gooey (*sl.*); foggy, smoky, hazy; hoarse, guttural, throaty; slow[-witted], witless. See BREADTH, DENSITY, MULTITUDE.

thicket, *n.* brush, underbrush; grove, coppice, covert. See VEGETABLE.

thickset, *adj.* dense; stout, stocky. See DENSITY, WEIGHT.

thick-skinned, *adj.* insensitive, callous[ed], hard. See INSENSIBILITY.

thief, *n.* robber (see STEAL).

thin, *adj.* slender, lean, narrow (see NARROWNESS); watery, weak, diluted; attenuated; faint, dim, threadlike; fine, delicate; poor, lame (*as an excuse*); flimsy, sheer, filmy. See RARITY, WEAKNESS, TRANSPARENCY, INSIPIDITY.

thing, *n.* affair, matter, circumstance; deed, act, occurrence; entity, person; possession, belonging, chattel; item, object, detail, article. See SUBSTANCE.

think, *v.* See THOUGHT.

third degree, *informal,* grilling, cross-examination, interrogation. See INQUIRY.

third estate, general public, common people. See POPULACE.

third world, developing *or* underdeveloped country (see POPULACE).

thirst, *n.* DRYNESS; craving, DESIRE; dipsomania, thirstiness, parchedness.

thirsty, *adj.* dry, parched, unslaked, un-quenched, arid; greedy, avid. See DRYNESS, DESIRE.

thistle, *n.* cactus, bramble (see SHARPNESS).

thong, *n.* strip, lace; sandal; string bikini. See FILAMENT, CLOTHING.

thorn, *n.* spine, prickle, briar, bramble; annoyance, irritation. See SHARPNESS, DISCONTENT.

thorough, *adj.* thoroughgoing, painstaking, exact, careful; complete, absolute, unqualified, arrant, out-and-out; exhaustive, deep, sweeping. See COMPLETION.

thoroughbred, *adj.* purebred, full-blooded, pedigreed; blue-blooded, noble, aristocratic; to the manor born; well-bred *or* -mannered. See PURITY, FASHION, NOBILITY.

thoroughfare, *n.* avenue, highway, street; PASSAGE, way; thruway, stop street, boulevard, turnpike.

though, *conj.* although, even if, nevertheless, yet. See COMPENSATION.

THOUGHT
Mental activity

Nouns—1, thought, thoughtfulness; reflection, cogitation, consideration, meditation, study, lucubration, speculation, deliberation, pondering; headwork, brainwork; cerebration; deep reflection, rumination, close study, application, ATTENTION; abstract thought, abstraction; doublethink (see ABSURDITY); contemplation, musing, preoccupation, brown study, reverie, Platonism; self-counsel, self-communing, self-consultation; association, succession, *or* flow of ideas; train *or* current of thought, stream of consciousness; lateral *or* vertical thinking; positive thinking, mind over matter. See JUDGMENT, INTELLECT, REASONING.

2, *(rethinking)* afterthought, mature thought, reconsideration, second thought; retrospection, hindsight; MEMORY; excogitation; examination (see INQUIRY); invention (see IMAGINATION).

3, *(subject for thought)* idea, concept, notion; opinion, conceit, belief, impression; principle; topic, subject of thought, material *or* food for thought; subject [matter], matter, theme, thesis, text, business, affair, matter in hand, argument; motion, resolution; head, chapter; case, point; proposition, theorem (see SUPPOSITION); field of inquiry; moot point, problem.

Verbs—1, think, reflect, cogitate, cerebrate, excogitate, consider, think over, deliberate, lucubrate; rationalize, speculate, contemplate, meditate, ponder, muse, dream, ruminate; brood upon; animadvert, study; bend *or* apply the mind; digest, discuss, weigh; realize, appreciate; fancy; think on one's feet. *Slang,* beat one's brains (out), use one's head, bean, noodle, *or* noggin.

2, take into consideration; see about *or* to; take counsel, commune with oneself, bethink oneself; collect one's thoughts; revolve, turn over *or* run over in the mind; sleep on; rack one's brains; set one's wits to work; puzzle *or* pore over; take into one's head; bear in mind; reconsider, think better of; put on one's thinking cap. *Informal,* sweat over, chew the cud, mull over. *Slang,* kick around.

3, occur, present, *or* suggest itself; come into one's head; strike one, cross *or* pass through the mind, occupy the mind; have on one's mind; make an impression; sink

. in, penetrate the mind; engross the thoughts; come to think of it. *Informal,* take a notion.

Adjectives—thinking, thoughtful, pensive, meditative, reflective, musing, wistful, contemplative, speculative, deliberative, studious, sedate, introspective, platonic, philosophical, metaphysic[al]; rational; lost in thought, engrossed, absorbed, rapt, preoccupied; in the mind, under consideration; on one's chest. *Slang,* on the brain.

Adverbs—thoughtfully, reflectively; all things considered.

Phrases—there is one thing stronger than all the armies in the world, and that is an idea whose time has come; great minds think alike; two heads are better than one; penny for your thoughts.

Quotations—Yond Cassius has a mean and hungry look; he thinks too much: such men are dangerous (*Shakespeare*), I think, therefore I am (*René Descartes*), Stung by the splendor of a sudden thought (*Robert Browning*), How can I tell what I think till I see what I say? (*E. M. Forster*), A man of action forced into a state of thought is unhappy until he can get out of it (*John Galsworthy*), The real question is not whether machines think but whether men do (*B. F. Skinner*), Being and thought are one (*Jean Dubuffet*), There is nothing either good or bad but thinking makes it so (*Shakespeare*).

Antonyms, see RASHNESS, INATTENTION.

---

thoughtful, *adj.* considerate, kind, tactful; meditative. See THOUGHT, ATTENTION, CARE.

thoughtless, *adj.* rash, reckless, heedless; casual; inconsiderate, unthinking, mindless; unreasoning; careless, indifferent. See RASHNESS.

thought-provoking, *adj.* stimulating, provocative. See THOUGHT.

thousand, *n.* fifty score, M, thou (*sl.*), yard (*sl.*), grand (*sl.*), G (*sl.*). See NUMERATION.

thrall, *n.* slavery, bondage, SERVILITY.

thrash, *v.t.* beat, spank, whip, flog, strike; defeat, overcome, conquer; thresh. See SUCCESS, PUNISHMENT.

thread, *n.* FILAMENT, fiber, hair; string; yarn; linen, cotton, silk, lisle, nylon, *etc.*; course, drift, train (of thought). See CONTINUITY, NARROWNESS.

threadbare, *adj.* frayed, tattered, worn[out]; jaded, weary; trite, hackneyed; scanty. See DETERIORATION, DIVESTMENT, WEARINESS.

THREAT
Declaration of intention to harm

Nouns—1, threat, menace, intimidation, commination, minacity, TERRORISM; empty threat, fulmination, sword- *or* saber-rattling; DEFIANCE; yellow menace *or* peril; blackmail, extortion. See FUTURITY, FEAR, WARNING.

2, thunder[bolt], gathering clouds, red sky in the morning; foreboding, imminence, omen, WARNING; bad eye; notice; peril, jeopardy, DANGER.

Verbs—1, threaten, menace, intimidate, comminate, fulminate; terrorize, frighten, hector, cow, bully, browbeat; snarl, growl, mutter, bark, thunder, bluster, brandish; jeopardize, imperil, endanger; blackmail, extort; talk big, look daggers, shake the fist at; carry a big stick. *Slang,* shake down, buy a woof *or* wolf ticket, mau-mau, heavy.

2, portend, presage, augur, omen, [fore]bode, foreshadow (see PREDICTION), impend, be imminent, overhang, lower, lour, loom, hang over one's head.

Adjectives—threatening, menacing, intimidative, denunciatory, fulminatory, bullying; WARNING, cautionary, dangerous, perilous, jeopardous; ominous, foreboding, lowering, looming, *etc.*; baleful, baneful, thundery, dire[ful], awful, sinister, dark, black.

Phrases—threatened men live long.

Quotations—Injustice anywhere is a threat to justice everywhere (*Martin Luther King, Jr.*).

Antonyms, see SAFETY.

three-dimensional, *adj.* stereoscopic; realistic, lifelike. See BREADTH, VISION.

threshold, *n.* sill, doorsill, entrance; outset, BEGINNING; limen, threshold of pain, *etc.* See EDGE.

thrift, *n.* thriftiness, ECONOMY, frugality, saving; providence, husbandry; vigor, growth, thriving.

thrifty, *adj.* frugal, saving; sparing; economical; foresighted; provident. See ECONOMY.

thrill, *n.* EXCITEMENT; tremor, vibration; sensation; tingle, kick (*sl.*), charge (*sl.*). —*v.* throb, tingle, shiver; stir, excite, move deeply; vibrate, tremble. See FEELING, SENSIBILITY.

thriller, *n.* chiller, shocker; pulp story, dime novel, cloak-and-dagger *or* spy story, whodunit (*sl.*); swashbuckler. See DESCRIPTION.

thrive, *v.i.* prosper, batten, succeed, grow, flourish, bloom, flower. See PROSPERITY.

throat, *n.* neck, gullet, gorge, maw; windpipe; throttle. See OPENING.

throb, *v.i.* beat, pulsate, vibrate, palpitate; quiver, shudder, tremble; ache, hurt. See AGITATION, FEELING.

throe, *n.* pang, spasm, paroxysm, PAIN, AGITATION.

throne, *n.* royal seat, chair; sovereignty, scepter. See AUTHORITY.

throng, *n.* multitude, crowd, mob, horde; army, host. See ASSEMBLAGE.

throttle, *v.* choke, strangle, suffocate; silence, stifle; close. See CLOSURE, KILLING.

through, *prep. & adv.* among, via, by way of; during, throughout; by, with. See DIRECTION, MEANS. —*adj.* finished, completed. See END.

throughway, *n.* thruway, turnpike, superhighway. See PASSAGE.

throw, *v.* pitch, toss, cast, fling, hurl, sling; propel, project, unhorse, unseat; *slang,* stop, disconcert, confound. See PROPULSION. —**throw away** *or* **out**, discard, reject (see EJECTION). —**throw up**, vomit, upchuck (*sl.*). See EJECTION.

throwback, *n.* atavism, REVERSION.

thrust, *v.* push, drive, shove, propel; lunge, plunge, ram; stab, pierce; compel, drive, force; interpose, interject. —*n.* blow, jab, poke; ATTACK, sortie; dig; repartee; POWER. See IMPULSE.

thud, *n.* bump, thump (see SOUND).

thug, *n.* cutthroat, assassin, killer; ruffian, hooligan, tough, hoodlum, mugger, hood (*sl.*), goon (*sl.*), yegg (*sl.*), torpedo (*sl.*), gorilla (*sl.*). See EVILDOER.

thump, *n.* blow, punch; thud. See IMPULSE, SOUND.

thunder, *v.* shout, bellow; resound, peal, boom, roar, roll, crash. See LOUDNESS.

thus, *adv.* so; consequently, hence. See CIRCUMSTANCE.

thwart, *v.t.* oppose, baffle, foil, frustrate, defeat, block, contravene. See HINDRANCE.

tiara, *n.* diadem, coronet. See ORNAMENT.

tic, *n.* twitch, jerk, rictus. See AGITATION.

tick, *n.* click, beat; check, dot; mite; *informal,* score, account. See INDICATION, CREDIT, ANIMAL.

ticket, *n.* notice, memorandum, record; license; label, tag; list, slate, ballot; admission ticket. See INDICATION, CHOICE.

tickle, *v.t.* excite; gladden, delight, overjoy; please; titillate; amuse, gratify, divert. See PLEASURE.

ticklish, *adj.* tickly, excitable, sensitive; unstable, touchy; delicate, critical, risky, dangerous. See SENSIBILITY, DANGER.

tidal, *adj.* littoral, estuarine, coastal. See WATER.

tidbit, *n.* morsel, bite, snack; goody, treat, bonbon; gem, pearl, jewel; news, INFORMATION, juicy bit. See FOOD.

tide, *n.* flow, current, flood, riptide. See WATER.

tidings, *n.pl.* NEWS, message, intelligence, INFORMATION.

tidy, *adj.* neat, orderly, trim, prim; *informal,* sizable, considerable (see GREATNESS). —*v.* arrange, put in order, straighten. See CLEANNESS, ARRANGEMENT, ORDER.

tie, *n.* bond, obligation; shoelace; necktie, cravat, four-in-hand *or* bow tie; fastening, ligature; draw, tied score, dead heat; beam, post; sleeper. —*v.t.* fasten, attach, join; bind, restrict, constrain, confine; knot; equal. See CLOTHING, DUTY, JUNCTION, CONNECTION, EQUALITY.

tier, *n.* rank, row, level, LAYER; gallery, boxes, balcony.

tie-up, *n.* halt, stoppage, blockade, impediment, snarl, [traffic] jam, impasse; *informal,* association, connection, tie-in, liaison. See COOPERATION, HINDRANCE.

tiff, *n.* temper, fit, tantrum; squabble, spat, miff (*inf.*). See CONTENTION, DISCORD.

tight, *adj.* close, compact, hermetic, impervious; snug, close-fitting; hemmed-in; strict, stringent; scarce, in short supply; *informal,* stingy, parsimonious; *slang,* intoxicated, inebriated, loaded. See CLOSURE, CONTRACTION, NARROWNESS, PARSIMONY, DRINKING.

tight-fisted, *adj.* stingy, frugal, parsimonious, grudging, niggard[ly], miserly, moneygrubbing, avaricious, tight (*inf.*), cheap (*inf.*). See PARSIMONY.

tight-lipped, *adj.* secretive, reticent. See TACITURNITY.

tights, *n.pl.* leotards (see CLOTHING).

tightwad, *n., slang,* skinflint, cheapskate. See PARSIMONY.

till, *prep.* until, up to, down to. See TIME. —*v.* cultivate, plow, farm. See AGRICULTURE.

tilt, *v.* tip, slant, incline, slope; joust. —*n.* joust, tournament; altercation, dispute; speed; slant, slope; awning, canopy. See CONTENTION, OBLIQUITY, COVERING.

timber, *n.* wood, lumber, log, beam; forest, woodland, stand of timber, timberland. See MATERIALS.

timbre, *n.* resonance, tonal quality, SOUND, tone color, ring, clang.

TIME
Measurement of duration

Nouns—1, time, duration; period, term, stage, space, span, spell, season; fourth dimension; the whole time; era, epoch, age, aeon; time of life; moment, instant, INSTANTANEITY, SYNCHRONISM; anachronism; course, progress, flow, march, stream, *or* lapse of time; slow *or* standard time, real time, elapsed time; free time, white space; Time, Father Time, ravages of time; time's arrow. See PAST, FUTURITY. *Informal,* donkey's years, many moons, a month of Sundays.

2, intermediate time, while, interim, interval, pendency; intermission, intermittence, interregnum, interlude; time frame; leisure, spare time; respite. See DISCONTINUANCE, BETWEEN.

3, anniversary, jubilee, recurrence (see REGULARITY).

4, timekeeper; timepiece, watch, clock (see CHRONOMETRY).

5, timing, clocking, chronology.

Verbs—continue, last, endure, go on, remain, persist; intervene, elapse, lapse, pass, flow, advance, roll on, go by, go on; flit, fly, slip, slide, *or* glide by; take [up] time, fill *or* occupy time; pass, spend, waste, while away, *or* consume time; live out; talk against time; tide over; seize an opportunity, take time by the forelock; make a day *or* night of it.

Adjectives—continuing; permanent, perpetual, eternal; regular, steady, periodic, intermittent; elapsing, passing, aoristic; timely, untimely, punctual, fast, slow, leisurely, unhurried, early, late. See EARLINESS, LATENESS, SLOWNESS, HASTE.

Adverbs—during, pending; in passing, during the time; during the time *or* interval; in the course of time; for the time being, day by day; in the time of, when; from time immemorial; meantime, meanwhile; in the meantime, in the interim, from day to day, from hour to hour; hourly, always; for a time *or* season; till, until, up to, yet, as yet; the whole time, all the time; all along; throughout, for good; hereupon, thereupon, whereupon; then; anno Domini, A.D., before Christ, B.C., once upon a time; in a time, in due time, in season, in the fullness of time, some fine day; out of season.

Phrases—there is a time for everything; time will tell; time works wonders; time is a great healer *or* the great physician; time is money.

Quotations—To everything there is a season, and a time to every purpose under heaven (*Bible*), Time the devourer of everything (*Ovid*), I am Time grown old to destroy the world, embarked on the course of world annihilation (*Bhagavad Gita*), I wasted time, and now doth time waste me (*Shakespeare*), Tomorrow, and tomorrow, and tomorrow, creeps in this petty pace from day to day (*Shakespeare*), Time, like an ever-rolling stream, bears all its sons away (*Isaac Watts*), Remember that time is money (*Benjamin Franklin*), Time is the great physician (*Benjamin Disraeli*), As if you could kill time without injuring eternity (*Henry David Thoreau*), The distinction between past, present and future is only an illusion, however persistent (*Albert Einstein*), The inaudible and noiseless foot of Time (*Shakespeare*), Time is a great teacher, but unfortunately it kills all its pupils (*Hector Berlioz*).

Antonyms, see PERPETUITY.

---

timeless, *adj.* endless, perpetual, everlasting, deathless, immortal; dateless, ageless, immemorial, prehistoric, legendary. See PERPETUITY.

timely, *adj.* well-timed, seasonable, opportune; auspicious, right. See TIME, EARLINESS, OCCASION, EXPEDIENCE.

timepiece, *n.* clock, watch, chronometer (see CHRONOMETRY).

timetable, *n.* schedule, timeline (see CHRONOMETRY).

timeworn, *adj.* out-of-date; worn, impaired. See OLDNESS, DETERIORATION.

timid, *adj.* fearful, cowardly, afraid, fainthearted, timorous; shrinking, bashful, shy, retiring, diffident; irresolute, hesitant; weak. See FEAR, MODESTY.

timing, *n.* synchronization; chronology. See TIME, MEASUREMENT.

timorous, *adj.* timid, fearful. See FEAR, MODESTY.

tincture, *n.* trace, vestige, touch, dash; tinge, tint, shade; soupçon. See COLOR, MIXTURE.

tinder, *n.* touchwood, punk, amadou. See FUEL.

tine, *n.* prong, branch, point, tip; skewer, spike, bodkin, barb. See SHARPNESS.

tinge, *n.* tint, shade, COLOR, dye, stain; flavor, cast. See MIXTURE.

tingle, *v.i.* sting, prickle; thrill. See PAIN, FEELING.

tinhorn, *n.* gambler, piker. See CHANCE.

tinker, *n.* handyman, jack-of-all-trades, Mr. Fixit (*inf.*); blunderer, bungler. —*v.* mend, repair; botch; tamper, putter, doctor; fiddle, fuss, play, *or* monkey with. See RESTORATION, UNSKILLFULNESS.

tinny, *adj.* flimsy, poor; metallic. See INFERIORITY, SOUND.

tinsel, *n.* tawdriness, gaudiness, frippery, show; baubles, gewgaws. See ORNAMENT, DECEPTION, OSTENTATION.

tint, *n.* COLOR, tinge, hue, dye, shade; tone, cast, nuance.

tiny, *adj.* minute, miniature, small, diminutive, wee, half-pint (*sl.*); microscopic. See LITTLENESS.

tip, *v.* overturn, capsize, upset; incline, slant, tilt, topple; reward. See PAYMENT. —*n.* point, END; apex, summit; clue, hint, warning, pointer; gratuity, gift, fee, perquisite, pourboire. See HEIGHT, GIVING, COVERING.

tipple, *v.* drink (see DRINKING).

tipsy, *adj.* intoxicated, high (*sl.*), tight (*sl.*). See DRINKING.

tiptoe, *v.i.* steal, sneak, walk on tiptoes; creep, sidle. See CAUTION, TRAVEL.

tiptop, *adj.* top-quality, topnotch, tops. See SUPERIORITY.

tirade, *n.* harangue, screed, diatribe, jeremiad; SPEECH, sermon; outpouring, flood, spate. See DISAPPROBATION.

tire, *v.* weary, fatigue, bore, exhaust, jade, fag. See WEARINESS. —*n.* recap, retread; snow, spare, radial, tube, tubeless, *or* bias-ply tire.

tireless, *adj.* untiring, indefatigable, unwearied. See RESOLUTION.

tiresome, *adj.* tedious, wearying, boring. See WEARINESS.

tissue, *n.* gauze, fabric, web, net, mesh; membrane, cartilage, muscle; tissue *or* crepe paper; structure. See CROSSING, TEXTURE.

tit, *n.* teat, nipple (see BODY).

titillate, *v.t.* tickle; excite. See TOUCH, DESIRE, EXCITEMENT.

title, *n.* name, handle (*inf.*); form of address; subheading, subtitle; appellation, designation, caption; legend; epithet; honorific, peerage; status, degree; cognomen, surname. —*v.* name, call. See NOMENCLATURE, NOBILITY, AUTHORITY, POSSESSION, RIGHTNESS.

titled, *adj.* noble, aristocratic; named, termed. See NOBILITY, NOMENCLATURE.

toady, *n.* fawner, sycophant, truckler, bootlicker (*inf.*). See SERVILITY, FLATTERY.

toast, *v.t.* brown, heat, warm; drink to, pledge, honor. —*n.* toasted bread, zwieback, rusk; health, pledge. See HEAT, CELEBRATION.

tobacco, *n.* smoking; leaf, perique, Burley,

latakia, Turkish, Havana, Virginia; cigar, cigarette, caporal; snuff, plug, chew, weed (*inf.*), Lady Nicotine (*inf.*). See PUNGENCY.

today, *n.* now, the present, here and now (see PRESENT).

to-do, *n.* ado, turmoil, bother, bustle, commotion. See EXCITEMENT.

together, *adv.* mutually, reciprocally, unitedly; coincidentally, concurrently, simultaneously. See ACCOMPANIMENT, SYNCHRONISM.

toil, *n.* labor, drudgery; task, work; effort, exhaustion. —*v.* work, drudge, moil, labor; strive. See EXERTION.

toilet, *n.* toilette, prinking, makeup; powder room, washroom, bathroom, lavatory, restroom, comfort station, water closet, W.C., cabinet; outhouse, latrine, privy, john (*sl.*), head (*sl.*), can (*sl.*); chamber pot, bidet, slop pail. See UNCLEANNESS.

toils, *n.pl.* snare, net, trap, mesh, web; grip, clutches. See DECEPTION.

token, *n.* sign, symbol, emblem; feature, trait; souvenir, memento, keepsake; badge, evidence; slug; earnest, INDICATION. See MEMORY.

tolerable, *adj.* endurable, bearable; passable, not bad. See CONTENT, GOODNESS, LENIENCY.

tolerance, *n.* toleration, allowance; MODERATION, temperance, endurance, forbearance, sufferance, laxity; clemency, LENIENCY. See PERMISSION, FEELING, INEXCITABILITY, LIBERALITY.

toll, *n.* tax, import, charge, fee. See PAYMENT, PRICE.

tomb, *n.* grave, sepulcher, mausoleum, vault, catacombs. See INTERMENT.

tomboy, *n.* hoyden, romp. See FEMALE.

tome, *n.* volume, BOOK.

tomorrow, *adv.* on the morrow, the next day, henceforth, mañana. See FUTURITY.

tone, *n.* SOUND; quality; accent, pitch, inflection, modulation, intonation; strain, key, spirit; elasticity, resilience; tension, firmness, tonus; condition; frame of mind, mood; ELEGANCE, stylishness; tint, shade, hue. See COLOR, FEELING, METHOD.

tongs, *n.pl.* pincers, nippers, pliers, forceps. See RETENTION.

tongue, *n.* communication, SPEECH, language, dialect; pole; flap, projection. See SUPPORT, CONVEXITY.

tongue-in-cheek, *adv.* facetiously, jokingly. See AMUSEMENT, RIDICULE.

tongue-lashing, *n.* scolding (see DISAPPROBATION).

tongue-tied, *adj.* silent, mute, inarticulate, STAMMERING; bashful, shy.

tongue twister, see STAMMERING.

tonic, *adj.* invigorating, bracing, refreshing; voiced, sonant; stressed, accented. See HEALTH, REMEDY. —*n.* medicine, stimulant; quinine; key, keynote. See STRENGTH.

tony, *adj., informal,* stylish, modish (see FASHION).

too, *adv.* also, likewise; over; additionally, excessively. See ADDITION. —**too much,** overabundance (see SUFFICIENCY); intolerable, unbearable (see DURABILITY).

tool, *n.* instrument, implement, utensil, device, machine; cat's-paw, dupe, henchman, intermediary. See INSTRUMENTALITY.

toot, *n., slang,* revelry, binge, bender. See DRINKING.

tooth, *n.* fang, tusk, canine, incisor, molar, cuspid, bicuspid, eyetooth, grinder (*inf.*), chopper (*inf.*); tine, cog; TASTE, relish; fondness. See SHARPNESS, CONVEXITY.

toothsome, *adj.* toothy, palatable, appetizing; delicious, luscious, dainty, delectable. See TASTE.

top, *n.* crown, head; acme, summit, pinnacle; pick, elite; lid, cover. —*v.* crown, cap; prune, excel, dominate. See SUPERIORITY, HEIGHT.

topcoat, *n.* overcoat, greatcoat. See CLOTHING.

topflight, *adj.* first-rate, superior. See SUPERIORITY.

topic, *n.* subject, theme, thesis, subject matter; item, question; business, point [of argument]; proposition, statement. See INQUIRY, INFORMATION, THOUGHT.

topless, *adj.* seminude, half-dressed. See DIVESTMENT.

topnotch, *adj., informal,* first-rate, superior; excellent. See SUPERIORITY.

topping, *n.* sauce, coating; layer, COVERING. See FOOD.

topple, *v.i.* fall over *or* down, tumble, somersault, pitch, plunge; fail, collapse, go bankrupt, fold (*sl.*). —*v.t.* push, trip, knock over *or* down; overturn, upset; overthrow, subvert, defeat, smash. See DESCENT, DESTRUCTION, FAILURE.

tops, *adj., slang,* first-rate (see SUPERIORITY).

topsy-turvy, *adj.* upside-down; disorderly, in a mess. See DISORDER.

torch, *n.* LIGHT, torchlight, brand; flambeau; flashlight; *slang,* firebug, arsonist. See HEAT, FUEL.

torment, *n.* languish, distress; torture, agony, PAIN —*v.t.* torture, distress, agonize, rack, afflict. See DISCONTENT, PUNISHMENT.

tornado, *n.* WIND, windstorm, twister, cyclone, typhoon. See VIOLENCE, ROTATION.

torpid, *adj.* dormant, sleepy; numb; inert, unmoving, still, stagnant; dull, stupid, apathetic, slothful, sluggish, lethargic; listless. See INACTIVITY.

torrent, *n.* cascade, deluge, downpour; current, rapids; outburst, outbreak, spurt, spate, surge, flood, Niagara. See VELOCITY, VIOLENCE, WATER.

torrid, *adj.* hot, burning, arid, parched, sizzling, scorching; equatorial, tropical; ardent, passionate. See HEAT, FEELING.

torso, *n.* trunk (see SUBSTANCE).

tortuous, *adj.* spiral, snaky, sinuous, serpentine; winding, crooked. See CONVOLUTION.

torture, *n.* PAIN, excruciation, agony, torment; martyrdom, crucifixion; anguish; cruelty. —*v.t.* punish; torment, rack, agonize, martyr; garble, distort, twist, misrepresent. See PUNISHMENT, BADNESS.

toss, *v.* fling, buffet, jerk; agitate, stir; throw, cast; tumble, sway; pitch, roll. See AGITATION, PROPULSION, EXCITABILITY.

toss-up, *n., informal,* toss of the coin, even chance. See CHOICE.

total, *adj.* complete, entire, utter, absolute, WHOLE. —*n.* sum, amount, aggregate, quantity, WHOLE. —*v.t.* add, reckon, tot up; amount to; constitute; *slang,* wreck, destroy. See NUMERATION.

totalitarian, *adj.* autocratic, authoritarian. See AUTHORITY.

totter, *v.* shake, tremble, rock, reel, waver; falter, stumble, stagger. See OSCILLATION, WEAKNESS.

touch, *v.t.* feel (see TOUCH); CONTACT; reach, equal, attain; pertain to, relate to; affect, move; tinge, imbue; *slang,* borrow from. See ARRIVAL, SENSIBILITY, RELATION, MIXTURE, BORROWING. —**touch up,** delineate lightly, refine, amend, improve, correct (see IMPROVEMENT).

TOUCH
Tactile sense

Nouns—1, touch, tact[us], CONTACT, impact, taction; tactility, palpability, tangibility, tangency; FEELING, sensation; manipulation, massage, fondling; stroke, tap, feel, brush, graze, glance, tickle, caress, kiss, osculation, lick, pat, rap, hit, handclasp. *Slang,* soft touch, feeling up.

2, hand, finger, palm, paw, toe, tongue; feeler, antenna, flipper, vibrissa, palp[us], barbel. See BODY.

3, reflexology, shiatsu.

Verbs—1, touch, feel, contact, handle, finger, thumb, palm, paw, toe; caress, kiss, lick, lap, pat, tap; fumble, grope; brush, graze, glance, skim; palpate, manipulate, wield, massage, rub, knead. *Slang,* cop a feel.

2, border on, be contiguous to, impinge, meet, reach, come to, abut, adjoin, neighbor, juxtapose. See NEARNESS, CONTACT.

Adjectives—touching, FEELING, tactual, tactile; tangible, touchable, palpable; lambent, licking; adjacent, bordering, tangent, abutting, neighboring, contiguous; affecting, moving, melting, distressing, heartrending, pitiable, tender, pathetic, impressive.

Quotation—Our Sense is such, that, spider-like, we feel the tenderest touch (*John Milton*).

---

touching, *adj.* moving (see FEELING).

touchy, *adj.* irritable; risky, delicate. See IRRITABILITY, SENSIBILITY, DANGER.

tough, *adj.* strong, firm; stiff, resilient; vigorous, robust, hardy; stubborn, intractable; violent, severe; unyielding, hardened, incorrigible; *informal,* vicious, rowdy, unruly, difficult, troublesome. See SEVERITY, STRENGTH, DIFFICULTY, EVILDOER.

toupee, *n.* hairpiece; wig. See ROUGHNESS.

tour, *n.* trip, journey, expedition, excursion, junket, jaunt; turn, shift, tour of duty. See TRAVEL, SUBSTITUTION.

tour de force, *Fr.,* feat of skill *or* strength. See SKILL, CUNNING.

tourist, *n.* traveler, voyager, sightseer; ugly American. See TRAVEL.

tournament, *n.* tourney, jousting, contest, match. See CONTENTION.

tousled, *adj.* disheveled, untidy, unkempt, rumpled, tangled, snarly. See DISORDER.

tout, *v.* boost, promote, pitch —*n.* booster, promoter, pitchman. See PUBLICATION).

tow, *v.t.* draw, pull, drag, haul; take in tow. See TRACTION.

toward, *prep.* See DIRECTION.

towel, *n.* dishtowel, bath *or* hand towel, *etc.* See DRYNESS, CLEANNESS.

tower, *n.* fortress, castle; skyscraper; campanile, belfry, spire. —*v.i.* rise, soar; loom, transcend. See DEFENSE, ASCENT, HEIGHT, STABILITY.

town, *n.* hamlet, burg[h], village. See ABODE.

toxic, *adj.* poisonous, venomous, virulent, noxious. See DISEASE, BADNESS.

toy, *n.* plaything, trinket, trifle; doll, puppet. —*v.* trifle *or* play (with); fiddle, dally. See AMUSEMENT, UNIMPORTANCE, ENDEARMENT.

trace, *v.* draw, sketch, delineate, COPY; track, trail, follow, scent, detect; investigate; deduce. See INQUIRY, REPRESENTATION, INDICATION. —*n.* course, path; track, footprint, trail; hint, shade, vestige. See INDICATION, RECORD, COPY.

track, *v.t.* trail, follow, scent; explore; traverse. See PURSUIT. —*n.* trace, trail, wake; vestige; footprints, spoor, scent; path, course; succession; rails; race track, [race]course, turf, cinders; footracing. See INDICATION, CONTENTION. —**track record,** *n. informal,* credentials, history. See RECORD.

tract, *n.* expanse, area, REGION; composition, DISSERTATION, treatise. See PUBLICATION.

tractable, *adj.* docile, well-behaved, manageable, adaptable, yielding, compliant; malleable, plastic. See FACILITY, SOFTNESS, OBEDIENCE.

TRACTION
Act of dragging

Nouns—traction; drawing, dragging, *etc.* (see *Verbs*); draft, draw, drag, pull, haul, tow, tug, jerk, twitch; suction (see EXTRACTION); grip, FRICTION; tension, ATTRACTION; tractor, traction engine, Caterpillar [tractor], skidder, tow truck, wrecker; tug[boat], towboat.

Verbs—draw, drag, draggle, haul, pull, tow, trail, lug, tug, take in tow; jerk, twitch, heave, wrench, yank.

Adjectives—tractional, tractive; tractile; attractive; in tow.

Antonyms, see PROPULSION, REPULSION.

trade, *n.* BUSINESS, profession, occupation; livelihood; craft; merchandising; commerce, traffic, BARTER; clientele; purchase and sale, deal. —*v.t.* BARTER, buy and sell, bargain. See SALE.

trademark, *n.* brand [name], cachet; logo[type], colophon, label. See INDICATION.

tradesman, *n.* shopkeeper, merchant. See SALE.

tradition, *n.* belief, practice, usage, custom, culture, folklore. See OLDNESS.

traditional, *adj.* conventional, customary, formal. See CONFORMITY.

traduce, *v.* slander, calumniate, vilify, defame, asperse, malign, disparage. See DETRACTION.

traffic, *n.* trade, BARTER, commerce, business. TRANSPORTATION; dealings, familiarity, intercourse, fraternization. —*v.* trade, deal, have dealings. See SALE.

tragedy, *n.* DRAMA; disaster, calamity, catastrophe; crushing blow. See EVIL.

tragic, *adj.* dramatic, melodramatic; dire, disastrous. See DRAMA.

trail, *n.* track, spoor, footprints; tire, *etc.,* tracks; vestige, scent; path, wake; train. —*v.* track, scent; hang; lag, dawdle, crawl, straggle; drag, draw. See SLOW-NESS, PURSUIT.

train, *n.* retinue, suite, entourage, procession, cortège; order, sequence, sequel, succession; railroad cars. See VEHICLE. —*v.t.* instruct, discipline, drill; educate. See TEACHING, DOMESTICATION, PENDENCY, CONTINUITY, PREPARATION.

traipse, *v.* saunter, amble, stroll. See TRAVEL.

trait, *n.* quality, characteristic, peculiarity, idiosyncrasy; custom; feature. See INDICATION, ATTRIBUTION, SPECIALITY.

traitor, *n.* betrayer, turncoat, renegade, deserter, conspirator; informer, Judas, fifth columnist, quisling. See EVILDOER.

trajectory, *n.* orbit, curve, arc, parabola; CIRCUIT, course.

trammel, *n.* net; tether, manacle, chain, fetter; impediment, shackle, HINDRANCE; confinement, RESTRAINT. —*v.t.* entangle, catch, trap; bind, hobble, tether, shackle, bridle, manacle, chain; restrain, imprison; impede, hinder.

tramp, *n.* traveler, vagabond, hobo, vagrant, bum, panhandler; jaunt, journey, hike, freighter; tread, walk, stroll;

slang, prostitute. See POPULACE, IMPURITY. —*v.i.* walk, tread, step, plod, trudge, travel, hike; trample, stamp. See TRAVEL.

trample, *v.t.* crush, tread, grind, squash, stamp on. See OVERRUNNING.

trance, *n.* daze, stupor; abstraction, ecstasy; somnambulism, sleepwalking; coma, catalepsy; hypnosis. See INSENSIBILITY, IMAGINATION.

tranquil, *adj.* calm, quiet, undisturbed, composed, serene, placid, peaceful. See MODERATION, REPOSE, INEXCITABILITY.

tranquilize, *v.* pacify, soothe, appease; calm, still. See PACIFICATION, CONTENT.

transact, *v.* negotiate, deal; CONDUCT, bring about, do, perform, execute. See BUSINESS, ACTION.

transaction, *n.* deal, proceeding, ACTION, affair; CONDUCT, act, deed. See BARTER, OCCURRENCE.

transcend, *v.* exceed, overpass, surpass, excel, outstrip, outdo. See SUPERIORITY, OVERRUNNING.

transcribe, *v.* COPY, write, reproduce, engross; decode, decipher; transliterate, RECORD. See INTERPRETATION.

TRANSFER
Convey from one person to another

Nouns—1, transfer, transference, transmission, transmittal, transmittance, consignment; transfusion, DISPLACEMENT, dislodgment; metastasis; shift, CHANGE, removing, removal, remotion, relegation, deportation, extradition; convection, conduction; contagion, infection. See TRANSPORTATION.

2, conveyance, assignment, assignation, alienation; enfeoffment, cession, grant, deed, quitclaim; conveyancing, bargain and sale, lease and release; exchange, INTERCHANGE, BARTER, SUBSTITUTION, delegation; succession, accession, REVERSION; demise, devise, bequest, legacy, gift.

Verbs—transfer, convey, assign, alienate; grant, cede, deed, confer (see GIVING), consign, enfeoff, sequester; sell, rent, let, lease, charter (see SALE); carry over; make *or* sign over, hand down, pass (on *or* down), transmit, negotiate, change hands; hand, turn, fork, *or* give over; demise, devise, bequeath, will, leave, give; devolve, succeed, come into possession, acquire (see ACQUISITION); rub off; substitute (see SUBSTITUTION). *Informal,* wish off on.

Adjectives—transferable, transmittable, assignable, conveyable; negotiable; contagious, catching, infectious, communicable; metathetic[al], metastatic.

Antonyms, see POSSESSION.

transfigure, *v.t.* transform, transmute; exalt. See CHANGE, ELEVATION.

transfix, *v.* pierce, fasten, impale. See OPENING, STABILITY.

transformation, *n.* CHANGE, alteration,

transmutation; conversion, transfiguration; metamorphosis; wig, switch.

transfuse, *v.t.* set into, insert, infuse, instill; pour, inject. See MIXTURE, TRANSFER.

transgression, *n.* trespass, sin, violation, fault, offense, crime, misdeed, slip, mis- demeanor; infraction, infringement. See ILLEGALITY, GUILT, WRONG.

TRANSIENTNESS
Temporary duration

Nouns—1, transientness, transience, evanescence, impermanence, fugacity, mortality, span; nine days' wonder, bubble, ephemerality; short term; spurt; planned obsolescence; temporary arrangement, interregnum; brevity, SHORTNESS; suddenness (see INSTANTANEITY); CHANGEABLENESS. *Informal,* half-life. *Slang,* flash in the pan.

2, transient, guest; bird of passage; migrant, part-timer, contingent *or* temporary worker, hired help. *Informal,* temp.

Verbs—be transient, flit, pass away, fly, gallop, vanish, evanesce, fade, evaporate; blow over; one's days are numbered.

Adjectives—transient, transitory, transitive; passing, evanescent, volatile, fleeting, elusive, elusory; flying, fugacious, fugitive; shifting, slippery; spasmodic; temporal, temporary; provisional, provisory; cursory, short-lived, meteoric, ephemeral, deciduous; perishable, mortal, precarious; impermanent; brief, quick, extemporaneous, summary; sudden, momentary, short and sweet.

Adverbs—temporarily, pro tempore; for the moment, for a time, for the nonce, for the time being; awhile, en passant, briefly.

Phrases—*tempus fugit* (time flies); here today, gone tomorrow; *sic transit gloria mundi* (thus passes the glory of the world).

Quotations—Like that of leaves is the generation of men (*Homer*), For a thousand years in thy sight are but as yesterday (*Bible*), All flesh is as grass (*Bible*), Gather ye rosebuds while ye may (*Robert Herrick*), They are not long, the days of wine and roses (*Ernest Dowson*), Ev'ry day a little dies (*Stephen Sondheim*), Unbidden guests are often welcomest when they are gone (*Shakespeare*).

Antonyms, see DURABILITY.

---

transit, *n.* passage, change, transition, conveyance, TRANSPORTATION, MOTION.

transition, *n.* passage, passing; CHANGE, development, flux, modulation; break, graduation, rise, fall; metastasis, metabasis.

transitory, *adj.* See TRANSIENTNESS.

translate, *v.* transfer; decipher, decode, render; construe, [re]interpret; transform, transmute, CHANGE.

translucent, *adj.* lucid, clear, diaphanous, hyalescent, semiopaque, frosty. See TRANSPARENCY.

transmission, *n.* conveyance, transference, sending, communication, conductance; gearshift, gears, torque converter. See PASSAGE, INSTRUMENTALITY, TRANSFER.

transmit, *v.* send, TRANSFER, convey, forward, post, mail, wire, telegraph; impart, hand down; admit, conduct; emit, broadcast, communicate. See TRANSPORTATION.

TRANSPARENCY
That which permits vision through

Nouns—1, transparency, translucency, transpicuity, diaphaneity, lucidity, pellucidity, limpidity, clearness, sheerness, thinness. See INVISIBILITY.

2, glass, crystal, Lucite, cellophane, [window]pane, prism, water, lymph, gauze, veil. *Informal,* goldfish bowl. See BUILDING.

Verbs—show through; be transparent, diaphanous, *etc.*

Adjectives—transparent, translucent, transpicuous, diaphanous, lucid, pellucid, lucent, limpid; glassy, hyaline, hyaloid, vitreous, crystal[line], clear as crystal, crystal-clear; gauzy, flimsy, see-through, thin, sheer, gossamer; serene, unclouded.

Antonyms, see OBSCURITY

transparent, *adj.* translucent (see TRANS-PARENCY); manifest, candid, obvious. See EVIDENCE, VISIBILITY, COHERENCE, SIMPLENESS.

transpire, *n.* transude, exhale, pass through, ooze *or* leak out, sweat, perspire; come to light, issue, unfold, crop up; occur, happen, come to pass, take place. See DISCLOSURE, OCCURRENCE, EXCRETION.

transplant, *v.t.* replant, repot, graft; relocate, resettle; colonize. See TRANSFER, AGRICULTURE.

transport, *n.* transformation, conveyance, movement; emotion, ecstasy, rapture; troopship; airplane, carrier. —*v.* convey, carry, move, ship; transfer; delight, overjoy. See TRANSPORTATION, PLEASURE.

TRANSPORTATION
Conveyance from one place to another

Nouns—1, transportation, transport, TRANSFER, transference, transmission, conveyance; movement, PASSAGE, transit, removal, delivery; carriage, portage, cartage, *etc.*, shipment, postage, express, messenger service; mass *or* public transportation; magic carpet. See TRAVEL, COMMUNICATION.

2, *(public transit)* a. common carrier, mass transit, commuter transport; cart, wagon, stagecoach; [omni]bus, coach, jitney, charabanc; car pool; taxicab, taxi, cab, hack, gypsy cab; truck, van; sledge, cart, dray, truck, trailer, semitrailer. See VEHICLE. b. railroad, railway, train; local, express, limited, freight [train], supply train, work train, wreck train, passenger train, milk train, parliamentary; streetcar, trolley [car], tram, subway, tube, el, elevated line, elevated [railway], interurban, metro, rapid transit; monorail, turbotrain; baggage train, bullet train, cannonball express, cog railway, rack-and-pinion railway, street railway, electric railway, funicular; horse railway. *Slang*, private varnish, rattler. c. airline, air shuttle, airliner, transport, airplane (see AVIATION); d. SHIP, ferry, troopship, transport. See NAVIGATION.

3, *(person who carries)* carrier, porter, bearer; redcap, skycap; stevedore; conveyer, conductor, transporter; freighter, shipper; courier, messenger, runner; coolie; postman, mailman, letter carrier (see COMMUNICATION); helper, expressman. *Slang*, bag person, black birder.

4, a. driver, coachman, whip, charioteer, postillion, postboy; cabdriver; engineer; chauffeur. b. rider, fare; commuter; ridership.

5, *(animal that transports)* beast of burden; horse, draft horse, packhorse, carthorse; ass, burro, jackass, hinny, jennet, donkey, mule; camel, dromedary, ox, llama, elephant; reindeer, dog, husky; carrier pigeon, passenger pigeon, homing pigeon.

6, shipment, traffic, freight, haul, cargo, lading, goods, baggage, luggage.

7, basket, box, carton, tray, *etc.* (see RECEPTACLE).

Verbs—transport, convey, transmit, TRANSFER, remove, move; carry, bear, cart, haul, truck, drive, ship, transship, ferry; fetch, call for, drop off; conduct, convoy, bring, take, pull, lug, pack, reach; run, smuggle (see ILLEGALITY); freight, express, railroad, forward, deliver, TRAVEL. See PASSAGE.

Adjectives—transportable, conveyable, transmittable; carry-on.

Antonyms, see STABILITY.

---

transpose, *v.* exchange, INTERCHANGE, reverse, rearrange, invert; substitute, transliterate; CHANGE. See INVERSION, MUSIC.

transsexual, *n.* epicene; hermaphrodite. See SEX.

transverse, *adj.* crossing, cross, athwart, oblique. See OBLIQUITY.

trap, *n.* pitfall, snare, net, deadfall; ambush; carriage; trapdoor; *(pl.)* equipment, luggage. —*v.* catch, entrap, [en]snare, net, enmesh, fool, ambush. See DECEPTION, VEHICLE.

trappings, *n.pl.* caparison, regalia, habiliments, outfit, rigging, panoply, vestments, decorations; indications, earmarks. See CLOTHING, ORNAMENT.

trash, *n.* rubbish, garbage, refuse, offal, litter, debris; junk, scrap, waste. See USELESSNESS, POPULACE.

trauma, *n.* traumatism, injury; shock. See DETERIORATION, DISEASE.

travail, *n.* labor, work, drudgery, toil; agony, pain. See EXERTION.

TRAVEL
Go from one place to another

Nouns—1, travel; traveling, wayfaring, itinerancy, tourism; journey, voyage, excursion, junket, expedition, safari, tour, [pleasure *or* business] trip, trek, crossing, cruise, grand tour, CIRCUIT; fact-finding trip; peregrination; procession, caravan; odyssey; discursion; sightseeing; pilgrimage; ambulation; sleepwalking, somnambulism. *Informal*, globe-trotting, flight-seeing. See NAVIGATION, PROGRESSION, AVIATION, MOTION, TRANSPORTATION.

2, *(travel by various means)* walk, promenade, stroll, saunter, tramp, ramble, jog-trot, turn, perambulation, pedestrianism; driving, riding, posting, motoring, touring; outing, ride, drive, airing, jaunt; constitutional, hike, spin; riding the rods *or* rails, riding blind. *Slang*, urban surfing. See VEHICLE.

3, *(aimless travel)* roving, vagrancy, nomadism; vagabondism; vagabondage; gadding; flitting; joyride.

4, *(travel across boundaries)* migration, emigration, immigration, intermigration.

5, *(travel route)* itinerary, course, route, road, path; bypass, detour, loop; handbook, road map; Baedeker, Michelin, guidebook.

6, traveler, wayfarer, voyager, itinerant, passenger, rider, motorist, tourist, excursionist; world traveler, globe-trotter; explorer, adventurer, mountaineer; peregrinator, wanderer, rover, straggler, rambler; bird of passage; gadabout, vagrant, tramp, vagabond, hobo, nomad, bindle-stiff, Bohemian, gypsy, Arab, Wandering Jew, hadji, pilgrim, palmer; peripatetic; somnambulist; emigrant, fugitive, refugee; runner, courier; pedestrian, walker, cyclist, passenger; rider, horseman *or* -woman, equestrian, jockey. *Informal,* road hog.

Verbs—1, *(aimless travel)* travel, journey, course; take a journey; voyage, cruise; take a walk, go for a walk, have a run; take the air; flit, take wing; migrate, emigrate, immigrate; rove, prowl, roam, range, knock about *or* around, kick around, go about, patrol, make rounds, pace up and down, traverse; perambulate, circumambulate; nomadize, wander, trek, ramble, stroll, saunter, go one's rounds, shamble, drift, dander, gad [about]; cover [the] ground. *Slang,* hit the road, hop a freight.

2, *(travel on foot)* walk, march, step, tread, pace, plod, wend; promenade, trudge, tramp, hike; stalk, stride, strut, foot it, bowl along, toddle; paddle; tread a path; frog-march, gallumph, amble, clomp, clump, footslog, scuffle; jog on, shuffle on; pace, walk the floor; bend one's steps; make, wend, pick, thread, plow *or* find one's way; slide, glide, skim, skate; march in procession; go to, repair to, hie oneself to, betake oneself to. *Informal,* hotfoot, stump, foot it, pound the pavement. *Slang,* stir one's stumps, hoof, ankle.

3, *(travel by animal or vehicle)* ride, take horse, drive, trot, amble, canter, curvet, prance, gallop; drive, fly; commute; go by car, train, rail, *or* air, ride the rails. *Informal,* joyride; hitchhike, thumb [a ride]. *Slang,* burn up the road.

Adjectives—traveling, ambulatory, itinerant, peripatetic, roving, rambling, gadding, discursive, vagrant, migratory, nomadic; footloose; equestrian; on the wing, on the road, on the move; locomotive, automotive; wayfaring; travel-stained.

Adverbs—on foot, on shank's mare, on horseback; abroad; en route.

Phrases—go abroad and you'll hear news of home; Thursday's child has far to go; travel broadens the mind.

Quotations—He disdains all things above his reach, and preferreth all countries before his own (*Thomas Overbury*), I travel for travel's sake. The great affair is to move (*R. L. Stevenson*), A man travels the world in search of what he needs and returns home to find it (*George Moore*), In America, there are two classes of travel—first class and with children (*Robert Benchley*), Men travel faster now, but I do not know if they go to better things (*Willa Cather*), Travelling is almost like talking with men of other centuries (*René Descartes*), He that travels much knows much (*Thomas Fuller*), He travels fastest who travels alone (*Rudyard Kipling*).

Antonyms, see REPOSE.

---

traverse, *v.* cross, ford, range, patrol; contradict, obstruct. See TRAVEL, PASSAGE.

travesty, *n.* caricature, burlesque, farce, parody, lampoon, takeoff (*inf.*), spoof (*sl.*); fiasco; ABSURDITY. See RIDICULE, IMITATION.

trawl, *n.* net, dragnet, seine. —*v.* beam *or* otter trawl, fish, net, haul, drag, seine. See TRACTION, PURSUIT.

tray, *n.* platter, salver, server, trencher; galley. See TRANSPORTATION, RECEPTACLE.

treachery, *n.* treason, perfidy, faithlessness, disloyalty, infidelity, falsity, falseness. See IMPROBITY, DECEPTION.

tread, *v.* walk, step, pace; trample, crush; stamp, tramp; dance. See TRAVEL, MOTION. —**tread water,** stand still, make no progress. See INACTIVITY.

treadmill, *n.* routine, rut (see HABIT).

treason, *n.* betrayal, disloyalty, faithlessness, sedition, treachery. See IMPROBITY.

treasure, *n.* hoard, STORE; wealth, riches. —*v.* value, prize, cherish, appreciate; remember. See MONEY, GOODNESS.

treasurer, *n.* bursar, purser; financier, banker, cashier, teller; receiver; steward, trustee; paymaster. See MONEY.

treasury, *n.* bank, exchequer; depository, vault, safe, safe-deposit box; till, strongbox, cash register; coffer, chest; purse, wallet, handbag, pocketbook. See STORE, MONEY.

treat, *v.* negotiate, bargain, deal, parley; entertain, pay for; deal with, discuss, teach; dose, attend, doctor. See REMEDY, PLEASURE, CONDUCT.

treatise, *n.* book, textbook; exposition, discussion, composition, commentary, tract, monograph, DISSERTATION. See PUBLICATION.

treatment, *n.* technique; discussion, examination; therapy, regimen, cure. See MEANS, CONDUCT, REMEDY.

treaty, *n.* compact, pact, covenant, concordat, entente, AGREEMENT.

tree, *n.* plant, sapling, scrub, shrub, bush; timber; whiffletree; stake; gibbet, gallows; family tree, pedigree, lineage. See VEGETABLE, ANCESTRY.

trek, *v.i.* walk, hike, TRAVEL, tramp, trudge. —*n.* journey, hike, migration, expedition.

trellis, *n.* lattice, grill[e]; network, screen, espalier, grid; arbor, bower, pergola, gazebo. See CROSSING, SUPPORT.

tremble, *v.* shake, shiver; vacillate; vibrate, totter, quake, quaver; shudder, pulsate. See FEAR, AGITATION, WEAKNESS.

tremendous, *adj.* stupendous, colossal, gigantic, huge; extraordinary. See SIZE.

tremolo, *n.* tremolando; trill, twitter, warble, crack. See OSCILLATION.

tremor, *n.* trembling, shivering, shaking, quivering, vibration. See FEAR, AGITATION.

tremulous, *adj.* trembling, unsteady; fearful, timid, irresolute. See AGITATION, FEAR.

trench, *n.* ditch, fosse, dugout; FURROW.

trenchant, *adj.* cutting, incisive, penetrating; thoroughgoing; clear-cut, keen, sharp, biting, crisp; energetic. See POWER, FEELING.

trend, *n.* direction, course, TENDENCY, inclination, drift, tide.

trepidation, *n.* quaking, trembling; alarm, FEAR, AGITATION, perturbation, dread, dismay.

trespass, *v.i.* sin, offend, transgress; encroach, infringe, intrude, invade. See IMPROBITY, BADNESS.

tress, *n.* strand, curl, ringlet, lock; (*pl.*) locks, hair. See ROUGHNESS.

trestle, *n.* [saw]horse; bridge. See CONNECTION, SUPPORT.

trial, *n.* test, EXPERIMENT, probation, hearing; hardship, ordeal; cross, tribulation, affliction; effort, attempt. See ADVERSITY, INQUIRY, LAWSUIT, PUNISHMENT.

triangle, *n.* trigon, delta, pyramid, triquetra; gore, gusset; triad, trio, threesome; the eternal triangle. See ANGULARITY, NUMERATION.

tribe, *n.* race, people, sect, group; clan, nation, society; lineage, family stock. See ASSEMBLAGE, ANCESTRY, CLASS.

tribulation, *n.* sorrow, woe; care, trouble, ordeal. See PAIN.

tribunal, *n.* court; board, forum; bench, judicatory; court of justice *or* law, court of arbitration, inquisition, kangaroo court (*sl.*); seat of judgment *or* justice, bar [of justice]; drumhead, court-martial. See JUDGMENT, COUNCIL.

tribune, *n.* dais, pulpit, rostrum; gallery. See SUPPORT.

tributary, *n.* stream, source, affluent; prayer of tribute. —*adj.* subject, subordinate; contributory. See WATER.

tribute, *n.* PAYMENT, tax, contribution; gift, offering, service; praise, encomium, compliment. See GIVING, APPROBATION.

trick, *n.* artifice, stratagem, craft; illusion; wile, ruse, subterfuge, fraud, imposture, DECEPTION; tour, shift, turn; trait, idiosyncrasy, peculiarity. See UNCONFORMITY.

trickle, *v.i.* drip, dribble, seep. See WATER, EGRESS.

tricky, *adj.* ticklish, intricate; deceitful, evasive, artful, shifty. See DECEPTION.

trifle, *n.* bagatelle, nothing, triviality; gewgaw, trinket, knickknack, gimcrack; particle, bit, morsel, trace. See LITTLENESS, UNIMPORTANCE.—*v.i.* toy, play, dally, fool. See NEGLECT.

trigger, *n.* lever; spark, CAUSE.

trill, *n.* vibration, tremor, quaver, tremolo, vibrato. —*v.* sing; quaver; warble. See MUSIC, OSCILLATION.

trim, *adj.* neat, well-ordered, compact, tidy, spruce, smart; slim, lean. —*v.* ORDER, tidy, adjust, dress, arrange; decorate, ORNAMENT, adorn; defeat; cheat; balance, equalize; cut, lop, shear, prune, barber; *informal,* defeat. See CLEANNESS, DISAPPROBATION, EQUALITY, NARROWNESS.

trinket, *n.* toy, plaything, bauble, gewgaw. See ORNAMENT.

trip, *n.* journey, excursion, voyage; slip, ERROR; *slang,* drug high. —*v.* skip; stumble; offend, err; obstruct, halt. See LEAP, IMAGINATION, DRUGS.

trite, *adj.* commonplace, ordinary; hackneyed, stale, old, corny (*sl.*), Mickey Mouse (*sl.*); boring, dull; banal. See HABIT, WEARINESS.

triumph, *n.* joy, exultation, celebration; success, victory, conquest; accomplishment. —*v.i.* win, conquer, succeed; celebrate, rejoice. See REJOICING, SUCCESS, CELEBRATION.

triumphant, *adj.* triumphal, victorious (see SUCCESS).

trivial, *adj.* insignificant, unimportant, trifling, picayune, paltry; mean, piddling, small, petty. See UNIMPORTANCE, CHEAPNESS.

troll, *n.* fairy, dwarf (see MYTHICAL DEITIES). —*v.i.* fish, angle; warble, lilt. See PURSUIT, MUSIC.

trolley, *n.* pulley, truck; trolley car, streetcar. See CIRCULARITY, TRANSPORTATION.

trollop, *n.* harlot, whore; slut, hussy, baggage. See IMPURITY.

tromp, *v.t., slang,* defeat, trounce. See SUCCESS. —*v.i.* stomp, tramp. See IMPULSE, TRAVEL.

trompe l'œil, (*Fr.*) optical illusion. See VISION, DECEPTION, PAINTING.

troop, *n.* group, number, party, company, crowd, ASSEMBLAGE.—*v.i.* march, tramp, go. See TRAVEL.

trooper, *n.* soldier; [mounted] policeman, state trooper, Mountie (*inf.*). See COMBATANT, SECURITY.

trophy, *n.* medal, prize (see APPROBATION, RECORD).

tropical, *adj.* torrid, hot, fiery; equatorial. See HEAT.

trot, *v.i.* run, jog, lope; hasten. See TRAVEL, VELOCITY. —*n.* lope; *informal,* crib, pony; (*pl.*) diarrhea. See TRAVEL, DECEPTION, DISEASE.

troubadour, *n.* trouvère, poet, bard, minstrel, jongleur, meistersinger, minnesinger, balladeer, street singer; laureate; serenader. See POETRY, MUSIC.

trouble, *n.* affliction, distress, misfortune, ADVERSITY, calamity; disorder, unrest; DIFFICULTY; pains, EXERTION, effort, anxiety, perturbation, sorrow, worry. —*v.* disturb, disquiet, perturb; annoy, molest, harass, agitate; worry, distress, grieve; afflict, ail, plague; inconvenience.

troublemaker, *n.* rabble-rouser, instigator; shit disturber (*sl.*). See CAUSE.

troubleshooter, *n.* repairer, fixer, fireman (*sl.*), Johnny-on-the-spot (*inf.*). See RESTORATION.

troublesome, *adj.* disturbing, annoying, distressing; vexatious, burdensome, grievous, worrisome; difficult. See DIFFICULTY.

trough, *n.* manger, hutch, bin; trench, ditch, FURROW. See RECEPTACLE.

trounce, *v.* thrash, beat, flog. See SUCCESS.

troupe, *n.* troop, band, group, party, company; dramatis personae. See DRAMA.

trousers, *n.pl.* breeches, pantaloons, pants; [blue]jeans, slacks, chinos, Levi's. See CLOTHING.

trousseau, *n.* bridal outfit, wardrobe. See MARRIAGE.

truant, *n.* shirker, absentee, deserter. See ABSENCE, AVOIDANCE.

truce, *n.* armistice, peace, respite, delay; cessation, lull. See PACIFICATION.

truck, *n.* VEHICLE, rig; lorry, van, pickup, dump, panel, rack; six-, *etc.* wheeler, half-track; cart, wagon, dray; barrow, dolly; dealings, BARTER.

truckle, *v.i.* grovel, kowtow. See SERVILITY.

truculent, *adj.* fierce, savage, deadly, bestial; vitriolic, scathing, mean; overbearing, cruel, with a chip on one's shoulder (*inf.*). See MALEVOLENCE.

trudge, *v.* march, slog, tramp, walk, plod. See SLOWNESS, TRAVEL.

true, *adj.* faithful, loyal, constant, sincere; certain, correct, accurate; truthful; sure, reliable; actual, genuine; legitimate, rightful; real, straight, undeviating. See PROBITY, TRUTH, STRAIGHTNESS.

truelove, *n.* sweetheart, lover. See LOVE.

truism, *n.* platitude. See MAXIM, UNMEANINGNESS.

trump card, *informal*, advantage, ace in the hole. See SUPERIORITY.

trump up, fabricate, fashion out of whole cloth. See DECEPTION.

trumpet, *n.* cornet, bugle, horn; ear trumpet. See MUSIC. —*v.* bellow, roar; blow, toot, blare; proclaim. See PUBLICATION.

truncate, *v.* abridge, reduce, shorten, curtail. See SHORTNESS, DEDUCTION, FORMLESSNESS.

truncheon, *n.* baton, staff, club. See AUTHORITY.

trundle, *v.* roll, wheel, revolve, rotate. See ROTATION.

trunk, *n.* stem, bole; body, torso; proboscis, snout; chest, box; circuit; (*pl.*) breeches, shorts. See RECEPTACLE, ANCESTRY, CLOTHING.

truss, *v.t.* gird[le], belt; tie, bind, *or* do up; lace, button, strap, buckle; skewer, sew, stitch; support, strengthen, bandage. —*n.* fasten, pack, bundle, bale; holder, fastening; supporter, belt. See JUNCTION, ASSEMBLAGE.

trust, *n.* reliance, confidence; CREDIT; holding company, monopoly. See BELIEF, BUSINESS. —*v.* rely on, believe in, give credit to. Se BELIEF.

trustee, *n.* guardian, fiduciary, overseer, supervisor. See POSSESSION.

trustful, *adj.* confiding, trusting. See CREDULITY, BELIEF.

trustworthy, *adj.* reliable, dependable, faithful, trusty, responsible, credible, believable; constant, true, loyal. See PROBITY, BELIEF, CERTAINTY.

TRUTH
Conformity to fact

Nouns—1, truth, fact, reality; verity, gospel, authenticity; plain, unvarnished, sober, *or* naked truth, matter of fact; the Gospel *or* naked truth; the truth, the whole truth and nothing but the truth. *Slang*, the [real] McCoy, the goods. See RIGHTNESS, MAXIM.

2, truthfulness, veracity; fidelity; accuracy, exactitude; exactness, preciseness, precision. See PROBITY, CERTAINTY.

Verbs—1, be true, be the case; stand the test; hold good *or* true, have the true ring; render *or* prove true, substantiate (see EVIDENCE); get at the truth. *Informal*, hold water, hit the nail on the head.

2, be truthful; speak *or* tell the truth; not lie; speak one's mind; make a clean breast (see DISCLOSURE); cross one's heart. *Slang,* say a mouthful, come across, word up, come off it.

Adjectives—1, true, factual, real, actual, existing; veritable, certain (see CERTAINTY); unimpeachable; unrefuted, unconfuted; genuine, authentic, legitimate; pure, sound, sterling, unadulterated, unvarnished, uncolored; well-grounded, well-founded; solid, substantial, tangible, valid; undistorted, undisguised, honest-to-goodness; unaffected, unexaggerated, unromantic, unflattering. *Informal,* all wool and a yard wide.

2, exact, accurate, definite, precise, well-defined, just, right, correct, strict; literal; undisguised; faithful, constant, unerring.

3, truthful, veracious; sincere, pure, guileless, bona fide, true blue. *Slang,* up front, outfront. See PROBITY.

Adverbs—1, truly, verily, indeed, really, in reality; with truth, certainly, actually, for real; exactly, verbatim, word for word, literally, sic, to the letter, chapter and verse, to an inch; to a nicety, to a hair, to a turn, to a T; neither more nor less, in so many words; in every respect, in all respects; at any rate, at all events; strictly speaking; de facto. *Informal,* on the nose, smack-dab. *Slang,* on the button.

2, truthfully, *etc.*; at heart, from the bottom of one's heart; honor bright.

Phrases—many a true word is spoken in jest; tell the truth and shame the devil; truth is stranger than fiction; truth will out; honesty is the best policy; what everybody says must be true; that's about the size of it.

Quotations—Great is Truth, and mighty above all things (*Bible*), Plato is dear to me, but dearer still is truth (*Aristotle*), And ye shall know the truth, and the truth shall make you free (*Bible*), I design plain truth for plain people (*John Wesley*), 'Tis strange—but true; for truth is always strange; stranger than fiction (*Lord Byron*), It is the customary fate of new truths to begin as heresies and to end as superstitions (*T. H. Huxley*), The truth is rarely pure, and never simple (*Oscar Wilde*), Truth is the most valuable thing we have. Let us economize it (*Mark Twain*), A platitude is simply a truth repeated until people get tired of hearing it (*Stanley Baldwin*), The aim of the superior man is truth (*Confucius*), There are truths which can kill a nation (*Jean Giraudoux*), A great truth is a truth whose opposite is also a truth (*Thomas Mann*).

Antonyms, see ERROR, FALSEHOOD.

---

try, *v.* essay, endeavor, attempt, undertake; test, examine, assay, EXPERIMENT; refine, purify, afflict, beset; strain, tax; judge, hear. See LAWSUIT, EXERTION, USE, UNDERTAKING.

trying, *adj.* dull, wearisome, boring; annoying, bothersome, galling, irritating. See WEARINESS.

tryout, *n.* trial; audition, hearing; test, dry run; EXPERIMENT. See HEARING.

tryst, *n.* assignation, meeting, appointment, rendezvous. See SOCIALITY.

tsar, *n.* See CZAR.

tub, *n.* pot, vat, cauldron; washtub, bathtub; *slang,* tramp, freighter (see SHIP). See RECEPTACLE.

tube, *n.* pipe, hose, conduit; tunnel, subway; *slang,* television. See PASSAGE.

tuck, *n.* FOLD, pleat, lap.

tuft, *n.* cluster, clump, wisp, bunch, brush; tussock; fetlock, topknot, crest. See ROUGHNESS.

tug, *v.* pull, strain, drag, haul, tow; toil, labor, strive, drudge. See EXERTION, TRACTION.

tuition, *n.* tutelage, training, coaching, education; fees, cost, charge, bill. See TEACHING, PRICE.

tumble, *v.* fall, roll; leap, spring; throw, overturn, disarrange, dishevel, tousle; toss, pitch. See DESCENT, AGITATION.

tumbler, *n.* glass, vessel, goblet; acrobat, gymnast, juggler; lever, cog, *etc.* See RECEPTACLE, DRAMA, INSTRUMENTALITY.

tumescent, *adj.* swelling, tumid. See CONVEXITY.

tumid, *adj.* turgid, swollen, distended, enlarged; protuberant, bulging; bombastic, pompous, inflated; teeming, bursting. See CONVEXITY, EXPANSION.

tumor, *n.* tumefaction, swelling, wen, cyst, tubercle, growth; neoplasm, sarcoma, cancer, carcinoma. See EXPANSION, CONVEXITY, DISEASE.

tumult, *n.* commotion, AGITATION, turbulence, DISORDER. See VIOLENCE.

tune, *n.* melody, air; harmony, concord. See MUSIC. —*v.* modulate, adjust, attune; harmonize. See AGREEMENT.

tunic, *n.* blouse. See CLOTHING.

tunnel, *n.* passageway, burrow, crosscut,

subway, tube. See OPENING, CONCAVITY, CONNECTION, CROSSING.

turbid, *adj.* roiled, muddy, cloudy, clouded, opaque; confused, muddled. See CLOUDINESS.

turbine, *n.* rotator, rotor, rotary wheel; propeller, turboprop *or* -jet. See PROPULSION, ROTATION, POWER.

turbulence, *n.* disorder, VIOLENCE, unrest, disturbance, EXCITEMENT, AGITATION.

turf, *n.* sod, sward; peat; racetrack; *slang,* territory, neighborhood (see REGION). See ARENA, VEGETABLE.

turgid, *adj.* See TUMID.

turkey, *n.* gobbler, tom; *slang,* failure, flop. See BIRD, FAILURE.

turmoil, *n.* confusion, tumult, turbulence, disturbance, AGITATION, commotion; DISORDER.

turn, *n.* ROTATION, revolution; twirl, twist; deflection, diversion; coil, CONVULSION; CHANGE; crisis; aptitude, ability, SKILL; act, skit; spell, shift, tour, trick. —*v.* revolve, rotate, pivot; reel; rebel, retaliate; shape, round, finish; CHANGE, move; invert, reverse; upset, derange; deflect, divert, veer, shift; pervert, prejudice, repel; avert; curdle, ferment, sour. See INVERSION, FORM, CURVATURE, OCCASION, DEVIATION, SOURNESS, REGULARITY. —**turn down,** *v.* reject, repudiate. See REJECTION. — **turning point,** *n.* crisis, crunch, moment of truth. See IMPORTANCE. —**turn on,** *v.* depend *or* be contingent on; *informal,* arouse, stir up; *slang,* get high, get a buzz on (*sl.*). See CIRCUMSTANCE, EXCITEMENT, DRUGS.

turnabout, *n.* reversal, return; reversion. See INVERSION.

turncoat, *n.* renegade, deserter, traitor; apostate, recreant. See EVILDOER.

turnout, *n.* output, PRODUCTION; attendance, box office, gate. See PRESENCE.

turnpike, *n.* tollroad, pike, throughway, thruway, skyway. See PASSAGE.

turpitude, *n.* depravity, baseness, wickedness. See IMPURITY.

turret, *n.* tower, gazebo, belvedere, cupola. See HEIGHT.

tussle, *n.* scuffle, struggle. See CONTENTION.

tutor, *n.* teacher, instructor, coach; guardian. See TEACHING.

tuxedo, *n.* dinner jacket, dress suit, smoking jacket, black tie, tux, tuck (*sl.*), monkey suit (*sl.*), soup-and-fish (*sl.*). See CLOTHING.

TV, television, boob tube (*sl.*). See COMMUNICATION.

twaddle, *n.* gabble, nonsense, fustian. See ABSURDITY.

tweak, *v.t.* twist, pinch; adjust. See CONTRACTION, CHANGE.

twice, *adv.* doubly, twofold. See NUMERATION.

twig, *n.* shoot, branch, tendril, slip, scion. See PART.

twilight, *n.* dusk, gloaming, nightfall; shade, shadow. See TIME, DIMNESS.

twin, *adj.* double, twofold; fraternal, identical; like. See SIMILARITY, NUMERATION.

twine, *n.* cord, string, line. See FILAMENT, CONNECTION, CONVOLUTION, CROSSING.

twinge, *n.* pinch, throb; qualm, doubt. See AGITATION, PAIN.

twinkle, *v.* blink, wink; scintillate, sparkle, shine. See LIGHT.

twirl, *v.* twist, spin, rotate, turn, whirl; wind, coil. See CONVOLUTION, ROTATION.

twist, *v.* wind, wreathe, twine, interlace; coil; wrench, contort; wring, screw; pervert; misinterpret, misapply; distort, warp. See CONVOLUTION, DEVIATION, DISTORTION.

twister, *n.* tornado, cyclone. See VIOLENCE, ROTATION.

twit, *v.t.* taunt, reproach. See ACCUSATION, RIDICULE.

twitch, *v.* jerk, writhe, shake, pull; tug, vellicate; pinch, squeeze; twinge. See TRACTION, EXCITABILITY, PAIN.

two-bit, *adj., slang,* cheap, worthless (see CHEAPNESS, USELESSNESS).

two-faced, *adj.* hypocritical, deceitful, double-dealing; faithless, false. See FALSEHOOD, DECEPTION.

two-time, *v.t., informal,* deceive, cheat (on), betray. See DECEPTION, IMPROBITY.

tycoon, *n.* shogun; *informal,* magnate, millionaire. See MONEY, AUTHORITY.

tympani, *n.pl.* kettledrums (see MUSIC).

type, *n.* sign, emblem; kind, CLASS, sort, nature; standard, model, example, ideal; group; letter, figure, character. See INDI-

CATION, PRINTING, FORM. —*v.* type, CLASS; symbolize; typewrite, touch-type, hunt and peck. See WRITING.

typewriter, *n.* teletype[writer], stenotype. See WRITING.

typhoon, *n.* hurricane, tornado, cyclone. See WIND.

typical, *adj.* emblematic, symbolic; characteristic, representative, model, ideal, conforming. See CONFORMITY, INDICATION.

typify, *v.* symbolize, exemplify, embody, represent; prefigure. See INDICATION, CONFORMITY.

tyranny, *n.* despotism, autocracy, totalitarianism; SEVERITY, rigor, harshness, oppression. See AUTHORITY, ILLEGALITY.

tyrant, *n.* despot, autocrat, oppressor. See AUTHORITY, SEVERITY.

tyro, *n.* beginner, novice, amateur, learner. See LEARNING.

U

ubiquitous, *adj.* ubiquitary, omnipresent; inescapable. See PRESENCE, DEITY.

U-boat, *n.* submarine. See SHIP.

udder, *n.* mamma, bag. See CONVEXITY.

UGLINESS
Repulsive appearance

Nouns—1, ugliness, deformity, disfigurement, blemish; INELEGANCE; want *or* lack of symmetry, DISTORTION; IMPRESSION; homeliness, plainness, unloveliness; grotesqueness; unsightliness, gruesomeness; loathsomeness, hideousness; sordidness, squalor (see UNCLEANNESS).

2, eyesore, sight, fright, specter, scarecrow, hag, harridan, satyr, witch, toad, baboon, monster; ugly duckling; Quasimodo, Caliban; gargoyle. *Slang,* buffarilla, beast, hog, pig, scag, witch, blister, bowser, gash, geech, ill-piece, mud puppy, paper bag job, one-bagger, triple-bagger, porker, mullion, face-ache, skunk, snag, zarf, drack, Zelda.

Verbs—be ugly, look unprepossessing; make faces; render ugly, uglify; deface; disfigure; distort, blemish.

Adjectives—1, ugly [as sin]; plain, homely, ordinary, unornamental, inartistic; squalid, unsightly, unseemly, uncomely, unshapely, unlovely; not fit to be seen; unbeautiful; beautiless; foul, dingy. *Slang,* coyote-, piss-, *or* plug-ugly, misty, beat, corroded, rugy.

2, gruesome, misshapen, repulsive, hideous, loathsome, disgusting, nauseating, misproportioned, deformed, disfigured, monstrous; gaunt, thin; dumpy, ill-made, ill-shaped, ill-favored, ill-proportioned; crooked, distorted, hard-featured; unattractive, unbecoming, ill-looking, unprepossessing.

3, grisly, ghastly; ghostlike, deathlike; cadaverous, frightful, repellent, grotesque, horrid, horrible.

Quotations—The great tragedy of science—the slaying of a beautiful hypothesis by an ugly fact (*T. H. Huxley*), Women who are either indisputably beautiful, or indisputably ugly, are best flattered upon the score of their understandings (*Earl of Chesterfield*), There is nothing ugly; *I never saw an ugly thing in my life*: for let the form of an object be what it may—light, shade, and perspective will always make it beautiful (*John Constable*).

Antonyms, see BEAUTY.

---

ugly, *adj.* repulsive (see UGLINESS); disagreeable, unpleasant; mean, hostile, quarrelsome. See UNSAVORINESS, CONTENTION.

ulcer, *n.* abscess, infection, sore, fistula. See DISEASE.

ulterior, *adj.* beyond, farther; further, remote; hidden, unavowed. See DISTANCE, FUTURITY.

ultimate, *adj.* farthest, most remote; extreme, last; maximum; terminal, final, conclusive; elemental; eventual. See END.

ultimatum, *n.* demand, requirement, exaction. See COMMAND, OFFER.

ultra, *adj.* radical, extreme; superlative, excessive. See SUPERIORITY.

ululate, *v.i.* howl, wail, CRY, hoot, bark, mewl, mew, meow, bellow, moo, roar, caterwaul.

umbrage, *n.* RESENTMENT, offense, dudgeon, huff; foliage, shade (see OBSCURITY).

umbrella, *n.* shade, screen; parasol, sunshade, bumbershoot; canopy, COVERING.

umpire, *n.* referee, arbiter, arbitrator, ump (*inf.*); linesman. See JUDGMENT.

unabashed, *adj.* shameless, brazen, unblushing, unashamed. See INSOLENCE.

unabated, *adj.* tireless, relentless, ceaseless, constant. See CONTINUITY.

unable, *adj.* incapable, unfit. See IMPOTENCE, UNSKILLFULNESS.

unabridged, *adj.* complete, unexpurgated. See COMPLETION.

unacceptable, *adj.* unsatisfactory; objectionable. See DISAPPROBATION.

unaccompanied, *adj.* alone, unattended, solitary, lone. See UNITY.

unaccountable, *adj.* inexplicable, mysterious, strange; not responsible, unanswerable. See UNCONFORMITY, UNINTELLIGIBILITY.

unaccustomed, *adj.* unwonted, unused (to); a stranger (to); uncommon, unusual, rare, strange. See UNSKILLFULNESS, DISUSE.

unacquainted, *adj.* ignorant, unknowing, uninformed; never introduced, strange. See IGNORANCE.

unadorned, *adj.* bare, severe, austere, unornamented, plain, simple; naked, blank; terse, trenchant. See SIMPLENESS.

unadulterated, *adj.* clear, simple, pure, undiluted; genuine, true. See PURITY, TRUTH, SIMPLENESS.

unaffected, *adj.* natural, simple, plain; genuine, sincere; ingenuous, artless; untouched, uninfluenced, unmoved. See INSENSIBILITY, SIMPLENESS.

unafraid, *adj.* See FEARLESS.

unaided, *adj.* unsupported; single [-handed]. See UNITY.

un-American, *adj.* anti-American, subversive, fascist, unpatriotic. See ILLEGALITY.

unanimity, *n.* agreement, consent, accord. See COOPERATION, UNITY.

unanticipated, *adj.* unexpected, unforeseen; surprising, startling. See SURPRISE, INSTANTANEITY.

unappetizing, *adj.* unsavory, distasteful, repugnant; tasteless, insipid. See DISCOURTESY, UNSAVORINESS.

unapproachable, *adj.* inaccessible; cold, cool, forbidding, distant. See IMPOSSIBILITY, TACITURNITY, SECLUSION.

unarmed, *adj.* weaponless, unprepared, defenseless. See IMPOTENCE.

unashamed, *adj.* shameless, unabashed, brazen. See INSOLENCE.

unasked, *adj.* voluntary, spontaneous; gratis, free; uninvited. See WILL, DISLIKE.

unassuming, *adj.* modest, retiring, reserved. See MODESTY.

unattached, *adj.* loose, independent, alone; unengaged, fancy-free. See DISJUNCTION, CELIBACY.

unattractive, *adj.* ugly, homely, plain, unsightly. See UGLINESS.

unauthorized, *adj.* unwarranted, unsanctioned; illegal; illegitimate, unconstitutional. See ILLEGALITY, PROHIBITION.

unavailable, *adj.* unattainable, not to be had for love *or* money. See IMPOSSIBILITY.

unavailing, *adj.* useless, vain, futile; ineffectual, bootless. See USELESSNESS.

unavoidable, *adj.* inevitable, certain, unpreventable, necessary. See CERTAINTY, NECESSITY.

unaware, *adj.* unwary, unwarned; oblivious, ignorant. See IGNORANCE.

unbalanced, *adj.* unpoised, lopsided, out of kilter; unhinged, deranged, off one's rocker (*sl.*). See INSANITY, INEQUALITY.

unbearable, *adj.* unendurable, intolerable, insufferable, odious. See PAIN.

unbeatable, *adj.* matchless, peerless; invincible, indomitable. See SUPERIORITY, STRENGTH.

unbeaten, *adj.* undefeated, unconquered. See SUCCESS.

unbecoming, *adj.* indecorous, unseemly, unfitting; ugly, unattractive, ill-suited, inharmonious. See UGLINESS, DISAGREEMENT.

unbelievable, *adj.* incredible; unthinkable, unimaginable, farfetched, implausible, impossible. See DOUBT.

unbeliever, *n.* skeptic, doubter, infidel, agnostic, heretic. See DOUBT, IRRELIGION.

unbiased, *adj.* impartial, unprejudiced, objective, dispassionate; fair, just, equitable. See JUSTICE.

unbounded, *adj.* boundless, limitless, unlimited, infinite. See SPACE, FREEDOM, INFINITY.

unbreakable, *adj.* indestructible; shatterproof, tough, durable. See HARDNESS.

unbridled, *adj.* unrestrained; violent, licentious; unruly, intractable. See FREEDOM, ILLEGALITY.

unbroken, *adj.* intact, WHOLE; continuous, constant, uninterrupted, even; untamed, unsubdued. See CONTINUITY, VIOLENCE.

unburden, *v.t.* unload; lighten, relieve; disclose, reveal. See EJECTION, LEVITY, DISCLOSURE.

uncalled-for, *adj.* undue, unnecessary, superfluous, gratuitous; ill-timed, untimely, inopportune. See USELESSNESS, INEXPEDIENCE.

uncanny, *adj.* mysterious, eerie, ghostly, weird, unnatural. See DEMON, DEATH, FEAR.

uncaring, *adj.* indifferent, uninterested; thoughtless, inconsiderate. See NEGLECT, INATTENTION.

unceasing, *adj.* continuous, uninterrupted; perpetual, eternal, endless. See CONTINUITY.

uncertainty, *n.* incertitude, DOUBT.

unchanged, *adj.* unaltered, *etc.* (see CHANGE); pristine, erstwhile, undiminished, good as new, the same, as of old; continuous, maintained. See PERMANENCE.

uncharted, *adj.* unfamiliar, unexplored. See UNCONFORMITY, NEWNESS.

unchaste, *adj.* lewd, incontinent, wanton, lascivious, lecherous, dissolute, immoral; unfaithful, adulterous. See IMPURITY.

uncivil, *adj.* rude, impolite, unmannerly. See DISCOURTESY.

uncivilized, *adj.* primitive, simple; barbarous, savage, barbaric. See VIOLENCE.

unclad, *adj.* unclothed, undressed, naked. See DIVESTMENT.

UNCLEANNESS
Dirtiness

Nouns—1, uncleanness, IMPURITY; filth, defilement, contamination, soilure; abomination; taint; MALODOROUSNESS; decay, putrescence, putrefaction; corruption, mold, must, mildew, dry rot; slovenliness, squalor, sordidness. See UGLINESS.

2, *(leavings)* offal, garbage, carrion; EXCRETION; feces, excrement, ordure, dung, biosolids; slough; pus, matter, gangrene, suppuration; sewage, sewerage; muck, guano, manure, compost. See DECOMPOSITION.

3, *(remainder)* dross, scoria; ashes, cinders, clinkers, scum, froth; swill, hogwash; ditchwater, dishwater, bilgewater; rinsings, offscourings, sweepings; scurvy, scurviness, scurf[iness]; dandruff, tartar. *Slang,* dreck. See REMAINDER.

4, *(grimy substance)* dirt, filth, soil, slop; dust, cobweb, smoke, soot, smudge, smut, grime; muck, mud, mire, quagmire, alluvium, silt, sludge, slime, slush. *Slang,* grunge.

5, *(unclean person)* drab, slut, slattern, sloven, slob, pig, riffraff; vermin, louse, flea, cockroach. *Slang,* litterbug, schlub, alley rat, grod(dess), trollymog, drap, mab, mopsy, swatchel.

6, dunghill, dungheap, midden, bog, sink, latrine, outhouse, head, privy, cesspool; sump, slough, dump, dumpheap, cloaca, scrapheap, junkyard, boneyard; drain, sewer; sty, pigsty, lair, den, Augean stables, sink of corruption; slum, rookery. *Slang,* rathole.

7, *(dirty mark)* spot, taint, mark, stain, blot; smear, smudge.

8, *(dirty thoughts)* foul-mindedness, obscenity, foulmouthedness; evil-mindedness, dirtiness; foul, evil, *or* dirty mind, filthiness; foul play. *Slang,* dirty fighting, dirty deal.

Verbs—1, rot, putrefy, fester, rankle, reek, stink (see MALODOROUSNESS); mold, go bad, spoil, become tainted.

2, dirty, soil, smoke, tarnish, spot, smear, daub, blot, blur, smudge, smirch; drabble, draggle; spatter, besmear, bemire, beslime, begrime, befoul; splash, stain, sully, pollute, defile, debase, contaminate, taint, corrupt (see DETERIORATION). *Informal,* foul.

Adjectives—1, unclean, dirty, filthy, grimy; soiled; dusty, smutty, sooty, smoky; thick, turbid, slimy; unclean, scruffy, slovenly, untidy, dingy, draggled, slatternly, sluttish, draggletailed; uncombed, unkempt, frowzy; unscoured, unswept, unwiped, unwashed, unpurified; squalid, rotten, seamy, nasty, coarse, foul, impure, offensive, abominable, nasty, piggish, beastly, reeky, sweaty, fetid, obscene; disgusting, nauseating, stomach-turning, revolting, sordid, corrupt. *Informal,* grubby. *Slang,* grungy, scuzzy, grotty, barnyard, yucky.

2, moldy, musty, mildewed, rusty, moth-eaten, rancid, bad, gone bad, fusty; scabrous, scrofulous, leprous; rotten, corrupt, tainted; gamy, high, flyblown, verminous, maggoty; putrid, putrescent, putrefied; purulent, carious, infected, infested, peccant, fecal, scurfy, impetiginous; gory, bloody; rotting, crapulous.

Phrases—poverty comes from God, but not dirt.

Quotations—While we spend energy and imagination on new ways of cleaning the floors of our houses, the Japanese solve the problem by not dirtying them in the first place (*Bernard Rudofsky*), Dirt is only matter out of place (*John Chipman Gray*).

Antonyms, see CLEANNESS.

---

unclouded, *adj.* unobscured, clear, LIGHT. See DISCLOSURE.

uncomfortable, *adj.* uneasy; cramped; disturbed, restless; embarrassing, difficult; unpleasant, distressing. See DISCONTENT.

uncommon, *adj.* unusual, rare, infrequent, sporadic; scarce; remarkable, extraordinary, strange; exceptional, original, unconventional. See RARITY, UNCONFORMITY.

uncommunicative, *adj.* taciturn, reticent; secretive. See TACITURNITY, SECRET.

uncomplicated, *adj.* simple, straightforward. See SIMPLENESS.

uncomplimentary, *adj.* unfavorable, unflattering. See DISAPPROBATION.

uncompromising, *adj.* inflexible, unyielding; rigid, strict. See SEVERITY.

unconcerned, *adj.* indifferent, uninterested, disinterested, detached, aloof; unmoved, uncurious. See INSENSIBILITY, INDIFFERENCE.

unconditional, *adj.* absolute, unreserved, unqualified; full, plenary; free. See FREEDOM.

unconfined, *adj.* unrestrained, free, unhampered. See FREEDOM.

UNCONFORMITY
Lack of conformity to convention

Nouns—1, unconformity, nonconformity, unconventionality, informality, abnormality; anomaly, anomalousness; exception, peculiarity, IRREGULARITY; infraction, breach, violation, *or* infringement of law, custom, *or* usage (see ILLEGALITY); eccentricity, oddity, twist, trick, quirk; conversation piece, something to write home about; DISAGREEMENT. *Informal,* one for the books. See DISSENT, HETERODOXY.

2, (*nonconformist nature*) individuality, SPECIALITY, idiosyncrasy, originality, mannerism; unusualness, strangeness; lunatic fringe; aberration; variety, singularity; EXEMPTION; mannishness, eonism, homosexuality, bisexuality, Lesbianism. *Slang,* third sex.

3, (*person*) nonconformist, nondescript, original; nonesuch, monster, prodigy, wonder, miracle, curiosity, rara avis; alien, foreigner (see EXTRINSIC); beatnik, hippie, yippie; enfant terrible; mongrel, hybrid (see MIXTURE); hermaphrodite; transsexual; homosexual, Lesbian; transvestite; bisexual; invert, pervert; monstrosity, rarity, freak, crank; maverick, misfit, fish out of water; freak of nature; neither one thing nor another; neither fish, [flesh,] nor fowl; one in a million; outcast, pariah, outlaw; outgroup. *Informal,* character, card. *Slang,* crackpot, screwball, oddball, flake, fluke, queer fish, wack, kook, airball, cornflake, cupcake, dingaling, dufus, space cadet, weirdo, fly ball, quoob; homo, fairy, nance, pansy, fag[got], queer, ladylover, dike; flower child.

4, (*unusual creature*) phoenix, chimera, hydra, sphinx, minotaur; griffin, centaur; hippogriff; cockatrice, roc, dragon, sea-serpent; mermaid; unicorn; Cyclops, Medusa, Hydra. See MYTHICAL DEITIES.

Verbs—leave the beaten track *or* path, go one's [own] way; baffle *or* beggar description. *Slang,* beat the Dutch.

Adjectives—1, unconformable, exceptional, abnormal, anomalous, out of place *or* keeping; irregular, arbitrary; alien, foreign; lawless, aberrant, peculiar, unnatural, eccentric, uncommon, extraordinary, outside the pale.

2, unusual, uncommon; rare, singular, unique, curious, odd, extraordinary, off the beaten track, out of the ordinary, strange, monstrous; wonderful, unaccountable; informal; unofficial; out of step, out of one's element; outré, out-of-the-way, remarkable, noteworthy; queer, quaint, sui generis; original, unconventional, unfashionable; unprecedented, unparalleled, unexampled, unheard of, nondescript; fantastic, grotesque, bizarre, kinky; pixilated; outlandish, exotic, offbeat, off-center, weird, out of this world; preternatural; superhuman, inhuman; unsymmetric. *Informal,* off-trail. *Slang,* far-out, wacky, flaky, kinky, kooky, off the grid, on tilt, way-out.

Adverbs—unconformably; except, unless, save, barring, beside, without, let alone; however, yet, but; against the grain *or* the hair.

Quotations—Whoso would be a man must be a nonconformist (*Ralph Waldo Emerson*).

Antonyms, see CONFORMITY.

---

unconquerable, *adj.* indomitable, invincible, irresistible, impregnable. See POWER, STRENGTH.

unconscionable, *adj.* unscrupulous, wrong, unethical; extravagant, excessive; immoderate, inordinate, intolerable. See IMPROBITY.

unconscious, *adj.* unaware, insensible; stupefied, asleep, out, blotto (*inf.*); uninformed, ignorant; submerged, subconscious, suppressed, repressed. See INSENSIBILITY.

unconstitutional, *adj.* illegal, unfair, unjust, against one's rights; un-American. See ILLEGALITY.

unconventional, *adj.* uncommon, unusual. See UNCONFORMITY.

uncooperative, *adj.* reluctant, resistant, recalcitrant, obstinate, stubborn, difficult, contrary. See OBSTINACY.

uncouple, *v.t.* unyoke, disconnect. See DISJUNCTION.

uncouth, *adj.* boorish, rude, crude, common, vulgar, uncultivated; ill-mannered, clumsy; strange, unusual; awkward, gauche, ungraceful. See VULGARITY, INELEGANCE.

uncover, *v.t.* open, unclose, unseal; disclose, discover; reveal, lay bare, expose; undress, denude, bare. See DISCLOSURE, DIVESTMENT.

unction, *n.* anointing; unguent, ointment; unctuousness, gushing; fervor. See FEELING.

uncultivated, *adj.* uncultured, unrefined, uncouth, rough; illiterate; wild, untilled, primeval. See IGNORANCE, UNPREPAREDNESS.

uncut, *adj.* unabridged, complete, unexpurgated. See COMPLETION.

undaunted, *adj.* courageous, undismayed; bold, intrepid, dauntless, cool, reckless. See COURAGE.

undeceive, *v.t.* disabuse, disillusion, correct. See INFORMATION.

undecided, *adj.* undetermined, unresolved, unsettled, uncertain, irresolute, doubtful, hesitant. See DOUBT, OBSCURITY.

undefeated, *adj.* unbeaten (see SUCCESS).

undemanding, *adj.* uncritical, lenient. See LENIENCY.

undemonstrative, *adj.* restrained, reserved; impassive, inexpressive, stolid, apathetic, calm. See TACITURNITY.

undeniable, *adj.* indisputable, incontestable, unquestionable, incontrovertible, irrefutable. See CERTAINTY.

under, *prep & adj.* below, beneath, underneath; subject to, controlled by; inferior, subordinate. See LOWNESS, SUBJECTION, INFERIORITY.

underage, *adj.* immature, premature; minor, in one's minority. See YOUTH.

underbrush, *n.* bush, thicket, brake, bracken, scrub, shrubbery, boscage; furze, gorse, heather. See VEGETABLE.

underclassman, *n.* freshman, frosh (*inf.*), sophomore; lowerclassman, plebe (*inf.*). See SCHOOL.

underclothes, *n.* See UNDERWEAR.

undercover, *adj.* masked, in disguise, incognito; [top-]secret, clandestine, sub rosa. See CONCEALMENT.

undercurrent, *n.* undertow; undertone, innuendo. See DANGER.

undercut, *v.t.* undersell. See SALE.

underdog, *n.* loser, victim. See FAILURE.

UNDERESTIMATION
Estimation of too low a value

Nouns—underestimation, underrating, undervaluing, *etc.*; depreciation, making light of. See DETRACTION, MISJUDGMENT, CONTEMPT.

Verbs—underestimate, underrate, undervalue, underreckon; depreciate, disparage, detract from; not do justice to; misprize, disprize; slight, neglect; slur over; make light of, play down, underplay, understate, take no account of; minimize, belittle.

Adjectives—underestimated, underrated, *etc.*

Quotations—No man ever went broke underestimating the intelligence of the American voter (*H. L. Mencken*), Let us not underrate the value of a fact; it will one day flower into a truth (*Henry David Thoreau*).

Antonyms, see EXAGGERATION.

---

undergo, *v.t.* suffer, experience, endure, sustain, bear, stand, withstand. See CIRCUMSTANCE, PAIN, OCCURRENCE.

undergraduate, *n.* freshman, frosh (*inf.*), sophomore, junior; lowerclassman, undergrad (*inf.*), plebe (*inf.*). See SCHOOL.

underground, *n.* subway, tube, Métro; [the] resistance, partisans, guerrillas, Maquis. —*adj.* subterranean, buried, interred. See CONCEALMENT, DEPTH.

underhand, underhanded, *adj.* hidden, secret; deceitful, fraudulent, unfair, tricky; stealthy, sly, clandestine, furtive, devious. See SECRET, DECEPTION, IMPROBITY.

underline, *v.t.* underscore; accent, emphasize, urge. See INDICATION, IMPORTANCE.

underling, *n.* subordinate, assistant, inferior, deputy, apprentice; SERVANT, menial, flunky, retainer. See INFERIORITY.

underlying, *adj.* hidden, latent, basic. See INTRINSIC.

undermine, *v.t.* excavate, mine, sap; honeycomb; subvert, weaken, demoralize, thwart, frustrate. See CONCAVITY, HINDRANCE, DETERIORATION, WEAKNESS.

underneath, *prep. & adv.* beneath, below, lower, under. See LOWNESS.

underpass, *n.* underwalk, tunnel, tube, viaduct. See CROSSING.

underprivileged, *adj.* impoverished, deprived, depressed, downtrodden, unfortunate; un[der]developed. See ADVERSITY.

underrate, *v.t.* undervalue (see UNDERESTIMATION); disparage, belittle. See DETRACTION.

underscore, *v.t.* See UNDERLINE.

underside, *n.* underneath, [under]belly, downside. See LOWNESS.

undersigned, *n.* signer, subscriber, endorser, petitioner. See ASSENT.

understand, *v.t.* know, comprehend, grasp, catch; perceive, discern, penetrate, apprehend; interpret, construe, fathom; gather, infer, assume; realize, believe; sympathize (with). See MEANING, INTELLIGENCE, SUPPOSITION.

understanding, *n.* discernment, comprehension, INTELLIGENCE, knowledge, insight, perception; sympathy; agreement. See INTELLECT.

understate, *v.* underestimate, undervalue, underrate; play *or* tone down, softpedal (*inf.*), palliate, belittle, degrade, deprecate, pull one's punches (*inf.*); whitewash. See DISTORTION, DETRACTION.

understudy, *n.* alternate, substitute, standby, stand-in, second, double. See DRAMA, SUBSTITUTION.

undertaker, *n.* funeral director, mortician; sexton; embalmer. See INTERMENT.

UNDERTAKING
Project

Nouns—1, undertaking; compact, engagement, PROMISE; enterprise, emprise, project; endeavor, venture, pilgrimage, adventure; matter in hand, BUSINESS; move, first move, beginning; caper. *Informal,* tall order. *Slang,* lay. See EXPERIMENT, INTENTION.

2, entrepreneur, man *or* woman of action, founder, launcher; contractor; adventurer.

Verbs—undertake, tackle; engage in, embark on; launch *or* plunge into; volunteer; apprentice oneself to, devote oneself to, take up, take in hand; set *or* go about; set to, fall to, fall to work; try one's hand, take the plunge, launch forth; set up shop; put in hand, put in execution; set forward; put *or* turn one's hand to, throw oneself into; begin; broach, institute, originate; put one's hand to the plow, put one's shoulder to the wheel; have in hand, have many irons in the fire; move heaven and earth. *Informal,* bite off more than one can chew, go in for, go off the deep end, give it a whirl, take the bull by the horns.

Adjectives—venturesome, adventurous. *Slang,* on the make.

Adverbs—on *or* in the fire. *Informal,* in the works.

Phrases—nothing venture, nothing gain.

Quotations—Fortune sides with him who dares (*Virgil*).

Antonyms, see REFUSAL.

---

undertow, *n.* riptide, undercurrent, backlash; eddy, vortex. See WATER, OPPOSITION.

underwear, *n.* underclothes, undergarments, underthings, unmentionables (*inf.*), lingerie, drawers, union suit, BVDs, briefs, panties, panty hose; foundation [garment], girdle, panty girdle, brassiere, bra, corset. See CLOTHING.

underworld, *n.* netherworld, infernal regions, HELL, Hades; world of crime, criminals, gangsters, gangland (*inf.*). See ILLEGALITY.

underwrite, *v.t.* insure, guarantee, warrant, indemnify; sanction, authorize; sponsor, finance, bankroll (*inf.*), subscribe to, support, back, stake (*inf.*), grubstake (*inf.*); defray, pay (for). See SECURITY, MEANS.

undeserved, *adj.* unmerited, unwarranted. See INJUSTICE.

undesirable, *adj.* disagreeable, distasteful, objectionable, disliked; inadvisable, inexpedient. See INEXPEDIENCE, DISLIKE.

undignified, *adj.* discreditable, inelegant, ludicrous, awkward, gauche; mean, degrading; indecorous, ill-bred. See INELEGANCE, VULGARITY.

undisciplined, *adj.* wild, chaotic; lawless, licentious; primitive, savage; spontaneous, capricious, erratic. See CHANGEABLENESS, ILLEGALITY.

undisguised, *adj.* true, genuine; evident, obvious; candid, frank, open. See TRUTH.

undisputed, *adj.* unchallenged, indisputable, accepted, agreed. See BELIEF, CERTAINTY.

undivided, *adj.* concentrated, exclusive, WHOLE, intact, entire; single, united.

undo, *v.t.* loose, unlock, unfasten, untie; release; annul, reverse, cancel, neutralize; spoil, destroy, ruin. See DISJUNCTION, DESTRUCTION.

undoing, *n.* downfall, defeat, ruin, reversal. See FAILURE.

undoubted, *adj.* undisputed, *etc.* (see DOUBT); accepted, sure, assured, certain. See CERTAINTY.

undress, *v.* strip, disrobe, unclothe, peel (*sl.*), dismantle, expose. See DIVESTMENT.

undue, *adj.* unjust, inequitable; improper, inappropriate; extreme, excessive, immoderate, inordinate, exorbitant, unwarranted. See INJUSTICE.

undulate, *v.* surge, fluctuate, ripple, pulsate, wave. See OSCILLATION, CONVOLUTION.

undying, *adj.* deathless, immortal, unending. See PERPETUITY.

unearth, *v.t.* exhume, disinter; expose, disclose, discover, uncover; eradicate, uproot, dig up. See EXTRACTION, INTERMENT, DISCLOSURE.

unearthly, *adj.* supernatural, uncanny, ghostly, spectral, eerie, weird, exceptional (*inf.*), unusual (*inf.*); appalling, hair-raising. See DEMON.

uneasy, *adj.* restless, restive; disturbed, perturbed, disquieted, uncomfortable; anxious, apprehensive, fearful; constrained; fidgety, jittery, on edge, jumpy; uncertain, unstable, touch-and-go. See AGITATION, EXCITEMENT, EXCITABILITY, FEAR.

uneconomical, *adj.* improvident, unthrifty. See WASTE.

uneducated, *adj.* ignorant, untaught, untutored, illiterate. See IGNORANCE.

unemotional, *adj.* apathetic, calm, cool, impassive, unfeeling. See INSENSIBILITY, INDIFFERENCE.

unemployed, *adj.* idle, jobless, out of work; loafing, at leisure, at liberty, free, available; looking [around]. See INACTIVITY.

unending, *adj.* endless, interminable; ceaseless, incessant. See PERMANENCE.

unequal, *adj.* disparate, disproportionate; inadequate; uneven, mismatched, one-sided; inequitable, unfair. See DIFFERENCE.

unequivocal, *adj.* unmistakable, unqualified; clear, definite, yes or no, black and white. See CERTAINTY.

unethical, *adj.* immoral, unprincipled, unscrupulous. See IMPROBITY.

uneven, *adj.* variable, odd, unequal, disparate; rough, lumpy, broken, rugged. See ROUGHNESS, INEQUALITY.

uneventful, *adj.* monotonous, humdrum, dull. See INACTIVITY.

unexceptionable, *adj.* faultless, beyond criticism. See PERFECTION.

unexceptional, *adj.* common, ordinary, unremarkable. See CONFORMITY.

unexpected, *adj.* unforeseen; sudden, SURPRISE, abrupt, accidental, coincidental, contingent, chance; from nowhere, out of the blue.

unfailing, *adj.* constant, steadfast, unfaltering, sure. See CERTAINTY, PERMANENCE.

unfair, *adj.* unjust, unreasonable, inequitable; unsporting; disingenuous; partial, biased, prejudiced, discriminatory. See WRONG, IMPROBITY, INJUSTICE.

unfaithful, *adj.* disloyal, faithless; adulterous, philandering, cheating, untrue, fickle; inaccurate, untrustworthy. See IMPROBITY, WRONG.

unfamiliar, *adj.* unknown, uncommon, strange, novel, new; unacquainted. See UNCONFORMITY, NEWNESS, IGNORANCE.

unfashionable, *adj.* dowdy, old-fashioned, out-of-date, old hat (*sl.*), out (*sl.*); passé, antiquated. See UNCONFORMITY, OLDNESS.

unfasten, *v.t.* loose[n], disconnect, unbind, unfix, unpin; liberate. See DISJUNCTION.

unfathomable, *adj.* fathomless, bottomless, unplumbed, unsounded; unintelligible, inexplicable, incomprehensible. See DEPTH, INFINITY, UNINTELLIGIBILITY.

unfavorable, *adj.* adverse, disadvantageous, inauspicious, unpropitious, unlucky; unfriendly, antagonistic; negative, contrary; inclement; inopportune, untimely. See INEXPEDIENCE, PREDICTION, ADVERSITY, DISAPPROBATION.

unfeasible, *adj.* impracticable, impossible, unthinkable. See IMPOSSIBILITY.

unfeeling, *adj.* hard[-hearted], cold [-blooded], cruel; heartless, inhuman, callous, dispassionate; merciless, pitiless, unmerciful, relentless, adamant. See INSENSIBILITY, MALEVOLENCE.

unfettered, *adj.* unchained, unrestrained, at liberty. See FREEDOM.

unfinished, *adj.* crude, raw, sketchy, rough; incomplete; amateurish, inept; unpainted, *etc.* See UNPREPAREDNESS, INCOMPLETENESS, UNSKILLFULNESS.

unfit, *adj.* incapable, unqualified, *etc.*; incapacitated, unhealthy, in poor condition; unsuitable, inappropriate, *etc.* See UNSKILLFULNESS, DISAGREEMENT.

unflappable, *adj.* cool (*inf.*), even-tempered, imperturbable. See INEXCITABILITY.

unflattering, *adj.* detracting, derogatory, abusive. See DETRACTION.

unfold, *v.* open, unroll, smooth out; disclose, expose, announce; develop, progress. See DISCLOSURE.

unforeseen, *adj.* unexpected, unanticipated, out of the blue; sudden. See SURPRISE.

unforgettable, *adj.* memorable, notable. See IMPORTANCE.

unforgivable, *adj.* inexcusable, unpardonable. See INJUSTICE.

unforgiving, *adj.* relentless, unrelenting, implacable, unappeasable, inexorable; merciless, pitiless; vengeful. See SEVERITY, RETALIATION.

unfortunate, *adj.* unlucky, hapless, ill-fated, ill-starred, star-crossed, luckless, unsuccessful, abortive, disastrous, ruinous; short *or* out of luck, SOL, behind the eight ball, jinxed, hexed (*all sl.*). See ADVERSITY, INEXPEDIENCE.

unfounded, *adj.* baseless, vain, groundless, ungrounded. See FALSEHOOD.

unfriendly, *adj.* hostile, inimical, antagonistic; unfavorable. See MALEVOLENT, DISAPPROBATION.

unfrock, *v.t.* dismiss, discharge, oust, disgrace. See PUNISHMENT.

unfruitful, *adj.* barren, unproductive, infertile, sterile; fruitless. See USELESSNESS.

unfurl, *v.t.* unroll, open, spread out, fly, wave; display. See OPENING, SMOOTHNESS.

ungainly, *adj.* awkward, clumsy; gawky, ungraceful, lumbering; grotesque. See UGLINESS, UNSKILLFULNESS.

ungenerous, *adj.* illiberal; mean, harsh, exacting. See SELFISHNESS, MALEVOLENCE.

ungodly, *adj.* godless, pagan, freethinking; profane, unholy, impious; satanic, diabolic; *informal,* bad, outrageous. See IRRELIGION, BADNESS.

ungovernable, *adj.* unbridled, irrepressible, unruly, headstrong, uncontrollable, unmanageable, incorrigible; licentious. See DISOBEDIENCE, OBSTINACY.

ungrateful, *adj.* unthankful, ingrate, unappreciative, thankless, forgetful; unwanted, unpleasing, unwelcome. See INGRATITUDE, DISCONTENT.

unguarded, *adj.* inadvertent, thoughtless, incautious; with one's guard down; not guarded. See DANGER, INATTENTION.

unhand, *v.t.* let go, release. See RELINQUISHMENT.

unhappy, *adj.* unlucky, unfortunate; sad, sorrowful, wretched, miserable, dolorous, despondent, disconsolate, inconsolable, gloomy, joyless; inappropriate, dismal; calamitous, disastrous, catastrophic. See DEJECTION, ADVERSITY.

unhealthy, *adj.* sickly, infirm, ailing, invalid; delicate, frail; undesirable, inauspicious, ominous. See DISEASE.

unheard-of, *adj.* unprecedented, unexampled; unbelievable, inconceivable. See UNCONFORMITY, IMPOSSIBILITY.

unhinge, *v.t.* unsettle, derange, unbalance, craze. See INSANITY.

unholy, *adj.* unhallowed, unconsecrated, unsanctified; wicked, profane; ungodly, impious, irreligious; *informal,* frightful, extreme, unseemly. See IRRELIGION, BADNESS.

uniform, *adj.* unchanging, even, regular; homogeneous, consistent. See UNIFORMITY, REGULARITY. —*n.* livery, outfit, caparison; regimentals, blues, whites, khaki, sailor suit, *etc.* See CLOTHING.

UNIFORMITY
Homogeneity

Nouns—uniformity, homogeneity, evenness, consistency, monotony, sameness; REGULARITY. See CONFORMITY, CONTINUITY, SYMMETRY, ORDER, UNITY.

Verbs—1, make uniform, homogenize, normalize, stabilize, even, level, balance.
2, remain uniform, persevere, persist.

Adjectives—uniform, homogeneous, homologous; of a piece, consistent, of a piece; monotonous, same; even, invariable, changeless; stable.

Quotations—Every body continues in its state of rest, or of uniform motion in a right line, unless it is compelled to change that state by forces impressed upon it (*Isaac Newton*), Constant labor of one uniform kind destroys the intensity and flow of a man's animal spirits, which find recreation and delight in mere change of activity (*Karl Marx*).

Antonyms, see DIFFERENCE, IRREGULARITY.

unify, *v.t.* consolidate, combine, amalgamate, join. See UNITY.

unimaginative, *adj.* uninventive, uncreative, uninspired; imitative, stereotyped, hack, pedestrian, prosaic. See WEARINESS, SIMPLENESS.

unimpeachable, *adj.* irreproachable, above reproach; innocent, faultless; reliable, authoritative. See INNOCENCE, CERTAINTY.

UNIMPORTANCE
Insignificance

Nouns—1, unimportance, insignificance, nothingness, immateriality, inconsequentiality, inconsequence; triviality, levity, frivolity, froth; paltriness, USELESSNESS; disempowerment; matter of indifference; no object. See FOLLY, MEDIOCRITY, SHALLOWNESS.

2, *(something unimportant)* trivia, trifle, minutiae, [minor] details; drop in the ocean *or* bucket, pinprick, fleabite, molehill; nothing [worth speaking of], nothing particular, nothing to boast *or* speak of, not the end of the world; bosh; small matter, no great matter, trifling matter; mere joke, mere nothing; hardly *or* scarcely anything; no great shakes; child's play; small beer *or* potatoes.

3, *(something of little value)* toy, plaything, gimcrack, gewgaw, bauble, trinket, bagatelle, kickshaw, knickknack, trifle; trumpery, trash, rubbish, stuff, frippery; chaff, froth, bubble, smoke, cobweb; weed, refuse, scrum; joke, jest, snap of the fingers; fudge, fiddlesticks; pack of nonsense, straw, pin, fig, button, feather, two cents, halfpenny, penny, [brass] farthing; peppercorn, jot, rap, pinch of snuff, old song. *Informal*, red cent, row of pins, hill of beans, fifth wheel. *Slang*, mickey, schmatte, chopped liver.

4, nobody, nonentity, nonperson, unperson, cipher, mediocrity, small fry, pipsqueak, nine days' wonder, flash in the pan, dummy, straw man; every Tom, Dick, and Harry. *Informal*, lightweight, no great shakes. *Slang*, squirt, zob, pencil dick, asswipe, chickenshit, fuckoff, schmendrick. See NONEXISTENCE.

Verbs—not matter, signify nothing, not matter a straw; trifle, palter, fiddle, mess around, idle; make light of; dispense with; underestimate, belittle, downplay, play down, think *or* make little of, minimize, set no store by, not care a straw about; catch at straws, overestimate, not see the wood for the trees. *Informal*, not be worth a damn, continental, rap, *or* hang, cut no ice, underwhelm. *Slang*, suck.

Adjectives—1, of little, small, *or* no account *or* importance, unimportant; inconsequential, immaterial, unessential, nonessential; indifferent; subordinate, inferior, mediocre, average; small-time.

2, trifling, trivial, slight; puerile; airy, shallow; frivolous, petty, niggling, picayune, piddling; inane, ridiculous, ludicrous, farcical; finical, namby-pamby, wishy-washy, milk and water; inappreciable. *Informal*, ditsy, footling. *Slang*, mickey mouse, jerkwater, nowhere, pissant.

3, poor, paltry, pitiful; shabby, miserable, wretched, vile, scrubby, niggardly, scurvy, beggarly, worthless, cheap; not worth the pains, not worthwhile, not worth mentioning, not worth speaking of, not worth a thought, damn, *or* straw; beneath notice *or* consideration; futile, vain. *Slang*, measly, punk, dog-ass. See CHEAPNESS.

Adverbs—slightly, rather, somewhat, pretty well, tolerably.

Interjections—no matter! tut-tut! pshaw! pooh[-pooh]! bosh! humbug! fiddlesticks! fiddlededee! never mind! what of it! what's the odds! stuff and nonsense! *Informal*, skip it! *Slang*, nuts! baloney! bunk! big deal!

Quotations—History, *n.* an account mostly false, of events mostly unimportant, which are brought about by rulers, mostly knaves, and soldiers, mostly fools (*Ambrose Bierce*), My country has in its wisdom contrived for me the most insignificant office [the vice presidency] that ever the invention of man contrived or his imagination conceived (*John Adams*), I demonstrate by means of philosophy that the earth is round, and is inhabited on all sides; that it is insignificantly small, and is borne through the stars (*Johannes Kepler*).

Antonyms, see IMPORTANCE.

uninhabited, *adj.* unpopulated, unpeopled, unsettled, vacant. See ABSENCE.
uninhibited, *adj.* unhampered, free [and easy], natural, spontaneous. See FREEDOM.

UNINTELLIGIBILITY
Incoherence

Nouns—1, unintelligibility, incoherence; OBSCURITY, ambiguity; uncertainty, intricacy, perplexity; confusion, DISORDER; mystification.

2, paradox, enigma, poser, mystery, riddle [of the Sphinx], [Chinese] puzzle (see SECRET); sealed book; cryptography, steganography, code, cipher; cacography (see WRITING); gibberish, jargon (see UNMEANINGNESS), Greek, Hebrew, Dutch, *etc.*

Verbs—1, pass comprehension; veil, obscure, obfuscate; confuse, perplex, mystify, speak in riddles.

2, not understand, lose [the clue], miss [the point]; not know what to make of, be able to make nothing of, give up; not be able to account for, not be able to make heads *or* tails of, be at sea; see through glass darkly, not understand one another, work at cross purposes.

Adjectives—1, unintelligible, unaccountable, incomprehensible, inapprehensible, unrecognizable, unfathomable, fathomless, undiscoverable, inexplicable, inscrutable, impenetrable, unsolvable, meaningless; incoherent, irrational; illegible, undecipherable, unexplained, as Greek to one; enigmatic[al], paradoxical, puzzling, baffling, intricate. *Informal,* clear as mud.

2, inconceivable, beyond comprehension, beyond one's depth, over one's head.

3, inarticulate, mumbled, confused. *Slang,* discombobulated.

Phrases—I don't understand; it's Greek to me.

Quotations—Metaphysics is almost always an attempt to prove the incredible by an appeal to the unintelligible (*H. L. Mencken*).

Antonyms, see MEANING.

---

unintentional, *adj.* accidental, involuntary, inadvertent, unpremeditated, spontaneous. See CHANCE.
uninteresting, *adj.* dull, dreary, tedious, humdrum. See WEARINESS.
uninterrupted, *adj.* continual, incessant, constant. See DURABILITY.
union, *n.* UNITY, concord, uniting, joining, connection; COMBINATION, fusion, coalescence; marriage; [con]federation, association, alliance. See AGREEMENT, JUNCTION, MIXTURE, PARTY.
unique, *adj.* sole, single; singular, only, sui generis; unequaled, matchless, unparalleled, unprecedented, unusual, rare. See UNCONFORMITY, EXCLUSION, INEQUALITY, UNITY.
unison, *n.* harmony, concord, AGREEMENT, union, unanimity, UNITY.

UNITY
Oneness

Nouns—1, unity, oneness, individuality; indivisibility, inseparability, homogeneity, integrality; solitude, isolation, SECLUSION; IDENTITY, sameness, uniformity, consistency, COHERENCE; unification, amalgamation, consolidation, integration, coalescence, fusion, JUNCTION.

2, harmony, concurrence, AGREEMENT, accordance, accord, concord, consonance, concert, peace; unison, union, unanimity, solidarity.

3, unit, one, ace, solo, monad, module, integer, integrant, figure, number; individual, person, entity, none else, no other; detail, particular; item, object, thing, article, WHOLE, ensemble.

Verbs—be one *or* alone, isolate, unite, unify, join, merge, mix, blend, fuse, weld, cement, consolidate, solidify; marry, wed; reconcile, harmonize, attune, fraternize.

Adjectives—1, one, single, sole, solo, solitary, monistic; individual, apart, alone, unaccompanied, unattended, unaided, unassisted; singular, odd, unique, azygous, unrepeated, first and last, three in one; isolated, insulated, insular; single-handed, single-minded.

2, inseparable, inseverable, indivisible, indissoluble, indiscerptible, irresolvable, integral, uniform, compact; unipartite, one-piece, unilateral, unilinear, unipolar, *etc.*, united, unified, joined, combined, connected, unseparated, undivided, homogeneous.

3, harmonious, concordant, unanimous. See AGREEMENT.

4, unifying, uniting, connective, conjunctive, combinative, coalescent.

Adverbs—singly, individually, independently, severally, separately; solely, simply, alone, by oneself, by the piece, each, apiece, by itself, only apart, per se; in the singular, in the abstract, one by one, one at a time, as an individual, as one man, in unison. *Informal,* high and dry.

Quotation—Unity in variety is the plan of the universe (*Swami Vivekananda*).

Antonyms, see MULTITUDE.

---

universal, *adj.* comprehensive, catholic, ecumenical; popular, general; cosmic; global, worldwide. See GENERALITY, UNIVERSE, KNOWLEDGE, THOUGHT.

UNIVERSE
Totality of existing things

Nouns—**1,** universe, cosmos, celestial sphere, macrocosm; infinity, span, [all] creation, earth and heaven, [all the] world, ether; ecosphere; catastrophism, catastrophe theory, big bang theory. See SPACE.

2, HEAVEN, the heavens, sky, empyrean, firmament, vault, roof, *or* canopy of heaven, celestial spaces, outer space, ceiling.

3, heavenly bodies, celestial body *or* object, luminaries, starry host, fires of heaven; nebula, galaxy, Milky Way; constellation, zodiac (Aries, Aquarius, Cancer, Capricorn, Gemini, Leo, Libra, Pisces, Sagittarius, Scorpius, Taurus, Virgo); Great *or* Little Bear, Ursa Major *or* Minor, Big *or* Little Dipper; Andromeda, Auriga, Boïtes, Canis Major *or* Minor, Cassiopeia, Centaurus, Cepheus, Cygnus, Draco, Hercules, Lyra, Orion, Perseus, Pleiades; star, Achenar, Alpha Centauri, Arcturus, Aldebaran, Altair, Antares, Betelgeuse, Canopus, Capella, Centauri, Pollux, Procyon, Rigel, Sirius, dog star, Vega, Polaris, polestar; falling star, neutron star, red giant *or* dwarf, pulsar, nova, binary *or* double star, visual binary, brown, white *or* black dwarf, cluster, black hole; metagalaxy, Milky Way, Andromeda galaxy, Magellanic Clouds, irregular, lenticular, starburst, elliptical *or* spiral galaxy, barred spiral, Great Wall; supernova; death star, nemesis; meteor, shooting star, fireball; comet, Halley's comet; planetoid, asteroid, asteroid belt; protoplanet, protostar.

4, solar system, sun, orb, eye of the day; planet, Mercury, Venus, Earth, Mars, Jupiter, Saturn, Uranus, Neptune, Pluto, gas giant, Vesta; Galilean satellite: Callisto, Europa, Ganymete, Io; Jovian satellites; Ariel, Ceres, Charon, Deimos, Miranda, Nereid, Oberon, Phobos, Titan, Titania, Triton, Umbriel; planetoid, asteroid, satellite; moon, Luna, man in the moon, new moon, half moon, crescent, first, *etc.*, quarter, change of the moon, man in the moon, mother of the months, queen of tides; comet, meteor[ite]; Earth, Terra, [terrestrial] globe, sphere, oblate, spheroid, world, Spaceship Earth, this earthly round; cosmic rays, sunspots, aurora borealis *or* australis, northern *or* southern lights; artificial satellite, bird, space station.

5, astronomy, astrometry, astrophysics, astrochemistry, spectroscopy, cosmography, cosmogony, cosmology, geography, geodesy, geology, geognosy, geophysics; almagest, ephemeris, star atlas *or* map, nautical almanac; observatory, planetarium.

Adjectives—**1,** universal, cosmic, empyrean, ethereal, celestial, heavenly; stellar, substellar, astral, sidereal, starry; solar, lunar, planetary, nebular; earthly, terrestrial, mundane.

2, astronomical, astrometrical, astrophysical, spectroscopic, *etc.*; geocentric, heliocentric, Copernican, Ptolemaic; 1st, 2nd, *etc.* magnitude.

Adverbs—under the sun.

Quotations—There is one outstandingly important fact regarding Spaceship Earth, and that is that no instruction book came with it (*Buckminster Fuller*), The moon's an errant thief, and her pale fire she snatches from the sun (*Shakespeare*), The evening star, Love's harbinger (*John Milton*), The heaventree of stars hung with humid nightblue fruit (*James Joyce*), There are more things in heaven and earth, Horatio, than are dreamt of in your philosophy (*Shakespeare*), The eternal silence of these infinite spaces terrifies me (*Pascal*), The world is disgracefully managed, one hardly knows to whom to complain (*Ronald Firbank*), Space isn't remote at all. It's only an hour's drive straight up if your car could go upwards (*Fred Hoyle*).

---

university, *n.* college, SCHOOL, academy, seminary, institute, institution [of higher learning]; campus, U (*sl.*).

unjust, *adj.* unfair, inequitable, undue, biased. See WRONG.

unkempt, *adj.* uncombed, disordered, ill-kept; slovenly, untidy, bedraggled. See VULGARITY, DISORDER.

unkind, *adj.* pitiless, merciless, hard-hearted, cruel, brutal, harsh, inhuman. See MALEVOLENCE.

unknown, *adj.* incognito, unrecognized, unperceived, unfamiliar. See OBSCURITY, LATENCY.

unlatch, *v.t.* open, unfasten. See OPENING.

unlawful, *adj.* See ILLEGALITY.

unleash, *v.t.* uncage, unshackle, [un]loose, release, set loose. See LIBERATION.

unless, *conj. & prep.* if [not], but, save, except[ing], other than, aside from, let alone, without, barring. See CIRCUMSTANCE, QUALIFICATION.

unlike, *adj.* dissimilar, diverse, different, disparate; distinct, separate. See DIFFERENCE.

unlikely, *adj.* improbable, doubtful, dubious; farfetched, inconceivable; impracticable, implausible; unpromising, inauspicious. See IMPROBABILITY.

unlimited, *adj.* undefined, indefinite, boundless, limitless, uncounted, infinite, full, absolute, unconfined, unconstricted, unrestrained. See FREEDOM, INFINITY.

unload, *v.t.* empty, disgorge, discharge, offload, unpack. See EJECTION.

unlock, *v.t.* unfasten, unbolt, disengage, undo; open; release, uncover, solve (a mystery, *etc.*). See LIBERATION, ANSWER.

unloved, *adj.* loveless, jilted, spurned. See HATE.

unlucky, *adj.* unfortunate, ill-starred, ill-omened, hopeless, disastrous; regrettable. See ADVERSITY, BADNESS.

unman, *v.t.* emasculate, devitalize, unnerve, enervate, weaken; effeminize. See IMPOTENCE, FEAR, DEJECTION.

unmanageable, *adj.* unruly, ungovernable, refractory. See OBSTINACY, DIFFICULTY.

unmanly, *adj.* cowardly; ignoble; effeminate. See COWARDICE, FEMALE.

unmannerly, *adj.* rude, uncivil, ill-mannered; caddish, discourteous. See DISCOURTESY.

unmarried, *adj.* bachelor, spinster, maiden, virgin; widowed, divorced; celibate, single, unwed. See CELIBACY.

unmask, *v.t.* disclose, lay bare, reveal. See DISCLOSURE.

UNMEANINGNESS
Lack of meaning or sense

Nouns—1, unmeaningness, meaninglessness, senselessness, *etc.*; ABSURDITY, inanity; ambiguity (see UNINTELLIGIBILITY); oxymoron.

2, nonsense, verbiage, mere words, empty sound, dead letter; gibberish, jargon, academese, jabber, babble, drivel, palaver, claptrap, double-talk, hocus-pocus, mumbo jumbo, gobbledy-gook, Jabberwocky; balderdash, rigmarole, flummery, humbug, moonshine, fiddle-faddle, wishwash, stuff [and nonsense]; fustian, rant, bombast, rodomontade; platitude, truism; scribble, scrabble, doodle. *Informal,* hogwash, eyewash, bushwah, horsefeathers, poppycock, flapdoodle, bunk, buncombe. *Slang,* tommyrot, applesauce, fudge, gas, yawp, baloney, hooey, blah, malarkey, bull[shit], horse[shit], crap.

Verbs—mean nothing, not mean a thing; jabber, babble, twaddle (see *Nouns*); scrabble, scribble, scrawl, doodle; drivel, slaver, drool. *Slang,* bull, gas, talk through one's hat, run off at the mouth.

Adjectives—unmeaning, meaningless, senseless, reasonless, nonsensical, void of sense, without rhyme *or* reason, for the birds; unintelligible, illegible, inexpressive, expressionless, vacant, blank, inane, vague, ambiguous; inexpressible, glassy, ineffable, undefinable, incommunicable. *Slang,* deadpan.

Antonyms, see MEANING.

---

unmentionable, *adj.* ineffable, unutterable, unspeakable, nameless, despicable. See DISREPUTE.

unmerciful, *adj.* merciless, pitiless, inhuman, cruel; unfeeling, relentless, unrelenting; stern, hard-hearted, cold-blooded, callous. See MALEVOLENCE, SEVERITY.

unmistakable, *adj.* obvious, evident, manifest, patent, clear, apparent, plain, open; downright, overt, certain. See CERTAINTY.

unmitigated, *adj.* unalleviated; downright, utter, sheer, out-and-out. See GREATNESS, COMPLETION.

unmoved, *adj.* unaffected, impassive, unsympathetic, *etc.*; unconvinced, firm, unwavering, unshaken, steadfast. See INSENSIBILITY.

unnatural, *adj.* artificial, factitious; affected, stagy, insincere; strange, abnormal, foreign; monstrous, freakish, misshapen; merciless, cold. See AFFECTATION, MALEVOLENCE, UNCONFORMITY.

unnecessary, *adj.* useless, needless, inessential, superfluous, dispensable. See USELESSNESS.

unnerve, *v.t.* unhinge, disconcert, frighten, rattle (*inf.*), give the jitters. See FEAR, IMPOTENCE, EXCITABILITY.

unnumbered, *adj.* uncounted; countless, innumerable. See INFINITY.

unobtrusive, *adj.* unassertive, unpretentious, shy, modest, retiring, timid. See MODESTY.

unoccupied, *adj.* empty, vacant, tenantless; unemployed. See ABSENCE, INACTIVITY.

unofficial, *adj.* unauthorized, unauthoritative; tentative; off the cuff *or* record, not for publication. See ILLEGALITY, UNCERTAINTY.

unopposed, *adj.* unanimous, unchallenged, uncontested. See UNITY.

unorthodox, *adj.* unconventional; heretical. See UNCONFORMITY, HETERODOXY.

unpack, *v.t.* unwrap, uncover, open; unload, put away. See EJECTION.

unpaid, *adj.* owing, due, unsatisfied; unsalaried, volunteer. See DEBT, NONPAYMENT.

unpalatable, *adj.* distasteful, unsavory, unappetizing; insipid; inedible, uneatable, tasteless. See UNSAVORINESS.

unparalleled, *adj.* unequaled, peerless, unmatched, inimitable. See SUPERIORITY.

unpardonable, *adj.* See UNFORGIVABLE.

unplanned, *adj.* unintentional, unpremeditated. See UNPREPAREDNESS.

unpleasant, *adj.* disagreeable, offensive, displeasing, unpleasing, bad, nasty, sickening; noisome; unattractive, unsatisfactory; surly, unfriendly. See DISCOURTESY, UNSAVORINESS.

unpopular, *adj.* disliked, unloved; distasteful; out of favor. See DISLIKE.

unprecedented, *adj.* new, novel, unheard-of, original. See UNCONFORMITY.

unprejudiced, *adj.* impartial, dispassionate, unbiased, uninfluenced. See LIBERALITY.

unpremeditated, *adj.* extempore, impromptu, extemporary, impulsive, spontaneous. See IMPULSE, UNPREPAREDNESS.

UNPREPAREDNESS
Lack of preparation

Nouns—1, unpreparedness, unreadiness, improvidence, imprudence; inadvertence (see INATTENTION); negligence; improvisation, unpremeditation (see IMPULSE); immaturity, prematurity. See EARLINESS, NEGLECT.

2, [state of] nature, absence of art; virgin soil, fallow ground, unweeded garden; raw material, diamond in the rough; rough copy; embryo, germ.

3, improvisation, extemporization; improviser. *Informal*, ad-lib. *Slang*, ear man.

Verbs—1, lie fallow, live from hand to mouth, take no thought of tomorrow; take aback (see SURPRISE). *Informal*, cook up, go off half-cocked.

2, extemporize, improvise, whip *or* cook up. *Informal*, ad-lib. *Slang*, wing it.

Adjectives—1, unprepared, unready, untutored, undrilled, unexercised; untaught, uneducated, uncultured; unqualified, disqualified, unfit[ted], ill-fitted, unsuited, ineligible; unorganized, unarranged, unfurnished, unprovided, unequipped, untrimmed. *Informal*, flat-footed.

2, immature, unripe, raw, green; uncooked, unboiled, unconcocted, undigested, ill-digested, unmellowed, unseasoned, unleavened; crude, coarse, rough[cast], rough-hewn, in the rough; unhewn, unformed, unfashioned, unwrought, unpolished.

3, rudimentary, rudimental, embryonic, in ovo, vestigial, inchoate, abortive, premature; undeveloped, unhatched, unfledged, unlicked, unnurtured; incomplete, imperfect.

4, fallow, unsown, untilled, uncultivated, unplowed, idle; in a state of nature, natural; undressed, in dishabille, en déshabillé.

5, shiftless, improvident, empty-handed; negligent, unguarded, thoughtless, caught napping.

6, unpremeditated, improvised, improvisatory, improviso, extemporaneous, extempore, extemporary, impromptu, offhand; unintentional; off the top of one's head, ad hoc. *Informal*, off the cuff.

Adverbs—unpreparedly, extemporaneously, extempore, impromptu, offhand, without preparation, on the spur of the moment.

Phrases—the unexpected always happens.

Quotations—Politics is perhaps the only profession for which no preparation is thought necessary (*R. L. Stevenson*).

Antonyms, see PREPARATION, EXPECTATION.

---

unprincipled, *adj.* unscrupulous, thievish, rascally; lawless, perfidious, dishonest, fraudulent; wicked, evil. See IMPROBITY.

unproductive, *adj.* inoperative; barren, unfertile, unprolific; arid, dry, sterile, unfruitful; fruitless, bootless; fallow; impotent, issueless; unprofitable, useless; null and void, of no effect. See USELESSNESS, IMPOTENCE.

unprofessional, *adj.* amateur (see UNSKILLFULNESS).

unprofitable, *adj.* profitless, unbeneficial, unproductive; useless, futile, bootless, fruitless; costly, expensive; unwise, inexpedient. See USELESSNESS.

unpromising, *adj.* discouraging, disappointing, hopeless. See PREDICTION.

unqualified, *adj.* unfit, unsuited, ineligible; straight, thoroughgoing; certain, out-and-out, outright, unconditional, consummate, complete. See CERTAINTY, UNSKILLFULNESS.

unquenchable, *adj.* quenchless, insatiate; thirsty, parched, arid. See DESIRE.

unquestionable, *adj.* indubitable, indisputable, certain, sure, undeniable, irrefutable, incontrovertible. See CERTAINTY.

unquiet, *adj.* disturbed, agitated; restless, unpeaceful. See AGITATION.

unravel, *v.t.* ravel, untwine, disentangle, untangle; develop, explain, unfold. See INTERPRETATION, DISCLOSURE, DISJUNCTION.

unread, *adj.* illiterate; unlearned, uneducated; unintellectual. See IGNORANCE.

unreal, *adj.* imaginary, illusionary, illusory, shadowy; imponderable, unsubstantial, fanciful, fictitious; ideal; *slang,* unbelievable. See IMAGINATION, NONEXISTENCE.

unrealistic, *adj.* impractical, idealistic. See IMAGINATION.

unreasonable, *adj.* irrational, illogical, absurd, senseless, preposterous, ridiculous; immoderate, excessive, extravagant, exorbitant; stubborn, obstinate. See FOLLY, IMAGINATION, CHANGEABLENESS, DEARNESS.

unrecognizable, *adj.* indistinct, unclear, indistinguishable. See DIMNESS.

unrefined, *adj.* unpurified, crude, raw, natural, native; unfastidious, uncultivated, rude, coarse, inelegant, vulgar, common. See VULGARITY, INELEGANCE, IGNORANCE.

unrelated, *adj.* unconnected; detached, discrete. See DIFFERENCE.

unrelenting, *adj.* relentless, inexorable, unyielding, rigorous, obdurate, remorseless, stern. See MALEVOLENCE, VULGARITY.

unreliable, *adj.* untrustworthy, irresponsible, unstable, treacherous, inconstant; unsure, uncertain, fallible. See IMPROBITY, CHANGEABLENESS, DOUBT.

unremitting, *adj.* unrelieved, unceasing, unending; endless, relentless, perpetual, continuous, chronic. See CONTINUITY.

unrequited, *adj.* unrewarded, unanswered; ignored, scorned. See INGRATITUDE, NONPAYMENT.

unreserved, *adj.* frank, outspoken; demonstrative, cordial; unrestricted, absolute. See COMPLETION, COMMUNICATION, PROBITY.

unresisting, *adj.* nonresistant, yielding, acquiescent, submissive, passive. See OBEDIENCE.

unrest, *n.* restlessness, disquiet, uneasiness; agitation, insurgence, rebellion. See CHANGEABLENESS, AGITATION.

unrestrained, *adj.* unbridled, unchecked, uncurbed, untrammeled, unbounded, free; inordinate, uninhibited, wanton, lax, loose, rampant. See FREEDOM.

unrestricted, *adj.* unlimited, unconfined, unqualified. See FREEDOM.

unrighteous, *adj.* wicked, ungodly; unjust. See EVIL, IRRELIGION.

unripe, *adj.* premature, immature; precocious, crude. See UNPREPAREDNESS.

unruffled, *adj.* serene, calm, placid, poised, undisturbed. See INEXCITABILITY, SMOOTHNESS, REPOSE.

unruly, *adj.* unmanageable, insubordinate, obstreperous, fractious, refractory, ungovernable, turbulent, boisterous, balky. See DISOBEDIENCE.

unsafe, *adj.* insecure, precarious, dangerous, risky, perilous; untrustworthy. See DANGER.

unsanitary, *adj.* unclean, polluted, contaminated; unhealthy. See UNCLEANNESS.

unsatisfactory, *adj.* inadequate; intolerable. See MEDIOCRITY, DISCONTENT.

UNSAVORINESS
Unpleasant taste

Nouns—unsavoriness, tastelessness, INSIPIDITY; unpalatableness, distastefulness, roughness, acridity, acridness, acerbity, SOURNESS; gall and wormwood. See DISLIKE, DISCONTENT.

Verbs—be unsavory *or* unpalatable; sicken, repel, disgust, nauseate, pall, turn the stomach.

Adjectives—1, unsavory, insipid, tasteless; unpalatable, ill-flavored, distasteful, harsh, rough, bitter, acrid, acerb, acrimonious.

2, offensive, repulsive, repugnant, obnoxious, unpleasant, objectionable, disagreeable, uninviting, nasty, sickening, nauseous, loathsome, disgusting, vile, foul, revolting. *Slang,* dorky.

3, disreputable, unprepossessing (see DISREPUTE, UGLINESS).

Antonyms, see TASTE.

unscathed, *adj.* unharmed, uninjured. See PERFECTION.

unscented, *adj.* odorless, scentfree, free *(inf.)*. See ODORLESSNESS.

unschooled, *adj.* uneducated, untaught. See IGNORANCE.

unscientific, *adj.* instinctive, intuitive, subjective; trial-and-error, untrue, unsound, unproved. See IMAGINATION, INTUITION.

unscramble, *adj.* untangle, disentangle, unmix; decode, decipher, disclose, solve, crack *(inf.)*, dope out *(sl.)*. See SIMPLENESS, ANSWER.

unscrupulous, *adj.* unprincipled, conscienceless, dishonest. See IMPROBITY.

unseasonable, *adj.* untimely, inopportune; inapt. See INEXPEDIENCE, DISAGREEMENT.

unseat, *v.t.* displace; depose. See DISPLACEMENT.

unseemly, *adj.* unbecoming, unsuitable, unfitting, improper, indecent, indecorous, tasteless. See UNCONFORMITY, VULGARITY.

unseen, *adj.* imperceptible, invisible. See INVISIBILITY.

UNSELFISHNESS
Generosity

Nouns—unselfishness, generosity, disinterestedness, selflessness, devotion (to others); LIBERALITY, liberalism, magnanimity; BENEVOLENCE; high-mindedness, nobility; impartiality, fairness, lack of prejudice; loftiness of purpose, chivalry, heroism (see COURAGE); altruism, self-denial, -abnegation, *or* -sacrifice; Good Samaritanism, good works; self-immolation, martyrdom, suttee; labor of love. See GIVING.

Verbs—be disinterested *or* generous, make a sacrifice, put oneself in the place of others, do as one would be done by, not have a selfish bone in one's body.

Adjectives—unselfish, disinterested, selfless, benevolent, altruistic; chivalrous, heroic; charitable, liberal, generous, magnanimous, large-hearted, high- *or* noble-minded; objective; self-denying, self-sacrificing. See BENEVOLENCE.

Quotation—Greater love hath no man than this, that a man lay down his life for his friends (*Bible*).

Antonyms, see SELFISHNESS.

---

unsettle, *v.t.* upset, disturb, disarrange, displace; unhinge, derange, unbalance. See DISORDER, SURPRISE.

unsettled, *adj.* outstanding, unpaid; disturbed, troubled; unfixed, indeterminate. See IRREGULARITY, CHANGEABLENESS, INSANITY, DOUBT, EXCITEMENT.

unsightly, *adj.* ugly, unattractive. See UGLINESS.

UNSKILLFULNESS
Lack of expertise

Nouns—1, unskillfulness, incompetence; inability, inexperience; quackery, maladroitness, ineptness, clumsiness, awkwardness, two left feet, black thumb.

2, mismanagement, misconduct; maladministration; misrule, misgovernment, misapplication, misdirection, misfeasance.

3, bungling, FAILURE; too many cooks, blunder, mistake, ERROR; gaucherie, act of folly, botch[ery]; bad job. *Slang*, snafu.

4, blunderer, bumbler, botcher, butcher, bungler, fumbler, duffer, klutz, country cousin; bull in a china shop; butterfingers; greenhorn, palooka; Mrs. Malaprop, sorcerer's apprentice. *Slang*, oaf, goofus, lobster, reject, schlemiel, schlub, cheechaks, clyde, galumph, lightfoot, gimp, gink, hacker, palooka, schmendrick, waldo.

Verbs—1, blunder, bungle, boggle, fumble, botch, flounder, stumble, trip, hobble; tinker, make a mess *or* hash of, play havoc with; make a fool of oneself; play the fool; lose one's head. *Informal*, put one's foot in it; foul up, be all thumbs. *Slang*, mess, ball, hash, *or* louse up, snafu.

2, err, make a mistake (see ERROR); mismanage, misconduct, misdirect, misapply, make heavy weather of; do things by halves; work at cross purposes; put the cart before the horse; not know what one is about; not know a hawk from a handsaw; kill the goose that lays the golden eggs; cut one's own throat, burn one's fingers; run one's head against a stone wall; fall into a trap, catch a Tartar, bring down the house about one's ears; too many irons in the fire.

Adjectives—1, unskillful, unskilled, inexpert, bungling, awkward, ungainly, clumsy, lubberly, gangling, gauche, maladroit; left-handed, heavy-handed, heavy-footed; inapt, unapt, inept; neglectful; all thumbs; stupid, incompetent; unqualified, ill-qualified; unfit; quackish; raw, green, inexperienced; amateur, jackleg; half-baked.

2, unaccustomed, rusty, out of practice, unused, untrained, uninitiated, unconversant, ignorant (see IGNORANCE); unadvised, ill-advised, misguided. *Informal,* wet behind the ears.

Quotations—In a hierarchy every employee tends to rise to his level of incompetence (*Laurence J. Peter*), Democracy substitutes election by the incompetent many for appointment by the corrupt few (*G. B. Shaw*).

Antonyms, see SKILL.

---

unsociable, *adj.* reserved, aloof, distant, shy, solitary, retiring. See SECLUSION.

unsolicited, *adj.* unsought (for), undue, unlooked for; voluntary. See WILL.

unsophisticated, *adj.* ingenuous, innocent, simple, guileless, artless. See INNOCENCE, SIMPLENESS.

unsound, *adj.* unhealthy, diseased, sickly; deranged, unbalanced, unsettled; invalid, unreliable; untrue, incorrect, faulty, imperfect, illogical; decayed. See DISEASE, ERROR, IMPERFECTION.

unsparing, *adj.* severe, harsh, unstinting. See SEVERITY.

unspeakable, *adj.* shocking, dreadful, horrible, execrable, unutterable, inexpressible, unimaginable. See WONDER, UNMEANINGNESS.

unspoiled, *adj.* perfect, intact, whole, wholesome; untouched, pristine; ingenuous. See PURITY.

unspoken, *adj.* tacit, implied; unsaid. See SILENCE, LATENCY.

unsportsmanlike, *adj.* unsporting, unfair (see INJUSTICE).

unstable, *adj.* irregular, fluctuating, unsteady; inconstant, vacillating, fickle, changeable, variable. See CHANGEABLENESS.

unsteady, *adj.* fluctuating, waving, shifting, vacillating, irresolute, shaky, tottery, wobbly, infirm. See INEQUALITY, CHANGEABLENESS, AGITATION.

unstinting, *adj.* unsparing, generous, lavish; unbounded. See LIBERALITY.

unstrung, *adj.* unhinged, unnerved, distraught, agitated. *Slang,* jittery. See EXCITABILITY.

unsuccessful, *adj.* unprosperous, unfortunate, unavailing, unproductive. See FAILURE.

unsuitable, *adj.* unsuited, inappropriate, unfitting, unbecoming. See DISAGREEMENT.

unsullied, *adj.* immaculate, spotless, unspotted, pure, flawless, untarnished. See CLEANNESS, INNOCENCE, PURITY.

unsung, *adj.* neglected, slighted, ignored. See LATENCY, NEGLECT.

unsure, *adj.* skeptical, uncertain; unconfident, hesitant. See UNCERTAINTY.

unsurpassed, *adj.* unexcelled, incomparable, nonpareil, nonesuch, preeminent, superlative, tops (*inf.*). See SUPERIORITY.

unsuspecting, *adj.* trusting, trustful, unsuspicious, credulous, unquestioning, artless. See BELIEF, CREDULITY, INNOCENCE.

unsympathetic, *adj.* unfeeling, apathetic, callous. See NEGLECT.

untangle, *v.* disentangle, [un]ravel, disengage; free, extricate; comb, tease, card, straighten [out]; clear up, interpret. See DISJUNCTION, ANSWER.

untaught, *adj.* illiterate, unlettered, uneducated. See IGNORANCE.

untenable, *adj.* indefensible, insupportable, inconsistent, illogical. See FALSEHOOD.

unthinkable, *adj.* inconceivable, unimaginable, impossible; repugnant, out of the question; beyond belief, unbelievable. See IMPOSSIBILITY.

untidy, *adj.* slovenly, careless, disorderly; messy, littered; dowdy, frumpy, slipshod; unkempt. See DISORDER, UNCLEANNESS.

untie, *v.t.* loosen, free, unbind, unknot. See LIBERATION, DISJUNCTION.

until, *prep.* till, to, up to [the time of]. See TIME.

untimely, *adj.* inopportune, unseasonable; intrusive; inexpedient, early, late, anachronistic. See DISAGREEMENT, EARLINESS, LATENESS, INEXPEDIENCE.

untiring, *adj.* tireless, indefatigable, unwearied, unremitting, unrelaxing. See RESOLUTION.

untold, *adj.* unknown, unrevealed, undisclosed; countless, measureless, legion, innumerable. See CONCEALMENT, MULTITUDE, INFINITY.

untouchable, *adj.* inaccessible, out of reach; immune, exempt, sacrosanct, taboo. —*n.* pariah, outcast[e]. See PROHIBITION.

untoward, *adj.* inconvenient, perverse, troublesome; vexatious; ungraceful, awkward; unfavorable. See ADVERSITY, BADNESS.

untrained, *adj.* unbroken, untamed; raw, inexperienced, green. See UNSKILLFULNESS.

untrue, *adj.*, untruth, *n.* See DECEPTION, FALSEHOOD.

unused, *adj.* See UNACCUSTOMED.

unusual, *adj.* uncommon, rare; out-of-the-way, curious, odd, queer, singular; abnormal, anomalous, exceptional, extraordinary; irregular, bizarre, peculiar; unwonted, unaccustomed. See UNCONFORMITY, RARITY, DISUSE.

unutterable, *adj.* See UNSPEAKABLE.

unvarnished, *adj.* plain, straightforward (see SIMPLENESS).

unveil, *v.t.* disclose, reveal, uncover. See DISCLOSURE.

unwanted, *adj.* unwelcome, uninvited, undesired. See INDIFFERENCE.

unwarranted, *adj.* unjustified, uncalled-for, unwarrantable, unjust. See INJUSTICE, ILLEGALITY, DEARNESS.

unwary, *adj.* rash, unwise, indiscreet, imprudent, unguarded, injudicious. See NEGLECT, RASHNESS.

unwashed, *n.* rabble, POPULACE.

unwell, *adj.* ailing, sick, indisposed, ill, invalid, diseased. See DISEASE.

unwieldy, *adj.* clumsy, awkward, cumbersome, ungainly, bulky, ponderous, hulking (*inf.*). See GRAVITY, SIZE.

UNWILLINGNESS
Indisposition

Nouns—unwillingness, indisposition, disinclination, aversion, DISLIKE; nolleity, nolition, renitence; reluctance; indocility, OBSTINACY, noncompliance, REFUSAL; scrupulousness, fastidiousness, delicacy; scruple, qualm, demur, shrinking; hesitancy, irresolution, indecision, UNCERTAINTY. See RESISTANCE, REFUSAL.

Verbs—be unwilling, grudge, DISLIKE, not have the stomach to; scruple, stickle, stick at, boggle at, shy at, demur, hesitate, hang back, hang fire, lag, RECOIL, shrink; avoid (see AVOIDANCE); oppose, refuse. *Slang,* duck.

Adjectives—unwilling, not in the mood *or* vein; loath, disinclined, indisposed, averse, renitent, reluctant, recalcitrant, balky, demurring, objecting, unconsenting, refusing, grudging, dragging, adverse, opposed, laggard, backward, remiss, slack, slow (to); scrupulous, squeamish, fastidious; involuntary, forced; repugnant.

Adverbs—unwillingly, grudgingly, with bad grace, with an ill will; against one's will, *à contre-cœur,* against one's wishes; against the grain, with a heavy heart; *nolens volens,* willy-nilly; in spite of oneself, *malgré soi;* perforce, under protest; no. See NEGATION.

Phrases—not for the world. *Informal,* not on your life.

Quotations—Then the whining schoolboy, with his satchel and shining morning face, creeping like a snail unwillingly to school (*Shakespeare*), There is nothing we receive with so much reluctance as advice (*Joseph Addison*).

Antonyms, see WILL, DESIRE.

unwind, *v.i.* relax, let down one's defenses, let one's hair down. See REPOSE, MODERATION.

unwise, *adj.* foolish, injudicious, imprudent, ill-advised; senseless, impolitic, indiscreet. See FOLLY.

unwitting, *adj.* unknowing, unaware, thoughtless, heedless; involuntary, inadvertent; blind, deaf. See IGNORANCE, NECESSITY.

unwonted, *adj.* unusual, uncustomary; unused, unaccustomed. See UNCONFORMITY, DISUSE.

unworkable, *adj.* inoperable, impractical; futile, no good. See IMPOSSIBILITY.

unworthy, *adj.* undeserving, worthless; unbecoming, disgraceful, shameful; despicable, discreditable, derogatory. See DISREPUTE.

unwritten, *adj.* legendary, traditional, folkloric. See SPEECH.

unyielding, *adj.* immovable, unbending, rigid, inflexible, firm; grim, indomitable, obdurate, stubborn, obstinate, relentless, uncompromising; pertinacious, resolute; intractable, perverse. See HARDNESS, OBSTINACY, SEVERITY.

up, *adv.* upward[s], aloft, higher. See ASCENT, HEIGHT.

upbeat, *adj., informal,* lively, brisk. See ACTIVITY.

upbraid, *v.t.* reprove, chide, admonish, rebuke, reprimand, scold; accuse, charge, revile. See DISAPPROBATION.

upbringing, *n.* rearing, breeding, training, education. See TEACHING.

update, *v.t.* make current, modernize; revise, reedit. See NEWNESS.

upgrade, *v.t.* improve, better; raise, increase; dignify. See IMPROVEMENT.

upheaval, *n.* cataclysm, debacle; agitation, unrest, REVOLUTION. See VIOLENCE, EXCITEMENT.

uphill, *adj.* ascending, rising; precipitous; laborious; difficult, strenuous. See EXERTION, OBLIQUITY.

uphold, *v.t.* maintain, sustain; champion, advocate, confirm; approve, encourage. See AID, SUPPORT, DEMONSTRATION.

upkeep, *n.* care, maintenance; sustenance; overhead, expenses; pension. See SUPPORT, PAYMENT.

uplift, *n.* ELEVATION; IMPROVEMENT, refinement, inspiration.

upon, *prep.* on, on top of, above; by, by the act of, through; touching, against; about, regarding, concerning. See CONTACT, COVERING, MEANS, RELATION.

upper, *adj.* higher, superior. See HEIGHT. **—upper hand,** *n.* advantage, edge. See SUPERIORITY.

upper-class, *adj.* fashionable, elite; moneyed, propertied; exclusive. *Slang,* classy. See NOBILITY, MONEY.

upperclassman, *n.* junior, senior. See SCHOOL.

uppish, *adj.* insolent, haughty, uppity. See INSOLENCE.

upright, *adj.* VERTICAL, perpendicular, erect; honorable, conscientious, upstanding, honest, righteous, straight (*inf.*). See PROBITY, RIGHTNESS.

uprising, *n.* revolt, REVOLUTION, rebellion, insurrection, [civil] war, coup.

uproar, *n.* tumult, hubbub, discord, pandemonium, bedlam, ado, bustle, din, clamor, hullabaloo (*inf.*). See DISORDER, LOUDNESS.

uproot, *v.t.* extirpate, eradicate, root out, abolish, destroy. See EXTRACTION, DESTRUCTION.

upscale, *adj.* luxurious, fancy; expensive, high-priced. See DEARNESS, OSTENTATION.

upset, *v.t.* overthrow, overturn, capsize; disturb, bother, discompose, disconcert; spoil; perturb; disarrange, unbalance; demoralize. **—n.** reversal, overturn, disorder. See DESTRUCTION, INVERSION, CHANGE, REVOLUTION.

upshot, *n.* outcome, conclusion, result, EFFECT, meaning. See JUDGMENT.

upside-down, *adj.* reversed, inverted, head over heels, standing on one's head, bottom-side up; upended, capsized. See INVERSION, DISORDER.

upstage, *v.* show up, overshadow, one-up (*sl.*). See SUPERIORITY.

upstanding, *adj.* upright, honorable. See PROBITY.

upstart, *n.* parvenu, pusher (*inf.*). See NEWNESS.

upswing, *n.* IMPROVEMENT, upturn, upsurge, uptrend, betterment, recovery, pickup (*inf.*). See ASCENT.

up-tight, *adj., slang,* tense, nervous. See EXCITABILITY.

up-to-date, *adj.* modern, new, fresh, current, timely; fashionable, modish, stylish; restored, renovated, revised, modernized. See NEWNESS, RESTORATION.

upward, *adv.* higher, aloft, upwards; more. See ASCENT, HEIGHT, INCREASE.

urban, *adj.* city, town, metropolitan, civil. See ABODE, REGION.

urbane, *adj.* suave, sophisticated, debonair; civil, polite, affable. See COURTESY.

urchin, *n.* hedgehog; child, imp, brat. See YOUTH, DEMON.

urge, *v.* solicit, plead, importune, advocate, exhort, incite, instigate; press, push. —*n.* IMPULSE, desire, ambition. See NECESSITY, REQUEST, CAUSE.

urgent, *adj.* important, imperative, exigent, necessary, critical; importunate, insistent, pressing. See IMPORTANCE, REQUEST, HASTE, NECESSITY.

urn, *n.* vase, vessel, pot, amphora, jardiniere; samovar; cinerary urn, canopic urn. See RECEPTACLE, INTERMENT.

USE
Employment for a purpose

Nouns—1, use, employ[ment]; exercise, application, appliance; adhibition, disposal; consumption; usufruct; recourse, resort, avail; utilization, service, wear; recycling; usage, function, practice, method, HABIT; usefulness (see UTILITY); exploitation, sexism. See POSSESSION.

2, user, employer, applier, consumer, buyer, purchaser, enjoyer; recycling center.

Verbs—1, use, make use of, utilize, harness, employ, put to use; put in action, operation, or practice; set in motion, set to work; ply, work, wield, handle, maneuver, manipulate; play [off]; play on; exert, exercise, practice, avail oneself of, make free with, seize on, make the most of, do with, profit by; resort to, look to, have recourse to, betake oneself to; take advantage of, exploit, trade on; try.

2, render useful, apply, turn to account, utilize; bring into play; press into service; bring to bear (upon), devote, dedicate, consecrate; apply, adhibit, dispose of; make a cat's-paw of; fall back upon, make shift with; make the most or best of.

3, use up, consume, absorb, dissipate (see WASTE); finish off, exhaust, drain; expend; tax, wear.

4, be used up or expended, run out.

Adjectives—in use, in effect; used, preused, preowned, nearly new; well-worn, well-trodden; functional, utilitarian, useful (see UTILITY).

Phrases—all is grist that comes to the mill.

Quotations—Use your health, even to the point of wearing it out. That is what it is for. Spend all you have before you die; and do not outlive yourself (*G. B. Shaw*), The value of life lies not in the length of days, but in the use we make of them; a man may live long yet live very little (*Montaigne*), Money is like an arm or leg: use it or lose it (*Henry Ford*).

Antonyms, see NEGLECT, WASTE, DISUSE.

USELESSNESS
Lack of utility

Nouns—1, uselessness, inutility; inefficacy, futility; impracticableness, impracticality; inefficiency, IMPOTENCE; worthlessness, vanity, inanity, UNIMPORTANCE. See UNSKILLFULNESS, HOPELESSNESS.

2, unproductiveness, unprofitableness; infertility, infecundity, barrenness, aridity; labor lost, wild-goose chase, voice in the wilderness.

3, WASTE; desert, Sahara, wilderness, wild, tundra, marsh; litter, rubbish, odds and ends, cast-offs; junk, dross, shoddy, rags, orts, trash, refuse, sweepings, scourings, rubble, debris; stubble, leavings; dregs; weeds, tares; white elephant; rubbish heap. See REMAINDER.

Verbs—1, be useless or unproductive; come to nothing; fall; seek or strive after impossibilities; roll the stone of Sisyphus; bay at the moon, preach to the winds, chase one's tail, tilt at windmills, plow the sand, chase rainbows; lock the barn door after the horse is stolen; cast pearls before swine; carry coals to Newcastle; cry over spilled milk; beat one's head against a wall, make bricks without straw. *Slang,* piss in the wind.

2, disable, hamper (see HINDRANCE); cripple, lame; spike guns, clip the wings; put out of gear; decommission, dismantle, disassemble, break up, tear down, raze, demolish, destroy; wear out; pull the fangs *or* teeth of, tie one's hands, put in a straitjacket.

Adjectives—**1,** useless, inutile, inefficacious, futile, unavailing, bootless; ineffectual, ineffective, effete; inoperative, unproductive, barren, infertile, sterile, fallow; unprofitable, null and void; inadequate, insufficient; unskillful (see UNSKILLFULNESS); superfluous, dispensable, disposable, throwaway; thrown away, wasted; abortive. **2,** worthless, nugatory, valueless, unsalable; not worth a straw; vain, empty, inane; gainless, profitless, fruitless; unserviceable, unprofitable; ill-spent; obsolete; good for nothing, no-good; of no earthly use; not worth having, not worth a cent, unnecessary, unneeded. *Slang,* not worth a tinker's damn.

Adverbs—uselessly, to little *or* no purpose; to no avail.

Phrases—dogs bark, but the caravan goes on; you cannot get blood from a stone.

Quotations—Everything exists, nothing has value (*E. M. Forster*), It seems that I have spent my entire time trying to make life more rational and that it was all wasted effort (*A. J. Ayer*), All dressed up [in their fighting clothes,] with nowhere to go (*William Allen White*).

Antonyms, see UTILITY, PRODUCTION.

---

usher, *v.t.* escort, introduce, announce, induct. —*n.* doorman; escort, groomsman, vestryman. See BEGINNING, RELIGION.

usual, *adj.* customary, accustomed, habitual, ordinary, wonted, normal, regular, everyday; traditional. See HABIT, CONFORMITY.

usurp, *v.t.* seize, expropriate, arrogate, appropriate; conquer, annex, snatch, grab. See ILLEGALITY, STEALING.

usury, *n.* overcharge, extortion. See DEARNESS, DEBT.

utensil, *n.* implement, instrument; vessel, container. See INSTRUMENTALITY, RECEPTACLE.

utilitarian, *adj.* See USE, UTILITY.

UTILITY
State of being useful

Nouns—utility; usefulness, efficacy, efficiency, adequacy; service, stead, avail, benefit; help, AID; convenience, availability; applicability, function, value; worth, GOODNESS; productiveness; utilization (see USE). See EXPEDIENCE.

Verbs—avail, serve; subserve; conduce, tend; answer *or* serve a purpose; bear fruit, produce (see PRODUCTION); profit, remunerate, benefit, do good; perform *or* discharge a function; do *or* render a service; bestead, stand one in good stead; be the making of; help, AID. *Informal,* come in handy.

Adjectives—useful, of use; serviceable, good for; instrumental, conducive, tending; convenient; subsidiary, helping, advantageous, beneficial, profitable, gainful, remunerative, worth one's salt; valuable, invaluable; prolific, productive; practical, practicable; at one's service; pragmatic, functional; adequate; efficient, efficacious, effective, effectual; expedient, applicable, available, ready, handy, at hand, tangible; commodious, adaptable, disposable.

Adverbs—usefully, efficiently, *etc.*; pro bono publico. *Informal,* on tap.

Quotations—Laws are always useful to persons of property and hurtful to those who have none (*Jean Jacques Rousseau*), A life spent in making mistakes is not only more honorable but more useful than a life spent doing nothing (*G. B. Shaw*).

Antonyms, see USELESSNESS.

utmost, *adj.* most, greatest, farthest, furthest; last, final; total, unlimited, full, complete. See COMPLETION, SUPERIORITY.

Utopian, *adj.* ideal[istic], optimistic, visionary, romantic; rosy; perfect; unrealistic, unworldly; quixotic, Arcadian. —*n.* utopianist; dreamer, idealist, optimist, visionary, romantic; Quixote. See IMAGINATION.

utter, *adj.* total, complete, entire; extreme, unusual; unqualified; stark, sheer, downright, absolute. See COMPLETION, GREATNESS, CERTAINTY. —*v.t.* speak, voice; pronounce, express, enunciate, deliver; issue, emit. See SPEECH, DISCLOSURE.

V

vacancy, *n.* emptiness, void, vacuum, space; inanity, stupidity, idleness. See ABSENCE.

vacant, *adj.* empty; open, free, untenanted, unoccupied, to let; blank, void, hollow; shallow, brainless, inane, idle, disengaged; stupid, vacuous. See ABSENCE, IGNORANCE, INATTENTION.

vacate, *v.* move out; leave, decamp; abandon, relinquish, surrender, quit; evacuate, leave empty; annul, cancel, invalidate, quash. See RELINQUISHMENT, DEPARTURE.

vacation, *n.* holiday, rest, time off, leave [of absence]; recess, respite; abandonment, DEPARTURE. See REPOSE.

vaccinate, *v.t.* jennerize, variolate; inoculate, inject, give a shot; immunize; prick, scratch, scarify. See REMEDY.

vaccine, *n.* bacterin, serum, antitoxin, immunotoxin. See REMEDY.

vacillation, *n.* uncertainty; fluctuation; hesitation, faltering, shilly-shallying. See DOUBT, OSCILLATION, CHANGEABLENESS.

vacuum, *n.* void, vacancy, emptiness, nothingness; space. See ABSENCE, NONEXISTENCE.

vade mecum, handbook, manual. See INFORMATION.

vagabond, *n.* hobo, tramp, vagrant, wanderer, idler, beggar. *Informal,* bum, knight of the road. See TRAVEL, POPULACE.

vagary, *n.* fancy, notion, caprice, whim; quirk, foible. See CHANGEABLENESS, IMAGINATION.

vagina, *n.* See BODY.

vagrant, *n.* tramp, hobo (see VAGABOND). —*adj.* wandering, aimless, wayward, roving; erratic, capricious. See TRAVEL, POPULACE.

vague, *adj.* unclear, blurred, blurry; amorphous, shapeless; undefined, uncertain, indistinct, inexact, indefinite, obscure. See FORMLESSNESS, OBSCURITY.

vain, *adj.* proud, conceited; futile, fruitless; trivial. See VANITY, USELESSNESS, UNIMPORTANCE.

vainglorious, *adj.* vain, proud, boastful. See VANITY, BOASTING.

valediction, *n.* farewell speech, valedictory; farewell, good-bye, adieu. See DEPARTURE, SPEECH.

valet, *n.* SERVANT; manservant, gentleman's gentleman, attendant.

valiant, *adj.* valorous, brave, courageous, gallant; daring, intrepid, dauntless, lionhearted; noteworthy. See COURAGE.

valid, *adj.* sound, logical; legal, binding, well-grounded, just. See DEMONSTRATION, TRUTH, LEGALITY, POWER.

validate, *v.t.* confirm; legalize. See LEGALITY, EVIDENCE, ASSENT.

valise, *n.* traveling bag, satchel. See RECEPTACLE.

valley, *n.* vale, river land, dale, dell, glen, canyon, hollow. See CONCAVITY, LOWNESS.

valor, *n.* COURAGE, intrepidity, fearlessness; prowess, heroism, gallantry; daring, derring-do.

valuable, *adj.* precious, costly; worthy, meritorious, estimable; useful. See UTILITY.

value, *n.* usefulness, worth; PRICE, cost, rate, rating; estimation, valuation, merit; import; significance; shade, tone, emphasis. —*v.t.* esteem, prize, treasure, regard highly; appraise, evaluate, assess, rate. See IMPORTANCE, GOODNESS, MEASUREMENT, APPROBATION.

valueless, *adj.* worthless (see USELESSNESS).

valve, *n.* damper, cutoff, cock, butterfly, pallet, poppet; ventil, side valve; plug, piston, cusp. See CLOSURE.

vamp, *n.,* *slang,* flirt, coquette. See ENDEARMENT.

vampire, *n.* bloodsucker, bat; ghoul; parasite; *slang,* siren, seducer, vamp, temptress. See EVILDOER, DEMON.

van, *n.* truck, lorry, moving van; forefront, vanguard, avant garde; FRONT, head. See VEHICLE.

vandalism, *n.* pillage, depredation, plundering; DESTRUCTION, mutilation, defacement; sabotage; desecration, profanation; barbarianism.

vane, *n.* girouette, anemometer; cone, sleeve, sock; arm, plate, fin, blade. See WIND, INDICATION.

vanguard, *n.* van; spearhead, front line, shock troops; marines; avant garde; forerunner, leader; innovators, modernists. See PRECEDENCE, FRONT, NEWNESS.

vanish, *v.i.* disappear, fade out; dissolve; *slang,* decamp, vamoose. See DISAPPEARANCE, DEPARTURE.

VANITY
Excessive pride

Nouns—1, vanity, conceit, conceitedness; immodesty, self-esteem, self-love, self-praise; complacency, smugness, amour-propre, hubris; ego trip. See BOASTING, SELFISHNESS.

2, [false] PRIDE, airs, pretensions; egotism, egoism; priggishness; coxcombery, vainglory, pretense, OSTENTATION; INSOLENCE.

3, egotist, egoist, prig, pretender, fop, coxcomb, know-it-all.

Verbs—be vain, put oneself forward; fish for compliments; give oneself airs; boast; presume, swagger, strut; plume *or* preen oneself; turn one's head, go to one's head, have a big head, flatter oneself. *Informal,* get on one's high horse. *Slang,* put on side, the dog, *or* the ritz, hot dog.

Adjectives—vain [as a peacock], conceited, immodest, overweening, pert, forward; haughty, puffed-up (see PRIDE); prideful, vainglorious, high-flown, ostentatious; self-satisfied, self-centered, full of oneself, smug, complacent, opinionated; imperious, arrogant, cocky, too big for one's britches, immodest, pretentious, priggish; ego[t]istic; soi-disant; unabashed, unblushing. *Informal,* swell-headed, stuck-up.

Adverbs—vainly, priggishly, pridefully, proudly, haughtily, *etc.*

Quotations—Vanity of vanities, saith the Preacher, vanity of vanities; all is vanity (*Bible*), Who does not detest a haughty man? (*Euripides*), Vanity is the greatest of all flatterers (*La Rochefoucauld*), The most violent passions sometimes leave us at rest, but vanity agitates us constantly (*La Rochefoucauld*), Vanity is only being sensitive to what other people probably think of us (*Paul Valéry*), The highest form of vanity is love of fame (*George Santayana*).

Antonyms, see MODESTY.

vanquish, *v.t.* conquer, subdue, subjugate, overcome; quell, silence; worst, rout; master. See SUCCESS.

vantage, *n.* advantage; rise, vantage ground *or* point. See SUPERIORITY, HEIGHT.

vapid, *adj.* flat, tasteless, insipid; tame, spiritless, lifeless, dull. See INSIPIDITY.

VAPOR
Visible gas

Nouns—1, vapor, vaporousness, vaporization, volatilization; gaseousness, gaseity; evaporation; distillation, aeration, sublimation, exhalation; fumigation, steaming; volatility. See INSUBSTANTIALITY, RARITY.

2, gas, elastic fluid; oxygen, ozone, hydrogen, nitrogen, argon, helium, fluorine, neon; natural gas, coal gas, illuminating gas; sewer gas, poison gas; damp, chokedamp; air, vapor, ether, steam, fume, reek, effluvium, miasma, flatus; flatulence; cloud (see CLOUDINESS). See FUEL.

3, vaporizer, atomizer, still, retort; spray, spray gun, airbrush, sprayer.

4, *(study of gasses)* pneumatics, pneumostatics; aerostatics, aerodynamics.

Verbs—vaporize, volatize, distill, sublime; evaporate, exhale, transpire, fume, reek, steam, fumigate; give off; atomize, spray.

Adjectives—vaporous, volatile, volatilized, gaseous, gassy, reeking; aeriform, evaporable, vaporizable.

Antonyms, see DENSITY.

---

variable, *adj.* changeable, alterable; inconstant. See CHANGEABLENESS, IRREGULARITY.

variance, *n.* change, alteration; DIFFERENCE, DISAGREEMENT, DISCORD; jarring, dissension; variation, UNCONFORMITY.

variation, *n.* variance, alteration, CHANGE, modification; diversification; divergence, deviation, aberration; innovation. See DIFFERENCE.

varicolored, *adj.* variegated, motley (see VARIEGATION).

VARIEGATION
Marking with different colors

Nouns—1, variegation, diversification, diversity, heterogeneity; spottiness, maculation, striation, streakiness, marbling, elaboration, discoloration; parti- *or* party-color, dichroism, dichromatism, polychrome; iridescence, iridization, opalescence, play of colors; counterchange. See COLOR.

2, stripes, bands, streaks, striae; vein, thread, line; check, plaid, tartan, motley, tricolor; marquetry, parquetry, mosaic, tessellation, tesserae; chessboard, checkerboard; confetti, patchwork, crazy quilt, harlequin, Joseph's coat [of many colors]; spectrum, rainbow, iris, tulip; peacock, chameleon, butterfly, zebra, leopard, piebald; tortoiseshell, mother-of-pearl, nacre, opal, marble, mackerel sky; kaleidoscope; color organ.

Verbs—variegate, vary, variate, varify, diversify; stripe, striate, streak, line, checker, counterchange; [be]spot, dot, mottle, dapple, brindle, pie, [be]speckle, freckle, [be]sprinkle, stipple, maculate, fleck, pepper, powder; inlay, tessellate, tattoo, damascene; vein, marble[ize], water; embroider, figure, braid, quilt, fret, lace, interlace.

Adjectives—variegated, varied, various, diverse, diversified; many-colored *or* -hued, multi- *or* varicolored, parti- *or* party-colored, divers-colored; bicolor, tricolor, versicolor, polychromatic, dichromatic, kaleidoscopic[al]; chameleonic; iridescent, opalescent, opaline, prismatic, rainbow-hued, rainbowlike, nacreous, nacre, pearly, chatoyant, cymophanous, tortoiseshell, shot; pied, paint, pinto, piebald; mottled, motley, harlequin, marbled, dappled, clouded, paned, pepper-and-salt, calico; spotted, spotty, dotted and speckled, freckled, studded, flecked, peppered, powdered, punctuated; striped, listed, streaked, streaky, banded, barred, cross-striped, grizzled; mosaic, tessellated, plaid, tartan, checkered, checked, embroidered, daedal; brindle[d], tabby; blotchy.

Antonyms, see UNIFORMITY, COLOR.

---

variety, *n.* variation, diversity, DIFFERENCE; assortment; kind, CLASS; brand; multifariousness; vaudeville. See MIXTURE, DRAMA.

various, *adj.* diversified, multiform, diverse; different; many, several, manifold, numerous, sundry; changeable, unfixed. See DIFFERENCE, MULTITUDE.

varnish, *n.* shellac, lac, lacquer; spar; gloss, mitigation, whitewash, excuse. —*v.t.* shellac, lacquer, *etc.*; palliate, glaze, gloss, excuse, whitewash; finish. See SMOOTHNESS, COVERING.

vary, *v.* CHANGE, alter; fluctuate; differ,

disagree; diversify. See DIFFERENCE, DISCORD, DISAGREEMENT.

vase, *n.* urn, cup, chalice, jug, amphora, ampulla. See RECEPTACLE.

vassal, *n.* liege, liegeman; thrall, bondman, subject; [feudal] tenant, serf. See SERVANT.

vast, *adj.* huge, immense; infinite, boundless, immeasurable; tremendous, enormous. See SIZE, SPACE, BREADTH.

vat, *n.* vessel, cistern, tank, drum, cauldron; tub, tun, puncheon, bac[k], barrel, cask, hogshead, keg, butt. See RECEPTACLE.

vaudeville, *n.* turns, acts, variety; burlesque, music hall. See DRAMA.

vault, *n.* arch, dome, cupola; bank vault, safe; tomb, sepulcher, catacomb; dungeon, cell, cellar; LEAP, jump, pole-vault. See INTERMENT, STORE. —*v.* arch; LEAP over, jump; pole-vault. See CONVEXITY, CURVATURE.

vaunt, *v.* boast, brag, vapor, talk big. See BOASTING.

veer, *v.i.* swerve, shift; deviate; jibe, come about, yaw. See CHANGE, DEVIATION.

VEGETABLE
Any plant

Nouns—**1,** vegetable kingdom, vegetation, vegetable life; plants, flora, verdure; growth, biome; weed.

2, vegetable, fungus, legume, fruit, nut, seed (see FOOD).

3, tree; acacia, alder, almond, apple, apricot, arborvitae, arbutus, ash, aspen, avocado, balsa, banana, banyan, baobab, basswood, bay[berry], beech, betel palm, birch, blackthorn, boxwood, Brazil nut, breadfruit, buckeye, buckthorn, butternut, cacao, candleberry, carnauba, carob, cashew, bassia, catalpa, cedar, cherimoya, cherry, chestnut, chinaberry, chinquapin, cinnamon, citron, citrus, clove, coconut, coffee tree, cornel, cottonwood, cypress, dogwood, dungon, ebony, elder, elm, encina, eucalyptus, fig, fir, frankincense, gardenia, ginkgo, grapefruit, guava, hum, hackberry, hawthorn, hazel, hemlock, henna, hickory, holly, hornbeam, horse chestnut, ironwood, jacaranda, juniper, kauri, kumquat, laburnum, lancewood, larch, laurel, lehua, lemon, lime, linden, litchi, locust, magnolia, mahogany, manchineel, mango, mangrove, maple, mastic, medlar, mesquite, mimosa, monkeypod, mulberry, nutmeg, nux vomica, oak, olive, orange, palm, palmetto, papaw, papaya, pawpaw, peach, pear, pecan, persimmon, pine, pistachio, plane, plum, pomegranate, pomelo, poplar, quince, rambutan, redwood, rosewood, rubber, sandalwood, sandarac, sapodilla, sappanwood, sassafras, satinwood, senna, sequoia, serviceberry, snowbell, soapberry, sorb, soursop, speedwell, spruce, sumac, sweetsop, sycamore, tacamahac, tamarack, tamarind, tangerine, teak, torreya, tupelo, upas, walnut, wattle, willow, witch hazel, yew.

4, shrub, bush, hedge; alder, allspice, aloe, arbutus, azalea, babasco, barberry, bayberry, bilberry, blackberry, blackthorn, blueberry, box, bramble, broom, buddleia, buttonbush, caper, cascarilla, cassia, cayenne, chokeberry, cinchona, climatis, cleome, coca, coffeeberry, cranberry, cubeb, currant, daphne, divi-divi, elderberry, erica, euonymus, farkleberry, firethorn, forsythia, frangipani, fuchsia, furze, genista, germander, gooseberry, gorse, grape, greasewood, greenbrier, guava, haw, heath, heather, hemlock, hibiscus, holly, honeysuckle, huckleberry, hydrangea, indigo, jojoba, jute, kalmia, kat, kumquat, laurel, lavender, lespedeza, lilac, ling, magnolia, manzanita, milkword, mistletoe, myrtle, nandina, ninebark, oleander, pepper, philodendron, photinia, poison oak, poison sumac, prickly ash, privet, quassia, raspberry, rhododendron, rose, sage[brush], serviceberry, sisal, sloe, smilax, spirea, strawberry, syringa, tamarisk, titi, toyon, veronica, viburnum, whin, winterberry, wisteria, yaupon, zenobia.

5, vine, creeper; actinidia, bean, bittersweet, bougainvillea, boxthorn, bramble, bryony, cantaloupe, casaba, chayote, slematic, cucumber, dewberry, dichondria, fleevine, gloryvine, gourd, grape, honeysuckle, hop, horsebrier, ipomoea, ivy, jasmine, kudzu, liana, loofah, melon, milkweed, moonseed, muscat, pea, peppervine, poison ivy, pokeweed, pumpkin, silvervine, similax, squash, stephanotis, string bean, vanilla, vetch, wandering Jew, watermelon, wintercreeper, wisteria, woodbine, yam.

6, herb[age]; ajuga, amaranth, angelica, anise, balm, basil, belladonna, bellwort, bergamot, betony, birthword, bitterroot, bladderwort, boneset, borage, bugle[weed], butterwort, calamint, calendula, caraway, cardamom, carrot, catmint, catnip, cauliflower, celery, chamomile, charlock, chervil, chicory, cilantro, clover, coleus, coriander, corydalis, cowbane, crowfoot, cumin, datura, dill, dittany, dropwort, eryngo, fennel, fenugreek, feverroot, figwort, finochio, fraxinella, germander, ginger, heliotrope, hemlock, hemp, henbane, henbit, honeywort, horehound, horsemint, hyssop, leadwort, lespedeza, licorice, lovage, lupine, mandrake, marijuana, marjoram, mint, monarda, monkshood, mullein, mustard, nutmeg, oregano, parsley, parsnip, patchouli, pennyroyal, peppermint, perilla, philodendron, rosemary, rudbeckia, rue, safflower, sage, salvia, samphire, sanicle, savory, sesame, sorrel, spearmint, spiderwort, tansy, tarragon, teasel, thyme, tobacco, trefoil, turmeric, wintergreen, woodruff, wormwood, wort, yarrow.

7, grass, furze, gorse, sod, turf; pasture, pasturage; [rush] sedge; alfalfa, bamboo, barley, bluegrass, bluejoint, bromegrass, broomcorn, buckwheat, bulrush, cane, chufa, corn, darnel, durra, durum wheat, eelgrass, fescue, foxtail, grama, hassock, hay, horsetail, khus-khus, lovegrass, maize, mesquite, millet, oat, paddy, papyrus, quitch, redtop, rice, rush, rye, sorghum, squitch, sugarcane, timothy, tule, vetiver, wheat, windlestraw, zoysia.

8, flower, flowering plant; annual, perennial, biennial, triennial; agave, ageratum, ailanthus, amaranth, amaryllis, anemone, arbutus, arethusa, arnica, arrowhead, artichoke, asphodel, aspidistra, aster, azalea, baby's-breath, bachelor's-button, begonia, berseem, betony, bird-of-paradise, bitterroot, black-eyed Susan, blazing star, bleeding heart, bluebell, bluebonnet, bluet, boltonia, broccoli, broom, buttercup, cactus, calendula, calypso, camass, camellia, campanula, candytuft, carnation, catalpa, cattail, century plant, chamomile, chysanthemum, cineraria, clematis, clethra, cockscomb, columbine, cornel, cornflower, corydalis, cosmos, cowslip, crocus, cyclamen, daffodil, dahlia, daisy, dandelion, delphinium, dogwood, duckweed, edelweiss, eglantine, erigeron, figwort, fireweed, flax, fleur-de-lis, forget-me-not, forsythia, foxglove, foxtail, frangipani, fuchsia, gardenia, gentian, geranium, gladiolus, goldenrod, groundsel, harebell, hawthorn, heather, hepatica, hibiscus, hogweed, hollyhock, honeysuckle, hyacinth, hydrangea, impatiens, indigo, iris, jack-in-the-pulpit, japonica, jasmine, jonquil, knotweed, lady's-slipper, larkspur, lavender, lehua, lilac, lily [of the valley], lobelia, lotus, lupine, magnolia, mallow, marguerite, marigold, mayflower, maypop, mayweed, mignonette, mimosa, morning glory, motherwort, mullein, narcissus, nasturtium, oleander, orchid, oxalis, pansy, pasqueflower, passionflower, pennyroyal, peony, periwinkle, petunia, phlox, pilewort, pink, pinxter, poinsettia, poppy, portulaca, primrose, pyrethrum, Queen Anne's lace, rafflesia, ragwort, ranunculus, rose, ruderal, safflower, saffron, saguaro, santonica, smilax, snapdragon, snowball, snowberry, snowdrop, spiera, stock, strawflower, sunflower, sweet pea, tamarisk, teasel, thistle, tidytips, trefoil, trillium, tulip, umbrella plant, vanilla, Venus's flytrap, verbena, vetch, viburnum, viola, violet, wallflower, water lily, wisteria, wolfbane, yarrow, yucca, zinnia.

9, timber, timberland, forest; wood[lands]; park, chase, greenwood, brake, grove, copse, coppice, thicket, spinney.

10, brush, underbrush, brushwood; jungle, prairie; heather, heath; fern, bracken, weed; fungus, mushroom, toadstool, chanterelle, crumblecap, deathcap, earthstar, milkcap, mottlegill, oyster cap, puffball, rust, scalecap; lichen, moss; growth. *Slang*, frog bread.

11, foliage, foliation, branch, bough, ramage, leaf; flower, bloom, blossom, bine; pulse, legume, bean, root, bulb.

12, botany, vegetable physiology, phytology; horticulture; AGRICULTURE, agronomy; silviculture; aquaculture (see WATER).

13, botanist, plant physiologist, horticulturist, *etc.*

14, botanical gardens, herbarium, arboretum.

Adjectives—vegetable, vegetal, vegetative, herbaceous, botanic; sylvan, arboreous, arborescent, dendritic, grassy, verdant, verdurous; floral; mossy; woody, lignous, ligneous, xyloid; deciduous; wooden; woodsy, leguminous; endogenous, exogenous.

Phrases—it is not enough for a gardener to love flowers—he must also hate weeds.

Quotations—What is a weed? A plant whose virtues have not been discovered (*Emerson*), All gardening is landscape-painting (*Alexander Pope*), He that plants trees loves others beside himself (*Thomas Fuller*), I like trees because they seem more resigned to the way they have to live than other things do (*Willa Cather*), I think that I shall never see a poem lovely as a tree (*Joyce Kilmer*).

Antonyms, see ANIMAL, INORGANIC MATTER.

vegetarian, *n.* cerealist, herbivore, granivore, nutarian, lactovegetarian; phytophagan; food faddist, health nut (*inf.*). —*adj.* Lenten, meatless; herbivorous, vegetivorous, plantivorous; grain-eating, granivorous; uncarnivorous. See FOOD.

vegetate, *v.i.* stagnate, exist. See EXISTENCE, INACTIVITY.

vegetation, *n.* VEGETABLE life; flora, verdure, greenery.

vehemence, *n.* VIOLENCE, VIGOR, impetuosity, force; ardor, fervor, warmth, zeal. See EXERTION, FEELING.

VEHICLE
Conveyance

Nouns—1, vehicle, machine, conveyance, equipage, turnout, cart, rig, car, wagon. See PASSAGE, TRAVEL, TRANSPORTATION.

2, (*animal- or human-drawn vehicle*) **a.** carriage, coach, chariot, chaise, phaeton, berlin, landau, barouche, victoria, hard-top, brougham, sulky; jalopy; two-wheeler, dogcart, trap, buggy. *Slang,* bucket of bolts. **b.** stage[coach], diligence, mailcoach; hackney, hack; omnibus, bus, cab, taxi[cab], hansom; jinrickishaw. *Informal,* jitney, ricksha. **c.** sled, sledge, pung, sleigh, bobsled, toboggan, travois, Alpine slide, luge. **d.** handcart, pushcart, barrow, wheelbarrow, handbarrow; sedan chair; go-cart, baby carriage, perambulator, stroller; wheelchair, litter, stretcher. *Informal,* pram.

3, cycle, bicycle, two-wheeler; tricycle, velocipede, three-wheeler; motorcycle, motor scooter, scooter; motor bicycle, moped. *Informal,* bike, trike, wheel, motorbike. *Slang,* hog, ass-hammer.

4, automobile, auto, car, motorcar; sedan, coupé, brougham, limousine, cabriolet, phaeton, convertible, hatchback, jeep, roadster, touring car; stock car, compact car, minicar, minibus; trailer, caravan; racing car; patrol car, squad *or* police car, patrol wagon, Black Maria; ambulance, hearse; station wagon, beach wagon, suburban; dune buggy; bus, motor coach, charabanc, kneeling bus; truck, four-by-four, minivan, pickup [truck], recreational vehicle, RV, sport utility vehicle, SUV, panel truck, monster truck, high-rider; lorry, tractor, van, moving van, semitrailer; wrecker; Tin Lizzie. *Informal,* paddy wagon. *Slang,* wheels, bus, flivver, [hot] rod, gas buggy; heap, jalopy, eggbeater, gas guzzler, junker, banger, rust-bucket, boat, beater; prowl car, pigmobile, roller; blood-box *or* -bucket, bonebox, meatwagon.

5, train, locomotive, passenger train, streamliner, turbo[liner], light rail vehicle, LRV; express, local, limited, freight train; subway [train], underground, tube, Métro; trolley, streetcar, cable car, interurban, tram, trackless trolley; freight car, boxcar, Pullman, sleeper, refrigerator car, tender, tank car, caboose; dining, smoking, lounge, *etc.,* car, day coach. *Informal,* iron horse.

6, space vehicle (see ASTRONAUTICS).

7, driver, operator, busman, cabbie, carter, coachman; engineer; [bi]cyclist. See TRANSPORTATION, DIRECTION.

Verbs—start, turn over; drive (see DIRECTION).

Adjective—vehicular, automotive, locomotive.

Quotations—The automobile changed our dress, manners, social customs, vacation habits, the shape of our cities, consumer purchasing patterns, common tastes and positions in intercourse (*John Keats*), To George F. Babbitt . . . his motor-car was poetry and tragedy, love and heroism (*Sinclair Lewis*), The car has become the carapace, the protective and aggressive shell, of urban and suburban man (*Marshall McLuhan*), Everything in life is somewhere else, and you get there in a car (*E. B. White*).

---

veil, *n.* net, mesh, curtain, screen, cloak, cover; film, haze, CLOUDINESS. —*v.t.* conceal, becloud, disguise, shield, cover, shroud. See CONCEALMENT, CLOTHING.

vein, *n.* blood vessel, rib (of a leaf); streak, stripe, marbling; [ore] deposit, lode, seam, ledge, leader; thread; bent, humor, disposition, temper. See FILAMENT, FEELING, NARROWNESS.

vellum, *n.* parchment, skin, sheepskin; papyrus; manuscript, document. See MATERIALS, WRITING.

VELOCITY
Speed

Nouns—1, velocity, speed, celerity, swiftness, rapidity, expedition (see HASTE); acceleration; hurry, spurt, rush, dash; smart, lively, swift, *or* spanking pace; flying, flight; gallop, canter, trot, run, scamper; race, horserace, steeplechase; sweepstakes, Derby; handicap; foot race, marathon, relay race. See HASTE, MOTION.

2, (*something rapid*) lightning, light, electricity, wind; cannonball, rocket, arrow, dart, quicksilver; whirlwind; telegraph, express train; torrent; hustler; eagle, antelope, courser, racehorse, gazelle, cheetah, greyhound, hare, deer, doe, jackrabbit, squirrel; jockey.

Verbs—1, speed, hasten, post, scuttle; scud, scour, scoot, scamper; run, fly, race, cut away, shoot, tear, whisk, sweep, whiz, skim, brush; bowl along; rush, dash, bolt; trot, gallop, bound, flit, spring, charge, dart; march in double time; ride hard, cover the ground. *Informal,* cut along, step along, step lively, zip, cut and run, make it snappy, cover ground, burn up the road, drive like Jehu. *Slang,* go all out, go hell-bent for election, go like a bat out of hell; watch one's dust *or* smoke; skedaddle; go hell-for-leather, burn up the road; hightail it, make tracks, lay rubber.

2, hurry, hasten (see HASTE); accelerate, quicken, step up; wing one's way; spur on; crowd on sail; gain ground; show a clean pair of heels; overtake, overhaul, outstrip. *Slang,* stir one's stumps, step on the gas, give her the gun, boot home, lay rubber, sandbag, streak.

Adjectives—fast, speedy, swift, rapid, quick, fleet; nimble, agile, expeditious, express; meteoric, breakneck, fast and furious; flying, galloping, light- *or* nimble-footed; winged, mercurial, electric, telegraphic; light of heel; swift as an arrow; quick as lightning *or* thought. *Informal,* flat-out.

Adverbs—swiftly, apace; at a great rate, at full speed, full tilt, posthaste; all sails crowding, heeling over, full steam ahead; trippingly; instantaneously; in seven league boots; with whip and spur; as fast as one's legs will carry one; at top speed, on the wings of the wind; by leaps and bounds. *Informal,* on the double, at a fast clip, like mad, like sixty, like all possessed, like greased lightning, to beat the band, like a [blue] streak, hell for leather, like wildfire. *Slang,* PDQ, lickety-split, like a bat out of hell; jet-propelled.

Phrases—the race is not to the swift, nor the battle to the strong.

Quotations—True hope is swift and flies with swallow's wings (*Shakespeare*).

Antonyms, see SLOWNESS.

---

velvet, *n.* silk, plush, velour, velure, velveteen; mossiness; SMOOTHNESS, SOFTNESS; *slang,* surplus, winnings, profit, graft. —*adj.* velvety, mossy; smooth, soft, mild, soothing, bland; light, caressing.

venal, *adj.* money-loving, mercenary, sordid; corrupt, bribable, purchasable (*of persons*). See IMPROBITY.

vend, *v.* sell, purvey (see SALE); publish, issue.

vendetta, *n.* feud, grudge fight, vengeance. See CONTENTION, RETALIATION.

veneer, *n.* facing, overlay, coating, shell; superficial polish, facade. See LAYER, SHALLOWNESS, COVERING.

venerable, *adj.* aged, hoary; patriarchal; respected, revered. See AGE, OLDNESS.

veneration, *n.* esteem, RESPECT; admiration, WORSHIP; awe. See PIETY.

venereal, *adj.* sexual, genital, coital; syphilitic, luetic; gonorrheal, chancrous; aphrodisiac, cantharidian. See IMPURITY, PLEASURE. **—venereal disease,** *n.* VD, social DISEASE, dose (*sl.*).

vengeance, *n.* RETALIATION, revenge; vengefulness; reprisal, retribution; nemesis.

vengeful, *adj.* vindictive, rancorous (see RETALIATION).

venial, *adj.* excusable, pardonable, slight, trivial. See VINDICATION.

venomous, *adj.* poisonous; envenomed, noxious, toxic, virulent, deadly; spiteful, malicious, malignant. See MALEVOLENCE, DISEASE, BADNESS.

vent, *v.t.* utter, express; let out, let off, emit, expel, discharge. **—***n.* ventilator, OPENING, airhole, air pipe, outlet, funnel; emission; blowhole; utterance, expression. See EGRESS, DISCLOSURE, WIND.

ventilate, *v.t.* AIR; freshen; disclose, publish. See WIND, REFRESHMENT.

venture, *v.* dare, risk; speculate; undertake; presume, hazard, stake, take a chance. **—***n.* enterprise, UNDERTAKING; adventure; speculation, hazard, risk. See CHANCE, COURAGE.

venturesome, *adj.* daring, enterprising; hazardous, dangerous. See COURAGE, DANGER.

veracity, *n.* See TRUTH.

veranda, *n.* porch, gallery, piazza, portico. See RECEPTACLE.

verbal, *adj.* spoken, oral, unwritten; literal, verbatim, word-for-word. See SPEECH.

verbalize, *v.* express in words, phrase; expatiate. See SPEECH, FIGURATIVE, DIFFUSENESS.

verbatim, *adj.* word-for-word, literal, verbal, letter-perfect; unchanged, unedited. **—***adv.* word for word, sic, literatim. See TRUTH.

verbose, *adj.* wordy, prolix, repetitive, talkative. See DIFFUSENESS.

verboten, *Ger.,* forbidden. See ILLEGALITY, PROHIBITION.

verdant, *adj.* green, grassy; fresh, spring-like; inexperienced, naive, artless. See COLOR, VEGETABLE, UNSKILLFULNESS.

verdict, *n.* JUDGMENT, ruling, finding, decision, opinion, decree; determination, conclusion; award, sentence. See LAWSUIT.

verdure, *n.* grass, growth, greenness, greenery. See VEGETABLE.

verge, *n.* EDGE, brink, rim, marge, margin; point, eve; LIMIT. **—***v.i.* be on the point (of); border, skirt, approach, touch; tend, incline. See TENDENCY, NEARNESS.

verify, *v.t.* corroborate, substantiate, confirm, prove, make certain, establish; identify. See EVIDENCE, DEMONSTRATION.

veritable, *adj.* real, genuine, authentic; proven, valid. See TRUTH.

vermin, *n.* pests, insects, rats, mice; scum, riffraff. See ANIMAL.

vernacular, *n.* tongue, dialect; argot, slang. See SPEECH.

versatile, *adj.* many-sided; adaptable; skilled. See SKILL, CHANGEABLENESS.

verse, *n.* versification; POETRY, prosody, poesy; line; stanza; meter, measure; poem, doggerel; passage. See PART.

versed, *adj.* skilled, skillful; knowledgeable; accomplished, trained, conversant. See SKILL, KNOWLEDGE.

version, *n.* rendition, account; translation. See INTERPRETATION.

versus, *prep.* against, in OPPOSITION to.

vertex, *n.* top, apex, head, cap, crown, pinnacle; HEIGHT; acme, zenith.

VERTICAL
Perpendicular to the earth's surface

Nouns—1, vertical, perpendicular, upright; verticality, plumbness, aplomb, perpendicularity, orthogonality, ELEVATION, erection; right angle, normal, azimuth circle; square, plumb, plumbline, plummet. See STRAIGHTNESS, OBLIQUITY.

2, *(something vertical)* wall, precipice, cliff, steep, bluff, crag, escarpment, palisade.

Verbs—stand up, on end, erect, *or* upright, be vertical, draw up, get up, get to one's feet; erect, rear, raise; set, stick, cock, *or* raise up; upraise, upend, raise on its legs; true, plumb, square.

Adjectives—vertical, upright; erect, perpendicular, plumb, true, straight, bolt upright, up-and-down; sheer, steep; rampant, standing up; normal, rectangular, orthogonal, longitudinal.

Adverbs—vertically, uprightly, erectly, up, on end, right on end, à plomb, endways, endwise; on one's legs *or* feet; at right angles, square.

Quotations—It is hard for an empty bag to stand upright (*Benjamin Franklin*), A man should be upright, not be kept upright (*Marcus Aurelius*).

Antonyms, see HORIZONTAL.

---

vertigo, *n.* dizziness, giddiness, vertiginous. See INSANITY, ROTATION.

verve, *n.* gusto, vivacity, dash, fervor, elan, VIGOR. See FEELING.

very, *adv.* exceedingly, highly; emphatically, decidedly, notably; unusually, remarkably, uncommonly; extremely, surpassingly. See GREATNESS.

vessel, *n.* container; vase, urn, jug; boat, SHIP. See RECEPTACLE.

vest, *v.t.* furnish, endow, invest; clothe; give the power *or* right, enfranchise, authorize. See GIVING. —*n.* waistcoat; bodice; weskit. See CLOTHING, PROVISION. —**vested interest,** *n.* special interest group, PAC (see PARTY).

vestibule, *n.* foyer, lobby, hall[way], reception hall; passage, entry[way]; anteroom *or* -chamber, alcove; narthex; porch, portico. See RECEPTACLE.

vestige, *n.* trace, REMAINDER, evidence, relic.

vestments, *n.pl.* canonicals (see CLOTHING).

vestry, *n.* vestiary, sacristy; chapel. See COUNCIL.

veteran, *n.* old man, elder, patriarch, graybeard, oldster (*inf.*), old-timer (*inf.*), codger (*inf.*), gaffer (*inf.*); grandfather, grandmother; old campaigner, seasoned *or* old soldier, ex-soldier; octogenarian, nonagenarian, centenarian. See COMBATANT, AGE.

veterinarian, *n.* veterinary, animal *or* horse doctor, vet (*inf.*). See DOMESTICATION.

veto, *n.* NULLIFICATION; no, *nyet*; pocket veto; disapproval, PROHIBITION. —*v.t.* turn thumbs down; forbid; disallow, prevent, disapprove, prohibit, negate; kill, quash. See REJECTION.

vex, *v.* tease, plague, harass, torment; roil, pique; fret, chafe, irritate, annoy, provoke, nettle. *Informal,* peeve, rile. See RESENTMENT, DISCONTENT.

via, *prep.* through, along, on, by way of, by means of, per. See DIRECTION.

viable, *adj.* fertile, capable; possible, potential; alive, living, vibrant; workable, practical. See LIFE, POSSIBILITY.

viaduct, *n.* trestle, bridge, span, arch. See CONNECTION.

vial, *n.* phial, flask, flacon, vessel, ampoule, test tube. See RECEPTACLE.

vibes, *n.pl., slang,* vibrations, intuition; vibraphone, vibraharp. See FEELING, MUSIC.

vibrant, *adj.* pulsing, athrob, seismic; resonant, sonorous; robust, healthy, dynamic, energetic, vital; vibratory. See VIGOR, OSCILLATION, AGITATION.

vibration, *n.* vibrating, shaking, shimmying; thrill, quiver, throb, pulsation; agitation, trembling; rattling. See OSCILLATION.

vicar, *n.* priest; deputy, AGENT. See CLERGY, SUBSTITUTION.

vicarious, *adj.* substitutive; once removed, secondhand, indirect; proxy, deputy; imaginary, fictive, fictional. See SUBSTITUTION.

vice, *n.* viciousness, evildoing, wrongdoing, wickedness, iniquity, sin, sinfulness; crime, criminality; prostitution; defect, vice; immorality, IMPURITY, looseness of morals; demoralization, [moral] turpitude, depravity, degradation; weakness [of the flesh], fault, frailty, error; besetting sin; delinquency; sink of iniquity. See EVIL, BADNESS, IMPROBITY, WRONG.

vice versa, oppositely, contrariwise, conversely, turnabout. See OPPOSITION.

vicinity, *n.* neighborhood, locality, vicinage; NEARNESS, proximity, environs, ENVIRONMENT.

vicious, *adj.* sinful, wicked, iniquitous, immoral, WRONG; criminal, disorderly; vile, felonious, nefarious, infamous, heinous; demoralized, corrupt, depraved, perverted; evil-minded, shameless; abandoned, debauched, degenerate, dissolute; reprobate, beyond redemption. See EVIL, IMPROBITY, IMPURITY.

vicissitude, *n.* CHANGE; change of fortunes; fluctuation.

victim, *n.* prey; sufferer, dupe, gull, cat's-paw; sacrifice, martyr. See CREDULITY, PURSUIT, RIDICULE.

victimize, *v.t.* cheat, dupe, swindle, hoax, fool, gull, deceive, hoodwink, sell (*inf.*), bamboozle (*inf.*). See DECEPTION.

victor, *n.* champion, winner; conqueror, vanquisher. See SUCCESS.

victory, *n.* conquest, triumph, SUCCESS; winning, mastery; the palm, laurel, wreath, award, trophy, prize, pennant.

victuals, *n.pl.* See FOOD.

video, *n.* television, TV. See COMMUNICATION.

vie, *v.i.* rival, emulate; contend, strive, compete. See CONTENTION.

view, *n.* sight; panorama, vista, prospect, scene; inspection, survey; purpose, aim; viewpoint, angle; opinion, BELIEF, notion; APPEARANCE, aspect. See VISIBILITY. —*v.t.* see; survey, scan; watch, witness; consider, regard, study. See VISION.

viewpoint, *n.* attitude, point of view, standpoint; outlook. See LOCATION, BELIEF, VISION.

vigil, *n.* watch, surveillance; wake; wakefulness. See CARE, ATTENTION, ACTIVITY.

vigilant, *adj.* alert, wary, watchful, wakeful, unsleeping; careful, cautious, circumspect; on the lookout, on the qui vive. See CARE.

vigilante, *n.* See SAFETY,

vignette, *n.* decoration, ornament; picture, illustration, depiction, sketch, squib, piece, DESCRIPTION.

VIGOR
Active strength

Nouns—1, vigor, force, might, vim, POWER, STRENGTH, ENERGY, potency, efficacy, ACTIVITY, vitality, virility; HEALTH, stamina; spirit, verve, warmth, exuberance, glow, sap, pith, bloom, tone, mettle, ELASTICITY. *Informal,* zip, get-up-and-go. *Slang,* pep, punch, starch, moxie.

2, ardor, fire, enthusiasm, piquancy, pungency, intensity, trenchancy; vehemence, point, cogency.

Adjectives—1, vigorous, strong, mighty, powerful, potent, energetic, mettlesome, active, virile; healthy, hardy, hearty, hale, robust, SOUND, sturdy, stalwart, muscular, lusty, strenuous, well, buxom, brisk, alert, glowing, sparkling, in good health; thrifty, fresh, flourishing. *Slang,* peppy, oatsy.

2, spirited, lively, racy, bold, nervous, trenchant, piquant, pungent, biting, slashing, sharp, severe; incisive, forcible, forceful, effective, cogent, pithy, pointed, full of point; picturesque, vivid, poetic. *Slang,* full of beans.

Adverbs—vigorously, powerfully, *etc.*; emphatically, in glowing terms.

Quotations—Even if the open windows of science at first make us shiver . . . in the end, the fresh air brings vigor, and the great spaces have a splendor of their own (*Bertrand Russell*).

Antonyms, see IMPOTENCE, WEARINESS.

vile, *adj.* base, debased, low, lowly, mean; repulsive, odious; foul, nasty; paltry; evil, villainous, corrupt, wicked, depraved. See BADNESS, DISREPUTE, UNIMPORTANCE.

vilify, *v.t.* vilipend, revile, calumniate, traduce, slander, libel, defame, decry, belittle, slur. See DETRACTION.

villa, *n.* mansion, chalet, château. See ABODE.

village, *n.* town, hamlet. See ABODE.

villain, *n.* blackguard, scoundrel; knave, rascal, rogue; badman; EVILDOER; *slang,* heavy, bad guy (see DRAMA).

villainy, *n.* roguery, rascality; criminality, depravity, wickedness, wrongdoing. See IMPROBITY.

vim, *n.* zest, ENERGY, VIGOR, pep, zip (*inf.*), ginger (*inf.*).

VINDICATION
Clearing from an accusation

Nouns—1, vindication, justification, warrant; exoneration, exculpation; acquittal; whitewashing; extenuation; palliation, softening, mitigation. See JUSTICE.

2, reply, defense, demurrer, exception; apology, plea, pleading; excuse, extenuating circumstances; allowance, argument. *Informal*, alibi.

3, vindicator, apologist, justifier, defender, defendant; proponent.

Verbs—1, vindicate, justify, warrant; exculpate, acquit (see ACQUITTAL); clear, set right, exonerate, whitewash; extenuate, palliate, excuse, soften; apologize, put a good face upon, smooth over, explain away; mince; gloss over, bolster up. *Informal*, give a clean bill of health.

2, defend; advocate; stand, stick, *or* speak up for; bear out, support; plead, say in defense; put in a good word for; talk up. *Slang*, go to bat for.

3, make allowance for, take the will for the deed, do justice to; give one his due, give the devil his due; make good; prove one's case.

Adjectives—vindicated, vindicating, vindicatory, vindicative; palliative; exculpatory; apologetic, vindicable; excusable, defensible, pardonable; venial, specious, plausible, justifiable.

Phrases—never complain, never explain.

Quotations—Laugh where we must, be candid where we can; but vindicate the ways of God to man (*Alexander Pope*).

Antonyms, see ACCUSATION, GUILT.

---

vindictive, *adj.* vengeful, spiteful, bitter; resentful; implacable, rancorous; bearing a grudge. See RETALIATION.

vine, *n.* climber, creeper, runner, twiner, tendril, vinelet; liana, bine, stem, shoot; grapevine, ivy, wisteria, *etc.* See VEGETABLE, AGRICULTURE.

vinegar, *n.* acetum, pickle; condiment, preservative. See SOURNESS.

vintage, *n.* crop, produce, harvest; viticulture, viniculture; [vintage] wine, vin du pays; time, age, style, period. See AGRICULTURE.

violate, *v.* break, breach; outrage, profane, desecrate; disrespect; transgress, infringe; usurp, encroach; rape, ravish. See ILLEGALITY, IMPURITY, BADNESS, DISOBEDIENCE, WRONG.

VIOLENCE
Characterized by physical force

Nouns—1, violence, vehemence, intensity, impetuosity; boisterousness; turbulence, riot, row, rumpus, devil to pay, the fat in the fire; turmoil, DISORDER; AGITATION; storm, tempest, rough weather; squall, earthquake, upheaval, cataclysm, volcano, thunderstorm, cyclone, tornado, hurricane; maelstrom, whirlpool. See ILLEGALITY, EXCITABILITY, IMPULSE.

2, (*wildness*) SEVERITY, ferocity, ferociousness, fierceness, rage, fury; fit, frenzy, paroxysm, orgasm; force, brute force; outrage, strain, shock, spasm, convulsion, throe; hysterics, tantrum, passion, EXCITEMENT.

3, (*violent reaction*) outbreak, outburst; burst, discharge, volley, explosion, blast, detonation, backfire, rush, eruption, blowup; torrent; storm center.

4, (*source of violence*) explosive, cap, fuse, proximity fuse, detonator; powder, gunpowder, smokeless powder, guncotton; cordite, melinite, lyddite, dynamite, nitroglycerine, TNT (trinitrotoluene).

5, (*violent person*) fury, fiend, dragon, demon, tiger; wild beast; fire-eater, hellion, hellcat, virago, termagant, beldame; madcap; rabble rouser, lynch mob, terrorist, agitator, agent provocateur; thug, tough, strongarm man, gunman, hooligan, hoodlum, hellcat, firebrand, hothead, hotspur, predator, ruffian, roughneck, exterminator, destroyer, berserker, aggressor; anarchist, urban guerrilla. *Slang,* tommy-buster, rough trade, bad actor; night rider, mad dog. See EVILDOER.

6, *(victim of violence)* battered child *or* spouse.

Verbs—1, be violent, run high; ferment, effervesce; rampage; run wild, run riot; break the peace; run amuck, raise a riot; lash out, make the fur fly; bluster, rage, roar, riot, storm; seethe, boil [over]; fume, foam, come in like a lion, wreak, wreck, spread havoc, ride roughshod, out-Herod Herod; spread like wildfire. *Informal,* make *or* kick up a row, raise the devil, raise Cain, raise the roof; roughhouse; fly off the handle; blow one's top, let off steam.

2, break, fly, *or* burst out; explode, implode, go off, fly, detonate, thunder, blow up, flash, flare, burst; shock, strain.

3, stir up, excite, incite, urge, lash, stimulate; inflame, kindle, foment, fulminate, touch off, set off; convulse, infuriate, madden, lash into *or* goad to fury; fan the flames, add fuel to the flames.

Adjectives—1, violent, vehement; ungentle, boisterous, rough-and-tumble, wild, untamed; impetuous, frenetic, bestial, barbaric; rampant; dog-eat-dog.

2, turbulent; disorderly, blustering, raging, troublous, riotous, tumultuous, obstreperous, uproarious; extravagant, unmitigated; ravening, frenzied, desperate (see RASHNESS); infuriated, furious, outrageous, frantic, hysterical; fiery, flaming, scorching, [red-]hot; seething; savage, fierce, ferocious, barbarous; headstrong, ungovernable, uncontrollable; convulsive, explosive; volcanic; stormy.

Adverbs—violently, *etc.*; amain; by storm, by force, by main force; with might and main; tooth and nail; with a vengeance; headlong.

Quotations—Force, unaided by judgment, collapses through its own weight (*Horace*), All they that take the sword shall perish with the sword (*Bible*), They have sown the wind, and they shall reap the whirlwind (*Bible*), A man may build himself a throne of bayonets, but he cannot sit on it (*William Inge*), Where force is necessary, there it must be applied boldly, decisively, and completely (*Leon Trotsky*), A riot is at bottom the language of the unheard (*Martin Luther King*), The only thing that's been a worse flop than the organization of non-violence has been the organization of violence (*Joan Baez*), In violence, we forget who we are (*Mary McCarthy*), Violence is good for those who have nothing to lose (*Jean-Paul Sartre*).

Antonyms, see MODERATION.

---

violin, *n.* fiddle; string; Amati, Stradivarius, Strad, Guarnerius; violinist; (*pl.*) string section. See MUSIC.

VIP, very important person, personage, somebody. See IMPORTANCE.

viper, *n.* adder, snake, serpent; traitor, turncoat, Judas [Iscariot], Iago, double dealer, rat *(sl.);* viperess. See ANIMAL, IMPROBITY.

virago, *n.* termagant, vixen, shrew, maenad, hellcat. See IRASCIBILITY.

virgin, *n.* maiden, celibate, vestal; spinster. —*adj.* chaste, untouched; maidenly, fresh, virginal, pure; new, uncut, unexplored, primeval. See CELIBACY, NEWNESS, PURITY.

virile, *adj.* manly, masculine, macho; vigorous, potent; fully sexed. See STRENGTH, VIGOR.

virtual, *adj.* practical; implied, implicit; substantial; true, veritable; potential. See INTRINSIC.

VIRTUE
Moral uprightness

Nouns—1, virtue; virtuousness, GOODNESS; morality; moral rectitude; integrity, PROBITY; nobleness; prudence; morals, ethics, DUTY; work ethic; cardinal virtues; merit, worth, excellence, credit; self-control; fortitude, self-denial; good deeds, good behavior; discharge, fulfillment, *or* performance of duty; chastity, INNOCENCE; meritocracy. See RIGHTNESS, GOODNESS, PIETY.

2, virtuous *or* good person. *Informal,* straight arrow, Mr. Clean.

Verbs—practice, virtue; do, fulfill, perform, *or* discharge one's duty; redeem one's pledge; behave; command *or* master one's passions; keep on the straight and narrow path; set an example, be on one's good *or* best behavior.

Adjectives—virtuous, good, innocent; meritorious, deserving, worthy, correct; dutiful, duteous, moral, right, righteous, right-minded; well-intentioned, creditable, laudable, commendable, praiseworthy; above *or* beyond praise; excellent, admirable; sterling, pure [as the driven snow], noble, exemplary, matchless, peerless; saintly, saintlike; heaven-born, angelic, seraphic.

Phrases—virtue is its own reward; he lives long who lives well.

Quotations—Morality is the herd-instinct in the individual (*Friedrich Nietzsche*), Morality is a private and costly luxury (*Henry Adams*), Moral indignation is jealousy with a halo (*H. G. Wells*), How far that little candle throws his beams! So shines a good deed in a naughty world (*Shakespeare*), Dost thou think, because thou are virtuous, there shall be no more cakes and ale? (*Shakespeare*), Virtue is like a rich stone, best plain set (*Francis Bacon*), When men grow virtuous in their old age, they only make a sacrifice to God of the devil's leavings (*Alexander Pope*), Virtue knows to a farthing what it has lost by not having been vice (*Horace Walpole*), My strength is as the strength of ten, because my heart is pure (*Lord Tennyson*), I used to be Snow White . . . but I drifted (*Mae West*), I know only that what is moral is what you feel good after and what is immoral is what you feel bad after (*Ernest Hemingway*), Our scientific power has outrun our spiritual power. We have guided missiles and misguided men (*Martin Luther King*).

Antonyms, see EVIL, IMPROBITY.

---

virtuosity, *n.* dilletantism, dabbling; SKILL, mastery, proficiency, technique, know-how, expertise, chops (*sl.*); finesse, flair, dexterity.

virtuoso, *n.* consummate ARTIST, artiste; connoisseur. See TASTE.

virulent, *adj.* poisonous, venomous; deadly; toxic, noxious; malignant, malevolent; caustic, acrimonious. See BADNESS, DISEASE, RESENTMENT.

virus, *n.* venom, poison, contagium, germ, microorganism. See DISEASE.

visa, *n.* endorsement, validation, stamp. See ASSENT.

visage, *n.* face, countenance, physiognomy; semblance, look, aspect, guise; puss, phiz, map (*all sl.*). See APPEARANCE, FRONT.

vis-à-vis, *adv.* face-to-face, tête-à-tête, facing. —*prep.* opposite, contra, versus, against; contrasted to, as opposed to. See OPPOSITION.

viscous, *adj.* viscid; ropy, glutinous, slimy; mucid; sticky, mucilaginous; oleaginous, greasy. See COHERENCE.

vise, *n.* clamp, gripper, clinch. See RETENTION.

VISIBILITY
Capability of being seen

Nouns—visibility, perceptibility; conspicuity, precision; APPEARANCE, manifestation, exposure [to view]; ocular proof, evidence, *or* demonstration; field of view, range; high *or* low visibility, visibility zero; view, prospect, horizon. See VISION.

Verbs—1, appear, show, gleam, glimmer, glitter, glare, meet *or* catch the eye, materialize; present, show, manifest, produce, discover, reveal, expose, *or* betray itself; stand out *or* forth, peep *or* peer out, crop out; start, spring, show, turn, *or* crop up; float before the eyes, be conspicuous, be prominent, attract the attention, speak for itself. *Informal,* stand out like a sore thumb.

2, expose to view; bring out; show, display, reveal, expose, disclose (see DISCLOSURE).

Adjectives—visible, visual, perceptible, perceivable, noticeable, observable, discernible, external, outward, seeable, to be seen; in [full] view, in sight, in the open, exposed to view; distinct; apparent, manifest, evident, obvious, unhidden, unclouded, conspicuous, prominent, in the public eye, in view, glaring, staring, standing out; before one; before one's eyes, under one's nose. *Informal,* plain as the nose on one's face.

Adverbs—visibly, perceptibly, *etc.*; in sight of, before one's eyes, *à vue d'œil,* as large as life.

Quotation—The visible is a shadow cast by the invisible (*Plato*).

Antonyms, see INVISIBILITY.

VISION
Sense of sight

Nouns—1, vision, sight, optics, eyesight, seeing; view, look, espial, glance, ken; glimpse, glimmer, peep, coup d'oeil; focus; gaze, stare, leer; perception, contemplation; regard, survey; observance, observation, examination, half an eye, surveillance; inspection (see INQUIRY); reconnaissance, watch, espionage, autopsy; ocular inspection; sightseeing; perspicacity, discernment. *Slang,* look-see; once-over; eyeful.

2, *(vision problems)* twenty-twenty vision, *etc.*; farsightedness, hyperopia, presbyopia, eagle eye; nearsightedness, myopia; myosis, astigmatism, presbyopia; double vision, diplopia; colorblindness, Daltonism, night *or* day blindness, nyctalopia, hemeralopia; strabismus, heterotropia, cross-eyes, cock-eyes, wall-eyes, squint, cast, cataract, ophthalmia; nystagmus; lazy eye; goggle-eyes. See OPTICAL INSTRUMENTS.

3, *(organ of vision)* visual organ; eye; eyeball; naked eye; optic nerve, retina, fovea centralis, pupil, iris, cornea, conjunctiva, sclera, choroid coat, ciliary body, epicanthus, white, canthus, vitreous humor. *Informal,* optics, orbs, peeper, peeled *or* weather eye. *Slang,* glim, blinkers, baby blues.

4, *(visual distortions)* refraction, distortion; illusion, optical illusion, mirage, phantasm, specter, apparition; reflection, mirror, image.

5, *(visual viewpoint)* point of view, viewpoint; vantage point; stance; observatory; gazebo, loophole, crow's nest; belvedere, watchtower; peephole, lookout post; field of view; grandstand, bleachers; theater, amphitheater, arena, vista, horizon; VISIBILITY; prospect, perspective (see APPEARANCE); commanding view, bird's-eye view; periscope; spectator, viewer (see PRESENCE).

Verbs—1, see, behold, discern, perceive, have in sight, descry, sight, make out, spot, lay *or* set eyes on, catch sight of, pick out, discover, distinguish, recognize, spy, espy, get *or* catch a glimpse of; command a view of; watch, witness, look on; cast one's eyes on; see at a glance.

2, look, view, eye; lift up one's eyes, open one's eyes, look around, survey, scan, inspect, contemplate, take the measure of; run one's eye over, reconnoiter, glance around, direct one's eyes to, observe, peep, peer, pry, take a peep; stare [down]; strain one's eyes; fix *or* rivet eyes on, feast one's eyes on; gaze; pore over; leer, ogle, glare; goggle, stare, gape, gawk, gawp; spectate; cock one's eye. *Slang,* get a load of, take a gander at, give the once-over, size up, eye-fuck.

3, dazzle, blind (see BLINDNESS); wink, blink, squint; screw up one's eyes; have a mote in the eye; see through a glass darkly.

Adjectives—visual, ocular, seeing; optic[al]; ophthalmic; shortsighted, blear; farsighted; clear-sighted; eagle-, hawk-, lynx-, Argus-, *or* keen-eyed; visible; misty, dim.

Adverbs—visibly; in sight of, with one's eyes open; at [first] sight, at a glance; out of the corner of one's eye; at first blush; prima facie.

Phrases—the eyes are the window of the soul.

Quotation—People see only what they are prepared to see (*Emerson*).

Antonyms, see BLINDNESS.

---

visionary, *adj.* idealistic, unpractical, quixotic, Utopian; imaginary, delusory, chimerical. —*n.* dreamer, idealist, theorist, theorizer. See IMAGINATION, HETERODOXY, NONEXISTENCE.

visit, *n.* call; interview, appointment;

stopover, sojourn. —v. call on, drop in; stop, stay, tarry; sojourn; afflict, assail. See ARRIVAL, SOCIALITY.

visitation, *n.* visit; calamity, misfortune; seizure, stroke, blow; disaster; bad luck, hardship. See ADVERSITY, DISEASE.

visor, *n.* beaver, vizard, mask, domino, [eye] shield, eyeshade, sunshade, peak, brim. See COVERING.

vista, *n.* view, prospect, scene; landscape; panorama. See APPEARANCE, VISION.

visual, *adj.* optical (see VISION). —*n.* picture, illustration. See REPRESENTATION. —**visual arts,** *n.* PAINTING, SCULPTURE, PHOTOGRAPHY, FILM.

visualize, *v.t.* picture, envision; imagine, project. See IMAGINATION.

vital, *adj.* essential, indispensable, necessary; life-supporting; vivifying, invigorating; alive, live, vibrant, animate; fatal. See LIFE, ORGANIC MATTER, NECESSITY.

vitality, *n.* LIFE; VIGOR, energy, virility; viability. See STRENGTH.

vitiate, *v.t.* adulterate, weaken; impair, spoil; destroy, void, invalidate; corrupt, contaminate, pollute; deteriorate. See DETERIORATION.

vitreous, *adj.* glassy, crystalline, vitriform; brittle, hard; transparent, translucent. See TRANSPARENCY, BRITTLENESS.

vituperate, *v.t.* vilify, abuse, revile; reproach, inveigh (against), rebuke, scold, upbraid; objurgate, tongue-lash. See DETRACTION, DISAPPROBATION.

vivacious, *adj.* lively, animated, sprightly; gay, breezy, spirited; frolicsome, sportive, cheerful. See ACTIVITY, CHEERFULNESS.

viva voce, Lat., aloud; orally. See SPEECH.

vivid, *adj.* striking; telling; picturesque; animated, bright; lifelike, realistic; lively, vital; vibrant, glowing; fresh, intense, unfaded, brilliant. See COLOR, LIGHT, VIGOR.

vixen, *n.* harridan, shrew, witch, scold, virago, harpy. See FEMALE, EVILDOER.

vocabulary, *n.* words, glossary, wordlist; dictionary, lexicon; language. See SPEECH.

vocal, *adj.* articulate; spoken, [to be] sung; choral, lyric; verbal, oral. See SPEECH, MUSIC.

vocalist, *n.* singer; tenor, alto, *etc.*; crooner, warbler, songstress, thrush, nightingale. See MUSIC.

vocation, *n.* profession; work, trade; calling, occupation. See BUSINESS.

vociferous, *adj.* loud, noisy, clamorous; blatant, obstreperous, loudmouthed. See LOUDNESS, CRY.

vogue, *n.* mode, style, FASHION; practice, custom, usage; favor, HABIT.

voice, *n.* vocality; speaking *or* singing voice; inflection, intonation; tone of voice; ventriloquism, ventriloquy; lung power; vocal cords, vocalization (see SPEECH); CRY, expression, utterance, vociferation, enunciation, articulation; accent[uation]; emphasis, stress; singer (see MUSIC); representation, vote, participation (see CHOICE). —*v.t.* speak, utter; give voice, utterance, *or* tongue to; shout, CRY, exclaim, ejaculate; express; vocalize, articulate, enunciate, pronounce, enounce, announce; accentuate; deliver, mouth. See PUBLICATION.

void, *adj.* empty, vacuous, blank; unoccupied, untenanted; devoid, lacking, unfilled; ineffectual; null, invalid; not binding; vain, unreal, unsubstantial. — *v.t.* vacate; abrogate, nullify, negate; evacuate, eject, cast off. See EJECTION. —*n.* emptiness, SPACE, nothingness; vacuum; abyss, chasm. See ABSENCE, NULLIFICATION, INSUBSTANTIALITY, NONEXISTENCE.

volatile, *adj.* gaseous, vaporizable; fickle, changeable, mercurial; unstable, transient; light, giddy; lively; capricious; buoyant, airy. See VAPOR, CHANGEABLENESS, TRANSIENTNESS.

volcanic, *adj.* eruptive, fiery, explosive. See VIOLENCE.

volition, *n.* WILL, CHOICE, voluntariness; option, preference, willingness.

volley, *n.* broadside, salvo, fusillade, raking, round; burst. See ATTACK.

volte-face, Fr., reversal. See INVERSION.

voluble, *adj.* talkative, verbose; fluent, glib. See LOQUACITY.

volume, *n.* book, tome; contents, capacity; bulk, mass, dimensions, SIZE, QUANTITY. See GREATNESS, PUBLICATION.

voluminous, *adj.* capacious, big, bulky; copious; prolix; ample. See SIZE.

voluntary, *adj.* free-will, volunteered, willing, spontaneous, willed, unasked; unforced; deliberate, intentional. See WILL, CHOICE.

volunteer, *n.* enlister; offerer. —*v.* enlist; OFFER, proffer; give, donate. See WILL, UNDERTAKING.

voluptuous, *adj.* sensual, carnal, fleshy, sexy (*sl.*), meretricious; epicurean, worldly. See PLEASURE, INTEMPERANCE.

vomit, *v.t.* throw up, disgorge; belch, spew, eject. See EJECTION.

voodoo, *n.* wanga, obeah, fetishism, witchcraft, black magic; witch doctor, shamanist, medicine man, sorcerer. See SORCERY.

voracious, *adj.* ravenous, omnivorous; rapacious; starving, famished, hungry; gluttonous, edacious. See GLUTTONY, DESIRE.

vortex, *n.* eddy, whirlpool; maelstrom; whirl; storm center. See ROTATION, WATER.

votary, *n.* votarist, devotee, disciple, follower, enthusiast, adherent, zealot, fan (*inf.*). —*adj.* votive, dedicated; consecrated; pledged; devoted. See DESIRE, AUXILIARY.

vote, *n.* poll, ballot; franchise, suffrage; CHOICE, voice, option, election; referendum, plebiscite. —*v.* cast a ballot; choose, select, elect, establish, enact, ratify, veto, nullify. See ASSENT.

vouch, *v.* guarantee, warrant; affirm, declare; answer for, attest; certify; support, back, bear witness. See AFFIRMATION, EVIDENCE, SECURITY.

voucher, *n.* receipt, stub; warrant, testimonium, EVIDENCE, record, support. See SECURITY.

vow, *v.* swear, take oath; vouch, affirm; pledge, PROMISE; dedicate, devote; take vows. —*n.* dedication, devotion; oath, swearing; pledge, PROMISE; consecration. See AFFIRMATION.

vox populi, *Lat.*, the voice of the people. See AGREEMENT, POPULACE, PUBLICATION.

voyage, *n.* cruise, sea trip, crossing, sail, excursion. See TRAVEL, MOTION.

voyeur, *n.* Peeping Tom; lecher, pervert, psychopath. See CURIOSITY.

VULGARITY
Bad taste

Nouns—1, vulgarity, vulgarism; barbarism; offense, bad taste; INELEGANCE, indelicacy; gaucherie, ill breeding, DISCOURTESY, incivility; coarseness, indecorum, boorishness; rowdyism, blackguardism; ribaldry, obscenity, pornography; risqué story, double entendre.

2, (*vulgar taste*) gaudiness, tawdriness, finery, frippery, brummagem, tinsel, gewgaws, knickknacks (see OSTENTATION).

3, (*vulgar person*) vulgarian, rough diamond; tomboy, hoyden, cub, unlicked cub; lout, churl, knave, clown, cad, roughneck, barbarian; snob, parvenu, frump, slattern, slut. *Informal*, bounder. *Slang*, pain in the ass, derriere, *or* neck, siwash, redneck, snot.

Verbs—offend, coarsen, vulgarize; misbehave, roughhouse. *Slang*, gross out.

Adjectives—1, vulgar, in bad taste, crass, crude; distasteful, fulsome, unrefined, coarse, indecorous, ribald, gross; unseemly, unpresentable; common, boisterous, loud, rough and ready; tasteless, obnoxious; backwoods.

2, uncourtly; uncivil, discourteous, ill-bred, bad-mannered, ill-mannered; ungentlemanly, unladylike, unfeminine; unkempt, uncombed, frowzy, unpolished, uncouth, rude, savage, blackguard, rowdy, barbarous, barbaric; low, vile, ignoble, monstrous, shocking; obscene. See POPULACE.

3, (*vulgarly flashy*) bizarre, outré, outlandish; affected, meretricious, ostentatious, extravagant; gaudy, tawdry, flashy, showy; cheap; shoddy; obtrusive; dressed like a dog's dinner.

Quotation—Vulgarity has its uses (*Max Beerbohm*), Nothing is more vulgar than haste (*Emerson*), You have all the characteristics of a popular politician: a horrible voice, bad breeding, and a vulgar manner (*Aristophanes*).

Antonyms, see TASTE.

vulnerable, *adj.* open (to attack); weak, defenseless, assailable, susceptible. See DANGER, WEAKNESS.

vulpine, *adj.* foxlike; foxy, crafty,

vulture, *n.* predator, scavenger; condor, buzzard, griffon; extortionist, bloodsucker, vampire, parasite, jackal, harpy. See EVILDOER, ANIMAL.

vulva, *n.* genitals, yoni, cunt (*sl.*). See BODY.

W

wacky, *adj.,* *slang,* erratic, odd, demented, wacko (*sl.*). See INSANITY, UNCONFORMITY.

wad, *n.* lump, plug, stuffing, filling, batting, wadding; bankroll. See SIZE, MONEY.

waddle, *n.* toddle, shamble, lurch, waggle, sway, duck walk. See SLOWNESS.

wade, *v.* walk through, traverse, ford; wallow, slog, slosh; stand up to one's ankles (in); *informal,* wade into, attack, undertake. See WATER, UNDERTAKING.

wafer, *n.* biscuit, cracker, cookie; lozenge, tablet, troche. See FOOD, NARROWNESS, LAYER, RITE.

waffle, *v.i.,* *informal,* vacillate, equivocate, fluctuate. See CHANGEABLENESS.

waft, *v.* float, buoy, convey, transport, carry; roll, wave. See WIND, TRANSPORTATION.

wag, *v.* wave, shake, sway, jerk, waggle, wigwag, nod. See OSCILLATION, AGITATION. —*n.* WIT, humorist; shake. See OSCILLATION.

wage, *v.t.* wager; conduct, make, carry on, engage in, undertake. See WARFARE, UNDERTAKING, CHANCE.

wager, *n.* & *v.* bet, stake, gamble, risk, hazard, gage. See CHANCE.

wages, *n.pl.* pay, PAYMENT, hire, compensation, remuneration; earnings, salary, income.

wagon, *n.* cart, dray, buckboard, wain; truck, lorry, car; van. See VEHICLE, TRANSPORTATION.

waif, *v.i.* stray, foundling; [street] Arab; homeless child; vagrant. See TRAVEL, RELINQUISHMENT.

wail, *v.i.* lament, CRY, moan, bewail; howl, ululate, caterwaul; complain. See LAMENTATION.

waist, *n.* girth, middle, midriff, loin, waistline; bodice, blouse, shirt, tunic. See CLOTHING.

wait, *v.* stay, linger, tarry, abide, remain, bide [one's time], sit tight, cool one's heels (*sl.*), sweat it out (*sl.*); dally, procrastinate, delay; serve, attend; await, expect, look for. See EXPECTATION.

waiter, *n.* SERVANT, garçon, attendant, steward, servitor, waitress, carhop; tray, salver (see RECEPTACLE).

waive, *v.* relinquish, renounce, give up, forgo, disclaim, surrender (a right *or* claim); defer. See DISUSE, RELINQUISHMENT.

waiver, *n.* quitclaim (see RELINQUISHMENT).

wake, *n.* path, track, trail, swath; vigil, watch. See REAR, INTERMENT, PASSAGE. —*v.* [a]rouse, awake[n]; stir, excite, animate. See ACTIVITY, EXCITEMENT.

wakeful, *adj.* alert, watchful, on guard, on the qui vive, vigilant; restless, sleepless, insomniac. See CARE, ACTIVITY.

walk, *n.* ramble, stroll, promenade, wander, saunter, TRAVEL (on foot), march, parade, tramp, hike, constitutional (*inf.*); path[way]; gait, carriage, tread, pace, step; calling, occupation; sphere, province, department, BUSINESS. See MOTION, SLOWNESS, PASSAGE.

wall, *n.* side, partition, bulkhead, flange, splashboard; rampart, DEFENSE; barrier; fence; cliff, precipice; levee, dike, seawall; (*pl.*) PRISON. See ENCLOSURE, HINDRANCE, VERTICAL, CIRCUMSCRIPTION.

wallet, *n.* purse, pocketbook, billfold; bag, pouch, sack, moneybag; pack, knapsack. See RECEPTACLE.

wallop, *v.* thrash, beat, strike, punch, hit, clout. See IMPULSE.

wallow, *v.i.* tumble, grovel, roll, flounder, welter, toss; revel, delight in, luxuriate in. See LOWNESS, PLEASURE, INTEMPERANCE.

wan, *adj.* pale, pallid, waxen, waxy, ashen, ashy, bloodless. See COLORLESSNESS.

wand, *n.* rod, caduceus, mace, scepter; staff, stick, baton; divining rod, dowsing stick; withe. See SORCERY.

wander, *v.i.* rove, ramble, stroll, walk, range; digress, swerve, deviate, stray; rave, maunder, be delirious; moon; straggle, forage. See TRAVEL, DEVIATION, INSANITY, MOTION.

wane, *v.i.* DECREASE, lessen, ebb, fade, diminish, peter out, dwindle; abate, subside; decline, sink, fail, slacken. —*n.* failure, ebb, decline, decay, DECREASE.

wangle, *v., informal,* wheedle, inveigle, coax; extort, wring, wrench; contrive, get by hook or crook, con (*sl.*), rustle up (*sl.*). See STEALING, ACQUISITION.

want, *n.* need; POVERTY, indigence; lack, dearth, deficiency, ABSENCE; shortage, inadequacy, scarcity; NECESSITY, requirement. —*v.* lack, need; be in need; require, DESIRE, wish, crave; fall short of, be deficient, miss, omit, neglect, fail. See INSUFFICIENCY.

wanting, *adj.* lacking, missing, absent. See ABSENCE.

wanton, *adj.* lewd, licentious, loose, dissolute, immoral; frolicsome, abandoned, capricious, willful; wild; heartless, malicious; heedless, reckless, wayward, perverse; luxuriant, rampant, exuberant. See IMPURITY. —*n.* libertine; flirt, baggage, hussy, trollop. See EVILDOER, FREEDOM.

war, *n. & v.* See WARFARE.

warble, *v.* trill, sing, quaver. See MUSIC.

ward, *v.t.* watch, guard, defend, protect; fend, parry, stave [off]. —*n.* watch, guard, DEFENSE, protector; CARE, charge, custody; protégé[e], dependent, minor; precinct, district; hospital room. See REPULSION, REGION, REMEDY, PRISON, SUBJECTION.

warden, *n.* keeper; game warden, church warden; custodian, curator; ranger; jailer, turnkey; superintendent. See SAFETY, AUTHORITY.

warder, *n.* keeper; gatekeeper; warden; guard; mace, staff. See SAFETY.

wardrobe, *n.* CLOTHING, outfit, togs, duds, apparel, attire, livery, uniforms, finery; clothes closet, cloakroom, vestry. See RECEPTACLE.

warehouse, *n.* STORE, depot, supply dump, storehouse.

wares, *n.pl.* merchandise, goods, commodities; products, stock in trade, provisions, kitchenware, tableware, *etc.* See SALE.

WARFARE
Act of war

Nouns—1, warfare, state of war, fighting, hostilities, act of war; war, combat, aggression; ARMS, force of arms, the sword, dogs of war; appeal to arms; baptism of fire, ordeal of battle; general warfare, war to the death, global thermonuclear war, limited conventional *or* strategic warfare, ground war, open war, internecine war, civil war, broken-back war, brushfire war, controlled war; world *or* global war, total war; war to end war; revolutionary war, REVOLUTION, religious war, crusade; underground warfare; guerrilla warfare; peace offensive, violent peace; chemical, biological, spasm, germ, *or* bacteriological warfare; trench warfare, war of position, war of attrition; scorched-earth policy; aerial, naval, conventional, economic, electronic, psychological, nuclear, *or* atomic warfare; Mars, Ares, Odin, Bellona; cold *or* hot war; nuclear deterrent, first-strike capability; balance of power, deterrence; police action. See KILLING.

2, (*military campaign*) call to arms, mobilization, deployment; operation, campaign[ing], crusade, expedition, invasion; investment; siege; air raid, strike, *or* support, amphibious operation; battle, fighting (see CONTENTION); withdrawal, retreat; trumpet, clarion, bugle, pibroch; slogan; war cry, war whoop; rebel yell, battle cry; beat of drum; tom-tom; password, watchword; muster, rally; service, active service, action; inactive service; war games; friendly fire. See ATTACK.

3, battlefield, battleground, field; theater [of war], front, battle line, beaten zone, combat zone; demilitarized zone, DMZ; camp, encampment, bivouac, billet, bunker, foxhole, laager; flank, center, salient, line; beachhead, airhead. See ARENA.

4, art of war, tactics, strategy, military science, generalship, soldiership; ballistics, ordnance, gunnery; chivalry; weapons (see ARMS); logistics.

5, warrior, soldier (see COMBATANT); camp follower.

6, warlikeness, belligerence, bellicosity, combativeness, contentiousness; militarism; chauvinism, jingoism (see PRIDE); warmonger.

Verbs—**1**, war, go to war; declare war, carry on *or* wage war, let slip the dogs of war; cry havoc; take the field, give *or* join battle; set *or* fall to, engage, measure swords with, cross swords; come to blows, come to close quarters; fight, combat; contend (see CONTENTION); battle with; fight it out, fight hand to hand; sell one's life dearly. *Informal*, flex one's muscles.

2, arm; raise troops, mobilize; enroll, enlist, sign up; draft, conscript, call to the colors, recruit; serve, be on active service; campaign; wield the sword, bear arms; live by the sword, die by the sword; take up arms; shoulder a musket, smell powder, be under fire; spill blood. *Informal*, join up. See COMPULSION.

Adjectives—**1**, warring, battling, contending, contentious; armed [to the teeth], sword in hand; in *or* under arms, up in arms; at war with; in battle array, in open arms, in the field; embattled, beleaguered, besieged.

2, warlike, belligerent, combative, bellicose, martial; military, militant; soldierlike, soldierly; chivalrous; strategic, tactical.

Adverbs—at war, in the thick of the fray, in the cannon's mouth; at swords' points; on the warpath.

Phrases—war will cease when men refuse to fight.

Quotations—We make war that we may live in peace (*Aristotle*), The sinews of war, unlimited money (*Cicero*), Wars begin when you will, but they do not end when you please (*Machiavelli*), There never was a good war, or a bad peace (*Benjamin Franklin*), War is nothing but a continuation of politics with the admixture of other means (*von Clausewitz*), It is well that war is so terrible. We should grow too fond of it (*Robert E. Lee*), I have a rendezvous with Death at some disputed barricade (*Alan Seeger*), War is too serious a matter to entrust to military men (*Georges Clemenceau*), The sword is the axis of the world and its power is absolute (*Charles de Gaulle*), Sometime they'll give a war and nobody will come (*Carl Sandburg*), Older men declare war. But it is youth who must fight and die (*Herbert Hoover*), Mankind must put an end to war or war will put an end to mankind (*J. F. Kennedy*), History is littered with the wars which everybody knew would never happen (*Enoch Powell*).

Antonyms, see PACIFICATION.

warhorse, *n.* charger, courser, destrier (archaic); *informal,* veteran, vet, war dog, old-timer; *slang,* standby, old reliable, chestnut (*sl.*). See SKILL, COMBATANT.

warlock, *n.* archaic, wizard, sorcerer, necromancer. See SORCERY.

warm, *adj.* hot, tepid, lukewarm; sunny, mild, summery; close, muggy; ardent, fervid, fervent, passionate; new, fresh; earnest, intimate; warmhearted, responsive, glowing, enthusiastic, hearty, affectionate, cordial; lively, excitable, feverish, hasty, quick; alive, living. See HEAT, FEELING, EXCITEMENT, BENEVOLENCE, FRIEND.

warm-blooded, *adj.* ardent, impulsive. See EXCITEMENT. FEELING.

warmonger, *n.* [war] hawk, war dog; war lord, militarist, mercenary; drumbeater, flag-waver, saber-rattler, firebrand, instigator; jingo[ist], xenophobe, rabble-rouser. See WARFARE, COMBATANT.

WARNING
Admonition

Nouns—**1**, warning, forewarning, CAUTION, caveat; notice; premonition, foreboding, PREDICTION; lesson; admonition, monition; alarm; advisory; THREAT. See DISSUASION.

2, warning sign, handwriting on the wall; mene, mene, tekel, upharsin; red flag; tip-off; foghorn; monitor, warning voice, wake-up call, Cassandra, signs of the times, Mother Carey's chickens, stormy petrel, bird of ill omen; shot across the bows; gathering clouds, clouds on the horizon; symptom; watchtower, beacon, lighthouse; a cloud no bigger than a man's hand; straw in the wind. See SAFETY, INDICATION.

3, *(guard posted to give warning)* sentinel, sentry, lookout; watch[man]; patrol, picket, scout, spy, advance guard, rear guard; watchdog, housedog; Cerberus.

Verbs—1, warn, caution; forewarn, prewarn; admonish, premonish, exhort; forebode; give notice *or* warning; menace; threaten, look black; put on one's guard; sound the alarm; cry wolf; ring the tocsin. *Informal,* tip off.

2, beware, take warning, take heed; keep watch; stop, look, and listen.

Adjectives—warning, premonitory, monitory, cautionary; admonitory, admonitive; symptomatic; ominous, foreboding; warned, on one's guard, careful, cautious.

Interjections—beware! take care! look out! watch out! *cave canem!* caveat emptor!

Phrases—a word to the wise [is sufficient]; fear the Greeks bearing gifts; forewarned is forearmed.

Quotations—Beware the ides of March (*Shakespeare*), Conscience is the inner voice that warns us somebody may be looking (*H. L. Mencken*).

Antonyms, see RASHNESS.

---

warp, *v.* twist, bend, serve, distort; bias, prejudice; pervert, deviate; incline. See DISTORTION. —*n.* bias; deflection, tendency; torsion, twist, malformation. See DEVIATION.

warpath, *n.* —**on the warpath,** bellicose; wrathful. See IRASCIBILITY, CONTENTION.

warrant, *n.* warranty, guaranty; pledge, SECURITY, surety; authority; summons, writ, permit, pass; sanction; justification. —*v.t.* guarantee, indemnify, vouch for, answer for, certify, secure; affirm; state, maintain; assure, support, sanction, authorize, justify. See PERMISSION, VINDICATION, AFFIRMATION, EVIDENCE.

warren, *n.* hutch, rabbitry; slum[s], tenement, shantytown. See ABODE.

warrior, *n.* See COMBATANT.

warship, *n.* See SHIP, ARMS.

wart, *n.* growth, blemish, excrescence, callous, protuberance. See CONVEXITY.

wary, *adj.* guarded, watchful, alert, cautious, suspicious, discreet, prudent, chary, scrupulous. See CARE, CAUTION.

wash, *v.* clean, cleanse, deterge, bathe, lave; wet, soak, rinse, drench; purify; irrigate, inundate, flood; scrub, swab, launder; paint, tint, COLOR; sweep; lap, lick; brim over, overflow. See CLEANNESS, PAINTING, WATER. —**washed up,** *informal,* through, spent, finished. See END, COMPLETION.

washout, *n.,* slang, FAILURE.

washroom, *n.* lavatory, wash-up, bathroom, rest room. See CLEANNESS.

washstand, *n.* sink, washbowl, washbasin, lavabo, lavatory, commode, washpot, water butt. See CLEANNESS, RECEPTACLE.

waspish, *adj.* snappish, petulant, irascible; slender-waisted. See IRASCIBILITY, NARROWNESS.

WASTE
Gradual loss or decay

Nouns—1, waste, wastage; dissipation; DISPERSION; ebb; leakage, LOSS; wear and tear; extravagance, wastefulness, prodigality, conspicuous consumption; waste of time; *jeunesse dorée;* misuse; wasting, DETERIORATION. *Slang,* pissing match. See USE, INSUFFICIENCY, WEAKNESS.

2, waster, wastrel, spendthrift, spender, prodigal, squanderer, profligate. *Informal,* sport.

Verbs—1, waste, spend, misspend, expend, USE, MISUSE, use up, consume, swallow up, overtax, exhaust; impoverish; spill, drain, empty; disperse; cast, fool, throw, fling, *or* fritter away; burn the candle at both ends; go *or* run through, squander; waste powder and shot, labor in vain; pour water into a sieve; leak, run out; ebb, melt away, run dry, dry up; deteriorate; throw to the winds; cast pearls before swine; throw good money after bad, play ducks and drakes with, spend as if there were no tomorrow. *Informal,* blow. *Slang,* jack *or* fart around, screw the pooch, piss away.

2, be wasted, give out; go to waste, go for nothing.

Adjectives—1, wasted, thrown away.

2, wasteful, prodigal, profligate, improvident, thriftless, unthrifty, extravagant, lavish, consumptive.

Phrase—easy come, easy go; penny wise and pound foolish; willful waste makes woeful want; waste not, want not.

Quotations—That's the way the money goes—pop goes the weasel! (*W. R. Mandale*), All decent people live beyond their incomes nowadays, and those who aren't respectable live beyond other people's (*Saki*), Half the money I spend on advertising is wasted, and the trouble is, I don't know which half (*John Wanamaker*), Each generation wastes a little more of the future with greed and lust for riches (*Don Marquis*), Full many a flower is born to blush unseen, and waste its sweetness on the desert air (*Thomas Gray*), I wasted time, and now doth time waste me (*Shakespeare*), No act of kindness, no matter how small, is ever wasted (*Aesop*), The national vice is waste (*Henry Miller*).

Antonyms, see STORE, PARSIMONY, ECONOMY.

---

wasteland, *n.* wilderness, desert, barren land. See USELESSNESS.

wastrel, *n.* spendthrift (see WASTE).

watch, *v.* look (at), scrutinize, examine; view, stare, ogle; regard, follow, survey; be alert, guard; chaperone, tend, baby-sit; oversee, superintend; wait, guard, patrol. —*n.* vigil, surveillance, sentry duty; guardianship, CARE; supervisor; guard, watchman, sentinel, lookout; timepiece, pocket watch, wristwatch. See SAFETY, VISION, CHRONOMETRY.

watchdog, *n.* bandog, bloodhound, mastiff; police dog; censor, monitor, policeman; guard[ian]. See DEFENSE, SAFETY.

watchful, *adj.* alert, vigilant, observant. See ATTENTION, CARE.

watchtower, *n.* beacon, lighthouse; lookout *or* observation post. See VISION, INDICATION.

watchword, *n.* countersign, shibboleth; password, catchword; slogan. See INDICATION.

WATER
A clear liquid and major component of all living things

Nouns—1, water, MOISTURE, wetness; drinking water, spring water, mineral water; sea *or* salt water, fresh water; serum, serosity; lymph; rheum; diluent; dilution, maceration, lotion; washing, immersion, infiltration, infusion, irrigation; douche, bath, hot tub, Jacuzzi; baptism, rain, deluge, spate, flood, high water, flood tide; balneology, limnology. *Informal,* Adam's ale, hobo cocktail. See FLUIDITY, CLEANNESS.

2, (*collections of water*) a. river, water system, waterway, stream, beck, tributary, branch, fork, creek, kill, brook, watercourse, bayou, spring, fount, fountain, rill, rivulet, streamlet, runnel, [dis]tributary, feeder; channel, swash, canal, cutoff, seaway, sound, strait, euripus (see PASSAGE); riverbed, wadi, arroyo; torrent, rapids, flood, freshet; current, tide, race. b. waterfall, falls, cascade, linn; cataract; jet, Niagara; rapids, white water, shoot, chute; fountain, geyser, [water]spout. c. gulf, bay, cove, inlet, ria, harbor, arm (of the sea), estuary, reach, firth, fiord. d. ocean, sea, great sea, high seas; the seven seas, [North *or* South] Atlantic, [North *or* South] Pacific, Indian, Arctic *or* Antarctic Ocean; mare nostrum; Mediterranean, Arabian, Caribbean, *etc.* sea; salt water, deep water, blue water; the [bounding] main, the [briny] deep; the Seven Seas, the frozen seas; the billow, wave, tide, *or* flood; the deep blue sea, wine-dark sea, Davy Jones's locker; Father Neptune, Poseidon; the watery waste; tidal basin, tide pool, tidewater, tideway; lake, salt lake, loch (*Scot.*), lough (*Irish*), nyanza, lagoon, laguna, [mill]pond, pool, tarn, lakelet, mere, puddle, water hole; polynya; undertow. e. marsh, swamp (see MOISTURE). f. well, cistern, tank; reservoir, dam.

3, rain, rainfall, precipitation; cloudburst, downpour; thunderstorm; shower, drizzle; rainstorm, monsoon, rainy season; deluge, flood, inundation, spate, torrent, cataclysm.

4, *(water current)* wave, billow, surge, swell, ripple, rollers, surf, breakers, heavy sea; undercurrent, eddy, vortex, whirlpool, maelstrom; waterspout; jet, spurt, squirt, spout; splash, plash; rush, gush, sluice. *Slang,* rhino, tube, zipper, hair ball, hollow wave, wacker, green monster, quaker.

5, *(water as energy)* hydraulics, hydrodynamics, hydrology, hydrokinetics, hydrostatics, hydroponics.

Verbs—**1,** be watery; be awash *or* afloat; swim (in), brim.

2, water, wet; moisten; dilute; dip, immerse, submerge, plunge, souse, douse, dunk, duck, drown; go under; drench, soak, steep, macerate, pickle; wash, sprinkle, lave, bathe, splash; slop; irrigate, inundate, deluge; syringe, douche, inject, gargle.

3, flow, run; issue, gush, pour, spout, roll, stream; rain, drizzle; drop, drip, dribble, drain, trickle, percolate; bubble, gurgle, spurt, ooze; spill, overflow. *Informal,* rain cats and dogs.

Adjectives—**1,** watery, liquid, aqueous, aquatic, lymphatic; balneal, diluent; brimming, drenching, diluted; weak; wet, moist, soppy, sopping, soaked, wet to the skin, waterlogged.

2, oceanic, pelagic, marina, maritime, briny; tidal, fluent, flowing, streaming, meandering; riparian, alluvial; lacustrine; marshy, swampy, boggy, paludal, miry, sloppy; showery, asea, under water.

Phrases—April showers bring forth May flowers.

Quotations—Water, water, everywhere, nor any drop to drink (*Samuel Taylor Coleridge*), The snotgreen sea. The scrotumtightening sea (*James Joyce*), The sea never changes and its works, for all the talk of men, are wrapped in mystery (*Joseph Conrad*), Water is best (*Pindar*), The people are like water and the army is like fish (*Mao Zedong*), Water is the principle, or the element, of all things. All things are water (*Thales of Miletus*), Though the seas threaten, they are merciful (*Shakespeare*).

Antonyms, see LAND, AIR.

---

watercourse, *n.* river (see WATER).

waterfall, *n.* cascade, falls (see WATER).

waterproof, *adj.* water-repellent *or* -resistant, watertight; leakproof, impermeable; seaworthy, hermetic, sealed. See DRYNESS, SAFETY, CLOSURE.

watershed, *n.* runoff, catchment basin; basin, reservoir; crisis, crux, crossroad[s], milestone. See HEIGHT, IMPORTANCE.

watertight, *adj.* water-repellent, waterproof; airtight, safe, binding, legal, ironclad, unbreakable. See DRYNESS, CLOSURE.

waterway, *n.* channel (see WATER).

watery, *adj.* aqueous, aquatic, liquid; wet, dripping; thin, diluted. See WATER, FLUIDITY.

wave, *v.* wag, shake, sway, flutter, stream (in the wind); signal, motion, gesture, indication; roll, undulate; ripple, swell, billow, flood, surge; flaunt, flourish. — *n.* sea, tide, WATER, ripple, billow, *etc.,* wavelet, undulation; signal, gesture, flourish; CONVOLUTION, curl; marcel, permanent, finger wave. See OSCILLATION, FASHION.

waver, *v.i.* vacillate, fluctuate, hesitate; sway, tremble, totter; undulate; teeter. See DOUBT, OSCILLATION.

wax, *v.* cere, grease, coat, smooth, polish; grow, INCREASE, strengthen. See SMOOTHNESS. —*n.* tallow, paraffin, beeswax, cerumen, OIL.

way, *n.* PASSAGE, road, route, path, roadway, highway, channel, street, avenue; journey, progression, transit; trend, tendency; approach, access, gateway; METHOD, manner, mode, style, fashion; SPACE, interval, stretch, distance; usage, custom, HABIT, practice, wont; course, routine; PLAN; CONDUCT, form; behavior; scheme, device; knack; charm, winsomeness. —**give way,** *v.* make way, step aside; break down, collapse. See FAILURE, MOTION.

wayfarer, *n.* traveler, walker, hiker, rambler, wanderer, pilgrim, journeyer. See TRAVEL.

waylay, *v.t.* accost, buttonhole, detain; attack, SURPRISE. See HINDRANCE.

wayward, *adj.* perverse, willful, forward; delinquent; capricious, changeable, wanton; rebellious; irregular, accidental. See CHANGEABLENESS, DISOBEDIENCE.

weak, *adj.* feeble (see WEAKNESS); faulty, unsatisfactory; uncertain, unsure, irresolute; watery, diluted, attenuated; faint, soft. See IMPERFECTION, UNCERTAINTY, COWARDICE, CHANGEABLENESS, SOFTNESS.

weak-minded, *adj.* moronic, idiotic, imbecilic, feebleminded; brainless, foolish, witless, empty-headed, vacuous; vacillating, irresolute, fickle. See IGNORANCE, DOUBT.

WEAKNESS
Lack of strength

Nouns—**1,** weakness, feebleness, debility, debilitation, infirmity, decrepitude, inanition; WEARINESS, enervation, IMPOTENCE; paleness, COLORLESSNESS; disability, attenuation, senility, superannuation, malnutrition, atony, asthenia, adynamia, cachexia, hyposthenia, anemia; invalidity, delicacy, frailty, foible, fragility, flaccidity, vapidity; invalidation, adulteration, dilution; vulnerability, perishability, accessibility; milk and water; Achilles' heel. See DETERIORATION.

2, *(something weak)* reed, thread, rope of sand, house of cards, house built on sand; child, baby, kitten, cat, chicken; water, milk and water, gruel.

3, *(weak person)* weakling, softling, poor specimen, wimp; invalid, asthenic, hypochondriac; deficient, defective, dunce, imbecile, lackwit, wreck, runt; faintheart, jellyfish, broken reed; weathercock. *Informal,* sissy, softy, betty, baby, crybaby, whiner; pantywaist, mollycoddle, milksop, namby-pamby, softhead, weak sister, half-pint, nebbish. *Slang,* doormat, pushover, fancy pants, schnook, wuss, creampuff, dork, dweeb, nerd, punk, marshmallow.

Verbs—**1,** be weak, faint, drop, crumble, droop, sag, fade, fail, flag, pine, decline, languish, give way, give in; deteriorate, waste, falter, halt, limp; black out; soften, relent, relax, yield, submit, succumb; totter, tremble, dodder, potter, shake, have one foot in the grave. *Informal,* keel over, cave in. *Slang,* wuss out.

2, weaken, enfeeble, debilitate, enervate, emasculate, devitalize, etiolate, take the edge off, take the starch out of, wear down; deplete, WASTE; bate, soften up, slacken, blunt; disintensify; undermine, sap, impair, damage, cripple, lame, maim, disable, paralyze.

3, dilute, thin, cut, water [down], attenuate, adulterate, debase; reduce, depress, lower, lessen, impoverish, invalidate.

Adjectives—weak[ly], feeble, infirm, invalid, debile, senile, decrepit; sickly, poorly, unhealthy, unsound; weakened, enfeebled, *etc.;* strengthless, impotent, defenseless; anemic, asthenic, atonic, cachectic, hyposthenic, adynamic, bloodless, short-winded; out of shape; faltering, doddering, drooping, *etc.;* unsteady, shaken, palsied, laid low, weak as a child, baby, *or* kitten; flimsy, flabby, frail, fragile; effeminate; vulnerable, assailable, indefensible; unsupported, unaided, unassisted. *Informal,* namby-pamby, wishy-washy; on one's last legs, on one's knees. *Slang,* woozy, limp-wrist *or* -dick, wussy.

Phrases—the weakest go to the wall; a chain is no stronger than its weakest link; faint heart never won fair lady.

Quotations—The concessions of the weak are the concessions of fear (*Edmund Burke*), The weak are strong because they are reckless. The strong are weak because they have scruples (*Henrik Ibsen*), Ambition, old as mankind, the immemorial weakness of the strong (*Vita Sackville-West*), The Spirit indeed is willing, but the flesh is weak (*Bible*), Frequent punishments are always a sign of weakness or laziness on the part of the government (*Jean-Jacques Rousseau*), The weak, in fact, always prevail over the strong, not only because they are in the majority, but also because they are the more crafty (*Friedrich Nietzsche*), If we resist our passions, it is due more to their weakness than our own strength (*La Rochefoucauld*), Only silence is great; all else is weakness (*Alfred de Vigny*), Three things are weakening: fear, sin, and travel (*Talmud*).

> *Antonyms,* see STRENGTH, POWER, VIGOR, RESOLUTION.

---

wealth, *n.* riches, fortune, opulence, affluence; PROSPERITY; MEANS, resources, property, MONEY; plenty, plenitude, luxuriance, excess, plethora, sufficiency.

wealthy, *adj.* rich, affluent, opulent, moneyed; worth a fortune; well-to-do, well-off; rich as Croesus, made of money, rolling in money, flush, in funds, well-heeled, in the chips, in the money, loaded, filthy rich (*sl.*), rolling in dough (*sl.*), in the big time (*sl.*), rolling high (*sl.*). See MONEY, PROSPERITY.

wean, *v.* separate, withdraw, deprive; estrange, grow up; alienate. See DISUSE.

weapon, *n.* See ARMS.

wear, *v.* last, endure; USE, show, display; tire, fatigue, weary; bear, don, put on; carry, have on; waste, consume, spend; rub, chafe, fray, abrade; jibe, tack, veer, yaw. See WEARINESS, FRICTION. —*n.* CLOTHING, garb; USE, usage, hard usage; impairment, wear and tear. See DETERIORATION.

WEARINESS
Exhaustion

Nouns—1, weariness, tiredness, exhaustion, lethargy, lassitude, fatigue; drowsiness, languor, languidness; WEAKNESS, faintness. *Slang,* rack attack, three-o'clock syndrome. See DEJECTION, INDIFFERENCE.

2, (*tiring person*) bore, proser, nuisance. *Informal,* wet blanket. *Slang,* drip, creep, pain in the neck, deadhead, plonk, dweeb, nudge, drone, Irving.

3, (*tiresomeness*) wearisomeness, tedium, tediousness, dull work, boredom, ennui, sameness, monotony, twice-told tale; heavy hours, time on one's hands. *Slang,* snooze.

Verbs—1, weary; wear, wear *or* tire out, tire, fatigue, jade; bore, weary, *or* tire to death; send *or* put to sleep; wear thin, frazzle, exhaust; run ragged, burn out; weigh down; harp on, dwell on. *Slang,* do in.

2, be weary of, never hear the last of; be tired of; gasp, pant; yawn. *Informal,* peter out. *Slang,* climb the wall, be fed to the gills *or* teeth, have had it, crump out.

3, bore [to tears]. *Slang,* bore stiff.

Adjectives—1, wearying, wearing, arduous, fatiguing, tiring; wearisome, tiresome, irksome; uninteresting, stupid, bald, devoid of interest, dry, monotonous, dull, drab, dreary, tedious, trying, humdrum, flat, wooden; prosy, soporific, somniferous.

2, weary, tired, spent, fatigued; toilworn, footsore; winded, out of breath; drowsy, played out, sleepy; uninterested, flagging; used up, worn out; dog-tired, ready to drop, more dead than alive, played out; exhausted, breathless, short-winded, dead tired, dead on one's feet; prostrate, on one's last legs, hors de combat. *Informal,* fed up, all in. *Slang,* done up, pooped [out], bushed, fagged, beat, tuckered out, zonked out, wasted, fucked.

3, bored, sick and tired, blasé, jaded.

Adverbs—wearily, boringly, tiresomely, *etc.;* ad nauseam.

Quotations—He is an old bore. Even the grave yawns for him (*Beerbohm Tree*), The secret of being a bore . . . is to tell everything (*Voltaire*), The plowman homeward plods his weary way, and leaves the world to darkness and to me (*Thomas Gray*), Once upon a midnight dreary, while I pondered, weak and weary . . . (*Edgar Allan Poe*), It is weariness to keep toiling at the same things so that one becomes ruled by them (*Heraclitus*).

> *Antonyms,* see ENERGY, AMUSEMENT.

weasel, *n.* ermine, suck-egg; sneak, skulker, trickster, hedger. See ANIMAL, AVOIDANCE. —*v., informal,* equivocate, bandy words, hem and haw, hedge, renege, pussyfoot (*sl.*), welsh (*sl.*). See FALSEHOOD.

weather, *n.* clime, climate. See AIR. —under the weather, *informal,* sick, ill; drunk. See DISEASE, DRINKING.

weatherbeaten, *adj.* weathered, seasoned, inured, acclimatized, casehardened. See DETERIORATION.

weathercock, *n.* girouette, weathervane; opportunist. See CHANGEABLENESS.

weatherman, *n.* meteorologist, weather forecaster. See PREDICTION.

weave, *v.* interlace, intertwine, twine, entwine; loom, spin, fabricate; plait, pleat, pleach, braid, mat; contrive, construct. See CROSSING, PLAN.

web, *n.* cobweb, spiderweb; weaving, TEXTURE, mesh, net; network, hookup; trap, snare, scheme, plan; tissue, gossamer. See CROSSING.

wed, *v.* marry, espouse; couple, blend, join. See MARRIAGE, UNITY.

wedge, *n.* quoin, chock, sprag, block, shim. See ANGULARITY.

wee, *adj.* tiny, little, minute, small; infinitesimal, microscopic; diminutive, petite, teeny-weeny (*inf.*). See LITTLENESS.

weed, *v.t.* root out, extirpate, clear (of weeds); cull; remove, eliminate. See CLEANNESS, EXCLUSION. —*n.* pest, nuisance; *informal,* tobacco, smoking. See VEGETABLE, AGRICULTURE, PUNGENCY.

weeds, *n.pl.* mourning, black, widow's weeds. See LAMENTATION.

week, *n.* seven-night (see TIME).

weep, *v.* shed tears, CRY, lament, wail, sob, blubber; mourn, grieve; rain, flow, drip. See LAMENTATION.

weigh, *v.* measure (weight); lift, heft; balance, scale, counterbalance; examine, ponder, consider, mull over, estimate; tell, count; weigh down, be heavy, drag, load, press; oppress, burden, depress; overbalance, bear down. See GRAVITY, MEASUREMENT, ELEVATION, INFLUENCE.

weight, *n.* heaviness; heft; overweight, avoirdupois, tonnage, poundage; GRAVITY; ballast; measurement; IMPORTANCE, INFLUENCE; significance; pressure, load, burden. See QUANTITY. —*v.* ballast, load, burden; favor; adjust, compensate. See COMPLETION.

weightless, *adj.* light, feathery; disembodied, immaterial, incorporeal, intangible; floating, drifting, lighter than air. See LEVITY, INSUBSTANTIALITY.

weighty, *adj.* ponderous, heavy; burdensome, onerous; influential. See GRAVITY, IMPORTANCE, INFLUENCE.

weird, *adj.* uncanny, eldritch, eerie, spooky (*inf.*); ghostly, spectral, unearthly; supernatural. See UNCONFORMITY, DEMON.

welcome, *n.* greeting, salutation, cordial reception, glad hand (*sl.*). —*v.t.* greet, salute; embrace, receive (gladly), hail. —*adj.* pleasing, agreeable, acceptable, wanted, gratifying. See COURTESY, SOCIALITY, PLEASURE.

weld, *v.t.* fuse, unite, join, fasten; blend. See JUNCTION, UNITY.

welfare, *n.* well-being; PROSPERITY, advancement, profit, sake, benefit; social work *or* service, dole, relief; happiness, success. See GOODNESS, PAYMENT.

well, *adj.* healthy, robust, strong, hale, hearty, in good health. —*adv.* rightly, properly; thoroughly, skillfully, accurately; amply, sufficiently, fully, adequately; favorably, worthily; very much; quite, considerable; easily, handily. See HEALTH, SUFFICIENCY; SKILL. —*n.* fount, font, wellspring, wellhead, reservoir, spring; source, origin; hole, pit, shaft. See WATER, CONCAVITY. —*v.i.* issue, gush, brim, flow, jet, rise. See EGRESS.

well-being, *n.* good, PROSPERITY; euphoria, good health, SANITY, robustness, CONTENT, PLEASURE, contentment.

well-bred, *adj.* well-behaved *or* -brought-up; noble, wellborn, gentle; courteous, polished, sauve, polite. See COURTESY, NOBILITY.

well-heeled, *n., slang,* see WEALTHY.

well-informed, *adj.* well-read, well-versed. See KNOWLEDGE.

well-known, *adj.* familiar, recognized, famous, renowned; notorious. See KNOWLEDGE.

well-meaning, *adj.* well-intentioned, with the best intentions, kind[ly], well-disposed, sympathetic. See BENEVOLENCE.

well-nigh, *adv.* very nearly, almost. See NEARNESS.

well-off, *adj.* prosperous, fortunate; wealthy. See PROSPERITY, MONEY.

well-read, *adj.* learned, erudite, scholarly, bookish, educated; well-informed. See LEARNING, KNOWLEDGE.

well-rounded, *adj.* complete, thorough. See COMPLETION.

wellspring, *n.* fountainhead, wellhead, *fons et origo,* source. See CAUSE.

well-to-do, *adj.* comfortable, well-off; prosperous, affluent, wealthy, rich. See MONEY.

welsh, *v.* welch; default on, fail, hedge, renege; leave high and dry, leave holding the bag. See NONPAYMENT.

welt, *n.* wale, weal; edging, rim; binding; cord, ridge, rib. See EDGE, CONVEXITY, DISEASE.

welter, *n.* confusion, turmoil; jumble, hodgepodge, mishmash; ruck, masses; ferment. —*v.i.* wallow. See DEPRESSION, ROTATION, AGITATION.

wench, *n.* girl, maiden, lass[ie]; servant; maid; slut, slattern, tart, trollop, harlot, broad (*sl.*), piece (*sl.*). See IMPURITY, FEMALE.

werewolf, *n.* wolf-man, lycanthrope, loup-garou; changeling. See DEMON.

west, *n.* Occident; Europe; Wild West. See DIRECTION.

wet, *adj.* damp, moist, dewy; clammy, dank, humid, dripping; rainy, showery, foggy, misty; soaked, drenched, saturated; watery, waterlogged. —*v.t.* soak, moisten, dampen, drench, saturate; immerse, dip, sprinkle; rain upon. —*n.* wetness, WATER; rain, fog, dew, mist; dampness, MOISTURE, clamminess, *etc.*; anti-Prohibition. —**wet blanket,** *n. slang,* spoilsport, killjoy; Cassandra, pessimist, alarmist; prophet of gloom *or* doom, crepehanger, party pooper (*sl.*). See DEJECTION, HINDRANCE, WEARINESS.

whale, *n.* cetacean; finback; blue, humpback, killer, sperm, sulphur-bottom, *or* right whale; orca, rorqual, narwhal, blackfish, dolphin, porpoise, grampus; Moby Dick; *informal,* whopper. See SIZE, ANIMAL.

whammy, *n., slang,* hex, spell, curse. See IMPRECATION, SORCERY.

wharf, *n.* dock, pier, quay, landing; waterfront. See EDGE.

what, *pron.* that which; sort of, kind of; which; how; whatever, whatsoever, whichever. See GENERALITY.

whatnot, *n.* thing, something, what have you, whatever, contraption, doodad (*inf.*), thingumabob (*sl.*), blankety-blank (*sl.*), doohickey (*sl.*), dingbat (*sl.*), gismo (*sl.*); cabinet, étagère, china closet. See RECEPTACLE.

wheedle, *v.t.* coax, cajole, persuade; court, humor, flatter. See SERVILITY, FLATTERY.

wheel, *n.* disk, circle, roller; roulette *or* fortune's wheel; bike, bicycle; *slang,* VIP, big wheel, bigwig. See CIRCULARITY, VEHICLE, IMPORTANCE. —*v.* roll; trundle, cycle; rotate, revolve, spin, twirl; pivot, about-face, turn, gyrate, whirl, wind. See ROTATION, DEVIATION.

wheelbarrow, *n.* pushcart, barrow. See TRANSPORTATION.

wheeler-dealer, *n., slang,* operator, player, power broker. See INFLUENCE.

wheeze, *v.* breathe hard, gasp, puff, choke. —*n.* old joke, gag, chestnut. See WIND, WIT.

when, *adv.* at what time?, at the same time; whereupon, just then, whenever. See TIME.

whence, *adv.* See ATTRIBUTION.

where, *adv.* in what place; whereabouts, whither; in what direction, from what source, place, *etc.* See LOCATION, INQUIRY.

whereabouts, *n.* locality, LOCATION.

whereas, *conj.* inasmuch as, since, while, as, in view of, forasmuch as, in consideration of, considering that, seeing that. See ATTRIBUTION, CAUSE.

whereupon, *adv.* whereat, after which. See SEQUENCE.

wherewithal, *n.* MEANS, resources; MONEY, funds, cash, capital, assets, the stuff (*inf.*), the goods (*inf.*), what it takes (*inf.*); power, ability, competence.

whet, *v.t.* sharpen, hone, whetstone, grind; excite, stimulate, provoke, stir up, kindle, quicken, inspire. See SHARPNESS, EXCITEMENT, DESIRE.

whether, *conj.* if, in case; if it is so; in either case. See QUALIFICATION.

whiff, *n.* puff, waft, blast; inhalation. See ODOR, WIND.

while, *conj.* during, as long as, whilst, whereas; although. —**while away,** *v.* pass the time, kill time. See TIME.

whim, *n.* caprice, fancy, DESIRE, vagary; notion, quirk, crotchet, whimsy; freak; impulse. See WIT, IMAGINATION.

whimper, *v. & n.* cry, whine. See LAMENTATION.

whimsical, *adj.* curious, odd, peculiar, freakish; humorous, waggish, droll; crotchety, capricious, queer, quaint. See CHANGEABLENESS, WIT.

whine, *v.i.* CRY, whimper, complain, moan, snivel, gripe (*sl.*), bellyache (*sl.*). See LAMENTATION.

whip, *n.* lash, scourge; quick motion, snap. —*v.t.* lash, beat, flog; thrash; conquer, subdue; defeat. See SUCCESS.

whippersnapper, *n.* brat, pipsqueak. See YOUTH, EVILDOER.

whir, *v.i.* buzz, hum. See SOUND.

whirl, *n.* spin[ning], gyration, turn; flutter, tizzy, confusion; pirouette. —*v.* spin, twirl, turn, rotate, revolve, gyre, gyrate; dance, pirouette. See ROTATION.

whirligig, *n.* merry-go-round, carrousel; rotor, roller, *etc.*; top. See ROTATION.

whirlpool, *n.* eddy, swirl; vortex, maelstrom. See WATER, ROTATION.

whirlwind, *n.* tornado, twister, cyclone, typhoon, hurricane, windstorm. See WIND. —*adj.* fast, speedy, headlong, breakneck, dizzying. See VELOCITY.

whisk, *n.* [egg]beater; whiskbroom. —*v.* whip, froth, beat; sweep; swish, whish; zip. See AGITATION, VELOCITY.

whiskers, *n.pl.* beard, hair, stubble; hirsuteness; mustache, sideburns, goatee, Vandyke, muttonchops, *etc.*; bristles; feelers, antennae. See ROUGHNESS.

whiskey, *n.* [hard] liquor, spirits; booze, moonshine, bootleg (*all inf.*); hooch,

white mule, rotgut, red-eye (*all sl.*); bourbon, rye, corn; firewater. See FOOD, DRINKING.

whisper, *n.* murmur, whispering, sigh, breath; hint, intimation, rumor, gossip, plot; aside, stage whisper. See INFORMATION, NEWS, SPEECH, SOFTNESS. —*v.* murmur, breathe, divulge, reveal, hint, intimate. See DISCLOSURE, CONCEALMENT.

whistle, *n. & v.* pipe, piping, flute. See WIND, LOUDNESS, SOUND, MUSIC.

white, *adj.* snow-white (see COLOR, COLORLESSNESS); cleansed, purified; Caucasian, Caucasoid. See HUMANITY. —*n.* whiteness, purity; hoariness, grayness (of age); lime, paper, milk, ivory, snow, sheet, alabaster; albinoism, blondness, fairness; pallor, ashiness, waxiness, bloodlessness; bleach, etiolation; silveriness; glare, LIGHT, lightness; INNOCENCE, stainlessness. —**white elephant,** nuisance, embarrassment; dead weight, deadwood, drag, burden, impediment, lemon (*sl.*); plague, cross. See GIVING, USELESSNESS.

whitewash, *v.t.* calcimine, kalsomine; whiten; vindicate, exonerate; *informal,* shut out, blank, skunk (*sl.*). See COVERING, VINDICATION, FLATTERY.

whittle, *v.* shape, carve; pare, cut, slice, shave; deduct, curtail, dock, diminish; dwindle, eat away, erode. See DISJUNCTION.

whiz, *v.i.* rush, scoot (see HASTE). —*n., slang,* expert, ace, crackerjack. See SKILL.

who, *pron.* which one?; that. See INQUIRY.

WHOLE
The complete thing

Nouns—1, whole, totality, totalness, integrity; entirety, ensemble, collectiveness; UNITY, completeness, indivisibility, integration, embodiment; integer.

2, the whole, all, everything, total, aggregate, one and all, gross amount, sum, sum total, tout ensemble, length and breadth of, alpha and omega, be-all and end-all; bulk, mass, lump, tissue, staple, body, trunk, bole, hull, hulk, skeleton. *Informal,* ball game. *Slang,* whole [kit and] caboodle, whole show, whole shebang, whole shooting match; the works, whole bag of tricks, every Richard *or* Tom, Dick, and Harry.

Verbs—form *or* constitute a whole; integrate, embody, amass; aggregate, assemble; amount to, come to, add up to.

Adjectives—1, whole, total, integral, entire, all, complete; one, individual; wholesale, sweeping.

2, unbroken, uncut, undivided, unsevered, unclipped, uncropped, unshorn; seamless;

undiminished; undemolished, undissolved, undestroyed; indivisible, indissoluble, indissolvable.

Adverbs—wholly, altogether; totally, completely, entirely, all, all in all, wholesale, in a body, collectively, all put together; lock, stock, and barrel; in the aggregate, in the mass, in the main, in the long run; en masse, on the whole, bodily, throughout, every inch, substantially, by and large.

Quotations—The whole of science is nothing more than a refinement of everyday thinking (*Albert Einstein*), All are but parts of one stupendous whole, whose body nature is, and God the soul (*Alexander Pope*), The highest wisdom has but one science—the science of the whole—the science explaining the whole creation and man's place in it (*Leo Tolstoy*).

Antonyms, see PART.

---

wholehearted, *adj.* sincere, earnest; enthusiastic. See RESOLUTION, FEELING.

wholesale, *adj.* bulk, job-lot, jobbing; extensive, indiscriminate; at a discount, cheaper; mass, sweeping, general, widespread. See WHOLE, GENERALITY, BARTER.

wholesome, *adj.* healthy, beneficial. See HEALTH, PURITY.

whopper, *n.*, *informal*, shamefaced *or* barefaced lie. See FALSEHOOD.

whore, *n.* prostitute, harlot, bawd, strumpet, streetwalker, call girl, B-girl, daughter of joy. See EVILDOER, IMPURITY.

whorehouse, *n.* brothel, cathouse, bordello. See IMPURITY.

why, *adv.* wherefore? what for? for what cause? how come? (*sl.*). See CAUSE, ATTRIBUTION.

wicked, *adj.* EVIL, bad; criminal, depraved, iniquitous; cruel, heartless, sinful, vicious, immoral; difficult, disagreeable; *informal*, mischievous. See WRONG.

wicker, *n.* twig, vimen, shoot, rod, osier, willow, withe, sallow; rattan, straw, buri, raffia; wickerware. See CROSSING.

wicket, *n.* gate, door; window; hoop, arch; turnstile. See OPENING.

wide, *adj.* spacious, widespreading, comprehensive; generous, ample, all-embracing; broad, large, roomy, extensive; vast, open; general. See BREADTH, EXPANSION.

widespread, *adj.* general, common, rife, universal, prevalent; ubiquitous; extensive, inclusive, all-embracing; global. See GENERALITY, DISPERSION, EXPANSION.

widow, *n.* survivor (of a husband), relict, dowager; divorcée, grass widow. See DIVORCE.

width, *n.* BREADTH, broadness; wideness, span, beam; extent, expanse.

wield, *v.t.* handle, manipulate, ply; brandish, flourish, wave, shake; employ, control, manage. See USE, OSCILLATION.

wife, *n.* married woman; mate, spouse, Frau, the Mrs., madam, little woman, old lady, ball and chain (*sl.*), better half; housewife, helpmeet, helpmate. See MARRIAGE.

wig, *n.* toupée, toupet, doily (*sl.*), divot (*sl.*), rug (*sl.*); peruke, periwig, switch, transformation; fall; headdress. See COVERING, ORNAMENT.

wiggle, *v.i.* squirm, shake, wriggle, wobble, wag, shimmy. See AGITATION.

wigwam, *n.* hut, lodge; teepee. See ABODE.

wild, *adj.* savage, untamed, uncivilized; feral, bloodthirsty, fierce; uncontrolled, amuck, frenzied; inaccurate, intemperate, unwise, foolish; eager, impetuous, stormy, violent, unrestrainable, desert, uninhibited; rank, thick, junglelike, luxuriant; untended, uncultivated; shy, skittish; daring, reckless, rash, breakneck; freak. See VIOLENCE, EXCITABILITY.

wildcat, *n.* lynx, puma, mountain lion, panther, ocelot. See ANIMAL. —*adj., informal*, risky, speculative, venturesome, shoestring; unauthorized, splinter, spontaneous. See DANGER, ILLEGALITY, RASHNESS.

wilderness, *n.* wasteland, waste[s], wilds, badlands; desert, sands, Sahara. See SPACE, USELESSNESS.

wild-goose chase, fool's errand, chasing rainbows; red herring, snipe hunt, chasing one's own tail, tilting at windmills. See USELESSNESS.

wildlife, *n.* animal kindgom, fauna. See ANIMAL.

wile, *n.* stratagem, subterfuge, ploy; trick, dodge. See CUNNING.

will, *n.* volition, purpose, determination

(see WILL); testament, bequeathal (see GIVING).

WILL
Volition

Nouns—will, free will, volition, conation, velleity; FREEDOM, discretion; option, CHOICE; voluntariness, spontaneity, spontaneousness; pleasure, wish, mind; frame of mind, disposition, proclivity, inclination, willingness, readiness, willing mind *or* heart; INTENTION, predetermination; self-control, determination, RESOLUTION.

Verbs—will, see fit, think fit; determine, resolve, settle, choose, volunteer; have a will of one's own; have one's own way; exercise one's discretion; take responsibility; take upon oneself, find it in one's heart; do of one's own accord.

Adjectives—1, voluntary, volitional, willful, intentional; free, optional; discretionary; prepense; intended; arbitrary; autocratic; unbidden, unspontaneous; original (see CAUSE).

2, willing, minded, disposed, inclined, favorable; favorably inclined *or* disposed to; nothing loath; in the mood *or* humor; ready, forward, earnest, eager; bent upon, desirous, predisposed; voluntary, unasked, unforced.

Adverbs—1, voluntarily, at will, at pleasure; ad libitum, as one thinks proper, according to one's lights; with good grace; of one's own accord *or* free will; by choice, purposely, intentionally, deliberately.

2, willingly, fain, freely; heart and soul; with pleasure, nothing loath, graciously, without reluctance, of one's own accord.

Phrases—a willful man must have his way; where there's a will there's a way; you can take a horse to [the] water, but you can't make him drink.

Quotations—The good or ill of man lies within his own will (*Epictetus*), If you will it, it is no dream (*Theodor Herzl*), Will and wisdom are both mighty leaders. Our times worship will (*Clarence Darrow*), We have to believe in free will. We've got no choice (*Isaac Bashevis Singer*).

Antonyms, see NECESSITY, UNWILLINGNESS.

---

willful, *adj.* self-willed, arbitrary; headstrong, wayward, obstinate, stubborn, unruly; intentional, deliberate, premeditated. See WILL.

willing, *adj.* minded, disposed (see WILL); bent upon, desirous, predisposed; docile, agreeable, easygoing, tractable, pliant; cordial, hearty; content, assenting, voluntary, gratuitous, spontaneous. See ASSENT.

willingness, *n.* voluntariness (see WILL); penchant, DESIRE; docility, pliability; goodwill; alacrity, eagerness; ASSENT, compliance, CONSENT; PLEASURE.

will-o'-the-wisp, *n.* ignis fatuus; illusion, chimera. See IMAGINATION, LIGHT.

willpower, *n.* self-control, self-discipline; CHOICE, determination. See WILL.

willy-nilly, *adv.* will I, nill I; *nolens volens*; like it or not, whether or not; perforce, inescapably. See COMPULSION, NECESSITY.

wilt, *v.i.* droop, sag; weaken, languish, wither; collapse. See DETERIORATION.

wily, *adj.* designing, tricky, crafty, foxy; deceitful, crooked, Machiavellian; clever, subtle, CUNNING.

wimp, *n.* weakling (see WEAKNESS, IMPOTENCE).

win, *v.* beat, conquer, master; gain, obtain, get; achieve, accomplish, reach; persuade, sway, convince, influence; succeed, triumph, surpass. See ACQUISITION, SUCCESS, BELIEF.

wince, *v.i.* flinch, RECOIL; shy, quail, shrink. See FEAR, PAIN.

winch, *n.* See WINDLASS.

wind, *v.* twist, [en]twine; coil, curl, spiral; bandage, loop; enfold, infold; wreathe, roll; crank, reel; sinuate, meander, wander. See CONVULSION, DEVIATION, ROTATION. —*n.* See WIND.

WIND
Current of air

Nouns—1, wind, windiness, draught, draft, flatus, afflatus, AIR; breath [of air]; puff, whiff, blow, drift; aura; stream, current, undercurrent; [in]sufflation, inflation; blowing, fanning, ventilation.

2, *(natural winds)* austral *or* boreal wind, prevailing wind; breath, [gentle, moderate, fresh, stiff, *or* strong] breeze, [gentle, moderate, fresh, strong, *or* whole] gale, violent storm, hurricane; zephyr, sea breeze, waft; gust, blast, flurry, squall, half a gale, storm, tempest, whirlwind, tourbillion, vortex, tornado, [anti]cyclone, twister, typhoon, neutercane, simoom, haboob, el niño; nor'wester, sou'wester, nor'easter, sou'easter, easterly, westerly; harmattan, ghibili, pampero, khamsin, williwaw, zonda, bora, chinook, monsoon, puna, samiel, Santa Ana, Montreal express, berg, trade wind, sirocco, solano, mistral, bise, tramontane, foehn, levanter; capful of wind; dust storm, sandstorm; stiff breeze; blizzard; rough, foul, *or* dirty weather; dirty sky, mare's tail, tailwind; microburst, stadium effect; firestorm, nuclear winter.

3, *(wind measurement)* anemography, aerodynamics; wind gauge, anemometer, pneumatics; weathercock, [weather]vane; Beaufort scale, Fujita-Pearson scale.

4, breathing, respiration, sneezing, sternutation; hiccough, hiccup; catching of the breath. *Slang,* fart. See EXCRETION, EJECTION.

5, *(wind gods)* Aeolus, Boreas, Eurus, Zephyr, Notus, cave of the winds.

6, air pump, lungs, bellows, blowpipe, fan, ventilator, vacuum cleaner, wind tunnel; air pipe (see PASSAGE); funnel; sailboat, windjammer (see SHIP).

Verbs—1, blow, waft; stream, issue; freshen, gather; storm; blow up, bluster; sigh, moan, scream, howl, whistle; breeze.

2, breathe, respire, inhale, exhale, puff, pant; whiffle, gasp, gulp, wheeze; snuff[le], sniff[le]; sneeze, cough; expire.

3, fan, ventilate; inflate; blow up, pump up.

Adjectives—windy, blowing, breezy, gusty, squally; stormy, tempestuous, blustering; boisterous; pulmonic, pulmonary, pneumatic; onshore, offshore.

Phrases—may the wind be always at your back; it's an ill wind that blows no good.

Quotations—Winter is icumen in, lhude sing Goddamm, raineth drop and staineth slop, and how the wind doth ramm (*Ezra Pound*), Rough winds do shake the darling buds of May, and summer's lease hath all too short a date (*Shakespeare*), Who has seen the wind? Neither you nor I: But when the trees bow down their heads the wind is passing by (*Christina Rossetti*), O Wild West Wind, thou breath of Autumn's being (*Percy Bysshe Shelley*), Sweet and low, sweet and low, wind of the western sea (*Lord Tennyson*), The answer, my friend, is blowin' in the wind (*Bob Dylan*), You throw the sand against the wind, and the wind blows it back again (*William Blake*), There is no wind that always blows a storm (*Euripides*), They have sown the wind, and they shall reap the whirlwind (*Bible*), I have forgot much, Cynara, gone with the wind (*Ernest Dowson*), The wind of change is blowing through this Continent (*Harold Macmillan*), The human heart is like a ship on a stormy sea driven about by winds blowing from all four corners of heaven (*Martin Luther*), The roaring of the wind is my wife and the stars through the window pane are my children (*John Keats*).

Antonyms, see REPOSE.

---

windbag, *n., slang,* bag of wind, gasbag, gasses (*sl.*), big mouth (*sl.*), blabbermouth (*sl.*); braggart, blusterer; gossip, chatterer. See LOQUACITY, BOASTING.

windfall, *n.* bonus, prize, blessing, boon; treasure trove, find; pennies *or* manna [from heaven], godsend, discovery. See ACQUISITION.

windjammer, *n.* sailboat, sailing SHIP; sailor (see NAVIGATION).

windlass, *n.* hoist, lifter; moulinet, reel, capstan, pinion, winch, crank. See ELEVATION.

window, *n.* casement, dormer, OPENING; pane; bay window, oriel; port[hole]; skylight; embrasure, loophole.

windpipe, *n.* airpipe, trachea; throat, throttle; weasand. See PASSAGE.

windup, *n., informal,* END, termination, conclusion, closure, settlement, climax, denouement, resolution, outcome, upshot; preliminaries, preparation. See COMPLETION.

windy, *adj.* See WIND.

wine, *n.* the grape; drink, liquor; DRINKING, intoxication; stimulant, alcohol; nectar.

wing, *n.* pinion, [feathered] limb, pennon, ala; arm, sail; flank; ell, annex, extension; airfoil; flight, flying. —*v.* fly; disable, wound. See ADDITION, AVIATION, COMBATANT, DRAMA, SIDE. —**wing it**, *v. inf.,* extemporize, improvise, ad-lib, fake (*inf.*). See UNPREPAREDNESS.

wink, *v.* blink, nictitate, nictate, squint, twinkle; overlook, ignore, condone. See VISION, FORGIVENESS, NEGLECT, INDICATION.

winning, *adj.* conquering, victorious, triumphant; winsome, captivating, charming, engaging, entrancing, prepossessing, comely, attractive; persuasive, convincing. See LOVE, SUCCESS, BEAUTY.

winnow, *v.t.* select, cull, sift, separate, glean, pick; ventilate, fan. See CHOICE, CLEANNESS.

winsome, *adj.* gay, merry, lively, sportive; charming, winning, captivating; lovable, adorable, pleasant, attractive. See LOVE, ENDEARMENT.

winter, *n.* wintertime, COLD; hibernation. See CHRONOMETRY.

wintry, *adj.* raw, brisk, COLD.

wipe, *v.t.* clean, rub, brush, dust, mop; dry, towel. See CLEANNESS, DRYNESS.

wire, *n.* (metal) thread, FILAMENT; flex, cord, line; telephone, telegraph, cable; cablegram, telegram. See COMMUNICATION.

wireless, *n.* radio; radiogram, marconigram. See COMMUNICATION.

wiry, *adj.* filamentous, filar, threadlike; strong, muscular, sinewy; tough; flexible. See FILAMENT, STRENGTH.

wisdom, *n.* sagacity, understanding; conventional wisdom. See KNOWLEDGE.

wise, *adj.* sage, sagacious; learned, profound, deep; judicious, well-advised; *informal,* impudent, rude. See KNOWLEDGE, INSOLENCE. —*n.* manner, METHOD. —**wise guy**, *slang,* wiseacre; gangster, mafioso. See WIT, EVILDOER. —**wise man**, sage, intellectual (see KNOWLEDGE).

wisecrack, *n., slang,* crack, quip, witticism, comeback, answer. See WIT.

wish, *n.* DESIRE, WILL; pleasure; craving, yearning, want, hankering; INTENTION. —*v.* want, long for, dream of, hope for, ask [for], yearn, crave, hanker. See HOPE, DESIRE.

wishful thinking, fantasy, wistfulness, nostalgia. See HOPE.

wishy-washy, *adj.* washed-out, anemic, colorless; weak-kneed *or* -willed, spineless, irresolute, feeble, vacillating. See INSIPIDITY, WEAKNESS.

wisp, *n.* bundle; tuft, lock. See ASSEMBLAGE.

wistful, *adj.* musing, pensive, thoughtful; desirous, wishful, hopeful; eager; craving, yearning. See DESIRE, FEELING, THOUGHT.

WIT
Cleverness

Nouns—1, wit, wittiness; Atticism; salt; sense of humor, funny bone, esprit, point, fancy, whim, humor, drollery, pleasantry; comedy; jocularity, jocosity, jocoseness; levity, facetiousness; waggery, waggishness, quipstering; comicality; laugh track. *Informal,* crazy bone.

2, (*broad humor*) farce, buffoonery, clowning, fooling, tomfoolery; harlequinade; broad farce, broad humor, slapstick; fun; smartness, banter, badinage, retort, repartee, riposte; RIDICULE; horseplay. *Slang,* monkey business, barrel of laughs.

3, (*joke*) witticism, jest, joke, conceit, quip, one-liner, quirk, quiddity, pleasantry; sally, wheeze; flash of wit, scintillation; mot, bon mot, smart saying, epigram; dry wit, cream of the jest. *Informal,* hoot. *Slang,* comeback, gag, [wise]crack, running gag, zinger.

4, wordplay, play on words, pun, punning, double entendre, equivocation; conundrum, riddle (see SECRET); trifling. *Slang,* chestnut.

5, wit, wag; joker, jester, buffoon; comedian, comic, humorist, punster; merry-andrew, fool; practical joker, fun maker. *Informal,* gagman. *Slang,* wisecracker.

Verbs—**1,** be witty, joke, jest; crack a joke; pun; make fun of, make sport of; retort; banter. *Informal,* kid. *Slang,* wisecrack, come back at.

2, be funny *or* amusing. *Informal,* crack one up, have people rolling in the aisles.

Adjectives—witty, Attic, quick-witted, nimble-witted; smart, jocular, jocose, droll, funny, waggish, facetious, whimsical, humorous; playful, merry, pleasant, sprightly, sparkling, epigrammatic, pointed, comic.

Adverbs—jokingly, jestingly, *etc.*; in jest, in sport, in play; in fun; not seriously, with tongue in cheek.

Quotations—We are not amused (*Queen Victoria*), Everything is funny as long as it is happening to Somebody Else (*Will Rogers*), Humor is emotional chaos remembered in tranquillity (*James Thurber*), Nothing is so impenetrable as laughter in a language you don't understand (*William Golding*), Brevity is the soul of wit (*Shakespeare*), Wit is the epitaph of an emotion (*Friedrich Nietzsche*), Impropriety is the soul of wit (*W. Somerset Maugham*), Better a witty fool than a foolish wit (*Shakespeare*), Wit makes its own welcome and levels all distinctions (*Emerson*), The wit makes fun of other persons; the satirist makes fun of the world; the humorist makes fun of himself (*James Thurber*).

Antonyms, see WEARINESS.

---

witch, *n.* hag, beldam[e], crone; shrew, scold, dragon; sorceress, enchantress; charmer. See UGLINESS, BEAUTY, SORCERY, EVILDOER.

witchcraft, *n.* SORCERY.

witch-hunt, *n.* vigilantism, persecution, baiting; purge, investigation, inquisition, McCarthyism, red-baiting, super-patriotism. See WRONG, INQUIRY, INJUSTICE.

with, *prep.* by, by means of, through; accompanying, alongside, among[st], amid[st], beside, plus; upon, at, thereupon, *etc.* See ACCOMPANIMENT, MIXTURE.

withdraw, *v.* remove, separate, subduct; retire, retreat, disengage, draw off; abstract, subtract; recall, rescind, recant; resign, relinquish; abdicate, decamp, depart; shrink, recoil, drop out, back out. See DEPARTURE, RECESSION, SECLUSION, RELINQUISHMENT.

wither, *v.* waste, decline, droop, wilt, fade, decay; contract, shrivel, pine, decline, languish; blast, destroy, burn, scorch; cut, scathe. See DETERIORATION, DRYNESS.

withhold, *v.t.* keep back, restrain, detain; check, hold back; hinder; suppress, repress, reserve. See CONCEALMENT, RESTRAINT.

within, *adj. & prep.* outside, outdoor[s], indoor[s]; internal. See INTERIOR.

without, *adv. & prep.* outside, outdoor[s], outward, beyond; minus. See EXTERIOR, ABSENCE, CIRCUMSTANCE, DEDUCTION, EXEMPTION.

withstand, *v.t.* face, confront; fight off, oppose, defy. See OPPOSITION.

witless, *adj.* senseless, brainless; silly, foolish, pointless, idiotic, moronic, imbecilic, dumb (*sl.*); half-witted, dull, thick, stupid, scatterbrained, muddle-headed, dopy (*sl.*). See IGNORANCE.

witness, *n.* testimony, proof, EVIDENCE, corroboration; deponent, eyewitness; testifier, attestor; beholder, observer. —*v.t.* see, observe; attest, sign, subscribe to, bear witness to. See PRESENCE.

witticism, *n., witty, adj.* See WIT.

wizard, *n.* wonder-worker, conjuror; Merlin, magician, sorcerer; *informal,* master, expert. See SORCERY, SKILL.

wobble, *v.* roll, rock, stagger, reel, lurch, yaw, sway; teeter, totter, flounder; hesitate, waver, quaver. See OSCILLATION, AGITATION.

woe, *n.* trouble, tribulation; sorrow, grief; unhappiness, misery. See PAIN, DEJECTION.

woebegone, woeful, *adj.* sorrowful, unhappy. See DEJECTION.

wolf, *n.* canid, wolfkin, cub, whelp; hyena; werewolf, wolfman; *slang,* philanderer, rake, roué, woman chaser, lady-killer. See ANIMAL, LOVE. —*v.t.* raven, gulp, bolt, gobble. See FOOD.

woman, *n.* FEMALE, lady, gentlewoman; wife. See HUMANITY.

womanish, *adj.* effeminate, emasculated; unmanly; shrill, vixenish; soft, weak. See FEMALE.

womanize, *v.* feminize; *slang,* philander, chase after women. See FEMALE, IMPURITY.

WONDER
Surprise or admiration or its cause

Nouns—1, wonder, wonderment, marvel, miracle, miraculousness, astonishment, amazement, bewilderment; amazedness, admiration, awe; stupor, stupefaction; fascination; SURPRISE. See UNINTELLIGIBILITY, SECRET.

2, sensation, phenomenon, marvel, prodigy; eighth wonder. *Slang,* lollapalooza.

Verbs—1, wonder, marvel, admire; be surprised, start; stare, open *or* rub one's eyes; gape, hold one's breath; look *or* stand aghast, stand in awe of; not believe one's eyes, ears, *or* senses.

2, be wonderful, beggar *or* baffle description; stagger belief.

3, SURPRISE, astonish, startle, shock, take aback, electrify, stun, stagger, bewilder.

Adjectives—1, wonderful, wondrous; miraculous; surprising, unexpected, unheard of; mysterious, indescribable, inexpressible, ineffable; unutterable, unspeakable; monstrous, prodigious, stupendous, marvelous; inconceivable, incredible; unimaginable, strange, uncommon, passing strange, striking, overwhelming. *Slang,* out of sight, hellacious, fantastic.

2, surprised, aghast, agog, breathless, agape; openmouthed; awestruck, thunderstruck; round-, wide-, *or* large-eyed; spellbound; speechless, at a loss [for words]; lost in amazement, wonder, *or* astonishment; unable to believe one's senses. *Slang,* bugeyed.

Adverbs—wonderfully, fearfully; for a wonder; strange to say, mirabile dictu, to one's great surprise; with wonder.

Interjections—lo! lo and behold! O! what! wonder of wonders! will wonders never cease! what will they think of next!

Phrases—wonder is the beginning of wisdom.

Quotations—Wonder is the foundation of all philosophy, inquiry the process, ignorance the end (*Montaigne*), Wonder is the feeling of a philosopher, and philosophy begins in wonder (*Plato*), Philosophy begins in wonder, and at the end, when philosophic thought has done its best, the wonder remains (*Alfred North Whitehead*), Wonder is the basis of worship (*Thomas Carlyle*), Men love to wonder, and that is the seed of science (*Ralph Waldo Emerson*), America is a land of wonders, in which everything is in constant motion and every change seems an improvement (*Alexis de Tocqueville*), O wonderful, wonderful, and most wonderful! and yet again wonderful, and after that, out of all whooping! (*Shakespeare*), Wonders are many, and none is more wonderful than man (*Sophocles*), A man is a small thing, and the night is very large and full of wonders (*Lord Dunsany*).

Antonyms, see EXPECTATION.

---

wonderful, *adj.* miraculous, marvelous, amazing, astounding;. great, swell, dandy; colossal, terrific (*all inf.*). See WONDER, GOODNESS.

wont, *n.* custom, use, HABIT, routine, practice, usage.

woo, *v.* court, make love to; seek, pursue, solicit; importune. See ENDEARMENT.

wood, *n.* forest, grove, timber, copse, coppice, thicket, spinny, bosque, bois; woods, woodland; board, plank, log, lumber. See MATERIALS.

woodcut, *n.* wood block, woodprint; xylograph, lignograph, pyrograph, wood ENGRAVING.

wooded, *adj.* sylvan, forested, timbered. See VEGETABLE.

wooden, *adj.* wood[y], ligneous, xyloid; oaken, mahogany, ash, pine, teak, walnut, *etc.;* frame, clapboard, shingle[d]; stiff, rigid, inflexible; expressionless, lifeless, unimaginative. See MATERIALS, UNMEANINGNESS, HARDNESS, WEARINESS.

woodshed, *n.* See RECEPTACLE. —*v.i.,* *informal,* study, cram, practice. See INQUIRY, LEARNING.

woodsman, *n.* woodcutter, lumberman, lumberjack, logger, timberjack; conservationist, forester, ranger; frontiersman, backwoodsman. See AGRICULTURE.

woodwind, *n.* flute, clarinet, oboe, bassoon, saxophone. See MUSIC.

woodwork, *n.* molding, paneling, baseboard, didoes, frames, jambs, sashes; doors. See ORNAMENT.

woof, *n.* weft, filling; fabric, TEXTURE. See CROSSING.

wool, *n.* fleece; down, hair; worsted, yarn. —*adj.* woolen; knitted; woolly, hairy, fleecy, downy, fluffy, flocculent. See COVERING, SOFTNESS, MATERIALS.

woolly, *adj.* fleecy; *informal,* confused, blurred, fuzzy. See MATERIALS, UNINTELLIGIBILITY.

woolgathering, *adj.* absentmindedness, daydreaming. See IMAGINATION, INACTIVITY.

woozy, *adj., slang,* confused, befuddled; shaky, groggy. See UNINTELLIGIBILITY, INATTENTION.

WORD
Written communication

Nouns—1, word, term, expression, locution, linguistic unit *or* form, word form, lexeme; homonym, synonym, antonym, heteronym, homophone; syllable, monosyllable, polysyllable; stem, root, derivative, inflected form (see GRAMMAR); particle, article; affix, prefix, suffix, combining form, element, proclytic, enclitic. See WRITING, NOMENCLATURE, LANGUAGE, NEWS, INFORMATION, PROMISE.

2, compound, back formation, phrase, cognate, etymon, ghost word, holophrase; phone, ideophone, phoneme, utterance (see SPEECH); neologism, neoterism, coinage, nonce word, sniglet; archaism; borrowing, paronym, loanword, calque, loan translation, pochismo; ink-horn term; portmanteau word, macaronicism, hybrid; colloquialism, informalism, localism, dialect, slang; barbarism, spoonerism, corruption (see ERROR); password, watchword (see INDICATION); technical term, jargon, cant. *Informal,* jawbreaker.

3, dictionary, lexicon, glossary, vocabulary, thesaurus, word treasury, word hoard, lexis, direct *or* linguistic atlas; concordance; definiens, definiendum.

4, lexicography, lexicology, [folk] etymology, derivation, comparative linguistics.

5, lexicographer, lexicologist, etymologist; neologist; phrasemaker; wordsmith, writer (see WRITING).

Verbs—coin a word *or* phrase; put into words, express.

Adjectives—verbal; lexicographical, lexicological, etymological; neological; morphological, inflectional, derivative.

Phrases—all words are pegs to hang ideas on; sticks and stones may break my bones, but words will never hurt me; talk is cheap; one picture is worth ten thousand words; the pen is mightier than the sword.

Quotations—Words are, of course, the most powerful drug used by mankind (*Rudyard Kipling*), Words are chameleons, which reflect the color of their environment (*Learned Hand*), There is no use indicting words, they are no shoddier than what they peddle (*Samuel Beckett*), Man does not live by words alone, despite the fact that he sometimes has to eat them (*Adlai Stevenson*).

---

word game, acrostic, palindrome, anagram[s], crossword puzzle, ghosts, riddles, word square, double acrostic; spelling bee; rebus, charades; Scrabble,

Jotto, Boggle, *etc.*; Guggenheim, categories, wordplay, *etc.* See AMUSEMENT.

wording, *n.* phrasing, expression, phraseology. See FIGURATIVE, SPEECH.

wordy, *adj.* verbose, talkative, loquacious, prolix, garrulous; rambling, circumlocutory, windy, long-winded. See DIFFUSENESS.

work, *n.* job, occupation, calling, trade, profession; task, stint, employment; drudgery, toil, moil, grind, routine; function; craftsmanship, workmanship; arts and crafts, craft, handicraft; opus, PRODUCTION, WRITING, book PUBLICATION; office; management; manufacture. See BUSINESS. —*v.* toil, moil, labor, plod, plug, drudge, use elbow grease (*inf.*); run, act, operate, function; leaven, ferment, yeast; use, employ; succeed, perform, do; effect, exert, strain; embroider, embellish, decorate. See ACTION, SUCCESS, EXERTION, AGENCY, EFFECT.

workable, *adj.* feasible, practicable; tractable. See POSSIBILITY, SOFTNESS.

workaday, *adj.* everyday, quotidian, common[place], matter-of-fact, homespun, humdrum; routine, orderly. See BUSINESS, EXERTION, SIMPLENESS.

workaholic, *n., slang,* overachiever, beaver. See EXERTION.

worker, *n.* laborer, workman; artisan, craftsman; operator, doer, performer; journeyman, yeoman; Trojan; drudge; mechanic; toiler, moiler. See EXERTION.

workhorse, *n., informal,* hard worker; drudge, hack. See EXERTION.

working, *adj.* effective; operational. See UTILITY. —*n.pl.* works, parts, action. See COMPOSITION.

working class, *n.* proletariat, wage-earners, blue-collar workers. See POPULACE.

workmanlike, *adj.* well-done, expert, professional. See SKILL.

workmanship, *n.* craftsmanship, handiwork, SKILL, technique, expertness; competence; performance, execution, construction; finish, polish, art. See PRODUCTION.

workout, *n.* trial, essay; practice, rehearsal, run-through. See EXERTION, EXPERIMENT.

works, *n.pl.* factory, plant, mill, workshop, shop; mechanism, machine; fort, rampart, breastworks, earthworks, barricade; *informal,* everything. See AGENCY, PUNISHMENT, COMPLETION.

workshop, *n.* workhouse, sweatshop; laboratory, factory, manufactory, mill, rolling mill, sawmill; works, steelworks, ironworks, foundry, furnace; mint; seminar, clinic; forge, loom; cabinet, atelier, studio, bureau, office, store, shop, plant. See BUSINESS.

world, *n.* creation, nature; earth, cosmos (see UNIVERSE).

worldly, *adj.* experienced, sophisticated; earthly, mundane; terrestrial; profane, secular, carnal; sordid, mercenary; proud, selfish, material, materialistic, unspiritual, irreligious. See SELFISHNESS, IRRELIGION.

worldwide, *adj.* universal, widespread; general, all-embracing, unlimited. See GENERALITY.

worm, *n.* earthworm, angleworm; maggot, larva, grub, caterpillar; insect; crawler, nightcrawler; flatworm, platyhelminth, tapeworm, cestode, nematode, roundworm, ascarid, pinworm, annelid; wretch; screw, spiral. See ANIMAL. —*v.* crawl; creep, belly; insinuate (oneself), bore; writhe, wriggle. See CONVOLUTION, INSERTION.

worn, *adj.* used, secondhand; frayed, shabby, threadbare; shopworn; weary. See DETERIORATION, WEARINESS.

worry, *n.* care, anxiety, mental anguish, uneasiness, FEAR, apprehension; concern, misgiving. —*v.* tease, plague, vex; disturb, fret, upset; torment, torture, trouble, bait, badger; maul, chew, mangle; get gray hairs. See MALEVOLENCE, DISCONTENT, CARE.

worrywart, *n., informal,* worrier, nervous Nellie (*inf.*), Cassandra. See CARE, FEAR.

WORSHIP
Reverence

Nouns—1, worship, adoration, devotion, homage, service; religious rites *or* observance; RESPECT, reverence, veneration; cult; deification, idolization. See IDOLATRY, GRATITUDE, RELIGION, RITE.

2, *(service ritual)* a. liturgy; prayer, orison, invocation, supplication, devotion[s], rogation, intercession, beseeching, entreaty, petition (see REQUEST); thanksgiving, grace; praise, laudation, exaltation, glorification, blessing, benediction, benison; Magnificat, doxology, hosanna, hallelujah, alleluia, Te Deum, Trisagion; paean, psalm, psalmody, hymn, anthem, plainsong, chant (see MUSIC). b. *(Christian:)* collect, litany, miserere, Lord's prayer, paternoster, Ave Maria, Hail Mary, rosary, prayer wheel, missal. c. *(Jewish:)* Shoma, Kol Nidre, Kaddish. d. *(Moslem:)* Aliahu akbar, Fatihah, shahada, rak'ah. e. *(Hindu:)* Ram, Siva.

3, *(service)* divine service, office, duty; Mass, Eucharist, Communion, Lord's Supper; morning prayer, matins, evening prayer, evensong, vespers, vigils, compline, prime [song], tierce, lauds, sext, nones; prayer meeting, revival. See RITE.

4, worshiper, adorer, venerator, reverer, glorifier; religionist, churchman, churchgoer, devout person, congregation; communicant, celebrant, votary, pietist; idolizer, devotee, deifier, deist; idolator, idolatress, fetishist, pagan. *Informal,* psalm singer. See CLERGY, RELIGION, PIETY.

Verbs—1, worship, adore, reverence, revere, inspire, aspire, lift up one's heart; pay homage, humble oneself, kneel, genuflect, bend *or* bow one's knee, fall on one's knees, prostrate oneself, bow down and worship; be devout.

2, RESPECT, adulate, idolize, lionize; deify, enshrine, immortalize.

3, pray, invoke, supplicate; offer up prayers, tell one's beads; return *or* give thanks, say grace, bless; praise, laud, glorify, magnify, exalt, extol, sing praises; give benediction, lead the choir, intone; go to church, attend service, attend Mass, communicate; daven.

Adjectives—worshipful, adoring, prayerful, devout, devotional, pious, reverent, religious, spiritually minded, paying homage; pure, solemn, fervent, fervid, heartfelt; reverential, venerating, obeisant.

Interjections—hallelujah! alleluia! hosanna! praise the Lord! Deo gratias! glory be to God! pray God that! lift up your hearts! sursum corda!

Phrases—the family that prays together stays together.

Quotations—Ask, and it shall be given you (*Bible*), One single grateful thought raised to heaven is the most perfect prayer (*Doris Lessing*), More things are wrought by prayer than this world dreams of (*Lord Tennyson*), Often when I pray I wonder if I am not posting letters to a non-existent address (*C. S. Lewis*).

Antonyms, see IRRELIGION, DISRESPECT, IMPRECATION.

---

worst, *v.t.* best, defeat, conquer. See SUCCESS.

worth, *n.* merit, value, PRICE, cost, estimation; worthiness, importance, VIRTUE, credit; character. See MONEY, UTILITY, GOODNESS.

worthless, *adj.* useless, no good, good-for-nothing, no-account (*inf.*), lousy (*sl.*); base, vile; valueless; poor, miserable; trashy; unserviceable; trifling; characterless. See USELESSNESS, CHEAPNESS, UNIMPORTANCE.

worthwhile, *adj.* beneficial, salubrious, good; gainful, profitable, lucrative; meritorious, worthy. See EXPEDIENCE, USE.

worthy, *adj.* deserving, meritorious; virtuous, good; estimable, honest, upright, reputable. See VIRTUE, SKILL, REPUTE.

would-be, *adj.* hopeful, aspiring; pretended, so-called, self-styled, soi-disant; fraudulent. See PRIDE, NOMENCLATURE, DECEPTION.

wound, *n.* injury, hurt; painfulness. —*v.t.* injure, hurt, lame, cripple; PAIN; shoot, stab, cut, lacerate, tear, wing; insult, offend, gall, mortify. See DETERIORATION, RESENTMENT.

wraith, *n.* ghost, specter. See DEMON, IMAGINATION.

wrangle, *v.i.* quarrel, bicker, squabble, dispute, altercate, argue, brawl. See DISCORD, CONTENTION.

wrap, *n.* robe, shawl, serape, cloak, coat, cape, cover, wrapper, blanket. —*v.t.* swathe, swaddle, clothe, cover, envelop, enclose; hide, muffle, conceal; fold, lap, wind; pack[age]. See COVERING, ENVIRONMENT.

wrap-up, *n.* summary, précis. See SHORTNESS.

wrath, *n.* choler, anger, ire, indignation; vengeance; fury, rage. See RESENTMENT.

wreath, *n.* garland, lei, chaplet, festoon; laurel wreath, garland of bays; floral ring, decoration. See ORNAMENT, APPROBATION, CIRCULARITY.

wreck, *n.* DESTRUCTION, ruin, undoing; accident, collision, crack-up, smash-up, crash; shipwreck; derelict; ruined person, human wreckage; breakup; ruins, demolition, wreckage, junk. —*v.t.* smash, crash, crack up, bust up (*sl.*); ruin, tear down, demolish, raze, destroy; shipwreck, strand, cast away; shatter, blight, blast. See REMAINDER.

wrench, *v.t.* twist, wring; yank, pull; extort, wrest, snatch; sprain, strain, dislocate; distort. —*n.* monkey wrench, spanner; twist, yank, *etc.* See EXTRACTION, DISJUNCTION, RETENTION.

wrest, *v.t.* turn, pull, twist; tear away, snatch, grab. See DISTORTION, ACQUISITION, EXTRACTION.

wrestle, *v.* grapple, strive, struggle with, contend. See CONTENTION.

wretch, *n.* sufferer; beggar, outcast, pariah; knave, villain; rogue, rascal. See EVILDOER, DISCONTENT.

wretched, *adj.* beggarly, worthless, miserable; paltry, mean, pitiful; unhappy, unfortunate; woebegone, tormented, afflicted; shabby, disreputable, deplorable. See BADNESS, UNIMPORTANCE.

wriggle, *v.* wiggle, shake, squirm, writhe, shimmy. See AGITATION.

wring, *v.t.* wrench, twist; rack, PAIN; squeeze, compress; extort. See CONVOLUTION, EXTRACTION, ACQUISITION.

wrinkle, *n.* FURROW, crease, pucker, FOLD, corrugation, rumple; crinkle, crow's-foot; *informal,* angle, development, gimmick. —*v.t.* crease, rumple, FOLD.

writ, *n.* process, summons, warrant. See LAWSUIT.

writhe, *v.i.* wriggle, squirm, twist, contort. See DISTORTION, PAIN.

WRITING
Graphical representation of sounds

Nouns—1, writing, chirography, calligraphy, pencraft, penmanship, hand, handwriting, script, longhand, shorthand, picture writing, uncial writing; boustrophedon, Cyrillic, Devanagari, Hangul, Kufic, kana, kanji, romaji, Wade-Giles, pinyin, cuneiform, rune, hieroglyph[ic], ideogram, ideograph, graffiti; epigraphy; romanization, transliteration; letter, grapheme, logogram, phonogram, phraseogram, pictograph, syllabary; alphabet; black and white; stroke of the pen, pen and ink; shorthand, stenography, typewriting; cryptography, code, steganography; pneumatography, spirit writing; graphology; *cacoethes scribendi.* See SPEECH, PUBLICATION, DESCRIPTION.

2, *(bad penmanship)* cacography, bad hand, illegible hand, scribble, scrawl; writer's cramp. *Slang,* hen tracks. See UNINTELLIGIBILITY.

3, WORD, syllable, phrase, sentence, paragraph; prose, POETRY.

4, manuscript, codex, document, ms., mss., COPY, transcript, rescript, typescript, rough copy *or* draft; fair copy; autograph, monograph, holograph.

5, **a.** writing paper, parchment, manila [paper], newsprint, onionskin, rice paper, bond [paper]; papyrus; tablet. **b.** pencil, pen; fountain, ball[point], felt-tip, laundry, *etc.* pen; manual, electric, *or* electronic typewriter, printer, dot-matrix *or* daisy-wheel printer, draft- *or* letter-quality printer.

6, a. writer, author[ess], litterateur, essayist, novelist, short-story writer, playwright, dramatist, poet; editor; lexicographer, annotator, commentator; journalist, newspaperman, critic, reviewer, correspondent; hack [writer], ghostwriter; librettist; screenwriter; scribe, amanuensis, scrivener, secretary, clerk, stenographer, stenotypist, penman, copyist, transcriber; typewriter, typist; calligrapher. *Informal,* freelance, inkslinger, penny-a-liner. *Slang,* bomber. **b.** authorship, composition.

Verbs—write, pen, COPY, engross; write out, transcribe; scribble, scrawl, scratch; interline; write down, record, sign; compose, indite, draw up, dictate; inscribe, dash off, draft, formulate; take pen in hand; typewrite, type; write shorthand.

Adjectives—writing, written, holographic, manuscript; shorthand, stenographic; in writing, in black and white; uncial, runic, cuneiform, hieroglyphic, hieratic; handwritten, cursive, printed, lettered; legible; Spencerian, backhand.

Phrases—the style is the man; the art of writing is the art of applying the seat of the pants to the seat of the chair.

Quotations—When we see a natural style, we are quite surprised and delighted, for we expected to see an author and we find a man (*Pascal*), The last thing one knows in constructing a work is what to put first (*Pascal*), Writing, when properly managed . . . is but a different name for conversation (*Lawrence Sterne*), A woman must have money and a room of her own if she is to write fiction (*Virginia Woolf*), I am a camera with its shutter open, quite passive, recording, not thinking (*Christopher Isherwood*), Writing is not a profession but a vocation of unhappiness (*Georges Simenon*), Good prose is like a window-pane (*George Orwell*), A good novel tells us the truth about its hero; but a bad novel tells us the truth about its author (*G. K. Chesterton*), There's nothing to writing. All you do is sit down at a typewriter and open a vein (*Red Smith*).

Antonyms, see SPEECH, PRINTING.

---

wrong, *adj.* immoral (see WRONG); mistaken, unfactual; unsuitable, improper. See ERROR, DISAGREEMENT. —*n.* evil, harm, injury. See WRONG, MALEVOLENCE.

WRONG
Deviation from moral right

Nouns—**1,** wrong, wrongfulness, INJUSTICE, imposition, oppression, corruption, foul play; ILLEGALITY, miscarriage of justice. See ERROR.

2, wrongdoing, wickedness, sinfulness, BADNESS, EVIL, sin, vice, iniquity, immorality, GUILT, reprehensibility, miscreancy, IMPROBITY; blackguardism; transgression, felony, trespass, misdeed, misbehavior, misdoing, indiscretion, crime, violation, offense, misdemeanor, tort, injury, grievance, outrage, the matter, malefaction, shame, blame.

3, wrongdoer, transgressor (see EVILDOER).

Verbs—**1,** wrong, harm, injure, damage, maltreat, mistreat, ill-treat, abuse, hit below the belt, oppress, persecute, outrage, offend, dishonor, misserve, do wrong to, do injury to, do injustice to, get at, treat unjustly, sin against; scandalize.

2, do wrong, transgress, be unjust, be inequitable, show partiality.

Adjectives—**1,** wrong[ful], bad, EVIL, immoral, sinful, wicked, vicious, grievous, iniquitous, scandalous, reprehensible, blameworthy, guilty, criminal; harmful, deleterious, injurious, hurtful, detrimental, pernicious, perverse, perverted.

2, unjust, unfair (see INJUSTICE); unreasonable, unallowable, impermissible; unjustified, unlawful, illegal; illegitimate.

Adverbs—wrong[ly], falsely, in the wrong; improperly, faultily, amiss, awry, bad; mistakenly, erroneously, inaccurately, incorrectly, in error.

Phrases—no peace for the wicked; the more you stir the worse it stinks; two wrongs don't make a right.

Quotations—The wages of sin is death (*Bible*), Commit the oldest sins the newest kind of ways (*Shakespeare*), We have erred and strayed from thy ways like lost sheep (*Book of Common Prayer*), For the sin ye do by two and two ye must pay for by one and one! (*Rudyard Kipling*).

Antonyms, see RIGHTNESS.

---

wrongful, *adj.* injurious; erroneous; unlawful; unjust, unfair. See EVIL, ERROR, ILLEGALITY, WRONG.

wrongheaded, *adj.* misguided, stubborn, obstinate. See OBSTINACY.

wry, *adj.* crooked, twisted; askew, awry; ironic, distorted, contorted; warped. See DISTORTION, OBLIQUITY.

X

xanthic, *adj.* yellow[ish]; fulvous, tawny. See COLOR.

xanthous, *adj.* blond[e], fair, light-skinned; fair-, yellow-, *or* golden-haired; yellowish; Mongolian. See COLOR.

x-rated, *adj.* racy, lewd; salacious, erotic, pornographic; adult, for adults only. See IMPURITY.

X-ray, *n.* Roentgen ray; radiation; radiograph. See REMEDY.

xylograph, *n.* woodcut, wood engraving. See ENGRAVING.

xyloid, *adj.* wood[y], ligneous. See VEGETABLE.

xylophone, *n.* marimba, gamelan[g], vibraphone, vibraharp, glockenspiel, orchestra bells, sticcado-pastrole, gigelira, straw fiddle. See MUSIC.

Y

yacht, *n.* sailboat, pleasure boat; houseboat; sloop, yawl, ketch; cruiser. See SHIP.

yahoo, *n.* lout, knave. See VULGARITY.

yammer, *v.,* *informal,* complain, wail, gripe (*sl.*), grouse (*sl.*), whine, whimper, pule; cry, howl; desire, crave, yearn; lament. See LAMENTATION.

yank, *n. & v.* pull, twist, jerk. See TRACTION.

yap, *v.i.* See YELP.

yard, *n.* ENCLOSURE, court[yard], patio.

yardstick, *n.* ruler; standard, criterion, rule, test, measure. See MEASUREMENT.

yarn, *n.* thread, worsted, spun wool; tale, fib, tall story. See FILAMENT, DESCRIPTION, EXAGGERATION.

yaw, *v.i.* drift, deviate; jibe, tack. See DEVIATION, NAVIGATION.

yawn, *v.i.* gape, open wide; split, part. See OPENING, WEARINESS.

yea, *adv.* yes; indeed, truly. See ASSENT.

year, *n.* twelvemonth; fiscal year, calendar year. See CHRONOMETRY.

yearbook, *n.* annual, annuary, calendar, almanac; journal, diary, RECORD.

yearling, *n.* teg; youngling, colt, filly, whelp, cub. See YOUTH, ANIMAL.

yearn, *v.i.* pine, long, hanker; grieve, mourn. See DESIRE, LAMENTATION.

yeast, *n.* leaven, ferment, barm; spume, froth, foam. See AGITATION.

yell, *v. & n.* shout, CRY, scream, shriek, bawl, call; yelp, bark; bellow, roar, hoot, squawk (*sl.*), holler (*sl.*).

yellow, *adj.* fair, blond[e], flaxen, light-haired (see COLOR); Mongolian, Mongoloid; jaundiced; jealous, envious, *informal,* cowardly, craven, fearful, lily- *or* white-livered, afraid, unmanly, pusillanimous; lurid, sensational, melodramatic, scandal-mongering. See COWARDICE.

yellowbelly, *n.,* *slang,* coward (see COWARDICE).

yelp, *n. & v.* bark, squawk, CRY, yap, yip.

yen, *n.,* *informal,* DESIRE, craving, longing, hankering, yearning; taste, hunger, relish; passion; tendency, appetite.

yeoman, *n.* freeholder, commoner, farmer; guardsman, beefeater; attendant, retainer; petty officer. See POSSESSION, AGRICULTURE, MALE.

yes, *adv.* yea, aye; indeed, true, verily; agreed, surely, certainly, of course, that's right. See ASSENT, CONSENT.

yeshiva, *n.* Talmudic academy, rabbinical seminary; Hebrew SCHOOL.

yesterday, *n.* day before; the PAST.

yet, *conj.* nevertheless, notwithstanding, still, however. See COMPENSATION. — *adv.* still, besides, thus far, hitherto, till now, up to now *or* this time. See PRIORITY, PAST.

yield, *n.* crop, harvest, product. See AGRICULTURE. —*v.* surrender, cede, abandon, give up; give in, succumb; produce, bear, bring; furnish, supply, afford; soften, relax, give [way]; assent, comply, obey. See RELINQUISHMENT, CONSENT, RECEIVING, RESIGNATION, SUBMISSION.

yielding, *adj.* soft, pliant, tractable, docile; submissive, compliant, acquiescent; supple, plastic, flexible; productive, fertile. See SOFTNESS, FACILITY.

yodel, *v.i.* warble (see MUSIC).

yoke, *n.* union, bond, chain, link, tie; bondage, slavery, oppression, servitude, enslavement, thralldom, vassalage; couple, pair, team. See SUBJECTION. —*v.t.* couple, join, pair, wed; bind, tie, link; bracket, connect, associate. See JUNCTION.

yokel, *n.* rustic, peasant, countryman; hick, hayseed, rube, bumpkin, yahoo (*all inf.*). See POPULACE.

yonder, *adj.* yon, that. —*adv.* in that place, thither, there, beyond; in the distance, afar, far away. See DISTANCE.

yore, *n.* antiquity, old times, olden days, good old days (*inf.*), time immemorial; yesterday; bygone[s], history, the PAST.

young, *adj.* youthful; puerile; ageless; green; foundling; adolescent, juvenile, teenage; fresh, new; inexperienced, immature. See YOUTH. —*n.* offspring, children. See POSTERITY.

YOUTH
Condition of being young

Nouns—1, youth, juvenility, juvenescence, immaturity, juniority; childhood, boyhood, maidenhood, girlhood, youthhood; minority, nonage, teenage, teens, tender age, bloom; prime of life, flower of youth *or* life; heyday of youth; school days; terrible twos; adolescence, puberty, the awkward age; rite of passage; growing pains; greenness, callowness; jeunesse dorée; inexperience, puerility; me decade. See NEWNESS, POSTERITY.

2, babyhood, infancy, cradle, nursery, apron strings.

3, infant, newborn, baby, babe, suckling, chrisom child, nursling; bairn, enfant, papoose; preemie; offspring, young; brat, tot, toddler; the patter of tiny feet. *Informal,* kid[dy], chick, bambino, mudlark; big baby, thumbsucker, crybaby. *Slang,* mama's boy, carpet *or* rug rat, ankle-biter, pickney.

4, child, boy, girl, muchacha, lad, maid, youth, hobbledehoy, stripling, subteen, tween, teen[ager], benjamin, adolescent, preppie, angry young man, enfant terrible; cherub, brat, imp, gamin, urchin; sapling; child prodigy, Wunderkind; foster child, fosterling; killcrop. *Informal,* bobby soxer, juvenile. *Slang,* spring chicken; boarder baby, zero-parent children, squeegee kid, banda; [jail]bait, forbidden fruit, juve, teenybopper; toyboy, punk kid, young fogy, shavetail, bimbo, colt, puppy, faun[l]et; bantam, quail, cover, crack, fluff, leg, tuna, zimmer.

5, bassinet, cradle, crib, rocker; day care *or* nursery; diaper, pacifier, teether, pottychair, swaddling clothes; diaper rash.

6, (*young animal*) pup, whelp, kitten, cub, foal, colt, lamb. See ANIMAL.

Verbs—rejuvenate, make young; rob the cradle.

Adjectives—young, youthful, juvenile, tender, immature, wet behind the ears, green, callow, budding, sappy, unfledged, underage, prepubescent, preteen, preadolescent, teenage, in one's teens; hebetic, adolescent, pubescent; immature; younger, junior; boyish, beardless; maidenly, girlish; infant, infantile, newborn, babyish, childish, puerile; knee-high to a grasshopper.

Phrases—children should be seen and not heard; if youth knew, if age could; little pitchers have big ears; never send a boy to do a man's job; out of the mouths of babes; adolescence: a stage between youth and adultery.

Quotations—A child is not a vase to be filled, but a fire to be lit (*Rabelais*), The child is father of the man (*Wordsworth*), My salad days, when I was green in judgment (*Shakespeare*), The Youth of a Nation are the trustees of Posterity (*Benjamin Disraeli*), I'm not young enough to know everything (*J. M. Barrie*), Youth would be an ideal state if it came a little later in life (*Herbert Asquith*), There is always one moment in childhood when the door opens and lets the future in (*Graham Greene*), Children's games are hardly games. Children are never more serious than when they play (*Montaigne*), What do we ever get nowadays from reading equal to the excitement and the revelation in those first fourteen years? (*Graham Greene*), Crabbèd age and youth cannot live together; youth is full of pleasance, age is full of care (*Shakespeare*), Uncontrolled violence is a fault of youth (*Seneca*), The young are permanently in a state resembling intoxication; for youth is sweet and they are growing (*Aristotle*), Youth is the pollen that blows through the sky and does not ask why (*Stephen Vincent Benét*), Youth is like spring, an overpraised season (*Samuel Butler*), Youth is something very new: twenty years ago, no one mentioned it (*Coco Chanel*), They are not long, the days of wine and roses (*Ernest Dowson*), No young man believes he shall ever die (*William Hazlitt*), Youth is quick in feeling but weak in judgment (*Homer*), It is only an illusion that youth is happy, an illusion of those who have lost it (*W. Somerset Maugham*), The American ideal is youth—handsome, empty youth (*Henry Miller*), Youth condemns; maturity condones (*Amy Lowell*).

Antonyms, see AGE.

---

yowl, *v.i. & n.* howl, scream, squawk. See CRY.

yummy, *adj., informal,* delicious, tasty, delectable. See GOODNESS.

yuppie, *n.* bourgeois, middle-class person. See MEDIOCRITY.

Z

zany, *n.* clown, madcap, buffoon, comic, fool, comedian, jester, merry-andrew, Punch, pickle-herring; nitwit, dunce. See FOLLY, WIT.

zeal, *n.* earnestness, devotion, dedication; passion; soul, spirit, ardor, fervor, verve, enthusiasm, eagerness, warmth, energy; zealotry, fanaticism. See ACTIVITY, FEELING.

zealot, *n.* fanatic, addict, fan (*inf.*); visionary, dreamer, enthusiast; bigot; devotee, partisan. See HETERODOXY, PIETY.

zenith, *n.* summit, top, acme, apex, pinnacle, apogee; climax, culmination; prime, heyday. See HEIGHT.

zephyr, *n.* breeze, breath, gentle wind, west wind. See WIND.

zeppelin, *n.* dirigible [balloon], airship. See AVIATION.

zero, *n.* nothing; naught, nought; cipher, none, zip (*inf.*), goose-egg (*sl.*), zilch (*sl.*); (*in games*) love, blank; nobody, not a soul. See INSUBSTANTIALITY. —**zero hour,** turning point, crunch, deadline. See LIMIT.

zest, *n.* relish, gusto, appetite, enthusiasm, enjoyment, thrill, titillation, exhilaration; tang, twang, PUNGENCY, piquance, savor, sauce, edge, kick (*inf.*), zip (*inf.*). See TASTE, PLEASURE, EXCITEMENT.

zigzag, *adj.* back-and-forth, tacking, serrated, jagged; crooked, tortuous. See DEVIATION, ANGULARITY.

zip, *n., informal,* zero; VIGOR, zest, ENERGY, ginger (*inf.*), whiz (*inf.*), ping (*inf.*), swish (*inf.*), pep (*sl.*). —*v.* flash; swish, whiz; close (a zipper). See VELOCITY.

zipper, *n.* slide fastener. See CONNECTION.

zither, *n.* zitter, cittern, cithara; koto. See MUSIC.

zodiac, *n.* constellations; horoscope, circle, circuit. See UNIVERSE.

zombie, *n.* walking dead, living ghost; automaton, stooge (*sl.*); monster; eccentric, oddball, nut, weirdo (*all sl.*). See DEATH, DEMON.

zone, *n.* REGION, clime, climate; district, ward, area; belt, girdle, band, girth, cincture. See CIRCULARITY, LAYER.

zoo, *n.* zoological park *or* garden; menagerie; vivarium, vivary; aviary, birdhouse; serpentarium; bear pit; aquarium. See ANIMAL, DOMESTICATION.